Goethe's *Faust I* Outlined

Library of the Written Word

Editor-in-Chief

Lisa Kuitert (*University of Amsterdam*)

Editorial Board

Bill Bell (*Cardiff University*)
Lisa Gitelman (*New York University*)
Henning Hansen (*UiT The Arctic University of Norway*)

VOLUME 113

The Industrial World

Series Editor

Lisa Kuitert (*University of Amsterdam*)

VOLUME 8

The titles published in this series are listed at *brill.com/lww*

Goethe's *Faust I* Outlined

Moritz Retzsch's Prints in Circulation

By

Evanghelia Stead

BRILL

LEIDEN | BOSTON

This is an open access title distributed under the terms of the CC BY-NC-ND 4.0 license, which permits any non-commercial use, distribution, and reproduction in any medium, provided no alterations are made and the original author(s) and source are credited. Further information and the complete license text can be found at https://creativecommons.org/licenses/by-nc-nd/4.0/

The terms of the CC license apply only to the original material. The use of material from other sources (indicated by a reference) such as diagrams, illustrations, photos and text samples may require further permission from the respective copyright holder.

This study is published with the generous support of an Institut Universitaire de France grant.

Library of Congress Cataloging-in-Publication Data

Names: Stead, Evanghélia, author.
Title: Goethe's Faust I outlined : Moritz Retzsch's prints in circulation / by Evanghelia Stead.
Description: Leiden ; Boston : Brill, 2023. | Series: Library of the written word, 1874–4834 ; volume 113 | Includes bibliographical references and index.
Identifiers: LCCN 2023025029 (print) | LCCN 2023025030 (ebook) | ISBN 9789004518551 (hardback ; acid-free paper) | ISBN 9789004543010 (ebook)
Subjects: LCSH: Goethe, Johann Wolfgang von, 1749–1832. Faust – Illustrations. | Retzsch, Moritz, 1779–1857.
Classification: LCC PT1924 .S74 2023 (print) | LCC PT1924 (ebook) | DDC 832/.6–dc23/eng/20230616
LC record available at https://lccn.loc.gov/2023025029
LC ebook record available at https://lccn.loc.gov/2023025030

Typeface for the Latin, Greek, and Cyrillic scripts: "Brill". See and download: brill.com/brill-typeface.

ISSN 1874-4834
ISBN 978-90-04-51855-1 (hardback)
ISBN 978-90-04-54301-0 (e-book)

Copyright 2023 by Evanghelia Stead. Published by Koninklijke Brill NV, Leiden, The Netherlands.
Koninklijke Brill NV incorporates the imprints Brill, Brill Nijhoff, Brill Hotei, Brill Schöningh, Brill Fink, Brill mentis, Vandenhoeck & Ruprecht, Böhlau, V&R unipress and Wageningen Academic.
Koninklijke Brill NV reserves the right to protect this publication against unauthorized use.

This book is printed on acid-free paper and produced in a sustainable manner.

An outline frequently stirs the spirit more pleasantly than the most elaborate picture.

EDGAR ALLAN POE (1842)

• • •

As a book is a sort of individual representation, not a solitary volume exists but may be personified, and described as a human being.

BENJAMIN D'ISRAELI (1820)

Contents

Acknowledgments   XI
List of Figures   XIII
Abbreviations   XXVIII

Introduction: Air View and Ant Perspective   1
Moritz Retzsch's Etchings after Goethe's *Faust I*   7

1   **Retzsch in the German States, a Borderline Celebrity**   25
   1.1   Profile in Contrast   25
   1.2   Romantic Pranks and Rituals   28
   1.3   Portraits and Sociability   34
   1.4   A Poetic Mind   35
   1.5   The Toils of Fancy and Melancholy   36
   1.6   Fluctuating Fate in Nineteenth-Century German States   39
   1.7   Plights and Plusses of Comparison (Retzsch, Cornelius & Naeke)   45
   1.8   German Amendments in the Twentieth Century   49
   1.9   Conclusion   50

2   ***Faust I* Outlined and the Original Retzsch Effect**   52
   2.1   A Modern Fourfold Device   52
   2.2   Goethe's Gifts   55
   2.3   In Goethe's Orb   59
   2.4   Retzsch at Work: Early Correspondence   63
   2.5   A Speculation on Relics   67
   2.6   "Full of Spirit"   80
   2.7   Outline Reformation   86
   2.8   Retzsch in Colour   89
   2.9   To Conclude   92

3   **German Editions and Copies: The Bait of Rich Morsels**   95
   3.1   Avowable (and Uncertain) Cotta Portfolios   95
   3.2   From Portfolios to Albums   99
   3.3   Pirated Goods   107
   3.4   Styled for the Ladies   112
   3.5   Valuing Copies in Visual Circulation   115

4   **First Steps in Britain**   120
   4.1   A Momentous Gift from Perthes to Crabb Robinson   121
   4.2   Imported Wares and Motley Exemplars   124
   4.3   Media Coverage and Publicity (A Mediated Launch)   126
   4.4   A First English Point of View (George Soane's Letterpress)   127
   4.5   Books as Cultural Objects: Readers and Cultural Representation   128
   4.6   Dibdin in Action   133

5 Retzsch Copied in Britain and Beyond 137
5.1 Attractive and Collectable 137
5.2 Cultural Adaptability 139
5.3 Boosey's 1820 Edition Re-issued? 146
5.4 "A More Careful Abstract" 148
5.5 *Faustus* as Template 154
5.6 Retzsch Gains Ground in Other Garb and Guises 159
5.7 Retzsch Wielded by Illustration 166
5.8 Competing Formats 168
5.9 "Bound to Please" 170
5.10 First Conclusions on Foreign Circulation 175

6 Retzsch in France and Belgium 177
6.1 Retzsch by Muret for Artists, Readers, and Print Collectors 181
6.2 Three Little Audot 184
6.3 A Francized Original Retzsch 190
6.4 Copies vs. Originals? The Brussels Case 197
6.5 Retzsch in French Nineteenth-Century Print Culture 201
6.6 Retzsch's Diffuse Influence 206
6.7 Conclusion 210

7 Extensive and Intensive Iconography 212
7.1 Loose Leaves 212
7.2 Copies, Copies, Copies ... 215
7.3 Bowdlerizing 222
7.4 A Kiss's Exceptional Fortune 232
7.5 Spread and Sway on Style, Form and Set 239
7.6 Extensive vs. Intensive Iconography 242
7.7 Extensive Rations 242
7.8 Intensive Inspiration 245
7.9 Recycling and Authorship in Image Circulation 252

8 The Power of Parody: A Crow amongst Nations 255
8.1 A Crow's Quill 258
8.2 Travesties 259
8.3 Mischief in Images 262
8.4 Homecoming and "Who Loves a Laugh" 262
8.5 A Mocking Deity with a Meerschaum Pipe 268

9 Outlines in the Limelight 270
9.1 Aptitudes and Assets 270
9.2 Weimar Trials 274
9.3 Staging: German *Décors* 277
9.4 British and French *Décors* 281
9.5 Time, Stage and the Arts 286
9.6 Performance: Fixed, Inviolable Instants? 288

CONTENTS

9.7 Outfits: Models and Embodiment   291
9.8 Creating Types   297
9.9 In the Limelight over Time   301

10 **Ink Worlds**   303
10.1 Devilish Relish of Converted Israelites   303
10.2 Théophile Gautier from Travelogue to Aesthetics   306
10.3 Visual Traps in Prose   309
10.4 Pictures within the Picture in Illustrated Books   313
10.5 Games of Fiction, Tricks and Screens   321

11 **Two Gifted Women**   323
11.1 Goethe's and Byron's Gifts   323
11.2 The Book as a Rose   325
11.3 Twelve Apostles and a *Faust*   329

12 **Artefacts: Poetics of Everyday Life**   333
12.1 Treasures of Gold and China   334
12.2 Porcelain for the Many   338
12.3 Moulded and Backlit   343
12.4 In Tin and Frail Paper   347
12.5 Conclusion   352

Conclusion: Grains of Sand as Cities   355

**Appendix 1: Moritz Retzsch's 26 *Umrisse* in Original and
Copied Editions**   359
Appendix 2: Moritz Retzsch's Prints Remediated   370

Bibliography   379
Index on Moritz Retzsch   412
General Index   422

Acknowledgments

My Faust adventures began years ago, at the outset of my academic career, when I devised a classically comparative literature programme around Goethe's *Faust I*, Marlowe's *Doctor Faustus*, spiced up with Frank Wedekind's *Franziska*, an unexpected (and still underestimated) she-Faust.

Faustian iconography would promptly reveal the impact of Retzsch's outlines and more visual Faustiana currently object of further or forthcoming publications. Over the years, other figures and programmes claimed attention and elbowed for space, pushing the Doctor aside, yet never for long. Mephistopheles and he (metaphorically *jeder Mensch*, everyman), kept coming back, puppet-like and sturdy, impudently pointing their noses at inappropriate moments.

This book may never have materialized at Brill without Arjan van Dijk's enthusiastic response and some strange coincidences. Certainly, due attention could never have been granted, nor the lavish reproductions envisaged, but for three meaningful turns allowing research in Germany and overseas and into special collections: first, a EURIAS fellowship took me to Freiburg's Institute for Advanced Studies (FRIAS) in 2014–15, close to Faust's legendary death-stage, Stauffen, in Baden-Württemberg. From Freiburg University's fortuitous *Gasthaus* location in Goethestrasse, I made five trips to Weimar (eight in all, to date), one to Frankfurt, and a last to Knittlingen, all remarkably fruitful, and organised an international conference with *Reading Books and Prints as Cultural Objects* as an outcome. Closely following suit, an Institut Universitaire de France fellowship in 2016–21 gave me time to further delve into barely fathomable Goethe bibliography and return several times to Germany, particularly Dresden, and Marbach's Deutsches Literatur Archiv; latterly, Beinecke's Hermann Broch fellowship in 2019 enabled me to pace my work on the rich Goetheana of the Speck Collection. I am very grateful to these institutions for their help, trust, and the many opportunities generously offered. The cost of reproducing images has been covered both by my IUF research endowment and by copyright-holders courteously waiving their rights.

Beyond sponsorship, detail research was furthered thanks to the following custodian institutions' deposits and the thorough dedication of their staff. I am delighted to acknowledge the help of the following: at Abbotsford Trust, Abbotsford, Claudia Bolling; at the Beinecke Rare Book and Manuscript Library, New Haven, Mary Ellen Budney, Paul Civitelli, Moira Fitzgerald, Anne Marie Menta, John Monahan, Kevin Repp, Natalia Sciarini, Adrienne Leigh Sharpe, all keen to satisfy my numerous requests; at the Berg Collection, New York Public Library, Emma Davidson; at the Blair Museum of Lithophanes, Ohio, Julia LaBay Darrah; at the Bodmer Collection, Geneva, Nicolas Ducimetière, Yoann Givry, and Sonia Manaï; at the British Library, Karen Limper-Herz and Paul Terry; at Columbia University, Rare Book and Manuscript Library, Jane Siegel; at the Deutsches Literatur Archiv, Marbach am Neckar, Helmuth Mojem; at Dr Williams's Library, London, Jane Giscombe; at the Faust-Museum, Knittlingen, Denise Roth and her collaborators; at the Free Library of Philadelphia, Caitlin Goodman; at the Freies Deutsches Hochstift, Frankfurter Goethe-Museum, Frankfurt am Main, Anne Bohnenkamp-Renken, Sonja Gehrisch, Carina Koch, Joachim Seng, Nina Sonntag, Andreas Wehrheim, and Esther Woldemariam; at the Galerie David d'Angers, Angers, Véronique Boidard and Fabrice Rubiella; at the Goethe- u. Schiller-Archiv, Weimar, Gabriele Klunkert, Johannes Korngiebel, Ariane Ludwig, and their colleagues who promptly pursued queries and answered questions; at the Goethe-Museum, Düsseldorf, Heike Spies; at the Herzogin Anna Amalia Bibliothek, Weimar, custodians and staff who attended requests, reserved a booth and relentlessly convoyed books, prints, and other material; at the Hochschule für Bildende Künste, Dresden, Simone Fugger von dem Rech; at Johns Hopkins University, Milton S. Eisenhower Library, Amy K. Kimball; at the London School of Hygiene & Tropical Medicine, Victoria Cranna and Claire Frankland; at the Médiathèque, Angers, Marc-Édouard Gautier; at the Robert B. Haas Family Arts Library, Yale University, Jen Aloi and staff; at the Sächsische Landes- u. Universitätsbibliothek (SLUB), Dresden, Kerstin Vogl; at Sidney Sussex College, Cambridge, Nicholas Rogers; at the Staatliche Kunstsammlungen Dresden, Kupferstich-Kabinett, Petra Kuhlmann-Hodick and Angela Rietschel; at the Städtische Galerie Dresden, Cornelia Fünfstück, Kristin Gäbler, Carolin Quermann, and Andrea Rudolph; at the Stiftung Preußische Schlösser und Gärten Berlin-Brandenburg, Michaela Völkel and Eva Wollschläger; at the University of Minnesota Libraries, Timothy J. Johnson; at the Vienna Theatre Museum, Rudi Risatti; at the Yale Center for British Art, Elisabeth Fairman, Amelia Giordano, and Francis Lapka; at the Yale University Art Gallery, Suzanne Greenawalt; and at Yale University Library, Genevieve Coyle and Judith Ann Schiff.

I express sincere thanks to collectors Andrew Cook, Detlev Dauer, and Peter-Christian Wegner for having liberally shared their treasures and knowledge, and agreeing to see them reproduced in this book. The present owners of the two later versions of Francesco Hayez's *Il Bacio* being unidentified, but the place of these versions in art history being critical to the argument set out here, it is hoped the new insights into Hayez's inspiration and their origins that this book purveys will amply make up for any omissions.

For permissions to reproduce prints, books, drawings and objects, I am indebted to the Adolf and Luisa Haeuser Foundation, Frankfurt am Main; the Beinecke Rare Book and Manuscript Library, Yale University; the Bibliothèque nationale de France and the Bibliothèque-musée de l'Opéra, Paris; the Blair Museum of Lithophanes, Toledo, Ohio; the Deutsches Literatur Archiv, Marbach; the Faust-Museum, Knittlingen; the Free Library of Philadelphia; the Freies Deutsches Hochstift and Goethe-Museum, Frankfurt; the Harvard Art Museums and Houghton Library, Harvard; the Heidelberg University Library; the Käthe Kollwitz Museum, Cologne; the Klassik Stiftung Weimar; the Kunsthistorisches Museum, Vienna; the Kupferstich-Kabinett, Staatliche Kunstsammlungen Dresden; the London School of Hygiene & Tropical Medicine and Ross family; the Martin Bodmer Foundation, Geneva; Hergé-Tintin*imaginatio* S.A. for Hergé's creations; the Museum Georg Schäfer, Schweinfurt; the New York Public Library; the Prussian Palaces and Gardens Foundation Berlin-Brandenburg; the Pinacoteca di Brera, Milan; the Réunion des Musées Nationaux, Paris; the SLUB and the Staatliche Kunstsammlungen, Dresden; the Staatliche Museen zu Berlin; the Städtische Galerie Dresden; the Stiftung Weimarer Klassik, Weimar; and the V&A Theatre Collection, London.

I am particularly indebted to Gudrun Bernhardt for careful manuscript transcriptions; to Andreas Schlüter and his team (HAAB, Weimar), as well as Mary Ellen Budney and the photographic studio at Yale University, for their lavish contribution to this book's iconography; I am pleased to record the testimony of Sandra Markham re. her ancestor Catharine Potter Stith and the latter's offspring, and thank both Michael Tichatschke and son Nils Seifert, family proprietors of Retzsch's vine slopes and house (*Retzschgut*), for their welcome in Radebeul.

Without the publishing team's dedication and love for books, this volume would have looked very different. I gratefully acknowledge the guidance of Ivo Romain and particularly my desk editor, Gera van Bedaf, for painstakingly steering this book through realisation. Any oversights remain my own.

My special thanks go to fellow scholars who have generously given of themselves: Paul Aron, Jean-Louis Backès, Andreas Beck, Jens Bergner, Patrick Berthier, Laurel Brake, Matheusz Chmurski, Robyn Creswell, Jean-Charles Geslot, Tom Gretton, Antony Griffiths, Rudolf Henning, Petra Kuhlmann-Hodick, Graham Jefcoate, Edmund M. B. King, Ralf Klausnitzer, Catriona MacLeod, Michel Melot, Helmut Mojem, Jean-Yves Mollier, Élisabeth Parinet, Paola Pallottino, Joëlle Raineau, Viera Rebolledo-Dhuin, Ruth-Ellen Saint-Onge, Bethan Stevens, Jolanta Talbierska, Michael Twyman, Gerd-Helge Vogel, and countless others for information exchanged.

Friendship and affection have escorted me throughout. It is a great pleasure to mention here fellow translator, close friend and aviator Gernot Krämer for discussing nuances and gradations in translation from German into English and for an inspiring flight over Berlin; and my American friends Anna Sigridur Arnar, Ellen Gruber Garvey, and Kristen Ghodsee, for precious guidance in seeking a publisher suitable for this book. Others were good enough to release peer reviews of the manuscript, and I thank all those involved for their constructive comments.

I have been guided in English with extra husbandry and care. Christopher Stead knows better than anybody else what the result would have been without his unflinching dedication and enthusiasm.

Evanghelia Stead
Paris, 4 November 2022, 20 March 2023

Figures

1.1   Moritz Retzsch stopping little Christel on her way to water duty with the complicity of Julie Renovanz and siblings watching from the upstairs window, coloured drawing in *Weinbergs Scenen, aus dem Leben der beiden Brüder August und Moritz Retzsch*. SKK, Inv. Nr. Ca 53 v 98, Dresden, photo Caterina Micksch   29

1.2   Julianne Henriette (Julie) Renovanz, hand-made silk embroidery accompanied by verse as a friendship gift, 12 January 1806. Friendship album of Moritz Retzsch. SLUB / Deutsche Fotothek, Mscr.Dresd.App.3044, 103r., Dresden   30

1.3   Moritz Retzsch courting Christel, coloured drawing in *Weinbergs Scenen, aus dem Leben der beiden Brüder August und Moritz Retzsch*. SKK, Inv. Nr. Ca 53 v 99, Dresden, photo Caterina Micksch   31

1.4   Moritz Retzsch, *Carl Boromäus von Miltitz and Auguste von Miltitz*, double portrait lost in World War II. Reproduced in *Der Cicerone. Halbmonatsschrift für die Interessen des Kunstforschers & Sammlers* 16, no. 11 (1924): 508. Heidelberg University Library   32

1.5   Moritz Retzsch, self-portrait, signed and dated 1811, black chalk on tinted paper, heightened with white, 24.3 × 18.8 cm, from the so-called "Carus album." SGK, Inv.Nr. 1978/k 182, Museen der Stadt Dresden, photo Franz Zadniček   35

1.6   Moritz Retzsch, *Fancy*, wood engraving by Dalziel in the series "Selections from the Portfolio of Moritz Retzsch," *Art Journal*, n.s., 4 (July 1852): 224. BnF, V-3101, Paris   38

1.7   *Silenus*, drawing by Moritz Retzsch engraved by Krüger, first plate contributed to Wilhelm Gottlieb Becker, ed., *Augusteum: Dresden's antike Denkmäler enthaltend* (Leipzig: Auf Kosten der Verfassers und in Commission, C. A. Hempel et al.), 2 (1808): fig. 71. SLUB Dresden / Deutsche Fotothek, 23.2.83-2,Taf, Dresden   41

1.8   Moritz Retzsch, Faust meeting Gretchen, *Umrisse zu Goethe's Faust gezeichnet von Retsch* (Stuttgart & Tübingen: Cotta, 1816), pl. 8. Courtesy HAAB, F 3487, Weimar   46

1.9   Gustav Heinrich Naeke, *Faust and Gretchen*, lost painting, c.1812. Repr. in *Katalog zur Ausstellung deutscher Kunst aus der Zeit von 1775–1875 in der Königlichen Nationalgalerie Berlin* (Munich: F. Bruckmann, 1906), 2:401, no. 1234. Courtesy HAAB, Ku 4° II A—210 (2), Weimar   46

1.10   Peter Cornelius, *Scene upon Leaving the Church. Faust Proffers Gretchen his Arm*, in *XII Bilder zu Göthe's Faust gezeichnet von Peter von Cornelius* (Frankfurt am Main: Johann Friedrich Wenner, n.d.), pl. 5. Courtesy Beinecke, Yale University, Folio Speck Ck99 C7 816   46

1.11   Gustav Heinrich Naeke, preliminary pencil and ink sketches, n.d., 19.6 × 31.8 cm. Courtesy Beinecke, Yale University, YCGL Mss. 26, box 2, folder 23   47

1.12a   *Faust. Scene in the Street. Faust and Margaret, Mephistopheles in the Background*, engraved by C. A. Schwerdgeburth after Gustav Heinrich Naeke, 10.5 × 7.3 cm. Insert plate in *Urania: Taschenbuch für Damen auf das Jahr 1815 mit neun Kupfern* (Leipzig & Altenburg: Friedrich Brockhaus, [1814]). Courtesy HAAB, F 9144, Weimar   47

1.12b   Faust Meeting Gretchen after Gustav Heinrich Naeke, lithographed by Johann Nepomuk Strixner, 1822, chalk lithograph, 28.5 × 18.8 cm. Courtesy HAAB, F 8052 gr [b] (45), Weimar   47

2.1a–b	*Umrisse zu Goethe's Faust gezeichnet von Retsch* (Stuttgart & Tübingen: Cotta, 1816). Original yellow portfolio with green flaps, shut and open with contents. Courtesy HAAB, F 3487, Weimar 53
2.2	*Umrisse zu Goethe's Faust gezeichnet von Retsch* (Stuttgart & Tübingen: Cotta, 1816). Label with Goethe's autograph, 7 December 1818, and Tsarina Maria Feodorovna's inscription. Courtesy Beinecke, Yale University, Speck Ck99 R3 +816 Copy 2 56
2.3	*Umrisse zu Goethe's Faust gezeichnet von Retsch* (Stuttgart & Tübingen: Cotta, 1820). With Goethe's dedication to L. John Vigoureux, 3 July 1827. Courtesy Martin Bodmer Foundation, Geneva 57
2.4a–b	(*top*) Moritz Retzsch, *Faust*, preliminary pencil drawing, n.d., 15.8 × 15 cm; (*bottom*) same scene further developed, n.d., 14.2 × 12.3 cm Courtesy HAAB, F gr 9228, Weimar; and: SKK, C 5056, Dresden, photo Andreas Diesend 68
2.5	Moritz Retzsch, Faust drinks the potion in the witch's kitchen, chemical-stained preliminary pencil drawing, n.d., 14.8 × 16.4 cm. SKK, C 5060, Dresden, photo Andreas Diesend 70
2.6	Moritz Retzsch, double strip of several drawings, n.d., overall 28.6 × 34.3 cm. SKK, C 1937–1500, Dresden, photo Andreas Diesend 71
2.7	Moritz Retzsch, Margaret at the spinning wheel, final pencil drawing, n.d., 13 × 14.7 cm. SKK, C 5074, Dresden, photo Andreas Diesend 72
2.8	Moritz Retzsch, Valentine dying accuses his sister, *Umrisse zu Goethe's Faust gezeichnet von Retsch* (Stuttgart & Tübingen: Cotta, 1816), pl. 20. Courtesy HAAB, F 3487, Weimar 73
2.9	Moritz Retzsch, Faust and Mephistopheles in Margaret's chamber with Margaret also present, blotched preliminary pencil drawing with Mephistopheles stylus-retraced, n.d., 16.1 × 17.8 cm. SKK, C 5063, Dresden, photo Andreas Diesend 74
2.10	Moritz Retzsch, Faust and Mephistopheles in Margaret's chamber, *Umrisse zu Goethe's Faust gezeichnet von Retsch* (Stuttgart & Tübingen: Cotta, 1816), pl. 10. Courtesy HAAB, F 3487, Weimar 75
2.11	Engelbert Seibertz, composition inspired by Retzsch, in *Faust: Eine Tragödie von Goethe. Mit Zeichnungen von Engelbert Seibertz* (Stuttgart & Tübingen: J. G. Cotta, 1854), 93, wood engraving in text. Courtesy HAAB, F gr 11196, Weimar 76
2.12	August von Kreling, composition inspired by Retzsch, in *Faust von Goethe, erster Theil. Mit Bildern und Zeichnungen von A. v. Kreling* (Munich: F. Bruckmann, [1875]), 85, wood engraving in text. Courtesy HAAB, F gr 5787, Weimar 76
2.13	Moritz Retzsch, preliminary drawings for Faust and Margaret kissing, n.d., 16.1 × 18.1 cm. SKK, C 4890, Dresden, photo Andreas Diesend 78
2.14	Moritz Retzsch, drawing for Faust and Margaret kissing, n.d., 13.6 × 15 cm. SKK, C 5073, Dresden, photo Andreas Diesend 78
2.15	Moritz Retzsch, Faust and Margaret kissing, drawing, n.d., 13.6 × 12 cm. SKK, C 5071, Dresden, photo Andreas Diesend 79
2.16	Moritz Retzsch, Faust and Margaret kissing, final drawing used for the etched plate, n.d., 14 × 16.3 cm. SKK, C 5070, Dresden, photo Andreas Diesend 79
2.17	Moritz Retzsch, Final prison scene, *Umrisse zu Goethe's Faust gezeichnet von Retsch* (Stuttgart & Tübingen: Cotta, 1816), pl. 26. Courtesy HAAB, F 3487, Weimar 81

FIGURES

2.18   Moritz Retzsch, The witch's kitchen, *Umrisse zu Goethe's Faust gezeichnet von Retsch* (Stuttgart & Tübingen: Cotta, 1816), pl. 6. Courtesy HAAB, F 3487, Weimar   82

2.19   Moritz Retzsch, Faust drinks the potion in the witch's kitchen, *Umrisse zu Goethe's Faust gezeichnet von Retsch* (Stuttgart & Tübingen: Cotta, 1816), pl. 7. Courtesy HAAB, F 3487, Weimar   83

2.20   Moritz Retzsch, Faust and Mephistopheles galloping past the Rabenstein, *Umrisse zu Goethe's Faust gezeichnet von Retsch* (Stuttgart & Tübingen: Cotta, 1816), pl. 24. Courtesy HAAB, F 3487, Weimar   84

2.21   Moritz Retzsch, Faust and Mephistopheles in Faust's study, *Umrisse zu Goethe's Faust gezeichnet von Retsch* (Stuttgart & Tübingen: Cotta, 1816), pl. 4. Courtesy HAAB, F 3487, Weimar   85

2.22   Moritz Retzsch, The poodle appearing in open country, coloured version, n.d., 14.6 × 19.4 cm. *Umrisse zu Goethe's Faust gezeichnet von Retsch* (Stuttgart & Tübingen: Cotta, 1816), pl. 2. FDH, Frankfurter Goethe-Museum, III-13099, Frankfurt   90

2.23   Moritz Retzsch, Faust's study with the poodle growing, coloured version, n.d., 13.9 × 15.8 cm. *Umrisse zu Goethe's Faust gezeichnet von Retsch* (Stuttgart & Tübingen: Cotta, 1816), pl. 3. FDH, Frankfurter Goethe-Museum, III-13098, Frankfurt   90

2.24   Moritz Retzsch, Margaret discovers the jewels, coloured version, n.d., *c.*14 × 16.7 cm. *Umrisse zu Goethe's Faust gezeichnet von Retsch* (Stuttgart & Tübingen: Cotta, 1816), pl. 11. FDH, Frankfurter Goethe-Museum, III-13100, Frankfurt   91

2.25   Moritz Retzsch, At the neighbour's house, coloured version, n.d., 23 × 31 cm. Courtesy FDH, Frankfurter Goethe-Museum, III-13929, Frankfurt   91

2.26   In Martha's garden, anonymous coloured version, n.d., 14.5 × 15.3 cm, after Moritz Retzsch, *Umrisse zu Goethe's Faust gezeichnet von Retsch* (Stuttgart & Tübingen: Cotta, 1816), pl. 14. Courtesy HAAB, F gr 9228, Weimar   93

3.1a   *Umrisse zu Goethe's Faust, gezeichnet von Retzsch in 26 Blättern* (Stuttgart & Tübingen: Cotta, 1830), pl. 16. Exemplar from Franz Glück's library. DLA, Glück: HH/Goethe: D, Marbach   98

3.1b   Moritz Retzsch, Margaret at the spinning wheel, *Umrisse zu Goethe's Faust gezeichnet von Retsch* (Stuttgart & Tübingen: Cotta, 1816), pl. 16. Courtesy HAAB, F 3487, Weimar   98

3.2   Moritz Retzsch, Faust and Gretchen, pencil drawing, n.d., 13.5 × 9.3 cm. Courtesy Beinecke, Yale University, YCGL Mss. 26, box 1, folder 12   100

3.3   Moritz Retzsch, *Faust*, pencil and chalk double portrait drawing with highlights on tinted paper, n.d., 35.9 × 31 cm. Courtesy HAAB, F gr 5824 (5), Weimar   100

3.4   Moritz Retzsch, Faust and Gretchen(?), double portrait, pencil drawing on tinted paper, n.d., 27.6 × 36.5 cm. Courtesy HAAB, F gr 5824 (4), Weimar   100

3.5   Moritz Retzsch, Faust and Gretchen in the garden, pencil drawing, 1847, 16.7 × 20.6 cm. FDH, Frankfurter Goethe-Museum, III-02828, Frankfurt   100

3.6   *Umrisse zu Goethe's Faust, zweiter Theil. Gezeichnet von Moritz Retzsch. Elf Platten, nebst Andeutungen* (Stuttgart & Augsburg: J.G. Cotta, 1836). Original blue portfolio with fuchsia flaps. Courtesy Beinecke, Yale University, Speck Ck99 R3 +836b   103

3.7   Moritz Retzsch, Mephistopheles lulls Faust to sleep, *Umrisse zu Goethe's Faust, erster Theil. Gezeichnet von Moritz Retzsch. Von dem Verfasser selbst retouchirt und mit einigen neuen Platten vermehrt* (Stuttgart & Tübingen: J. G. Cotta, 1834), insert pl. 5. Courtesy HAAB, F 3478, Weimar   104

3.8	Final full-page Cotta advertisement dated October 1836, in *Umrisse zu Goethe's Faust, zweiter Theil. Gezeichnet von Moritz Retzsch. Elf Platten, nebst Andeutungen* (Stuttgart & Augsburg: J. G. Cotta, 1836). Courtesy Beinecke, Yale University, Speck Ck 99 R3 + 836c 105
3.9	Christian Votteler, coloured lithographic cover, *Umrisse zu Goethes Faust, erster und zweiter Theil gezeichnet von Moritz Retzsch. Erster Theil neunundzwanzig Platten, Zweiter Theil elf Platten* (Stuttgart: J. G. Cotta, n.d. [1884?]. Courtesy HAAB, F gr 3493, Weimar 107
3.10a	Back cover with title and publisher's imprint of *Faust von Goethe in 26 Umrissen* (Göttingen: Dieterich, n.d. [c.1827]). Courtesy HAAB, F 3489, Weimar 111
3.10b	Front cover of the same with an outline reproduction after Johannes Riepenhausen. Courtesy HAAB, F 3489, Weimar 111
3.11	Johannes Riepenhausen, *Faust's Meeting with Gretchen in front of the Church*, 1811, black chalk, heightened with white, paper mounted on cardboard, 47.1 × 38.1 cm. Courtesy Museum Georg Schäfer, MGS 1148A, Schweinfurt 111
3.12	Eberhard Emminger, chalk lithograph in black on light beige plate after Johannes Riepenhausen, *Faust's First Meeting with Gretchen*, with relevant verses from Goethe's *Faust* as captions, 1827, 48.2 × 38.2 cm (Stuttgart: G. Ebnerschen Kunsthandlung). FDH, Frankfurter Goethe-Museum, III-04375, Frankfurt 111
3.13	*Kleines Geschenk zum neuen Jahr für 1818* and *Kleines Geschenk zum neuen Jahr für 1820*, almanacs published in Frankfurt by Jaeger. FDH, Frankfurter Goethe-Museum, Library, XI T 124 (1818) and XI T 124/2 (1820), Frankfurt 112
3.14a–c	*Kleines Geschenk zum neuen Jahr für 1818* (Frankfurt: Jaeger), three of the five copied and re-focussed plates after Moritz Retzsch's outlines. Page numbers in the *Faust* quotes used as captions refer to the 1816 *Faust* pocket edition issued by Cotta, as in the *Umrisse* edition. FDH, Frankfurter Goethe-Museum, Library, XI T 124 (1818), Frankfurt 113
3.15a–c	*Kleines Geschenk zum neuen Jahr für 1820* (Frankfurt: Jaeger), three of the seven copied and re-focussed plates after Moritz Retzsch's outlines. FDH, Frankfurter Goethe-Museum, Library, XI T 124/2 (1820), Frankfurt 114
3.16a–b	*Kleines Geschenk zum neuen Jahr für 1820* (Frankfurt: Jaeger), frontispiece, title-page vignette, and pl. 3. FDH, Frankfurter Goethe-Museum, Library, XI T 124/2 (1820), Frankfurt 115
3.17a	Wilhelm Eytel, *Faust Handing over the Pledge to the Devil*, woodcut after Moritz Retzsch, in *Das ärgerliche Leben und schreckliche Ende des vielberüchtigten Erz-Schwarzkünstlers Johannis Fausti. Erstlich vor vielen Jahren fleißig beschrieben von Georg Rudolf Widmann. Hernach übersehen und wieder herausgegeben von Pfitzer*, new edition decorated with 16 woodcuts (Reutlingen: Kurtz, 1834), 34. Compare with Retzsch's pl. 4, Fig. 2.21. Courtesy HAAB, F 456, Weimar 116
3.17b	Wilhelm Eytel, *The Holy Angels as Servants before God's Throne*, woodcut after Moritz Retzsch but deleting Mephistopheles, in *Das ärgerliche Leben und schreckliche Ende des vielberüchtigten Erz-Schwarzkünstlers Johannis Fausti*, new edition decorated with 16 woodcuts (Reutlingen: Kurtz, 1834), 54. Compare with Retzsch's pl. 1, Fig. 5.1. Courtesy HAAB, F 456, Weimar 117
3.18	Unique compound volume, with (*right*) Henry Moses's English engraving copied after Retzsch entitled *Mephistopheles Leaves Rich Ornaments in*

	Margaret's Chamber, and (*left*) two pages from the 1816 *Faust* pocket edition by Cotta carefully cut and inlaid (pp. 179 and 180). Courtesy HAAB, F gr 5276, Weimar 118
4.1	Charles Murton, black calf binding with rich gilt decorations showing Faust in his study with the poodle. The bound volume coalesces *Extracts from Göthe's Tragedy of Faustus, Explanatory of the Plates, by Retsch, Intended to Illustrate that Work. Translated by George Soane* (London: Printed for J. H. Bohte, 1820) and *Umrisse zu Goethe's Faust, gezeichnet von Retsch* (Stuttgart & Tübingen: Cotta, 1820). Pages inlaid to create a uniform objet. Courtesy Beinecke, Yale University, Speck Ck99 R3 +820b 130
4.2	Albrecht Dürer, *Saint Jerome in his Study*, 1514, engraving, 24.6 × 18.7 cm. BnF Est., Réserve CA-4 (+, 4)-Boîte Ecu, Paris 131
4.3	Moritz Retzsch, Faust's study with the poodle monstrously growing, *Umrisse zu Goethe's Faust gezeichnet von Retsch* (Stuttgart & Tübingen: Cotta, 1816), pl. 3. Courtesy HAAB, F 3487, Weimar 132
4.4a–c	Thomas Frognall Dibdin, *A Bibliographical, Antiquarian and Picturesque Tour in France and Germany* (London: Printed for the Author by W. Bulmer and W. Nicol, Shakspeare Press, 1821), 3:122–27. Three openings with woodcuts by John Byfield reproducing Dibdin's cutouts as set in his commentary. Courtesy Beinecke, Yale University, X350 +821 (3) 134–35
5.1	Moritz Retzsch, Prologue in Heaven, *Umrisse zu Goethe's Faust gezeichnet von Retsch* (Stuttgart & Tübingen: Cotta, 1816), pl. 1. Courtesy HAAB, F 3487, Weimar 141
5.2	Henry Moses, *Introduction*, engraved copy after Moritz Retzsch, in *Retsch's Series of Twenty-Six Outlines, Illustrative of Goethe's Tragedy of Faust* (London: Boosey & Sons, Rodwell and Martin, 1820), pl. 1. Courtesy HAAB, F gr 5785, Weimar 142
5.3	John Flaxman, *Il sol degli angeli* or *Circle of Angels around the Sun*, outline drawing engraved by Tommaso Piroli after Dante's *Paradise*, canto 10. *La Divina Commedia di Dante Alighieri* (Rome, 1802), pl. 10. BnF Est., Ta-32-4, Paris 143
5.4	(*top*) Henry Moses, *Faust and Mephistopheles in the Witch's Cave*, engraved copy after Moritz Retzsch, in *Retsch's Series of Twenty-Six Outlines, Illustrative of Goethe's Tragedy of Faust* (London: Boosey & Sons, Rodwell and Martin, 1820), pl. 6; (*bottom*) Moritz Retzsch, The witch's kitchen, *Umrisse zu Goethe's Faust gezeichnet von Retsch* (Stuttgart & Tübingen: Cotta, 1816), pl. 6. Courtesy HAAB, F gr 5785 and F 3487, Weimar 144
5.5	Henry Füssli, *The Night Mare (Le Cauchemar)*, 1782, coloured etching and stippled engraving. BnF Est., Ca18C-1 (Füssli, Johann Heinrich)-Fol, Paris 145
5.6	Henry Moses, *The Witches' Revel*, engraved copy after Moritz Retzsch, in *Retsch's Series of Twenty-Six Outlines, Illustrative of Goethe's Tragedy of Faust* (London: Boosey & Sons, Rodwell and Martin, 1820), pl. 22. Courtesy HAAB, F gr 5785, Weimar 146
5.7	Moritz Retzsch, Walpurgis Night, *Umrisse zu Goethe's Faust gezeichnet von Retsch* (Stuttgart & Tübingen: Cotta, 1816), pl. 22. Courtesy HAAB, F 3487, Weimar 147
5.8	Peter Cornelius, *Prelude in the Theatre, with the Painter's Dedication*, in *XII Bilder zu Göthe's Faust gezeichnet von Peter von Cornelius* (Frankfurt am Main: Johann Friedrich Wenner, n.d.), pl. 2. Courtesy Beinecke, Yale University, Folio Speck Ck99 C7 816 150

5.9	Henry Moses, *Frontispiece*, outline etching after Peter Cornelius facing the title-page, with the inscription "Drawn and Engraved by Henry Moses," in *Faustus: from the German of Goethe* (London: Boosey and Sons, Rodwell & Martin, 1821). Courtesy Beinecke, Yale University, Speck Ck99 R3 +821 Copy 1 151
5.10a	Circular ornament with vignettes after Moritz Retzsch, pasted on petrol-green paper boards, *Faustus: from the German of Goethe* (London: Boosey and Sons, Rodwell & Martin, 1821). Courtesy HAAB, F gr 5288, Weimar 152
5.10b	Circular ornament inserted between half title and frontispiece, in *Faustus: from the German of Goethe* (London: Boosey and Sons, Rodwell & Martin, 1821). Exemplar owned in turn by C. Wood, Amos Niven Wilder, American poet, minister and theology professor, and his bother, the novelist and playwright Thornton Niven Wilder. Courtesy Beinecke, Yale University, Speck Zab W 6445+Zz 821 G 153
5.11a–c	Kinetic effect in *Faustus: From the German of Goethe. Embellished with Retsch's Series of Twenty-Seven Outlines, Illustrative of the Tragedy, Engraved by Henry Moses. Third edition* (London: Boosey and Sons, 1824), plates inserted between pp. 30–31. Courtesy Beinecke, Yale University, Speck Ck99 R3 +824 155
5.12	Title-page of *Faustus: From the German of Goethe. Embellished with Retsch's Series of Twenty-Seven Outlines, Illustrative of the Tragedy, Engraved by Henry Moses. Third edition* (London: Boosey and Sons, 1824). Courtesy Beinecke, Yale University, Speck Ck99 R3 +824 158
5.13	Title-page of *Faustus: From the German of Goethe. Embellished with Retsch's Series of Twenty-Seven Outlines, Illustrative of the Tragedy, Engraved by Henry Moses. New edition. And An Appendix Containing the May-Day Night Scene Translated by Percy Bysshe Shelley* (London: Edward Lumley, 1832). With "The Kiss" plate mounted as frontispiece. Courtesy HAAB, F 3495, Weimar 158
5.14	Moritz Retzsch, Faust and Mephistopheles ascend the Brocken, *Umrisse zu Goethe's Faust gezeichnet von Retsch* (Stuttgart & Tübingen: Cotta, 1816), pl. 21. Courtesy HAAB, F 3487, Weimar 159
5.15	*Mephistopheles Obtains from God Permission to Tempt Faustus*, lithographic copy after Moritz Retzsch, in *Faustus: Illustrated in Twenty-Six Outlines by Retsch* (London: H. Berthoud, 1825), pl. 1. Courtesy HAAB, F 3496, Weimar 160
5.16	*Faustus with the Dog in the Cabinet*, lithographic copy after Moritz Retzsch, in *Faustus: Illustrated in Twenty-Six Outlines by Retsch* (London: H. Berthoud, 1825), pl. 3. Courtesy HAAB, F 3496, Weimar 161
5.17	(top) Pictorial pink cover by John Berryman for *Retzsch's Outlines to Goethe's Faust, Adapted to Illustrate Any Edition of FAUST, But Particularly the Translation of Lord F. L. Gower to Whom They Are Most Respectfully Dedicated* (London: James Bulcock, 1827; (*bottom*) Moritz Retzsch, The witch's kitchen, *Umrisse zu Goethe's Faust gezeichnet von Retsch* (Stuttgart & Tübingen: Cotta, 1816), pl. 7. Courtesy Beinecke, Yale University, Speck Ck99 R3 +827b; and: courtesy HAAB, F 348 7, Weimar 164
5.18	Johann Wilhelm Frey, six vignettes after Moritz Retzsch, cover and title leaf of *Faust: dramatisch Dichtstuk van Goethe. Nagevolgd door H. Frijlink. Met een zestal schetsen, naar teekeningen van Moritz Retzsch* (Amsterdam: Frijlink / Spin, 1865). Courtesy HAAB, F 3988, Weimar 165

FIGURES

XIX

5.19   Green commercial binding with gilt pictorial title for *Goethe's Faust by Retzsch, Engraved by Henry Moses* (London: Tilt and Bogue, 1843). Courtesy Beinecke, Yale University, Speck Ck99 R3 +843   171

5.20   Green commercial binding with gilt pictorial title for *Illustrations of Goethe's Faust by Moritz Retzsch, Engraved by Henry Moses* (London: Tilt and Bogue, 1843). Courtesy HAAB, F 3477, Weimar   171

5.21   John Leighton, decorative spine design, industrial cloth binding for both parts of *Faust: A Tragedy, by J. Wolfgang von Goethe. Translated into English Verse by J. Birch, Esq.* (London: Black and Armstrong, 1839; Chapman and Hall, 1843). Courtesy Beinecke, Yale University, Speck Rc37 +c839   172

5.22   Moritz Retzsch, outline engraving from *Faust II*, in *Umrisse zu Goethe's Faust, erster und zweiter Theil. Erster Theil neun und zwanzig Platten. Zweiter Theil elf Platten gezeichnet von Moritz Retzsch* (Stuttgart: Cotta, 1836), pl. 10. Courtesy HAAB, F 3479 Weimar   173

5.23   Bookplates of Robert Hoe III and gift of James Laughlin, front pastedown of *Faust: A Tragedy, by J. Wolfgang von Goethe. Translated into English Verse by J. Birch, Esq.* (London: Black and Armstrong, 1839; Chapman and Hall, 1843). Courtesy Beinecke, Yale University, Speck Rc37 +c839   174

6.1a–b   Eugène Delacroix, freehand copies of Moritz Retzsch's outline engravings, pl. 16 (Margaret at the spinning wheel), pl. 18 (woman, cathedral scene), pl. 11 (Margaret admiring the jewels) and pl. 12 (proffering her arm to Martha). ML, RF 10215 recto and verso. Courtesy RMN GP, photo © Michèle Bellot   177

6.2   Eugène Delacroix, freehand copies of Margaret (pl. 13), Martha (pl. 12, 13, 14), and a lady from the cathedral scene (pl. 18, visible rotating the image 180°) by Moritz Retzsch. ML, RF 10340, courtesy RMN GP, photo © Michèle Bellot   178

6.3   Eugène Delacroix, early sketches for Goethe's *Faust* after Moritz Retzsch, c.1821, pencil on wove paper, 19.6 × 30.8 cm. HAM / FM, 1929.308, Gift of Dr. Charles L. Kuhn, photo President and Fellows of Harvard College   178

6.4   Pinéas, *Faust signe le pacte avec Méphistophélés*, engraved copy of Moritz Retzsch's pl. 4 used as frontispiece to Nerval's translation, in *Faust: Tragédie de Goëthe, nouvelle traduction complète, en prose et en vers, par Gérard* (Paris: Dondey-Dupré, 1828). BnF, Réserve 8-Re-13257, Paris   181

6.5   Jean-Baptiste Muret, *Méphistophélès obtient de Dieu la permission de tenter Faust*, lithographic copy of Moritz Retzsch's pl. 1, in *Faust* (Paris: Auvray, n.d. [1824]). BnF, 8-RIC-71, Paris   182

6.6   Jean-Baptiste Muret, *Marguerite dans sa chambre*, lithographic copy of Moritz Retzsch's pl. 9, in *Faust* (Paris: Auvray, n.d. [1824]), to compare with Fig. 9.6. BnF, 8-RIC-71, Paris   183

6.7a–b   Front and back orange paper covers of Nerval's translation advertising Muret's second edition by Auvray Frères. *Faust: Tragédie de Goëthe, nouvelle traduction complète, en prose et en vers, par Gérard* (Paris: Dondey-Dupré, 1828). BnF, Réserve 8-Re-1325, Paris   185

6.8   *Faust. Vingt-six gravures d'après les dessins de Retzsch*, second and third edition with the Voïart preface (Paris: Audot, 1828 and 1829). BnF, Paris, author's photograph   186

6.9   Anonymous eye-catching Audot cover to *Faust. Vingt-six gravures d'après les dessins de Retsch* (Paris: Audot, 1828). BnF, 8-RIC-2, Paris   187

6.10   Trueb, engraved copy of pl. 1 after Moritz Retzsch replacing God by beaming rays, in *Faust. Vingt-six gravures d'après les dessins de Retsch* (Paris: Audot, 1828). BnF, 8-RIC-2, Paris   190

6.11	*Être suprême, Peuple souverain, République française*, coloured engraved print, 41.5 × 51.5 cm (À Paris: chez Basset, [*c.*1794]). De Vinck, 6288. BnF, Réserve QB-370 (46)-Ft 4, Paris 191
6.12	Etched title-page in *Faust: Esquisses dessinées par Retsch* (Paris: Giard, 1830). Courtesy Beinecke, Yale University, Speck Ck99 R3 +830b Copy 1 192
6.13	Cover for the Giard edition, lithographed by Alphonse Bichebois, 18.5 × 25 cm. BMO, Estampes scènes Faust (23), Paris 193
6.14	Spine with four interlocked double Ls surmounted by a count's crown between raised bands. Courtesy Beinecke, Yale University, Speck Ck99 R3 +830b Copy 1 194
6.15a–b	Trial lithograph and etching to best render Moritz Retzsch's outlines, after plates 23 (Faust accusing Mephistopheles) and 16 (Gretchen at the spinning wheel) in the Laborde exemplar. Courtesy Beinecke, Yale University, Speck Ck99 R3 +830b Copy 1 196
6.16a–b	Two versions of Goethe's portrait by Delacroix, lithographed by Dominique Vincent (later Meulenbergh) and by the Williaume brothers, in *Faust: Tragédie Ornée de 26 Gravures, d'un Beau Portrait de l'auteur, et accompagnée de notes de M. de Goëthe. Traduite par M. A. Stapfer* (Bruxelles: Librairie Romantique / Weissenbruch, 1828). Courtesy HAAB, G 349 and F 3858, Weimar 199
6.17	*Acht Umrisse zu den merkwürdigsten Scenen Faust's gezeichnet von M. Retzsch, c.*27.5 × 18 cm, eight outlines after Moritz Retzsch for *Faust I* and *II* as synoptic frontispiece for various editions of Goethe's works (Paris: Baudry, 1840s and 1850s). BnF & BMO, Estampes scènes Faust (14), Paris 202
6.18	Four woodcuts after Moritz Retzsch, in *Faust par Wolfgang Goethe: Traduit de l'allemand par Gérard de Nerval, précédé de la légende populaire de Johann Faust, l'un des inventeurs de l'imprimerie, illustré de jolies vignettes par Éd. Frère* (Paris: J. Bry aîné, 1850), 12–13. Courtesy HAAB, F gr 5293, Weimar 204
6.19	Anonymous vignette of Margaret undoing her hair in "Abend" after Moritz Retzsch, in Goethe, *Faust: Avec introduction, notes et commentaires par P. Labatut*, third edition (Paris: Masson, 1951), 168–69. Courtesy HAAB, N 10700, Weimar 205
6.20	Tony Johannot, Mephistopheles (after Moritz Retzsch) between Faust and Margaret in the prison scene, in *Le Faust de Goethe: Traduction revue et complète, précédée d'un essai sur Goethe par M. Henri Blaze. Édition illustrée par M. Tony Johannot* (Paris: Dutertre, 1847), insert engraving facing p. 192. BnF, Rés. M-Yh-2, Paris 207
6.21	Martha adorns Margaret with the jewels. Two images cut out and mounted by Achille Devéria opposite the corresponding *Faust* passage: (*left*) Muret's lithographic copy after Moritz Retzsch and (*right*) Johann Heinrich Ramberg's rendition of the scene engraved by J. Axmann (*Minerva: Taschenbuch*, 1828). BnF Est., Tb-55 (C)-Pet. fol., Paris 209
6.22	Unsigned cover for Goethe, *Faust: Traduction de Gérard de Nerval* (Paris: Librairie Gründ, 1938), republished within "La Bibliothèque précieuse" series. After Retzsch's pl. 14 (garden scene) following Édouard Frère's version. Author's collection and file 210
7.1	Moritz Retzsch, Faust and Gretchen on a bench with eavesdropper Mephistopheles, *Umrisse zu Goethe's Faust, erster Theil. Gezeichnet von Moritz Retzsch. Von dem Verfasser selbst retouchirt und mit einigen neuen Platten vermehrt* (Stuttgart & Tübingen: J. G. Cotta, 1834), insert pl. 19. Courtesy HAAB, F 3478, Weimar 214

FIGURES

7.2	Moritz Retzsch, Faust and Gretchen on a bench, stipple engraved by [Friedrich] Wagner, *Kupfersammlung zu Göthe's sämmtlichen Werken in vierzig Blättern* (Leipzig: Fleischer, 1829–34), plate meant for vol. 12 of the *Ausgabe letzter Hand*. Courtesy HAAB, F 3469, Weimar 215
7.3a	Moritz Retzsch, *Umrisse zu Schiller's Lied von der Glocke: nebst Andeutungen von Moritz Retzsch* (Stuttgart & Tübingen: J. G. Cotta, 1833), pl. 19. Courtesy HAAB, Bh 66, Weimar 216
7.3b	Charles Heath, *The German Lovers*, engraved after Moritz Retzsch, 22 × 15.2 cm, in *The Keepsake for 1835*, ed. by Frederic Mansel Reynolds (London: Longman, Rees, Orme, Brown, Green, and Longman; Paris: Rittner and Goupil; Berlin: A. Asher, 1835), insert plate between pp. 168–69. NYPL, New York 217
7.4	Faust and Gretchen kissing, signed and dated "G. R. 1822," ink drawing lifted from Moritz Retzsch's pl. 15, 38 × 16.9 cm. FDH, Frankfurter Goethe-Museum, III-10749, Frankfurt 218
7.5	Sheet of tracing paper with pencil copies of four Gretchen scenes and other outlines after Moritz Retzsch, n.d., 30 × 21.2 cm. FDH, Frankfurter Goethe-Museum, VIIId-kI, no. 14847, Frankfurt 219
7.6	(*top*) Ronald Ross, Faust and Mephistopheles smoking pipes, drawing lifted from Moritz Retzsch's pl. 7. From Ross landscape sketchbook in half leather, post 1872, 13.2 × 25.8 cm; (*bottom*) Moritz Retzsch, In the witch's kitchen, *Umrisse zu Goethe's Faust gezeichnet von Retsch* (Stuttgart & Tübingen: Cotta, 1816), pl. 7. Courtesy LSHTM, Gb 0809/Ross/158, © Ross Family / LSHTM, and: Courtesy HAAB, F 348 7, Weimar 222
7.7	(*top*) Ronald Ross, Mephistopheles sitting in a landscape, lifted from Moritz Retzsch's pl. 6. From Ross landscape sketchbook in half leather, post 1872, 13.2 × 25.8 cm; (*bottom*) Moritz Retzsch, The witch's kitchen, *Umrisse zu Goethe's Faust gezeichnet von Retsch* (Stuttgart & Tübingen: Cotta, 1816), pl. 6. LSHTM, Gb 0809/Ross/158, © Ross Family / LSHTM, and: Courtesy HAAB, F 348 7, Weimar 223
7.8	John Massey Wright after Moritz Retzsch, *The Kiss*, engraved by W. Humphreys, in *The Literary Souvenir; or, Cabinet of Poetry and Romance*, ed. Alaric A. Watts (London: Hurst, Robinson Co., 1826), insert plate between pp. 280-81. BnF, Z-33733, Paris 225
7.9	John Massey Wright after Moritz Retzsch, *The Decision of the Flower*, engraved by Charles Heath, used as frontispiece in *The Literary Souvenir; or, Cabinet of Poetry and Romance*, ed. Alaric A. Watts (London: Hurst, Robinson Co., 1825). BnF, Z-33732, Paris 225
7.10	Alexandre Colin, Faust and Margaret in the garden in troubadour style, lithographic print cut out and mounted by Achille Devéria in his *Faust* compendium. BnF Est., Tb-55 (C)-Pet. fol., Paris 226
7.11	Nicolas Maurin, *Marguerite consulte une fleur pour savoir si elle est aimée de Faust*, lithographic print cut out and mounted by Achille Devéria in his *Faust* compendium. BnF Est., Tb-55 (C)-Pet. fol., Paris 228
7.12	Édouard Robert, *La Décision de la fleur*, reverse lithographic print after Moritz Retzsch, cut out and mounted by Achille Devéria in his *Faust* compendium. BnF Est., Tb-55 (C)-Pet. fol., Paris 229
7.13	Friedrich August Zimmermann after Moritz Retzsch, *Scene from Goethe's Faust. Gretchen: "He loves me, he loves me not,"* lithograph, n.d., 35.5 × 49 cm, printed by G. Braunsdorf, published by Eduard Pietzsch and Co., Dresden. Courtesy HAAB, F gr 5822 (1), Weimar 230

7.14	Karl Müller after Moritz Retzsch, *Scene from Goethe's Faust. Gretchen: "He loves me, he loves me not,"* lithograph, n.d., 37.5 × 43.5 cm, printed by Carl Pohl and published by Eduard Pietsch [*sic*] and Co., Dresden. Courtesy HAAB, F gr 5822 (4), Weimar 230
7.15	Heinrich Ferdinand Grünewald after Moritz Retzsch, *Scene from Goethe's Faust. Gretchen: "He loves me, he loves me not,"* lithograph, n.d., 43 × 50 cm, printed in Grünewald's establishment. Courtesy HAAB, F gr 8052 [a] (39), Weimar 230
7.16	Unknown artist, embossed colour postcard after Goethe's garden scene, posted [19]07, 14 × 9 cm. Courtesy Faust-Museum, Moosmann Collection, Ill. 568, Knittlingen 231
7.17	Moritz Retzsch, Faust and Gretchen kissing, *Umrisse zu Goethe's Faust gezeichnet von Retsch* (Stuttgart & Tübingen: Cotta, 1816), pl. 15. Courtesy HAAB, F 3487, Weimar 232
7.18	Four prints on Faust and Margaret (three of their embrace) cut out and mounted post 1847 by Achille Devéria in his *Faust* compendium opposite the corresponding passage. BnF Est., Tb-55 (C)-Pet. fol., Paris 234
7.19	Nicolas Maurin, *Réunis dans un pavillon du jardin, Faust reçoit de Marguerite l'aveu du plus sincère amour*, lithographic print, n.d., cut out and mounted by Achille Devéria in his *Faust* compendium. BnF Est., Tb-55 (C)-Pet. fol., Paris 235
7.20	Friedrich Zimmermann after Retzsch, *Scene from Goethe's Faust. Gretchen: "Dearest of men, I love thee from my heart!"* lithograph, n.d., 35 × 50 cm, published by Eduard Pietzsch and Co., Dresden. Courtesy HAAB, F gr 5822 (7), Weimar 236
7.21a	Édouard Schuler after Moritz Retzsch, *Faust and Gretchen*, engraving, 1837, 12.5 × 19.5 cm, cut out by Alexander Tille, provenance unknown. Courtesy HAAB, F gr 8052 [b] (8), Weimar 237
7.21b	After Moritz Retzsch and following Édouard Schuler, *Faust and Gretchen*, steel engraving, post 1849, *Album aus der Damenzeitung Iris*, engraved and printed by the Art Institute of the Austrian Lloyd, published by E. Ludwig in Graz. Available in Paris and Vienna. Courtesy Peter-Christian Wegner 237
7.22	Carl Friedrich Patzschke after Moritz Retzsch, *"Dearest of men, I love thee from my heart!"* coloured lithographic copy, c.1880, 27 × 29 cm, printed in Berlin by L. Zöllner and commercialized by C. G. Ende. Courtesy HAAB, F gr 5822 (8), Weimar 238
7.23	Édouard Frère after Moritz Retzsch, *Quelle céleste image se montre dans ce miroir magique!*, woodcut by François Rouget, (enlarged) detail vignette of Faust contemplating the magic-mirror woman, in *Faust par Wolfgang Goethe: Traduit de l'allemand par Gérard de Nerval* (Paris: J. Bry aîné, 1850), 12b. Courtesy HAAB, F gr 5293, Weimar 243
7.24a	Édouard Frère after Moritz Retzsch, two woodcuts by François Rouget, in *Faust par Wolfgang Goethe: Traduit de l'allemand par Gérard de Nerval* (Paris: J. Bry aîné, 1850), 24–25. Courtesy HAAB, F gr 5293, Weimar 244
7.24b	Édouard Frère after Moritz Retzsch, four woodcuts by François Rouget, in *Faust par Wolfgang Goethe: Traduit de l'allemand par Gérard de Nerval* (Paris: J. Bry aîné, 1850), 34–35. Courtesy HAAB, F gr 5293, Weimar 244
7.25	Édouard Frère, front-page scene after Retzsch and series header, in *Faust par Wolfgang Goethe: Traduit de l'allemand par Gérard de Nerval* (Paris: J. Bry aîné, 1850), 1. Courtesy HAAB, F gr 5293, Weimar 245

FIGURES XXIII

7.26 Gaston Jourdain, photogravure by J. Chauvet, in *Le Faust de Goethe, traduction de Gérard de Nerval, préface de M. Frantz-Jourdain, illustrations inédites de Gaston Jourdain* (Paris: Imprimé pour la Société de Propagation des Livres d'Art, 1904), insert plate 8, between pp. 60–61, telling detail of frogs after Moritz Retzsch (cf. Fig. 2.18–19). BnF, Rés. M-Yh-4, Paris   246

7.27 (*top*) Eugène Delacroix, lithograph, in *Faust, tragédie de M. de Goethe, traduite en français par M. Albert Stapfer* (À Paris: Ch. Motte & Sautelet, 1828), insert plate between p. 72–73; (*bottom*) Moritz Retzsch, Faust meeting Gretchen, *Umrisse zu Goethe's Faust gezeichnet von Retsch* (Stuttgart & Tübingen: Cotta, 1816), pl. 8. BnF, Rés.-Yh-17, Paris, and: Courtesy HAAB, F 3487, Weimar   248

7.28 Francesco Hayez, *Il Bacio. Episodio della giovinezza. Costumi del secolo XIV*, oil on canvas, 1859, 112 × 88 cm, first version. Courtesy Pinacoteca di Brera, Milan   249

7.29 Francesco Hayez, *Il Bacio*, oil on canvas, 1861, 127 × 95 cm, second version, private coll. All rights reserved   251

7.30 Francesco Hayez, *Il Bacio*, oil on canvas, 1867, 116.8 × 80 cm, third version, private coll. All rights reserved   251

7.31a Federico Seneca, *Baci: ciocolato Perugina*, in *Tavole di Federico Seneca con prefazione di Leonardo Borgese* (n.p.: Edizioni Vendre, n.d. [*c.*1950]). Courtesy Paola Pallottino   252

7.31b Present-day display of Baci Perugina in Venice airport. Author's photograph 10 June 2022   253

8.1a Alfred Crowquill, *Faust Sees Margaret for the First Time*, in *Faust: A Serio-Comic Poem with Twelve Outline Illustrations* (London: B. B. King, 1834), large paper edition, pl. 5. Courtesy Beinecke, Yale University, Speck Sg8a F6 +834b   256

8.1b Alfred Crowquill, *Margaret Refuses to Leave the Prison*, in *Faust: A Serio-Comic Poem with Twelve Outline Illustrations* (London: B. B. King, 1834), large paper edition, pl. 12. Courtesy Beinecke, Yale University, Speck Sg8a F6 +834b   256

8.2 Alfred Crowquill, "The German in an English dress," in *Faust: A Serio-Comic Poem with Twelve Outline Illustrations* (London: B. B. King, 1834), p. viii (author's portrait-signature). Courtesy Beinecke, Yale University, Speck Sg8a F6 +834b   259

8.3a Alfred Crowquill, *Margaret Admiring the Present Left by the Devil*, standard version, in *Faust: A Serio-Comic Poem with Twelve Outline Illustrations* (London: B. B. King, 1834), pl. 6. Courtesy HAAB, F 3487, Weimar   260

8.3b Alfred Crowquill, *Margaret Admiring the Present Left by the Devil*, coloured version, in *Faust: A Serio-Comic Poem with Twelve Outline Illustrations* (London: B. B. King, 1834), pl. 6. Courtesy Beinecke, Yale University, Speck Sg8a F6 +834b   260

8.4 Moritz Retzsch, Faust blaming Mephistopheles, *Umrisse zu Goethe's Faust gezeichnet von Retsch* (Stuttgart & Tübingen: Cotta, 1816), pl. 23. Courtesy HAAB, F 3487, Weimar   263

8.5 Alfred Crowquill, *Faust Hears that Margaret is in Prison*, in *Faust: A Serio-Comic Poem with Twelve Outline Illustrations* (London: B. B. King, 1834), pl. 11. Courtesy HAAB, F 3482, Weimar   263

8.6 Alfred Crowquill, *Faust Signs Over his Soul to the Devil*, in *Faust: A Serio-Comic Poem with Twelve Outline Illustrations* (London: B. B. King, 1834), pl. 1. Courtesy HAAB, F 3482, Weimar   265

8.7	*Mephistopheles: Nur eins! Um Lebens oder Sterbens willen. Bitt'ich nur ein Paar Zeilen aus*, in *Bilder zu Goethes Faust von Anselmus Lachgern* (Leipzig: C. F. Doerffling, 1841), pl. 1. Courtesy HAAB, F 3467, Weimar 265
8.8	*Bilder zu Goethes Faust von Anselmus Lachgern* (Leipzig: C. F. Doerffling, 1841), front cover. Courtesy HAAB, F 3467, Weimar 266
8.9	*Bilder zu Goethes Faust von Anselmus Lachgern* (Leipzig: C. F. Doerffling, 1841), back cover. Courtesy HAAB, F 3467, Weimar 267
9.1	Moritz Retzsch, Cathedral scene, *Umrisse zu Goethe's Faust gezeichnet von Retsch* (Stuttgart & Tübingen: Cotta, 1816), pl. 18. Courtesy HAAB, F 3487, Weimar 271
9.2	August and Moritz Retzsch, Home theatricals, ink and wash coloured drawing, 1800, in *Weinbergs Scenen, aus dem Leben der beiden Brüder August und Moritz Retzsch*. SKK, Inv. Nr. ca 53 v 74, Dresden, photo Caterina Micksch 272
9.3	(*top*) Johann Wolfgang von Goethe, *Prologue in Heaven*, pen and ink drawing, *c.*1811, 21.5 × 33.4 cm; (*bottom*) Moritz Retzsch, Prologue in Heaven, *Umrisse zu Goethe's Faust gezeichnet von Retsch* (Stuttgart & Tübingen: Cotta, 1816), pl. 1. Courtesy SWK, Weimar; and: Courtesy HAAB, F 3487, Weimar 275
9.4	(*top*) Johann Wolfgang von Goethe, *Conjuring the Poodle*, pen-and-ink drawing, wash, *c.*1811, 29.9 × 20 cm; (*bottom*) Moritz Retzsch, Faust's study with the poodle monstrously growing, *Umrisse zu Goethe's Faust gezeichnet von Retsch* (Stuttgart & Tübingen: Cotta, 1816), pl. 3. Courtesy SWK, Weimar; and: Courtesy HAAB, F 3487, Weimar 276
9.5	Karl Friedrich Schinkel, *Margaret's Chamber*, 1820, *décor* design after Moritz Retzsch, watercolour over preliminary drawing, graphite and compass on vellum, 23.5 × 36.3 cm. © Staatliche Museen zu Berlin, Kupferstichkabinett, SM 22d.95, Berlin 278
9.6	Moritz Retzsch, Margaret in her chamber, *Umrisse zu Goethe's Faust gezeichnet von Retsch* (Stuttgart & Tübingen: Cotta, 1816), pl. 9. Courtesy HAAB, F 3487, Weimar 278
9.7	Peter Cornelius, *Scene in the Prison. End of the Tragedy*, in *XII Bilder zu Göthe's Faust gezeichnet von Peter von Cornelius* (Frankfurt am Main: Johann Friedrich Wenner, n.d.), pl. 12. Courtesy Beinecke, Folio Speck Ck99 C7 816, Yale University 280
9.8	Moritz Retzsch, Margaret in the prison, *Umrisse zu Goethe's Faust gezeichnet von Retsch* (Stuttgart & Tübingen: Cotta, 1816), pl. 25. Courtesy HAAB, F 3487, Weimar 282
9.9	Louise Bertin, *Ultima scena di Fausto/Dernière Scène de Faust, Composée et Arrangée pour le Piano-Forte* (Paris: Maurice Schlesinger, [*c.*1831]), scroll cover with illustration after Moritz Retzsch. Courtesy HAAB, F 5598, Weimar 283
9.10	Édouard Despléchin, stage set for Gounod's *Faust*, 5, 4 after Moritz Retzsch, 1859, pen, watercolour and gouache highlights on blue cardboard, 26.8 × 40 cm. BnF, Esq. Desplechin-5, Paris 284
9.11	(*top*) Joseph Thierry, *Faust and Mephistopheles Riding in front of the Montfaucon Gallows*, 1866, oil on canvas, 95 × 125 cm, previously design for the stage curtain of Gounod's *Faust*, 5, 1, [1859]; (*bottom*) Moritz Retzsch, Faust and Mephistopheles galloping past the Rabenstein, *Umrisse zu Goethe's Faust gezeichnet von Retsch* (Stuttgart & Tübingen: Cotta, 1816), pl. 24. BMO, Paris; and: Courtesy HAAB, F 3487, Weimar 285

FIGURES

XXV

9.12 Meyerheim, *I'd give a deal if I could say who was that gentleman today!*, 29.8 × 40.2 cm, in *Scenen aus Goethes Faust in acht lithographirten Bildern* (Berlin: Zum ausschliesslichen Debit in Commission bei T. Trautwein, [1835]), pl. 7. Drawing of the room after a sketch by Prince Ferdinand Radziwill, the figure by Biermann. Faust-Museum, Moosmann Collection, B 70, Knittlingen, photo Christopher Stead   289

9.13 *Mr. Terry as Mephistopheles the Devil in "Faustus,"* portrait print, undated (*c.*1825). Harvard, Houghton Library, MS Thr 933, Box 3   292

9.14 Actress Julie Gley as Margaret in a costume by Philipp von Stubenrauch, Hofburgtheater, 29 May 1839, Vienna. © KHM-Museumsverband, Theatermuseum, HZ HM805, Vienna   293

9.15 Cäcilie Brand, *Herr und Madame Schütz (als Faust und Gretchen)*, print, n.d., various formats. Courtesy HAAB, F gr 5748 (18), Weimar   294

9.16 Maleuvre, *I would never dare to adorn myself with all these jewels,* showing Marie Dorval as Margaret, coloured etching, *c.*1828, 23 × 14.5 cm, published by Hautecœur. BnF, 4-Ico Cos-1 (7,637), Paris   295

9.17 Moritz Retzsch, The wine prodigy at Auerbach's tavern, coloured version, n.d., 15.2 × 19.8 cm. *Umrisse zu Goethe's Faust gezeichnet von Retsch* (Stuttgart & Tübingen: Cotta, 1816), pl. 5. FDH, Frankfurter Goethe-Museum, III-13102, Frankfurt   296

9.18 John Bernard Partridge, *Mr Irving in the character of Mephistopheles*, watercolour, pencil and ink on paper, *c.*1885, 31 × 20.5 cm. © V&A, Gabrielle Enthoven Collection, S. 321–2011, London   300

9.19 John Bernard Partridge, Irving as Mephistopheles in the witch's kitchen, print of proof sketch, dated 24 April 1894, 18.1 × 13 cm. Illustration to A Student of Goethenburg, "On Faust," *Punch; or, The London Charivari,* CVI (28 Apr 1894): 193, with the caption *Betting Mephistopheles; or, The Magic Ring-Man.* © V&A, Theatre Collection, S. 3766–2013, London   300

9.20 Phil May, Henry Irving as Mephistopheles in *Faust*, colour print, *c.*1885–88, 24.5 × 32.5 cm. © V&A, Gabrielle Enthoven Collection, S. 965–2017, London   301

9.21a–b Hergé, *Coke en stock* (Bruxelles: Casterman, 1958), 39, vignettes A3 and C3. © Hergé-Tintin*imaginatio* 2023   302

10.1 Gabriel Max, *"Es ist ein Zauberbild, ist leblos, ein Idol,"* in *Faust-Illustrationen von Gabriel Max: Zehn Zeichnungen, in Holz geschnitten von R[ichard] Brend'amour und W. Hecht* (Berlin: G. Grote, 1880), pl. 10. Courtesy HAAB, F gr 5768, Weimar   312

10.2 Phiz (Hablôt Knight Browne), *I make the acquaintance of Miss Mowcher,* etching, final plate C, Dec 1849, 12.8 × 10.78 cm, in Charles Dickens, *David Copperfield,* Ch. XXII, "Some Old Scenes, and Some New People." Author's collection and file   314

10.3 Moritz Retzsch, Garden scene, *Umrisse zu Goethe's Faust gezeichnet von Retsch* (Stuttgart & Tübingen: Cotta, 1816), pl. 14. Courtesy HAAB, F 3487, Weimar   315

10.4 Phiz (Hablôt Knight Browne), *I make the acquaintance of Miss Mowcher,* pencil and crayon sketch A with extra sketches, added to the original edition of Dickens, *The Personal History of David Copperfield* (London: Bradbury and Evans, 1850), copy 9, facing p. 232. NYPL, Berg Collection   316

10.5 Phiz (Hablôt Knight Browne), original illustration for *I make the acquaintance of Miss Mowcher,* version B of the final plate, graphite on paper, image 13 × 10 cm. Courtesy Rare Book Department, Elkins-Copperfield cdc389917, Free Library of Philadelphia   317

10.6	Moritz Retzsch, Martha adorns Margaret with the jewels, *Umrisse zu Goethe's Faust gezeichnet von Retsch* (Stuttgart & Tübingen: Cotta, 1816), pl. 12. Courtesy HAAB, F 3487, Weimar 320
11.1a	Corolla and calyx of Lord Byron's rose given to Catharine Potter Stith, 3 × 3 cm, dried and pressed between two sheets of glass in painted wood frame 38 × 36 × 4 cm. Courtesy Beinecke, YCGL MSS 54 (Art), Yale University 326
11.1b	Lord Byron's rose under the cracked glass pane. Courtesy Beinecke, YCGL MSS 54 (Art), Yale University 326
11.2	Henry Moses, *The Decision of the Flower*, engraved copy after Moritz Retzsch, in *Retsch's Series of Twenty-Six Outlines, Illustrative of Goethe's Tragedy of Faust* (London: Boosey & Sons, Rodwell and Martin, 1820), pl. 14. Courtesy HAAB, F gr 5785, Weimar 328
11.3	Henry Moses, *Margaret Meets Faust in the Summer House*, engraved copy after Moritz Retzsch, in *Retsch's Series of Twenty-Six Outlines, Illustrative of Goethe's Tragedy of Faust* (London: Boosey & Sons, Rodwell and Martin, 1820), pl. 15. Courtesy HAAB, F gr 5785, Weimar 328
11.4	Käthe Kollwitz, *Gretchen*, 1899, line etching, dry point, aquatint and burnisher, green-black on Japanese paper, 26.7 × 21 cm, Knesebeck 45 IV. Cologne, © Käthe Kollwitz Museum Köln 331
12.1	Königliche Porzellan-Manufaktur (KPM), eight of the twelve surviving painted and gilded plates with scenes after Moritz Retzsch's outlines, 1822. FPPGBB, Inv. Nr. XII 10069–10080, Berlin, photo Wolfgang Pfauder 335
12.2	Königliche Porzellan-Manufaktur (KPM), twenty-four painted and gilded plates with scenes after Moritz Retzsch's outlines, 1822–23. FDH, Frankfurter Goethe-Museum, IV-2021-001, Frankfurt, permission of Adolf and Luisa Haeuser Foundation 336–37
12.3	Unmarked china plate, painted and signed by G. Koch, Mephistopheles lulls Faust to sleep after Moritz Retzsch's outline, *c.*1850–60, diameter 22.6 cm. Courtesy Peter-Christian Wegner collection 339
12.4	Meissen pipe bowl, *c.*1820?, Faust and Margaret in the garden scene with Martha and Mephistopheles passing, painted after Moritz Retzsch, framed in gold, 12.1 cm, Berlin form. Courtesy Detlev Dauer collection D2152 341
12.5a	KPM pipe bowl, *c.*1830–40, with Margaret and Faust kissing and Mephistopheles spying, painted after Moritz Retzsch, framed in gold. Courtesy Peter-Christian Wegner collection 342
12.5b	KPM pipe bowl, *c.*1830–40, hinged ornate lid, with Margaret and Faust kissing and Mephistopheles spying, painted after Moritz Retzsch, framed in gold, 13.7 cm, Berlin form. Courtesy Detlev Dauer collection D2479 343
12.6a	Julius Nisle, outline of Faust and Margaret kissing in the garden combining two outlines by Moritz Retzsch, in *Göthe-Gallerie: Stahlstiche zu Göthe's Meisterwerken nach Zeichnungen von Julius Nisle*, 4th fasc., *Faust, erster Theil* (Stuttgart: Literatur-Comptoir, [June 1840]), pl. 15, steel engraved and printed by W. Pobuda. Courtesy HAAB, F 3337 (d), Weimar 344
12.6b	Sepia painted Nathusius pipe bowl framed in gold, Margaret and Faust kissing in garden approached by Mephistopheles, 1840, 14.5 cm, Berlin form, with *Faust* quote and friendship inscription. Courtesy Detlev Dauer collection D1133 345
12.7	Jacob Petit (attributed to), five-sided *veilleuse théière*, French, 19th century. Faust and Gretchen in the garden scene after Moritz Retzsch. Courtesy Blair Museum of Lithophanes, acc. no. 2512, Toledo, Ohio 348

12.8	Kretzschmar, Bösenberg & Co., commercial postcard advertising candle screens, Dresden, 19th century, picturing screen with Faust and Margaret after Moritz Retzsch. Courtesy Archives of Blair Museum of Lithophanes, Toledo, Ohio 349
12.9	Woburn window, large oak frame (213.36 × 91.44 × 16.51 cm) with a mosaic of 1834–41 acquired lithophanes in brass grids. Lithophane of Faust and Margaret's "Kiss" after Moritz Retzsch featuring under the Vesuvius eruption. Private coll., image courtesy Andrew Cook 350
12.10	Tin showcase figurines, Faust and Margaret on bench, Mephistopheles eavesdropping, after Retzsch's 1834 insert plate 19 (cf. Fig. 7.1), produced by Werner Fechner, July 1979. Author's coll., photo Christopher Stead 351
12.11	Cover printed in red, picturing Faust, Margaret, Martha and Mephistopheles in the garden scene after Moritz Retzsch, *Goethe's Faust Translated by J. Birch* (Lancashire, St. Helen's: Published by T. Beecham, [1886]). Courtesy HAAB, F 7665, Weimar 353
12.12	Last page of Goethe's *Faust* in black and advertisement of Beecham's Cough Pills in red, in *Goethe's Faust Translated by J. Birch* (Lancashire, St. Helen's: Published by T. Beecham, [1886]). Courtesy HAAB, F 7665, Weimar 353

Abbreviations

AKL	*Allgemeines Künstlerlexikon Online/Artists of the World Online*
AlH	*Ausgabe letzter Hand*
Analysis 1820	"An Analysis of Goethe's Tragedy of Faust" (Boosey et al., 1820)
Arsenal	Bibliothèque de l'Arsenal, Paris, France
Beinecke	Beinecke Rare Book and Manuscript Library, Yale University, New Haven, USA
BHVP	Bibliothèque historique de la ville de Paris, France
BL	British Library, London, UK
BM	British Museum
BMO	Bibliothèque-musée de l'Opéra, Paris, France
BMPD	British Museum Prints and Drawings, London, UK
BnF	Bibliothèque nationale de France, Paris, France
BnF ASP	Bibliothèque nationale de France, Arts du spectacle, Paris, France
BnF Est.	Bibliothèque nationale de France, Estampes et Photographie, Paris, France
BnF Musique	Bibliothèque nationale de France, Département de la Musique, Paris, France
Bodmer	Martin Bodmer Foundation, Cologny, Geneva, Switzerland
BwGZ	*Briefwechsel zwischen Goethe und Zelter in den Jahren 1799 bis 1832*
DCHA	*Dictionnaire critique des historiens de l'art actifs en France de la Révolution à la Première Guerre mondiale*
DiNB	*Dictionary of National Biography*, 1885–1900, online
DLA	Deutsches Literatur Archiv, Marbach, Germany
DLA C-R	Cotta-Retzsch correspondence, Deutsches Literatur Archiv, Marbach, Germany
DLA Co	Cotta Contracts (by name), Deutsches Literatur Archiv, Marbach, Germany
Düsseldorf	Goethe-Museum, Anton-und-Katharina-Kippenberg-Stiftung, Düsseldorf, Germany
Engel	Engel, Karl, *Zusammenstellung der Faust-Schriften vom 16. Jahrhundert bis Mitte 1884*
F	*Faust, eine Tragödie*, subsequently *Faust I* (in German)
F II	*Faust, der Tragödie zweiter Teil*, subsequently *Faust II* (in German)
FA	Goethe, *Sämtliche Werke: Briefe, Tagebücher und Gespräche*, Frankfurter Ausgabe
Faustus 1824	*Faustus: from the German of Goethe,* 3rd ed. (Boosey, 1824)
Faustus 1852	*Faustus; or, The Demon of the Drachenfels* (Purkess, 1852)
FDH	Freies Deutsches Hochstift, Frankfurter Goethe-Museum, Frankfurt, Germany
FPPGBB	Foundation Prussian Palaces and Gardens Berlin-Brandenburg
GAug	*Goethes Briefwechsel mit seinem Sohn August*, ed. Gerlinde Ulm Sanford
GBW	Goethe, *Sollst mir ewig Suleika heißen. Goethes Briefwechsel mit Marianne und Johann Jakob Willemer*, ed. Hans-J. Weitz
GCB	*Goethe und Cotta, Briefwechsel*, ed. Dorothea Kuhn
GG	*Goethes Gespräche*, ed. Flodoard Frhr. von Biedermann et al.
GLTT	*Goethes Leben von Tag zu Tag: eine dokumentarische Chronik*, ed. Robert Steiger, later Angelika Reimann
Goedeke	Goedeke, Karl, later Edmund Goetze, *Grundrisz zur Geschichte der deutschen Dichtung aus den Quellen*, 4, 2, 3rd ed.
GSA	Goethe und Schiller Archiv, Weimar, Germany
HAAB	Herzogin Anna Amalia Bibliothek, Weimar, Germany
HAM / FM	Harvard Art Museums / Fogg Museum, Boston, USA
HCR, MS D	Henry Crabb Robinson, MS Diary, Dr Williams's Library, London, UK

ABBREVIATIONS

Introduction 1821	In *Faustus: from the German of Goethe* (Boosey, 1821)
Introduction 1877	In *Illustrations to Goethe's Faust: Twenty-Six Etchings by Moritz Retzsch* (Estes and Lauriat, 1877)
Kippenberg	*Katalog der Sammlung Kippenberg*
LM	*London Magazine* (*The*)
LSHTM	London School of Hygiene & Tropical Medicine, London, UK
ML	Musée du Louvre, Paris, France
MLA	*Monthly Literary Advertiser* (*The*)
NDB-online	*Neue Deutsche Biographie* (Duncker & Humblot, 1953–), online resource
Neubert	Neubert, Franz, ed. *Vom Doctor Faustus zu Goethes Faust*
Niessen	Niessen, Carl, ed. *Katalog der Ausstellungen "Faust auf der Bühne"*
NYPL	New York Public Library, New York, USA
OC	Théophile Gautier, *Œuvres complètes*, pts. 1–7 (Honoré Champion, 2003–)
ODNB	*Oxford Dictionary of National Biography*, online edition
RA	*Briefe an Goethe. Gesamtausgabe in Regestform*, ed. Klassik Stiftung Weimar, Goethe- und Schiller-Archiv
RA online	Royal Academy of Arts Collection, London, UK
RMN GP	Réunion des musées nationaux Grand Palais, Paris, France
SGK	Städtische Galerie, Kunstsammlung, Dresden, Germany
SKK	Staatliche Kunstsammlungen, Kupferstich-Kabinett, Dresden, Germany
SLUB	Sächsische Landesbibliothek – Staats- und Universitätsbibliothek Dresden, Germany
St D	Stadtarchiv, Landeshauptstadt Dresden, Dresden, Germany
Sterling	Sterling Memorial Library, Yale University, New Haven, USA
Steuer MS.	Dation Steuer, Médiathèque d'Angers, Angers, France
SWK	Stiftung Weimarer Klassik, Weimar, Germany
Tg	Goethe, *Tagebücher: Historisch-kritische Ausgabe im Auftrag der Stiftung Weimarer Klassik*
V&A	Victoria & Albert Museum, London, UK
WA	*Goethes Werke*, Weimarer Ausgabe
Wegner	Wegner, Wolfgang, *Die Faustdarstellung vom 16. Jahrhundert bis zur Gegenwart*

INTRODUCTION

Air View and Ant Perspective

On 10 April 1822, the great Romantic Percy Bysshe Shelley was grappling with a translation of Goethe's *Faust I* from the original German verse into a poet's English. He could hardly suspect he would drown when his sailing boat, the Don Juan (or Ariel), met three months later with an ill-fated accident. His main concern was how to drive a deep ocean of briny German words and metres into English anchorage. As the later publication of his fragmentary efforts would show, he had given himself an arduous task most translators had spurned or would spurn: to render the very two *Faust* passages that most offended British taste, beliefs, and feelings of propriety and measure. The first of these is the opening dialogue in Heaven, when God allows Mephistopheles to tempt Faust. The second is the witches' Sabbath, or Walpurgis Night, an orgiastic scene oscillating between ribald carrousel and political or literary satire. The endeavour despaired him all the more, the only possible translation seeming to be through images, not words, as he eagerly wrote to John Gisborne:

> What etchings those are! I am never satiated with looking at them, and I fear it is the only sort of translation of which Faust is susceptible—I never perfectly understood the Har[t]z Mountain scene, until I saw the etching.—And then, Margaret in the summer house with Faust!—The artist makes one envy his happiness that he can sketch such things with calmness, which I dared only to look upon once, and which made my brain swim round only to touch the leaf on the opposite side of which I knew that it was figured.—Whether it is that the artist has surpassed Faust, or that the pencil surpasses language in some subjects, I know not; or that I am more affected by a visible image—but the etching certainly excited me here more than the poem it illustrated.[1]

Our poet was poring not over Goethe's original text, but re-engraved German prints, proxy amongst many. The English letterpress that supplemented them summed up Goethe's play and partly translated it, but utterly failed to impress the Englishman who observed: "the translations are miserable." The printed outlines, compositions

based solely on contour and devoid of colour, fulfilled the task far better. Yet Shelley did not refer to the cribber and perpetrator of the London copies, but to their original conceiver, the German artist Friedrich August Moritz Retzsch. This name, little known but to specialists today, was at the time a big favourite with the English public, to such extent that, when asked for *Faust* editions, Gisborne would send derivative prints to the Italy-resident Shelley with the play's adjoining English synopsis and translated extracts. A full English translation would yet be long in coming (1833).

It is striking how one great Romantic found hard to understand the poetic work of a contemporary equal while himself involved in its very translation. Shelley was not the only one. Nearly a decade earlier, Germaine de Staël, *Faust*'s interpreter of European prominence both in France and German lands, had in her *Germany* given in English (1813), then in French (1814), an influential chapter assessing the play thus:

> Certainly, we must not expect to find in it either taste, or measure, or the art that selects and terminates; but if the imagination could figure to itself an intellectual chaos, such as the material chaos has often been painted[,] the "Faustus" of Goëthe should have been composed at that epoch. It cannot be exceeded in boldness of conception, and the recollection of this production is always attended with a sensation of giddiness.[2]

The oblique and puzzling structure of Goethe's *Faust, eine Tragödie* (1808, subsequently *Faust I*) had baffled readers on publication. Devoid of partition into acts and scenes, the play moved elliptically from one episode to the next as if lacking structure. It required explanation, if not interpretation. Goethe's previous offering on the subject had been *Faust: Ein Fragment* (1790), and this new poetic gesture

---

1 *The Letters of Percy Bysshe Shelley*, ed. F. L. Jones (Oxford: Clarendon Press, 1964), 2:407.

2 Staël, "Faustus," in *Germany*, trans. from the French (London: John Murray, 1813), 2:181–82. On the debate between countries launched by this important book and its presentation of *Faust*, see John Claiborne Isbell, "The First French *Faust: De l'Allemagne's Faust* Chapter, 1810–1814," *French Studies* 45 (1991): 417–34; Isbell, *The Birth of European Romanticism: Truth and Propaganda in Stael's "De l'Allemagne," 1810–1813* (Cambridge: Cambridge University Press, 1994); Axel Blaeschke, "*De l'Allemagne*: Prolégomènes à une nouvelle édition," *Cahiers staëliens*, no. 64 (2014): 187–97.

© EVANGHELIA STEAD, 2023 | DOI:10.1163/9789004543010_002

This is an open access chapter distributed under the terms of the CC BY-NC-ND 4.0 license.

(or version) resembled a splinter as well. Admittedly written in rich and varied verse, it smacked of the unfinished and read shockingly incomplete. Unresolved, its finale in a prison condemned tender Margaret, forsaken, to a tragic fate. Disaster and doom awaited Faust himself, clutched away by Mephistopheles as he tried to free his adorable paramour, albeit tardily. Such intrigues shocked public sensibility and hinted at Faust's damnation. *Faust, der Tragödie zweiter Theil* (subsequently *Faust II*) would be published twenty-four years later (1832), shortly after Goethe's passing, as an enigmatic heritage item European culture would have to reckon with. In *Faust I*, the "Prologue in Heaven" and the wager proposed to God by Mephistopheles would both make sense only later. Significantly, Gérard de Nerval, himself deeply inspired by the Faust myth as Goethe's most famous translator in France, did not acknowledge Faust's remittance and salvation before 1840, foreshadowing the German revival under Prussian leadership.

Such an unlikely emissary of Goethe's sensibility appeared undiplomatically amid cultures, nations, and political systems in conflict. *Faust I* was issued at the time of the Napoleonic wars that had brought the German States, the British Empire and post-revolutionary Republican France into fierce rivalry. The three contenders would further challenge, provoke and oppose each other for a long time hence, while Goethe's play infiltrated languages and cultural traditions. In such European context, his *Faust* was not *any* text nor *plain text*. As embodiment of an old Germanic myth, it was not to be ignored; as epitome of the most recent German literature, it was fraught with ideological and symbolic value. A strange ambassador between cultures, it told the tale of a learned man, discouraged by knowledge, despairing at the approach of old age, but trusted by God who permitted the devil to tempt him. This particular Faust seemed a weird and wonderful embodiment of any cultured European man, well educated, knowledgeable, the very representative of a dominant civilization, inheritor of a brilliant past, at present discouraged and dejected. The story echoed of course the geopolitical situation of the waning and recently dissolved Reich (1806). The latter word was charged with significance, indeed laden with *Angst*, as it designated both the Holy Roman Empire and, in spiritual terms, the kingdom of God. Moreover, in the industrial era, a growing number of books augured a formidable challenge to Goethe's deeply melancholic protagonist.

Were it not for the images! Amongst these, Moritz Retzsch's set of twenty-six etchings merit pride of place. Retzsch had early turned the tragedy into a silent picture story, shaping characters, places and plot by using the outline aesthetic. His frames, devoid of captions, in landscape format and slow succession, had strengthened the narrative. A prime practice to illustrate major poetic compositions at the time, already used by John Flaxman to European renown, the outline technique invited the reader into the picture to elaborate upon the play. To this Retzsch cleverly added numerous details and fanciful creatures, further opening up storyline vistas, as yet without words. As his compositions amply circulated, Goethe's *Faust I* came to be appreciated by peers, Shelley offering a remarkable example amongst others. Lord Byron, Samuel Taylor Coleridge, Charles Dickens and his chief illustrator Phiz (Hablôt K. Browne), Benjamin Disraeli, Thomas Frognall Dibdin, Théophile Gautier, Heinrich Heine, Gérard de Nerval, Henry Crabb Robinson, and John Ruskin are all involved in the story this book relates. Also Felix O. C. Darley, Eugène Delacroix, Edgar Allan Poe, and many others. In September 1810, Retzsch had already crafted drawings after Goethe's script published by Johann Friedrich Cotta in April 1808. As this book shows on new evidence, he had completed all twenty-six plates by April 1812, although Cotta only issued them nearly four years later, in October 1816. They were proffered in a small appealing portfolio with accompanying elements, and would go through many transformations.

The initial series travelled from country to country and from publisher to publisher, and often changed shape, meaning, and purport. It carried off a major achievement, making of Goethe's aesthetically shocking and morally disreputable play one of the works of German literature most respected abroad. It did not address the same public nor attract homogeneous readership. It spawned a run of multiple printed goods that would leave numerous and telling testimonials in the press, libraries, repositories, and readers' books; they would impress and influence Faustian iconography; they would further affect and inspire literary texts, parodies, stage sets and costumes; they would even adorn ordinary and extraordinary decorative objects. From the beginning, they would involve social rituals of giving (generosity), acceptance (grace), and commentary (involvement), even enhancing personal intercourse. They would later welcome undistinguished merry-makers by way of illuminated panels for a Saint Petersburg summer show and musical attraction. In short, they lie at the tangled centre of knotty questions on the function of printed cultural objects that this book will attempt to unravel. *Goethe's "Faust I" Outlined* focuses on Moritz Retzsch's twenty-six outline engravings after Goethe's *Faust, eine Tragödie* (1808), traces their trajectories in multiple forms, and tracks how these largely disregarded images founded and shaped the reception of Goethe's play in the German States, Europe and overseas.

Retzsch's outlines circulated in three manners: between countries; print genres and categories, shaping hybrid items; and as typical expressions of culture. The first concerns geography and commercial relations; the second, modified printed formats and readers' understanding over time; and the third, Retzsch's influence on fiction, theatre, and precious goods or popular artefacts, including an array of consumer items. Combining such perspectives, I pursue a number of divergent paths, seeking to contribute, through Retzsch's case, to a cogent overview of print culture in Europe. The means: a close-up of specific editions, exemplars, and copies, comprising their owners, stature, and relative worth. The prints would travel widely, but also meet the *Faust* text in manifold and intriguing ways.

Importantly, as they partnered with text in various forms (excerpts in a separate brochure, later captions, summaries, even *Faust I* in full or partial translation), these pictures worked very differently from massive commentary. As this book shows in detail, they turned into inter-semiotic tools, making numerous claims on a text they borrowed from but also changed, all the while contributing to understanding, appreciating, and establishing it as canon. They replaced its fragmentary construction by a more or less structured and uninterrupted narrative, strung together scenes and events, brought forward characters, and highlighted situations. The combined effect made different demands on readers' faculties—textual linearity on one hand, over-intricate and silent representations on the other, either in succession, or echoing a motif within the series.

Studies on Retzsch are surprisingly few in number, relate to one context only, and focus on his set as an unchanging entity. Prior investigations have mainly examined his presence in two countries, German lands (V. Hildebrand-Schat) and Great Britain, as in an innovative chapter by William Vaughan.[3] All other terrains are unexplored but for a first venture into comparative reception I attempted nearly twenty years ago[4] with material since copiously enhanced. Text-image approach has additionally privileged Retzsch's relation to Goethe's text or aesthetic questions of the time as in Viola Hildebrand-Schat's comprehensive book on Retzsch's overall outline work.[5] The diverse impact of printed items prone to transformation has not been explored. Retzsch's precedence in *Faust* iconography has also been contested and his pervasiveness sidelined in an art history dominated by artists more conspicuous thanks to painting commissions, monumental assignments or institutional positions (Peter Cornelius being an exemplary case). The importance of Retzsch's etchings as an intercultural tool has thus remained invisible. By accurately dating his production, tracking in many transformations its relation to Goethe's text, and by comparatively following its circulation, this book reinstates the true rank of Retzsch's *Faust*. It brings forward the part the artist played in several countries' understanding, translating and acceptance of Goethe's play. It further sets Retzsch's work in cultural negotiation and showcases its weight in reproduction and media circulation as the prints spawn other prints, portfolios turn into albums and illustrated books, and further inspire commercial and artistic bindings, travesties, theatre sets, twists in literary plots, three-dimensional artefacts, and objects in a fashionable consumerist culture.

Retzsch's all-embracing role in media negotiation shows how already prevalent is media culture from the onset of the nineteenth century. Beyond Goethe's *Faust*, his complex case illustrates in depth the potency and aura of print culture in diffusion. It opens new perspectives in evaluating cultural practices and tendencies.

His fortunes in Europe read as an uneven story of flamboyant albeit relatively brief celebrity (Great Britain, mainly England), established but unacknowledged presence (France), and popularity of the prints, yet scarce and faint prestige for the artist himself (German States). His reception—always interlinked with Goethe's *Faust*—prompts a series of queries. To what purpose would outline etchings be offered to the public in German-speaking territories of the time after the poet's major work had occasioned more than one edition? Once Goethe's *Faust* left German-speaking terrain, which translation would prove more effective? Pen or stylus? Translation into words or rather engravings? Who best captures and renders the emotions and movement of a scene? Poet or

---

3 Vaughan, "F. A. M. Retzsch and the Outline Style," in *German Romanticism and English Art* (New Haven: Yale University Press, 1979), 123–54.

4 Stead, "Les tribulations d'une série gravée d'après le *Faust I* de Goethe: le cas de Moritz Retzsch entre l'Allemagne, l'Angleterre et la France," in *Interkulturelle Kommunikation in der europäischen Druckgraphik im 18. und 19. Jahrhundert*, ed. Ph. Kaenel and R. Reichardt (Hildesheim: Olms, 2007), 689–716.

5 Hildebrand-Schat, *Zeichnung im Dienste der Literaturvermittlung: Moritz Retzschs Illustrationen als Ausdruck bürgerlichen Kunstverstehens* (Würzburg: Königshausen und Neumann, 2004). For a fuller overview of recent criticism, see section 1.8 "German Amendments in the Twentieth Century" in Chap. 1.

artist? What has greater pull on the reader? A powerful passage in verse or the image it instigates? Retzsch's outlines already raised such interrogations at the time, not in an absolute or abstract sense, but in relation to understanding and interpreting a text, not least appropriating it.

Since the reception of Goethe's play proved awkward, the immediacy of images came to the fore as major currency in exchange. *Iconography* means literally *writing with/through images* and in religious art connotes a singular emulative constant, i.e., a repeated pattern or tradition both emulative and singular. As such, it constitutes an influential part in a major work's reception, as significant as the texts (translations, prefaces, reviews, etc.), yet rarely considered in scholarship. Françoise Forster-Hahn early made the point in *Faust* iconography,[6] although only through deluxe prints, whose exclusive reading may be diversely challenged. Still, Retzsch's outlines *always* met with text in one way or another. They gave birth to multifaceted printed articles combining differential readings: *reading text* as well as *reading with images*; and images' prominence both *as* translation and *in* translation. We 2014 explored the argument in a special issue of *Word & Image* thanks to an array of cases from the late eighteenth to early twentieth centuries.[7] The dual dimensions involve dissimilar parts of the brain, responsiveness and awareness that lie poles apart, close reading of a page from top to bottom, and leafing through a volume or an album to take in the images. When examined in combination and comparatively, their subtle interaction reveals the several cultural levels the outlines worked on and sustained, as they appealed to artists, literati, travellers, and collectors alike.

Retzsch's outlines were not *illustrations* in the common sense of reproduced artworks set within a printed text. As this study shows, they freely jostled company first with a few excerpts, later with synopses, afterwards with the play itself, never merging with it. They worked as an exchange voucher or a bargaining chip. A circulating medium, they mingled variously with translations from language to language—sometimes provoking them, often accompanying them—and engaged interaction between figural and textual effects. The original compound object further materialized in a wide-ranging series of print media of bourgeois and industrial contrivance. They themselves tell many stories about books and prints. They also bear in their pages the pattern and purport of their use, while specific exemplars often reveal what they may have meant to individual owners: hence my second motto (by Benjamin Disraeli) on the book as individual.

Several dozen offshoots of distinct significance in several countries form the basis for this book's investigations. In 1925, to establish the catalogue *raisonné* of Retzsch's graphic works, Leopold Hirschberg had from the outset dismissed examining them. Adamant in trusting only originals, true to his faith in graphic works, he fobbed off all Retzsch clones, particularly English ones, as "wretched imitative scrawls" (*klägliche Nachkritzelungen*) and "reduced tangled (litt. cobweb) images" (*verkleinerte Spinnewebebilder*).[8]

Extensive copying blighted Retzsch's reputation to a certain extent. The artist benefitted from industrialized printing as much as his cloned and changed *œuvre* suffered from it. He had originally crafted and engraved himself an artwork printed in numbers. Others' copies lack the subtlety and refinement of his original prints. He has frequently been examined through *reproductions* of not always the best kind, or compendia of *Faust* images, and evaluated using later issues of his work (mainly albums from the 1830s). In addition, his drawings and etchings lose out in the process of digitization that flattens his nuance of line. His minute detailing, subtlety, and personal use of the outline aesthetic present a challenge to faithful reproduction. Extra care has been taken in this volume to do his polyvalence justice. Nevertheless, besides being a multiple artwork, his own *œuvre* and technique harnessed the copying process, was clearly achieved with reproduction as endgame in mind, further evolving under its influence. His art surfed a powerful wave of rapidly expanding early nineteenth-century print culture.

In following original and extensive copying, careful assessment here of what *seems to be the same* (but *is not*) suggests ways to understand these printed items and to reconstruct, imagine, evoke, and conceptualize their function. In more than two hundred years, they have changed hands many times and undergone various treatments. Their primary artistic aim or social and aesthetic function has been lost or obscured, in many ways now unrecognizable. Yet comparison between exemplars allows for reconstruction in several cases. Leopold Hirschberg's reaction was logical as an art historian and book lover, to whom only original editions and prime exemplars mattered.

---

6 See Françoise Forster-Hahn, "Romantic Tragedy or National Symbol? The Interpretation of Goethe's *Faust* in 19th-Century German Art," in *Our "Faust"? Roots and Ramifications of a Modern German Myth*, ed. R. Grimm and J. Hermand (Madison: University of Wisconsin Press, 1987), 82–95; Forster-Hahn, "A Hero for All Seasons? Illustrations for Goethe's *Faust* and the Course of Modern German History," *Zeitschrift für Kunstgeschichte* 53, no. 4 (1990): 511–36.

7 Évanghélia Stead and Hélène Védrine, eds. "Imago & Translatio," special issue, *Word & Image* 30, no. 3 (July–Sept 2014).

8 Hirschberg, *Moritz Retzsch: Chronologisches Verzeichniss seiner graphischen Werke* (Berlin: Heinrich Tiedemann, 1925), 6.

Diffuse print culture was of little concern to him. Besides, why should it be important, in times such as ours, when digitized availability and free-to-all access are paramount considerations? Yet, as we shall see, digitization has further transformed Retzsch's work—it has *remediated* it, and digitization entails a kind of blindness that proves treacherous in book and print culture studies.

In his notes on Bernard Shaw (1951), Jorge Luis Borges contrasted conceptions of literature: as an endless experience of interactions or as a formal game, an *algebra* of words, indeed, literally a *reunion of broken parts* (from the Arabic *al-jabr*). For Borges, a book is not a closed or settled entity, but the very centre of innumerable relations and interactions. The text may not vary, what essentially varies is the way we read it. If we could, as Borges argued back then, read any present-day page in the way it might be read in 2000, we would know what makes literature in 2000.[9] In their many metamorphoses, Retzsch's originals, copies, and copies of copies introduce just such numerous relations, evidencing how print culture evolved, harnessed to new technologies and book genres. Comparison is in this sense a prime tool in evaluation, an initiation to *Faust* readings within print culture as it was in the nineteenth century, not to *Faust* as a play of broken parts. Retzsch's prints also admit us to a series of *Faust* interpretations as *outlined* in at least two aspects. First, delineated, bordered and defined in linear compositions—drawings capturing essential aspects of it, which allow the reader-spectator his own imaginings and interpretation; and second, epitomized, generalized, mapped, and summarized, affording interpretation errors and mishaps.

This book is about a pictured *Faust* that reveals many others and may even conceal a *Faust* yet to be discovered.

Goethe's Faust *Outlined* offers an interdisciplinary and comparative framework for evaluating the importance of Retzsch's outlines in *Faust* reception and print circulation from 1816 to the beginning of the twentieth century. It combines art history, book history, print culture, comparative literature, semiotics and aesthetics. Items and texts in this book have always been examined and compared first hand and in their original language. Unless otherwise stated, translations are by this author. In text, F refers to Goethe's *Faust I* in the original German. Given the difficulty to translate *Faust*, I have chosen to offer studied passages in the English translation that best renders the particular excerpt's meaning and style when compared to Goethe's original, and retained the following three as

largely read in *Faust's* long trajectory: Albert G. Latham's for "Everyman's Library" (1908), Walter Arndt's in the Norton critical edition (2nd ed., 2001), and David Luke's for "Oxford World's Classics" (1987, reissued 2008). I have purposefully limited cross-references and devised two detailed indexes for specific enquiries.

Following Retzsch's images in their many metamorphoses, the book bids unexplored investigation of a major text travelling between cultures engaged in political antagonism and commercial rivalry. Focusing on circulation and comparing prints with book genres challenge three dominant narratives of *Faust* reception. These have promoted textual translation and theatre performances as principal tool; extolled images by major artists as particularly influential; and tied scholarship to stable geo-linguistic limits. Whereas these narratives insist on isolated and specialized evaluations, I propose to gauge prints and books by calling on several disciplines and show why a differential grasp of comparative reception is important in *Faust's* fortunes. I argue that an assessment embedded within compared cultural practices and reading experiences throws light on the nineteenth-century phenomenon of duplicate printing.

In this book, I propose an innovative way of considering books and prints as objects, media, and symbols. I first tested the method in French, in my monograph *La Chair du livre* on fin-de-siècle books and prints,[10] and subsequently prolonged it in English, by editing a collection of papers from late medieval manuscripts to e-readers in *Reading Books and Prints as Cultural Objects*.[11] In a nutshell, I take into account materiality, reading modes, readers' personalities, as well as representation and imaginative heft. Materiality is seen as a vehicle of and testimony to ideas, specific material objects examined in a number of ways ultimately revealing cultural trends. This book thus addresses both high-end and popular editions, copies and replicas, compares noble and ordinary items, and challenges the limits of the much-abused term "illustration," which inadequately captures the range and function of imagery in books, albums, and other media. Images do not only lead to dual text-and-image relations based on interpretation. They point to the many-sided stories told by books and prints, three-dimensional objects that reveal publishing trends and reading publics.

Embracing Edgar Allan Poe's definition of the outline as "stir[ing] the spirit more pleasantly than the most

---

9 Borges, "Nota sobre (hacia) Bernard Shaw," *Otras inquisiciones*, in *Obras completas*, vol. 2, *1952–1972* (Barcelona: Emecé, 1996), 125–26.

---

10 Évanghélia Stead, *La Chair du livre: matérialité, imaginaire et poétique du livre fin-de-siècle* (Paris: PUPS, 2012), repr. 2013.

11 Evanghelia Stead, ed., *Reading Books and Prints as Cultural Objects* (Cham: Palgrave / Macmillan, 2018).

elaborate picture," I also call attention to the creative faculties of *Faust* readers and Retzsch's hold on their (our) imagination to shape intellectual inquiry and interact with a modern mythical figure. By outlining *Faust*, Retzsch initiates us to a series of interpretations: he bordered and defined the play in linear compositions. He captured essential aspects that coaxed reader-spectators' inner imaginings and own meanings. However, by admitting interpretational errors and mishaps, he also charted, condensed, and typified *Faust*. Minor accidents and major misfortunes occur in the life of all masterpieces. If Goethe's play is a great work, its complex reality makes us understand what art and literature may be all about: both

a complex constellation offering food for thought and a stark synopsis spotlighting main features, while making explicit opportunities to read, imagine, and see diversely. *Goethe's "Faust 1" Outlined* demonstrates how Retzsch's twenty-six prints met both challenges.

By comparing multiple language editions and media stemming from Retzsch, this book shows how his outlines worked as strategic complements in differing cultures. They were pivotal in adopting *Faust* as a major heritage text while superseding the potentially restrictive medium of the printed book. An extensive range of popular or refined derivatives, analysed as cultural messengers, would empower readers as independent creative agents.

Moritz Retzsch's Etchings
after Goethe's Faust I

∴

© EVANGHELIA STEAD, 2023 | DOI:10.1163/9789004543010_003

This is an open access chapter distributed under the terms of the CC BY-NC-ND 4.0 license.

Umrisse zu Goethe's Faust gezeichnet von Retsch (Stuttgart & Tübingen: Cotta, 1816).
COURTESY HAAB, F 3487, WEIMAR

In 1834, Retzsch further added 3 plates to his 26 engravings, inserted as plates 5, 7 and 19. These are reproduced in the wake of the original set after *Umrisse zu Goethe's Faust, erster Theil. Gezeichnet von Moritz Retzsch. Von dem Verfasser selbst retouchirt und mit einigen neuen Platten vermehrt* (Stuttgart & Tübingen: J. G. Cotta, 1834).
COURTESY HAAB, F 3478, WEIMAR

RETZSCH'S ETCHINGS AFTER GOETHE'S *FAUST I* – PLATES 1 & 2

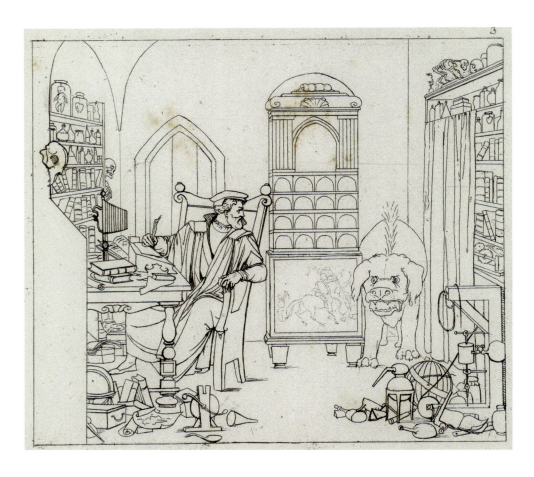

RETZSCH'S ETCHINGS AFTER GOETHE'S *FAUST I* – PLATES 5 & 6

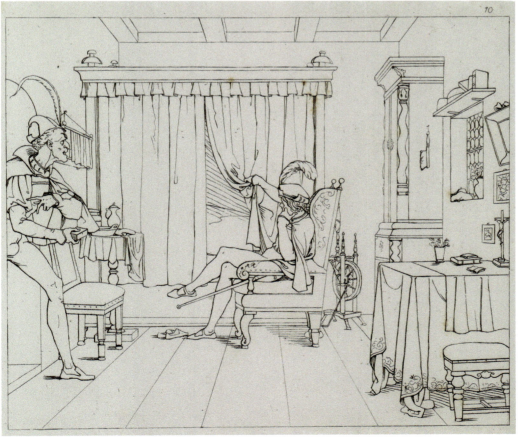

RETZSCH'S ETCHINGS AFTER GOETHE'S *FAUST I* – PLATES 13 & 14

RETZSCH'S ETCHINGS AFTER GOETHE'S *FAUST I* – PLATES 25 & 26

RETZSCH'S EXTRA ETCHINGS AFTER GOETHE'S *FAUST I* – INSERT PLATE 7

CHAPTER 1

Retzsch in the German States, a Borderline Celebrity

How present an artist, nearly 250 years after his birth, in the wake of homeland criticism? The persona of Friedrich Moritz August Retzsch (Dresden, 9 December 1779–Oberlößnitz near Dresden, 11 June 1857) comes to us in a hazy halo of contradictory information. In short supply, period German prose on him is motley: few obituaries, an 1858 hagiographic bio-sketch shortly after his demise by a cryptic intimate contemporary, Th. S., an assortment of belittling criticisms, and some embryonic attempts to assess his work. In the twentieth century, documented German contributions are surprisingly few, academic inquiries and a shift in appreciation being relatively recent. Compared with the early nineteenth-century fame of his outlines abroad, particularly Britain, the contrast is arresting. Yet delving through mostly forgotten German pages, occasionally compared with English or French counterparts, grants a contrasting picture of Retzsch's persona and work, his life vs. career choices. This chapter hardly takes stock of his entire *œuvre*. It first cuts a lively figure of Moritz Retzsch when he turned to Goethe's *Faust* shortly after publication (1808), and refutes his reputation as a "recluse," alien to sociability. It then offers an overview of his later life, and suggests reasons that have obscured metamorphic, grotesque, erotic or fanciful aspects of his art in favour of sentimentality. It also reviews the causes for his neglect and disparagement in nineteenth-century German criticism. It opens a new direction by comparing his treatment of a key *Faust* scene, Faust meeting Gretchen, to Cornelius's and Naeke's, concluding with a synopsis of new twentieth- and twenty-first-century approaches to his art in Germany.

1.1   Profile in Contrast

One striking feature, recurrent in criticism, is Retzsch's aloofness and estrangement from Dresden's social life, often mixed with diffidence of academic work and rules. Was he verily an outsider or a solitary artist, a loner grappling with Goethe's *Faust*? Dreamy nineteenth-century portraits have shaped a made-up figure and even rubbed off on present-day evaluations. It is helpful to compare them with data from period correspondence, Uwe Hellwig's thorough archival research and 2018 thesis, and other documents.

Retzsch's 1857 obituary in the *Crayon*, an American journal, portrays him as a romantic "gentle youth, roaming about in the adjacent woods with a gun on his shoulder, shooting birds and hunting the deer," engrossed more in nature than art.[1] The December 1851 French *Magasin pittoresque* underscores his ardent desire to become a forester-cum-huntsman (*Jäger*) yet also stresses "keen and tenacious diligence to draw, model clay, and carve wood" since childhood.[2] Curiously, a similar verdict occurs more than a century later in William Vaughan's authoritative 1979 study on Retzsch in England: "something of a recluse by nature," he retired shortly after his professorship "to a country cottage in the neighbourhood." His lack of stylistic evolution is even ascribed to his isolation from the artistic movements of his time, particularly historical illustration, since he "did not move beyond an early Romantic sensationalism," a harsh judgment yet not entirely unfounded.[3] That Retzsch never went to Italy, deemed then an essential requirement for artists, may have influenced such evaluations, echoing quixotic nineteenth-century press reports. Such renouncement would have a Faustian resonance as suggested below.

Art would finally have the upper hand, enhancing Retzsch's and elder brother August's inbred predispositions. For leisure, their artistically inclined father carved objects in spindle wood, drew horses and landscapes. Yet, Moritz's late formal training and lack of formative residence abroad are often cited. Both stress the importance of official instruction at the time and his unfettered artistic temperament. A short examination of the period's academic drill sheds further light on the matter.

An innate lover of nature, having briefly contemplated life as a *Jäger*, Retzsch first entered the Dresden Academy of Arts at eighteen to study draughtsmanship (1798–1880) under assistant tutor Caetano (Cajetan) Toscani. From 1803, he drew from plaster casts and antique originals studying oil painting after the Dresden Gallery pictures under Professor Josef Grassi. Courses, based on replication, were schematic and mechanical, as Caspar David Friedrich and

---

1   "Maurice Retzsch," *Crayon* 4, no. 10 (1 Oct 1857): 305b.
2   "Moritz Retzsch," *Le Magasin pittoresque* 19, no. 49 (Dec 1851): 388b.
3   Vaughan, *German Romanticism and English Art*, 126, 128.

© EVANGHELIA STEAD, 2023 | DOI:10.1163/9789004543010_004
This is an open access chapter distributed under the terms of the CC BY-NC-ND 4.0 license.

Ludwig Richter complained.[4] Retzsch mixed academic schooling with withdrawal into self-regulated practice. In Th. S.'s supportive biography, his education strings out a series of such spells: engagement and disengagement with the Academy, and retreats to Oberlößnitz closer to nature. Hypotheses vary: misconstruing his tutor's approval, finding imitative drawing tedious, losing faith, declining unpaid understudy work, hopes thwarted, promises broken, or simply lack of financial means.[5] The latter would prove decisive.

From 1806 the Napoleonic wars had swarmed over German territory. Retzsch's widowed mother's short resources evaporated when she had to support French soldiers billeted in their dwelling and two other inherited buildings.[6] A petition letter Retzsch addressed to War Secretary von Carlowitz in 1815 pictures a harrowing period, and was later published as documenting post-Napoleonic Dresden.[7] In truth, financial predicaments had started early on, when in 1789 his father died in a riding accident, Retzsch being by then nearly ten, not just eight, as the biographic devotee would have it. Youngest of three siblings, he would become his family's only breadwinner, drawing antiquities for Wilhelm Gottlieb Becker's *Augusteum* (1804–11) and painting commissions, particularly portraits, from 1803. The usual artist's tour in Italy had to be renounced in favour of family bonds and duties. He took students on early and pursued oil painting.[8] Emerges the figure of a hardworking young artist at odds with that projected of a hermit. Hitches in affiliation with the Dresden Academy of Arts are also revealing.

End 1816, Director general Count Heinrich Vitzthum von Eckstädt pleaded Retzsch's appointment as Academy member with Friedrich August I, King of Saxony, aka Frederick Augustus the Fair, alluding to Retzsch's miniature portraits of all three court princes and other appraised paintings.[9] Also supported by Christian Ferdinand Hartmann, Retzsch was allotted a yearly salary of 100 Reichsthaler instead of the proposed and usual 150,[10] as received by Academy member Caspar David Friedrich for landscape

painting.[11] Was it that miniatures ranked lower than landscapes? Despite the meagre wage, prestigious Dresden Academy membership provided a stepping-stone and a commendation, bettered Retzsch's livelihood and brought him further students. His attempt to secure a professorship, twice thwarted in the 1820s, was felt as an offence.[12] He was finally appointed "extraordinary" or associate Professor (*außerordentlich Professor*) in 1824 under Director general von Eckstädt and Art director Hartmann, which principally granted him title. He may not have been on a par with regular professors, and no painting, habitually donated to the royal collections as counterpart for Academy admission, has ever been traced on his account.[13] Interestingly, if, on application, the substantial lack of historical painting was signalled as a shortcoming in his work, the main commendation was the acclaim of his outlines abroad.[14] Vaughan likewise noted in 1979 Retzsch's absence of historical illustration, echoing the period argument. Retzsch's claim to a distinguished rank lay far beyond Saxony. It also ran on an *imported technique*, the outline, diverging from Dresden's academic canons. His appointment was therefore somewhat out of step with the Academy's 6 February 1764 founding document expecting members to increase prestige for Saxon artists.[15] In terms of success and style, he was an outsider in his home country, hardly attuned to his contemporaries' artistic options, and this local period view has left an enduring mark on German criticism.

Accounts and documents suggest a different narrative if highlighted otherwise.

The French *Magasin pittoresque* for instance knew better than publicize an artistic education based only on Italy: "thanks to its museum and inhabitants' taste," Dresden was "an excellent school of art."[16] There, promising youth could find ample artistic nourishment. Even by today's standards, its Gallery may be considered one of the richest in Italian art throughout Europe. It had been enhanced in 1746 by the most significant pieces from Modena and further eighteenth-century acquisitions. For art historian Anna Jameson in 1834, its 534 Italian pictures could

---

4   Uwe Hellwig, "Studien zu Moritz Retzsch (1779–1857) und seinen Umrissillustrationen im verlegerischen Kontext," (PhD diss., Göttingen, 2018), 19, 44–45, 50–51.

5   Th. S., "Moritz Retzsch. Ein Lebensbild," *Deutsches Kunstblatt* 9 (Jan 1858): 5–7.

6   Hellwig, "Studien zu Moritz Retzsch," 41, 54–55.

7   "Aus dem Leben Moritz Retzsch's," *Dresdner Geschichtsblätter*, no. 3 (1896): 280. Cf. Mscr.Dresd.t,3097.

8   Th. S., "Ein Lebensbild," 7b.

9   Cf. Jean-Louis Sponsel, ed., *Fürsten-Bildnisse aus dem Hause Wettin* (Dresden: Wilhelm Baensch, 1906), 67, 85.

10   Hellwig, "Studien zu Moritz Retzsch," 62.

11   Gerd Spitzer, "Caspar David Friedrich, Johann Christian Dahl und die Professur für Landschaftsmalerei an der Kunstakademie," *Dresden Hefte*, no. 120 (2014/4): 24, n. 4.

12   Th. S., "Ein Lebensbild," 8a.

13   Katrin Bielmeier, "Die Rezeptionsstücke der Professoren und Mitglieder der Dresden Kunstakademie seit deren Grundung im Jahre 1764" (Master thesis, Universität Dresden, 2001), 51.

14   Hellwig, "Studien zu Moritz Retzsch," 67–68.

15   Founding script, fol. 5v. I particularly thank Ms. Simone Fugger von dem Rech for researching this point in Academy records.

16   "Moritz Retzsch," 389a.

compete with "no gallery, except that of Florence."[17] The riverbank city itself, endowed with new glory by Augustus II the Strong (1670–1733), a convert to Roman Catholicism, followed an Italian model studded with baroque buildings, rivalling Venice or Rome as a major centre for the arts. It is no accident that it was called "Florence of the Elbe" (*Elbflorenz*). Nor that Bernardo Bellotto (1722–80), pupil and nephew of Canaletto and court painter to the Saxon Elector, left of it numerous *vedute* alongside those of prominent Italian art capitals. Still, the perceived need for an artistic training in Italy, a strong nineteenth-century prerequisite for an artist of status, had a bearing.

Was Retzsch closer to nature than to the city? The exact year he left Dresden to settle in vine country is a moot point. Th. S.'s devout sketch has him bid adieu to the city in 1828 for reasons of health and heavy workload. Already in 1813, he had suffered from a nervous disease.[18] By the 1830s, his numerous outline commissions for Cotta in Stuttgart and the *Shakespeare Gallery* for Ernst Fleischer in Leipzig weighed on him. When painting, he was subject to trembling fits.[19] In a contrasting version, he would only have left the city after the 1848 upheaval.[20] Other accounts lie in between. His professorial duties seem to have been no sinecure, and he was a practising and committed artist to the end. From 1810 to the late 1830s, his business correspondence with the Cottas father and son is always from "Dresden." In his first 10 October 1810 missive, contracting with Johann Friedrich Cotta, he writes from the old town (*auf den breiten Gaße im | Mohrenkopfe 1. Treppe*).[21] In January 1823, he addresses Cotta from "his own house" (*Neustadt. No 16 am Palaisgarten | im eignen Haus*).[22] "From 1819 he lived for thirty years at Kohlmarkt in the new town," notes well-informed Ernst Sigismund.[23] The latter, a teacher at the Academy, a member of the Saxon Art Association, and author of two Retzsch articles, of which the Thieme-Becker entry, collected Retzsch's work. Yet, on 10 June 1831, Karl Förster writes to Ludwig Tieck that Retzsch "has been living at his vine slopes (*Weinberg*)

for some time" and comes into town for one or two days per week.[24]

When Anna Jameson visited him in November 1833, Retzsch warmly received her and showed his work in two lodgings, first "a small house in the Neustadt," where he had a "painting room," obviously an artist's studio, then his "*campagna*—for whether it were farm-house, villa or vineyard, or all together, I could not well decide."[25] This version occurs in Jameson's travelogue on Germany. When the same text is tailored as part of her preface to Retzsch's *Fancies* for the English public, the city abode is omitted and the picturesque has crept in: "His usual residence is at his own pretty little farm, or Weinberg, a few miles from the city."[26] Crafting Retzsch's portrait, particularly for his English audience, favoured an artistic personality as close to nature as possible. David d'Angers who visited him in October 1834 joins in to strongly nuance the myth of an antisocial life: "he comes into town every Thursday, to give his lessons."[27] Assuredly frustration and disappointment had later crept in, and cast many a shadow.[28] Yet, in 1810, at the time of the *Faust* outlines, Retzsch was an urbane thirty-year-old artist of growing fame, mainly for his paintings, hindered mostly by social shortcomings and a mesh of family obligations.

Retzsch's large country house in nearby Oberlößnitz, on Radebeul's vine hills overlooking Dresden and the river Elbe, today home to three families, was his mother's inheritance, further extended by a vineyard, his wife's heirloom. A nature-lover, frequently departing from the city to seek inspiration, he had spent the happiest moments of his youth there, regularly painting with brother August, a landscape artist. This likely became his permanent and only abode after 1849 (confirming Sigismund) until his death in 1857. Until then, he seemingly kept a house-cum-studio in new Dresden. He was buried in the Neustadt-Dresden cemetery but his grave is effaced.

An 1850s visit is worth mentioning in some detail for its conflicting views at a late date. It is in Oberlößnitz that successful but conservative Irish novelist Anna Maria Hall called on him, with her husband Samuel Carter Hall, writer and editor of the *Art Journal*, a major nineteenth-century publication on artistic matters. The periodical, an 1849 renaming of the *Art Union Monthly Journal*, grew to be

---

17   Jameson, *Visits and Sketches at Home and Abroad* (New York: Harper and Brothers, 1834), 1:217.

18   Hellwig, "Studien zu Moritz Retzsch," 58.

19   Th. S., "Ein Lebensbild," 8b.

20   Klaus J. Lemmer, "Moritz Retzsch und seine Illustrationen zu Goethes *Faust*," *Börsenblatt für den deutschen Buchhandel* 44, no. 69 (1988), *Aus dem Antiquariat*, no. 8: A322a.

21   DLA Co: Retzsch.

22   DLA C-R, no. 2.

23   Sigismund, "Moritz Retzsch," *Neueste Nachrichten, Beilage*, no. 15 (15 Jan 1901): (15 Jan 1901).

---

24   Karl Holtei, ed., *Briefe an Ludwig Tieck* (Breslau: Eduard Trewendt, 1864), 1:196.

25   Jameson, *Visits and Sketches*, 1:223, 225.

26   Jameson, "Introduction," in *Fantasien: Fancies. A Series of Subjects in Outline* (London: Saunders and Otley, 1834), x.

27   *Les Carnets de David d'Angers,* ed. André Bruel (Paris: Plon, 1958), 1:308.

28   Hellwig, "Studien zu Moritz Retzsch," 70.

popular and influential,[29] particularly in the context of the 1851 Crystal Palace Great Exhibition of the Works of Industry of all Nations, the very first of World Fairs to mark the second half of the nineteenth century. A day before the visit, Mrs Hall expressively wrote of a dwelling mysteriously hidden in the hills, seen far away from central Dresden against the setting sun.[30] Such an overture, penned in a diffuse naïve tone, was intended for a broad magazine-reading public, who mostly knew Retzsch's work from copies and reproductions. The growing moral allegories in his work begged for a face and personality to match. The article appeared in January 1851 with a portrait of ageing Retzsch and a sketch of his "cottage-house" by Edwin Williams. By June, the portrait, in "a green cloak over the usual homely attire in which he is accustomed to tend his vineyard," claimed pride of place in the Royal Academy annual display, between the likenesses of sculptor John Gibson and poet William Wordsworth.[31] The RA event attracted the World Fair's international public but the buoyant effect had already been boosted: in March, Mrs Hall's article had appeared in *Harper's New Monthly Magazine* for a substantial American audience, yet without any images.[32] It must have spread further in the press, fostering the hermit's tale, and even rubbed off on Vaughan's expert analysis. Yet reality is in the eye of the beholder. Samuel Carter Hall, Anna Maria's husband, was rather more down to earth: Retzsch, he wrote, "seemed mightily to enjoy the retirement that supplied him with pure air, quiet, and the means of enjoying healthful exercise."[33] The Halls had visited Germany to secure manufacturing drawings, yet again as a Crystal Palace exhibition offshoot, and profited from the journey to pay calls on prominent artists. By then the Retzsch-hermit legend was well fleshed out. However, all this occurs forty years later than 1810 and *Faust*, to which I shall now turn.

1.2 Romantic Pranks and Rituals

Retzsch enjoyed painting from an early age. An illuminated diary in seven notebooks, drawn and coloured with his brother August between 1795 and 1809, is a rare

pictorial chronicle revealing the happy moments they shared outdoors. It has been published under the title *Bilder einer Kindheit* (*Images of a Childhood*) but in numerous pictures the brothers are well over twenty. Many of the scenes corroborate Caspar David Friedrich's pranks, well past his first youth. Friedrich was also in his late twenties when he egged on the Retzsch brothers and other artists in self-amusement by targeting an old pot and glass bottle on the Elbe banks after visiting an exhibition.[34] The Retzsch brothers' painted diary reveals a kindred spirit. Charming days out in the open unfold leaf by leaf but not only. A witty perception of social rituals pervades scenes of frolic, dance, and music making. Pastime performances in company, whimsical staging of chivalrous battles and sports (cf. Fig. 9.2), and eerie or fantastical episodes follow on each other. "They also knew how to entertain themselves for hours with fantastic plays for which they had created and cut out landscapes, buildings, and figures," enhances Th. S. Gay spirit, the power of imagination, artistic implements, and the performances themselves refute the very legend of solitude and withdrawal. Retzsch's youthful occupations included devising and illuminating tales, carving male and female heads from clothes' pegs, and decking playing cards with witty heads and figures.[35]

Love and desire lurked around the corner. Plates from October 1807 (Moritz was nearly twenty) to December 1808 (over twenty by then) depict his budding idyll with Christel Miersch (Johanna Christiana Mürisch or Mirisch), the twelve- to thirteen-year-old daughter of a neighbouring vinedresser. In one of these, Moritz has waylaid her on some pretext, and she listens abashed to his eager talk as he bends over, taking her hand, one arm over her shoulders (Fig. 1.1). August's diary entry reads: "Here stands little Christel Miersch, taken aback by Moritz. He had begged Julie Renovanz[36] to go down and keep talking to Christel, who was on water duty—until Moritz came! My sister and I are eavesdropping behind the window shutter of the corner room."[37] In a frock coat, curly young Moritz takes Christel unawares and traps her in conversation, just as his rejuvenated Faust, in his future plate 8 (cf. Fig. 1.8), would forcefully approach and offer his company to juvenile Margaret, "past her fourteenth year," as Goethe has it (F 2627). Albeit with allowances, his cognizant, prying siblings behind the window shutter, also prompt future comparison with his lurking Mephistopheles in

---

29   Maureen Keane, *Mrs. S. C. Hall: A Literary Biography* (Gerrards Cross: Colin Smythe, 1997), 19.

30   Mrs S. C. Hall, "A Morning with Moritz Retzsch," *Art Journal*, n.s., 3 (1 Jan 1851): 21.

31   "The Royal Academy—The Eighty-Third Exhibition—1851," *Art Journal*, n.s., 3 (1 June 1851): 156a.

32   *Harper's New Monthly Magazine* 2, no. 10 (Mar 1851): 509b–13a.

33   Samuel Carter Hall, *Retrospect of a Long Life, from 1815 to 1883* (New York: D. Appleton and Co., 1883), 238.

---

34   Herrmann Zschoche, ed., *Bilder einer Kindheit: Das malerische Tagebuch der Brüder Retzsch 1795–1809* (Husum: Verlag der Kunst, 2007).

35   Th. S., "Ein Lebensbild," 5.

36   "Rendvang" in Zschoche, corrected.

37   Zschoche, ed., *Bilder einer Kindheit*, 79.

FIGURE 1.1   Moritz Retzsch stopping little Christel on her way to water duty with the complicity of Julie Renovanz and siblings watching from the upstairs window, coloured drawing in *Weinbergs Scenen, aus dem Leben der beiden Brüder August und Moritz Retzsch*
SKK, INV. NR. CA 53 V 98, DRESDEN, PHOTO CATERINA MICKSCH

FIGURE 1.2   Julianne Henriette (Julie) Renovanz, hand-made silk embroidery accompanied by verse as a friendship gift, 12 January 1806. Friendship album of Moritz Retzsch
SLUB / DEUTSCHE FOTOTHEK, MSCR.DRESD.APP.3044, 103R., DRESDEN

plate 8, not to mention his own bearing, akin to Faust's in the garden scene to come (cf. Fig. 10.3). Julianne Henriette Renovanz, surely a neighbour and close friend, contributed two elaborate embroideries with inscriptions to both Moritz's and August's friendship albums (*Stammbücher*).[38] The busy bees besieging a florid bush in her wonderful needlework for Moritz along with rhymed wishes (not reproduced here), comment on his fertile creativity as divine gift and testify to the cultural refinement of the Oberlößnitz community (Fig. 1.2). In another diary picture, Moritz stands at an open door ardently declaring his love to the maiden-child Christel whose transparent porcelain features and clear blue eyes depict an ideal Gretchen (Fig. 1.3). It seems no coincidence he took to Goethe's *Faust* from 1808.[39] Both diary plates, painted in March 1809, look at events dated "30th October 1807" and "Spring 1808." His falling in love intersects with his reading of Goethe's play but also frames it in a manner that Borges would later spell out.[40] It may well be that Goethe's *Faust*, personal recollections, and image making have mutually shaped each other already in this diary. In young Moritz Retzsch's case, life and literature blend.

Friedrich La Motte Fouqué's knight Huldbrand also comes to mind, riding through the enchanted forest to secure Undine, his child wife. Fouqué compares him to Pygmalion gratified by Venus in his chapter 8. Retzsch, who painted an *Undine* after Fouqué, a close friend, may be similarly seen as a Pygmalionic husband educating and grooming the young girl before marrying her: "She was the daughter of a vinedresser, whom Retzsch fell in love with while she was yet almost a child, and educated for his wife—at least so runs the tale," writes Jameson.[41] *Tale* stresses the extent to which life and literature mix and match. It is not by chance that, upon meeting her, Jameson called Christel "as pretty *a piece of domestic poetry* as one shall see in a summer's day."[42]

The way Retzsch forwent artistic training in Italy also relates to Goethe's *Faust* as described by Th. S. with first-hand access to intimate details: "The phrase 'you must renounce' (*Das Wort 'Du sollst entbehren'*) was impressed in his sensitive artist's mind amid much pain, and this wound did not heal so long as he lived, although in this renunciation he devoutly and tacitly honoured

---

38   Mscr.Dresd.App.3044, Bl. 102v–103r (Moritz's album) and Mscr.Dresd.App. 3043, Bl. 51v–52r (August's).
39   Sigismund, "Retzsch, Moritz," in Hans Vollmer, ed., *Allgemeines Lexikon der Bildenden Künstler* (Leipzig: E. A. Seemann, 1934), 38:193b.
40   See Introduction, p. 5.

---

41   Jameson, *Visits and Sketches*, 1:225–6.
42   Ibid., 1:225, my emphasis.

FIGURE 1.3   Moritz Retzsch courting Christel, coloured drawing in *Weinbergs Scenen, aus dem Leben der beiden Brüder August und Moritz Retzsch*
SKK, INV. NR. CA 53 V 99, DRESDEN, PHOTO CATERINA MICKSCH

God's will as well."[43] Goethe's line "*Entbehren sollst du! sollst entbehren!*" ("Abstain! it calls, You shall abstain!," F 1549, trans. W. Arndt) inevitably comes to mind, with Faust stating to Mephistopheles the unappeasable thirst that no "renouncement" or "self-denial" will ever quench. In reading Goethe's tragedy, this key line must have made a strong impression on Retzsch, a pious man, by contrast.

Merging literature and life was a romantic predilection. So was reciprocal portrait painting and drawing as a pledge of friendship. Fellow artist Caspar David Friedrich's portrait is assumed to have figured amongst Retzsch's works. In quest of knowledge, Friedrich himself was drawn to Goethe's *Faust*, as in his 1810–11 poem on the two souls inhabiting his breast.[44] His famous oil painting *The Monk by the Sea*, crafted in Dresden in 1808–10, while Retzsch was at work on his own *Faust* outlines, has been discussed as based on Retzsch's *Faust Umrisse*

43   Th. S., "Ein Lebensbild," 7a.

44   Caspar David Friedrich, *Die Briefe*, ed. H. Zschoche (Hamburg: ConferencePoint, 2005), 73–74.

FIGURE 1.4
Moritz Retzsch, *Carl Boromäus von Miltitz and Auguste von Miltitz*, double portrait lost in World War II. Reproduced in *Der Cicerone. Halbmonatsschrift für die Interessen des Kunstforschers & Sammlers* 16, no. 11 (1924): 508
HEIDELBERG UNIVERSITY LIBRARY

that Friedrich likely knew.[45] Other prominent Romantics were friends of Retzsch. From 1812 to 1816 he belonged to the Castle Scharfenberg circle.[46] The castle regulars included Friedrich de La Motte Fouqué, warrior, poet, novelist, literary review editor, and author of *Undine*; poet Johann August Apel, co-editor of the famous *Gespensterbuch*, whose French translation inspired Mary Shelley of the Diodati group to write *Frankenstein*; and host Carl Borromäus von Miltitz, a man of many talents and strong musical inclination. The double portrait of Miltitz and his wife, Auguste, with both of whom Retzsch corresponded, is a masterpiece lost during World War II (Fig. 1.4). It had belonged to Count Vitzthum von Eckstädt.[47] Figured in intense interaction and traditional German dress against Scharfenberg's daunting towers, whither they had intentionally moved, Auguste and Carl von Miltitz make the

---

45 Werner Busch, *Caspar David Friedrich: Ästhetik und Religion* (Munich: C. H. Beck, 2003), 61–64; Friedrich, *Die Briefe*, 74f, 66.

46 Otto Eduard Schmidt, *Fouqué, Apel, Miltitz: Beiträge zur Geschichte der deutschen Romantik* (Leipzig: Dürr, 1908); Hans Joachim Neidhardt, "Der Scharfenbergerkreis—ein Freundschaftsbund der Romantik," in *Caspar David Friedrich und die Malerei der Dresdner Romantik* (Leipzig: Seemann, 2005), 76–77; Neidhardt, *Die Malerei der Romantik in Dresden* (Leipzig: Seemann, 1976), 36–42.

47 M. R. Möbius, "Romantik und Biedermeier," *Der Cicerone* 16, no. 11 (1924): 508.

past come alive in pure romantic fashion and dress. The painting deliberately omits the castle's ruins to show dwellers and abode united:

Das stille, sinnige Wesen der schönen Frau, die geistig erregtere, ein wenig lehrhafte, fast nervöse Art des Mannes—kurz das innerste Seelenleben der beiden Gatten ist auf diesem Bilde mit solcher Treue und Tiefe gemalt, daß es uns—der höchste Triumph des Malers—im Innersten packt und zwingt, den dargestellten Personen, ja sogar dem "Gehause ihres Daseins" unsere lebhafteste Teilnahme zu schenken.[48]

The motionless, thoughtful nature of the beautiful woman, the more mentally excited, a little didactic, almost nervous manner of the man—in short, the innermost soul life of husband and wife is here painted with such faithfulness and depth that the picture—such is the painter's greatest triumph—affects us at the utmost and forces us to grant our most lively sympathy to the people portrayed, and what is more, to the "house of their being."

Castle life, a continuation of the social gatherings and theatricals of Retzsch's youth (cf. Fig. 9.2), further blended life and literature. Some thirty-five years later, in an 1847 letter to Luise von Watzdorf, cousin of Auguste Miltitz and her most intimate friend, herself part of the circle, memories of such community life still held sway over Retzsch's imagination:

Die Stunden, welche im Thurmzimmer bei Lampenlicht und singender Theemaschine im lieben Familienkreis traulich verbracht, sowie die, welche in der reizenden Umgebung des Schlosses gemeinschaftlich verlebt wurden, sie ziehen an meinem inneren Auge nicht selten vorüber; dort, im Thurmzimmer, glaube ich mein Zeichenbuch aufgeschlagen vor mir liegen habend, noch Miltitzen vorlesen zu hören, sie [sic] und die gute Miltitz wirtschaftlich beschäftigt zu sehen, ausserhalb die Töne des Nachtwindes und der Eulen zu vernehmen und die Phantasiegebilde, welche mir vorschwebend die Räume durchzogen und alles belebten, zu erschauen.[49]

The hours intimately spent in the cherished household circle in the tower room by lamplight and the singing tea kit, as those spent in company in the charming surroundings of the castle, often fleet before my inner eye; there, in the tower room, it seems to me, my sketchbook open before me, I can still hear Miltitz reading aloud, I see you and the goodly [Auguste] Miltitz busy with the housekeeping, I perceive outside the wail of the night wind and the owls, and I behold the fantastic images that, floating afore me, pervaded the rooms and enlivened everything.

The artist's sketchbook did not lie open in vain. Letters from fellow circle members refer now to "our Retzsch," or again "excellent Retzsch," endorsing his outlines or requesting them for numerous literary works. Fouqué's short novels and stories, a play extract, and a tale by Caroline de La Motte Fouqué figure conspicuously in 1816–17 almanacs with engravings after Retzsch, along with an 1820 Miltitz story.[50] Portraitwise, Retzsch painted Apel's in oil and pencilled Miltitz's.[51] The latter would in turn comment several of Retzsch's creations: his *Chess Players* using the artist's own remarks (dated 1831, actually beyond 1834), his Shakespeare-inspired *Romeo and Juliet* (1836) and *King Lear* (1838), his outlines for Gottfried August Bürger's poems (1840).

Relations between Retzsch and Fouqué are even stronger. At the 1814 Dresden Academy exhibition, Retzsch's *Undine* after Fouqué's novel (published 1811) gave to the knight carrying Undine across the river Fouqué's features and up-turned whiskers. Twenty years later, in Retzsch's trilingual *Fancies* (1834), his plate 3, *The Fate of the Poet*, also known as *The Poet and the Undines*, pictures a young naked rider on a powerful horse, assaulted by a rowdy crowd of water nymphs, eager to bag their prey. He again sports Fouqué's features[52] but the romantic story is a darker allegory. Poetry almost drowns under waves like the assailed poet. In a "rhymed salute" (*Liedergruß*), Fouqué in turn celebrated Retzsch as "noble wizard" (*edler Magier*) and "magically fashioning comrade" (*zaubrisch bildender Genosse*). In this, Retzsch's creative power outmatches the luminous pageants born of a magic ring, namely Fouqué's own 1813 three-volume romance *Der Zauberring*.[53] Fouqué's creations emerge in a mist while Retzsch's craft turns imaginings into live

---

48   Schmidt, *Fouqué, Apel, Miltitz*, 48.
49   Qtd. ibid., 218.

---

50   Hirschberg, *Chronologisches Verzeichniss*, 22–24, 27.
51   Schmidt, *Fouqué, Apel, Miltitz*, 51, 33.
52   Ibid., 20–21.
53   Fouqué, *Gedichte, zweiter Band* (Stuttgart: Cotta, 1817), 179.

embodiments. The tribute hails Retzsch's gift for bringing imaginary creatures to life *through etching*. Such close interactions contest the fiction of an unsociable recluse. Although Retzsch made a living through painting, for Fouqué his most gripping images were engravings.

1.3 Portraits and Sociability

His 1811 self-portrait shows how Retzsch saw himself in the very years he conceived and etched his *Faust* outlines. It figures in the so-called "Carus album," a collection of eighteenth- and nineteenth-century artists' self-representations compiled in Dresden by Jacob Seydelmann and Italian-born wife Apollonia, née de Forgue. They both were accomplished artists: Josephus Johannes Crescentius, known as Jacob, a pupil of Anton Raphael Mengs, was reputed for his sepia copies of Dresden paintings, drawn to original size. Apollonia excelled in miniature and sepia copies of the same, but also in portraiture, held a weekly salon, and cherished artistic gatherings. The Seydelmann collection, put together between 1805 and 1816, during the Napoleonic domination and ensuing war of liberation, testifies to bonds of friendship and social connections. A credential of artistic work, it also harks back to the new standing of a recently empowered middle class.[54]

Retzsch's self-portrait severally pays tribute to sociability, artistry and friendship within a cultured circle of which he was an integral part. Attitude, dress, and expression display sophisticated choices and "the peculiar skill with which he expresses the mental characteristics of his sitters," as praised in a London article.[55] In his thirty-second year in 1811, he pictured himself as a brisk young man, still in his twenties, self-confident and lively, full of desire to please and will to succeed (Fig. 1.5). Features, hair, coat and shirt are firmly drawn in black chalk on tinted paper. White highlights bring forward large, willing eyes, dense, curly locks, and an open neck with a *jabot* frill. The background adds to the portrait's keen forwardness, and his full initials form a decorative signature above the date. His coat, typical of the time, matches at first sight that worn by his friend and fellow student Gustav Heinrich Naeke in his own self-portrait, also part of the Seydelmann collection. Yet Retzsch's M-point collar is distinctly modern, his

ruffles more fashionable than Naeke's formal cravat. His markedly romantic character gainsays the cliché of the solitary youth in the woods. It posits him in an urbane and social context of artistic dynamism.

Sociability is writ large in his artistic commitments. The ritual of portraiture was a sure sign of standing and vehicle of social intercourse at the time. Constrained to earn his family's and own living through commissions, Retzsch proved an able portraitist for the court, nobility and army officers, including the Saxon court's own princes allegedly visiting him in his town studio. Portraits gained him admittance to Dresden's aristocratic and upper classes, providing protection and introductions.[56] The public display of General Joseph Adolf Thielmann (Thielemann) and wife Wilhelmine's life-size portraits, judged first-rate for conception and colouring, brought him further assignments.[57] The sitters also provided the necessary introduction to Goethe during his September 1810 Dresden visit. Yet, like numerous other paintings by Retzsch, their portraits are no more traceable.[58] Beyond these highly placed acquaintances, Retzsch also took to miniature painting. In Napoleonic post-war times of mourning and grief, well before photography, portraiture was the customary way to remember the departed and pay tribute to their memory. Retzsch seemingly developed, to their relatives' satisfaction, a speciality in portraying the busts of defunct persons he had seen only once or fleetingly.[59] If true, such an assertion compliments his keen eye and shows an exceptional visual memory. However, several miniatures, as well as the double Miltitz portrait, are lost since World War II.[60] Indeed Retzsch's career and work were blighted by war from the nineteenth through the twentieth centuries.

In parallel, he declared himself to have chosen "history painting" (*geschichtliche Malerei*),[61] an official label that set him within an established genre while allowing for a broad choice of subjects. His submissions to the Academy exhibitions followed suit: they not only disclose a distinct preference for mythology and religion but were also stirred by literature. A passionate reader, his inclination for ardent romantic ideals of the heart and senses, his delight in fancy, and a fertile imagination found ample food for thought in penetrating texts of the time. Besides *Undine*, he painted after Fouqué's *Sintram*, felt close to Salomon Gessner's enchanted nature and made

---

54 Angela Böhm, *Carus Album. Die Wiederentdeckung einer Porträt-sammlung* (Dresden: Städtische Galerie Dresden Kunstsammlung, 2009), 7.

55 "Literary and Scientific Intelligence," *LM* 6, no. 33 (Sept 1822): 287.

56 Lemmer, "Moritz Retzsch," A333b.

57 Th. S., "Ein Lebensbild," 7a.

58 *Tg* 4, 2:1088.

59 Th. S., "Ein Lebensbild," 7a.

60 See Lost Art Internet Database, Stiftung Deutsches Zentrum Kulturgutverluste: Retzsch, nos. 27, 28, 29.

61 "Aus dem Leben Moritz Retzsch's," 280.

FIGURE 1.5
Moritz Retzsch, self-portrait, signed and dated 1811, black chalk on tinted paper, heightened with white, 24.3 × 18.8 cm, from the so-called "Carus album"
SGK, INV.NR. 1978/K 182, MUSEEN DER STADT DRESDEN, PHOTO FRANZ ZADNIČEK

a painting after his *Idylls*, just as he would after Goethe's *Egmont*, the *Fisherman*, the *Erlking*, and *Wilhelm Meister's Apprenticeship* (Mignon at the feet of Wilhelm Meister).

1.4 A Poetic Mind

Still more essentially, Retzsch also conceived and created after his own imaginings. He has been repeatedly credited with a personal gift for conjuring up poetic subjects in his art.

Such qualities stood out early in his *Faust* outlines. The unsigned preface to the 1816 German original edition, actually by Therese Huber, editor of Cotta's *Morgenblatt für gebildete Stände*, saw in his plates a second poem reinvented from Goethe's. Resumed in the 1820 Boosey English edition, with Retzsch's plates copied by Henry Moses, her words flatteringly resounded in both German and English: "The artist seems to *have created the work once again*," said her German italics attracting attention (*Der Künstler scheint das Werk* noch einmal gemacht *zu haben*), while the English translation went a step further: "so as it were to renew the work itself." Both introductions insisted on the "ingenious translator" (*ein geistvoller Uebersetzer*) though his achievement slightly differed. In German, his craft and instrument led the way as he had "intimately fitted the creation of his etching needle to the spirit of his poet" (*so innig hat er die Schöpfung seines Griffels dem*

Geist seines Dichters angeeignet) while the English advantaged adaptation: "by most intimately adapting his Plates to the very genius of the author."[62] In both cases Retzsch's *geistvoll* originality mirrored Goethe's own *Geist*, a keyword to which I will return, since Goethe also used it to describe Retzsch's work.

Although undoubtedly written with the commercial success of *Faust* in mind, Huber's preface is an important text that circulated widely: promptly reprinted in the *Morgenblatt*, it would be reissued in all German *Umrisse* editions to at least 1836 and influence introductions to the English copied outlines. Her *translation* claim was not chance. It prophetically met Shelley's view. In Retzsch's outlines, she argued, *Faust* was not so much *illustrated* (an invasive term I will later address) as *transposed* or *transferred* from word to image. Apprehended by the artist's vivid imagination, the play was *interpreted* through visual media. These outlines were also the first to attract attention to Retzsch. The fact that his name is misspelt on the German label (*Retsch*) and initially spread to Britain and France in that form reflects how inconspicuous he was beyond Dresden in 1816. Things would rapidly change after 1820. The growing success of his *Faust* in Britain prompted Johann Friedrich Cotta to commission him with interpreting Schiller, leaving him free choice of text. Outlines for Schiller came out in as quick succession as several other commissions would allow for: between 1823 and 1833, Retzsch conceived, drew and etched four sets after Schiller's poems, ranging from eight to forty-three plates. His choice of *Pegasus in Harness* (*Pegasus im Joche*, 12 plates) surely reflects his own feeling of bondage and servitude, akin to the fetters set on poetry's winged horse in Schiller. He also authored eight sets after Shakespeare's plays in bilingual editions 1827–46, an enlarged *Faust I* in 1834 and *Faust II* in 1836. Outlines after Bürger's poems followed in 1840. Numerous illustrations in almanacs, outlines for Dante's *Divina Commedia*, thirteen frontispieces issued to grangerize Goethe's renowned *Ausgabe letzter Hand*, and Retzsch's unpublished *Bürgschaft* after Schiller's ballad, form a rich list of accomplishments. Beyond growing confidence and a financial boost, success and fame abroad brought to the fore in the 1830s an able interpreter not only in contour but also in words, poet at heart.

In his own 1833 prose "suggestions" (*Andeutungen*) for Schiller's *Song of the Bell*, poetic thoughts interspersed with Schiller's verse bind Retzsch's forty-three plates in a twin *œuvre* of engraving needle and pen. Self-crafted etched allegories with own texts would be printed in multilingual editions. They were but a small choice from albums filled with drawn reveries and notebooks packed with musings.[63] Numerous commentators typically saluted his gift. Jameson's appraisal is nevertheless exaggerated and over-worded: "Retzsch is himself a poet of the first order, using his glorious power of graphic delineation to throw into form the conceptions, thoughts, aspirations of his own glowing imagination and fertile fancy."[64] Mrs Hall calls him "the poet painter," echoing again Jameson's "both poet and designer."[65] Reviewing his Schiller outlines, Sigismund chimes in: "More poetic commentaries (*poetische Commentare*) than just transfers into another art (*Übertragungen in andere Kunst*), these images are also finely modelled and independently spun out."[66] How come such a double talent has been largely unacknowledged? Retzsch's varying propensities, changeable moods, and a strong bent towards moral allegory are part of the answer.

1.5 The Toils of Fancy and Melancholy

Personal sacrifice under the demands of life left a defining mark on Retzsch's inspiration. Disappointments, existential hardships, disenchantment, frustration and regret all added to a dejected disposition, frequently observed: "He said he was often pursued by dark fancies, haunted by melancholic forebodings, desponding [*sic*] over himself and his art."[67] "Often a deep melancholy (*tiefe Schwermut*) seized upon him; his eyes wet when he saw others, who were not his betters either in talent or education, walking unhampered to the top."[68] This mood predominated as he advanced in years, particularly after August died from a stroke in 1835. Twelve years later, Retzsch wrote to Luise von Watzdorf: "Since the good Lord [...] took away my only true friend, my dear brother, I stand without the male friend whom my soul requires, all alone." At sixty-seven, he hoped for a quick exit from life. "I am in a high degree what is called weary of life (*lebensmüde*)," he added, a word that may also translate as *suicidal*.[69] He lived to be seventy-eight.

Several eyewitnesses and visitors however credit him with an amiable manner that belies a dark and downcast mood. His European fame attracted to Dresden numerous

---

62   [Huber], "Vorrede," in *Umrisse zu Goethe's Faust, gezeichnet von Retsch* (Stuttgart: Cotta, 1816), 5; Analysis 1820, 2.

63   Hirschberg, *Chronologisches Verzeichniss*, 105–21.

64   Jameson, *Visits and Sketches*, 1:222.

65   Hall, "A Morning with Retzsch," 21b; Jameson, "Introduction," v.

66   Sigismund, "Moritz Retzsch."

67   Jameson, *Visits and Sketches*, 1:224.

68   Th. S., "Ein Lebensbild," 7a.

69   Schmidt, *Fouqué, Apel, Miltitz*, 219.

visitors, among whom David d'Angers and Theodor von Holst. In his 1834 notes, the French artist recorded a man welcoming them "with a Frenchman's vivacity and the frank gestures of an artist," echoing Jameson's "open-hearted frankness." His "impatience," his "extremely sudden and quick movements," showed in his curly mane "constantly thrown back like the women do when they throw back their veils." All his gestures indicated "the free independence of a genuine artist."[70] David's medal of Retzsch (possibly helped by an autograph outline profile of the artist now in Angers) emphasizes his moving wavy locks. In turn, after an idealized portrait (toned down in the German translation), Jameson added: "In his deportment he is a mere child of nature, simple, careless, saying just what he feels and thinks at the moment, without regard to forms; yet pleasing from the benevolent earnestness of his manner, and intuitively polite without being polished."[71] Even fifteen years later, once Retzsch had had his share of sadness and discouragement and old age had set in, Mrs Hall could add: "Nothing can be more frank and cordial than Retzsch's manner, mingling, as it does, much simplicity with promptness and decision." Resembling a bipolar intriguing Janus, the melancholic recluse had another face. The Bacchus feasts and Radebeul's vinedressers' festival floats (*Winzeraufzuge*) involved him and August in a festive spirit, the antipode of darker tempers, and have been skilfully studied.[72] Sorrowful moments were surely alleviated by joyous diversions.

Retzsch regularly set aside a day per week to receive visitors, to least disturb his strenuous work rhythm and alleviate an increasing workload.[73] Such a busy life did not prevent him from communicating with penfriends and contacts in Europe and across the Atlantic. Relay posts and publishers acted as go-betweens, witness his 1840s correspondence with young Francis Lieber. Financially constrained to work in the US, Lieber wrote enthusiastically to Retzsch through the agency of his Hamburg-based wife Mathilde and the middlemen publishers Perthes and Besser.[74] Years back, Friedrich Christoph Perthes had sent the first known copy of Retzsch's *Umrisse* to London three months after publication (Chapter 4).

By 1834, though famous abroad, Retzsch was not officially recognized in German lands. Success had brought his graphic art to the fore, nudging painting aside, which clashed with established artistic hierarchies. His compositions from the inner mind privileged allegory with recurrent moral overtones. Such a penchant did not always show him at his best. In his "Statements", Caspar David Friedrich assessed his 1824 painted allegory on man's life and nature's cycle—presumably *Die vier Jahreszeiten* (*The Four Seasons*) after a cycle by Fouqué—in the following terms: "I already know these Four Seasons, and freely admit that I am sorry to have seen something like it by this otherwise so excellent, so sophisticated, ingenious artist (*sonst so außgezeichneten, so geistreichen, jenialen Künstler*). Everything else he has already done, and hopefully will continue to do, makes us easily overlook these four images."[75] Retzsch had been inspired by Friedrich's own 1803 and 1807 cycles on the theme, as well as Philipp Otto Runge's 1803 allegory conceived in Dresden,[76] but his art was also prone to mawkishness, of which his better work is devoid.

The international market however favoured the trend of etched poetic allegories. *Phantasien und Wahrheiten/Fancies and Truths/Fantaisies et Réalités* was issued as a sophisticated album by Leipzig publisher Ernst Fleischer in 1831 with Retzsch's comments in three languages. The emblematic bent was backed by the artist's personal feelings. He had married Christel in 1818 and would annually present her with the birthday gift of a visionary drawing. In the trilingual *Fantasien: Fancies, a Series of Subjects in Outline* (1834), Mrs Jameson introduced six of these to great appraise in England: "to address the moral faculties through the medium of the imagination" was, she argued, to renew allegory through graphic art and poetry. Fable and fancy had educational merit in her eyes, and the public needed such genuine moral, religious and poetical qualities. Her preface was styled for a principled Victorian audience, a growing middle class of artists' devotees. Apologetic moralizing may have bolstered Retzsch's English success during his lifetime but certainly carried a price. It led to oblivion and significantly concealed other facets of his art, primarily its grotesque, satirical and comic aspects.

Earlier in 1834, Jameson had given a different view of his genius: it "embraces at once the grotesque, the comic, the wild, the wonderful, the fanciful, the elegant!"[77] Quoted by

---

70 *Les Carnets de David d'Angers*, 1:308.

71 Jameson, *Visits and Sketches*, 1:283.

72 See *Das Winzerfest der Weinbaugesellschaft im Königreich Sachsen am 25.10.1840* (Dresden: G. G. Meinhold & Söhne, 1840), 6; also Jutta Bäumel's and Gerd-Helge Vogel's articles, in Heinrich Magirius, ed., *600 Jahre Hoflößnitz: Historische Weingutsanlage* (Dresden: Sandstein, 2001), 125–39 and 154–62.

73 Th. S., "Ein Lebensbild," 8b.

74 Claudia Schnurmann, *A Sea of Love: The Atlantic Correspondence of Francis and Mathilde Lieber* (Leiden: Brill, 2018), 577; Schnurmann, *Brücken aus Papier: Atlantischer Wissenstransfer in dem Briefnetzwerk des deutsch-amerikanischen Ehepaars Francis und Mathilde Lieber* (Berlin: LIT, 2014), 43, n. 179.

75 Friedrich, *Die Briefe*, 73.

76 Neidhardt, *Die Malerei der Romantik*, 78.

77 Jameson, *Visits and Sketches*, 1:225.

FIGURE 1.6 Moritz Retzsch, *Fancy*, wood engraving by Dalziel in the series "Selections from the Portfolio of Moritz Retzsch," *Art Journal*, n.s., 4 (July 1852): 224
BnF, V-3101, PARIS

Mrs Hall, artist Vogel von Vogelstein, who had introduced her to his friend Retzsch's household, joined in: "there is always a discovery to be made,—some allegory, half hidden under a rose-leaf; some wise and playful satire [*sic* for *satyr*], peeping beneath the wing of a Cupid, or from the fardel of a traveller."[78] Hall herself worded the drawings' qualities through genre: "triumphs of pure Art, conveying a poetical idea, a moral or religious truth, a brilliant satire, brilliant and sharp as a cutting diamond, by 'graphical representation'; each subject was a bit of the choicest lyric poetry, or an epigram."[79] The *epigram*, a short surprising, satirical, even sarcastic piece, originally carved in stone, comes from the Greek *graphein*, both to *draw* and to *write*. Comparison with the cutting diamond stresses the sharp edge of Retzsch's work. Etching, the technique he mastered, signals abrasive inspiration, not to be toned down for the sake of decorum. As with personal choices and inspiration, Retzsch's perception is binary, just as his mood was double and his media paired.

The grotesque side of his art, gradually put out of sight, has passed almost unnoticed. Yet, one of the twenty-four drawings the Halls had come away with, and partly reproduced in wood engravings in the *Art Journal*, was a composition based on grotesque (Fig. 1.6). The caption ran:

> FANCY, a ruling and creative power, borne onward by a Swan, Pegasus, and Eagle (Poetry, Inspiration, and Aspiration), is surrounded by the beings of her own world whom she calls forth with her magic wand, in heterogeneous shapes, indicative of her restless creative faculty all ending in a manner different from the beginning, all full of meaning yet abounding with apparent contradiction.

---

78 Hall, "A Morning with Retzsch," 21c.
79 Ibid., 22a.

Fancy, mounted on a three-form mongrel, dominates a parade of incongruous creatures, a carnival of beings that would have thrilled the Surrealists. Max Ernst's collages, recycling old etchings and woodcuts, spring to mind. No shape (animal, mineral, vegetable) belongs to just one reign, and no creature stands alone. They jumble and cross-fertilize as they pull wry faces, fight, kiss, push, prod, plague, stab, and colonize each other. A picture of Retzsch's complex creativity, the composition acknowledges his awareness of Fancy's "restless activity," as he critically assesses his own delivery: "all ending in a manner different from the beginning, all full of meaning yet abounding with apparent contradiction." Here is proof of a multifaceted artist, unfathomable in few words.

Already in 1810, metamorphosis and mingling of man and animal with obvious sexual overtones had been the core subject of his first known thirteen outline etchings, named by Hirschberg "Mythological Depictions."[80] Nine out of the surviving twelve summon mutation and passion, perhaps spurred by reading Ovid: Lycaon in profile, half-man, half-animal, turns into a wolf; swan-like Zeus and Leda unite; naked Danae's lap receives Zeus as golden rain; Zeus as Artemis fervently kisses a naked-breasted Callisto in homosexual love; Cadmus-as-snake coils lovingly round bare Harmonia's body; Zeus-into-bull carries away Europe; cursing Hera changes Callisto into a she-bear; Arkas and she-bear Callisto become stars; Zeus in flames clasps Semele (who will perish in his fiery embrace).[81] The plates are a set for art enthusiasts, simply numbered above left, as the concurrent *Faust* plates would be. Retzsch's classical training under Grassi is manifest in line and form, but transformation, the magnetism of romantic literature, and the impetus of imagination would stimulate his fluidity of line.

1.6 Fluctuating Fate in Nineteenth-Century German States

What makes or breaks a reputation? Beyond temperament and talent, in Retzsch's time an artist's fortune depended strongly on social origin, patronage, commendation, and official recognition. Hierarchy prevailed in fine art, with painting—itself ruled by graded genres—ranking far above the graphic arts, even though the Romantics had started to rock standards. Within the graphic arts

themselves, styles and preferences waxed and waned. A rising force was the press. Its acclaims, on either exhibitions or publications, mattered. However, harvesting reviews on Retzsch in the German-language press yields no bumper crop. Articles from abroad had to be marshalled for notoriety. Anna Jameson's pages, for instance, were promptly translated in the art supplement of Cotta's *Morgenblatt*[82] and their sway over Georg Kaspar Nagler's 1843 *Neues allgemeines Künster-Lexicon* is obvious. Not to mention the disarray of the former German empire: the budding artist's career was strongly handicapped by the Napoleonic legacy and his name spread unequally among small religiously and politically chequered German States. Nevertheless, across nineteenth-century Europe, Retzsch's work, associated with two major poets' names, Goethe and Schiller, was a mediation card with a strong bearing on their repute. His uneven German reception is therefore the outcome of assorted causes. Comparisons help: with his brother, the landscape painter August; with his friend and fellow student Gustav Heinrich Naeke; with the particular prestige that Moritz enjoyed in Britain and France; lastly, with Peter Cornelius's *Faust*, a regular association in need of adjustment.

The evolution of Retzsch's historiography mirrors fluctuating fortunes. His first reviews by influential Johann Georg Meusel praise the paintings of Josef Grassi's pupil at the annual Dresden exhibitions between 1805 and 1808. The mentions are concise, yet precise in description, and, due to the wealth of exhibits, a clear commendation. They reflect Retzsch's swift evolution from classical (under Grassi's influence) to religious and literary subjects, and portraits. His art is judged superior (*vorzüglich*). In 1805, he is singled out as the foremost of students mentioned, while in 1807 and 1808 Naeke enjoys pride of place.[83] Already in 1805, Meusel demands a clear separation of painting from drawing or etching. Retzsch's *Diana* canvas, exhibited alongside his drawings (considered foundation work at the time), is deemed jarring,[84] which evidences prevailing hierarchies and, more importantly, Retzsch's

---

80 Hirschberg, *Chronologisches Verzeichniss*, 12–13.

81 See https://skd-online-collection.skd.museum/Details/Index /1078193 and following. Last checked 28 Feb 2023.

82 Jameson, "Biographisches. Moritz Retzsch als Mensch und Künstler geschildert," trans. Dr Vogel, *Morgenblatt für gebildete Stände*, no. 252, *Kunst-Blatt*, no. 84 (21 Oct 1834): 333–34; *Morgenblatt*, no. 254, *Kunst-Blatt*, no. 85 (23 Oct 1834): 338–39. Their hold is also obvious on a French article by Philarète Chasles, *La Revue britannique*, 3rd ser., 12, no. 11 (Nov 1834): 104–21.

83 Meusel, "Schreiben über die von der Königl. Sächs. Akademie der Künste," *Archiv für Künstler und Kunstfreunde* 2, no. 3 (1808): 8:2, no. 4 (1808): 144.

84 "Die Künstausstellung in Dresden betreffend," *Archiv für Künstler und Kunstfreunde* 1, no. 4 (1805): 114–15.

classless conception of his art as a dynamic whole. In 1809, his first list of works in Meusel's *Teutsches Künstlerlexikon* grants him an already significant entry.[85] The same year, in Haymann's account, he excels in portraiture as much as Naeke in historical painting, both still under Grassi.[86] This promising *début* hinges on authoritatively recognizable parameters: entering the Academy as a pupil in 1798, studying under a master, and exhibiting oil paintings on praiseworthy genres. His brother August (1777–1835) did not comply with this pattern: more self-learned than academic, his training was backed by younger Moritz's tuition and the guidance of nature itself. He also copied landscapes after the Gallery models (Claude Lorrain and seventeenth-century Dutch masters). Although praised by Meusel in 1805 for a Hoflößnitz landscape, August lacked patrons, and obviously preferred watercolours to oils. The want of "encouraging recognition" finally discouraged him, as Nagler recorded.[87]

Moritz disposed by comparison of a broader range of genres and an exceptional imagination. He signs an 1823 letter to Cotta as "history and portrait painter" (*Historie u Portraitmaler*),[88] a phrase allowing for broad interpretation, but he kicked over the traces of academic training. He disliked imitative drawing (*Nachzeichnen*) and took pride in submitting to the Academy exhibitions not only skilful genre paintings but individual work. Yet, he complied with expected training under Grassi's taste for the neoclassic, and lent himself to lucrative tasks, such as his forty-four contributions to Becker's royal *Augusteum: Dresdens antike Denkmäler enthaltend* (*Augusteum: Containing Dresden's Ancient Monuments*, 1804–11), recording Dresden's antique statues collection in 154 plates with commentary. Influential Becker was Director of both the Dresden Gallery of Antiques and famous Green Vault. Still, these were not purely potboilers for Moritz: seven of them picture Silenus, Dionysus, Silvanus, and Pan, all forest- and wine-related creatures that would nurture his *Parade of the Vinedressers* (1840). In the latter, analysed by Gerd-Helge Vogel, the mythological tradition of triumphal bacchanalia meets Christian pageants and a modern-day vinedressers' parade.[89] Tellingly, Retzsch's first *Augusteum*

figure, an arresting Silenus (Fig. 1.7), represents in Becker's lengthy comment a forest-demon, the spirit of death, and the very dance of Proteus's transfigurations.[90] Retzsch certainly enjoyed the dark euphoria such incarnations stood for.

Yet, moving on from painting and the Academy, Retzsch struggled to satisfy German criticism. Ironically, what strengthened his reputation abroad weakened it at home. His 1816 *Faust* outlines are a turning point: an important success, they gradually made his name known across Europe. Later chapters will show how and along which paths. To turn a play, deemed offensive in Britain, into an accepted masterpiece is no small or casual feat but a form of alchemy. Yet, the aura-gaining outline medium was much more severely assessed amongst his own.

Indeed, throughout the German States, the situation was diametrically different. It was not *Faust*, but the artist who was in need of promotion. Goethe's commendation would prove essential. A multi-talented engineer of the picturesque, collector, practitioner and arbiter of the arts, Goethe was an admired writer, princely minister, and reorganiser of the formerly small and indistinct Weimar court into a glowing centre of flourishing arts. Concurrently, artistic hierarchies still held strong and outlines could hardly stake a claim over painting. Besides, Retzsch etched his own plates without resorting to a job-engraver or skilled hand, a task perhaps viewed as a sub-standard or low-grade occupation for an artist. Evidence shows that he paid rare attention to the slightest details of the process, as in his 1830s letters to Georg von Cotta pleading the need to have the *Faust* plates cleaned and re-engraved by none other than himself. He knew that much of the expressivity of his prints lay in the effect of line he had mastered with a firm delicacy.

His precise, idiosyncratic style is attentive to detail and particularities, without flamboyant, flowing gestures. This may have been deemed a weakness, indicating unexceptional talent and run-of-the-mill qualities. Moreover, his penchant for nature rather than the worldly duties of society, his predilection for reading in solitude, his need of important patrons, a dearth of means, even his condition as semi-orphan-cum-breadwinner, make for a strangely unfashionable figure, out of step with usual patterns of social promotion. He had a clear calling for art but his personality and tastes did not quite marry with the regular cut of an appointed artistic career. The oft-cited lack of training in Italy is telling. Other details support such

---

85   Meusel, *Teutsches Künstlerlexikon*, 2nd rev. ed. (Lemgo: Meyer, 1809), 2:200–01.

86   Christoph Johann Gottfried Haymann, *Dresdens theils neuerlich verstorbene theils ietzt lebende Schriftsteller und Künstler* (Dresden: Walther, 1809), 374.

87   Nagler, *Neues allgemeines Künstler-Lexicon* (Munich: E. A. Fleischmann, 1843), 13:52.

88   DLA C-R, no. 2.

89   See Vogel, "Moritz August Retzschs Winzerzug," in Magirius, ed., 154–62.

---

90   Wilhelm Gottlieb Becker, ed., *Augusteum: Dresden's antike Denkmäler enthaltend* (Leipzig: Auf Kosten der Verfassers, 1808), 2:68–74.

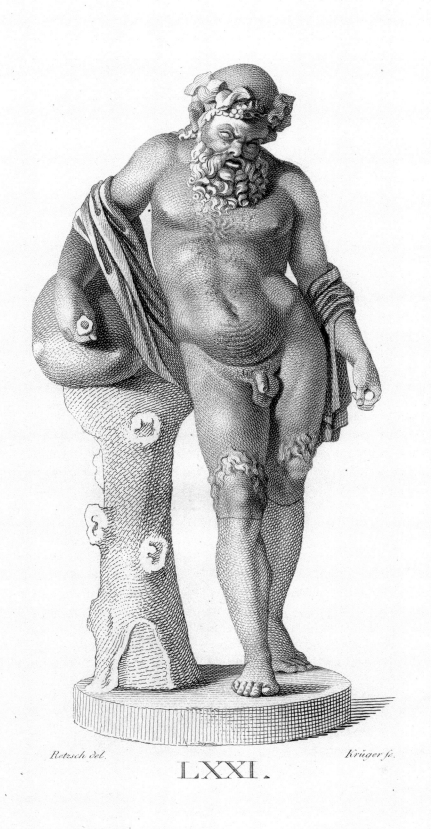

FIGURE 1.7
Silenus, drawing by Moritz Retzsch engraved by Krüger, first plate contributed to Wilhelm Gottlieb Becker, ed., *Augusteum: Dresden's antike Denkmäler enthaltend* (Leipzig: Auf Kosten der Verfassers und in Commission, C. A. Hempel et al.), 2 (1808): fig. 71
SLUB DRESDEN / DEUTSCHE FOTOTHEK, 23.2.83-2, TAF, DRESDEN

speculation: his first deliveries to Johann Friedrich Cotta through a Leipzig representative are neglected; Goethe's sight of the *Faust* drawings is not recorded in the poet's diary despite his alleged warm approval; and Johann Heinrich Meyer in *Über Kunst und Althertum* is conspicuously lacking information on his origins, training or current occupation, unlike Naeke and Cornelius whose biography is more complete.[91] Compared to them, he appears artistically undefined and professionally indecisive.

On issue, his *Faust* outlines hardly attracted attention in the German press. Traced articles amount to only three (which, on closer examination, proves just one), and are spread apart: 1816, 1818 and 1824. Conversely, the English press brims with reviews. The first, in Cotta's October 1816 *Morgenblatt*, is but a duplicate of the unsigned *Umrisse* preface by Huber. It promotes in-house goods, and its qualification of the outlines as "exquisite" (*trefflich*) is of no legitimate consequence. The third, attributed to a French art critic, Pierre-Alexandre Coupin, advocate of neoclassicism and expert on lithography, criticizes Goethe's *Faust* and Schiller's *The Robbers* before applauding Cornelius over Retzsch. Its presence in Cotta's *Kunst-Blatt*, *Morgenblatt*'s art supplement to which Coupin regularly contributed, is due to the success of Jean-Baptiste Muret's copy of Retzsch's *Faust* in France. The scarcity of German articles may have turned it into an indirect tribute, used by Cotta to boost the original etchings' sales. Coupin praises Cornelius's "sublimity of thought" and "great talent," recognizing however Retzsch's rendering of the entire tragedy with "lively and rich imagination" (*lebhaften und reichen Einbildungskraft*). He also admits his renown abroad, and praises the moderate price of the January 1824 French copies, already sold out by April 1824.[92]

We are left with one genuinely German article, an anonymous lukewarm critique in the 1818 *Leipziger Literatur-Zeitung*. Although its author considers impossible for a sensitive artist to neglect a work so admired as *Faust*, foreseeing cases in which art surpasses poetry, Retzsch's prints are merely "well worked out" (*brav gearbeitet, gut gearbeitet*).[93] Several are sternly criticized for gawky expressions, deceptive surroundings, theatricality or overcrowdedness. Restrained exaggeration, where imagination usually goes wild (as in the witch's kitchen and the witches' Sabbath), can hardly be considered praise, but stands for this critic's eulogy. Such mealy-mouthed

appreciation is at odds with English or French acclaim of the time. On his 1834 visit, David d'Angers considered Retzsch's outlines admirable, "devoid of the aridity common to Germans," and the grace of his figures of women and children worthy of Correggio. His distinctive feature is "sensuality" (*la sensualité*) as in his Mephistopheles, "the man embittered by his passions" (*l'homme aigri par ses passions*), contrasted with Caspar David Friedrich's "sombre melancholy."[94] In an unpublished letter to Victor Pavie, David called Retzsch "the man of genius, of great genius, as great as he is good" (*l'homme de génie, de grand génie, aussi grand qu'il est bon*).[95]

German coverage is at best meagre and prone to foreign impact. From 1820 Cotta had entrusted the *Kunst-Blatt* to Ludwig Schorn, who would turn it into a leading art periodical. Its columns, open to news from abroad, mostly England, regularly recorded the success of Retzsch's copies. Significantly, Retzsch's *Faust* first met with sheer applause in two 1824 and 1825 *Kunst-Blatt* articles by Schorn on the German *Fridolin* (1823) and *Fight with the Dragon* (1824), yet only once they had been copied by Moses in London. It had taken almost ten years for the *Faust* outlines to receive overt admiration in a roundabout way. Schorn called Retzsch "the Poet in reproduction" (*reproducierenden Dichter*), a phrase that captured spot-on two main qualities: the outlines' poetic facet and adaptability.[96] Even then, the favour acknowledged was somehow marred by Schorn's interview of John Flaxman, who declared that he knew Retzsch's *Faust* but preferred Cornelius's.[97] Although a commercial success, as shown later, Retzsch's outlines were thus credited only thanks to third parties. Even in the 1830s, once the *Shakespeare Gallery* and Goethe's delight had established him, review editors would welcome foreign comments. Witness, Jameson's pages translated in the *Kunst-Blatt* in 1834, and the 1835 article "Urtheil eines Engländers über die deutschen Malerschulen" ("An Englishman's Judgment on the German Schools of Painting") in the progressive Frankfurt review *Phönix*.[98] The foreign vs. domestic preference would be regularly either mentioned by Retzsch himself or chronicled in past and recent studies.

---

91   FA, pt. 1, 20:169.

92   [Coupin], "Paris, April 1824. Lithographie," *Kunst-Blatt*, no. 256 (13 May 1824): 154–55.

93   "Bildende Künste: *Umrisse zu Göthe's Faust*, gezeichnet von *Retsch*," *Leipziger Literatur-Zeitung*, no. 91 (10 Apr 1818): 725.

94   *Les Carnets de David d'Angers*, 1:308–09, 311.

95   Steuer MS., 1:85.

96   S. [Schorn], "Neue Kupferstiche," *Kunst-Blatt*, no. 45 (3 June 1824): 177.

97   Schorn, "Besuch bey Flaxman im July 1826," *Kunst-Blatt*, no. 30 (12 Apr 1827): 120.

98   Jameson, "Biographisches"; *Phönix: Frühlingszeitung für Deutschland* 1, no. 37 (12 Feb 1835): 146–48; no. 38 (13 Feb): 154b–55a; no. 41 (17 Feb): 162–64a.

The anonymous 1818 *Leipziger Literatur-Zeitung* reviewer had somewhat alleviated his harshness by pointing out that the effect often lost in outline should produce significant paintings.[99] The outline technique implied an artistic low key rhyming with obscurity. Karl August Böttiger in the *Zeitung für die elegante Welt* early praised Retzsch's "definite talent," "prolific imagination," and "rich individual invention."[100] Still, the applause is buried in a compound paragraph on *Faust* in the graphic arts with Retzsch nestling between the Riepenhausen brothers, Ludwig Nauwerck, and Viennese artists Karl Heinrich Rahl and Vincenz Raimund Grüner. By contrast, Naeke's *Faust and Margaret in the Garden*, a painting that had attracted all eyes at the 1811 Dresden Academy exhibition, earned a full page. Any contest between brush and engraving needle was clearly to the latter's disadvantage.

Retzsch's mistake was therefore to have chosen drawing or "illustration," that lowly category under which, from the nineteenth century, diverse undertakings would be regularly bundled, as is still the case. In *History of Modern German Art* written in French (with concomitant German translation), Atanazy Raczyński credited him with "the highest reputation for his outlines" but admitted not knowing any of his paintings. Consequently, in this critic's influential three-volume work, Retzsch earned only three lines despite due appreciation of his Gretchen compared with a Genoveva painting.[101] Raczyński's concise acclaim is exceptional. Retzsch remains outside the artistic mainstream. His German commentators either stand aloof or scrutinize him harshly.

Regular nineteenth-century German judgments of his *Faust* form an almost military list of tickings-off, cold reprimands or diffident reproofs. Hardly the main subject under discussion, they are asides regularly comparing him with Cornelius or Flaxman. Taken in chronological order they prove obvious changes in taste. For Carl Gustav Carus, Retzsch represents the "poetical romantic tendency" of an "insipid period of art (*flaue Kunstperiode*)," definitively outmoded by the 1860s.[102] Outline, favoured for poetry, had fallen out of fashion as realism and historicism had taken over. For Theodor Kutschmann in 1899, his outlines are "dry," his heroes lacking "individuality and character," an unsurprising judgment for the *Jugendstil*

period, ending: "Today one asks in vain how it was possible that there was still an audience for such things back then."[103] At best, Franz von Reber grants him personality in a satirical drawing analysed in opposition to Overbeck. Still, open scorn surfaces in "the empty illustration style of old M. Retzsch."[104] Kutschmann and Reber even wonder at Goethe setting him on a par with Cornelius. The poet's mark of esteem was of no consequence for these pundits, and by 1876 Cornelius's established hegemony allowed for no challenger. The absence of critical evaluation, distance, and cultural awareness of historical breaks in style that such statements reveal is surprising for today's reader as much as these writers' pretence to often arbitrate on the mere basis of personal taste.

Georg Kaspar Nagler's 1843 *Neues allgemeines Künstler-Lexicon* and its four-page Retzsch entry is a landmark in his praise, no doubt widely read, and reprinted (unaltered) in 1909. A major nineteenth-century reference for art history, it does not flinch to call Retzsch an "epoch-making" artist (*als Künstler Epoche machen werde*), recalling the blights of the war and his commitment to family. It frequently echoes Mrs Jameson, describes in detail the painter's *œuvre* and lists his graphic work, yet with inaccuracies that would remain in later accounts. Nagler's misdating the *Umrisse zu Faust* as 1828 is particularly unfortunate since it belittles the first artist to shape the iconography of Goethe's *Faust* throughout. In his *Monogrammisten*, Nagler further calls him an "ingenious draughtsman and etcher" (*genialer Zeichner und Radierer*), an uncommon endorsement at such a late date.[105]

Nagler apart, the scarce nineteenth-century German commentators favourable to Retzsch were not strictly art historians. Franz Kugler for instance, author of the often reprinted and influential *Handbuch der Kunstgeschichte* (*Handbook of Art History*, 1841–42), had interdisciplinary training and was attracted to cultural history. He had studied literature, music, the visual arts, and architecture, wrote verse, frequented artists and romantic writers, and himself practised drawing. Jacob Burckhardt, the would-be prominent historian of art and culture, was his student. Yet even Kugler demanded proper stylization for outline, to attain the quality he admired in Flaxman, but found "rarely and accidentally" in Retzsch. To make his point, he turned to Dibdin's woodcuts of the *Faust* main figures inserted in his *Tour in France and Germany* (1821),

---

99   "Bildende Künste," 726.

100   Böttiger, "Bilder nach Wieland, Göthe und Schiller," *Zeitung für die elegante Welt*, no. 80 (22 Apr 1811): 636.

101   Raczynski, *Geschichte der neueren deutschen Kunst*, trans. from the French by F. H. von der Hagen (Berlin: Auf Kosten des Verfassers, 1836–41), 3:219 and 1:132.

102   Carus, *Lebenserrinerungen und Denkwürdigkeiten* (Leipzig: F. A. Brockhaus, 1865), 1:292–93.

---

103   Kutschmann, *Geschichte der deutschen Illustration* (Goslar: Franz Jäger, 1899), 159.

104   Reber, *Geschichte der neueren deutschen Kunst* (Stuttgart: Meyer & Zeller, 1876), 211 and 454.

105   Nagler, *Die Monogrammisten* (Munich: Georg Franz, 1871), 4:665.

on which more in Chapter 4. When singled out as in Dibdin (cf. Fig. 4.4a–c), Kugler stressed, these groups would "gain extraordinarily from the removal of other surroundings" and the suppression of "disruptive factors," carping at Retzsch's mannerisms, details, and penchant for "theatrically historical costumes" that he found superficial.[106]

All such nuances were simply swept aside in Hans Wolfgang Singer's 1901 diatribe in the *Allgemeines Künstler-Lexikon* that he continued on succeeding Hermann Alexander Müller:

> Bis zu welchem Grade die Kunst in Deutschland einstens gesunken war, ersehen wir aus dem Umstand, dass dieser hohle, bombastische Pfuscher, so unglaublich es uns auch jetzt erscheinen mag, ehedem nicht nur unter die Künstler, sondern unter die bedeutenden gerechnet wurde. Es gibt nichts Affektirteres, Alberneres als die fad geistreichelnden Illustrationen zu den deutschen Klassikern, zu Shakspere [*sic*], etc. des R., der nicht einmal genügend Können besass, um seine Platten selbst zu ätzen. Einigermassen erträglich ist er noch in seinen Bildnissen in Miniatur, von denen die Dresdener Galerie zwei besitzt. Dem dortigen Kupferstichkabinet wurde R.'s gesammter zeichnerischer und radierter Nachlass gestiftet.[107]

> We perceive the extent to which art had once sunk in Germany from the fact that this hollow, bombastic bungler, incredible as it may even now seem to us, was formerly not only counted among the artists but among the important ones. There is nothing more affected and absurd than the insipidly witty illustrations for the German classics, Shakespeare, etc. by R., who did not even have enough skill to etch his plates himself. He is still to some extent bearable in his miniature portraits, two of which are in the Dresden Gallery. R.s overall drawing and etched legacy was donated to the Prints Cabinet there.

It was all the fiercer as it stood for the whole entry (but for two lines of biographical data). Singer was speaking with the authority of the Dresden Prints collection where he worked from 1891 to 1932, and had personally dealt with the 1892 bequest of Retzsch's work. In 1922, the sixth edition of his dictionary had not taken back one word, even

though in 1914 he had tried to make amends. In an article on August and Moritz's pictorial diary, he invokes his inexperience, claiming he was twenty-one (whereas he had turned thirty-two); the exertion of "ploughing through" a legacy that required "the patience of Job" (of which he had none); and the dominant naturalistic bias of the day that blinded him. The overture quotes verbatim the above lines, "amongst the earliest of my occasional rants" (*eine der ersten meiner weniger Philippiken*), to the same shocking effect, devoid of any curatorial level-headedness.[108] Nonetheless, Singer's *Lexikon* is still a readily accessible tool in scholarly libraries or on Internet. It has been much consulted and Retzsch scholars repeatedly felt the need to refer to the inescapable quote.[109]

Across time, Retzsch's German critics form an arena of split opinion. Curt Glaser concedes him "numerous art lovers until late in the [eighteen] thirties,"[110] as will be substantiated and furthered by German editions and copies, scrutinized in Chapter 3. German nineteenth-century criticism is reticent, to say the least. Retzsch's complaints to Francis Lieber about his compatriots' sparse interest correspond to a genuine reality: his *Faust* outlines were indeed, and still are, less prized in his country than abroad. It took nearly two centuries for a German article to redeem him. "Moritz Retzsch is unjustly dismissed as a small master and forgotten," wrote Bernhard Fischer, Cotta specialist and former director of successively the Marbach and Weimar Goethe and Schiller archives, only to continue: "there was hardly a more successful German illustration artist in the first half of the nineteenth century."[111]

Foreign acclaim stands in strong contrast. In a splendid 2017 Philadelphia Museum of Art catalogue of German prints, Cordula Grewe gauges Retzsch "king of the Romantic version of pure contour" no less.[112] John Michael Cooper has called his outlines "remarkable for the tension that resulted between the taut crispness of their flowing lines and the absence of any emphasis on light and shadow."[113] Such novel endorsements meet with Bernhard

---

106 Kugler, *Kleine Schriften und Studien zur Kunstgeschichte* (Stuttgart: Ebner & Seubert, 1854), 3:36, 56, 78.

107 Singer, ed., *Allgemeines Künstler-Lexikon*, 3rd rev. and enlarged ed. (Frankfurt: Rütten & Loening, 1901), 4:47.

108 Singer, "Die Weinbergsszenen von Moritz Retzsch," *Mitteilungen aus den sächsischen Kunstsammlungen* 5 (1914): 82.

109 For instance, Lemmer confronts Singer's tirade with Nagler's entry in 1980 and 1988.

110 Glaser, *Die Graphik der Neuzeit* (Berlin: Bruno Cassirer, 1922), 164.

111 Fischer, "Aus Moritz Retzschs unveröffentlichten Kupferstichen zur 'Bürgschaft' von Friedrich Schiller," *Marbacher Magazin*, no. 107 (2004): 89.

112 Grewe, "Outline and Arabesque: Simplicity and Complexity in German Prints," in *The Enchanted World of German Romantic Prints, 1770–1850*, ed. J. Ittmann (Philadelphia: Philadelphia Museum of Art / Yale University Press, 2017), 237.

113 Cooper, *Mendelssohn, Goethe, and the Walpurgis Night* (Rochester: University of Rochester Press, 2007), 172.

Fischer's. Indeed, the beginning of this twenty-first century marks a turning point in re-evaluation. By contrast, Retzsch's outline engravings "are little known today, and even less appreciated," had written Vaughan in 1979, adding that his nineteenth-century fame in England seemed "astonishingly great."[114] Reservation still lingered in the air until the millennium.

German praise's nineteenth-century rise and fall thus sync with the artist's contrasted portrait. They both reflect the extent to which past artists' repute has heavily depended on cultural context and periodic trends in evaluation, as affected by critics' sanction. Periodicity, *Zeitgeist* and cultural framework are indicators of first importance. Retzsch therefore allows us to grasp an interesting paradigm shift. Crucially, art criticism depended on established hierarchies and shifting styles, while his outlines were promptly diffused in a changing world, hooked on visual media, amongst multiple categories of readership, thanks to an expanding book trade. Retzsch's nineteenth-century German reception, typically negative, struggled with the first, while his good fortune would lie enduringly with the second.

Yet, his purport lies not only in the way his work helps us understand changes in cultural history but also in interpretation of Goethe. He is the only German artist of his time to mediate, beyond the bundled confines of individual German States, a text central to their one-nation ambitions and representative literature. His set offered *Faust* a passport to a wider public, domestic and foreign, through a pliable medium reaching other cultures. A comparison with his main nineteenth-century rival, Peter Cornelius, throws light both on the conditions of *Faust* reception and Retzsch's particular merits.

1.7 Plights and Plusses of Comparison (Retzsch, Cornelius & Naeke)

Comparison, if commendable as a method for nuanced results when cautiously wielded on close yet dissimilar data across time, may also be prone to preconception. Even good methods have drawbacks when applied unfittingly. Partisan comparison with gifted artist Cornelius has been fatal to Retzsch's own *Faust*. For a long time, the former's fame and outstanding career overshadowed the latter's artistic skill and lower visibility. The way histories of art were written moulded Cornelius's prominence: early entrusted with prestigious fresco decorations, he enjoyed eminence amongst the Nazarenes he had joined

in Italy in 1811; summoned by the crown prince (future King Ludwig I of Bavaria) from 1823 to Munich to decorate the Glyptothek, he directed the Munich Academy from 1824 (having been offered an analogous position in Düsseldorf). At the origin of a burgeoning national style, based on Old German masters, and feted for his grand conceptions and large-scale allegories synthesising Greek classicism with Christianity, he enjoyed fame Europe-wide. His *Faust* drawings are indeed admirable and have given a superlative text unparalleled interpretation. However, the chorus of such appraisal, belittling Retzsch, his precursor, is grounded on frequency (Cornelius) vs. scarcity of comment (Retzsch), preconceptions in art historiography, and unclear, even flawed, chronology. Günter Busch usefully put matters into perspective by recalling Sulpiz Boisserée's active backing of young Cornelius from the outset, and replacing Goethe's declarations in context.[115]

Was Retzsch influenced by Cornelius in his *Faust*? Comparison of similar scenes by both has often suggested Retzsch's debt to the Nazarene, Viola Hilderbrand-Schat's being the latest to date.[116] The point is regularly made in *Faust* iconography. Certainly, in several episodes, tricky parallels occur in setting—yet not in spirit and manner. It may well be that the Dresden artist had seen the work of his Düsseldorf counterpart. Yet, tellingly, nobody has inverted the question, namely, might not Cornelius himself have seen Retzsch's drawings? Richard Benz was more poised: "Cornelius was not the first among the Faust illustrators, but whether rightly or wrongly he became the most famous."[117] In Thieme-Becker, Sigismund was more direct: "Immediately after the first part of Goethe's *Faust* became known (1808), that is, before Cornelius, R. had produced a series of sketches."[118] Neidhardt followed suit.[119] On new evidence, Chapter 2 shows that Retzsch had already delivered to Cotta 12 *Faust* plates by May 1811, when Goethe saw Cornelius's first drawings. Retzsch had also completed his *Faust* set by April 1812.

Who was first? is a tantalizing question, and may be unanswerable if renderings are seen only in terms of influence. Right from publication, *Faust* prompted a copious flux of serial graphic works based on Goethe's scenes. Seen from such an angle, similarities would be expected, if not the rule. All German artists vied to embody their own vision of a play by an eminent author, the latest expression

---

114   Vaughan, *German Romanticism*, 123.

115   Günter Busch, *Eugène Delacroix: Der Tod des Valentin* (Frankfurt: Klostermann, 1973), 39f.

116   Hildebrand-Schat, *Moritz Retzschs Illustrationen*, 28–37.

117   Benz, *Goethe und die romantische Kunst* (Munich: R. Piper & Co., 1940), 160.

118   Sigismund, "Retzsch, Moritz," 38:193b.

119   Neidhardt, *Die Malerei der Romantik*, 78.

FIGURE 1.8 Moritz Retzsch, Faust meeting Gretchen, *Umrisse zu Goethe's Faust gezeichnet von Retsch* (Stuttgart & Tübingen: Cotta, 1816), pl. 8
COURTESY HAAB, F 3487, WEIMAR

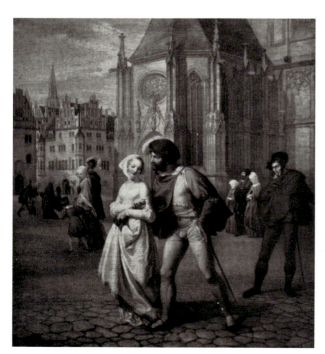

FIGURE 1.9 Gustav Heinrich Naeke, *Faust and Gretchen*, lost painting, c.1812. Repr. in *Katalog zur Ausstellung deutscher Kunst aus der Zeit von 1775–1875 in der Königlichen Nationalgalerie Berlin* (Munich: F. Bruckmann, 1906), 2:401, no. 1234
COURTESY HAAB, KU 4° II A—210 (2), WEIMAR

FIGURE 1.10 Peter Cornelius, *Scene upon Leaving the Church. Faust Proffers Gretchen his Arm*, in *XII Bilder zu Göthe's Faust gezeichnet von Peter von Cornelius* (Frankfurt am Main: Johann Friedrich Wenner, n.d.), pl. 5
COURTESY BEINECKE, YALE UNIVERSITY, FOLIO SPECK CK99 C7 816

FIGURE 1.11
Gustav Heinrich Naeke, preliminary pencil and ink sketches, n.d., 19.6 × 31.8 cm
COURTESY BEINECKE, YALE UNIVERSITY, YCGL MSS. 26, BOX 2, FOLDER 23

FIGURE 1.12A *Faust. Scene in the Street. Faust and Margaret, Mephistopheles in the Background*, engraved by C. A. Schwerdgeburth after Gustav Heinrich Naeke, 10.5 × 7.3 cm. Insert plate in *Urania: Taschenbuch für Damen auf das Jahr 1815 mit neun Kupfern* (Leipzig & Altenburg: Friedrich Brockhaus, [1814])
COURTESY HAAB, F 9144, WEIMAR

FIGURE 1.12B Faust Meeting Gretchen after Gustav Heinrich Naeke, lithographed by Johann Nepomuk Strixner, 1822, chalk lithograph, 28.5 × 18.8 cm
COURTESY HAAB, F 8052 GR [B] (45), WEIMAR

of a home-grown myth, not least their very conception of art in dialogue with prevalent models, whether German or not. Yet, differing artistic outcomes are as numerous as potential readings of *Faust*. Influence proves less important than other shaping factors: effective scenes, the storyline behind a metaphysical drama, arraying a reputedly unruly poetic composition, gradual typification, and, last, but not least, image circulation.

If, instead of loosely comparing Retzsch to Cornelius, we focus on a pivotal scene, Faust's first meeting with Gretchen, the main candidates are at least three: Retzsch (Fig. 1.8), Naeke (in a lost painting, Fig. 1.9), and Cornelius (Fig. 1.10). Comparison is enlightening. All three show the rejuvenated Faust approaching the young girl in public space but all differ in particulars: depiction of protagonists, treatment of Mephistopheles, and crucially the setting. Naeke paints a lively, alluring, and coy Margaret, Cornelius draws a bareheaded girl fleeing away. Retzsch's Gretchen wavers between surprise, restraint and inclination. Eager in all three, Cornelius's Faust is a dazzling, determined, robust and statuesque cavalier, Naeke's and Retzsch's slenderer, intense yet tentative. Everywhere Mephistopheles lurks in the background, with a difference. In both Naeke and Cornelius, he loiters on the right, in contrast to a couple, child (and dog) on the far left, an image of family happiness that would be denied to Faust and Gretchen, alluded to at the moment they meet. The background has dramatic overtones. In Naeke's preparatory sketches, the couple gives alms to a beggar, and there is no child apart from that accompanied by a lone female (Fig. 1.11). As for the dog, it was added in retouched, first engraved (C. A. Schwerdgeburth) later lithographed (J. N. Strixner) versions (Fig. 1.12a–b), probably after the Cornelius detail. Naeke's and Cornelius's Mephistopheles is a prowling evil spirit keeping an eye on Faust. Only Retzsch builds an analogy between doctor and devil through identical costume and swords in parallel—a clever detail that will not be lost on Delacroix (see Chapter 7, Fig. 7.27).

It is the setting that highlights a major disparity in their reading of Goethe. The lines alluded to by Faust's gesture are but two (F 2605–6) and the scene title "A Street." Cornelius and Naeke project the meeting against a cathedral, a sure way to anchor it within the medieval past—Cornelius with Boisserée's project to restore Cologne's cathedral as a national monument in mind, Naeke picturing churchgoers after mass. There is no such celebration in *Faust* but Mephistopheles stresses Gretchen's untouchable purity as she returns from confession. In both Cornelius and Naeke, the background (whose social and emotional overtones affect the imagination of an audience identifying with the setting) arises from Mephistopheles's subsequent lines

(F 2621–22). Only Retzsch has set the scene in a simpler, urban space. The choice literally respects Goethe's title, "A Street," and stresses the relationship between protagonists, two in the fore, one at the rear. On the far right, three tiny figures afore a building (but no conspicuous cathedral), remind us they are not alone. Likewise, on the left, on either side of a front door, two basins may ambivalently identify as decorative flowerpots or indeed as holy-water stoups, alluding to Gretchen's ablution and absolution of sins. Typical of Retzsch's subtlety, the treatment shows fine-tuning of images with the play. It stirs interpretation of the slightest pictorial detail, stimulates perusing the text, and construes new meaning by fostering analogies. Just as Goethe's *Faust* empowers an active reader, it provides scope for reading between image and text. Naeke's and Cornelius's are demonstrative standalone compositions, the first a painting, the second a king-size print. They work on immediate emotions, while Retzsch's single plate from the series is initiatory and insinuating.

If we further focus on only graphic media, stylistic and aesthetic differences loom even greater in Cornelius's and Retzsch's chosen vocabulary. Titling is identifying and classifying. Neither adopts *Illustration*, long absent from German dictionaries, although recurrent in modern scholarship.[120] Instead, *Bilder zu ...* (Cornelius) and *Umrisse zu ...* (Retzsch) allude to distinct stances, and target separate spaces. The Düsseldorf-raised Cornelius followed the gallery model (*Bildreihe*)—and may have been inspired by the celebrated Düsseldorf Gallery of which his own father, Aloys, was an inspector. The size of his prints is designed to compete with paintings. Retzsch on the other hand conformed to Flaxman's outlines after the *Iliad*, the *Odyssey* and Aeschylus's tragedies, well diffused in Europe thanks to Tommaso Piroli's etched multiples. Rather than the Elector's Gallery, his small portfolio is meant for the library or the drawing room of the upwardly mobile classes. Above and beyond these, a fundamental, and to my knowledge altogether neglected difference, lies in other choices, such as format, modes of use, circulation, and reproduction.

Retzsch's small and easy to handle set ($c.17 \times 21.5$ cm) begs touch: folder opening, perusing, flipping through, browsing, or variously poring over the contents. An unpretentious format, it travels easily. Engraved by the artist, the prints will be widely copied, re-engraved, reproduced, and even parodied in the German States, Great Britain (mainly

---

120   See Stead, "*Faust*-Bilder: Uses and Abuses of 'Illustration' in Faust Literature and Faust Collecting. The Case of Alexander Tille," in *Faust-Sammlungen: Genealogien—Medien—Musealität*, ed. C. Rhode (Frankfurt: Klostermann, 2018), 151–56.

England), France, and beyond, as following chapters show. Inserted in Goethe's text in translation, they will give birth to illustrated books in the literal sense. Their broad circulation set the basis of an extensive iconography (see Chapter 7). By contrast, Cornelius's double folio adopts a monumental format (*c*.59.3 × 75 cm), requiring strenuous manhandling. Rivalling Boisserée's grand *Geschichte und Beschreibung des Doms von Köln* (*History and Description of the Cologne Cathedral*) in two Cotta editions in German and French (1821–23), it is meant to throne on a large table or a connoisseur's lectern. Generally taken as a full set of 12 published in one go, in fact it came out in instalments at various dates, the first two including but 8 prints. Issued between Easter 1816 and early 1817, they were completed only in the 1820s. Most were engraved in Rome between 1813 and 1816 by Ferdinand Ruscheweyh, the last by Julius Thaeter in 1825, none by Cornelius himself. The original 1816 fascicles are rarer than Retzsch's folder, and the first set of all twelve published by Wenner has been dated 1826.[121] A smaller edition in plain outline after the pen drawings (*c*.30 × 44 cm), with missing publication data (probably Mey and Widmayer, 1841), has none of the original prints' stylistic effects.[122] Crucially, due to grand format and delayed completion, the set circulated much less. April 1824, Coupin knew of only one Cornelius set in Paris's Royal Library, no longer traceable. By then, Retzsch's outlines had been imported, re-engraved, thrice issued in England and once in Washington; their French January 1824 lithographic copy by Muret had already sold out.[123] Size also translated into a substantial difference in price. As Abraham Hayward put it in his English translation, Cornelius's "illustrations of Faust have great merit; but being in the largest folio, and three or four pounds in price, they are comparatively little known."[124] Hence, their influence was inevitably slighter, and their circulation diametrically at odds with that of Retzsch.

In point of fact, comparisons between Retzsch and Cornelius are often based on later editions, reproductions, or image compendia, such as Franz Neubert's *Vom Doctor Faustus zu Goethes Faust* (1932). The latter reproduces the images in homogenized format and size, rubbing out significant variances of intent, layout, and usage. Different treatments become all the more meaningful when such parameters are gauged. In its oversize scale Cornelius's *Faust* addresses princely museography whereas Retzsch's reproducible prints suit everyman. In Cornelius's *Faust*, strength, size, epic treatment, and typification rhyme in, but these very qualities also make for a lack of life: "it almost seems that in these characters the circulation of blood has stopped."[125]

1.8 German Amendments in the Twentieth Century

Discerning articles and specialist studies would gradually gauge Retzsch's *Faust* merits and shortcomings in the twentieth century in more nuanced ways, from bashful observation to apology, and from vindication to a plea for recognition. Despite inaccuracies, Arthur Dobsky's 1908 article (with fine outline reproductions in sepia, green, and red) set Retzsch in historical perspective, showed his impact on the theatre, and hailed his simple yet surprising manner. Completing several detailed articles, Leopold Hirschberg's catalogue *raisonné* (1925) is still the only full survey of Retzsch's graphic work. With Arthur Rümann's 1930 study on the illustrated book in the first half of the nineteenth century across three countries, we move towards more comparative ground and a proper account of German outline artists. Yet, even in this context, the artist fails to convince completely: "Retzsch sought to do justice to the great poem with a nearly ascetic meagreness of means and good taste. Monumental effects were alien to him, and lyrical scenes mattered more than dramatic ones."[126] Rümann's refrain from rebuke, and notable rhetorical balance between compliment and coolness, may have been impelled by Eckermann's eulogy and Goethe's view, dutifully recorded. A sample of Retzsch's style, plate 15 from the *Umrisse*, known as "The Kiss," harbours a lyrical, intimate scene, although more complex and symbolically crucial (cf. Fig. 7.17). It had a distinct fortune and influence I will turn to later. Rümann has merit. He distinguishes Retzsch from German artists closer to Flaxman's classical trend, notes his romanticism, records his popularity, his clear draughtsmanship, and justly remarks that both he and Cornelius had made of *Faust* a Gretchen tragedy. To his eyes Retzsch's art is not first-rate, and his penchant for "the sentimental and the gruesome romance of chivalry" questionable.[127] Delacroix's *Faust*

---

121 Stephan Seeliger, "Zur Editionsgeschichte der Faust-Bilder von Peter Cornelius," *Aus dem Antiquariat*, no. 7 (1988): A277–83.

122 Beinecke: Speck Folio Ck99 C7 830; BnF Est.: Tb. 56 pet. folio; FDH: VIII d (mi) 13260. Unfortunately Seeliger does not account for this. Publication details in Engel, no. 1807.

123 [Coupin], "Paris, April," 155.

124 Hayward, "Appendix, no. II," in *Faust: A Dramatic Poem by Goethe*, 4th ed. (London: Edward Moxon, 1847), 245.

---

125 Raczyński, *Geschichte der neueren deutschen Kunst*, 2:188.

126 Rümann, *Das illustrierte Buch des XIX. Jahrhunderts in England, Frankreich und Deutschland, 1790–1860* (Leipzig: Insel, 1930), 225.

127 Ibid., 226.

is the acclaimed masterpiece against which Retzsch and Cornelius had produced "bloodless figures, bordering on the puppet-like."[128] Still, his study is based on degrees of artistic ability, overall knowledge and techniques, less so on personal taste. He would never have denied Retzsch artistic worth.

The 1930s was a turning point. Faust iconography, hitherto promoted by Alexander Tille, became a standard topic of discussion on Goethe's *Faust*, sanctioned by Neubert's compendium (1932), itself based on previous publications I will not detail. The celebrations of Goethe's centenary in 1932 and the Leipzig international exhibition on Goethe's illustrated editions changed the perspective. Benz's levelheaded and informative study on *Goethe und die romantische Kunst* gave Retzsch due praise by relative comparison.[129] Academic research joined in from World War II onwards, treating Retzsch diversely: unsympathetically in Clösges's 1942 thesis and unemotionally in Odenkirchen's 1948 Master diploma on Retzsch's reception in England. Amongst inclusive studies on *Faust* iconography, Wolfgang Wegner's in 1962 is particularly illuminating. In his 1973 Delacroix study, Günter Busch considers Retzsch as an important influence in a fine and fair discussion considering the work of art in all its uses. In the last sixty years, all-embracing German studies on *Faust* iconography have granted Retzsch regular attention and gradually changed the perspective. They are used in this book with nuances. In the last twenty-five, German academic enquires have proven definite turning points. Already in 1994, Sigrun Brunsiek signalled Retzsch's primacy and stressed his evolution from classical to romantic outline.[130] In a 1998 unpublished dissertation, Sebastian Giesen offered a new interpretation of his Gretchen, stressing the *Outlines*' aesthetic effect and influence on the stage.[131] Albeit second-hand slip-ups, Doris Schumacher also 2000 recognized his prevalence, pointing to the fanciful treatment of Faust's study.[132] In her 2004 detailed expert study, Viola Hildebrand-Schat approached the *Faust* etchings in relation to Goethe's

text as expressive of middle-class art appreciation: first as a cycle, studying stilisation, characterisation and use of space, secondly as technique and aesthetics between classicism and romanticism. She thus compared Retzsch to Flaxman, Cornelius or Neureuther, and outline to arabesque.[133] Comparatively, this book stresses the social range of Retzsch's readers and enthusiasts, follows the transformations of his outlines across cultures, repeatedly discusses their relation to translation, and measures their appeal on reproduction within a diffused print culture. In six articles (1999–2008), well-known art historian and exhibition curator Gerd-Helge Vogel has contributed revealing aspects of Retzsch's art in context, offering new data and an approach that benefitted from international expertise. By comparing Retzsch and Dante Gabriel Rossetti, Eva Krüger 2009 showed his influence on a major pre-Raphaelite artist and poet. Finally, Uwe Hellwig's 2018 archival research has considerably reviewed facts and dates in Retzsch's life, studying in detail relations with his publishers.

1.9 Conclusion

All the above shows an intricate creative temperament to be probed in context without biases by comparison with broader cultural concerns. Melancholic and despondent by 1835, Retzsch had been the opposite of a recluse when he worked on Goethe's *Faust*. A thirst for nature and need for solitude, essential for dedication to his art, were yoked to a lively cordiality and openness to artists and family, patrons and clients. A refined, dynamic, and skilled craftsman, he took pains to develop his art and dual creativeness in numerous ways, genres, and techniques. He had talent and commitment, perseverance and brilliance, ability and flair. A dedicated son, brother, and adoring husband, he was bent on success, yet had to struggle for official recognition.

Art and literature early mingled with personal life and vice versa. Imagination held sway over his sensibility and ideas, and it would be artificial to separate one from the other. The magnetism and success of his *Faust* lie as much in fancy and craving as in tenderness and feeling. Frequently stressed, the latter have screened desire, ingenuity, and wit. With due allowance, moralization also curbed his somewhat acerbic mockery, the droll and more grotesque side of his later creations.

In his *œuvre*, drawing and etching overshadowed painting. His 1816 Academy membership finally enhanced his

---

128 Ibid., 122.

129 Benz, *Goethe und die romantische Kunst*, 170, 175–78, 180.

130 Brunsiek, *Auf dem Weg der alten Kunst. Der "altdeutsche Stil" in der Buchillustration des 19. Jahrhunderts* (Marburg: Jonas, 1994), 174–79.

131 Giesen, "'Den Faust, dächt'ich, gäben wir ohne Holzschnitte und Bilderwerk': Goethes *Faust* in der europäischen Kunst des 19. Jahrhundert" (PhD diss., Technische Hochschule Aachen, 1998), 60–74.

132 Schumacher, *Kupfer und Poesie: Die Illustrationskunst um 1800 im Spiegel der zeitgenössischen deutschen Kritik* (Cologne: Bölhau, 2000), 187–89.

---

133 Hildebrand-Schat, *Moritz Retzschs Illustrationen*, 17–117.

status and freedom as an artist, and his 1824 "extraordinary" or associate professorship wrested a much-awaited title. By then, fame abroad and publishers' contracts on further outlines after major texts that provided an income, had already given free rein to his imaginings, turned his penchant for literature into a bond, and tied him professionally to the outline technique. While art evaluation in his country hinged on long-standing hierarchies, his outline engravings summoning later developments, easy to transfer, copy and transform, made a difficult play accessible and, as we shall discover, attained new publics through reproduction processes.

This book does not however pit his domestic inconspicuousness against his celebrity abroad. Circulation begins already in his homeland states (Chapter 3). German editions, when appropriately documented, show his popularity through the favour granted to his prints spreading in varied formats. Let us now turn to his *Umrisse* and his outline technique. Before we proceed with reproductions, the originals lay their own claim.

CHAPTER 2

Faust I Outlined and the Original Retzsch Effect

In mid-twentieth-century German evaluations, the merits of Retzsch's *Umrisse zu Goethe's Faust* were typically gauged as text-dependent artwork in "thin and dry" style (*dünn und vertrocknet*) and "pale lifeless abstractions" of scenes and figures, using detailed explanatory analysis plate by plate;[1] or as "too cool, too deprived of genuine feeling" (*zu kühl, zu stimmungsarm*).[2] In 1990 it was even deemed that "the clarity, even flatness, of these simple line drawings, their lack of any shading—literal or metaphorical—emptied the depicted events of all internal and external connotations."[3] As noted, new approaches are recent and limited in number, based on an engraved set considered unvarying, on middle-class sensibility, and text-image relations.[4]

This chapter sheds new light on Retzsch's outlines by scrutinizing originals and considering how they were made and how they work. The process adopts a number of complementary angles. It first considers the agency and efficacy of the original set issued by Cotta, an artefact hitherto unheeded through shape and format, including Goethe's own evolving appreciation and gifts. Second, it retraces the history of the outlines' making, using new data and cross-referencing correspondence, including Goethe's with Cotta. Third, re-evaluation signals their potency: relative independence from text and revelatory interpretation. The artist's fanciful and playful disposition, his latent or open suggestiveness, veiled eroticism, even special sensitivity, I argue, should be measured against an established characteristic of the set, identified as sentimental.

2.1 A Modern Fourfold Device

What did Retzsch's *Umrisse zu Goethe's Faust* originally look like? Comparison between available items that carry the same content (yet appear not identical) helps us better understand the set, and probe its purpose and function. In over two hundred years, it often changed hands privately and underwent various treatments in public repositories.

The primary aim was obscured, nearly lost. In many ways, the initial object has become unrecognizable. Digitization has further remediated it, transformed it, and entailed a kind of treacherous blindness regarding its modernity.

The 1816 set may for instance come to us as an overview display of letterpress and outline prints in a brown half-binding as visible on the Heidelberg website.[5] Or as a uniform landscape album with twenty-six images, headed by an unsigned introduction and twenty-six *Faust* quotes in German. Or even, as a combined *Faust I* and *II* on HathiTrust, in a Google-scanned scroll-down pdf of dubious quality, dated 1836 on the label, 1837 on the title-page. It totals a longer run of introductory letterpress and 40 successive plates.[6] Such regimented and homogenized e-objects are light years apart from the handy fourfold contrivance that the *Umrisse* originally were.

The user of the initial 1816 edition first encountered a yellow or buff wrapper (*c*.17 × 21.5 cm), indeed a portfolio with green flaps, fastened by a tongue-shaped strip inserted to a slit. This disclosed two *loose* parts: 26 etchings, engraved by Retzsch himself, simply strung together on the left-hand side, and a slender, smaller letterpress brochure with green back echoing the flaps (Fig. 2.1a–b). The 26 small etchings were artist's proofs (no captions) with narrow margins close-cropped to the image frames. The letterpress brochure comprised all textual elements: a title-page, an anonymous introduction (by Therese Huber), and 26 excerpts referring not to the original 1808 but a 1816 *Faust* pocket edition by Cotta. A label in Gothic print, pasted to the wrapper, ran: *Umrisse | zu | Goethe's Faust. | Gezeichnet | von | Retsch* (*Outlines after Goethe's Faust. Designed by Retsch*). All in all, wrapper, prints, letterpress brochure and label brought together distinctly significant functions.

Rarely preserved intact, the full artefact was hybrid. Neither illustrated booklet, nor artist's portfolio with stand-alone images as for Cornelius's grand format, it involved opening and handling, reviewing the images, perusing the letterpress, and reading from one to the other. Users might open to check the contents in diverse ways:

---

1 Elisabeth Clösges, "Die Illustration von Goethes Dichtung in seiner Zeit" (PhD diss., Friedrich-Wilhelms-Universität zu Bonn, 1942), 179ff.

2 Neubert, 241a.

3 Forster-Hahn, "A Hero for All Seasons?" 515b.

4 See "Air View and Ant Perspective," p. 3 and Chap. 1, p. 49 & 50.

5 Heidelberg Historic Literature—Digitized, last accessed 28 Feb 2023, https://digi.ub.uni-heidelberg.de/diglit/retzsch1816/0012/thumbs.

6 HathiTrust, https://babel.hathitrust.org/cgi/pt?id=mdp.39015005464311&view=1up&seq=1. Original from the University of Michigan. Last accessed 28 Feb 2023.

© EVANGHELIA STEAD, 2023 | DOI:10.1163/9789004543010_005

This is an open access chapter distributed under the terms of the CC BY-NC-ND 4.0 license.

FAUST I OUTLINED AND THE ORIGINAL RETZSCH EFFECT 53

FIGURES 2.1A–B *Umrisse zu Goethe's Faust gezeichnet von Retsch* (Stuttgart & Tübingen: Cotta, 1816). Original yellow portfolio with green flaps, shut and open with contents
COURTESY HAAB, F 3487, WEIMAR

prints in succession composed a story like a silent strip cartoon; the prints-cum-quotes worked as *Faust* excerpts with potential illustration; the prints with extracts and a do-and-don't introduction posed *Faust* as a guide for life and spirited conversation; and the excerpts alone helped memorize noteworthy passages. Further uses are open to conjecture. Loosely associated with the text, the images had special agency thanks to the outline aesthetic, as we shall see. The decorative importance of packaging was an asset publisher Johann Friedrich Cotta was developing,[7] and evidence from the production and release context shows that he used this prompt to attract buyers to the 1816 pocket and subsequent *Faust* editions at hardly any cost.[8] The pocket *Faust*, a cute little volume, almost square in shape (12.7 × 10.5), proffered 309 pages of fine dense print in the same Gothic type as the brochure letterpress.[9] Along with the affordable little portfolio, it intended to allure new readers. Bibliophile Thomas Frognall Dibdin would be seduced by it in Cotta's very Stuttgart bookshop (see Chapter 4).

We may assume then that the enticing item successfully promoted sales. Its colourful formula was again used in the 1820s and 1830s with slight differences. In 1823, Retzsch's eight outlines after Schiller's *Fridolin* or *The Road to the Iron-Foundry* materialized in a pale yellow portfolio with petrol green flaps (20.6 × 25.3 cm). In 1836, *Faust II* sat in an analogous blue portfolio with bright fuchsia flaps and a blushing pink label (cf. Fig. 3.6). The template obviously caught on, even though Retzsch, first artist to ever interpret the second part of *Faust*, had to markedly reduce the number of plates to only 11. Cotta father's trademark portfolios branded Retzsch's outlines after Goethe and Schiller, freely accompanying the visual narrative with a selection of excerpts. Then son Georg von Cotta launched both Retzsch's enlarged *Faust I* (1834, 29 pl.) and combined *Faust I* and *II* (1836, 40 pl.) in cloth-bound albums, in which homogeneous letterpress-cum-prints endorsed linear reading and image-text dependence. The last of these corresponds to the 1836–37 Google file on the HathiTrust cyber-library.

Retzsch's first publicized artwork coupled his name with a text of great consequence in German and European literature. It made him widely famed outside the German States, while he had to compete for recognition at home. The set worked very differently from the oil paintings of literary inspiration he had exhibited at Dresden: as a multiple graphic work, it spread further than single canvases sparsely exhibited; it could enter collectors' and noblemen's galleries or *Sammlungen*, and a variety of abodes; as a serial work on the print market, it chaperoned the tragedy with a picture story from beginning to end, the visual account substituting its own message for the verse. Occasionally altered, easily moving across states and from country to country, it promoted Goethe's *Faust* thanks to image circulation and transfers.

In single-line frames, free of captions, simply numbered above right 1 to 26, the outlines would be named differently according to destination and context: the 1851 *Magasin pittoresque* called them "a series of sketches" (*une suite d'esquisses*). In contrast, their first English recipient, Henry Crabb Robinson, noted "Outlines à la Flaxman a very interesting little work," recognizing an aesthetic class via its pioneer, his own personal friend, to whom he would present them. In modern art historians' discourse,[10] they have been labelled "German neoclassical prints," although Retzsch had by then freed himself from Grassi's model paradigm in favour of romanticism.

Compared to other visual renderings of *Faust*, Retzsch's set was the broadest, cheapest, and easiest to reproduce or copy outright. These merits also make it the more influential, albeit this quality struggled to impose itself in the German States. As Mrs Hall diplomatically stated "those wonderful 'OUTLINES' which have been the admiration of the world for half a century, [...] are scarcely better known in Germany than they are in England."[11]

Except for Christian Friedrich Osiander's clumsy prints that could be sparsely added to individual copies,[12] Cotta's 1808 *Faust* had been issued with no images, to Goethe's explicit wish. In a well-known and often quoted, albeit rarely commented, 1805 letter to his publisher, the poet had expressed this in colourful language:

---

7   Helmuth Mojem and Barbara Potthast, eds., *Johann Friedrich Cotta: Verleger—Unternehmer—Technikpionier* (Heidelberg: Winter, 2017), 11. On Cotta and cultural prestige, see Daniel Moran, *Toward the Century of Words: Johann Cotta and the Politics of the Public Realm in Germany, 1795–1832* (Berkeley: University of California Press, 1990).

8   Dorothea Kuhn, "Verleger und Illustrator. Am Beispiel der J. G. Cotta'schen Verlagsbuchhandlung," in *Buchillustration im 19. Jahrhundert*, ed. R. Timm (Wiesbaden: Otto Harrassowitz, 1988), 225.

9   HAAB: F 705.

10 Katharine Lochnan, "Les lithographies de Delacroix pour *Faust* et le théâtre anglais des années 1820," *Nouvelles de l'estampe*, no. 87 (July 1986): 6.

11 Hall, "A Morning with Retzsch," 21a.

12 Hirschberg, "Über vier wenig bekannte Kupfer der 1808-Ausgabe von Goethes Faust," *Zeitschrift für Bücherfreunde* 11, no. 4 (July 1907): 174–76. Hirschberg refers to a single exemplar that I have not been able to trace. Schumacher relates a similar experience, *Kupfer und Poesie*, 184–85.

Den Faust, dächt' ich, gäben wir ohne Holzschnitte und Bildwerk. Es ist so schwer, daß etwas geleistet werde, was dem Sinne und dem Tone nach zu einem Gedicht paßt. Kupfer und Poesie parodieren sich gewöhnlich wechselweise. Der Hexenmeister soll sich allein durchhelfen.[13]

I'm rather minded we give Faust without woodcuts or pictures. It is so difficult to achieve something fitting to the spirit and tone of a poem. Copper and poetry generally parody each other. The chief sorcerer will have to fend for himself.

The entire letter addresses matters of proofing, printing, and choosing the right typeset for the best possible reading effect of his forthcoming *Works*. Print technologies mattered to Goethe to the highest degree. Yet for *Faust*, he uses modal verbs (in caution or hesitation) and vocabulary oddly mixed: specialized (*Holzschnitte*), inclusive (*Bildwerk*), and informally technical (*Kupfer* for *Kupferstiche*, copper plates). He was at ease with graphic techniques he had either himself practised or used, and had previously commissioned from Johann Heinrich Lips a frontispiece after Rembrandt for *Faust: Ein Fragment* (1790). Strikingly, his paragraph ends with a fanciful portrait of protagonist merged with printed object, of magician Faust being one with the to be-published text. Implied is the innate force of the sole word, yet both Goethe's phrasing and tropes hint at artworks' special enchantment and agency. Cotta's promotional use of Retzsch's outlines implies that the "chief sorcerer" struggled somewhat on his own, particularly without images. Retzsch's *Umrisse* paved the way to recognition for a work deemed unfathomable, and influentially branded by Germaine de Staël an "intellectual chaos."[14]

2.2 Goethe's Gifts

The conniving ways in which the author himself used the *Umrisse* as gifts make, to my knowledge, for a new turn in Goethe (and Retzsch) studies. Collectible data are not always as complete as one might desire, subsequent to library dispersals, undetected correspondence, untraceable or vanished items. Yet postures are significant: Goethe's is no private economy of intimate gifting but a public persona's conspicuous transmission of an interpretative artistic rendering of his lifetime's major work. His gracious gestures extend into the public sphere. Handing

over Cotta's clever portfolio highlights another singularizing feature of its function. A nifty, transportable offering, the set acts as a flexible envoy. By changing hands, it is a go-between with a message, and Goethe was not the only one to use it so. German publisher Perthes followed suit (Chapter 4). Gifting and sending are integral to circulation, a key mechanism critical to Retzsch's reception within and beyond Germany.

The earliest transmission I have been able to trace is exceptional in more ways than one. The *Umrisse* were addressed to Jakob and Marianne von Willemer in Frankfurt on 8 November 1816, twelve days after a dozen exemplars had reached Weimar on 28 October.[15] Goethe only perused them on 7 November, forwarding one to the Willemers directly on the morrow.[16] In response to a present from Jakob (a case of an incomparable wine) and as a gift to Marianne (Goethe's Suleika in the *West-östlicher Divan*), the dispatch carries complex values as a token of special friendship, a souvenir of happier times, and a pledge of love. It is also part of the trio's relationship and correspondence, prompting recipients' reactions from both. In Chapter 11, "Two Gifted Women," I compare it with yet another special item given by a poet to a lady, an English offshoot of Retzsch given by Lord Byron to an American diplomat's spouse. In both cases, the boundary between private protocol and public gesture was elastic.

Another remarkable specimen donned social, gendered, charitable, and political garb. Well aware of the value his signature carried, Goethe lent weight to Retzsch's *Umrisse* by leveraging for them, to philanthropic ends, a hefty price. On 7 December 1818, shortly before Christmas, he employed the apposite stuck-on label to autograph a dedication running "To the most honourable Women's Association" (*Dem verehrtesten Frauenverein*) with the date, and presented it to the Jena Patriotic Women's Association for their bazaar. Ladies were no less attuned than famous authors to social ritual and active charity work. Goethe's carefully penned dedication boosted auctionability (Fig. 2.2). Below his, a scribbled line in a tiny hand pursued the undertaking: it was purchased by Tsarina Maria Feodorovna,[17] née Sophia Dorothea of Württemberg, second wife to Tsar Paul I, herself mother of ten siblings, including two future tsars (Alexander I and Nicholas I) and a princess, herself an accomplished patron of the arts and letters.[18] Her daughter, Maria

---

13   GCB 1:133.
14   Staël, "Faustus," 2:181.

15   RA 7:no. 533; *Tg* 5:425, 14.
16   *Tg* 5:429, 3, 23.
17   Carl F. Schreiber, "Coleridge to Boosey—Boosey to Coleridge," *Yale University Library Gazette* 22, no. 1 (July 1947): 6–7.
18   Kazimierz Waliszewski, *Paul the First of Russia, the Son of Catherine the Great*, 1911; repr. ed. (Miami, Fla.: Hardpress, [2013]), 17f.

FIGURE 2.2 *Umrisse zu Goethe's Faust gezeichnet von Retsch* (Stuttgart & Tübingen: Cotta, 1816). Label with Goethe's autograph, 7 December 1818, and Tsarina Maria Feodorovna's inscription
COURTESY BEINECKE, YALE UNIVERSITY, SPECK CK99 R3 +816 COPY 2

Pavlovna, as Grand Duchess of Saxe-Weimar-Eisenach, had launched in 1814–17 the Patriotic Women's Association in the homonymous Grand Duchy to help the population cope with damage caused by the Napoleonic wars. The welfare concern she brought to Weimar's state affairs, in her mother's footsteps, is a spirit she would pass on to her own daughter-in-law Sophia, her daughter Augusta (future Queen of Prussia and German Empress), and her granddaughter Luise von Baden.[19] The Retzsch portfolio, adorned with Goethe's and the tsarina's prestigious signatures, stands at the crossroads of multiple connections, transmissions, and public achievements as a charitable godsend.

Unique, due to its social and public status, to its early date and political circumstances, the Retzsch set shows Goethe endorsing practices that bridged social rifts between aristocracy, middle-classes and the poor. Such promotional fundraising parallels Cotta's marketing tool. Trading and publicizing were in the air along with a growing conscience of symbolic object value.

The *Umrisse* also testified to cultural, artistic and literary practices. Goethe discussed them within his circle and presented them to friends, acquaintances and visitors, frequently linked with the arts, as his diary and correspondence show.

Among others, two folders of the 1820 edition were used as tokens "to remember" shared moments. In one, infringing the confines of the label, the poet's writing covers the wrapper's lower part. The warm inscription irregularly scrolled, perhaps under the effect of emotion, suggests a parting moment: "To the dear Bracebridge spouses in

---

19 Ramona Burkhardt, *Der Frauenverein in Jena im Spannungsfeld zwischen höfischen Impulsen durch Maria Pawlowna und der städtischen Gesellschaft* (Munich: GRIN, 2009).

FIGURE 2.3 *Umrisse zu Goethe's Faust gezeichnet von Retsch* (Stuttgart & Tübingen: Cotta, 1820). With Goethe's dedication to L. John Vigoureux, 3 July 1827
COURTESY MARTIN BODMER FOUNDATION, GENEVA

fond souvenir Weimar 1 March 1826 Goethe" (*Den theuren Gatten | Bracebridge | zu geneigtem Andencken*).[20] In another, a more formal dedication is neatly traced beneath the label, a balanced spatial effect akin to its demure wording: "to Mr L. John Vigoureux in cordial souvenir Weimar 3 July 1827 Goethe" (*Herren L. John Vigoureux | zu freundlichem Andenken*) (Fig. 2.3). The said individual had visited Goethe thanks to the Weimar merchant and forwarding agent Johann Gabriel Wilhelm Münderloh on the very day he must have departed with the autograph.[21] In his case, further construal is hardly possible for lack of evidence.[22] Not so for the Bracebridges.

Selina, née Mills, and her husband, the English writer and traveller Charles Holte (Holt) Bracebridge, are better known for taking up residence in Athens in the 1830s and their later connexion to Florence Nightingale. Widely travelled, the couple had also wintered in Weimar 1825–26. Goethe admired their "ardent, collected life," likened to Carlyle's in opposition to Weimar's "dispersion." He saw in them "people who amid the ocean are united on a narrow barge, unperturbed by the din and the turmoil around them,"[23] and his dedication reflects high regard. Selina was close to Ottilie, Goethe's daughter-in-law, with whom she corresponded, but her relation to Goethe is of aesthetic

---

20 Christie's, live auction 6521, 28 Nov 2001, lot 97. <https://www.christies.com/en/lot/lot-3822764>. Last accessed 28 Feb 2023.
21 GLTT 7:757.
22 In 1826, the Hon. Percy Jocelyn, a former Anglican Bishop, caught in homosexual practices in London and forced from his position in 1822, used the name L. John Vigoureux to sign a hotel register

in Leukerbad, Switzerland (see Kevin Laheen, "Further Letters of Robert Haly, S. J., 1810-29, in Irish Jesuit Archives," *Collectanea Hibernica*, no. 44–45 (2002–3): 197). To be sure that Jocelyn was indeed Goethe's visitor would require further investigation.
23 GG 3:447.

importance. Painter, draughtswoman, and talented former student of Samuel Prout, she authored several works now in the V&A Collection, and Goethe mentions her drawings on 1 November 1825.[24] Seven months later, on 14 June 1826, he discussed her portrait of Countess Julie von Egloffstein with the sitter, a beautiful member of the Weimar Court, herself a talented artist, whom he had greatly encouraged in her artistic undertakings. The discussion must have reflected his criticism of Selina's manner in portraying Julie, as expressed to Friedrich von Müller four days later: it had been an error to follow "the infamous manner of the Nazarenes."[25] Beyond the link to his *Faust*, Goethe's choice was certainly designed to appeal to Selina's artistic talents, perhaps as an invitation to move away from the coldness, dryness and flatness that Nazarene style represented to his eyes.

The outlines toured well beyond Weimar with the Bracebridges. Thus dispatched by Goethe the diplomat, they would journey to other lands. End February-beginning of March 1819, they were part of a small parcel handed over by Goethe to Heinrich Karl Ernst von Köhler (Egor Egorovič Köhler) in Weimar and subsequently opened by him in Saint Petersburg. Writer, renowned specialist of cameos and engraved stones, Köhler, a member of several Academies of science, was the keeper of the tsar's cabinet of stones and medals at the Hermitage.[26] His long 1817–19 trip to Germany, France and Italy, visiting museums and studying art collections, had taken him to Weimar, whence his leave-taking present. In expressing his thanks for "the beautiful outlines after Faust" and an exemplar of *Hermann and Dorothea*, he called the latter, in a verbal lapse indicative of his genuine passion, a "master stone" (*Meisterstein*) instead of masterpiece (*Meisterstück*).[27] The gifts may also have been advance compensation for the pains he would take to provide Goethe with sulphur casts and reproductions of cameos from Saint Petersburg collections. If he had taken away a small parcel, Goethe would expect a chest of samples, indeed delivered to Weimar by his son in August 1820.[28] Polished manners rhymed with donating art treasures between royal and personal collections. In this exchange diplomacy, Retzsch's outlines were also for Privy Councillor von Goethe a precious asset.

A thank-you gift to any artist may carry aesthetic prize (so with Selina Bracebridge) but also provokes a benchmark effect. In Mary Margaret Dawe's case, Retzsch's

Umrisse became a touchstone by which to judge English copied prints against German originals. She and her brother, George Dawe, had been taught the trade by their father, the mezzotint engraver Philip Dawe. Yet, regardless of the quality of his engravings, George had turned to more profitable tasks. He moved to Saint Petersburg (spring 1819–May 1828) to portray more than 300 Russian army leaders who had beaten Napoleon, while Mary continued business in London. He would be named first painter to the Russian court in 1826. The portraits of Goethe and Prince Bernhard II, Duke of Saxe-Meiningen, were to be engraved by Thomas Wright, George Dawe's associate in his "portrait factory." In order to thank Miss Dawe for preparing them for engraving, Goethe asked Johann Christian Hüttner, a London-based German writer, journalist and translator, literary agent to Grand Duke Karl August, to present her with Retzsch's *Umrisse* in November 1820. By then, he well knew English copies by Henry Moses, sent to him by the publishers Boosey and Sons, and today still part of his preserved library (Chapter 5). Yet, he valued the German originals as "more striking" (*merkwürdiger*) than Moses's ersatz.[29] Subtle competition engaged between original and copy. Hüttner endorsed his choice with a nuance. To him, the *Umrisse* also had value by virtue of promoting and transiting between countries. In Miss Dawe's circle, they "would be seen by many connoisseurs" (*kämen* [...] *unter die Augen vieler Kenner*).[30] Yet, instead of answering the call, Miss Dawe's thanks for "the handsome present from Mr de Goëtha" [*sic*] disclose her veritable condition. Overcome by duties and in imperfect spelling, yet impeccable third-person formal style, she responded to Hüttner on Boxing Day, a Sunday:

> It is a present, that she most highly values, as illustrating with so much feeling, and talent, the very interesting tragedy intitled [*sic*] Faust, but which she shall always esteem much more, as a mark of attention from Mr de Goëtha, whom she has ever been taught to think of with admiration, and to whom she is indebted for some of the greatest delights, that the power of Genius, and humain emagination [*sic*], can to afford [*sic*].

> Miss Dawe would have had the pleasure of answering Mr Hutners [*sic*] polite note sooner, but till now she has not had one moment's leisure. Nor has she yet had the opportunity, of comparing the original Etchings, with the copies by Mr Moses; it is

---

24   GLTT 7:550.
25   GLTT 3:275.
26   See Karl Morgenstern, *Heinrich Karl Ernst Köhler* (St Petersburg: Buchdruckerei der Kaiserlichen Akademie der Wissenschaften, 1839).
27   GSA 28/88, 375–80.
28   GLTT 6:760; GLTT 7:179.

29   WA 4, 33:247.
30   WA 4, 34:312.

FAUST I OUTLINED AND THE ORIGINAL RETZSCH EFFECT

however easy to discouver [*sic*] the superiority ~~as to~~ as to the sentiment and spirit, with which the work is both conceived & executed in those impressions which Mr de Goëtha has honored [*sic*] Miss Dawe with.[31]

Sketchily drawn, her comparison favoured the German artist, more on behalf of Goethe's fame than *per se*. Mary Margaret Dawe would fortunately marry Thomas Wright, her brother's associate, in Saint Petersburg in 1825 and better her condition. Her case proves a crucial point, namely that the *Umrisse* transcended social rank and educational grade.

It would have of course been gratifying to close this investigation on Goethe managing the *Umrisse* in diverse ways by a last exceptional sending, a so-called *Umrisse* copy given by Goethe to Sir Walter Scott, the early translator of *Götz von Berlichingen* into English (1799). The claim—reported unquestioningly by Lillian Atkins in her Yale thesis[32]—was originally made by Hermann Kindt in 1869. In a 15 May *Notes & Queries* memorandum, Kindt chronicled the following passage from a letter by painter William Bewick (1795–1866):

> I am reminded of an extremely interesting evening at Sir Walter Scott's at Abbotsford, when he was good enough to show me and the company present a copy of the original illustrations to Faust, that had been sent to him by the poet Goethe, and which had just arrived. And I still remember with what delight, as an artist, I examined for the first time those beautiful works, and that too in the house of a mutual friend and brother poet, as well as a correspondent of Goethe—for Sir Walter was an excellent German scholar.[33]

The passage is not included in *Life and Letters of William Bewick* (1871), which repeatedly records memories of Walter Scott at Abbotsford. In the 1874 German version of his study, Kindt affirms quoting from a letter "under [his] eyes," which could be possible since he seems to have been an autograph fan, but deliberately substitutes Cornelius for Retzsch.[34] He mentions no date for the Bewick letter. The Abbotsford library catalogue, compiled by John Lockhart, records under Retzsch the still extant "*Umrisse* zu Goethe's Faust. *oblong 4to*," with the curious mention "Leipzig" and

no date.[35] Upon inspection, the object, a bound version of only the prints, with neither title-page nor publisher's imprint, is possibly part of the 1820 Cotta edition and no English ersatz. In any case, it shows no trace of Goethe, whose correspondence with Scott dates from 1828. It must have come to Abbotsford through some other channel, perhaps Scott's protégé, the actor Daniel Terry, who was to interpret Mephistopheles in a costume after Retzsch in 1825 (cf. Fig. 9.13). If Bewick's letter is genuine, the narrated scene might readily bear on easy confusion, superimposing Scott's interest for Goethe and circulation of the *Umrisse* in Britain. Until further elucidated, the scene described testifies mainly to the appeal of Retzsch's work for a gathering of art lovers around the Scottish author.

The inconclusive episode does not mar the fact that procedures developed by Goethe in genuine presentations of Retzsch's *Umrisse* vest them with a particular aura. A vehicle of ideas and credos, the easily transportable item is not only a palpable symbol of give-and-take in cultural relationships, but also a medium, a material object in cultural practices, which plays even into such hands as those of *Faust*'s own author.

2.3 In Goethe's Orb

Yet, when fathoming the Goethe-Retzsch relationship in the spangled firmament of European fame, author and artist seem worlds apart: a bright sun orbited by a stray planet, a mere satellite.

There is no known letter from Goethe to Retzsch although they met in Weimar (see *infra*). Author-artist communication on the making of the *Umrisse* was mostly indirect. After his Dresden visit, Goethe was informed of the etchings' progress by Heinrich Ludwig Verlohren, a managing agent of the Dresden Court, whom he used as middleman for sundry commissions and purchases. His own letters to Verlohren, though recorded, have not been saved. Abiding in turn by Retzsch's preference for "a local commissioner," publisher Cotta used a go-between in their transactions, the Leipzig bookseller Paul Gotthelf Kummer,[36] who seemed neither keen nor prompt to answer Retzsch's eager requests. Exchange of letters, sheet-proofs and metal plates mostly adopted a roundabout fashion. Contrariwise, art collector and archaeologist Sulpiz Boisserée directly introduced Cornelius to

---

31   GSA 28/92, 110.

32   Atkins, "Fragmentary English Translations of Goethe's Faust" (PhD diss., Yale University, 1937), 16, n. 2.

33   Kindt, "English Versions of Goethe's *Faust*, Part I," *Notes & Queries*, 4th ser., 3 (15 May 1869): 453–54.

34   Kindt, "Goethes Faust in England," *Die Gegenwart*, no. 24 (13 June 1874): 376b.

35   *Catalogue of the Library of Abbotsford* (Edinburgh: [T. Constable], 1838), 232. All Cotta editions I know bear either the imprint "Stuttgart" or "Stuttgart & Tübingen."

36   Identified as Paul Georg Kummer by Hellwig, "Studien zu Moritz Retzsch," 89, n. 408. I have followed the Cotta archive indication (DLA).

Goethe. His pert diary descriptions of the poet's reactions, and Goethe's 1811 letter to Cornelius, full of approval and advice, set from the beginning Retzsch's relation to the author of *Faust* in a very different light.

Given the above, the concision of Goethe's remarks on Retzsch's *Faust* hardly comes as a surprise. Initially encouraging, in Goethe's oral or written exchanges with others, in unpublished third parties' accounts, or by way of comparative evaluation (with Cornelius or Delacroix), they prove mostly incidental but for August Retzsch's diary inscription. A cool view, presumed to reflect Goethe's, is in the 1817 issue of *Über Kunst und Altertum*, authored by Johann Heinrich Meyer, Cornelius being set above Retzsch. Goethe is more direct in his letters to Hüttner, who regularly apprised Weimar of English literary life via reports to the Grand Duke, frequently transmitted to his Privy Counsellor, keen to follow UK literary affairs.[37] Arguably, that *Faust* drew benefit from the *Outlines* in Britain, still at hostile grips with Goethe's writings (due to the suicide craze after *Werther*) and where Retzsch's own fame was speedily rising, fostered the politically savvy poet's enthusiasm. Moreover, alterations to the prints as copied by Moses, must have attracted his mind to some of their exact merits, hardly conspicuous at first glance. Their cross-border circulation within Europe will additionally have helped win his definitive support. While in Goethe's 1816 yearly notes Retzsch is on a level with Cornelius, praise for the former rises in the 1820s to the latter's detriment. Unreserved admiration for Retzsch's *Hamlet* outlines, noted for their intrinsic qualities, follows on 24 March 1828. Interestingly, Goethe's oft-quoted predilection for Retzsch over Cornelius, expressed to Joseph Karl Stieler, dates from only a few months later (May–July 1828). Contemporary comparison with Delacroix's *Faust* also advantages Retzsch, to the young romantic Victor Pavie's astonishment on his 1829 Weimar visit.[38] Goethe's blessing of Retzsch had developed over the years in accordance with a shift in his aesthetic preferences.

The statesman-poet first saw Retzsch's drawings in the course of his Dresden stay, 16–25 September 1810. His diary mentions "Portraits of Gen. Thielmann and wife by Retsch [*sic*]" on 20 September.[39] Although nothing on the artist himself appears, August Retzsch's unpublished

diary fills in the blanks on Goethe's two meetings with Moritz, providing unpublished information on the drawings' reception.[40] Having been informed by Thielmann (upon viewing the double portrait) of the artist's *Faust* drawings, Goethe expressed the desire to see them. Retzsch visited him early morning on 22 September. In the course of an amiable reception, Goethe praised his work ("which is something extraordinarily rare," notes August within brackets), expressed his desire to see the drawings etched, and invited Moritz to visit him in Weimar. The welcome seems to have been out of the ordinary, as shows Thielmann's reaction, also recorded by August: "the fact of being treated so extraordinarily by this otherwise haughty man, was proof of how much this great art connoisseur must have liked Moritz's work" (*er sey von dießem sonst stolzen Mann, auf eine außerordentliche Art von ihm behandelt worden, ein Beweiß wie sehr dießem großen Kunstkenner Moritz[ens] Arbeiten gefallen haben müßten*). No Retzsch visit to Weimar seems to have been recorded. Further, Moritz was invited to Thielmann's (who received Goethe on 24 September *en soirée* as noted in Goethe's diary)—August adding that Hartmann was also present. This corroborates (and explains) Hartmann's mention in Retzsch's first letter to Cotta as well as the devised medium: a set of etchings was certainly discussed by the parties as in Goethe's first interview with Retzsch. The preface in Retzsch's *Outlines to Bürger's Ballads*, later published in Boston and obviously translated from L. Hermann's introduction to the homonymous 1872 German album, gives the story in the following terms: "Retzsch made the personal acquaintance of Goethe through General Thielemann, whose portrait he had painted. To them and to Professor Hartmann of Dresden, he owed a commission from Cotta, the publisher, to design a series of outlines for Faust."[41] Beyond its overall laudatory appreciation and minor inaccuracies, it proves exact.

Indeed, it was not the publisher who commissioned Retzsch but the artist who contacted Cotta. In an 1810 introductory contract-like letter, Retzsch twice mentioned Hartmann, a freemason advocate of classicism, recently appointed Professor of History Painting at the Dresden Academy.[42] *Das Hartmannsche Haus*, his father's influential salon in Stuttgart, Cotta's new Württemberg seat, received major literary personalities, hence a more than fortuitous connexion for the Dresden artist residing in easterly Saxony. Goethe himself had known Hartmann

---

37 See Walter Wadepuhl, "Hüttner, a New Source for Anglo-German Relations," *Germanic Review* 14 (1939): 23–27; Catherine W. Proescholdt, "Johann Christian Hüttner (1766–1847): a Link between Weimar and London," in *Goethe and the English-Speaking World*, ed. N. Boyle and J. Guthrie (Rochester, NY: Camden House, 2002), 99–110.

38 Pavie, *Voyages et promenades romantiques*, ed. G. Trigalot (Rennes: PUR, 2015), 81–82.

39 *Tg* 4, 1:183–85.

40 St D, Hs Biogr. II 4925, notebook 25 (1810), 70–73.

41 "Moritz Retzsch and Bürger," in *Outlines to Bürger's Ballads* (Boston: Roberts Brothers, 1873), 2; L. Hermann, "Moritz Retzsch und Bürger," in *Umrisse zu Bürgers Balladen* (Leipzig: Ernst Fleischer, 1872), 2.

42 DLA Co: Retzsch.

since the latter's 1801 Weimar visit and his three submissions to the local "Friends of the Arts" competition between 1799 and 1801. In Dresden, Christian Gottfried Körner noted down their amiable intercourse at the Thielmanns' 24 September *soirée*, although Hartmann had recently criticized a Weimar exhibition.[43] Retzsch's letter to Cotta mentions his fee, again agreed upon via Hartmann. As Art director, Hartmann is also the very man who would later advocate Retzsch's Academy membership and professorship along with Count Vitzthum von Eckstädt. Yet, nothing indicates that Goethe visited the artist. Dorothea Kuhn's assertion that "according to the diary" Goethe "paid Retzsch a visit in his studio" has created a conviction that no record substantiates.[44] Presumably an oversight, it has been repeated in later scholarship,[45] and has even given rise to fictional conjecture, for instance, Goethe reporting to Cotta from Retzsch's studio.[46] Whether or not the poet saw "twelve plates" at Dresden, as Ernst Sigismund has it,[47] is discussed later.

Following the Dresden visit, Goethe first mentioned Retzsch in a 6 November 1810 letter to Cotta brimming with news on artistic undertakings often related to his writings (Riepenhausen, Boisserée, Nauwerk, etc.): "I have seen really interesting and ingenious outlines by Retzsch in Dresden. If he sets them just like that on the [metal] plates, they will make quite a delightful booklet." (*Recht interessante und geistreiche Umrisse zu Faust von Retzsch habe ich in Dresden gesehen. Wenn er sie ebenso auf die Platten bringt, so wird es ein gar erfreuliches Heft geben.*)[48] Both medium and format had been resolved. Desired by Goethe (perhaps with Flaxman's designs in mind), outline etchings also corresponded to Retzsch's endeavours. In 1810, his very first set of thirteen mythology-inspired prints were precisely etched outlines, simply numbered above right as the *Faust* ones would be. He was apt to adopt but also adapt Flaxman's manner.

When synthetically examined, his acclaimed features or alleged failings pertain to three major issues. First and foremost, a key aesthetic preoccupation of the time, the substantiation of a proper visual art to render German culture. Faust being a genuinely German figure,

Goethe's tragedy provided a paragon against which artistic endeavours would be gauged. Meyer's "Neu-deutsche religios-patriotische Kunst" ("Neo-German Religious and Patriotic Art") in *Über Kunst und Altertum* (1817) is in this sense typical. It mentions numerous artists inspired by *Faust* but names only three, with Retzsch second after Naeke and before Cornelius.[49] Order of appearance and progressively expanding comments set a grading scale. For Meyer (and Goethe?), Retzsch deserves attention by virtue of a sequence extending over the whole text, etched by his own hand. However, although Cornelius's *Faust* amounted to only 8 of the final 12 plates at the time, his dexterity and art, inspired by Dürer, received maximum praise. Both his *Faust* and much-acclaimed graphic sequence on the Nibelungen saga, another prototype for German art, fitted the article's title. By contrast, Retzsch remained obscure. The "Remarks and Evidence" added that the author had "no further information on his activities."[50] Much later, in conversation with Stieler, the ageing Goethe would sceptically criticize Cornelius's renderings as too "*alt-deutsch*," and prefer Retzsch as having captured "what was really depictable" (*das wirklich Darzustellende*) in *Faust*. In point of fact, Meyer's 1817 discrimination between the two had already been revised by Goethe in his 1816 *Tag- und Jahres-Hefte als Ergänzung meiner sonstigen Bekenntnisse* (*Daily and Yearly Booklets Supplementing my Other Confessions*):

> Zeichnungen zum Faust von Cornelius und Retzsch wirkten in ihrer Art das Aehnliche: denn ob man gleich eine vergangene Vorstellungsweise weder zurückrufen kann noch soll, so ist es doch löblich sich historisch praktisch an ihr zu üben und durch neuere Kunst das Andenken einer älteren aufzufrischen, damit man, ihre Verdienste erkennend, sich alsdann um so lieber zu freieren Regionen erhebe.[51]

> Drawings for Faust by Cornelius and Retzsch had a similar effect in their diverse way: for although one neither can nor should call back a past way of depicting, it is however praiseworthy to train historically and practically in it, refreshing a more recent art through the memory of an older art, so that, recognizing its merits, one would then rise all the better to freer regions.

---

43   *Tg* 4, 2:1086, 1091.

44   GCB 3, 1:294.

45   Doris Schumacher, *Kupfer und Poesie*, 187; Giesen, "Goethes *Faust* in der europäischen Kunst," 61–62; Peter-Christian Wegner, *Literatur auf Porzellan und Steingut* (Lönneker, Stadtoldendorf: Jörg Mitzkat Holzminden, 2012), 212.

46   Alexander Rosenbaum, "Bildende Kunst," in *Faust-Handbuch*, ed. C. Rohde, Th. Valk and M. Mayer (Stuttgart: J. B. Metzler, 2018), 178.

47   Sigismund, "Retzsch, Moritz," 193b.

48   GCB 1:216.

49   FA 1, 20:119–20.

50   FA 1, 20:169.

51   WA 1, 36:104.

In 1816, Goethe still saw Retzsch's work as historical style and encouraged artistic liberty. As the endeavour towards a freer art would grow, Retzsch's complex yet simple-looking depictions would loom higher in the poet's eyes. From the outset, his particular merits were mainly two: his 26 plates converted *Faust* into a continuous and detailed visual story, investing each protagonist with an identifiable personality. The latter's recognizable features and particular character had been cast: they would accompany *Faust* through incomprehension or perplexity as much as they would gradually become *visibly personified*, yet *fictional* characters cherished by readers. Retzsch had thrown the basis for typifying, a priceless passport to *Faust*'s European reception. The play's fortune and poet's recognition in Britain pointed that way, and, as mentioned, Goethe followed English literary matters through Hüttner's reports. When Meyer compared German artists' merits to Delacroix's plates in an 1828 issue of *Über Kunst und Altertum*, he retained only two: Cornelius excelled in drawing "the figures with great care and more scientifically," but Retzsch "paid more attention to the cyclical sequence of the images," and had succeeded "in bearing the characters with more continuity through the whole series" (*mehr auf cyklische Folge der Bilder geachtet, mag es gelungen seyn die Charaktere mit mehrerer Stetigkeit durch die ganze Reiche durchzuführen*).[52] German artists, Meyer concluded, could defend themselves against the Frenchman.

Competition bred comparison. That, I believe, also triggered initiation of the eye and finer perception of graphic art, leading to greater discernment of two features in Retzsch's style: subtlety of line and veiled imaginative brio. Goethe's trained taste may have already detected both, yet comparison with the Moses copy brought them dramatically to the fore. Receiving both English initial instalments by Thomas Boosey and Sons as they came out in June and July 1820, he noted three critical changes that I will come back to: the non-representation of God in pl. 1, the expunging of explicit male forms in several plates, and *a contrario* overtly elaborated female charms in pl. 6. He noted laconically but eloquently in his response to Hüttner: "These originals become all the more striking since certain changes appreciated in the copy give food for thought." (*Diese Originale werden dadurch merkwürdiger, weil man gewisse Veränderungen bey der Copie beliebte, welche zu denken geben.*)[53] Bowdlerization had sparked his fathoming of Retzsch's understatement, hardly noticeable when compared to Cornelius's grandiloquence and Delacroix's brio. Retzsch was merely *noteworthy* or simply *significant* (*merkwürdig*), yet instructive for eye and imagination alike. Moreover, his minimalism was commercially viable and reflected upon the play as Boosey was quick to point out: "Perhaps it would be gratifying to Mr de Goethe to know, that in consequence of the extensive Sale of the Outlines in this Country, great curiosity has been excited respecting the tragedy, and of course has had a great Sale lately." What had actually benefitted from a great sale was *not* Goethe's *Faust* in English translation (which did not yet exist) but an extensive prose summary, "merely a literal translation of a portion of the Tragedy to explain the Outlines" (Boosey again).[54] What drove the sales was Retzsch's copied outlines. Goethe instantly knew that his repute in Britain was rapidly improving thanks to Retzsch.

For similar reasons, I argue, also intrinsic to Goethe's insight and imagination, Retzsch had one quality hitherto neglected in criticism. It is summed up in a single adjective, *geistreich*, a term easily translated and yet richer than any equivalent. An alternative to *geistvoll*, it literally means *full of spirit*, and is translatable by *ingenious*, *witty*, *clever*, *gifted*, *brilliant* or even *sophisticated*. It would return now and again under Goethe's pen as an appropriate term, both critically indisputable and wilfully persistent, just as emotional reflexion works. In Goethe's first letter to Cotta, it is already there: "I have seen really interesting and ingenious outlines (*geistreiche Umrisse*) by Retzsch in Dresden." It sneaks into the sparse praise of Meyer's 1817 article: "Many pieces in this sequence are to be praised as brilliant compositions (*geistreiche Compositionen*)." It finds its way again into Goethe's 6 March 1820 letter to Hüttner: "Retzsch's small plates are witty (*geistreich*); in bookseller Bohte's hands, they will make *Faust* known in England."[55] Captivatingly, it reappears in Caspar David Friedrich's notes, highlighting one of the three facets of Retzsch's personality: "this otherwise so excellent, so sophisticated, ingenious artist" (*diesem sonst so ausgezeichneten, so geistreichen, jenialen Künstler*).[56] Mrs Jameson's remark comes to mind: "he is peculiar, fantastic, even extravagant—but never false in sentiment of expression."[57] All concur that the reader's intellectual and emotional stimulation was rooted in the artist's gifted treatment. Retzsch's outlines call for our distinct attention, perhaps even an initiation. But before that, a factual chronicle of the work's development and completion is necessary, as consistent as evidence allows.

---

52   FA 1, 22:488.
53   WA 4, 33:247.
54   GSA 28/89, 415.
55   WA 4, 32:181.
56   Friedrich, *Die Briefe*, 73.
57   Jameson, *Visits and Sketches*, 1:224.

2.4 Retzsch at Work: Early Correspondence

Goethe's *Faust* had come out in April 1808 and Retzsch was quick to act. He translated the play into pictures early enough for Goethe to see several in Dresden thirty months later. Closely following on Goethe's September visit, he wrote on 10 October 1810 to Cotta in clearly contractual terms:

Wohlgebohrner Herr
Hochgeehrtester Herr
Mit Ew: Wohlgebh: in eine schriftliche Unterhandlung zu treten, verdanke ich der Güte meines Freundes, dem Hr: Profeßor Hartman, auf deßen Veranlaßung ich wünschte mit Ew: Wohlgeb: wegen der von mir zu radirenden 26 Blatt Umriße zum Gedichte Faust von Göthe, ein näheres zu bestim[m]en. Zur baldigen Publicirung dieser Sam[m]lung nicht allein schon mehreremals vor verschiedenen Seiten ersucht und gebeten; als vorzüglich ermuntert durch den ungetheilten Beifall des Hr: GeheimRath v Göthe selbst, während seines Hierseyns, und auch von ihm zum radiren verschiedendlich aufgefordert, wäre ich geson[n]en, da mir es meine Zeit jetzt einigermaßen erlaubt diese Arbeit vorzunehmen. Der Versicherung des Hr. Profeßor Hartman zu Folge, ist Ew: Wohlgeboh: der Preiß jeder Platte, 20 Thlr:, schon bekan[n]t. Ich über laße es übrigens Ew: Wohlgebh: in wiefern Dieselben die Zahlung gefälligst einzurichten gedenken, und machen denselben nur bemerklich, daß es mir lieb seyn würde, wen[n] ich die Zahlung auf drey, fünf oder sechs Platten durch Anweisung hier beziehen, u dagegen die Platten an einen hiesigen Com[m]ißionair abliefern kön[n]te. Oder wollen Dieselben allemal, der manigfachen Auslagen wegen die Hälfte auf sechs, acht oder zehn Platten voraus gegeben, das stehet bey Ew. Wohlgeb. In jedem Falle erwarte ich von Ew: Wohlgeb: über die zu treffende Einrichtung gefälligst einige Nachricht. Ich empfehle mich übrigens Deroselbe Wohlwollen und bin mit vollkom[m]ener Hochachtung
        ergebener Diener M Retzsch[58]

Most gracious Sir,
Very honourable Sir,
I owe the kindness of entering into written negotiation with your excellent self to my friend, Professor Hartmann, at whose instigation I would like to define more closely with your excellent self what relates to the 26 sheets of outlines to be etched by me after the poem *Faust* by Gœthe. Not only often requested and asked by various parties to speedily publish this collection, but also excellently encouraged by the full praise of Mr Privy Councillor v Gœthe himself, during his presence here, and also repeatedly asked by him to engrave them, I would be disposed to do so, since my time now allows me to undertake this work to some extent. According to Professor Hartmann's assurance, the price for each plate, 20 Thalers, is already known to you. Incidentally, I leave it to your excellent self [to decide] to what extent you may intend to kindly arrange the payment, and only wish to point out that it would be agreeable to me if I were to receive it here by money-order per three, five or six plates, and could in return deliver the plates to a local commissioner. Or else if you prefer to always advance, because of the multiple expenses, half [of the sum] per six, eight or ten plates, that rests with your excellent self. Incidentally, I recommend myself to your benevolence and remain very respectfully at your service, M. Retzsch.

Behind the customary well-mannered formulas of respect, Retzsch's matter-of-fact and business-like tone shows himself sure, determined to publicize an assignment he highly valued, and to require due payment of his inexpensive fee (it would later rise substantially). Several turns of phrase merit comment or explication: "often requested and asked by various parties to speedily publish this collection" implies his *Faust* sequence was well advanced and already had its devotees. Was it complete? The assertion would be rash: it seems gainsaid by drawings for the "Witch's Kitchen" and "Outside the City Walls" that reached Weimar only late December 1810. Pauline Gotter, Friedrich Wilhelm Schelling's second wife, recorded Goethe's "high satisfaction" with them at the time of her visit.[59] Yet, in her phrasing, Goethe's approval lay with a series of compositions, not just individual drawings. It is possible that Retzsch had extended, even completed the set between meeting Goethe and writing to Cotta. At least fleshed out in general conception, perhaps not finalized in every detail, as we shall see. The proposed contract already stipulates 26 plates, and exactly 26 plates would be published. His zeal is obvious, not least in his contractual epistle, which *precedes* by nearly a month Goethe's own 6 November missive to the publisher, mentioning the outlines for the first time (amongst others' endeavours to visually interpret *Faust*). Once Cotta's agreement confirmed,

---

58   DLA Co: Retzsch. Transcriptions follow original manuscripts as faithfully as possible. I have restored current spellings in my translations.

59   GG 2:103.

Retzsch must have set to work on the metal plates without further delay. On the 2 December, Verlohren informed Goethe that Retzsch was in the process of etching "the drawings he had made." He added: "as soon as he will have finished this work, he will send the [metal] plates (*die Blatten*) over to bookseller Cotta for the sale of prints (*zum Verkauf der Abdrücke*); should Sir however wish to see the drawings (*die Zeichnungen*), he would gladly send them over for a few days for you, Sir, to see and I therefore expect your orders."[60] It could also well be that the drawings received late December corresponded to such a desire on Goethe's part.

The choice of number of plates per batch and corresponding payment had been left with Cotta who must have settled on four since none of Retzsch's extant convoying notes to Kummer gives another figure. Retzsch will have been hard at work as the New Year set in. For his part, Goethe will have expressed concern about the faithfulness of the etchings to the drawings seen, as may be inferred from Verlohren's 20 January 1811 response:

> Sir, Mr Retsch [*sic*] recommends himself to you, he would very gladly send over proof-sheets of his drawings (*Proba Abdrücke seiner Zeichnungen*) or, once the whole thing is completed, a copy of it, but, since Mr Cotta has taken over the whole work, he would prefer it, if Sir had the goodness to turn to the aforesaid Mr Cotta for a copy. I saw some sample prints of his drawings (*einige Abdrücke seiner Zeichnungen*), they seemed very perfect to me.[61]

Crucially, the letter no longer offered *drawings* but *sample sheets* pulled from the plates. By then, Retzsch, fully engaged in the etching process of a likely settled series, was developing an object for issue in large numbers. As such, it no longer belonged to him but the publisher. The artist clearly decided to keep the exchange on a professional basis, and, aware of treading new ground, to keep Cotta actively involved. He may also have intended to lever Goethe's influence and use his request for trial proofs to accelerate publication.

On the very morrow of Verlohren's letter to Goethe, Retzsch dispatched the first four metal plates to Leipzig, but Kummer did not know what to do with them. He wrote to Cotta on Retzsch's own note asking: "Should I keep these plates here? or send them to you by *post* or *carrier*?"[62] Proper arrangements had not yet been made on Cotta's side, let alone a production line, which had not been

decided. Kummer remained in the dark. On 9 March 1811, the second batch ready, Kummer having informed the artist that the first still lay in his hands, Retzsch turned to Cotta. His anxiety is revealed in his long zigzagging sentence of knotty syntax:

> Ew. Wohlgebohr.
> Habe ich die Ehre zu melden, dass zur Zeit abermals vier Platten zu Göthens Faust vollendet parat liegen; und bitte zugleich, dass da ich von Hr: [Herrn] Kummer in Leipzig an welchen Dieselben mich gewiesen, auf meine kürzliche Anfrage wegen der an selbigen schon bereits vor 10 Wochen abgeschikten vier ersten Platten, wobei sich auch zu jeder ein Abdruck befindet, zur Antwort erhalten habe, dass zwar die Platten sich seit dieser Zeit in seinen Händen befänden, er aber noch bis jetzt keines weges wisse, was damit werden solle, ihm gefälligst von unserm Contrakt zu unterrichten und anzuweisen, damit ich nicht allein in der Arbeit ununterbrochen fortfahren und sonach in Stand gesetzt werde Herrn Göthe, welcher desshalb schon einigemale an mich geschikt, und der übrigen Interessenten eine ohngefähre Zeit der Vollendung des ganzen Werks angeben zu können, als auch meiner anderweitigen Geschäfte darnach einzurichten vermag, weil ich im Spätjahr verreisen werde.
> Ew Wohlgebohr. empfiehlt sich
> ergebenst Moritz Retzsch.[63]

> Honourable Sir,
> I have the honour to announce that at the moment four plates for Gœthe's *Faust* are again ready: and at the same time I pray you to kindly inform and instruct of our contract Mr Kummer in Leipzig; indeed, to my recent request concerning the first four plates sent to him already 10 weeks ago, with a proof impression for each, Kummer, to whom you have yourself referred me, responded that the plates have been in his hands, but he did not yet know in any way what to do with them, so that I am enabled to pursue uninterruptedly my work not alone, and therefore be in a position to give Mr Gœthe, who has already contacted me several times to this end, and all other interested parties, an approximate time for the completion of the whole work, as well as to arrange my other business accordingly because I will travel later on this year.
> I remain, Honourable Sir,
> very respectfully, yours M. Retzsch.

---

60 GSA 26/934, 3.
61 GSA 26/934, 4.
62 HAAB: F gr 5019, document 9, Kummer's emphasis.

63 Beinecke: YCGL MSS 6, box 14, folder 555.

FAUST I OUTLINED AND THE ORIGINAL RETZSCH EFFECT

Letters are fascinating in research because they bring us briskly back in time and usher us there and then into the reality of the artist's life and creation. Yet they are often infinitesimal documents abruptly torn out of context, containing indistinct and unclear indications. They beg to be completed and corroborated by other minutiae perhaps forever lost. Till now, two letters have been most used by scholars in relation to Retzsch's *Faust 1*: his contract-like letter to Cotta, and the above epistle to Cotta, asking the publisher to duly inform his representative (oddly confused in Giesen's appreciation with the printer[64]) and urging him for a publication date.

I do not consider here correspondence with J. F. Cotta posterior to 1823 as in Hildebrand-Schat's book, irrelevant to the 1810s. Retzsch's adroit argument that Goethe and "other interested parties" were anxious to announce a publication date for the *Umrisse* may have mirrored Goethe's inquiries through Verlohren, whose letters have not been preserved. The argument may also have been devised to compel Cotta: it well confirms the artist's willingness to publicize his *Faust*.

The first of these letters is in the Deutsches Literatur Archiv in Marbach, the second at the Beinecke Library in Yale University. Neither alone provides the picture, if not completed by six authentic documents in Retzsch's hand, three dated 1811, another three 1812, dates either specified on emission or recorded on reception. They are part of an artificially assembled and bound volume of variously signed autograph material, now at the Herzogin Anna Amalia Bibliothek in Weimar. The volume's bulk itself is an interesting example of copies *after* Retzsch to which I shall come back later (Chapter 7). As for the six documents, although digitized, they appear not to have been signalled before. Four are brief delivery notes, documenting Retzsch's transactions with Kummer in 1811–12. One, already mentioned, escorts the first 21 January 1811 consignment. The fourth, dated 8 April 1812, is an autograph receipt reading: "I hereby certify that I received 520 Thalers cash for 26 plates after Goethe's *Faust* at 20 rt [Reichsthaler] apiece from the bookseller Kummer."[65]

The settled account could hardly reflect the order more accurately. The diligent Retzsch had indeed already completed his task. His swift processing transpires in Böttiger's assertion in the 22 April 1811 *Zeitung für die elegante Welt*: "he is engraving at this moment a series of figures, of his own rich invention, after Goethe's *Faust*, with which Goethe himself is said to have been satisfied when the drawings were presented to him" (*radirt in diesem Augenblick eine Reihe von Darstellungen nach Göthe's*

Faust, von seiner eigenen reichen Erfindung, womit Göthe selbst, als ihm die Zeichnungen vorgelegt wurden, zufrieden gewesen seyn soll.)[66] Böttiger and Retzsch's Scharfenberg friends were certainly among the "other interested parties," mentioned in Retzsch's 9 March 1811 letter. In his devout biography, Th. S. dates the engraving process as 1812 and dramatizes Retzsch's efforts under French occupation in Dresden in an account that hardly stands the evidence of a payment receipt.[67] To cut a long story short, four months after Goethe's visit, the artist had to all intents and purposes completed drawings, etched and delivered the first batch of four metal plates. Thirteen months later, he had etched, proofed and supplied the remaining twenty-two. His work was done with, and paid off, at a sustained pace of four plates every ten weeks or so. Yet, as is well known, his *Umrisse* only came out in October 1816. What had happened in between?

Before I attempt an answer, let me point out that strong affirmations, such as the following, need to be revised: "The late publication date is probably not due to the publisher, who was constantly taking care of the publication, but to the illustrator, whose correspondence betrays hesitation and uncertainty and who suffered from an eye ailment," all the more so as it concludes by opposing Retzsch's "reserve" to Cornelius's "actionism."[68] Nothing substantiates constant care by the publisher, quite the reverse. Retzsch's eye complaint occurs much later (1828 and 1834) as record his letters to both Cottas.[69] As for a hesitant stance, besides Retzsch's obvious eagerness, another letter to Cotta dated 30 April 1812, just after the Leipzig book fair, shows that problems and delays lay indeed with the publisher's representative:

> Da das Werk von 26 Platten zu Göthens Faust schon längst beendigt ist, u ich dieselben, wie Sie wünschten jedesmal zu 4 Platten an Hr. Kum[m]er in Leipzig schickte, wogegen ich auch, nach Ihrer Anordnung, die Bezahlung für selbige sogleich erhielt, wie Ihnen die Hauptquittung, die derselbe über das Ganze von mir nun in Händen hat, auch beweisen wird; so kan[n] ich nicht einsehn, wie das zugehen muß, daß Sie sämtliche Platten noch nicht empfangen haben. Sollten Sie dieselben bei Ihrer Rückkehr nicht alle vorfinden, was ich nicht hoffen will, so wird Hr: Kummer Ihnen hierüber die beste Auskunft geben kön[n]en.

---

64 Giesen, "Goethes *Faust* in der europäischen Kunst," 62, n. 339.

65 HAAB: F gr 5019, document 6.

66 Karl August Böttiger, "Bilder nach Wieland, Göthe und Schiller," *Zeitung für die elegante Welt*, no. 80 (22 Apr 1811): 636.

67 Th. S., "Ein Lebensbild," 7a.

68 Giesen, "Goethes *Faust* in der europäischen Kunst," 62.

69 DLA C-R, no. 12 and no. 40.

Die Zeichnungen, welche ich zu dem Werke gemacht hatte, bestanden säm[m]tlich in einem leichten Umriß, u ich habe, nachdem dieselben auf den Firnis der Platten abgedrückt waren, mich nicht ferner darnach gerichtet, weil ich die Ausführung gleich mit dem Radieren verband; sie würden daher ohne den mindesten Nutzen für Nachhülfe, die etwan mit der Zeit nöthig werden dürfte, seyn, zu welchem Zweck übrigens die guten Abdrüke, deren zu jeder Platte einer hinzugefügt ist, am besten dienen werden.[70]

Since the work of 26 plates on Gœthe's *Faust* has long been completed, and I sent it, as you requested, by [batches of] 4 plates a time to Mr Kummer in Leipzig, against which, according to your order, I received immediate payment, as my general receipt, that he now has in his hands for the whole thing, will also prove to you; I therefore cannot see how it may happen that you have not yet received all the plates. Should you not find them all on your return,[71] which I hope not, Mr Kummer will be in a position to best inform you on the matter.

The drawings which I had made for the work were all in slight outline, and once they had been impressed on the plates' varnish, I did not pursue in that direction because I closely associated their execution with the etching; they would therefore be of no use whatsoever for retouching, should this ever prove necessary over time; by the way, the good impressions, one of which is attached to each plate, would best serve that purpose.

The HAAB documents are a valuable source of information. Kummer's negligence and perhaps Cotta's belated or hazy instructions were to blame for the delay. Retzsch's recourse to a local agent (to save post costs and perhaps anguish) had taken the wind out of his sail. His very proposal had turned against him. As the letter shows, he was a keen artist, attentive to the slightest detail, and even foresaw that extensive use of the plates would need refurbishing, to which his sample proofs would serve. A last note to Kummer, delivering another 4 plates on 21 May 1812, would have completed the sequence, presumably replacing the lost ones.[72]

Yet available documentation also has limits. Two years elapse before references to Retzsch's *Umrisse* emerge again in Goethe's diaries, recording on 30 June 1814 the arrival in Weimar of "drawings from Faust," attributed to Retzsch.[73] They were examined and discussed by the poet, his close friend and correspondent Carl Friedrich Zelter, perhaps the historian Georg Freiherr Sartorius von Waltershausen, and Friedrich Wilhelm Riemer, by then Goethe's amanuensis, who noted in his unpublished diary on 1 July: "In the evening at Goethe's, Zelter present. Examined Retzsch's drawings after Faust, fascinating (*reizend*)."[74] It is impossible to say whether these were meant to replace lost plates; whether Goethe had requested changes or even rejected plates (leaving no trace); whether Retzsch had reviewed some of his compositions while awaiting publication; or added further drawings.

One thing is certain, further delays occurred, on the publisher's side. Cotta solicited in vain Goethe's comment on the *Umrisse*. He well knew that such endorsement would boost the value of his publications and attract buyers. His first entreaty to Goethe along with a set of all 26 proofs, construed as "[Stuttgart October 1815]" in the Goethe-Cotta correspondence, dates clearly back to 1814, as Dorothea Kuhn notes.[75] It received no response. A second plea followed on 31 October 1815,[76] this time favourably received: "As for *Faust*, I have given it some thought, and hope to be able to deliver something, although it would be but a page, something that could be inserted as an inscription after the title, either printed or engraved." (*An den Faust habe ich gedacht und hoffe etwas liefern zu können, doch würde es etwa nur ein Blatt seyn, welches man als Dedication hinter den Titel entweder gedruckt oder gestochen einheften könnte.*)[77] A year later, nothing having come, the *Umrisse* were finally issued in October 1816 with the (anonymous) preface by Therese Huber, by then editor of the *Morgenblatt für gebildete Stände*. Cotta's argument was that the publication had been announced in book fair catalogues (*Messekataloge*) and already charged to the booksellers.[78] He was under the obligation to bring it out. Curiously, I find no trace announcing Retzsch's *Umrisse* in Leipzig book fair catalogues between 1812 and 1818, not even after the *Umrisse* had been published. However, Cotta had indeed announced them under Goethe's name in the 1 January 1816 "Circulaire" he sent out to booksellers as "Faust, (with outlines by Retsch [*sic*])," although text

---

70 HAAB: F gr 5019, document 5.
71 The phrase refers to the 1812 Leipzig book fair, from 13 Apr to 1 May.
72 HAAB: F gr 5019, document 4.

73 *Tg* 5, 1:160 & 31–32.
74 Qtd. in *Tg* 5, 2:682.
75 GCB 1:282; 3, 1:349.
76 GCB 1:282.
77 GCB 1:284.
78 GCB 2:28.

was reduced to a few excerpts. From his point of view, the work was subordinate to Goethe's. His first announcement of Retzsch's outlines vaunting the artist's name would occur only in the 1 January 1831 "Circulaire" regarding Schiller's *Song of the Bell* (issued 1833). The book fair catalogues would register Retzsch's work under his name only in 1840 (outlines after Bürger).

Despite his efforts and energy, Retzsch had had to wait nearly four years before his *Faust* at last addressed a German public in October 1816. Unluckily for him, Cornelius's first instalment had come out at Easter 1816 according to Seeliger, and further sample proofs sent by Friedrich Wenner reached Weimar in August.[79]

2.5 A Speculation on Relics

How many *Faust* drawings and precisely which did Goethe see in Dresden? How many of them are today preserved in Dresden's Prints Cabinet collection? In the Thieme-Becker dictionary, Ernst Sigismund set the record—potentially a moot point—by way of a diminutive, parenthetic indication, defying detection: "R. had delivered a series of Faust sketches, which Goethe saw with great interest in September 1810 in Dresden (12 sheets, Prints Cabinet, Dresden)."[80] The greater part of the present-day Retzsch collection came to the Dresden Prints Cabinet in autumn 1892 through J. M. C. Hildebrand's bequest (*Vermächtnis*), 35 years after Retzsch's demise. It contains a large number of *Faust* drawings, none of which is dated, let alone accredited as presented to Goethe. Comparison with the etched prints shows that they may be roughly divided into five categories:

a) Early draft sketches
b) Preliminary studies of complete scenes at various stages
c) More complete studies showing alternative details
d) Detailed finished drawings close to the etched versions
e) Drawings traced from the final etchings.

When dealing with an artist's primary creation, it would be unwise to set strict limits through classification. The first and last of these notional groupings are the easiest to identify and interpret. Otherwise, they easily overlap, particularly (b) and (c) in this case. Nevertheless, roughly classifying them prompts insights into the evolution of Retzsch's work and his aesthetics.

Early draft sketches (a) is a rather inadequate term for Retzsch's outlines and their firm contours. However, this group involves no comprehensive scenes. Six drawings are but early designs capturing the core of an episode. Leaving out settings, and focussed on the protagonists, they seize key actions and gestures, turning points, and scenes of despair, devilry or desire: the covenant (C 5056); Faust in the witch's kitchen, engrossed in the magic mirror (with an ensnaring Mephistopheles slouching in an armchair, fire fan in hand) (C 5059); accosting Margaret (C 5061); raising the bed drapes in her chamber (C 5064); ascending with Mephistopheles the Brocken (C 5086); and exhorting Margaret to leave prison (C 5081). In most, an appropriate backdrop will be subsequently added, but the fitting atmosphere is already there. Three are inscribed *Faust* in a neat Roman hand, exactly as on a likewise entitled Weimar drawing. An earlier version of the Dresden covenant scene, the latter sports on the same sheet two male nudes wrestling and a third climbing. Comparison between the Weimar and Dresden drafts shows that the tension between protagonists will hardly subside. In the earlier Weimar (cf. Fig. 2.4a), Mephistopheles's fierce expression already fleets over the animal features of his widened triangular face as in the later etching (cf. Fig. 4.3). In the further developed Dresden sketch (C 5056, cf. Fig. 2.4b), Retzsch still wavers over the final position of one of Faust's legs and sparely indicates furniture. Still, he will only have to set the partners in context. His depiction of a capital moment is already there.

This part of his *Nachlass* evidences his ability to fix chief moments in an interactive minimal scene. In the final etchings, he slightly reinforces protagonists' contours, enabling the viewer to differentiate levels of image gradation. This slightly emphasized line weight, a key feature of his graphic work, is lost in later reproductions such that several items replicated appear flat.

Drawings traced after the final etchings (e) are later additions, a consequence of plying the drawings into the etching process itself. He had alluded to this in his 30 April 1812 letter to J. F. Cotta: instead of pursuing drawing, he associated it "with the etching" itself by imprinting drawings "onto the plates' varnish." Had the plates been lost, his drawings would be of no assistance but sample proofs would. He employed the same process in his Schiller outlines and subsequent assignments. In a 13 July 1831 letter to Georg von Cotta, who had asked him for drawings, he explicitly writes:

> So gern ich Ihnen die Zeichnungen, Ihrem Wunsche gemäß zustellen möchte, so wiederhole ich doch da offene Geständniß, daß dieselben gewöhnlich aus der Druckerei durch das Aufpausen vermittelst

---

79 See Seeliger, "Faust-Bilder von Peter Cornelius," A278; *Tg* 5, 2:978–79; RA 7:no. 447.

80 Sigismund, "Retzsch, Moritz," 193b.

FIGURES 2.4a–b
(*top*) Moritz Retzsch, *Faust*, preliminary pencil drawing, n.d., 15.8 × 15 cm; (*bottom*) same scene further developed, n.d., 14.2 × 12.3 cm
COURTESY HAAB, F GR 9228, WEIMAR, AND: SKK, C 5056, DRESDEN, PHOTO ANDREAS DIESEND

der Preße, in einem so verbleichten u zum Theil schmuzigen Zustand zu mir zurück kehren, daß die mehrsten davon gänzlich unbrauchbar geworden von mir gar nicht aufbewahrt worden sind u werden kön[n]en, wovon sich män[n]iglich augenscheinlich überzeugen würde.[81]

As much as I would like to send you the drawings following your wishes, I however repeat my frank confession that they usually come back to me in such a bleached and partly dirty state from the printer's because of the tracing through the press, that most of them, having become completely unusable, have not and could not have been kept by me, a fact of which anybody would be plainly convinced.

Later, he recorded the final etchings by tracing them in light outlines: three of the Dresden *Faust* drawings (C 5055, C 5058 and C 5075) are pencil copies of his extra etchings for the 1834 enlarged *Umrisse zu Faust* edition (29 instead of 26 plates). As post-production replicas, they are not reversed like the originals transferred to the plates. Such is also a pencil tracing of pl. 9, Margaret in her chamber (C 1937–1495), which joined the Dresden *Nachlass* later from Johann Friedrich Lahmann's collection, perhaps a cherished art lovers's copy (see Chapter 7).

Detailed finished drawings close to the etched versions (d) form an instructive group, albeit tricky to substantiate. Read in a certain way, they might amount to twelve, as per Sigismund's remark. Given their nearly finished status, that well-informed art historian and collector of Retzsch's work may have been tempted to see in them an ideal series of "12 plates," perhaps even those shown to Goethe. No documents uphold or gainsay such a theory, and, according to other parameters, their number ought to exceed twelve.

Far more thought-provoking than grappling with what Sigismund actually meant, is the way they have been wielded by the artist while etching. Straight lines or geometrical shapes are often not drawn in pencil. Instead, traced through the paper by means of a blunt stylus or etching needle, they directly impressed the plate's varnish beneath. Some bear slightly varying details, although they do not seem incomplete nor resemble setting-out drafts: they have been finalized via the etching process itself, as evidence blotches or chemical stains. In others, the stylus has retraced pencil contours to similar effect (C 5066,

Martha adorns Margaret with the jewels). In several, remarkably detailed, fanciful minutiae are lacking and appear to have been imprinted directly onto the plates. For instance, whereas Faust drinks the potion in the witch's kitchen in C 5060 (Fig. 2.5), the drawing, clearly used for etching, includes neither the tiny creatures in the cauldron's vapours nor the string of frogs of the final plates (cf. Fig. 2.18–2.19); in Margaret imploring Our Lady of Sorrows (C 5076), the bricks and roof tiles are missing, again drawn onto the plate. Although the first plate, Prologue in Heaven (C 5052), is part of this group (with hatched clouds added on the plate), the majority corresponds to plates beyond the cycle's mid-point and includes complex crowded scenes: the cathedral (C 5085), Valentine dying (C 5083), Faust and Mephistopheles ascending the Brocken (C 5087), the witches' Sabbath (C 5077). In a drawing from group (b), extant in many versions, Faust contemplates Margaret's bed while Mephistopheles briskly enters with the jewels' casket (C 5063), yet only the latter has been traced onto the varnished plate (cf. Fig. 2.9). This suggests etching by trial and error, the final plate coalescing a choice of the most engaging drawn figures.

In the presently preserved presentation, all drawings are pasted. None of the reverse sides is accessible, although they seem to bear further indications. Yet, excitingly, this part of the *Nachlass* allows exploration of Retzsch's approach to outline etching.

It is of course possible that the artist, anxious to promptly execute the work, chose such a method to gain time, skipping the transfer of a detailed finished drawing onto the polished and varnished plate before etching. Yet, his recurrent preference over time for such practice shows he consciously capitalized on a multiplication process to get his work known. He was not anxious to preserve original drawings. He rather used them for the ultimate purpose of reproduction. Since he turned the etched plates over to a publisher (the prints belonged to Cotta, as he stressed to Goethe via Verlohren), he was wielding etching as *a medium to which industrializing features would be applied*. He will have been aware of the fact that his *Faust* interpretation was a burgeoning vehicle. He may not have yet suspected to what extent it would proliferate, but knew that the medium would propel his designs far beyond Dresden.

Retzsch thus appears as a craftsman, designer, and artist in one. He mastered engraving to the last detail, as evidence his later correspondence with Georg von Cotta and his resolve to retouch and re-engrave the plates himself, a task he considered tedious, yet necessary, for his work to show at its best. He wielded engraving both as an art and a reproduction vehicle. This shows in a bidirectional

---

81   DLA C-R, no. 21.

FIGURE 2.5 Moritz Retzsch, Faust drinks the potion in the witch's kitchen, chemical-stained preliminary pencil drawing, n.d., 14.8 × 16.4 cm
SKK, C 5060, DRESDEN, PHOTO ANDREAS DIESEND

strip-like cartoon, unfortunately undated, in the Dresden Prints Cabinet (C 1937–1500) (Fig. 2.6).

The lower half hosts four small *Faust* pencil drawings. All four are reduced, rougher outline copies of prints taken from the *Faust* sequence and recomposed as a small storyboard. Set in a run, frame by frame, they recall the eight lithographs in sequential reproduction that would form the long *Parade of the Vinedressers* (1840), albeit with several differences. This is no march (for which the plate-to-plate device would be expected) but a wilful selection. The mounting repurposes the outlines, creating a novel effect, perhaps as a prospectus design or a publishing crib.

It is no satirical or caustic sequential narrative either, as in Hogarth's *The Harlot's* or *The Rake's Progress* (1732 and 1735)—famous eighteenth century etched six-plate precedents, to be viewed plate by plate in larger format, albeit later turned into picture stories on a tiny scale with German commentaries.[82] Retzsch's four images are selected, positioned, and re-structured to make a lay Margaret tetraptych, hence with Christic overtones, recalling memorable

---

82 See David Kunzle, *History of the Comic Strip*, vol. 1, *The Early Comic Strip* (Berkeley, Ca.: University of California Press, 1973), 393b.

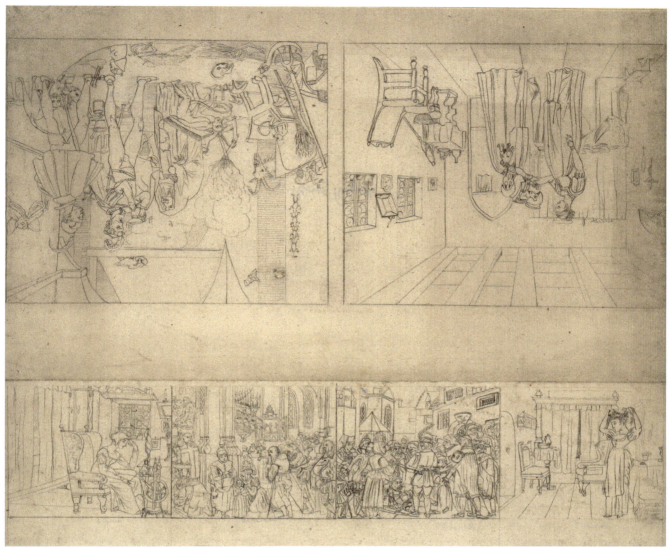

FIGURE 2.6   Moritz Retzsch, double strip of several drawings, n.d., overall 28.6 × 34.3 cm
SKK, C 1937–1500, DRESDEN, PHOTO ANDREAS DIESEND

moments from her story, yet not in chronological order, either from the right or from the left. Working on antithesis, they neatly counterbalance Margaret solitary at both ends with crowd scenes in the centre. The former show her loveliness in private (at the spinning wheel and musing in her chamber), the latter set in public her sense of guilt (cathedral) and disgrace (Valentine dying).

The upper half bears upside-down two other drawings of larger size that may also have been considered for reproduction in a diptych on temptation: Margaret donning the jewels at Martha's, and Faust drinking the potion in the witch's kitchen. As with Hogarth, they may have been "modern moral subjects," conceived as sequential or complementary displays for larger circulation. It is possible Retzsch had in mind Daniel Chodowiecki's visual etched narratives for almanacs.[83]

Extant graphite drawings in groups (b) and (c), *preliminary or more complete studies at various stages*, afford comparative exploration of versions, shedding light on Retzsch's reading of Goethe. Multiple versions of the same scene exemplify what enticed the artist's responsiveness or tried his ability to graphically convert his inspiration, emotions or imagination. They betray either dissatisfaction with the result or particular attraction. Here interpretation has to rely on surviving drawings. It

---

83   On Chodowiecki, see ibid., 393–401.

FIGURE 2.7 Moritz Retzsch, Margaret at the spinning wheel, final pencil drawing, n.d., 13 × 14.7 cm
SKK, C 5074, DRESDEN, PHOTO ANDREAS DIESEND

cannot be excluded that versions of *other* scenes may have been lost or destroyed. The sketch of Faust entreating Margaret to leave prison (C 5081) figures for instance on a crumpled piece of paper as if thrown away, then retrieved. Precaution thus taken, five scenes have at least one variant, drawing attention to passion and desire.

Not surprisingly, all five picture crucial moments: Faust in his study (one), Faust and Margaret (two), Margaret's sad fate (two). The latter aroused more interest than the former. In a first version of Faust's study with the poodle appearing (C 5053), Retzsch drew a ferocious bare-fanged canine barking at Faust, later abandoned for the final nightmarish beast ominously swelling by the stove on which

Saint George symbolically kills the dragon (cf. Fig. 4.3). His two initial versions of the garden (C 5069 actually preceding C 5068) capture the antithetic structure of couples promenading (cf. Fig. 10.3), as in Goethe's opposed disposition. The second (C 5068) momentously catches the devil's glaring eye. Retzsch's dissatisfaction must have lain with the lovers' posture and details of Margaret's clothing, ultimately changed. His initial design of Faust entreating Margaret to leave prison unconvincingly attempts to render her madness rather than his pleading, and was abandoned for good reason (C 5081). The tension built into the final plate, as Mephistopheles pulls away Faust desperately trying to carry off Margaret, who herself lifts arms

FAUST I OUTLINED AND THE ORIGINAL RETZSCH EFFECT 73

FIGURE 2.8 Moritz Retzsch, Valentine dying accuses his sister, *Umrisse zu Goethe's Faust gezeichnet von Retsch* (Stuttgart & Tübingen: Cotta, 1816), pl. 20
COURTESY HAAB, F 3487, WEIMAR

heavenward, is more dramatically effective (cf. Fig. 2.17). The first version of Margaret dejected at the spinning wheel differs from the final by an important detail: in the cast-off version, she still wears her hair in braids and ringlets as a girl (C 5072). In the final version C 5074 (as in the set) it has disappeared under a neat coif, as for a married woman, implying her loss of virginity (Fig. 2.7). The first version of Valentine dying in public poses Margaret weeping over her brother, while slanting glances publicly stigmatize her (C 5084). In the final version, lost from view within the crowd, her face concealed, but pointedly accused by Valentine, she is symbolically overwhelmed by social dishonour and indifference (two boys badger each other, oblivious to the calamity, Fig. 2.8).

Comparisons between discarded and later versions bring to the fore central features to Retzsch's art: overall image planning in which everything matters, a wealth of detail, and important symbolic implications—all meaningful changes proving his reading of Goethe's *Faust* to be sophisticated.

Moreover, expression of desire and passion in *Faust* tested Retzsch's pencil. Two episodes show complex handling in multiple drafts: entering Margaret's chamber and the lovers' kiss. They both obviously appealed to the artist and bring libido to the fore—a daring aspect for the time. His final conceptions had lasting appeal and even inspired the marketing of English albums.

The trespass on Margaret's chamber is a symbolic penetration of privacy. A first draft orchestrates the incursion itself, fusing together three distinct moments from "Evening. A small well-kept room" (C 5063, Fig. 2.9). Foreground left, Margaret standing half-turns away from

FIGURE 2.9 Moritz Retzsch, Faust and Mephistopheles in Margaret's chamber with Margaret also present, blotched preliminary pencil drawing with Mephistopheles stylus-retraced, n.d., 16.1 × 17.8 cm
SKK, C 5063, DRESDEN, PHOTO ANDREAS DIESEND

her mirror as if already sporting the jewels. She is shown to be present and taken aback, whereas she should be absent and chronologically the last to appear and find the jewels (F 2753f). Mid-ground, Faust draws aside her bed curtain, his back to the viewer, lost in musings as reflected in his words some fifty lines previous (F 2709f). In the play, he discovers Margaret's virginal nature. His former sudden lust at first sight ("Look, you must get that girl for me!" F 2619, trans. D. Luke) changes suddenly into ardent love mingled to thoughts on nature ("I was resolved, my lust brooked no delay— | And now in dreams of love I wilt and melt away!" F 2722–23, trans. D. Luke). In Retzsch's drawing, with his back turned and no caption, his expression is unfathomable, and the viewer may project upon the picture a different reading. In the text, this moment also *precedes* Mephistopheles who abruptly breaks in from the left, jewel casket in hand, calling: "Quick! I can see her by the gate." (F 2729, trans. W. Arndt). Conflating three instants in simultaneous action, C 5063 stresses the forcefulness of the devil's irruption to the male lover's pondering and the girl's intimacy. Retzsch's draft also mirrors his fervour as he attempts to capture Faust's longing in yet another sketch astride the bed top. We may consider the draft as a matter-of-fact sketching sheet, in which the artist has simply tried his hand at three different poses. Yet, he later imprinted to the final etching the irruptive

FIGURE 2.10   Moritz Retzsch, Faust and Mephistopheles in Margaret's chamber, *Umrisse zu Goethe's Faust gezeichnet von Retsch* (Stuttgart & Tübingen: Cotta, 1816), pl. 10
COURTESY HAAB, F 3487, WEIMAR

Mephistopheles sectioned by the frame, a visual metaphor of erotic invasion as the vertical cuts through his crotch (Fig. 2.10). Not by chance: libido is the devil's part in the story.

This drawing shows Retzsch intuitively combining forms, shapes, and distinct moments to hint at the scene's sexual overtones. His design reflects emotion. While drawing, he broods on the text. Margaret's presence here belongs and yet does not belong to literal interpretation. Her genuine presence stresses the violation; her imagined self symbolizes her assaulted purity. Another draft of the same scene (C 5064) shows only Faust pondering and Mephistopheles stepping in, yet lacks the force and brutality of this one, and will be discarded. In the final set, the bed hangings will be changed and the two moments separately treated—Faust and Mephistopheles in plate 10 (Fig. 2.10), Margaret trying on the jewels in plate 11 (cf. Fig. 2.24).

The arresting translation, steering the lover's gaze towards Margaret's bed, first seized in *Faust* iconography, will thereafter never be lost. Engelbert Seibertz will recycle it in a woodcut inserted to his monumental edition of 1852–54. His reclining Faust's attitude is commented by a lusty plant on the left, ending in disorderly arabesque, a sign of eroticism in his iconographic programme (Fig. 2.11).[84] So will August von Kreling in his own monumental and fully illustrated *Faust* edition of 1875–76,

---

84   See Stead, "Les deux *Faust I* d'Engelbert Seibertz," *La Lecture littéraire*, no. 5–6 (2002): 55; Stead, "Monumental German *Faust* Editions in International Circulation and Multimedia Modernity," *Quaerendo* 50, no. 4 (2020): 388.

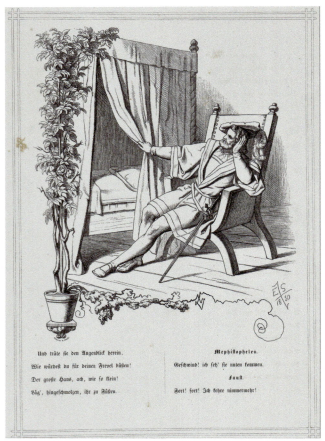

FIGURE 2.11   Engelbert Seibertz, composition inspired by Retzsch, in *Faust: Eine Tragödie von Goethe. Mit Zeichnungen von Engelbert Seibertz* (Stuttgart & Tübingen: J. G. Cotta, 1854), 93, wood engraving in text
COURTESY HAAB, F GR 11196, WEIMAR

FIGURE 2.12   August von Kreling, composition inspired by Retzsch, in *Faust von Goethe, erster Theil. Mit Bildern und Zeichnungen von A. v. Kreling* (Munich: F. Bruckmann, [1875]), 85, wood engraving in text
COURTESY HAAB, F GR 5787, WEIMAR

FAUST I OUTLINED AND THE ORIGINAL RETZSCH EFFECT 77

granting Faust historical costume and demonstrably placing a crucifix above Gretchen's couch, as if to protect her from intruding eyes (Fig. 2.12). The intimate meaning of the scene will not be lost on English book traders either. A gilt reproduction of Retzsch's design will ornate the green cover of an album of his outlines, turning the item itself into the favourite object for any book lover to keep and cherish. Inviting to purchase the album itself, the device will be packaged as a tangible substitute for Gretchen's coveted body (cf. Fig. 5.20).

Retzsch's maximum effort was further granted to Faust and Margaret kissing in four drawings prior to the final etching. In two early drafts on the same sheet, the artist's focus is on the lovers clasping each other as their lips meet (C 4890, cf. Fig. 2.13). Their tender hug shows abandonment as they fondle each other's hair or neck. Still, their decorous silhouettes remain distinct, with no overt signs of arousal. Retzsch however redrew them in complex surroundings (C 5073, cf. Fig. 2.14). He cornered their uninhibited embrace between an open door and a casement giving onto dense foliage. Gretchen yields to Faust's grasp and his male specifics become visible. Vague hangings either side enhance the scene's theatricality. Their passionate kiss is robbed of a fleeting moment. Likewise, in Goethe's text, their breathless half-lines reflect passion, especially on Gretchen's part, that of a willing paramour (F 3205–06). Yet, their privacy is open to the four winds as a third person or prying voyeur appears on the left. Perhaps inspired by Flaxman's *The Lovers Surprised*, rendering the kiss of Paolo Malatesta and Francesca da Rimini in Dante's *Inferno*, as Krüger astutely remarks,[85] Retzsch's conception shows two important differences.

That Retzsch borrowed Flaxman's idea is of course possible but Goethe's text is equally suggestive with Mephistopheles and Martha breaking in on the amorous couple. The first line following their embrace, sundered in four (F 3207), accentuates Faust and Mephistopheles' violent verbal exchange:

Faust, *stamping his foot.*
    Who's there?
MEPHISTOPHELES.
    A friend!
FAUST.
    A beast!
MEPHISTOPHELES.
    We must take leave now, come!
    (trans. A. G. Latham)

Thus prompted, Retzsch merged the two moments in one, in another pair of drawings and the final engraving. He first depicted the two prowlers through the open door, at a small distance, approaching, with Martha hanging off Mephistopheles's arm (C 5071, cf. Fig. 2.15). On the left, the ample casement affords the lovers breathing space. In the final drawing, however, to be impressed upon the plate, the door is under assault as the intruders attempt to burst in (C 5070, cf. Fig. 2.16). Verbal violence is transferred to movement, underpinning the scene's erotic overtones. Mephistopheles's pelvis is thrust against the door while Martha lifts her skirts as if to cross the threshold. Such vigour is absent from Goethe's text where the lovers must part at the onset of dark, and the short scene ends with Gretchen wondering: "What a poor untaught child am I! | I know not what he can find in me!" (F 3215–16, trans. A. G. Latham). Contrariwise, Retzsch has Mephistopheles's glaring look encroach while in the foreground hovers a mask with similar slanting features. The devil's expression itself was likewise retouched on the metal plate giving him a disturbing, indiscreet mien (cf. Fig. 7.17).

The result, attained by small touches, is a brilliant instance making us aware, by contrast, of the lovers' passionate sexual mutual consent, and forces opposing their happiness. In accomplishing it, Retzsch surpassed Flaxman's Paolo and Francesca, by far one of the most famous embraces in literature. Intruding viewers set aside, Paolo's kiss on Francesca's cheek by Flaxman has none of Retzsch's intensity in bringing into full view Faust and Gretchen's rapture, riveted in each other's arms. Their kiss as *pars pro toto* is a metonymy for lovemaking and a turning point in the story. No contemporary kiss image displays such ardour, astonishing to viewers of the time. Examples abound: we may think of Huldbrand and Undine's decorous kiss as they hardly touch lips in an idyllic landscape in plate 7 from C. F. Schultze's 14 outlines for Fouqué's *Undine*, published in Frankfurt *c.*1818. Or even Retzsch's own *Der Kuß* (*The Kiss, Le Baiser*), plate 4 in his trilingual *Fancies and Truths* (1831) with his own comments. In this, a young priest leans towards the girl, caressing her chin, but the viewer grasps from the title, although does not see, that he kisses her on the cheek. Retzsch's own comment stresses moral and social aspects as in his subtitle *Altes und neues Coelibat* (*Old and New Celibate*):

> Ein junger Priester umarmt und küßt an den Kirchenmauer ein sich nur wenig sträubendes Mädchen. Das in die Mauer eingelassene Steinbild einer die Hände faltenden, fast ganz verhüllten Matrone scheint einen strafenden Blick auf das Paar zu richten. Auf dem Sarkophag eines Bischofs (im Hintergrund) wälzt sich ein höhnisch lachender Teufels-Satyr.

---

85 Eva Krüger, *Bilder zu Goethes "Faust": Moritz Retzsch und Dante Gabriel Rossetti* (Hildesheim: Olms, 2009), 33.

FIGURE 2.13
Moritz Retzsch, preliminary drawings for Faust and Margaret kissing, n.d., 16.1 × 18.1 cm
SKK, C 4890, DRESDEN, PHOTO ANDREAS DIESEND

FIGURE 2.14
Moritz Retzsch, drawing for Faust and Margaret kissing, n.d., 13.6 × 15 cm
SKK, C 5073, DRESDEN, PHOTO ANDREAS DIESEND

FIGURE 2.15
Moritz Retzsch, Faust and Margaret kissing, drawing, n.d., 13.6 × 12 cm
SKK, C 5071, DRESDEN, PHOTO ANDREAS DIESEND

FIGURE 2.16
Moritz Retzsch, Faust and Margaret kissing, final drawing used for the etched plate, n.d., 14 × 16.3 cm
SKK, C 5070, DRESDEN, PHOTO ANDREAS DIESEND

A young priest by the church wall hugs and kisses a young girl who is but little resisting. The effigy of an almost completely veiled matron folding her hands, set into the wall, seems to direct a reproving glance at the couple. On a bishop's sarcophagus (in the background) a mockingly laughing devil-satyr exults.

Hollywood screen close-ups of kissing actors had not yet dulled sensibilities. Retzsch's treatment caused a stir and thrilled audiences. Faust and Gretchen's kiss is one of his best-known images from *Faust*, vowed to ulterior treatment and numerous handlings as will be later discovered.

2.6   "Full of Spirit"

What did Goethe mean by *geistreich*? What gave him, when comparing the originals to the English copies, "food for thought"? Retzsch's treatments of *Faust* episodes and his inventing images by "simultaneousness of effect and concurrence of meaning"[86] have already illustrated such points. Yet an overall view could further highlight a few aspects.

Conspicuous features have been stressed over and again: William Vaughan, assessing the reception of German romanticism in England, showed that Retzsch appealed to an English audience by "the clarity and dramatic power of his visualizations."[87] His treatment combined narrative vigour, moral symbolism, and sentimentality.[88] On this score, Viola Hildebrand-Schat delved in detail into Retzsch's stylization and means of characterization, and highlighted formal aspects from a German art historian's point of view, considering his designs as "mediating literature" for the bourgeoisie.[89] In three insightful articles, Gerd-Helge Vogel replaced Retzsch within German romanticism and set in perspective the artist's reading of Goethe in the tradition and renewal of *exempla amoris*.[90] In gauging Retzsch's influence on Rossetti, Eva Krüger studied text-image relations, though the weight she gives to the brochure excerpts confuses publisher's choices with those of the artist.[91] Retzsch clearly read Faust *in extenso*. There seems little left to say. Yet, further singularities of

Retzsch's spirited art need to be added. They stand out on closer examination of original, not later, *Umrisse* editions.

His first major and recognized achievement was turning Goethe's tragedy into a picture story circumscribed and delimited, bordered and defined, accessible to audiences albeit Staël's dismissal. Retzsch abridged it and redrafted its main features. He left out key passages (Faust's night monologue, his invocation of the Earth Spirit, his near suicide, long exchanges with Mephistopheles, etc.). Metaphysical considerations beat a retreat, even disappeared, in favour of a poignant love story at Margaret's expense. Plot shifted from the dejected doctor to Gretchen: more than half the lines (F 1–2604) correspond to only seven plates, while nineteen follow Faust and Margaret from their meeting to the very end (2,008 lines). Retzsch charted Goethe's perplexing textual geography and epitomized the protagonists' personae. Still, he did not idealize Margaret's purity. In the kiss, she is an amorous female yielding to desire and her youthful shape will develop into that of a full-grown woman. When, in prison, she lifts her arms heavenward, her full round breasts and deep lap are no more that of demure innocence (Fig. 2.17).

Hitherto unremarked, in unfolding events according to Goethe, Retzsch also displays personal liberty by swapping the cathedral (pl. 18) for the duel and Valentine dying scenes (pl. 19–20). In Goethe, Gretchen haunted at the cathedral *follows* on Faust and Valentine's deceitful duel and her brother's murder. Attending a requiem (taken to be her mother's, as in *Urfaust*), resonant with *Dies irae*, she is accused by an evil spirit for calamities: her mother's passing, her brother dying on her threshold struck by her lover's hand, and herself being with child. In Retzsch (and Goethe's own *Urfaust*), Gretchen in the cathedral *precedes*. That the artist preferred the previous version to the 1808 *Faust* is implausible. He rather sought viewers' sympathy by setting her pangs in a triptych just after the ardent kiss: pensive at her spinning wheel (pl. 16), imploring Virgin Mary as a *Mater dolorosa*-to-be herself (pl. 17), crushed by guilt in the cathedral (pl. 18). A sort of a lay altarpiece within the set, the three prints track Gretchen from intimate guilt and dejection to public stigma and shame. Through this device, Retzsch discreetly affirms his artistic independence while faithfully following Goethe in detail. The subtle reversal of order became a distinctive mark of *his* interpretation, particularly in its reception abroad: the sequence of 18 (cathedral)–19 (duel)–20 (Valentine's contempt) shows the degree, as we shall see, of his plates' assimilation in British, North American, French and Continental culture. It also proved a sure sign of his set's resistance to an altogether alien medium, the

---

86   Vaughan, *German Romanticism*, 123.
87   Ibid.
88   As summarized by Kevin J. Hayes, "Retzsch's Outlines and Poe's 'The Man of the Crowd,'" *Gothic Studies* 12, no. 2 (Nov 2010): 36.
89   Hildebrand-Schat, *Moritz Retzschs Illustrationen*, 37–64, 112–7.
90   See in bibliography Gerd-Helge Vogel 1999 (twice) and 2008.
91   Krüger, *Retzsch und Rossetti*, 18–24.

FAUST I OUTLINED AND THE ORIGINAL RETZSCH EFFECT   81

FIGURE 2.17   Moritz Retzsch, Final prison scene, *Umrisse zu Goethe's Faust gezeichnet von Retsch* (Stuttgart & Tübingen: Cotta, 1816), pl. 26
COURTESY HAAB, F 3487, WEIMAR

illustrated book, which would impose on the images obedience to text, instead of the artist's own order.

The popularity he gained rests on his gift for pulling the reader into the story thanks to simple devices: a continuum of images at viewer's eye level, and unpretentious yet careful landscape framing. Horizontal presentation gave viewers width of space, a hold on the image, and fostered their possession of setting and background. It corresponds to the eye's natural movement, taking in the middle-band at a glance. It allows for scene breadth, accommodates outside and inside, and engages reading in an evolving chain. It offers a proscenium vista, a continuous theatrical run, threaded as distinct spaces, each hosting a small sequence of events. Faust's study houses the poodle's mutation, the devil's advent, and the covenant.

The witch's kitchen cements Faust's temptation and rejuvenation. Gretchen's bedroom catches her musings, her find of the jewels, and subsequent dejection. Martha's home lodges the jewels' decoy and Mephistopheles's visit. Space identity is attained by consistent viewing, bordered by a thin linear frame, unchanged furniture and objects, and, discreetly yet crucially, *distinct image dimensions*: Faust's study, the witch's kitchen, Gretchen's chamber, Martha's interior, even the prison, each possess, in their own right, their proper width and height. This hitherto unremarked trait explains why image sizes differ within the series all the while strengthening graphic narrative. Space identity conceals a potential kinetic quality that will later transpire in an English edition with new typeset and layout (cf. Fig. 5.11a–c). Typical features foreshadowing an

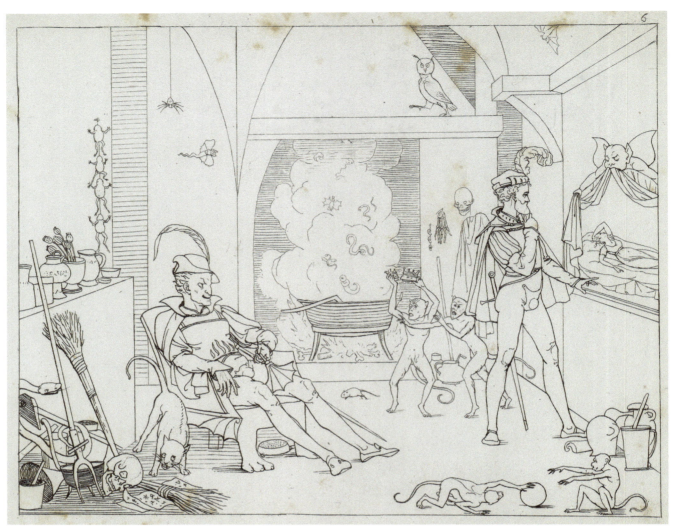

FIGURE 2.18 Moritz Retzsch, The witch's kitchen, *Umrisse zu Goethe's Faust gezeichnet von Retsch* (Stuttgart & Tübingen: Cotta, 1816), pl. 6
COURTESY HAAB, F 3487, WEIMAR

original story, conveyed via multiple framed images, emerge in Retzsch some twenty years before Rodolphe Töpffer's *Story of Mr. Jabot* (1833) and the birth of the comic strip.

Retzsch varies inside and outside events, alternates individual and group scenes, and peppers the sequence with dramatic hints. Scenes are treated close-up or remotely, individuality and uniqueness offset by over-crowded symbolic spaces: the cathedral stages piety; Valentine's demise, public contempt; the witches' Sabbath, the orgiastic nature of devilry. The two former underline the share of society in Margaret's decline, conviction, and death. Such treatment diverges from the play, based on individual confrontation, while encouraging sympathy for the heroine. Retzsch may have been judged sentimental but did not lack humour (Fig. 2.18 & 2.19). When he pictured the witch's kitchen in two successive plates, he drew tiny creatures bobbing in the vapours of the witch's cauldron, an inquisitive-looking owl strutting on the mantelpiece (pl. 6), then bewildered at what it saw (pl. 7), a spider at the end of its thread dropping from the ceiling, and a string of frogs hanging from the wall. He wittily deflated the hocus-pocus with whimsical creatures, mock-macabre trappings, and cavorting monkeys.

His numerous details open up further possible story lines and make room for personal interpretation beyond Goethe's text. Such is his rendering of the witches' Sabbath with its sprawling grotesque bodies, swarming crowds, bizarre animals, irrepressible individuals, erotic interludes, wild dances, and rowdy scenes, while Faust and Mephistopheles, perceiving Margaret's spectral apparition, still cut a clear figure (cf. Fig. 5.7). The combination in one single sheet of chaotic goings-on in strong contrast

FAUST I OUTLINED AND THE ORIGINAL RETZSCH EFFECT

FIGURE 2.19   Moritz Retzsch, Faust drinks the potion in the witch's kitchen, *Umrisse zu Goethe's Faust gezeichnet von Retsch* (Stuttgart & Tübingen: Cotta, 1816), pl. 7
COURTESY HAAB, F 3487, WEIMAR

to Gretchen, a thin line marking her would-be severed head, pays credit to his artistic efficacy. Commenting on this plate's copy by Moses (cf. Fig. 5.6), Shelley gives him due praise: "I never perfectly understood the Har[t]z Mountain scene, until I saw the etching."[92] The subjective treatment of his short riding scene, between Faust's clash with Mephistopheles (pl. 23) and the prison (pl. 25), also shows subtlety. While the text stresses urgency (horses galloping in the foreground), Retzsch's background hosts a dance of death, a Sabbath residue, around the combined image of the gallows and an execution wheel. The murder of Margaret's illegitimate child and her chastisement haunt it. The impatient stampede of horses reworks dark romantic motifs, yet the backdrop billets a show of quirky gesticulating skeletons (cf. Fig. 2.20). In both scenes, Retzsch develops an elusive spectacular dimension. His minute treatment, fit to capture the spectators' imagination, also includes a grim kind of comic relief.

His twenty-six prints may look simplistic or poor to an eye avid for grand spectacular effects. True, they offer an interpretation based on *Faust* events, and he had better grasped "the merely depictable" (Goethe to Stieler). The poem was little suited to fine art, Goethe had added, because "it was too poetic" (*wenig für die bildende Kunst geeignet ist, weil es zu poetisch ist*).[93] Retzsch's minute chronicling and multiplication of objects develops however interpretation of character and feeling, but also symbolism. There is poetry in his art, for instance, in the

---

92   *The Letters of Percy Bysshe Shelley*, 2:407.

93   GG 3: no. 2586.

FIGURE 2.20   Moritz Retzsch, Faust and Mephistopheles galloping past the Rabenstein, *Umrisse zu Goethe's Faust gezeichnet von Retsch* (Stuttgart & Tübingen: Cotta, 1816), pl. 24
COURTESY HAAB, F 3487, WEIMAR

depiction of Margaret's neat and orderly chamber, every single object on her table reflecting her inner life. Her lamp (a neoclassical *lucerna*) follows her even inside her prison cell, a metaphor of light and love (cf. Fig. 2.17). In place of the absent monologue, Faust's crammed study pictures his dead-end science and despair. Its disorder and disarray reveal anguish and desolation. Two jars contain a foetus and a conserved heart, bleak symbols of the future drowning of Margaret's baby and their doomed love affair (Fig. 2.21). Delacroix, who loved these plates, would take the hint and develop it into an overladen shelf of paraphernalia, sagging under the weight of the doctor's melancholy as Mephistopheles appears in his lithograph no. 5. As Benz recorded, Retzsch was often the first to treat an episode in a genuinely typifying way.[94] The devil's cunning smirk and sinewy silhouette are amongst the most remarkable ever devised in outline (see Chapter 9).

Yet Retzsch's imaging may strongly diverge from Goethe's intention and promote inconsistent interpretation. In plate 4, Faust hands a sheet of paper to Mephistopheles while his open palm touches his breast. His expressive gesture (meant to stress the weight of the given word as opposed to any signed document, F 1716–19) is lost on the reader as Mephistopheles eagerly grips the document. Retzsch has failed to depict the most significant aspect of *Faust*, the wager proffered to God by the devil, even though his set opens with their dialogue (pl. 1). That wager has become a written pledge. The lines credited to the scene do not resolve the ambiguity: "But one thing still, come life, come death, I prithee | Give me a written line or two." (F 1714–45, trans. A. G. Latham). English copies by Moses unambiguously name it "Faust makes over his soul to Mephistopheles," and French ones

---

94   Benz, *Goethe und die romantische Kunst*, 176.

FAUST I OUTLINED AND THE ORIGINAL RETZSCH EFFECT 85

FIGURE 2.21   Moritz Retzsch, Faust and Mephistopheles in Faust's study, *Umrisse zu Goethe's Faust gezeichnet von Retsch* (Stuttgart & Tübingen: Cotta, 1816), pl. 4
COURTESY HAAB, F 3487, WEIMAR

"Faust signs the covenant with Mephistopheles" from Muret's lithographs (1824) to the frontispiece of Nerval's translation (1828). The wager has vanished, damnation is on the books.

Nevertheless, depicting desire and the devil's eye are particular achievements. Retzsch chose attire with particular care. In his preface to Retzsch's outlines after Bürger's poems (1840), Carl Borromäus von Miltitz quotes a long letter from the artist, responding to criticism and explaining his choice of outfits. Epoch considerations and aesthetics come into play in his *exposé*.[95] We

may be certain he devised Faust's and Mephistopheles's tight leggings and bulging codpieces after Renaissance models. The Dresden Armoury (*Rüstkammer*) and the collections of historical weapons and costumes put together by Augustus the Strong were precious material to hand. Several Renaissance items respond to the clothing adopted. Drastic expurgation of codpiece specifics in English and French copies evidences how disturbing the detail was. It thrust Faust's desire under spectators' eyes, often at the centre of the picture, in no less than fifteen plates (pl. 4–10, 13–15, 21–26). Its suppression, and that of a few others, gave Goethe "food for thought." Blatant sexuality pervaded the witch's kitchen (Faust enthralled by a reclining female in the magic mirror), in Gretchen's

---

95   *Retzsch's Outlines to Buerger's Ballads/Umrisse zu Buerger's Balladen* (Leipzig: Ernst Fleischer, 1840), III–IV.

bedroom (Faust poring over her bed), in the summer-house, at the Sabbath. The prying devil's eye intrusively spiced the garden and summerhouse scenes.

Full of spirit: Retzsch plied images, in detail as in sequence, in complex ways. Recurrent disparagement of his "thin and dry" style and of his figures as "pale lifeless abstractions,"[96] merits refutation. I have stressed here aspects of his *Faust* rendering that have hardly been noticed in the hope that further nuanced assessments, such as Gretchen's reading by Gesa von Essen, based on Giesen's analysis, will help to evaluate Retzsch's subtlety:

> Auffallend an den Illustrationen von Retzsch ist jedenfalls insgesamt, dass Margarete in der Proportionierung des Körpers, mit dem klassisch geschnitten Gesicht sowie der kunstvoll hochgesteckten Frisur beinahe antikisierend gezeichnet ist und im weiteren Verlauf des Geschehens als beherzt handelnde Frau auftritt, die in der Beziehung zu Faust einen eigenen aktiven Part übernimmt, sodass hier erstmals ein Mitwirken bzw. eine Mitschuld Margaretes im Fortgang der Handlung deutlich wird.[97]

> In any case, what is altogether striking about Retzsch's illustrations is that Margaret's bodily proportions, her classically cut face and the artful hair get-up, are drawn in an almost classicizing style, and in the further course of events she appears as a boldly acting female who, in her relationship to Faust, takes her own active part, so that here for the first time an involvement, if not complicity, of Margaret in the course of the plot becomes clear.

2.7 Outline Reformation

Retzsch's privileged technique, the outline drawing (*Umriss, dessin au trait*), had made a remarked entry into European stylistic vocabulary at the end of the eighteenth century. Flaxman's outlines after great poets of antiquity (Homer, Aeschylus, Hesiod), but also decisive works at the origins of modern literature such as Dante's *Divina Commedia*, had been well diffused thanks to Tommaso Piroli's engravings across Europe. Their success grew on ground well prepared by neoclassical theories of art. They launched a vogue, studied in depth since Robert

Rosenblum's pioneer 1956 thesis, published only twenty years later,[98] and the 1979 joint English and German exhibitions on Flaxman. The historical birth of outline, and its impact on German, French, Spanish and Danish artists has been recorded.[99] Outline has also been studied in relation to arabesque as a major contribution to the German art of the book in the first nineteenth century.[100] Like other German artists, Retzsch followed Flaxman, but more decisively adapted him. His *Umrisse* show key differences to identify.

In the 1799 German-speaking world, Goethe's veiled criticism of Flaxman as "all dilettanti's idol" (*der Abgott aller Dilettanten*)[101] jousted with August Wilhelm Schlegel's *Athenaeum* essay on Flaxman and the outline style. Goethe's reservation itself was ambiguous.[102] Schlegel mockingly evoked the declining art of illustration in Germany and critically contrasted it to the potency of Flaxman's outlines, calling for a renewal. Although, influenced by Lessing's concept of beauty, he dismissed Hogarth and Chodowiecki as crude and prosaic,[103] Schlegel's views clashed with Lessing's celebrated *paragone* regarding competition of text with image. In his *Laocoon* (1766), Lessing had opposed text as art of sequence to images, considered synchronic, timeless, and fixed, while words were diachronic and in motion. Schlegel undermined such strong antitheses, opening new paths in romantic art. Three key characteristics of outline (meaningful abstraction, liberation of the imaginative powers, and initiation) bade new ways of reading as reflected in this well known passage, here newly translated and commented:

> Ihre Zeichen werden fast Hieroglyphen, wie die des Dichters; die Phantasie wird aufgefodert zu ergänzen, und nach der empfangenen Anregung selbständig

---

96   Clösges, "Die Illustration von Goethes Dichtung," 179f.

97   "Gretchen," in *Faust-Handbuch*, 248a; Giesen, "Goethes *Faust* in der europäischen Kunst," 63.

98   Robert Rosenblum, *The International Style of 1800: A Study in Linear Abstraction* (New York: Garland, 1976); Rosenblum, *Transformations in Late Eighteenth Century Art*, 3rd repr. (Princeton, NJ: Princeton University Press, 1974).

99   Werner Hofmann ed., *John Flaxman: Mythologie und Industrie* (Munich: Prestel, 1979), and David Bindman, ed., *John Flaxman* (London: Thames and Hudson, 1979); Sarah Symmons, *Flaxman and Europe* (New York: Garland, 1984).

100   Werner Busch, "Umrißzeichnung und Arabeske als Kunstprinzipien des 19. Jahrhunderts," in *Buchillustration im 19. Jahrhundert*, ed. R. Timm (Wiesbaden: Otto Harrassowitz, 1988), 119–48; Grewe, "Outline and Arabesque," 228–47.

101   WA 1, 47:245–46.

102   See Peter-Klaus Schuster, "'Flaxman der Abgott aller Dilettanten.' Zu einem Dilemma des klassischen Goethe und den Folgen," in Hofmann ed., 32–35; Symmons, *Flaxman and Europe*, 208–211.

103   Symmons, *Flaxman and Europe*, 203.

FAUST I OUTLINED AND THE ORIGINAL RETZSCH EFFECT

fortzubilden, statt daß das ausgeführte Gemählde sie durch entgegen kommende Befriedigung gefangen nimmt. [...] So wie die Worte des Dichters eigentlich Beschwörungsformeln für Leben und Schönheit sind, denen man nach ihren Bestandtheilen ihre geheime Gewalt nicht anmerkt, so kommt es einem bey dem gelungenen Umriß wie eine wahre Zauberey vor, daß in so wenigen und zarten Strichen so viel Seele wohnen kann.[104]

Their signs almost become hieroglyphs, like those of the poet; from the stimulus received, imagination is encouraged to complete and continue to create independently, whereas, finished paintings hold it prisoner through a gratifying sense of satisfaction. [...] Just as the words of the poet are inherently bewitching formulae for life and beauty, even if one does not perceive the secret power of their components, it turns out, as if by true magic, that in a successful outline so much soul can dwell in so few delicate lines.

Goethe's ideal of Faust as "chief sorcerer" (*Hexenmeister*), having "to fend for himself" without images, springs again to mind.[105] In Schlegel's essay, true magic (*wahre Zauberey*) had no more to do with Faust's labours. In Retzsch's work, it became the means of evoking the "sorcerer" through the outlines' power as poetry's *analogon*. However, Schlegel's was not just a statement of equivalents but an active prompting of *movement* between word and image. Like the poet's verse, contours thrived on economy of means. Focused on the truly characteristic, in opposition to the completeness and detail of stipple engravings, the delineated forms worked by allusion, championing symbolism and connotation. Evocative and secret, they roused creative faculties. Likened to the poet's incantatory formulas, they were initiatory, pulling the viewer into the drawing and directing him back to the poem that had instigated the images. A new form of reading was implied for reader-spectators, drawn in as active co-participants, mind's eye stirred and interpretative faculty kindled. Unlike the engraved versions of Flaxman's compositions, Retzsch's etchings were not captioned. Simple numbering led readers from one frame to the next, while excerpts met in the separate letterpress brochure (cf. Fig. 2.1b).Reviving the experience of how the set devoid of captions worked

at the time, the present reader may peruse Retzsch's images in this book's initial booklet (p. 9–21).

If Cotta's portfolio thus prompted interactive reading, outline further nurtured fantasy. Although based on neo-classical ideal and archetype, it was a theatrical invention through which the dream effect could unfurl. "The outline's tyrannical presence, which may seem an impoverishment, imposes on the other hand evidence of a second world, alleviated of its reality attributes, deprived of broad daylight's sun, and docile to the transcription of desire," writes Jean Starobinski. An art of delicate poise, hovering between boldness and submission, "the graphic dream may well take the most daring shapes: it will find its defence in the illustrious text it claims adhering to."[106]

It is to this art that Retzsch had subscribed, shifting from classicism to romanticism, yet in personal manner at variance with Schlegel's ideal conceptions. He enhanced outline with detail, pleased and intrigued the eye, making his work quickly known. "His reputation in England briefly exceeded that of Flaxman," states the 2001 *Oxford Companion to Western Art*.[107] Let us try to understand how, especially since Flaxman himself had declared to Crabb Robinson that Retzsch "did not properly understand the nature of an Outline," and avowed to Schorn that Cornelius's were "thought out in a grander sense and with a deeper spirit" than Retzsch's.[108]

A close comparison of Retzsch's pl. 1 (Prologue in Heaven) with Flaxman's assembly of the Gods in Homer's *Iliad* led Hildebrand-Schat to skilfully conclude on two main formal differences between their respective treatments: on the one hand, Flaxman uses flatness in bodies and space but attains shape even in blank areas thanks to structuring, while Retzsch combines two-dimensional manner with volumes and perspective elements, achieving forms proportionally. The former casts characters as academically idealized figures, whereas the latter imparts to them an array of emotions through posture, gestures and facial expression. On the other, Flaxman's compositions correspond to an illustrative abstraction of poetic plot, blurring episodes, while Retzsch's maintain narrative precision from beginning to end.[109] Let me add that Retzsch's detailed conceptions privileged a story of dramatic colouring at the expense of philosophical and

---

104   Schlegel, "Über Zeichnungen zu Gedichten und John Flaxman's Umrisse," *Athenaeum* 2, no. 2 (1799): 205.

105   See p. 55.

106   Jean Starobinski, "La vision de la dormeuse," in *Trois fureurs* (Paris: Gallimard, 1974), 151, 153.

107   *The Oxford Companion to Western Art*, ed. H. Brigstocke (Oxford: Oxford University Press, 2001), 630c.

108   Schorn, "Besuch bey Flaxman," 120. On Crabb Robinson and Flaxman, see pp. 121, 123–24.

109   Hildebrand-Schat, *Moritz Retzschs Illustrationen*, 82–87.

certain poetical aspects. Yet, his was neither melodramatic nor excessively sentimental. Absence of dialogue and wording repressed emotions. Although English reviews frequently stressed the compositions' pathos, witty and quirky elements pepper his scenes alongside sexual yearning. Vogel, for instance, emphasized Retzsch's handling as counterpart to Goethe's, and argued that his work successfully responds to the poet's incisiveness (*Prägnanz*) and forcefulness (*Eindringlichkeit*).[110]

Contrariwise, English articles of the time comparing Retzsch with Flaxman were engaged in disputes over aesthetic principles, evidencing period preferences. A prominent 1825 article featured in the first issue of a new fine-arts periodical, *The Parthenon: A Magazine of Art and Literature*, "the first journal to be produced anywhere entirely by lithography," using both right-reading (reverse) types impressed on the stone, and illustrations, autographs or music reproduced via transfer paper.[111] "Remarkable for its ambitious and technically daring foray into typolithography," the *Parthenon* nonetheless supported a classicist stance, faithful to its title. Flaxman's "sublime conceptions" were championed over Retzsch's "puerile extravaganzas," "showy dashes," "tricks of mannerism," and "ostentation." The English artist prevailed thanks to "chaste models of antiquity." Yet, when the writer (signing in cipher and Greek initials Φ. Χ. Ψ.) considered Retzsch's feats on their own merit, he largely praised their "exuberance of fancy," "power of combination and versatility," and "creative faculty" adapting "with admirable facility" to the wildest subjects (such as produced by "Goethe's imagination"). Subject matter constrained Retzsch more than style *per se*. However, there is more to his case than meets the eye; his example served a distinction between fanciful and imaginative art as Vaughan has shown,[112] but also a discussion on the value and efficacy (or not) of outline in art. Ruskin's discussion of Retzsch shows how the artist's appreciation evolved in the course of the nineteenth century.

In his second volume of *Modern Painters* (1846), John Ruskin examined in detail three kinds of imagination (penetrative, associative, and contemplative) opposing them to fancy. Fancy consisted of the outside, of what was clear, brilliant, and full of detail. Retzsch was thus opposed to Turner, true master of the imagination, like Dante to Milton. Eleven years later, in *The Elements of Drawing* (1857), Ruskin somewhat imperiously wrote off outline as bad, on the basis of a perceived deficiency in rendering artistic subjects: "The published works of Retzsch, and all the English translations of them, and all the outline engravings from pictures, are bad work, and only serve to corrupt the public taste," he asserted.[113] Yet, later on in the same work, he conceded: "Retzsch's outlines have more real material in them than Flaxman's, occasionally showing true fancy and power; in artistic principle they are nearly as bad, and in taste, worse."[114] It was only several years later that differences eased as Ruskin wrote in "The Black Arts: A Reverie in the Strand" (1887): "a man of imaginative power can do more and express more, and excite the fancy of the spectator more, by frank outline than by completed work; and that assuredly there ought to be in all our national art schools an outline class trained to express themselves vigorously and accurately in such manner."[115] He thus aligned himself with Schlegel's views, albeit late in the day. By then, he had been overwhelmed by the mass proliferation of images and new reproduction technologies.[116] His attitude to outline had considerably changed: "the value of outline is in its power of suggesting quantity, intricacy, and character," he added,[117] all qualities perhaps taught him through Retzsch.[118] He had considered the German artist in *The Art of England* (1883) as the master of "only grotesque or terrible fancies" with "a very real gift of making visibly terrible such legend as that of the ballad of Leonora, and interpreting, with a wild aspect of veracity, the passages of sorcery in *Faust*."[119] In the same text, he had disparaged *The Genius of Poetry* (in fact *The Fate of the Poet* or *The Poet and the Undines* from Retzsch's *Fancies*) as lacking dignity and beauty. Retzsch represented "states of gloomy fantasy" but ranked alongside with Blake's *Book of Job*, Dürer's *Apocalypse*, and Rethel's dances of death. By at last recognizing the

---

110 Gerd-Helge Vogel, "Faust und Gretchen—Goethes Drama in den Umrissstichen und -zeichnungen von Moritz August Retzsch," in *"Man halte sich ans fortschreitende Leben …": über Goethe und Goethezeitliches aus Güstrower Sicht*, ed. E. Neumann, D. Pocher, V. Probst (Güstrow: Heidberg, 1999), 19; Vogel, "Moritz August Retzschs Annäherung an Goethe im poetischen Motiv der 'exempla amoris'," *Anzeiger des Germanischen Nationalmuseums* (2008): 61.

111 Michael Twyman, *Early Lithographed Books* (London: Farrand Press & Private Libraries Association, 1990), 54, 56.

112 Vaughan, *German Romanticism*, 126.

113 *The Works of John Ruskin*, ed. E. T. Cook and A. Wedderburn (London: George Allen, 1903–12), 15:83.

114 Ibid., 225.

115 *The Works of John Ruskin*, 14:360.

116 See Jonah Siegel, "Black Arts, Ruined Cathedrals, and the Grave in Engraving: Ruskin and the Fatal Excess of Art," *Victorian Literature and Culture* 27, no. 2 (1999): 395–417.

117 *The Works of John Ruskin*, 14:360.

118 Attempts to illustrate his own written works may have reconciled Ruskin to the utility of outline.

119 *The Works of John Ruskin*, 33:334.

FAUST I OUTLINED AND THE ORIGINAL RETZSCH EFFECT

value of outline in "The Black Arts," Ruskin admitted that, although Retzsch and Adrian Ludwig Richter would never have become painters, "their countrymen owe more to their unassuming instinct of invention than to the most exalted efforts of their historical schools."[120]

The last two qualities, Retzsch's inspiration from gloomy fantasies and his capacity for invention, are also two of his distinctive contributions to outline art. Goethe's *Faust* was such a gloomy fantasy, arresting by its novel elliptical and unorthodox structure. Frequent gaps in plot, based on the disconnected and piecemeal quality of twenty-five episodes, were mostly labelled after succinct, spatial and occasionally time markers. The whole play seemed but a gigantic splinter in a variety of language levels and metres, made of somewhat erratic shards in moods changing from tragedy to comedy, embracing irony and bitter sarcasm. An abstruse creation by period standards, it seemed a nocturne or winter's tale from Faust's first night monologue to the prison scene immersed in darkness. Retzsch had translated its blackness into clear sequential picturing to dramatic effect.

Moreover, by early treating it in outline, Retzsch had made a claim for Goethe's play in international classification: thanks to his technique, it would rank with the great poems of antiquity and Dante's *Comedy*, with which *Faust* compares as "disguised comedy" in Dieter Borchmeyer's brilliant study.[121] What has been repeatedly called the "simplicity" of Retzsch[122] is misleading. The term conceals the concentration of his abridged compositions and their synthetic qualities. These resound in the etched prints. Yet, they themselves invited reproduction and copying, steering off dissemination of the reinterpreted poetic text.

2.8   Retzsch in Colour

The vogue of outline did not last long in Germany. By the end of the 1830s, outlines already looked outmoded while Retzsch kept producing his work (and means of living) in engraved sets as before. Line reproductions in his favourite technique had gained him worldwide fame, yet its very aesthetics prepared the weakening of his appeal and his

falling into oblivion and critical silence. Although he persevered, it is dismissive to suggest he was a belated artist and his productions out-dated,[123] as refutes an exceptional document in colour, originating from Dresden and attributed to Retzsch himself.

It currently consists of fourteen of his prints carefully coloured, now at Frankfurt's Freies Deutsches Hochstift. They carry strong theatrical assumptions that seem uncertain. As late as July 1951, twelve of them were offered by antique bookseller Gerd Rosen to Ernst Beutler, then director of the FDH, as a "likely basis for a production get-up" with reference to Klingemann's Braunschweig *Faust*.[124] Another two (pl. 13 and 14, Mephistopheles at Martha's, and the garden scene) were likely added later. All fourteen had belonged to Stumme as shows a seal someone vainly tried to mask or erase. They also differ from Carl Niessen's detailed listing who had traced them to Stumme with a stronger Braunschweig postulation: Niessen includes a (non-extant) Walpurgis Night, while omitting the (extant) poodle's appearance.[125] Shading and hues indeed resemble closely the use of colour in the Retzsch brothers' early diary and all correspond to startling scenes: the poodle appearing in flat country; swelling to monstrous size in Faust's study; Auerbach's cellar; Faust accosting Margaret; Gretchen with the jewels; Martha adorning Gretchen; Margaret, Martha and Mephistopheles; Margaret plucking the daisy; the kiss; Margaret pensive at the spinning wheel; imploring the Mater dolorosa; in the cathedral; Valentine dying; and Faust entering the prison.

The original etchings, carefully trimmed down to their thin line frames, have been pasted on a backing sheet, given a redrawn double frame, and coloured. A sophisticated use of pigments, shadows and light produces an atmospheric, supernatural dimension. Twilight descends on the fields, on Faust's black mantle and white shirt (a deck of clothes signalling his melancholic disposition in contrast to Wagner's russet and brown) while the poodle's smouldering breath, red eyes, and incandescent trail highlight the supernatural (Fig. 2.22). Faust's study is a remarkable night scene. A bright lamp projects the strong shadows of his armchair and stove unto the black poodle, towering with glowing eyeballs and foaming jowls (Fig. 2.23). In Auerbach's cellar, the light comes in from

---

120   Ibid., 14:361.

121   See Borchmeyer, "*Faust*—Goethes verkappte Komödie," in *Die großen Komödien Europas*, ed. F. N. Mennemeier (Tübingen: Francke, 2000), 199–225.

122   Peter W. Guenther, "Concerning Illustrations to Goethe's *Faust*," in *The Age of Goethe Today: Critical Reexamination and Literary Reflection*, ed. G. Bauer Pickar and S. Cramer (Munich: Wilhelm Fink, 1990), 106.

123   Vaughan, *German Romanticism*, 128–29. He states inaccurately that the subscription list to Retzsch's *Chess Players* "remained pathetically small." Recurrent reports from Fleischer in Retzsch's SLUB *Nachlass* show the opposite. Hellwig provides a long list of booksellers involved in its diffusion, 202–4.

124   FDH: VIIId-gr, 13098/13109, item data file.

125   Niessen, no. 515–28.

FIGURE 2.22   Moritz Retzsch, The poodle appearing in open country, coloured version, n.d., 14.6 × 19.4 cm.
Umrisse zu Goethe's Faust gezeichnet von Retsch (Stuttgart & Tübingen: Cotta, 1816), pl. 2
FDH, FRANKFURTER GOETHE-MUSEUM, III-13099, FRANKFURT

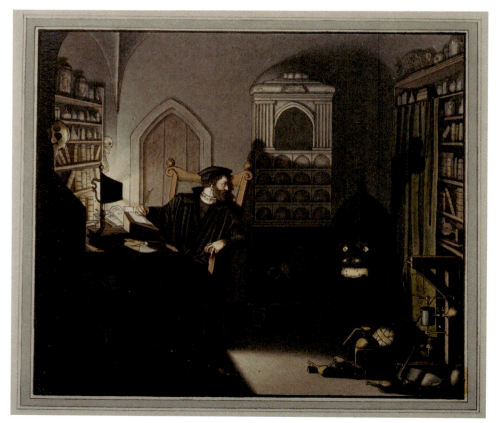

FIGURE 2.23   Moritz Retzsch, Faust's study with the poodle growing, coloured version, n.d., 13.9 × 15.8 cm.
Umrisse zu Goethe's Faust gezeichnet von Retsch (Stuttgart & Tübingen: Cotta, 1816) pl. 3
FDH, FRANKFURTER GOETHE-MUSEUM, III-13098, FRANKFURT

FAUST I OUTLINED AND THE ORIGINAL RETZSCH EFFECT 91

FIGURE 2.24   Moritz Retzsch, Margaret discovers the jewels, coloured version, n.d., *c*.14 × 16.7 cm.
Umrisse zu Goethe's Faust gezeichnet von Retsch (Stuttgart & Tübingen: Cotta, 1816), pl. 11
FDH, FRANKFURTER GOETHE-MUSEUM, III-13100, FRANKFURT

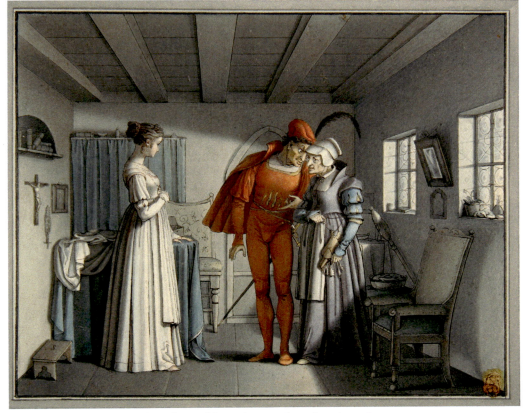

FIGURE 2.25   Moritz Retzsch, At the neighbour's house, coloured version, n.d., 23 × 31 cm
COURTESY FDH, FRANKFURTER GOETHE-MUSEUM, III-13929, FRANKFURT

the right, revealing Mephistopheles's red costume full centre and Faust's worried mien. On meeting, the couple stand in full light: Margaret's expression of defence and surprise surfaces delicately, while Faust parallels a lurking Mephistopheles, whose ominous sword pointing downward grants him a third lower member. Finding the jewels, Margaret is doubly lit by the lamp on the table and an external source that uncannily, yet significantly, projects her drawn-out shadow onto the bed behind her (Fig. 2.24). White becomes Margaret, and interiors around her are shaded, cool and blue. One of the palest versions shows her imploring the Virgin, the shadow of her clasped hands and uplifted body falling on the white statue, raising arms in entreaty. Her chamber in dark green, blue and grey is attuned to her melancholic resignation. Half-light reigns in Martha's lodging while she lays the gems on Margaret and Mephistopheles intrudes in red, tingeing violet Martha's blue dress (Fig. 2.25). In the garden, plucking the daisy's petals, or in Faust's arms in the summerhouse, Margaret is fair-haired and rosy-cheeked. A large tree shadows Mephistopheles and Martha, and the devil's eye lights up either in the gathering dark or as he pushes open the summerhouse's door. For Valentine expiring and Faust finding Margaret prostate in prison, Retzsch's source of light is an antique oil lamp carried by hand, subtly shining on Margaret's public disgrace and private misery, whilst the cathedral's vaults are lit by high Gothic windows in alternate glow and gloom.

The expert rendering of atmosphere, protracted shadows and subtle glow are striking. They bring the compositions forward vividly and make them theatrically explicit. Conversely, the uncoloured outlines lead the reader into the poem to imagine situations, invent feelings, and suppose effects. Such an important difference in function and purport may have led to believe that the coloured version was meant for stage production at a time of developments in gas lighting. The 1825 advent of the limelight, fascination with the magic lantern and optical effects,[126] the soft grey ambiance suffusing the coloured prints show responsiveness to emotions raised by the play. The finely layered wash—whether diluted ink or watercolour—is evenly spread, devoid of brush marks. Depth and volume seem to echo profundity of feeling.

Far from the theatre, the coloured set corresponded to Friedrich Daniel Schleiermacher's contemporary theories on the expressiveness of colour, Goethe's own research on chromatics (1810), and Philipp Otto Runge's investigation of colour symbolism, as Viola Hildebrand-Schat has

expertly shown.[127] Sensing that outline, his privileged means of expression, was aesthetically on the wane, Retzsch probably ventured a painted version of the work that had made him known. It is further tempting to think that his subtle colouring rebutted regular criticism alleging poor or inadequate use of colour as one of his artistic failings. Mrs Hall for instance mentioned two paintings "both exquisitely drawn and designed, but so unlike what we had expected in colour, that for a moment we felt disappointed;"[128] David d'Angers noted: "We recognize, however, that this painter is not experienced colour-wise" (*n'est pas rompu au mécanisme de la couleur*).[129] Could it also be that his shadows and clever darkening were a response to Delacroix's lithographs' fantastic atmosphere and deep blacks? The question has to remain open.

Whatever the case, it would be false to consider the FDH coloured series "unique" as repeatedly assumed. Weimar's HAAB also preserves a coloured copy of the garden scene—not an original print carefully tinted, but an outline redrawn and coloured by an unknown hand (Fig. 2.26). Like the numerous copies of Retzsch's *Faust*, achieved freehand or thanks to tracing paper (see Chapter 7), it confirms Retzsch's appeal but also the unknown artist's desire to pep up the scene, while introducing slight yet meaningful interpretative changes. Colour is used symbolically: Faust's sword is tinted with the blood of Valentine yet to flow, Mephistopheles's is black like night or Hell (and placed on the other side of his body to reveal his skin-tight costume in all its blazing splendour); luxuriant vegetation marks this earthly paradise (complete with serpent) while the true-to-life background shows a day's end in a real garden: a wall catches the afternoon sun, clouds cover the sky. In the foreground, Faust and Margaret, with expressions delicately changed, have been treated in grisaille, a clever rendering of the original's slight relief of both characters thanks to enhanced line. The grey monochrome grants them a ghostly presence as of figures brought into a well-known painted scene, the recognizable temptation scene in a garden.

2.9 To Conclude

New archival evidence highlights in Retzsch a resourceful young artist, keen to deal with *Faust* on professional grounds with promptness and inventiveness. He is verily

---

126 Burwick, "Stage Illusion and the Stage Designs of Goethe and Hugo," *Word and Image* 4, no. 3–4 (July–Dec 1988): 694.

---

127 Hildebrand-Schat, *Moritz Retzschs Illustrationen*, 103–11.
128 Hall, "A Morning with Retzsch," 21c.
129 *Les Carnets de David d'Angers*, 2:216.

FIGURE 2.26   In Martha's garden, anonymous coloured version, n.d., 14.5 × 15.3 cm, after Moritz Retzsch, *Umrisse zu Goethe's Faust gezeichnet von Retsch* (Stuttgart & Tübingen: Cotta, 1816), pl. 14
COURTESY HAAB, F GR 9228, WEIMAR

the first to graphically turn a play, unruly in contemporaries' eyes, into a silent story with rich interpretative potential. Despite his inventiveness, his artistic identity remains inconspicuous in his native land. In his *Faust Umrisse*, original remediated authorship looms higher than hitherto appreciated in all stages of their devising. The Cotta product is a clever marketing tool, when fathomed in its initial materiality and potential uses. Its diffusion starts with *Faust*'s author himself, as Goethe plies the set to philanthropic, political, cultural and relational expenditure. He also turns it into a benchmark medium to assess the first English copy against the German original. Most importantly, originality drives Retzsch's own creative inspiration.

The artist's studio drawings reveal not only his keen reading, attentive to dramatic effect and close to story line, but also an open-minded responsiveness to the play's suggestive and ardent aspects, capable of nuance and counterpoise. Retzsch masterly renders an effective alliance of narrative with moving, fantastic, yet also droll effects all the while potently involving imaginative readers as inventive agents. As his cycle draws them in, it provides them with a wealth of detail they may invest according to their own creative capacities, as we shall see. Yet such qualities do not loom in his work as either evident or immediate. They depend on initiation. Retzsch had seized the nature of outline as medium and aesthetic to which he conferred a personal twist and particular brio. He left his own mark in the original *Faust* set thanks to a displaced plate, Margaret in the cathedral, which stresses his independence from text, and the multifaceted value of his interpretation. If seen for its true complexity, his *Faust* worked well beyond appearances of simplicity. Retzsch's appeal was real, evidenced by burgeoning editions of the *Umrisse* in German lands.

CHAPTER 3

German Editions and Copies: The Bait of Rich Morsels

Mapping out German editions of Retzsch's *Umrisse zu Goethe's Faust* is a meander, like adventuring into a copse. Bibliographies do not concord with each other. They sometimes do not even match with dates given on printed items. Portfolios and albums also provide fluctuating and conflicting data. What to make, for instance, of the retouched and enlarged *Faust I* edition totalling 29 etchings, issued by Georg von Cotta, when the front cover label reads 1830 and the title-page 1834? Further editions and copies give rise to other queries, turning the researcher-cum-bibliographer into a makeshift interpreter and archive detective.

There are several reasons behind this, starting with their initial publication. Between 1816 and 1820 Johann Friedrich Cotta's publishing firm was still growing. His competitive business was keen to satisfy a rapidly growing middle-class public and meet its educational needs at a time of democratic and technical advances. Cotta owned a paper factory and printing premises, engaged early with lithography, and introduced techniques of modern journalism to his press publications.[1] Yet his announcements concerned either on-going series (mainly Goethe's and Schiller's works whom he exclusively published) or novelties (*Neuigkeiten*) but not reprint editions, even when initial and later issues slightly differed. A proper account of how many *Umrisse* editions he published, and exactly when, thus proves trickier than expected. Export of Retzsch's outlines to Europe further complicates tracing. A resourceful German bookseller in London, Johann Heinrich Bohte, was quick to import them. He advertised in his catalogues a "Tübingen 1818" edition still unmatched by any item I have yet to see. Was there a special print run of the letterpress brochure (along with impressions pulled from the metal plates) for the foreign market? The postulate cannot be ignored, and Cotta aimed at internationalisation. Yet, copperplates are not suitable for extensive printing. Accidents apart, they could provide about 1,500 copies before lines faded or blurred. Refurbishing would be necessary. Retzsch's letters to Georg von Cotta in the 1830s stress the importance of proper re-engraving and printing

by a master printer to guarantee his outlines' quality and effect on viewers. Yet, he had also claimed in January 1824, while working on *Fridolin*, that good and light handling of the plates could deliver several thousands.[2] Still, the impressions' quality fluctuates between editions, and background features, thin lines, or minute trivia are—in cases as early as 1820—faint. Cotta's ledgers hardly deliver any information on this, and are awkward to decipher. Competing with his wares, re-engraved copies and lithographs were also produced in German lands, particularly in the 1820s when the artist's fame grew. The outlines were evidently in demand whereas press reviews remained scarce. Their success abroad held sway over German circulation as well, producing a series of intriguing items. Last, but not least, they were revised as early as 1818 and 1820 and restyled for a female audience in two miniature almanacs with a series of sonnets. Remodelling into other formats and genres started early, was not exclusive to the foreign market, and is revelatory of reception.

In short, it is worth attempting, however tricky, to account chronologically for German *Umrisse zu Faust* and their ersatz editions as best possible. As they start being copied, remediated, repurposed, and circulated, their consequent influence completes the puzzle of their agency in Germany. Their transformations, even when of inferior or dubious quality, point at several readers' categories.

I have here cross-referenced first-hand data across repositories and countries: printed exemplars and editions in comparison, Cotta's order book (*Auftragbuch*) and commercial announcements (*Circulaire*), Bernhard Fischer's directory of Cotta's production 1787–1832, Retzsch's manuscript letters to Cotta father and son over a long period,[3] other correspondence, commercial and press notices, extant bibliographies, and scholarly studies.

3.1 Avowable (and Uncertain) Cotta Portfolios

At first sight, the core German Cotta editions of the *Faust I* outlines could only have been three: the original in 1816; a second impression in 1820; and a "retouched" and enlarged edition (*retouchirt und mit einigen neuen Platten vermehrt*) in 1834. Problems arise when further data more

---

1   Max Bach, *Stuttgarter Kunst 1794–1860* (Stuttgart: Adolf Bonz & Comp., 1900), 185–87; Liselotte Lohrer, ed. *Cotta in Tübingen* (Tübingen: [Bürgermeisteramt], 1959), and Lohrer, *Cotta: Geschichte eines Verlags, 1659–1959* (Stuttgart: J. G. Cotta, 1959); Mojem and Potthast, eds. *Johann Friedrich Cotta*, 9–11; Moran, *Toward the Century of Words*, 1–9.

2   DLA C-R, no. 6.
3   DLA C-R, Oct 1810–Jan 1837.

© EVANGHELIA STEAD, 2023 | DOI:10.1163/9789004543010_006

This is an open access chapter distributed under the terms of the CC BY-NC-ND 4.0 license.

than double the list: an 1816 original; an 1818 version (for the foreign market?); a second impression in 1820; perhaps a further 1828 edition; an extra 1830 impression; the retouched and enlarged edition of 1834, also corresponding to a drastic change in format. Extant scholarship on the subject records them puzzlingly as follows: "New editions (*Neuauflagen*) were published in 1820, 1828, and 1834";[4] "New German editions of the *Outlines to Goethes Faust* appeared in 1818, 1820, 1825, 1828 and 1830";[5] "new editions of his prints, whose sales spanned practically without breaks the entire 19th century";[6] Retzsch's cycle "went [in the German States] through 13 editions until 1837";[7] "the cycle had a large reception and went through several new (1820, 1830, 1834) as well as pirated editions (1818, 1820)."[8]

The *Umrisse* were certainly first printed in 1816 and reprinted in 1820. Both are aggregate items bringing together the 26 etched plates and the letterpress brochure in a small portfolio with a pasted-on label (cf. Fig. 2.1a–b). Though matching in content, and based on the same design and colour scheme (yellow or buff and green apart from exceptions), the two editions are not identical. The main differences concern plate margins, but also the crafting of a composite object. Their making was not machine-standardised throughout, as slight dissimilarities between exemplars indicate. In the 1816 original, the paper is cropped close to the etchings' frames. On the basis of Retzsch's much later (18 [not 16] November 1833) letter to Georg von Cotta, Hildebrand-Schat attributed this to "English taste" in an attempt to conceal any trace of copperplate indenting.[9] The explanation seems unlikely for several reasons. Retzsch's letter refers to the international Fleischer edition of his outlines for Shakespeare on fine-grained paper. There, to avoid print marks, copperplates larger than the sheet had been used at considerable expense, extra cost being recovered in sales. The artist interpreted it as "not following necessity but rather falling prey to an English whim" (*der mehr einer Englischen Marotte als der Nothwendigkeit anheim fällt*).[10] While working on Schiller's *Fridolin* and *The Dragon*, his letters to Johann Friedrich Cotta on 15 January 1824 and

12 January 1827 mentioned that art lovers at home and abroad regretted the poor editions of his much admired etchings and pointed out that the close-cropped paper did not allow for a fine art issue.[11] As noted, the very frames' dimensions deliberately differ from the outset between depicted scenes, notably interior vs. exterior, occasionally by 1.50 cm. Individual spatial identities, an important characteristic of the set, is no chance upshot, but the *intentional* outcome of Retzsch's design by episode. It would therefore prove unfeasible to conceal indented marks throughout. Furthermore, wider margins in the 1820 set clearly improve the etchings' perception and appearance. The sturdy English copy, re-engraved by Henry Moses in imperial 4to on fine white paper, must have had a bearing on the second German edition, upgraded by Cotta. The initial cropped margins of 1816 are easily explained by paper shortages in the post-Napoleonic-war economies of German States, nor exclude the scarcer value attributed to Retzsch's work compared to others'.

Expected dissimilarities thus occur in the size of the overall portfolio (17.8 × 22.1 cm in 1816 vs. 19.5 × 24.7 cm in 1820), engravings and letterpress booklet. The form of the tongue-tipped fastening may vary, although not consistently (pointed in 1816, rounded in 1820), along with the shape and size of the label. In the 1816 edition, brochure and prints tend to match in height but not in width. Bound copies of both may look like homogeneous albums but are by no means original. They result from fine binders' interventions compensating size discrepancies in ulterior treatment to meet individual bibliophilic choices or preservation purposes. The original was manifold and invited further manipulation.

Such descriptions are both confirmed and contradicted by published data from the Cotta archive. The first 1816 run of 1000 copies concerns the letterpress rather than the prints "partly pulled on demand" (*Die Kupfer wurden in Partien nach Bedarf abgezogen*).[12] The etchings, some of which still exist as a single series, were also traded distinctly from the letterpress. The second run of 1820, also estimated at 1000 copies, did not seemingly meet with growing demand, although it is unclear whether the data concern letterpress or prints. By 1824, the letterpress stock had been reduced by roughly only one third. More than half the brochure sheets lay unfolded at Cotta's ("*510 roh + 178 brosch.*"), half were still available in 1826, and decreased

---

4   Neubert, 241b.

5   Stella Esther Odenkirchen, "Moritz Retzsch, Illustrator, with Special Reference to his Relation to England" (Master diss., University of Chicago, 1948), 32.

6   Hildebrand-Schat, *Moritz Retzschs Illustrationen*, 38.

7   Waltraud Maierhofer, "Die Titelkupfer von Moritz Retzsch zu Goethes *Ausgabe letzter Hand*," *Goethe Yearbook* 21 (2014): 222.

8   Rosenbaum, "Bildende Kunst," in *Faust-Handbuch*, 178b.

9   Hildebrand-Schat, *Moritz Retzschs Illustrationen*, 42.

10   DLA C-R, no. 35.

---

11   DLA C-R, no. 5 & 8.

12   Bernhard Fischer, *Der Verleger Johann Friedrich Cotta. Chronologische Verlagsbibliographie 1787–1832* (Marbach: Deutsche Schillergesellschaft; Munich: K. G. Saur, 2003), no. 1050.

GERMAN EDITIONS AND COPIES: THE BAIT OF RICH MORSELS

to 45 brochures only by 1829.[13] Those sales were probably boosted by Retzsch's outlines after Shakespeare's plays, published from 1828 [1827] by Ernst Fleischer in Leipzig, to Goethe's acclaim, and the Braunschweig *Faust* production, which explicitly used Retzsch. Goethe openly encouraged all superintendents of reading circles and literary societies to buy the *Hamlet* outlines.[14] Such unstinting praise will have beneficially rebounded on the *Faust* etchings.

In the 1820 edition, batches of engravings are likely to have been several since their overall dimensions might differ by several millimetres, although this may have also resulted from shrinkage or stretching of paper as it dried after impression. Take for instance two 1820 exemplars in the HAAB, both in original portfolios with green flaps (N 28602 and F 3488). Differences in height vary from 1 mm (brochure) to 5 mm (prints) and 13 mm (portfolio), while width fluctuates by 6 mm (brochure), 7 mm (prints) and 11 mm (portfolio). Even more striking is the variably applied colour scheme. The first (N 28602) sports a watery version of the 1816 original, the portfolio being an off-white light-weight paperboard while its label seems a leftover. The second (F 3488) sits in a warm yellow portfolio, albeit of haphazardly glued paperboard. As if to divert the eye, the label's corners are bevelled. The tongue-shaped fastener is triangular and pointed whilst it tends to be rounded in most "second" editions, etc. In both, the etchings' background details are attenuated, at times nearly evanescent. The plates had obviously not been re-engraved for reprint, but the larger plates match an earlier print run with a more sophisticated fastening. The letterpress brochure shows slight variations in printing the same text, revealing a second print run. The British Museum Prints and Drawings holds an exemplar with prints on wove paper, finer and smoother than the one used for the letterpress, watermarked "Jacob Bick in Egelstall." The paper appears to be quarter-sheets.[15] The specimen given to Vigoureux by Goethe (cf. Fig. 2.3) sports lilac flaps and a finely spun string holding the plates. Were samples meant for the author more refined? If available, comparative inspection of similar exemplars should deliver further information.

All this points to complex unrecorded publishing deals in response to foreign and domestic demand. Engel and Goedeke date a "third" Cotta edition from 1828.[16] Several other writers simply date the original *Umrisse* from that

same year.[17] Such ulterior dating reinforced Clösges's mistaken belief that Retzsch's designs heavily depended on Cornelius. However, she convincingly demonstrates that a Retzsch detail in the Mater Dolorosa plate derives from Cornelius.[18] Not traceable, the putative 1828 edition could have related to volume 12 of *Goethe's Werke* in the renowned *vollständige Ausgabe letzter Hand*, namely *Faust* in "pocket" 16° size, issued then. Odenkirchen's intriguing statement, "New German editions of the *Outlines to Goethes Faust* appeared in 1818, 1820, 1825, 1828 and 1830," may simply be based on flawed bibliographies.[19] In brief, since unrecorded in Fischer's authoritative catalogue, these raise puzzling questions.

Just so is a "Tübingen 1818" edition of Retzsch's *Umrisse*. Unconfirmed by Fischer, nor recorded in either digitized or printed catalogues, it is referenced by former studies as imported to London by Bohte where it had "found a ready sale,"[20] and met "with much success in spite of the high import duty which at that time greatly hindered the free flow of books across the channel."[21] It would be rash to dismiss such statements as defective or mimicking of each other. Bohte's printed catalogues for his English clientele regularly list "J. Retsch [*sic*], *Umrisse zu Goethe's Faust in 26 Blättern*, 4to, Tübingen 1818 (12 shillings)" from 1819 to 1821. The inaccurate initial is undoubtedly a misprint but not so the surname, which mirrors the very spelling on Cotta's portfolios (*Retsch* in both 1816 and 1820 editions). Bohte's imports of the original German sets had given birth to composite half-English half-German exemplars, of which I have been able to collate seven (see Chapter 4). On two of them the German title-page reads 1816, on the other five 1820, but none borrows from a putative 1818 edition. Bohte had presumably imported Cotta's stock shortly after 1816. Unluckily, his catalogues between 1814 and 1819 concern classical authors, not modern books. Launching Retzsch in London would benefit him through an intense campaign in the *London Magazine*, which deliberately mentions numbers, allowing for a rough estimate of some 400 imported items. The *LM* campaign started in January 1820 and it is not clear whether the 1820

---

13 Ibid., no. 1256.
14 WA 1, 49:356.
15 BMPD: 1862,1213.92–117. I am particularly grateful to Dr Antony Griffiths for this information, as unable to re-examine this exemplar myself due to recent restrictions.
16 Engel, no. 1809; Goedeke, 765, 4. Heinrich Kopp couples it with the Braunschweig staging the following year: *Die Bühnenleitung*

August Klingemanns in Braunschweig (Hamburg: Leopold Voss, 1901), 52.
17 Nagler, *Neues allgemeines Künstler-Lexicon*, 13:51; Bach, *Stuttgarter Kunst 1794–1860*, 203; Arthur Dobsky, "Moritz Retzsch, der Klassiker-Illustrator," *Bühne und Welt* 10, no. 12 (Mar 1908): 494, also reducing the prints to only fifteen; etc.
18 Clösges, "Die Illustration von Goethes Dichtung," 184f, 199–201.
19 Odenkirchen, "Moritz Retzsch, Illustrator," 32.
20 William Frederic Hauhart, *The Reception of Goethe's Faust in England in the First Half of the Nineteenth Century* (New York: The Columbia University Press, 1909), 32.
21 Odenkirchen, "Moritz Retzsch, Illustrator," 32.

FIGURE 3.1A
Umrisse zu Goethe's Faust, gezeichnet von Retzsch in 26 Blättern (Stuttgart & Tübingen: Cotta, 1830), pl. 16. Exemplar from Franz Glück's library
DLA, GLÜCK: HH/GOETHE: D, MARBACH

FIGURE 3.1B
Moritz Retzsch, Margaret at the spinning wheel, *Umrisse zu Goethe's Faust gezeichnet von Retsch* (Stuttgart & Tübingen: Cotta, 1816), pl. 16
COURTESY HAAB, F 3487, WEIMAR

Cotta edition was already available. Fischer's indication of "prints on demand" begs speculation, and it could well be that the "Tübingen 1818" met foreign orders. It is further authenticated by a December 1818 statement in London's *Literary Panorama and National Register* under the regular heading "Foreign Literary Gazette": "At Tubingen has lately been published, a work consisting of engraving in outline, representing scenes from Faustus, a tragedy of Goethe: they are designed by Retsch, on 26 plates."[22] The October 1820 *LM* also listed it in German amongst Bohte's imports, dating it "Tübingen 1819."[23] Although such data may suggest an edition aimed at the foreign market, a corresponding item has yet to emerge.

The burgeoning of Cotta's wares, recorded or not, reflects growing demand from both German States and abroad in the 1820s, while English and French copies flourished in parallel, as following chapters show. Cotta issued the portfolio again in 1830. By then, several pirated editions were also vying for the German-speaking market, lithographed or re-etched. The 1830 Cotta portfolio is recorded[24] but extant samples show the extent to which the publisher had exploited the copperplates, disregarding Retzsch's finesse and etching technique. Exemplars dated 1830, with engravings still in their earliest (1816 and 1820) order, and plate 18 (Margaret in the cathedral) preceding her brother's fatal duel, are few and flawed in one way or another. The Speck exemplar sits in a yellow and vivid green portfolio but eight plates are missing.[25] Another, from the collection of Austrian museum director, literature and art history critic Franz Glück, friend to Karl Kraus and Adolf Loos, previously belonged to the well-known Hungarian politician József Ürményi.[26] Its successive owners well illustrate the extensive appeal of Retzsch's *Umrisse* beyond German borders. However, its poor condition and crumpled and frayed edges suggest second-rate material: the portfolio is pale, its green flaps terribly faded; its front cover label irregularly trimmed; in several engravings, details and thin lines are hardly visible, weakened by repetitive printing from exhausted plates (Fig. 3.1a to compare with Fig. 3.1b). Another oddity, the title label (correctly spelling the artist's name at last) adds "In 26 Plates" (*In 26 Blättern*), but gives no date, while the title-page adopts the regular *Umrisse zu Goethe's Faust gezeichnet von Retzsch* above the 1830 imprint. This is not the case everywhere. The FDH exemplar recycles an old label (from the 1816 or 1820 edition), still with the early spelling *Retsch*, while the title-page carries 1830 and the correct spelling.[27] Haphazard combination of new and older parts expedited demand. The formula inciting the reader to acquire the tragedy's text still prevails: the letterpress excerpts refer to yet another 1830 *Faust* pocket edition but the prints still respect initial order (the cathedral preceding the duel). Is the addition "In 26 Plates" a peculiarity or a publisher's device of necessary distinction? Cotta would also issue ornate labels with further details and the 1830 imprint. In a double frame, with corner embellishments and full edition references, the latter would be pasted onto covers of the retouched and enlarged 1834 *Umrisse* in 29 plates, repeatedly delayed and with some title tags printed earlier. "In 26 Plates" would prove a clever addition to differentiate the earlier from the enlarged, all the while pulling prints from the elderly metal plates for the imperfect 1830 issue, although not for the revamped 1834 album.

3.2 From Portfolios to Albums

The wear and tear of Cotta's acknowledged versions and unacknowledged runs, the gradual obliteration of copperplates' incisions and deteriorated print quality, were good reasons for a new edition of restored material, the outcome of several factors. Between 1816 and the end of the 1830s, Retzsch's fame had achieved European resonance. His outlines for Goethe and Schiller were widely copied in Britain as well as France and Belgium. The ambitious chart of 400 projected compositions after Shakespeare, announced by Leipzig's Ernst Fleischer (starting with 16 *Hamlet* plates and a title vignette in 1827), of which almost only a quarter would ensue, met with substantial acclaim in the German States and the UK. The edition was bilingual, Fleischer making good use of his German and English commercial networks. It was high time Cotta caught up. He should offer nobler wares. Goethe announced *Faust, Part Two*, and, as prime *Faust* illustrator, Retzsch was early object of contention between Fleischer and Cotta from May 1827.[28] He would be the first to interpret *Faust II* in his favourite technique, and had asked Cotta for the galley proofs, as the play was being printed shortly after Goethe's demise in 1832—further evidence of how prized his work was.

---

22   "Want of Character in the Devil and Doctor Faustus," *Literary Panorama and National Register* 8, no. 51 (Dec 1818): 1490.

23   "Foreign Books," *LM* 2, no. 9 (Oct 1820): 464b.

24   Kippenberg, no. 1874; FDH: III-15973; not in Fischer, *Chronologische Verlagsbibliographie*.

25   Beinecke: Speck Ck99 R3 +830.

26   DLA: Glück: HH/Goethe: D.

---

27   FDH: III-15979.

28   DLA C-R, no. 9. See Hildebrand-Schat, *Moritz Retzschs Illustrationen*, 42.

FIGURE 3.2 Moritz Retzsch, Faust and Gretchen, pencil drawing, n.d., 13.5 × 9.3 cm
COURTESY BEINECKE, YALE UNIVERSITY, YCGL MSS. 26, BOX 1, FOLDER 12

FIGURE 3.3 Moritz Retzsch, *Faust*, pencil and chalk double portrait drawing with highlights on tinted paper, n.d., 35.9 × 31 cm
COURTESY HAAB, F GR 5824 (5), WEIMAR

FIGURE 3.4 Moritz Retzsch, Faust and Gretchen(?), double pencil portrait drawing on tinted paper, n.d., 27.6 × 36.5 cm
COURTESY HAAB, F GR 5824 (4), WEIMAR

FIGURE 3.5 Moritz Retzsch, Faust and Gretchen in the garden, pencil drawing, 1847, 16.7 × 20.6 cm
FDH, FRANKFURTER GOETHE-MUSEUM, III-02828, FRANKFURT

Retzsch's own interest in *Faust I* had not dwindled over the years. According to his diary, on 4 October 1823, Goethe received from Retzsch *Faust* "drawings" (*Zeichnungen zu Faust*), of which little is known except that he perused them in the company of Chancellor Friedrich von Müller, architect Clemens Wenzeslaus Coudray, and Count Karl Friedrich Reinhard.[29]

Several drawings in Retzsch's hand, mostly undated, offer tamer versions of Faust and Margaret in historical costume. One is a small full-length portrait in pencil outline and etched frame, showing Faust leading Margaret, as in a dance, one hand in hers, the other on her hip (Fig. 3.2). The second is a pencil and chalk double portrait in Renaissance headdress, with highlights on tinted paper, capturing their gaze as they peer in amorous contemplation of each other (Fig. 3.3). The third, likely as not from *Faust*, focuses in subtle pencil lines on the expressions of a gracious female and spirited male, again on tinted paper. The female has the finest eyelashes possible and wears an earring; the male boasts curly hair, a light beard and a moustache (Fig. 3.4). His features and shocks match the 1816 outlines' rejuvenated Faust, perhaps Retzsch's projected self-image, the most striking traits being the curly locks and the amorous gaze on a graceful blond-haired damsel, evocative of his own Christel. The fourth, dated 1847, has them both promenading in the garden, another curly Faust tenderly eyeing Margaret as fair maiden with lowered gaze. Their rich traditional costume may have been influenced by theatrical performances, while their countenances depict delicate feelings. Favoured by Retzsch for its idyllic spirit, the garden stroll earns picturesque treatment with background trees and shrubbery, and even a mill on the left (Fig. 3.5). It is further confirmed in several prints of the garden scene I will return to. Such predilection is yet again obvious in three depictions now in Berlin, of which a pen, ink and wash drawing of Faust and Gretchen on a garden bench.[30] Undated and lacking the expressive maturity of the corresponding 1816 outline (pl. 14), these—particularly the ink and wash drawing

commented by Vogel—may indicate preliminary attempts at rendering a striking episode. Retzsch had indeed used a similar technique (pen, ink and wash over pencil) for a study of the cathedral, in an uneven octagonal shape.[31] All record *Faust*'s lasting appeal for Retzsch. Th. S.'s laudatory memoir of his life also logs a full-size painting of Faust and Gretchen in half figure, once his major commitments were over.[32] Except for the champion garden scene, none of these has a direct bearing on Cotta editions of the 1830s, but confirm a sustained challenge throughout the artist's lifetime. His 1816 outlines crystallized *Faust* as a powerful work that later editions promoted in their own right.

Reasons for the delay in producing the planned new *Faust* editions piled up. In line with his artistic commitment, fees, and self-confidence, Retzsch's workload had substantially increased. He continued not only to conceive and compose but also to etch himself, "most solemnly rejecting interference from a stranger's hand in my works," as he characteristically put it in October 1833, even for the most tedious and menial retouching of *Faust* plates (*ich gegen alles Einmischen einer fremden Hand in meine Wercke feierlichst appelliren müßte*).[33] Committed to Cotta for numerous Schiller editions, he was severally engaged with Fleischer: the vast *Shakespeare Gallery*, his own *Chess Players* by subscription, six plates for his *Phantasien und Wahrheiten* (*Fancies and Truths*), both with his own comments in three languages. In 1833, Cotta published the forty-three plates of *The Song of the Bell* and twelve plates with explications on *Pegasus im Joche* (*Pegasus in Harness*), both after Schiller, while Fleischer gave thirteen plates after *Macbeth*. In 1834, another six plates of Retzsch's own conception, in the trilingual *Fancies* prefaced by Mrs Jameson, was published by four firms: Saunders and Otley, as well as Black, Young and Young (London), Treuttel and Würtz (Paris and Strasbourg), and Fleischer (Leipzig). Simultaneously, Georg von Cotta urged Retzsch hard to finish off *Faust II*, read from proofs as early as 1832. His own re-etching of old *Faust I* plates proved a major task, indeed a chore, since the printer's ink had set and solidified into the grooves due to careless repetitive printing.[34] By now in his fifties, the cumulative assignments must have tried his stamina. Old ailments set in, and an eye complaint.[35] Last, but not least, Johann Friedrich's demise in December 1832 had left him to deal with his son, Georg

---

29 WA 3, 9:125.

30 Berlin, Kupferstichkabinett. Three artworks of Faust and Gretchen in historical costume, two of which on either side of the same sheet, 16.2 × 20 cm; the third in ink and wash, 23 × 24,4 cm. Gerd-Helge Vogel comments on two, "Moritz August Retzschs Annäherung an Goethe," 68; "Das Spiel der Könige. Ein Bild von M. A. Retzsch—eines in Vergessenheit geratenen Künstlers aus dem Umfeld von König Johann von Sachsen," *Sächsische Heimat Blätter*, no. 6 (1999): 362; Vogel, "Bildhafte Sprache und sprechende Bilder: Anmerkungen zum Einfluß der Werke Goethes auf Bildfindungen der Dresdener Romantiker," *Anzeiger des Germanischen Nationalmuseums* (1999): 180–81.

---

31 FDH: III-11851, https://goethehaus.museum-digital.de/object/2711.

32 Th. S., "Ein Lebensbild," 10a.

33 DLA C-R, no. 34.

34 DLA C-R, no. 36, May 1834.

35 DLA C-R, no. 37, 41–3.

von Cotta, who ran the business on profit-making expectations rather than personal relations of confident incentive. Cotta son was moving with his times. Tellingly, he initially conceded only 6 plates for *Faust II*.[36] Upon receiving several larger plates for this, he severely criticized the diverse size of the frames in *Faust I*, unable to perceive the desired effect.[37] He contested the artist's price for re-engraving the *Faust I* plates with the argument that he could find a much cheaper job-engraver for the task. Harsh negotiations followed. Retzsch ardently defended his work, commitment and craft, made a slight concession on the requested fee, took offense at the allegation he might be dishonest, finally leaving Cotta to decide.[38] His long letters are a precious source of information on his aesthetics, technique and artistic credo, as shows one telling passage, selected amongst many:

> die Buchhandlung ganz u gar keinen Unterschied darin zu machen scheint *wem* die Retouche zu übertragen gewesen sey, und es derselben gleich giltig ist, ob der Künstler, von welchem das zu retouchiren gewesene Werk herrührt, den schwierigen Aufstich der Platten selbst übernom[m]en habe, oder ob, wen[n] man[n] den Unterschied des Honorares gekan[n]t hätte, eine fremde Hand in die Arbeit hin[n]ein gepfuscht hätte; daß der Umstand übersehen oder wenigstens nicht der Beachtung werth gefunden zu werden scheint, daß vom Autor der zu retouchirenden Umriße, mehr Sorgfalt u Mühe, mehr Liebe zur Sache, mehr Ambition bei dieser Arbeit voraus zu setzen sey, daß nur er allein im Stande seyn kan[n], mit gleichem Geiste das Fehlende wieder zu ersetzen, die schwächsten Linien richtig zu verstehn u mit gleichem Gefühl da nachzuhelfen wo es Noth thut, während von einer fremder Hand, Keins von alle dem zu erwarten stand u daher wohl ein Unterschied im Honorar hervortreten mußte.[39]

the publishers seem to make absolutely no distinction as to *whom* retouching might be entrusted, and could not care less whether it is the artist, from whom the work to retouch originates, and who has himself undertaken the tough restoring of the plates, or whether a foreign hand would bungle the work, had the difference in fee been known; it seems that no notice is taken, or at least it is not considered worthy to grant attention to the event that extra care and effort, extra love for the matter, extra ambition in the task would be presumed from the author of the outlines to be retouched, that only he is in a position to do it, to replace what is missing in the same spirit, to grasp the weakest lines correctly, and to retouch with the same feeling where needs be, while, if in a foreign hand, none of these could be expected and therefore a fee difference necessarily stood out.

All this complicated and adjourned publication of both the enlarged *Faust I* (26 + 3 plates in 1834) and *Faust II* (finally 11 plates, issued in 1836). The artist had completed the latter only on 15 May 1836.[40] Further discrepancies in the new *Faust I* concern: a) the date: the title-page consistently prints 1834 vs. the label's 1830, even 1836 when corrected by hand; b) the label's wording itself, with or without the indication "retouched and enlarged edition in 29 plates"; and c) the plates' irregular array.

Retzsch's *Faust I*, as issued by Cotta, had up to 1834 been in the initial portfolio's colour scheme, a separate letterpress brochure and strung together prints (cf. Fig. 2.1b). The flexible arrangement appealed to readers, while working as a recognisable tool of public marketing. Georg von Cotta did not hesitate to style *Faust II* on a similar model. It came out in a blue portfolio with fuchsia flaps holding prints and letterpress, the latter a simple folded sheet including the title-page (Fig. 3.6). Due to the plates' remarkably low number, loose summaries, drafted by Retzsch himself,[41] alluded to acts and scenes instead of precise excerpts. Dense data on the pink label formed an attractive front cover advert. Cotta commercialized it with partners in Paris (Veith and Auzer [*sic* for Hauser]) and London (Black and Armstrong). The latter used their own label, promptly adding a double sheet in English to anglicise it.[42] International appeal held sway and Georg von Cotta's fine edition had joined the bandwagon.

However, now that Georg von Cotta had spotted what he considered a major inconsistency on the artist's part, i.e., dimensional differences between scenes, he strongly wished to deal with the issue. His idea of a work of art was standardized, to say the least, and his ambition, to compete with the Shakespeare albums issued by Fleischer. The enlarged *Faust I* would thus be shaped as an *album*, bound in either black, lilac or grey-green cloth, and printed on a stronger and thicker paper than ever previously used by

---

36   DLA C-R, no. 32, July 1833.
37   DLA C-R, no. 34, Oct 1833.
38   DLA C-R, no. 39–40.
39   DLA C-R, no. 39, 4 Sept 1834, Retzsch's emphasis.

40   DLA C-R, no. 44.
41   See DLA C-R, no. 45.
42   Beinecke: Speck Ck99 R3 +836c, with two letterpress sheets in German and English.

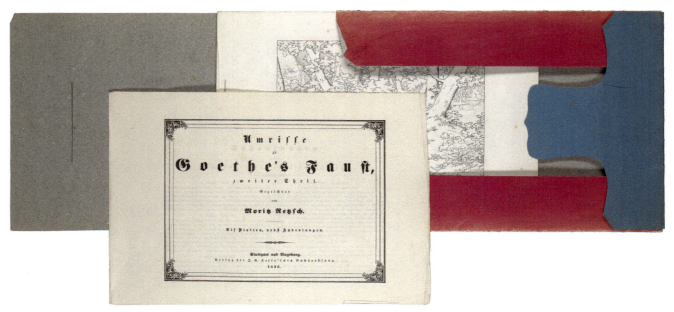

FIGURE 3.6 *Umrisse zu Goethe's Faust, zweiter Theil. Gezeichnet von Moritz Retzsch. Elf Platten, nebst Andeutungen* (Stuttgart & Augsburg: J. G. Cotta, 1836). Original blue portfolio with fuchsia flaps
COURTESY BEINECKE, YALE UNIVERSITY, SPECK CK99 R3 +836B

Cotta for Retzsch's work. The idea had come from the artist himself, who, under the stimulus of Fleischer's plush editions, had proposed to his publisher several means of repairing so-called irregularities. Retzsch wrote: "One uniform external format, namely the paper on which to print both parts' plates, should, with good equipment, compensate, overlook and render insignificant everything that is in itself beyond the limits of petty criticism." (*Ein gleiches Format in der äußern Form, nehmlich des Papiers worauf die Platten beider Theile gedruckt werden, dürfte bei guter Ausstattung, vieles ausgleichen, übersehen u. unwesentlich finden laßen, was an u für sich schon außer den Grenzen kleinlicher Critick liegt.*).[43] It bolstered Georg von Cotta's conception of a regulated creation and allowed him to vie with Fleischer's stylish albums. The plates' margins and overall size of *Faust I* dramatically grew (new binding 24.1 × 33.7 cm vs. 17.8 × 22.1 cm for the 1816 portfolio) rivalling fine art reproductions (overall 23.9 × 33.4 cm vs. 16.8 × 21.6 cm for the 1816 plates). Thanks to retouched plates on pristine paper, the prints would have looked impeccable, except for … order.

Retzsch had indeed requested and etched three extra plates. Mephistopheles lulling Faust to sleep surrounds the doctor in his study with lithe erotic figures, a sensual fantasy that would consequently influence other artists (insert pl. 5, Fig. 3.7); a second Auerbach's tavern with drunken students grabbing at each other's noses (insert pl. 7, influenced by Cornelius); and Faust handing Gretchen a small phial with the potion that would put her mother to eternal sleep with Mephistopheles spying on them (insert pl. 19, cf. Fig. 7.1). In strengthening the narrative with additional scenes, Retzsch had enhanced the role of dream and magic, counter-played temptation against tenderness, and pointed at tragedy, all the while placing his former pl. 18 (the cathedral) as renumbered pl. 21 *before* the duel (pl. 22). Significantly however, the publisher henceforth subjugated the order of prints to the excerpts, themselves re-arranged according to strictly textual sequence. Retzsch's mute inventiveness could hardly resist word-based supremacy. Although renumbered 21, the cathedral curiously found itself exiled beyond pl. 22 and 23. Other mishaps had to do with incongruously placing the extra plates themselves, partly the result of inexperience at binders' hands. It would be tedious to give examples. Not all exemplars are concerned, and those affected diverge. The artist had gained in standing but his ambition was once again vexed.

Not so the publisher. Georg von Cotta made sure that a small printed advert was affixed to the front pastedown, listing as correspondents Black, Young and Young in London, and Piéri-Bénard in Paris. He proudly announced Retzsch's forthcoming *Faust II*, hoping "to soon delight the public," and listed all Retzsch's *Umrisse* he was commercializing

---

43   DLA C-R, no. 34.

FIGURE 3.7   Moritz Retzsch, Mephistopheles lulls Faust to sleep, *Umrisse zu Goethe's Faust, erster Theil. Gezeichnet von Moritz Retzsch. Von dem Verfasser selbst retouchirt und mit einigen neuen Platten vermehrt* (Stuttgart & Tübingen: J. G. Cotta, 1834), insert pl. 5
COURTESY HAAB, F 3478, WEIMAR

with their prices, along with other art wares. The pasted ad timidly promoted him as an art publisher and would become a full-page supplement. *Faust I* sold at 4 Florins, the price of the outlines for Schiller's *Fight with the Dragon*, although the former contained 29 plates against the latter's 16. The original *Faust* had cost very little, Cotta had taken into account the expense of the retouched plates, but was still making a tidy profit. To further boost sales, he had Mrs Jameson's chapter on Retzsch translated into German and published in two *Kunst-Blatt* issues on 21 and 23 October 1834.[44] Böttiger followed suit with a laudatory article in Dresden's *Artistisches Notizenblatt*.[45] The album championed yet another textual edition of *Faust*, issued in 1833 and footnoted in the excerpts. The latter cost only 4 Groschen more, Böttiger touted, and included Goethe's portrait—an eloquent grading scale of an ancillary relationship maintained between Retzsch's prints and the text that had inspired them.

Thanks to the campaign, Retzsch's 1834 *Umrisse* must have sold very well. Cotta issued them again in 1837, still with the 1834 imprint on the label. It really did not matter to anyone whether dates be accurate throughout, that

---

44   Jameson, "Biographisches," 333–34, 338–39.

45   Karl August Böttiger, "Retzsch: Umrisse nach Göthe's Faust 1ster Theil," *Abend-Zeitung. Artistisches Notizenblatt*, no. 23 (Dec 1834): 92.

contents match the enlarged *Faust I* edition as announced or abut in a joint album *Faust II*, launched in the meantime. What mattered was to occupy the field and attract customers. By 1925, when Hirschberg published his catalogue *raisonné* of Retzsch's graphic work, the enlarged *Faust I* edition was unobtainable. Copying the title from another catalogue, Hirschberg noted: "All editions known to me have been published without a date" (*Alle mir bekannten gewordenen Ausgaben sind ohne Jahreszahl erschienen*).[46] Yet another assertion to muddy the waters.

The packaging of the enlarged *Faust I* was so effective that it even informed the recently issued colourful portfolio of *Faust II* (*Umrisse zu Faust, zweiter Theil*). In 1836, Cotta exploited the album format to amalgamate both, peddling their availability in London (Black and Armstrong) and Paris (his correspondent was by now Veith and Auzer [Hauser]). The label's pull grew. Its treble frame with curlicues announced a comprehensive "First Part 29 plates, Second Part 11 plates, with guidelines" (*Andeutungen*), an immaculate set of 40 prints Cotta could be proud of. He varied the label's colour (blue, beige, slight grey, light yellow) to distinguish it from the 1834 tag. In truth, he fairly effortlessly put together the matching parts of both *Faust* already issued. All letterpress sheets were at the outset due to accompany the 40 prints in succession, that is, when the haphazard assemblages allowed for order. Indeed, exemplars might sport two title-pages, marked 1837 compared to the label's date 1836,[47] or even carelessly include the original blue *Faust II* portfolio itself with pasted label.[48] The combined album might include scraps, remnants and vestiges of separate previous editions.

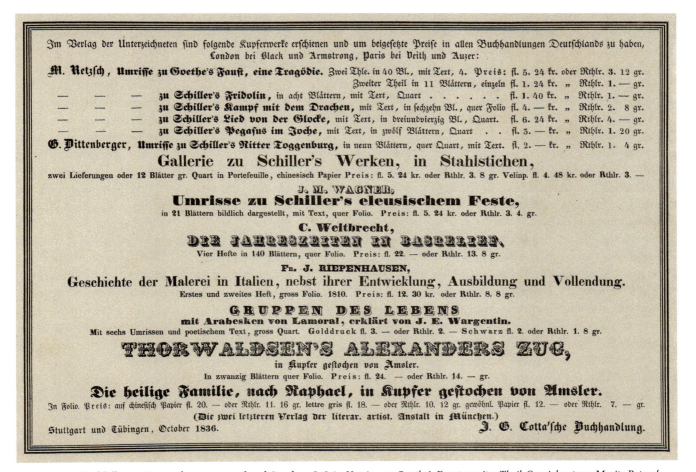

FIGURE 3.8   Final full-page Cotta advertisement dated October 1836, in *Umrisse zu Goethe's Faust, zweiter Theil. Gezeichnet von Moritz Retzsch. Elf Platten, nebst Andeutungen* (Stuttgart & Augsburg: J. G. Cotta, 1836)
COURTESY BEINECKE RARE BOOK AND MANUSCRIPT LIBRARY, YALE UNIVERSITY, SPECK CK 99 R3 +836C

46   Hirschberg, *Chronologisches Verzeichniss*, 60.

47   Library of the University of Michigan, with the bookplate of Lawrence B. Evans (class of 1894). Digitized by Google (accessed 1st Apr 2021).

48   BMPD: 1927,1231.37.1–40.

By then, the small commercial pastedown of 1834 had grown into a full-page ad appended at the very end of several (but not all) exemplars. Thus developed, in a variety of typesets, it aggrandized Georg von Cotta as art publisher. Three consecutive versions, dated December 1835, October 1836, and January 1837, illustrate how pushy the practice had become, how precipitated the issuing must have been, also reflecting swift sales of Retzsch's *Faust I* in album format. In December 1835, only the *Umrisse* after *Faust I* were available, *Faust II* yet to come, and the combined album not even envisaged (despite the very same ad featuring in just such an album as well as in a portfolio exemplar of *Faust II*).[49] By October 1836, the ad no more includes the *Faust I* album, by then presumably out of print; it promotes the combined *Faust I* and *II* at 5 Florins 24 Kreutzer, alongside *Faust II* at 1 Florin 24 Kreutzer (Fig. 3.8).[50] Interestingly, Cotta also announces two fine art editions of Retzsch outlines for a "Schiller Gallery" in steel engravings. Printed on either Chinese or vellum paper, obviously for collectors, the project, much discussed in correspondence with Retzsch, hardly materialized. The January 1837 ad reads identical.[51]

Detailed examination and comparison of several exemplars point at three conclusions.

First, Georg von Cotta used Retzsch's *Umrisse* to increase sales of Goethe's *Faust* time and again, after the fashion of his father, certainly with his skill but not his prepossessing style. Cotta father had managed the task in parallel with Goethe's active steering of his own works' publication. He had brought out three voluminous editions of Goethe's *Works* during the poet's lifetime. The very last, *Ausgabe letzter Hand*, was already selling poorly in an oversupplied market.[52] Retzsch's *Umrisse* will have lent a useful promotional hand as spirited mediators between intricate poem and cultivated, yet miscellaneous, aristocratic and upper middle-class readers. With his father's and Goethe's demise, and international competition growing, Cotta son faced new challenges. In his hands the Retzsch set became a pliable marketing tool thanks to its confirmed appeal and European demand. Its enrichment and elevation to an art edition not only further inveigled collectors and a growing middle-class public with finer requirements and

pretences, but also confirmed Cotta as a significant fine art publisher with European connexions.

Secondly, beyond commercial considerations, still at stake was the intellectual probing of the play, especially with an even more mysterious second part now in print. Who else but Retzsch, the in-house *Faust* illustrator, could face the task? Deployed in order, his prints enhanced public awareness of *Faust*'s potential for further categories of readers, while flattering their feelings and caressing the eye. They proved an integral part of *Faust* reception in the German States especially in the 1830s.

Thirdly, and most importantly, they displayed a marked resilience to printing adventures and mishaps and a degree of adaptability that placed them in the book trade simultaneously high-brow, midrange, and lower-scale. Such pliability would be a major asset in their advancement.

Witness another cohesive album of both parts, issued by Cotta with no date, perhaps from copperplated or plain steel engravings. Yet another brainteaser, this corresponds to dual versions, diverse readership, and two periods of the firm's publishing history. Dissimilarities are threefold: the presence or not of Cotta's griffin on the title-page, designated printer, and external appearance. Both versions refer to an 1840 *terminus ab quem* textual *Faust*, referenced in the excerpts. The older is plainly hardbound, printed on strong paper with wide margins at Cotta's own printing works in Stuttgart (Buchdruckerei der J. G. Cotta'schen Buchhandlung), and lines up the contents under a plain printed cover.[53] The griffin, used from 1839 as publishing mark, ought to have figured on the title-page but does not. The fine volume addresses a choice clientele. It was also published as a portfolio with plates in varying sizes.[54]

The second, printed in Stuttgart by "Druck von Gebrüder Kröner," a trade name only extant from 1877, is certainly posterior. The Cotta firm was in business relations with Adolf Kröner from 1877, and leased to the Kröner brothers (Adolf and Paul) from 1879, before the firm's transfer to them on 1 January 1889.[55] The album has a colourful cover, designed and lithographed by master draughtsman, illustrator and lithographer Christian Votteler, active in Stuttgart, in point of fact a simple printed colour sheet carefully applied to a robust commercial binding (Fig. 3.9). Its elaborate frame and traditional grotesque motifs, vaguely pointing at devilry (face-to-face griffins, youths with spindly limbs, a naked-breasted siren

---

49 Beinecke: Speck Ck99 R3 +836. See also Beinecke: Speck Ck99 R3 +836b (portfolio *Faust II*).

50 It figures however in the portfolio of the combined German (1836) and English (1837) *Faust II* edition.

51 DLA: Cotta Hss Slg.

52 Regine Otto, "Editionen als Instrumente der Goethe-Rezeption," in *Spuren, Signaturen, Spiegelungen: zur Goethe-Rezeption in Europa*, ed. B. Beutler and A. Bosse (Cologne: Böhlau, 2000), 212.

53 Beinecke: Speck Ck99 R3 +884.

54 Engel, no. 1813.

55 Paul Heichen, ed., *Taschen-Lexikon der hervorragenden Buchdrucker u. Buchhändler* (Leipzig: Moritz Schäfer / Schäfer & Koradi, 1884), 169; *NDB*-online, s.v. "Kröner, Adolf von" (by Franz Menges), last accessed 1 Mar 2023; Lohrer, ed., *Cotta in Tübingen*, 37.

GERMAN EDITIONS AND COPIES: THE BAIT OF RICH MORSELS 107

FIGURE 3.9 Christian Votteler, coloured lithographic cover, *Umrisse zu Goethes Faust, erster und zweiter Theil gezeichnet von Moritz Retzsch. Erster Theil neunundzwanzig Platten, Zweiter Theil elf Platten* (Stuttgart: J. G. Cotta, n.d. [1884?])
COURTESY HAAB, F GR 3493, WEIMAR

between angry swans, snakes elaborately coiling round fruit-laden cornucopias and urns), drew in knowledgeable post-Biedermeier readers proud of their classics. The central image, copied from Retzsch, lodged Faust's treacherous duel with Valentine, revealing how his sword, warded off by Mephistopheles, exposed his breast to Faust's blade. A paradoxical choice, appealing to youthful rather than adult imagination, the image may have engaged with newly imperial Germany's resentment that had led to the Franco-Prussian war of 1870—Valentine standing for the valorous German soldier, Mephistopheles, for the French enemy. Allegedly dated 1884, it could be from a few years earlier, and bears the marks of a growing trade in marketed commodities for a wider novelty-wise public. In this last version, sumptuous thick paper and wide margins reinstate Retzsch's work on a par to Goethe's poem but the fine lines of the original prints have solidified and stiffened. Line nuances are no more visible. Interestingly,

the very first plate, of God and Mephistopheles in Heaven (cf. Fig. 5.1), has been detached as a frontispiece to both sequences. This meets the scene's purpose and Goethe's overall structure, significantly conditioning the meaning of both parts, particularly Faust's salvation. The wager proposed by Mephistopheles presides now over a sustained ensemble, as does "The Prologue in Heaven" in the text. No extra sheets separate *Faust I* from *II*, the engravings unfold to ensure continuous reading. Luxury has been achieved by new technology, and Retzsch's *Umrisse*, again revamped, had become profit-generating yet ideology-invested wares.

3.3 Pirated Goods

A lack of legislation binding copyright and the high price that fine prints would fetch both facilitated plagiary in the

German States at the time. Böttiger had expressly noted in the *Artistisches Notizenblatt* reviewing Cotta's enlarged 1834 *Faust*: "The price of this new edition is deliberately set so low that the reproduction is safe from any predatory handling." (*Der Preis dieser neuen Ausgabe ist absichtlich so niedrig gestellt, daß dadurch vor jedem Diebsgriff des Nachdrucks gesichert wird.*)[56] Publishers and cultural analysts were all aware of the market's unwritten laws. As plenipotentiary representative of the German book trade, J. F. Cotta had taken part in the 1814–15 Vienna congress, championing protection of authors' rights and advocating the prohibition of pirated editions, along with Friedrich Christoph Perthes, also an advocate of Retzsch's *Umrisse* (Chapter 4). Both believed that fair trade, underpinning authorship and national literature, was needed throughout the German-speaking territories. Yet those were early times and their efforts inconclusive since the 1806 dissolution of the Reich. The lack of a unified or centralized state suited a multifaceted market. Wherever introduced, any copyright ruling could easily be circumvented, since a book, if deemed illegal here, could be freely accessible elsewhere. The road was open for licit duplication and illicit forgery and it has been argued that such a state of affairs favoured economic progress, nurtured industrialisation, and spread knowledge.[57]

Retzsch's outlines bore none of the usual formal imprints, neither *del.* for *delineavit* (identifying the artist) nor *sc.* for *sculpsit* (naming the engraver). Despite accomplishing both tasks, his only trace was on the portfolio's label that advertised them as "drawn by Retsch" (*gezeichnet von Retsch*) without even inserting "and engraved." With no further sign than a mere numeral above right, his 26 prints appeared an anonymous multiple set from the outset. The copying business had favourable ground on which to thrive.

Replication accrued Retzsch's popularity and reputation. Indeed, his *œuvre* was based on multiplication. Its notoriety benefitted from reproduction even though plagiarized. In his case, copies became the very means to impact, stimulate, inspire and foment ever larger numbers of users. Copying furthered a largely shared conception of Goethe's tragedy. It has often been stated that Retzsch's impact on the stage was considerable, and Chapter 9 will return to this. Yet diffusion of his cloned *Umrisse* wielded their power no less favourably and earlier than theatre performances. Both acknowledged and unacknowledged copies ensured flow and boosted rotation. Extensive

circulation also exploited their conception as a run of twenty-six. It promoted typification and exemplification, gradually dispossessing the inventor's hand. As they netted audiences, the copies captured and translated various aspects of contemporary *Zeitgeist*. In short, they worked as a flexible, impressionable mould, recording public sensitivity and understanding.

Interestingly, replicas have come to us as valuable collectables, despite their uncertain status. Collectors have favoured scarcity over their possibly fake origin. Such is a lithographed duplicate, dated *c.*1825, from the former Faust Collection of Alexander Tille (characteristically called *Faustbücherei*),[58] the first to collect, study in length, and exhibit Faust iconography in the nineteenth century, indistinctly mingling originals with replicas.[59] Its dummy cover bears in pencil, seemingly in his hand, "Rare lithographed edition, the other German editions are engraved!" Its call mark shows it fitted into part B of Tille's 1899 exhibition catalogue, *Bode-Tilleschen Faust-Galerie*, but was acquired at a later date since it does not figure in his initial inventory. It is a typical example of a new hardwearing technology, faster and friendlier than engraving, wielded to achieve numerous impressions devoid of the inevitable wear that extensive use of copperplates would have produced. As noted, several exemplars of Cotta's 1820 and 1830 engraved editions show such blurring (cf. Fig. 3.1a). Naturally, the lithographed plagiary has neither title-page nor imprint and offers the (now unreferenced) *Faust* excerpts on four initial pages in dense Gothic type. The prints closely reproduce Retzsch's conceptions, details and plate order, although protagonists' face expressions may differ and line intensity vary. Slightly bigger than Cotta's 1820 edition, they proffer wide collectors' margins, destined for extensive distribution at a lower price.

Another unique copy in Martin Bodmer's Collection, seemingly lithographed by an unidentified hand, is distinct for the expurgation of explicit male attributes throughout. The *Faust* excerpts, anonymously calligraphed in Gothic script on extra inserted pages, face the plates.[60]

The duplicate engravings are more complicated to categorize due to unrecorded publishing deals, although all sustain the genuine and extensive foreign and domestic public demand. Fischer lists for instance an 1827 reprint or pirated edition (*Nachdruck*[61]) published by "Jäger," so far untraced.[62] Established 1762 in Frankfurt by Johann

---

56 Böttiger, "Retzsch: Umrisse," 92.

57 See Eckhard Höffner, *Geschichte und Wesen des Urheberrechts* (Munich: VEW, 2010), 2:337f.

---

58 HAAB: F 8099.

59 See Stead, "*Faust*-Bilder," 151–74.

60 Bodmer catalogue under construction.

61 *Nachdruck* means both *reprint* and *pirated copy* in German.

62 Fischer, *Chronologische Verlagsbibliographie*, no. 1256.

GERMAN EDITIONS AND COPIES: THE BAIT OF RICH MORSELS

Wilhelm Abraham (1718–90), and pursued by his son Johann Christian (1754–1822), publisher, bookseller and cartographer, the Jaeger firm was a flourishing business that also owned a paper mill. Like Perthes, it traded with Cotta to wit the latter's "Circulaire" ledger. Their book, paper and map store (*Jaegersche Buch- Papier- und Landkartenhandlung*) published two almanacs in 1818 and 1820 with several of Retzsch's *Faust* outlines clumsily copied, re-centred and supplemented by poems for a female readership (see below). It may be that the firm also copied the outlines themselves in 1827.

Items labelled "bad re-engraving of the 26 outlines for the first part (Göttingen: Dieterich, *c.*1825)"[63] form a singular category. In his catalogue *raisonné* of Retzsch, Hirschberg included and dated two editions of the artist's *Fight with the Dragon* and *Fridolin* as published 1814 in Göttingen by Dieterich,[64] preceding Cotta's larger publications of the same in 1824 and 1823. These are considered as erroneously attributed to Retzsch.[65] A reduced pirate copy, dated *c.*1827 by collector Gerhard Stumme,[66] transpires to be a bootleg item and again testifies to growing demand. Two specimens of this, preserved in the HAAB and the Beinecke, of analogous size, bear the Göttingen Dieterich imprint.[67] A slightly smaller exemplar, presented to the historical "library of Weimar" by legal scholar, law Professor, writer, and literary historian Alfred Nicolovius, son to one of Goethe's nieces, and considered by himself as a reduced copy of the first edition, bears no imprint, but comes from the same hand.[68] Interestingly, on 8 April 1828 Goethe showed an unidentified *Faust* by Riepenhausen along with Retzsch's *Hamlet* to Princess Augusta, future Queen of Prussia and consort to William I, German Emperor.[69] This could be Emminger's fine lithograph after the Riepenhausen brothers' chalk drawing (see below). On 21 May 1831, Goethe noted in his diary: "The Faust outlines from Göttingen had arrived" (*Die Umrisse von Faust von Göttingen waren angekommen*).[70] Deneke takes the latter to be a Riepenhausen father etched copy of Retzsch ordered by Goethe. In an August 1828 letter,

Riepenhausen father writes to an art-dealer that he would have sold twenty-five *Faust* exemplars to Göttingen students, had he any left.[71] He likely printed further exemplars to satisfy demand in the following years and it may well be that the May 1831 entry in Goethe's diary corresponds to such a case. By then, Cotta's poor printing surely corresponded to scenes with faint details from the wearied-out plates, and Goethe may have fallen back on the cruder engraved Riepenhausen ersatz. Prints from Retzsch's own revamped plates would still be long in coming (1834). Deneke further elaborates on other engravings presented by Riepenhausen father to Goethe.

Whatever the exact circumstances, the poet's diary entries and his descendant's gift to the Weimar library testify to the part played by bootleg goods exploiting Retzsch's prominence. Goethe is reported to have had "much sympathy" for Nicolovius, his niece's son,[72] and the latter's gift to the Weimar library smacks of his relationship to the poet and personal interest in related iconography. He had compiled in 1828 a volume of literary and artistic information on Goethe, including a first list of copper engravings of his portraits and after his works.[73] Although a variety of other proposed dates besieges the Göttingen Retzsch copy,[74] it deserves a commentary. It showcases Retzsch's creation as subject to versions very different from his, but still informative of the ways Goethe's play was perceived. It is also fully part of print circulation.

Stumme identified the Retzsch replicated set as engraved by Ernst Ludwig Riepenhausen, engraver for Göttingen University and father to the romantic artists Friedrich Franz (known as Franz) and Christian Johann (known as Johannes). Goethe had come to know both brothers thanks to Weimar's artistic competitions and sustained their efforts before their attraction to old-Germanic style and religious symbolism repelled him.[75] The

---

63 Kippenberg, no. 1873.

64 Hirschberg, *Chronologisches Verzeichniss*, 17–19.

65 Otto Deneke, *Göttinger Künstler, zweiter Theil* (Göttingen: beim Herausgeber, 1936), 75f; Hellwig, "Studien zu Moritz Retzsch," 87, n. 403.

66 Stumme, "Über den Göttinger Nachstich der Retzschschen Umrisse zu Goethes Faust," *Archiv für Buchgewerbe und Gebrauchsgraphik* 69, nos. 11–12 (1932): 548c.

67 HAAB: F 3489 (overall 15.8 × 22.7, plates 13.5 × 21.4 cm); Beinecke: Speck Ck99 R3 +827 (overall 14.9 × 22.5 cm, plates 13.5 × 21.2 cm).

68 HAAB: Th N 2: 11 (bound, overall 13 × 17,9 cm).

69 WA 3, 11:203.

70 WA 3, 13:81.

71 Qtd. by Deneke, *Göttinger Künstler*, 76.

72 *Henriette Herz: Ihr Leben und ihre Erinnerungen*, ed. J. Fürst (Berlin: Wilhelm Hertz, 1850), 214.

73 Nicolovius, "Kupferstich-Sammlung auf Goethe's Person und Werke bezüglich," in *Über Goethe: Literarische und artistische Nachrichten* (Leipzig: J. F. Leich, 1828), 413–20. Concerning Retzsch, he only lists the Cotta 1820 *Umrisse* edition (417).

74 The authoritative edition of Heine's works (*Historisch-kritische Gesamtausgabe der Werke*, 6:614) refers to an 1823 reprint of Retzsch's *Faust* outlines issued in Göttingen, where Heine studied, implying this would be the one known to Heine before his Harz journey alluding to Retzsch. On Heine and Retzsch, see Chap. 10. Rümann (*Das illustrierte Buch*, 358) dates a Göttingen ed. from 1814 seemingly by confusion with *Fridolin* and *The Fight with the Dragon*.

75 Benz, *Goethe und die romantische Kunst*, 42–43, 46; *Illustrationen zu Goethes Werken*, ed. H. Haberland (Frankfurt.a.M.: Freies Deutsches Hochstift, 1962), 21; Werner Busch, "Goethe,

Riepenhausen brothers had conceived in Rome a series of fourteen chalk drawings after *Faust* before Cornelius's contract with Wenner brought their plans to a close. In the past, their father had copied for Johann Christian Dieterich, a personal friend and patron of his, two major artists' works: Hogarth's plates, and Flaxman's outlines for the classics and Dante, as engraved by Piroli. Goethe had shown strong interest in the father's reduced version of Hogarth. Indeed, Ernst Ludwig had become a reference in engraving. Limited financially, he engraved for almanacs, an extensive activity, along with trading in prints from his own collection.[76] Both profiles of father (engraver) and sons (*Faust* artists) must have offered a plausible guarantee for a pirated engraved copy of Retzsch, reduced in size to 4/5ths of the original.[77] They may also have banked on the copied prints' success to garner financial support. In surviving exemplars, margins differ, particularly in height, and prints may have been issued in two formats. Intense research on the publisher, Dieterich, has returned no results.[78] Order and treatment in the replica follow Retzsch (including the cathedral before the duel) but expressions are altered, outline nuances ironed out, fantastic or witty elements prominent, and details modified. The animalized Mephistopheles looks fiercer, and Margaret appealing heavenward more ethereal. A copy is but a copy, and this one mars the original's subtlety, as show its design and the cover's final touch.

Indeed, the plates, again merely strung together, sit somewhat roughly between unassuming blue cardboard flaps. On the reverse, title and publisher's imprint feature on erratically cut-and-pasted paper slips (Fig. 3.10a). The unprepossessing object also bears on the front cover an outline lithographed reproduction (Fig. 3.10b) of Johannes Riepenhausen's drawing *Begegnung Fausts mit Gretchen vor der Kirche* (*Faust's Meeting with Gretchen in front of the Church*, 1811, Fig. 3.11). The latter is one of the two brothers' *Faust* chalk drawings, also known in several versions and even painted in oil.[79] In the original work, Johannes had grafted a religion-inspired allegory onto the scene, absent from both Goethe's play and Retzsch's

renderings. A naked, horned and dark Mephistopheles, donning the powerful wings of an evil spirit, whispers temptation into chaste Gretchen's ear. As beseeching knight, Faust approaches, his vertical sword reassuringly pointing downwards. Above the trio, Gretchen's guardian angel wrings hands (Fig. 3.11). At the crossroads of good and evil, Gretchen is trapped between Mephistopheles and Faust. Johannes's stylistic choices—old-Germanic costumes, a Renaissance angel and mannerist Satan[80]—burden Goethe's play with a heavy mantle of moral implications. These outdo Margaret's surprised attraction for the knight and Faust's sudden passion.

As outline lithograph on the cover of the plagiarized Retzsch copy (Fig. 3.10b), the reverse reproduction further testifies to duplication technologies and bears as caption the play's matching lines (F 2605–8). It was attributed by Stumme to Stuttgart lithographer Eberhard Emminger, but is in fact unsigned with two intriguing adjustments. First, the original's cathedral has given way to a square with a fountain in an urban background, which tallies with Retzsch's analogous choice in his pl. 8 of an ambiguously rendered simple street and covert allusion to cathedral stoups (cf. Fig. 1.8). Both the detail and lack of signature point again to Riepenhausen father, author of the replicated and engraved Retzsch outlines. Second, the tuft of Mephistopheles's animal tail skilfully masks his genitalia. In Johannes's original drawing, these are part of his robust anatomy, a detail the outline, meant for a larger audience and as cover decoy, cannot explicit. Such is again the case in a much larger chalk lithograph in black (48.2×38.2 cm) printed on light beige paper (60×45.1 cm) by the Stuttgart art publishing firm of Georg Ebner, with both Riepenhausen's credentials on the left and "Emminger lith. 1827" on the right, along with the same *Faust* lines as captions (Fig. 3.12). Its black and grey tints further dramatize the scene, the cathedral again figuring prominently in the background as in the original chalk drawing. Eberhard Emminger, mainly known as a landscape artist, apprenticed from 1821 to Georg Ebner as reproduction engraver, was mostly self-taught in lithography, yet his first landscape portfolio in 1825 had been a great success. Likewise, his 1827 lithograph of Faust and Gretchen, although the earliest of its kind, and seen as bread work,[81] is a fine piece. It could well be that Goethe showed Princess Augusta, Empress to be, this very print along with Retzsch's outlined *Hamlet* he so valued, although Dieterich's pirated

---

die Gebrüder Riepenhausen und deren Empfang in Rom," in *Rom-Europa: Treffpunkt der Kulturen 1780–1820*, ed. P. Chiarini, W. Hinderer et al. (Würzburg: Königshausen & Neumann, 2006), 43–57.

76 See Brigitte Kuhn-Forte, "Ernst Ludwig Riepenhausen, Kupferstecher," in *Zwischen Antike, Klassizismus und Romantik: Die Künstlerfamilie Riepenhausen*, ed. M. Kunze et al. (Mainz: Philipp von Zabern, 2001), 1–6.

77 Stumme, "Über den Göttinger Nachstich," 548c.

78 See Hellwig, "Studien zu Moritz Retzsch," 86–88.

79 Jens Christian Jensen, ed., *Deutsche Romantik: Aquarelle und Zeichnungen* (Munich: Prestel, 2000), no. 68.

80 Ibid.

81 Rudolf Henning and Gerd Maier, *Eberhard Emminger: Süddeutschland nach der Natur gezeichnet und lithographiert* (Stuttgart: Konrad Theiss, 1986), 12–17.

GERMAN EDITIONS AND COPIES: THE BAIT OF RICH MORSELS 111

FIGURE 3.10A Back cover with title and publisher's imprint of *Faust von Goethe in 26 Umrissen* (Göttingen: Dieterich, n.d. [c.1827])
COURTESY HAAB, F 3489, WEIMAR

FIGURE 3.10B Front cover of the same with an outline reproduction after Johannes Riepenhausen
COURTESY HAAB, F 3489, WEIMAR

FIGURE 3.11 Johannes Riepenhausen, *Faust's Meeting with Gretchen in front of the Church*, 1811, black chalk, heightened with white, paper mounted on cardboard, 47.1 × 38.1 cm
COURTESY MUSEUM GEORG SCHÄFER, MGS 1148A, SCHWEINFURT

FIGURE 3.12 Eberhard Emminger, chalk lithograph in black on light beige plate after Johannes Riepenhausen, *Faust's First Meeting with Gretchen*, with relevant verses from Goethe's *Faust* as captions, 1827, 48.2 × 38.2 cm (Stuttgart: G. Ebnerschen Kunsthandlung)
FDH, FRANKFURTER GOETHE-MUSEUM, III-04375, FRANKFURT

Retzsch, with the modified outline on the cover, cannot be excluded either.

Circulation was even more telling: a sonnet from Zacharias Werner's *Nachlass*, i.e., written before 1823, but published on the front page of Cotta's *Morgenblatt* on 18 January 1828, refers to the Riepenhausen composition under the generic term "image" (*Bild*). This could allude to Emminger's chalk lithograph but also the repurposed outline cover of the Retzsch copy, which again beckons to Goethe's relation to either, this time through his very publisher. In his *Morgenblatt*, Cotta introduced indeed a larger public to fine prints through Gottlob Heinrich Rapp's agency.[82] Issued together, sonnet and lithograph signpost a refined inter-arts dialogue, although Werner's sonnet favours Faust instead of Gretchen. The lithograph was also one of the three 1828 annual gifts of the recently founded Stuttgart art club (Württembergischer Kunstverein Stuttgart) to its members, a cultivated audience of art enthusiasts.[83] German art clubs were a growing forum of sponsoring, mediating and diffusing artworks in numbers, among which Goethe's *Faust* iconography held pride of place. Selected for *Bürger* and *Kleinbürger* subscribers alike, the choice prints promoted distribution networks, later to be developed photomechanically through a powerful periodical press.[84]

Given the above, the Retzsch spin-off relates to an intricate case of circulation both wide and loose, implicating the *Faust* outlines, Zacharias Werner's sonnet, and interventions by Emminger, as well as Riepenhausen father and sons. The spin-off (cf. Fig. 3.10a–b) is itself an object fashioned by three hands (Retzsch, Johannes Riepenhausen, and the copyist of both, seemingly Riepenhausen father). It merges images of varied origin, reshuffles extant iconography and reformulates *Faust*'s message to stimulate readers' emotions. In its two versions (outline cover of the ersatz and nobler standalone print by Emminger), the lithograph itself and the correlated sonnet testify to multimedia dissemination. Involved were a writer, lithographers, booksellers and sophisticated connoisseurs, Cotta's daily, and a larger bourgeois public, presumably attracted by cheaper simulated publications.

In the late 1820s, Retzsch's prints had already entered a complex pattern of circulation through German lands. Further Retzsch re-workings indicate alteration of print formats and genres.

3.4 Styled for the Ladies

In a puzzling lure for female readers, Margaret's grim fate was exploited as a warning in two diminutive almanacs issued by Jaeger in Frankfurt in 1818 and 1820. Bound in turquoise blue and pink leather, daintily decorated (Fig. 3.13), they sit in the palm of a hand (9.9 × 5.9 cm and 9.8 × 6 cm). In both, a coarse reworking of Retzsch's engravings has re-centred protagonists and been darkened by shading, as if an ominous fate hovered over the scenes. The reduced copies are embedded in a complex apparel of sonnets, poems and images honed to revise meaning. Rather than the often-cited four, the first contains five Retzsch copies, starting with Mephistopheles grimly absorbed in Faust, himself enticed by the female apparition in the witch's magic mirror. The four ensuing plates compose a sequel from so-called real life, based on the altered significance of Margaret's story. Fulfilment of a vicious threat, they mark four fatal steps in the young girl's temptation: accosted by Faust, musing in her chamber, she considers the jewels, before donning them at neighbour Martha's house (Fig. 3.14a–c).

The idea that an enticed Margaret fall victim to vanity is foreign to Goethe's tragedy. Yet these scenes are now twisted into delivering a moral message. They reveal

FIGURE 3.13   *Kleines Geschenk zum neuen Jahr für 1818* and *Kleines Geschenk zum neuen Jahr für 1820*, almanacs published in Frankfurt by Jaeger
FDH, FRANKFURTER GOETHE-MUSEUM, LIBRARY, XI T 124 (1818) AND XI T 124/2 (1820), FRANKFURT

---

82   Bernhard Fischer, "Cotta und die Brüder Riepenhausen: Zur Publikationsgeschichte der Riepenhausenschen Zeichnungen im *Morgenblatt*, im *Taschenbuch für Damen* und in der *Geschichte der Mahlerei*," in *Zwischen Antike, Klassizismus und Romantik*, ed. M. Kunze, 149–51.

83   Uwe Degreif, *Eberhard Emminger, 1808–1885: Werkverzeichnis der druckgrafischen Arbeiten* (Biberach: Uwe Degreif, 2021), 53.

84   See John Ittmann, "Glazed and Framed: *Kunstverein* Prints for the Parlour," in *The Enchanted World of German Romantic Prints*, 108–23; and Stead, "*Faust-Bilder*," 171–73.

GERMAN EDITIONS AND COPIES: THE BAIT OF RICH MORSELS 113

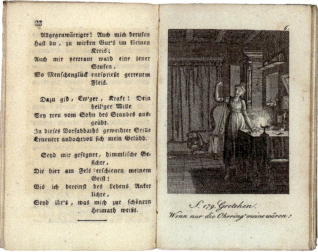

FIGURES 3.14A–C *Kleines Geschenk zum neuen Jahr für 1818* (Frankfurt: Jaeger), three of the five copied and re-focussed plates after Moritz Retzsch's outlines. Page numbers in the *Faust* quotes used as captions refer to the 1816 *Faust* pocket edition issued by Cotta, as in the *Umrisse* edition
FDH, FRANKFURTER GOETHE-MUSEUM, LIBRARY, XI T 124 (1818), FRANKFURT

Zeitgeist perception of women as feeble creatures drawn to trinkets and presents, such as the diminutive calendar to hand, signposted by its very title: *Kleines Geschenk zum neuen Jahr für 1818* (*Little Gift for New Year 1818*). The rough plates are set well before the escorting poetry as cogent gratifying images. In their wake, five explanatory sonnets by Georg Döring drive the message, dotting the i's and crossing the t's for any candid female perchance enticed by gems. Döring's moralistic verse, hammering home that futile self-love is an infernal snare, is however mildly interlaced. A recurrent weaver's metaphor substantiates action by Mephistopheles, Hell or Martha as trap in sonnets two, four and five: *Spinnt* (weaves), *verweben* (woven into), *ein andres Netz* (another web), *umstrickt* (ensnared). The annual's emphatic image of virtue is further completed by three anonymous etchings after Schiller's popular, yet often harshly criticized *Die Jungfrau von Orleans* (*The Maid of Orleans*, 1801), itself first issued in almanac form.[85] In the play, Schiller has Joan of Arc victoriously lead troops into battle, unpredictably fall in love at first glance with adversary Lionel, and direly treated as witch in the woods, once her heroic status is lost. The Jaeger booklet intriguingly works the double paradigm of a beguiled Gretchen and enamoured Joan into a mythical compound portrait of the expectedly worthy female. As suggests the expression "Fear of God and Ancestral Virtue" (*Gottesfurcht und Vätertugend*) in the opening poem, mind-sets are traumatised by the Napoleonic wars. The booklet opens with Theodor Körner's portrait, an untimely victim on the field of honour, considered the German Tyrtaeus, elegiac poet known in Greek legend as sire of martial poetry. A wealth of patriotic verse by Christian Karl Ernst Wilhelm Buri further presses the point. To put the last touch, a paragraph from Therese Huber's *Umrisse* preface has been recycled as "Explanation to the Images from Goethe's Faust," introducing Döring's sonnets. In her preface, Huber had presented Goethe's *Faust* as the book of experience commonly shared at any stage and age in life, recommended as any young man's guidebook, the modern counterpart of Fénelon's *Telemachus* and Joachim Heinrich Campe's *Theophron*. Slightly paraphrased in the almanac, the principle extends to the ignored fairer sex. Jaeger's microscopic publication claims to be a toy *Faust* for females, a pocket vade mecum for mature and younger ladies alike.

---

85 Lydia Schieth, ed., *Fürs schöne Geschlecht: Frauenalmanache zwischen 1800 und 1850* (Bamberg: Staatsbibliothek, 1992), 131; Maria Lanckorońska and Arthur Rümann, *Geschichte der deutschen Taschenbücher und Almanache aus der klassisch-romantischen Zeit* (Munich: Ernst Heimeran, 1954), 56.

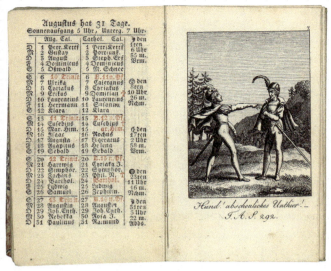

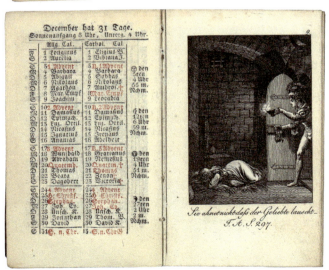

FIGURES 3.15A–C *Kleines Geschenk zum neuen Jahr für 1820* (Frankfurt: Jaeger), three of the seven copied and re-focussed plates after Moritz Retzsch's outlines
FDH, FRANKFURTER GOETHE-MUSEUM, LIBRARY, XI T 124/2 (1820), FRANKFURT

The attempt must have proved successful since Jaeger renewed the bid two years later in a pink version adorned with an arabesque border, a wreathed lyre on the front, a star on the back cover, and marbled pastedowns. It offered seven copies after Retzsch from Gretchen's toils in the cathedral, through Valentine treacherously wounded, then luridly upbraiding his sister, Faust charging Mephistopheles, their nightly cavalcade, to Gretchen's despair in the prison (Fig. 3.15a–c). As in 1818, all images referred to Cotta's 1816 pocket *Faust* (*Taschenausgabe*), inviting she-readers to purchase it. Another anonymous verse sequence (perhaps by Döring who again signed a poem elsewhere in the almanac), described in detail the torments of "poor Gretchen," addressing her directly in the initial sonnet, and stressed her heap of misfortune. Yet the poet's inspiration fell short of her hardships and trials. Plate 5 gave only six verses, and plates 6 and 7 inspired a single sonnet. The poetic vein was running out, and the New Year gift (reduced in page length, packed with monthly charts absent from the first version) worked by contrast. The frontispiece presented two children hand in hand with the caption "Shared Innocence." A four-line stanza revealed that a pure mind's "loveliest jewellery" was chastity itself, as distant reminder of the 1818 jewels that had brewed ruin. A title vignette flashed a child Eros aiming his arrow at she-readers while another stanza invited them to beware of the "God of hearts," even if the wounds of love prove sweet (Fig. 3.16a). In yet another engraving, an aged potbellied gentleman, bending towards a stately young lady in a garden arbour, asked "Have you already had a sweetheart goddaughter?" The corresponding poem commented on the beautiful girl prey to his riches as he himself falls victim to his self-conceit and foolishness (Fig. 3.16b). Gretchen's story set the seal. She was the very image of irreproachability, lacking in guile, yet, because she and Faust had "one day found each other in love | To land in the magic realm of lust" (*Denn daß sie sich in Liebe einstens fanden, | Um in dem Zauberreich der Lust zu landen*), she lost everything. Still, the "Most High" smiled down on her from Heaven.

Neither almanac nor pocket calendar, the two Jaeger booklets may best qualify as hybrid print wares. Of the former, they borrow only two of three characteristics, minute size and probably fair price, but they were neither published regularly nor as a series, not even as instalments. The second's composition testifies to a dearth of contents while developing attractive features by way of compensation. As printed products reflecting a fleeting moment, they are particularly interesting. They concentrate commercial interest, evolving public gusto for tiny objects, responsiveness to emotional imagery and verse; last, but not least, the re-purposing and re-fashioning of wares in a

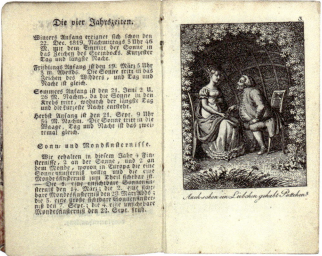

FIGURES 3.16A–B   *Kleines Geschenk zum neuen Jahr für 1820* (Frankfurt: Jaeger), frontispiece, title-page vignette, and pl. 3
FDH, FRANKFURTER GOETHE-MUSEUM, LIBRARY, XI T 124/2 (1820), FRANKFURT

highly mobile and flexible environment not yet subject to copyright rules and strict law.

Intense scholarship on German annuals and the weight of illustration as essential component of book culture have stressed the importance of almanacs for both cultivated aristocratic and educated middle-class readers in Germany.[86] Jaeger's wares might not have been the most outstanding (indeed they are never mentioned in scholarship), still, their small size, fine binding, artwork, and variety of literary texts accurately satisfy the genre. With

---

86   See in bibliography Lanckorońska and Rümann, 1954; York-Gothart Mix, ed., 1986 and 1996; Karl-Heinz Fallbacher, 1992; Schieth, ed., 1992; Paul Gerhard Klussmann, in Mix, ed., 1996; Beate Reifenscheid, in Mix, ed., 1996; Klussmann and Mix, eds., 1998; Schieth, in Klussmann and Mix, eds., 1998; Catriona MacLeod, in Ittmann, ed., 2017.

impropriety expelled, middlebrow sentimentality crept in, true to the governing template. Yet, Jaeger's second booklet makes timid allusions to love's appeal as well. Its singular mixture of scruples and soft talk, of morality and attraction for Eros's pointing arrow (cf. Fig. 3.16a), definitely increased female readership. An unadulterated *Faust* was perhaps not the most palatable text for she-readers. Yet its reworking through substitute texts and stand-in images introduced it to wider audiences. The rougher copies of Retzsch were a key part of such redrafting.

3.5   Valuing Copies in Visual Circulation

Jaeger's wares for female readers favour imperfect approximate copies and crucially raise the question as to the value attributed to substitutes in growing nineteenth-century visual culture. In recent years, art history, grounded on past worth and appeal of originals, has shown accrued awareness of the weight of widely circulating print wares. Recycled images and reproduction in print have been re-evaluated as central to heritage and gained a place in cultural history.[87] As key visual *Faust* translations replicated, Retzsch's outlines and their miscellaneous destinies contest the dominant paradigm of originality. Their impact has yet to be measured in this sense, which confers on them greater strength and significance. I argue that the Dresden artist is not just one of the first to significantly shape Goethe's *Faust* iconography alongside Christian Friedrich Osiander, Vincenz Raimund Grüner, Christian Ludwig Stieglitz, Peter Cornelius, Gustav Heinrich Naeke, or Ludwig Nauwerck. He shared with them indeed the same motley business, modelling *Faust* on visual grounds. Yet, especially unique in having translated *Faust* into a continuous narrative sequence, as Meyer and Goethe had been quick to point out, even more decisively, Retzsch produced multimedial images, disseminated throughout nineteenth-century visual culture. *Faust* illustrators may have been legion but their images rarely spread as did Retzsch's—indeed, by comparison, most of the above-mentioned artists' productions hardly circulated at all.

Retzsch's graphic conceptions spread widely, both within and beyond the German States. In so doing, they played many roles. They exposed, divulged, propagated, and publicized. They proved an effective translation of the tragedy both in the same tongue (ironing out obscurities and ambiguities) and across languages. As visual ciphers of cumulative information, they introduced *Faust*'s overall storyline, but also packed it with detail. They captured

---

87   For instance, Georges Roque and Luciano Celes, eds., "L'Image recyclée," special issue, *Figures de l'art*, no. 23 (2013).

FIGURE 3.17A   Wilhelm Eytel, *Faust Handing over the Pledge to the Devil*, woodcut after Moritz Retzsch, in *Das ärgerliche Leben und schreckliche Ende des vielberüchtigten Erz-Schwarzkünstlers Johannis Fausti. Erstlich vor vielen Jahren fleißig beschrieben von Georg Rudolf Widmann. Hernach übersehen und wieder herausgegeben von Pfitzer*, new edition decorated with 16 woodcuts (Reutlingen: Kurtz, 1834), 34. Compare with Retzsch's pl. 4, Fig. 2.21
COURTESY HAAB, F 456, WEIMAR

readers' attention, stirred their interest, and incited them to purchase the text. They contributed to portfolios, standalone prints, almanacs, albums, books and other print wares spanning social categories. The audiences they targeted diverge and fluctuate much more than bookish and textual culture generally admit. Indeed, images open up wider vistas for literary reception and interpretation when texts themselves prove demanding. *Faust* is just such a case. Not everybody could read and follow it but anybody could grasp at a glance what was at stake in Faust and Margaret's first meeting or be gripped by the intricacy of the witches' revelry. Yet, the role of images extends even further, since they "perhaps more poignantly than interpretative readings, mirror the changing cultural role that literary works and their authors play beyond their own time," as Françoise Forster-Hahn argues. She studied *Faust* illustrations as "intricate links to the political and cultural fabric" of late nineteenth- and early twentieth-century culture.[88] The argument is valid for the *early* nineteenth century as well. Since Retzsch's copies also addressed less sophisticated readers, presumably of fewer means (although they come to us as collectors' treasures), they provide an interesting perception of the social aspects of Goethe's *Faust* diffusion and propagation. Even when detached from Retzsch's set to fare on their own, they remain a dynamic part of visual heritage, fundamental to understanding Goethe's *Faust* reception within an extended cultural history.

---

88   Forster-Hahn, "A Hero for All Seasons?" 511.

FIGURE 3.17B   Wilhelm Eytel, *The Holy Angels as Servants before God's Throne*, woodcut after Moritz Retzsch but deleting Mephistopheles, in *Das ärgerliche Leben und schreckliche Ende des vielberüchtigten Erz-Schwarzkünstlers Johannis Fausti*, new edition decorated with 16 woodcuts (Reutlingen: Kurtz, 1834), 54. Compare with Retzsch's pl. 1, Fig. 5.1
COURTESY HAAB, F 456, WEIMAR

For all these reasons, the status that copies occupy in this book is on a par with originals. Chapter 7 on extensive and intensive iconography will turn to the question of evaluation and proportionate assessment where great variety and diversity of artefacts are involved. At present, let us close this investigation into the artist's fortunes in the German States with two telling examples. The first exemplifies his extended influence. No more is Retzsch the interpreter of Goethe's *Faust*, but rough outlines inspired by his are summoned to illustrate a historical *Faustbuch*, proving his *Umrisse*'s ascendancy, impact and authority. The second, amalgamated, shows how foreign copies of his work espoused the German text.

In 1834, the abridged version of two historical Faust chapbooks by Georg Rudolf Widmann (1599) and Johann Nicolaus Pfitzer (1674) trimmed off the lengthy comments and additions that had burdened them to give readers access to popular versions of the legend. It also offered woodcuts by Wilhelm Eytel, a clergyman and amateur draughtsman.[89] Two of Eytel's woodcuts are unmistakably copied after Retzsch. In *Faust übergiebt dem Teufel die Obligation* (*Faust Handing Over the Pledge to the Devil*) (Fig. 3.17a), Eytel imitated Retzsch picturing Mephistopheles and Faust in the latter's study. In *Die heiligen Engel as Diener vor Gottes Thron* (*The Holy Angels as Servants before God's Throne*) (Fig. 3.17b), he followed

---

89   Bernd Mahl, ed., *Das ärgerliche Leben und schreckliche Ende des vielberüchtigten Erz-Schwarzkünstlers Johannis Fausti*, facsimile ed. (Kirchheim: Jürgen Schweier, 1990), 269.

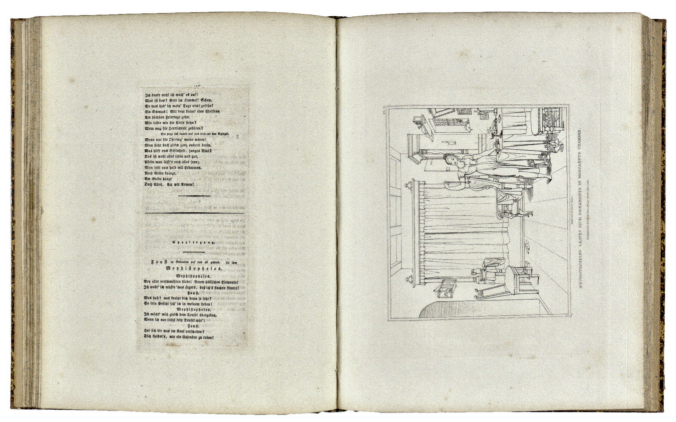

FIGURE 3.18   Unique compound volume, with (*right*) Henry Moses's English engraving copied after Retzsch entitled *Mephistopheles Leaves Rich Ornaments in Margaret's Chamber*, and (*left*) two pages from the 1816 *Faust* pocket edition by Cotta carefully cut and inlaid (pp. 179 and 180)
COURTESY HAAB, F GR 5276, WEIMAR

Retzsch's Prologue in Heaven although his piety banned Mephistopheles. The sense-laden shift from engraving to woodcuts aped the aesthetics of the sixteenth-century *Faustbücher*. The style is much cruder and blunt, yet Retzsch's compositions provide an unmistakable basis. Moreover, the very first woodcut, *Unter der Leitung des Christoph Hayllinger gräbt Faust nach dem Crystalspiegel* (*Under Christoph Hayllinger's Guidance, Faust Digs to Get the Crystal Mirror*), again recalls Retzsch and Cornelius in the Rabenstein background detail with a figure hanging and two soaring witch-like shapes. Similar details had been purposefully added to an engraving by Julius Thaeter after Moritz von Schwind, illustrator of Ludwig Bechstein's poem *Faustus*, published 1832 in the press, and in book form the following year.[90] These images are loosely related to the texts to which they are inserted, and all alterations seek to adjust them to script. Pursuing a lasting impression on readers, they connect early nineteenth-century Faust iconography with its mythical past. Such popularity, covering German retrospective and prospective Faust literature, reveals how prominent Retzsch's work had become in publishing and artistic cycles, although treated harshly by critics. If nothing else, he appears to be the champion titleholder of sustainable recycling.

To the second concluding example now: a unique compound copy in Weimar's HAAB (Fig. 3.18) shows how English copies of Retzsch's images were wielded to consort with the German pocket *Faust* quoted in Retzsch's set. The intriguing item is no chance piece but proficient work, knowledgeably put together by an excellent bookbinder to precise instructions. It combines: a) the text of Cotta's 1816 pocket *Faust* in Gothic script (the *Taschenausgabe* to which the original Retzsch outlines referred), b) interleaved plates from the first English 1820 Boosey edition (Moses's copies of Retzsch), c) the English "Analysis" from the same Boosey edition which had two title-pages, both included, and d) mounted as frontispiece, a portrait of Goethe engraved by Heinrich Lips.[91] The latter does not belong to any of the above, yet its inscription "Züllichau

---

90   Wegner, 85, fig. 68.

91   See https://haab-digital.klassik-stiftung.de/viewer/!thumbs/820 465712/1/.

bey Darnmann" shows it predates all three, from 1791.[92] The cut-out and carefully inlaid pages from the German edition have been set to match the copied English plates as accurately as possible. A faked assemblage, it nevertheless recalls a project harboured by Johann Heinrich Bohte, who had intended to bring together the original Retzsch outlines with an English translation. The unique hybrid HAAB exemplar operates inversely, merging English outline replicas with the genuine German text. It demonstrates intense interaction of Retzsch's heritage with foreign editions, to be examined in turn.

---

92   Peter Mortzfeld, ed., *Die Porträtsammlung der Herzog-August-Bibliothek Wolfenbüttel* (Munich: Saur, 1998), 2, 3:A7915.

CHAPTER 4

First Steps in Britain

Retzsch's *Umrisse* met with booming and blossoming success in the UK. Data salient to their reception were first established by Stella Esther Odenkirchen in her MA thesis (1948) and furthered in a first-rate analysis of Retzsch's aesthetic and artistic impact in William Vaughan's *German Romanticism and English Art*.[1] This chapter and the next, "Retzsch Copied in Britain and Beyond," extend exploration by reading books as "bearing in their pages and lines the boundaries of their possible reception."[2] Books and prints are further explored as cultural objets. The parametres of such an approach have been embodied and variously illustrated in a collection spanning from late medieval manuscripts to e-books I have edited.[3] Reading processes and tendencies, readers' personalities, as well as representational value and imaginative heft combine with telling material details and how items solicit perusal and prompt reactions. In diverse shapes and several ways these printed objects met with text to reveal publishers' expectation and readers' reception. As crucial components of meaning when they shift hands, change scope, and vary in shape, books and prints are given, shown, championed, re-published, repurposed and remediated. Cultural trends, ideas, and personal considerations reflect onto the broader significance of Goethe's play. New evidence accrues. In both chapters, originals, copies, and exemplars of copies that *seem* the same *but are not* have been compared, sorted, and whenever possible identified, thanks to first-hand research at several repositories in Europe and overseas.

In Britain Retzsch's set met a context quite unfriendly to Goethe. It provided adjustment and provoked a craze. *The Sorrows of Young Werther*, highly favoured for its sentimentality yet blamed for the suicide wave of lovesick youths across Europe,[4] had left strong negative impressions in the UK.[5] Hitherto *Faust's* reception ("impure trash") had principally depended on the blunders and rebuff of William Taylor of Norwich in the 1810 *Monthly Review*;[6] Madame de Staël's widely read *Germany*;[7] and the English translation of Friedrich Schlegel's *Lectures on Dramatic Art and Literature*.[8] Doubts, scruples and objections hung over *Faust*, based on ethical, social and theological grounds. Samuel Taylor Coleridge for instance styled it "a work in bad repute with the religious part of the Community" in reponse to Boosey's translation proposal.[9] Lord Byron pointed out its boldness in defense of his own *Cain*.[10] In a country where readers of German language and literature were few and the post-Napoleonic wars' financial restraints considerable, Retzsch's outlines succeeded in making *Faust* one of the most respected works of Teutonic letters, and eased out difficulties in grappling with its complex message. Retzsch's clarity, stirring compositions, and transposition of disparate scenes into a steady visual account were keys to success. Before the term was ever coined, his was a silent *bande dessinée* on an unhappy love affair, which involved the supernatural—an alluring formula by period standards.

Retzsch's introduction to Britain is full of unpredicted turns, vivid personalities, and colourful individuals, bringing dates and events to life. It begins with a *foreign object*, the German portfolio, first a gift fraught with commercial and political symbolism, social and aesthetic implication; then imported, flamboyantly advertised and commercialized in random versions; ultimately purchased in Stuttgart, scissored, plundered and merged into another's English book. In this Chapter, I follow three mediators: a renowned diarist and Anglo-German go-between; a resourceful book merchant, favoured by a literary periodical with articles in an idiosyncratic style; and a bibliomaniac touring Europe. Meanwhile other individuals appear: booksellers, binders, artists, book and art lovers,

---

1 Odenkirchen, "Moritz Retzsch, Illustrator"; Vaughan, *German Romanticism*, 123–54.

2 Roger Chartier, "Du livre au lire," in *Pratiques de la lecture*, ed. R. Chartier (Marseille: Rivages, 1985), 79.

3 Stead, "Introduction," in *Reading Books and Prints as Cultural Objects*, ed. E. Stead (Cham: Palgrave / Macmillan, 2018), 1–30.

4 Hauhart, *Reception of Goethe's Faust*, 2.

5 William Rose, "Goethe's Reputation in England during his Lifetime," in *Essays on Goethe*, ed. W. Rose (London: Cassell & Co., 1949), 151–53; Timothy Webb, *The Violet in the Crucible: Shelley and Translation* (Oxford: Clarendon Press, 1976), 169.

6 "Faustus, a Tragedy, by Goethe," *Monthly Review, Appendix* 62 (May–Aug 1810): 492.

7 Isbell, *The Birth of European Romanticism*, 2; Axel Blaeschke, "*De l'Allemagne*: Prolégomènes à une nouvelle édition," *Cahiers staëliens*, no. 64 (2014): 187–90.

8 Catherine Waltraud Proescholdt-Obermann, *Goethe and his British Critics: The Reception of Goethe's Works in British Periodicals* (Frankfurt: Peter Lang, 1992), 161.

9 *Collected Letters of Samuel Taylor Coleridge*, ed. E. L. Griggs (Oxford: Clarendon Press, 1971), 5:44.

10 *Medwin's Conversations of Lord Byron*, ed. E. J. Lovell, Jr. (Princeton: Princeton University Press, 1966), 130.

© EVANGHELIA STEAD, 2023 | DOI:10.1163/9789004543010_007

This is an open access chapter distributed under the terms of the CC BY-NC-ND 4.0 license.

FIRST STEPS IN BRITAIN

an English peer, and a translator, whose frames of mind echo the spirit of the time.

4.1 A Momentous Gift from Perthes to Crabb Robinson

The first known exemplar of Retzsch's *Umrisse* to reach London was sent in January 1817 to Henry Crabb Robinson, a key mediator for all things German—language, literature, philosophy, and culture—who had built vital acquaintances and friendships over the years.[11] An established fact in scholarship,[12] its multiple implications need unfolding and illuminating. Past slips regarding dates and persons are here amended, since accuracy is crucial.[13]

An avid reader, Robinson features threefold in this preview as renowned intercessor between English- and German-speaking lands, early champion of Goethe's *Faust*, and (neglected) art connoisseur. Already an early advocate of extracts among sceptics, such as Charles Lamb in August 1811, or grudging adherents, such as Coleridge a year later,[14] he read *Faust* in November 1811 with delight and shocked bewilderment.[15] Less than three months after publication in October 1816, Retzsch's outlines as gift from abroad therefore have special weight. Context and the individuals involved surpass the prints' physical relocation. They assert complex instances of Anglo-German exchange, signal social, symbolic and trade rituals, avow cultural interactions, and hint at literary, artistic and aesthetic negotiations.

In his pioneer study, Vaughan somewhat dismissively portrays Robinson's passion for literature as a limitation upon the reception of Retzsch's prints: "he does not appear to have anything to do with gaining them a wider public—his interests lying mainly in the sphere of German literature."[16] This needs to be nuanced. While Retzsch's public circulation clearly depends on Bohte importing his prints, Robinson's mediation may hardly be restrained to literature alone, not least because it elicits a key comment from Flaxman. Once elucidated, data and identities read suggestively.

On 3 January 1817, the set from Friedrich Christoph Perthes is given to Robinson via Johann Martin Lappenberg, a young German known to Walter Scott and much appreciated by William Wordsworth. For the second time in two years, Lappenberg is seeking a position in England, relying on political backers.[17] Seeking local introductions, his first 2 January call on Robinson bears on German political and social news. Robinson invites him to breakfast on the morrow with a third party, his friend Karl (Charles) Aders, an influential German merchant and collector of old Dutch and German masters. His open house would seal numerous cross-cultural exchanges from 1821. No less pointedly, the sender, Perthes, prominent in the German book trade and an old acquaintance from Robinson's second Hamburg trip in 1807, is a representative of the Hanseatic city's intellectual bourgeoisie. His was the first retail bookshop (*Sortimentbuchhandlung*) in the German States, the rallying point of a knowledgeable elite providing him with financial support and influence.[18] Perthes had resisted Napoleonic occupation and sought from 1814 to overcome war penalties.[19] All three individuals meeting around Retzsch's *Umrisse* moved in political and cultural networks of the time.

Presented to Robinson by Lappenberg at the 3 January breakfast, the *Umrisse* conform to social rites, the date underscoring them as a seasonal offering, a New Year's gift. Laden with cultural implication, they stir a discussion on romanticism as Robinson notes: "Aders and Mr L. both belong to the new school of poetry,"[20] a statement implicitly evoking the absent donor, Perthes, patron, past associate and friend of major romantic artist Philipp Otto Runge.[21]

---

11 Eugene L. Stelzig, *Henry Crabb Robinson in Germany: A Study in Nineteenth-Century Life Writing* (Lewisburg, Pa: Bucknell University Press, 2010).

12 Hertha Marquardt, *Henry Crabb Robinson und seine deutschen Freunde: Brücke zwischen England und Deutschland im Zeitalter der Romantik* (Göttingen: Vandenhoeck & Ruprecht, 1967), 2:50; Vaughan, *German Romanticism*, 130 & 280, n. 31–32.

13 The 3 January gift is not from *Mrs* Perthes (Vaughan) but from her husband, the bookseller F. C. Perthes with manifold connotations (see main text). Robinson does not show it to Flaxman either on the 4 (Marquardt) or the 5 (Vaughan) but only the 7 January (MS Diary). In the increased time lapse between reception and discussion with Flaxman it may have been viewed by others.

14 Frederick Norman, *Henry Crabb Robinson and Goethe* (London: Alexander Moring, 1930), 1:66–67.

15 Edith J. Morley, ed., *Henry Crabb Robinson on Books and their Writers* (London: J. M. Dent and Sons, 1938), 1:45, and 1:107–09.

---

16 Vaughan, *German Romanticism*, 130.

17 Marquardt, *Robinson und seine deutschen Freunde*, 2:50, n. 130.

18 Dirk Moldenhauer, *Geschichte als Ware. Der Verleger Friedrich Christoph Perthes (1772–1843) als Wegbereiter der modernen Geschichtsschreibung* (Cologne: Böhlau, 2008), 81, 88–90; Karen Junod, "Crabb Robinson, Blake, and Perthes's *Vaterländisches Museum* (1810–1811)," *European Romantic Review* 23, no. 4 (Apr 2012): 441.

19 Moldenhauer, *Geschichte als Ware*, 269f.

20 HCR, MS D, 3 Jan 1817, 120v.

21 Mary E. Gilbert, "Two Little-Known References to Henry Crabb Robinson," *Modern Language Review* 33, no. 2 (Apr 1938): 269–70; Vaughan, *German Romanticism*, 18.

They are also an engaging tradesman's sample. Perthes's 1816 sales catalogue advertises Retzsch's set for 2 Reichsthaler under "Ueber redende und bildende Künste" ("On Rhetorical and Fine Arts"), a sundry list of twelve, including print assortments by Hogarth, German masters, and plates after the Elgin marbles, all of which heighten its artistic merit. It vanishes from Perthes's register over the next three years, either due to swift success (being no longer available) or Perthes's agreements with Cotta, maybe even trade issues. As token of the bookseller's wares, it carries transactional value. It recalls Robinson's 1814 assistance in London of Johann Heinrich Besser, Perthes's associate, in negotiations with English booksellers for an ambitious plan: promote German and French in schools, found a German reading club, and establish *Deutsche Miscellen*, a newspaper with literary supplement. The project had been conceived to help the Hamburg bookstore overcome the Napoleonic aftermath from abroad while strengthening Anglo-German ties.[22] In an 1814 letter to Perthes, Besser had enthusiastically mentioned a certain *Hans* Lappenberg whose youthful first-rate company had been a comfort amidst his London hardships.[23] This vests Retzsch's set as symbol of past relations, pointedly brought to London by one Lappenberg. It is inconsequential whether Besser had mistaken *Hans* for 20-year-old Johann Martin, present in London in 1814, or was referring to a different Lappenberg, since the family had many Hamburg ties with Perthes. His choice of a Lappenberg[24] to bring to London an item from his catalogue looms large as a thank-you present for past help, perhaps hinting at future ventures.

A closer analysis further illuminates the context. Perthes's pursuits are to be seen within the general framework of a tension "between a European, cosmopolitan Germanic-ness and a much narrower, nationalistic German-ness," considered as "two opposite, yet reconcilable, affiliations,"[25] in a period when "nationalism and cosmopolitanism overlapped."[26] Perthes believed in establishing a fair book trade for booksellers and authors to ground national literature agin undercutting, bootlegging, and censorship. Witness his often referred-to 1816 memorandum, eloquently entitled *Der deutsche Buchhandel als Bedingung des Daseyns einer deutschen Literatur* (*The German Book Trade as a Condition for the Existence of German Literature*). In his intellectual circles, Germany still being a patchwork of small states, provinces, principalities and free cities, literature was deemed a favoured ethnic bond with poets assuming a herald's or emissary's role. Goethe's *Faust* revisited a myth rooted in the anonymous *History of Dr Johann Faust*, printed and published by Johann Spiess in 1587. Its introduction to England through Retzsch surfed on the Flaxmanic model of outlines after major European verse. In the context, Retzsch's designs not only made *Faust* accessible; they promoted Goethe as a major creator. The gift carried national and transnational value, and its graphics had transforming significance.

Like Flaxman's renderings that knew no borders, Retzsch's prints, devoid of captions, convert Goethe's *Faust* into a language that needed no translation. Linear interpretation becomes an early rival to interlingual translation. As pointed out, the set's German preface promotes Retzsch as ingenious *translator*, endorses *Faust* as any man's companion, and compares it to well-known educational narratives of the time. Yet, the Flaxman reference checks and reviews this paradigm, ably transferring *Faust* as text from didactic to poetical canon. Flaxman had rendered major literary texts in internationalised language. In turn, Retzsch's mediating outlines pave the way for Goethe to par with Homer, Aeschylus, Hesiod, and Dante, all re-interpreted by Flaxman.

They also act as inspired poetry visually correlated. In an 1811 article translated for the German public, Robinson had upheld William Blake's art and poetry in Perthes's *Vaterländisches Museum*, a successful Hamburg periodical. As present, Perthes's bond and counter-bond of cultural exchange brings Retzsch's interpretation of *Faust* to Britain via the very same mediator as had sponsored Blake in Germany, bridging visionary poetry and art in a ritual of give and receive. Robinson's brief comment, "Skchethes [*sic*] for Faust—Outlines à la Flaxman a very interesting little work," displays stark aesthetic recognition and instant translation into a "home" style that had spread over Europe. The choice of words pits unimportance (*sketches, little*) against distinction (*Outlines, very interesting*). This rapid judgment and his presentation to Flaxman four days later prove him a competent art evaluator, a skill his much-commented literary or philosophical mediation has left in the dark. It further attracts attention to Retzsch's pictorial, aesthetic and relational worthiness regarding a play of which Robinson was a keen pitcher.

---

22   Clemens Theodor Perthes, *Friedrich Perthes Leben* (Hamburg: F. und A. Perthes, 1855), 2:10f; Marquardt, *Robinson und seine deutschen Freunde*, 2:30–31.

23   Perthes, *Friedrich Perthes Leben*, 2:14.

24   F. C. Perthes later backed J. H. Lappenberg's historical work through his publications (Moldenhauer, *Geschichte als Ware*, 571–74). One of Lappenberg's books would bear on the history of printing in Hamburg (1840).

25   Junod, "Robinson, Blake," 442.

26   Mark Hewitson, "Preface," in *Nationalism versus Cosmopolitanism in German Thought and Culture*, ed. M. A. Perkins and M. Liebscher (Manchester: The Edwin Mellen Press, 2006), III.

FIRST STEPS IN BRITAIN

First to greet Blake's kinsmanship with early German Romantics, Robinson had efficiently noted his capacity to translate and even rival poetic thought. His own art criticism, stressing Blake's use of line and outline, is deemed more poignant than that literary.[27] Perthes's choice of Retzsch may also have targeted his friend's keen perceptiveness, duly appreciated by publishing Robinson's article in his magazine. If such had been the intention, it worked marvellously, given the adjacent diary entries showing Robinson's involvement with art and engravings.

On the evening of 3 January, Robinson briefly calls again on Aders. On the morrow, he takes his friend John D. Collier, editor of the *Monthly Register* he had provided with various articles on German lands, to "see some painting by Albert Durer [sic] purchased by Aders."[28] This would later prove not to be by Dürer, but remarkably first mentions Aders's collection in Robinson's diary. His friend and editor's son, John Payne Collier, would translate into English Schiller's *Fridolin* and *The Fight with the Dragon* with Retzsch outlines copied by Moses in 1824 and 1825. Aders's presence at breakfast the day before related to his numerous social and business connections that could profit Lappenberg, yet ultimately to Goethe's reception in England: in the past Aders had repetitively lent Robinson new editions of Goethe's works.[29] He and Robinson had spent time cross reading to each other British and German poetry, occasionally comparing Goethe's *Faust* "Dedication" to "A Vision" by Burns.[30] No doubt Retzsch's *Umrisse* had granted this relationship a new artistic radiance.

Similarly, Robinson spends the evening of 5 January at the home of topography and architecture specialist John Britton, a book lover and collector, whose substantial library would be later dispersed in four different auctions, each lasting several days.[31] His comment on the party gathered at Britton's (including the poet John Thelwall, the would-be lexicologist Peter Mark Roget, the printer Arthur Taylor, son of John Taylor, the Unitarian hymnist, and several others) symptomatically stresses such exchange in art circles: "And they are enticed by each others [sic] company as well as by a large collection of books of engravings which give the cue to the conversation"—just as Retzsch's set had kindled two days before "a very agreeable [long] conversation" with Lappenberg and Aders.[32]

Retzsch's *Umrisse* will have further been evoked with John Collier, Anthony Robinson, and Isaac Aldebert, German merchant and close friend with whom Crabb Robinson had first crossed over to German lands in 1800, as well as Thomas Edward Amyot who supported Robinson's interest in German literature. Robinson frequently discussed with his friends his diary topics.[33] As Norman put it: "Crabb never read anything without talking about it to somebody."[34]

While the above are deductions not substantiated in Robinson's diary, the connexions surrounding Perthes's gift all point to negotiations in Anglo-German cultural dialogue. Perthes's pregnant choice wins Retzsch's *Faust* as a cultural infant to be adopted within an international community. The graphic rendering of the tragedy assumes rhetorical and translational weight in joining a group of works that revise the frontiers of cultures in dialogue. It sheds light on Robinson not only as mediator within a diverse political, literary and artistic framework, but as connoisseur and collector: he subscribed to Blake's *Job*, owned other Blake works, bought further prints,[35] and kept acquiring such through Aders.[36] In his later friendship with Aders's wife, Eliza, daughter of the London engraver Raphael Smith, he frequently refers to art. He also brings to the Aders' circle not only men of letters but artists and art critics, among whom Flaxman is to become one of the household's regulars. His recording of Flaxman's appreciation of Retzsch on 7 January again stresses Retzsch's value in aesthetic arbitration where three countries meet in comparison:

> I then went to Flaxman whom I had not seen for a long time—I spent a pleasant 2 hours with him I took to him Retsch's Outlines to Gothes Faust[.] F expressed himself well pleased with them. They are the best he has seen since the public[ation] of his Homer. The French have produced nothing of the kind—These are full of merit. But he objected to the [number of the] minuteness of the detail[.] The artist, he says, did not properly underst[an]d the nature of an Outline—Every line should be significant—Instead of a var[iet]y of articles in Faust's study, there sho[ul]d be just a volume or two and a crucible to indicate Faust's [habits] pursuits, but no more.[37]

---

27   Junod, "Robinson, Blake," 440, 446–47.
28   HCR, MS D, 4 Jan 1817, 120r.
29   Marquardt, *Robinson und seine deutschen Freunde*, 2:14.
30   Ibid., 2:22–23, n. 30.
31   The last auction catalogue of Britton's library shows that he owned the third edition of Retzsch's parody by Crowquill (1835). Unfortunately not all the catalogues are available.
32   HCR, MS D, 6 Jan 1817, 121v, and 3 Jan 1817, 120v.

---

33   Marquardt, *Robinson und seine deutschen Freunde*, 2:14, n. 3.
34   Norman, *Robinson and Goethe*, 1:67.
35   Gerald Eades Bentley, *Blake Records*, 2nd ed. (New Haven: Yale University Press, 2004), 785–86, 431n.
36   Marquardt, *Robinson und seine deutschen Freunde*, 2:44, 46.
37   HCR, MS D, 7 Jan 1817, 121r–122v.

That Flaxman compare the *Umrissse* to his own first out-lines heralds a successful start for Retzsch, a newcomer in the very art form to which Flaxman owed his European fame. His censure insists on pure outline, minimal vocabulary and simplification—the ideal and symbolic permanence that helped to shape a new world born from ruins, "rejection of illusionistic Baroque traditions," and preference for "wilful two-dimensionality."[38] Retzsch's *Umrisse* challenge this model of timeless Greek art through Renaissance abundance. The advent of consumer profusion was furthermore on the industrial horizon. Retzsch's accumulation of objects in Faust's study was the deliberate translation of the doctor's initial monologue, his fruitless review of many sciences. The heap of objects and spirited details exemplify Retzsch's capacity to adapt a celebrated art form to interpreting a different poet, his very contemporary. In fact, the elements Flaxman reproaches in Retzsch are the ones that pleased Goethe, as reflected in his repetitive use of *geistreich* to qualify the *Umrisse*.

In a nutshell, the *Umrisse*'s British debarkation, three months after publication, already reads as a multifarious cultural adventure as Retzsch plays absent host to commercial hopes and literary trends, humours an intricate representational agenda, and stirs aesthetic debate. Once in public circulation, several such considerations will come to the fore.

4.2 Imported Wares and Motley Exemplars

Retzsch's introduction to England by German bookseller Johann Heinrich Bohte has been precisely dated, and assigned not only a year, but a month: January 1820.[39] Although no reason is given, this dating presumably relied on English letterpress imprints and the February 1820 *London Magazine* article that brought Retzsch to public attention. Bohte's item and catalogues reveal however a different story, and this should come as no surprise. What we deal with here is neither fish nor fowl, neither wholly German nor entirely English, neither just text nor individual prints, but a crossbreed, in which two countries, two imprints, two typographies, and two media mingle.

As described, the original German portfolio was a buff or yellow wallet-like wrapper with green flaps holding:

a) a 12-page letterpress booklet composed of title-page, preface, and 26 *Faust* excerpts, and b) 26 etchings without imprints or letterpress, strung and numbered 1–26 in upper right-hand corners (cf. Fig. 2.1a–b). Bohte's item is an additional 8 pages of letterpress, printed in London by his regular printer Gottlieb Schulze and dated 1820. This offers in English a title-page, a single page preface, and a different selection of excerpts, translated by George Soane. The imported German portfolio contents, either complete (booklet and etchings) or in parts (only etchings), combine(s) with the 8-page Bohte letterpress in diverse ways as shown *infra*. Some German contents may *pre-date* the English letterpress. Whatever the combination, it would be misleading to speak of "a Bohte edition,"[40] since the outcome mutates.

Bohte's extant catalogues, offering the original German set, precede the English letterpress by one year. The 1816 issue does not include it, and regrettably those of 1817 or 1818 only offer German editions of Greek and Latin authors. As noted, from 1819 to 1821, they advertise "J. Retsch" [*sic*]: the initial is doubtless a misprint yet the name mirrors the German title's misspelling. In "*Umrisse zu Goethes Faust in 26 Blättern*, 4to, Tübingen 1818 (12 shillings)," the "quarto" may indicate plates with margins larger than in the 1816 edition, sometimes used in the subsequent combinations. Both Odenkirchen and Hauhart, along with two English periodicals, record a "Tübingen 1818" edition, while none of the surviving exemplars match such an imprint. If only for these data, Bohte clearly started importing the German folder earlier than January 1820.

Extant exemplars further extend the time span. They are generally catalogued under the short English title, *Extracts from Göthe's Tragedy of Faustus*, yet seven of them, collated and compared, deliver dissimilar importation scenarios.[41] While paired for certain characteristics, no two read identically throughout, which makes every one unique in its own version. Two of them are based on the original 1816 Cotta set (Grenville and Elmer L. Andersen Library) with added 1820 English letterpress. In another two, there is no German letterpress: the 1820 English text accompanies the German etchings only. However, in one of them, English text and German prints sit in the originally devised German portfolio, complete with title ticket in German but without flaps (Leonard L. Mackall exemplar). Four out of the seven, including Goethe's own, mostly

---

38 Rosenblum, *Transformations in Late Eighteenth Century Art*, 182, 162–64.

39 Frederick Burwick and James C. McKusick, eds., *Faustus: From the German of Goethe, Translated by Samuel Taylor Coleridge* (Oxford: Clarendon Press, 2007), XI; Burwick, "On Coleridge as Translator of *Faustus* from the German of Goethe," *European Romantic Review* 19, no. 3 (July 2008): 250.

40 Graham Jefcoate, *An Ocean of Literature: John Henry Bohte and the Anglo-German Book Trade in the Early Nineteenth Century* (Hildesheim: Olms, 2020), 309, 387–89; Burwick and McKusick, *Faustus*, XIX, 142.

41 See references in Appendix 1, under no. 2.

combine (in order) German letterpress/English letterpress/German etchings, but may vary: English letterpress/etchings/German letterpress (Elmer L. Andersen Library). In one of them, the etchings still feature in blue flysheets, used by Bohte at the time to protect printed matter, due for binding.[42] In another, the blue pastedown of the binding may be a faded version of such flysheets. In a third, all contents sit in the original German portfolio. Most seem based on etchings with wide margins, with the English letterpress printed to match. However, the presence of bindings, trimmed and inlaid pages oblige us to postulate rather than assert. The hybrid upshot, half German, half English, is the first in a long series of conversions and metamorphoses of the initial artefact.

Without further turning the above into a dry list of material particularities, a few importation scenarios may be construed, without forgetting that, whatever the material evidence, all items are now more than two hundred years old. Some of them have been through several lives and random readers' hands. However, importation to England possibly started straight after the original October 1816 publication. Bohte was the most resourceful German bookseller in London, also dealing in illustrated books, prints, maps, and music. In the London reading room (*Deutsche Lesebibliothek*) he founded 1814, German books and periodicals were available on an annual subscription. He further offered to take on any request for books, music, copper prints or maps, also issued in Holland, Sweden and Denmark.[43] From 1814, he was regularly present at Leipzig's Easter book fair, where he kept a representative, and had been appointed in 1819 "Foreign Bookseller to George III."[44] No lesser man than August Wilhelm Schlegel considered his untimely death in 1824 "a real loss to the literary commerce of the two countries."[45] In his obituary, Schlegel also stressed the levy of "duty on the introduction of foreign thoughts, which ought to be free as light and air," which burden represented import taxes to England and the commercial risk for booksellers who could not return imported books to the Continent without heavy losses.[46] The *London Magazine* campaign of 1820 (see below) confirms that Retzsch's *Umrisse* were

imported in batches, some of them "bespoke." Target publics must have included print collectors, continental expats (which included the royal Hanoverian dynasty), and German literature enthusiasts, whether proficient or not in the language. Thomas Grenville was one of the latter: not linguistically competent, he could probably make out words.

However, the German item was not only imported, but added to, thanks to the 1820 English letterpress especially devised for the English reader. It could be offered in the original wrapper; or without it, in provisional sheets; the etchings and letterpress might derive from either the 1816 or the 1820 edition, depending on imports and stock availability. Binders' mediations (some of them telling, as we will see) treated it variously: in the original portfolio or not, with the German letterpress or not, the etchings preceding or following. In all these variants, the English letterpress and German prints are the two staple (yet incomplete) elements. When complete, particularities are telling. Goethe's exemplar, from the poet's personal library, a full set based on the 1820 Cotta edition, results from careful handling. With German parts occasionally foxed and wrapper remounted and reinforced, it is the work of a binder who adjoined *separate* items. The English letterpress in nearly prime condition was previously *folded in four* (with creases still visible, yet ironed out in the digitised version). Indeed, it had been sent to Goethe from London on 28 January 1820 by Hüttner, who explicitly wrote: "The enclosed printed sheet is presented by J. H. Bohte" (*Inliegendes gedrucktes Blatt überreiche J. H. Bohte*).[47] It then joined other 1820 parts whose German provenance cannot be fathomed.[48] In brief, each exemplar represents *one* instance only. None should screen, disguise or distort the *plasticity* and *intermediality* of the intermingled and bilingual assortments at hand. Conclusively, there was no "Bohte edition,"[49] but eight pages printed by Schulze and variously added to the German imports.

All this portrays Bohte as an early dynamo, gifted in marketing wares for various audiences, albeit behind the scenes. "It was due to Bohte's propaganda" that Retzsch "was to become the best-selling German artist in England," notes Vaughan.[50] Further broadcasting would follow from press columns and Wainewright's playful pen, both boosted by Bohte.

---

42 For instance, Edmund Henry Barker, *Aristarchus Anti-Blomfieldianus* [...] *Translated from the German* (London: Printed for J. H. Bohte, 1820), still in its original blue flysheets. BL: 12923.dd.16.(2.).

43 Bohte, *Verzeichniss deutscher Bücher welche um beygesetzten Preisen zu haben* (London: Gedruckt bey G. Schulze & J. Dean, 1814), announcement.

44 Patrick Bridgwater, *De Quincey's Gothic Masquerade* (Amsterdam: Rodopi, 2004), 39.

45 Schlegel, "Vorrede"/"Introduction," in J. H. Bohte, *Handbibliothek der deutschen Litteratur* (London: G. Schulze, 1825), XXI.

46 Ibid., XXIII.

---

47 GSA 28/434, 30.

48 The original 1816 *Umrisse* are not in Goethe's library.

49 Jefcoate's description (*Ocean of Literature*, 388) of the Cambridge exemplar as "an 'enhanced' state" with Bohte's printed label on the cover hardly corresponds to the item, an original German portfolio with Cotta's label.

50 Vaughan, *German Romanticism*, 26.

4.3 Media Coverage and Publicity (A Mediated Launch)

The *London Magazine*, most literary of all urban journals, and favourable to the Romantics and foreign literature,[51] was the main contemporary vehicle of the pro-Retzsch lobby, thanks to the buoyancy of its fine arts columnist Janus Weathercock. His backer, the editor John Scott, had rooms at the rear of Bohte's bookshop, 4 York Street, Covent Garden, in 1820–21.[52] The pseudonym is one of the spirited disguises of Thomas Griffiths Wainewright, writer, painter, forger, and alleged future poisoner of several members of his family to inherit funds and settle debts, yet "one of the first critics to praise Goethe's *Faust* in England."[53] Wainewright, twenty-six in 1820, had been raised by his maternal grandfather, Ralph Griffiths, founding editor of the *Monthly Magazine*. He knew the power of the printed word, ostensible in his pen name.[54] Indeed, what better tutor for a multifaceted import than Janus? Guardian of doors and thresholds like the Roman deity, revolving and pirouetting to the news, Weathercock follows the wind as he senses novelty. He is the man who launches Retzsch in London. Four vibrant pages, his second piece in the *London Magazine*, bear entirely on Retzsch. He does even more: from one issue of the periodical to the next and from February to September 1820, he forges the object's desirability as he stirs up and sensationalizes the fashion.

To start with (February 1820), he urges art devotees to acquire the portfolio by using persuasion, rebuke, and even disdain, as any able manipulator of buyers' psychology might do.[55] In June, he feigns dejection: his article has had no effect, and art lovers' inept choices of prints make him despair. Fortunately, Bohte appears to whisper in his ear a figure, the number of sets sold, and reassures him: he has just ordered more from abroad. A handful of asterisks and dots veils their dialogue as the (possibly genuine) incident is evoked. Nothing arouses curiosity

better than hush-hush exchange, and Janus knows it too well.[56] In July, the editor, John Scott, lends a hand: in his opening column, "The Lion's Head," a long note confirms "a large sale," triggered by the cognizant view of the penetrating Janus, and announces a new arrival of sets from the Continent.[57] In passing, Scott reports on a future *Faust* translation and drops the name of Coleridge. The August number devotes an anonymous, extensive and knowledgeable article to *Faust*. Known to be by Rev. George Croly,[58] it is an important weapon wielded in the periodical's strategy of initiating the public to an arduous play,[59] an operation launched under the aegis of Retzsch's images. The August issue reached Weimar and is still part of Goethe's library, preserved with an autograph inscription by Bohte.[60] In September, Weathercock hammers it in: a hundred German sets have just passed customs and will be envied since sixty are already "bespoke," further praising Retzsch.[61] Over eight months, this effective ploy spurs collectors and galvanizes potential readers. Indeed, since June 1820, Retzsch (and Bohte) have a genuine rival in the market place, the English copyist Henry Moses working for publishers Boosey and associates. Bohte's wares need upholding. Weathercock however is a skilled strategist. In Retzsch, he defends a thoroughbred, an unadulterated original with charm and charisma, worthy of the fray.

Are the figures he announces correct? If reliable, the imported German items would range *c.*400 between February and September 1820—which explains the frequent use of German 1820 editions in the seven hybrid assemblages previously discussed. The English vogue must have absorbed a substantial number, and Cotta surely profited from orders from abroad. Yet importation surely started earlier. Bohte had met Johann Friedrich Cotta at the 1814 Leipzig fair and they were closely connected: Cotta had even sent his son to London as booktrade understudy with Bohte.[62] The English assemblage was not cheap. The price given by Weathercock, twelve shillings sixpence (12s 6d), equaled four days' wages for a skilled worker. Higher than the one mentioned in Bohte's sales catalogues between 1819 and 1821 (12s), it priced the English letterpress at an additional sixpence. But Janus knew advertising and was a dab hand at marketing.

---

51   Josephine Bauer, *The London Magazine, 1820–29* (Copenhagen: Rosenkilde and Bagger, 1953), 153–76, 332–34.

52   Patrick O'Leary, *Regency Editor: Life of John Scott* (Aberdeen: Aberdeen University Press, 1983), 125; Jefcoate, *An Ocean of Literature*, 147.

53   Bauer, 167–74; *ODNB* online, s.v. "Wainewright, Thomas Griffiths" (by Annette Peach), accessed 3 Jan 2020; Andrew Motion, *Wainewright the Poisoner* (London: Faber and Faber, 2000), 79. On Wainewright's dire reputation challenged by Motion, see Ian H. Magedera, *Outsider Biographies* (Amsterdam: Rodopi, 2014), 115–19, 121–49.

54   Joanna Gilmour, *Elegance in Exile. Portrait Drawings from Colonial Australia* (Canberra: National Portrait Gallery, 2012), 153–54.

55   Weathercock, "Sentimentalities on the Fine Arts (To be Continued when He Is in the Humour) No. 1," *LM* 1, no. 2 (Feb 1820): 136–40.

56   Weathercock, "Janus's Jumble: Enterlaced with Hys Iourney to Town, etc.," *LM* 1, no. 6 (June 1820): 629.

57   "The Lion's Head," *LM* 2, no. 7 (July 1820): 6.

58   Bauer, 288–90.

59   "Goethe and his Faustus," *LM* 2, no. 8 (Aug 1820): 125–42.

60   HAAB: Ruppert 371(1).

61   Weathercock, "Mr. Weathercock's Private Correspondence, Intended for the Public Eye," *LM* 2, no. 9 (Sept 1820): 229[*sic* for 299]–301.

62   Jefcoate, *Ocean of Literature*, 91, 226.

Did he also know German? Had he read *Faust*? His first chronicle (Feb 1820) provides a narrative connecting the plates. His quirky explanations vie for highest ranking: in pl. 2, when the poodle appears, Wagner does not see it, and Faust rants away. Blanks are filled: Margaret's mother falls ill; her son's death, her daughter's pregnancy, and the administered potion finish her off—pathos at its peak. Two visits by Mephistopheles are merged into one. In the witch's kitchen, the monkeys' parody of power and the devil's ironic comments become Faust the philosopher's contempt for crowns and jewels. Faust raising the drapes of Margaret's bed is daringly interpreted: "he sits, in one of the finest attitudes invented, contemplating his sleeping mistress." It hardly matters that Faust's darling is absent, or that love is not yet consumed, Weathercock would have the inner eye imagine intercourse. Such lapses are common at the table of cultural negotiation. But it is another matter altogether when the play's finale is altered. In Janus's comment, the wager between Faust and Mephistopheles, crucial to Goethe's *Faust*, disappears in favour of a pact the doctor signs with his blood; Margaret's complexity (in the cathedral scene) is reduced to fleshly sin alone; her tale-telling neighbour reveals she killed her child, she is inculpated and imprisoned. Cause and stunning effect are plausible, such scenes apt to attract clients to Bohte. Besides, Janus's readers likely knew Christopher Marlowe's *Dr Faustus*, ending in bleak damnation.

Although increasingly discussed by July 1820, Goethe's *Faust* remained "very imperfectly known" in Britain.[63] Non-Germanophone collectors and readers required to be accompanied in their discovery of Retzsch. The English letterpress was meant for them, a few companion pages entrusted to the younger disinherited son of the prestigious establishment architect Sir John Soane, who had fallen out with his parents to find himself deeply in debt. The English appropriation of Retzsch's *Umrisse* begins with George Soane's comments.

4.4   A First English Point of View (George Soane's Letterpress)

Despite limited page length, Soane's English letterpress is rich in significance. The long title, *Extracts from Göthe's Tragedy of Faustus, Explanatory of the Plates, by Retsch, Intended to Illustrate That Work; Translated by George Soane*, bears a special touch. It weds three concepts (explanation, illustration, translation) distributed between texts and images, which make roles spin. All three apply to the imported prints, which explain, illustrate and translate

the play in another medium, but also to Soane's use of text. The preface displays modesty ("The Translator neither seeks nor deserves credit; his task has been a simple one") but the capitalized Translator implies professional authority or rank, perhaps a desire to set the rules. The item has intermedial importance. Its appeal is shaped in-between, each cog borrowing something from the next and gearing it. The idea that the etchings urge and steer an English translation suggests itself by implication. The latter would soon come to be in more extensive versions. Still, the short letterpress already reveals an eloquent stance.

An independent nature, rebuffed by his talented father, and rejected by his peers, George Soane had enrolled 1806 in Cambridge and earned a BA from Pembroke College in 1811. He wed soon afterwards the daughter of a playwright against paternal wishes (thwarting Sir John's plans), and turned to writing novels and sensational melodramas. Two scathing anonymous 1815 articles on Sir John caused a family rupture.[64] His own genius being overshadowed by his father's omnipotence, George has occasionally been assimilated, by dint of his thinking and mores (he served a prison sentence for debt and fraud and had an adulterous relationship with his wife's sister), to the libertine of *The Rake's Progress*, the Hogarth series Soane father famously owned. Yet, he knew German, French and Italian well, and the 8-page English letterpress, his first treatment of Goethe's *Faust*, proves him a smart commentaror. He firmly shortens the German extracts, chooses otherwise, handles and pilots the prints towards a different meaning. He also introduces the quotes by italicized prods as in stage directions or a nascent summary. All this reads as the chart of a play he knows well, all the while asserting its originality in his one-page preface. In a total of just five pages, his rendition reads as a feat.

Goethe's originality lies in his demon, he notes with reason in the "Preface": *exit* Marlowe's despicable devil or Milton's fallen angel. Not only does the demon take on human looks, he is interiorised, dwells moreover within the mind: "doubt is the very essence of his being." Although elaborating on Huber's idea of Faust and demon as being one, this remarkably heralds later psychoanalysis and Carl Gustav Jung's writings. In the lines chosen, Soane seems to favour Mephistopheles or Margaret, whose sayings are shorter and more fervent. Prints likely to upset the English reader are cautiously treated: in Heaven (pl. 1), Soane's deity speaks (contrariwise, in the German excerpt,

---

63   "The Lion's Head," 7.

64   Gillian Darley, *John Soane: An Accidental Romantic* (New Haven: Yale University Press, 1999), 234–36; ODNB online, s.v. "Soane, George" (by Emma Plaskitt), accessed 4 Jan 2020; Burwick and McKusick, eds., *Faustus*, 141–44.

sharply adressed by the devil, God is silent); apropos the raised bed hangings (pl. 10), Faust refers only to the ancestral armchair. Conversely, the dying Valentine (pl. 20) no longer addresses the crowd, as in the German, but covers his sister with shame. Melodrama lies in wait. The wager is not explicited, and the agreement reads suspiciouly like a pact ("Mephistopheles binds himself to serve Faustus on earth on condition that Faustus makes over to him his soul"). However, it is no longer the demon asking for a signature, as in the German excerpt, but Faust protesting: "Is it not enough that my given word disposes of my eternal life?" Any other choice would prove difficult, as Retzsch's etching sets a sheet of paper at the centre (cf. Fig. 2.21). Last, but not least, tension between salvation and damnation hovers over the finale as in Goethe, despite the closing stage direction "The Demon carries off Faustus"— inevitably evoking Marlowe for an English audience.

Soane's introduction of Goethe's *Faust* to Great Britain would not end there. He is contentiously credited with authoring the rival "Analysis," published by Thomas Boosey and partners six months later to accompany Moses's copy of Retzsch's etchings, but the anonymous text proves rather by Daniel Boileau.[65] By contrast, Soane authored a far more accomplished piece of work, a partial translation of Goethe's *Faust* in verse. Pursuing Retzsch's promotion in rivalry with Boosey, who had joined the running in the meantime, Bohte planned a bilingual *Faust*, interleaving Retzsch's etchings, and commissioned no other than George Soane to provide the English translation. The *London Magazine* publicized the event.[66] In December 1821, Janus Weathercock mulled over thirty-two pages in proofs: "Ah! this is a very good idea, the inserting of the original on one side in oblong quarto so as to bind with the genuine etchings."[67] In frisky style, he pictured to himself in London the imagined words of Goethe's enthusiastic praise in Weimar. Fiction had merged with fact: the information is first-hand and comes from Bohte—as probably does Weathercock's much improved knowledge of *Faust* itself in this article. An extract of Soane's translation would indeed reach Weimar early 1822, since Bohte, due at the Leipzig fair, would himself bring the galley proofs, paginated 3–32. They are still part of Goethe's library,[68] and correspond to the pages Weathercock (supposedly) pored over, just as Goethe himself must have done. In twin columns and two typesets, Gothic for German, Antiqua for English, it fits three landscape quires, probably by Bohte's

printer Schulze, precisely dimensioned to lodge the 1820 Cotta etchings by Retzsch. It comprises the "Dedication" (published in English by Goethe in *Über Kunst und Altertum* the following year), the "Prelude on the Stage," "Prologue in Heaven," and Faust's first night monologue down to line 576. By June 1822 Goethe would applaud Soane's translation.[69]

The ingenious idea never materialized: Soane's private difficulties and Bohte's death put an end to the projected bilingual-cum-etchings edition.[70] Yet, some clever hand did the same with correspondingly inverse material, as previously shown: Moses's copied engravings mounted with the 1816 German pocket *Faust* (cf. Fig. 3.18). As for Soane, he co-authored (with actor Daniel Terry) *Faustus: A Romantic Drama*, also known as *The Devil and Dr Faustus*, the very melodrama that would impress Delacroix at Drury Lane in 1825 and set off his own lithographic interpretation of *Faust*. In a way, George Soane's bustling *Faust* activity, starting with the introduction to Retzsch's prints, matched his work for the theatre. The 1820 title-page of the English letterpress accumulated accreditations, begging for recognition (and income): "by George Soane, A. B., Author of 'The Innkeeper's Daughter'—'Falls of Clyde'—'The Bohemians,' &c. &c. &c." Retzsch's first steps in the UK had met with colourful individuals, to say the least.

4.5 Books as Cultural Objects: Readers and Cultural Representation

At least two of the above seven hybrid exemplars further read as cultural objects. The individuals behind them, a renowned bibliophile and a bookbinder, bestow on them special worth. Although by common standards such identifications are marketable, I do not refer to monetary value. More significantly, a name, whether of purchaser or craftsman, gives any book identity and context. It also brings together not so much owner with prized object as person with medium.

Among such, Thomas Grenville (1755–1846) is salient. The second son of Prime Minister George Grenville, he was an important diplomat, whose career took him to France (where he notably danced with Marie-Antoinette) and Germany (whose language he did not speak). Well read in classical authors, he spoke Latin, and established a Greek

---

65   Burwick and McKusick, *Faustus*, 177–78.
66   "Works Preparing for Publication," *LM* 3, no. 5 (May 1821): 578.
67   Weathercock, "C. Van Vinkbooms, his Dogmas for Dilettanti, No III," *LM* 4, no. 24 (Dec 1821): 657.
68   HAAB: Ruppert 1916.

69   WA 4, 36:61.
70   Leonard L. Mackall, "Soane's *Faust* Translation, Now First Published, from the Unique Advance Sheets Sent to Goethe in 1822," *Archiv für das Studium der neueren Sprachen und Literaturen* 112, no. 3–4 (1904): 277–97; Burwick and McKusick, eds., *Faustus*, 143–44.

edition of Homer. He had put together "one of the largest single collections of beautiful specimens of printing and binding," now in the British Library, of which he was a trustee.[71] His exemplar, part of the prestigious legacy, is kept today in the glass tower housing the King's Library. It has an elegant unsigned binding with no features designed to flaunt wealth or status. Like others in his collection, it bears centrally his discreet coat of arms on both covers and inside the front cover, with a gilt double-line frame. All edges of the text block are also gilded, a commonplace refinement, his priorities being stability and usability.[72]

Several hallmarks of this first cultural object are to be noted: first, Retzsch's *Umrisse* had joined a prestigious gentleman's collection, whose library was dominated by Greek, Latin, and high-status texts (manuscripts, First Folio Shakespeare, editions of historical value). The item does not belong to its most extensive sections (French, Italian and Spanish books) but to a mixed "foreign" category ranging from Arabic to Japanese, Romansh to Russian.[73] Second, this is the earliest example I know of the original 1816 German contents with the 1820 Bohte letterpress belonging to an Englishman. Grenville presumably acquired them in London: by 1816 he had stopped travelling abroad and was leading a scholarly life around his collection. He was frequently advised on acquisitions to make and may have been one of "the circle of English Literati" "with whom [Bohte] was on terms of friendship," as mentioned in the latter's obituary.[74] The 1816 Cotta part in Grenville's book, ostensibly one of the first imported by Bohte, relates to the rarities favoured by Grenville. Third, Retzsch's admittance to the collection may be explained by Grenville's interest in the Faust figure,[75] but also signals growing curiosity for Goethe's work and Retzsch's prints. Fourth, the exemplar's structure and internal organization are intriguing: Retzsch's *Faust* is bound with Carl Friedrich Schultze's 1818 outlines after *Undine* by La Motte Fouqué.[76]

Grenville was a demanding bibliophile: he collated his possessions, had them washed, and asked binders to restore shortcomings and deficiencies.[77] In this certainly post-1820 binding, pages have been carefully inlaid and/ or remounted but the result is perplexing. Instead of choosing a landscape format, and ordering materials in sequence (as in all other hybrid cases), the quarto chosen is higher than it is wide (24 × 19.2 cm). Landscape and portrait formats alternate. For full perusal, the exemplar must be pivoted. Surprisingly, the English letterpress and all *Faust* and *Undine* plates are to be viewed swivelling the book, which stresses, if nothing else, the amalgamated and intermedial nature of its parts. Its three components (1816 *Faust Umrisse* with German letterpress brochure, Bohte's English letterpress, and Schultze's *Undine*) may have baffled the anonymous binder. Conversely, the decision to have *Faust* and *Undine* bound together was almost certainly Grenville's. It bonded two works from analogous literary stock, of same trend (romanticism), atmosphere (supernatural), and aesthetic (outlines). A poetical visual interpretation of *Faust* had met *Undine*, a literary fairy tale (*Kunstmärchen*) also in favour.

George Soane (who had freely translated *Undine* in 1818 and would adapt it for the English stage in 1821) and the *London Magazine* (in which Weathercock had also referred to Schultze's outlines[78]) also connected the two. Again in December 1826, the two outline works would be associated by Thomas De Quincey in *Blackwood's Magazine*: Fouqué's *Undine* "has been a good deal read, chiefly in connexion with the Outline Illustrations of it, in the manner of those which accompanied the Faust of Goethe."[79] Interest in outline rendering of literary works met a growing awareness of modern German literature. Last, but not least, Grenville's library was semi-public, "accessible to friends, family, scholars, and fellow collectors, but also to relative strangers," either at his premises or by lending his books out, as his correspondence reflects.[80] His *Faust*-cum-*Undine* was not only a covetable item but also a volume probably seen and perused by others, including aristocracy.

A sumptuous binding comes second. A ticket and address show this object to be the work, from his 1821 London beginnings, of Charles Murton.[81] Contrary to Grenville's anonymous binder's quaint arrangement, Murton has inlaid the German and English letterpress, followed

---

71 Karen Limper-Herz, "A Monument of the Love of Letters: The Right Honourable Thomas Grenville and his Library" (PhD diss., University College London, 2012), 11.

72 Ibid., 111–13.

73 Barry Taylor, "Thomas Grenville (1755–1846) and His Books," in *Libraries within the Library: The Origins of the British Library's Printed Collections*, ed. G. Mandelbrote and B. Taylor (London: The British Library, 2009), 321–24.

74 "Mr J. H. Bohte," *Gentleman's Magazine* (Oct 1824): 379.

75 Grenville owned an English translation of the anonymous German *History of Dr Faust* by P. F. Gent (1608) and *The History of Dr John Faustus*, a rhymed English version (1696).

76 *Undine von de la Motte Fouqué, componirt von C. F. Schultze* (Nürnberg: Friedrich Campe, n.d. [1818]).

77 Taylor, "Grenville and His Books," 324.

78 "C. Van Vinkbooms, His Dogmas for Dilettanti, no. II. Giulio Romano," *LM* 4, no. 22 (Oct 1821): 420.

79 "Gillies's German Stories," in *The Works of Thomas De Quincey*, ed. D. Groves and G. Lindop (London: Pickering & Chatto, 2000), 6:15n.

80 Limper-Herz, "Grenville and his Library," 100–03.

81 Charles Ramsden, *London Bookbinders, 1780–1840* (London: B. T. Batsford, 1956), 109.

FIGURE 4.1 Charles Murton, black calf binding with rich gilt decorations showing Faust in his study with the poodle. The bound volume coalesces *Extracts from Göthe's Tragedy of Faustus, Explanatory of the Plates, by Retsch, Intended to Illustrate that Work. Translated by George Soane* (London: Printed for J. H. Bohte, 1820) and *Umrisse zu Goethe's Faust, gezeichnet von Retsch* (Stuttgart & Tübingen: Cotta, 1820). Pages inlaid to create a uniform objet
COURTESY BEINECKE, YALE UNIVERSITY, SPECK CK99 R3 +820B

by the prints, with regard to easy viewing: the reader turns from text to plates (protected by added tissue paper) or vice-versa, and may compare them at leisure. Such manifest extra care favours a particular reading of *Faust*.

Although Murton rather specialised in blind stamping, the polished black calf binding is bedecked on both sides with a large block showing Faust in his study (Fig. 4.1). The lavish aesthetic suggests a particular responsiveness to a play that lends itself to neo-Gothic interpretation, since Faust's monologue opens in "a highly-vaulted, narrow Gothic room" (*In einem hochgewölbten, engen gotischen Zimmer*). Dormant tomes of knowledge sum up the doctor's misery and desolation. The binding instead glorifies Goethe's work, along with its interpretation by Retzsch. The central scene, elaborate and detailed, is enhanced by an impressive frame richly decorated in arabesque (2.1 cm in width), festooned by blind tooling, four corner flowerets, and turn-ins also gilt, obviously for a library of standing.

A library is indeed the theme of the central composition, Faust translating into German the beginning of John's Gospel. The scene corresponds to Faust's four versions of the line "In the beginning was the Word," the poodle's growing turmoil, its transformation, and the exorcism, culminating with Mephistopheles appearing in the doctor's study (F 1220f). The dog, crouched sphinx-like at Faust's feet and lifting its head towards him, supports such a reading. On an item *translating* the text into etchings (Retzsch), and in which a few German lines are also translated into English (Soane), the impressive decoration creatively couples the elaborate binding with contents. It is also styled on an illustrious model, Albrecht Dürer's masterly engraving *Saint Jerome in his Study* (1514), translating the Bible into Latin, lion crouched before him

FIGURE 4.2 Albrecht Dürer, *Saint Jerome in his Study*, 1514, engraving, 24.6 × 18.7 cm
BnF Est., RÉSERVE CA-4 (+, 4)-BOÎTE ECU, PARIS

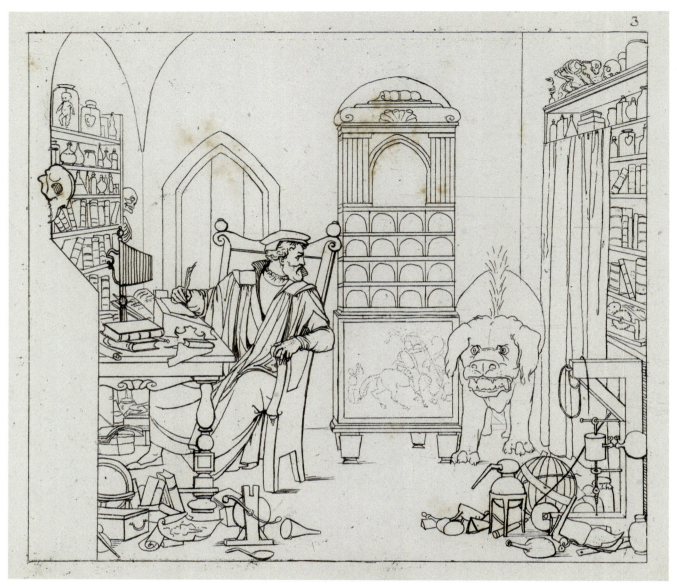

FIGURE 4.3 Moritz Retzsch, Faust's study with the poodle monstrously growing, *Umrisse zu Goethe's Faust gezeichnet von Retsch* (Stuttgart & Tübingen: Cotta, 1816), pl. 3
COURTESY HAAB, F 3487, WEIMAR

(cf. Fig. 4.2). The prestigious precedent clarifies the cultural depth and daring of Goethe's conception, while the binder's composition suggests by opposition the agitation and havoc of the devil's intrusion as counter-model to Saint Jerome, the Christian scholar, peacefully translating Scripture at his desk, his lion subdued in the foreground. Retzsch's plate 3 shows the devil, a hybrid swelling canine monster by the stove, on which Saint George kills the dragon in dotted outline (Fig. 4.3). Murton's arrangement, perhaps simply made to order, reveals a bold understanding of *Faust* beyond the binder's usual task. It explicits cultural transfer and develops a tension oscillating between good and evil. Costly in execution and exceptional in conception, the device will not be lost. "Such a block would have been expensive to make, Murton may well have produced a number of these bindings, although we have not traced any other example," notes expert Peter Harrington on his bookselling website apropos the 1821 *Faustus from the German of Goethe*, decked with the same block in a much simpler frame.[82] The binding block on the hybrid Retzsch exemplar is not only another example, but also earlier, and has indeed been used several times.[83]

82 https://www.peterharrington.co.uk/faustus-from-the-german-134583.html (last accessed 1 Mar 2023).
83 See pp. 146–47, 173, 359–60.

4.6 Dibdin in Action

By including a "gossiping epistle" in his *Bibliographical, Antiquarian and Picturesque Tour in France and Germany*, Thomas Frognall Dibdin offers another arresting example of the uses made of Retzsch's original. In characteristically demonstrative and inflated manner, the episode unfolds in Cotta's own Stuttgart bookshop.[84] The date (4 August 1818) makes of Dibdin an early patron of Retzsch, tailing Crabb Robinson by twenty months. He dates Retzsch as "published about eighteen months ago" but is notorious for inaccuracy. He predicts the etchings' future success, remark which may have been added since his book only came out in spring 1821. By then, Henry Moses's copies, proudly cited in a lengthy footnote by Dibdin, had already been issued (June and July 1820) and successfully re-included in a second edition, titled *Faustus* (1821), as the next chapter shows in detail. While Dibdin's letters are written *en voyage*, the notes are said to follow his return, which would explain the case. However, even if the foresight had been fostered in hindsight, the traveller's perception of the tragedy is revealing of period mindsets while the boundaries of bibliophilia suddenly shift.

Unlike Robinson, convinced of its poetry and originality, Dibdin sees in *Faust* an incomplete "dramatic fragment." It is unclear whether his limited "analysis" builds on the tragedy, the German letterpress (or Boosey's homonymous "Analysis" published in the meantime!), but it certainly banked on unnamed help, since he read no German. Dibdin characteristically omits the Prologue in Heaven and the weary scholar's soliloquies, overlooks all disturbing facets (intercourse, childbirth, infanticide, unintended matricide, and witches' Sabbath), and turns *Faust* into a sentimental drama that ensnares the protagonist and dooms Margaret. Philosophical concerns and the wager have vanished: Faust is oddly cast as "a young, virtuous, and hard-fagging student," whose intense curiosity is abused by Mephistopheles, the cunning demon common to both his and Margaret's ruin. Dibdin's reading is symptomatic of his failure to fully take in the questions at stake. His patent pathos pities the pure: Margaret is his heroine. Even so, the sketchy plot is "purposely made […] subservient to the decorations," that is, the outlines. Retzsch carries the day as standards move.

Anxious to inform, impress and charm antiquarians and bibliophiles, Dibdin presents his visit to Cotta's bookshop as impromptu while awaiting consent from Stuttgart's chief librarian to peruse local antiquarian rarities. Out of kilter with his usual haunts and preoccupations, Cotta's is "a house of business, for the sale of common and useful publications," "the Longman and Co. of this part of the world." True to his passion, even at Cotta's modern premises, Dibdin asks for "M. Engelhardt's projected work." This refers to an acclaimed opus, Christian Moritz Engelhardt's pioneering treatise on Herrad von Landsberg's famed *Hortus deliciarum* (twelfth century), published by Cotta in 1818. A Germanist and archaeologist, Engelhardt had published his lengthy study on the *Garden of Delights*, the first medieval encyclopaedia compiled and painted by an abbess for the nuns of her monastery, along with twelve copperplates in outline to the dimensions of the manuscript, four of full pages, seven composed by himself from sundry miniatures, and one with sample texts and musical notation.[85] Engraved by Willemin and Aubert fils, it was dedicated to Maximilian I, King of Bavaria. Yet Dibdin turns away in "disappointment" from this partial modern reconstruction of the medieval masterwork only to succumb to the charm of Retzsch: "These designs are inimitable. I became rivetted by them. I had never before seen any thing more original and more exquisitely tender." Engelhardt's twelve thematic and colourless displays, a handful of the original's some 346 illuminations,[86] obviously carry less weight. Dibdin could not know that Herrad's manuscript would be destroyed by fire during the 1870 Franco-Prussian War, nor that Engelhardt's and another nineteenth-century projected edition's copies would become particularly valued. His comparison of Engelhardt with Retzsch is therefore all the more interesting as Herrad's colourful miniatures lead the way in the *Hortus*. The pictures are to be read afore the text,[87] just as Retzsch's plates set a similar trend for *Faust*. Overtly favouring Retzsch, the book lover spurns antique treasures for something tenderer and closer to the heart, covertly upsets standards, defies hierarchies, and ranks Retzsch's *Umrisse* a masterpiece. It is perhaps no concidence that *Philosophy and the Liberal Arts*, a frequently reproduced plate from the *Hortus*, is an allegory of wise learning, sacred and profane, diametrically contrasting

---

84 Dibdin, "Letter XXXVII. Stuttgart, August 4, 1818," in *A Bibliographical, Antiquarian and Picturesque Tour in France and Germany* (London: Printed for the Author by W. Bulmer and W. Nicol, Shakspeare Press, 1821), 3:120–30.

85 Rosalie Green, "The Miniatures," in Herrad of Hohenbourg, *Hortus deliciarum*, ed. R. Green et al. (London: The Warburg Institute; Leiden: E. J. Brill, 1979), 1:17.

86 Green (ibid., 23) notes that the count "should not be taken as a firm figure."

87 Fritz Saxl, "Illustrated Mediaeval Encyclopaedias, 2. The Christian Transformation," in *Lectures* (London: The Warburg Institute, 1957), 1:253.

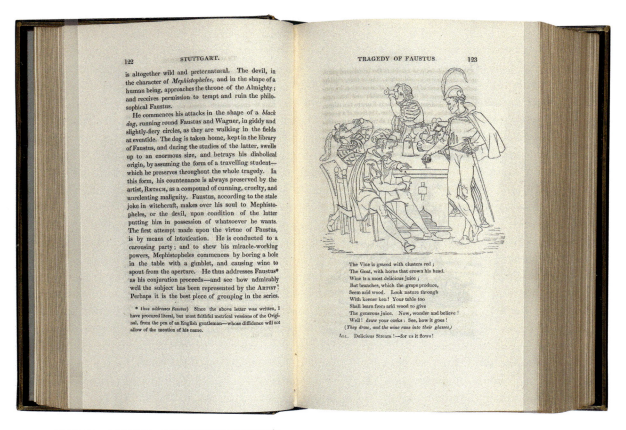

FIGURES 4.4A–C Thomas Frognall Dibdin, *A Bibliographical, Antiquarian and Picturesque Tour in France and Germany* (London: Printed for the Author by W. Bulmer and W. Nicol, Shakspeare Press, 1821), 3:122–27. Three openings with woodcuts by John Byfield reproducing Dibdin's cutouts as set in his commentary
COURTESY BEINECKE, YALE UNIVERSITY, X350 +821 (3)

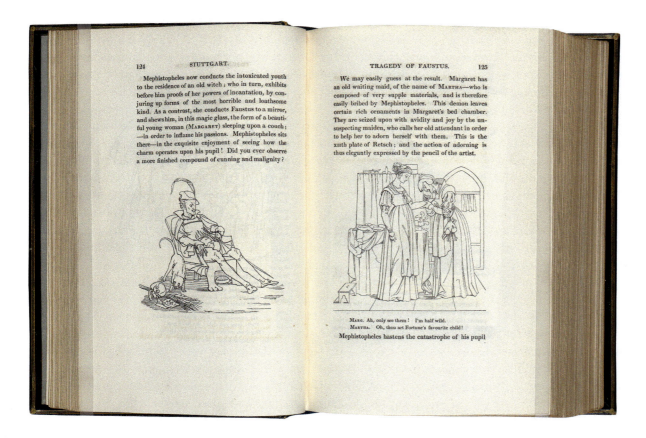

Faust, a tragedy of disheartened knowledge. Nor that "pride and fall" are Herrad's opening theme.[88]

Dibdin further enhances the overturn with incisive action in Stuttgart. His book offers the reader a proper text-image-and-verse display (as if he were Herrad) based on cut-and-paste (Engelhardt-fashion). He does not turn to artist George Robert Lewis, who travels with him to regularly enhance his *Tour* with inserted plates (landscapes, portraits, monuments). He himself edits and incorporates Retzsch clippings into the *Tour* by collage. While he connects the *Faust* scenes with both his prose and some verse translations, most integrated images (yet not all) are enlarged details of Moses's reworked Retzsch etchings (with several telling expurgations), centred on the protagonists, particularly his favoured Gretchen. "The book is cheap enough (about ten shillings English) to justify such a measure" [i.e., cutting up], he tells his actual or fictive correspondent. If ever traced, the manuscript mock-up should confirm or refute the reported manoeuvre. In the published book, the cutouts are redrawn by [John] Byfield, one of the Byfields regularly contributing woodcuts to Dibdin's works.[89] Dibdin explicitly compares his with Boosey's wares in the footnote: "The plates are upon copper, and were executed by the skilful burin of Mr. Moses. The fac-similes, in the above text [i.e., his text], are executed upon wood—by Mr. Byfield: and I think they have *rather* more tenderness of outline line than those of Mr. Moses; but I may be wrong in this conclusion."[90] To a theatrical flip of document hierarchies, choice of techniques brings novelty. Copperplates are more valued than woodcuts and Dibdin knows it only too well. He has been advertising his book's costly plates, yet turns to woodcuts for comfortable in-text layouts. Four of his seven *Faust* openings are careful displays around six symmetrically magnified insert groups, cleverly underlined by verse, and starting or finishing with a woodcut (Fig. 4.4a–c). Faust is present in only one; Mephistopheles and above all Margaret have stolen the show. The fine lines cited appear in neither 1820 nor 1821 *Faust* English summaries. Another footnote states: "Since the above letter was written, I have procured literal, but most faithful metrical versions of the Original, from the pen of an English gentleman—whose diffidence will not allow of the mention of his name."[91] Both expression and desire for anonymity recall the

---

88 Green, 25.
89 ODNB online, s.v. "Byfield family (per. c.1814–1886)" (by Susanna Avery-Quash), accessed 8 Jan 2020.
90 Dibdin, "Letter XXXVII," 3:121n, his emphasis.
91 Ibid., 3:122n.

heated Coleridge debate on which more later, yet Dibdin's "metrical translations" do not match any of those I know.

More significantly, a series of manipulations elucidate why Retzsch, in the spotlight, leads interpretation of *Faust*. Most are emotional, technical and aesthetic: first, sensibility; Dibdin stresses that images speak more to the heart than the intellect; second, the synoptic value of outline; it summarizes forms and silhouettes for easy pull-outs, reinsertions, and strong typification; third, it is tempting to think that the disjointed nature of the *Faust* text, stressed by Dibdin and enhanced by his uneven analysis, is taken on by the plates themselves as they function by suggestion, inter-connexion, and reading between the lines (which recalls Schlegel's essay on the outline aesthetic); fourth, Retzsch's plates are highly malleable, a compliant medium easily accommodating intermedial arrangements, as Dibdin's prose-cum-verse collages show. Fifth, Dibdin's chapter showcases shifting rules in reproduction techniques and the book trade, affecting the love of books and romantic reinterpretation. Lastly, while signalling Retzsch's value for modern collectors, by his clever arrangement, Dibdin indirectly rivals Boosey's successful books and plates, already on the market. The display was not reprinted in his *Tour*'s second edition (1829), based on lower costs, textual abridgments, and new updated material. Neither did its French translation allow for these pages since it is curtailed and stops at Strasbourg without crossing the Rhine. It is strange that the low cost of his *Faust* pages did not make it to the second English edition. But the choice is understandable: by 1829, many *Faust* editions rivalled for recognition in the UK market, all pirating Moses's already pirated prints.

Mutability, converting power and remediating agency prove key notions in the above, beyond usual conceptions of purely lingual translation. The latter's prominence in reception studies regularly obscures and even dismisses other facets when printed items move to a country from abroad or shift within an influential capital such as London. Retzsch's original *Faust* has multiple conversion capacity. As a gift to Henry Crabb Robinson, it carries national, literary, commercial and aesthetic value. As Bohte's import, it mixes and amalgamates, spawning a series of crossbreeds, hardly ever the same. As John Scott's and Weathercock's thoroughbred, it underscores early advertisement techniques in a first-rate literary magazine that consolidates knowledge of Goethe in Britain. Due to its hybrid nature (prints and text), the notional stability of translation itself mutates to reveal a trading token of variable exchange. Faust in his library poised as scholar counterpart of the Christian Saint Jerome, explicits the profound inversion of key cultural icons here at stake. Translation itself mutates with profligate yet knowledgable George Soane: it may lodge in choice of excerpts, comment, or full-blown verse translation. It metamorphoses, through genre conversion, into a theatre play. The original's composite materiality invites multifaceted handling and change. Owners' personalities and a binder's extraordinary composition show how early and intensely *Faust* items took on and reflected cultural and imaginative trends. Comparison with past treasures is even more dramatic as Retzsch's simple set ousts Herrad of Landberg's *Garden of Delights*.

In Dibdin's hands, Retzsch was fourfold remediated (original cutout, set in new layouts, Moses copy partly copied, and cut in wood). Reproduction of Moses's copies and mushrooming of *his* by-products was under way, appropriation of Retzsch in Britain as well.

CHAPTER 5

Retzsch Copied in Britain and Beyond

In a key metamorphosis Retzsch's *Umrisse* became *Outlines* in Britain. This chapter narrates the switch by comparing surviving items first hand in European and overseas depositories. Comparison applies both to editions (to distinguish them) and exemplars from the same edition (with differentiating results). Up to now, the bulk of such material has loosely been referred to as a series of dates without probing the very evidence of printed objects. When detail is provided, data prove incomplete and occasionally flawed. Typically, differing editions are merged and dates confused. Such practice may reflect on our understanding of which edition Shelley or Byron actually read. Yet, my main scope here is to unravel the story of Retzsch acclimatizing Goethe's *Faust* through books and prints, step by step.

The core conversion is from an original *twofold device* (Cotta's clever portfolio) to *illustrated English book*. This does not occur before 1839 at the earliest, when Moses's copies, re-engraved on steel by John Brain, pair with Jonathan Birch's translation of both *Faust* parts. Before that, from 1820 and for over nineteen years, intermediary items variously imply customized imitations, pirated copies, and copies of copies, disclosing diverse audiences.

Anglicising the *Outlines* also involves texts in English. By moving to another country, the initial visual translation of *Faust* provokes the key question of its verbal corollary. This gainsays traditional conceptions of the subsidiary role ascribed to image vs. text; it also begs scrutiny of related versions. A heated debate was kindled in 2008 around the verbal translation attributed to Samuel Taylor Coleridge of parts of one of these texts. The discussion, mostly in Coleridge studies and on philological grounds, tellingly shifted the attention from intermedial items to literary analysis, occasionally progressing Retzsch scholarship. I will not add to that debate but reset the printed object in truer light, i.e., within a series published by Boosey and Co. That series quickly spread east and west, one item at least showing influence from France. I have followed others well beyond Britain, to Polish-speaking Lithuania, the Netherlands, and the US, even Australia.

The account meets more books than men. Yet colourful personalities also appear behind the printed items, and period stances emerge through the *Outlines'* many mutations.

5.1 Attractive and Collectable

The importation of his *Umrisse* had sparked Retzsch's welcome in Britain. The artist had not signed them and no international legislation was in place to protect them. Excitement and success followed through pirating. Between June and July 1820, in clear competition with Bohte, publishers Thomas Boosey and Sons issued in association with printsellers Rodwell and Martin copies of Retzsch by English master engraver of antiquities Henry Moses (1781–1870), famous for his meticulous technique and Flaxmanic manner. Rivalry between the imported (German) and copied (English) *Faust* ensued on many fronts: the collectability and readability of plates depending on dimension and format; presentation and promotion of the play to readers by strongly increasing textual elements; last, but not least, the appeal of price.

The very first English issue of Retzsch is made of several components, five in all, even seven, if sundry parts are to be taken into account: engravings in two batches (26 in all), a textual "Analysis" in two parts (a final 60 pages), a "List of Plates," plus *two* title-pages. The latter by printer W. Wilson, identical in type, imprint, and layout, are parallel, one for the plates, the other for the "Analysis." They "could be had separately" (publisher's inserted slip). Even if reduced from five (or seven) to three, parts still commingle in a number of ways. No exemplar perused resembles another. Plates may take the lead, and "Analysis" follow, or vice-versa. Plate one, labelled atop INTRODUCTION (all other captions are as usual below the images), could be detached as frontispiece. In most bound exemplars, text leads, with plates either following as a unit or interleaved. A "List of Plates" offered (text) page numbers, and could in turn appear upfront, midway or at the end of the bound book. Assemblages show how subservient prints become once a text is provided. They make believe that this is an *illustrated* edition of *Faust*, which it could hardly be. Boosey, Sons and partners had crafted a twofold object likely to please readers, perplex curators, and possibly contrast collectors' whims and wishes with binders' commendations. Retzsch first anglicised is therefore another crossbreed, no longer formed from Bohte's (Soane's) English excerpts variously added to the German original, but from coupled ways of conveying meaning: text and image, literature and art, visual and textual conversion.

© EVANGHELIA STEAD, 2023 | DOI:10.1163/9789004543010_008

This is an open access chapter distributed under the terms of the CC BY-NC-ND 4.0 license.

Boosey and Co issued the plates in two batches of thirteen between customary wraps: plates 1–12 and plate 15 on June 1, plates 13–14 and 16–26 on July 1, witness the tiny italicized lettering and publisher's imprint beneath captions. A first-page announcement in Bent's *Monthly Literary Advertiser* aroused curiosity as did the visual lure, the primacy given to plate 15, Faust and Gretchen kissing. The prints were favoured, not so the text, despite its length. In periodicals, the advert characteristically appeared under "Fine Arts."[1]

Moses had stuck to Retzsch's sequence with insubordinate plate 18, "The evil spirit whispers despair to Margaret while at Mass," followed by "Valentine fights with Faust" (pl. 19), contrary to Goethe's (still little known) *Faust*. Faust's soliloquies thrilling less, as in Retzsch, he poignantly tracked Margaret. Yet, in the interleaved versions performing as text-and-image runs, rebel plate 18, pulled out of order, was relegated beyond 19 and 20.

Whatever the resulting assemblage, it never failed to attract. Dimensions were enhanced: ordinary quartos measure overall 27.5 × 21.7 cm, imperial ones 34 × 26.2 cm, doubling the height of Cotta's original. In imperial quartos, the copperplate indentations gave Retzsch's images ample breathing space. Moses's double frame (instead of Retzsch's single line) also upped their rank. Format, paper, precision and realistic accuracy were valued with typical collector's zeal by Gerhard Stumme: "The extremely impressive edition (*äußerst eindrucksvoll*) was issued in large formats, on the best paper, and the comparison with the very modest (*sehr bescheidenen*) German original also shows differences in living standards between the English and German peoples of the time. Various minor errors were improved, e.g., the rod of the distaff in Gretchen's room is extended to the floor."[2]

Adverse arguments were nevertheless heard in London. Editor Scott defended Retzsch: "But the originals have a spirit which has not been transfused into the copies, and we are therefore glad to hear that a fresh supply from the Continent has been received."[3] Weathercock gave vent to explicit criticism: "How is it that Mr. Moses, the etcher, takes it into his head, in engraving from antique pictures and vases, to fancy that he improves the originals, by substituting for their wonderfully harmonious, though apparently careless lines, his own stiff-drawing?"[4] Both defended Bohte's interests. Opinions varied, but one fact remains: Shelley's enthusiastic praise of Retzsch benefitted

from Moses's clarity (he certainly had the English plates to hand). In the meantime, Cotta may have lent an ear to Retzsch's remarks on fine art sets, enhanced margins, and improved the 1820 German set's paper quality.

Boosey and Sons sent their wares to Weimar, and Goethe acknowledged receipt of the first batch to Hüttner on 30 July 1820.[5] Yet the batches do not correspond in format (large paper for the first, ordinary for the second). Had success depleted the publishers from imperial quartos of the second batch or were they sparing? In Goethe's library today, all four parts are kept separate. Without previous knowledge, it is hardly possible to see how they worked together, not to mention that pl. 1 has been bound with the second batch by mistake.[6] Yet, the quality of the paper is stunning. No wonder Goethe judged them "extremely neat and precise" (*höchst reinlich und genau*).[7]

In the combined Boosey outcome, texts astutely surround Moses's prints starting with descriptive captions (Retzsch's had none). The latter fix the meaning and annex the prints to the "Analysis" with a governing function. More importantly, the two title-pages would set translation and illustration at loggerheads with each other:

[PLATES' TITLE-PAGE:] *Retsch's Series of Twenty-Six Outlines, Illustrative of Goethe's Tragedy of Faust, Engraved from the Originals by Henry Moses. And an Analysis of the Tragedy*

["ANALYSIS" TITLE-PAGE:] *An Analysis of Goethe's Tragedy of Faust, in Illustration of Retsch's Series of Outlines, Engraved from the Originals by Henry Moses*

In both, the equivocal term *illustration* increases uncertainty. At the time, *illustration* regularly qualified *textual clarifications and elucidations*. As such, the "Analysis" "in Illustration of Retsch's Series of Outlines" offers indeed a textual explanation deemed necessary to understand a work of art. Concurrently, what *we* may now take as the current meaning of *illustration* in the plates' title, that is, text-bound images, is in fact ahistorical. The term referring to images in books was commonly "embellishments," only very rarely "illustration." "Illustrative of Goethe's Tragedy of Faust" means that the plates add *lustre* and *aura*. The definite visual turn in print culture that images implied did not tally with their ancillary dependence.[8]

---

1 "New Publications," *Quarterly Review* 24, no. 47 (Oct 1820): 271.

2 Stumme, *Faust als Pantomime und Ballett* (Leipzig: Poeschel & Trepte, 1942), 92.

3 "The Lion's Head," *LM* 2, no. 7 (July 1820): 6.

4 "Mr. Weathercock's Private Correspondence," 301.

---

5 WA 4, 33:137.

6 HAAB: Ruppert 1918 (1–2) text only, Ruppert 1947 (1–2) plates only. Ruppert 1947 (2) is the only bound exemplar.

7 WA 4, 36:169.

8 See Ian Haywood, Susan Matthews, and Mary L. Shannon, "Editors' Introduction," in *Romanticism and Illustration* (Cambridge: Cambridge University Press, 2019), 2–4.

Recalling historical meaning and clarifying such ambiguity highlight the several purposes of the twofold object. The newly engraved set, adapted to English taste, built on Retzsch's growing public fame by seducing potential clients away from Bohte thanks to quality. A "connected view of the whole drama"[9] astutely outshone Soane's twenty-six excerpts as long textual addendum. It bade a considerably lengthier approach to Goethe's *Faust* that had raised public interest, but was still largely unknown. The first protracted and accurate article by Rev. George Croly on it would only appear in the 1820 *London Magazine*, once Boosey's binary device had been published.[10]

Whether separate or united, Boosey's parts promoted divergent readings. When separate, the plates were the tragedy's proxy, favouring the underline narrative. In his much-discussed correspondence with Boosey, who approached the poet for advice (if not translation), Coleridge reflects: "What have the Purchasers of *the Prints* to do with the poetic or moral merits or demerits of the Poem? All, they want, is the *Story*." When united, the "Analysis" grew in importance, less so in quality, begging for proper translation, a formidable task, as critics observed. Still, as inferred from Coleridge's response, Boosey "wish[ed] to have no more *Leaves* of Letter-press, than Prints, allowing only two or three additional for the introduction." Retzsch's copied plates should carry all the glory. The text was markedly ancillary, a strong enough reason for Coleridge to feel bound to refuse: "but to give my *name* to the mere Letter-press subservient to productions of an Art, not connected with my own pursuits—this, I more than fear, my Friends & Family will regard as a sort of Job-work."[11]

Boosey's pricing also seduced users away from Bohte's package. In October 1820 press advertisements, quarto plates sold for only a crown (5s.), each part for 2s. 6d., which more than halved the price of Bohte's, who faced irretrievable import duties, as Schlegel stressed.[12] Bohte's was offered at 12s. 6d. (13s. with added English text). Even if the 60-page "Analysis" upped Boosey's price, his twofold item remained cheaper. The "Analysis" sold for only 6s. (3s. per part), the combined plates-with-Analysis for 11s., again lower than Bohte's 13s. Of course, collectors' proof impressions in imperial quarto made a marked difference, being pricier by a third. The plates went for a guinea (21s., 10s. 6d. per part), the large paper "Analysis" for 8s., the complete set for £1 9s., or nine days' wages for a skilled tradesman

at the time. Tellingly, as demand grew, the "Analysis" price remained stable for both formats, while the quarto plates rose dramatically from 5s. (July) to 14s.[13] Sustained demand and retouching the plates for finer printing are likely to have increased the price, their production cost being higher than for typeset. Yet, the imperial quarto price did not change. As the increase bears only on the more affordable quarto, not the costly imperial, attracted readers were surely not only select aficionados: in Moses's version Retzsch appealed to the average bourgeois. Building on strong commercial spurs, Boosey had broadened the circle of end-users: print collectors, German literature amateurs, literati, critics and poets, neophytes and connoisseurs, whether educated aristocrats or the learned of upper and middle classes.

5.2 Cultural Adaptability

Dibdin's treatment of Retzsch's outlines in his *Tour* proves their plasticity and malleability as, cut-out and reset, they signify differently (cf. Fig. 4.4a–c). Conversely, Boosey's edition is the very first of an extended series to exemplify cultural compliance: it adopts, rejects or accustoms a new public's demands and expectations both in text and plates.

Composition and type were done in haste as show a list of seven errata and captions' spelling. Typically all captions omit the genitive apostrophe (e.g., "Mephistopheles Leaves Rich Ornaments in Margarets [*sic*] Chamber") and the witch's kitchen is oddly called "cave." Time pressed, demand had been swelling, and Bohte's imports could not meet it. This radically impacted the clumsy translation. Scenes are merely sketched out, incompletely summarized or curtailed. When translations do occur, they are literal and generally in prose. Many songs and crucial elements, such as Margaret's question on religion (*Gretchenfrage*) and a fair part of the Walpurgis, are omitted. "The 'Analysis' may be termed innocuous, for the most part being a literal prose translation, interrupted by miserable verse," states Atkins while commenting several blunders.[14] There is not much to add to this conviction. Coleridge's dismissal of it as "Job-work" or "mere Letter-press" is accurate. Burwick and McKusick, noting further mishaps, attribute the translation to Daniel Boileau, and append his remarks on Abraham Hayward's 1833 *Faust* translation.[15] Yet, even if a

---

9 Analysis 1820, 2.
10 "Goethe and his Faustus," *LM* 2, no. 8 (Aug 1820): 125–42.
11 Beinecke: YCGL MSS 6, box 2, folder 87, autograph letter, his emphasis; Schreiber, "Coleridge to Boosey," 8–9; *Collected Letters of Samuel Taylor Coleridge*, 5:44.
12 Schlegel, "Vorrede" / "Introduction," XXI–XXIII.

13 "New Publications," *Quarterly Review* 24, no. 47 (Oct 1820): 271 (published only on 19 Dec 1820).
14 Atkins, "Fragmentary English Translations," 13–15.
15 Burwick and McKusick, eds., *Faustus*, 177–79, 218–22.

broad summary, no way is this an "extensive literal translation of *Faust*."[16] It sold not on account of the text but the prints. Still, both image and letterpress well reflect English mentalities, emotions, and ideas, public or personal. In the acclimatized item cultures meet.

More than once, the English text echoes Huber's German foreword. *Faust*, a book for any age, chaperones male readers from youth to old age; again the artist acts "the part of an ingenious translator;" and still the rock in plate 21 resembles "a veiled woman."[17] Adaptions are few. Lord Chesterfield's *Letters to His Son on the Art of Becoming a Man of the World and a Gentleman* (first published 1774), more familiar to British readers, yet still remote, has replaced Campe's *Theophron*. Just as Xenophon's *Cyropaedia* and Fénelon's *Telemachus* sound distant from "man as he is," "the creature which is a riddle to itself, an enigma" is baffling to philosophers. In Britain, the German States, indeed worldwide, "this creature 'MAN'" is a modern conundrum, to which classical literature has only conjectural answers. Inversely, *Faust* is the up-to-date response.

Following Huber (and Soane), tempter and tempted become "*one* person, represented symbolically, only in a two-fold shape,"[18] although *Faust* is a "didactic fiction" in which God and good will prevail. The romantic tradition explores man's duality. It is tempting to think that Huber's preface had a protracted bearing. Evil as integral to good would be one of Carl Gustav Jung's seminal ideas more than a century later. Jung would define the self as "a *complexio oppositorum*, a union of opposites," or "united duality," "the hero and its adversary (arch-enemy, dragon), Faust and Mephistopheles."[19] In *The Development of Personality* (1934), he heard in the legendary antique demon none other than "the voice of the inner man," the strong vocation that animated exceptional individuals,[20] which oddly echoes again the 1820 *Faust*: "Let youth detect the Demon within himself."[21] In *Memories, Dreams, Reflections* (1968), split personality was a way for Jung to interpret himself ("The dichotomy of Faust-Mephistopheles came together within myself into a single person, and I was that person"), but also a myth for a "collective experience that

[...] prophetically anticipated the fate of the Germans."[22] In the "Analysis," hatred of mankind turns a far more traditional "goaty" Mephistopheles into "furious destroyer." Metaphysical *Faust* questions on God, the devil, and man as passionate seeker, marked Daniel Boileau and his readers, even if the witches' Sabbath is cast simply as "revel." The "Analysis" summarizes the "Prologue in Heaven" and shows the devil asking God for permission to tempt Faust, which is granted as in Job.

Moses's replicas are even better sensors, the very touchstone of alterations that raise questions inherent to British propriety and public sensitivity. Two of these have been early and repeatedly noted, which neither exhausts the subject nor adequately explains it.[23] I discuss briefly and further complete them, drawing attention to period comments, and refer to likely visual sources. Two sensitive categories, the representation of the divine and the erotic, had given Goethe in Weimar "food for thought."[24]

At the very opening, pictured in plate 1 by Retzsch amidst angels (Fig. 5.1), Moses's God simply vanishes, replaced by a radiant void (Fig. 5.2). Had Moses's biblical namesake resounded within in deference to the second commandment? "Thou shalt not make thee any graven image" (Deut. 5:8) was on the tablets that the Hebrew leader and lawgiver had brought back from Sinai. For scholar William Heinemann in 1886, God's disappearance already smacked of prohibition, recalling "the English feeling of piety."[25] Coleridge had avowed it in a private literary debate with Crabb Robinson on 24 June 1817: "He spoke with great love of Goethe—yet censored the impious prologue to Faust."[26] Even the *London Magazine*'s Janus felt qualms: The Germans "do not hesitate to introduce the person of the Deity in compositions of a mixed nature." Their "freedom of manner" smacked "of innocence or of impudence," of which the scandalized analyst was quite undecided.[27] Tille peculiarly argued that the removal of the august figure was an improvement, yet only in the

---

16   Ibid., 178.

17   Analysis 1820, 1–3.

18   Ibid., 2, author's emphasis.

19   Jung, *Psychological Types*, trans. H. G. Baynes, revised by R. F. C. Hull, in *Collected Works* (London: Routledge and Kegan Paul, 1971), 6:460, §790.

20   Jung, *The Development of Personality*, trans. R. F. C. Hull, in *Collected Works* (ibid., 1954), 17:175–56, §300.

21   Analysis 1820, 2.

---

22   Jung, *Memories, Dreams, Reflections*, ed. A. Jaffé, trans. R. and C. Winston, 3rd repr. (New York: Pantheon Books, 1963), 235 & 234.

23   William Heinemann, *Goethes Faust in England und Amerika* (Berlin: August Hettler, 1886), 1; Alexander Tille, "The Artistic Treatment of the Faust Legend," *Publications of the English Goethe Society, No VII* (London: David Nutt, 1893), 189; Jean-Marie Carré, *Bibliographie de Goethe en Angleterre* (Lyon: Impressions des Deux-Collines, 1920), 80; Kippenberg, no. 1878; Atkins, "Fragmentary English Translations," 11–12; Schreiber, "Coleridge to Boosey," 6, etc.

24   WA 4, 33:247.

25   Heinemann, *Goethes Faust in England*, 1.

26   Morley, ed., *Robinson on Books*, 1:208.

27   Weathercock, "Sentimentalities," 137.

FIGURE 5.1 Moritz Retzsch, Prologue in Heaven, *Umrisse zu Goethe's Faust gezeichnet von Retsch* (Stuttgart & Tübingen: Cotta, 1816), pl. 1
COURTESY HAAB, F 3487, WEIMAR

German version of his 1893 study.[28] He was still working in the UK, with a career in Germany yet to unfold.

Goethe had drawn poetic inspiration from the oldest biblical scripture, the Book of Job, but public devoutness must have felt relief. Moses's censored version was probably also prompted, if not authorized, by an illustrious precedent. In *Il sol degli angeli* or *Circle of Angels around the Sun* for Dante's *Paradise* canto 10, Flaxman had outlined angels in gracious attitudes intoning praise around bright sunlight (Fig. 5.3), a plausible model for Moses, religiously and artistically discharged in making the change. This amendment hallmarks the anglicised Retzsch. The suppression would bear on Audot's French copies, albeit with a different meaning as later discussed, but occurs first in Moses. Proescholdt-Obermann's strange claim that a first English plate with God present was modified under pressure, hardly supported by evidence, is perhaps explicable by confusion with Bohte's import.[29]

Erotic tenure, on the other hand, is subject to expansive and meaningful negotiation. A cavalier rejuvenated, Faust adopts Mephistopheles's stylish apparel after Goethe (F 1535–41). Retzsch clothed both in close-fitting Renaissance hoses that bring bulging codpieces more or less into full view, depending on the scene depicted. This authentic male fashion accessory appears in sixteen of the twenty-six plates and concerns either Mephistopheles, Faust, or both. On sixteen occasions, Moses carefully erases it. He is not alone. "If dangerous thoughts could

---

28 Tille, "Die Bilder zu Goethes Faust," *Preußische Jahrbücher* 72, no. 2 (May 1893): 284.

29 Proescholdt-Obermann, *Goethe and his British Critics*, 162, n. 57. Her information on Retzsch proves otherwise unreliable.

FIGURE 5.2 Henry Moses, *Introduction*, engraved copy after Moritz Retzsch, in *Retsch's Series of Twenty-Six Outlines, Illustrative of Goethe's Tragedy of Faust* (London: Boosey & Sons, Rodwell and Martin, 1820), pl. 1
COURTESY HAAB, F GR 5785, WEIMAR

be presented in corporeal forms, [...] the engravings of Mr Stone [...] do not contain what offends in those of Retsch," circuitously states [Jules de] Wallenstein, Russian Secretary of Legation in Washington DC, prefacing the American re-engraved copy.[30] Retzsch's fame had already crossed the Atlantic in 1824, preceding that of Goethe's *Faust*, and Henry Stone's plates are similarly self-censored. Tellingly, his suppressions affected neither God in heaven nor the magic mirror's female. "His sense of decency, however, must have been outraged by the laxities of the orgy on the Brocken (plate 22), for he has clothed the two most flagrant of the naked witches."[31] Moreover, *no later Retzsch copy* (with the remarkable exception of Giard in 1830) will ever fall short of the task: male crotches remain strangely innocuous.

In counterpart, Moses has stripped to the waist an unruly female sprawling in the magic mirror of "The Witch's Kitchen" (pl. 6, Fig. 5.4), replacing Retzsch's decently-clad damsel, decorously and modestly reclining (cf. Fig. 2.18). With regard to sexual hierarchies, males, projecting themselves onto the plates, might cower at their manly parts

30 "Retzsch's Illustrations of Faust," in *Illustrations of the Celebrated Tragedy of Faustus by Goethe Engraved & Published by Henry Stone* (Washington City: H. Stone, 1824), 4.

31 Atkins, "Fragmentary English Translations," 29.

RETZSCH COPIED IN BRITAIN AND BEYOND 143

FIGURE 5.3 John Flaxman, *Il sol degli angeli* or *Circle of Angels around the Sun*, outline drawing engraved by Tommaso Piroli after Dante's *Paradise*, canto 10. *La Divina Commedia di Dante Alighieri* (Rome, 1802), pl. 10
BnF Est., TA-32-4, PARIS

being paid attention, while female representations developed their appeal unabashed to please collectors' and experts' eyes. Moses's female not only exhibits a buxom bosom, she also appears totally naked beneath a sheet that hardly covers her, as she gesticulates wildly. Another illustrious model knew Moses's mind: Füssli's erotically haunting evocation in *The Nightmare* (1781, exhibited 1782 at the Royal Academy), renowned through numerous engraved versions (Fig. 5.5), and the Swiss artist's emphasis on outline in lectures. In his preface to Bohte's leaflet, Soane had reportedly asserted: "The praise of *Fuseli* would alone put the stamp of fame upon his [Retzsch's] work."[32] Moses's choice was indirectly hallowed. Heinemann again sensed the analogy: "throwing her head aside, as if in feverish dreams" (*als ob in wirren Fieberträumen*).[33] To clinch the parallel, Füssli's demon crouching on the woman's breast could well match Retzsch's (and Moses's) with draperies between his teeth.

Noting in a roundabout way the absent codpieces, Janus Weathercock mused: "As to these copies [Moses's], they affectedly alter the peculiar fashion of Faust's '*unmentionables*';" He must have compared original and copy with a magnifying glass, since he added: "and, at the same time, in the witch-feast, on the Harz mountains, [they] bring many things, 'nice but vicious,' into light, which were properly left in mystic dimness by the German artist."[34]

---

32 Soane, "Preface," in *Extracts from Göthe's Tragedy of Faustus* (London: Printed for J. H. Bohte, 1820), 3, his emphasis.

33 Heinemann, *Goethes Faust in England*, 1.

34 "Mr. Weathercock's Private Correspondence," 301a.

FAUST AND MEPHISTOPHELES IN THE WITCHES CAVE.

FIGURE 5.4
(*top*) Henry Moses, *Faust and Mephistopheles in the Witch's Cave*, engraved copy after Moritz Retzsch, in *Retsch's Series of Twenty-Six Outlines, Illustrative of Goethe's Tragedy of Faust* (London: Boosey & Sons, Rodwell and Martin, 1820), pl. 6; (*bottom*) Moritz Retzsch, The witch's kitchen, *Umrisse zu Goethe's Faust gezeichnet von Retsch* (Stuttgart & Tübingen: Cotta, 1816), pl. 6
COURTESY HAAB, F GR 5785 AND F 3487, WEIMAR

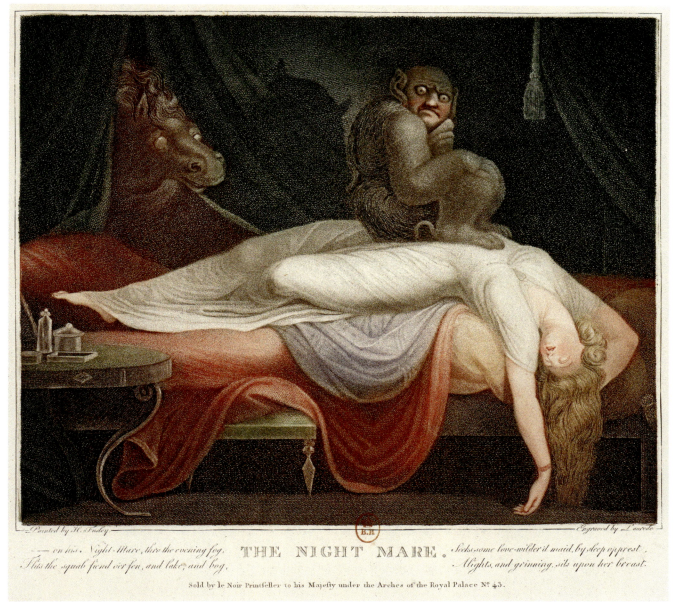

FIGURE 5.5 Henry Füssli, *The Night Mare* (*Le Cauchemar*), 1782, coloured etching and stippled engraving
BnF Est., CA18C-1 (FÜSSLI, JOHANN HEINRICH)-FOL, PARIS

A minute comparison (lens in hand) proves how accurate the remark was: the outburst of violence and passion are strengthened in Moses's plate 22 (cf. Fig. 5.6). On the left, Retzsch had represented a tangle of sexes in a free-for-all erotic romp (cf. Fig. 5.7). Moses overemphasizes. By redrawing every genital, limb and curve, he stresses carnality. Keeping a distance, Retzsch had vaguely drafted creatures overlapping, tossing and tumbling, witches riding a sow or a snail, orgying around a barely indicated goat. Moses adds nothing if not meticulous lines. The implied becomes crudely overt. On his dense surface, shapes congregate and the unspeakable erupts: animal intercourse, defecation, wild carousing. The protagonists' expressions have all been changed. Faust's questioning and concern are visible, the devil's nervousness and ruse more obvious. Margaret is no longer a ghostly spirit; her face is redrawn, her loose amply floating hair turns serpentine, her belly swells, underlined by her thigh, all details indeterminate in Retzsch. It is such features that made Shelley assert: "I never perfectly understood the Har[t]z Mountain scene, until I saw the etching."[35] Prudish souls, states Stumme, had veiled plates such as this by inserting screens in an exemplar he owned.[36] No longer traceable in Weimar, where his collection ended up, might not he himself have censored such acts?

---

35   *The Letters of Percy Bysshe Shelley*, 2:407.
36   Stumme, *Faust als Pantomime*, 92–93.

FIGURE 5.6 Henry Moses, *The Witches' Revel*, engraved copy after Moritz Retzsch, in *Retsch's Series of Twenty-Six Outlines, Illustrative of Goethe's Tragedy of Faust* (London: Boosey & Sons, Rodwell and Martin, 1820), pl. 22
COURTESY HAAB, F GR 5785, WEIMAR

5.3 Boosey's 1820 Edition Re-issued?

All this sped success, but did Boosey re-issue the item within the year? "Extraordinarily enough, there were at least four issues published by Boosey in 1820," states Atkins uncorroborated.[37] Yet, evidence is hard to come by on *any* edition's further issues. If her affirmation is based on the four variant exemplars in Beinecke's Speck Collection, all with an 1820 imprint, yet catalogued as "another issue," it should be taken with caution. Three of these are bound (two in opulent versions by Murton, cf. Fig. 4.1), the fourth in firm cardboard wrappers.[38] Both practices allow for inserts to enhance the items' value. The Murton bindings can be dated 1822 from his mechanically stamped signature and address, "9 Broad St. Golden Sq."[39] They postdate the *second* 1821 Boosey edition (which offers extras). A Weimar exemplar, in a similar green long-grain morocco binding by Murton, also allows for additional plates to join an authentic 1820 imperial quarto, under the

---

37 Atkins, "Fragmentary English Translations," 11.

38 Beinecke: Speck Ck99 R3 +820c (Murton); Speck Ck99 R3 +820d (Murton); Speck Ck99 R3 +820e; Speck Ck99 R3 +820f. For further details, see Appendix 1, no. 4.

39 Ramsden, *London Bookbinders*, 109.

FIGURE 5.7 Moritz Retzsch, Walpurgis Night, *Umrisse zu Goethe's Faust gezeichnet von Retsch* (Stuttgart & Tübingen: Cotta, 1816), pl. 22
COURTESY HAAB, F 3487, WEIMAR

same binder's address.[40] Tooling on the spine, *Outlines to Faust with Analysis*, combines both titles, but only one title-page (*Retsch's Series of Twenty-Six Outlines Illustrative of Goethe's Tragedy*) has been retained, the other discarded, and plates interleaved. Differences in Beinecke's four Speck items result therefore from bibliophiles' habits of garnishing their exemplars with add-ons to increase their customized appeal, but do not *per se* testify to further issues. Plates are interleaved in all four, three are grangerized with a frontispiece or further addenda, all from the 1821 (second) Boosey edition, entitled *Faustus*. At this stage it is difficult to prove that the twofold 1820 Boosey item was re-issued within the year. Besides, the *European Magazine* called the "first edition" of the "Analysis" already "out of print," deeming it "rather rare," only in October 1821.[41]

Though evidence may yet turn up, it seems more important to stress how differently Boosey's package worked from Bohte's. In open competition, the former promoted propriety and piety, while conveying new ideas on the relation of good to evil. By chaperoning the reformed prints, the "Analysis" founded and fostered textual transition. It introduced causality and urged explanation. As in the original German, *Faust* in outline was still in two parts, combined or separate, twofold or interleaved. The object boosted circulation with Goethe's text gaining importance. Appropriation of Goethe was on the move, but the sought-after translation still proved difficult to secure.

40   HAAB: F gr 5785 (T. W. Glanville's heraldic bookplate).

41   R., "*Faustus: from the German of Goethe*," *European Magazine and Monthly Review* 80 (Oct 1821): 364b.

5.4 "A More Careful Abstract"

Boosey's 1820 edition of copied prints-with-Analysis attracted buyers as the London publisher apprised Goethe via Hüttner on 19 August 1820: "in consequence of the extensive Sale of the Outlines in this Country, great curiosity has been excited respecting the tragedy, and of course has had a great Sale lately."[42] In reality, the plates led the way, furthering the text. Before the first edition was out, Boosey had even written to Coleridge aiming at a second, offering a slightly enlarged text and requesting advice (his proposal is inferred from Coleridge's answer, the original has not been preserved). The poet eschewed involvement on 10 May 1820 and bade "My Advice & Scheme" on 12 May instead.[43] Careful analysis of his reply shows him hesitant, and Boosey responded in a preserved recorded response.[44] He had been far-sighted, to say the least. Bohte's ringing success may have taught him anticipation. Both publishers had had ample proof that the attractive prints steered the market while *Faust* intrigued. Readers would hunger for more.

Further competition ensued. Using strikingly analogous phrasing, press announcements as early as April and May 1821 publicized that "from the pen of Mr. George Soane" Goethe's *Faust* was "shortly to appear in an English dress," presumably for Bohte.[45] Yet, from July, counter-announcements stressed that "a Gentleman of Literary Eminence" was preparing "a Translation of a considerable portion of the wild and singular play into English Blank Verse" for competitor Boosey.[46] Such ambition boded greater literary scope than the plain "Analysis." Under preparation in September,[47] the new Boosey "translation" was out in October 1821, both as a plain text octavo and a book with Moses's copied plates increased from twenty-six to twenty-seven.[48] It is the latter that both Shelley and Byron had to hand (see below). Bohte instead continued banking on Retzsch's imported etchings. As noted, to avoid disruption of reading in two formats, he devised a bilingual landscape quarto with interleaved prints, briefly reviewed by Weathercock.[49] His planned issue did not go further than the first 576 lines translated by Soane opposite the German text, the very galley proofs received by Goethe who found the translation highly effective.[50] His 10 June 1822 letter to Count Reinhard avers: "a Mr Soane has admirably understood my Faust (*bewundernswürdig verstanden*) and translated its particularities (*Eigenthümlichkeiten*) with those of his language."[51] He republished Soane's English "Dedication" in his 1823 *Über Kunst und Altertum*.[52] Even by twentieth-century standards, Soane's is "one of the best English translations of the poem, as far as it goes."[53] Such appraisals undermine attribution of the weak 1820 "Analysis" to Soane in favour of Boileau's hand. Boosey's publication hype would however prove confusing.

Mixing promising small caps and uppercase, the October 1821 *Monthly Literary Advertiser* heralded it as a complete version: "A TRANSLATION of | FAUSTUS, from the German of GOETHE." Preceding lines baited bibliophiles: "on fine Paper, hot-pressed, and embellished with a correct and highly finished Portrait of the Author." In reality it had not cost much. The portrait, of Goethe in profile by Ferdinand Jagemann, was already part of the 1820 catalogue of Boosey and his printseller associates Rodwell and Martin.[54] As for the text, it fell clearly short of the promise: "It is not pretended that the following pages contain a full translation of this celebrated play," stated more realistically the quarto itself, calling the translation "a more careful abstract."[55] A subsequent publisher's catalogue at the end of another quarto joined in unison: "A NEW TRANSLATION OF THE MOST STRIKING PASSAGES AND SCENES, Connected by a Detailed Description in Prose."[56] Contrariwise, the *Monthly Literary Advertiser* repeatedly touted the translation of a famous play while covertly paralleling it with the English canon. Cleverly swapping *Faustus* for *Faust*, Boosey alluded to Marlowe's tragedy, familiar to the British public. That same month, the *Monthly Magazine* proffered discontented criticism of the presumed "translation," deeming the title "unfair," the

---

42   GSA 28/29, 415.

43   *Collected Letters of Samuel Taylor Coleridge*, 5:42–44.

44   Beinecke: YCGL MSS 6, box 2, folder 87, pencilled response on Coleridge's letter; Roger Paulin, William St Clair, and Elinor Shaffer, "Goethe's *Faust* and Coleridge," 7.

45   "Literary Intelligence," *European Magazine and London Review* 79 (Apr 1821): 354b; "Works Preparing for Publication," *LM* 3, no. 5 (May 1821): 578 ("about to appear in an English dress").

46   "Works Preparing for Publication," *LM* 4, no. 7 (July 1891): 104.

47   "Works Preparing for Publication," *LM* 4, no. 9 (Sept 1821): 341.

48   *MLA*, no. 198 (10 Oct 1821): 75a (advertisement).

---

49   Weathercock, "C. Van Vinkbooms, his Dogmas for Dilettanti, No III," 657.

50   The proofs are still part of his library (HAAB: Ruppert 1916).

51   WA 4, 36:61; Mackall, "Soane's *Faust* Translation," 277–97.

52   "Faustus. Dedication," in FA 1, 21: 447–48. Unfortunately, the editors Stefan Greif and Andrea Ruhlig further obscure the quality of Soane's work by erroneously attributing his translation to Francis Leveson Gower, a poor translator (p. 936).

53   Atkins, "Fragmentary English Translations," 11.

54   BL: C.57.h.2, publisher's catalogue inserted at the end of the 1820 edition, still in original wrappers.

55   Introduction 1821, VII.

56   Beinecke: Speck Ck 99 R3 +824.

RETZSCH COPIED IN BRITAIN AND BEYOND

publication misleading, and denouncing the transformation of "the usual quantity of letter-press" into "a quarto form" as a publisher's sleight of hand. It emitted a definite "*caveat emptor*" (Let the purchaser beware).[57] The widely read *European Magazine* also published a long carping review of the translation attempt.[58] The seller certainly knew better than buyers. The portrait was a first booster, promoting Goethe along with a text doubly outlined: in plates copied after Retzsch (increased to twenty-seven) and précised in a reader's digest interspersed with blank verse. Other extras would follow.

A threefold marketing strategy was at work at Boosey's: a) recycling the (enlarged) formula of prints-with-text; b) varying printed items and formats (the octavo "translation" in boards along with the quarto prints-with-text); and c) refurbishment by addition. Variability of set-ups and add-ons astutely occupied the publishing field with an array of printed objects all sustaining interest in *Faust*. By October 1824, three *Faustus* variants were available at Boosey and Sons: a) the quarto, offering the new text with 28 plates (Goethe's portrait included); b) a separate quarto of the sole outlines in boards; and c) the text "translation" with the author's portrait in octavo.[59]

The new text is the one edited by Frederick Burwick and James McKusick as *Faustus. From the German of Goethe. Translated by Samuel Coleridge* in the standard Oxford series of major English texts (2007). The shortcomings of this edition and its attribution have been largely debated.[60] There is no need to return to the textual discussion here. Its value had been enhanced by character analysis and passages translated into blank verse. The *London Magazine* did not hesitate to brashly call it "Boosey's prose, which is very prose,"[61] and Atkins, after detailed study, concluded on "the limpness of the entire translation."[62] Submitting to decorum, the Prologue in Heaven and the Walpurgis had been bypassed, revealing perceptions of public mind-set and belief, but also societal pressure to protect official religion.[63]

Faustus from the German involved characteristic features of the illustrated book typology: a frontispiece, the author's portrait, and interleaved plates opposite textual synopses intensifying graphic effect. Nevertheless, once again, this was *not* an illustrated book, but a post-production marketing spin-off, a template of etchings set amongst type. The landscape prints had been rotated alongside the vertically printed text, coercing the user desirous to consider both into swivelling the volume time and again. Rebel plate 18, pulled out of order, now appeared *after* 19 and 20, all ancillary to text, none renumbered, while Wilson's "List of Plates" still followed initial order. It had been recycled with no changes but page numbers referring to the new textual version. Plates were interleaved haphazardly with the caption either towards the inner gutter or the outer edge. Only plate 11, "Mephistopheles Leaves Rich Ornaments in Margaret's Chamber," had become "Margaret Admiring the Jewels Left by Mephistopheles," better matching the scene. Captions maintained patent errors in the prints (witch's "cave" instead of "kitchen").

Significantly, lone prints were also offered apart from the book. Their varied destinations and purposes have been singled out: objects of conversation, joining others in a cabinet or portfolio; multiple handling from lap to desk, passed around in company; perused in order or returned to, independently from the text; and efficient as substitute to "actually being present at a performance of Goethe's *Faust*."[64]

Add-ons further confirm the importance of images as *Faust*'s main driver. The author's portrait is of course common practice, especially in an octavo, Boosey's edition being no exception. Publisher William Heinemann read *Faust* in one of these.[65] The finely incised version of Goethe's portrait after Jagemann enhanced aura. Often wanting in surviving exemplars, it likely served as wall or cabinet ornament. Subsequently it found its way from the octavo to the quarto as a complementary enrichment.[66]

An added frontispiece, signed "Drawn and Engraved by Henry Moses" (Retzsch's pirated copies were only marked "Engraved by Henry Moses"), is yet another replica, plagiarizing this time Peter Cornelius's dedication plate from his *Bilder zu Goethes Faust* (1816). The first two instalments of Cornelius's monumental set had reached London and been briefly criticized in the *London Magazine*, alongside

---

57 "New Books Published in September," *Monthly Magazine* 52, no. 359 (1 Oct 1821): 260a–61b.

58 R., *"Faustus: from the German,"* 362–69.

59 *Examiner*, no. 871 (10 Oct 1824): 656b (advertisement).

60 See in bibliography Kelly Grovier, 2008; Paulin, St Clair, and Shaffer, 2008; Ritchie Robertson, 2008; Burwick, 2008; Joyce Crick, 2008; Chris Murray, 2009; James Engell, 2010; Stefan H. Uhlig, 2010; J. C. C. Mays, 2012; Refat Aljumily, online Version 1.0, 2015.

61 "Lord F. L. Gower's Faust," *LM*, n.s., 6, no. 10 (Oct 1826): 165.

62 Atkins, "Fragmentary English Translations," 23.

63 Paulin, St Clair, and Shaffer, "Goethe's *Faust* and Coleridge," 24.

64 Ibid., 21–22.

65 Sterling: Hkg8 162. MS ex libris on front pastedown "Wm Heinemann | 10 Lancaster gate Hyde Park | W," corresponding to his 1890 address. Belonged previously to Henry G. J. Parsons. Pencilled date "Oct. 12, 1868" on title-page verso.

66 Beinecke: Speck Ck 99 R3 +82of (extra-illustrated 1820 Boosey ed., with the finely engraved Goethe portrait pasted in a blind-stamped frame).

FIGURE 5.8 Peter Cornelius, *Prelude in the Theatre, with the Painter's Dedication*, in *XII Bilder zu Göthe's Faust gezeichnet von Peter von Cornelius* (Frankfurt am Main: Johann Friedrich Wenner, n.d.), pl. 2
COURTESY BEINECKE, YALE UNIVERSITY, FOLIO SPECK CK99 C7 816

Retzsch's, in February 1820.[67] Perhaps emboldened by the success of his Retzsch copies, Moses now adapted Cornelius's inspired *mise en abyme*, which referred to Goethe's "Prelude on the Stage."

Cornelius's ingenious composition is in three parts, with a raised stage in the middle, complete with curtain and prompter in his box, an audience gathered to see the play on the left, and a laurel-wreathed Goethe composing on the right (Fig. 5.8). The poet is beset by a gesturing man, presumably the theatre owner, driven by cash concerns as his conspicuous money-pouch suggests, asking, as in *Faust*, how he may fill the playhouse. Next to an onlooker, a painter with the instruments of his trade leans towards the poet, ready to render the play (as Cornelius does graphically), while *Faust* is composed—and simultaneously performed by the characters on stage in theatrical attire. Faust rehearses his part, Valentine looks on, Margaret does up her hair in the mirror Martha proffers, while the *ignis fatuus* that will lead the way to the witches' Sabbath appears backstage. From atop the stage set, decorated with allegorical creatures and devices, a leaning angel pulls a trap-cord and lets Hell's creatures loose to leap and gambol, while Mephistopheles, grabbing the curtain, surveys sharply the spectators, musing whether they are ready for it all.

It is these interconnected incidents that Moses adapts for Boosey readers (Fig. 5.9). His somewhat wooden lines make the scene sharper while Cornelius's costumes have been switched for Retzsch's. The astute updating is backed by significant changes in depicted spectators' attitudes:

---

67 Weathercock, "Sentimentalities," 136.

FIGURE 5.9 Henry Moses, *Frontispiece*, outline etching after Peter Cornelius facing the title-page, with the inscription "Drawn and Engraved by Henry Moses," in *Faustus: from the German of Goethe* (London: Boosey and Sons, Rodwell & Martin, 1821)
COURTESY BEINECKE, YALE UNIVERSITY, SPECK CK99 R3 +821 COPY 1

Cornelius's hat-clad lady, talking over her shoulder to a companion, has become Moses's be-hatted young man who invitingly waves to us; a young child with some adult parent (Cornelius) now gazes at us (Moses). The frontispiece has become a mediating device, beckoning readers to enter and peruse the book. Staging furthers imaginative mutability of standpoints, and readers now face themselves as spectators. Subtle interaction, social exchange and aesthetic experience chain author to user at the threshold of Boosey's second edition. The artist was not called Moses for nothing; he offered the god Goethe audiences who now felt involved.

In reddish brown or dark green paper-covered boards, the same 4to *Faustus* hosts yet another decoy: a circular woodcut, 17.2 cm in diameter, in neoclassical style (as show the palmettos), presumably again by Moses (Fig. 5.10a).[68] Separately printed, carefully cut out, and centrally mounted, it presents the title in decorative lettering and whorls with choice scenes at cardinal points. All four vignettes, redrawn from Retzsch's plates 2, 8, 14 and 24 to fit the allotted spaces, bring attention to significant turns (the poodle appearing, Faust meeting Margaret, the daisy scene, Faust and Mephistopheles galloping away). If text sequence is applied, they are to be read in zigzag, darkening the clarity of the conception. If read clockwise, literal meaning recedes in favour of a constellation, suggestive of occult sciences, or of Faust summoning the devil in a magic circle, a scene lifted from Marlowe. Despite its clarity, it is an enigmatically tantalizing ornament. Insertions in collectors' exemplars show that it became a prized extra-illustrating item (Fig. 5.10b).[69]

Exciting, albeit unsatisfactory text-wise, *Faustus from the German* also passes through the hands of three foremost Romantics, Coleridge, Shelley and Byron, whether through publication, translation, or social intercourse. Boosey and Sons sought Coleridge's help and advice in May 1820, as mentioned. A year later, in August 1821, *Faustus* lay in Coleridge's bed-cum-book room at Highgate, in one of the formats, possibly proofs. It inspired him to such an illuminated speech that the episode triggered John Moultrie's conversion to the clergy.[70] Early 1821, Shelley

---

68 The same woodcut on front cover occurs later, particularly in the 3rd 1824 edition. In FDH: IV e/2, dated 1820 by hand, the publisher's slip on Schiller's *Fight with the Dragon* is certainly later than end July 1825.

69 Beinecke: Speck Ck 99 R3 +820d (Boosey, 1820, bound by C. Murton in 1822); Beinecke: Speck Zab W 6445+Zz 821 G (Boosey, 1821). See Fig. 5.10b.

70 Mays, "*Faustus* on the Table at Highgate," 119–27.

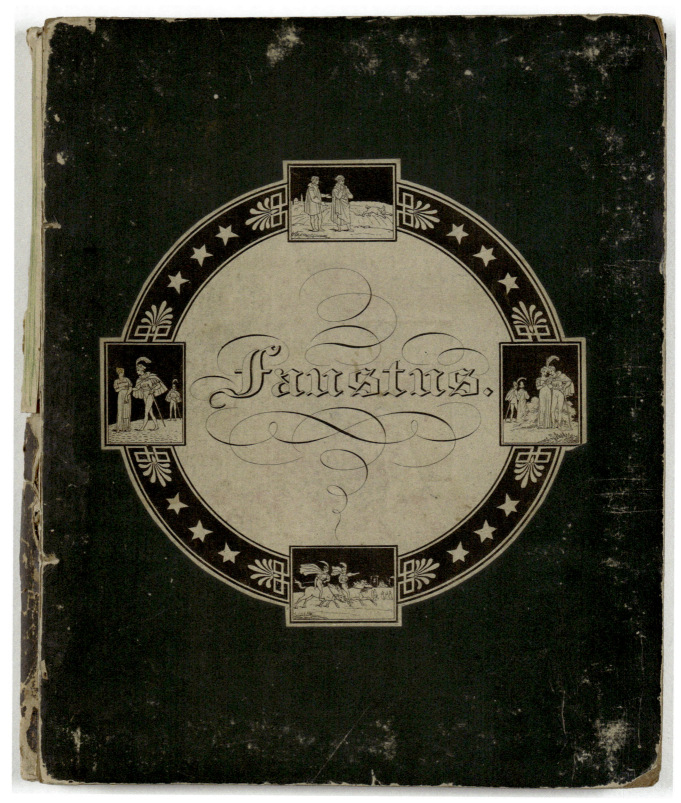

FIGURE 5.10A   Circular ornament with vignettes after Moritz Retzsch, pasted on petrol-green paper boards, *Faustus: from the German of Goethe* (London: Boosey and Sons, Rodwell & Martin, 1821)
COURTESY HAAB, F GR 5288, WEIMAR

FIGURE 5.10B Circular ornament inserted between half title and frontispiece, in *Faustus: from the German of Goethe* (London: Boosey and Sons, Rodwell & Martin, 1821). Exemplar owned in turn by C. Wood, Amos Niven Wilder, American poet, minister and theology professor, and his bother, the novelist and playwright Thornton Niven Wilder
COURTESY BEINECKE, YALE UNIVERSITY, SPECK ZAB W 6445+ZZ 821 G

discovered *Faust* in German thanks to John Gisborne,[71] but received his copy only on 12 January 1822,[72] by which time Boosey's 1820 edition was out of print. It is in the 1821 *Faustus from the German* that he had excitedly found *The Kiss* that made him almost pass out, and the witches' revel that made him grasp Walpurgis. He certainly translated "The Prologue in Heaven" and "The May-Day Night Scene" by reference to that edition since he "only attempted the scenes *omitted* in this translation."[73] Indeed, the 1820 Boosey contained (imperfect) summaries of both,[74] while in 1821 the first would be utterly suppressed, the second only very partially translated. One month later, on 21 May 1822 at Leghorn, Catharine Potter Stith would pluck a red rose from Byron's lapel. He acquiesced and sent her on the morrow his own exemplar of this very *Faustus*,[75] a "memorial less frail" but laden with metaphor. As heady as a red rose, if not more. Chapter 11 in this book reflects on the episode in comparison to a significant Retzsch gift imparted by Goethe to Marianne and Jakob von Willemer.

In short, while the "careful abstract" failed to meet the high literary standards of the German *Faust*, Retzsch's compositions, pirated by Moses, were still the most attractive part of the package. The visual add-ons confirm *Faust*'s visual success. Were they lures for bibliophiles alone? They certainly gladdened a few collectors as bonus material to 1820 exemplars sumptuously bound by Murton in 1822. Still, their prime significance rather lies in their manifold shaping of printed matter into mediating, tempting objects. "To live by the book" (to obey rules or the law) takes a novel significance: it points at meaning- and emotion-laden possessions. These were not just editorial packages for consumption, but multifaceted pieces of a technological revolution granting material bibliography social, symbolical and poetic value.

Even more prominently, Boosey was yet to deliver a third attempt, based on the printable durability of a stereotype edition.

5.5 *Faustus* as Template

In issuing a third edition in 1824, Boosey and Sons made no mystery about the visual success of *Faustus*: "Retsch's outlines have given to the eye the very essence of the leading occurrences in this tragedy." "We have never repeated so frequently the inspection of any publication

of Engravings," admitted the preface, quoting lengthily from "a celebrated weekly paper."[76] It borrowed heavily from an 1821 review by R. H. [Richard Horne] in the *Examiner*, shortened and water-downed for *La Belle Assemblée*, then reprinted even in the British Empire's 1822 *Calcutta Journal*.[77] By taking on board this excerpt as preface, Boosey inserted his "third edition" into both the print network of the time and within a mythological continuum that looked back to Ovid, as Horne's perspicacity had spotted. In its newest re-embodiment, the German *Faust* turned *Faustus* had become an Englander, thanks to Moses's replicas and Marlowe's precedent. It straddled novelty and the past. No accident Ovid was benchmarked: another significant metamorphosis was under way, though far from complete.

In point of fact, only one element had changed. Boosey's printer, W. Wilson, had *reset* the text in denser layout. He used the same type and repeated everything with remarkable, if not obdurate, constancy. The 1820 "List of Plates" had hardly changed (except for page numbers, *Faust* became *Faustus*, yet not in the captions, and the added top line "Head of Goethe to face the frontispiece"). The caption of plate 11, improved in 1821, had reverted back to the 1820 version, and the kitchen scene still read "in the witch's cave." Yet, the new technology had a notable outcome. Sheer quantity of letterpress dramatically dropped by a quarter (from 86 to 64 pages), its place now taken by the 26 prints interleaved at considerably diminished intervals. The latter still suffered from oscillating portrait/landscape formats, with plate 18 again sited *after* 19 and 20. However, the reduced ratio of letterpress to plates infused the volume with novel tempo. A fresh rhythm of swapping text for image and vice versa urged page-turning in a motion boosted by abridged scenes. The 64-page quarto earned a kinetic dimension to greater dramatic effect. The theatrical quality of Retzsch's conceptions and his plates' capacity to foster events were brought forward. For example, between pages 30 and 31, a much-condensed text chaperones three interleaved plates, all staged in Margaret's chamber. She undoes her tresses (pl. 9), Faust lifts the drapes and amorously contemplates the bed, while the devil intrudes with a casket (pl. 10), whose contents Margaret discovers and admires (pl. 11). Before readers' eyes a short teaser pinpoints crucial turns of the play, sixty-three years before movies would be invented (Fig. 5.11a–c). True, the book has to be swivelled

---

71   Webb, *Shelley and Translation*, 144, 147–48.
72   *The Letters of Percy Bysshe Shelley*, 2:376.
73   Ibid., 2:407, my emphasis.
74   Analysis 1820, 4, 51–53.
75   Beinecke: Speck Ck99 R3 +821, copy 2 (Byron's MS ex libris, inscribed "Presented by him to Mrs Stith").

---

76   *Faustus: from the German of Goethe*, 3rd ed. (London: Boosey and Sons, 1824), III–IV.
77   R. H. [Richard Horne], "Fine Arts," *Examiner*, no. 719 (14 Oct 1821): 648–49a; *La Belle Assemblée* (Nov 1821): 183; *Calcutta Journal of Politics and General Literature* 3, no. 104 (1 May 1822): 7.

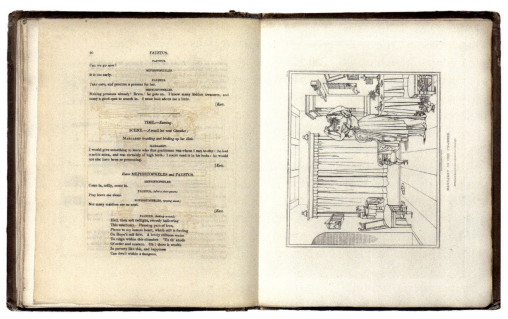

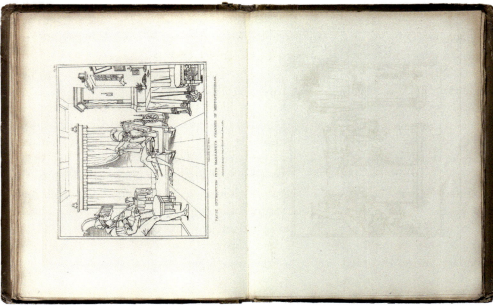

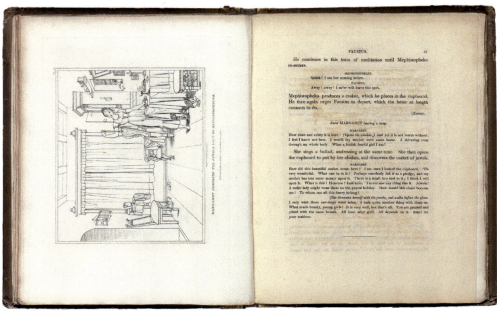

FIGURES 5.11A–C
Kinetic effect in *Faustus: From the German of Goethe. Embellished with Retsch's Series of Twenty-Seven Outlines, Illustrative of the Tragedy, Engraved by Henry Moses. Third edition* (London: Boosey and Sons, 1824), plates inserted between pp. 30–31
COURTESY BEINECKE, YALE UNIVERSITY, SPECK CK99 R3 +824

and every image flipped shows a blank reverse. The agile reader must improvise as cameraman-cum-film editor to flick images in succession. Still, this occurs instantly with Margaret at Martha's house (pp. 32–33); again in Faust's study and the witch's kitchen to a lesser degree, since the device bears on only two plates. Sequence may also lead to poignant disparity (pp. 52–53) as when Margaret swoons at the cathedral on the right (pl. 18) and, after turning the page, on the left, Faust ascends the Brocken with Mephistopheles (pl. 21). Conversely, Gretchen plates marooned in copious typeset read more pathetically, such as at the spinning wheel (pl. 16) or before the Mater Dolorosa effigy (pl. 17), both dolefully mid-chant, harping on emotions.

If Moses's copies had proven a graphic matrix, Wilson's set-up turned out as print template. The crafty publishers had traded the by now stereotyped contraption to others. It became foundational for later editions and furthered Goethe's *Faust* as inseparable from Retzsch.

Two cases are illuminating. The first entails the resourceful Septimus Prowett who published Milton's *Paradise Lost* in 1825 with John Martin's superb mezzotints, having paid the artist a substantial 3,500 guineas. Reputedly a "mysterious publisher," Prowett emerges as a significant professional in the London book market, and shaper of public taste in graphic matters, with accomplished results in a variety of genres.[78] In 1824 and 1825 respectively, he published Schiller's *Fridolin, or The Road to the Iron-Foundery: A Ballad*, and *The Fight with the Dragon: A Romance*. Both were bilingual, just as Bohte had imagined for *Faust*, but with Retzsch's outlines re-engraved by Moses, after Boosey's model. Effective recipes were not to be discarded. Borrowing from both their clever ideas prompted a third, even more effective. In Prowett's two books, translations were by John Payne Collier, son of John D. Collier, who, as Henry Crabb Robinson's lodger and friend, was likely one of the first, back in 1817, to have seen the original *Umrisse*, Perthes's gift to Robinson (see Chapter 4). Prowett offered *Fridolin* (by May 1824) and *The Dragon* (by end July 1825) to the British public only one year after Cotta's corresponding originals. Aware of the foreign Retzsch craze, the Stuttgart publisher had indeed issued eight prints by Retzsch after *Fridolin* with C. A. Böttiger's comments in 1823, and sixteen others after *Der Kampf mit dem Drachen* in 1824, for all three markets, German, British and French. In London, press reviews inescapably related Prowett's well-designed and bilingual albums, offered at even more

competitive prices,[79] to Boosey's *Faustus*. Yet, the bond was not only intellectual or aesthetic but conspicuously material. Boosey's third *Faust* had predicated *a format*. Prowett significantly advertised *Fridolin* as published "uniformly with Retsch's Designs to Goethe's *Faust*."[80] This materialized 1824 in a threefold volume with Boosey's third "kinetic" *Faustus*, printed by W. Wilson, next to Prowett's cloned 1824 *Fridolin* and 1825 *Dragon*, printed by S. and R. Bentley.[81] In this, the template was not altered, not even by a hair's breadth. The crossbreed, juxtaposing three outlined works copied from Retzsch, uses a common matrix decreed by Wilson. Cloned formats had come to be and would set the trend.

Prowett's clever exploit, which undoubtedly enhanced sales, also provoked rivalry and stimulated competition. A Boosey flyer, *post* end July 1825, touts in turn *The Fight with the Dragon* "uniform with Faustus," at a sharp "14s. boards." Its rhetoric deploys innuendo, uppercase and small caps to lure clients away from Prowett towards Retzsch's imported German prints:

> A Series of Sixteen spirited OUTLINES by M. RETSCH, to | SCHILLER'S FIGHT with the DRAGON, have been imported | by Boosey and Sons, Broad-Street, Royal Exchange, who have added | a Translation of the Poem, and an Explanation of the Plates. | We think it right that the admirers of Faustus and Fridolin should | be informed that these Outlines are designed and engraved by Retsch | himself, and are to be had uniform with the Faustus, price 14s. boards. | Sold also at T. Boosey and Co's Foreign Music Warehouse, Holles-|Street, Oxford-Street.[82]

Prowett had out-Booseyed Boosey, but Boosey would not let himself be imposed upon. He reverted to Bohte's formula of importation, having already out-Bohted Bohte with a vengeance.

In the second case, the *Faustus* template works not by juxtaposition, but inclusion or addition. Indeed, yet another *Faustus: from the German of Goethe* was issued in 1832 by Edward Lumley. It offered as "Appendix" Shelley's translation of "The May-Day Night Scene," that is the

---

78 Howard J. M. Hanley, Margaret Cooper, and Susan Morris, "The Mysterious Septimus Prowett: Publisher of the John Martin 'Paradise Lost'," *British Art Journal* 2, no. 1 (Autumn 2000): 20–25.

79 Ordinary runs for *Fridolin* cost 8s sewn, 9s 6d in boards, and 16s in royal 4to on India paper and extra boards. The ordinary *Dragon* cost 8s sewn, 16s in boards, 12s in royal 4to on India paper, 24s in India paper boards. A few were offered as separate proofs on India paper, royal 4to, at £1 10s.

80 *Literary Chronicle* 6, no. 250 (28 Feb 1824): 144; same advert *Examiner*, no. 841 (14 Mar 1824): 175.

81 Sterling: Hkg8 020 (Noah and Jared Linsly Fund).

82 HAAB: F 3494; FDH: IV e/2 (ticket of Alfred Lorentz, University bookseller, Leipzig).

witches' Sabbath, another disturbing element for the British, either absent, severely abridged, or bowdlerised in previous *Faust* translations. Shelley's translations had already been published first in the *Liberal*, shortly after his untimely death, then in *Posthumous Poems* edited by his wife Mary (June 1824). In transferring Goethe's *Faust* into English, Shelley had precisely chosen to render in blank verse the two most shocking passages, the "Prologue in Heaven" and the Walpurgis.[83] Nearly all anglicised *Faust* editions had turned away from the first, and Lumley would be no exception. But the second was not to be spurned. Quite the reverse. As a version by a morally reproved and politically disreputable modern poet, who had recently met with a tragic death, it was bound to attract.

Lumley's case reveals how book materiality may be charged with symbolic, aesthetic, and poetical substance. The third Boosey *Faustus* is composed of quarto gatherings A to I, followed by a single sheet K listing plates. In Lumley 1832, extra K, K2, L and L2 gatherings in smaller type (pp. 65–79) have been either *inserted* (between end of I and list of plates K) or added onto K to slot Shelley's translation into the template. Evocative plates, pulled out, have become eye-catching frontispieces (cf. Fig. 5.13).[84] Printers Davison, Simmons, and Co, in charge of this extra at Whitefriars, seem also to have adjusted the title-page to the new content. Indeed, the 1824 *Faustus* title-page (Fig. 5.12) has been tampered with to accommodate the lines "An Appendix | Containing the May-Day Night Scene | Translated by | Percy Bysshe Shelley" (Fig. 5.13). The insertion in small print and various types is almost tongue-in-cheek as it mirrors the *physical* insert to the body of the book using supplementary gatherings. Symbolic irony lurks in that, thanks to Shelley, one of the most expurgated *Faust* scenes returns to restore some of Goethe's wildest pages to Boosey's tamer version. As acclaimed winner repeatedly published, Boosey's anglicised and standardised *Faustus* embodied a newly prosperous literary community of romantic persuasion. Shelley, the rebel compelled to leave England, paradoxically returns, piggybacking Goethe's play, not only to integrate this British community but also rank with its national poets.

All the above surfs on L. H.'s [Leigh Hunt] brief introduction to the translation.[85] The editor of the *Liberal* praises Shelley's genius, poetry, and translation talent, which stand the challenge of Goethe's "work of creation" and re-form it in another idiom. Deliberate insistence on *creation* and *formation* not only styles Shelley "true representative of his author [Goethe]," but also creator of pages English dramatists such as Webster and Middleton would gladly have endorsed. A poetic pantheon forms, welcoming Shelley and Goethe as equals to eminent dramatic English-language poets. Hunt's symbolism makes of Shelley's Walpurgis not just a version or a rendition, but an original and vibrant work infused with a dynamic of its own. Shelley has met the challenge of Goethe's world growing "like the animated rocks and crags which he speaks of." By translating it, and measuring himself against the poem's wildest verse, Shelley is part of this undertaking, an uncontrollable spirit, the very essence of poetry.

Romantic metaphor is not innocuous. It reflects a Walpurgis passage, in which Shelley not only has enlivened the cliffs but speeded up the version. It is quite possible that the animation was inspired by "a personification in the German" as Timothy Webb has it.[86] Yet it could also be that Shelley's *visual* imagination, a strong component of his poetic *fiat*,[87] was roused by the huddled-up old woman, pictured as a rock on the left of Retzsch's plate 21 (Fig. 5.14), faithfully copied by Moses, and singled out in English reception. In both cases, Shelley stirs emotion thus: "How, clift by clift, rocks bend and lift | Their frowning foreheads as we go." In Hunt's preface, the enhanced image of animated rocks and crags represents Goethe's "work of creation." The motif is strongly reminiscent of a key vision in Staël's appreciation of Goethe's tragedy: "if the imagination could figure to itself an intellectual chaos, such as the material chaos has often been painted, the 'Faustus' of Goethe should have been composed at that epoch."[88] The orgiastic and organic nature of Walpurgis is indeed material chaos; to translate it into English is to come to terms with an intellectual chaos through poetry; it is to be a poet, the welcome prodigal son riding home witch-like on a wild foreign composition, thanks to this supplement. Shelley's posthumous homecoming afore the British public, thanks to the popular *Faustus*, may even have more genuine worth than his incorporation to the glorious pantheon of the past (Webster, Middleton, and Marlowe, all mentioned by Hunt). It acquires common reference status, typically valued. Had not Boosey's device

---

83   Webb, *Shelley and Translation*, 148–49.

84   Beinecke: Speck Ck99 R3 +832 (translation inserted); BL: 11746.l.4 (translation added); HAAB: F 3495 (translation added on; "Kiss" plate mounted as frontispiece). Further details in Appendix 1 under 1832 and 1834.

85   L. H., "Addenda: May-Day Night," in *Faustus: from the German of Goethe. New edition*, trans. P. B. Shelley (London: Edward Lumley, 1832), 65–66.

---

86   Webb, *Shelley and Translation*, 194.

87   Nancy Moore Goslee, *Shelley's Visual Imagination* (Cambridge: Cambridge University Press, 2011); Matthew P. M. Kerr's review highlights Retzsch, *Notes & Queries* 61, no. 2 (June 2014): 310–11.

88   Staël, "Faustus," 2:181.

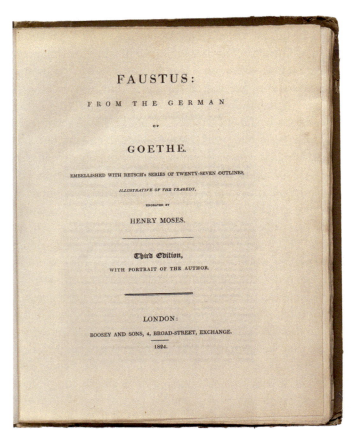

FIGURE 5.12
Title-page of *Faustus: From the German of Goethe. Embellished with Retsch's Series of Twenty-Seven Outlines, Illustrative of the Tragedy, Engraved by Henry Moses. Third edition* (London: Boosey and Sons, 1824)
COURTESY BEINECKE, YALE UNIVERSITY, SPECK CK99 R3 +824

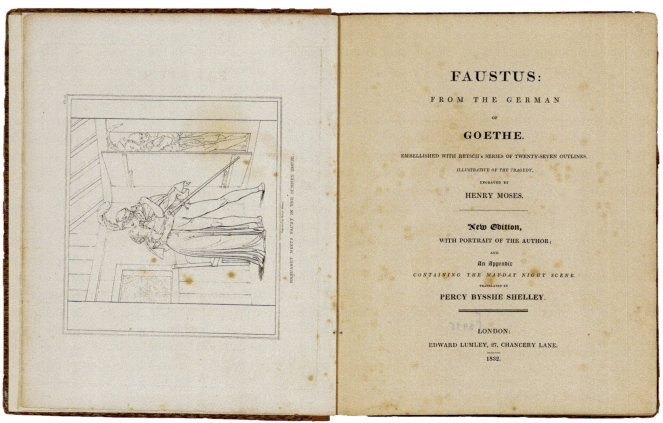

FIGURE 5.13
Title-page of *Faustus: From the German of Goethe. Embellished with Retsch's Series of Twenty-Seven Outlines, Illustrative of the Tragedy, Engraved by Henry Moses. New edition. And An Appendix Containing the May-Day Night Scene Translated by Percy Bysshe Shelley* (London: Edward Lumley, 1832). With "The Kiss" plate mounted as frontispiece
COURTESY HAAB, F 3495, WEIMAR

FIGURE 5.14   Moritz Retzsch, Faust and Mephistopheles ascend the Brocken, *Umrisse zu Goethe's Faust gezeichnet von Retsch* (Stuttgart & Tübingen: Cotta, 1816), pl. 21
COURTESY HAAB, F 3487, WEIMAR

by then become *canon*? Omitting the "objectionable parts of the original" had rendered from October 1821 "that curious work fit *for general perusal*" as a magazine "addressed particularly to the ladies" would confirm.[89]

5.6 Retzsch Gains Ground in Other Garb and Guises

Other publishers vied for rank, putting their weight behind copies of Retzsch. Commercial strategies experimented with alternative techniques, size, and quality of plates, while examples of fine printing, proofs for collectors (before lettering), and deluxe paper stayed. Theatrical success reflected on the book market as *Faust* versions multiplied. Textual translations into English, even German editions published in London, embodied a commercial potential for extra-illustration not to be neglected by enterprising printsellers and makers. A hub spreading over the Channel to the Continent, the London market also supplied France with a godsend. Southeast Lithuania and the Netherlands would follow.

Lithography, still nascent, proved a suitable technique to readily copy and reinterpret Retzsch. English painter and engraver Henry Berthoud Jr (1794–1864) operated from the early 1820s in Nash's fashionable Regent's Quadrant, initially as printmaker, subsequently as full partner of Henry Berthoud Sr, his father's publishing business. The firm published without any text in 1825 *Faustus: Illustrated in Twenty-Six Outlines by Retsch*, lithographically printed by Charles Joseph Hullmandel.

---

89   "Literary Intelligence," *La Belle Assemblée*, n.s., 24 (Oct 1821): 183a, my emphasis.

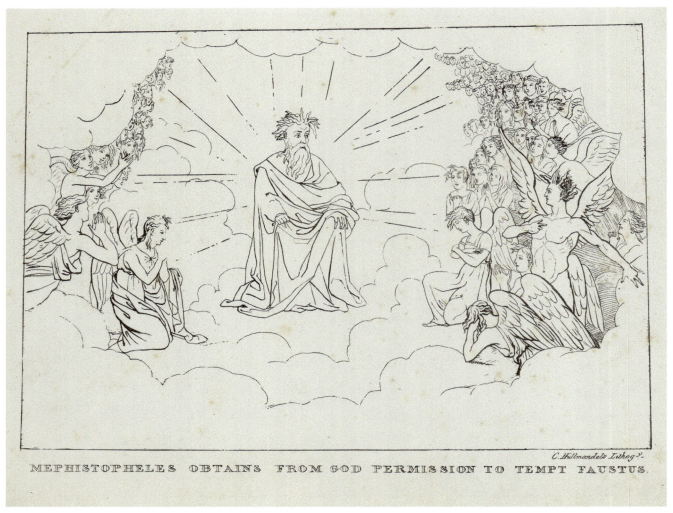

FIGURE 5.15   *Mephistopheles Obtains from God Permission to Tempt Faustus*, lithographic copy after Moritz Retzsch, in *Faustus: Illustrated in Twenty-Six Outlines by Retsch* (London: H. Berthoud, 1825), pl. 1
COURTESY HAAB, F 3496, WEIMAR

The latter, "the only scientific lithographer" in England according to his *Art Journal* obituary,[90] famously experimented with the process Senefelder had introduced to England in 1801. Berthoud's prints coincide with a turning point in Hullmandel's career. Originally an artist, drawing on the stone himself, he 1819 set up his press in Great Marlborough Street, a pebble's throw from Regent's Quadrant, and turned in parallel to lithographing others' work. His decisive mid-1820s change coincided with publishing *The Art of Drawing on Stone* (1824) and printing Géricault's lithographs.[91]

Intriguingly, Berthoud's publication does not seem to have left traces in the press or be listed in standard catalogues. Prints in landscape octavo oddly follow cover and title-page in portrait format. The cover, framed in neoclassical running spirals, adds the price (25s) to bait bargain hunters.[92] A pencilled statement on an exemplar's mock wrapper runs: "Hullmandel's lithographs (to accompany the 8° ~~ed of~~ <vol. of 1821 called> Faustus from the German of Goethe." *Faustus*, Berthoud's main title nods at Boosey's octavo *Faustus* (adorned only with Goethe's portrait), inviting readers to complete it with his lithographic prints. However, the pencil note, perhaps by reliable collector Stumme, is twice contradicted by inconsistencies in size and price. Larger than Boosey's octavo (either 20.5 × 13.4 cm or 22 × 13 cm), the prints (27.3 × 21.9 cm) would have

---

90   "Mr C. J. Hullmandel," *Art Journal*, n.s., 13 (Jan 1851): 30; repr. *Gentleman's Magazine* 189 (1851): 209–10.
91   Michael Twyman, "Charles Joseph Hullmandel: Lithographic Printer Extraordinary," in *Lasting Impressions: Lithography as Art*, ed. P. Gilmour (Canberra: Australian National Gallery, 1988), 42–90.

---

92   HAAB: F 3496, Stumme's Collection. https://haab-digital.klassik-stiftung.de/viewer/!thumbs/1335564675/1/.

RETZSCH COPIED IN BRITAIN AND BEYOND   161

FIGURE 5.16   *Faustus with the Dog in the Cabinet*, lithographic copy after Moritz Retzsch, in *Faustus: Illustrated in Twenty-Six Outlines by Retsch* (London: H. Berthoud, 1825), pl. 3
COURTESY HAAB, F 3496, WEIMAR

been closely cropped to fit it—a practice clashing with bibliophilic wide-margin protocol. The combined price of Boosey's octavo (6s) and Berthoud's prints (25s) exceeds by 11s that of Boosey's 1824 *Faustus*, offering the text with "Retzsch's Series of 27 exquisite Outlines" by Moses at £1.[93] Why buy costlier prints by Berthoud, cruder and more naïve than Moses's, besides the extra binding expenditure to bring it all together? An alternative response to growing demand, the pirated substitute sold in central London as plates only.[94]

Other peculiarities occur in the treatment itself. Although offered in London, the first plate represents (shockingly for English piety) God in Heaven (Fig. 5.15). All captions eccentrically name Gretchen "Marguerite" instead of Margaret. Altered details match Jean-François Muret's lithographed Retzsch copy issued 1824 in Paris, on which more in the next chapter. Stumme calls them "a rather sloppily executed lithograph copy by Hullmandel" without questioning this attribution.[95] Were these printed or both copied and printed by the lithographer? Rough treatment suggests an unknown hand, the plagiarist's stones simply printed by Hullmandel. His imprints

---

93   *Examiner*, no. 854 (13 June 1824): 393 (advertisement).
94   Beinecke: Speck Ck99 R3 +825b. Details in Appendix 1.

95   Stumme, *Faust als Pantomime*, 93.

on only two of nine plates (the others not lettered) correspond to diversely dated uses, further muddying the waters.[96]

The publisher's motivations seem threefold. Previously expunged by Moses in all Boosey editions, re-representing God in pl. 1 would attract amateurs as a rarity. The imitator may have ingeniously suggested it by carefully decorating all the spines of Faust's volumes in his study as if they were elegantly bound and gilt (Fig. 5.16). Retzsch had simply outlined them since they worked by implication (cf. Fig. 4.3). The detail is already in Muret, enhanced in the Berthoud version. Acquiring these prints, any bibliophile likely projected their self into the picture. Many nineteenth-century book lovers identified with Faust in their own library, as bespoke bookplates testify.

More importantly, this Retzsch duplicate is twice lifted. It is based on Muret, himself copy-lithographing Retzsch in Paris, whence the spelling "Marguerite." Hullmandel, himself half French, had improved his technique in France with the guidance of both François Delpech and Godefroy Engelmann. His French connexions were numerous. Berthoud Jr too would move to Paris after 1828 and die in France. *Tartini's Dream*, a print by Louis Boilly in the V&A Collection, dated *c*.1824, is similarly published by Berthoud Jr and printed by Hullmandel. Had Retzsch been roughly copied in France, the stones exported for printing? The Berthoud would tempt their London clientele with French morsels. That market was the nerve centre of a commercial network spreading over the Channel to and from the Continent.

A last strong driver was the English stage. From 1822, Berthoud Jr published full-length coloured prints of famous actors and dancers in full attire. An expensive *British Theatrical Gallery: A Collection of Whole Length Portraits with Biographical Notices* by Daniel Terry would follow in 1825, sold at £3 13s 6d coloured or £1 plain. Berthoud had himself worked at length with Terry, author, actor and playwright, gathering visual material and engraving the plates, occasionally to great effect, such as the print of Mrs Siddons as Lady Macbeth.[97] Terry and Soane's resounding success at Drury Lane in June 1825, the very play that electrified Delacroix, was *Faustus: A Romantic Drama*, with Terry performing Mephistopheles in a costume after Retzsch (cf. Fig. 9.13). "Seeing that play which, however distorted, was extremely well arranged, inspired me in doing my lithographic compositions. *Terry* who did *the devil* was perfect," noted Delacroix.[98] Between the theatre and Boosey's octavo *Faustus from the German*, Berthoud's *Faustus: Illustrated in Twenty-Six Outlines by Retsch* doubled the catch. Retzsch replicas had fully entered the cultural arena and already crossed the Channel from France.

Inversely, James Bulcock (fl. 1826–35) swore authenticity by banking on fine prints, variety and inserts. Also centrally established at 163, Strand, he boasted on his wares "11 doors East of Somerset House," which accommodated at the time the Royal Academy, the Royal Society, and the Society of Antiquaries. Bulcock traded in lithographs, highly finished engravings, and steel engravings in mezzotint after paintings, monuments, and works of art. Intermittently featured in the *Gentleman's Magazine*, they were offered as prints, collectors' proofs, India proofs, and on paper sometimes tinted. He commissioned John Kennerley, a skilful artist in line- and stipple engraving, to re-engrave from Retzsch's originals. Kennerley imprinted two footers, marking "Retzsch" on the left and "J. Kennerley" on the right. Yet, he only restored the demure female in the witch's mirror. Again God and codpieces fell victim to prudery. In fact, his copy fused Retzsch with Moses.

Two batches of prints were issued with descriptive captions, following on Boosey: ten mostly around Margaret (pl. 2, 5, 8–14, 23) on 1 August, and the remaining sixteen on 22 September 1826, developing bolder episodes around Faust and Mephystopheles [*sic*]. In 1827, a delightful pink cover (cf. Fig. 5.17) hyped *Retzsch's Outlines to Goethe's Faust*, twenty-seven plates in all, including Goethe's portrait by Jagemann, also on 22 September. Their cleverest feature is diminutive size. Images in ordinary runs (average 7.2 × 9.2 cm), hardly larger in India proofs (7.4 × 9.7 cm), offer conspicuous margins (overall 19.2 × 24.3 cm). The expedient worked marvellously well: it could fit the requirements of collectors' portfolios, and prove ready seasoning for book lovers to spice up their cherished octavos.[99] The subtitle touted the bid: "Adapted to Illustrate Any Edition of FAUST, but Particularly the Translation of Lord F. L. Gower to Whom They Are Most Respectfully Dedicated." Lord Francis Leveson Gower's translation, *Faust, a Drama by Goethe* (1823), had by then run into a second enlarged

---

96   Used in eight plates, "C. Hullmandel's Lithog^y" is considered as used up to mid-1821, followed by "Printed by C. Hullmandel," used later. The latter occurs only in pl. 25. See Felix H. Man, *150 Years of Artists' Lithographs* (London: William Heinemann, 1953), XXIII. I am indebted to Michael Twyman for several suggestions on Hullmandel.

97   Tessa Maria Kilgarriff, "Reproducing Celebrity: Painted, Printed and Photographic Theatrical Portraiture in London, *c*.1820–1870" (PhD diss., University of Bristol, 2018), online pdf, 147–48.

98   Delacroix, *Journal*, ed. M. Hannoosh (Paris: Corti, 2009), 1:918, his emphasis.

99   Beinecke: Speck Ck99 R3 +827b (ordinary); Speck Ck99 R3 +826 ("Quarto, on Indian paper, of which there are only 50 Taken, One Guinea"). See further Appendix 1.

edition (1825). Although savaged in the *London Magazine* and the *Quarterly Review*, it was prized and suited Bulcock's prints. Other suitors included yet again Boosey's octavo, but also Bohte's *Faust, eine Tragödie*, printed in London by his regular printer Gottlieb Schulze in 1823. The latter, a remnant from Bohte's failed bilingual *Faust* with Retzsch etchings, readily matched Bulcock's prints.[100]

Intriguingly though, the pink cover was not by Kennerley but a little-known wood engraver, John Berryman, who, posing as "ingenious," had printed in 1808 his cuts on separate sheets as "wondrous specimens of the art."[101] Whether conceived by publisher or engraver, his composition has mediating power (Fig. 5.17). It acts as cover, title-page and small poster, advertises prints, formats, and paper tints-cum-prices, and pulls together fantastic ingredients from Retzsch's witch's kitchen in a fresh arrangement around an open book perched on the monkey's back. The title *Retzsch's Outlines* appears on the magic mirror's drapery. Proscenium-like, three winged demonic heads (based on Retzsch's) hold it in their teeth. Bulcock's title, subtitle and imprint are pressed into the fumes of the witch's cauldron, while Mephistopheles summons Faust, now a reverse figure boldly facing him, to quaff the rejuvenating potion. The enclosed prints are meant to have undergone a similar transformation: they have been refreshed by reverting to Retzsch's originals—though the promise is uncertain. Hocus-pocus works better than pretence. On the pink cover, the witch is no more. The volume on the monkey's back, poised with other bogus paraphernalia amid beldam bric-a-brac, insinuates to any potential book lover that a rejuvenating force lurks precisely in this very publication—ready to be seized. In pink, like Faust's youthful flush; all the same, a little fake, as the cover hints and data confirm.

The Kennerley version advertised by Bulcock would have an extended effect on Faustiana in and beyond Great Britain. Time and again in the 1830s, presumably after Bulcock's death in 1835, London publisher W. W. Gibbings of 18 Bury St, issued it as *Illustrations to Goethe's Faust in Twenty-Six* (or *Twenty-Seven*) *Outline Engravings by Moritz Retzsch*, depending on whether or not he includes Goethe's portrait. In an album of varying size with an ornate cover, the wee prints sat in ample margins opposite condensed and rhymed excerpts. Corresponding to none of the ten or so extant translations, all checked,

the formula dramatized hustle and bustle. *A contrario*, the radiant void (supplanting God), cautiously entitled "Introduction," faced no translation, recalling that the initial plate and scene were taboo. The title's inaugural *Illustrations* shows that change was in the air. Coerced by print technologies and a spawn of *Faust* texts, Retzsch in English version was entering a new phase, soon to be endorsed by Jonathan Birch's translation and John Brain's steel engravings in an officially sanctioned edition.

Still the prints stood their own ground far and wide. The three small items published by Audot in Paris in 1828–29 look indebted to Kennerley's copies and Bulcock's clever cover, as the next chapter shows. Yet Retzsch's compositions were to spread further. A *Faust* translation issued 1844 in Vilnius by Józef Zawadzki (1781–1838), founder of one of the most important publishing houses of the city, recycled Bulcock's plates with captions in Polish. Or did it rather reprocess Audot's diminutive prints inspired by Bulcock's? Their lengthy and explicit captions read after the French Audot, not Boosey-cum-Bulcock. The tragedy had been translated "from the German" by Alfons Walicki, major Polish translator of the Greek tragic poets and works by Goethe and Hoffmann, also professor at Kharkiv University from 1835. Fifteen plates were re-engraved (and slightly modified) by a certain P. Keppel, unrecorded in German or Polish art dictionaries, perhaps a job-engraver. With characters' expressions altered, they were gathered in succession at the very end as an extra ornament, again askance to the textual sequence. Meaningfully, four scores of lyrics, choral or other, by the Polish Prince Anton von Radziwill, interleaved and folded with care, are set close to apposite passages, an homage to his musically interpreted *Faust*, partial readings, and pioneer Berlin performances in private and court circles (see Chapter 9).[102] In distant Vilnius, under Russian occupation at the time, the book addressed a prominent Polish-speaking community. Thanks to Radziwill's music and Retzsch's outlines partly reinterpreted, by 1844, in subjugated Lithuania, Goethe's *Faust* was already much more than a mere play: an intermedial exponent of trans-European culture, mingling Goethe, Radziwill, Bulcock and Audot, the crossbred outcome of German, British and French editions alike.[103]

John Berryman's inventive 1826 idea for a striking cover also emerged in a Dutch version in Amsterdam thirty-nine years later. Vesting a *Faust* translation albeit with

---

100   Beinecke: Speck Rb1 823b copy 2 (extra-illustrated with Bulcock's prints, beautifully bound, with Harry Bagot's MS ex libris, dated 5 May 1840).

101   F. W. Fairholt, "William Harvey, and the Wood Engravers of His Era," *Art Journal* 28 (1 Mar 1866): 89.

102   Digitized at <https://polona.pl/item/faust-tragedya-gothego,Mz c3MzE3/4/#info:metadata> (last accessed 3 Mar 2023).

103   Radziwill's score for the piano had been published as *Compositionen* (Berlin: T. Trautwein, 1835), the ornate title-page frame partly influenced by Retzsch.

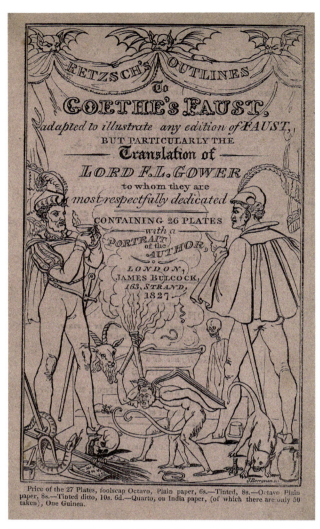

FIGURE 5.17
(*top*) Pictorial pink cover by John Berryman for *Retzsch's Outlines to Goethe's Faust, Adapted to Illustrate Any Edition of FAUST, But Particularly the Translation of Lord F. L. Gower to Whom They Are Most Respectfully Dedicated* (London: James Bulcock, 1827); (*bottom*) Moritz Retzsch, The witch's kitchen, *Umrisse zu Goethe's Faust gezeichnet von Retsch* (Stuttgart & Tübingen: Cotta, 1816), pl. 7
COURTESY BEINECKE, YALE UNIVERSITY, SPECK CK99 R3 +827B, AND: COURTESY HAAB, F 3487, WEIMAR

RETZSCH COPIED IN BRITAIN AND BEYOND 165

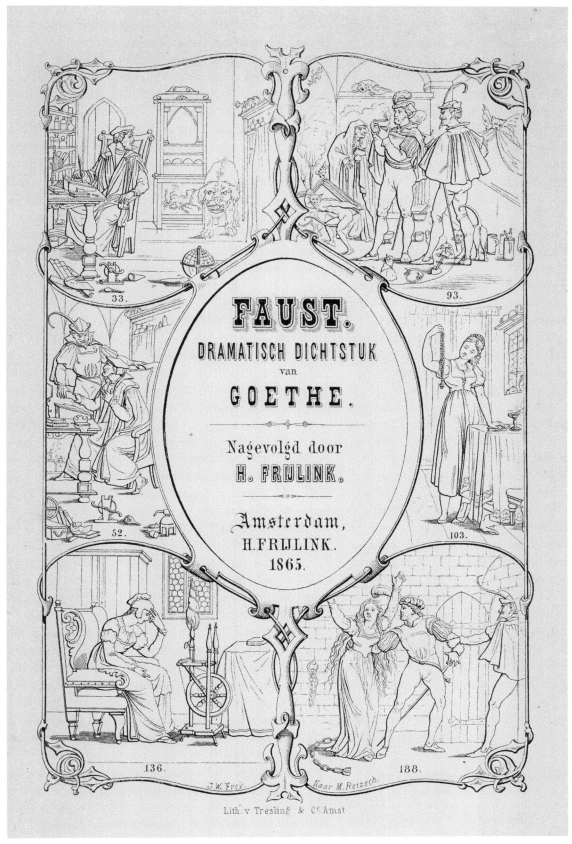

FIGURE 5.18   Johann Wilhelm Frey, six vignettes after Moritz Retzsch, cover and title leaf of *Faust: dramatisch Dichtstuk van Goethe. Nagevolgd door H. Frijlink. Met een zestal schetsen, naar teekeningen van Moritz Retzsch* (Amsterdam: Frijlink / Spin, 1865)
COURTESY HAAB, F 3988, WEIMAR

omissions into Dutch by Hendrik Frijlink (1800–86), also the book's publisher, it claimed primacy.[104] This self-taught quick-witted young man had grown from errand boy to severally occupy the book trade via children's books, adaptations and translations, a reading cabinet, a 1834 periodical, *Het Leeskabinet*, that would attain 40,000 readers by 1847, and publishing. He is credited with extra attention "in the care of outward form, neatness, taste, art feeling" (*in het behartigen van uitwendige vormen, van net-heid, van smaak, van kunstgevoel*).[105] His 1865 *Faust* "with six sketches, after drawings by Moritz Retzsch" tallies the assessment, however derivative. Six focused vignettes by German lithographer and graphic artist Johann Wilhelm Frey (1830–1909), trained in Amsterdam, encircle the printed title on the front cover. Page numbers, alluding to the text, work as summary when read piecemeal rather than clockwise (Fig. 5.18). Duplicated on thicker paper as compound frontispiece or ornamental title leaf, the device serves as cover and ornate title-page in two colour variants (buff or light grey, the latter complementing the book's red edges). However retouched, outline performs at its strongest as iconographic skeleton flagging key scenes and referring the roused reader to Frijlink's translation. A single drawing of Faust and Gretchen in historicist costume, a far cry from Retzsch, decorates the back cover, all figures lithographically reproduced. Though incomplete in conception, the effective Dutch book ran to a second edition (with revised and enlarged text) a year later.

From London to Paris, Vilnius or Amsterdam, and from 1819 to 1865, Retzsch's outlines spread across Europe in more guises than the seven ages of man's or a book's life. Berthoud's prints beg questions that cannot be addressed without measuring exchanges between France and Great Britain in a complicated period of rapid technological evolution, swaps and borrowings, hardly yet researched. Bulcock's wares, another sample of the many paths the prints followed, indicate European circulation. Within London and the UK, both Berthoud's and Bulcock's goods signpost multiple uses (free-standing or interleaved), a diversity of consumers, and interplay between book, print trade, and stage.

Boosey had anglicised and in a way standardised Retzsch. This might have side-lined the etchings or led to

a dead-end, yet their plasticity and adaptability resisted. Their main strength lies in resilience, their capacity to adjust and transform into diversified print artefacts. As the latter branch out, customized by innovative technologies and tradesmen's clever plans, our very idea of the printed book, the graphic set, or the work of art, changes. In Great Britain, within just a few years, Goethe's *Faust* had first found in Retzsch a forerunner that played an active role in intellectual and social barter, who influenced perception, and paved the way to textual translations. Once the text itself had acquired a genuine, however imperfect, status in English, its connection to Retzsch called for dependence. The prints yielded, pursuing in parallel their own route yet again. In all printed versions up to now, they had always been crucial, but even so, *none* of the above was yet *an illustrated book*.

5.7 Retzsch Wielded by Illustration

Present-day readers may wonder at the forcefulness of my argument nor even support it. In point of fact, in recent academic discourse, *illustration* has become an umbrella term for almost *any* image related to text. One of the consequences of intense and unequal digitization, it results in material flatness and disingenuous assimilation of items, which neither read alike nor are of same ilk. Such failure to differentiate, bundling dissimilar objects or situations without nuance, is ahistorical and demonstrably so. It ignores and obscures the meaning and function of images in printed artefacts.[106] In Retzsch's case, that Boosey's 1821 *Faustus* be chiefly considered a translation, and an illustrated edition to boot, is an outcome of such levelling.[107] Significantly, the authenticity debate was also primarily steered on textual merits (with rare exceptions) by specialists of Coleridge or romanticism.

Previous sections of this chapter establish quite the opposite: in all Boosey editions, texts are ancillary to the prints. Synthetically recalling their wording will suffice. We have seen that, in alternate 1820 title-pages (*An Analysis/Retsch's Series* or *Retsch's Series/An Analysis*), *illustrative* and *illustration* refer autonomously to both text and prints, *not* to text-bound images; besides, two thirds of the "Introduction" bear on the plates, not the text. The 1821 *Faustus from the German* identifies its textual content as "[t]he slight analysis drawn up as an accompaniment to Retsch's Outlines," and refers to itself as "a book of reference and explanation for the use of the purchasers of the

---

104 Engel no. 1002 records an earlier trans. published by C. Van der Post (Utrecht, 1842). Another trans. and fragments by Lodewijk Joachim Vleeschouwer had also been issued 1842 in Antwerp and Brussels. See *Faust-Bibliographie*, ed. H. Henning (Berlin: Aufbau-Verlag, 1968), 2, 1:164–68.

105 Arie Cornelis Kruseman, *Bouwstoffen voor een Geschiedenis van den Nederlandschen Boekhandel, gedurende de halve eeuw 1830–80* (Amsterdam: P. N. van Kampen & Zoon, 1887), 2:337.

---

106 See Stead, "*Faust*-Bilder," 151–56.

107 Burwick and McKusick, eds., *Faustus*, XX, XXXV–XLVII, 5.

plates," which "might also possess some claims to interest the general reader as an independent publication."[108] The reset 1824 *Faustus from the German* (3rd ed.) repeats this in its own "Introduction." The latter almost opens with "Retzsch's Outlines have given to the eye the very essence of the leading occurrences in this tragedy," quoting "a celebrated weekly paper, a considerable portion of which is usually devoted to the fine arts" (i.e., the *Examiner*). The last page calls the captions' record (labelled "List of Plates") a "Table of Reference," emphasizing that it is *not* an illustrated book feature, since "this little publication" is considered "an accompaniment" to the prints, not the reverse.[109] Such is again the 1832 Lumley edition, recycling the 1824 *Faustus* template. In all of them, *translation* is visual, not textual. The "translating language" is graphic, and "the graver" is Moses copying Retzsch.[110] The prints prompted, even modelled, textual translation: "the first full translation [by Abraham Hayward, 1833] appear[ed] as a direct result of the success of Retzsch's outlines," concluded Vaughan. Adolf Ingram Frantz recorded that Retzsch was one of the "many prominent German scholars, friends, and contemporaries of Goethe" whom translator Hayward had visited in Germany "to make sure he did not misconstrue *Faust* in the original and translate it accurately".[111] Translating *Faust* was indeed an awe-inspiring task, duly noted in period comment. The original carried metric complexity, breadth of language registers, stature of thought, loftiness of metaphor, Mephistopheles's biting irony and sarcasm, not to mention symbolism and metaphysics.

Jonathan Birch (1783–1847) was manifestly not daunted by the task, quite the contrary. While working for a timber merchant, he had spent eighteen months during the Napoleonic wars at Memel (then the Northernmost part of East Prussia, today part of Lithuania) with the three elder sons of the King of Prussia, including he who would bear the crown in 1840 as Frederick William IV. Returning to the UK in 1812, Birch took to literary pursuits, addressing copies of his endeavours to the crown prince. His full translation of *Faust I* in 1839 is dedicated to his patron, who granted him on the occasion the "great gold medal of homage" and was presumably instrumental in having him elected in 1841 as "foreign honorary member of the Literary Society of Berlin," the only other Briton after

Thomas Carlyle.[112] The first *Faust* edition truly *illustrated by Retzsch* is his translation, more than twenty years after Retzsch's first introduction to Britain. In point of fact, this 1839 *Faust* musters so many emblematic features of the illustrated book genre, and conforms so markedly to its typology that it looks almost artificially created to stress the difference with previous Retzsch editions variously worded ad hoc.

Text-wise, it is an unabridged verse translation of *Faust I* with extra closing "Notes and Remarks," dedicated to the newly crowned King of Prussia. *Faust II* followed in 1843. Volume I opens with a four-page "Dedication" to his benefactor, followed by a six-page preface justifying the translation, and a three-page ranking of illustrious subscribers, mostly in double file. Birch's aspiration to textual completeness goes hand in hand with a display of knee-crooking homage to the king, over-laudatory exaltation of Goethe, and humbling of self before "the arduous task," all of which rather underline his self-esteem in achieving the feat. Although deemed by third parties "uniformly mediocre," he had been bold enough to send the translation to August Wilhelm Schlegel, "the inimitable Translator of Shakespeare," for approval.[113] In comparing nine extant *Faust* translations in November 1840, the *Dublin Review* did not mince its words: "As a translation it is bad; as a poetical translation, it is worse; but as a translation of *Faust* it is worst of all," "falling into the grossest blunders."[114] It is however his text that won medals, *illustration* implying, as noted, embellishment, lustre, and worthiness.

The octavo (*c.*25 × 15.7 cm), often bound and gilt-edged (25.8 × 17.2 cm), hosts half titles listing characters and summarizing the plot (a Birch deluxe trait, enhancing dramatization). Birch did not scruple to introduce genre (and subtitles), renaming "The Prologue in Heaven" for instance "A Dramatic Mystery." Thanks to his contacts, perhaps at his own expenditure, *Faust I* was jointly issued by F. A. Brockhaus in Leipzig, and Black and Armstrong in London. Foreign Booksellers to the King (as Bohte had been), the latter had released in English Cotta's *Umrisse zu Faust, zweiter Theil* by Retzsch in 1837. Both facts were of assistance. However, negative reviews of *Faust I* and the cost involved (reflected in Birch's abortive attempt to

---

108   Introduction 1821, VII.

109   *Faustus: from the German of Goethe*, 3rd ed., 1824, VI, III, 64.

110   Ibid., III.

111   Vaughan, *German Romanticism*, 132; Adolf Ingram Frantz, *Half a Hundred Thralls to Faust: A Study Based on the British and the American Translators of Goethe's Faust, 1823–1949* (Chapel Hill: University of North Carolina Press, 1949), 20.

112   *DiNB*, s.v. "Jonathan Birch" (by Thompson Cooper), online wikisource; Frantz, *Half a Hundred Thralls to Faust*, 140–42.

113   Hauhart, *Reception of Goethe's Faust*, 126–27; Frantz, *Thralls to Faust*, 142–45.

114   Charles William Russell, "Faust; a Tragedy," *Dublin Review* 9, no. 18 (Nov 1840): 492.

publish *Faust II* by subscription[115]) may have refrained them from pursuing. His *Faust II* would be published by substitute Chapman and Hall in association with F. A. Brockhaus.

A typical case of text annexing prints as dependent images, the book displays the same desire for exhaustiveness. It takes over not the initial 26, but 29 (of 40) Retzsch plates from the joint 1836 Cotta album. Askance to text, in diminutive format protected by tissue paper, they are copied by John Brain, mainly known as steel engraver (fl. 1838), witness his small plates in sharp lines. Compared to Moses, his treatment of God and male crotches has no variants. In contrast, the magic-mirror lady, stripped to her pelvis, presents two inviting orbs as she meekly lays head on bare arm—a decoy for male readers (the support list shows no female subscriber but for "Her Majesty the Queen Dowager," first to be mentioned). Along with the tissue paper and captions (lifted from Birch's translation), another giveaway of the illustrated book typology is the placement of rebel plate 18 (re-numbered 23), subordinate to text. The early leaf "The plates to be placed as follows," customary in deluxe editions in fascicles, was for binders. The (later) expression "embellished with eleven (or forty) engravings on steel," on the title-page of either *Faust II* or both parts combined, also appears standard. Last, but not least, copper is replaced by cheaper and harder-wearing steel, which allowed thousands of prints before re-engraving would become necessary. Steel's sharper and more distinct lines seemed well suited to outline compositions. However, reduced dimension of plates, lost nuance of line weight, and general flatness countersign Retzsch's domestication.

5.8 Competing Formats

From Birch's translation onwards, Retzsch's fortune in Britain observed a forked pathway. Its distinct prongs defined two print artefacts, two layouts, and two user categories: the portfolio or the album for connoisseurs, and the upper- or middle-class general reader's standard octavo.

Like Birch's translation, octavos set Retzsch's copied plates sideways as a supine embellishment to the fully translated *Faust*. Not only is text dominant, it is also increasingly treated as a recognized and reputable work of fitting tradition. In these editions, Goethe's *Faust* pertains to a distinctly German myth, a text in need of historical, philological or analytical explanation. Introductions on Faust the magician and German developments of the legend explain Goethe's play and compare him with Marlowe. Notes prosper.

A typical example, oscillating between standard item and refined object for the connoisseur's library, is Anna Swanwick's metrical translation, first published in 1850 and praised for "talent of versification" and her "ear for rhythm." Swanwick had knowledge of the classics and perfected her German on location. She dedicated her literary efforts to translation, chiefly of ancient Greek and German literature. Her professional translator's deontology faithfully followed textual quality, including of parts she did not agree with or that shocked her.[116] Her *Faust I* translation, not much noticed, came out in *Dramatic Works of Goethe*, with *Iphigenia in Tauris*, *Tasso*, and *Egmont*, as part of "Bohn's Standard Library" in 1850, a sure sign of Goethe having entered the literary canon. In 1878, George Bell and Sons republished a revised version of Swanwick's *Faust I*, along with "Scenes from the Second Part of the Tragedy of Faustus." The quarto of meticulous quality (25.3 × 19.2 cm) adopted mechanised technology from its binding in Mephistophelean red and its gilt spine to insert steel-engraved plates on heavier creamy paper with wide margins. The "Publishers' Note" unashamedly stated: "The illustrations are accurate copies of the original designs; they have undergone a slight reduction in size, which has tended to improve their effect." Print collectors had to be on their guard. The "originals" were by Brain, and he stuck to the usual alterations. As Kennerley had done, he doubly foot-marked the plates "M. Retzsch" on the left and "J. Brain" on the right, not so much insignia of loyalty to the German artist as need to differentiate himself from Moses's supremacy. However, in Bell and Sons' 1893 volume, finally reduced to a regular octavo (19 × 13.2 cm), Brain's plates were baptized "Retzsch's illustrations." A last refined feature was the title-page in red and black inks, a traditionally elegant feature in typography, re-symbolized in this case as strongly reminiscent of Faust's parody of a covenant signed in blood.

Numerous editions multiplied the octavo template, decked with copies after Retzsch, often affixed either as frontispiece, disorderly combinations in twos, or reduced

---

115 Birch's letter to Schlegel refers to "outlay of money." *Faust II* in instalments by subscription was a fiasco. Potential subscribers were invited to write to Birch care of Black and Armstrong (Frantz, 145–46). Attempts for a Black and Armstrong *Faust II* in fascicles subsist in HAAB: F 3591(b). The Beinecke preserves a *Faust I* Cotta edition (1831) with Birch's interleaved MS translation (YCGL MSS 6 Vol 806a–c) and a sizeable Birch file with various MS translation attempts of *Faust II* (YCGL MSS 6 Vol, folder 807).

---

116 Hauhart, *Reception of Goethe's Faust*, 132.

to head and tail vignettes. The craftsmen involved are never mentioned, the plates may not be complete, and it would be tedious to record them as they speckle the last quarter of the nineteenth well into the twentieth century, expanding from the UK westwards to the US and eastwards to Melbourne. Retzsch had become a fixture of Goethe's illustrated *Faust*, a predictable component taken for granted.

On the other hand, the landscape album of prints facing apposite extracts sports fine paper, increasingly industrialized, with broad margins. The plates may be copper or steel engraved, the latter gradually superseding the former as the century moves on and print runs lengthen. Both idea and format look back to W. W. Gibbings's oblong *Illustrations to Goethe's Faust in Twenty-Six* (or *Twenty-Seven*) *Outline Engravings by Moritz Retzsch* (1830s) with few variations.

Tilt and Bogue's 1843 *Illustrations of Goethe's Faust* aptly shows the album's appeal. An ingenious contrivance, its 32 pages adapt Boosey's 1824 template *Faustus* (text and interleaved plates) to an even more kinetic form by resetting the text in double column. Josiah Fletcher, originator and chief editor of the *Norwich News* as well as printer of the *Norwich Magazine*, printed it there. The new item, closer to the aesthetics of the fleeting press, sets text and plates opposite each other, undeniably heightening dramatic effects. No need to swivel the book any more, nor rotate combinations of text and matching image. High-tension scenes such as Faust and the poodle, Margaret with Martha and Mephistopheles, the duel, or the witches' Sabbath evolve before the user's eyes as alternate visual/textual or textual/visual language, leaf after leaf, switching page for plate. The climax (3 plates for 4 pages) tallies with the play's unresolved end and heart-rending prison scene. Conversely, long pauses created by blank versos underline episodes ominous (the covenant), amorous (the kiss), or adversarial (pl. 23, cf. Fig. 8.4).

At the time, Tilt and Bogue's plates (after Moses) evidently competed with Brain's, issued in portfolio as *Goethe's Faust: Retzsch's Forty Illustrations. Engraved by J. Brain*, a spin-off of the 1839 and 1843 two-part illustrated Birch translation. Forty larger free-standing steel engravings (max. 22.3 × 30 cm) on thicker paper sat either in a royal or a quarto landscape portfolio meant for collectors.[117] They paraded as classy prints without captions or dates. Although issued after completion of Birch's two-part *Faust*, they aspired to ahistorical artistic status,

free from the fetters of illustrated text. The mention of Birch's version on a larger vertically printed double sheet (24.5 × 15.8 cm) served contextualization purposes alluding to an absent text.[118]

Still, within the album format, *Faust* interpretations and readings differ between the United States and Great Britain as in two artefacts published Boston and London two years apart.

Back in the 1820s, Retzsch's plates had been a visual narrative, reconstructing the story and doctoring the plot of a play deemed obscure. An American album, *Illustrations to Goethe's Faust. Twenty-six Etchings by Moritz Retzsch with Illustrative Selections from the Text of Bayard Taylor's Translation*, published 1877 in Boston by Estes and Lauriat from steel plates,[119] interestingly redeems initial aesthetics. Paying tribute to "the celebrated outlines of Retzsch," it captures "the very essence of the leading occurrences in this tragedy."[120] The term *essence* suggests sequential distilling: the designs abstracted Goethe's thought, rendering it in visual terms; they were also shapes, contours, virtually mental forms *initiating* the onlooker to the poet's ideas and a masterpiece. Eighty years after Schlegel's far-sighted remarks, this stress echoed the crucial idea of the outlines as magic formulas (or heady potions), inviting the Boston reader to complete images and create independently. Wide margins, sparse letterpress and blanks stir the mind. Selected passages from Bayard Taylor's recent metrical translation (1870) serve as incidental *suggestions*. Although Moses is still favoured, with the identical "Faust and Mephistopheles in the Witches Cave" [*sic*!], this striking object, beautifully confectioned at Cambridge (Ma.) by renowned master printers John Wilson and Son,[121] prompts the mind's eye. Visually and textually applied, the idea of abstraction addresses *Faust* as a quintessential epitome. An excellent example of fine printing, the album reverts to Retzsch, and may have nurtured the American transcendentalists' sustained interest in Goethe, particularly that of Ralph Waldo Emerson.

Retzsch had found a new public across the Atlantic, in post-civil war US. Meanwhile his UK fortune had dramatically declined. Reviewing four outline gift books, issued 1875 by Sampson Low, Marston & Co., including a *Faust* album advertised at 10s 6d with etchings after Moses and extracts from John Anster's translation, the *Athenaeum* did not hide its annoyance. Flaxman was

---

117 Beinecke: Speck Ck 99 R3 +843b (royal 4to). Landscape 4to at Bow Windows Bookshop (Lewes, Sussex), cat. 197, no. 217, £100, Mar 2015.

118 Beinecke: Speck Ck99 R3 +843b (title after gilt label on portfolio).

119 Beinecke: Speck Ck99 R3 +877.

120 Introduction 1877.

121 "John Wilson and Son," *Cambridge Chronicle* 31, no. 6 (5 Feb 1876): 5d–e.

sternly criticized for outlining such a "Gothic poem" as Dante's *Divine Comedy*, and Retzsch did not fare better, *Faust I* being superlatively un-Greek. The spirit of his designs was "stagey, sentimental, and occasionally foolish. To critics of these days, all his labour, his affectation of learning, his enormous care, are nought."[122] For Christmas 1871, Sampson Low, Marston & Co. had strongly promoted *Faust* silhouettes by Paul Konewka in royal octavo, previously earning the *Examiner*'s praise for their "remarkable vigour."[123] Remembering Retzsch's past glory, the publishers probably thought that the shift from pure black silhouettes to clear shapes would be welcome. It was not so. From then on, Retzsch would almost solely crop up in illustrated books. Amusingly, the only feature that found favour with the *Athenaeum* was the mechanical red cloth binding, copiously bordered in black and gilt. To us, this seems unnecessarily florid. Similarly, a *Faust* might seem an ill-chosen Christmas present, given its open end and Mephistopheles's imperative "Hither! To me!" (F 4611, trans. W. Arndt). But just as the choice gift would rank Goethe's *Faust* a masterpiece, ultimately canonizing it, so did the plush binding match Victorian interiors.

5.9   "Bound to Please"

The appeal, nevertheless, of Retzsch's prints before favour would decline, also branded both octavos' and albums' commercial bindings in the 1830s and 40s. Several of Retzsch's designs inspired stamped and embossed motifs. Calico triumphed: alongside decorous ladies' hats, eye-catching gilt cloth bindings held sway. Ornate volumes with embellishments gradually expanding (on upper board, both boards, and/or spine), all edges gilt, with "numerous illustrations," were treasured. Gift inscriptions show they were appreciated as presents.

Retzsch took indirect part in the fun through publishers' signal choices. Traces left by outlines on bindings are carefully picked, contained in place and size. Three telling samples date from the 1840s: two for the same album, the third for the full Birch *Faust*.

The first two apply to the kinetic version from Tilt and Bogue as an extra binding decoy. One of them plunders five Retzsch plates, the other adopts a single capital scene. As mentioned, Tilt and Bogue's *Illustrations of Goethe's Faust by Moritz Retzsch, Engraved by Henry Moses* is the most kinetic template of them all, with plates bang opposite

the 1824 *Faustus from the German* letterpress in double columns. From 1826, publisher and bookseller Charles Tilt was based at 86 Fleet Street, a major thoroughfare to and from the City, at the heart of literary and journalistic London. As part of his thriving undertakings, he published in 1829, in association with Rudolph Ackermann's renowned *Repository of the Arts*, a *Fridolin* album by Retzsch with a new translation by J. W. Lake, to compete with J. P. Collier's for Prowett (1824). The new *Fridolin* was printed in Paris by Rignoux, Audot's printer, with English and French captions for a European market, like Retzsch's *Gallery of Shakspeare, or Illustrations of His Dramatic Works* (1828–32), also in association with Ackermann. Compared to the bilingual *Fridolin*, the kinetic 1843 *Faust* echoed a dynamic of news-borne images, and motion clips from steam railway windows. Tilt, newly partnered with his former assistant David Bogue, needed to attract the eye in busy Fleet Street. Gilt design served the purpose, stamped on the same green blind-embossed cloth. Tellingly, the spine bears neither title nor publishers' insignia, again drawing the eye to the upper board designs with two distinct titles for identical contents. The album was meant for display, not to be lodged on a bookshelf.

Sitting in the centre of a devilish interlude, the gilt title *Goethe's Faust by Retzsch* assimilates it to a magic object (Fig. 5.19). Two howling canine monsters (Retzsch, pl. 3, cf. Fig. 4.3) frame either side the witchery scene (R, pl. 6–7, cf. Fig. 2.18 and 2.19). A hovering demon biting drapery, the tiny monkey rolling a skull, the snake writhing, and dried-up frog, some amusingly retouched, all inhabit Retzsch's fanciful kitchen. Instead of the witch, a toothless hag with a pitchfork from the Sabbath (pl. 22, right, cf. Fig. 5.7) faces Mephistopheles in profile, himself a figure from Auerbach's cellar (pl. 5, cf. Fig. 9.17). His casket of jewels looks suspiciously like a book. A steaming phial alludes to alchemy and the frog jumping above is deviously reminiscent of a homunculus. The green and gold collage arouses curiosity, titillates and amuses (the skull gawps at the monkey, the demon ogles Mephistopheles) to draw the purchaser into the shop with the message: you won't discover *Goethe's Faust by Retzsch* unless you buy it.

Retzsch's Illustrations of Faust, the second title, is even cleverer (Fig. 5.20). In a suggestive parallel, Faust lifts the hangings of Gretchen's bed to ponder his paramour, compelling the reader-spectator to raise the album's cover and peek at images, their own object of desire. The word "Illustrations" is half-hidden half-revealed by the bed drapes. "Cover, uncover, discover" prompts this covert title by analogy. It spurs a craving that only acquisition will sate. Modern marketing has hardly invented anything better since.

---

122   "Gift Books," *Athenaeum*, no. 2509 (27 Nov 1875): 716.
123   "Books of the Week," *Examiner*, no. 3327 (4 Nov 1871): 1101.

FIGURE 5.19
Green commercial binding with gilt pictorial title for *Goethe's Faust by Retzsch, Engraved by Henry Moses* (London: Tilt and Bogue, 1843)
COURTESY BEINECKE, YALE UNIVERSITY, SPECK CK99 R3 +843

FIGURE 5.20
Green commercial binding with gilt pictorial title for *Illustrations of Goethe's Faust by Moritz Retzsch, Engraved by Henry Moses* (London: Tilt and Bogue, 1843)
COURTESY HAAB, F 3477, WEIMAR

Touting wares in such expert fashion stresses how powerful Retzsch's images were: not only eye-catching and narrative-efficient, but also garbed in albums as symbolic objects imbued with fantastic or erotic power.

The third is the decorative spine design of an industrial binding for both parts of Birch's *Faust* translation, a simplified task since they had the same dimensions (Fig. 5.21). The motif is inspired by Retzsch's etching 10 in *Faust II* (Fig. 5.22), shortly before the *dénouement* (F II 11,676f). Heaven and Hell both claim Faust's soul. In Retzsch's print, hovering above an assembly of hideously grimacing, gaping, gripping, howling, farting and vomiting Bosch-inspired devils, angels shower them with roses, which become ardent flames as they fall. On the left, Mephistopheles fights the roses off, while Faust's venerable head, eyes shut, remains sunken in a darkened void, both tomb and Hell. Demonic creatures sprawl across the plate. In contrast, the decorative spine, focused on select elements, accentuates the ascendant symbolism of salvation, turning the roses into falling stars. The angels, soaring above the title with hallowing gestures and floating hair, linger over the lettering, drawn into a gothic casement. A small cross, pointing downwards dagger-like, evokes the flaming heart of Jesus. Erect and allegoric, the spine is the minute stained-glass window of book as cathedral. Faust has vanished from this dispute between good and evil. At the edge of the gaping pit, cloven-footed Mephistopheles (defeated), half-blinded by fiery roses, is on the verge of falling into it with the monstrous demons. In a small vertical surface, the spine sums up the finale of numerous verses. Once lodged in the bookcase, that most visible part of the book spells volumes.

For such an industrialized stamped binding, the spine would have been created using brass dies to the design of a talented artist. The binding was commercialised by Josiah Westley, whose establishment, adjoining the *Times* office until February 1852, flourished through ads. At the 1851 Crystal Palace World Exhibition, Westley had filled a case with publishers' bindings, favourably received.[124] The talented and prize-winning John Leighton, aka Luke Limner, worked for him at the time. That the spine is by Leighton is confirmed by his monogram, a crossed J and L in the final central curlicue above "London." The binding may be dated 1849, thanks to Westley's pasted-in binder's ticket and the *London Gazette*.[125] Ordered from Westley,

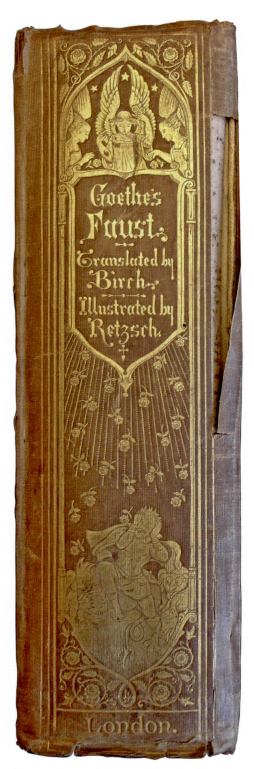

FIGURE 5.21
John Leighton, decorative spine design, industrial cloth binding for both parts of *Faust: A Tragedy, by J. Wolfgang von Goethe. Translated into English Verse by J. Birch, Esq.* (London: Black and Armstrong, 1839; Chapman and Hall, 1843)
COURTESY BEINECKE, YALE UNIVERSITY, SPECK RC37 +C839

---

124 *Tallis's History and Description of the Crystal Palace and the Exhibition of the World's Industry in 1851* (London: John Tallis and Co., 1852), 1:220.

125 Josiah Westley, Frederick Westley and William Clark dissolve their partnership (as Westleys and Co.) by mutual consent, *London Gazette*, pt. 4 (1848): 4683. Josiah Westley 1849 is confirmed

FIGURE 5.22　Moritz Retzsch, outline engraving from *Faust II*, in *Umrisse zu Goethe's Faust, erster und zweiter Theil. Erster Theil neun und zwanzig Platten. Zweiter Theil elf Platten gezeichnet von Moritz Retzsch* (Stuttgart: Cotta, 1836), pl. 10
COURTESY HAAB, F 3479 WEIMAR

presumably after a deal between the publishers of *Faust I* (Black and Armstrong, 1839) and *Faust II* (Chapman and Hall, 1843), it offers together both unsold volumes translated by Birch to an extensive readership at a time when books were "on every table, the *necessaries* as well as the *monitors* of life."[126] If Charles Murton's gold-blocked composition on leather was for choice custom, this elaborate spine suggests industrial volumes, amortizing design and dye costs. Paradoxically, while five instances of Murton's precious leatherwork subsist, I know of only one industrial sample of Leighton's, still unfamiliar to specialists. Additionally, the exemplar has a splendid pedigree, reflected in the bookplates (Fig. 5.23). One of the owners was Robert Hoe III (1839–1909), prominent printing-press maker and collector of rare books and manuscripts, one of the founding presidents of the Grolier Club, as well as author of *A Lecture on Bookbinding as a Fine Art* (delivered 1885, published 1886). In his lecture, Hoe described binding in detail with "gold tooling," heritage techniques and trends.[127] He did not touch on modern ornate cloths, finished in a single stamp, but this exemplar was part of his collection. Another proprietor was the American poet

---

by the RA online. Westleys and Clark (London): Bookbinders, trading under this name 1842–48; as Josiah Westley 1849; as J. & F. Westley 1850–52; as Westleys & Co. 1850–99. See Douglas Ball, *Victorian Publishers' Bindings* (Williamsburg, Va.: The Book Press, 1985), 190–92.

126　"Ornamental Bookbinding," *Art Journal*, n.s., 12 (July 1850): 229, author's emphasis.

127　Hoe, *A Lecture on Bookbinding as a Fine Art* (New York: Grolier Club, 1886), 11–12.

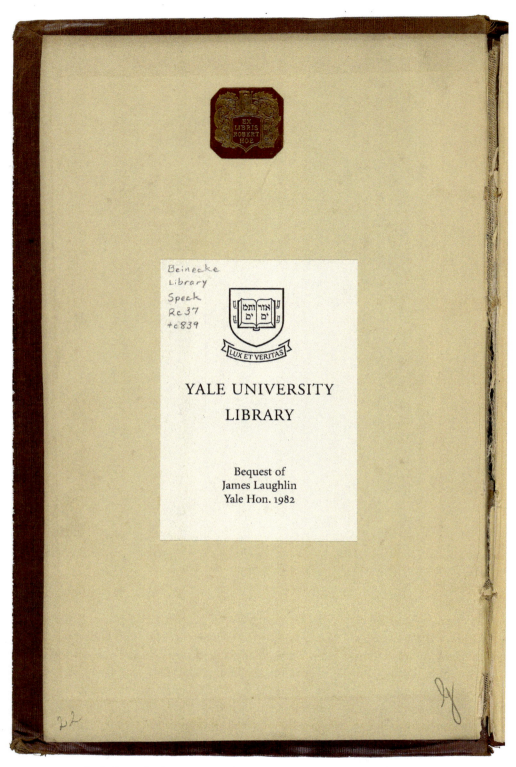

FIGURE 5.23 Bookplates of Robert Hoe III and gift of James Laughlin, front pastedown of *Faust: A Tragedy, by J. Wolfgang von Goethe. Translated into English Verse by J. Birch, Esq.* (London: Black and Armstrong; Leipzig: F. A. Brockhaus, 1839)
COURTESY BEINECKE, YALE UNIVERSITY, SPECK RC37 +C839

and literary publisher James Laughlin (1914–97), founder of New Directions Publishing, who edited *Faust* with Richard Smyth for the series "New Directions College Books" in 1949. Laughlin studied at Harvard but was granted an honorary degree from Yale in 1982 (as the bookplate reflects). The book is one of the two (from twelve) thousand, bequeathed by Laughton to Yale, that reached the Beinecke by curator's selection.[128]

John Leighton, a man with wide interests, "possessed of a powerful imagination," created "designs often in keeping with a book's subject."[129] Apart from his apparently Catholic take on *Faust*, his spine design renders the key outcome of a tragedy that many failed to grasp. Faust would be saved, Mephistopheles defeated. A book spine is a confined lay space. The cascade of fiery roses Leighton condensed and adapted to it, suggests greater symbolic and sacred forms. He admirably followed Goethe's poetic idea that had travelled to England thanks to Retzsch. The mosaic on the south side of his family tomb at St. Mary, Harrow, shows a red lion rampant within a shield above the words "Light On" (a pun on Leighton). One inevitably thinks of Goethe's last words, "Mehr Licht!"

5.10 First Conclusions on Foreign Circulation

Cotta's artefact had been a stylish small portfolio with an unsophisticated label and binary contents. I stressed here how it kindled a plethora of artefacts beyond German terrain. It changed into templates of text/image groupings; sculpted formats implying ways of reading; enlarged readers' categories; and excited imaginative creation. While collective German editions of Goethe's works in the 1820s shaped a broad audience of readers and a national body politic at home (Andrew Piper),[130] Retzsch's book-bound prints were the driving force operating abroad. They distributed, disseminated, spread and circulated outlined *Faust* surrogates that worked powerfully for foreign audiences in large numbers. The stand-ins inveigled their way into literary, symbolic, spiritual and social interaction.

Parallelograms figure awkwardly in books. Retzsch's landscape etchings—both hardy (the rebel plate 18, out of textual order from the beginning) and pliant (easily copied and altered)—caused disorder. Since they set the pace, and text was subservient, publishers had to find ways to respond to collectors' desiderata and readers' growing curiosity in *Faust*. The primacy and mutual subordination of contending parts was twofold: either associated or in competition with each other. The visual vs. textual reel unravels as alternating prints/text or text/prints (Boosey, 1820); prints-with-associated text (Boosey, 1821); a typecast text and askance plates interleaved to kinetic effect (Boosey, 1824), with additions (Lumley, 1832); an album of prints with matching excerpts (Gibbings, c.1835); lastly, an album of text with prints and an ever-increasing mobile reading effect (Tilt and Bogue, 1843). All this spawned rival formats: octavo, quarto, royal or imperial quarto, portfolio or album. In a nutshell, it took the British market some twenty-three years to hit upon what Bohte had projected in 1821: collocation of (translated) text and prints in landscape quarto with original German to boot. The fact brings precursor Bohte's foresighted resourcefulness to light, even though his own project was never finalized.

The outlines were ambassadors to *Faust*, and, as pertains that role, negotiation helped avoid conflict. This led to an unusually wide range of diverse reading effects over a short period (1820–24, c.1835, 1843) before regular octavos domesticated the plates to produce a run of illustrated books, depriving Retzsch's prints of their congenital assets. Coaxing translation, stimulating poets such as Shelley, Retzsch's copies founded Goethe's and *Faust*'s reputation in a hostile context. Ironically the text's consecration, i.e., its introduction into celebrated series from 1846, rhymed with the prints' capitulation (save exceptions). Yet, as important book trade hub, Britain disseminated prints bearing the text east and west, over the Continent, to the US and Australia.

Assorted forms and shapes call for development of skills to fathom items now over two hundred years old. Comparison of several resembling exemplars conveys information regarding originals. That printed items undergo no alteration is a myth.[131] Semblances that appear or are itemized identical, actually accrue with differences. Inscriptions, dedications, slip-ins and add-ons, along with correspondence, diaries, archives, book scholarship, and

---

128 Patricia C. Willis, "'Luz y Verdad:' J. Laughlin and Yale," *Paideuma* 31, nos. 1–3 (Spring-Fall-Winter 2002): 275.

129 Edmund M. B. King, *Victorian Decorated Trade Bindings, 1830–1880* (London: The British Library; New Castle, Del.: Oak Knoll Press, 2003), XIV; Ball, *Victorian Publishers' Bindings*, 69–81; ODNB online, s.v. "Leighton, John" (by E. M. B. King), accessed 26 Mar 2020.

130 Piper, *Dreaming in Books: The Making of the Bibliographical Imagination in the Romantic Age* (Chicago: University of Chicago Press, 2009), 58–59.

---

131 Leslie Howsam, "An Experiment with Science for the Nineteenth-Century Book Trade: The International Scientific Series," *British Journal for the History of Science* 33, no. 2 (2000): 187–207.

the invaluable backing of periodicals provide further insights into cultural and publishing practices.

No other country than Great Britain gave Retzsch such ringing applause and welcome. In his pioneer study, William Vaughan underscored the artist's publishing fortune throughout the nineteenth century: "the Faust illustrations were republished in 1834 and 1839, twice in 1843, 1852, 1875, 1879 and 1893."[132] In chain succession, the Retzsch fashion spanned nearly a century. More closely examined, the period of enthusiastic favour rather indicates twenty odd fervent years that set artists, print-sellers, publishers and collectors athirst (*c.*1818–1843). Its most important effect lies not so much in duration or vogue, as in its numerous literary, artistic and cultural consequences. Retzsch's work lent itself to easy copying and left a long-lasting mark on Goethe's *Faust* iconography (see Chapter 7). It also inspired numerous artists in Britain from Theodore von Holst to Daniel Maclise, John Everett Millais, and Dante Gabriel Rossetti.[133] This chapter explored ways of reading his hallmark on printed items as cultural objects. Material evidence (formats, layouts) and publishing trends were related to reading and translation practices, and analysed as imaginative cultural elaborations on Goethe's Faust as figure and myth. Retzsch in

---

132   Vaughan, *German Romanticism*, 139. I do not know of an 1852 English edition. Maybe confused with the 1852 French one?

133   Ibid., 145f; Krüger, *Retzsch und Rossetti*; Stephen Calloway, "John Everett Millais, James Wyatt of Oxford and a volume of Retzsch's *Outlines to Shakespeare*: A Missing Link," in *Burning Bright: Essays in Honour of David Bindman*, ed. D. Dethloff et al. (London: UCL Press, 2015), 160–70.

Britain carries us to the heart of what *Reading Books and Prints as Cultural Objects* means.

Further chapters will elaborate on several reception aspects. Social and cultural rituals have been disclosed in Chapter 4, particularly in relation to Crabb Robinson and Perthes. I further discuss Retzsch's wide-ranging adherents at the end of chapter 6, "Retzsch in France and Belgium," comparing contextually different readership. Elaborate miscellany of Retzsch copies is addressed in Chapter 7 "Extensive and Intensive Iconography." Parodies, theatre, literature, courtship, and three-dimensional artefacts follow on.

Remarkable imagination would be applied to English printed artefacts inspired by Retzsch. These books, albums or portfolios are regularly objects wrought by the mind's eye, recalling in every day life man's relation to paradise, evil, knowledge, and desire. Charles Murton's lush block (cf. Fig. 4.1), adaptable to various editions and formats, but only surviving on a few bindings, looks back to Saint Jerome translating the Bible. Moses's circular *Faustus* title with Retzsch-inspired vignettes and stars, separately printed and applied on paper-covered boards, alludes to a magic ring (cf. Fig. 5.10a–b). John Berryman's pink cover for Bulcock epitomizes rejuvenation (cf. Fig. 5.17). Gilt titles on green Tilt and Bogue cloth enticingly beckoned the Fleet Street passer-by (cf. Fig. 5.19 and 5.20). Last, but not least, John Leighton's gothic spine showers roses harking back to God and the firmament (cf. Fig. 5.21). "God is the myriad of insects and the real roses" (*Gud är insekternas myriader och rosornas extas*) would later write the Scandinavian poet Edith Södergran.

CHAPTER 6

Retzsch in France and Belgium

In an 1862 letter to Philippe Burty, some forty years after his splendid *Faust* lithographs, Eugène Delacroix listed various stimuli on his work. He wrote *inter alia*: "I saw, towards 1821, compositions by Retzsch that rather struck me."[1] What had the French artist seen? Delacroix research has successfully established Retzsch's impact,[2] although the extent of his aesthetic and compositional bearing on the lithographs needs gauging. To judge by his freehand copies of Retzsch, an original set either lay beneath his eyes or was vividly remembered (Delacroix willingly drew from memory). Whatever the case, on the recto of a now short-cropped sheet, he emulated a pensive Margaret in her armchair and the pious woman against a pillar from the cathedral (Fig. 6.1a, cf. Fig. 3.1b and 9.1). He pursued on the verso with Margaret admiring the jewels, and proffering an arm to don them (Fig. 6.1b, cf. Fig. 2.24 and 10.6). An intact sheet, used diversely again and again, further shows Martha twice at home with the casket, once in the garden seen from the back, and other feminine figures from Retzsch's plates (Fig. 6.2). Delacroix's earliest sketches even take stock of the witches' Sabbath, a winged Mephistopheles, and treacherous duel, after Retzsch's plates 22, 1, and 19 (Fig. 6.3).[3] Still, we may ask, to precisely what had Delacroix access? An art lover's item brought to

FIGURES 6.1A–B   Eugène Delacroix, freehand copies of Moritz Retzsch's outline engravings, pl. 16 (Margaret at the spinning wheel), pl. 18 (woman, cathedral scene), pl. 11 (Margaret admiring the jewels) and pl. 12 (proffering her arm to Martha)
ML, RF 10215 RECTO AND VERSO, COURTESY RMN GP, PARIS, PHOTO © MICHÈLE BELLOT

---

1   *Correspondance générale d'Eugène Delacroix*, ed. A. Joubin (Paris: Plon, 1938), 4:303.
2   Guinevere Doy, "Delacroix et Faust," *Nouvelles de l'estampe*, no. 21 (May–June 1975): 18–23; Delacroix, *Journal*, 1:120, n. 54.
3   Agnes Mongan, *David to Corot*, ed. M. Stewart (Cambridge, Ma: Harvard University Press, 1996), 128.

© EVANGHELIA STEAD, 2023 | DOI:10.1163/9789004543010_009
This is an open access chapter distributed under the terms of the CC BY-NC-ND 4.0 license.

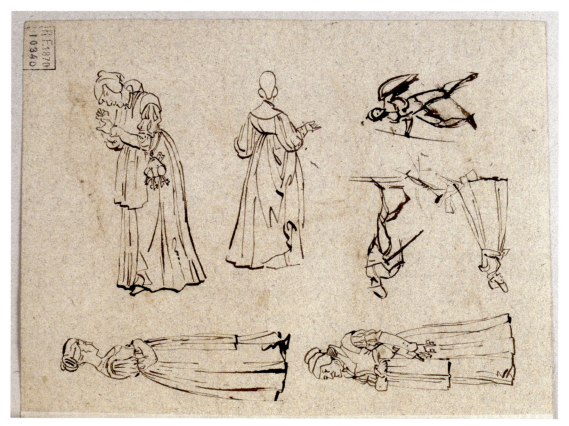

FIGURE 6.2   Eugène Delacroix, freehand copies of Margaret (pl. 13), Martha (pl. 12, 13, 14), and a lady from the cathedral scene (pl. 18 , visible rotating the image 180°) by Moritz Retzsch
ML, RF 10340, COURTESY RMN GP, PARIS, PHOTO © MICHÈLE BELLOT

FIGURE 6.3   Eugène Delacroix, early sketches for Goethe's *Faust* after Moritz Retzsch, c.1821, pencil on wove paper, 19.6 × 30.8 cm
HAM / FM, 1929.308, GIFT OF DR. CHARLES L. KUHN
PHOTO PRESIDENT AND FELLOWS OF HARVARD COLLEGE

France? A Bohte ware from London? Had perhaps English copies by Moses been a catalyst during his London stay as much as the surrogate *Faustus* he saw in Drury Lane?

References to Retzsch in French journals begin only January 1824 regarding Jean-Baptiste Muret's lithographic copies. In one of the very first press quotes, "A very distinguished artist from Stuttgart" locates rather Cotta's publishing house than Retzsch's native Dresden.[4] While the first two French reviews follow German and English credits calling him "Retsch," in March his identity curiously vanishes behind a double mask: geographically and chronologically closer, the French lithographer Muret steals the show; on his heels, a nameless party appears, an anonymous "English engraver" (surely Henry Moses).[5] Even a year later, Retzsch is still the "unknown draughtsman."[6] Proper (yet scarce) information and correct name spelling would come to France only with the 1828 Audot copies, thanks however to the second edition established by Élise Voïart who read (and translated) German. Retzsch's 1824 launch was hesitant, to say the least. Even Amédée Pichot in his 1825 travelogue simply styled him "a German artist."[7]

Inversely, his penetrating influence held sway north of the Channel. In May 1825 the London *Literary Gazette* expertly noted "Retsch's *Faust* and *Fridolin*, (especially the former) have spread his fame over Britain, as well as over the Continent." It added that Retzsch offered a good opportunity for British artists to "distinguish themselves by copying foreign works," and thanked "Mr. Moses for his rapidity in making *that* English, which but ten days before was a German curiosity in the hands of amateurs."[8] Like comments give reason to believe that British copies were effective in making him known in France. For all that, did such adjustments make the plates *specifically English*? As shown, the 1825 Berthoud London edition bears French features.

Similar questions are central from the viewpoint of cultural transfers and mediation instances, which often prioritize lingual translation rather than graphic culture. For such a vast and diversely mapped subject, prints' distribution and circulation in Europe play numerous parts: when related to works of literature, they disclose unexpected literary readings. Diversely, as international language seldom requiring translation, cultural negotiation of images knows no borders. Nevertheless, images themselves undergo visible or subtle changes, more often than imagined, not only in content and captions but also

in target public and meaning.[9] Chapter 5 dwelt on the extent of this, crucially relating to translation and interpretation. Are these changes valid elsewhere? How do the German-language territories relate to Britain and France?

To establish the depth of historic trilateral relationships is demanding, due to disruptive events, commercial rivalry and social variances. This chapter first addresses them in the wake of the Napoleonic wars, diversely interpreted by historians: John Harold Clapham considers that economically and socially France developed slowly during the Bourbon Restoration after two decades of political disruption,[10] while David Todd stresses its economy's reactionary policies, particularly in rejection of "British" free trade.[11] In a debatable context, might the direct trade of prints between German States and France have prospered at the beginning of the 1820s? Or was it supplemented by British deals? Paris clearly had no equivalent of the risk-taking Bohte. In 1830, a Giard *Faust* advert hailed Retzsch's prints "until today almost unknown because of the difficulty in obtaining them."[12] Publishers' characteristic puff aside, such phrasing is revelatory of the salesmanship involved. Strasbourg booksellers and publishers Treuttel and Würtz, dealing in contemporary French and foreign books, prints and maps, also active in Paris from 1795, established themselves in London from 1817. By comparison, they kept agents in Leipzig, Frankfurt and Stuttgart only from the 1830s.[13] Whence the importance of asking how Delacroix actually laid eyes on the original, or whether what seemed Anglicised was verily English.

Reasons abound for surveying all three cultural contexts or adopting a broader view: Retzsch's French copies may hark back to the English renderings, yet not always. Even so, some are also designed for Germany, meant for a bilingual or a German-language public, and even go back to the original prints in triangulated circulation. They trigger comparison: French copies neither boost translation of the play, as English ones did, nor predate translations, but follow, escort or supplement extant Francophone translations, occasionally acting as substitutes. Beyond collectors' and readers' practices, they reveal an intentional culture of imitation with variation. In social use,

---

4   *Gazette de France*, no. 7 (7 Jan 1824): 4.

5   "Beaux-Arts. Faust," *La Pandore*, no. 244 (15 Mar 1824): 5a.

6   H., "Faust," *Le Mercure du dix-neuvième siècle* 10 (1825): 244.

7   Amédée Pichot, *Voyage historique et littéraire en Angleterre et en Écosse* (Paris: Ladvocat et Charles Gosselin, 1825), 1:393.

8   *Literary Gazette*, no. 435 (21 May 1825): 329c, author's emphasis.

---

9   See for instance, Alberto Milano, "Change of Use, Change of Public, Change of Meaning: Printed Images Travelling through Europe," in *Reading Books and Prints as Cultural Objects*, ed. E. Stead, 137–56.

10   Clapham, *The Economic Development of France and Germany 1815–1914* (Cambridge: Cambridge University Press, 1921), 53f, 121.

11   Todd, *Free Trade and its Enemies in France, 1814–1851* (Cambridge: Cambridge University Press, 2015).

12   *Journal des débats* (7 May 1830): 3.

13   Giles Barber, "Treuttel and Würtz: Some Aspects of the Importation of Books from France, c. 1825," *Library*, 5th s., 23, no. 2 (June 1968): 118–44; Jefcoate, *Ocean of Literature*, 70–74.

they parallel the stage, whereas English copies introduced theatrical features to readers' protocol and the book itself, like Moses's use of Cornelius's "Dedication" as frontispiece (cf. Fig. 5.9). Conversely, connections of British editions with the stage are scarce, but for Hullmandel's version for Berthoud Jr, a likely sequel to Soane and Terry's *Faustus: A Romantic Drama*. Although material aspects of the French-language copies are less diverse or flamboyant and their time span contained (1824–30), their effect endures throughout the nineteenth century and into the twentieth. Britain's more intense craze (*c.*1818–43) ended up serially standardized after the 1840s as illustrated books (see Chapter 5).

Retzsch's reception in France thus points at triangular relations in print culture, intricate to fathom in the absence of specialized period research into printmaking and trade exchanges between France, the German States, and Britain. Book and print trade are mostly studied apart. Frédéric Barbier and Jean-Yves Mollier have led, directed or codirected expert comparative studies on book networks in industrialised Germany, France and Europe;[14] Helga Jeanblanc fathomed Germans in the Parisian book industry and trade;[15] yet study of trilateral relations is singularly lacking. Similarly, close printmaker links between London and Paris after 1815 form an under-investigated commercial terrain. Tim Clayton and Sheila O'Connell address the subject to 1815, bearing on caricature.[16] Rolf Reichardt's work is centred on the French Revolution. Stephen Bann newly discusses French print culture yet from 1863.[17] Noteworthy exceptions are Antony Griffiths's numerous expert studies on comparative print culture. Two excellent books have straddled new ground, drawing attention to the prints' numerous uses, including copying.[18] Some of the details reported here may contribute to a field of research where much remains to be addressed.

Retzsch in France also needs better mapping. Regular catalogues of *Faust*-related material mostly limit themselves to the Audot and Giard editions, neither fittingly nor fully. This may be due to French bibliographies of the time (by Jacques-Charles Brunet, Joseph-Marie Quérard, Georges Vicaire) mentioning only one Audot edition. The first French copy of Retzsch by Muret is at present (March 2023) diversely dated by the BnF catalogue, and generally considered tardier. Atkins notes "in 1823 there appeared in Paris a reprint of the outlines in octavos and 16mos," attributing them to Audot (after former references),[19] which hardly fits issued items. French translations of Goethe's *Faust* have been regularly studied since 1902.[20] However, that a Retzsch plate serve as frontispiece to Nerval's celebrated translation in 1828 has been much neglected (Fig. 6.4). Tellingly, it first emerges as late as 1898, as a rarity in discussion between cognoscenti in France, simply because the frontispiece of that translation's *second* edition (more commonly after Rembrandt) is investigated.[21] In the 1828 Motte-Sautelet folio decked with Delacroix lithographs, Stapfer (echoing Goethe) mentions Retzsch as the artist who best captured the salient scenes of *Faust*. Still, he considers his plates "mere outline sketches, generally a little cold" (*de simples croquis au trait, en général un peu froids*) of Flaxmanic rigidity.[22] Such mentions are seldom acknowledged, save by Ségolène Le Men.[23] In a long "Art Note" on Faust, more preoccupied with painting than graphic works according to characteristic nineteenth-century standards, A.-J. Pons considers only Cornelius (to whom he oddly attributes twenty-four prints) and Delacroix, with no mention of Retzsch.[24] There is something peculiar about this denial of Retzsch in France. Lea Marquart's thorough study, one of the latest on *Faust* reception in French theatre, is typical in this sense: it signals only one Audot edition,

---

14 See in bibliography Barbier 1987 (PhD); Barbier 1995 (enlarged published version); Barbier, Jurratic and Varry, eds., 1996; Barbier, ed., 2005; Barbier and Monok, eds., 2008; Michon and Mollier, eds., 2000; Mollier, 2005; Cooper-Richet, Mollier, and Silem, eds., 2005.

15 Jeanblanc, *Des Allemands dans l'industrie et le commerce du livre à Paris (1811–1870)* (Paris: CNRS Éditions, 1994).

16 Tim Clayton and Sheila O'Connell, *Bonaparte and the British: Prints and Propaganda in the Age of Napoleon* (London: British Museum Press, 2015).

17 Bann, *Distinguished Images: Prints in the Visual Economy of Nineteenth-Century France* (New Haven: Yale University Press, 2013).

18 Antony Griffiths and Frances Carey, *German Printmaking in the Age of Goethe* (London: British Museum Press, 1994); Griffiths, *The Print Before Photography: An Introduction to European Printmaking, 1550–1820* (London: The British Museum, 2016). On copying, 114–31.

---

19 Atkins, "Fragmentary English Translations," 28. Based on Engel, no. 1809, and Neubert, 241b.

20 Martha Langkavel, *Die französischen Übertragungen von Goethes "Faust"* (Strassburg: K. J. Trübner, 1902); Karl Heinz Kube, *Goethes Faust in französischer Auffassung und Bühnendarstellung* (Berlin: E. Ebering, 1932); Lea Marquart, *Goethes Faust in Frankreich: Studien zur dramatischen Rezeption im 19. Jahrhundert* (Heidelberg: Winter, 2009).

21 *L'Intermédiaire des chercheurs et des curieux* 37, no. 788 (10 Feb 1898), 166; no. 796 (30 Apr 1898), 624–25; no. 799 (30 May 1898), 760.

22 Albert Stapfer, "Préface," in Goethe, *Faust*, trans. A. Stapfer (Paris: Ch. Motte et Sautelet, 1828), I.

23 Le Men, *La Cathédrale illustrée de Hugo à Monet* (Paris: CNRS Éditions, 1998), 39.

24 A.-J. Pons, "Notice artistique," in Goethe, *Faust*, trans. Blaze de Bury (Paris: A. Quantin, 1880), 264–66.

FIGURE 6.4 Pinéas, *Faust signe le pacte avec Méphistophélés*, engraved copy of Moritz Retzsch's pl. 4 used as frontispiece to Nerval's translation, in *Faust: Tragédie de Goëthe, nouvelle traduction complète, en prose et en vers, par Gérard* (Paris: Dondey-Dupré, 1828)
BnF, RÉSERVE 8-RE-13257, PARIS

never tackling Retzsch's impact on stage sets, costumes or actors' bearing.[25]

This chapter will engage these questions with evidence: again and again, from 1824 to 1830, French publishers Auvray, Audot and Giard had Retzsch's plates copied for the French market either by lithography or engraving. Three editions in six years (of which one twice republished with textual additions) prove all the more considerable as they read diversely and addressed distinct publics. Although they mostly come to us as bound albums, they were originally either prints in wrappers or booklets with adjacent text, smaller or wider margins. As a stepping-stone to the Continent, they lead us further, to nearby Belgium. Retzsch's European reception was on the cards.

6.1 Retzsch by Muret for Artists, Readers, and Print Collectors

The first of these is a set of twenty-six loose landscape prints, lithographed by water-colourist Jean-Baptiste Muret (1795–1866) for printseller Auvray. In plain,

Retzsch-like frames, numbered top right as previously, and on buff paper with wide margins, they elegantly bear short italicized captions. Systematically signed "Muret," they are sometimes marked "Lith. printed by Villain," i.e., François Villain who would prove industrious in reissuing Delacroix's lithographs after Charles Motte. On the front cover of their plain brown wrap (23 × 29.2 cm), the title *Faust* and the publisher's imprint appear within a palmetto-decorated rim.[26] Most exemplars traced have since been bound.[27] No introduction nor title refer to either Goethe or Retzsch, and initial order is respected (the cathedral precedes the duel). The witch's kitchen (pl. 6) is altered in a way similar to Moses's, the naked damsel amorously sprawling on her bed, but God amongst angels does appear in Heaven (pl. 1). The handling blends British and German treatments.

Muret, a well-chosen French counterpart to Moses, had a skilful, linear style, ideal for rendering Retzsch. He contributed *c.*30 of the 315 lithographs to Baron Vivant

---

25 Marquart, *Goethes Faust in Frankreich*, 404.

26 Beinecke: Speck Ck99 R3 +840 copy 2. See further Appendix 1, no. 6.

27 Beinecke: Speck Ck99 R3 +840 copy 1, half-bound, devoid of title-page and covers, plates foxed. Some of the plates show vestiges of having been mounted (exhibited?) at top or bottom.

FIGURE 6.5 Jean-Baptiste Muret, *Méphistophélès obtient de Dieu la permission de tenter Faust*, lithographic copy of Moritz Retzsch's pl. 1, in *Faust* (Paris: Auvray, n.d. [1824])
BnF, 8-RIC-71, PARIS

Denon's grand project *Monuments des arts du dessin chez les peuples tant anciens que modernes* (between 1816 and 1820), which acquainted him with a large number of artists and numerous styles. Muret was employed at the Numismatic Cabinet from 1830 to his death, and copiously drew antiquities from various collections across Europe for the *Recueil des monuments antiques*, a large assortment of original drawings, critically edited online at present.[28]

If in style Muret is akin to Moses, the lithographic medium brings him closer to the 1825 London copies by Hullmandel for Berthoud Jr with all significant details (God, the magic-mirror sylphid, male private parts, and location of pl. 18) perfectly matching Berthoud's. As said, Hullmandel himself is related to France in a number of ways. In which direction was influence exerted? Accurately dating Muret's version proves all the more vital, as at present and for no apparent reason this copy is inaccurately dated 1820, 1830, or c.1840 (BnF). The correct *Bibliographie de la France* date of 3 January 1824 is corroborated by several press reviews.[29]

Influence is then as bi-directional as trilateral: it is rather Muret who inspired the smaller and cruder London version, lithographed by Hullmandel. A telling Muret detail shows two horn-like locks above God's brows, strongly reminiscent of Michelangelo's Moses descending from the Sinai with the Tables of the Law, *karan* in Hebrew (both *horned* and *radiant*). A year later, Berthoud's deity (cf. Fig. 5.15) refers back to Muret's and his wild tufts of hair (Fig. 6.5), rather than the opposite. Still, Muret's version has in turn been shaped both by Moses's copies (in gender and sexualised issues) and the original German (by showing God in Heaven, contrary to Moses). Since the Counter-Reformation, Roman Catholicism encourages

---

28   Digital Muret: https://www.inha.fr/fr/ressources/outils-documentaires/digital-muret.html.

29   Press reviews in chronological order: *La Gazette de France* (7 Jan 1824); *Le Constitutionnel* (8 Jan 1824); *La Gazette de France* (12 Mar 1824); *La Pandore* (15 Mar 1824); *Le Corsaire* (19 Mar 1824).

FIGURE 6.6   Jean-Baptiste Muret, *Marguerite dans sa chambre*, lithographic copy of Moritz Retzsch's pl. 9, in *Faust* (Paris: Auvray, n.d. [1824]), to compare with Fig. 9.6
BnF, 8-RIC-71, PARIS

representation of the divine, particularly significant in France where it must compete with Republican iconography. One press review mentioned God "as he is pictured everywhere, in images of Catholic faith."[30] When God vanishes in Audot's versions, his fading has an altogether different significance.

Egged on by financial incentive, emulation culture was effective. Muret's pen lithographs answered connoisseurs' demand to have the "London engraver's work" copied at a cheaper price.[31] Praised for charm and accuracy, Muret imposed his own personality. He brings forward Margaret's appeal by heightening her bodily charms, stresses objects of piety, and introduces subtle ornamental details to her room (Fig. 6.6). He grants extra tension to the kiss scene by retouching facial expressions and hair. His characters are more passionate and expressive, Mephistopheles is doted with further malevolence and animalism.

Print collectors' demand was one stimulus, another was publication of the first two French translations. The very first, by Albert Stapfer son, in a collected edition of Goethe's plays, issued partly by Auguste Bobée, partly by Auguste Sautelet, had come out one year before, in January 1823. The second, by Louis-Clair Beaupoil Comte de Sainte-Aulaire, was published in Ladvocat's famous theatre series (October 1823).[32] Both Pierre-François Ladvocat and Sautelet were associated with the romantic school. Thanks to them, *Faust* in translation was in vogue, being read and talked about. *La Pandore*'s review opened with a double reference to foreign literature admirers and the play's originality, Muret granting it extra presence. His prints did not have to take up cudgels for *Faust* as Moses's had done in London; they visually heightened rather than triggered readers' awareness. Still, depending on

30   H., "Faust," 242.
31   "Beaux-Arts. Faust," 5.

32   Robert Vilain, "*Faust* and France: Stapfer's Translation, Delacroix's Lithographs, Goethe's Responses," *Publications of the English Goethe Society* 81, no. 2 (June 2012): 75–76.

journalists' culture and acuteness, reviews might typically echo Germaine de Staël on the play's audacity and wildness. The genre of "this extraordinary poem" was blatantly unstable. The abandonment of dramatic conventions erred beyond "tragedy" or "drama," advanced "melodrama" with much circumlocution, and "dramatic novel" seemed appropriate. In a safer chronological perspective, French commentators turned to Doctor Faust's fabled biography by Widman (*sic* for Georg Rudolf Widmann), and Faust as inventor of printing. Literary references piled up, sporadically fuelling new and older myths. Whether bogey narrative, Goethean scenario, or marvellous tale, Margaret always provided a first-rate storyline for writers with verve.

Little is known about Auvray, one of the "Rue Saint-Jacques" printsellers, who also dealt in maps, occasionally in partnership, from fluctuating Paris addresses. A namesake had been active in Nantes, Petite Rue des Carmes, around 1784.[33] To imagine his premises as a fashionable gallery-like shop after Henry Monnier's delightful *Marchand d'estampes* (1826) seems far-fetched. Auvray operated from n° 5 quai Voltaire, on the left bank of the river Seine, directly across from the Louvre, an area well known for its antique dealers and *bouquinistes*. His *Faust* prints were also available at Lecouvey's, under the "great vault" close to Palais-Royal shopping arcades that attracted the wealthy elite and genteel middle class, amid theatres, eating-houses, gambling dens, and brothels. The *Gazette de France*, regularly printed at 5 Rue Christine by Pillet aîné, ran a long article, footnoting that Pillet also held Muret's prints for sale. At 12 Francs (more than twice a worker's daily salary) their price drew customers in vagrant markets. Slightly reduced, the lithographs were reissued by "Auvray Frères," this time with two addresses, 11 quai Malaquais and 5 quai Voltaire, yet no date. They belong in fact to the 1827–28 *Faust* craze as shows an ad on the back cover of Nerval's translation, already printed in November 1827 (cf. Fig. 6.7b). As produced by "Villain and Muret from the original German," they obviously competed with Audot. The previous error "Villin" on plate 11 was corrected to "Villain".

The lithographs attracted a varied public of collectors, artists, and *Faust* enthusiasts (one Speck exemplar bears pencilled references on nearly every plate, perhaps to a translation) and introduced new readers to *Faust* with the help of articles recapping the story. Several press reviews used the expression "for the gentleman's portfolio" in response to connoisseurs' demand for a French version,

and pointed to yet another category: artists looking for striking scenes and curious incidents might thereby *train their hand*. More than graphic artworks explaining or illuminating the play, they had become archetypes, models, templates. In 1821 Dibdin had embraced that task with his *Tour*, employing scissors and John Byfield's woodcuts (cf. 4.4a–c). Copying, the very reason for Retzsch's flow and circulation, would be *de rigueur*, a drill to practise.

Uncertainty on how to name them ("sketches," "futile lithographs," "a graphic poem") may reflect French commentators' relative linguistic uneasiness with the outline manner. Muret's prints may not have met with the fervour Retzsch had kindled in the UK. When praised, aesthetic standards differed, yet one reviewer mentioned "Gérard, Horace, and Charlet,"[34] and swore he would be damned if these "*poets* did not subscribe to so fertile compositions"—an indirect allusion to the outlines' philosophical or poetical purport.[35] Giard's edition, and later Théophile Gautier's comments on avant-garde theatre genres, would revive the poetic concern. Some regretted a lack of shadows (*Le Corsaire*), others spoke of "engravings" (*gravures*) overlooking their lithographic technique. Theatre was to follow with further applications and fresh remediation of the pliable Retzsch.

6.2 Three Little Audot

"*Faust* will be successively represented on every Parisian stage," wrote Gérard de Nerval introducing his translation in 1828, by then third on the market, "and it will probably be a curious thing, for all those who will see it performed, to access in parallel the German masterpiece." The stage versions, he added, would bank on dramatic effect, hardly developing either the philosophy "in the first part" or "original passages of the second part."[36] Both parts referred to one and the same play, *Faust I*, comprised in Nerval's view of two destinies, the protagonist's truth-seeking tragedy and young Gretchen's story. The argument was sound. By November 1827, when his own translation as by "M. Gérard" appeared (dated 1828), "the Faust year" (*l'année Faust*) was still in full swing.[37] Delacroix had sent *Mephistopheles Appearing to Faust* to the Salon and was completing his lithographs; composers

---

33   Pierre-Louis Duchartre and René Saulnier, *L'Imagerie parisienne. (L'Imagerie de la rue Saint-Jacques)* (Paris: Gründ, [1944]), 191.

34   Probably intended are Henri-Gérard Fontallard, Horace Vernet, and Nicolas-Toussaint Charlet.

35   H., "Faust," 245, author's emphasis.

36   *Faust, tragédie de Goëthe: nouvelle traduction complète, en prose et en vers, par Gérard* (Paris: Dondey-Dupré, 1828), V–VI.

37   Claude Pichois, *Philarète Chasles et la vie littéraire au temps du romantisme* (Paris: J. Corti, 1965), 1:264.

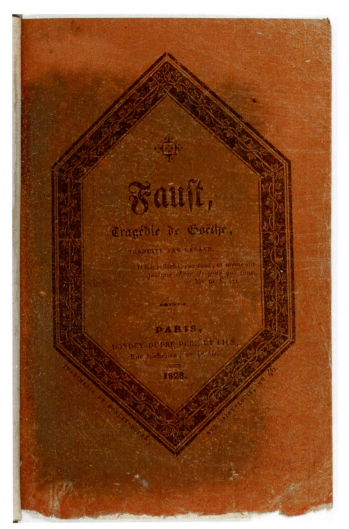 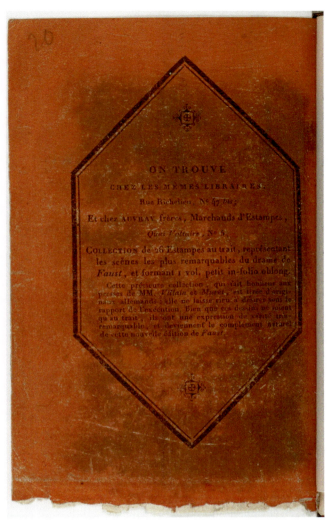

FIGURES 6.7A–B   Front and back orange paper covers of Nerval's translation advertising Muret's second edition by Auvray Frères. *Faust: Tragédie de Goëthe, nouvelle traduction complète, en prose et en vers, par Gérard* (Paris: Dondey-Dupré, 1828)
BnF, RÉSERVE 8-RE-1325, PARIS

François-Adrien Boieldieu, Giacomo Meyerbeer and Hector Berlioz were engrossed with the subject; three open letters on Goethe had appeared May and June in *Le Globe* newspaper; and the stage had been quick to follow suit. Emmanuel Théaulon's *Faust*, a "lyrical drama in three acts," had opened at the Nouveautés on 27 October 1827.[38] In a few years, Paris had become a "Faustian junction" and Goethe's script a new resource for commercially successful melodrama as well as a reference in French romanticism.[39]

Given the taste for drama, Retzsch's set, of numerous theatrical virtues, was a sure card in publishers' hands. Nerval's very translation promoted its visual appeal. Its original bright orange covers caught the eye, tendering the title in a particular setting of elongated hexagons (Fig. 6.7a). The back cover touted the second edition of Muret's lithographs (by Auvray Frères) as a precious complement to the translation (Fig. 6.7b): "Although the designs are only in contour, they possess a very remarkable truth of expression, and become the natural match of this new *Faust* edition." Dondey-Dupré served as yet another commercial outlet for Auvray. The translation itself opened on Retzsch's plate 4 as engraved frontispiece (cf. Fig. 6.4), a copy shamelessly signed "Pineas fec." (for *fecit*, i.e., *made* or *conceived*). An obscure illustrator, Pinéas would self-publish in 1848 twenty lithographic plates as exercises on linear drawing and ornament.[40] Press

---

38   Ginette Picat-Guinoiseau, *Une œuvre méconnue de Charles Nodier: "Faust," imité de Goethe* (Paris: Didier, 1977), 52–54.

39   Emmanuel Reibel, *Faust: La musique au défi du mythe* (Paris: Fayard, 2008), 112–13.

40   Pinéas, *Dessin linéaire, ornement: Exercices gradués de dessin linéaire et de dessin d'ornement. 1ère série* (Paris: Chez l'auteur, 1848).

FIGURE 6.8 *Faust. Vingt-six gravures d'après les dessins de Retzsch*, second and third edition with the Voïart preface (Paris: Audot, 1828 and 1829)
BnF, PARIS, AUTHOR'S PHOTOGRAPH

recommendations of Retzsch's outlines as excellent drill tools had not been lost. Yet, despite Nerval's claims that his translation would enhance the play's philosophy, the frontispiece was captioned "Faust signs the covenant with Mephistopheles," ignoring the wager proposed by Mephistopheles in Heaven and its parodied version in Faust's study. In his preface Nerval himself had used the term *pledge* (*pacte*).

French reception was openly biased but already richly intercultural, aligning book and print trade with theatre. Nerval's long-life attachment to the stage precedes even his translation, which would go through several versions and corrections. In point of fact, young Gérard was not above imitation or reference. His introduction quotes heavily from Germaine de Staël (he owes her his motto), and his translation partly echoes Stapfer's.[41] As Dédéyan has shown, Goethe's flattery on Nerval's translation ("I never better understood myself but thanks to reading you") is a legend upheld by his close friend, Théophile Gautier.[42] *Ars simiae* was in the air, not only in graphics. Text preyed on precedent.

Hence prominent demand for Audot's *Faust. Vingt-six gravures d'après les dessins de Retsch* in social, literary and artistic contexts. Nerval's intuition proved correct. The 29 October 1828 *première* of *Faust* by Antony Béraud, Jean-Toussaint Merle and Charles Nodier triumphed at Porte-Saint-Martin theatre with Marie Dorval (Toussaint's wife) as an exquisite Marguerite and Frédérick Lemaître an awe-inspiring Mephistopheles. In a letter to Weimar chancellor Friedrich von Müller, Count Karl Friedrich Reinhard, Goethe's friend, described the impact Retzsch's prints had had on the actors.[43] Retzsch's icons, however

---

41 Jean Malaplate, "La traduction de *Faust* par Gérard de Nerval, vérité et légende," *Cahiers Gérard de Nerval*, no. 13 (1990): 9–17; nuanced in Stephen Butler, *The Fausts of Gérard de Nerval: Intertextuality, Translation, Adaptation* (Oxford: Peter Lang, 2018), 23–26, 81–82, 166–69, 186–88.

42 Charles Dédéyan, "Vocation faustienne de Gérard de Nerval," *La Revue des lettres modernes*, no. 25–26 (1er trimester 1957): 52–53; Gautier, "Gérard de Nerval," in *Portraits et souvenirs littéraires* (Paris: Michel Lévy Frères, 1875), 12.

43 Helmut Spiess, *Goethe, Eckermann und "Faust auf der Bühne"* (Dingelstädt: Josef Heinevetter, 1933), 95n. More on this in Chapter 9.

FIGURE 6.9
Anonymous eye-catching Audot cover to
Faust. Vingt-six gravures d'après les dessins de Retsch (Paris: Audot, 1828)
BnF, 8-RIC-2, PARIS

reworked by others, proved a key to onstage events especially since they had inspired sets and costumes. Other fanciful, even tongue-in-cheek, *Fausts* were to follow, such as the Gaîté extravaganza *Le Cousin de Faust* (*Faust's Cousin*, 13 March 1829) with a "ballet of winged creatures" (*ballet des Volatiles*); *Faust, ou Les Premières Amours d'un métaphysicien romantique* (*Faust; or, The First Love Affairs of a Romantic Metaphysician*, Pélicier and Chatet, 1829), a cascade of adaptations: adapted from Goethe by Rousset, who adapted Barbier; Lesguillon's *Méphistophélès*, rehearsed but censured, would only be staged in 1832 under the reign of Louis-Philippe. Spohr's *Faust* opera premiered on 20 April 1830, and Louise Bertin's half-French half-Italian *Fausto: Opera semi-seria in quattro atti* at Théâtre Italien on 8 March 1831.[44] Audot's landscape booklets were ideal for the theatre vogue: they would fit a pocket, hide in a pouch, tuck into a suit, in marked contrast to Delacroix's lithographs, set in the luxury Motte-Sautelet folio published February 1828.

Indeed, they were minute (*c.*11.6 × 13.6/14.1 cm) in the mostly cropped bound versions of preserved exemplars (Fig. 6.8), although Audot also issued a large paper version.[45] In all cases images are diminutive, from 7.3 × 9.6 cm for the biggest to 6.6 × 7.5 cm for the smallest. Motif handling mirrors Kennerley's plates, issued 1826 in London by Bulcock to accompany any octavo *Faust*. The first edition in May 1828 was an instant success, a second following in September, a third in 1829. The copies, with longhand captions, were advertised as "lovely engravings" (*jolies gravures*) executed by Trueb, an unidentified craftsman, and illustrator Jean-Antoine Branche, "one of our best engravers."[46] Branche was close to the theatre to wit his outline lithographs after the 1831 production sets for *Robert le Diable*.[47] His copies after Retzsch may have spawned the latter commission.

Louis-Eustache Audot, a bookseller and scribbler in one, had a goal, vulgarisation. His *Encyclopédie populaire, ou Les sciences, les arts et les métiers* was patently *Available to All Classes* (*mis à la portée de toutes les classes*) (1828–29), and his *Musée de peinture et de sculpture*, one franc par fascicle, with texts in English and French, gave visual access to Louvre and other European museums' treasures. His few extant announcements-cum-catalogues between 1826 and 1829 show he had specialized in horticulture, good husbandry, sundry practical and technical subjects, adding art to his wares, particularly Canova's and Goujon's outlines. Once he had tested a product's success, he printed at Rignoux's for a European market. In May 1828, with the first edition out, he tried an eye-attracting cover (Fig. 6.9) on the same principle as Berryman's pink version

---

44 Picat-Guinoiseau, *Une œuvre méconnue*, 54 (adjusted).
45 BnF Musique: RES-1443. Auguste Vincent's exemplar of 3rd Audot ed.; French-German captions and large paper plates.
46 F., "Faust et Hamlet," *Journal des artistes et des amateurs*, 2nd ser., 2, no. 23 (7 Dec 1828): 354.
47 Catherine Join-Diéterle, *Les Décors de scène de l'Opéra de Paris à l'époque romantique* (Paris: Picard, 1988), nos. 94, 96–97, 99.

for Bulcock (cf. Fig. 5.17). Four motifs meet: Faust and Margaret kissing (pl. 15); the magic-mirror demon with drapery (pl. 6–7); and Mephistopheles grinding his teeth at Faust (pl. 23) while the witch's cat rubs against his leg (pl. 7). In a dramatized gothic triptych or lay *rétable*, the demonic drapery serves as proscenium. Niched in an apse, the lovers abandon themselves to a passionate embrace, Mephistopheles taunts and menaces them on the right, the demon hovers centrally above the very title, threatening disaster. This mock altarpiece sums up Margaret's fate. Audot's booklet is a fake shrine to her lost virginity, and a sure lure.

The first edition still misspelt the artist's name (Retsch), offering an unsigned 4-page note. In fewer than three months, the tables turned thanks to Élise Voïart, writer of historical works, fiction and children's books, and prolific translator from German and English into French. She quoted Nerval's translation and, using the plates, elaborated on key scenes in a long "Introduction." Herself a water-colourist, she knew the pull of pictures. The price climbed from 2 to 2.50 Francs, confirming that text sold for less than images. Voïart's interpretation, available as a separate brochure to "the purchasers of the first edition at 50 centimes," will also have served as a universal and widespread digest of the play's obscurer passages. The booklets coupled with trustworthy translations, and echoes of Böttiger's approval of Retzsch, correctly named, trickled in. Paralleling the press, Audot touted expressive and graceful drawings, low price and Retzsch's European fame. Obviously, at only 2 Francs, *Faust* was a gold mine, while the press boosted extensive demand. Audot's catalogue still offered it along with Retzsch's *Hamlet*, *Fridolin* and *The Dragon* in 1838, *Faust* gripping the Francophone market for a long time yet.

Inside, Gretchen's story gained new subtitles. Auvray had inaugurated in 1824 a longhand caption for every Muret print, contrasting with the brief Boosey labels also bunched together in a "List of Plates." Yet several look suspiciously matter-of-fact as if translated from the English and loosely sketching the plot, toning down the supernatural but elaborating on Mephistopheles, cast as schemer. Audot's seamless captions marked a difference: they expound plot, present characters, offer explanation, tip in psychology, and link consequence to cause. Comparison by translation of a Margaret sequence in all three versions is telling:

> (pl. 8). Faust sees Margaret for the first time. (Boosey = Auvray)
> Faust meets Marguerite for the first time and offers her his arm and company, which she refuses. (Audot)

(pl. 9). Margaret in her chamber. (Boosey = Auvray)
> Marguerite, back home, thinks of the handsome cavalier she has met. (Audot)

(pl. 10). Faust introduced into Margaret's chamber by Mephistopheles. (Boosey)
> Mephistopheles introduces Faust to Marguerite's room and leaves a casket in her wardrobe. (Auvray)
> Faust enters Marguerite's room in her absence. Mephistopheles leaves a casket in her wardrobe. (Audot)

(pl. 11). Mephistopheles Leaves Rich Ornaments in Margaret's Chamber. (Boosey) (Changed in 1821: Margaret admiring the jewels left by Mephistopheles)
> Marguerite discovers the casket. (Auvray)
> Marguerite admires her jewels. (Audot)

(pl. 12). Margaret shews her treasures to Martha. (Boosey)
> Marguerite shows her jewels to her neighbour Martha. (Auvray)
> Marguerite's mother having given the casket to the church, Faust has introduced a new one. Marguerite shows it to her neighbour Martha, who advises her to keep it. (Audot)

(pl. 13). Mephistopheles informs Martha of her husband's death. (Boosey = Auvray)
> Mephistopheles visits Madame Martha and commits her to receiving Faust in the presence of Marguerite. (Audot)

(pl. 14.) The decision of the flower. (Boosey)
> Marguerite plucks a flower to see whether Faust loves her. (Auvray)
> Marguerite in Madame Martha's garden plucks a flower to see whether Faust loves her. (Audot)

(pl. 15). Margaret meets Faust in the summerhouse. (Boosey)
> Faust and Marguerite in a summerhouse. (Auvray)
> Marguerite has hidden in the garden lodge. Faust has followed her. They are told that it is time to separate. (Audot)

(pl. 16). Margaret disconsolate at her spinning wheel. (Boosey)
> Marguerite despairs of Faust's absence. (Auvray)
> Marguerite weeps after the absent Faust. (Audot)

As Nerval had pointed out, text was crucial, and the Audot booklets built on that, expanding the product's appeal. Audot probably wrote himself the first edition's "Note on Faust" (though Nerval might just be to blame), mingling legend, praise of Goethe, and Nerval catchphrases. The doctor's evil deeds culminated in magical books he "had composed with Beelzebub's help and infinitely multiplied" and "a list of his books on magic" compiled by "a bibliographer." Nerval was fascinated by the motif. Beware of books ... but buy one! Touted as "the German Shakespeare," Goethe had presented in his dramatic poem "the vanity of human knowledge, the peril of delving too far into studies too strange, lastly how a man acts under the demon's influence." Audot counted on readers' curiosity and cultural transfer. Assimilating Goethe to Shakespeare, Homer and Dante, had already emerged in Stapfer's preface. Hagiography was in the air.

Audot had captured the market, each further release offering something special, as Boosey had done in London. The second edition (September 1828) met with the success of the Porte-Saint-Martin *Faust* (premièring 29 October 1828): the press recommended the booklet as "indispensable to familiarity with *Faust*," publishing etching ads and stage reviews in parallel.[48] The booklet was available at the publisher's, from bookseller Bezou on Boulevard Saint-Martin, close to the theatre, or 7 Cour des Fontaines, outlet for Barba, who also published theatre annals. Etchings and stage worked hand in hand, scene by scene.

The third bilingual edition combined French captions with original German lines for a multilingual audience, and travelled outside France to bring home a distinct echo of the French craze.[49] Retzsch's appeal met that of Voïart, who had adapted in translation many a sentimental novel by Auguste Lafontaine. Also in 1828, Audot launched Retzsch's *Shakespeare Gallery*, immediately triumphant in London, with *Hamlet* issued first, copied on steel by Branche to better effect than the *Faust* plates.[50] In 1829, he imported (via the UK rather than from the German States) Schiller's *Fridolin* with Retzsch's outlines on the same formula (copies after Retzsch, line per line Voïart translation, French and English captions). The idea mimics Charles Tilt's *Fridolin*, published in London in J. W. Lake's translation (1829), with captions in English and French, but printed in Paris by Rignoux, Audot's very

same printer. For enterprising booksellers with scribbling skills such as Audot, books and engravings were less the outcome of intellectual exchange than an upshot of editorial patterns validated by inter-continental exchange: manipulated artefacts, critical for reception.

The 1829 French *Fridolin* consolidated Retzsch's reputation and referred to Cotta's commission of the artist. Retzsch's art resonated in all three countries. Voïart hyped his idiosyncrasies in a somewhat affected style: "the clever draughtsman did not impose on himself the order adopted by the poet, he took delight in painting scenes Schiller had not at all described." He "made up for silence" and "characterized with singular vigour that very kind of monstrous creature, half human, half demon." Even his dragon (in *Le Dragon de l'île de Rhodes* after Schiller's *Der Kampf mit dem Drachen*) was typical of Germany's sublime and naïve poetry.[51] Contrariwise, for Ralph Waldo Emerson "Retzch [*sic*] is a Gothic genius [—] not the Greek simplicity but the Gothic redundancy of meaning & elaboration of details."[52] Although appreciation diverged either side of the Atlantic, French papers now spelled Retzsch correctly, and the *Journal des artistes* even talked of "the great drawings of the German artist, almost equally estimated to the ones by Flacmann [*sic*, meaning Flaxman] for Dante." Flaxman had only been recently published in France. True, as pointed out, the booklets' low price also counted. By contrast, Delacroix's drawings were "incorrect" and "extravagant," Goethe's poem overestimated, a "shapeless" or "failed work."[53] Retzsch alone held the key to understanding and appreciating *Faust*.

Meanwhile, rays had replaced God surrounded by angels in adoration on clouds, strongly hatched to indicate depth. They gave a strange woodcut quality to the engravings (Fig. 6.10), criticized in the *Journal des artistes* and contrasted with Branche's delicate engravings on steel for Retzsch's *Hamlet*. The *Journal* did not wish to mar Retzsch's growing fame without clarifying however why the representation of God had vanished, in the likes of Kennerley's prints, yet not exactly to respect piety, as in Britain. Beaming celestial radiance represented the Supreme Being in the iconography of the French Revolution (Fig. 6.11), noted 1836 Karl Rosenkranz, German pedagogue and Hegelian philosopher, who

---

48   *L'Écho de Paris* (29 and 30 Oct 1828): 1, 4.

49   Pasted on lilac backing sheets, the re-engraved prints with French captions form part of the Theatersammlung, Universität Köln, n.d.

50   F., "Faust et Hamlet," 354.

---

51   Voïart, "Avertissement," in *Fridolin: 8 dessins de Retzsch* (Paris: Audot, 1829), 6–7.

52   Emerson, *The Journals and Miscellaneous Notebooks*, vol. 5. *1835–1838*, ed. M. M. Sealts, Jr (Cambridge, Ma.: The Belknap Press of Harvard University Press, 1965), 298. Journal C, between 16 and 20 Apr 1837.

53   F., "Faust et Hamlet," 353–54.

FIGURE 6.10
Trueb, engraved copy of pl. 1 after Moritz Retzsch replacing God by beaming rays, in *Faust. Vingt-six gravures d'après les dessins de Retsch* (Paris: Audot, 1828) BnF, 8-RIC-2, PARIS

further attributed the change to a natural leaning of the French towards abstraction.[54] Another possible explanation might be "God is the sun!" in the *Illuminati* tradition opposed to (religious) obscurantism and superstition. Illuminism was dear to Gérard de Nerval, who had discovered early in life many an occult volume in the library of his uncle, Antoine Boucher.[55] The Audot copies, reliant on Nerval's translation, reflected his recognizable prose. English religious courtesy on the one hand disputed a radical breach with it on the other. A similar iconographic treatment was of diametrically opposed significance, depending on which side of the Channel one stood. *A posteriori*, to a modern viewpoint, this could translate as the un-representable, which shows how dependent images are on concept.

Despite the praise he gained, Retzsch's finer forms had however become gross and blunted in these booklets. His whimsical details now spawned a proliferation of oddities. The suggestiveness of his outline style, giving the reader free rein to imagine the play's poetry and metaphysics, was ceding to realism anchoring the characters in a crude and tangible world. All three Audot substitutes reduced *Faust* to a graph oscillating between devilry and pathos. Reaction was quick, as shows the last French copy from Giard.

6.3 A Francized Original Retzsch

Competition between Giard and the third Audot is flagrant. Notwithstanding the possibility that Audot antedate his last edition, or the checklist defer recording it, the *Bibliographie de la France* dated both issues 13 February 1830. Audot's booklet, still available in 1838, may have been reissued by one of his sons, either Louis-Désiré or Louis-Joseph, who took over their father's license in 1832, before he himself returned to the book trade in 1835.[56] More decisively, a contest engaged noiselessly, yet unmistakably, on graphic and printing grounds.

The name Giard belongs to a long genealogy since the 1760s when Antoine Giard, succeeding his uncle Jean Quesnel, established himself as bookseller at Valenciennes in Northern France, to François Giard at present in Lille. From Valenciennes to Cambrai via Lille and Paris, the

---

54 Rosenkranz, *Zur Geschichte der deutschen Literatur* (Königsberg: Gebrüder Bornträger, 1836), 260–61.

55 Charles Dédéyan, *Gérard de Nerval et l'Allemagne* (Paris: Société d'Édition d'Enseignement Supérieur, 1957), 1:20.

---

56 BnF: Q-10B-1834, Q-10B-1818–1900 (publishers' catalogues).

FIGURE 6.11 *Être suprême, Peuple souverain, République française*, coloured engraved print, 41.5 × 51.5 cm (À Paris: chez Basset, [c.1794]). De Vinck, 6288
BnF, RÉSERVE QB-370 (46)-FT 4, PARIS

Giard family line embraces most aspects of the book trade: grocer-booksellers, pedlars, street vendors, and experts. In 1830s Paris close to the Mint, Institut de France, and French Academy, at 5 Rue Pavée-Saint-André-des-Arts, currently Rue Séguier, Giard dealt mainly in engravings, prints after museum galleries, maps, and topographic prints. He is listed in an 1829 trade catalogue as publisher of "all the works of Count [Alexandre] La Borde; picturesque travels in Spain, etc."[57] One of these, Laborde's major heritage assortment *Monuments de France* (1816–36) was printed by top printers Pierre and Jules Didot, alias P. Didot aîné and J. Didot aîné, while Giard issued the plates and ornaments. Similar bonds also tag the 1830 *Faust* copy.

Faust: Esquisses dessinées par Retsch reveals a double intent: to honour Goethe's master play and revert specifically to the original German set in the finest possible way. Giard promptly marketed it as a much-desired rarity for collectors, aiming to oust the altered Audot wares. In French terminology of the time, *esquisses* was the closest to *Umrisse*, currently named *gravures/dessins au trait*. Giard's title championed Retzsch, instating ascendance over Goethe himself, whose name had simply disappeared. As advertised, the edition reproduced the plates "in exactly the same format as the [Cotta] original," while "adding a brief account of the subject and the plot's progress."[58] Manifestly referring to the 1820 Cotta edition in larger margins, Giard's item further enlarged these, both for letterpress (20.6 × 27.8 cm for Cotta's 17.8 × 22.9 cm)

---

57 M.-A. Deflandre, *Répertoire du commerce de Paris* (Paris: Au Bureau du Répertoire du Commerce de Paris, 1829), 2:471.

58 *Journal des débats* (7 May 1830): 3; *La Semaine* 3 (23 May 1830): 3.

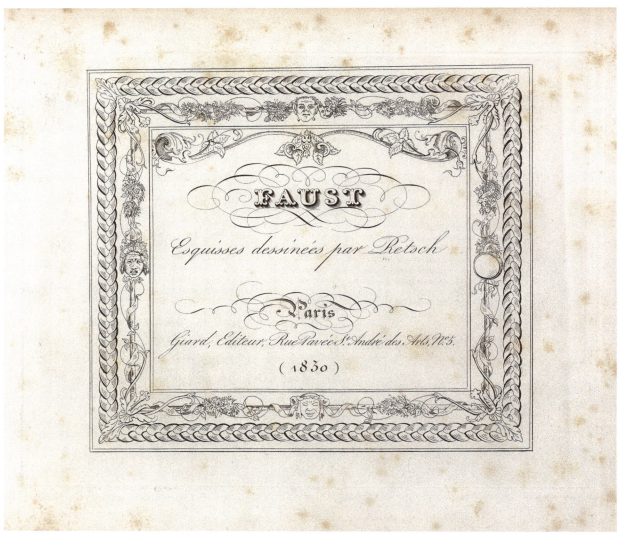

FIGURE 6.12 Etched title-page in *Faust: Esquisses dessinées par Retsch* (Paris: Giard, 1830)
COURTESY BEINECKE, YALE UNIVERSITY, SPECK CK99 R3 +830B COPY 1

and plates (23.9 × 31 cm for Cotta's 19.2 × 24.3 cm). Their difference in size is noticeable, the initial 8-page leaflet being smaller—a Parisian imitation of Cotta's letterpress brochure, yet not designed to stand alone. It does not hold translated excerpts (a note stresses the difficulties of *any* translation, indirectly praising Nerval without naming him), but sizeable *Faust* abstracts per plate (with pl. 18, now subservient to the plot, renumbered 20, out of kilter with the Cotta set). Akin to detached captions in longhand, brief italicized sentences in abstracts allude to the plates, themselves neat proofs in thin frames, numbered atop right as the originals. The deftly designed item cost 5 Francs in paper wraps, 6 Francs in boards, under a sensational cover and a title-page I will come to.

Despite best intentions, *restoration* of any original is seldom done without the process reflecting later period and restorers' mindsets. The Giard version is no exception. Like numerous hitherto neglected artefacts discussed here, it provokes analysis of its strong textual, typographical and graphic motivation—three aspects closely interrelated, seldom so prominent at the time. They beg the question of the originator's identity.

Textually, the anonymous "Introduction" sanctions Goethe as a great poet and *Faust* "as that remarkable work whose merit has been recognized by Europe's universal approval." Such a firm conviction sounds novel for France. Much could be said about certain other interpretations, I shall not linger on those. Vitally, this unnamed writer knows *Faust* first hand—having certainly read it in German. The foreword focuses on Faust as inventor of print type, and explains how two distinct historical facts (Faust or Fust, printer and Gutenberg's associate, and doctor Faust, former Wittenberg student) meet and merge in a single legend, before introducing Lessing, then Goethe, and the protagonist's possible redemption. The recurrent French emphasis on Faust and printing is of particular weight and further supported, I argue, by typography and printing choices.

FIGURE 6.13   Cover for the Giard edition, lithographed by Alphonse Bichebois, 18.5 × 25 cm
BMO, ESTAMPES SCÈNES FAUST (23), PARIS

One of his last, the letterpress leaflet is by Jules Didot aîné, a descendant of the illustrious printing house. Himself an unconventional printer-bookseller and typefounder, Jules introduced bands, border ornaments and vignettes to romantic editions.[59] After 1830 he transferred his printing business and foundry to Brussels and sold them to the Belgian government, before losing his reason in 1838. Both letterpress and plates, printed with particular care in the Giard set, tout Faust as forebear printer and this modern *Faust* as instance of legendary printing. Emmanuel Théaulon's *Faust* (1827) also bore on Faust's printing activity, and Nerval's "Observations" to his translation ended with the same motif. By no coincidence, one act and a summary of August Klingemann's 1815 popular romantic play, *Faust*, again featuring a damned Faust as inventor of printing type, would soon be presented to French readers in the *Gazette littéraire*, a review issued by Sautelet, also publisher of Stapfer's *Faust* translation.[60]

The Giard edition adds to the Retzsch copies an etched title-page and sensational cover, lithographed by Alphonse Bichebois at Saint-Denis. The title-page's mix of hand-drawn romantic lettering symptomatically combines diverse fonts and flourishes within a threefold frame (Fig. 6.12). An eye-catching plaited motif is amended by an inner arabesque of vine leaves, ivy sprigs, blossoming clusters, corner embellishments and four vignettes at cardinal points. The grotesque masks of comedy (bottom) and tragedy (left) take on demonic features atop middle (faun ears and horn-like tufts of hair). A round mirror on the right-hand side invites the reader to look at himself and consider his self-portrait as the composition's finale. The uncanny sequence reads stylistically close to Bichebois's

---

59   André Jammes and Françoise Courbage, eds., *Les Didot: Trois siècles de typographie et de bibliophilie, 1698–1998* (Paris: [Agence culturelle de Paris], 1998), 29, 53.

60   *Gazette littéraire* 2, no. 18 (31 Mar 1831): 276–79.

FIGURE 6.14
Spine with four interlocked double Ls surmounted by a count's crown between raised bands
COURTESY BEINECKE, YALE UNIVERSITY, SPECK CK99 R3 +830B COPY 1

title-page for Jacques Milbert's *Itinéraire pittoresque du fleuve Hudson* (1828–29), where the same densely plaited motif is used.[61] However, the sequence's complexity of meaning is unusual for Bichebois, a painter who obtained a lithographic licence from Saint-Denis (where the cover was also printed) only after several requests by mayors and members of the nobility. Bichebois, known for landscapes and antiquities, lithographically transposed others' motifs, for instance Milbert's.[62] He probably transposes here somebody else's composition. Indeed, the inner arabesque reveals a finer understanding of *Faust*. The comic and tragic masks echo its twofold purport, voiced by the Poet and the Merry Person in the introductory "Prelude on the Stage," a scene rarely understood, commented, or even published at the time. Similarly, the demonic mask reflects devilish sway over the protagonist, while the mirror invites individual readers to consider themselves, underscoring the play's universal bearing on mankind. Such subtle interpretation is rare for the time, in this case also secret, depending not on words but a cryptic graphic motif, the mirror. Its multifaceted toying demands identification of the prefacer and his novel approach to Goethe's play. The same may be said of the cover.

The latter is based on Retzsch's plate 1, dramatically swapping an infernal assembly for the original celestial scene (Fig. 6.13). Beneath the title in bold capitals, a gigantic fist grips as if to fling a tiny naked and agonizing human into Hell. Around it, three harpies (a pun on *harpadzo*, in ancient Greek *to seize*) gape in awe, threat or mourning, while two dragon-like canines guard the gates Cerberus-like, alongside two other diabolical creatures, one of which also contemplates the central scene in dread. The grim message is played down by comic undertones, as in the gawp of terrified monsters. The clutched hand may yet be another pun on *die Faust*, literally *the fist* in German, pointing again to the mysterious author reading the play in the original. A further assembly appears at all four corners: men in dense groups glaring at Faust's infernal punishment engage in passionate discussion. The disorderly gatherings evoke contemporary depictions of the romantic school, such as the battle pitched by partisans and opponents at the *première* of Victor Hugo's *Hernani* (Théâtre-Français, 25 February 1830). A few turbaned heads among these may cite the fanciful dress of several

---

61 http://elec.enc.sorbonne.fr/imprimeurs/node/21884, digitized cover; digitized version of the volume https://gallica.bnf.fr/ark:/12148/bpt6k10485756.

62 *Dictionnaire des imprimeurs-lithographes du XIXe siècle*, s.v. "Bichebois, Louis, Pierre, Alphonse" (by Élisabeth Parinet), <http://elec.enc.sorbonne.fr/imprimeurs/node/21884> (7 Sept 2018).

Hernani's supporters, again alluding to *Faust*'s pertinence for all humanity.

Further printing of the Giard version throws up surprises. The half-morocco binding of a Speck exemplar bears four interlocked double Ls surmounted by a count's crown between the spine's raised bands (Fig. 6.14). It contains 68 plates on thick paper, and reads as a series of experiments in reproduction techniques, trial prints and/or artists' proofs.[63] These are: the copy's etched title-page in its ornamental border; a first set of all 26 numbered plates etched as proofs (before letters); plates 1–21 and 23–26 lithographed and captioned (the witches' Sabbath is missing); a proof of the sole title-page border; finally, 15 etched plates without numbers or letters. Several lithographs signed (presumably C.) Magnenat, an obscure draughtsman, are printed by George Frey, well-known lithographer for the review *L'Artiste*, Charles Philipon's satirical prints, and illustrations.[64] They are captioned after Muret, as if a cheaper lithographic version of Retzsch's images had been considered (still with alterations) to succeed Muret's, by then out of print. As in Muret and the original, plate 18 is not renumbered and precedes the duel. A few are not signed, and may be by a different hand. Whatever the case, they show that other ways of framing had been tried, modifying the scenes and their reading. Last, but not least, the final cluster of 15 corresponds to selected plates at various stages of etching. Trials explored how to highlight a scene's main character and best render Retzsch's slightly stronger outlines (Fig. 6.15a–b). The exemplar (with count's crown), which does not include the sensational cover printed by Bichebois, clearly belonged to an aristocrat keen on engraving and printing techniques.

In 1830 (the year he launched the *Faust* copy) Giard started issuing fascicles of Léon de Laborde and Louis Maurice Adolphe Linant de Bellefonds's well-known *Voyage de l'Arabie Pétrée*, including 23-year-old Léon's own drawings that first acquainted the Western world with the since famous rock-carved tombs of Petra. Two of these were also engraved by Léon. Solidly trained in classics, modern languages, and later Arabic, born into a family of aristocratic intellectuals, Léon de Laborde (1807–69) was a young archaeologist, traveller, and draughtsman, keenly interested in engraving and printing. Oriented by his father towards the diplomatic service from 1828, he had studied in Germany, and *Voyage de l'Arabie Pétrée* is dedicated to William II, Elector of Hesse. A fine German scholar, he

also authored essays on engraving.[65] The Speck exemplar of printing samples strongly points at Léon as owner, also authoring the 1830 *Faust* "Introduction" and synopsis, and possibly conceiving the uncommon title-page and cover, revelatory of complex *Faust* readings.

Indeed, the second part of the 1872 auction catalogue of Léon de Laborde's library mentions 40 exemplars of the Giard set, either in paper covers or in boards (as in the two options published), in a section titled "Works by MM. Alexandre and Léon de Laborde (in numbers)," while the first part includes yet another exemplar of proofs before and after letters, which may identify with the Speck volume.[66] In neither Léon's nor Alexandre's bibliographies does this title appear. Alexandre might conceivably have also been candidate to the attribution. A polyglot with perfect command of German, a writer of richly engraved publications and wide interests, an independent-minded Empire statesman, Laborde father was connected to all three individuals, Giard, Didot, Bichebois. In fact, Blanc's *Protestation des députés réunis chez Alexandre de Laborde* (De Vinck 11052), a lithograph printed by Bichebois in 1830, shows political figures meeting at his house in opposition to Jules de Polignac, ministerial leader of the Ultraroyalists. Alexandre had been made a *comte* of the Empire under Napoleon (9 January 1810) but assumed the title of *marquis*, purchased by his father, at the Bourbon Restoration (1815). In 1830, the title (and crest) of count already belonged to his first-born, Léon, and the two interlaced Ls on the Speck volume are the latter's initials. Although book expert Jean-Baptiste de Proyart advertised four prime copies of books with the same crest and spine design as from their former shared library, the Speck exemplar may be safely attributed solely to Léon. He, not Alexandre, was keenly interested in engraving and lithography. In 1833, through Jules Didot, he published *Essais de gravure pour servir à une histoire de la gravure en bois*, starting with a daring experimental plate, "Chisel Tests" ("*Essais de burin*"). Several other wood engravings by himself or others, outlines and maps, along with his sketches of turbaned figures (as in the Giard *Faust* cover) evoke his travels. A distinct interest in grotesque, tragic or macabre atmosphere and surprising incidents, confirmed

---

63 Digitised at my request https://collections.library.yale.edu/catalog/16712419.

64 *Dictionnaire des imprimeurs-lithographes du XIXe siècle*, s.v. "Frey, Jean George" (by Élisabeth Parinet) <http://elec.enc.sorbonne.fr/imprimeurs/node/22337> (16 Apr 2019).

65 Bertrand de Villeneuve-Bargemon, *Alexandre de Laborde* ([Neuilly-sur-Seine]: IBAcom, 2011), 129; Christian Augé and Pascale Linant de Bellefonds, "Présentation," in Alexandre de Laborde and L.-M.-A. Linant de Bellefonds, *Pétra retrouvée* (Paris: Pygmalion / Gérard Watelet, 1994), 9–13; DCHA, s.v. "Laborde, Léon-Emmanuel-Simon-Joseph (vicomte, comte, puis marquis de)" (by Geneviève Bresc-Bautier), online (last accessed 5 Mar 2023).

66 *Catalogue des livres composant la bibliothèque de feu M. L. J. S. E., Marquis de Laborde* (Paris: Adolphe Labitte, 1871–72), 2:no. 3464, 1:no. 643 respectively.

FIGURES 6.15A–B
Trial lithograph and etching to best render Moritz Retzsch's outlines, after plates 23 (Faust accusing Mephistopheles) and 16 (Gretchen at the spinning wheel) in the Laborde exemplar
COURTESY BEINECKE, YALE UNIVERSITY, SPECK CK99 R3 +830B COPY 1

by his library holdings, permeates this "first fascicle" on engraving, due to be continued but without suit. Although Alexandre also had dealings with Giard, evidence mostly points to Léon. Further, his father's opposition to Polignac, in self-designed uniform leading a popular insurrectional movement during the July Revolution's troubled times, the overthrow of King Charles X, and the 1830 July Monarchy under Louis-Philippe, hint as to why the Giard edition had little echo in press reviews. It also explains why 40 exemplars may have been left untouched in the Laborde library, later to be sold at auction.

Thus, the finest Retzsch renderings in France, accompanied by a novel understanding of the play, met little demand, despite the spirited title-page, lithographic cover, and Léon's plausible eager involvement in their making. It is the Audot booklets that many artists and writers would add to their library: to name but a few, no lesser luminaries than the English poet Bryan Waller Procter (pseud. Barry Cornwall, 1787–1874), Byron's Harrow school fellow; French composer Auguste Vincent, pianist virtuoso, teacher and bibliophile; modernist poet Guillaume Apollinaire, playwright and art critic; and modernist theatre practitioner Edward Gordon Craig.[67]

6.4   Copies vs. Originals? The Brussels Case

Post-Waterloo Brussels deserves special attention. From 1810, it had become the growing centre of Belgian counterfeit editions (*contrefaçon belge*) thanks to Napoleonic and post-Napoleonic political censorship and surveillance, as well as considerable financial barriers in the French book trade.[68] This expedient business, backed by successive governments, created a flourishing knockoff activity that dominated foreign markets and boosted the public's taste for reading, regardless of whether the industrialised process endorsed or demoted the emergence of "Belgian" publishers.[69] The Brussels book trade popularized mainly French literature abroad in two ways: by launching French books from the serialized novels in journals, prior to their publication in France (*préfaçons belges*), and by *reprinting* texts (as opposed to forging editions) in a different type

and layout.[70] Accompanying images belonged to three categories: a) copies of original images; b) engraved or lithographed prints acquired by agreement; and c) original Belgian illustrations in counterfeit editions.[71] However, a school for wood engraving on a commercial basis was not founded in Belgium before 1836 with the chair for steel engraving remaining vacant.[72] The Belgian Retzsch editions bring further light to this and spark aesthetic, political or commercial repercussions.

In 1828, shortly before the Belgian Revolution led to the creation of a modern state in 1830, Brussels was a bilingual city, where Latin-rooted French and Germanic Dutch met. Part of the United Kingdom of the Netherlands, under an enlightened Protestant monarch, William I (1815–40), it represents a buffer zone against the threat of French expansionism. In such a political and social context, *Faust: Tragédie de Goëthe* [*sic*], a "new edition" issued by La Librairie Romantique, matched romantic stance with genuine business concerns. La Librairie Romantique, at various Brussels addresses and a London branch, was a typical bookseller-cum-stationer, created in 1828 and run by Sylvain Van de Weyer with a French exile, Auguste Feuillet (who styled himself Feuillet-Dumus), would-be administrator of revolutionary journal *Le Libéral*.[73] It also imported architecture and art books from Paris, Florence, Rome and Naples, and engaged in reprinting, mostly by instalments with alluring images, occasionally coloured. It promoted romantic Francophone writers, such as Charles Nodier, Prosper Mérimée, Benjamin Constant or Germaine de Staël, and also launched the drama series "Théâtre romantique."

Printed in-18° on satin wove paper by Weissenbruch, "Printer to the King," *Faust* bears on the title-page the political allegory "Freedom" (*Liberté*), a vignette of an eagle in flight against a flaring sun emerging from clouds. It relates to pre-marxist political activities by Feuillet-Dumus,[74] and sponsors a romantic watchword well before Hugo's *Hernani*. Feuillet-Dumus's wife had inherited a part of the printing business from August Karl Wilhelm

---

67   Beinecke: Speck Ck99 R3 +828 (Cornwall); BnF Musique: RES-1443 (Vincent); BHVP: 8-APO-1566 (RES) (Apollinaire); BnF ASP: P16-EGC-368 (Craig).

68   Odile Krakovitch, *Les Imprimeurs parisiens sous Napoléon Ier* (Paris: Paris-Musées, 2008); Marie-Claire Boscq, *Imprimeurs et libraires parisiens sous surveillance (1814–1848)* (Paris: Classiques Garnier, 2018), 19–24.

69   Jan van der Marck, *Romantische Boekillustratie in België* (Roermond: J. J. Romen & Zonen, 1956), 269.

70   [Charles Hen], *La Réimpression: Étude sur cette question considérée principalement au point de vue des intérêts belges et français* (Bruxelles: Auguste Decq, 1851); Herman Dopp, *La Contrefaçon des livres français en Belgique, 1815–1852* (Louvain: Librairie Universitaire, 1932).

71   François Godfroid, *Aspects inconnus et méconnus de la contrefaçon en Belgique* (Bruxelles: Académie Royale de Langue et de Littérature Françaises, 1998), 693.

72   Marck, *Romantische Boekillustratie*, 273–74.

73   Dopp, *La Contrefaçon*, 27.

74   Jacques Grandjonc, *Communisme/Kommunismus/Communism: Origine et développement international de la terminologie communautaire prémarxiste des utopistes aux néo-babouvistes* (Trier: Schriften aus dem Karl Marx Haus, 1989), 1:125.

Weissenbruch, one of the first Encyclopaedists, whose son, Louis, was patented "Printer to the King" in Brussels. This entitlement, and Goethe's lithographic portrait in the book from the court studio, effectively set this *Faust* under the monarch's protection. Feuillet-Dumus profited from the first fifteen years of prosperity under William I and the southern provinces' industrial revolution that strengthened the liberal bourgeoisie. The King had adopted French Revolution principles in order to subjugate the Catholic south, such as equal protection for religious creeds (in effect privileging Protestants) and the same civil and political rights for every subject. *Faust* thus addressed middle and upper educated classes of liberal spirit, upheld by the powers-that-were as the right of every citizen.

As such, it is a thought-provoking object since it blends material and ideas from *two* separate French editions on the very year of their publication. Issued in October and December 1828 at 1.25 Florins or 2.64 Francs per part,[75] it adapts the Audot plates copied by Trueb and Branche in two versions (either with French or French-German captions[76]) to the Stapfer translation (as re-published by Motte and Sautelet in folio with Delacroix's lithographs). Its small format (*c.*14.1 × 9.7 cm) confirms Audot's primacy abroad, borrowing from the Motte-Sautelet folio a text-and-image combination prototype along with the Stapfer translation. Feuillet-Dumus had garnered inspiration from both.

Indeed, the Brussels *Faust* distributes the Audot plates opposite (and askance to) the matching passages, as the French folio had done with Delacroix's lithographs. Choice prints with French captions are always on the right-hand side, those bilingual being allocated left or right to suit correlation. Whatever the result, the extensive captions oddly recap the adjacent text, the images evidencing the publisher's sleight of hand. Variance in placing could result from the binding (all examined exemplars are bound) or from two diverse issues, as confirms Goethe's effigy as frontispiece in two versions. In these, Feuillet-Dumus uses yet another copy, the portrait Delacroix lithographed for Motte after Johann Joseph Schmeller's 1826 drawing of the poet.[77] In one issue (HAAB: G 349), the effigy, printed by the court's lithographic studio, is signed D. V ..., identified by a note as "M. Vincent, distinguished Brussels artist." Dominique Vincent (later Meulenbergh), half-brother of Frères Williaume, was a painter specializing in likenesses,

often of court figures (Fig. 6.16a). In the other (HAAB: F 3858), the effigy is printed by the Williaume brothers, Joseph and François, who dealt in sundry counterfeit lithographs.[78] The privy counsellor's expression, romanticized to fit "an imaginative recreation of Delacroix's idea of Goethe-the-poet,"[79] has been further modified each time. Vincent gives Goethe an intense, pensive and firmer expression as he fixes the reader with a piercing glance, the Williaume deliver a gentler and sunnier rendering of broader appeal (Fig. 6.16b). A lithographed Goethe signature, reproduced below his portrait as in the French edition, but much enlarged, seals the attempt with brio, as if the author himself had authenticated it in person.

Feuillet-Dumus thus put on the market two issues of Retzsch partially copied at origin (Audot < Bulcock), now inserted to an edition reprinted from the French, as counterfeit Belgian editions usually did. The Motte-Sautelet folio had also initially included a Delacroix copy of Goethe's effigy, again copied with variations in Brussels. Into what category do these adjustments fall? A counterfeit *Faust*? A reprint *Faust*? Or an *original* work? If their organizing principle was original, all parts were copied. Feuillet-Dumus certainly displays a nascent *publisher*'s intense preoccupation to provide a romantic *Faust* for a new audience in a Francophone context. He combined Audot's theatrical appeal with Stapfer's text and Motte-Sautelet's blend of image with text (without though the "wild" Delacroix lithographs, presumably too daring for Brussels). As such, through variation (in two differing issues), the item stands for a new creation. In a vulgarized Retzsch-copying industry, the care spent to invent yet another *Faust* by mustering sundry parts and ideas, indicates keenness to represent the romantic school, as Feuillet-Dumus's catalogue repeatedly states.

In a study on illustration in counterfeit Belgian romantic editions, Marij Lambert has argued that lack of attention to the material aspects of a book and absence of illustrations confirm a perceived dearth of modern publishers in Belgium.[80] Feuillet-Dumus's *Faust* points however to a more complex reality. From a cultural point of view, this *"nouvelle édition"* (title-page) appeals to its readers quite differently from both French prototypes, even

---

75 *Revue bibliographique des Pays-Bas et de l'étranger* 7, no. 37 (17 Oct 1828): 435; no. 41 (11 Dec 1828): 491–92.

76 HAAB: G 349 (French captions) and HAAB: F 3858 (bilingual captions). Both, named *"nouvelle édition,"* are dated 1828.

77 Vilain, "*Faust* and France," 113.

78 On D. Vincent and the Williaume brothers, see Marie-Christine Claes, *Répertoire des lithographes actifs en Belgique sous la période hollandaise et le règne de Léopold Ier (1816–1865)*, 3rd ed. (IRPA, 2022), 503–04 and 512–20, http://balat.kikirpa.be/lithographes/claes_lithographes.pdf (last accessed 8 Mar 2022).

79 Vilain, "*Faust* and France," 113–15.

80 Lambert, "L'illustration dans les contrefaçons belges: Une approche systémique," *Image [&] Narrative*, no. 7 (Oct 2003), http://www.imageandnarrative.be/inarchive/graphicnovel/marij lambert.htm.

RETZSCH IN FRANCE AND BELGIUM　　　　　　　　　　　　　　　　　　　　　　　　　　　　　199

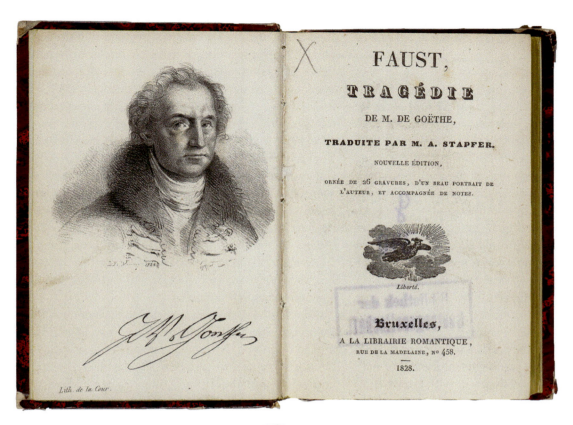

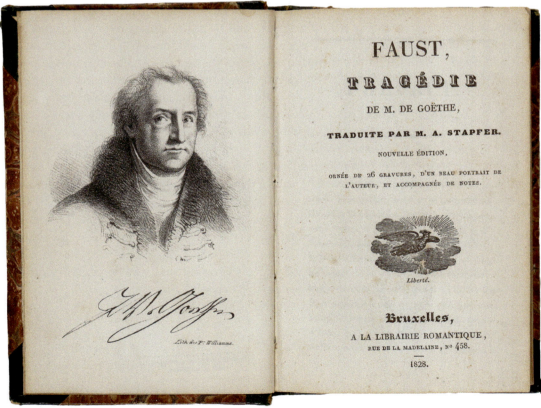

FIGURES 6.16A–B　Two versions of Goethe's portrait by Delacroix, lithographed by Dominique Vincent (later Meulenbergh) and by the Williaume brothers, in *Faust: Tragédie Ornée de 26 Gravures, d'un Beau Portrait de l'auteur, et accompagnée de notes de M. de Goëthe. Traduite par M. A. Stapfer* (Bruxelles: Librairie Romantique / Weissenbruch, 1828)
COURTESY HAAB, G 349 AND F 3858, WEIMAR

though strictly speaking it may be considered reprinted, even legally forged. At the time, copyright does not exceed a nation's boundaries.

Its singularity stands out when compared to another two Brussels *Faust* editions, first by Jean-Paul Meline alone in 1833, then with associates "[Léon] Cans et Compagnie" in 1838, both well-known counterfeit publishers but also book exporters.[81] Meline, born in Livorno, first established himself as bookseller in that city, then in Leipzig, before becoming one of the most important publishers in Belgium. Also benefitting from royal protection of the book trade, he printed at Adolphe Wahlen's, "Printer-Bookseller to the Court." By 1838 the associates had their own bookselling, printing and foundry business. With his initial bureaux in Livorno and Leipzig, Meline had covered a large part of the European market, his Leipzig antenna "supply[ing] Germany, Poland, Denmark and Russia."[82] In such an extended distributive flow of prints, Retzsch copies are to be spotted.

The 1833 edition pirates the Feuillet-Dumus *Faust* within Belgium itself, shamelessly naming it "third edition," with the Audot plates either on yellow paper with French titles or white paper with French-German ones (variation persists).[83] Lithographed either at the court studio or by Frères Williaume, Goethe's likeness is reversed in some, not in others. Vincent's name has disappeared and three lists of characters introduced (afore "Prelude on the Stage," "Prologue in Heaven," and the "Tragedy"). Feuillet-Dumus's *Faust*, obviously deemed original—in a way it surely is—, was worth pirating and clearly in demand. Still, in the 1838 *Faust*, again based on the Feuillet-Dumus template, the Stapfer translation was "revised and corrected by Doctor C[arl] M[artin] Friedländer, director of the German Institution in Brussels, member correspondent of the Historical Institute of France," and may have spread in France. Dissimilarity and variation countered publishers' possible claims. Publishing contention accompanied the reception of *Faust* across Europe, Retzsch's plates being always a coveted attraction.

It may then come as something of a surprise to see how popular would prove Meline's counterfeits in very different and learned context. A Speck exemplar of the 1833 *Faust* belonged to Kuno Meyer, distinguished Celtic philologist. Founder and editor of four journals on Celtic studies, Meyer taught at Liverpool and in Ireland (he introduced

the Irish public to ancient Irish poetry, entered the Royal Irish Academy, and was made a freeman of both Dublin and Cork), before joining Friedrich Wilhelm University in Berlin. In his exemplar, pencilled manuscript comments refer mostly to the final translation notes by Stapfer, but one of them reveals that he used his book to cross-compare iconography with the first edition of Nerval's translation (1828) and Birch's English *Faust*. Another exemplar, from Harvard's Widener library, belonged to American romantic and abolitionist poet James Russell Lowell, who succeeded Longfellow in modern languages at Harvard (teaching Spanish and French, 1855–86), edited the *Atlantic Monthly* (1857–61), and served as US ambassador (Spain, UK).[84] As for the 1838 edition, it has entered the Germanic Collection at Princeton, founded by American businessman, weapon historian, and collector Carl Otto Kretzschmar von Kienbusch.

None of these possessors seems to have doubted their exemplars' quality or authenticity. It may of course be argued that none were seeking genuine prototypes. They doubtless wanted to read *Faust* in Stapfer's original or corrected translation (though all of them could read it in another language, and Meyer in German). In point of fact, all three specimens evince varying compilation rationales: didactic (Lowell), connoisseurship (Meyer) or putting together a collection (Kretzschmar von Kienbusch). The latter's was based nevertheless on the expertise of Theo Feldman, "one of the best-known dealers in works related to German literature."[85] Even more surprisingly, the 1838 *Faust* features in a French bibliophile's library sold at auction. Abel Giraudeau, a medical doctor, was founding member of the renowned Société des Amis des Livres, and his library held illustrated books, original editions, and art publications. His uncut copy was in a Japanese binding, the last word in bookish refinement at the end of the nineteenth century.[86]

It is ostensibly in various disguises (copied editions), in several garbs (materiality), and through diverse channels (provenance) that Retzsch's copies circulated Goethe's text freely, disregarding set ideas. Retzsch's prints trespassed on preconceived categories.

---

81 René Fayt, "Les contrefacteurs belges étaient des 'étrangers'," *Cahiers du Cédic*, no. 2–4 (Jan 2003): 165–70.

82 Dopp, *La Contrefaçon*, 40, 79; Marck, *Romantische Boekillustratie*, 33.

83 Appendix I, no. 22.

84 Digitized by Google, https://babel.hathitrust.org/cgi/pt?id=hvd .hwk7uh&view=1up&seq=15.

85 Victor Lange, "The Kretzschmar von Kienbusch Germanic Collection," *Princeton University Library Chronicle* 19, no. 1 (Autumn 1957): 56.

86 *Catalogue de livres modernes [...] composant la bibliothèque de feu M. le docteur Abel Giraudeau* (Paris: Librairie Techener, 1898), 2nd pt., 133:no. 612.

6.5 Retzsch in French Nineteenth-Century Print Culture

English print culture around Retzsch is prolific, with novel printed items situated in a condensed time frame, but results in standardisation. Sparser but further-reaching, Francophone culture vests objects and publics with different functions both spatially and temporally. Having fathomed the first three French editions and the Brussels case in ant-like detail, let us consider a century (1840s–1940s) from a bird's eye view.

Retzsch's images often condition book reception for a fluctuating readership: the educated urbane German of the 1840s and 1850s; the broad (including the less fortunate) French base, enticed by cheap reading-room materials in the 1850s and 1860s; and *lycée* (secondary school) pupils or undergraduates from 1940 onwards. Such diversity again substantiates Retzsch's plasticity and compliance, though with significant dissimilarities.

In 1840, eight Retzsch outlines (six from *Faust I* and two from *Faust II*) nestled on one single sheet with captions in German (cf. Fig. 6.17), a synoptic frontispiece in two columns for two ponderous editions of Goethe's works, one selected (*auserlesene*), the other complete (*sämmtliche Werke*). The first a hefty tome, the second of five volumes, both in double-columned pages and Gothic type, plus a single, slightly smaller one-volume *Faust*, were all published by Baudry in Paris. By then, his European Bookstore (*Baudry's europäische Buchhandlung*) had considerably expanded to an adjacent reading room and balcony overlooking the Seine river, at 3, Quai Malaquais. A bookseller and publisher active from 1815, Louis-Claude Baudry (1793?–1853) specialized in foreign books as Galignani's main Paris rival in importing books from Britain. His *Télémaque* "in the six most utilized European languages" (Paris, 1837) was also available to clients' language(s) choice, along with handbooks to study modern languages. In 1831 (or 1833) Baudry founded a "European Bookstore" series, following on his "Foreign Languages Library." In the early 1840s, as trade in German books grew, he launched the "Library of the Best Old and New German Writers" (*Bibliothek der besten ältern und neuern deutschen Schriftsteller*). Goethe's *Works* were volumes II to VI, issued with three portraits, eight grouped subjects after other titles, and the eight *Faust* outlines "after Reitsch" [*sic* in catalogues, yet correctly spelt in the published works], all for 50 Francs. The series would comprise "205 tomes" by first-rate writers "in 15 large in-8° volumes printed in two columns on wove paper, with portraits, engravings and facsimile" for 196 Francs.

In dense gothic type for the educated gentleman's library, all five tomes sit in half-leather publisher's bindings with spines elegantly decorated in gilt arabesques and crowned by a minute *chinoiserie* of period taste. A vast German-speaking community in Paris of 30,000 in 1841, 60,000 in 1848, and over 100,000 in 1866, although their numbers would dwindle due to political upheavals,[87] was also a target public. Intellectuals, printers, book traders and other educated types would gladly read a by then consecrated author. They might not afford any classy series, but peruse it in Baudry's reading room, then be only too happy to acquire the single *Faust* for 4.50 Francs.

In all three cases, the outlines grouped cartoon-like meaningful episodes (Fig. 6.17). Smaller than Retzsch's own prints and slightly altered, they respect the German originals in detail (male crotches are unadulterated, the condensed formula resulting in miniaturization surely offering less offence to prudish eyes). They line up Faust's pledge, his meeting Margaret, the kiss, the duel, Faust's and Mephistopheles's cavalcade, and Margaret's refusal to leave prison, along with the Classical Walpurgis Night and Faust's burial from *Faust II*. Centred on Margaret's story and tragic fate, concluding with the doctor's doom, they alter the overall meaning to emphasize a sorry state of affairs for both protagonists. Short italicized lines from *Faust I* enhance dramatization, contrasting the merely descriptive slogans for *Faust II* depictions.

Inserted to every *Faust* by Baudry, the single-page theatrical synopsis burgeoned. By 1843, the separate *Faust* had been through eight reprints.[88] Under Louis-Philippe, last king of France, it was available, as touted its title-page imprint, at Baudry's, Quai Malaquais (near the Pont des Arts, the Institut de France, and the Louvre), and further afield.[89] A manuscript ex libris, signed L., clearly a member of the German community in Paris, bears a hybrid script for the date, "19. Juin 48," half in German (19. instead of 19), half in French (*Juin*), the very year of the February 1848 Revolution and only a few days before the 23 June uprising.[90] The publisher's vignette by [Charles] Marville (a small angel sits atop a seething urn held by a siren and a triton with a bat-winged dog at their feet) may be a political cryptogram. An exemplar with copious notes, possibly by a different hand, sports the manuscript

---

87   Jeanblanc, *Des Allemands*, 9.
88   Engel, no. 726.
89   At Stassin and Xavier's at Rue du Coq (previously Baudry's own premises); Amyot's at Rue de la Paix near the Palais-Royal; Truchy's on Boulevard des Italiens; Théophile Barrois's on Quai Voltaire, "and in all good bookshops in France and abroad."
90   Beinecke: Speck Rb41 843b copy 1.

FIGURE 6.17   *Acht Umrisse zu den merkwürdigsten Scenen Faust's gezeichnet von M. Retzsch*, c.27.5 × 18 cm, eight outlines after Moritz Retzsch for *Faust I* and *II* as synoptic frontispiece for various editions of Goethe's works (Paris: Baudry, 1840s and 1850s)
BnF & BMO, ESTAMPES SCÈNES FAUST (14), PARIS

ex libris of N. J. Wyeth, probably Nathaniel Jarvis Wyeth (1802–56), the American merchant inventor of the Boston ice industry and explorer of Oregon and the Northwest.[91] The book travelled widely, and *Faust* (especially *Faust II*) must have matched Wyeth's herculean efforts and modernizing ambitions in real life.

The synoptic frontispiece still held sway in 1855, when Baudry's widow put to an already oversupplied market all three editions "entirely revised and corrected" with a new date and her imprint, dropping the price of *Selected Works* to 25 Francs. Even before that, three Goethe portraits and 16 grouped subjects sold independently as advertised at 5 Francs. This explains the detached frontispiece, which found its way into the Paris Opera collection "Prints after *Faust* scenes," conveniently on file for stage and set arrangements. The impressive cover of the Giard edition (cf. Fig. 6.13) belongs to the same collection.

Joseph Bry's popular "Literary Illustrated Evenings" series ("Les Veillées littéraires illustrées," 1849–56) was meant for broad readership, in popular and bourgeois circles thirsting after literature. Eugène Sue's hugely successful *The Mysteries of Paris*, published in the *Journal des débats* between June 1842 and October 1843, had stirred demand. Five years later, J. Bry aîné (1822–64), a print shop worker turned publisher, developed the *roman de quatre sous*, a quarto gathering of 16 thin pages in two columns with two wood engravings on pages one and nine at 20 centimes (*quatre sous*) per part. Sold weekly or monthly at modest cost, his fascicles delivered democratic reading in unhampered batches, inviting readers to compose from them bespoke volumes according to their own interests.[92] The offer combined several recognized authors such as Rabelais, Tasso, Jean-Jacques Rousseau, Samuel Richardson or Oliver Goldsmith, with modern celebrities, including Walter Scott, Lord Byron, Charles Dickens, and even Charles Baudelaire, whom Bry contributed to popularize. Between 1848 and 1856, thirteen volumes of fascicles, richly "illustrated by Édouard Frère," opened with *Werther*, *Faust* following in July 1850.

Sandwiched between Walter Scott novels, the latter is based on Nerval's 1840 reviewed translation, his last *Faust I* interpretation, and a partial translation of *Faust II* interspersed with abstracts. For the first time, Nerval added to the *Faust II* ending the protagonist's redemption through divine grace, which alters the overall meaning and importantly amends the damnation scenario. He also included Goethe's 1830 appreciation of his own rendering,

only recently brought to public attention in France, as a meaningful endorsement of his own toils. Perhaps surprisingly the humble edition is deemed pivotal in Nerval studies, since it marks a vital shift from his journalism to later inspirational work.[93] It also subjugates *Faust* to an anonymous legendary text (in a sixteenth-century French translation by Palma Cayet) incorrectly attributed to Widmann, as if Goethe's text itself were a fabulous continuation, particularly in Nerval's rendering. The complex mix of legend, translation, additions, and Goethe's commentary made for a successful marketing formula, while the cheap brochure marks a turning point in French *Faust* reception. Iconography grants it extra weight thanks to Frère's reworkings and Bry's clever layout. The high figure of its distribution (12,000 prints) benefitted from Bry's association with Maresq and Pelvey's "Librairie centrale des publications à 20 centimes."[94]

To accommodate all *Faust I* material, Bry's original formula had become a 44-page dense quarto in two columns with eleven in-text illustrations, cut by Belgian wood engraver [François] Rouget. The hyped "drawings by Édouard Frère" were in point of fact shamelessly copied from Retzsch via Muret or some other go-between at a time when, pressed by necessity, Frère (1819–86), painter, water-colourist and etcher, provided Bry's series with some 800.[95] Creating a sensation, Frère bowdlerized Retzsch, focusing on the main scenes, in black and white contrast with astute gradual shadowing, laid out to enhance effect. Appealing to the average reader, he heightened sentimental drama, and tempered grotesque, erotic or unruly details. One exemplary opening suffices here, these images being further commented in Chapter 7 as typical of extensive iconography. Four revamped Retzsch scenes, inserted to Goethe's translated "Outside the Town Wall," titillated well prior to related textual events: a bevy of intoxicated students supervised by a grinning Mephistopheles; Faust absorbed by the half-naked magic-mirror vision; he accosts Margaret; she studies an opulent necklace astonished (Fig. 6.18). Nerval's note on "Widmann," an abridged introduction to both parts, his translator's note with Goethe's praise, and additional *Faust II* paragraph on divine grace, completed the offer.

Results ensued. The fascicle was reprinted in 1852 and 1854. Baldensperger dates the original edition 1851, while

---

91   Beinecke: Speck Rb41 843b copy 2.
92   Georges-André Vuaroqueaux, "L'édition populaire au milieu du XIXe siècle: L'exemple de la famille Bry," (Master diss., Université Paris X-Nanterre, 1989), 162–68.

93   Nerval, *Œuvres complètes*, ed. J. Guillaume and Cl. Pichois (Paris: Gallimard, 1989), 1:1694–99, 1930–31 (by Lieven D'Hulst).
94   Vuaroqueaux, 185–91, and his Appendix I.
95   Flor O'Squarr, "Édouard Frère," *Galerie contemporaine, artistique, littéraire* 1, 2nd ser. (Paris: Ludovic Baschet, 1876), 1; Daniel Baduel, Aude Bertrand, and Christian Dauchel, *L'École d'Écouen: Une colonie de peintres au XIXe siècle* (Écouen: Office de Tourisme d'Écouen, 2012), 147–48; 2nd enlarged ed., 2018, 14–15.

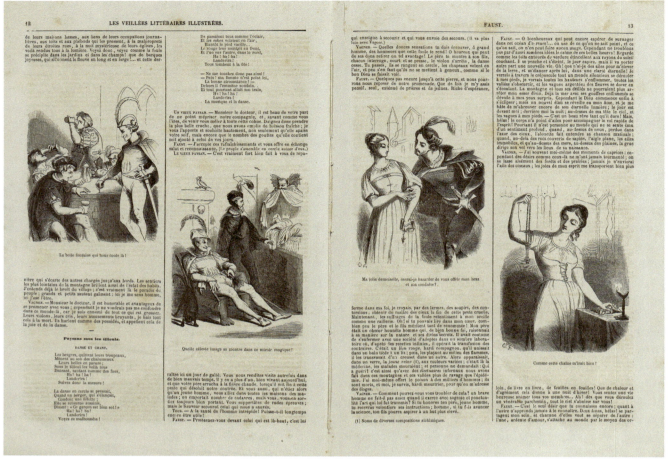

FIGURE 6.18   Four woodcuts after Moritz Retzsch, in *Faust par Wolfgang Goethe: Traduit de l'allemand par Gérard de Nerval, précédé de la légende populaire de Johann Faust, l'un des inventeurs de l'imprimerie, illustré de jolies vignettes par Éd. Frère* (Paris: J. Bry aîné, 1850), 12–13
COURTESY HAAB, F GR 5293, WEIMAR

Henning avers four editions instead of three 1850–54, and another three 1858–64.[96] Joseph Bry went bankrupt on 10 May 1855 but the fascicle resuscitated in 1858, along with *Werther*, under the corporate name "Librairie centrale des publications illustrées à 20 centimes." The latter was more distributor than publisher of numerous cheap publications, including "Complete Works" by Balzac, Hugo, Sand, and Sue. Bry's price however now fetched 90 centimes. A dramatically changed header conceived by Charles Mettais disclosed a portrait of Walter Scott amid a motley collection of figures, probably from his best-selling novels, above Faust's covenant. Mettais's recycled image was often used as series header. In fact, popular fiction at the time (as in Paul Lacroix, alias Bibliophile Jacob's numerous penny novels) is infused with Faustian iconography. Alchemists' studios, prison scenes, men hanging in a row, or dark riders galloping away by night are period props influenced by Retzsch and revamped in France by Delacroix's dark imagery. However cost-effective, images were also printed separately on fine paper as artists' proofs for gentlemen's and collectors' print portfolios.[97] In Bry's fascicles, emotional iconography spices up the tales.

The significant rise in price of the 1858 *Faust*-cum-*Werther* impression draws on the work's popularity. "Bry aîné" is given as printer with a different address. Odd caption inversions in the first four woodcuts evidence hasty printing. Gounod's 1859 *Faust* also rekindled interest in Goethe's play. The fascicle was again reissued in 1860 with fitting image captions, now printed by Jouaust et fils at 338 Rue Saint-Honoré. Interestingly, this is Charles Jouaust, whose son, Damase, would later become a reference for bibliophilic editions. As for the last Nerval translation, the fluidity of print culture resists set ideas about exclusive volumes.

Conquest of the masses in the 1850s and 1860s, thanks to such as Bry and associates, is matched nearly a

---

96   Fernand Baldensperger, *Bibliographie critique de Goethe en France* (Paris: Hachette et Cie, 1907), no. 774; *Faust-Bibliographie*, ed. H. Henning, no. 1097.

97   Arsenal: EST-Pet. fol.-I (1).

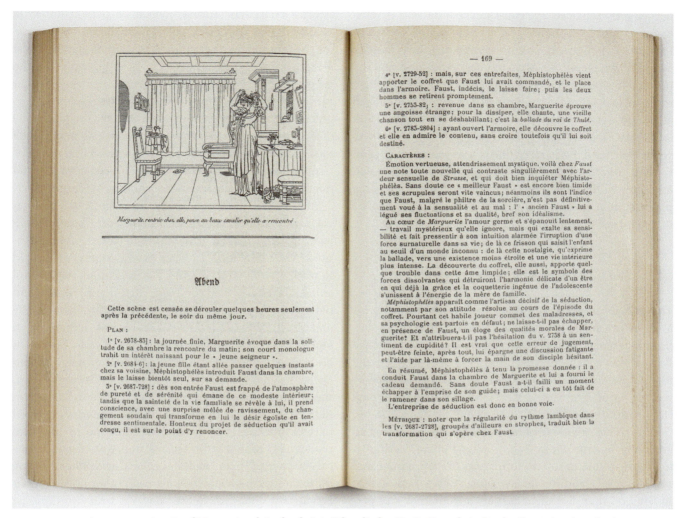

FIGURE 6.19 Anonymous vignette of Margaret undoing her hair in "Abend" after Moritz Retzsch, in Goethe, *Faust: Avec introduction, notes et commentaires par P. Labatut*, third edition (Paris: Masson, 1951), 168–69
COURTESY HAAB, N 10700, WEIMAR

century later in 1940s educational publishing. P. Labatut's *Faust* edition in publisher's boards is part of the "New Collection of German Authors" released in 1940 under the aegis of prominent secondary education teachers, two from Paris's prestigious *lycée* Montaigne, a third being headmaster of the French *lycée* in Mainz, Gutenberg's own city. The editor, P. Labatut, himself *agrégé de l'Université*, regional academic inspector, and a highly qualified tutor at Carcassonne's *lycée*, had previously published *Werther* in this same collection with silhouette illustrations throughout (1929). The edition was launched by a key publisher in medical and scientific books, Masson et Cie, run by various members of the family since 1836, and still active under the name Elsevier Masson. Dense and informative, Labatut lengthily introduced *Faust*, based on focused bibliography and several reliable German and French editions of the time. Bountiful notes in Gothic print fathom language, ideas and poetry, in all likelihood for higher *lycée* classes and university undergraduates. Among the painters and engravers mentioned, Retzsch is first referred to. Well-known Faust iconography illustrates the introduction (after Rembrandt, Delacroix, Kaulbach, etc.), yet only Retzsch's outlines pace the text, each scene illustrated by smallish double-framed copies mostly to Audot's captions. If Muret's details have much suffered, imaginable reformations observe scholastic notions of respectability: even Margaret's complicated hair-do in plate 9 was subdued in Labatut's edition (Fig. 6.19). This leads to censorship in two cases: outlines for the Prologue in Heaven and the Walpurgis Night have vanished to avoid tempting excitable young minds. Audot's caption for plate 1, "Mephistopheles obtains permission from God to tempt Faust," perhaps disturbed, the textbook serving in Catholic institutions.[98] All scholastic things considered,

---

98 Exemplar given by P. Labatut to "Father Salvat (i.e., Joseph Salvat, chair of Occitan language and literature), professor at the Catholic Institute, in highly respectful homage" on 9 Jan 1946. Book withdrawn from the Institut catholique de Toulouse (ICT) library.

it was aptly replaced by "Faust devotes himself by covenant to Mephistopheles" (pl. 4). Still, in the course of Labatut's introduction, a reproduction of Julius Oldach's *Mephistopheles and the Student* (1828) will have made a peculiar impression on youths poring over Goethe's verses, more or less ardently studious of Germany. Published at the onset of World War II, Labatut's *Faust* would run to at least four editions (1940, 1947, 1951, 1959), and was still widely used in the 1960s and 70s, as prove French and German reference textbook bibliographies. Diminished and altered, Retzsch's *Faust* art however made a lasting impression in France, particularly on the formative years of several generations.

6.6 Retzsch's Diffuse Influence

The last three examples (Baudry, Bry and Labatut for Masson et Cie) best map the fortune of Retzsch's outlines in France. Due to new artistic trends holding the floor, these were otherwise sparsely used between the 1850s and the 1940s. The outline aesthetic was eclipsed by realism, impressionism, aestheticism, photography, even stereoscopic views, as by Charles Gaudin in 1868. Besides, Goethe's *Faust* was no more the utter reference it had gradually become. From 1859, Gounod's opera overtook it in France, totalling 500 performances in 1886, a thousand in 1894, and Gaudin's stereoscopic images refer rather to Gounod than Goethe. Faustian melodramas still prevailed, and music vied for first place as well,[99] although Hector Berlioz's *Damnation de Faust* would not have come to light but for Goethe's play.[100] Nor are to be neglected earlier or fin-de-siècle parodies, giving an unexpected bearing to Retzsch's and Goethe's reception, even reading *Faust* itself, as Chapter 8 on Crowquill and Lachgern argues. If, by the nineteenth century's dusk, Faust was "in decadence" as Jean de Palacio has claimed,[101] Retzsch, however belittled, survived such fate.

True, evidence of dwindling interest in Retzsch is provided by Champfleury's *Les Vignettes romantiques* (1883) in an early chapter reviewing German influence on French romantic art. Champfleury, keener to criticize Delacroix in a highly impressionistic way than explain Retzsch, treats the former artist as "possessed," calling Devéria's front cover for the Motte-Sautelet folio "the

pencil's Walpurgis." Citing "Retsch" "a patient and cold worker," after *Faust* "fascicles" (*cahiers*) he claims possessing, he reproduces a very poor imitation of plate 6 (Faust absorbed in the magic mirror, cf. Fig. 2.18), copied for the umpteenth time after Muret or Trueb with the peculiar caption *Faust's Laboratory*. Both display and comment suggest he sourced material well out of context. Judging by the derivative and clichéd iconography likely passing through his hands, he concludes: "It should be noted that romanticism in Germany was classical, orderly, conservative, and not excessive, violent and demolishing as in France."[102]

All things considered, might his pages reflect nevertheless a period stance? They rather signal Champfleury's lack of care, indeed messy rule-of-thumb approximations. They also show to what extent copies underrated Retzsch's work and marred his reception, while still spreading *Faust's* fame abroad. Stereotypes were compelling to shape and outlines helped both aesthetically and practically. Champfleury's book was influential in tackling vignettes and has been widely read by historians both of art and literature. His judgment of Retzsch (and Delacroix) has permeated. Conversely, in December 1851, the highly popular *Magasin pittoresque*, in a short note on Retzsch bearing portrait and facsimile signature, stressed that his drawings after Goethe and Shakespeare were "less translations than interpretations, and, so to speak, poetical comments,"[103] all qualities lost on Champfleury. Pitting these contrasting views against each other bodes no fair conclusion either. Evidence may yet turn up. Contrast hardly encourages nuance, and such finesse is critical in fathoming Retzsch's work and diverse readership. Still, a noticeable disparity in Retzsch's French reception distinguishes first and second halves of the nineteenth century.

Retzsch's *Faust* outlines left a recognizable trace on early and late romantic motifs. In 1847, Tony Johannot's flimsy, sinuous, elongated devil, suddenly springing like jack-in-the-box betwixt Faust and Margaret in prison (Fig. 6.20), marks Retzsch's influence, and was re-used.[104] Even before Johannot, several Delacroix lithographs bear Retzsch's influence in general composition or in detail, as well as Gaston Jourdain's synthetic iconography that I further discuss in "Extensive vs. Intensive Iconography."

A most arresting instance of Retzsch's impact informs the "Goethe" section of Achille Devéria's extensive visual registry. Eloquently described by Thierry Laugée as "an

---

99   Reibel, *Faust: La musique*, 10–11.

100 Claude Paul, *Les Métamorphoses du diable: Méphistophélès dans les œuvres faustiennes de Goethe, Lenau, Delacroix et Berlioz* (Paris: Honoré Champion, 2015), 9, 164–69.

101 Palacio, "Décadence de Faust," in *Mythes de la décadence*, ed. A. Montandon (Clermont-Ferrand: Presses Universitaires Blaise Pascal, 2001), 37–46.

102 Champfleury, *Les Vignettes romantiques* (Paris: E. Dentu, 1883), 54–56.

103 "Moritz Retzsch," *Le Magasin pittoresque* 19, no. 49 (Dec 1851): 389b.

104 By Michel Lévy Frères in 1868; four of the engravings also entered a cost-effective translation into Spanish, decked with varied plates, including German ones (Barcelona: Olivares, 1876).

FIGURE 6.20 Tony Johannot, Mephistopheles (after Moritz Retzsch) between Faust and Margaret in the prison scene, in *Le Faust de Goethe: Traduction revue et complète, précédée d'un essai sur Goethe par M. Henri Blaze. Édition illustrée par M. Tony Johannot* (Paris: Dutertre, 1847), insert engraving facing p. 192
BnF, RÉS. M-YH-2, PARIS

immense visual encyclopaedia classified by disciplinary fields, themes, historical period or geographic area," it originally comprised 569 volumes of which less than 200 survive today.[105] Tellingly, Devéria's "Goethe" file relates only to *Faust I*. The material assembled dates from 1824 to the early 1850s, although the general compilation date is recorded as much later.[106] Alaric Watts already mentions Devéria's collection in an 1832 article: "His library contains no less than three hundred quarto volumes of prints, drawings, and tracings of costume, referring to all ages and countries, and to all ranks, from the prince to the peasant."[107] Devéria had invented an adroit binding system allowing him to easily insert or remove sheets as work progressed (used for the Bibliothèque nationale's catalogue of Prints and Drawings of which he became a keeper). For "Goethe," he starts with a gallery of *Faust I* iconography in nearly textual order. He extends by mounting images opposite a dismantled copy of Stapfer's translation as issued 1828 by Motte and Sautelet (Motte was Devéria's father-in-law). Between the two, as if to superimpose protagonist and author, he has lodged the Ciartes portrait of Faust with two Goethe portraits by Delacroix and Obrest Kiprinksi lithographed by H. Grevedon, and Seibertz's final full-page vignette of a griffin-riding Goethe from the monumental Cotta *Faust I* (1852–54).[108] The assortment combines items French (mainly sixteen Delacroix lithographs along with prints by Nicolas Maurin, Alexandre Colin, and Devéria himself), German (Ramberg's 1828–29 *Minerva* engravings and random Seibertz material), and English (from Alaric Watts's *Literary Souvenir; or, Cabinet of Poetry and Romance*). Rather than his original set, Retzsch copies prosper as lithographed by Muret (1824), re-engraved by W. Humphreys (or Humphrys) after John Massey Wright's version (1825–26), or wood engraved by Rouget (1850), on whom all more in the next chapter. Mounted opposite corresponding *Faust* passages, they compare with other artists', as in Margaret at Martha's by Muret (after Retzsch's pl. 12, cf. Fig. 10.6) juxtaposed with Ramberg's rendition (Fig. 6.21).

Devéria's compendium reveals that Retzsch's copied and mediated iconography early did the rounds of French romantic circles. Delacroix was a close friend and fellow student of both Devéria brothers. Achille designed the spine, front and back covers of the 1828 folio *Faust* with Delacroix's lithographs, as well as the poster advertising it. Hardly deriving from Retzsch, his sensational conceptions promote melodrama. Yet, in matching visual material encyclopedically, Devéria reveals covert relationships and courts Retzsch's favour.

Another two instances epitomize how broadly Retzsch's images spread in France from rebel fin-de-siècle aestheticism to middle- and lower middle-class bathos in the 1930s.

Notwithstanding Champfleury's disparagement, detached plates still found their way into visual repertories. Lavishly produced 1900 by La Maison d'Art under directors François Jollivet-Castelot, Paul Ferniot and Paul Redonnel, a 206-page compilation on esoteric sciences, occultism and magic, *Les Sciences maudites*, printed on pink, white and blue paper, has two in-text vignettes and a half-page illustration after Retzsch. Unsurprisingly, the vignettes replicate Faust's pledge, and Mephistopheles leading him to the witches' revel, the illustration reproducing (an attenuated version of) the Sabbath itself.[109] In November 1900, the first issue of *Les Partisans. Revue de combat, d'art, de littérature et de sociologie*, edited by Ferniot and Redonnel, predictably trumped the third image full-page to evoke *Les Sciences maudites*. The review was in fact advertising illustrated books by La Maison d'Art, a short-lived venture, which itself issued between 1900 and 1901 some twelve bibliophilic editions of anarchist propensity along with *Les Partisans*. Paul Redonnel (1860–1935), a poet and writer keen on Occitan culture, *félibres*, and alchemy, was involved in numerous art and literature magazines, occasionally as secretary of Léon Deschamps's *La Plume*. He directed *La Plume* for a month and half after Deschamps's demise on 28 December 1899, followed by little-known Paul Ferniot, editor for a sole 1 March 1900 issue (before the review was bought by Karl Boès) and would-be author of an ample illustrated volume on India (1900).[110] Following setbacks with Boès, the duo had founded the short-lived *Partisans*. Fascination for the occult and rebellious attitudes ultimately blended with alchemic practice—Jollivet-Castelot was a Martinist and Rosicrucian, general secretary of the French Alchemic Association—in celebrating a few Retzsch compositions.

On the flip side, Librairie Gründ, art publisher of Bénézit's dictionary from 1920, reissued Nerval's revised translation of *Faust* in 1936, prefaced by his life-long friend Théophile Gautier. By 1938, idealistic or maudlin

---

105   Thierry Laugée, "Achille Devéria et son herbier de femmes," in *L'Invention du geste amoureux: Anthropologie de la séduction dans les arts visuels de l'Antiquité à nos jours*, ed. V. Boudier, G. Careri and E. M. Kelif (Bruxelles: Peter Lang, 2019), 92.

106   Between 1853 and 1870. The collection entered the BnF Prints department in 1858, of which Devéria had become adjunct curator in 1848 (Laugée, 91–92).

107   Alaric A. Watts, "The Deveria Family," *Literary Souvenir* (1832): 326.

108   On the latter (and the griffin), see Stead, "Les deux *Faust I* d'Engelbert Seibertz."

---

109   Jollivet-Castelot, *Les Sciences maudites* (Paris: Édition de la Maison d'Art, 1900), 25, 26, 27.

110   Philipp Leu, "Les revues littéraires et artistiques, 1890–1900. Questions de patrimonialisation et de numérisation" (PhD diss., Université Paris-Saclay, 2016), 1:71, 109.

RETZSCH IN FRANCE AND BELGIUM 209

FIGURE 6.21   Martha adorns Margaret with the jewels. Two images cut out and mounted by Achille Devéria opposite the corresponding *Faust* passage: (*left*) Muret's lithographic copy after Moritz Retzsch and (*right*) Johann Heinrich Ramberg's rendition of the scene engraved by J. Axmann (*Minerva: Taschenbuch*, 1828)
BnF Est., TB-55 (C)-PET. FOL., PARIS

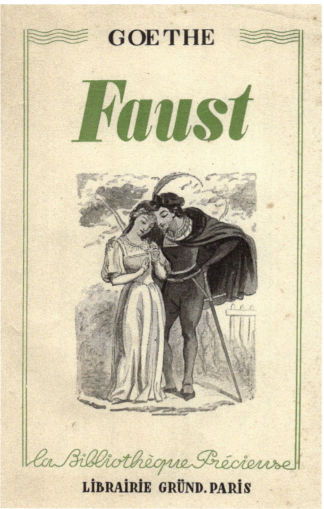

FIGURE 6.22 Unsigned cover for Goethe, *Faust: Traduction de Gérard de Nerval* (Paris: Librairie Gründ, 1938), republished within "La Bibliothèque précieuse" series. After Retzsch's pl. 14 (garden scene) following Édouard Frère's version
AUTHOR'S COLLECTION AND FILE

readers would be treated to one of several pictorial covers of a book for broad readership, an anonymous copy of Retzsch's plate 14 with Faust leaning over Margaret and her daisy, noticeably after Édouard Frère's already derivative and repurposed image (Fig. 6.22 to compare with Fig. 7.24a). In its message, the image obliterated all tragic tension or devilry (Mephistopheles and Martha are absent), cut a definite success with the public, and was regularly reissued within the "Bibliothèque précieuse" series from 1936 well into 1941 and World War II.

6.7 Conclusion

This chapter starts by pinpointing Retzsch's French reception in time (1824–30). The time band spans the first three editions by Auvray, Audot and Giard that launched Retzsch in France, yet his fortune there well exceeds any English-language counterpart. More varied than standardized octavos, popular with British, American or all-inclusive Anglophone readers, French and Belgian publishing ventures stud the nineteenth and overflow into the twentieth century with variety.

Thanks to variable scales in reproduction and a range of techniques, Retzsch's outlines met with a comparatively broader Francophone readership, comprising print collectors and artists (Auvray), upper middle- to middle-class literati, men of letters, theatre enthusiasts, stage directors (Audot), and the progressive aristocracy keen on engraving and lithography (Laborde, Bichebois and *alii*'s experiments). It embraced the German community in France (Baudry), and spread to the United States (Kuno Meyer, Wyeth). French items spawned counterfeit Belgian editions and allow us to nuance set ideas about *contrefaçons belges*. They appealed to the general reader and the masses thanks to Frère's and Rouget's variants for the dime brochures of the time (J. Bry aîné). Retzsch marked romantic iconography (Johannot and Delacroix), interested fin-de-siècle aesthetes and younger writers (*Les Partisans*), appealed to middle-class readers in the 1930s (Gründ), and became accessible to *lycée* pupils and undergraduates in the 1940s (Labatut for Masson). Last, but not least, his icons served to drill draughtsmen in copying exercises.

Without France equalling the striking variety of prints and books of Retzsch's British vogue, the first French lithographed and engraved copies, often re-used, establish his public awareness. The interest of Auvray and Audot editions lies in their early transformation of the engraved set into a captioned picture story (*Bildergeschicht*). Both revived, via more recent means of reproduction (lithography, engraving), the long-standing dialogue of the Faust myth with brochures and *Bilderbogen*, which brought together several small captioned scenes on the same Épinal-like sheet.[111] Scarce awareness of Retzsch in France, and his near invisibility in specialist literature, stem from translation-based scholarship that mask the purport and weight of non-textual printed culture. Indeed, Retzsch's prints either followed on translations (Muret), escorted or supplemented them (Auvray and Audot's relation with Nerval), or rivalled the Motte-Sautelet folio. I have flagged up diverse points also to show the medallion's reverse side.

Last, but not least, behind Nerval's translation that hallmarks this chapter lies a French fascination with Faust as mythical inventor of printing. Théaulon's Faust is a printer, and the anonymous legend attributed to Widmann by

---

111 Neubert, 32–37, 80.

Nerval celebrates printing. The unsigned preface to the Giard edition I attribute to Louis de Laborde expands on Faust as its inventor. Several period reviews refer to the same myth. The variety of editions that welcomed Retzsch form a vista of printing cases illustrative of the French fusion of Fust, Gutenberg's companion, with Goethe's Faust in print culture. Both the frontispiece and the cover of Nerval's 1828 translation deserve then a few remarks as they reflect such speculative concerns.

Pinéas's print, facing the title-page of Nerval's translation, has two foci: the demon's malignity and the doctor's library (cf. Fig. 6.4). Pinéas reworked Muret's matching plate. The devil leans over Faust, in a different poise, glaring avidly at the covenant, his triangular face exaggerated. A fierce expression runs over his animal-like features. His long claw-like fingers are ready to clutch. The bookshelves are filled with precious tomes, row after row of ornate spines, a motif echoing the cover's composition signalling a choice book. On orange paper, an elongated ivy-clad hexagon frames the title in Gothic type, the subtitle in small caps, a motto signed Germaine de Staël, and the publisher's imprint (cf. Fig. 6.7a). Ivy symbolising printing, the publisher re-emerges as printer with his address along the two lower sides. The *hedera*, a small sign of theoretically no particular meaning in the shape of an ivy leaf, was mainly used in Latin epigraphy to separate words or fill an empty space or a short line. Manuscript copyists used it, then printers re-appropriated it. As printer's ornament, assimilated to the fleuron, it often adorns elegant nineteenth-century printed books such as Dondey-Dupré's. Its sophisticated cover, echoed by the doctor's impressive library, mirrors the end of Nerval's preface on Faust as inventor of printing. The devil's irony, Nerval had specified, echoing Mme de Staël, "judges the universe as a bad book with the devil as *censor*" (his emphasis). Several of the French editions discussed in this chapter toyed with just such an idea.

CHAPTER 7

Extensive and Intensive Iconography

The Hoflößnitz Museum of Saxon Viticulture sits midway up a hill in Radebeul overlooking the vineyards of Saxony, down on the river Elbe, and beyond to the city of Dresden. Hoflößnitz, Retzsch's choice abode, is no hermit's hideaway. Viticulture dates back to 1401 here, where the Electoral House of Wettin would later enjoy a winery and formal rural retreat. In the ballroom of a remarkable 1650 pavilion, over eighty painted Brazilian and African birds vividly parade alongside allegories of good regency. Birds and virtues soared over court festivities celebrating the wine harvest in the seventeenth and eighteenth centuries. The pavilion today houses the better part of the Museum collection.

Retzsch's *Parade of the Vinedressers* (*Winzerzug*) opens any tour of its exhibits. A run of eight consecutive coloured lithographs marks the first national festival for Saxon vintners on 25 October 1840. Retzsch, owner of a large vineyard nearby, had been made its honorary member. In his sophisticated pageant, local lore blends with mythological fauns, bacchantes, Silenus, and wine-related biblical figures (Caleb's grapes from the Holy Land), ending with congregations of citizens.[1] The eight lithographs prompt our steps towards a vibrant inscription: "Nothing lives here but pleasure, but freedom, banter and rest | grief be banished, you guests, come to me." An invitation to "luxury, calm and delight," it recalls Henri Matisse's painting *Luxe, calme et volupté*, while "you guests, come to me" evokes Jesus's beckoning of children. The vineyards summon their own, just as the eight sheets set the tone for bourgeois wine festivities, local and past traditions, antique and biblical figures. Duly credited as their designer and original conceiver, Retzsch himself leads an artisan parade of three: lithographer E. Otto, printer E. Böhme, and Käthe Bernardt, who had carefully coloured them in 1958. Art-wise, the crafted item ranks as the work of many hands.

Across the way from the pavilion, the main building houses in line with tourists' expectations a modern information desk, cashier's till, display stand, and gift stall, all in one. Again Retzsch's *Parade*, wood-carved in low relief, but unsigned, adorns its imposing fascia. His authorship is surprisingly unacknowledged. When asked, the young girl

at the counter saw no problem in that. Just an imitation, a replication, an apery (*Nachahmung*), she readily replied. As such it required no signature. Authenticity merits a name, genuineness earns a mark, she seemed to say, counterfeit does not. Yet, the carved parade, neither imitation nor bogus picture, reproduces Retzsch's lithographs down to their very captions.

Both carved relief and coloured prints testify to a culture of replication, inseparable from Retzsch's own practice. His technique lent itself uncommonly well to copying by himself and others. Intrinsic to his permeation is the rationale of a remarkable response to reproduction processes and his work's resilience to imitations. The difference between the anonymously carved *Parade* and the eight signed lithographs lies not in the imitation process (both copies are accurate) but in the divergent needs of radically different clientele. The counter welcomes the passer-by who would enjoy the view and a glass of wine, and perhaps peruse exhibits before buying a few bottles to carry home. He would not be bothered with signatures, nor does the carved frieze bear one. It is simply part of the *décor*, an iconic label. The pavilion museum caters for the more inquisitive, who savour historical, cultural and artistic detail. Retzsch's work answered both requirements. It lives on at the centre of an ample reproduction apparatus that made his icons widely known, just as it lent itself to an equally sizeable imitation craze that led to duplicates, simulations, and even ersatz clones. This chapter considers both processes, while it also shows how genuine interpretations may occur within repetition. It particularly aims at discussing the implications of extensive and intensive iconography.

7.1 Loose Leaves

No mention has been made—notes Atkins—of the countless ways in which Retzsch's plates were employed singly or in small numbers to illustrate anything connected with the Faust legend. His designs were copied in the numerous almanacs, which circulated widely among the public. They were sold as separate sheets with a quotation from *Faust* to illustrate the scene. They were lithographed, and reproduced accurately and inaccurately in various countries. The frescoes in Auerbach's Keller were

---

1 See Vogel, "Moritz August Retzschs Winzerzug," and visit "Winzerzug," *Wikipedia*, last modified 4 June 2022, https://de.wikipedia.org/wiki/Winzerzug.

© EVANGHELIA STEAD, 2023 | DOI:10.1163/9789004543010_010

This is an open access chapter distributed under the terms of the CC BY-NC-ND 4.0 license.

EXTENSIVE AND INTENSIVE ICONOGRAPHY

modelled on Retzsch's drawings, which have in turn been used for menus and other practical purposes. New editions of the old *Faustbuch* have been decorated with Retzsch's work.[2]

She attempted no excursus into such diffuse material, whose every issue I do not undertake either, but rather indicate dominant tendencies in cultural terms.

Reprocessing Retzsch images may be broadly addressed through the productive metaphor of *fliegende Blätter* (*loose* or *scattered leaves*), a significant yet undervalued extension of a well-known trend, the interpretation of key literary texts in outline. I do not refer here to the popular humoristic magazine published 1845–1944 in Munich, but to the meaningful expansion and agency of Retzsch's twenty-six prints. These harnessed both prototype and duplicate, original and reproduction, genuine article and ersatz print. They launched the 1808 *Faust* and instituted it as a major work by introducing it in the honoured pantheon instituted by Flaxman's outlines after Homer, Aeschylus, Hesiod, and Dante.

Replication and circulation marked them genuinely. As an engraved series, the set thrived on multiplication, spread swiftly, and was much in demand. Novel processes prevalent in the nineteenth century (lithography, wood and steel engraving, later photomechanical reproduction) made of it insert or interleaved plates, in-text images, standalone prints or colour replicas. By not even signing them, the artist himself hardly opposed their multifarious fortunes. Their modest price and availability made them ready cut-and-paste material, as Dibdin early shows. They were no longer outlines according to August Wilhelm Schlegel's aesthetic and poetic definition, inciting the reader's imagination to complete the picture. In their many metamorphoses, they became unpretentious contours: they sketched for an untried eye, pictured, and summed up *Faust*, offering a synoptic digest variously reinterpreted.

Retzsch's loose leaves are twofold: free-standing prints based on previous templates; and prints copied, remediated, yet productively imitated as well.

A good example of their free-standing mobile agency is Retzsch's own involvement in Goethe's *Ausgabe letzter Hand* (*AlH*), published 1827–30 by Cotta without illustrations. Meant as Goethe's legacy to the nation, hallowing him as a classic author, the edition exercised the power of words only, a founding textual monument as Andrew Piper has shown.[3] Yet, Friedrich Fleischer visually trailed

Cotta's undertaking 1828–34, offering a total of fifty-six prints for extra-illustration of the memorable edition in two formats and two successive issues under the title *Kupfersammlung zu Goethes sämmtlichen Werken* (*Collection of Copper Prints for Goethe's Collected Works*). As emblematic interpretations per title, these were frontispieces by a variety of artists. A showcase of the period's visual culture, they exemplify popular styles in literary illustration around 1830.[4] Within the same print artefact, opposite aims met: the extra-illustrated tomes established text yet grangerized it, instituted for all yet personalized it, standardized and singled out, textually coalesced and visually teased, all the while calling on the imagination.

As Fleischer's pet artist at the time, Retzsch is the second issue's champion with thirteen plates. Contrary to his artistic principles, but due to workload and his eye complaint in those years, the task of engraving was not done by him, but a third party. His prints are literally *fliegende Blätter*: unconnected yet assorted sheets cut by another, commercialised in unbound sets, they invited readers to ornate their Cotta exemplars with bespoke visual material.

As if fostering what would be a much-loved scene with the public, Retzsch chose Martha's garden for the *Faust* frontispiece. As noted, two of his surviving drawings (one in pencil, the other in ink) also revolve around this episode, again twice rendered in his printed *Faust I* set: first in 1816, in plate 14 centred on the plucked daisy (cf. Fig. 10.3), then, in plate 19 of the 1834 enlarged edition with Faust handing Gretchen the potion phial (cf. Fig. 7.1). The 1829 *AlH* frontispiece repeats the phial instant, in historical costume with differences: there is no eavesdropper Mephistopheles, and the plate, stipple-engraved by [Friedrich] Wagner, is a close-up of Faust and Gretchen on the bench (cf. Fig. 7.2). A few border details of lush foliage reveal their blossoming desire and longing for each other, in contrast with imminent tragedy. Faust hands the potion that will lull Gretchen's mother to sleep, granting them an hour of amorous intercourse, yet the mother's sleep will be eternal.[5] Posture and clothing hint at lovemaking as Waltraud Maierhofer notes of Gretchen: "She holds her other hand parallel to the noticeable fold of her dress that marks her lap. A strand of her hair pinned up Biedermeier-fashion has already come loose and, like the broad neckline, indicates her willingness, in contradiction with her facial expression." As for Faust, he "looks youthful and confidence-inspiring but in both engravings the tight stockings and the almost bare legs with a distinctive flap emphasize his male sexuality, underlined by the

---

2 Atkins, "Fragmentary English Translations," 36–37.
3 Piper, *Dreaming in Books*, 58–59.

4 See Maierhofer, "Die Titelkupfer von Moritz Retzsch," 219–45.
5 For this and following copied material, see Appendix 2.

FIGURE 7.1   Moritz Retzsch, Faust and Gretchen on a bench with eavesdropper Mephistopheles, *Umrisse zu Goethe's Faust, erster Theil. Gezeichnet von Moritz Retzsch. Von dem Verfasser selbst retouchirt und mit einigen neuen Platten vermehrt* (Stuttgart & Tübingen: J. G. Cotta, 1834), insert pl. 19
COURTESY HAAB, F 3478, WEIMAR

boldly towering hat feather."[6] No longer a middle-class backyard, the lovers' niche has also been upgraded. The detail better matches the technique: stipple engraving (emulating paintings) was deemed nobler than plain outline. Fleischer's aesthetic and technical choices were in subtle accord with Cotta establishing a textual Goethe monument.

This double of Retzsch's own production suggests replication as integral to his practice. In parallel, it is a typifying device, extracting characteristic traits of the main characters and condensing them. Repetition and epitome prepare Retzsch's prints for wider circulation. The print flow would again single out the garden scene as a choice moment with template-like value. Proof comes again from Retzsch himself as plate 19 from his engraved set after Schiller's *Song of the Bell* in 1833 (cf. Fig. 7.3a). The outline pictures another amorous couple on a bench under a tree, in verdant yet placated nature, lifting their eyes to the sky and a diaphanous crescent moon after Schiller's lines 74–75: "The eye sees the heavens open | The heart falls silent in bliss" (*Das Auge sieht den Himmel offen; | Es schweigt das Herz in Seligkeit*). Its exemplary quality is confirmed by *The German Lovers*, the new title it acquired in a repurposed version, re-engraved by Charles Heath and published in *The Keepsake for 1835* with a poem by Lord Pierrepont, Viscount Newark (cf. Fig. 7.3b). By focusing on the lovers, lowering the moon, and turning the light atmosphere into a quiet nocturne, Heath suffused Retzsch's image with romantic emotion and brought forward typical characters, dialoguing as Bertha and Albert in Newark's poem. Independently from Schiller's *Bell*, poem

---

6   Ibid., 226.

FIGURE 7.2
Moritz Retzsch, Faust and Gretchen on a bench, stipple engraved by [Friedrich] Wagner, *Kupfersammlung zu Göthe's sämmtlichen Werken in vierzig Blättern* (Leipzig: Fleischer, 1829–34), plate meant for vol. 12 of the *Ausgabe letzter Hand*
COURTESY HAAB, F 3469, WEIMAR

and print (also extant as standalone) gained emblematic value for British readers. Several pictures by Retzsch held similar archetypal value that would come forward under appropriate treatment.

We may justly see the above as exceptional, even though based on circulation, and boosting in turn distribution and trade abroad. It is indeed but an instance. Far more frequently, Retzsch's loose leaves do not originate from himself. They were leaves detached and lifted, sheets reworked, and plates remediated by many another. They may be free-standing or enter editions; gather meaning per user category; subsist as flying separate pages; autograph duplicates; etc. They form a vast catalogue of Retzsch copies testifying to his long-lasting influence not only on imitated scenes and motifs, but also on style, treatment and format in well-known artists' work.

7.2 Copies, Copies, Copies …

Copies of Retzsch's outlines cover several categories. First and foremost, they were part and parcel of the European book trade and print selling industry, hitherto investigated in detail through mainly three hubs in print circulation, Britain, France and the German States, themselves spearheading other markets (Belgium, Polish-speaking Lithuania, the Netherlands, etc.). Their agency nurtures variability and embraces a large scale of print genres as

FIGURE 7.3A   Moritz Retzsch, *Umrisse zu Schiller's Lied von der Glocke: nebst Andeutungen von Moritz Retzsch* (Stuttgart & Tübingen: J. G. Cotta, 1833), pl. 19
COURTESY HAAB, BH 66, WEIMAR

they shape and respond to diverse readers' uses. The core phenomenon is the prints' flexibility, resilience and adaptability. In this context, Retzsch copies emerge as driven by the wave of European print culture and one of the forces driving it.

Second, they form a vast ensemble of outline copies drawn by various hands in diverse shapes: complete scenes whether standalone or in series; imitations re-worked in other techniques (watercolours, oils); groups detached or details re-ordered; incidents modified in detail or inserted to other scenes. Most are anonymous but not always. Interpretation largely depends on tell-tales of use inferred by material condition, although assumptions are not always guesses. Clusters are loose but intriguingly arresting because of their extensive range and alleged applications.

Demand for copies may stem from any of the following: safeguarding and conservancy, as when Retzsch traces in pencil his three extra plates from the 1834 enlarged *Faust*; intense interest in the outline technique and probing Faust stock, as in Delacroix's freehand replicas (cf. Fig. 6.1a–b to 6.3); as drill doubles for draughtsmen to train their hand in contour (the English and French press encouraged artists to do so); enthusiasts' hunt for Retzsch figures for personal adornment of walls or portfolios; collectors' harvest of original piecemeal material bound together; industrial applications responding to the demand for transfer figures onto other surfaces and materials; ultimately the phenomenon known as *remediation* of an artwork, that is, transformed and reinterpreted through a different medium. Creative sketching may be coupled with copying and trigger re-appropriation, as in

FIGURE 7.3B
Charles Heath, *The German Lovers*, engraved after Moritz Retzsch, 22 × 15.2 cm, in *The Keepsake for 1835*, ed. by Frederic Mansel Reynolds (London: Longman, Rees, Orme, Brown, Green, and Longman; Paris: Rittner and Goupil; Berlin: A. Asher, 1835), insert plate between pp. 168–69
NYPL, NEW YORK

the case of Ronald Ross. Copying then turns approval, responding to aesthetic and emotional undercurrents of desire. When springing from individual incentive, it discloses inclination, preference, even predilection. More than a wish to retrace the play's touching heroine, to possess her by one's own hand, or catch the villain's wily expressions and tortuous silhouette, it signals a personal ritual of intimate adoption—perhaps indeed, a *Faust* staging in the inner playhouse of one's own heart.

The Knittlingen Faust-Archiv has a copy of plate 13 (Mephistopheles at Martha's with Margaret present) completed in great detail after the original and dated 1948. On the back, another (undated) copy of Gretchen pondering in her bedroom has been haphazardly added. Frankfurt's Goethe-Museum collection is even richer. Four sheets disclose replicas of a diverse kind, allowing for speculation on a range of practices. One of them is a highly finished ink drawing of Faust and Gretchen kissing, lifted from Retzsch's plate 15, with a wealth of staged details (cf. Fig. 7.4). The artist has reworked all timber specifics (wall panelling, soffit, door planks), deepened the vista into the garden through the window, and added a small flowerpot on the windowsill. He has constrained the observer's view between side-wings of decaying walls, highlighting the intensity of the kiss, and altered Mephistopheles's and Martha's prying expressions. Dimensions (13.8 × 16.9 cm) show that he respected height to one millimetre's difference but enlarged width by ten to accommodate his extra

FIGURE 7.4 Faust and Gretchen kissing, signed and dated "G. R. 1822," ink drawing lifted from Moritz Retzsch's pl. 15, 38 × 16.9 cm
FDH, FRANKFURTER GOETHE-MUSEUM, III-10749, FRANKFURT

effect. Albeit concealing the name, the signature "G. R. 1822" inscribed on a little shield at lower left begs authorship and authenticity. Further, at the FDH, a pencilled sheet of tracing paper groups several instances from four arresting scenes of Gretchen: a) thoughtful in her chamber (traced almost complete); b) bejewelled by Martha; c) admiring the necklace; and d) conspicuously absent (with sundry figures copied from the cathedral print) (Fig. 7.5). The duplicate is from the original etchings. The sheet has been turned in all directions to lift as many figures as possible. Now creased and crumpled with numerous little dots and holes, it has probably been pinned, re-applied repeatedly, and used on both sides to borrow or transfer several figures, not just from *Faust*. Three details on the recto are further picked from Retzsch's 1833 compositions after Schiller's *Song of the Bell* (arm and hand details from the Hours' dance in pl. 1, and the central male figure from pl. 2). Like other replicas after or by Retzsch,

it has been pasted down. Any revealing particulars on the verso are for the moment beyond reach.

Lastly, two sheets of thicker paper, signed "ar 1830," carry smaller grouped pen-and-ink figures, pinched from Retzsch, distinctly isolated, clearly altered, and marshalled like templates for toy theatre figures. Due to their diminutive size and changes, they are believed to be "traced designs from the French 1829 edition or another," i.e., the prints re-engraved by Trueb and Branche for Audot. Kennerley (published by Bulcock) could also be a candidate. Emulating Retzsch was clearly not limited to the German States or the original prints, but pursued with zest abroad or after copies once or twice removed. Both sheets were previously mounted, possibly for interior decoration—another form of cherishing with a distinctly social dimension. In both, the layout roughly follows the *Faust* intrigue, and the somewhat wooden style aims at

EXTENSIVE AND INTENSIVE ICONOGRAPHY 219

FIGURE 7.5
Sheet of tracing paper with pencil
copies of four Gretchen scenes and
other outlines after Moritz Retzsch,
n.d., 30 × 21.2 cm
FDH, FRANKFURTER
GOETHE-MUSEUM, VIIID-KI,
NO. 14847, FRANKFURT

a growing intensity: standalone figures (mostly on one sheet) recede to an array of dramatized group events (on the other). Two exciting items from the Kippenberg Collection, a finished replica and its draft, also point at templates for the stage. The finalized pen drawing, distinctly after Retzsch, bears a long caption in French, close to the stage directions in "The Witch's Kitchen," allegedly for a theatre performance.

The gem of such loot is a half-cloth landscape volume of sundry autograph material now in Weimar. Besides Retzsch's very letters testifying to his regular deliveries to Kummer from 21 January 1811 and completion of the task on 8 April 1812, its miscellaneous contents include a cloned set of all 26 outlines on tracing paper. They strictly abide by the dimensions of the original but for a millimetre's difference in very limited cases and respect original order (the cathedral scene *is* pl. 18). Occasionally they slightly modify characters' expressions. A hand-drawn title-page in overformal black and red Gothic script, signed "R. Jäger 1928," is a later addition, possibly added on binding. This has obfuscated the primary date, place and signature, which feature however at the end of the introduction to the cloned plates, which fully reproduces by hand the original Cotta letterpress brochure (Huber's preface and *Faust* excerpts) in regular Gothic script. Obviously, no pains were spared to replicate as accurately as possible the printed Cotta prototype, yet hand-written (text) and retraced (images). Dated "Muskau 3rd February 1836," the textual parts were noticeably completed *after* the plates, giving them pride of place. These are also dated lower centre of the first, "Muskau 21 January 36," and lettered "Retsch" on the left and "John" on the right. The same holograph "John" appears on yet another plate (Mephistopheles at Martha's, pl. 13), the last in fact completed. Collation of dates substantiates that they were copied in piecemeal order from 21 January to 3 February [18]36 with brief breaks. A carefully posited "J" also marks plate 2 to ascertain authorship, a single incidence that validates the unknown copyist's confirmed production and extreme discretion, given that the entire set is but a duplicate.

Gerhard Stumme, who acquired this in 1936, oddly overlooks such tell-tale detail and notes that the copy's author is unidentified.[7] A potential accreditation might be the Polish-Austrian printmaker and etcher Friedrich John (1769–1843). Active over borders in diverse places and contexts, John distinguished himself by his many engravings after well-known master painters, conspicuous personalities' portraits, or other artists' drawings for various illustrated editions.[8] *Inter alia*, he cut Johann Heinrich Ramberg's drawings and Veit Hans Schnorr von Carolsfeld's designs for Wieland's and Klopstock's deluxe *Works* (Leipzig, Göschen), and also worked for Cotta.[9] John is of course mainly recognized for stipple engraving and portraiture, and it may seem odd to attribute outline technique to him. He had retired from his artistic occupations in 1832 to today's Slovenia. His autograph signature at the end of a 22 December 1824 letter from Vienna does not match the carefully stylized moniker in the re-traced Muskau prints, although an artist's signature in correspondence may differ from his authenticating sign on a drawing or painting. Yet the "John" signature, the Muskau provenance, today Bad Muskau, on the border of Germany and Poland, as well as his many relations within aristocratic circles, for whom he diligently copied, still plead

for a possible ascription.[10] Last, but not least, he seems to have engraved Retzsch's portrait.[11]

Whatever the case, more significantly than any precise attribution to a documented artistic hand, the cloned object speaks of cultural trajectory. It originates from an artistically important borderland, typically known for its park, today a Unesco-classified World Heritage Site, created to the design of renowned landscape gardener, traveller and writer Prince Hermann von Pückler-Muskau (1785–1871) and centred on his princely residence. Pückler-Muskau had seen one of Radziwill's *Faust* performances in Berlin, and also enjoyed the Porte-Saint-Martin *Faust* in Paris, as record his profuse memoirs. In an unpublished 17 April 1817 letter to an unidentified correspondent, who is clearly J. F. Cotta, he inquires about purchasing original *Faust* drawings from Retzsch.[12] The carefully made replica could be related either to him, his family, or his wider circle. Reproducing by hand the initial Cotta folder (down to the faulty spelling of the artist's name—"Retsch" after the original, rather than "Retzsch") at a time (1836) when the market was flooded by Georg von Cotta's industrialized albums (whose 1834 *Faust I* set had been extended from 26 to 29 plates) signals the wish to revert to an archetype, a unique hand-made item after an original source, since superseded by machine-produced contraptions. It points to the nostalgia of an art enthusiast or refined upper-crust circles with the means to commission both manuscript introduction and outline replicas against remuneration. At an unknown date, autograph letters by Retzsch (the latest is dated 4 October 1846) joined the replica drawings-cum-manuscript-introduction, and an unfathomable "R. Jäger" (given the name's frequency in German) contrived the 1928 title-page. This individual may have been a collector or a scribe working to order. It is likely the tome was bound at this date, given the binding's average quality. Had they ever wished to have them bound, the original patrons would have gone for top-notch garbing of the hand-copied contents. By 1928 indeed, the precious tome had entered collectors' orbit: it belonged to

---

7   Stumme, *Meine Faust-Sammlung*, ed. H. Henning (Weimar: Jahresgabe der Nationalen Forschungs- und Gedenkstätten der klassischen deutschen Literatur in Weimar, 1957), 85.

8   *AKL Online*, s.v. "John, Friedrich" (by Susanna Partsch), https://www-degruyter-com.proxy.rubens.ens.fr/database/akl/html (accessed 16 September 2021).

9   Dorothea Kuhn, Anneliese Kunz, and Margot Pehle, eds., *Cotta und das 19. Jahrhundert: Aus der literarischen Arbeit eines Verlages* (Munich: Kösel, 1980), 14.

---

10   Other candidates might be (Carl) Wilhelm John or Johne (1782–1840), architect in Dresden, or (August) Wilhelm John (1813–81), landscape painter in Düsseldorf and Berlin. Prince Pückler-Muskau also knew Eugenie John (1825–87), successful magazine writer under the pen name E. Marlitt. Might the signature refer to one of her family? See Ulf Jacob, Simone Neuhäuser, and Gert Streidt, eds., *Fürst Pückler: Ein Leben in Bildern* (Berlin: Bebra / SFPM, 2020), 419.

11   See https://de-academic.com/dic.nsf/dewiki/975898 (last accessed 14 Mar 2023). Regrettably it has not been possible to retrace the original engraving up to now.

12   Beinecke: YCGL MSS 6, box 14, folder 546. There is no recorded answer in the Cotta archive.

EXTENSIVE AND INTENSIVE ICONOGRAPHY

Hans Kasten's Bremen collection in 1929[13] before entering Gerhard Stumme's vast assortment in 1936, whence it reached Weimar's HAAB.

Replica making would take us even further. "The copies of the set are innumerable inland and abroad," states Wolfgang Wegner, who groups several indiscriminately: lampooning or not, standalone or in sequence, including second-hand bibliographical references.[14] Retzsch copies in various techniques still crop up in contemporary auctions.[15]

Let us however turn to the noteworthy re-appropriation of two Retzsch prints by Ronald Ross (1857–1932), a tropical medicine specialist and 1902 Nobel-prize winner for discovering the role of the *Anopheles* mosquito in malaria transmission. *Anopheles* in ancient Greek first means *unprofitable, useless*, and second *hurtful, prejudicial*. The first designation ironically fits like a glove Ross's own fate, whose ambition to become an artist had been thwarted by his father, but whose *Nachlaß* archive and *Memoirs* testify to his vital interest in Byronic and Faustian literature. Byron's *Manfred*, frequently compared in scholarship to Goethe's *Faust*, had been his unyielding father's favourite text before becoming his own. Taken with blowpipe chemistry in his youth, and dissecting mosquito after mosquito in India, himself contracting malaria in 1897, it is no coincidence that scientist Ross had turned to Goethe's alchemic and ultimately God-driven scientist and researcher Faust. As a teenager he had also avidly read Elizabethan tragedies (including Marlowe's hell-condemned hero in *Faustus*).[16] His interest in Goethe's *Faust* dates well earlier than his seminal malaria discovery, as revealed by a sketchbook inscribed on the endpaper "R. Ross | September 10th. | 1872," and entitled "Sketches in Isle of Wight etc." It had already been variously used from 1870, to judge by the inscription "Walking tour through Isle of Wight with Gerald Lowder? in 1870," a couple of 1881 entries, and neat additional 1920 ink tags.[17]

Ink lettering (later added to the endpaper) runs "Figures copied from Retsch's Outlines of Faust," a title defying identification. It figures once on a Murton binding, but the wording may have been lifted from "Retsch's Series of Twenty-Six Outlines" (Boosey, 1820).[18] It is certainly based on Moses's copies, as show attenuations and corrections, yet combined with an original, since one drawing features codpieces. Three (pencilled or more finished) Faust compositions seem to result from the friendly Isle of Wight hike according to a brief description ending "We have had *plenty of time* for sketching." These are however difficult to date. A pencilled 1870 would correspond to Ross's puberty, while on the same page the inked 1920, a full half-century later, records his mature 63 years. All three compositions show male figures, in obvious self-identification and vibrant or spirited interactions with the models.

In copying Faust rebelling against Mephistopheles from plate 23 ("A Gloomy Day. Open Field"), Ross has reinforced the outline's profile, stripping Faust of his floating short cloak, and prolonged his outstretched arm by a sword, as if the blade now carried his vocal passion. The other two are jubilant, even jokey, doubtless reflecting the tour's jovial atmosphere. Faust and Mephistopheles, lifted from the draught-drinking scene in the witch's kitchen (pl. 7), smoke pipes (cf. Fig. 7.6). It is unclear what Faust holds in his raised hand (the witch has evaporated). The last, and most interesting, oddly identified by Oxford art historian Martin Kemp as "Faust sits brooding in a landscape, while an owl, a symbol of night, hovers nearby,"[19] pictures rather Mephistopheles (cf. Fig. 7.7), seated comfortably before the witch's blazing hearth, fire fan in hand from Retzsch's plate 6. Ross has banished the trappings of witchery and set him in a shorescape, perhaps after nature. The owl, winging towards him in determination, replaces the avian that originally marched facetiously along the beldam's mantelpiece or peered from it to ogle events in dismay. Kemp, nebulously influenced by Faust-lore, claims dark overtones that Ross's ambiguity hardly supports. His ironic Mephistopheles's smile, taking in the landscape, is hard to interpret with certainty and his witty transformation of the stunned night bird into live airborne fowl may simply remodel sombre deathly details according to ancient iconic symbols of virility. Copying Retzsch rarely was a servile task, and toadying to the model included a fair part of (occasionally tongue-in-cheek) bemusement.

---

13   Niessen, no. 3095.

14   Wegner, 58, n. 226.

15   Copy of the garden scene in oils, Artnet auction, 2017: http://www.artnet.fr/artistes/friedrich-moritz-august-retzsch/gretchen-and-faust-in-the-garden-Px4JU5a_24KpokiAJ41v8A2 (last accessed 14 Mar 2023).

16   Ross, *Memoirs, with a Full Account of the Great Malaria Problem and its Solution* (London: John Murray, 1923), 21–22.

17   LSHTM: Ross/158, file 69. Ross's question mark makes the date uncertain. References in his *Memoirs* are also vague (pp. 22–23).

18   Beinecke: Speck Ck99 R3 +820b. "Retzsch's Outlines engraved by Henry Moses" also figures in arabesque on a sham file from Tille's Collection (HAAB: F 8078).

19   Kemp, "A Feverish Imagination," *Nature* 451 (28 Feb 2008): 1056.

FIGURE 7.6 (*top*) Ronald Ross, Faust and Mephistopheles smoking pipes, drawing lifted from Moritz Retzsch's pl. 7. From Ross landscape sketchbook in half leather, post 1872, 13.2 × 25.8 cm; (*bottom*) Moritz Retzsch, In the witch's kitchen, *Umrisse zu Goethe's Faust gezeichnet von Retsch* (Stuttgart & Tübingen: Cotta, 1816), pl. 7
COURTESY LSHTM, GB 0809/ROSS/158, © ROSS FAMILY / LSHTM, AND: COURTESY HAAB, F 3487, WEIMAR

7.3 Bowdlerizing

A third category includes a wide range of Retzsch copies of special scenes, re-purposed, and further spawned through media culture or home decorations. Amending Retzsch by abridging, correcting, editing and extra-embellishing his compositions to please bourgeois taste inevitably spurred his European fame. For their emotional charge, two

EXTENSIVE AND INTENSIVE ICONOGRAPHY 223

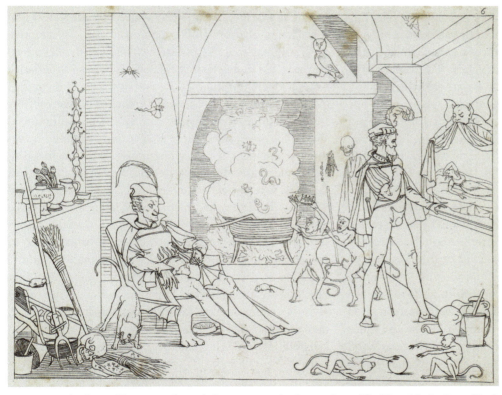

FIGURE 7.7 (*top*) Ronald Ross, Mephistopheles sitting in a landscape, figure lifted from Moritz Retzsch's pl. 6. From Ross landscape sketchbook in half leather, post 1872, 13.2 × 25.8 cm; (*bottom*) Moritz Retzsch, The witch's kitchen, *Umrisse zu Goethe's Faust gezeichnet von Retsch* (Stuttgart & Tübingen: Cotta, 1816), pl. 6
COURTESY LSHTM, GB 0809/ROSS/158, © ROSS FAMILY / LSHTM, AND: COURTESY HAAB, F 3487, WEIMAR

choice scenes fell victim to such undertakings: the garden with Gretchen plucking the daisy, and the lovers kissing. As 1841 lithographs by F. A. and F. Zimmermann (presumably the same artist), they were printed and published by Dresden's Eduard Pietzsch and Company in imperial folio and similar dimensions.[20] In both, Gretchen echoes fervent lines from *Faust*. First of amorous qualm in "He loves me—he loves me not" (*Er liebt mich—liebt mich nicht*,

20 Hirschberg, *Chronologisches Verzeichniss*, nos. 402 & 403.

F 3181), then yielding to passion in "Dearest of men, I love thee from my heart!" (*Bester Mann! Von Herzen lieb'ich Dich!*, F 3206), as she readily returns his kiss. The capital D in *Dich* reflects social disparity, equally stressed by Gretchen's blonde and white-gowned innocent beauty. In both, priority of feeling works to the expense of the play's metaphysics. Concurrently, Gretchen's second statement is piquant, even bold, for a young girl expected to conform to more rigid behaviour. It moves the viewer, excites her or his expectations, and corrects the first line's latent mawkishness with zest. The same print pars desire with prowling danger, embodied by a lurking Mephistopheles. Printsellers' and publishers' acute market intelligence mutually promoted both, in an array of techniques and media inland and abroad.

Their expansive use had premièred foremost in Britain with the two 1820 batches of Moses's copies after Retzsch, each of 13 plates, published by Boosey and Sons and printsellers Rodwell and Martin. Instead of releasing plates 1 to 13 on 1 June 1820, concluding the sequence with "Mephistopheles informs Martha of her husband's death," Boosey and Co shrewdly distinguished "The Kiss" (pl. 15). Extricated and specially offered as an enticing prompt, it came out to sensational effect with plates 1–12, just after "Margaret shews her treasures to Martha." For readers unfamiliar with *Faust*, it looked as if barging into the maiden's room, contemplating her bed with raised drapes (pl. 10), and the devil's jewels (pl. 11 & 12), had all pushed chaste Margaret into Faust's arms. More would come, but smitten customers need purchase the second batch a month yon. The set appointment on 1 July disclosed an ominous pander's scene, Mephistopheles stooping to Martha's ear (suggesting a second troth) afore bejewelled Margaret (pl. 13, cf. Fig. 2.25), directly followed by the daisy-plucking garden episode. Both already enjoyed an English title. Plate 15 had been cautiously named "Margaret meets Faust in the Summer House," at times simply "Embrace," but rapidly renamed "The Kiss," and plate 14 "The Decision of the Flower," a title that would stick. Even today, as web-surfer's keyword, it corresponds to girls holding an oversize yellow daisy and suggestively soft-eyeing the viewer. In the interleaved version of Boosey's 1821 edition, "The Kiss" was further enhanced museum fashion by blank sheets on either side.

Painter and book illustrator John Masey Wright (1777–1866) reworked both plates "after the original by Retzsch" according to the imprint, more credibly after Moses's copies. In the summerhouse, Moses had cautiously tempered the bulging "unmentionables" flaunting Faust's desire bang in the middle of the page. Wright followed on,

additionally giving Margaret a fair, purer, yet unrestricted surrender of self to her lover (Fig. 7.8). Similarly, in the garden, Wright's blond Gretchen rapt in the flower took on a more suave and gentle look, again in white gown, confidently leaning against Faust, as if nothing else mattered in the world (Fig. 7.9). Respectively engraved by W. Humphreys (or Humphrys) and Charles Heath for the flourishing keepsake market, both also featured as standalone prints copyrighted by Hurst, Robinson and Co. in London. Indeed, in 1825 and 1826, these publishers' *Literary Souvenir; or, Cabinet of Poetry and Romance*, edited by Alaric A. Watts, a master of the genre, offered both prints facing apposite verse. The garden instant inaugurated the new publication as frontispiece with a delicate poem by L. E. L. after the etching's title.[21] This was a publisher's choice, not Watts's.[22] A year later, the summerhouse scene with "The First Kiss: A Poetical Sketch," Watts's own lengthy composition with Mephistopheles encroaching as any man's foe, became the keepsake's allegorical and moralizing finale.[23] Hurst, Robinson and Co. exulted: both volumes sold like hot cakes. The first (6,000 copies) was extolled in fourteen press reviews, whose superlative excerpts were reprinted at the end of the second volume. Watts described in a "Postscript" following its success how he had been showered with submissions, and announced two of his own forthcoming collections, sustained by yet another assortment of gushing praise to his talents. Hidden under bashful initials, L. E. L., was Letitia Elizabeth Landon, whose poetry collections, *The Troubadour* and *The Improvisatrice*, had respectively been through three and six editions by 1826. The *Literary Gazette*, cheering *The Troubadour*, thought her "the greatest name in the annals of elegant and imaginative female literature, whether of modern or ancient times," and added that *The Improvisatrice* marked "an era in our country's bright style of female literary fame."[24] Detached, transformed, and versified into poignant scenes for (mainly female) sensibilities, Retzsch's plates, numerously replicated, had

---

21 L. E. L. [Letitia Elizabeth Landon], "The Decision of the Flower," *Literary Souvenir*, ed. A. A. Watts (1825), 1–2.

22 Alaric Alfred Watts, *Alaric Watts: A Narrative of his Life by his Son* (London: Richard Bentley and Son, 1884), 1:173.

23 *Literary Souvenir*, ed. A. A. Watts (1826), 280–84. Watts subsequently republished his composition as "A Scene from Faust" with an image of quite a different ilk, *Gretchen at the Spinning Wheel* by Madame Colin, in harmony with his collection *Lyrics of the Heart: And Other Poems* (London: Longman, Brown, Green, and Longmans, 1851), 141–45, also issued for the American market (New York: D. Appleton & Co., 1852). The adjustment shows how disturbing the kiss scene was.

24 Publishers' catalogue at the end of the *Literary Souvenir*, 1826.

EXTENSIVE AND INTENSIVE ICONOGRAPHY 225

FIGURE 7.8 John Massey Wright after Moritz Retzsch, *The Kiss*, engraved by W. Humphreys, in *The Literary Souvenir; or, Cabinet of Poetry and Romance*, ed. Alaric A. Watts (London: Hurst, Robinson Co., 1826), insert plate between pp. 280–81
BnF, Z-33733, PARIS

FIGURE 7.9 John Massey Wright after Moritz Retzsch, *The Decision of the Flower*, engraved by Charles Heath, used as frontispiece in *The Literary Souvenir; or, Cabinet of Poetry and Romance*, ed. Alaric A. Watts (London: Hurst, Robinson Co., 1825)
BnF, Z-33732, PARIS

integrated gift-book culture. Goethe had penetrated the foreign market for keepsake literature, a thriving industry of the time.

Britain was not unique in such undertakings. Further variation ensued. In France, Édouard Robert, a deaf and mute lithographer, also reworked both scenes with French titles echoing the English ones (*La Décision de la fleur*, *Le Baiser*) for lithographer and printseller E. Ardit, who commercialized them as twinned prints. He specified "d'après Restech," yet another bizarre francization of Retzsch's Magyar name, attributable to Robert's handicap.[25] Robert had produced for Charles Motte a collection of colourful Turkish army costumes in 1828, and

Achille Devéria was one of his friends. Precisely, in the "Goethe" volume from Devéria's eclectic visual encyclopaedia, a precious period iconographic repertoire, several prints attest Retzsch's impact, including Robert's copies. The lithograph of a contrapuntal garden composition by Alexandre Colin (1798–1875) sports Faust and Margaret in medievalist attire, loyal to "troubadour style" and an already antiquated romantic agenda (cf. Fig. 7.10), but also with facetious details (Faust's long blade amusingly and unnaturally dangles between his legs, a hook-nosed horned creature leers from a corner urn). It can be identified as plate 6 from *Album composé et dessiné sur pierre* by Colin issued in 1829, in full Parisian *Faust* craze, with the

---

25 This identifies with Wolfgang Wegner's curious mention "A. Phil. Ed. Robert lith. d'après Restech" (Wegner, 58, n. 226).

Kippenberg, no. 1887, accurately lists it as a lithograph by Ed. Robert, published by E. Ardit.

FIGURE 7.10 Alexandre Colin, Faust and Margaret in the garden in troubadour style, lithographic print cut out and mounted by Achille Devéria in his *Faust* compendium
BnF Est., TB-55 (C)-PET. FOL., PARIS

inevitable text quote serving as caption. A further print pictured Valentine dying. Colin, a close friend of Delacroix and Bonington, was well known to the Devéria brothers from their student years. He had spent several months of 1825 in London (according to other sources, accompanying Delacroix during his trip) and was certainly acquainted with the local craze for Retzsch prints. Less convincingly, painter-lithographer Nicolas Maurin (1799–1850), in an opulent flowery frame intertwined with snakes, snubs any salutary irony with an over-decorous Margaret idiotically eyeing Faust to whom she offers the devastated flower but for one petal—his love pledge (cf. Fig. 7.11). One

EXTENSIVE AND INTENSIVE ICONOGRAPHY

of twelve, dated 1830 by the BnF, it heralds typical lower middle-class over-romanticizing, as if to correct the spicy *croquis de mœurs*, for which Maurin is cited by Baudelaire among the painters of modern life under the Bourbon Restoration.

In the second part of Devéria's compilation, which extra-illustrates the Motte-Sautelet dismantled folio of 1828, Édouard Robert's reverse lithographic version, with tenderer protagonists and a spooky antithetic couple in the gathering evening darkness, has been mounted opposite the garden passage (cf. Fig. 7.12). Comparison between these versions powerfully proves how French romantic artists' keen understanding of *Faust*'s complex messages gradually gives way to empty medievalism and galloping soppiness. Such European expansion heralds the spread of Retzsch's twinned scenes in the German lands in the late 1830s and early 1840s, this time developing rather patriotic overtones.

Nagler lists "Faust und Gretchen" as "two lithographs by H. F. Grünewald and C. Müller" in large oblong folio format, then, "the same, lith. by F. Zimmermann" in oblong folio.[26] In reality, their formats and framing make for several versions, while Nagler's single, impenetrably loose title doubtless camouflages two different scenes. In his 1899 exhibition catalogue, Tille imparts their titles as "after Retzsch."[27]

Of those inspected, "He loves me—loves me not" corresponds to three distinct, reframed and repurposed lithographed versions. Two of them are by F[riedrich] A[ugust] Zimmermann (1805–76) and Karl Müller (1807–79). Based respectively in Dresden and nearby Meissen, the artists prepared these prints for the Dresden firm of Eduard Pietzsch and Co. Interestingly, at the Dresden Academy, Zimmermann had "pushed himself" into Ferdinand Hartmann's class, Retzsch's friend and protector, before turning to porcelain painting as a potboiler and assiduously producing lithographs, mainly portraits, for the Dresden periodical *Saxonia* from 1834 to 1841.[28] Karl Müller is not to be confused with Carl Müller (1818–93), later close to the Nazarenes and the Düsseldorf Association for the diffusion of religious images (*Verein zur Verbreitung religiöser Bilder*).[29] Also a former student of the Dresden Academy, he tirelessly worked for the Meissen porcelain factory where he was promoted chief painter from 1860. The third lithograph with the imprint "executed and

lithographed by H[einrich] Ferd[inand] Grünewald," was made in Grünewald's own Dresden lithography studio according to the imprint, either in competition or in association with Müller. Even more interestingly, Grünewald, painter and lithographer (1802–49), studied from 1822 at the Dresden Academy under Retzsch himself, executed large oil versions of Retzsch's compositions after Goethe, Schiller and Shakespeare, brought out lithographs after Horace Vernet and Jean-Antoine Gros with the printer Ludwig Theodor Zöllner (see below), and is reported to have made "with Karl Müller two images after Retzsch (Faust and Gretchen)."[30] All three versions date from the early 1840s (as mentioned, Hirschberg dates both "Faust and Gretchen" scenes 1841).

Twenty-five years after the Cotta original, remediated lithographic reproduction had then originated, from Retzsch's very hometown, in a technology catering for long print runs. Zimmermann's print subsists in at least four variants, given inking, size, printing, framing, conditioning, and other technical details, while Müller's is in at least two formats. All three are close-ups, centred foreground hip-high on Margaret and Faust, with Martha and Mephistopheles passing background left (cf. Fig. 7.13 to 7.15). Frames are elaborate, double or treble, highlighting the scene, and marshalled by prompts within the image. Margaret is always given an elaborate white dress with either embroidered cuffs or gigot sleeves and mid-arm puffs, and an amply pleated full skirt, which converts her youthful slender figure into that of a latent matron. In both Pietzsch versions, a decorative sash or girdle enhances her ample lap, promising that her capable flanks will bear the nation-to-be a brood. Her face is fuller and rounder, her intricate hairstyle loosens blond curls over the shoulders. Her expression, mild and serene (Zimmermann), earns large Madonna-like features and a vague smile (Müller), or a remote angelical aspect (Grünewald). Contrasting and complementing her mellow beauty, Faust in terrific dark attire at her side sports a cavalier's sober but costly costume with a short mantle under a spectacular plumed hat. Of his daunting blade, concealed by reframing, only an elaborate hilt remains, an opulent jewel rather than a weapon, matching his cape's chain. His ample locks, sideburns and stylish moustache mirror any handsome young man's return from the wars to happily live with his beloved in an Eden-like garden. A paradise with parasites however, since the devil's eye flashes and burns in the background, unrelentingly ogling the lovers. Whatever the treatment of the garden (realistically urban in Grünewald, lusher in

---

26   Nagler, *Neues allgemeines Künstler-Lexicon*, 13:52.

27   Tille, *Bilderverzeichnis der Bode-Tilleschen Faust-Galerie* (Cologne: J. G. Schmitz, 1899), nos. 112 & 113.

28   Sigismund, "Zimmermann, Friedrich August," in Thieme-Becker 36 (1947): 510b.

29   Pieske, *Bilder für Jedermann: Wandbilddrucke 1840–1940* (Berlin: Keyser, 1988), 60.

30   *AKL Online*, s.v. "Grünewald, Ferdinand" (by Andreas Quermann), https://www-degruyter-com.proxy.rubens.ens.fr/database/akl /html (accessed 7 Oct 2021).

FIGURE 7.11　　Nicolas Maurin, *Marguerite consulte une fleur pour savoir si elle est aimée de Faust*, lithographic print cut out and mounted by Achille Devéria in his *Faust* compendium
BnF Est., TB-55 (C)-PET. FOL., PARIS

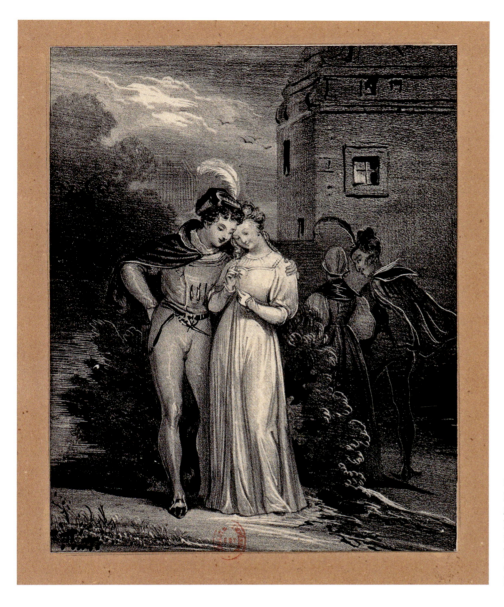

FIGURE 7.12
Édouard Robert, *La Décision de la fleur*, reverse lithographic print after Moritz Retzsch, cut out and mounted by Achille Devéria in his *Faust* compendium
BnF Est., TB-55 (C)-PET.FOL., PARIS

Müller, blurred and hazy in Zimmermann, as if from a faraway legendary past), the devil's pupil lights up, and his sword's hilt portentously matches Faust's in anticipation of Valentine's doom.

By the 1830s and 1840s, when standalone prints swarmed the market, Goethe's *Faust* had become a commonly shared story of pathos with German readers sorrowing for pure and comely Margaret. Identification processes strongly worked on public sensitivity and these images were for everyone as Christa Pieske has amply shown in *Bilder für Jedermann* (1988). Households "lived with images," walls were covered in them, illustrated magazines distributed them as premium samples, art societies gave their members costly first-class prints as annual gifts, and travelling sellers varied routes to spread, circulate and deliver prints to secluded spots. The three garden scene lithographs belong to the lower-grade wares of such implementation. Pieske's valuable roll of art publishers lists neither Pietzsch's Dresden firm nor the lithographers or printers concerned, since it mostly covers the second half of the nineteenth and early twentieth centuries. The phenomenon, object of her seminal study, can be antedated by ten years thanks to these prints that document an extensive use of Goethe's *Faust* as widespread reference. The garden scene quickly typified consumer goods: it decorated for instance porcelain pipe bowls (see Chapter 12) or became a picture postcard in the 1870s, when the ever-expanding German card industry adopted illustrated versions.

Such is an embossed specimen with gilt impression (*Goldtiefdruck*) recapping the garden scene, now in Knittlingen (Fig. 7.16). Faust in a cavalier's brown doublet with slashed and puffed sleeves, breeches to match, and knee-high white stockings, hat in hand, stands as if

FIGURE 7.13   Friedrich August Zimmermann after Moritz Retzsch, *Scene from Goethe's Faust. Gretchen: "He loves me, he loves me not,"* lithograph, n.d., 35.5 × 49 cm, printed by G. Braunsdorf, published by Eduard Pietzsch and Co., Dresden
COURTESY HAAB, F GR 5822 (1), WEIMAR

FIGURE 7.14   Karl Müller after Moritz Retzsch, *Scene from Goethe's Faust. Gretchen: "He loves me, he loves me not,"* lithograph, n.d., 37.5 × 43.5 cm, printed by Carl Pohl and published by Eduard Pietsch [*sic*] and Co., Dresden
COURTESY HAAB, F GR 5822 (4), WEIMAR

FIGURE 7.15
Heinrich Ferdinand Grünewald after Moritz Retzsch, *Scene from Goethe's Faust. Gretchen: "He loves me, he loves me not,"* lithograph, n.d., 43 × 50 cm, printed in Grünewald's establishment
COURTESY HAAB, F GR 8052 [A] (39), WEIMAR

EXTENSIVE AND INTENSIVE ICONOGRAPHY 231

FIGURE 7.16
Unknown artist, embossed colour postcard after Goethe's garden scene, posted [19]07, 14 × 9 cm
COURTESY FAUST-MUSEUM, MOOSMANN COLLECTION, ILL. 568, KNITTLINGEN

proposing to an azure-gowned Gretchen leisurely seated on a bench. Not by chance, instead of Martha's, we now see the devil's back (his fiery look has disappeared). *Her* aged profile, as worried matchmaker, casts a spying glance over the youthful couple and the outcome. The front caption in German unmistakably identifies the very *Faust* episode, yet the commercials on the back are in fourteen European languages.[31] That of the Universal Post Union, established 1874 by the Bern Treaty, testifies on the reverse in three languages to a worldwide postal system, analogous to the potential commercialization of such a card. By 1874 then, the garden episode was common currency across Europe, if not the world. A staple of Retzsch copies had fed its spreading. The postcard's message, from her Dorfen mother (50 km to the east) to Theres Moshofer, cook to Baroness von Schacky in Munich's central Türkenstraße 31, is revelatory. Sublimating the scene's potency, the mother had chosen the image to write "One hears that the Lenz girl is getting married do not know more [to] write to you" (*Man hört daß die Lenz-dirn heiratet wißen nicht mehr schreiben dir*), no doubt wishing her daughter the same. The card may be dated [19]07 from the incomplete postmark. Far removed from Retzsch's original, the postcard, typical of nineteenth-century remodelling, had been sent to the address of a noble household that had given Bavaria several public servants. It made ends of the social ladder meet at an address close to royal palaces, embassies and the Gallery of Old Masters (Alte Pinacothek), yet also the 1903-inaugurated Simplicissimus cabaret at Türkenstraße 57.

31 German, French, English, Italian, Dutch, Norwegian, Austrian (naming the postcard differently from the German), Czech, Slovenian, Polish, Hungarian, Spanish, Portuguese, and Russian.

FIGURE 7.17   Moritz Retzsch, Faust and Gretchen kissing, *Umrisse zu Goethe's Faust gezeichnet von Retsch* (Stuttgart & Tübingen: Cotta, 1816), pl. 15
COURTESY HAAB, F 3487, WEIMAR

7.4   A Kiss's Exceptional Fortune

"The Kiss" met with an even wider fortune as it titillated viewers' imagination in a still more intricate way. In order to fully capture its enticing pull, we need to view it with period sensibility, long before Hollywood kisses and deep embraces anesthetized our inner eye. To judge by his numerous preliminary drafts (see Chapter 2), Retzsch had spared no effort to capture the right atmosphere for one of the shortest and most tumultuous passages in *Faust*—eleven lines of curt responses, interjections, cries, yells, and outbursts, enlacing four characters (F 3205–16). The artist finally left aside playfulness, friskiness, yearning, fervour, annoyance, disgust, meddling, fear, apprehension, and prohibition, which end with Margaret at a loss, asking herself what Faust might find in her. Retzsch's image retained fervour instead of commotion and confusion. Even when isolated, framed, revised, and mounted, it still works powerfully.

In the prototype, enraptured Margaret and passionate Faust ardently kiss in full embrace. Bareheaded Margaret features in neat attire, while Faust in short cape, plumed hat, and protuberant sword cuts a lordly, domineering figure drawing close his paramour (Fig. 7.17). Bosoms cling but limbs keep cautiously apart from the waist down, to stay decorum, a clever detail that fully displays Faust's strong legs and robust thighs in a tight-fitting hose, his secret parts swelling with desire. The couple's self-surrender to love speaks unambiguously of sex shortly to be consummated. Slightly off centre, they stand

EXTENSIVE AND INTENSIVE ICONOGRAPHY

in a wood-panelled space overlooking a fully-grown garden (a transparent symbol of lush fertility), while the door, violently pushed inwards, yields to Mephistopheles and Martha. Love is spied and intruded upon with glee and guile as show Martha's sly grin and Mephistopheles's sharp look and raised brow. No end kissing meets with curt interruption. The display indiscernibly turns *us*, whether readers or spectators, into nosy trespassers. Our full viewing is indeed no different from the devil's wild eyeing and the procuress's door ramming. In British consciousness, De Quincey's "On the Knocking at the Gate in *Macbeth*" (*London Magazine*, October 1823) hovers inescapably over the scene. Even without that souvenir, our glare, riveted on the lovers—Retzsch tells us—might be different in intention, if not in deed, from the devil's. Yet is it? We infringe privacy, and like it or not, become peeping Toms. If we ourselves violate the exclusiveness of a closeted affair, plate 15 throws it open to public view.

It is this plate that made Shelley almost swoon. His reaction reflects the exhilaration and tension that Retzsch's vista could trigger at the time. What Shelley saw of course was Moses's smoothed-out 1820 copy, republished in the 1821 *Faustus*, similar to most engraved and lithographed English, French, and American editions (but for the 1830 Giard one). Nevertheless remain the intimate setting, the passion, the unwelcome invasion, the prying, the prurience. In Shelley's case, the print's impact engaged his souvenir of reading Jean-Jacques Rousseau's *La Nouvelle Héloïse* and meshed with personal qualms for forsaking wife Harriet, as Timothy Webb has subtly suggested.[32] One exemplar of Lumley's 1832 edition (the first to include Shelley's translations next to Boosey's *Faust*) strangely mirrors his troubled feelings: the kiss plate is elected frontispiece (cf. Fig. 5.13), as if the poet's vivid sensibility had dictated the volume's structure at the binder's. It is unfortunately impossible to attribute.[33] More widely than this unique case, publishing evidence shows that men of the trade and readers alike felt the kiss's pull on all accounts, and rightly so.

Achille Devéria's self-devised "Goethe" compendium stands as best proof of romantic artists' tributes to the scene (cf. Fig. 7.18). The collector-cum-compiler has carefully cut, framed and mounted four reproductions in comparison, of which three are identifiable Retzsch copies: top left, Wright's English version engraved by Humphreys, either taken from the *Literary Souvenir* or a detached print of the same; next to it, Édouard Robert's reverse lithograph "Le Baiser," in which Faust has removed

his sword, while an evil-looking Mephistopheles knocks the door inwards; bottom left, Tony Johannot's title vignette to Blaze de Bury's *Faust* translation into French (1847) with a gloomy, desperate Faust pulling to him a white, distant Margaret; and Muret's 1824 lithographic version. Devéria's assemblage shows no trace whatsoever of Retzsch originals. Perhaps by the time he put together this particular sheet (1847 at the earliest), the original set was hard to come by. The compendium's first part, mostly of full-page prints, also shows Nicolas Maurin's version. Over-sentimentalizing Maurin had sacrificed the kiss to a startled Margaret clinging at Faust's neck for protection, as the door, more agape than ajar, discloses at low angle a cock-eyed Mephisto, ready to leap at the reader (cf. Fig. 7.19). Martha follows innocuously on, an explicit caption running: "United in a summer house, Faust receives from Margaret the avowal of the purest love." Male prominence and sensationalist mawkishness were fast gaining ground.

German lithographs of the 1840s grant characters, theme and mood further such development, although a c.1850 steel engraving by August Hoffmann after Wilhelm von Kaulbach clearly exemplifies the impact of Retzsch's scene on the nineteenth-century German master.[34] Karl Müller's is missing from the four versions inspected, but must be extant, as his and Zimmermann's will have formed a twin set with the garden scene, commercialized by Dresden's Pietzsch. Besides, Müller is supposed to have produced two "Faust and Gretchen" scenes with Grünewald. In Zimmermann's version, the framing, again hip-high, bears the same imprints and type, Margaret and Faust sport the same historical attire (cf. Fig. 7.20). Now in profile, they offer a pleasant match-cum-variation of the frontal garden view. Passion is toned down, composed bodies keep apart, lips hardly touch (Gretchen targets Faust's nose, he tentatively kisses her lower lip). Margaret wears a pear-shaped earring closely resembling the one she displays on one of Retzsch's own fine drawings (cf. Fig. 3.4).

Had Zimmermann tiptoed into Retzsch's Academy courses, diligently followed by Grünewald? Had he bartered with the master, laboured in oils for him or after him? The question is all the more important as, from the very beginning of the *Faust* adventure, Retzsch himself seems to have been aware of the value of reproduction techniques. As shown, he used his own original etchings as reproduction tools. If the moderated Zimmermann lithograph, repurposed in Dresden, perhaps with the master's consent, takes on features of other Retzsch compositions,

---

32   Webb, *Shelley and Translation*, 153–55.

33   HAAB: F 3495, digitized: https://haab-digital.klassik-stiftung.de /viewer/epnresolver?id=1335575138.

34   See https://www.oblivion-art.de/index.php/malerei-grafik /19-jahrhundert/kaulbach-w-1805-1874.

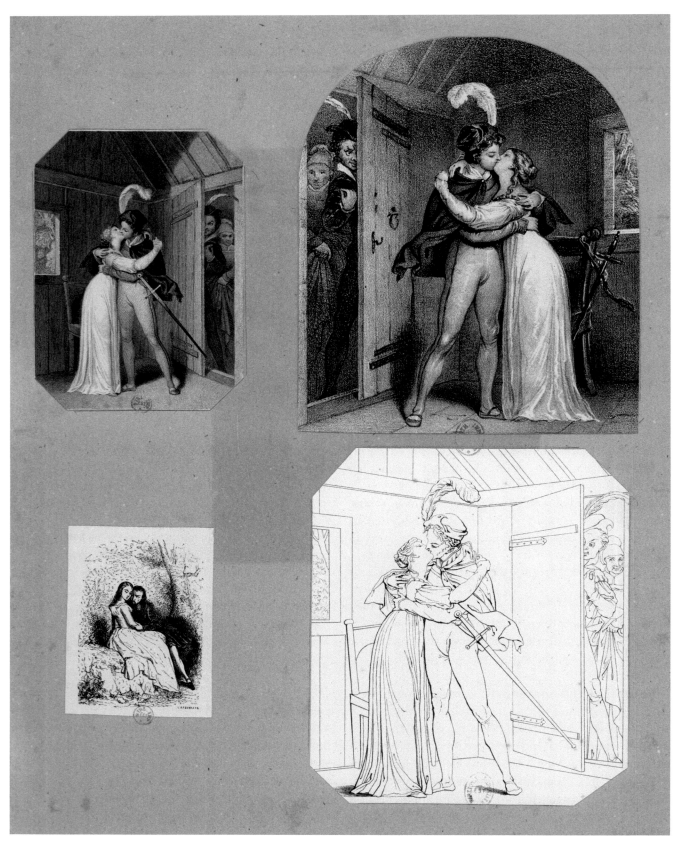

FIGURE 7.18 Four prints on Faust and Margaret (three of their embrace) cut out and mounted post 1847 by Achille Devéria in his *Faust* compendium opposite the corresponding passage
BnF Est., TB-55 (C)-PET. FOL., PARIS

EXTENSIVE AND INTENSIVE ICONOGRAPHY 235

FIGURE 7.19   Nicolas Maurin, *Réunis dans un pavillon du jardin, Faust reçoit de Marguerite l'aveu du plus sincère amour*, lithographic print, n.d., cut out and mounted by Achille Devéria in his *Faust* compendium
BnF Est., TB-55 (C)-PET. FOL., PARIS

FIGURE 7.20 Friedrich Zimmermann after Retzsch, *Scene from Goethe's Faust. Gretchen: "Dearest of men, I love thee from my heart!"* lithograph, n.d., 35 × 50 cm, published by Eduard Pietzsch and Co., Dresden
COURTESY HAAB, F GR 5822 (7), WEIMAR

it may be considered not plagiarized but simply derivative. In Peter-Christian Wegner's knowledgeable book on lithophanes—a fascinating industry of the time I turn to in the last chapter—two of these prints are considered as plagiaries (*Plagiate*).[35] Grünewald's lithograph was however exhibited in the 1932 Dresden Goethe centenary exhibition as a collector's piece.[36] Categories and hierarchies therefore shift with the times, and we ourselves, under copyright law, have become hypersensitive to surrogate prints, previously considered part of an artist's legacy—surrogate, yet still a part.

Whatever the case, in these reworkings, one important lithographic revision is the background: the initial opening onto the fully-grown garden (cf. Fig. 7.17), offering the lovers air, light and the protection of verdant nature, akin to their passion, has given way to oppressive stonework with the only opening blocked. Zimmermann's lithograph walls them in, and the only casement opening towards them discloses Mephistopheles prying (Martha has vanished), a rather ghostly figure emerging from a hazy past.

These changes are not however Zimmermann's own. They originate from an image dated 1837 and attributed to E. Schuler, that is, Édouard Schuler (1805/06–82). An Alsatian steel and copper engraver, also a lithographer

---

35 Wegner, *Literatur auf Porzellan*, 115–16.
36 *Goethe Ausstellung: Sächsischer Kunstverein zu Dresden* (Dresden: Wilhelm und Berta von Baensch Stiftung, 1932), 159, no. 839, from Puppel's Berlin collection.

FIGURE 7.21A
Édouard Schuler after Moritz Retzsch, *Faust and Gretchen*, engraving, 1837, 12.5 × 19.5 cm, cut out by Alexander Tille, provenance unknown
COURTESY HAAB,
F GR 8052 [B] (8), WEIMAR

FIGURE 7.21B
After Moritz Retzsch and following Édouard Schuler, *Faust and Gretchen*, steel engraving, post 1849, *Album aus der Damenzeitung Iris*, engraved and printed by the Art Institute of the Austrian Lloyd, published by E. Ludwig in Graz. Available in Paris and Vienna
COURTESY PETER-CHRISTIAN WEGNER

FIGURE 7.22 Carl Friedrich Patzschke after Moritz Retzsch, *"Dearest of men, I love thee from my heart!"* coloured lithographic copy, c.1880, 27 × 29 cm, printed in Berlin by L. Zöllner and commercialized by C. G. Ende
COURTESY HAAB, F GR 5822 (8), WEIMAR

active in Strasburg and Karlsruhe, he also authored prints after Flaxman's *Iliad* and *Odyssey*. The image, definitely smaller (12.5 × 19.5 cm) and in sharp lines (cf. Fig. 7.21a), was cut out by Alexander Tille perhaps from a gift-book or periodical, without any leads to its potential provenance, for use in his exhibition.[37] As a steel engraving from the *Album aus der Damenzeitung Iris*, commercialized by E. Ludwig in Graz, it further circulated in France and Austria after 1849 (cf. Fig. 7.21b). Unless further evidence emerges, Schuler seems to be the inventor of the dungeon-like walls encircling Faust and Margaret, while a demonic gaoler pushes the casement. Zimmermann and Grünewald followed suit, both watering down details for a broader public.

A further lithographed version by self-taught reproduction lithographer Carl Friedrich Patzschke (1813–71), printed in Berlin by Ludwig Zöllner (active c.1840), and commercialized by C. G. Ende, coloured the scene, a final touch to attract further clients (Fig. 7.22). With the canonical quote *"Bester Mann, von Herzen lieb' ich dich!"* in ornate lettering, prints survive in several formats, and—more importantly—various stencil-applied colour schemes, as shows variance in tints. These are not always

---

37   Tille, *Bilderverzeichnis*, no. 111. See on this, Stead, "*Faust*-Bilder," 163–67.

successful (in one, Gretchen's rosy complexion has turned apoplectic mauve) but chromolithography using several stones was still costly and chancy. All four testify to Retzsch's appeal and many metamorphoses. Additionally, it has proven rather complicated to find precise information on the artists who followed Retzsch and produced proxy work.[38] But at the same time, such an excursus into the sparsely and unequally mapped area of reproduction shows how much remains to be done in an area indispensable for understanding how prints circulated in the nineteenth century.

7.5 Spread and Sway on Style, Form and Set

Retzsch's influence on other artists would fill volumes. In the German context, Peter-Christian Wegner's expressive metaphor is that of an admiralty flagship, all sails set, cruising on the iconographic *Faust* ocean and steering other artists' creations: "Retzsch stands for a milestone (*Markstein*) in *Faust* iconography, and *Faust* illustrators, from Nisle to Stassen, follow time and again in the wake (*in den Sog*) of his pictorial creations."[39] From Julius Nisle's *Göthe-Gallerie* in steel-engraved outlines, and his third 1840 issue entirely on *Faust I*, to the 163 *Faust* pen drawings by Franz Stassen (1919) republished in 1980, the (non-exhaustive) list would include the Brandenburg draughtsman, painter and lithographer Theodor Hosemann (1807–75) and Meyerheim,[40] active in *Scenen aus Goethe's Faust in acht lithographirten Bildern*, an 1835 homage to Prince Radziwill's *Faust* performances; Gustav Nehrlich; Retzsch's friend Carl Vogel von Vogelstein; Ferdinand Rothbart who worked as lithographer, engraver, and illustrator; and historicist painters such as Wilhelm von Kaulbach, Engelbert Seibertz or August von Kreling. Taking stock of Busch, Giesen and Wegner, Viola Hildebrand-Schat mentions in her own right Eugène Delacroix, Moritz von Schwind, Gustav Heinrich Naeke, as well as Gustav Nehrlich, A. Riedel, August Ferdinand Hofgarten, Louis Freiherr von Pereira-Arnstein, and Ludwig Ferdinand Schnorr von Carolsfeld.[41]

Even in the 1920s, after the Great War, when *Faust* iconography underwent major changes, Retzsch's influence may still be seen among expressionist artists. Such is prominent set designer Ernst Stern's elongated Mephistopheles in a *Faust* edition for the "Booklets of German Theatre" series.[42] All the more so, Willi Jaeckel's 1925 masterly engraving of a naked Gretchen, prostrate on her cell's straw bedding, stems from Retzsch's penultimate plate.[43]

We may be tempted to see Retzsch's Faustian sway limited only to black and white iconography. *Faust* graphics, repetitive and dull for certain scholars,[44] already form a sub-category in graphic arts. Invested with scant esteem, the latter themselves were underrated in traditional art hierarchies, before a comprehensive media stance repetitively stressed their weight. Yet, Retzsch's stimulus is also traceable in renowned contemporaries' paintings. Art historian Werner Busch, for instance, lengthily discusses the meaning of Caspar David Friedrich's famous *Der Mönch am Meer* (*The Monk by the Sea*, 1808–10) in the light of Retzsch's plate 2, i.e., Faust's walk and discussion with Wagner (cf. Fig. 2.21). His reading opens up a newly interpretative perspective touching on methodology in art history, and enriching our understanding of Friedrich's pursuits. Friedrich commented on Retzsch's work, developed interest in the Faust legend, and himself nourished Faustian preoccupations. Busch refers to a first version of Friedrich's painting, examined with imaging techniques and X-rays, revealing two figures in old-style German clothing, closely resembling Faust and Wagner's promenade, as in Retzsch's plate.[45] One of the figures was finally erased, leaving in a vast and unruly landscape the solitary form, back turned to the viewer, as if he, Faust-like, faced the world's sea of tumult and unrest. Busch reads the early version of this painting as a palimpsest in "direct response to the *Faust* illustrations"[46]—despite *illustrations* being inappropriate to define Retzsch's artefacts.

However concealed in Germany, Retzsch's repute and influence was standard proof abroad. When Rümann, a knowledgeable scholar, asserted in 1932 "Stylistically however Retzsch had not won any kind of influence on English artists,"[47] his assertion can only be explained by

---

38   I have used several art dictionaries to collate information provided without detailing in footnotes. Sigismund's 1947 article on Zimmermann (in Thieme-Becker, 36:510b) is however particularly arresting, as he knew well both the milieu, the work of Retzsch, and Dresden.

39   Wegner, *Literatur auf Porzellan*, 113.

40   Perhaps Friedrich Eduard Meyerheim (1808–79). Several of the Meyerheim family were however artists.

41   Hildebrand-Schat, *Moritz Retzschs Illustrationen*, 38, n. 83.

42   Goethe, *Faust: der Tragödie erster Teil. Mit Federzeichnungen von Ernst Stern*, Die Bücher des Deutschen Theaters 3 (Berlin: Verlag der Bücher des Dt. Theaters, 1920).

43   *Faust, eine Tragödie von Goethe* (Berlin: Erich Reiss, n.d. [1925]).

44   Thomas Fusenig and Sebastian Giesen, "Goethes *Faust* in Bildern," *Börsenblatt für den deutschen Buchhandel* 166, *Aus dem Antiquariat*, no. 7 (1999): A378–88.

45   Werner Busch, *Caspar David Friedrich*, 46–81, particularly on Retzsch 61–64.

46   Beate Allert, "Goethe, Runge, Friedrich: On Painting," in *The Enlightened Eye: Goethe and Visual Culture*, ed. E. K. Moore and P. A. Simpson (Amsterdam / New York: Rodopi, 2007), 88, 90.

47   Rümann, *Das illustrierte Buch*, 55.

period views and his own diffident stance. Vaughan's ample chapter on Retzsch in English art has proven the contrary,[48] and his proficient example may be extended to numerous other cases. In the last twenty years of his life, for instance, Thomas Stothard (1755–1834) adopted in his outlines intricate detailing, minutiae, and a staccato rhythm, the outcome of Retzsch's popularity in England. His parsimonious patron George Thomson of Edinburgh asked him to imitate Retzsch's style when he altered in 1821 Scottish artist David Allan's designs to suit his sponsor's whim.[49] Imitative style was one of the ways Retzsch's influence spread, and in Stothard's case, the exceptional aesthetic appeal of his designs proved certainly a plus.

More often, however, than desirable, British artists domesticated Retzsch's inventions. Two occurrences from the nineteenth-century press mirror how wide and recognisable was this impregnation. It did not escape the critics' eye, trained in the German artist's widespread *œuvre* thanks to reproduction. In 1879, the *Saturday Review* commented on Charles Bell Birch's outlines thus: "M. Birch has made what are called illustrations of [Byron's] *Lara*, more obviously than commendably imitated from Retzsch."[50] The innuendo veils frank criticism, yet the plates, published by the Art Union of London, were a premium product of the time. The 1902 *Athenaeum* followed on in the obituary of eminent painter Sir Joseph Noël Paton: his 1863 outlines for *Coleridge's Rime of the Ancient Mariner*, a set of 20 lithographs again for the Art Union of London, were "in the manner of Retzsch, but conventionalized and tamed."[51]

"By precisely following the *Faust* scenes," the "modest" Retzsch[52] had not then only found for many of them "the first *typified* conceptual representation" [*den ersten* Typus *der Verbildlichung*], as Richard Benz had early noted[53] and Wolfgang Wegner corroborated;[54] nor just invented "deeply abstract types" for the characters by opposition to the "pretentious Cornelius";[55] he had importantly spread a style, borrowed from Flaxman, further developed, and expanded in countries in which printing industries thrived—delays, deferrals, and seasonal discrepancies

being explicable by circumstances pertaining to their national histories.

On returning to London after their German tour, the Halls themselves were utterly convinced. As the 1851 Crystal Palace exhibition was attracting multitudes to London, Samuel Carter Hall stated in an *Art Journal* review of a recently published pictorial life of Martin Luther: "The Faust of our friend Moritz Retzsch has given an ever sensible impulse, especially to the small plate and vignette works of Germany. After the Faust plates nothing, without impressive character, perfect drawing, and full and appropriate composition, would be at all successful."[56]

Retzsch's legacy then had not only affected image construction, but inadvertently determined book ornaments, even portfolio or album shape. From a wealth of examples, I will develop here only one case, which takes us over the ocean to the United States. There, lithographer Henry Stone had turned to engraving and re-cut Retzsch's twenty-six plates as early as 1824 in Washington. His work was apparently not reissued but it is possible that English or European surrogates were early imported as well. Aesthetic infiltration was such that Ralph Waldo Emerson, deeply interested in Goethe, noted in his diary between 16 and 20 April 1837: "Retzch [*sic*] is a Gothic genius [—] not the Greek simplicity but the Gothic redundancy of meaning & elaboration of details. His pictures are like Herbert's poems hard to read[,] for every word is to be emphasized."[57] Such detailed ability proved rewarding for several North American artists.

Illustrator Felix O. C. Darley (1822–88), Emerson's contemporary, would devote several full-page large-format outlines to Sylvester Judd's *Margaret*, a novel of transcendentalist breed. Ultimately embracing wide-reaching fame, his case typically combines initial obscurity, when working for Philadelphia periodicals, then quick recognition, characteristic outline aesthetic choices, and on moving to New York, celebrity with commissions from an art society. Flaxman's feted style and Retzsch's notoriety "clearly inspired" Darley to illustrate in outline,[58] although several of his plates also recall Nehrlich's or Nisle's more detailed designs, both already strongly influenced by Retzsch. Being born into a theatrical family may

---

48   Vaughan, *German Romanticism*, 123–54.

49   Shelley M. Bennett, *Thomas Stothard: The Mechanisms of Art Patronage in England circa 1800* (Columbia: University of Missouri Press, 1988), 55–57, 98.

50   "Minor Notices," *Saturday Review* 47, no. 1224 (12 Apr 1879): 473.

51   "Sir Joseph Noël Paton," *Athenaeum*, no. 3871 (4 Jan 1902): 24c (obituary).

52   Günter Busch, *Eugène Delacroix*, 38.

53   Benz, *Goethe und die romantische Kunst*, 176, my emphasis.

54   Wegner, 58.

55   Busch, *Eugène Delacroix*, 38.

---

56   "Reviews," *Art Journal*, n.s., 4 (1 Jan 1852): 35b.

57   Emerson, *The Journals and Miscellaneous Notebooks*, vol. 5. *1835–1838*, 298.

58   Nancy Finlay, *Inventing the American Past: The Art of F. O. C. Darley* (New York: New York Public Library, 1999), 15a. Cf. Sue W. Reed, "F. O. C. Darley's Outline Illustrations," in *The American Illustrated Book in the Nineteenth Century*, ed. G. W. R. Ward (Winterthur, Del.: Henry Francis du Pont Winterthur Museum, 1987), 113–35.

EXTENSIVE AND INTENSIVE ICONOGRAPHY

also account for his attraction to Retzsch's silent stage-like views. A self-taught draughtsman, he began working for illustrated magazines in the early 1840s, yet first attracted attention thanks to fifteen full-page outlines of a fictional Sioux chief for *Scenes in Indian Life* (1843). His career was verily launched in 1848–49 thanks to two outline sets after Washington Irving commissioned by the American Art-Union (1838–52). The latter represented a remarkably ambitious attempt to furnish many of the elements of a nascent art world: large-scale patronage, an exhibiting venue, criticism, and even rudimentary education for artists and the public in order to encourage US art and artists.[59] At its height in 1849, the society boasted "nearly 19,000 members from almost every state in the country." Period descriptions show consorting of social classes to the venues. The Darley years also tally with the Union's decision to combine premium prints for members, coupling historic with popular themes.

Distinctly on the popular side, Darley was entrusted with Irving's *Rip Van Winkle* and its companion tale, *The Legend of Sleepy Hollow*. The second's German gothic atmosphere and Headless Horseman (supposedly a Hessian trooper, beheaded by a cannon ball during the American War of Independence and pursuing lanky schoolmaster Ichabod Crane) may have settled his choice on Retzsch. Similarly, *Rip Van Winkle* was a legend "transplanted from Germany to the banks of the Hudson."[60] Both light-hearted and cherished, they were a resourceful attempt to spread contour graphics in the US. Once outlined, they addressed a large audience of mixed social origin, appreciative of fine quality printing as an upgrading social plus.

Both in landscape format (*c.*32 × 39 cm) and tan paper wrappers, they sport refined title-pages in black and red, and frame Irving's abridged texts, finely printed in double column and followed by Darley's prints with large margins on thicker creamy white paper. Layout and content sequence mirror the Retzsch albums issued by Georg von Cotta and Ernst Fleischer in the 1830s. Title-pages publicize the plates (engraved on stone) as "Designed and etched by Felix O. C. Darley," the American turning both into designer and printmaker, contrary to national tradition.[61] Both were printed in New York by Sarony &

Major, one of many lithographic partnerships involving Napoleon Sarony (1821–96), lithographer and would-be popular photo-portraitist. Coupled with a fine landscape engraving, they were reserved for American Art-Union's members under the annual five-dollar subscription. Press announcements harped on the pains taken in sixfold printing to achieve a fine result, while insisting on the Art-Union "putting to press in all an edition of some twenty thousand."[62] The *Bulletin of the American Art-Union* concluded its praise of Darley's *Rip Van Winkle* on "scatter[ing] these leaves, in tens of thousands, from the St. John to the Rio Grande."[63] *Fliegende Blätter* meant not just words. The metaphor materialized in circulation and imitations in the late 1840s even beyond the European publishing market. New modes of consuming books and prints had been established.

Choosing Retzsch and outline marked a brilliant beginning to Darley's career before he turned to wood, steel engraving, and three-dimensional style. Best-known illustrator of his time, even outside the United States (in 1853 Goupil and Co published large tinted lithographs by him in Paris, and Prince Napoleon commissioned watercolours), the fluid, expressive line for which he has been much praised draws on Flaxman and Retzsch.[64] A variety of techniques would allow him to illustrate over a hundred texts, several in deluxe editions. Among them, let me single out *Compositions in Outline from Hawthorne's Scarlet Letter*, with a full-page dedication to "Henry W. Longfellow | in memory of | a friendship of many years" in 1879. Under a front cover in fancy lettering, the album reiterated the formula of the set with large margins, offering twelve of Darley's fifteen outline compositions after Hawthorne with corresponding excerpts facing the plates. By then, heliotype printing had taken over and albums were widespread commodities issued by Houghton, Osgood and Co. in Boston, in association with the Riverside Press in Cambridge. Finely engraved sets belonged to the past. The Hawthorne album would be re-issued the following year in a smaller format, and under the heading of Houghton, Mifflin and Company in an elegant Japanese stab binding (Boston and New York, 1884), before becoming a large paper octavo with sideways-inserted photogravure plates (The Riverside Press, 1892). All three sets are stock illustration for Irving's tales and Hawthorne's novel even today.

---

59   Kimberley Orcutt, "The American Art-Union and the Rise of a National Landscape School: Scholarly Essay," in Orcutt and Allan McLeod, "Unintended Consequences: The American Art-Union and the Rise of a National Landscape School," *Nineteenth-Century Art Worldwide* 18, no. 1 (Spring 2019): 3.

60   "The Fine Arts. Mr. Darley's Rip Van Winkle," *Bulletin of the American Art-Union* 1, no. 14 (10 Nov 1848): 29.

61   Finlay, *Inventing the American Past*, 20a; Reed, 120–21.

---

62   "The Fine Arts," 28.

63   Ibid., 30.

64   *AKL Online*, s.v. "Darley, Felix Octavius Carr" (by Georgia B. Barnhill), https://www-degruyter-com.proxy.rubens.ens.fr/database/akl/html (accessed 3 Oct 2021).

We might be tempted to think that Darley's Retzsch inspiration appealed most to an East coast WASP audience retaining strong ties with Europe, but the Art-Union's vast membership roll and recent mapping per state[65] contradicts such a narrow view. As Retzsch and others had done for *Faust*, Darley was granting American literary texts pride of place nationwide, building the US canon.

7.6 Extensive vs. Intensive Iconography

The main question is then: how to evaluate these *fliegende Blätter*, what tools to use to assess their importance and malleability?[66]

I suggest using extensive vs. intensive iconography. I coined the terminology in 2005 by reference to Ségolène Le Men's article on "extensive" and "intensive culture of the image" in Jean-François Millet's work.[67] Le Men expertly studies, against the backdrop of an internationalized art market and competition between nations (his painting *L'Angélus* was acquired by the United States outbidding France), how Millet is extensively diffused thanks to reproduction from the 1850s, through popular objects of everyday life. She also shows how the artist expertly condensed and reduced an overabundance of images and materials into iconic compositions, his work preserving a tension between extensive and intensive culture. The incentive derives in turn from Roger Chartier's notion of "intensive" and "extensive reading," borrowed from German and American reading theories.[68] Intensive reading, following Chartier and his peers, corresponds to periods in which books are sparse, valuable, and infused with (often religious) aura within family or church circles. Reading communities might gather around a key mentor, who would read aloud for a group. Conversely, extensive reading matches the age of multiple printed books, negligible by-products of the industrial era, easily discarded, often destroyed.[69] Le Men proposed to import "intensive"

and "extensive" from history of reading to other cultural areas, particularly image production and art reception. The pattern is readily applicable from books to images, especially in the nineteenth century, rich in novel techniques of multiplication and reproduction.

I follow suit, specifically transferring the concept from a text to its iconographic interpretations; from author (Goethe) to artist-cum-engraver (Retzsch); from one such key figure to several others, either named or anonymous; from Retzsch's originals to their multiple re-workings, reception, and aftermath. Application of the concept is obviously not confined to Retzsch and may span Goethe's several visual interpretations through their gradual establishment as iconographic canon, Retzsch serving as showcase model.

In this sense, extensive iconography applies to the "veritable flood of images" (*eine wahre Bilderflut*)[70] across the German lands, then Europe, with which artists hailed Goethe's 1808 *Faust*, and strove to interpret, transpose or illustrate it. It underlines the role of images, active in the migration of motifs from artist to artist, while showing how they gradually constitute a collective orientation of imagination. To take but an example, images and motifs pass from one edition to another, as when Édouard Frère (1850) or Gaston Jourdain (1904) copy, highlight, and rework key scenes by Retzsch. An intensive iconography however persists within the extensive trend, allowing for genuine reinterpretation within characteristic books. Such is the case of Delacroix's brilliant development of Faust's meeting with Gretchen, on the basis of a Retzsch plate, in his celebrated *Faust* issued by Auguste Sautelet and Charles Motte in 1828. An equally arresting example is Italian master Francesco Hayez's painting *Il Bacio*, a powerful picture construed, I argue, from Retzsch's "The Kiss." Gradually endowed with national overtones and grown duly iconic, *Il Bacio* extensively nurtured items, even banal, for everyday life. A closer look will elucidate what I mean.

7.7 Extensive Rations

Édouard Frère's copied, focussed and enhanced images for Joseph Bry's "Les Veillées littéraires illustrées" ("Literary Illustrated Evenings," 1849–56) are a meaningful example of extensive iconography based on Nerval's last *Faust*

---

65 Orcutt, "The American Art-Union," 6–7.

66 A first version of some of the following pages appeared open access in *Artl@s Bulletin* 10, no. 1 (2021): Article 4, <https://docs.lib.purdue.edu/artlas/vol10/iss1/4/>.

67 Stead, "Le voyage des images du *Faust I* de Goethe: Lecture, réception et iconographie extensive et intensive au XIXe siècle," in *L'Image à la lettre*, ed. N. Preiss and J. Raigneau (Paris: Paris-Musées / Les Éditions des Cendres, 2005), 137–68; Le Men, "Millet et sa diffusion gravée, dans l'ère de la reproductibilité technique," in *Jean- François Millet (Au-delà de l'Angélus), colloque de Cerisy*, ed. G. Lacambre (Paris: Éditions de Monza, 2002), 370–87.

68 Chartier, "Du livre au lire," 69–70.

69 Chartier recalls Rolf Engelsing, *Der Bürger als Leser: Lesergeschichte in Deutschland, 1500–1800* (Stuttgart: J. B. Metzler,

1974), and David D. Hall, "Introduction: The Uses of Literacy in New England, 1600–1850," in *Printing and Society in Early America*, ed. W. L. Joyce et al. (Worcester: American Antiquarian Society, 1983), 1–47.

70 Petra Maisak, "Illustrationen," in *Goethe Handbuch*, vol. 4, 1, *Personen, Sachen, Begriffe A- K*, ed. H.-D. Dahnke and R. Otto (Stuttgart: J. B. Metzler, 1998), 518a.

EXTENSIVE AND INTENSIVE ICONOGRAPHY 243

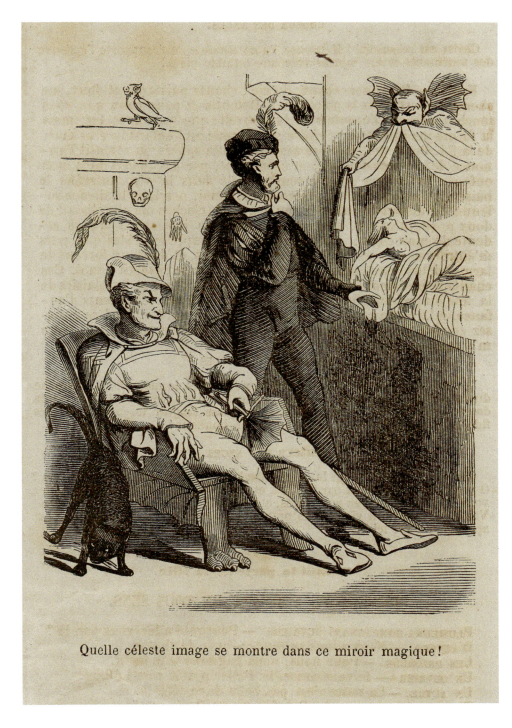

FIGURE 7.23
Édouard Frère after Moritz Retzsch, *Quelle céleste image se montre dans ce miroir magique!*, woodcut by François Rouget, (enlarged) detail vignette of Faust contemplating the magic-mirror woman, in *Faust par Wolfgang Goethe: Traduit de l'allemand par Gérard de Nerval* (Paris: J. Bry aîné, 1850), 12b
COURTESY HAAB, F GR 5293, WEIMAR

translation. Frère's ten in-text illustrations adopt astute gradual shadowing. Black and white contrasts dramatically offset effect by preceding, paralleling or finishing the most touching or gripping parts of *Faust* with engraver [François] Rouget's help. Amongst the four revamped Retzsch copies in pp. 12–13, well before the text, one focusses on Retzsch's plate 6 of Faust contemplating the reclining young woman, chastely dressed, in the witch's magic mirror. As in Moses's English and Muret's French renderings, the comely figure has become a feverish sheet-clad female with bared breasts, passionately gesturing in a fantastic amorous embrace (Fig. 7.23, cf. Fig. 6.18 for the page layout). Two further wood engravings, set in matching passages (pp. 24–25), oppose a malignant Mephistopheles, muttering to Martha, to a tender Faust, leaning over a petal-plucking Margaret, his arm over her shoulders (cf. Fig. 7.24a). Nearly ninety years later, Gründ would copy this for the cover of their *Faust* edition (cf. Fig. 6.22). A fourfold climax, ending with the text (pp. 34–35), hammers home Margaret's suffering (at the spinning

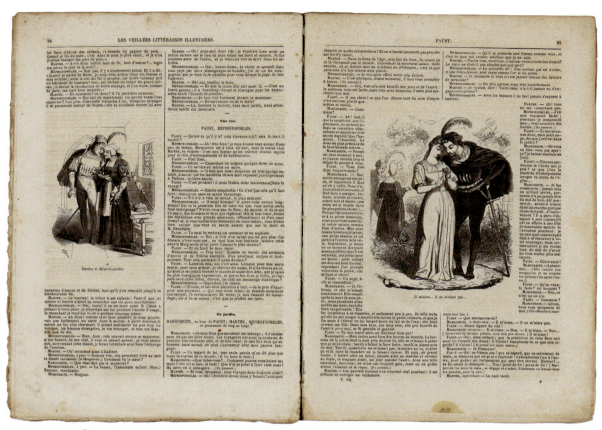

FIGURE 7.24A   Édouard Frère after Moritz Retzsch, two woodcuts by François Rouget, in *Faust par Wolfgang Goethe: Traduit de l'allemand par Gérard de Nerval* (Paris: J. Bry aîné, 1850), 24–25
COURTESY HAAB, F GR 5293, WEIMAR

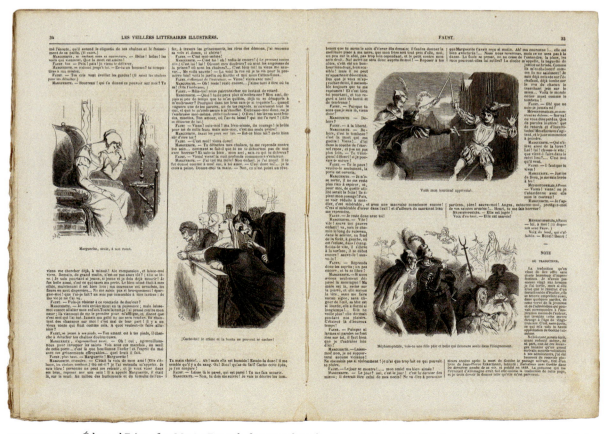

FIGURE 7.24B   Édouard Frère after Moritz Retzsch, four woodcuts by François Rouget, in *Faust par Wolfgang Goethe: Traduit de l'allemand par Gérard de Nerval* (Paris: J. Bry aîné, 1850), 34–35
COURTESY HAAB, F GR 5293, WEIMAR

FIGURE 7.25 Édouard Frère, front-page scene after Retzsch and series header, in *Faust par Wolfgang Goethe: Traduit de l'allemand par Gérard de Nerval* (Paris: J. Bry aîné, 1850), 1
COURTESY HAAB, F GR 5293, WEIMAR

wheel, then at the cathedral), and Faust's torments (killing Valentine, aghast at Margaret's spectre) (Fig. 7.24b). Front page, full centre, Faust pledges to a white, phantom-like Mephistopheles, also reproduced on the cover. Above it, the "Veillées littéraires illustrées" header, with two suave ladies nonchalantly reading, promises a brighter future to the consumer for the modicum of 50 centimes (Fig. 7.25).[71]

Conversely, the book illustrated by Gaston Jourdain, issued after his premature death, pertains to fin-de-siècle book collecting. Jourdain's compositions in photogravures (*héliogravures*) by J. Chauvet are insert plates in a deluxe private publication, again based on Nerval's translation and prefaced by Frantz Jourdain, his architect brother, Art Nouveau theoretician, and author. A four-page list of noble and literati subscribers underpins its prestige. The dramatized introduction implicitly parallels Gaston's toils and early demise with Nerval's own tragic fate. According to the preface, both artists are bonded through a common creative idealism and passionate vision. The iconography opens with a quasi-erotic scene—a shapely female nude in a meditative Faust's dark study—an intensified idea borrowed from the opening plate of Gabriel Max's 1880 portfolio. In the latter, a body lies foreground concealed beneath a veil.[72] Frantz Jourdain's preface stresses how Gaston toiled ten years for these compositions, commissioned by Paul Gallimard, although he knew *Faust* by heart: "Each drawing summarizes a mound of documents, research, sketches, studies, attempts, trials and errors that exhausted him."[73] Indeed, the plates read as a compendium of Faustian iconography where Retzsch, hailed, is subject to fantastic or burlesque treatment and gender reversal. When the poodle mutates in Jourdain's plate 4, Gaston's ferocious monster has swollen to extraordinary proportions, his muzzle revealing terrifying fangs, but both the creature and the room's layout are based on Retzsch's plate 3. A male sorcerer is swapped for the witch in her kitchen, but strung frogs hang from the ceiling (cf. Fig. 7.26), clearly a graphic citation of Retzsch (cf. Fig. 2.18 & 2.19). A true compilation, this book shows to what extent nineteenth-century iconography rests on pliable amalgams, at the heart of which Retzsch occupies pride of place.

7.8 Intensive Inspiration

An impressive 1828 *Faust* folio was imposed on Delacroix (who himself drew his creations on stone and would have preferred a portfolio of lithographs[74]) by lithographer and printseller Charles Motte. It is now hailed as an important romantic book responding to Goethe's opus, yet period realities differed.

Delacroix knew Retzsch well since 1821, both directly and indirectly, mentioning him in his diary and correspondence.[75] His freehand sketched copies show he had studied his work (cf. Fig. 6.1 to 6.3), lifting at least fifteen figures from some ten Retzsch plates, including the witches' Sabbath and the Prologue in Heaven, not all

---

71 A fully digitized version of *Faust* illustrated by Frère in a later edition (1860) is of poor quality, as it is based on a previous microfilm, not the printed item: https://gallica.bnf.fr/ark:/12148/bpt6k692289.

72 Max, *Faust-Illustrationen: Zehn Zeichnungen, in Holz geschnitten* (Berlin: G. Grote, 1880), pl. I, https://goethehaus.museum-digital.de/singleimage.php?imagenr=2882.

73 Jourdain, "Préface," in *Le Faust de Goethe, traduction de Gérard de Nerval, illustrations inédites de Gaston Jourdain* (Paris: Imprimé pour la Société de Propagation des Livres d'Art, 1904), III.

74 *Correspondance générale d'Eugène Delacroix*, 4:304.

75 To Burty he writes having seen Retzsch's outlines *c.*1821; Delacroix, *Journal*, 1:120–21 (20 Feb 1824).

FIGURE 7.26   Gaston Jourdain, photogravure by J. Chauvet, in *Le Faust de Goethe, traduction de Gérard de Nerval, préface de M. Frantz-Jourdain, illustrations inédites de Gaston Jourdain* (Paris: Imprimé pour la Société de Propagation des Livres d'Art, 1904), insert plate 8, between pp. 60–61. Telling detail of frogs after Moritz Retzsch (cf. Fig. 2.18–19)
BnF, RÉS. M-YH-4, PARIS

EXTENSIVE AND INTENSIVE ICONOGRAPHY

of which have been identified. Moreover, in *The Devil and Doctor Faustus*, the Drury Lane play that triggered Delacroix into action, Daniel Terry had performed Mephistophiles (*sic* in the play) in a costume after Retzsch (cf. Fig. 9.13).[76]

Retzsch's set is therefore an important iconographic matrix for Delacroix. It inspires numerous scene compositions and details: the poodle's twisting tail in his lithograph 4, as it alights at Faust and Wagner's feet in open country, harks back to the trailing strokes of Retzsch's plate 2. The upper diagonal of the Brocken scene, as Mephistopheles and Faust ascend the mountain in Delacroix's lithograph 14, is similarly based on Retzsch's plate 21.[77] The Dresden artist was first to compose the layout, to order the characters and their ascent, even though there are substantial differences in atmosphere and feeling between Delacroix's superb dark lithographs and Retzsch's fanciful, energetic, yet clear outlines. In several other plates, similarities and distinctive traits would infringe on the scope of the point discussed.

Here, I neither seek an artist's source of inspiration nor discuss creations in terms of originality. Conception of creation—whether in literature or other arts—as pure originality or the elaboration of talented genius-cum-unique spirit is largely the outcome of a romantic myth, farfetched from artistic or literary realities.[78] Artists and writers create their work not only through talent, but also grasping knowledge. Delacroix grasped what he knew. What is remarkable in his case is his capacity to extract the dramatic potential from a scene by Retzsch. Intensive iconography builds on this. Let me briefly revert to a telling Faust scene, the protagonist's first meeting with Margaret.

Exceedingly short in the play, yet momentous in Faustian iconography, it brings together the two main characters of Gretchen's story, setting the tone for what will subsequently be developed. Retzsch's plate 8 could itself be based on extensive iconography, or indeed set the rules for such future development. As shown in Chapter 1, comparison with Cornelius and Naeke suggests that the original for such parallel treatment can hardly be pinned down (cf. Fig. 1.8 to 1.10). Ostensibly, all three artists were stimulated by Goethe, whose several details can easily be conveyed into a picture. Each of their renderings however

creates a special atmosphere and builds on variant symbolism. Delacroix's conception however poses the question differently since he creatively transforms Retzsch's plate.

As Faust approaches Margaret, Retzsch subtly parallels Faust in the foreground and Mephistopheles in the background through identical costumes and corresponding swords. Delacroix projects this very analogy to the fore, partly masking one of the swords under Faust's ample cloak while each figure lines up with the other, either side of Gretchen (cf. Fig. 7.27). In his lithograph, the male bodies become a narrow trap, into which an alluring, disdainful, yet frightened Margaret falls. The partners close in on her in a powerful grip, both real and fantastic, in which each is the other's double as suggest their strongly similar profiles shown in parallel. Here, Faust turns devil, the physical embodiment of Mephistopheles's spectral form, while the contrapuntal movement of their legs and feet on the ground builds a metaphor of the road to destruction. Delacroix's intensive scene clearly transcends Retzsch's inspiring plate, adding a fantastic dimension and dark symbolism to the scene.

A last case shows how intensive iconography, again triggered by Retzsch, gives in turn birth to extensive iconography in its own right.

Il Bacio by Italian painter Francesco Hayez (1791–1882) is probably Italy's best-known nineteenth-century painting (cf. Fig. 7.28), which I argue takes after Retzsch's "The Kiss." Shelley was not alone in being impressed by the latter, a most popular image indeed, due to its numerous copies and repurposed versions as amply shown.

To my knowledge, neither Hayez studies on *The Kiss* (mostly by Fernando Mazzocca) nor general studies on the theme refer to Retzsch's print. Regular interpretation of Hayez in Italian scholarship is strongly based on his own previous conceptions, mainly the painting *L'ultimo bacio dato a Giulieta da Romeo* (*The Last Kiss Given to Juliet by Romeo*, 1823), a sensational romantic work with scandal overtones at the time, differing though from *Il Bacio* in dimensions, atmosphere and formal treatment. Conversely, Retzsch's influence on Hayez seems highly plausible for at least three reasons. First, the iconographic kinship between images, both thematic and aesthetic. Thematically, the lovers are isolated between open door and sinking stairwell (the scene intimates leave-taking), while an indefinite third disappears down the steps. In consecutive versions, this figure is occasionally further dimmed. What remains is the passionate riveting of both figures clasping each other, lost in the kiss, as in Retzsch. If Carlo Carrà insists in his 1919 *Pittura metafisica* on the

---

76   Christopher Murray, "Robert William Elliston's Production of *Faust*, Drury Lane, 1825," *Theatre Research* 11, no. 2–3 (1971): 108, n. 25; Doy, "Delacroix et Faust," 19.

77   Doy also makes this comparison, 22.

78   Isbell, *The Birth of European Romanticism*, 1–2.

FIGURE 7.27
(*top*) Eugène Delacroix, lithograph, in *Faust, tragédie de M. de Goethe, traduite en français par M. Albert Stapfer* (À Paris: Ch. Motte & Sautelet, 1828), insert plate between pp. 72–73; (*bottom*) Moritz Retzsch, Faust meeting Gretchen, *Umrisse zu Goethe's Faust gezeichnet von Retsch* (Stuttgart & Tübingen: Cotta, 1816), pl. 8
BnF, RÉS.-YH-17, PARIS, AND: COURTESY HAAB, F 3487, WEIMAR

FIGURE 7.28   Francesco Hayez, *Il Bacio. Episodio della giovinezza. Costumi del secolo XIV*, oil on canvas, 1859, 112 × 88 cm, first version
COURTESY PINACOTECA DI BRERA, MILAN

picture's "linearities," its "sensitive, definite lines," and the "engraved crystallisation" (*cristallizzazione incisa*) of all Hayez's compositions,[79] Mazzocca stresses the arabesque of the couple as resolving the strong colour contrast. He summons both Venetian colour treatment and the Munich school's purist abstraction as in the work of Schnorr, Kaulbach and Feuerbach.[80] Line accuracy, arabesque and abstraction all recall Schlegel's comments on the outline and bring forward the painting's delineated underpinning. Second, Hayez, mostly known as a painter, also was a printmaker for Milanese publishers. He lithographed Walter Scott's *Ivanhoe*, illustrated Andrea Maffei's translations of Schiller, and also was briefly a candidate to illustrate Manzoni's *I promessi sposi* (*The Betrothed*, first published 1827) with vignettes.[81] His printmaking achievements in the late 1820s are deemed a major feat of his romantic period.[82] Such contexts would have readily acquainted him with Retzsch's set. And thirdly, his numerous contacts with German painters and 1830s trip to Munich were further opportunities for familiarity with Retzsch, although cited bibliographies rather stress the influence German historicist artists had on him. This is not however the case of *Il Bacio*, the lesser dimensions of which (112×88 cm) contrast with its wider fame. Precisely, its intimate quality works emotions while subtly donning patriotic and commonly shared symbolism.

Hayez's painting gave four oil versions, proliferation being also a telling feature. A first from 1859, *Il Bacio. Episodio della giovinezza. Costumi del secolo XIV* (*The Kiss. An Episode of Youth. Costumes of the 14th Century*), exhibited the very year of its making at Milan's Brera Academy annual art exhibition, instantly brewed patriotic significance as Mazzocca has shown.[83] Hayez was by then a prophet-painter, whose work signalled turning points in his native land's history. His *Bacio* post-dated by only three months Vittorio Emmanuele II's and Napoleon III's triumphant entry to Milan, after liberating Lombardy of Austrian rule. Not by chance, already in 1862, reproduction of *Bacio* prints are referentially embedded in two further Italian paintings. Gerolamo Induno's *Triste presentimento* (*Sad Premonition*) shows a young girl contemplating the

portrait of her departed lover to fight for Italy's liberation at Garibaldi's side: a small coloured *Bacio* hangs on the wall close to Garibaldi's bust. The same year, in Giuseppe Reina's *Triste novella* (*Sad News*), a young lady melancholically considers another larger *Bacio* print by the window, while the colours of sparse objects on the table recall the Italian flag.[84] The two maidens belong to different social backgrounds. By 1862 then, Hayez's coloured *Bacio* reproduction had spread among diverse social strata. His painting was fast becoming an Italic icon.

In the meantime, it had itself been through at least one further version in 1861 with the embracing couple's colour scheme (red and green for the young man, dazzling white for the damsel) manifesting the Italian flag, and sponsoring explicit national fervour (Fig. 7.29). The kiss was of leave-taking. An ominous shadow fell on the steps to the right, and the mysterious figure sliding down the shadowy, stately stairwell, spoke of threat. Hayez sent a last version in oils, entitled simply *Il Bacio* (*The Kiss*), to Paris's 1867 Universal Exhibition, which quickly entered princely collections, and is still today in private hands (Fig. 7.30). In this, even more portentously, the kiss occurs between two open doors with the descending figure dimmer than ever. Disquiet and dread hover over the parting while a white veil or stole, fallen on the stairs, stresses urgency and fervour. The meaning-laden colours (azure blue dress, brilliant green doubling of the man's mantle, red hose, and white fallen wrap) allude to the flags of two nations, France and Italy, bonding in Italy's future unification. The painting does not represent just any departing young man's kiss to his beloved, but precisely the Garibaldi volunteer's goodbye kiss to a *fiancée* he may never see again, in a painting celebrating the strong friendship and political alliance between "two friendly nations that embrace each other with a view to a common destiny of intention" (*due nazioni amiche che si abbracciano verso un commune destino di intesa*).[85] Already at the time, the painting was named *Il Bacio del volontario* (*The Volunteer's Kiss*). Its symbolism and public exhibition at the Paris Universal Exhibition, shortly before the Franco-Prussian war, make of it a manifesto, the Italian version of Overbeck's *Italia und Germania*.

Hayez's successive renderings show how extensive iconography may acquire strong ideological and political importance, all the more paradoxical as it originates from

---

79   Carlo Carrà, *Pittura metafisica* (Florence: Vallecchi, 1919), 281–82.

80   Mazzocca, *Francesco Hayez: Catalogo ragionato* (Milan: Federico Motta, 1994), 334–35.

81   Mazzocca, "L'illustrazione romantica," in *Storia dell'arte italiana*, pt. 3, *Situazioni momenti indagini*, vol. 2, *Grafica e immagine*, 2, *Illustrazione, fotografia* (Turin: Einaudi, 1981), 394, 406.

82   *Grove Art Online*, s.v. "Hayez-Francesco" (by Mazzocca), https://doi-org.janus.bis-sorbonne.fr/10.1093/gao/9781884446054.article.T037051 (accessed 21 Jan 2021).

83   Mazzocca, *Hayez. Dal mito al Bacio* (Venice: Marsilio, 1998), 178.

---

84   Mazzocca, *Francesco Hayez: Il Bacio* (Milan: Silvana Editoriale, 2009), 13–18; and Susanna Zatti, "Amore e morte, passione e patriottismo nell'iconografia del bacio tra Ottocento e Novecento," in *Il bacio tra Romanticismo e Novecento*, ed. S. Zatti and L. Tonani (Milan: Silvana Editoriale, 2009), 31.

85   Mazzocca, *Hayez. Dal mito al Bacio*, 180c.

EXTENSIVE AND INTENSIVE ICONOGRAPHY 251

FIGURE 7.29   Francesco Hayez, *Il Bacio*, oil on canvas, 1861, 127 × 95 cm, second version, private coll.
ALL RIGHTS RESERVED

FIGURE 7.30   Francesco Hayez, *Il Bacio*, oil on canvas, 1867, 116.8 × 80 cm, third version, private coll.
ALL RIGHTS RESERVED

German-speaking territories (Retzsch's print) at the very moment fledgling Italy was fighting to throw off Austro-Hungarian dominion, and unite. But, as is well known, most travelling images have no indelible ethnic, national or religious identity. Retzsch's "The Kiss" is one of such. Revamped by Hayez, it entered yet another cycle of transmutations, "from engravings to chromolithographs and the covers of chocolate boxes" (*dalle incisioni alle oleografie ai coperchi delle scatole di cioccolatini*).[86]

In present-day Italy's standard culture, the faraway reminiscence of Hayez's painting subtly informs a commonly shared industrialized product, known as chocolate kisses or *baci*. Based on a special recipe invented by Luisa Spagnoli after the Great War, the small, round, somewhat irregular sweets, using hazelnut and chocolate filling, are topped with a bulging hazelnut, all covered in chocolate. They are always accompanied by a text with a twist, proverb or apophthegm on the meaning of life or love. Due to the uneven shape recalling a fist, they were initially named *cazzotti* (punches), rechristened kisses (*baci*), or Perugina kisses (*Baci Perugina*), and astutely advertised as "a kiss on every Italian's mouth" by La Perugina firm.[87] An industrial yet elegant product, an inexpensive yet succulent present, they reply to the immediately recognizable image of a forlorn couple in elegant dress, kissing against the sky. The iconic image is based on a 1923 logo by Federico Seneca (1891–1976), Perugina's artistic director at the time, who shaped both the image and the marketing campaign with Hayez's painting in mind (Fig. 7.31a). The reversed contrast of the couple in silhouette is reminiscent of transfer techniques (engraving, lithography, etc.). It suggests a brighter perspective as the couple kisses under a blue sky and the promising *Baci* inscription. Their clothing is voided of Hayez's nationalistic symbolism although still vaguely historic and refined. Yet this is a post-World War I image. Based on an iconic template, it subliminally talks of togetherness rather than heroic parting. In any event, wrapped in silver paper decked with stars, both axiom

---

86   Ibid., 178a.

87   Luca Masia, *Buitoni, la famiglia, gli uomini, le imprese* (Milan: Silvana Editoriale / Volumnia, 2007), 118–21.

FIGURE 7.31A   Federico Seneca, *Baci: ciocolato Perugina*, in *Tavole di Federico Seneca con prefazione di Leonardo Borgese* (n.p.: Edizioni Vendre, n.d. [*c*.1950])
COURTESY PAOLA PALLOTTINO

and chocolate kiss are far-flung upshots of Doctor Faust's wisdom or folly (Fig. 7.31b).

Within extensive and intensive iconography, the interaction and reinterpretation of iconographic motifs and circulation of images re-evaluated from country to country thus involve famous and less conspicuous artists in the comparative process. Illustration studies traditionally privilege exceptional cases but sideline composite cultural objects. By contrast, the extensive/intensive concept allows us to address circulation of images in larger corpora through an interdisciplinary approach.

7.9   Recycling and Authorship in Image Circulation

In an article on the recycling of Théodore Géricault's *The Raft of the Medusa* reproductions, Tom Gretton has pointedly opposed the notion of authorship, relating intentional agency (individual or collaborative gestation), to the effect of pictures' post-partum life and their power over onlookers' imagination.[88] We may be inclined to consider some of these proxies as sub-products lacking "aura," as in Walter Benjamin's well-known 1935 essay "The Work of Art in the Age of Mechanical Reproduction." Yet what Benjamin names "aura" is to be viewed in terms of authorship, specifically individual, which serves to grant artworks a precise place in space, time, personal career, and national history. It also later feeds the competition of nations for cultural recognition within an international arena.

---

88   Gretton, "Reincarnation and Reimagination: Some Afterlives of Géricault's *Raft of the Medusa* from c. 1850 to c. 1905," in "L'Image recyclée," ed. L. Cheles and G. Roque, *Figures de l'art*, no. 23 (2013): 77–94.

FIGURE 7.31B Present-day display of Baci Perugina in Venice airport
AUTHOR'S PHOTOGRAPH 10 JUNE 2022

However, aura barely resists the mass culture phenomenon and the effectiveness of pictorial motifs in circulation, particularly when subject to combination, modification, or profound alteration. For Ségolène Le Men, Jean-François Millet's work gained aura in reproduction through Millet's ability to condense images into icons, emblems or symbols. Yet Retzsch's case differs entirely.

Customized copies of his twenty-six plates reveal intentional agency. In most cases, this does not reflect on Retzsch himself, but on Goethe's *Faust*. The aura pertains to the author of a singular text, gradually canonized and treasured as paragon of heritage. In this sense, Retzsch's outlines, much abused through copying, are an "outline" bait, that is, a fishing line cast out by publishers to pull in clientele: small fry as well as big fish. In Frère's case, tailored as mass production publications, the focussed and repurposed Retzsch copies reveal diverse artistic intentions and the combined agency of authorship by publisher Bry, the French artist, and Belgian wood engraver François Rouget. The item thus produced gains further aura, this time for both Goethe and Nerval, his translator, publicizing, with the German author's approval and endorsement, his own translation.[89] In Gaston Jourdain's recycling of details, we perceive an ironic reference-packed fin-de-siècle compendium of culture, reflecting yet again on the play's aura, but also his brother Frantz's clever intention to parallel Gaston's and Nerval's common path for a choice audience. Extensive iconography prompts analysis of publishing context, readers' reactions, public sensitivity to images, and imaginative processes. It reveals that books and prints are largely cultural objects, relegating authorship to a *de facto* subordinate position. In considering their circulation, we are led to see those dimensions, and can hardly consider copied images in isolation.[90]

In intensive iconography, intention is still manifest but strongly engages with the re-imaginative process of

---

[89] Goethe, *Faust: Traduit de l'allemand par Gérard de Nerval*, 35–36.
[90] Further on this approach, see Stead, ed., *Reading Books and Prints as Cultural Objects*, index entries under *circulation*.

different communities. Delacroix's *Faust* only acquired aura in the second half of the twentieth century, when the artist himself emerged as a major master. In the 1950s, Jacqueline Armingeat would refer to it as "a forgotten book."[91] In its own time, this *Faust* was a commercial failure, for both publishers and artist, dismissed as "one of the leaders of the school of ugliness" (*un des coryphées de l'école du laid*).[92] Conversely, Hayez's celebrated image quickly became an early icon, which it still is, having strongly gripped the collective imagination of Italians. It gave in turn birth to products of arguably uneven artistic merit, which nevertheless strongly connect with a nation's modern history.

---

91 Armingeat, "Un livre oublié," *L'Œil*, no. 12 (Noël 1955): 54.
92 *Correspondance générale d'Eugène Delacroix*, 4:304.

In all cases, historical, artistic, and ideological context is still to be taken into account, if we wish to properly evaluate image circulation.

This book might have ended here, the influence of print culture on other arenas affording no suit. Other matters, such as parody, literature, inspiration for the stage, romantic gifts by poets to exceptional women, or popular three-dimensional objects, may seem secondary to prints, outlines and their circulation. Yet to consider outlines "beyond outlines" is crucial, if we wish to fathom cultural history. The appeal of Retzsch on such contexts poses critical aesthetic questions and flags up nations' ambitions, time and again. Hence, beyond such a turning point, this book tracks burlesque, stage designs, actors' bearing and costumes, authors' scheming and plot, literary barter, even decorative trivia, all after Retzsch. However differently illuminated, are the latter to be dismissed as trivia?

CHAPTER 8

The Power of Parody: A Crow amongst Nations

A parody only works with that already known; and one only parodies what is well known. Hardly a guarantee, both constraints challenge the parodist, who must excel in the art of faking and spice it up as well. Such science demands requisite zest. A successful parody means mastering both a multi-layer culture and an ironic or critical, even self-critical, distance from the parodied work. In so doing, parody achieves the cultural clout of a double-edged sword. One false move, one verbal slip-up, one skewed graphic, and the author risks failing abysmally. But parody also offers the possibility of revising the initial work's target and even revealing some of its hidden aspects. That is what stands out in a now nearly forgotten work: Alfred Crowquill's *Faust* (London, 1834) and its transformation into a German album (1841).[1]

To parody Goethe's *Faust* (1808) in Great Britain as early as 1834, with an amended version of the English spoof entering the German States in 1841, was no trouble-free operation. If, at his 1832 demise, Goethe was a revered and quasi-untouchable author in his own country, the intricate European reception of his *Faust* had been strongly dependent on images. Amongst these, Retzsch's set was, as shown, the darling of town and many a country with seven copied diverse editions in the English-speaking world from 1820 to 1832 (six in London, one in Washington DC), often reissued,[2] in addition to standalone prints, copies of select episodes, reproductions in other media, and staged applications. A distinctive feature was the simultaneous presence of text in various forms: a textual synopsis gradually growing into a form of translation of Goethe's play itself; translated excerpts from it; explanatory introductions; or plain captions. In whatsoever form, text convoyed Retzsch in textual and visual chitchat confronting and supporting each other, always upwelling from Goethe's *Faust*.

Alfred Crowquill's parody naturally targeted Retzsch's *Faust*, far better known in Britain than Goethe's, via images, yet supplemented with Crowquill's own particular (and much neglected) text. Indeed, his burlesque iconography alone attracted little attention, nor praise in scholarship. Rümann calls it a "travesty (*Travestie*),"

"suitable to mention for the sake of historic rather than artistic interest."[3] More than forty years later, Vaughan caustically adds: "In 1835 A. H. Forrester published a rough parody of the *Faust* illustrations that served to damage his rather than Retzsch's reputation."[4] Yet, Crowquill's parody proved popular enough to run through three editions in two years. Besides ordinary exemplars, a large paper edition with hand-coloured plates and gilt edges for collectors further indicates public appeal and approval (Fig. 8.1a–b).[5] If only for this, it integrates *Faust* readings of the time, albeit through a distorted lens. What may the latter reveal?

In tackling Goethe's *Faust* via Retzsch, Crowquill's parody evinces *Faust*'s composite reception. A case of nested reading through the original's iconographic surrogate, the parody works by deputy thanks to a twofold screen. An anonymous Edinburgh press review stated at the time:

> We are not sure that we relish the scoffing and malicious mockery of travesties of this kind. *Faust* is, however, becoming such a *bore* to the merely English reader, that one is glad of the relief of seeing him in Harlequin clothes. One may therefore give up Faust, Martha, and Mephistopheles, to the mocking fiend, Caricature;[6]

More than a weapon violating Retzsch, I argue, a *Faust* "in Harlequin clothes" proves a refined means of reading Goethe, revealing in the process concealed trends of thought. Crowquill's dual travesty should also be read as the result of images *and* text combined. Both art historians, Rümann and Vaughan, evaluate only images (rather crude indeed). Examining the text however discloses unexpected views on the conflict of nations in post-Napoleonic Europe. Furthermore, Crowquill's parody travelled and metamorphosed in displacement, producing another unexpected reading of Goethe's *Faust* in Germanic contexts themselves. It emerges as a complex intermedial and intercultural work testing our capacities to read between the outlines.

---

1 A first version of this Chapter was published in French online in 2019, https://www.revue-textimage.com/17_blessures_du_livre/stead1.html.

2 See Appendix 1, nos. 4, 5, 7, 9, 11, and 21.

3 Rümann, *Das illustrierte Buch*, 225.

4 Vaughan, *German Romanticism*, 136.

5 Large paper edition, 37.6 × 27.6 cm. Ordinary exemplars 26.3 × 17.4 cm.

6 "Faust, a Serio-Comic Poem, with Twelve Outline Illustrations," *Tait's Edinburgh Magazine* 1, no. 11 (Dec 1834): 852b, author's emphasis.

© EVANGHELIA STEAD, 2023 | DOI:10.1163/9789004543010_011

This is an open access chapter distributed under the terms of the CC BY-NC-ND 4.0 license.

256   CHAPTER 8

FIGURE 8.1A
Alfred Crowquill, *Faust Sees Margaret for the First Time*, in *Faust: A Serio-Comic Poem with Twelve Outline Illustrations* (London: B. B. King, 1834), large paper edition, pl. 5
COURTESY BEINECKE, YALE UNIVERSITY, SPECK SG8A F6 +834B

FIGURE 8.1B
Alfred Crowquill, *Margaret Refuses to Leave the Prison*, in *Faust: A Serio-Comic Poem with Twelve Outline Illustrations* (London: B. B. King, 1834), large paper edition, pl. 12
COURTESY BEINECKE, YALE UNIVERSITY, SPECK SG8A F6 +834B

Before we turn to it, a brief comparison with *Faust*-inspired music proves useful from a chronological perspective. In the German-speaking world, Goethe's text inspired Beethoven's and Schubert's *lieder*, both entitled *Margaret at the Spinning Wheel* (1803 and 1814). Like Retzsch's set, they displace the attention from Doctor Faust to the young girl. Though only *lieder*, this melancholic and touching scene would inspire a high number of them: about fifty.[7] Inversely, more sizeable musical creations turned to Goethe much later. Louis Spohr's opera *Faust* (1813) is closer to Friedrich Maximilian Klinger's novel *Fausts Leben, Thaten und Höllenfahrt* (*Faust's Life, Deeds and Journey to Hell*, 1791) than to Goethe.[8] Analogous large-scale musical compositions in France are all posterior, witness Berlioz's "dramatic legend" *La Damnation de Faust* (1845) and especially *Faust*, Charles Gounod's opera (1859), a huge success, which also naturalized German under the title *Margarete* (Darmstadt, 1861). By comparison, between 1824 and 1830, Retzsch's copies were lithographed or re-engraved six times in France, and Nerval's 1828 translation, already the third into French, uses a copy after Retzsch as frontispiece (cf. Fig. 6.4). Retzsch was by far a more conspicuous interpreter in reception.

As a result, while a *Faust* parody may certainly have aimed at *mocking* Goethe by distorting or violating *his* play (deemed "a bore"), in the early days of *Faust's* European reception, it could only do this *at a second level of interpretation* and by relying on Retzsch as well-known intermediary. The latter, as basis for the adaptational foundation in the host country, served as the parody's springboard. The layered process also implied twin-headed arts, prevailing images and contiguous texts. The intermediary, like a cutting grafted onto Goethe's plant or a shoot sprouting from the *Faust* tree, was the first to pay the price; the affront would attain the original *Faust* only later, in a second moment. Yet images, immediately appealing and swiftly diffused from one country to the next by easy copying and widespread use of prints, naturally, yet insufficiently, caught the specialist eyes of Rümann and Vaughan. Moreover, Crowquill's parody of *Faust* ended up entering German territory, where its humour hit the mark, all the while laughing up its own sleeve.

In such superposition, the mocking imitation of a major work presupposes an even higher degree of cultivation, creative methods, and parodist ingenuity. Also implied is a degree of ironic or critical distance, including

self-deprecation. In the case of Crowquill, who parodied Goethe's *Faust* via a British Retzsch copy and an indigenous poetic form, one intended violation became manifold: (a) His spoof is of a play not only transferred from one culture to the next, but also from one medium to another. The parodist more or less uses the same technique as the caricaturist, and the odds are that the text-image association of pen and pencil (or stylus) grant Crowquill great impact in Britain. Conceived for a British audience, his parody originally bears on Retzsch's imagery, the hyped and most publicized forms of Goethe's play. Yet, given its transmedial nature, its text and images do not necessarily work together. (b) Since Crowquill added a poem of his own, his spoof also undermines the original register by substituting one genre for another. As a literary form of expression, it deflates the original pitch, all the while commending a great deal of technical dexterity and skill in an exaggerated form of art. (c) The original's content and form are displaced in a composition laden with cultural connotations, mixed with vernacular references, and based on material previously reworked and already redirected, multiplying the layers of cultural stratification. (d) In addition to the alterations it inflicts on the original, the parody itself takes into consideration several elements: the original's reception in the country where it is parodied and that parody's context; the variation in codes of meaning from one culture to the next; and the prior cultural tradition of parody in the country where the new caricatured version is proffered.

In Crowquill's work, we deal of course with the tongue-in-cheek humour specific to parody, implying a *second level of interpretation*—the tension between high and low, sublime and grotesque, enthusiasm and mockery, insult and compliment, all blended together. But the multi-layered context provokes a *third level* of interpretation based on the intermediary (Retzsch), indeed a *fourth level* involving Crowquill's text, and ultimately a *fifth level* when the parodied set penetrated Germany. It thereupon returns to the source of this piled-up chain reaction, directly targeting Goethe's *Faust*. In this final stage, the parody's critical impact ends up by stripping away, like a caustic paint remover, parasitic appended layers of meaning to ultimately reveal the original work in all its vigour.

Subsequently, all media are under tension and cultures confronted. Interpreters show up, more numerous than the target (Goethe) and the parodist (Crowquill). Historical contexts play a role. Last, but not least, the cultural referents in each country are summoned, which process leads to a deeper, yet disguised, reading of the original.

Let us then take things step by step.

---

7   Reibel, *Faust: La musique*, 64; Walter Aign, *Faust im Lied* (Stuttgart: Ausgabe der Stadt Knittlingen / Enzkreis, 1975), 45–47.

8   Reibel, *Faust: La musique*, 28–37.

8.1 A Crow's Quill

Alfred Crowquill's *Faust: A Serio-Comic Poem, With Twelve Outline Illustrations* was published in London in 1834 by B. B. King, a publisher active between 1835 and 1839 and specializing in engravings (notably mezzotints). It sold for six shillings. Thirty-two pages under a light green (symbolically acid) letterpress cover (26.1 × 17.4 cm) offer twelve short cantos and twelve images, possibly lithographed, albeit the imprint "Drawn and Eng[rave]^d by Alf. Crowquill." Alfred Henry Forrester, artist, humourist and younger brother of the polygraph Charles Robert Forrester, had composed the poem and drawings, which he reputedly also etched. Both brothers shared the pseudonym "Alfred Crowquill" in works pairing Charles's texts with Alfred's drawings. *Faust*, however, was exclusively the work of Alfred, if we are to believe the handwritten note figuring in English and Latin in the Bibliothèque nationale de France exemplar: "This Poem, was written by Mr. Forester [*sic*], who also designed the drawings and engraved the plates: a fecundity of arts, tria juncta in uno. || Markham Sherwill."[9] According to another manuscript inscription, the exemplar was given by B. B. King, the publisher, to Sherwill himself, who must have had direct information on the techniques employed. The prints however show no indentations (perhaps larger plates had been used), and a press review of the time runs: "Alfred Crowquill has well designed his plates, but the outlines are not sufficiently sharp and clear. They should have been cut in copper, for they really deserve it."[10]

Alfred Henry Forrester began his career in the City alongside his brother, a notary, but quickly turned to the illustrated press, the widespread medium of the time. He studied drawing, modelling, wood and steel engraving. A prolific illustrator, he drew for works by his brother and others, was an early contributor to *Punch; or, The London Charivari*, and often published texts illustrated with his own images in the influential *Illustrated London News*. In addition, he painted profusely (landscapes, pastoral scenes, interiors), was interested in the applied arts (he is a well-known designer for ceramic and porcelain ornament), and designed theatre posters, backdrops for pantomimes, calling cards, and comic postcards. He conceived numerous hardcovers and dust jackets for yellow-backs— garishly coloured chromolithographed paper covers. He also devised children's books and stage plays with brio. In short, he cuts a multi-talented figure, also capable of improvising and singing. His work is largely neglected in British criticism, which has instead focused on more popular draughtsmen (Robert Seymour, George Cruikshank, Kenny Meadows, H. K. Browne and so on). Although he did not equal them in draughtsmanship, he excelled in comic depth and conceptualization.[11]

This shifting artistic shape is reflected in his alias, "Crowquill," literally a crow's quill, but also, technically speaking, the steel-tipped pen of his ink drawings, which also references both piquant writing and art, more specifically the fine characteristics of outline. Simon Cooke cleverly observes that in English "Crowquill" sounds similar to *croquis*, the quickly drawn sketch that instantly captures satirical moments. Let me add that the term refers to failings in need of correcting. The expression *to have a crow to pluck with somebody* means "to find a fault in someone," and the verb *to crow* connotes perceived superiority. Both expressions could be used to describe the satirist, a close observer of humanity's shortcomings—who could again also be a critical reader of *Faust*. The "crow" in "Crowquill" also harks back to the extensive tradition of unpleasant and disgraceful animals—deemed unpoetic—often used in parodies. This includes, for example, the frogs and mice in two of the genre's well-known ancestors, the *Batrachomyomachia* or *Battle of the Frogs and Mice*, a mock epic parodying the *Iliad*, and Aristophanes's *The Frogs*, which spoofed the tragic poets. Indeed, just what would such a crow do with Goethe's *Faust*?

As Cooke observed, the polysemy of "Crowquill" also offers the reader a useful tool for deciphering Alfred Forrester's art on three levels: the creation of visual conceits, distortions and elisions; the production of nimble jokes and amusing situations; and an interest in the falsely naive, a humour celebrating awkwardness, while favouring anything disturbing, inconvenient or annoying, according to a coded form (such as "the hook that bites when it is least expected"[12]). Conscious of these layered meanings, Forrester published tongue-in-cheek *A Bundle of Crowquills, dropped by A. Crowquill in his Eccentric Flights*

---

9 BnF Est.: Tb 58 in-4°. Captain Markham Sherwill (1787?–1845), one of the originators of mountaineering and co-author of *Ascent to the Summit of Mont Blanc* (trans. into French in 1827), had a keen interest in literature and lived in France for much of his life.

10 *Metropolitan Magazine* 12, no. 45 (Jan 1835): 17.

11 Sarah Dickson, *Alfred Crowquill: A Few Words about Pipes, Smoking and Tobacco* (New York: New York Public Library, 1947); Simon Cooke, "'If Not a Genius'? Alfred Crowquill as an Illustrator and Applied Artist," *Victorian Web*, last modified 27 May 2017, http://www.victorianweb.org/art/illustration/crowquill/cooke.html.

12 Cooke, "'If Not a Genius'?"

over the Fields of Literature in 1854. Similarly, his parody of *Faust* was a sophisticated exercise and *pas de deux*.

8.2 Travesties

Trite elements in the twelve images and twelve cantos combine to deliberately make the tragedy dull and vulgar. The plates refer to key episodes in Goethe's *Faust*, modified and reinterpreted: the signing of the covenant (not the wager); Auerbach's tavern (where cognac and rum flow freely); Faust in the witch's grotto (not the kitchen), where the image of a plump Margaret appears in the mirror; Faust drinking the magic potion; the first encounter between Faust and Margaret (armed with an umbrella, cf. Fig. 8.1a); Margaret admiring the devil's gift (see below); Margaret showing the gift to the neighbour; "The Decision of the Flower" (a title taken from Retzsch's English copies of the dual garden scene); the travestied scene in the summerhouse; Faust's duel with Valentine (now a pugilist); Faust's confrontation with the devil; and Margaret's refusal to leave the prison (she menaces Faust with a beer stein, cf. Fig. 8.1b). The images distort twelve of Retzsch's twenty-six plates and add jarring details.

Other means contribute to the devaluation, such as reflecting on translation, choosing a significant British poetic line, self-commenting on the style employed, and inserting English cultural signifiers.

The preface introduces the work as a spiced-up *translation* of a poem *dulled* by canonical renderings: "The fact is, our precursors have, one and all, only done this wild poem into tame English."[13] In order to recover the initial ferocity, the new author systematically inserts material and prosaic marks (food, drink, tobacco) to the intellectual drama. Referred to as "the German in an English dress," he is promptly drawn at the end of the preface instead of the usual signature: a character in period costume holding an umbrella and smoking a long meerschaum pipe (Fig. 8.2). This is Crowquill himself, as comparisons with extant portraits show. He stands in a circle (perhaps the magic circle of conjuration from the Faustian vulgate or Marlowe's tragedy, not in Goethe's work) and has a shadow (perhaps the parodied original). He could well be a modern-day Momus, the god of derision, sarcasm and mockery, the son of Nyx or Night in Greek mythology (who was in turn related to Erebus or Darkness).

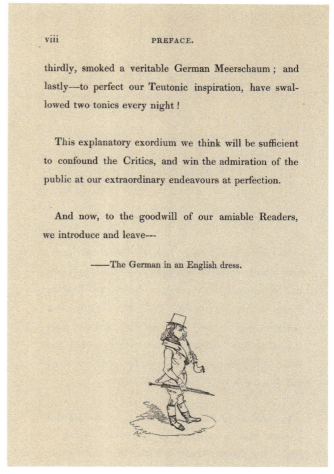

FIGURE 8.2 Alfred Crowquill, "The German in an English dress," in *Faust: A Serio-Comic Poem with Twelve Outline Illustrations* (London: B. B. King, 1834), viii (author's portrait-signature)
COURTESY BEINECKE, YALE UNIVERSITY, SPECK SG8A F6 +834B

The textual content plays belittlingly on values and borrows modern details that anchor the universal drama in the most immediate British and German trappings. Crowquill's Faust is thick-lipped. Besides an umbrella, his short and chubby Madge (Margaret) sports on her chest a prominent cross. The jewels are replaced by sausages, devoured by the priest and coveted by the neighbour (Fig. 8.3a–b). These elements come as no surprise. Retzsch's plates are Crowquill's primary victims. The reader faces a steady visual reworking of metaphysics via grub and frippery. What is surprising, however, is the form of the text. Crowquill inserts such elements into a challenging poetic structure, the stanza of eight iambic pentameters rhyming *abababcc*, derived from the *ottava rima* used in the Italian epics of Ariosto and Tasso. Edmund Spenser had used the latter to create the Spenserian stanza

---

13   Crowquill, *Faust: A Serio-Comic Poem with Twelve Outline Illustrations* (London: B. B. King, 1834), VII.

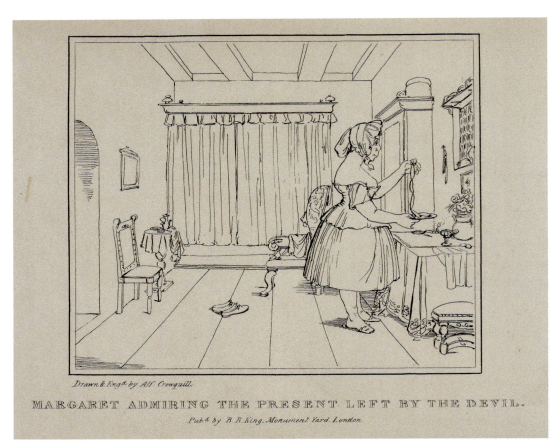

FIGURE 8.3A
Alfred Crowquill, *Margaret Admiring the Present Left by the Devil*, standard version, in *Faust: A Serio-Comic Poem with Twelve Outline Illustrations* (London: B. B. King, 1834), pl. 6
COURTESY HAAB, F 3487, WEIMAR

FIGURE 8.3B
Alfred Crowquill, *Margaret Admiring the Present Left by the Devil*, coloured version, in *Faust: A Serio-Comic Poem with Twelve Outline Illustrations* (London: B. B. King, 1834), pl. 6
COURTESY BEINECKE, YALE UNIVERSITY, SPECK SG8A F6 +834B

THE POWER OF PARODY: A CROW AMONGST NATIONS

for his great English epic *The Faerie Queene*. Without going so far as Spenser's nine verses, Crowquill's stanza draws on the scholarly tradition of heroic-comic poetry. It becomes the chamber housing a series of mix-ups, words with dual or triple meaning, clashes between linguistic registers, and dubious associations between noble and trivial. The result is a sharp and strident resonance that drags the tragedy towards the burlesque. Such an overhaul recalls Samuel Butler's *Hudibras* (1663, 1664, 1678). The great seventeenth-century burlesque poem ridiculed courtly poetry through Sir Hudibras, a wandering knight based on Don Quixote, with one major difference: *Hudibras* was written in rhyming couplets, or flat rhymes, which *flattened* the form. This is hardly the case here.

In addition to asides, moments of self-correction, and talking to oneself, Crowquill's poem includes a number of ironic comments on style and genres, each tested in turn, then discarded. The frequent and conscious display of an ironic stance in the composition itself shows the author fully aware of what he is carrying out. His narrator adopts a meta-literary position, while the reader is invited to consider both the sardonic reworking of the original and the expertise behind its production, as well as the ability of an author-draughtsman conscious of his conceptual skills.

The complex result is to be set in historical and political perspective. Crowquill's composition was published before the *Gründerzeit* in the German-speaking lands, the period extending from the 1848 revolutions to the Viennese stock market crash in 1873. During this time, the German bourgeoisie expanded, grew in economic power, and sought cultural strength in foundational myths. Faust would prove one such myth, and Goethe's tragedy a founding national text. It would end up becoming heavily Germanized via a nationally inspired iconography already developing, produced by Wilhelm von Kaulbach and his disciples in the 1840s or Engelbert Seibertz in the first fully illustrated and luxuriously printed *Faust I* (1852–54).[14] The myth of Faust, the tragedy of universal man for Goethe, would be heavily re-orientated, readjusted, and re-symbolized. Illustrated editions would echo such a strong propensity. By a significant phenomenon of cultural transfer, printed items—especially of major "national" texts—would reflect the rivalry between European nations either fully industrialized or in the process of industrialization.[15]

In such context, parody assumes an unexpected role, at once poetic and political. Crowquill's creation is particularly interesting as the *early* expression of a two-fold

inversion: the distortion of Goethe's play through burlesque excess exorcised in advance the nationalistic appropriation yet to come but *already at work in German iconography*; the parody also announced the disruptive power of cultural highjack and a violent transfer. Caricaturing *Faust* for a British readership profoundly revived the original.

Crowquill gives certain German lines a concrete implication, updates and politicizes them. In the tragic climax of the prison cell, a delirious Margaret does not recognize Faust, who has come to free her. She moans that her beloved abandoned her. In *Faust*, Goethe remains relatively vague: "Far is my friend, who once was nigh" (*Nah war der Freund, nun ist er weit*, F 4435, trans. W. Arndt). In the parody, the lover who left her has become a soldier: "No! '*He has gone to fight the French*,'" cries Madge. Who could be this Faust who went to war to fight the French? Is it one of the German volunteers who stood up against Napoleon's troops in 1813? Goethe's play was published as these wars were taking place (1808). If the play were in the process of becoming nationalized, this Faust would indeed appear to be a brave Teuton soldier resisting the French, ironically viewed through an English lens. Yet Madge jeers the Germans. The stanza ends with the following vehement words: "All *Germans* spill at once that make ungrateful man." The final verse has however nothing to do with Goethe. It is taken from King Lear's curse on the heath, in which he entreats the storm to destroy the earth and all humanity. Crowquill has made a very slight but witty change, quite apparent in the note he has added, *Germans* having replaced the *germens* of Shakespeare's lines: "all *germens* spill at once | That make ingrateful man."[16] The alteration casts Germans as despicable beings who should disappear from earth, just as Margaret rejects this lover who turns out to be German. The soldier left to fight the French is therefore rather English, or even a "German in an English dress" (such as the author), since she hates the Germans whom she vilifies. Upended and updated, the Elizabethan bard becomes catalyst to acclimatize the perennial Franco-British dispute in a parody of the German *Faust*. Madge's lover appears an Englishman who fought the French—at Waterloo, perhaps. A typical spoof-specific characteristic of the burlesque update thus de-Germanizes Faust in a work born of Goethe's *Faust*. The minimal adjustment is no less powerful. The "German in an English dress" is a little cosmopolitan Momus who proves very disruptive indeed.

---

14   Forster-Hahn, "Romantic Tragedy or National Symbol?" 511–36.
15   Stead, "Monumental German *Faust* Editions," 362–94.

16   *King Lear*, 3.2.8–9. Crowquill also uses "ungrateful" instead of "ingrateful," but such variations on spelling are current in Elizabethan tragedies.

8.3 Mischief in Images

The presentation of Crowquill's *Faust* harbours two reading orientations. The engravings, in landscape format like Moses's copies, fit sideways in the vertically printed book. Two routines and two directions make reading a hybrid exercise, pulling the viewer one way or the other. While the insertion of plates results from technical constraints, the push-me-pull-you effect is an additional distortion stressing rivalry between text and image.

Twelve selected and travestied scenes from Retzsch, mostly in outline, more detailed and smaller than either the originals or Moses's copies, use frontal layouts, which lend the parody one of the most notable characteristics of Retzsch's engraved set: theatricality and dramatization. Within this stylistic mould, Crowquill inserts caricatured faces, bodies, and fixtures to grotesque effect. Such are the jewels changed into a chain of sausages, rendering his stocky Margaret a lover of *andouillettes* (cf. Fig. 8.3). The crow's quill also focuses on four supernatural episodes (signing the covenant, Auerbach's tavern, the female apparition in the witch's mirror, the potion rejuvenating Faust) before devoting (just like Retzsch) most of the storyline to Madge's tale (plates V–XII). Madge—the commonly used hypocorism of both Magdalene and Margaret in English—is not only a small scale Margaret but could also be a Magdalene, a name commonly associated in Britain at the time with fallen women and even prostitutes.[17] Despite perfectly knowing her own story (that of Gretchen) and explicitly admitting the fact, she still ends up its victim. Curtain.

One character emerges unscathed from this treatment, bearing well his English name "Old Nick." Compared to Retzsch's devil (Fig. 8.4), he has hardly grown in size (unlike Margaret), and his sharp silhouette, crowned with his long Retzschian feather, leads the dance. Crowquill endows him with yet another trait: a long German pipe, which he dispassionately smokes in plates III and XI (Fig. 8.5), the very accessory that Crowquill had adopted for his double self-portrait as "German in an English dress" at the beginning of the booklet (cf. Fig. 8.2). The meerschaum pipe had signalled a new attempt at translation, meant to restore the true spirit and meaning of the wild poem that had been blunted: "Now we propose, not to give a dull and literal Translation of our Author, but the true spirit and meaning of the Poem in the vernacular."[18]

---

17   Susan Haskins, *Mary Magdalen: Myth and Metaphor* (London: Harper Collins, 1993), 317–19.
18   Crowquill, *Faust*, VII.

We may then trust that if Faust has been anglicized, and if this dubious Madge defends her virtue using that symbolic British accessory, an umbrella, then the only true German spirit at the heart of the parody is the devil with his meerschaum pipe. As the English saying goes, *the devil is in the details*—to which the German answers *der Teufel sitzt im Detail*, much like the French *le diable est dans les détails*. The fact that he shares his trademark pipe with the author, the "German in an English dress," suggests that a diabolical German imp lives on in this parody. The latter is both a caricature of the German play via text and image and an Anglo-Germanic hoax. The pipe turns Old Nick into another facet of Momus by association with the author. Or is it the opposite? A review published in the *Weekly True Sun*, and recited by the publisher on the second edition's back cover, highlights both the devil's polymorphic nature and his distinctly German character by playing on the words "germane" (i.e., relevant, appropriate) and "German":

> The many-figured tempter of Faust never took more shapes than Faust himself has assumed, literary and pictorial. Here is another version of his story, quite as "germane to the matter" as the most German of them all.

While it cannot be said that the on-going play on words (germane, germen, German) was an invitation to return to the country of origin, what happened has the flavour of a piquant sequel, inseparable from the spirit of parody.

8.4 Homecoming and "Who Loves a Laugh"

Seven years later, in 1841, a parody of Crowquill emerged in the form of a small landscape album under absinthe-coloured cover (14.7 × 19 cm), reduced to the sole images, entitled *Bilder zu Goethe's Faust*, and issued by Carl Friedrich Doerffling (Dörffling) in Leipzig, the heart of German publishing. It is signed Anselmus Lachgern, literally "who loves a laugh," a pseudonym that several catalogues on the posterity of Goethe's *Faust* attribute to Crowquill. Although this is unlikely, the author's real identity has to date proved impossible to unmask.

In reality, "Lachgern" is simply a German translation of "Philogelos," or "friend of laughter," a collection of colloquial jokes or humbugs in ancient Greek, often targeting highbrows. It was first drafted in the third or fourth century CE and has frequently been republished since the seventeenth century. As for the plates, a comparison

THE POWER OF PARODY: A CROW AMONGST NATIONS 263

FIGURE 8.4
Moritz Retzsch,
Faust blaming
Mephistopheles, *Umrisse zu Goethe's Faust gezeichnet von Retsch* (Stuttgart & Tübingen: Cotta, 1816), pl. 23
COURTESY HAAB,
F 3487, WEIMAR

FIGURE 8.5
Alfred Crowquill, *Faust Hears that Margaret is in Prison*, in *Faust: A Serio-Comic Poem with Twelve Outline Illustrations* (London: B. B. King, 1834), pl. 11
COURTESY HAAB,
F 3482, WEIMAR

between Crowquill's set and the new (probably litho-graphed) version reveals several varying details. The German album is composed of retouched copies, not strict reproductions of Crowquill's compositions. The unknown artist who produced it adopted the German *Umriss* tradition. In several instances, he even referred to Retzsch's original prints. His line is much more precise than Crowquill's, and he adds to his drawings several details either simply sketched or roughly depicted in the English booklet. The contents of Faust's jars are imprecise in Crowquill's drawing (Fig. 8.6) but they contain a foetus and a heart in Lachgern's plate of the study (Fig. 8.7). The synecdoche sums up Margaret's story, as it did in Retzsch's set. Several other details differ, for instance, Lachgern's Gothic arch to the back is more pointed, the stove more carefully decorated. Reversing Crowquill's skeletal left-facing animal, the bones of perhaps a monkey, turned right atop the right-hand bookcase, hovers over a leftward-gazing human skull, again imitating a scene conceived by Retzsch (cf. Fig. 4.3 and 2.21). It is quite possible that the malicious pairing of man and animal reflect the spirit of copy and countertype figuring on the back cover as a final signature (see below). Aping has long been associated with distorted imitation.

At the time, Doerffling, a Leipzig publisher later in partnership with Franke, published works translated from English,[19] and portfolios of prints by region, featuring panoramic views and landscapes (*vedute*). These medium-sized steel-engraved plates (26 × 31 cm) focused on a central view surrounded by smaller outline images depicting other landscapes, urban prospects, monuments, and typical local scenes. In one of them, entitled *Unter-Italien* (Southern Italy),[20] the main view—a panorama of Naples—is embellished by a series of quaint goings-on. According to Andreas Beck, two of them are end-grain wood engravings by John Jackson, published in the 1833 *Penny Magazine* and later reprinted in *Le Magasin pittoresque* and *Das Pfennig-Magazin*.[21] Doerffling's activ-

ities and commercial exchanges with Great Britain support the idea that Lachgern's album is a lithograph copy of Crowquill's imported and retouched plates, probably by a German artist.

No specific intention is revealed, yet the components speak for themselves. Both the nickname "Lachgern" and the caricatures copied from Crowquill, who was spoofing Retzsch, form a parody of parody, not only of Retzsch's set but also of Goethe's play, achieved by way of *new captions* and the *omission* of one plate. Instead of translating Crowquill (whose lettering imitated Boosey's), the captions are now lines taken straight from Goethe's own *Faust*, which serves as first and foremost target. Furthermore, all of the original jeering plates have been used except for the final, the prison cell that Margaret refuses to leave. Thus, the slim German set opens with the covenant (pl. 1) and ends with Faust confronting the devil (pl. 11, cf. Fig. 8.5), in other words, with an unresolved tension. The omission of the prison scene, in which Margaret is redeemed by celestial voices, deprives the German copy of any glimpse of redemption, no matter how caricatured. The item seems to suggest that the story could begin all over again with Faust enslaved to the contract signed in the first plate. This is no less piquant.

Further elements appear to be encoded. The title duplicates Cornelius's, *Bilder zu Goethe's Faust*, while the copied (and enlarged) plates recover the dimensions of Retzsch's originals (Crowquill's are smaller). They are enclosed in double frames characteristic of Retzsch's English copies by Moses, and not the initial thin line. Without insisting on this detail, present after all in Crowquill, and which could simply signal targeting the English popular copies, the plates sport top left an easily recognizable element from Retzsch's prototype: simple numerals followed by a full stop. Strongly recalling Retzsch, the detail works as a hallmark of authenticity in a clashing context. In other words, Lachgern's German copy of Crowquill's plates pours the intentionally inflated English parody into a graphic mould combining the first two German sets (Cornelius and Retzsch) that helped read Goethe's *Faust* through iconography.

The German parody tried to pass as a British product, and succeeded, convincing most compilers of *Faust*

---

19   For example, *Die Frau, nach dem Englischen der Mistress Norton von T. Vockerode* (Leipzig: C. F. Dörffling, 1835), one of many works by the feminist and polygraph Caroline Sheridan Norton, or the anthology *The English Novelist: A Collection of Tales by the Most Celebrated English Writers* (Leipzic: William Engelmann / C. F. Doerffling, 1837 or 1839).

20   *Italien, Neapel: Golf von Baja*, etc., c.1844, steel engraving, 26 × 31 cm, Antiquariat Murr, Bamberg.

21   "Neapolitan Maccaroni-Eaters," *Penny Magazine* 2, no. 87 (10 Aug 1833): 305, repr. "Scènes italiennes: le marchand de macaroni," *Le Magasin pittoresque* 1, no. 51 (1833): 401, repr. "Die neapolitanischen Maccaroniesser," *Das Pfennig-Magazin*, no. 38 (18 Jan

1834): 297; "The Carriages of Naples," *Penny Magazine* 2, no. 90 (31 Aug 1833), repr. "Les voitures à Naples," *Le Magasin pittoresque* 2, no. 33 (1834): 257, and "Die neapolitanische Kalesche," *Das Pfennig-Magazin*, no. 48 (29 Mar 1834): 350. Both comic incidents feature on either side of the Naples panoramic view in *Unter-Italien* (kindly communicated by Andreas Beck).

FIGURE 8.6
Alfred Crowquill, *Faust Signs Over his Soul to the Devil*, in *Faust: A Serio-Comic Poem with Twelve Outline Illustrations* (London: B. B. King, 1834), pl. 1
COURTESY HAAB, F 3482, WEIMAR

FIGURE 8.7
Mephistopheles: Nur eins! Um Lebens oder Sterbens willen. Bitt'ich nur ein Paar Zeilen aus, in *Bilder zu Goethes Faust von Anselmus Lachgern* (Leipzig: C. F. Doerffling, 1841), pl. 1
COURTESY HAAB, F 3467, WEIMAR

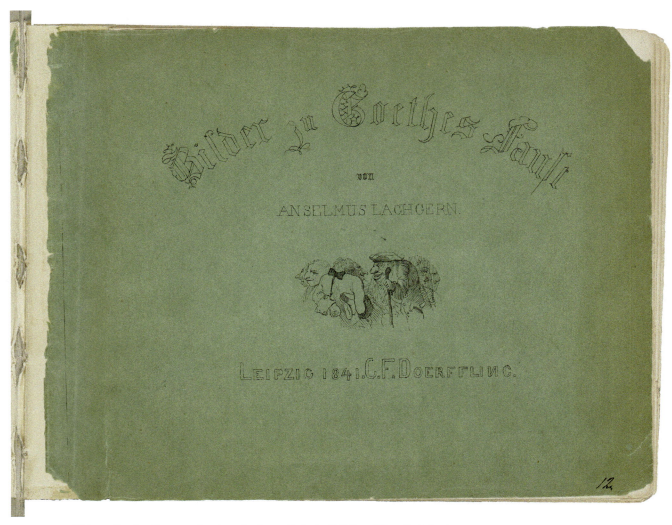

FIGURE 8.8 *Bilder zu Goethes Faust von Anselmus Lachgern* (Leipzig: C. F. Doerffling, 1841), front cover
COURTESY HAAB, F 3467, WEIMAR

catalogues to attribute it to Crowquill. Its lithographed front cover (probably by two different hands as the differing lettering suggests) introduces a new element specifically made to drive home the idea of its English identity: a vignette of grouped Englishmen with features distorted in a style reminiscent of Hogarth or 1830s English satirical drawings (Fig. 8.8). And yet it only parades as English. In truth, it is a "(masked) German in an English dress," astutely inversing the very process used by Crowquill.

Lachgern's Germanized copy of Crowquill is to my knowledge the first iconographic set to assail Goethe's *Faust* only nine years after Goethe's demise. While *Faust* textual parodies (only two earlier than Lachgern, and some illustrated, but later) will flourish in Germany over the years and have attracted copious scholarly attention, the satirical iconography of Goethe's *Faust* has been considered only in examples tardier than the complex masked distortion offered by this anonymous Momus.[22]

Lachgern's creation is a shrewd and powerful tool. It cleverly uses easily recognizable and standardized scenes (as initially epitomized by Retzsch), and its violent

---

22 Theodor Verweyen and Gunther Witting, *Die Parodie in der neueren deutschen Literatur: Eine systematische Einführung* (Darmstadt: Wissenschaftliche Buchgesellschaft, 1979); Verweyen and Witting, *Die Kontrafaktur: Vorlage und Verarbeitung in Literatur, Bildender Kunst, Werbung und politischen Plakat* (Konstanz: Universitätsverlag, 1987); Waltraud Wende-Hohenberger and Karl Riha, eds., *Faust Parodien: Eine Auswahl satirischer Kontrafakturen, Fort- und Weiterdichtungen mit einem Nachwort* (Frankfurt: Insel, 1989); Waltraud Wende, *Goethe-Parodien: zur Wirkungsgeschichte eines Klassikers* (Stuttgart: J. B. Metzler, 1999). See the early textual parodies by Franz Grillparzer (1811–22) and Friedrich Theodor Vischer (1835), in *Faust-Parodien*, 11–20.

FIGURE 8.9 *Bilder zu Goethes Faust von Anselmus Lachgern* (Leipzig: C. F. Doerffling, 1841), back cover
COURTESY HAAB, F 3467, WEIMAR

message is driven home unswervingly. The image stocks and supplies a conglomerate distortion of the play's key scenes that directly clash with Goethe's *Faust* excerpts used as captions. In Crowquill's virulence Rümann had symptomatically discerned "the intention to denigrate" Retzsch, but left it to the reader and his own appreciation of "the German artist" to decide whether Crowquill had succeeded. He took no account of the offense to Goethe.[23] What would he have thought of Lachgern? The latter's parody is also a pioneering attempt. Indeed, the only examples I know of sharp *Faust* spoofs using disruptive images are not only posterior by at least twenty years, but also miscellaneous. Such is the "humoristic album" by Charles Benoit, Adam West and Roland Weibexahl, *Neue Bilder zu deutschen Dichtern* (*New Images after German Poets*), whose range is broader with only its third fascicle aiming at *Faust*. Lithographed in Leipzig, and published by Adolph Werl in Grimma and Leipzig, it postdates Lachgern by sixteen years (1857). An earlier attempt, still later than Lachgern by eight years, is again an assortment in periodical form, the *Humoristich-satirisches Bilder-Album oder Bilder mit und ohne Worte* (*Album of Humorous-Satirical Images or Images with or without Words*), reported to be by "several Rhine artists," lithographed by David Levy Elkan (1808–65) in Cologne, and published by F. Wengler in Aachen. Its second fascicle (1849) opens on a parody of Faust as Prussian dragon officer tailing a mincing Gretchen. Both the latter use a standard process in heroic-comic poetry, the displacement of well-known original verses to comment on trite,

---

23   Rümann, *Das illustrierte Buch*, 98.

vulgar or hackneyed incidents. Lachgern adopts a similar technique, yet the verses of the original comment scenes, twice perverted and twisted, of Retzsch's originals via his English copies. The gesture is exceptionally arresting: it amply proves how venerated was the poet Goethe, since the parody adopts such a circuitous and thrice deformed contrivance; yet, it is also because of these twice-warped disguises that its violation is all the more effective.

Indeed, the filching was diabolically complex. It apes an original translated in images (Goethe's *Faust* viewed through the dual lens of Retzsch and Cornelius). By further altering, pilfering even, it leads astray an English parody of Retzsch's plates as had been copied in Britain. Still, it may also be interpreted as the outcome of irreverent humour, of second-degree readings, i.e., drollness and jeering—an offbeat biting spirit integral to Goethe's *Faust*. Lachgern's back cover (Fig. 8.9) reproduces indeed the *countertype* of "the German in an English dress," the visual signature of Crowquill's preface to his *Faust* parody (cf. Fig. 8.2). Lachgern's last image is a *reverse* copy. This English Momus, with his meerschaum pipe, stoically echoes Mephistopheles, also depicted in the *penultimate* plate of Crowquill's parody as an unwaveringly evil spirit calmly smoking a similar pipe (cf. Fig. 8.5). The latter is however Lachgern's *last* plate, since he had rejected Crowquill's final, depriving his own *Faust* of (even mock) redemption. Is this Mephistopheles a malicious critic? A phlegmatic mocking god or demon? The taciturn son of carnival nights is perhaps grafting the poetics of English caricature onto the benchmark German images by Retzsch and Cornelius. These are recognizable beyond bombastic inflation—just like Goethe's verses quoted beneath them.

8.5   A Mocking Deity with a Meerschaum Pipe

Goethe's *Faust* opens with a key introductory scene, a "Prelude on the Stage" in which the Theatre Director converses with a Poet and a Merry Person on plays and genres liable to fill playhouses. Goethe's *Faust* itself, with its ample variety of keys, shades, and pitches, could well be an answer to the question. Besides, the successive introductory parts and their chain of spectacles and audiences make of *Faust I* a play within a play within a play.[24] In historicist nineteenth-century Faustian iconography, strongly jingoistic in inspiration, the Poet is frequently given Goethe's features and the Merry Person those of Mephistopheles, the irreverent cunning spirit that is as much at home in *Faust*

as gravity. Crowquill's parody reveals this among other things through the meerschaum pipe, as does the set's homecoming to Germany thanks to the "lover of laughter."

The several facets of this *Faust* parody ultimately favour Mephistopheles.[25] In Crowquill's version, the devil embodies an ironic poetic, the burlesque spirit of farce, and the flip side of a solemn composition. Goethe's *Faust*—canonized in the nineteenth century by commentary, monumental editions, or excessively heroic and Germanized iconography—will end up becoming a sedate work. Contrariwise, Crowquill brings his composition to an end because, once imprisoned, his Muse grows gloomy—and this is what is unbearable.[26]

The first-degree mechanism of parody is maybe just that: an externalized display of travesty assaulting its model in excessive spirit. When parody works, the model inevitably suffers under the weight of distortion. Reduced to a mere pattern, it is flaunted precisely to be satirized—and satire may at times sound or seem thin. The case is different for this work, which exploits parody to the fifth degree.

Furthermore, Faust has long been linked to burlesque elements, before even his legend was arranged into a story in the unsigned *History of Dr Johann Faust* (1587). In 1559 he figures among the characters of a carnival show; and in a 1588 description of the Nuremberg carnival, Gretchen is abducted by Faust.[27] According to legend, he dreadfully perishes in Staufen, south of Freiburg-im-Breisgau, with its vivid Alemannic tradition of carnivals, witches' revels, and fools' parades. Such forms of expression nonetheless reflect more popular, widespread, and sometimes toned down versions. Conversely, Crowquill's and Lachgern's *Faust* manifest heavily political, social, and ideological cultural confrontations. They are born from and contribute to a widespread phenomenon of relocating, copying and reformulating, characteristics specific to centuries of media-driven modernity among nations in political conflict and commercial rivalry. Crowquill's burlesque booklet critically re-reads the initial play from over the Channel thanks to a distorting English lens and dual means of expression. But prints and texts travel, and circulation accrues their impact, one outcome being Lachgern's album.

---

24   See p. 272.

25   Cf. Helmut Schanze, *Faust-Konstellationen: Mythos und Medien* (Munich: W. Fink, 1999), 95–97.

26   Crowquill, *Faust*, 32.

27   Wegner, 125.

Revising, thanks to parody, a myth compelled to gradual and excessive national appropriation, ends up revealing an aspect neatly enclosed in Goethe's very *Faust*: Mephistopheles's potential, not so much as a tempting demon, but a sharp and mocking force against national—even nationalistic—canonization. This is what Lachgern achieved in German terrain by importing and reworking Crowquill's burlesque prints and by labelling them after Goethe's original *Faust*. His booklet has been much read since most surviving copies come to us in very poor condition. "The role of burlesque," wrote Pierre Mac Orlan in relation to Faust, "is the demon's strength and the secret of his resistance to all the seductions of sentimentality."[28] He could have also added "the seductions of jingoism."

---

28 Mac Orlan, "Daragnès et les livres," in *Œuvres complètes*, vol. 12, 2, *Masques sur mesure*, ed. Gilbert Sigaux (Évreux: Cercle du Bibliophile, 1970), 206.

CHAPTER 9

Outlines in the Limelight

En route to Marburg in 2010, I visited Frankfurt's cathedral between two trains. Under the July sun, over glistening rooftops, its spire attracts the eye from the quays of the river Main, as it drew crowds and pilgrims from afar over the centuries. I did not know then that the imposing building had become during the nineteenth century a symbol of national unity. No merely impressive construction, *Kaiserdom* is the imperial cathedral where coronations of monarchs of the Holy Roman Empire had been held.

Oddly I felt, turning from the crossing into a chapel, as if I had walked into Retzsch's plate 18, the artist's response to Goethe's "A Cathedral." This is Retzsch's rebel print, purposely placed out of textual order. It stages an evil spirit torturing Margaret while *Dies Irae* resounds below lofty vaulting. A mass for the dead tolls her mother's funeral and blame has been laid on Gretchen. Goethe's demon powerfully evokes God's wrath to burden the girl with guilt and despair (Fig. 9.1).

Retzsch's perspective view is a ploy harbouring multiple vistas. He has combined the side view of a priest officiating at a main altar on the left with a drawn-out bench on the right. Far right, three further priests under a polyptych create the illusion of a second populous congregation celebrating mass. In an ornate gallery, a choir of singing monks perch between scenes of the Nativity (main altar, left) and Crucifixion (altar far right), two pictures framing Jesus's Gospel of salvation. Between them, high up on the left-hand pillar, a half-truncated figure, the resurrected Christ crushing the dragon's head, is designed to echo Saint George spearing the dragon on the stove of Faust's study, when the poodle monstrously transmutes and Mephistopheles appears (pl. 3 & 4, cf. Fig. 2.23, 4.3, & 2.21). Retzsch links Faust and Gretchen through related symbols, but the key move here is to quit intimacy for the common ground of public space. His cathedral scene stages the universal dimension Goethe's play possesses from the outset. The artist knows it too well, being the first to open his *Faust* set with the Prologue in Heaven. In the cathedral, he brings Gretchen (and through her Faust himself) into humanity's common plight and relates them to an audience's variegated destinies yet shared sense of piety. He animates the multi-vista space with hotchpotch figures. Nobles, the middle class and poor, weak and strong, modest and proud, infirm and vigorous, all mingle. (Delacroix copied both pious female afore left pillar and devout lady with book afore far-off altar, cf. Fig. 6.1a and

6.2). Margaret is just one of them, and her torture by an evil spirit is but an episode in the common predicament, either of damnation or redemption. Still, her veiled figure swooning on the bench upfront right, while the faun-like spirit waves an ominous finger, will not be lost on either Delacroix or Ary Scheffer. Her fallen prayer book, lain open resurfaces in Delacroix's lithograph of Margaret's dejection and tedium.

Recollection of Retzsch's use of space hosting diverse parallel events, explains my impression inside Frankfurt's *Kaiserdom* of having walked right into his setting. I have no means to ascertain that the composition was stirred by this particular minster's plan; nor even that Retzsch intended it as an allusive tribute to Goethe's native city. Besides, the cathedral I myself visited has been twice reconstructed since a devastating 1867 fire and heavy World War II bombardments. Most probably the artist had in mind other consecrated interiors (his friend Naeke had recourse to Meissen cathedral, closer to Dresden). Yet, by the wealth and symbolism of his designs, he imposes himself as Goethe's stage manager-cum-assistant playwright in one.

As stage manager, he bestows and allots space, devises fittings, and contrives underpinnings; as assistant playwright, he plies together several deeds and infuses the still mute picture with potential performance. True, this singular cathedral scene *rewrites* Goethe and his exclusive focus on Gretchen's trials, replaced here by multiple *dramatis personae* in various stances. The assortment of Retzsch's particularities gives his viewer food for thought, hinting at the tragedy's collective meaning. The scene is also an exception. In Retzsch an episode usually evolves in two or three frames of shared background with player-like characters carrying the plot either through action or strong emotion. His entire set may be seen as a playhouse in print, yet with a discrepancy lurking between staging and performance. Indeed, its double hold over *mise en scène* and acting engaged with period concepts of theatre and aesthetics. It backed, enhanced, and superseded them, marking a definite turn or surrender, whose yield, I argue, was typification.

9.1 Aptitudes and Assets

Specific qualities were needed for such agency and Moritz did not lack them. Home theatricals staged with his

---

© EVANGHELIA STEAD, 2023 | DOI:10.1163/9789004543010_012

This is an open access chapter distributed under the terms of the CC BY-NC-ND 4.0 license.

FIGURE 9.1 Moritz Retzsch, Cathedral scene, *Umrisse zu Goethe's Faust gezeichnet von Retsch* (Stuttgart & Tübingen: Cotta, 1816), pl. 18
COURTESY HAAB, F 3487, WEIMAR

siblings in fantastical costumes after weird self-devised plots were a youthful pastime as the Retzsch brothers' illustrated journal shows (Fig. 9.2). Performances were not limited to their youth either: Moritz's own *Chess Players* composition would be enacted at his home by relatives and long-time friends. In costumes borrowed from the Dresden court theatre, a *tableau vivant* in rosy light and to music would honour a birthday of his later years.[1] In 1840, he staged the Radebeul vinedressers' parade, consecrated in eight sequential lithographed sheets, skilfully blending mythology, biblical displays, triumphal bacchanalia and a modern show.

His prints became the surest templates for *Faust* to gain access to the limelight. Scholarship has stressed now and again the practical difficulty of producing *Faust*, a play rich in supernatural episodes, showing Heaven, God himself and the Earth Spirit, and an overwhelming number of settings in breath-taking succession. From Julius Petersen and Carl Niessen to Bernd Mahl, critics stress how the graphic arts settled unresolved questions.[2] Clarity, contour and definition are remarkably prominent in their words:

> The visual arts jumped to the place of the absent stage; they turned the visible side of theatrical content into perceptible coinage; they brought to life the vision of *sharply outlined appearances* (*scharf umrissenen Erscheinungen*); they granted Faust, Mephistopheles, Gretchen and Madam Martha their

---

1 Th. S., "Ein Lebensbild," 9b.

2 Petersen, *Goethes Faust auf der deutschen Bühne* (Leipzig: Quelle & Meyer, 1929), 7–8; Niessen, "Faust auf der Bühne," *Westermanns Monatshefte* 146, no. 871 (1929): 55; Mahl, *Goethes "Faust" auf der Bühne, 1806–1998: Fragment, Ideologiestück, Spieltext* (Stuttgart: J. B. Metzler, 1999), 8–9.

FIGURE 9.2 August and Moritz Retzsch, Home theatricals, ink and wash coloured drawing, 1800, in *Weinbergs Scenen, aus dem Leben der beiden Brüder August und Moritz Retzsch*
SKK, INV. NR. CA 53 V 74, DRESDEN, PHOTO CATERINA MICKSCH

characteristic miens and costumes; they grouped these figures afore a stage backdrop: in this way they gave the smallest detail of the spectacle *such a definite outline* (*einen so bestimmten Umriß*) that later stage tradition could at first do nothing but give way to the guidance of the visual arts.[3]

Graphic artistry referred to by stage directors made up for deficient stage flexibility and adaptability, mostly using Cornelius, Delacroix, Ramberg, and Retzsch, a record-holder with a complete scenario in twenty-six views: Retzsch's outlines "are probably the noblest and the surest to abide by. I will seek to obtain them and send them for you to inspect," wrote Eckermann to actress Auguste Kladzig in 1829.[4]

There is however more to *Faust* than just a crushing sequence of technical difficulties to overcome. Beyond the initial opening discussion between Theatre Director, Poet and Merry Person comparing views on any play's aim and latitude and how to attract crowds to the performance, *Faust* discloses an intricate structure of "theatre within the theatre within the theatre." Nobody has better expressed it than Frederick Burwick: "The 'Prelude in the Theatre' is used to introduce the 'Prologue in Heaven', which in turn introduces the 'Tragedy'. We are to understand that Poet, Director, and Merry Person are witnesses to the wager between God and Mephistopheles, and that God himself becomes a spectator of the 'Tragedy.'"[5] With this in mind, Retzsch's cathedral scene gains substance. Influenced by Goethe's text and later iconography in isolating Gretchen's plight with commiseration, we may ask: *Why look for her in a crowd?* When put to the test, most students overlook her. Yet Retzsch enhances the tragedy's

---

[3] Petersen, *Goethes Faust auf der deutschen Bühne*, 7–8, my emphasis.
[4] L. G. [Ludwig Geiger], "Eckermann an eine Schauspielerin," *Goethe-Jahrbuch* 17 (1896): 261.

[5] Burwick, "Goethe and Hugo," 695.

collective dimension and implications, whence the importance of his cathedral scene.

Other major advantages, aptly identified by Sigrun Brunsiek and Viola Hildebrand-Schat, stress the careful construction of a dramatic viewpoint, a frontal view, and a slightly elevated position from beginning to end. The spectator embraces the depth of scene (or stage) from back- to fore-ground at a glance, as if in a theatre, while the close association (*Verklammerung*) of characters and *milieux* contradicts traditional use of outline.[6] Let me add that specific frame dimensions per location and special details create ambiance. Faust's study, the witch's kitchen, Margaret's bedroom, Martha's house, and the prison, stage-set the prospect to a potent emotion or a key event: the devil's advent, Faust's rejuvenation, intrusion into the virgin's chamber, Margaret's temptation, her forebodings, guilt, and refusal to flee. Emotion and action carry the plot. Interiors are thoroughly furnished, the objects multiple, the outfits delineated as upcoming props. Exterior settings and prospects further action: flat country for the poodle's appearance, a street to meet, a garden where courting couples cross, a square for a deadly duel, the witches' mountain, a bare landscape where Faust reprimands Mephistopheles. As potential production kits, they re-emerged here and there on theatre plateaux after silently pleasing armchair reader-spectators at home. In both cases, a play impossible to stage had become visible and memorable.

Faust I on stage marked a decisive step in making Goethe's tragedy known, albeit with barefaced changes. Zelter's 1820 letters to Goethe see the major benefit of Radziwill's Berlin anniversary (partial) performance as "having brought to light this poem until then swathed in the thickest shadows."[7] Tellingly, in 1819–20 the text was not yet available in Berlin and had to be sent for in Leipzig. Nine years later, "the play was terribly mutilated," wrote young Victor Pavie to his father from Weimar on 20 August 1829.[8] As handbook, readers still relied on it for the show: in 1829 Weimar, engrossed students piously followed the text and its "mysteries" line after line, "more devout on their benches than catechumens," wrote Pavie.[9] However imperfect, every staging secured Goethe's notoriety and imposed *Faust*'s popularity.

Throughout the first half of the nineteenth century Retzsch's prints led such developments in supplying settings, props, backdrops, and costumes. Yet, Arthur Rümann still recognized their dominance over the stage in the 1930s.[10] Such remarkable endurance with respect to twentieth-century theatre's radical changes in aesthetics raises many questions. As modern spectators, we would expect them to transmute, acquire a second life in a three-dimensional playhouse. Still, they sponsored theatre choices both romantic and neoclassical down to actors' poses and attitudes. There is no paradox here: the latter modelled repetitive fixed elements, the former borrowed heavily and transformed.

Eckermann's 1829 oft-quoted letter to actress Auguste Kladzig on the forthcoming Braunschweig *Faust* is revealing. He had discussed specifics with Goethe, meaning *costumes* and *décors*.[11] On stage, illustration and depiction dominated. Everything written for the imagination's sake was left aside (*alle undarstellbaren, für die Imagination geschriebene Scenen weggelassen sind*).[12] Eckermann's main concern was clarity, and outlines delineated unmistakeably, with trades working to predesigned patterns: "the physical aspect of the main characters, as well as their costumes, surroundings, and background, is brought to the senses in a special and clear manner (*speziell und deutlich vor die Sinne gebracht ist*), so that from stage-set painter to theatre dressmaker no one can be unsure about what he has to do."[13] Unsurprisingly, Retzsch and his world-famous outlines (*weltberühmt*) are mentioned first by Eckermann, before Ramberg, and—despite his "somewhat wild talent" (*etwas wildes Talent*)—Delacroix. However, the 1829 Braunschweig performance, historically the first *Faust* staged in German lands, had substantially changed Goethe's finale with Faust ultimately damned. Ernst August Klingemann's version had altered Goethe's grandiose and cosmic dimensions and the Prologue in Heaven was suppressed. As if to react, the poet would not attend the 1829 Weimar performance after Klingemann in his honour. Eckermann's taxonomy of artists (above) mirrors both Goethe's 1829 judgment of Retzsch as "tidy" (*geleckt*), seizing "the merely depictable," and his ambiguous appraisal of Delacroix. What satisfied Eckermann was the outline's agency shrunk to explanatory function. Perhaps Goethe's detached comment to Stieler echoed disappointment at such theatre trappings.

In the Anglophone world Retzsch's prints had accelerated linguistic translation of *Faust*. They also crucially

---

6   Brunsiek, *Auf dem Weg der alten Kunst*, 178–79 and n. 512; Hildebrand-Schat, *Moritz Retzschs Illustrationen*, 216–17.

7   BwGZ, 1:610.

8   André Pavie, *Médaillons romantiques: Lettres inédites* (Paris: Émile Paul, 1909), 84.

9   Ibid., 85.

10   Rümann, *Das illustrierte Buch*, 225.

11   Hans Gerhard Gräf, *Goethe über seine Dichtungen*, vol. 4, 2, *Die dramatischen Dichtungen* (Frankfurt: Rütten & Loening, 1904), 479n.

12   [Geiger], "Eckermann an eine Schauspielerin," 261.

13   Ibid., 260–61.

translated it into performance within and beyond German borders. Still, fittings and fixtures were not the only concern. One would expect costumes to be pliable; that overpowering romantic characters flesh out genuinely passionate individuals, not present themselves frontally, in profile, or in characteristic gestures frozen in time à la Flaxman. Theatre's elasticity and ebullience challenge set countenances, airs, and stances. How could Retzsch's prints resist movement, expression or action on stage?

Such questions prompt several answers, some novel, even surprising, starting with Retzsch's impact on Goethe himself.

9.2   Weimar Trials

Seven sketches in Goethe's "Theatre Drawings" bear on *Faust*. The 1812 *Tag- und Jahreshefte* show him "induced," as if against himself, to "even design stage sets and other requisites" (*ja sogar Decorationen und sonstiges Erforderniß zu entwerfen*).[14] The 1810–12 Weimar production, initiated by actor Pius Alexander Wolff and Goethe's secretary Friedrich Wilhelm Riemer, never came about but has left several traces.[15] One of these, a dynamic stage diagram in swift pencil strokes, partly heightened in ink, pictures God, Mephistopheles and three angels amid clouds (Fig. 9.3). The tragedy's grandiose opening is rare in *Faust* iconography but for Retzsch's pl. 1, consciously responsive to its importance in the play and a most probable model (cf. Fig. 5.1). In Goethe's diary the first entry for the inconclusive theatre attempt dates 13 November 1810, shortly after he had seen Retzsch's compositions in Dresden (September). Cornelius's synthetic title page, also picturing God atop middle, is posterior. In another three drawings, uncanny or demonic presences in Faust's study (a witch on a broom, the Earth Spirit, and the poodle gigantically transmuting) emerge within a frontal wide window, as in Rembrandt's *The Alchemist* (renamed *Faust*), in towering Gothic style as in Nauwerck, yet are always framed by bookcases, as in Retzsch. Lips's retouched frontispiece after Rembrandt shows but one bookcase. The artist's prescience further reflects on Goethe's own poodle's massively rendered muzzle within the study's large bay (Fig. 9.4). His gleaming eyes and wide nostrils are strongly

reminiscent of Retzsch's formidable shape next to Faust's stove (cf. Fig. 4.3).

Similarities are obvious in the Heaven drawing (God's centrality, angels' praise), yet differences tell of aesthetic stances at variance. In Goethe's design, a bearded, naked-breasted Jupiter solemnly sits full centre, confronted by an erect and robust Mephistopheles emerging from drapery bottom left. Three seraphim, hailing or reverentially bowing, hint at a larger crowd. In striking opposition, Retzsch's Mephistopheles, with Lucifer's wings, defies a fully draped, quietly majestic Judeo-Christian God. As in his other *Faust* compositions, Goethe pursues a vivid dramatic atmosphere and his free strokes establish an impression. Conversely, Retzsch's arrangement is of careful rendering. Both have presumably been influenced by Flaxman's frontal, central and domineering Olympian, in two of his *Iliad* outlines, *Jupiter Sending the Evil Dream to Agamemnon* and *The Council of the Gods*.[16] Yet, Goethe owes Flaxman only his central figure; his conception of Heaven is of no other than Retzsch.

Research into the Weimar performances yields further food for thought. On 3 January 1821, painter, engraver and restorer Carl Lieber asked Goethe's permission via Meyer to present *Tableaux from Faust* for eight successive days in Weimar's Harmonie, a social circle of the time. The venture was under preparation by an artistic trio: the same Lieber, court engraver Carl August Schwerdgeburth, and *décor* painter, engraver and actor Carl Holdermann.[17] Lieber asked in parallel for Cornelius's prints from the library because his partners thought Retzsch's plates 8, 18 and 20 "should be left aside" (*wegbleiben sollen*). The latter are all pivotal scenes in public space (the meeting, Gretchen at the cathedral, Valentine dying), the first in a plain street with no cathedral background, the latter two excessively crowded. Cornelius's would help replace them with significant differences. Lieber, Schwerdgeburth and Holdermann had joined skills to produce a selection of *tableaux vivants* from *Faust*, further enhanced in 1822, as attests a Riemer letter to Goethe inviting him to a "much praised performance" not always open to the public. Extra scenes had been added.[18] Such a choice may have satisfied Goethe's desire to see the play enhanced rather than belittled by stage snags. He had himself meaningfully used *tableaux vivants* in his *Elective Affinities* and their specific aesthetics.

The example fascinatingly shows how a group of artists' grasp of *Faust* piloted selection and combined prints

---

14   WA 1, 36:75.

15   *Die sieben Zeichnungen Goethes zu seinem "Faust"*, ed. H. Wahl (Weimar: Den Freunden des Goethehauses, 1925); Petra Maisak, *Johann Wolfgang Goethe: Zeichnungen* (Stuttgart: Philipp Reclam Jun., 1996), 249.

16   Maisak, *Goethe: Zeichnungen*, 251.

17   GSA 28/92, 12, 19.

18   GSA 28/96, 75.

OUTLINES IN THE LIMELIGHT 275

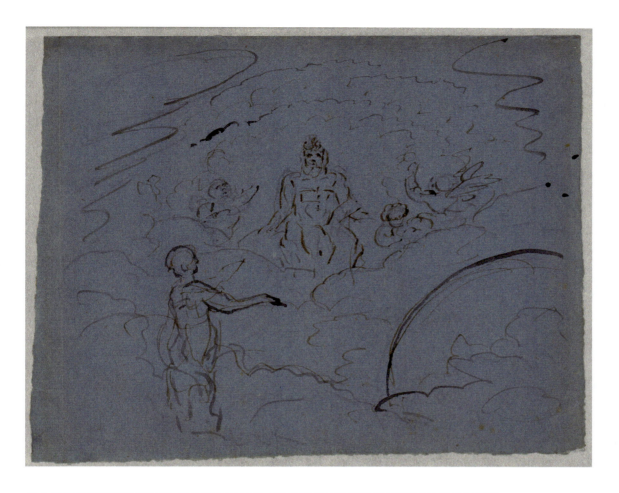

FIGURE 9.3 (*top*) Johann Wolfgang von Goethe, *Prologue in Heaven*, pen and ink drawing, *c*.1811, 21.5 × 33.4 cm; (*bottom*) Moritz Retzsch, Prologue in Heaven, *Umrisse zu Goethe's Faust gezeichnet von Retsch* (Stuttgart & Tübingen: Cotta, 1816), pl. 1
COURTESY SWK, WEIMAR; AND: COURTESY HAAB, F 3487, WEIMAR

FIGURE 9.4 (*top*) Johann Wolfgang von Goethe, *Conjuring the Poodle*, pen-and-ink drawing, wash, *c*.1811, 29.9 × 20 cm; (*bottom*) Moritz Retzsch, Faust's study with the poodle monstrously growing, *Umrisse zu Goethe's Faust gezeichnet von Retsch* (Stuttgart & Tübingen: Cotta, 1816), pl. 3
COURTESY HAAB, F 3487, WEIMAR

with respect to stage requisites. It also evidences that their pull on theatrics was based on close tracing (*durchbausen* for *durchpausen*) Retzsch's etchings.[19] On more than one occasion, prints materialised on stage. Today neither Retzsch's nor Cornelius's original sets figure in Weimar collections, although Goethe had received both, as if over-use had caused their disappearance. Extant exemplars are from later collectors' bequests.

9.3   Staging: German *Décors*

A major aesthetic invention took the cue in 1820 via Karl Friedrich Schinkel, the Prussian architect and designer who left a lasting mark on neoclassical, romantic and neo-Gothic styles. Prevented from building by the Napoleonic wars, Schinkel had enthusiastically turned to stage design, backed by Count Karl Friedrich von Brühl, the court theatre manager keen to radically revamp productions and renew theatre tradition in Berlin.[20] Music also played its part. Between 1816 and 1820, composer and Polish Prince Anton von Radziwill gave partial *Faust* readings and performances there as intermedial creations. Initially based on Faust's despair, his monodrama on Goethe's partially reworked and expanded text was rehearsed either privately or for splendid gatherings of blue-blooded guests. Two performances on the occasion of his wife's 24 May birthday are well documented. The 1819 show was a pre-production with orchestra and a portion of the Singing Academy at Monbijou palace theatre, attended by Goethe's son, August, and described in letters by him and Count Brühl.[21] Recapped on 13 July, this time to celebrate Prince Radziwill's own birthday, it proved such a success that it prompted further *Faust* fragments whose aim became completion. Monbijou would also host a general rehearsal on 20 May and a grand anniversary production on 24 May 1820 for a select audience and the Prussian court. Letters to Goethe from Zelter, present at both, give numerous details, mainly on Gretchen scenes performed for the first time.[22]

Schinkel's watercolour of Margaret's chamber, with stage set carried out by Johann Karl Wilhelm Zahn, is reputedly his only surviving *Faust* design (Fig. 9.5). It harks back to Retzsch's plate 9 (Fig. 9.6) and has been widely

noted as a major development in theatre aesthetics.[23] Contrary to stage decks of the time, open overhead and devoid of side-wings, it is enclosed on three sides. Closed stage versions had been experimented 1774 by Friedrich Ludwig Schröder in Hamburg or 1800 by Jean-Baptiste Pujoulx in Paris without catching on.[24] Now Schinkel, steered by Retzsch, blazed a trail. Count Brühl emphasized the innovation already in 1819 describing Faust's study to Goethe, and stressing the "small theatre" and the "small stage," with himself literally "cramped for room" (*Impressario in Angustie*):

> Um Ihnen eine anschauliche Idee von der kleinen Bühne selbst zu geben, auf welcher die Vorstellung statt findet, lege ich Ihnen hier die Zeichnung der Decoration bei. Es sind gar keine *Coulissen* gemacht worden, sondern das Theater ist durch fünf mehr oder weniger breite oder schmale Wände abgeschloßen, und gleichfalls mit einem verschloßenen *Plafond* versehen, so daß also das Ganze vollkommen einem Zimmer ähnlich ist.[25]

> In order to give you a clear idea of the small stage itself on which the performance takes place, I am enclosing here the drawing of the stage set. No *coulisses* whatsoever have been made, instead the stage is closed off by five more or less wide or narrow walls, and equally provided with a closed *Plafond*, so that the whole thing looks completely like a room.

His letter has drawn attention for his suggestions on a tricky subject (how to represent the Earth Spirit). Yet it also documents a turning point in staging, of which Goethe was instantly aware: "The theatre you built will certainly open a new epoch for the German stage, provide and prompt an opportunity for many good things." (*Auch wird Ihr hergestelltes Theater gewiß eine neue Epoche der deutschen Bühne eröffnen und zu manchen Guten*

---

19   GSA 28/92, 19.

20   Ulrike Harten, *Die Bühnenentwürfe*, ed. H. Börsch-Supan and G. Riemann (Munich: Deutscher Kunstverlag, 2000), 50–64.

21   GAug, n° 348; Rüdiger Wartusch, "Neue Spuren der ersten Aufführungen von Szenen aus dem *Faust*," *Goethe-Jahrbuch*, 113 (1996): 309–13.

22   BwGZ, 1: 605–11 (no. 343 & 345).

---

23   Alfred Gotthold Meyer, "Schinkels Theaterdekorationen," *Berliner Architekturwelt* 6, nos. 11–12 (1904): 360–68, 398–408; Paul Zucker, *Die Theaterdekoration des Klassizismus, eine Kunstgeschichte des Bühnenbildes* (Berlin: Kaemmerer, 1925), 20f; Helmut Börsch-Supan and Lucius Grisebach, *Karl Friedrich Schinkel: Architektur, Malerei, Kunstgewerbe* (Berlin: Staatliche Museen Preussischer Kulturbesitz, 1981), n° 224; Harten, *Die Bühnenentwürfe*; Anna Marie Pfäfflin, "Bühnenbild und inszenierter Raum: Zum Konzept des Theatralischen im Werk von Karl Friedrich Schinkel," *Jahrbuch der Berliner Museen* 56 (2014): 111–21.

24   Zucker, *Die Theaterdekoration*, 18.

25   Wartusch, "Neue Spuren," 311, French terms in italics.

FIGURE 9.5　Karl Friedrich Schinkel, *Margaret's Chamber*, 1820, *décor* design after Moritz Retzsch, watercolour over preliminary drawing, graphite and compass on vellum, 23.5 × 36.3 cm
© STAATLICHE MUSEEN ZU BERLIN, KUPFERSTICHKABINETT, SM 22D.95, BERLIN

FIGURE 9.6　Moritz Retzsch, Margaret in her chamber, *Umrisse zu Goethe's Faust gezeichnet von Retsch* (Stuttgart & Tübingen: Cotta, 1816), pl. 9
COURTESY HAAB, F 3487, WEIMAR

Gelegenheit geben und nöthigen).[26] Neither Brühl's drawing nor Schinkel's design are unfortunately attested but Petersen's description favours again a Retzschian font for Faust's studio: "The picture of Radziwill's performance is brimming with odds and ends of instruments, books, and stuffed animals; it represents a veritable caveman's hollow (*Wolfsschlucht*) of singular signs."[27]

Flaxman's objection to Faust's study crammed by Retzsch comes to mind, and Petersen, a sharp critic with a wide knowledge of stage versions, likely knew Brühl's drawing. To be sure, Schinkel's surviving watercolour (Gretchen's chamber) evidences the ground-breaking shift. The rafters and floor planks of Retzsch's pl. 9 to 11 have become a joisted ceiling, orderly floorboards, and chamber walls. The stage is the boxed volume of a quadrangle, an echo chamber for the players' recital. From then on, stressed for good, performances would unwind inside a cubicle, open to the orchestra, pit and gallery. In borrowing from Retzsch theatre's invisible "fourth wall" had been devised. Acting and shows would empower spectators' senses. I argue that Faust's study read analogously.

Beyond specifics and location (a bed with hangings, the grandfather's chair, the mirror, table, crucifix, and window with bull's-eye panes),[28] Retzsch's art of detailing *also stirred* in Schinkel *a style of meaningful decoration*. He decked room and table with props for further events. His set is a synthetic platform for Faust to easily lift the bed drapes, Gretchen to find the jewels, later sadly sing at the spinning wheel or piteously address the Mater Dolorosa hanging on the wall. In Retzsch, abundance of objects supported character; in Schinkel, it fuels action. Zelter, impressed, sent Goethe a full description but wished the chamber to be much smaller, more thrifty, and darker. All "was so cheerful and naive that precisely for this reason a highly tragic Gretchen did not seem at home" (*so heiter und naiv aufgestellt daß eben aus diesem Grunde ein hochtragisches Gretchen nicht zu Hause erschien*).[29] Harten justly stressed a bourgeois interior at variance with Gretchen's "poverty" (*Armut*, F 2693).[30] Yet, the discrepancy was theatrics' inevitable consequence. Staging had to please the eye and impress the select Monbijou audience that included the king, his family, and several princes. Such adaptability ruled the way Retzsch's prints were plied with remarkable endurance. Gretchen's room by both

Gilbert Lehner for the Viennese Hofburgtheater in 1891 and set designer Amable for a 1908 French performance of Gounod's opera has a Retzschian bed with hangings.[31] The stage designers proved quite conservative.[32]

Schinkel's set was used with slight changes over and over again: in the Berlin Opera *Faust* in six parts on 15 May 1838 with the late Radziwill's music completed; a detailed watercolour with gouache highlights preserved in France confirms its extensive diffusion.[33] The same year it served the first Berlin *Faust* at the Royal Theatre with bespoke sets, an exception, since (unlike opera) plays typically used extant scenery. For over a hundred years, Gretchen's bedroom remained unchanged.[34] Théophile Gautier, shocked at the dusty negligence of a different Munich *décor* in 1854, longed for Retzsch.[35] Called "conservative," and modelling "a type" (*einen Typus vorgebildet hatte*), it had even adapted to the requisites of proscenium and revolving stage.[36]

Turned run-of-the-mill patterns for theatre, Retzsch's prints set the tone. For the famed 1829 *Faust* Braunschweig production (strongly rearranged), Ernst August Klingemann, "at a loss," and Hermann Neefe, his set designer, let themselves be "guided."[37] The Dresden *Abend-Zeitung* ran: "we were also pleasantly surprised to repeatedly recognize, without appearing inflexible and pre-prepared for it, the tableaux of Retzsch's outlines, in which particularly Mr Schütz [Faust] had truly conceived (*treu aufgefaßt*) his character."[38] Intriguingly, the Braunschweig cathedral

---

26   *Johann Valentin Teichmanns literarischer Nachlass*, ed. F. Dingelstedt (Stuttgart: J. G. Cotta, 1863), 250.

27   Petersen, *Goethes Faust auf der deutschen Bühne*, 44.

28   Harten, *Die Bühnenentwürfe*, 357–58.

29   BwGZ, 1: 606 (no. 343).

30   Harten, *Die Bühnenentwürfe*, 358a.

31   Gilbert Lehner, *Theater-Decorationen zu W. v. Goethe's Faust* (Wien: Hessling & Spielmeyer, [1891]), C.8; Chassaigne de Néronde, "La nouvelle mise en scène de *Faust* à l'Opéra," *Les Annales politiques et littéraires*, no. 1284 (2 Feb 1908): 108. Bruno Hessling issued a second more comprehensive edition of Lehner's theatre *décors* in Berlin and New York.

32   Mathias Auclair and Pauline Girard, "Les décors de *Faust* à l'Opéra de Paris (1869–1908)", in *L'interprétation lyrique de la fin du XIXe au début du XXe siècle*, online, http://www.bruzanemediabase.com/Parutions-scientifiques-en-ligne/Articles/Auclair-Mathias-Girard-Pauline-Les-decors-de-Faust-a-l-Opera-de-Paris-1869-1908.

33   BnF, Décors Allemands-11, https://gallica.bnf.fr/ark:/12148/btv1b53068363s/f1.item.

34   Mahl, "Die Bühnengeschichte von Goethes *Faust*," in *Goethe Handbuch*, vol. 2, *Dramen*, ed. Th. Buck (Stuttgart: J. B. Metzler, 1996), 525.

35   See p. 308.

36   Petersen, *Goethes "Faust" auf der deutschen Bühne*, 45.

37   Mahl, "Die Bühnengeschichte von Goethes *Faust*," 525; cf. Richard Daunicht, "August Klingemanns Inszenierung von Goethes *Faust 1. Teil*: Zur ersten Berufstheater-Aufführung des Stückes am 19. Januar 1829 in Braunschweig," *Braunschweigisches Jahrbuch* 61 (1980): 55–74.

38   *Abend-Zeitung*, no. 24 (28 Jan 1829): 96.

FIGURE 9.7 Peter Cornelius, *Scene in the Prison. End of the Tragedy*, in *XII Bilder zu Göthe's Faust gezeichnet von Peter von Cornelius* (Frankfurt am Main: Johann Friedrich Wenner, n.d.), pl. 12
COURTESY BEINECKE, FOLIO SPECK CK99 C7 816, YALE UNIVERSITY

scene *preceded* the duel. Retzsch then had left his mark even on scene sequence, a point insufficiently stressed,[39] yet all the more important as the historical *première* unfurled within the year from one German state to the next in honour of Goethe's eightieth birthday. Dresden, Hanover, Leipzig, and Weimar celebrated a Retzschian *Faust*, along with Frankfurt, where scenes were only recited onstage. Depending on the reporter, Bremen, Hamburg, Magdeburg, Munich and Stuttgart may also join the list.[40] Retzsch's name had become superfluous. An article on the Weimar performance mentions, *inter alia*, Gretchen's bedroom and the witch's kitchen "very ingenious and true, following acknowledged models (*nach den bekannten Mustern*)."[41] In Leipzig and Dresden, Ludwig Tieck also resorted to Retzsch for Faust and Wagner returning from the Easter promenade with poodle. The stage booklet reads "Scene after Retzsch."[42] The list comprises Carl Seydelmann's Stuttgart show in 1832 that long triumphed; and the 1838 Royal Theatre production in Berlin, which lured Seydelmann-Mephistopheles away from Stuttgart. Seydelmann's acting outline (*Spielplan*) was still being used in 1892.

Repetition need not be dreary. Klingemann swore by Retzsch, plundering other artists such as Cornelius or Ramberg only exceptionally.[43] It is easy to grasp why. When Tieck resorted to Cornelius's and Ramberg's prison scene in the *dénouement*, following Klingemann and his damned Faust, an angel hovered over Gretchen. In

---

39   Daunicht, "August Klingemanns Inszenierung," 68.
40   Heinz Kindermann, *Theatergeschichte der Goethezeit* (Wien: H. Bauer, 1948), 838.
41   Spiess, "Faust auf der Bühne," 93.
42   Mahl, *Goethes "Faust" auf der Bühne*, 23.
43   Ulrich Parenth, *Wie Goethes "Faust" auf die Bühne kam* (Braunschweig: Gerd J. Holtzmeyer, 1986), 64; Mahl, *Goethes "Faust" auf der Bühne*, 18.

Cornelius's masterly polarised ending between Margaret's salvation and Faust's damnation, the devil is about to carry the hero away, while Margaret kneels with prayer book, cross, rosary and skull on a mat (Fig. 9.7). Such a template is however not of Gretchen but of Mary Magdalene mourning in the desert, the very image of sinner and former prostitute that Margaret never was. The rush matting beneath her, still unrolled at her back and conjured out of thin air, stresses the oddity of a foreign image embedded in the prison scene, as if Cornelius was purposefully pursuing a tongue-in-cheek iconographic game. Applied to the stage, the pictorial device would float over Margaret a pasteboard angel, palm in hand, while a dragon-winged devil clutches Faust away. What would happen to the mat? Retzsch's simpler conception (cf. Fig. 2.17), more faithful to the play, did not allow for such dubious props.

Beyond borders, his prints were also a passkey to stage productions in Britain and France.

9.4 British and French *Décors*

London and Paris had preceded Braunschweig in *Faust* adaptations, exalting love at the expense of metaphysics, in melodrama with suggestive titles. *Faust* (or *Le Docteur Faust*) by Antony Béraud, Jean-Toussaint Merle and Charles Nodier, the blandest of these headings, opened in 1828 at the Porte-Saint-Martin with two superstars of the time, Marie Dorval as Margaret and Frédérick Lemaître as Mephistopheles. Henry M. Milner's 1824 *Faustus; or, The Demon's Victim* rivalled it in London. George Soane and Daniel Terry tailed it in 1825 with *The Devil and Dr Faustus*, also by the milder title *Faustus: A Romantic Drama*. Milner's version, strongly based on the 1821 Boosey edition and Shelley's translation of the witches' Sabbath, had stage sets, scenery and costumes closely following Retzsch as copied by Moses. The plates literally materialized on stage.[44] Inversely, *The Devil and Doctor Faustus* only hosted a costume for Mephistophiles [*sic*] after Retzsch and launched diorama into serious drama for the first time with ever-changing sets and scenery. Crabb Robinson noted: "As a spectacle the piece is admirable—I recollect no piece of equal splendour and beauty—The scenery sweetly painted and the machinery better contrived than in any pantomime."[45] It again triumphed 1827 in New York

with spectacular revival at Broadway Theatre in 1851.[46] Daniel Terry's close-fitting gear, "admirably modelled from the outlines of RETSCH" (cf. Fig. 9.13),[47] would epitomize Goethe's play (see below).

London had pre-empted Paris and may have influenced the Porte-Saint-Martin show. As one of the most popular boulevard theatres, attended by workers, shopkeepers and the middle class, the latter had imported stage machinery to France from London in 1824. Its priority was spectacular melodrama complete with singing, dancing, contest, and mime acts. Two years before *Faust*, chief set designer Charles Lefèvre had worked with English head-rigger and sceneshifter Tomkins to produce *Le Monstre et le Magicien* after Mary Shelley's *Frankenstein*. Machineries, stunning scenes and marvellous events swarmed the stage.[48] Press articles on *Faust*, gauging Lemaître's Mephistopheles, still referred to *Le Monstre* two years later. Béraud, Merle and Nodier's *Faust* opened on the 29 October 1828 in a fully refurbished theatre after three months of building works. A huge success, it won over the public but forsook philosophy and poetry for a mere melodramatic plot. A pact with the devil had replaced Goethe's wager, and the *dénouement* contrasted Margaret's ascent to Heaven with Faust condemned to fire and brimstone. Yet, in the brand new auditorium, seventeen quick-change scenes stunned 2,000 spectators and fire rained on the witches' Sabbath.[49] Set designer and sceneshifter were deemed far more important than any author, and both swore by Retzsch. In press reviews Lefèvre was the instigator of the success for instance, more than three months after the *première*, in *L'Album national*:

> For the devotees of theatrical souvenirs, Retzsch's engravings are, in a way, doubly appealing; for they reproduce the drawings of several of the beautiful stage sets that contributed to the glory of *Faust* at the Porte Saint-Martin theatre. The German artist's work was not wasted on Mr Lefèvre. He used it particularly to paint the witch's kitchen, Margaret's chamber, the witches' Sabbath, the prison, and several other stage set effects.[50]

---

44   Frederick Burwick, "*Faust* Translations of Coleridge and Shelley on the London Stage," *Keats-Shelley Journal* 59 (2010): 32.

45   Eluned Brown, ed., *The London Theatre 1811–1866: Selections from the Diary of Henry Crabb Robinson* (London: The Society for Theatre Research, 1966), 110–11.

46   Christopher Murray, "Elliston's Production of *Faust*," *Theatre Research* 11, no. 2–3 (1971): 109–10, 113.

47   Q., "Drury Lane," *Examiner*, no. 903 (23 May 1825): 321.

48   Marie-Antoinette Allevy, *La mise en scène en France dans la première moitié du dix-neuvième siècle* (Paris: E. Droz, 1938), 64–68.

49   Y., "Théâtre de la Porte-Saint-Martin," *Diogène*, no. 32 (6 Dec 1828): 3a–4b.

50   E. R...x, "Faust," *L'Album national*, no. 27 (14 Feb 1829): 214–15; see also *Le Corsaire*, no. 2090 (30 Oct 1828): 2.

FIGURE 9.8 Moritz Retzsch, Margaret in the prison, *Umrisse zu Goethe's Faust gezeichnet von Retsch* (Stuttgart & Tübingen: Cotta, 1816), pl. 25
COURTESY HAAB, F 3487, WEIMAR

Similarly, in an enthusiastic 23 March 1829 letter on Parisian life, would-be composer Ferdinand Hiller avowed to Eckermann in Weimar that the production was making the fortune of a play "not that good." (*Die mise en scène war sehr schön und machte das Glück des Stückes was an sich nicht viel taugt*).[51] In truth, the published version of this *Faust*, promoted on the title-page as "after Goethe," must have been conceived with Retzsch's plates to hand, to judge by stage directions. Goethe's epigrammatic "A Prison" was for instance replaced by this: "The Theatre represents a dungeon. A pillar to which are attached chains, which end in an iron belt that retains Margaret. She is lying on the straw."[52] A truthful précis of Retzsch's pl. 25 could hardly be better phrased (Fig. 9.8). A surviving copy of "The Witch's Kitchen" after Retzsch with a long French caption may also relate to this.[53] Audot's booklets, advertised in parallel with the play, sold like hot cakes, recommended to theatregoers both as souvenir and elucidation of Goethe's obscurities.

Three years later, an early *Fausto: Opera semi-seria* in four acts, by a 25-year-old she-composer, Louise Bertin, daughter of *Le Journal des débats* editor, premièred at the Parisian Théâtre Italien on 8 March 1831 with the royal

---

51 Düsseldorff: Nachlass Johann Peter Eckermann.

52 Antony Béraud et ***, *Faust, drame en trois actes, imité de Goethe* (Paris: J.-N. Barba, 1828), 57.

53 Düsseldorf: KK 1863 and 1864 (Kippenberg, nos. 1863–64).

family present, yet in the middle of Republican turmoil. It was bold and confident to attempt that *magnum opus*, to render in French and Italian a Germanic subject, to compose an opera in a professional arena dominated by men, let alone choose such a daring subject.[54] Except for a few press reviews and the bilingual libretto, Bertin's work "remains a curiosity" and the score is supposedly lost.[55] At the time, it was buried under misogynist and caustic comment, witness Ludwig Borne writing from Paris: "The music is at times not boring, and if one is not dead, he comes round again."[56] Yet, if one only crosses the Channel or the Rhineland border, the British Library and Weimar collections turn up three noteworthy scores: two correspond to the last scene arranged for the piano by Bertin herself, one of which bears an autograph dedication to Meyerbeer, himself a *Walpurgisnacht* composer.[57] The third, a longer version for the harpsichord by "signor Rifaut," is part of Goethe's music collection with a dedication penned by Bertin in French (*À Goethe*).[58] Three voices bid to enliven the piano score, and the libretto's stage direction yet again describes Retzsch's pl. 25: "The Theatre represents a gloomy prison. Margaret lies down at the far end. Faust enters holding a lamp." (cf. Fig. 9.8) Even Borne was forced to scathingly admit: "The most beautiful thoughts first come to the she-composer at the opera's end, despite the apparently female quality of the signature. The last scene, Gretchen in prison, makes a good impression."[59] The cherry on the cake is both its cover and title-page, an alleviated lithographic version of Retzsch's last plate (Fig. 9.9): Faust grips Margaret to free her from prison, himself seized by Mephistopheles to a darker reign. Margaret lifts her arms heavenward and her Retzschian oil lamp still burns on three boulders (cf. Fig. 2.17). The convict's jug of water stands nearby, calling to mind the stage apparel. The opera has coincidentally just revived in Paris as this book goes to press.

Even Gounod's *première* at Théâtre Lyrique would fall under Retzsch's influence as late as 1859. A set design for act 5, scene 4, offered again the prison after Retzsch.

---

54   Reibel, *Faust: La musique*, 109–12.
55   Ibid., 110.
56   Borne, *Briefe aus Paris*, ed. A. Estermann (Frankfurt: Insel, 1986), 203.
57   BL: Music Collections H.450; HAAB: F 5598 (inscribed to Meyerbeer, Fig. 9.9).
58   GSA 32/100 (Goethes Notensammlung). Gräf erroneously records it as referring to the piano score, *Goethe über seine Dichtungen*, 570, n. 2.
59   Borne, *Briefe aus Paris*, 203.

FIGURE 9.9   Louise Bertin, *Ultima scena di Fausto/Dernière Scène de Faust, Composée et Arrangée pour le Piano-Forte* (Paris: Maurice Schlesinger, [c.1831]), scroll cover with illustration after Moritz Retzsch
COURTESY HAAB, F 5598, WEIMAR

No coincidence, the celebrated Édouard Despléchin had trained with Porte-Saint-Martin's Lefèvre. More than thirty years had elapsed since the 1828 *Faust*, yet both Lefèvre's and Tomkins's influence is felt in his work, also supported by his Dresden experience. From 1836, engaged indeed in Dresden and considered the best stage designer by Richard Wagner, Despléchin had worked for twenty years in Gottfried Semper's opera finished in 1841.[60] Intriguingly, if Retzsch's sway long prevailed in Paris, the European city most in the public eye, it had turned full circle thanks to a Parisian working in Retzsch's native city.

---

60   Jean-Maxime Lévêque, *Édouard Despléchin, le décorateur du grand opéra à la française, 1802–1871* (Paris: L'Harmattan, 2008), 70–71, 108–09.

FIGURE 9.10　Édouard Despléchin, stage set for Gounod's *Faust*, 5.4 after Moritz Retzsch, 1859, pen, watercolour and gouache highlights on blue cardboard, 26.8 × 40 cm
BnF, ESQ. DESPLECHIN-5, PARIS

Despléchin has enlarged Retzsch's vaulted ceiling, amplified Gretchen's cell, and multiplied the massive ashlars, meticulously drawing mortar joints, chains, and jug of water on stone block (Fig. 9.10). His Margaret prostrate on the straw adopted the dejected position Retzsch had devised (cf. Fig. 9.8). Through a clerestory window on the left, light filters in, illuminating the stained glass—a weird invention for a prison. It flickers on the outcast and glimmers towards the open door. Despléchin combines Retzsch's penitentiary and Gounod's optimistic finale, again at odds with Goethe's play. The poignant ending answered a stage curtain for act 5 that gave cause to shudder (Fig. 9.11): Joseph Thierry's Faust and Mephistopheles wildly galloping on horses past the gallows with hanging corpses—echoes Retzsch's plate 24 with skeletons and veiled witches attenuated, and scraggy gibbet replaced by portentous white pillars. Gautier in *Le Moniteur universel* and later in *Portraits contemporains* eagerly commented the sensational design, also a painting in the 1866 Salon. Jean-Dominique Ingres, Eugène Delacroix, Gustave Doré, and several other French artists were associated with this luxurious production.[61] Retzsch's presence, perhaps unexpected in such context, has not been traced before. It strikes a chord, since *Faust* stage sets grew intensely more realistic in France towards the end of the nineteenth century. The impact of his linear depictions, adapted to aesthetics a far cry from his own, was felt beyond Germany even in the 1850s.

However, not everything was in the eye of the beholder. As with Schinkel, innovations in handling of time, representation and performance art were yet in store.

61　Auclair and Girard, "Les décors de *Faust* à l'Opéra de Paris," 11–14.

FIGURE 9.11 (*top*) Joseph Thierry, *Faust and Mephistopheles Riding in front of the Montfaucon Gallows*, 1866, oil on canvas, 95 × 125 cm, previously design for the stage curtain of Gounod's *Faust*, 5.1, [1859]; (*bottom*) Moritz Retzsch, Faust and Mephistopheles galloping past the Rabenstein, *Umrisse zu Goethe's Faust gezeichnet von Retsch* (Stuttgart & Tübingen: Cotta, 1816), pl. 24

BMO, PARIS; AND: COURTESY HAAB, F 3487, WEIMAR

9.5 Time, Stage and the Arts

Onstage treatment of transition from one *Faust* scene to another was a crux for writer and dramatic producer Karl Eduard von Holtei. He ambitioned to abruptly jump from Margaret, wildly mimicking the murder of her child, to Faust, defying Mephistopheles in woodland. In order to "symbolically help the spectator over the [time] rift," he planned a change of musical theme, a dark forest on stage, to lower the backstage wall, and, float in "allegorically and phantasmagoria-like the shapes from the Blocksberg scenes, which would show themselves without words at their sharpest (*welche sich ohne Worte am karsten bezeichen lassen*)." Outlines had caught his eye (cf. Fig. 5.7) and he would use them to catch others' notice. He added pointedly: "The excellent sketches by Retzsch must come to assistance. Think of the colourful swarming, like a dream, accompanied by wild, swaying music!"[62] Moving images and gimmicks of stagecraft would bridge the abolished time gap. Retzsch's compositions had a double gift: provide motionless scenery and come to life as fragmented, hovering visions, endowed with duration, a trait that supplied shimmering and time-spanning *tableaux vivants*. Regrettably, Holtei did not obtain Goethe's approval for the Berlin production he was planning, feeling rather bitter about it.[63] Goethe's refusal was however not for aesthetic reasons but due to the antagonism of Brühl, who laid exclusive claim to high tragedy in Berlin.[64]

To mediate performances and blend the staging of *Faust* with the visual arts also meant turning to Retzsch. On the 25 April 1838 the Coburg Court Theatre welcomed a spectacle labelled *Lebende Bilder aus Faust nach den Umrissen von Moritz Retzsch mit Declamation aus Goethes Tragödie* (*Tableaux vivants from Faust following Moritz Retzsch's Outlines with Recitatives from Goethe's Tragedy*). On 7 May 1838 that same year, noting how popular *tableaux vivants* were in Germany, Théophile Gautier commented on the oddity of the process apropos a Parisian spectacle: live pictures, a "rather singular entertainment," consisted "in dressing in clothes similar to those of the characters in the performed painting, copying their attitude and physiognomy, in short, inverting the ordinary process (*prendre l'inverse du procédé ordinaire*), which is to reproduce nature with colours."[65] The idea, originating in medieval performances and adopted in eighteenth-century theatrics, had considerable aesthetic clout in German lands. Goethe himself, impressed by the 1787 Caserta performance of Emma, future Lady Hamilton, managed numerous *lebende Bilder* performances in Weimar with Johann Heinrich Meyer and Friedrich Wilhelm Riemer.[66] By no coincidence, Lord Hamilton, galvanized by Greek antiquities, was instrumental in bringing Flaxman's outlines to light and the beautiful Emma to London. Goethe's own description of three *tableaux vivants* and a nativity scene performed by Ottilie and Luciane in his *Elective Affinities* (1809) was the occasion to launch a new form of representation, making "low" and "high" culture fuse. After all, mutual attraction between aristocrat and commoner could even result in wedlock as in Hamilton's case. Scholarship has thoroughly studied the meaning of these passages, stressing their value in character depiction,[67] and evaluating the high/low cultural and masculine/feminine divide they epitomize. As Peter McIsaac has shown, originating in popular culture and performed by women, yet staged and vocalized by men, *lebende Bilder* earned a complex cultural status in nineteenth-century novels.[68] From my point of view, they importantly challenge Lessing's well-known divide between the visual and the verbal in questioning nature, art, and representation.

Goethe had not survived to either guide or see the Coburg performance. Six years after his demise, the impersonations, staffed and crewed in Retzschian costumes, poise, props and scenery theatrically lit, enlivened the prints. As complex incarnate artefacts, they avoided full theatrical trappings—an ideal solution for a tragedy in which the supernatural has the lion's share. In Goethe's *Elective Affinities*, the templates needed for the socialites are noticeably supplied by etchings after famous paintings (*man suchte nun Kupferstiche nach berühmten Gemälden*, II, V). By comparison, Retzsch presented two advantages: his engravings were prototypes, not replicas; and their long career as pliant models in the European copying industry best qualified them for live reproduction. Nonetheless, the *tableaux vivants* in Goethe's novel obey subtle gradation. Imitation of painting is at first imperfect

---

62   Max Hecker, "Karl Eduard von Holtei im Goethekreise," *Jahrbuch der Goethe-Gesellschaft* 4 (1917): 192–93.

63   Spiess, *"Faust auf der Bühne,"* 41.

64   Petersen, *Goethes "Faust" auf der deutschen Bühne*, 14–15.

65   Gautier, "Feuilleton de *La Presse*," in *Œuvres complètes*, pt. 6, *Critique théâtrale*, vol. 1, *1835–1838*, ed. P. Berthier (Paris: Champion, 2007), 489.

66   Tanvi Solanki, "A Book of Living Paintings: Tableaux Vivants in Goethe's *Die Wahlverwandtschaften* (1809)," *Goethe Yearbook* 23 (2016): 245–70.

67   Birgit Jooss, "Lebende Bilder als Charakterbeschreibungen in Goethes Roman *Die Wahlverwandtschaften*," in *Erzählen und Wissen: Paradigmen und Aporien ihrer Inszenierung in Goethes "Wahlverwandtschaften*," ed. G. Brandstetter (Freiburg-im-Breisgau: Rombach, 2003), 111–36.

68   McIsaac, "Rethinking Tableaux Vivants and Triviality in the Writings of Johann Wolfgang von Goethe, Johanna Schopenhauer, and Fanny Lewald," *Monatshefte* 99, no. 2 (Summer 2007): 152–76.

(reality distressfully transpiring beneath make-believe), then perfectly matching, finally superior to the original. His incisive treatment also playfully toys with the *reading analogy* of such showmanship. At the height of Luciane's third *tableau-vivant* success, her back to the assembly, Goethe's French insert "*tournez s'il vous plaît*", explicitly refers to readers' prompts in printed books as well as her stage posture. The novel's finale also deviously alludes to deceased Ottilie as art's most perfect incarnation. The charades that swarmed across Germany, endowing prints with life and pepping them up with costumes in many dyes, are thus puzzling, hybrid creations, straddling a middling space between "material painting" (*cette espèce de peinture matérielle*)[69] and "natural picture-making" (*natürliche Bildnerei*, II, V).

Was the Coburg performance a realization of poetry at its best while plot provided storyline? Or just an umpteenth conversion of *Faust* into dramatic outline, merely for pathos and damnation? Little has survived. Niessen refers to the same coloured prints as those supposedly used in Braunschweig, whose Faust was ultimately damned.[70] As noted, whether the latter were devised for stage is a moot point (cf. Fig. 2.22 to 2.25). Moreover, the Coburg storyline turns even more pathetic than Braunschweig (and again contradicts the theme of the coloured prints): 1. Faust in his Study, 2. Faust and Mephistopheles, 3. Auerbach's Cellar, 4. The Witch's Kitchen, 5. Faust and Gretchen, 6. The Amorous Confession, 7. Gretchen, the Culprit, 8. The Murder, 9. Faust and the Child Murderess, 10. Faust's End. The playbill shows that the ten *tableaux* were highly contrasted *pièces de résistance* on the heels of a short comedy by C. W. Koch after Heinrich Zschokke's "Love and Hate." Evidence has yet to emerge on this production though deductions may be extrapolated.

The Coburg show was neither domestic evening amusement for upper- or middle-class salons of the *Elective Affinities* vogue, nor pure entertainment; no popular show by commoners (as seen by Goethe in Naples), nor private performance (like those to which Lord Hamilton himself held the artistic light). A professional company adapted a still unfamiliar yet famed title, shaping it for another destiny as German national drama. The show had reached the planks of a small court theatre. The Saxe-Coburg and Gotha dynasty, critical for the political history of Europe, would run its own politics until World War I. Under Duke Ernst I (1806–44), theatre had greatly developed in rivalry with other small courts' stages (like nearby Weimar) to

become "the expression of the rising bourgeoisie."[71] Ernst's son, Prince Albert, would marry his cousin, Victoria, the British imperial sovereign. Commissioned by the Prince of Coburg, Retzsch made several artworks for Queen Victoria that found their way into the British royal collections.[72] In such context, the 1838 Coburg performance of *lebende Bilder* bridge the aristocracy and the bourgeoisie. They express the cultural ambition of a small duchy that sought to impress Europe from central Germany.

Faust's standing on the stage (and beyond) was quickly changing. By 1859, with Retzsch still in the lead, his prints became the basis of popular entertainment. Conclusive proof is the Saint Petersburg *Faust* in one of the pleasure establishments founded by Johann Luzius Isler (in Russian Ivan Ivanovič Izler, 1810–77). This Swiss confectioner, first active on the Nevsky Prospect, had turned leisure entrepreneur through several successive and successful attractions, primarily his "mineral water and summer establishment" (*Islerische Mineralwasser-Sommermonaten Anstalt*) that had opened in 1848 as a vast pleasure ground with dance balls, promenades, bowling, jugglers, conjurers and acrobats, regattas, *variété* shows, waterworks, ornamental fountains, and fireworks.[73] In 1859, in yet another establishment, "Villa monde brillant," Isler twice staged a singular *Faust*, ending with "resplendent fireworks" (*glänzendes Feuerwerk*) and followed by big band accompaniment (*großes Musik*).[74] Inspiration possibly sprang from Goethe's *Faust* itself, with Mephistopheles promptly dragging Faust away from the witches' Sabbath and Gretchen's disturbing spectre to the "Intermezzo": "Come up that hillock there— | Here's quite a merry Prater fair!" (F 4210–11, trans. W. Arndt). But also from Vienna's Prater itself, where a popular *Faust*, heavily bent on the damnation scenario and ending with fireworks, had

---

69   Gautier, "Feuilleton de *La Presse*," 489.

70   Niessen, n° 2127. See pp. 89–92.

---

71   Jürgen Erdmann, "Ein Stück deutscher Theaterhistorie. Zur Geschichte des ehemaligen herzoglichen sächsischen Hoftheaters Coburg-Gotha und seiner Notensammlung," in Rudolf Potyra, *Die Theatermusikalien der Landesbibliothek Coburg* (Munich: G. Henle, 1995), 1:XIV; Erdmann, *Die Herzogliche Privatbibliothek Coburg als markantes Zeugnis nationaler und internationaler fürstlicher Kulturbeziehungen ab dem späten 18. Jahrhundert bis 1918*, (Coburg: [Landesbibliothek], 2009).

72   L. Hermann, "Moritz Retzsch and Bürger," 2a; documented in Hellwig, "Studien zu Moritz Retzsch," 59–60.

73   Hugo Hafferberg, *St. Petersburg in seiner Vergangenheit und Gegenwart* (Saint Petersburg: Friedrich Assmann, 1866), 177–79; Erik Amburger, *Ingermanland* (Köln: Böhlau, 1980), 1:549–51; Roman Bühler, "Von der Konditorei zum Vergnügungspark: Ivan Ivanovič Izler, ein Petersburger Vergnügungsunternehmer um die Mitte des 19. Jahrhunderts," *Bündner Monatsblatt*, no. 4 (1994): 274–82.

74   *St. Petersburger Zeitung*, no. 150 (12 July 1859): 657; no. 156 (19 July 1859): 681.

already materialized in 1829.[75] Isler too swore by Retzsch. A surviving poster in Russian advertises *Faust* as a "grand fantastic poem" after Goethe "in two parts." In the first, thirteen tableaux after thirteen Retzsch prints developed in rightful order except for a conclusive witches' Sabbath (placed after the prison) to validate the fireworks.[76] The poster faithfully reproduces the corresponding excerpts from the Cotta letterpress brochure (or rather, by then, from a Cotta album). The second part, away from Goethe and including a dwarf, unrolls Faust's travels, a pretext for the band's assorted picturesque melodies. In bad weather, the *fête* would be replaced by a "Grand Musical Evening." Indeed, the performance reads more like a garden party with images transferred onto vast transparent screens.[77] Guests, potentially drunk like the Auerbach cellar's students on the clear liquid, may have enacted the Faustian plot themselves: by circulating among sets, flirting with Faust, Margaret or Martha, or rejuvenating thanks to witches' magic potions. Engel even provides the rhymed recipe for a *Faust* cake for devotees. Arguably, Tieck, as writer and inventor concerned amongst other things with art and theatrical innovation, might have approved the middle-of-the-road show. One can hardly avoid Coleridge's formula: "The scenes are mere magic-lantern pictures."[78] In his mind, the phrase postulated *Faust*'s lack of unity. In Isler's, it had become a vast public holiday resort enhancing the popularity of Goethe's *Faust* as everyman's own.

9.6 Performance: Fixed, Inviolable Instants?

At the opening of his novel *L'Ève future* (*The Eve of the Future*, 1886), Villiers de L'Isle-Adam lamented that the phonograph had not yet been invented to record the initial *fiat*, God's voice creating the universe. On that cue, we may deplore that cinema and video never registered Mephistopheles proposing a wager to God, appearing to Faust, Faust and Gretchen's garden tête-à-tête, nor Margaret finding the jewels. What expressions might her mirror have reflected? Self-admiration, wonder, desire, dread, or resignation?

Our motion-educated eye doubts the prints' reign over the stage. If Retzsch's engravings modelled *décors*, could

they also sculpt "characteristic miens"?[79] Did they actually dictate "the bearings of the main characters" (*das Körperliche der Hauptcharaktere*)?[80] Did not acting itself animate, ply, and alter expressions and postures?

The album *Scenen aus Goethes Faust in acht lithographirten Bildern* (*Scenes from Goethe's Faust in Eight Lithographic Prints*), commemorated in 1835 remarkable instants from Prince Radziwill's staging. Margaret at her table (Fig. 9.12), a lithograph by Meyerheim, combining a sketch by Radziwill's son, Ferdinand, and the figure by Bierman, echoes in detail Retzsch's pl. 9 (armchair, high-backed seat, mirror, crucifix and book, even bed with hangings, although draped differently, cf. Fig. 9.6). The impact of Schinkel's design is also obvious in the table on the opposite side of the room and his extra fittings (spinning wheel, Mater Dolorosa, elaborate cabinet). Here Gretchen cuts a double figure between stage and lithograph in a much richer garment than her Retzschian attire. She sports velvet sleeves and bodice. An elaborate pouch billows her skirt around her hips, baring ankles and feet in open pointed dress shoes. She loosens her hair (unerringly after Retzsch) but is no longer engrossed in thought. She eloquently turns her face to the audience. Her performance will acquaint them with her concerns. What we see is a still, poised in time, as tricky to maintain as an actress's get-up compliant with stage directions.

Evidence in both classical tradition and romantic practice privileges moments frozen in time, yet for dissimilar reasons. To model actors' poise on statuary, that of antique sculpture, was one of the rules that Goethe had imposed on neoclassical theatre in Weimar. In principle, Goethe's stage should resemble a painting and the disposition match a mural, although research has explored contradictions apparent in his theories.[81] Neoclassicism had resorted to the principle of analogy and models of expression handed down by history. Tragedy was conceived as a portico of paintings impregnating a fine artist's imagination. In an important 1783 letter to Italian tragedian Vittorio Alfieri, the theatre theoretician Ranieri de' Calzabigi, lyrical drama reformer and Gluck's librettist, praised the efficacy of Antiquity's mime acts. A gripping tragedy was founded neither on recitation nor narrative, he argued, but on "a series and continuity of pictures." Alfieri should be a

---

75   *Abend-Zeitung*, no. 156 (1 July 1829): 624.

76   HAAB: F gr 5817, items 386–87. Warm thanks to Jean-Louis Backès for translations from the Russian.

77   Engel, 455.

78   *The Collected Works of STC*, vol. 14, *Table Talk, recorded by Henry Nelson Coleridge (and John Taylor Coleridge)*, ed. C. Woodring (Princeton: Routledge / Princeton University Press, 1990), 339.

79   Petersen, *Goethes "Faust" auf der deutschen Bühne*, 7–8.

80   [Geiger], "Eckermann an eine Schauspielerin," 260.

81   Günther Lohr, "Inskription des Szenischen: Zum Kontext von Goethes 'Regeln für Schauspieler' (1803)," and Irene Ruttmann, "Goethes Modell eines antinaturalistischen Theaters," in *Goethe et les arts du spectacle*, ed. M. Corvin (Bron: CERTC, 1985), 162–77, 180–202.

FIGURE 9.12 Meyerheim, *I'd give a deal if I could say who was that gentleman today!*, 29.8 × 40.2 cm, in *Scenen aus Goethes Faust in acht lithographirten Bildern* (Berlin: Zum ausschliesslichen Debit in Commission bei T. Trautwein, [1835]), pl. 7. Drawing of the room after a sketch by Prince Ferdinand Radziwill, the figure by Biermann
FAUST-MUSEUM, MOOSMANN COLLECTION, B 70, KNITTLINGEN, PHOTO CHRISTOPHER STEAD

poet-painter (*farvisi poeta-pittore*).[82] For an actor, exalting individual passions and character in chosen key episodes would offset freedom lost in movement. Acting in the first third of the nineteenth century pursued an ideal of immobile gesturing, seeking all the while to free itself from it, as by Schinkel and Seydelmann in Berlin, Klingemann in Braunschweig, even more so Tieck in Dresden, who privileged pathos. Diderot's idea of drama had made its way to the German States and defied motionless attitudes on stage. However, France's François-Joseph Talma, major tragedian of the Napoleonic era who had introduced natural gestures and onstage expression of emotions, still worked to classical reference, styling costume, gait and gestures on period documents. Charles Nodier would comment on his "numismatic physiognomy to the point of beguiling the eye of the most trained antiquary," when he played Nero in Racine's *Britannicus*.[83]

Emerging from the classical model, romantic theatre was slowly hatching. History met with a new, modern sensibility but production realities influenced expression on stage. In London's larger theatres (Drury Lane held 3,060 seats in 1812), verses easily became inaudible and face expressions lost. Extravagant gestures, attitudes in profile,

---

82   "Lettera di Ranieri de' Calzabigi all'autore sulle quattro sue prime tragedie" [1783], in *Il teatro italiano*, vol. 4, Vittorio Alfieri, *Tragedie*, ed. Luca Toschi (Torino: Einaudi, 1993), 349.

83   "Théâtre français," *Journal des débats* (8 July 1814): 2b (not 14 July as often stated).

actors detaching themselves from the backdrop were the solution for the public to follow the plot.[84] It is in such conditions and with extravagant diorama effects that Delacroix saw Soane and Terry's *Dr Faustus* in 1825.

Yet, modelling posture, expression or attitude on a print rather than statuary differed. The era of speedy publications was in full development. As the number of prints and books rose, it became increasingly difficult to long maintain a fixed attitude. Flexibility on the stage echoed mobility in printed matter, motion in society, change in politics. The nineteenth century's sense of time was fast evolving. Acting followed suit, particularly outside German States. Still, the indelible impression the etchings left in spectators' minds pleads the case.

In Béraud, Merle and Nodier's melodramatic adaptation of Goethe's *Faust* at Porte-Saint-Martin, Marie Dorval's interpretation of Margaret was much praised but less than Frédérick Lemaître's much discussed rendering of Mephistopheles. Commenting the fourth performance, Count Karl Friedrich Reinhard, Württemberg-born French diplomat and Goethe's friend, wrote, half seduced half miffed, to chancellor Müller:

> It is the Goethean Faust, it is Gretchen, Mephistopheles, Martha, yet misrepresented, materialized, limited to Earth and Hell, everything spiritual blurred. All the scenes from the original are there— but thrown together and mixed up—, the walk in the garden, the fiery wine but in a peasants' inn, the prison, the scene of the witches, even the Blocksberg. Gretchen's arrival, Mephistopheles's laugh are faithful to Retzsch's drawings. He has kept the laugh, still, it is a wild mocking laugh, besides he is a Catholic devil.[85]

When he notes that Gretchen is seen "writhing with horror on her straw," Retzsch's plate 25 (cf. Fig. 9.8) comes again to mind. Yet her "tugging at the chains, maddened by pain" is further romantic expression to be expected. The press echoed Reinhard's comment on Lemaître with a remarkable constancy: "infernal laugh," "that diabolical fury characteristic of the spirit of evil," impressed spectators and journalists.[86] One of them even alluded to "this

Jesuit laugh, which grants to the joy of this demon such fierceness."[87] Interpreting it proves however thorny.

Lemaître had trained as a mime artist at the Funambules and the *Faust* melodrama drew on that tradition. His acting was stylized and excessive, studiedly taking time for the spectators to appreciate his attitudes.[88] A press report pointedly mentioned "his statuesque pose" "when he seeks to subdue Faust to his power by his persuasive satanic speeches."[89] He himself narrates in his *Memoirs* that he had to spice up a part he considered insipid by introducing, with ballet master Coralli's help, a hypnotic "infernal waltz".[90] In his colourful study of the actor, L.-Henry Lecomte relates how Lemaître searched lengthily for the appropriate devilish expression in front of his mirror, slamming his shutters at neighbours' indiscretion. His successful finds, abundantly praised in a letter from mute and deaf individuals invited to the performance, show his modelling was effective.[91] Had he pored over Retzsch's etchings? It seems highly unlikely and his *Memoirs* make no allusion to prints. Is then Count Reinhard projecting *his own* recollection of the prints onto the theatrical display? Might it not rather be that the engravings had longer lasting effect than the very show evolving beneath his eyes?

Intriguingly, Retzsch re-emerges as a reference in Victor Pavie's 1874 travelogue. For three weeks in 1829, young Pavie accompanied to Weimar sculptor David d'Angers for his monumental Goethe bust. They both attended Goethe's eightieth birthday festivities and *Faust* performance (after Klingemann), Karl von LaRoche refining a spiritual Mephistopheles. Goethe himself had taken extra care to coach LaRoche in his part after a memorable *Faust* reading he had personally given.[92] The poet had left his mark on an actor in a performance he would ultimately not attend. Nearly a year later, the souvenir of the Porte-Saint-Martin was still vivid in young Pavie's mind. Compared to LaRoche's, he judged Lemaître's insolent and bizarre act tasteless and crude. In his narrative more than forty years later (presumably from earlier notes), he would give Weimar the upper hand. Goethe's radiance certainly influenced him, yet the key to such prominence is again Retzsch. Pavie's recollection of the Porte-Saint-Martin

---

84   Brian Dobbs, *Drury Lane: Three Centuries of the Theatre Royal, 1663–1971* (London: Cassell, 1972), 124.

85   BwGZ 3:967.

86   *Le Corsaire*, no. 2090 (30 Oct 1828): 2; *Le Courrier des théâtres*, no. 3616 (31 Oct 1828): 3–4; *L'Écho de Paris* (31 Oct 1828): 1; *Le Fashionable*, no. 3 (2 Nov 1828): 2.

87   *Nouveau journal de Paris*, no. 460 (2 Nov 1828): 1, author's emphasis.

88   Picat-Guinoiseau, *Une œuvre méconnue*, 32.

89   *L'Écho de Paris* (3 Nov 1828): 1.

90   *Souvenirs de Frédérick Lemaître, publiés par son fils avec portrait* (Paris: Paul Ollendorff, 1880), 101.

91   Louis-Henry Lecomte, *Un comédien au XIXe siècle: Frédérick-Lemaître, étude biographique et critique, d'après des documents inédits* (Paris: Chez l'Auteur, 1888), 1:126–28.

92   Mahl, *Goethes "Faust" auf der Bühne*, 30.

Faust surprisingly met Count Reinhard's description, although the latter was in Paris, the former in Weimar: "So it goes without saying that the ironic and curious accent with which Retzsch the draughtsman had marked his characters, dominated the scenic [Weimar] interpretation, and that Mme Dorval's pathetic outbursts could not have responded better to the genius of the audience than the freakish flippancy and devilishness of Frédérick."[93] Retzsch's prints had made a far more lasting impression than any famous actor's performance on stage.

Their effect impressed imaginations even independently of Goethe's *Faust* as in Amédée Pichot's 1825 travelogue through England and Scotland. Pichot refers to Retzsch's *Faust* but comments on actor Charles Mayne Young, Shakespeare's Iago in a London theatre. Obviously *Othello* had nothing to do with *Faust*. Yet Pichot recognized in Young's acting none other than Retzsch's Mephistopheles to the point of noting down: "You would say that Young has moulded (*calqué*) the facial features and attitudes of his Iago after those of this astute messenger of Satan." The identification was seemingly made during the performance itself. But also, *beyond it*, while Pichot leafed through the prints: "I was looking again this morning at these etchings [Retzsch's] at Conalghi's [*sic*], and in each one of them I recognized Young."[94] The prints both prepared and tracked down the acting, as if the latter had no proper weight, no bearing, no plasticity. The engravings had somehow been etched onto actors' and viewers' minds. Similarly, a major actor, such as Ernesto Ristori performing Hamlet, would serve as template for yet another Retzsch set: "Of his poses, in the main scenes, one could make an outline album like Retsch's *Faust*, and these simple contours would render the entire meaning of the drama."[95]

9.7 Outfits: Models and Embodiment

Theatrical costume followed Retzsch with adaptations. Dress is one of the standard means of positing a character on stage. Harvard's Theatre Collection has a pair of full-length portraits in stage costume of the 1825 Drury Lane protagonists, notably *Mr. Terry as Mephistopheles* strongly impressing Delacroix. Though not coloured in this print (Fig. 9.13), Daniel Terry in a "bottle-green double and hose, tight to the skin" with a "little red cloak to

his back" and "a red cock's feather" on his "very small hat" (after the Cumberland edition of the play) had come to life from Retzsch's outline, tailing Goethe's description:

> [...] To cheer
> You up, I've come dressed as a cavalier:
> In scarlet, with gold trimmings, cloak
> Of good stiff silk, and in my hat
> The usual cock's feather; take
> A fine long pointed rapier,
> And one's complete. So, my dear sir,
> Be ruled by me and do just that:
> Wear clothes like mine, strike out, be free,
> And learn what the good life can be.
> (F 1534–43, trans. D. Luke)

Not so for Faustus himself, in "Oxonian gown and trencher cap," a costume submitting to English dress codes and a different agenda in a plot at odds with Goethe's. Splendour and variety were secrets of successful melodrama. Lavish theatrics compelled most characters' diversity (and enhancement of actresses' feminine charms) performance after performance.

Take for instance Margaret, the role that moved all nineteenth-century hearts to the point of dispossessing Faust's tragedy as her own. Retzsch's Margaret is unaffectedly dressed: her only gown is simple and neat with tapering cuffs barely covering the hands. Beneath her humble bodice, with chemise's high neckline and sleeves occasionally slashed (arms raised), her bosom is hardly perceptible, her sexuality scarcely manifest. The skirt, with apron of subordinate status, conceals the lower members and falls decorously over the shoes. The most daring images show her at toilet in her chamber. In plate 9, she releases her plaits that take on an elaborate, serpentine, animated look, while she intensely dwells on remembering Faust (cf. Fig. 9.6). As she considers the jewels, in mere petticoat in plate 11, her thigh and leg show (cf. Fig. 2.24 and 5.11c), exactly as in the garden scene (plate 14), when amorously plucking the daisy (cf. Fig. 10.3). Forlorn at her spinning wheel in plate 16, her hair disappears under a simple coif and a plain flat collar covers her shoulders (cf. Fig. 3.1b). Only in prison does she emerge as a mature woman, with an ample bosom and generous lap. She lifts arms in despair as her unbridled mane swarms over her back in plate 26 (cf. Fig. 2.17). Using a limited vocabulary of postures and a single costume, Retzsch has courted an intriguingly nuanced scale of characteristic stances. His measured, indeed controlled, list of attitudes duplicated itself onstage. Kindermann reports that in a remarkable 24 May 1832 Vienna performance of Margaret in honour

---

93   Pavie, *Voyages*, 93.
94   Pichot, *Voyage historique et littéraire*, 1:393.
95   Théophile Gautier, "Revue des théâtres" *Le Moniteur universel*, no. 148 (28 May 1866): 1.

FIGURE 9.13 *Mr. Terry as Mephistopheles the Devil in "Faustus,"* portrait print, undated (c.1825)
HARVARD, HOUGHTON LIBRARY, MS THR 933, BOX 3

FIGURE 9.14
Actress Julie Gley as Margaret in a costume by Philipp von Stubenrauch, Hofburgtheater, 29 May 1839, Vienna
© KHM-MUSEUMSVERBAND, THEATERMUSEUM, HZ HM805, VIENNA

of Goethe's decease (22 March), actress Julie Gley undid Gretchen's braids in Retzschian fashion. Did she maintain the gesture over the years? The period picture corroborating the scene refers in fact to a 29 May 1839 première.[96] Her costume details, designed by Philipp von Stubenrauch, even her acting (Fig. 9.14), exactly mirror Meyerheim's 1835 lithograph after Retzsch and Schinkel (cf. Fig. 9.12).

Yet actresses also gained fame thanks to bold and opulent stage outfits. Such is Sophie Schütz-Höffert's attire when Eduard Schütz offers his arm as Faust, 1836 in Braunschweig (Fig. 9.15). "Correspondence" or "conformity" with

---

96 Kindermann, *Theatergeschichte der Goethezeit*, 872. Inversely Theatre Museum Vienna (with thanks to Dr Rudi Risatti).

FIGURE 9.15　Cäcilie Brand, *Herr und Madame Schütz (als Faust und Gretchen)*, print, n.d., various formats
COURTESY HAAB, F GR 5748 (18), WEIMAR

Retzsch's seem hardly convincing terms.[97] While Schütz's pose and mien imitate Retzsch's etching of the meeting (cf. Fig. 1.8), his wife's tight-fitting, elaborately front-laced bodice with plunging neckline expose her shoulders, lavish bosom, and naked arms to advantage. An hourglass corset, shaping her figure, complements an elaborate hairdo and long earrings. She smiles promisingly at Faust whose hand already grips her waist. Magnetic accomplices, they are drawn close whereas Retzsch had hitherto shown them keeping respectable distance. Moreover the actress holds a flower, their meeting already fusing with the garden scene on the print. Further patent differences may be noted. Marie Dorval discovers the jewels in a low-neck dress curtailed to reveal her ankles (Fig. 9.16). Two ornately knotted ribbons garnish the puffed sleeves. A forehead band, with a precious stone, signs off the high mounting braids, the only element still reminiscent of Retzsch's coiffure. The Porte-Saint-Martin had reopened after more than three months' refit, and impersonations had to be highly seasoned. Three coloured prints published by printer and bookseller Herménégilde-Honorat Hautecœur commemorate the fanciful costumes and appealing scenes, including the hypnotic waltz from act 1 extolled in the press. Success had depended on actors' attire and delivery, phantasmagoria, *coups de théâtre*, and choreography.

The Drury Lane disparity between Faustus in Oxonian gown and a Retzschian Mephistophiles [sic] served to set the latter's distinct style. The fiend cut a unique figure. His was a "parade role," an exceptional occasion for an actor's expression of brilliance and range.[98] Retzsch's stylus had incised a thin, drawn-out and lithe form, a lanky and lean

---

97　Mahl, *Goethes "Faust" auf der Bühne*, 17.

98　Petersen, *Goethes "Faust" auf der deutschen Bühne*, 25.

FIGURE 9.16 Maleuvre, *I would never dare to adorn myself with all these jewels,* showing Marie Dorval as Margaret, coloured etching, *c.*1828, 23 × 14.5 cm, published by Hautecœur
BnF, 4-ICO COS-1 (7,637), PARIS

FIGURE 9.17 Moritz Retzsch, The wine prodigy at Auerbach's tavern, coloured version, n.d., 15.2 × 19.8 cm. *Umrisse zu Goethe's Faust gezeichnet von Retsch* (Stuttgart & Tübingen: Cotta, 1816), pl. 5
FDH, FRANKFURTER GOETHE-MUSEUM, III-13102, FRANKFURT

figure, crowned by a smallish, triangular head with animal features that snakes its way between episodes. Irony incarnate, his glove-like costume sheaths sardonic, scathing lines. Three rudiments persistently shape his pointed silhouette: his cloak's rigidity, the spiky prominence of his cockerel's feather, and long pointed blade, as in the Drury Lane print (cf. Fig. 9.13). His invitation to Faust to replicate his own attire gives the tragedy a powerful clone. Scarlet stresses his infernal symbolism but also his sturdiness, durability and agility as he elastically glides from scene to scene. Retzsch appropriately applied scarlet throughout his carefully coloured prints as in Auerbach's tavern or at Martha's (Fig. 9.17 & Fig. 2.25). The tint he chose kowtows to older established traditions, particularly the devil's attire at the witches' Sabbath (*scharlachne Kleider*),[99] but also the Viennese eighteenth-century theatre that had inspired Goethe.[100] Red would prevail.

The devil's costume, "entirely red, with the ironical feather curved on his head, was of the best taste," penned Victor Pavie from 1829 Weimar.[101] Much later, Edward Gordon Craig would note on the flyleaf of his original

---

99 Lily Weiser-Aall, "Hexe," in *Handwörterbuch des deutschen Aberglaubens*, ed. E. Hoffmann-Krayer and Hanns Bächtold-Stäubli (Berlin: Walter de Gruyter & Co, 1930–1931), 3:1888.
100 André Dabezies, *Le mythe de Faust* (Paris: Armand Colin, 1972), 50.
101 Pavie, *Médaillons romantiques*, 84.

1828 Audot edition in a hotchpotch of English, French and Italian:

> Mephisto here shown as a gallant.
> Bien! but he has to be distinguished.
> & always the master—commanding—
> quiet—self possessed of course as
> dignified as an ascetic.
>> Occasionally daemonic & fearful
>> but more often masked by perfect manners.

> This amore was Irving in the 19th century
> at the Lyceum 1885–1886.[102]

Then seventeen years old, Craig, engaged by actor Henry Irving at the Lyceum in 1889, had certainly witnessed his triumph in *Faust*, on which more shortly. "Mr Irving's Mephistopheles is more like Retzsch's than that of any other illustrator," had corroborated in December 1886 the writer and critic Walter Herries Pollock, who used Retzsch in one of his own novels (see Chapter 10). Irving was his best friend. His Mephistopheles was his "best achievement in expression," he added, a type "taken" by Irving and "improved on by touches of his own genius." The effect was again as much the result of Retzsch styling Irving as that of Irving recalling Retzsch—just like Amédée Pichot's grasp of Young's Iago sixty years hither: "Here indeed Retzsch's Mephistopheles comes nearest to Mr Irving's in its diabolical and humorous nonchalance."[103]

9.8   Creating Types

The keyword for such workings was *type*. Type obsessed nineteenth century writing and type-making haunted nineteenth century graphics. Kenny Meadows's *Heads of the People* (1839–40), translated into French as *Les Anglais peints par eux-mêmes* (1840–41), met with a major type-making venture in France, *Les Français peints par eux-mêmes* (1840–42). Great Britain in turn would welcome Jules Janin's *Pictures of the French: A Series of Literary and Graphic Delineations of French Characters* (1840). This all-embracing literature of *physiologies* has been extensively studied. Its main purpose was a social cartography of all professions and walks of life but it contributed to furthering national stereotypes.

From 1830, the idea also gained special weight and significance in literature and media multiplication. *Type* derives etymologically from the Ancient Greek *typto*, litt. "to make a strong, indelible impression," by extension, "to print" as in the printing press. *Type* and *image* related by printing and reprinting, and the proliferation of his images through copied prints, made of Retzsch an exemplary template, a matrix for media cloning.

Literature played second fiddle to the idea. In a well-known 1830 essay, creating types was for Charles Nodier the hallmark of genius. Types were symbolic characters, the quintessence of ideas, stamped and moulded. They embodied "an original but striking individuality" that made the type "familiar to all," therefore "a true image, a typical image of man."[104] In the process, proper names, dispossessed of their capitals, turned into simple nouns, commonly shared. Passing through everybody's hands, they were the widespread coinage of intellectual transaction. Writers like Goethe cast such, as Nodier knew: "everybody admits that Faust and Mephistopheles are admirable *types*."[105] Steeped in books and print matters, had Nodier intuited the importance of printed duplication? In his *Human Comedy* foreword, twelve years after Nodier, Honoré de Balzac, himself a publisher and printer who ambitioned to create a literature representative of the lifestyle and mores of his time, stated that types were cast by "gathering together the distinctive features of several homogeneous characters."[106] An alchemy of distillation, extraction, and composition presided over Balzac's Faust-like broodings, as he nightly combined types in his study. If God was writing (*logos*), as Goethe's *Faust* spread through Retzsch's burgeoning prints into other arts and media, the devil was setting the type and printing.

More precisely, Nodier put forward that seizing prototypes hinges on *invention* (condensed features in a dazzling individual), whereas perpetuating fine antique types hinges on *reproduction* (copies). The given names that become "nouns in every language" (substantives commonly shared), brought forward by Nodier as evidence of

---

102   BnF ASP: 16-EGC-368, MS inscription front flyleaf.
103   Pollock, "Illustrations of *Faust*," *Temple Bar* 78 (Dec 1886): 528–29.

104   Nodier, "Des types en littérature," in *Œuvres de Charles Nodier*, vol. 5, *Rêveries* (Paris: Eugène Renduel, 1832), 52, 56.
105   Ibid., 64, his emphasis.
106   "Avant-propos à la Comédie Humaine," in *Œuvres complètes de H. de Balzac* (Paris: A. Houssiaux, 1855), 1:22. Text dated July 1842.

the type-making process, are exemplary of the inherent relation between types ("great literary figures chosen to become human symbols") and stereotypes.

Retzsch's secret in creating types was simple and manifold. On the one hand, his treatment was exemplary. He followed scenes closely and launched vivid representations. He was the first to schematize the plot, use recurrent oppositions, and bring forward the three types Goethe had moulded: dejected genius (Faust), betrayed purity (Margaret), and ironic negation (Mephistopheles). Delacroix did not err when he freehand copied Retzsch's Gretchen at the spinning wheel, a delicate figure encapsulating charm, purity, beauty, innocence, appeal, modesty, and melancholy, all that Gretchen stood for in the play (cf. Fig. 2.7, 3.1b and 6.1a). He noted in his diary on 20 February 1824:

> Every time I see the *Faust* engravings again, I feel seized by the desire to make a brand new form of painting, which would consist in tracing, so to speak, from life. One would render interesting, through the extreme truth of brevity, the most simple postures. One could thus, for the small pictures, draw the subject and sketchily model it on the canvas; then copy the right posture from the sitter.[107]

Reviews of the time had encouraged artists to copy Retzsch in order to train their hand. Delacroix had turned that method into an aesthetic consideration, not just treadmill work. He would calque the postures on canvas (like outlines traced in the etching process), then complete them from life—just as an actor, directed on stage, would take the poise from a graphic still.

On the other hand, Retzsch's work was not only published and republished but also transferred and re-mediated (Chapter 7). Its added value lay in reproduction and extension through other arts. Replicas, genuine or counterfeit, enhanced its aura. Imitations, engraved or faked copies turned the originals into a well-worn mould. The copying process in itself, by burrowing into types and repeating them, reduced them to replicas, stereotypes, clichés. When considered an archetypal narrative, with countless versions and forms demoted, myth itself does not function otherwise. Once established on patterns or around great human symbols (types), myth is rolled out at the risk of reducing itself—through repetition, simplification, and reduction—to a stereotype. In numerous myths

we may observe multiplication, brushing aside story lines and versions, reducing complex circumstances to a simplified pattern, turning a given name into a common noun (the opposite proves true but less frequent). Similarly, Retzsch's series did not only work as a synoptic substitute for Goethe's tragedy made accessible to all. It became a stronghold foundation for the play's iconographic repertoire. The literary work, unique and hard to access, was assisted, surrounded, escorted by a replicate genealogy of the twenty-six originals spawned by multiple reproduction techniques.

Once they materialized on stage, by that decisive, intensifying effect, they turned the graphic portrayals into well-known figures that impregnated public imagination, as Craig's, Reinhard's, Pichot's and Pollock's examples show. Close, familiar personae came alive in the limelight. None cut a sharper figure than Mephistopheles.

As actor, dramatic producer (*Dramaturg*), and stage director all in one, Carl Seydelmann incarnated from 1832 the Mephistophelean role to perfection in Stuttgart. His performance strongly differed from that of Duke Charles of Mecklenburg, who had set the tone in top hat, tailcoat and silk stockings 1819–20 in Monbijou. Thanks to his acting prowess, Seydelmann's costume and scenery after Retzsch served as a basis to artfully elaborate an influential character, leaving his imprint even on toy theatre.[108] Six years later, enticed to Berlin, he would perform Mephistopheles at the Royal Theatre.[109] His interpretation would set a standard in Germany for over half a century, yet not without difficulties. In Berlin they would prefer to "have the devil as civilized as possible, i.e., Voland the *Junker* with his cock's feather, the 'Baron,' rather than the fearful elementary spirit, who is not simply the devil, but Hell as well."[110] Seydelmann was no elegant cavalier, nor ironic man of the world. Demonization ruled his physiognomy, his cloven hoof, clutches, and drooping nose.[111] Added, artificial devices were scarce, Seydelmann's twisted facial muscles did all. Was it indeed surprising to see devil and man merge? Therese Huber, stressing the moral facet, and

---

107   Delacroix, *Journal*, 1:120–21.

108   August Lewald, *Seydelmann und das deutsche Schauspiel* (Stuttgart, 1835), qtd. in Grosse and Vogelsang, eds., *Faust und Mephisto: Goethes Dramenfiguren auf dem Theater* (Cologne: Theatermuseum der Universität Köln, 1983), 67; Georg Garde, *Theater-Geschichte im Spiegel der Kinder-Theater* (Herning: Borgens Forlag, 1971), 65.

109   Mahl, *Goethes "Faust" auf der Bühne*, 31–33.

110   Karl Gutzkow, *Öffentliches Leben in Deutschland, 1838–1842* (Leipzig 1842), qtd. in Grosse and Vogelsang, eds., *Faust und Mephisto*, 68.

111   Petersen, *Goethes "Faust" auf der deutschen Bühne*, 26.

her English follower had previously noted that Goethe's devil (through Retzsch) was intensely human, the *alter ego* of Faust *sapiens*.[112] A new Mephistopheles had come into being in the very preface presenting Retzsch. Similarly, for Craig, blending demonization with "perfect manners" was the secret of a distinguished Mephistopheles. Devilry met gentility in Retzsch, who had also tailored the attire.

Costume would style Mephistopheles for the masses. A prose summary of Soane and Terry's 1825 play, published for a wide and modest public sometime in the 1850s as *Faustus: or, The Demon of the Drachenfels*, sums it up, recapping Terry's outfit that had brought Retzsch's drawing to life (cf. Fig. 9.13): "A tall red feather rose from his conical hat, and a short cloak hung from his shoulders."[113] As late as July 1887, Pollock affirmed noting Irving, yet pointing again to Drury Lane's Terry: "Until quite recent years, Mephistopheles was known to the English public as a name, and to the French public by Terry's performance of the part in a kind of olla-podrida of Goethe's play, which olla-podrida led to one very striking result—the great Delacroix's very unequal and very powerful designs."[114] The model had escaped Britain to France, perhaps infiltrated Europe. En route to the United States, it discovered in Irving a powerful relay.

Dozens of signed or anonymous nineteenth-century prints, now in the Theatre and Performance collections of the Victoria and Albert Museum, show Irving's slim red silhouette expanding from the stage to cover all printed media. In yet another adaptation of Goethe's *Faust* by William Gorman Wills, Irish playwright, novelist and painter, actor-cum-manager Irving met with one of his greatest successes as Mephistopheles. His tall, skinny build abetted the identification. His dazzling production opened at London's Lyceum Theatre on 19 December 1885, ran until 1888, then played on Broadway, and toured the United States that same year. It was revived in 1894, reached its 500th performance on 30 June, remaining in the company's repertoire until 1902, the end of Irving's partnership with Ellen Terry (who played Margaret). Immensely popular and appraised by critics, the loose version introduced a chilling interpretation of Mephistopheles along with new sound and lighting effects. The variety of media that record the performance (and costume) speak for

themselves—limited here to only three artists but further expanded by countless artworks.

Painter and illustrator John Bernard Partridge, later chief cartoonist of *Punch*, also acted with the Lyceum company. His several portrayals of Irving-Mephistopheles include: a watercolour (Fig. 9.18); a pencil, charcoal and gouache drawing; numerous sketches in a compilation page of the 23 January 1886 *Illustrated London News*; and even a witty drawing after the witch's kitchen published in *Punch* in April 1894 (Fig. 9.19). One instance of the compilation page ("Mephistopheles on the Brocken top"), wood engraved in dim red, became a stock item for the London Stereoscopic and Photographic Company, and was further reproduced on posters and cards. In a black and red sketch, Phil May, famous for economy of line, captured Irving's expression incisively (Fig. 9.20). An oil painting by William Henry Margetson, *Henry Irving as Mephistopheles and George Alexander as Faust in "Faust" by W. G. Wills, adapted from Goethe*, dated as 1885 by the V&A, can only have been painted in 1886 or later, since the witch's kitchen it shows had only then been added to the adaptation. In the same database, an unidentified press sketch shows Irving in his dressing room, still totally identifying with Mephistopheles. In another one, Queen Victoria placidly observes the character on stage. As Albert of Saxe-Coburg's widow, she is bound to have remembered her father-in-law's taste for theatre and politics independent of the second Reich, which Great Britain regarded as a rampant menace.

Irving's vast gallery forms a culminating point, preceded and followed by several other depictions. Opera had paved the way. In 1869, the year Gounod's *Faust* entered the official repertoire of the Paris Opera (then named Académie Impériale de Musique), A. Morlon lithographed Jean-Baptiste Faure as Mephistopheles in a red costume with an offensive double feather on his cap. Faure had already triumphed in a July 1864 London performance as show several sepia photographs by Leonida Caldesi. Alfred Concanen in turn pictured in chromolithography Howard Paul as Mephistopheles in a similar red costume on a score's cover advertising *Faust in Five Minutes*, Henry Walker's "Musical Medley Historiette" of 1868. Another score cover for J. Meredith Ball's 1887 *Mephistopheles: March*, dedicated to Irving (in unmistakable costume amid Brocken crags), is a lithograph by Hugh Concanen, Alfred's son. Music halls were at the zenith of popularity and music sheet covers were instrumental in propagating the Mephistophelean type. Even Mademoiselle Debreux, photographed in 1870 as Lyceum Theatre's Mephistopheles for *Le Petit Faust*, wears a similar costume. German toy theatre exploited the craze. When coloured popular prints

---

112   [Huber], "Vorrede," 4–5; Analysis 1820, 2. See p. 127 & 140.

113   *Faustus* 1852, 2.

114   [W. H. Pollock], "Mephistopheles at the Lyceum," *Longman's Magazine* 10, no. 57 (July 1887): 294.

FIGURE 9.18
John Bernard Partridge, *Mr Irving in the character of Mephistopheles*, watercolour, pencil and ink on paper, c.1885, 31 × 20.5 cm
COURTESY AND © V&A, GABRIELLE ENTHOVEN COLLECTION, S. 321–2011, LONDON

FIGURE 9.19
John Bernard Partridge, Irving as Mephistopheles in the witch's kitchen, print of proof sketch, dated 24 April 1894, 18.1 × 13 cm. Illustration to A Student of Goethenburg, "On Faust," *Punch; or, The London Charivari*, CVI (28 Apr 1894): 193, with the caption *Betting Mephistopheles; or, The Magic Ring-Man*
COURTESY AND © V&A, THEATRE COLLECTION, S. 3766–2013, LONDON

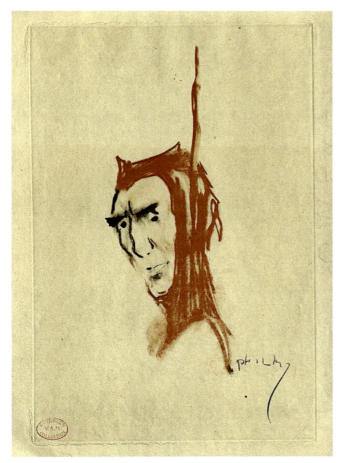

FIGURE 9.20   Phil May, Henry Irving as Mephistopheles in *Faust*, colour print, c.1885–88, 24.5 × 32.5 cm
COURTESY AND © V&A, GABRIELLE ENTHOVEN COLLECTION, S. 965–2017, LONDON

toned down costumed *Faust* figures, Mephistopheles's attire still flared up in rusty red slashed with yellow.[115] It reflected Seydelmann's impressive German Mephistopheles who rivalled Irving's hold on the English-speaking world.

It is these flourishing multiples of the Retzschian model, copied in turn, that hatched the devil's type, leaving an unforgettable mark on *Faust* iconography. In 1847, he is Tony Johannot's sinuous and skinny demon, appearing to Faust or springing (both fantastically and comically) between a startled Faust and desperate Margaret (cf. Fig. 6.20). Red costume, short cape and long feather are his trademark. In several images, the feather may even be double, ominously long and thin, hovering horn-like on the wedge-shaped head. Profuse prints, posters, press cuttings, photographs, postcards, caricatures, illustrations,

costume designs, even models, disseminated the template in France, helped by the popularity of Gounod's opera, Berlioz's *Damnation de Faust*, or even Hervé's spoof of Gounod, *Le Petit Faust*, which toured internationally. In a 1911 satirical sketch of *Rouen-Gazette*, a provincial French paper, such a typified Mephistopheles carries characters from two operettas off stage to usher in Franz Lehár's *The Merry Widow*, an enormous success at the time. In his Retzschian attire he had become the very mascot of Rouen's Théâtre des Arts. *Le Méphisto: Journal théâtral, musical, fantaisiste, illustré* was launched in Rouen on 7 January 1883. Its masthead adopted no other figure but yet another Mephistopheles of Retzschian ilk playing the mandolin under a tree, despite German repertoire being rarely staged in Rouen.[116] Dozens of similar *Méphisto* theatre periodicals covered fin-de-siècle French territory and even spread to Algiers.

9.9   In the Limelight over Time

In a merry 1968 *Faust*, staged in East Berlin by Adolf Heinz and Wolfgang Dresen, and in a *Faust* performed ten years later in Stuttgart by the same, Retzsch's design of the poodle growing elephant- and hippopotamus-like was used for a last time. In East Berlin, an enormous poodle was inflated during the performance. In Stuttgart, three actors on top of each other, covered by a large, black poodle's mantle, served as the creature.[117] This rarely used scene amusingly concludes a long series of Retzsch routines on stage, which pinpoint unexpected outcomes beyond their frequent employment by stage directors in the first half of the nineteenth century: the hold of outlines over our collective imagination; their shaping of actors' interpretation; and weight in creating stereotypes. To have engaged wittily with Retzsch in the 1960s and 1970s closed an era that is unlikely to return as theatre has since engaged with *Faust* experimentally. Yet the clever entertainment it produced could be seen as another tribute to its former glory.

In Gérard Oury's extremely popular 1966 film *La Grande Vadrouille (Don't Look Now … We're Being Shot At!)*, a full-chested Mephistopheles in the foreseeable red costume fleetingly responds to the central character, an opera conductor played by Louis de Funès. It is obvious that both type and its hallmark work by a cumulative repetition that has not yet waned for us.

---

115   Garde, *Theater-Geschichte*, 65.

116   Christian Goubault, *La musique, les acteurs et le public au Théâtre des Arts de Rouen: 1776–1914* (Rouen: CRDP, 1979), 69, 13, 64.

117   Mahl, *Goethes "Faust" auf der Bühne*, 205.

FIGURES 9.21A–B Hergé, *Coke en stock* (Bruxelles: Casterman, 1958), 39, boxes A3 and C3
COURTESY AND ©
HERGÉ-TINTIN*IMAGINATIO* 2023

Nor, when he reappears in a fancy-dress ball on a luxury yacht cruising the Red Sea in Hergé's *Coke en stock* (1958, translated as *The Red Sea Sharks* in 1960), is the interloper hard to recognize as Rastapopoulos (Fig. 9.21a–b). His clothing has turned out so emblematic that we instantly realize that the yacht, a potential refuge for the trio drifting on a raft (Haddock, Tintin and hireling pilot Piotr Szut), is the hotbed of threat and peril. Ironically, Rastapopoulos's allusions to Hell ("By Lucifer!" "Fire and brimstone!") are played-down metaphors for danger of (his own) detection. The tables are turned, and he has been identified. If the shipwrecked heroes lay eyes on him, he will be recognized any minute as himself and a diabolical villain. The use of *Faust* in *Les Aventures de Tintin* has been brilliantly analysed by Cormac Newark as a case of nested reception of Gounod's opera with La Castafiore singing Margaret's jewel song as centre of attention.[118] Let me add that the costumed Mephistopheles appears but twice in the Tintin set, in two subsequent albums, as a (genuine) opera character in *L'Affaire Tournesol* (1956, translated as *The Calculus Affair*) and as masked scoundrel in *The Red Sea Sharks*. In the latter, Hergé significantly uses the costume device when Captain Haddock and Tintin seek for refuge or flee to avoid their identity being exposed in a camouflaged context of imminent danger. By playing the identification card so closely to the Mephistophelean cliché, Hergé revives and renews the truism, uses the commonplace critically, stirs laughter, and furthers the hide-and-seek game of characters, leaving no time for his reader to reflect or analyse emotions.

On hot summer days, when competing cyclists wind through the country, the red "Devil," German cycling fan and bicycle inventor Didi Senft, escorts several *étapes* of the Tour de France in his red polyester suit. He also performs on Il Giro d'Italia. Adults and children rejoice when seeing him, so popular is he a symbol of the event. Nobody of course thinks of who first cut the figure, Moritz Retzsch, artist hardly recognized nowadays in Germany, let alone in France or Italy. His *Faust* outlines have however left their hallmark on popular imagination, as strongly, durably and recognizably as Rastapopoulos's red disguise on his yacht. Retzsch's influence is all embracing. To firebrand a well-known event, open to all comers, having launched a brilliant career in stage sets and props for the aristocracy (at Radziwill's Monbijou theatrics) is no small exploit for the impact of one man's imagination.

---

118 Newark, "Faust, Nested Reception and La Castafiore," *Cambridge Opera Journal* 25, no. 2 (July 2013): 165–84.

CHAPTER 10

Ink Worlds

To discuss Retzsch in literary texts blazes a trail. In his study on *German Romanticism and English Art*, William Vaughan derives from "the accounts of contemporary [nineteenth-century] novelists" the idea that the rather "peculiar attraction" of Retzsch's outlines was a sign "of mere superficial appeal," "an essential adornment of the cultivated lady's drawing-room."[1] Vaughan crucially addressed the intense interest of English artists and poets in Retzsch. Conversely, his summary view of novels hardly resists textual analysis and the intricate symbolism often emanating from writers' handling of Retzsch, especially in fiction. He did not name the "contemporary novelists," and his otherwise excellent critique refers only to Disraeli. Without pretending to exhaust the subject, I want to advance in this chapter several new names forming an array of cases, whilst re-investigating Disraeli's. I mean to show how and why Heinrich Heine, Benjamin Disraeli, Edgar Allan Poe, Théophile Gautier, Walter Herries Pollock, even Charles Dickens (in *David Copperfield*) and his regular illustrator, Phiz, all sampled Retzsch at various moments in their own creations. They did not just confirm or enhance a fashion. They exploited the graphic benchmark in intricate ways that show how literature turns to art to fortify or extend plot, complement style, and vie for prominence in aesthetic appeal.[2]

10.1   Devilish Relish of Converted Israelites

Two such uses occur in inaugural prose works by daring young men, Heine's *Die Harzreise* (*The Harz Journey*, written in 1824, published in 1826), and Disraeli's first novel *Vivian Grey* (1826). The former alludes to only two plates introducing the Brocken sequence as "Master Retzsch's pretty *Faust* images" (*auf den hübschen Faustbildern des Meister Retzsch*, 116).[3] The latter accommodates Retzsch's entire set in chapter x of Disraeli's Book Two of the novel and projects onto it several Château Desir characters. Although both allusions to Retzsch seem but minor

textual details, their multiple implications enrich analytical reading when examined more closely.

Heine only embarked on his own hike from 12 or 13 September to 11 October 1824, but in his playful account the narrator ascends the Brocken on the night of 30 April to 1 May. He makes a point of honour to match the date of ascent with the traditional Walpurgis Night, which gives *The Harz Journey* a mysteriously supernatural tinge. True to such playful deceit, Heine tricks his readers. The introductory reference to Retzsch is a picture (*Bild*) of what will neither *happen* nor *be shown* in his future *Travel Pictures* (*Reisebilder*). Irony is predominant, no witchery occurs. Instead, Heine parallels the Eucharist to a sunset, a scene contemplated from a platform by numerous students, craftsmen and middle-class holidaymakers, a lay gathering defiantly treated like a Catholic mass (119). Furthermore, the narrative *ends* with his arrival at Ilsestein, a locality cited by Goethe in the Walpurgis Night, yet only at the onset of the witches' congregation (F 3968). The pretence deflates the expectancy of a storyline centred on their revelry, and works rather as an X-ray of the motley poetics at work in a heterogeneous text. It critically substantiates its distinct design.

The Harz Journey lays claim to the status of fragmentary and rambling narrative, contrary to and competing with two of Goethe's travelogues, *Letters from Switzerland* and the *Italian Journey*, explicitly or implicitly mentioned (120 & 128). Besides, his actual hike took Heine further, to Weimar, where he indeed met Goethe on 1 October. *The Harz Journey* is therefore much more than the travelogue of a genuine journey. Its autobiographical facet, rich in associations of ideas, assesses Heine's Göttingen studies, mocks his tutors, refers to his recent opportunistic christening, and unravels his souvenirs of places, women, and books. It is also an analytical tour of opinions, beliefs, and judgments. It weaves a complex pattern of literary references and genres in which allusions are not to be taken at face value. It is tempting to see this varied array as a literary equivalent of Retzsch's Walpurgis orgy in plate 22 (cf. Fig. 5.7): an attempt to recompose the picture by learned means and through varying roles.

As the narrator ascends the Brocken amid animated nature, glimpses of tales that will never be, although he would have loved to write them, mingle with vibrant descriptions and cultural allusions. To take but one example, the souvenir (after a well-known German legend) of

---

1   Vaughan, *German Romanticism*, 123.

2   In this chapter, pages from the literary works in reference editions (including Théophile Gautier's fiction) appear in the main text, except for his press reviews referenced in footnotes.

3   Heine, "Die Harzreise," in *Briefe aus Berlin. Über Polen. Reisebilder I–II (Prosa)*, ed. Jost Hermand, in *Historisch-kritische Gesamtausgabe der Werke* (Hamburg: Hoffmann & Campe, 1973), 6:81–138.

© EVANGHELIA STEAD, 2023 | DOI:10.1163/9789004543010_013

This is an open access chapter distributed under the terms of the CC BY-NC-ND 4.0 license.

huge granite blocks thrown like magic bullets by evil spirits during the Walpurgis Night spurs the writer's desire to compete with Goethe (115–16). Mockingly, Heine chooses the most modern part of the witchery in *Faust*, the jeering allusions to several Enlightenment philosophers and thinkers, particularly Goethe's "Buttock Fantasist" or Proktophantasmist (F 4144–71). No coincidence that, in Goethe's blatant satire of this part of Walpurgis, "Buttock Fantasist" proudly asserts finding "travel-material" even in the orgy, and ambitions to control poets and devils. The prototype, Friedrich Nicolai, indeed a prolific travel-writer, supplies a counter-model. Yet, Heine's own satire is not aimed at persons but literary trends and self-irony. His is a gathering of bluestockings, a supremely literary high court, half-animal half-human, mildly drinking tea and judging poetic works, including two of Heine's own plays, favourably assessed, since he is henceforth deemed a pious and Christian author. The facetiousness is all the more obvious as this scene proves to be but a frightening nightmare. Extended to the full narrative, the sudden change of mood, taunting tone, piled-up references, and disorder reflect the wild and mixed carousing of Retzsch's plate 22, and its leering orgiastic devils at odds with the decapitated and pitiful Margaret.

Expelled from University and even excluded by the innkeeper, the narrator is an outcast. The Brocken becomes his individual revel, his appropriate tribune to act out an unruly threefold part: as traveller-cum-reader, he holds in check *Faust*, "the grand, mystical, German national tragedy" (116); as a performer, he joins in the action and dramatically stages it; and as an interpreter, he indirectly plans his own chapter on *Faust* in a future title tackling Mme de Staël. Indeed, Heine's *De l'Allemagne* (*On Germany*), initially published 1834 in French, includes a chapter on Johann Faust's legend, centred in point of fact on Mephistophela, the female devil of his ballet to be, *Der Doktor Faust, ein Tanzpoem* (first authored 1847). Years before, on his solitary Brocken tour, the pert narrator transpires as Faust a number of times. He ascends alongside a jocular, out-of-breath, Mephistopheles imparting to him his humorous "cloven foot" spirit (116). As professor-cum-huckster or silver-tongued devil, he gives lectures, particularly to a beautiful young lady met on the Brocken (118 & 120). And, in one of the closing paragraphs, he declares "But now it stirs again and presses in my breast" (137), citing Goethe's verses on the two souls dwelling and competing in *his* Faust's breast (F 1112–13).

One last striking feature is the optical dimension of these pages. They were perhaps influenced by a phenomenon known as the Brocken spectre (*Brockengespenst*),

the magnified shadow of an observer, surrounded by a halo and cast upon clouds heading into the sun. Heine's idiosyncratic treatment seems to play with this, yet again in a literary sense. He makes of the Blocksberg a map of Northern Germany that allows scrutiny of his *Vaterland* (and its foremost "national" tragedy, Goethe's *Faust*). He also turns Brocken, its highest summit, into a magic prism transforming the world at its feet. The panoramic view delivers two contradictory readings: the Blocksberg may be as calm and rational as a Philistine, and at the same time as wild and passionate as a Romantic, foremost proof being the 1 May anniversary, i.e., night of the Walpurgis revel itself (118). *The Harz Journey* is Heine's prose *début*. As such, it bears already the hallmark of a style surprising for his contemporaries but characteristically spanning the gamut from irony to sublime. Despite its derisive manner and abrupt changes of tone, it offers an original depiction of the country's complexity, emulating Retzsch's orgiastic print 22.

Disraeli too, like Heine, converted to Christianity for social advancement and professional advantage but, unlike Heine's variegated Walpurgis, introduced Retzsch's set (and the reader) to the exclusive English upper crust. In *Vivian Grey* (1826), the very name Château Desir pictures a sire's castle as a place of amorous and political cravings, amidst social gatherings and intrigues, with the ambitious Vivian Grey as main hero. Machinations revolve around electoral power and sexual gratification. With his sensational *début*, Disraeli had cut a winning *succès à scandale* in glittering style. In its richly woven pattern, frequent allusions to Goethe, nearly matching Disraeli's worship of Byron, foster his interest in German romanticism. Vivian, extoling Lord Alhambra (a Byron alias), follows "the oldest poet in Europe," that is, Goethe (70).[4] He even boasts recognizing his style in an anonymous article of "the Weimar Literary Gazette" (a fictitious title he subscribes to), pretending to read it in the original.

In such a context, Retzsch's outlines, hardly "an essential adornment of the cultivated lady's drawing-room,"[5] are a powerful cultural mediator (52–57). The scene does not take place in Julia's own salon but at an aristocrat's guest-filled summer mansion.[6] Ironically referring to the portfolio as "anything so old, and so excellent" (53)—

---

4   *The Early Novels of Benjamin Disraeli*, vol. 1, *Vivian Grey* (*1826–7*), ed. Michael Sanders (London: Pickering & Chatto, 2004).

5   Vaughan, *German Romanticism*, 123.

6   Vaughan's presentation has influenced the following report, even further than the scene staged in the novel: "She shows her sophistication by possessing and displaying a copy of Retzsch; he [Vivian Grey] shows his by recognizing it." See Kevin Hayes, "Retzsch's

in 1826 Boosey's version is only five years old but has already sold three editions—Vivian swears by a recent publication for several reader categories. The outlines' presence in the silver-spoon castle residence settles of course Retzsch's credit amongst aristocrats. Yet, more importantly, it also spreads the idea of its standing within a much larger middle class, fascinated by the fashionable world of Disraeli's novel itself, titillated by the anonymity of its first edition, and boosted by merchant publisher Colburn's puffed-up advertising. In 1826, Retzsch's copied prints feature crucially as cultural surrogate. They contribute to establishing Goethe in England, but also disclose the plot's Faustian thread. It seems no coincidence that the album sits cheek-by-jowl with *Tremaine; or, A Man of Refinement*, Robert Plumer Ward's novel, also published anonymously a year beforehand (1825), and known to be Disraeli's model for *Vivian Grey*. Retzsch provides the talisman surrogate any young man of refinement should rely on to succeed, and launches the Faustian track, hinting at the scene's meaning and characters' impulses.

Thanks to Retzsch's prints, Vivian stages his courtship of Julia Manvers after two patterns, a Faust with Margaret and a Faust with devil (52–57): "the fashion has gone out of selling oneself to the devil," boasts he (56). The course of the chapter invites us to deduct that young ladies, innocent or not, may well supply the fiend's part. Vivian, alone with fair Julia, is the scheming young Faust of this chapter, having driven off his potential rivals thanks to a Machiavellian trick. His flippant chat revolves around the prints more than once. Margaret's loveliness is a pretext to sit next to Julia and leaf with her through Boosey's *Faustus* (presumably third) edition. His comment actually pays *her* a compliment: "'How beautiful Margaret is!' said Vivian, rising from his Ottoman, and seating himself on the sofa by the lady. 'I always think, that this is the only Personification where Art has not rendered Innocence insipid.'" (54). Meaningfully, in the draft manuscript, this retort ended with "the only personification where Innocence does not look—insipid" (580). The adjunct on Art gratifies Retzsch's skill and conceptual talent. A sudden opening and closing of the door then disrupts the idyll, giving Disraeli's Vivian occasion to make of the intruder, the mysterious Mrs Felix Lorraine, a very incarnation of Retzsch's evil spirit: "'Mephistophiles, or Mrs. Felix Lorraine; one or the other,—perhaps *both*.'" (55) The prints also work as visual allusion, inciting readers to *picture* in their mind's eye the invasion just described.

The incident reads as Mephistopheles's brutal incursion on the lovers passionately kissing in the summerhouse (pl. 15, cf. Fig. 7.17) or spying on them in the garden (pl. 14, cf. Fig. 10.3), Moses duly attenuating. Still, even this obstacle is turned to advantage by Disraeli as Vivian resorts to a more general Faustian scheme, Julia's coax to Incantation. She plays the she-spirit that grants Faust-Vivian *his* wishes, culminating in a camouflaged marriage proposal, until a second (motherly) intrusion in the next chapter, induced by Mrs Lorraine, takes Julia away, bringing Vivian's courtship to an abrupt end.

Behind this spirited hoax, the scene confirms Vivian as a charmer; it exposes his rival, Mrs Lorraine, as an arch-schemer; more importantly, as the first to introduce a Faustian matrix, it provides a plausible reading of charmer's and schemer's incessant contention through that trend. To wit, Vivian is a flattering manipulator, a psychic Faust, conquering men's and women's souls and spirits. In the original edition, the Retzsch chapter is entitled "Marriage," but a later (spurious) heading in an American edition runs "Vivian Instructs an Ingénue,"[7] disclosing an editor's preconceptions, and predisposing other readers' reception. Mrs Lorraine, of German origin, imbued with German folklore, fantasies, and beliefs, laden with numerous Gothic tales, is a devious Mephistopheles, a "female fiend" (108 & 159), "a d—d odd woman!" (128). Later editions have dully filled in the unreported word: "deuced" (601), given that *deuce* is the devil. Intrigue replaces bargaining for souls. Yet, Vivian and Mrs Lorraine are each other's double, as Vivian admits ("I have met a kind of *double* of myself"). He muses: "the struggle between two such spirits will be a long and a fearful one" (108–9). In their deceitful hide-and-seek, they are interchangeable, Faust and Mephistopheles in turn. It comes as no surprise that upon finally defeating her, Vivian "watched his victim with the eye of a Mephistophiles" (161).

The citation of Retzsch's prints in *Vivian Grey* is tentacular. The chapter devises Mrs. Lorraine's sly marring of Vivian's amorous expectations, a foretaste of her wrecking his political ambitions. Still, this roguish female role does little justice to Disraeli's brilliance in contriving dramatic episodes after Retzsch. Since Mrs Lorraine is also a "negative double" of the protagonist,[8] the analogy stresses the inter-changeability of Faust and Mephistopheles. Parallel

---

Outlines and Poe's 'The Man of the Crowd'," *Gothic Studies* 12, no. 2 (Nov 2010): 31.

7   *The Works of Benjamin Disraeli, Earl of Beaconsfield*, vol. 1, *Vivian Grey, A Romance of Youth*, Intr. Edmund Gosse, Biographical Preface Robert Arnot (New York: M. Walter Dunne, 1904), 75.

8   Luisa Villa, "Mrs Felix Lorraine and Lady Caroline Lamb: Byronic Lore in *Vivian Grey*, Part I," *L'Analisi linguistica e letteraria* 27, no. 1 (2019): 41–52.

attitudes and comparable costumes in Retzsch (cf. Fig. 1.8 and 8.4) surely strengthened Disraeli's inspiration. Just as Heine cites Faust's soliloquy, Disraeli recalls Goethe's lines, later translated as "Two souls, alas! within my breast abide, | The one to quit the other ever burning" (F 1112–13, trans. A. G. Latham).

Disraeli and Heine alike feature a female fiend. Heine's Mephistophela is a complex poetic and aesthetic creation that renews the Faust myth and competes with Goethe. Contrariwise, Mephistopheles in skirts seems but a detail of Disraeli's dashing writing but confirms his talent for creating minor characters and promoting femaledom. Mrs Felix Lorraine substantiates the novel's feminine cast. It has been said that her "motivation remains a mystery,"[9] but the Faust template, subtly evoked through Retzsch's graphic medium, conceivably points at an elusive Goethe intertext backed up by Retzsch's prints, woven more finely than so far estimated.

10.2   Théophile Gautier from Travelogue to Aesthetics

Théophile Gautier's mentions of Retzsch are several and varied. Ranging from stereotype to core aesthetic idea, they form a challenging artistic assortment to investigate Retzsch's impact in France. Importance derives from the generous range of Gautier's writings (fiction, travel, theatre and art criticism) that have renewed critical assessment of his work.

His last mention of Retzsch to date[10] occurs in *Loin de Paris* (*Far from Paris*), certainly not the best nineteenth-century travelogue. Gautier penned its various sections on diverse occasions and put them together as a travel anthology only in 1865, presumably at his publisher Michel Lévy's request. A motley work, it has received sparse and unequal attention, in line with commentators' or editors' specific interests. *Loin de Paris* combines an 1845 picturesque tour of Algeria (critically edited in 1973 by Madeleine Cottin), an 1852–53 series of articles on Italy published in the newspaper *Le Pays*, and an account of Gautier's journey through German States after attending an August 1854 *Faust* performance in Munich.[11] As his boat descends the Rhine, narrative is random and cumulative, subservient to passenger incidents, sights, and landscape. A short description of ladies boarding the steamship closes with an unsophisticated Gretchen, recalling "the type of Margaret in Reschz's [*sic*] illustrations." As shown (Chap. 9.8), the choice of term (*type*) signals a characteristic shape, extorted from the prints, to be compared conversely with English and French maids, respectively a *lady* and a *soubrette*. Rather than a persona, this Margaret is a cast figure, an emblematic sample, a model incarnate.[12] As such, she has no bearings on the development. Still, she serves to elaborate a comparative European paradigm duly placed in a travelogue, which confirms the sway that the engravings held over collective imagination.

Gautier had already confessed to it while discussing Goethe's creativity in crafting female characters. On 17 November 1851, in a theatre review of a French comedy based on Mignon, he notes that all that Gretchen does or says in *Faust* would not fill ten pages, if put together. Yet by contrast she has made an "indelible impression" (*empreinte ineffaçable*) on imagination. Tellingly he adds: "Who would ever forget Margaret! You would sooner forget your first mistress." Her common retorts, simple songs, and attitudes are "yet so true, so right, yet so deeply female that they get to be *engraved* within the heart."[13] The verb seems not randomly chosen, Retzsch's originals or copies being mostly engravings. It endorses a blending of stereotype and genuinely significant details, hallmarking Gautier's figures after Retzsch.

Their return obeys a complex mechanism: the more characteristic the type, the more evanescent. It may be imprinted and reproducible, yet, hardly scrutinized, it vanishes, shadow-like. Disappearance and reappearance are watchwords for what is deeply engraved in the heart. The Gradiva complex works no differently. However, the same trope of figures carved in everybody's memory may also be conveyed by other than an *etching*, such as a "familiar sketch (*croquis familier*) drafted with the pencil tip," as in a comment on a French Charlotte and Werther drama,[14] or through sculptural metaphor—the artist's thumb modelling clay, while commenting Goethe's *Egmont*.[15]

---

9   Sanders, in the novel's introduction, LIV.

10   Unless the on-going critical edition of Gautier's theatre and art reviews should disclose further mentions. I have used Gautier's criticism up to May 1866 as edited by Patrick Berthier, also personally helpful.

11   Wolfgang Drost and Marie-Hélène Girard, eds., *Gautier et l'Allemagne* (Siegen: Universi, 2005), 8.

---

12   Gautier, *Loin de Paris* (Paris: Michel Lévy Frères, 1865), 314.

13   "Feuilleton de *La Presse* du 17 novembre 1851," in *OC*, pt. 6, vol. 10, *Novembre 1851–1852*, ed. P. Berthier (Paris: Champion, 2018), 46, my emphasis.

14   "Feuilleton de *La Presse* du 27 juillet 1846," in *OC*, pt. 6, vol. 6 (2015), 342.

15   "Feuilleton de *La Presse* du 15 août 1854," in *OC*, pt. 6, vol. 12 (2019), 166–67.

INK WORLDS

Have then Retzsch's etchings influenced Gautier's idea of Margaret as an "indelible impression" or not? On 22 August 1843, Gautier concluded his review of Delacroix's *Hamlet* lithographs, regretting that French artists hardly composed after the poets, and commended a literal application of *ut pictura poesis*: "The Germans have made numerous such drawings: Reshtz's [*sic*] outline engravings on *Faust*, on *Fridolin* are known by all." His first-hand acknowledgment of their notoriety shows cognizance of effect and efficacy of printed object on readers. He adds: "Nothing stirs the mind like leafing through one of these portfolios in which the idea of a poem or a play is summarized (*se résume*) in a few plates."[16] Although the etching and printing metaphor may seem either hackneyed or emblematic of his art-inspired store of tropes, Margaret is not just a typecast. In January 1847, its strong rebound ("they are etched in indelible lines in all memories") blends with the pictorial metaphor to convey again his admiration for Goethe, "the greatest painter of women ever extant," his creations spawning from only a couple of brushstrokes. His female characters are simple, Margaret is even "almost silly," yet nimble and vivacious: "They are not literary types, but live creatures we think we once met and knew."[17]

In Gautier's thinking, Goethe's blending of type with creative verve may well correspond to a sophisticated view on the creation of characters in literature. If a few meaningful strokes suffice to fix female personae, some of these appear in either writer's fiction. The idea that Gautier's are mainly cast as types, as upheld by Gautier criticism,[18] needs nuancing. In his "La Toison d'or" ("The Golden Fleece"), however suggestive, a heroine named "Gretchen" expertly blends with the Argonauts' myth and Rembrandt's Mary Magdalene, far from any Faustian template. Conversely, an encoded allusion within a text may hide a construction expertly devised.

Gautier's familiarity with Retzsch's work may have been from modified versions of the original series. His frequently flawed transcriptions of the artist's name (Reschz, Reztch, Reshtz, or even Roetzsch—the equally faulty Retsch being commonly used at the time, even on the original Cotta portfolio) suggest laxity, negligence, or plain incapacity to deal with five consonants in a row. Such are not only Gautier's trademark, and not all may be attributed to dodgy typesetting. In 1853 *La Presse* even once prints Kretzch (!). Misprints frequently occur either in the press or from the pen of other writers too, though rarely to such extremes. Yet, correct spelling in Gautier's case is negligible. In his *Les Beaux-arts en Europe—1855* (*The Fine Arts in Europe—1855*), the elaborate and over-detailed Retzsch plate of the witches' Sabbath (pl. 22, cf. Fig. 5.7) serves a comparison with the luxuriance and intricacy of Joseph Noel Paton's famous 1847 painting *The Quarrel of Oberon and Titania*.[19] The example testifies to Gautier's trained eye, grounded awareness, and masterly knowledge. In a theatre review of April 1852 on Palmyre Wertheimber, performing Pygmalion's part in a light opera (a sexual inversion that certainly enchanted the author of *Mademoiselle de Maupin*), the mention is latent, tacit, but unmistakable: "The young girl with a slender and supple waist, with a bowed head, like Marguerite in Martha's garden" can only correspond to Retzsch's plate 14 (cf. Fig. 10.3) and his petal-plucking heroine.[20] Goethe's play includes neither such stage direction nor textual hint. In 1853, commenting on another actress's "melancholic charm" and "ailing grace," Retzsch's prints become, as if Gautier owned them, "*our* delicate outline engravings by Reztch [*sic*] in the Goethe and Schiller illustrations."[21] Did he possess a set or merely wish to acknowledge the artist's adoption by the French public? Whatever the case, his ideal of the pure young German girl was incarnate in Retzsch's Margaret. As frequently cited in his theatre criticism, he knows particularly well Goethe's play (including *Faust II*), read in a translation by either Blaze de Bury or his bosom friend Gérard de Nerval. He is fascinated by Margaret's bedroom, by the cathedral and prison scenes. The scarlet line on her throat when appearing in the witches' revel has made an indelible impression on his mind. They are all regularly recalled or used in comparison. Evaluation of Retzsch was certainly backed by such familiarity, his exceptional memory, but also copies and other artefacts. He surely had in mind Pinéas's pirated copy of plate 4, the frontispiece to Nerval's 1828 translation of Goethe's *Faust* (cf. Fig. 6.4). When he assessed in 1854 the Munich *Faust* performance, he condemned the *décor* of Margaret's chamber, expanding on the appropriate furnishings in the following terms:

---

16   "Feuilleton de *La Presse*, 22 août 1834. *Hamlet* illustré. *Treize lithographies*, par M. Delacroix," in *OC*, pt. 6, vol. 4 (2012), 356.

17   "Feuilleton de *La Presse* du 25 mai 1847," in *OC*, pt. 6, vol. 6 (2015), 782.

18   Anne Geisler-Szmulewicz, "Gautier, lecteur du *Faust* de Goethe (1831–1841)," in *Gautier et l'Allemagne*, 34–36.

19   *OC*, pt. 7, *Critique d'art*, vol. 4, *Les Beaux-arts en Europe—1855*, ed. M.-H. Girard (Paris: Champion, 2011), 167.

20   "Feuilleton de *La Presse* du 19 avril 1852," in *OC*, pt. 6, vol. 10 (2018), 403.

21   "Feuilleton de *La Presse* du 2 mai 1853," in *OC*, pt. 6, vol. 11 (2019), 202, my emphasis.

A stage set badly made or badly chosen robs this adorable scene of all its intimacy. How would you have us accept this big bazaar deprived of its furnishings, where an old chest strolls along a dusty wall, for Margaret's chamber, that chaste and white retreat, that lilied interior, that paradise of freshness and innocence? It is in vain we look for the little virginal bed whose hangings Faust lifts, the oak armchair polished with such care, the wax-rubbed wardrobe, the figure of the Virgin, the two flower vases, the spinning wheel with its lustrous flywheel, all this poor household of a young girl, where mediocrity smiles with such a happy look, where the purity of a humble life shines with such artlessness, where love, abashed, dithers on the threshold. Retsch's [*sic*] outline engraving, with its minute details, so naively German, of such deep feeling, simply ought to have been reproduced. It has thwarted us to see Margaret take the earrings brought by Mephistopheles from a dirty and dusty piece of furniture, and walk about in such a room.[22]

What he missed, and lyrically craved for, was stirred by a stage set he had presumably observed in France, previously based on Schinkel (hence the Virgin, spinning wheel, and flower vases), and originally inspired by Retzsch (Fig. 9.5). As noted, that *décor* had travelled afar from Berlin and lasted a hundred years. Similarly, in his 1839 "La Toison d'or" ("The Golden Fleece"), he develops a detailed room description for his own Gretchen, his Antwerp Margaret rid of Faust and devil (793).[23]

Whether first- or second-hand, Gautier's grasp of Retzsch is indisputable and particularly wide-ranging in its applications. The inspiration he draws from the German artist concerns primarily Margaret (embodying Innocence) and Mephistopheles (epitomizing Cunning and Intrigue), the two characters prominent within the French tradition, rather than the titular figure. Similarly, Disraeli's Vivian Grey, while faking a Washington Irving autograph, flippantly blots the album entitled *Faustus*. The blot stains both title and protagonist. In his "Toison d'or," Gautier refers to Rembrandt's famous etching *The Alchemist*, related to Faust since Goethe's *Faust: Ein Fragment* (1790), only to incongruously compare a love letter received by his Antwerp Gretchen to a luminous

etched detail (800). As in Disraeli, both the disproportion and voiding of Faust connections are ironic in Gautier, successfully echoing the overall tone of the "Toison d'or" short story. Additionally, light-handed witty treatment of Goethe's *Faust* informs another 1841 short story, "Deux acteurs pour un rôle" ("Two Actors for One Part").[24] In this, the black poodle escorts Katy, a Viennese Margaret in satin and furs. Her lover Henrich (short of an *i* compared to Goethe's Heinrich), a young scholar rather than a disillusioned thinker, has merely studied theology, and spurned a learned and quiet existence to perform Mephistopheles on the stage. The tongue-in-cheek treatment excludes Goethe's protagonist. To square the circle, Mephistopheles in person contests Henrich his very part on stage. The demon incarnates it brilliantly himself, particularly thanks to his impressive laughter—rather more reminiscent of Frédérick Lemaître's performance than of Retzsch's sinister Mephistophelean grin. Gautier's genius thus draws on interdependent influences, of which Retzsch is certainly central, more or less prominent depending on plot and aim. Gautier's encrypted aesthetic inventions are thus particularly remarkable.

How to counter a "Werther-like sentimentality?" Gautier's *Les Roués innocents* (*The Innocent Profligates*) poses this very question and provides a crafty answer (1051).[25] This short novel in ten chapters, published 1846 by instalments in *La Presse*, twists the very style and scope of the sentimental genre. Over-hasty reading may explain why it has received scarce critical attention. Its apparent conventionality has discouraged more complex evaluations. The feigned sentimental narrative, ending offhandedly and in a somewhat burlesque manner with the happy marriage of two young people, is based on a well-kept mystery and a series of reversals and vagaries. The title builds on an oxymoron and the novel itself is a clever pastiche of mawkish creations of the time. By making opposites meet, it warns readers that nothing is really as it seems. Gautier plays here with stereotypes at the level of novel construction and genre, thanks to a subtle strategy that makes of *The Innocent Profligates* a much more complex work than meets the eye.

In the opening chapter, the traitor, Mr Rudolph, initiates proceedings by ordering the centrepiece to be taken off the dinner table during an overnight carousal. Once removed, the epergne discloses two rival beauties, apparently both of loose morals, in reality representing the

---

22   "Feuilleton de *La Presse* du 3 août 1854. Théâtre royal de Munich. *Faust*, de Goethe," in *OC*, pt. 6, vol. 12 (2019), 160.

23   "La Toison d'or," ed. J.-Cl. Fizaine, in *Romans, contes et nouvelles* (Paris: Gallimard, 2002), 1:773–815. All page references for Gautier's fiction in main text after this edition.

24   "Deux acteurs pour un rôle," ed. P. Whyte, in *Romans, contes et nouvelles*, 1:867–77.

25   "Les Roués innocents," ed. Claudine Lacoste-Veysseyre, in *Romans, contes et nouvelles*, 1:1025–118.

INK WORLDS 309

battle of good (Florence) and evil (Amine). Yet the reader will discover Florence's real role only in the last chapter. The sequence of events emulates this initial device thanks to a series of volte-faces and masks of character, situation, intention, and correspondence. Nothing is certain until the very end, except for the innocent profligates' love (Henri Dalberg and Calixte Desprez) and the villain's malignity. No coincidence, Rudolph is twice compared to Mephistopheles. He is the authentic rake of the story, a sophisticated devil rid of Faust, while Dalberg is but a guiltless *roué*. First, Rudolph is "the Mephistopheles of the Ghent boulevard" (1063), street-talk for the Boulevard des Italiens during the Hundred Days War, a meeting place for dandies in the heart of Paris. Second, confirming all Rudolph's devilish traits, "I detest him and represent him to myself as the Mephistopheles of the *Faust* illustrations" (1110) could point again to Retzsch. The phrase is typical of Gautier's nod at the outlines but for the explicit identification—a likely part of the novel's encrypted strategy.

Captivatingly, the simile emerges in a letter addressed by young Calixte Desprez to Florence, her long-standing friend from the convent, all along covertly defending Calixte's and her lover's interests against the malicious Amine, Rudolph's co-conspirator. While the analogy singles out Rudolph as the touchstone of malignity, Calixte's command of both Goethe's tragedy and the consecutive prints is clearly part of the novel's encoded design not so readily fathomed. Similarly, Calixte is no stereotype of respectable young girl, no "insipid" Margaret in her chamber (albeit a purposefully misleading description), but a knowledgeable and intelligent young female, a chaste *rouée*, matching the title. In chapter two, she collects clandestine correspondence through her prayer book and writes back messages in sympathetic ink, which should have alerted the reader. Besides, she reads poets in foreign languages (1043), and nothing could have hindered her familiarity with Goethe's *Faust*. Such a subtle use by Gautier, who puts no name to the *Faust* images, underlines their fame and the extent to which their diffusion had informed, even inspired young girls of the bourgeoisie.

More significantly, Retzsch's creations nourished Gautier's aesthetic defence of dumb shows and ballet. He was champion, promoter, and admirer of the performing arts, including those regularly deemed minor by mid-nineteenth-century standards, and authored himself ballets, six staged, two un-staged, including the famed *Giselle*. The associations implied in his arguments are therefore all the more meaningful. In December 1851,

condemning Saint-Léon's tempestuous and brilliant ballets,[26] that he deemed lacking in clarity and visibility of action, Gautier heralded Retzsch's outlines as a mode of writing: "A ballet libretto should be ably written through a series of outline drawings, like Rœtzsch's [*sic*] illustrations for Goethe's *Faust* and Schiller's *Fridolin*."[27] In just over a year, in January 1853, his critique had developed into an innovative poetical stance. Adolphe Adam's *Orfa*, a mime show-cum-ballet and its novel Nordic mythology belong to "those silent poems where the idea is only manifest through plastic appearances and which should be written alongside a series of outline drawings, like Kretzsch's [*sic*] illustrations on Goethe and Schiller."[28] Retzsch had become an aesthetic benchmark, the very example and mode of writing a "silent poem." Setting absent words off against plastic expressiveness and extolling outline as writing, Gautier had surpassed even August von Schlegel's view of the technique as hieroglyph in arousing readers' imaginations. He had seen in Retzsch the very expressiveness of avant-garde poetry without text, or even future film directors' and screenplay writers' modes of working. Ten years later, outline would provide an ideal mode of writing as bodies moved across the stage in action or passion devoid of words: "Surely the best ballet script would be an album of outline scenes like Retsch's [*sic*] illustrations for Goethe's *Faust*, whose story a child would understand from the pictures, without reading a word of the text."[29] Retzsch had found an advocate in a man and writer spellbound by animated statues.

10.3 Visual Traps in Prose

Setting subject matter aside, Gautier saw in Retzsch's outlines parameters for new creative modes: mute poems in gesture and action, and silent shows through motion and sequence. Modern art and silent film would occur half a century later. Still, Gautier's "writing through" (*écrire par*) and "writing alongside" or "with" outlines (*écrire avec*)

---

26   Saint-Léon (1821–70), born Charles Michel, a dancer and violinist, was the choreographer, business partner and husband of Fanny Cerrito, the renowned dancer.

27   "Feuilleton de *La Presse* du 1er décembre 1851," in *OC*, pt. 6, vol. 10 (2018), 67.

28   "Feuilleton de *La Presse* du 3 janvier 1853," in *OC*, pt. 6, vol. 11 (2019), 15.

29   "Revue des théâtres," *Le Moniteur universel*, no. 200 (18 July 1864): 1a (on Ludwig Minkus's ballet *Néméa*). Kindly imparted by P. Berthier.

heralded pioneering ways of combining visual, textual, and performing arts. He was not the only writer to gather inspiration from visual spurs or heighten prose with their effects. Edgar Allan Poe's "The Man of the Crowd" (1840) and Walter Herries Pollock's short novel *The Picture's Secret* (1883) both constructed character or triggered plot through Retzsch. In his 1799 *Athenaeum* essay on Flaxman and drawing after poetry, Schlegel had stressed outlines' suggestive power: they set spectators' and readers' imaginations in motion. Poe and Pollock epitomize how they also sparked *writers'* inspiration.

In a stimulating 2010 article on "Retzsch's Outlines and Poe's 'The Man of the Crowd'," Kevin J. Hayes drew on a variety of sources to show the extent of Poe's knowledge of Retzsch, the artist's cultural notoriety in the United States, and the place he holds in Poe's and other writers' criticism. His remarks on the "ramifications" of Retzsch's work "in terms of Poe's visual imagery and his aesthetic theory" are a welcome contribution to the points discussed in this chapter. Hayes stresses the appeal on Poe of "Retzsch's combination of clear outline with dense symbolism," the "dramatic quality" of his conceptions, and his capacity to depict "active, dramatic moments."[30] He aptly singles out a passage in Poe's review of Henry Wadsworth Longfellow's *Ballads and Other Poems*, in which Poe pits imaginative effect, suggestion and brevity against truth and realism, mentioning Retzsch and Flaxman in the following terms:

> That the chief merit of a picture is its *truth*, is an assertion deplorably erroneous. Even in Painting which is, more essentially than Poetry, a mimetic art, the proposition cannot be sustained. Truth is not even *the aim*. Indeed it is curious to observe how very slight a degree of truth is sufficient to satisfy the mind, which acquiesces in the absence of numerous essentials in the thing depicted. An outline frequently stirs the spirit more pleasantly than the most elaborate picture. We need only refer to the compositions of Flaxman and of Retzsch. Here all details are omitted—nothing can be farther from *truth*. Without even color the most thrilling effects are produced.[31]

Hayes also discusses the use Poe makes of suggestion, and the problematic relation between outline (exterior appearance) and inner self (true nature) to conclude on the visual and stylistic influence of the German artist on the American writer. In his words, "Retzsch's work taught Poe economy of style."[32] The remark is of course crucial in understanding the aesthetics of a writer whose fame rests on the bearing and power of the *short* story.

Hayes has convincingly established how Poe used outline in "The Man of the Crowd" and "Metzengerstein" by using shadow, illumination, and outlining with darkness. The former story bears on a mysterious individual, pursued by the narrator in overcrowded London streets without piercing his secret motivation, except that of his seeking swarming masses to mingle with them. Hayes's study may be extended further. Indeed, I argue that Poe did not only follow Retzsch, he competed with him, and implemented outline as a *screen* to thwart readers' attempts to solve the puzzle. In short, he constructed a mystery tale on an open challenge: to read what cannot be read, or rather "does not permit itself to be read," as per his own translation of the German opening the tale: "*er lasst sich nicht lesen*" (506).[33] Attracting the reader into it, the story makes him stumble over enigma. The narrator brings up Retzsch on discerning the protagonist in the throng, indeed presenting him, while the writer himself claims to out-Retzsch him:

> With my brow to the glass, I was thus occupied in scrutinizing the mob, when suddenly there came into view a countenance (that of a decrepid old man, some sixty-five or seventy years of age,)—a countenance which at once arrested and absorbed my whole attention, on account of the absolute idiosyncrasy of its expression. Any thing even remotely resembling that expression I had never seen before. I well remember that my first thought, upon beholding it, was that Retzch [*sic*], had he viewed it, would have greatly preferred it to his own pictural incarnations of the fiend. (511)

The plural "pictural incarnations" hints not only at Mephistopheles in *Faust* but also at Retzsch's allegorical *The Chess Players* (*Die Schachspieler*), widely reproduced, diffused, and well-known in the United States. No coincidence: the devil fights man for his soul over a game of chess and the overall meaning tallies with Goethe's tragedy.

Yet, in Poe's story, viewing has already been thwarted before these "pictorial incarnations" prompt recognition.

---

30   Hayes, 33.

31   Poe, "*Ballads and Other Poems*. By Henry Wadsworth Longfellow," in *Essays and Reviews*, ed. G. R. Thompson (New York: Literary Classics of the United States, 1984), 695.

32   Hayes, 39.

33   *Collected Works of Edgar Allan Poe*, ed. T. O. Mabbott (Cambridge, Ma.: The Belknap Press of Harvard University Press, 1978), 2:505–18.

Even so, the pictorial quality of "The Man of the Crowd" can by no means be denied. In *Le Peintre de la vie moderne* (*The Painter of Modern Life*, 1863), as Hayes recalls, Baudelaire called this very story "a painting (verily, it is a painting!)." The device employed, a large bow window in which the narrator sits, functions as a display case to view, inspect, and diagnose the various social groups and types by gaslight. To view them is to read them like as many stories: "and although the rapidity with which the world of light flitted before the window, prevented me from casting more than a glance upon each visage, still it seemed that, in my then peculiar mental state, I could frequently *read*, even in that brief interval of a glance, the history of long years" (511, my emphasis). Two details under the anonymous protagonist's cloak, the diamond and the dagger, build up tension, and tickle the reader's curiosity, suggesting enigma and crime. The narrator's stalking of the man, street by street, invites the reader into the story, incites him to build it alongside himself, while the central character's attitude and reasons remain obscure. The face that even Retzsch "would have greatly preferred to his own pictural incarnations of the fiend" works as a guiding device for deciphering, yet stimuli fail. Poe marshals visual qualities and rhetorical techniques to enigmatic purpose. They rouse the reader but to trip up on the undecipherable. Not only may the external *not* signify the exterior, as Hayes would have it, what is more, the exterior serves (outline-like) to deceive. It may lure but also elude. The story concludes with the very words it opened: "'*er lasst sich nicht lesen*'."

The riddle of "The Man of the Crowd" is the very inscrutability of everyman's story, the problematic legibility of the protagonist. The answer is there from the beginning, as in "The Purloined Letter" by Poe, hidden because it is extremely noticeable. Thomas Mabbott, Poe's reference editor, wondered whether he should substitute *er* (he) by *es* (it) in the opening and closing German phrase (518). He did keep *er*, and *es* could also be possible. Seemingly indicating a book's or this story's title (it), the phrase refers to the protagonist (he) as well. Beyond Poe's own cryptic translation "It does not permit itself to be read," another decoy, the translation could also run "*He* does not permit *himself* to be read." In "The Man of the Crowd" suggestion is a misleading veil, the outline a deceitful drapery, indeed perhaps a shroud. The central character is in Mabbott's felicitous phrase "unknowable apart from the crowd" (505): one *of* many and one *in* or *through* many, both *in* the crowd and *of* the crowd, everyman in the throng, ordinary and exceptional all in one.

A riddle also sits at the core of Walter Herries Pollock's *The Picture's Secret* (1883), a straight upshot of the Gothic

craze for animated or fatal pictures.[34] In Gautier, who had discarded the palette for the pen, visual imagery heightens impressions, enhances purple patches, and impacts the plot without being the only process. In Pollock, the visual leaning is central and decisive: the witches' Sabbath scene inspired by Retzsch (pl. 22, cf. Fig. 5.7) triggers the plot. Paintings, a painter, two art lovers, visual props, and symbolism all bear on storyline and riddle. What is the true nature of young Lilith, daughter to acclaimed painter von Waldheim? She grows into the typically destructive *femme fatale* of the story, heartbreaker of men: her talented musician husband, Cecil 13th Earl of Falcon; his bosom friend, Arthur Vane, lured into loving her, who proves treacherous to Falcon and dies tragically; and at the end of the story, even her own father, unremittingly "dabbling a dry brush on an empty canvas, and appealing to imagined crowds of admirers whether his work was not the best that he had ever done" (222–23). The disastrous end is carefully prepared.

Also an amateur fencer, Pollock wielded the stylus in a number of genres (fiction writing, songs, theatrical adaptations and amateur theatricals, criticism, biography, memoirs, and review editing). A translator from the French of Alfred de Musset and Denis Diderot, he was prominent in Victorian literary circles and lectured (among other subjects) on Théophile Gautier whose works he knew well. A close friend of Henry Irving, the sensational interpreter of Goethe's Mephistopheles in a memorable red costume after Retzsch at the Lyceum commented by himself (cf. Fig. 9.18 to Fig. 9.20), Pollock composed the detailed article on Faust illustrations already referred to. His novel's action is set both in aristocratic circles and a rich aesthetic context, recalling those of Disraeli, yet without the latter's vim. Several textual, pictorial or musical works on the fantastic, "*diablerie*" and the supernatural (59) are called to mind, contributing to the enigma of Lilith, the child of a painter, also born from a picture of his:

> "Yes," said Vane, "that is fine [Faure interpreting Gounod's *Faust*]. I see, Mr. von Waldheim, you have chosen the moment of Lilith's appearance for your picture. Retzsch, if I am not mistaken, has taken the apparition of Gretchen for his outline drawing."
>
> "Yes," replied the artist, "it may have been because I was afraid of copying Retzsch; but I think the real fact was, that the idea started into my head. A picture strikes me suddenly, and takes possession of

---

34 Pollock, *The Picture's Secret: A Story, to Which is added an Episode in the Life of Mr. Latimer* (London: Remington and Co., 1883), 3–224.

FIGURE 10.1
Gabriel Max, *"Es ist ein Zauberbild, ist leblos, ein Idol,"* in *Faust-Illustrationen von Gabriel Max: Zehn Zeichnungen, in Holz geschnitten von R[ichard] Brend'amour und W. Hecht* (Berlin: G. Grote, 1880), pl. 10
COURTESY HAAB, F GR 5768, WEIMAR

me until I have transferred it to canvas. Whether it is worth the trouble of transferring or not, is a question which never occurs to me at the time." (34–35)

The Retzsch reference may here seem a mere pretext, pure cultural innuendo, if it was not for a careful and crafty shift on the part of the novelist. Both Gretchen and Lilith are present at Goethe's Walpurgis. Lilith, "Adam's first wife" and her ensnaring hair, a "net" that "can catch young men," come into view as she features among the witches a she-demon (F 4118–23), long before Gretchen's disturbing spectre. In the opening pages of Pollock's novel, von Waldheim's substitution of his daughter for Retzsch's Margaret enriches Lilith's covert nature. In Waldheim's picture, doubly fathered, she is swathed in Gretchen's garb, in an elaboration on Retzsch's pl. 22. Subsequent works of art, such as Gabriel Max's ominous Gretchen (Fig. 10.1), may have also stirred Pollock's imagination, yet retouched in melodramatic fashion:

> In the very centre of the picture was a rift in the clouds, through which a ray of moonlight streamed

on to a woman's figure draped in long gauzy robes, from whom the surrounding goblins and witches seemed to have shrunk in terror or subjection, so that she walked entirely alone. Her face could not be distinguished; but the artist had infused a spirit of disdain into her attitude, which would by itself account for her solitude. (33)

Lilith von Waldheim is thus another combination of outline with dense symbolism but purposefully complicated and reworked to carry the figure's ambiguity *in absentia* and *in presentia* of both Gretchen and Lilith. In a way, Pollock outshines Goethe's Lilith, part and parcel of the witches' revel in *Faust*, and one of Retzsch's most complex prints, now infused with new symbolism. This is no chance sleight of hand but a game of hide-and-seek around the heroine's true identity, central to the novel, whose *dénouement* unravels itself again through a picture. Later on, Falcon, Lilith, and Arthur Vane, the trio bonded in love and betrayal, embody the fatal triad of husband, wife and lover shown in an old picture hanging in an allegedly haunted room in Falcontree Hall. They incarnate similar roles in life; they exemplify them when disguised for a masked ball; and fatally, play them out in a *tableau vivant* before the picture, precipitating Vane's tragic death and Falcon's separation from Lilith. In that second picture, the expression on the woman's face is the ultimate key to Lilith's cruel and deceitful nature, prepared by the clever subversion of Retzsch's composition. Pollock's novel, rather obvious but culturally rich, makes of Retzsch the very spark that prompts the narrative. Additionally (though this is an aside), the names Arthur Vane and Lady Emmeline Grey, Falcon's sister, pre-monitor James Vane, Sybil's brother in *Dorian Gray*, the famed novel by Oscar Wilde, a close friend of Pollock. *The Picture of Dorian Gray* (1891) was elaborated on well-tested foundations.

10.4 Pictures within the Picture in Illustrated Books

In illustrated editions, drawings and plates certainly add extra significance, when inserted, to the story. Gautier in *The Innocent Profligates*, Poe in "The Man of the Crowd," and Pollock in *The Picture's Secret*, all utilize Retzsch to hint at the hidden through merely textual means. The previously seen is put to work to show the presently unseen, and the capacity of outline to suggest is optimized in skilled narrative constructions. However, Retzsch's outlines may also be solicited as visual means, images within images in relation to fiction. They may even unexpectedly bring and knot together several symbolic trends of a novel in one seemingly secondary episode.

Such is the case in chapter XXII of Charles Dickens's *David Copperfield*, when Miss Mowcher, the dwarf dealer in cosmetics and beautifiers, grooms Steerforth's hair and whiskers while showering him and Copperfield with gossip on patrician society (271–90).[35] Hablôt Knight Browne, known as Phiz, has granted this scene an illustration, captioned "I make the acquaintance of Miss Mowcher," in which four other pictures hang on the wall (Fig. 10.2). However, what we see and read and what broods behind the scenes (and will eventually happen) do not coincide, the wall pictures being instrumental in hinting at covert purposes.

Dickens's plot meets indeed a turning point: David Copperfield looks bewildered at the embellishment of his friend's locks and listens to the dwarf beautician's curious lingo, while in preparation is little Emily's seduction by Steerforth and their elopement, aided by Littimer, his butler. In the foreground, Copperfield and Steerforth leave Yarmouth, while the text sparsely hints at the backstage fate of little Emily. As chapter XXXII of the novel will reveal, Miss Mowcher will herself be instrumentally deceived into approaching Emily with the letter that will ultimately cause her downfall (394–96). The "illustration" itself divulges the secret, thanks to the pictures on the wall.

In his study on *Victorian Novelists and their Illustrators*, John R. Harvey suggests that Miss Mowcher, standing on the table to spruce up Steerforth's locks, bears a direct analogy to Retzsch's garden scene (Fig. 10.3), best known in English as "The Decision of the Flower." Faust leans over the petal-plucking Margaret in the foreground, while Mephistopheles leers behind. In Phiz's "illustration," Mephistopheles has been brought forward and shadows Faust. Phiz represents this by the large framed picture in Miss Mowcher's immediate background, just above her head. Harvey astutely remarks that the feather on the dwarf's hat echoes a pictorial feature common to Faust's and Mephistopheles's headgear, a detail evident in the embedded picture.[36] The visual parallel presses ominous portent into a burlesque scene. The picture within the picture signals Emily as an innocent Margaret, Miss

---

35   Dickens, *David Copperfield*, ed. N. Burgis (Oxford: At the Clarendon Press, 1981).

36   Harvey, *Victorian Novelists and Their Illustrators* (London: Sidgwick & Jackson, 1970), 148–49.

FIGURE 10.2   Phiz (Hablôt Knight Browne), *I make the acquaintance of Miss Mowcher,* etching, final plate C, Dec 1849, 12.8 × 10.78 cm, in Charles Dickens, *David Copperfield*, Ch. XXII, "Some Old Scenes, and Some New People"
AUTHOR'S COLLECTION AND FILE

FIGURE 10.3   Moritz Retzsch, Garden scene, *Umrisse zu Goethe's Faust gezeichnet von Retsch* (Stuttgart & Tübingen: Cotta, 1816), pl. 14
COURTESY HAAB, F 3487, WEIMAR

Mowcher as a potential Mephistopheles, and Steerforth as Faust, the seducer. An important shift in use of outline is to be stressed. The mustered image discloses, rather than implies, unsavoury truths: the suggestive power of the medium (Schlegel) has been subverted, even overturned. The aesthetic reversal highlights the illustrated novel as a strong twofold instrument laden with complex meaning.

Such interpretation is all the more convincing as Dickens's novels came out serially, in illustrated monthly instalments on which both writer and artist cooperated closely.[37] The writer is known to have repeatedly given instructions to Phiz, his regular illustrator for the shilling-apiece parts, each containing three chapters and two full-page etched illustrations. These were not just luring adjuncts for their middle-class readers but combined media issues elaborating implicit meanings through word and image in lockstep. In Mowcher's instance, their joint agency lifts the veil on clandestine deeds and stealthy schemes revealed much later. The question as to which of the two, writer or artist, had the idea or took the lead becomes important (but is all the more tricky to determine) for three reasons: there have been a few changes both in the novelist's intention and the artist's preliminary

---

37   *David Copperfield* in monthly parts, May 1849–November 1850; *The Personal History of David Copperfield, with Illustrations by H. K. Browne* (London: Bradbury & Evans, 1850).

FIGURE 10.4   Phiz (Hablôt Knight Browne), *I make the acquaintance of Miss Mowcher*, original pencil and crayon sketch A with extra sketches, added to the original edition of Dickens, *The Personal History of David Copperfield* (London: Bradbury and Evans, 1850), copy 9, facing p. 232
NYPL, BERG COLLECTION

INK WORLDS 317

FIGURE 10.5 Phiz (Hablôt Knight Browne), original illustration for *I make the acquaintance of Miss Mowcher*, version B of the final plate, graphite on paper, image 13 × 10 cm
COURTESY RARE BOOK DEPARTMENT, ELKINS-COPPERFIELD CDC389917, FREE LIBRARY OF PHILADELPHIA

studies; direct evidence of who suggested what is lacking; and Harvey's reading has been at least partially challenged by Michael Steig.[38] The former's study insists on Dickens's exceptional visual memory, acute vision, and power in treating scenes as complete pictures. Harvey grants him the leadership of the writer-artist tandem, considers the illustrations as "produced to Dickens's specifications," and concludes: "The illustrations participate in a larger play of visual imagining which, in Dickens's writing, is inseparable from the total drama."[39] Conversely, in his expert study on *Dickens and Phiz*, Michael Steig concludes on "a high degree of independence on the part of Phiz." His view is supported by Phiz's emblematic use of embedded pictures laden with symbolism. Precisely in the background picture inspired by Retzsch, Phiz adds a crucial third character, Mephistopheles, between the initial and final versions, a detail not discussed by Harvey. Although the alteration cannot be attributed with certainty either to writer or artist, Steig inclines to think that "Browne invented it on his own" because "the *Faust* detail in the drawing would probably be unintelligible to Dickens when first submitted to him for approval."[40]

The actual situation proves however far more complicated. The small background change has major reading implications for the episode in hand, and depends on prior knowledge of further developments in the novel. Moreover, there are in fact three preserved stages of Phiz's plate, and not just the two considered by Steig: a) a preparatory drawing with marginal sketches, namely A, now in the Berg Collection, added to an original edition of *David Copperfield* (cf. Fig. 10.4); b) a first version of the final plate, namely B, now in the Free Library of Philadelphia (cf. Fig. 10.5), that Harvey and Steig have both compared to C, the latter with welcome additional remarks; and c) the published plate, namely C, that is, the final etching with three characters in the background picture, two of which wear a feather (cf. Fig. 10.2). All three show conceptual development of the four embedded wall pictures, never attributing agency to either Dickens or Phiz. In all three, the background treats differently Miss Mowcher's role, the novel's evolution, and the message intended for the reader. Last, but not least, both Harvey and Steig agree on the garden scene and its origins in Retzsch, which may however be challenged, if compared to the pictures' and the novel's elaboration.

On Dickens's side, "Mrs. Seymour Hill, a dwarf working as a chiropodist," the real-life model for Miss Mowcher,

protested upon recognizing herself in the novel (XLI). The writer had to tone down her intended part. He originally meant her to be a procuress but ultimately turned her into a duped figure. In the text, Mowcher's seemingly chance question on the prettiest woman in town answers to Emily, "the prettiest and most engaging little fairy in the world" in Steerforth's words. Details of name, employment, dwelling, and engagement are intended to give the shady beautician the information needed to approach her (283–84). Besides, Steerforth's "I'll quench the curiosity of this little Fatima [Miss Mowcher]" (284) pictures himself as a seducer, a Bluebeard with many conquests "done with" in a secret chamber. Dickens was a lover of fairy tales, often recycled in his own novels, and to name Fatima the inquisitive female is indeed typical of English versions of "Bluebeard."

In Phiz's preparatory sketch A, only the large frame behind Miss Mowcher displays an image. This cursorily reveals two rather than three figures, in female rather than male attire, facing each other. From the remaining three frames, one shows an unclear shape (a female sitting at a mirror?), the two others being nearly blank, as if awaiting inspiration, hints or instructions (cf. Fig. 10.4). In the more finished B drawing, the large frame distinctly shows only two figures in dresses, one bending towards the other, neither sporting a feather (cf. Fig. 10.5). The remaining three all now harbour a scene. Two of them show a female portrait full-frontally and a ship in the tempest, matching the published version C. In the fourth frame, yet another female figure has also taken shape perhaps with a companion. The main changes between B and C concern the "Mowcher frame," and this fourth image, finally replaced in C by a diminutive man on a table surrounded by giants.

Both Phiz and Dickens knew Retzsch's prints well. Steig defines Phiz as "a literate man, widely read and fully conscious of his predecessors in English graphic art, from Hogarth through John Doyle ('HB') and the Cruikshanks."[41] He backs Harvey's evidence of Phiz having previously used Retzsch's garden scene in illustrating Charles Lever's novel *Roland Cashel* a year before *David Copperfield*.[42] The illustration for Lever is literal: it corresponds to a scene of rose-petal plucking and indirect love-declaration on a visit to a picture gallery, one of the pictures being the very garden scene in *Faust*.[43] However, Lever's style, likened by Trollope to his conversation, has none of the subtleties involved in *David Copperfield*. Nevertheless, Phiz's image

---

38   Michael Steig, *Dickens and Phiz* (Bloomington / London: Indiana University Press, 1978).

39   Harvey, 159.

40   Steig, 19–20.

41   Steig, 5.

42   Harvey, 226; Steig, 19.

43   Charles Lever, *Roland Cashel* (London: Chapman and Hall, 1850), 204.

INK WORLDS

testifies to his good knowledge of Retzsch and ability to use him accordingly. In the frontispiece of Dickens's *Dombey and Son* (1848), he further borrows an outline from Retzsch's trilingual *Fancies and Truths*, published in 1831.[44] Dickens, on the other hand, was also well aware of Retzsch's prints, interestingly alluded to in personal and emotional circumstances. Joyously greeted by the family pets upon his return from the United States, he spiritedly writes in a 25 May 1868 letter about his elder daughter's dog, Mrs Bouncer by name, that she "tore round and round [him], like the dog in the Faust outlines."[45] This is a clear allusion to Retzsch's pl. 2 (cf. Fig. 2.22).[46] Further, in *David Copperfield*, the Mowcher scene is not the only one pregnant with Faustian allusions: Doctor Strong in his study with Annie at his knee, pictured by Phiz in chapter XVI, may be seen as a Faustian figure among his zoological samples high up on a shelf, his many books on the walls, the disordered folios on the floor, and a wall-hung world map replacing Faust's iconic globe. However the Mowcher scene is laden with pictorial and textual innuendo, the background outline bearing the key to the riddle. In the published plate, the four wall-hung pictures not only lift the veil on secret aims, they also foretell the conclusion of the Emily subplot. Steig's excellent comment runs: "The plate has three emblematic details: a ship in a storm (probably representing Emily's impending fall but also conceivably foreshadowing Steerforth's death in a shipwreck), a comic reference to Miss Mowcher's size and performance in a print showing Gulliver performing for the Brobdingnagians, and a scene from *Faust*."[47]

His fine reading may be extended: the uncommented fourth detail, the female portrait, answers to the "pretty woman in town" motif and points (along with the text) at little Emily. It is an additional illustrative device singling out the subplot's heroine. The Gulliver scene also alludes to Miss Mowcher herself performing for an aristocratic clientele, the social giants who condescendingly look on her as a fairground freak, albeit indispensable. Its comic side becomes touching when Dickens sets the social comment (and very image) in Miss Mowcher's mouth, as if to redeem her: "If I am a plaything for your giants, be gentle with me.'" (395). As for the *Faust* image, the insertion corresponds in fact to two differing versions. I argue indeed that any identification with the garden scene may be incorrect; and that versions B and C correspond to two

different Retzsch outlines suffusing Phiz's plates with two different meanings at distinct but successive stages of conception.

Retzsch's idyll in the garden (cf. Fig. 10.3), "The Decision of the Flower" in Moses's copy (cf. Fig. 11.2), pictures true love, harmony and union between the lovers. A strange match for Dickens's narrative line, it makes a rather poor candidate, though not to be excluded (a tree may be seen on the right-hand side). Instead, Phiz may have drawn inspiration from Faust approaching Margaret in the street, the scene of their first meeting, while observed by Mephistopheles in the background (Retzsch's pl. 8, cf. Fig. 1.8). Phiz has brought the devil closer for a telling parallel, as Harvey and Steig argue regarding the garden scene. In all the previous examples in this chapter, a free treatment of Retzsch's plates, to endow them with further connotations, is common. Such a conjecture fits better the meaning intended by the novel: Mowcher is circuitously asked by Steerforth to approach Emily, just as Faust approaches Margaret in Retzsch's etching.

Steerforth has of course already met Emily but there is no contradiction. The outline discloses the covert plan of a future secret meeting that Miss Mowcher is asked to set up. Such is never narrated (but, in the same chapter, the episode of Martha, pleading Emily for help, introduces the fallen-woman motif both textually and pictorially). Besides, Dickens went a long way to later restore a duped Miss Mowcher to the intrigue, once his life-model had complained of cruelty. Her indirect role of shadow Mephistopheles is finally played by Steerforth's butler, absent from the plate. Still, her care for Steerforth's looks recalls Mephistopheles's rejuvenation of Faust by the witch's potion, turned here to cosmetics, an allusion more playful than vile. Miss Mowcher could however also be Copperfield's Mephistopheles: Steerforth repetitively calls David "Daisy" ("Marguerite" in French!) to stress his youth and innocence. In English, Daisy is also an occasional diminutive for Margaret. In the published version, the background image hints at Copperfield's education inasmuch as the episode is also part of his *Bildungsroman*: an initiation to the subtle troika of temptation, seduction and abuse. By finely combining the inserted outline and slight textual allusions, Phiz's published plate brings these various options together. It does even more: it utters Steerforth's secret desire, reveals his covert intention, and weaves the hidden intrigue beneath the reader's very eyes thanks to a scene doubling the narrative: Faust (Steerforth) *will* meet Margaret (Emily) under the plumage of some Mephistopheles or other, the wicked intention of the lover connecting likewise with the malevolent action of his purveyor (whomsoever it may prove to be) under the same feather.

---

44   Steig, 111.

45   *The British Academy, Pilgrim edition. The Letters of Charles Dickens*, vol. 12, *1868–1870*, ed. G. Story et al. (Oxford: Clarendon Press, 2002), 119.

46   Alfred Heinrich, "Charles Dickens und die *Faust Outlines*," *Anglia: Zeitschrift für englische Philologie*, n.s., 37 (Jan 1926): 353–55.

47   Steig, 19.

FIGURE 10.6
Moritz Retzsch, Martha adorns Margaret with the jewels, *Umrisse zu Goethe's Faust gezeichnet von Retsch* (Stuttgart & Tübingen: Cotta, 1816), pl. 12
COURTESY HAAB, F 3487, WEIMAR

What then of version B, now in the Free Library of Philadelphia? This is further illuminating but in a different sense. It does not refer to Faust and Margaret (as Steig supposes), but to Goethe's Martha, Margaret's neighbour, who convinces her to keep the casket against her mother's advice. In Retzsch's pl. 12, Martha adorns Margaret with the jewels provided by Mephistopheles (Fig. 10.6). I argue that it is this outline that Phiz imported in version B. In his drawing both figures are female, the one on the left leans towards the other (as Martha bends towards Margaret in Retzsch), and none wears a feather. Phiz, who drew inspiration from Retzsch now and then, may have thought of this plate because it matches Dickens's text. Miss Mowcher's traffic in beauty wares is analogous to Goethe's Martha decking Gretchen with jewellery and textually arranging her first rendezvous with Faust. In addition, female trinket-pedlars and beauty suppliers have traditionally been bawds of loose morals. Such a background would allude to Miss Mowcher as procuress: easily approaching little Emily, she would introduce an offer from Steerforth, tempting the young girl desirous to be a lady. Understandably, Harvey could not detect the *Faust*-scene in B, and considered it "a late addition" to C.[48] It is nevertheless still there but cribs a different outline.

Such choice by Phiz may have incited Dickens to further spice up the scene by introducing an even clearer allusion to *Faust*, bringing into the picture two male figures, Faust and Mephistopheles, instead of Goethe's Martha, in the final version C. Version B had also sketched a plausible scenario. With its dramatic changes, the final illustration however alludes to a far more complex situation, involving three characters instead of two. It inverts and complicates the series of events in a way that further masks overt meaning. It is this last quality—along with the impact of the image on a subplot—that shows a sophisticated use of the image as a tantalizing screen, both veiling and unveiling what is not narrated, the quintessence of Anglo-Saxon eroticism indeed. The images hint at events that the reader may credit or not, while his own imagination speculates on how Emily's seduction came about.

---

48 Harvey, 150.

We may never know which of the two, Dickens or Phiz, authored the ingenious arrangements in either final (published) or B versions, but my intuition is that Dickens well understood the *Faust* allusion made by Phiz in the latter. He probably further enhanced it by suggesting the Faust-Margaret-Mephistopheles trio in C (whether meeting or garden scene) instead of the Martha-Margaret duo in B. Certainly the choice has added to the complex nature of this secondary episode. Phiz may have followed suit, elaborating in parallel Miss Mowcher as Gulliver amongst the Brobdingnagians, a detail taken up again by Dickens in the dwarf's pathetic textual appeal. The intricate and evolving development of implanted images as in *I make the acquaintance of Miss Mowcher* displays not only an expert use of iconographical tropes, but also awareness of later text developments, not to mention an acute use of the borrowed image to unveil masked realities. The C (published) image may safely be deemed the result of both writer's and artist's complex collaboration.

10.5 Games of Fiction, Tricks and Screens

Retzsch's outlines prove a sample case of pliable goods in fiction. Their remarkable resilience lies in easy recognition. Copies, and copies of copies, have established them as stereotypes, coined typecasts in writer-reader give-and-take. Disraeli's *Vivian Grey* and Gautier's *Les Roués innocents* share a (male or female) Mephistophelean figure, a malevolent snoop of Germanic origin. Although cultivated men in *Vivian Grey*, such as Frederick Cleveland, have a double education, English and German, Mrs Felix Lorraine bears the Anglo-French name for the disputed Rhineland territory of Teutonic origin (*Lothringen*). Her connexion with Mephistopheles operates through a prominent German text (Goethe's *Faust*) thanks to Retzsch's prints. No obvious double agent, her true character is ambiguously implied by the word "friend," a "monosyllable full of meaning" (154), the suggestion rather being *fiend*. Similarly, in Gautier's *Les Roués innocents*, Baron Rudolph is a sinister schemer, presumed German, two qualities that melodramatically underscore his diabolical nature. In Disraeli, a future Prime Minister, the political tinge takes stock of the Napoleonic wars' aftermath differently. It forebodes in Gautier proto-imperial Franco-German rivalry in an era of mounting anticipation of future hostilities. Yet, Gautier's reversible use of stereotypes in travelogues, reviews, or ironic fiction, shows their ability to metamorphose and adapt while they maintain a small stock of traits that make them recognisable.

Indeed, once replaced and analysed in complex worlds of fiction, Retzsch's outlines are not just visual accompaniments to text or commentaries. They belong to a vast array of visual and verbal techniques capable of bearing multifaceted allusion, symbolism, metaphor or analogy. Quoting a Retzsch in fiction is not just cultural sophistication. Beyond typing naive characters (villains and lovable maidens), his images prove a key to oxymoron as embodied by Calixte Desprez. The (literally) "fairest (*Calixte*) of the meadows" (*des près*) is a young chaste profligate hoarding in her virginal chamber not diabolic jewels but Retzsch's seminal prints.

Outlines cited in fiction also excel through their aesthetic qualities. They may be visual models for an impertinent and motley narrative emulating the depiction of a convoluted orgy (Heine). They expertly teach brevity, suggestion, and imaginative effect. As such, they have no realistic ambition and make no pretence at "truth." Their value is to make believe, and draw the reader into the game of fiction. Even so, their visual immediacy may stand at loggerheads with their rhetorical value. In Pollock's *The Picture's Secret* the plot may seem mechanically combined from one fatal picture to the next, were the novelist not an image-blurring trickster substituting a wicked for a harmless heroine, thereby making of her a conundrum. Edgar Allan Poe does not even bother with such devices (somewhat crude in Pollock's fiction). He uses the outline as a refined screen to bemuse, hoax, and puzzle readers with a riddle, only answerable to and solvable by his own text, an enigma devised to trick them.

The capacity of outline to suggest fiction and the ability of writers to use visuals and coax guesses at the unseen (Dickens and Phiz), are thus outshone by poetics of the hidden. That strategy is a sophisticated policy of authors to veil motivations and events, while dazzling through blatant visual means. If "It is the glory of God to conceal a thing," writers are indeed creators of worlds, and readers challenged as "kings [whose] honour is to search out a matter." (Prov. 25:2). The boldest of writers conceal and withhold in order to efficiently lure and ensnare in their fictional universes. They are Makers in competition.

Lastly, that inspired champion and promoter of performing arts, Théophile Gautier, still considered mere storyteller and inadequately assessed for the span of his creative capacities, saw in Retzsch's outlines a vanguard mode of writing dumb shows and ballet as silent poems, with ideas posturing as plastic apparitions. The way to early cinema, experimental shows, and abstraction was open.

This chapter establishes the *Faust* outlines' full capacity to convey veiled messages. Printed matter qualifies as cultural envoy in a literary bargain between the arts and in nations' political negotiations. So strong and complex were such visual symbols that they would also be tendered by hero-poets to lovable ladies. What more intimate messages, then, did outlines carry in Goethe's and Byron's hands?

CHAPTER 11

Two Gifted Women

11.1   Goethe's and Byron's Gifts

Apart from a singular exception (minute almanacs for the ladies in Chapter 3), female readership has played little part until now in this book. Now, the select gift—to a woman by a poet—of Moritz Retzsch's *Faust* prints lies at the heart of this chapter. The two editions offered differ in form and language and are no mere instruments of seduction, which renders their choice all the more interesting. However configured, they remain gift books. As proffered and accepted, they transmit a series of signs and translate into symbolic language, as though, delivered and opened, the book began to speak. The stories involve twelve bottles of wine, a rose, Johann Wolfgang von Goethe and Lord George Gordon Byron (who named himself Noel in order for his initials, N. B., to coincide with Napoleon's). Both poets harboured mutual esteem, even fascination, despite lack of German preventing Byron from reading Goethe in the original. Two women step up: Marianne von Willemer (1784–1860) and Catharine Potter Stith (1795–1839).[1]

At first glance, it seems that they have nothing in common and can be compared only in terms of their differences. Foremost is the nature of their ties with the male protagonists, fleeting on the one hand (Byron/Stith), enduring and profound on the other (Goethe/Willemer). Equally, their biographies diverge. Marianne Jung was the illegitimate child of an Austrian actress who had sought fortune in Germany. At the age of fourteen, she enchanted the audiences of Frankfurt's theatres with her ethereal dancing, acting, and singing (Clemens Brentano fell madly in love with her). The banker Jakob Johann von Willemer, twice a widower, took her aged eighteen into his family alongside his two daughters. When Goethe met her twelve years later in August 1814 in Wiesbaden, where he was taking the waters, he described Miss Jung to Christiane, his own wife, as Willemer's "little companion" (*kleine Gefährtin*).[2] Barely two months later, on 27 September 1814, the banker made Marianne his third wife, putting an end to gossip, possibly at Goethe's instigation. She was thirty years old. For Goethe—then sixty-five—she became the object of a great passion, centrally related to the composition of his lyrical collection *West-östlicher Divan* on which he was working at the time. In addition to being his amorous muse and inspiration for the famed Suleika of the *Divan*'s eighth book, Marianne also contributed at least three poems to it. The soul mates saw each other one final time in September 1815 but a three-way correspondence (between Goethe, Marianne, and Jakob) continued until the poet's death in 1832. Goethe's gift is set in this November 1816 context. So far as I know, Marianne and Jakob were the first among Goethe's friends to receive *Umrisse zu Goethes Faust*, an original exemplar of Retzsch's prints, sent by the poet himself from Weimar on 8 November 1816, only a few days after he himself had received it from his publisher Cotta. It is not known where this is now, nor indeed whether it has survived, but the Willemers responded to the dispatch with a joint letter. Marianne wielded the pen, Jakob made do with adding the postscript.

Catharine Potter Stith's situation was quite different. Born 1795 in Philadelphia, she married Townshend Stith in September 1818, and in June 1819 followed him to Tunis where he was to become American Consul. In May 1822, the Stiths found themselves in Leghorn, likely on a return journey to the United States (Townshend Stith would die 2 November 1823 in Gibraltar). They joined other Americans aboard the USS Constitution, to which Lord Byron had been invited as guest of honour. He wore a rose in his buttonhole, which was either *given to* or *taken by* Catharine Stith (versions differ) as a precious souvenir with which to return to her country. Today the rose, relic of eros (an established metaphorical anagram), lies under glass at the Beinecke Rare Book and Manuscript Library. It is even available for consultation, bearing, as it does, a shelf-mark, as though a book (cf. Fig. 11.1a–b). This rose also prompted the *gift* of a book. Indeed, the very next day, Byron sent a *Faust* to Mrs Stith, accompanied by a letter urging her to accept "a memorial less frail than that which you did me the honour of requiring yesterday."[3] The book was *Faustus: from the German of Goethe*, the second edition of the English version of Retzsch's outlines, copied by Moses and published by Thomas Boosey and Sons (1821). The book also contains, as noted, a long summary of Goethe's play interspersed with passages translated

---

1   A somewhat different French version of this Chapter, titled "Le *Faust* comme don," features in Aurélie Foglia, Georges Forestier, Juliette Kirscher, Henri Scepi, and Nicolas Wanlin, eds., *"Une transparence du regard adéquat:" Mélanges en l'honneur de Bertrand Marchal* (Paris: Hermann, 2023), 603–19.

2   WA 4, 25:14.

3   Beinecke: YCGL MSS 6, box 1, folder 38–39.

© EVANGHELIA STEAD, 2023 | DOI:10.1163/9789004543010_014

This is an open access chapter distributed under the terms of the CC BY-NC-ND 4.0 license.

into blank verse, controversially attributed to Coleridge (Chapter 5). It is with a view to producing this version that Boosey had approached Coleridge in May 1820. And it is this same edition, sent by John Gisborne, that Percy Bysshe Shelley, also in Italy, and close to Byron at the time, was consulting in 1822, as he himself went about translating Goethe's *Faust* into English. Whether this *Faustus* troubled (Coleridge), inspired (Shelley), or aroused curiosity (Byron), it relates to three major English Romantics beyond serving as a gift in epistolary exchange.

In his letter to Mrs Stith, Byron hastened to justify his choice (he had none of his own works to hand) but his reasoning appears all the more poignant. In parallel, he had almost certainly given his *Don Juan* to George Bancroft, who also witnessed his encounter with Catharine Stith. Proprieties had to be observed but proffering a Faust rather than a Don Juan (two figures connected in literature) remains an equivocal choice. A book in which Margaret loses her honour and her life, against a rose, the sensual symbol par excellence. Why this *Faustus*? And what of the flower? The episode raises questions, which, while they may offer no conclusive answers, encourage a flight of the mind, the results of which are worth setting out.

Despite differences in social status, context, and occupations, several features are common to Catharine Potter Stith and Marianne von Willemer: their literary talent and cryptic authorial status; musical aptitude; strong interest in the education of women; and their silence. Marianne is a well-known figure who has been studied from various perspectives. Catharine, on the other hand, remains elusive beyond what we know of her from Arthur Burnett Benson's short biographical study, based on correspondence and her papers. He describes her as "a woman of rare physical charm, twenty-seven years old, an accomplished musician on the piano, guitar, and harp, a linguist and student of considerable ability, and a person who possessed exceptionally broad intellectual attainments and interests."[4]

Both women were considered fascinating, whether for beauty (Catharine) or charm (Marianne), and both later taught music and singing. Catharine, an expert musician who sang, like Marianne, set several poems to music, including two by Friedrich Schiller. When she returned to the United States after her husband's death, she opened a school for young girls in Philadelphia in 1826 and advocated a liberal education in *Thoughts on Female Education* (1831). The songs she composed include "Our Friendship," of which the first line ("It died in beauty, a rose blown

from the parent stem") is, however fortuitously, evocative of Byron's token. As with Marianne in the *Divan*, her poems published in journals did not bear her name. And just as Marianne ceded her poems to Goethe, so would Catharine publish, independently of her relationship with Byron, under the dual mask of translation and anonymity. She spoke fluent French, knew Italian, and translated several German authors and poets into English without putting her name to these versions.[5] She even published a novella in *Godey's Lady's Book* of broad readership.[6] Which is all to say that Byron's gift (of a *Faustus* doubly translated into word and image) already hints at a hidden, but nevertheless fervent literary activity, as daring as the anonymous authoress's quite public pluck of a rose from the rebel poet's lapel. Benson supposes, with good reason, that their relationship was more prolonged. Byron's letter supports this hypothesis: "I feel much flattered and gratified by the interest which you have been pleased to take in my writings," he wrote, words which are difficult to explain simply by their meeting on the frigate Constitution. The letters written to Catharine Stith between 1832 and 1833 by the novelist-adventurer Edward John Trelawny, touring the United States, also reveal ties with the circle of English poets exiled in Italy.[7]

Both women refused to yield their secrets. The relationships, which linked them whether briefly or enduringly to Byron and Goethe, remain closed chapters. Catharine showed great reserve when invited by L. Gaylord Clark, editor of a New York journal, to write an article entitled "Recollections of Lord Byron" for the *Knickerbocker*, despite ingratiating compliments about her intellectual capacities and a good financial incentive. As for Marianne, upon Goethe's death, she thanked God for having honoured her with his long friendship and kept the secrets of her heart to herself alone. Their biographies are therefore a fit setting for paths opened up by Retzsch's outlines: a substitute for the rose (Byron), a thank-you offering in return for twelve bottles of wine (Goethe). Retzsch's *Faust*, whether in its original portfolio (*Umrisse zu Goethe's Faust*) or as an English copy (*Faustus: from the German of Goethe*), becomes a token of desire mediated by a flower (Byron) or the fruit of the vine (Goethe). Calling cards for chequered affection, these two outlined *Faust* serve as a link between the male poets and a female author, whether amorous or simply bold. Highly literary, they lend themselves to two readings: that of Marianne

---

4 Benson, "Catherine Potter Stith and Her Meeting with Lord Byron," *South Atlantic Quarterly* 22, no. 1 (Jan 1923): 12.

---

5 Ibid., 21.

6 Mrs Townshend Stith, "The Chest of Bones," *Godey's Lady's Book* (Apr 1833): 145–59a.

7 Benson, "Catherine Potter Stith," 14–17.

and Jakob, the readers of yesteryear, and my own reading, thanks to Catharine.

In both cases, that which is dictated by desire, stirring the imagination, transcends biography and the learned footnoting of correspondence. It goes so far as to suggest the hypothesis that *Umrisse zu Goethes Faust* and *Faustus: from the German of Goethe* serve to reflect, in the former case, the very different reactions to *Faust* stirred in both Jakob and Marianne, and in the latter case, Byron's timidity, his propensity for seduction, and the fascination he exercised over others.

11.2 The Book as a Rose

Did Catharine seize the rose? Or did Byron give it to her? Catharine Potter Stith's encounter with Lord Byron gave rise to at least six diverging accounts: a chapter by George Bancroft, passenger on the USS Constitution, who would become a renowned American historian;[8] three passages in Byron's correspondence (to his publisher John Murray, close friend and poet Thomas Moore, as well as friend, financial advisor, trustee and banker Douglas Kinnaird); the content of Byron's letter sent with the book; a short manuscript by Catharine Stith's granddaughter, Emily Brandegee;[9] and a later article by the historian William M. Sloane, Bancroft's personal secretary, who expanded upon the latter's memories.[10]

The brazen gesture was indeed her own, although her granddaughter, keen on propriety, would reverse the roles (claiming the poet held the flower out to her). As for Bancroft, he offered a vivid version of the scene, gracefully toned down:

> One lady, of great personal beauty, put out her hand, and saying, "When I return to Philadelphia, my friends will ask for some token that I have spoken with Lord Byron," she gently took a rose which he wore in the button-hole of his black frock-coat.[11]

Bancroft added, in terms reminiscent of Byron's letter to Catharine, which he no doubt consulted: "He was pleased with her unaffected boldness, and the next day sent her a charming note and a copy of 'Outlines to Faust' as a more durable memento." Byron, on the other hand, boasted of

the encounter. In two of the three passages, he emphasized the rose (in italics), placed himself at the centre of the scene, and ascribed different meanings to it. The Murray version sees him detached, the woman's gesture consigned to the background, but the homage to him magnified, much like the rest of the letter which provides a litany of tributes to his own renown. The intention was to impress his publisher: "an American lady asked for a *rose* which I wore—for the purpose she said of sending to America something which I had about me as a memorial." The Kinnaird version focused on the bold gesture and the way it reflected upon him: "an American lady took a *rose* (which I wore) from me—as she said she wished to send something which I had about me to America." Finally the letter to Moore offered a more detailed and personal account, adding a significant detail: the rose had been a gift from another woman that very morning ("given to me by a very pretty Italian lady"). As he pondered this keepsake, Byron added: "*There* is a kind of Lalla Rookh incident for you!"[12] Literary auspices sketch out a novel between the lines, to which Retzsch's *Faust* adds images.

It is some story. That most symbolic of flowers decorating Byron's lapel had been given to him by his lover, Guiccioli. Catharine had taken possession of another woman's declaration. *Lalla Rookh*, an oriental poem by Thomas Moore (1817) had already met with considerable success (Bancroft recounts that it had been lavishly represented on stage at the court in Berlin, and Goethe's *Über Kunst und Altertum* reports on the performance). It shows its eponymous heroine, the daughter of the Mughal Emperor Aurangzeb, falling in love with a poet while journeying to meet another man, her royal fiancé, who in fact turns out to be the poet in question. Was the allusion to *Lalla Rookh* the covert wish of an aroused poet? Byron's imagination creates a lovers' knot around the rose. He is no doubt also exploiting the image—in the nymph's song next to Azim, included in "The Veiled Prophet of Khorassan," the first part of *Lalla Rookh*—of faded roses, symbolising the passage of time, and blossoms distilled into the fragrance of reminiscence.[13] Implicit in the triumphant exclamation ("*There* is a kind of Lalla Rookh incident for you!") is the invitation to

---

8   Bancroft, "A Day with Lord Byron," in *History of the Battle of Lake Erie* (New York: Robert Bonner's Sons, 1891), 190–210.

9   Beinecke: YCGL MSS 6, box 1, file 32.

10 Sloane, "George Bancroft—in Society, in Politics, in Letters," *Century Magazine* 33, no. 3 (Jan 1887): 473–87.

11 Bancroft, "A Day with Lord Byron," 192.

12 For these letters, close in time (26 May 1822 to Kinnaird and Murray, 8 June 1822 to Moore), see *"In the wind's eye": Byron's Letters and Journals*, vol. 9, *1821–1822*, ed. L. A. Marchand (London: John Murray, 1979), 164, 162–63, and 171. In the first two *rose* is underlined by Byron in cognizance of the act's boldness and implications.

13 *The Poetical Works of Thomas Moore Collected by Himself*, vol. 6, *Lalla Rookh* (London: Longman etc., 1841), 77–78.

FIGURE 11.1A
Corolla and calyx of Lord Byron's rose given to Catharine Potter Stith, 3 × 3 cm, dried and pressed between two sheets of glass in painted wood frame 38 × 36 × 4 cm
COURTESY BEINECKE, YCGL MSS 54 (ART), YALE UNIVERSITY

FIGURE 11.1B
Lord Byron's rose under the cracked glass pane
COURTESY BEINECKE, YCGL MSS 54 (ART), YALE UNIVERSITY

imagine *another* romance poem. The rose is already an evocation of things past.

On the American frigate, however, the incident became the epicentre of frenzied women competing for the rose leaves: "the ladies on board of the ship begged the leaves," notes Emily Brandegee, "but the rose is still able to tell of that distinguished visitor." Today, all that remains of the flower, stripped of these leaves, is a shrivelled corolla and a withered calyx (2.5 cm × 3 cm), reverently pressed between two panes of glass in a gilt wooden frame (Fig. 11.1a). The glass is cracked (Fig. 11.1b), making the object, enclosed in a small case, an unexpected twin of Marcel Duchamp's famous glass *The Bride Stripped Bare by her Bachelors, Even*. The roles have been reversed with Byron and his rose in place of the bride ...

Another singular detail: filial piety and a sense of propriety prompted Emily Brandegee to insert children to the narrative in place of women fascinated by the poet's good looks and scandalous reputation. Indeed, the model granddaughter specified that Catharine's rose was "to show her children." The watered-down story met with the favour of William Sloane: "when the consul's wife laughingly said that her children would want some proof that she had seen Lord Byron, she was permitted to take the rose from his buttonhole."[14] But the justification is somewhat fanciful if not jarringly incongruous. In reality, Catharine Stith and Lord Byron had both just lost children. In Catharine's case, her first-born and only male heir, Bolling Buckner Africanus Stith, born in Tunis on 8 April 1820 (hence Africanus) and buried in Leghorn two months previous, on 18 March 1822; in Byron's case, Allegra, his illegitimate daughter by Claire Clairmont, had died at the age of five on 20 April 1822. Her remains were shipped to England on 26 May and the first part of the letter to Murray, mentioned above, outlined the poet's desired funeral arrangements. His paternal affection was said to be slight but he had just written to Moore: "I have lately lost my little girl Allegra by a fever, which has been a serious blow to me."[15] A few months earlier, in Florence, Catharine, for her part, had given birth to a daughter, Ann Florence Stith, born on 8 November 1821.[16] She would have a second daughter, Victorina Sprague Stith, born in Gibraltar, who would die at the age of twelve. This might explain the rewriting of the episode after the event, but there can be no doubt that adults were involved and not children.

The letter to Catharine is explicit. The book Byron asks her to accept from him "contains an outline and some designs from the famous Faust of Goëthe [*sic*]—which have been much admired both in Germany and England." "Outline" refers to the synopsis of the play but this is not the reason for the gift. It is Retzsch's copied prints ("designs") that steal the limelight. At the heart of the book (pp. 49–51 of a volume containing a total of 86), two of them depict Margaret's seduction through a flower whose petals she removes one by one: Gretchen plucks them off to discover the secret of her beloved's heart. In his *Faust*, Goethe structures this scene around a cunningly constructed antithesis that opposes two couples in an Edenic garden (F 3073–3204). While Faust is courting Margaret and learning about her simple life, Martha tries to extract a promise of marriage from Mephistopheles that would suit her down to the ground, given her recent widowhood. On the one hand, greed, cunning, and the circumlocutions of a language designed to entrap; on the other, innocent amorousness and passionate sincerity. Shameless calculation versus the giving of oneself without counting the cost: Margaret invests the naïve game of petal plucking with all her trust. Unlike in French, where the ritual has various degrees ("he loves me a little, very much, passionately, madly, more than anything, not at all"), in German as in English, it is binary: "he loves me, he loves me not." In Goethe's *Faust*, the final petal, removed, declares "He loves me" (F 3184). With a great flourish, Faust declares his passion, given over to a rapture that he would wish to last forever (*eine Wonne | Zu fühlen, die ewig sein muß!*, F 3191–2). Intimidated, unable to believe her happiness, stunned that a grand gentleman should have set his heart on her, embarrassed by the intensity of her feelings, Margaret flees. Then follows the brief scene in the summerhouse and their embrace.

In the *Faustus* with Retzsch's copied engravings that Byron gave to Catharine Stith, the synopsis is however quite different: a short introduction mentions the alternation between the couples but their dialogue is in fact suppressed. Foreshortened, the scene focuses on the plucked daisy as proof of love and Faust's passionate declaration. The fleeing Margaret is immediately found again by Faust in the summerhouse and, once in his arms, abandons herself to a passionate kiss that betokens sexual consent. The rougher adaptation renders her seduction more complete and rapid. Reduced to a set of contours without shading, the outline image emphasizes the immediacy and explicitness of desire. The two Moses re-engravings summarising this episode, *The Decision of the Flower* (pl. 14, Fig. 11.2) and *Margaret Meets Faust in the Summer House* (pl. 15, Fig. 11.3), both on the right-hand side of the opening, draw

---

14   Sloane, "George Bancroft," 478.

15   *Byron's Letters and Journals*, 160.

16   I am very grateful to Sandra Markham for precious information on her ancestry.

FIGURE 11.2
Henry Moses, *The Decision of the Flower*, engraved copy after Moritz Retzsch, in *Retsch's Series of Twenty-Six Outlines, Illustrative of Goethe's Tragedy of Faust* (London: Boosey & Sons, Rodwell and Martin, 1820), pl. 14
COURTESY HAAB, F GR 5785, WEIMAR

FIGURE 11.3
Henry Moses, *Margaret Meets Faust in the Summer House*, engraved copy after Moritz Retzsch, in *Retsch's Series of Twenty-Six Outlines, Illustrative of Goethe's Tragedy of Faust* (London: Boosey & Sons, Rodwell and Martin, 1820), pl. 15
COURTESY HAAB, F GR 5785, WEIMAR

the reader's gaze to the very heart of the book. Not surprisingly, as shown in Chapter 7, they both flourished independently of the full set.

The title-page of the exemplar that Byron offered to Mrs Stith bears his ex libris, "Noël Byron | Pisa—1822." Below, in paler ink and a different hand, the words: "Presented by him to Mrs Stith,"—the inscription that turned the book into a memento.[17] As it changed hands, it perhaps carried a message in its engravings. To retrieve it, the reader had to leaf through its pages, just as Gretchen plucks the daisy petals and the ladies on the USS Constitution grabbed at the rose leaves. The beautiful Mrs Stith was about to return home bearing a book and a rose—a book in which a flower leads to the flaring of passion, consummated love, and perdition. The poet's choice was just as singular as the 27-year-old woman's ardent gesture. Boldness had met with boldness. The petals had become the leaves of a book, endlessly turned, so much so that, as withered as the rose, it would require repair, unlike the rose, sheltered beneath its glass. This book is today one of the gems of the Speck Collection, despite its modest state. By dint of being perused, it has lost one leaf of text, has been rebound, and five of its engravings are placed nonsensically. These flaws reveal nevertheless its true value: its contribution to Byron's legend through an episode that, while marginal in many ways, is also central to what it has to say about literature as a living, ardent pulse, subject to the laws of desire and imagination.

But let us stick to reason. The legend should not overshadow the political dimension to Byron's visit aboard the USS Constitution.[18] This was not just any ship: her name, chosen by George Washington, made the frigate the symbol of the United States' liberation from the imperial British yoke. Launched in 1797, she is one of the first six American navy battleships and the third to be built. She distinguished herself during the 1812 war by capturing several British merchant ships and defeating five British warships, and was the flagship of the Mediterranean and African squadrons, hence the presence on board of Townshend Stith, the US Consul to Tunis. Affectionately known as "Old Ironsides," the ship is today the oldest commissioned naval vessel still afloat in the world and is used for important official occasions. In 1822, the visit of a rebel aristocrat—Byron, banished from Britain—was a deliberate snub to English dominance, as well as an explicit identification with the democratic ideals that animated him despite his lordly rank. Byron's letter to Mrs Stith echoes this: "I have also been ever a Wellwisher to your Country

and Countrymen in common with all unprejudiced minds amongst my own."

As if in jest, the Consul's wife approaches him, extends her hand, and takes the rose. The tension between the two countries evaporates with this act that emancipates her. With her, it liberates all women to come, whether fascinated or not by the magnetic charm of handsome poets. More than bold, her act was above all disarming. It demilitarised and depoliticised the visit, winning her the favour of a young god: "I found him unpretending, natural: he seemed to me like a sensitive, gracefully bashful boy,—a young Jove, hiding his thunderbolts," she would later declare, writing anonymously.[19] Had things been different, Catharine Potter Stith could well have met with the same fate as Semele, the mortal who wished to see Zeus (Jove) in full glory as proof of his divinity, and was consumed by flames. Yet, not a bit of it. And so it was that she came away with both book and rose: a book that perhaps enfolded secrets like a rose.

11.3 Twelve Apostles and a *Faust*

The rose could well have led to she who was "rose of all roses" and "lily of all lilies," her very image garlanded with gilded roses, were Marianne von Willemer a single woman.[20] Not only is she now wedded but her letter of November 1816 is not the only one of its kind. It adds to a body of correspondence struck between two men. Her reaction to Retzsch's prints was swift and spontaneous, as though finding her voice for the first time. Until then, she had only sent Goethe the poem "I count myself among the little ones" ("*Zu den Kleinen zähl ich mich*"), ascribing to each of them roles of diametrically opposed standing.[21] Alongside the grandest, *der Größte*, whose multiple connotations designated Goethe as poet and privy counsellor, this antithetical baptism endows *die Kleine*—the little one—Marianne's usual nickname in the Willemer household, with social and literary dimensions that refer to her physical stature to underscore it. For this reason, her immediate identification with Gretchen, in the Willemer correspondence that interests me here, is all the more striking.

The November letter itself orchestrates this transformation. Until then, with the exception of the 1 August 1816 missive (in which she speaks directly and anxiously after an accident had befallen Goethe), Marianne had only ever addressed the poet in the company of others (Jakob

---

17   Beinecke: Speck Ck99 R3 +821 copy 2.

18   Peter Cochran, *Byron's Romantic Politics* (Newcastle upon Tyne: Cambridge Scholars, 2011), 169–71.

19   Benson, "Catherine Potter Stith," 19.

20   GBW, 37 and 33.

21   GBW, 11–12.

and his daughter Rosine, or Jakob alone) and from the background. Her letter of 12 October 1816 testifies to this. Mostly flavouring the expressions of her husband, who wielded the pen, her voice is only discernable second or third hand, when her words are not sparingly relegated to the postscript. They recall the silver-bowled golden apples evoked by Goethe in one of the poems he sent her, on which Jakob comments: a gilt-like veneer of propriety covers their apple-core intent.[22] Customary good manners. In November 1816, however, on receiving Retzsch's original prints, her voice rings out, carried by Gretchen, little in years and rank, like Marianne herself. The simple refinement of the portfolio (cf. Fig. 2.1a–b), the economy of means, the starkness of the medium, its apparent modesty and delicate lines, all served to touch the heart of a poetess in love. What Schlegel had said about the hieroglyphic function of outline drawing, fit for emotion and poetry, triggering the imagination that reconfigures the poem, is traceable in Marianne's reading of the etched *Faust* outlines. Suddenly she takes up her pen and gives free rein to her impressions. It is Jakob who must fit his words into the postscript. Roles have been inversed.

There is more however than meets the eye. Goethe sent Retzsch's prints on 8 November in response to a gift from Jakob: twelve bottles of wine, likened to twelve apostles knocking on his door shortly before Christmas, or as Three Kings (the Three Magi), an image borrowed from a sextain by Jakob, a six-line stanza that accompanied the bottles.[23] Goethe's wife, Christiane, had died on the 6 June 1816 and the poet was in mourning. The comforting and enlivening tonic he received was Eilfer wine of 1811 "comet" vintage, well-known as an exceptional year in winemaking (the Great Comet having preceded the harvest). The consoling gift, neither the first nor the only one of its kind, rekindled in Goethe the spark extinguished by grief and the cold of winter. About this unique beverage, their correspondence took on a brilliant and animated tone, rich in literary allusions. Grateful for the precious present, Goethe reciprocated by sending the portfolio with Retzsch's outlines, which says much of his appreciation, while naturally he refers to his own *Faust*. The perfect opportunity had come to forget his pain an instant, especially since from the previous delivery only one bottle remained. Jokingly, he admits trying to multiply them without success. He forcefully alludes to pagan, even infamous, practices (*heidnische, ja noch schlimmere Handlungen*) in favour of a garden gnome who might assure multiplication, as well as to pierced tables (*die angebohrten Tische*). The one character

he singles out from Retzsch's set (*beikommende Figur*), namely Mephistopheles himself, refers to an episode from *Faust*: the devil's supernatural trick in Auerbach's tavern, figured in Retzsch's plate 5 (cf. Fig. 9.17). Mephistopheles famously drills holes in the tavern's tables to fulfil the wishes of drunken students. Three different wines flow copiously before turning into flames while Faust and Mephistopheles escape. Save that, by staging the devil, the banter in Goethe's letter changes. What had been a joke changes tone. A sniff of sulphur lends new colour to the desired multiplication. Goethe re-appropriates the biblical story of the multiplication of the loaves and fishes and figures the twelve apostles as bottles. His 8 November letter invokes a pagan Last Supper that borders on the sacrilegious: it well and truly subverts the mission of the twelve apostles and the status of wine in the Eucharist.

No doubt the joke exceeds the equivocal, but there is more to it. By placing Mephistopheles at the centre of the discourse (to the extent that certain commentators even thought that he had only sent Retzsch's pl. 5 to the Willemers), Goethe turned him, still jokingly, into his own messenger: a herald who would arrive before he himself could "play a dear song on the zither of a friend" (*eh ich noch das liebliche Lied zu einer freundlichen Zither vernommen habe*). We might think of the flea song struck up by the devil in Auerbach's tavern, were it not that the zither rather alludes to a much more troubling scene: Mephistopheles's mocking serenade at Gretchen's door, interrupted by her brother Valentine (F 3650ff). This sarcastic song to the sound of a zither (*Singt zur Zither*, F 3681) about Margaret's deflowering and her pregnancy provokes the duel rigged between Faust and Valentine and the latter's murder. Should one not point out that Goethe's letter, as grief-stricken as it is haunted by desire, ends with a ghost (*das Gespensterwesen*), a spectral figure embodying an ardent wish who comes knocking on the Willemers' door in the middle of the night (*wenn es in tiefer Nachtzeit am ernsthaften Tore zuweilen poltert und klingelt*) ... none other than Goethe himself?

The triangular relationship (which has given rise to much speculation) is spectrally projected through the depraved song at the windowsill of Margaret-Marianne. The allusive scene functions as an epithalamium, once again re-appropriated: no longer the song of the bridegroom's best man, extolling the groom's virtues to his future wife, but of the drunken and ghostly friend who knocks at the door in the middle of the night. Hoping perhaps to gain admittance to the bride with the connivance of the groom? Goethe as Mephistophelean intruder thanks to Retzsch's prints? Quite possibly so: 1811 Eilfer was after all an exceptional vintage.

---

22   GBW, 22–23.

23   GBW, 49.

FIGURE 11.4
Käthe Kollwitz, *Gretchen*, 1899, line etching, dry point, aquatint and burnisher, green-black on Japanese paper, 26.7 × 21 cm, Knesebeck 45 IV
© KÄTHE KOLLWITZ MUSEUM KÖLN, COLOGNE

Measuring readers' reactions in terms of reception is generally considered a tricky business for lack of specific period testimony. However, the Willemers' 16 November response is for such purpose a Grail, and provides a reading both double and antithetic: it would be difficult to find a better illustration of the different ways in which a man and a woman, of such different position and status at the time, might read Retzsch (and Goethe).

Jakob's postscript reveals a synthetic, shrewd, double reading: he immediately sees the value of the dual item and the impact it will have on iconography. Thanks to Retzsch, there is another way of looking at Goethe's tragedy. Henceforth, according to Jakob, there will be essentially two Faust: he of artists and he of philosophers, without either exhausting the story of good grappling with evil, well suited to this era of recurring spectres. The latter detail responds to Goethe's ghost knocking on the door, but everything that matters has already been said: posterity would vindicate Jakob's highly pertinent analysis.

Although Mephistopheles had been granted a starring role, Marianne, for her part, does not hesitate for a moment to give precedence to Margaret. Better still, she imposes on Mephistopheles a reign of happiness to which she alone has the key. Even the devil should make the best of it, and leave a joyful impression (*ja selbst Mephistopheles mußte sich gefallen lassen, den heitersten Eindruck zu machen*)! She had nevertheless perused the prints more than once and his diabolical portrait had struck her. She provides one of the earliest and most accurate comparisons between Retzsch and Cornelius, discerning a key feature of Retzsch's engraved set, namely its humanity. The tone is hurried. Dispensing with any opening address, the letter begins immediately with "the goodly Gretchen" (*Das gute Gretchen*), even though she only appears in the set from plate 8 onwards: Marianne clearly identifies with her. The neutral *Das* and the diminutive *Gretchen* are connected, since Marianne sees in the figure of Faust's "goodly" friend her own "little" self. Is she not the dear friend of an ageing poet, rejuvenated and regenerated by a miraculous wine—a substitute for a witch's potion? No sooner, though, has she given her aesthetic verdict, than she beats a hasty retreat, ashamed, and afraid that Goethe will laugh, or worse, at her brazenness. For her impertinence does not only take the form of spoken words (a child is forgiven for babbling nonsense). She has dared much more: she uses a pen to set out her opinions in writing, and has taken control of the letter by opening it with a comparison between two artists. The outrage is comparable to Catharine Stith's evasion through anonymity: in writing, wielding a pen, becoming an author. In Marianne's very words, there is an echo of those Gretchen utters at the beginning of the first garden scene: "I'm quite ashamed, I feel you're being so kind | And condescending, just to spare | My feelings, sir!" (F 3073–74, trans. D. Luke). The dependent and submissive relationship that Marianne forms with Goethe not only reflects the strong emotions his imposing figure inspires, but also her subordinate status as a woman, albeit one who—so deeply touched by these etchings—dares put forward her ideas.

Two further scenes from *Faust* project themselves onto the final paragraphs of Marianne's letter: the daisy petal-plucking game and a song. Say it with flowers ... women knew this language by heart, whether of daisies or of roses. Marianne has thought about the garden scene but doubts the flower oracle as reliable, for the fields are covered in frost and the rivers in ice, leaving no blossom to interrogate love from afar. The *Blumenorakel* only works in the spring, and *Faust* may ultimately be little more than a play about Spring endangered by the frost of old age.

A melancholic mind might project two further poignant images upon these lines. One is an engraving by Käthe Kollwitz (for whom Goethe was a key author) of her little Gretchen, a poor pregnant worker in a snow-covered landscape, contemplating the ghost of her drowned child in the river's flow (Fig. 11.4). This same sombre mind might read Margaret's lament at the spinning wheel, subject of a fine outline by Retzsch that Marianne herself must have contemplated (cf. Fig. 3.1b), into the song that she sends, and would like to sing for Goethe. But that would be morose. For Marianne, these two scenes offer a pretext to weave into her letter subtle allusions to her second reading of her great friend's *Italian Journey*, which had warmed both her imagination and her heart. Goethe is a sun that drives away any allusion to the winter. Similarly, her song charms: it transforms, as though by enchantment, the ghostly knock at the door into the bright light of truth (*Möge sich doch einmal die freundliche Dichtung vom ernsthaften Tore und dem nächtlichen Klingeln und Poltern in klare lichte Wahrheit verwandeln*).

Strengthened like Gretchen in her humble choices, Marianne, the writer and dear friend, was able to dispel with a play of allusion and expert hand the nightmares of men that follow in the footsteps of Mephistopheles. A previous letter from Jakob, sent from the spa town of Soden, was headed "Bad Soden and Gomorrah" in a clear allusion to the two cursed cities destroyed by fire and brimstone.[24] In Marianne von Willemer's happy gift for transforming the most disastrous of auguries, we may confidently discern a joyful disposition, a luminous personality, and the happiness she spread around her.

Exceptional examples, Marianne's and Catharine's, show the extent to which readers and Goethe lovers of the time may have invested *Faust* through prints. They represent a unique case, deserving choice treatment, indeed a chapter, evidencing how, within a broader cultural history, literature penetrated individual lives and circumstances. Most readers however could not enjoy such privileged relations. Alongside the play and its prints, they settled for substitutes, objects of variable value and status, as the following last chapter shows.

---

24   GBW, 42.

CHAPTER 12

Artefacts: Poetics of Everyday Life

Germany penetrated France, notes Victor Pavie, thanks to the arts, literature and University tenure. Referring to the late 1820s, he writes in 1874, in the wake of the short-lived Franco-Prussian war, when France lost Alsace and Lorraine to the second Reich. To merely study the German language or enthusiastically clap at a *Freyschutz* performance did not satisfy Pavie. With two of his friends he bought a fire screen representing Faust's duel with Valentine. German culture permeated the very core of French homes by way of decorative curios. Was their fire screen embroidered or metal embossed? Or perhaps a lithophane? Pavie's panel follows on Delacroix's particular manner of picturing Mephistopheles and a potent theatre souvenir: "Two Mephistopheles for one, relieved of their philosophical gear, each answered one another from one Paris junction to the next, in the disguises of Bouffé and Frédérick Lemaître."[1] His brisk narrative brings fine art, playhouse, and craftsmanship together. Domestic reminder of a vibrant onstage event, the fire screen has turned an admired romantic artist's interpretation of the fiend. The parallel bonds a key aesthetic depiction of Goethe's play (Delacroix's novel interpretation via a new medium, lithography) and what I would term Faustian "home poetics" in early nineteenth-century France.

This chapter may be read as a display of puzzle pieces. Contrived after Retzsch and inspired by Goethe's play, the things it contains strongly connect to literature, while often remaining part of mundane life, fashioned by devices, gestures and habits. Modern eyes may see such objects as keepsakes, agents of things past, but in most cases they feature only the visible part of a grander riddle. As such, they are maimed: their meaning appears lost. Connecting their past significance to lingering counterparts might conceivably restore their integrity. This is how *symbols* worked in ancient Greece. They were originally objects split between two ancestral allies, each of which passed a half on to their children; whenever reunited, the two parts' descendant bearers recognized themselves as bound by the mutual hospitality previously contracted. A *symbol* thus links etymologically to *sym-ballein, put* or *bring together, make a parallel between, compare,* by extension, *conjecture* or *interpret.* Such are the objects discussed in this chapter: they are riddles or clues as to how Goethe's *Faust* entered people's lives through Retzsch. Associated

rituals, projections and signalling, as guessed or inferred, furnish the missing or maimed significance.

Triviality (as in *Trivialliteratur*) or ephemera are frequent terms in scholarship to classify such adornments.[2] Triviality lacks value, importance, ability or moral quality; it smacks of the unscientific or popular; it rhymes with trifles or gewgaws, insignificant baubles. In such guise, objects of Faustian culture string out under our eyes like trinkets, an asyndeton gathering force from sheer enumeration and accumulation as in Karl Engel's or Alexander Tille's accounts. In 1885, Engel itemizes Faustian images reproduced on stage curtains, theatre ceilings, pipe bowls, cups, cigarette boxes and tobacco pouches, ball fans, lampshades, lithophanes, porcelain keys, and marzipan cakes.[3] Tille harps on: "Fausts, Mephistos, and Gretchens are seen on the insides of cigar-boxes, on tarts and fans, on albums and boxes for postage stamps, on inkstands, on silver spoons, on table services, and as window transparencies. [...] The heads of Faust and Mephisto appear on letter paper and on portfolios."[4]

Dumb-founding as lists, both point to routines and patterns, social and domestic life shared by the multitude. Yet, objects in this chapter are no trivial array. They span social categories from the aristocracy receiving kingly presents through upper-middle to lower-middle classes using mass-produced readymades. Some of them were expensive, celebratory artefacts bestowing status, now turned treasured collectables, hardly bric-a-brac. Then as now, they reveal practices charged with cultural significance, identification rituals, and mental patterns. The indiscriminate notion of triviality hardly allows a better grasp of what they meant, fathomable by differentiating their many functions in dissimilar contexts.

To note, Retzsch himself is no alien to precious handcraft. New York's Tiffany and Co. made to his design the elaborate *Intemperance Tankard*, a tapering cylindrical mug of *c.*23.5 cm in height, modelled all over with Bacchanalian figures in historical costume. The tankard, approximately dated 1856–70 for the 2008 Christie's auction, was probably made earlier, given the artist's demise in 1857.[5]

---

2   Carsten Rohde, *Faust-Ikonologie*, 79–95. Chap. 9 is subtitled "Kommerzialität und Trivialität."

3   Engel, 454.

4   Tille, "Artistic Treatment of Faust," 151.

5   *Important American Silver*, New York, Christie's, 17 January 2008, lot 146.

---

1   Pavie, *Voyages*, 61.

© EVANGHELIA STEAD, 2023 | DOI:10.1163/9789004543010_015

This is an open access chapter distributed under the terms of the CC BY-NC-ND 4.0 license.

Importantly, its buoyant carousing, exuberant vines and intoxicated children on the lid, joyfully struggling for a wine jug, defy the expansive American Temperance movement that swept over the country in the mid-1850s. For Tiffany to produce such an object (reminiscent of Retzsch's Höflößnitz *Parade of the Vinedressers*) was daring given the time and context. Similar examples therefore beg for greater nuance.

New approaches to objects have also taken us beyond considering them inconsequential. A Harvard exhibition, and joint seminars on *Tangible Things*, evoked material culture as lively parts of American history through stories to unfold.[6] In *Evocative Objects*, Sherry Turkle discloses things as "companions to our emotional lives or as provocation to thought." She uses Claude Lévi-Strauss's notion of *bricolage*, that is "goods-to-think-with and good-to-think-with," combining and recombining a closed set of materials to come up with new ideas.[7] Let me add that things may also guard an entry to the domain of everyday poetics: to what is to be done with them, dreamt and projected through them, or identified with them, since "as good poets know, common objects when looked at anew have a dazzle of their own."[8] Past human experience, thought, feelings, and suggestive worlds have also been built via *Faust* objects bearing Retzsch's hallmark.

12.1 Treasures of Gold and China

Two of the earliest are of royal lineage. According to their commissions' ledger, in 1821 and 1822 Prussia's Königliche Porzellan-Manufaktur (KPM) produced two sets of twenty-four porcelain painted plates, by order of Friedrich Wilhelm III, as royal presents with scenes painted after Retzsch's etchings. Neither service has passed through the rigours of time intact. Today only half of the first belongs to the palace collection in Charlottenburg, the other half's whereabouts remaining unknown (Fig. 12.1). The second (1822), auctioned as an inclusive lot of twenty-four items at Sotheby's in 2018 and ultimately at Frankfurt's Goethe-Haus, is not quite homogeneous (cf. Fig. 12.2).[9] As noticed by experts, the full gilt rim of one of the plates associates it rather with the 1821 set. Further, and

unremarked by experts, the scene itself is not by Retzsch but after fellow artist Naeke's now lost painting on *Faust and Gretchen* (cf. Fig. 1.9), already by then re-engraved and lithographed (cf. Fig. 1.12a–b). As prove the rim pattern and a quote on the reverse, the missing plate (since substituted by the Naeke view) is none other than Gretchen appealing to Mater Dolorosa, clearly after Retzsch, previously auctioned in Berlin and now in private hands.[10] Such dispersal variously reflects precious objects' odd fortunes and destinies over time, iconographic propinquity between Retzsch and Naeke, but also commercial practice in the sale of a full service despite apparent anomalies.

Notwithstanding partly deficient data, all plates' wells (Naeke excluded) reproduce focused scenes from twenty-four of Retzsch's twenty-six outlines. Retzsch's engravings were surely the models, as proves the 1820 Cotta edition, still in the KPM archive. Although time and use have left their mark, the archival item is complete with text brochure and all 26 prints sitting in the early small portfolio. It is not then by accident but deliberate choice that two prints have been rejected from the solely known comprehensive porcelain service—tellingly the Prologue in Heaven and the witches' Sabbath (cf. Fig. 12.2). It may well be that kingly Protestant reserve refrained from ordering God to be painted; or that the Sabbath's swarm of erotized crowds proved too profuse and bold, or both, for the restrained space of the plate well. Anyhow, the elimination seems fraught with intention. By discarding Heaven and Hell, the porcelain cycle deliberately covers a story with characters grown familiar and grants them new life in indelible bright glaze.

The two sets differ in colouring of the scenes (yet Mephistopheles glows red from top to toe in both) and quite strongly in rim decoration. The incomplete Charlottenburg service, more opulent, is fully gilded with no inscriptions at the back (Fig. 12.1). In the second, with individual tooled gilded borders in delicate gold and white designs (cf. Fig. 12.2), the undersides offer quotes lifted from the Cotta 1820 letterpress brochure. Both Retzsch's etchings and Cotta's text excerpts had therefore been put to good use. From 1820 already, they had passed through noble hands.

Fascinatingly, the purpose of such lavish creations, well known for both, links them to Prince Anton von Radziwill's *Faust* performances in Berlin.[11] The first, commissioned in 1821, was a royal present to Duke Charles

---

6   Laurel Thatcher Ulrich, Ivan Gaskell, Sara J. Schechner, and Sarah Anne Carter, *Tangible Things: Making History Through Objects* (New York: Oxford University Press, 2015).

7   Turkle, ed., *Evocative Objects: Things We Think With* (Cambridge, Ma.: MIT Press, 2007), 4–5.

8   Ulrich et al., *Tangible Things*, 2.

9   Sotheby's, *Of Royal and Noble Descent*, London, 17 January 2018, https://www.sothebys.com/en/auctions/ecatalogue/2018/of-royal-and-noble-descent-l18306/lot.17.html.

10   Lempertz, Berlin, 2 May 2015, auction 1047, lot 153.

11   Samuel Wittwer, *Refinement and Elegance: Early Nineteenth-Century Royal Porcelain from the Twinight Collection* (Munich: Hirmer, 2007), 73–75; Hannelore Plötz-Peters, "Porzellane der KPM Berlin für den polnisch-preußischen Fürsten Radziwill," *Keramos* 246 (2019): 25–34.

ARTEFACTS: POETICS OF EVERYDAY LIFE

FIGURE 12.1   Königliche Porzellan-Manufaktur (KPM), eight of the twelve surviving painted and gilded plates with scenes after Moritz Retzsch's outlines, 1822
FPPGBB, INV. NR. XII 10069-10080, BERLIN, PHOTO WOLFGANG PFAUDER

FIGURE 12.2 Königliche Porzellan-Manufaktur (KPM), twenty-four painted and gilded plates with scenes after Moritz Retzsch's outlines, 1822–23
FDH, FRANKFURTER GOETHE-MUSEUM, IV-2021-001, FRANKFURT, PERMISSION OF ADOLF AND LUISA HAEUSER FOUNDATION

ARTEFACTS: POETICS OF EVERYDAY LIFE

337

of Mecklenburg, presumably for his 1819–20 performance of Mephistopheles in Monbijou palace. As noted, in top hat, tailcoat and silk stockings, the Duke had turned the devil into a sophisticated *Junker* eliciting the court's and the monarch's praise. The second service, commissioned in 1822, was a two-part birthday gift to Princess Luise, Anton Radziwill's wife, on two successive years, 1822 and 1823. It was also on her 24 May birthday that *Faust* had been twice performed, first in 1819 then in 1820 (Chapter 9).

The gift in two moments perhaps commemorated those two occasions. It reciprocated pleasure given by bestowing further pleasure. Marcel Mauss's famous essay on reciprocity and gift exchange bears on archaic societies; still, his notions of "settling accounts" and stress on "a mix of spiritual bonds" between things and individuals or groups come to mind.[12] In both cases however, the precious plates after Retzsch carried further meaning. They were not only a distinct symbol of royal favour. They also were (and still are) splendid visual objects fraught with cultural history and chic appeal. They belong to the very first testimonies of *Faust*'s visual fortunes in select circles. They had already become exceptional aesthetic messengers. Through the vivid souvenir of the first onstage performances of that extraordinary play, they brought together the distant Dresden artist, the Prussian monarchy and its court, purveyors and manufacturers to the royal household, the court theatre manager Count Brühl, and the architect-cum-set-designer Schinkel. Inspired again by Retzsch, the latter two had broken with theatre conventions, adopted new stage sets, and inaugurated a transformation of the German stage (Chapter 9). Beyond a token of exchange, the costly presents launched that long trail of objects that would bring *Faust* to its diverse publics. They acted as go-betweens of Goethe's ambition, Cotta's printed products (Goethe's *Faust* and Retzsch's *Umrisse*), reading habits, and visual surrogates of the time. Past theatre, the staging of *Faust* was in the wider world. In such matters, the play's adoption passed through tangible, material artefacts.

12.2   Porcelain for the Many

As the century grew and Faust culture spread, porcelain allowed Retzsch's protagonists to address greater numbers in other attire. His compositions became part and parcel of literary scenes that bedecked bourgeois homes, thanks to porcelain knick-knacks. As the painters often used trimmed or cut-up prints to obtain handy working formats for colourful representations, Retzsch's engravings must often have been chosen to serve such reworking. They were both cheap and easy to manoeuvre. The spread of literary episodes and personae on china has been interpreted as a sure sign of the bourgeoisie's cultural penchant, self-confidence, and economic prosperity.[13] Let me add that the expanding book and print trades had enhanced such tendencies: objects, books and prints had all become commodities.

Yet, objects were not only "obvious, trivial" things satisfying basic needs, but also "strange", "mysterious" items "abounding in metaphysical subtleties and theological niceties." In *Capital: A Critique of Political Economy*, Karl Marx had reflected on the fetishism of the commodity and its secrets. He noted that useful things became odd as soon as they emerged as merchandise. They were no longer inert and lifeless, mere necessities. To show their weirdness, Marx used a lively picture, of a wooden table behaving like a grotesquely animated creature, that stood not only on its feet but also on its head and "evolve[d] out of its wooden brain grotesque ideas, far more wonderful than if it were to begin dancing of its own free will."[14]

In the case of Retzsch-inspired porcelain, Marx's imaginative figure fits the bill in two ways. On the one hand, porcelain items mass-made after Retzsch's plates are based on scenes copied and remediated, that is, twice or thrice removed from the artist's original compositions. The substitute scenes, typically endowed with middle-class sensibility and decorum, may be seen in a way as objects standing on their heads, evolving out of their china wits new ideas and emotions that embody their users' responses and propensities to identification.

Contrariwise, a faithful representation of a Retzsch scene in a colourful china plate 22.6 cm in diameter, now in Peter-Christian Wegner's collection, *eludes* industrialized manufacturing. According to the collector, while the plate itself may have come from a Thuringian manufacturer, it is unmarked, and interestingly decorated with a scene of home production, signed "G. Koch" in the lower right corner of the image. Datable 1850–60, or more cautiously second half of the nineteenth century, its painter must have known the colouring of the KPM plates after Retzsch, and have wanted to elaborate on a Retzsch scene not used in the KPM production.[15]

---

12   Mauss, *The Gift*, expanded ed., ed. and trans. Jane I. Guyer (Chicago: Hau, 2016), 75.

13   Peter-Christian Wegner, *Literatur auf Porzellan*, 10–11; Rohde, *Faust-Ikonologie*, 80–81.

14   Karl Marx, *Capital: A Critique of Political Economy*, trans. Ben Fowkes (London: Penguin Books, 1990), 1:163–64. Also referred to by Turkle.

15   Peter-Christian Wegner, e-mail message to author, 23 Feb 2022.

ARTEFACTS: POETICS OF EVERYDAY LIFE

FIGURE 12.3 Unmarked china plate, painted and signed by G. Koch, Mephistopheles lulls Faust to sleep after Moritz Retzsch's outline, c.1850–60, diameter 22.6 cm
COURTESY PETER-CHRISTIAN WEGNER COLLECTION

As a unique example however, it may also be interpreted as disclosing a very personal involvement with Goethe's tragedy by the very choice of scene (Fig. 12.3). The plate shows Faust in an armchair lulled to deep slumber by a sly Mephistopheles who slips away from the doctor's study. The scene changes into phantasmagoria of the scholar's unutterable cravings (cf. Fig. 3.7). The chosen composition is twice off-centre. On one hand, the template engraving, as published by Georg von Cotta in only 1834, belongs to the extra three plates Retzsch added much later to his 1816 *Faust*. It postdates the original *Umrisse* by some twenty years and perhaps captures, as shows its popularity with the individual who chose to paint after it, changes in public sensibility regarding *Faust*. On the other, choosing a dream scene is far from innocuous. A series of sensual naked female genii, vividly painted, fill the doctor's dark quarters with a clearly tempting composition, venting sensuous bodily needs. Out of kilter with current public perception, this exclusive item was another object standing on its head. It reflects its signatory painter's psyche, and his reading of the play through Retzsch as the very place of desired enticement and invitation to escape.

Retzsch's appeal extended to porcelain tobacco pipe bowls, treasured in the nineteenth century. As early *objets d'art*, these open perspectives for "a cultural, social, and behavioural branch of the social sciences," although authors admit that precise answers to the objects' countless messages of significance and motivation are lacking.[16] Introduced from the eighteenth century to France and Germany, the manufacture of such porcelain wares was far from negligible and well established by the nineteenth century. Their elaborate fashioning with silver or brass wind covers (hinged lids) and costly stems involved hand painting the chosen scene, adapting it to the bowl form, and customization on demand (personal touches, owner insignia, emblems and inscriptions). Their variegated *décors* honoured important public figures, commemorated historical events, and distinguished literary characters. They were far from cheap. A pipe bowl painted in detail and made at a well-known factory would cost about 500 euros today.[17]

Two treasured Retzsch scenes proved choice ornaments for such bowls. Unsurprisingly, the flower oracle with Margaret plucking the daisy (Fig. 12.4); and Margaret and Faust kissing in the summerhouse (cf. Fig. 12.5a–b). The bowls themselves were respectively made in Meissen *c.*1820? (flower oracle[18]) and by KPM 1830–40 (kiss[19]) but no date befalls the scenes on the bowls. Delicately painted by expert artists with the help of a magnifying glass, both relay the remediated versions in lithographs by Zimmermann and consorts dated 1841 by Hirschberg (Chapter 7). In both, these bowdlerized and emotionalized close-ups had supplanted Retzsch's originals as in the lithophanes discussed below. The flower scene, attributed to Naeke, is clearly by Retzsch as specified to the collector by this author. A close artist's greater notoriety has again obscured Retzsch's work, even when remediated.

Comparative chronology of prints and objects is a knotty issue. Knowledgeable collector Peter-Christian Wegner dates the "kiss" KPM pipe bowl 1830–35, which precedes Zimmermann's lithographs. One might plausibly think that the prints served as matrix rather than the opposite: that a wide-ranging and ever-spreading flux of print culture had set and crystallised into things. However, Édouard Schuler's 1837 etching (cf. Fig. 7.21a) could have been used from the late 1830s to decorate the bowl with an amorous scene.[20] A tempting surmise would then be that transfers and circulation between prints and valued objects occurred already in the 1830s, not necessarily from print to handcrafted goods but rather in a rotating chain of swapped imagery. Pipe bowls, lithographic prints and lithophanes would all be part of the same rife and rampant Faust culture pervading German interiors, following Goethe's demise in 1832. They join and share a major cultural trend making the tragedy familiar to all, thanks to the touching story of Margaret.

In both cases, pipe painters have made ingenious use of the surfaces available to their art beside careful rendering and colouring. While the front of the pipe (visible to comrades and onlookers) focuses on the protagonists' amorous intermezzo, the side discloses latent or lurking danger. In the summerhouse scene, Mephistopheles in red pushes open not the door (as in Retzsch's engraving) but the casement of a secluded dark recess (as in the Schuler engraving or the Zimmermann and Müller lithographs) while Martha has evaporated. In the garden scene, eyebrow raised, he cocks his fierce eye on the couple from backstage, while promenading. Full-blown love will find itself at any moment helpless. Let us imagine an instant the smoker's movements: as he draws at his pipe, both sides are set in motion in a diminutive theatre performance, privileging in turn bliss, then threat, again ecstasy, then again peril. Smoking a capacious porcelain pipe was a lengthy contemplative process. Georges Herment, recalls in *Traité de la pipe* (*Treatise on pipes*, 1952) that huge pipes, holding a "prodigious quantity of tobacco," were called by some smokers "their kitchen."[21] The scene

---

16   Sarunas (Sharkey) Peckus and Ben Rapaport, *The European Porcelain Tobacco Pipe: Illustrated History for Collectors* (Atglen, Pa.: Schiffer Publishing, 2014), 7.

17   Hartmut Berg, *Herrn Biedermeiers Rauchvergnügen*, auction cat., 2010, 12; Heiko Haine, ed., *Brennende Liebe: Thüringer Porzellanpfeife in alle Welt/Burning Love: Thüringer Porcelain Pipes Around the World*, unpublished exh. cat. (© Museum Eisfeld, 2013), 56.

18   Oblivion art D 2152, https://www.oblivion-art.de/index.php/porzellan/porzellanmalerei-im-biedermeier/pfeifenkoepfe/item/2432-gustav-heinrich-naeke-1785-1835-faust-szene-im-garten-porzellanmalerei-pfeifenkopf-d2152.

19   Oblivion art B 0136, https://www.oblivion-art.de/index.php/porzellan/kuenstler-der-motivvorlagen-auf-porzellan/retzsch-m-1779-1857/item/1295-moritz-retzsch-1779-1857-gretchen-und-faust-im-gartenhaeuschen-porzellanmalerei-pfeifenkopf-b0136.

20   Mr Wegner agrees that the colour application, dated "post 1843" in his book, is certainly earlier, as well as the "kiss" lithophane (Wegner, 114–16).

21   Qtd. in *The European Porcelain Tobacco Pipe*, 11.

ARTEFACTS: POETICS OF EVERYDAY LIFE

341

FIGURE 12.4   Meissen pipe bowl, *c.*1820?, Faust and Margaret in the garden scene with Martha and Mephistopheles passing, painted after
Moritz Retzsch, framed in gold, 12.1 cm, Berlin form
COURTESY DETLEV DAUER COLLECTION D2152

FIGURE 12.5A KPM pipe bowl, *c.*1830–40, with Margaret and Faust kissing and Mephistopheles spying, painted after Moritz Retzsch, framed in gold
COURTESY PETER-CHRISTIAN WEGNER COLLECTION

could easily be one of dreamy imaginings, intimate forebodings, if not fears. These were not only private but also social routines in smoking rooms, clubs or gatherings. Pipe bowl scenes had strong representational value. They decorated private interiors with racks of some dozen pipes or *Studentenbunden* (student unions), according to period depictions.[22] They bestowed kudos and gave status. They bred exaltation, triggered emulation, and activated projection. Every smoker could be Faust because Faust had become everyman. Striving for knowledge, disenchanted with science, sceptic about God, intensely melancholic amid a growing heap of books, yearning for love: such are to be found in every *Stube*. From the late 1830s, growing social categories identified with this major figure of German literature. Such context throws light on these items' intimate meaning and value. It illuminates a culture

---

22 Berg, *Herrn Biedermeiers Rauchvergnügen*, 12–13.

FIGURE 12.5B KPM pipe bowl, c.1830–40, hinged ornate lid, with Margaret and Faust kissing and Mephistopheles spying, painted after Moritz Retzsch, framed in gold, 13.7 cm, Berlin form
COURTESY DETLEV DAUER COLLECTION D2479

an elegant moustache and light brown beard under his tremendous double white and purple feather (Fig. 12.5b);[23] in a 1850–85 adaptation of the kiss scene to a bowl from Schney's porcelain factory in Bavaria, his towering plume is lopped by the lid but still curves proudly.[24] The scenes may even combine. In a particularly interesting example in the Dauer collection (D 1133), the flower oracle and the kiss have merged into one.[25] In 1840, Julius Nisle's *Faust* outlines, heavily inspired by Retzsch with some Cornelius additions, had been issued as steel engravings in three small popular brochures composing his *Göthe-Gallerie*, one of which shows the amorous pair kissing in a garden (cf. Fig. 12.6a). It was soon transferred onto a pipe bowl (cf. Fig. 12.6b). Drawn in sepia and framed in gold, the lovers tenderly embrace in a luminous garden against a low fence with trailing flowerets and vegetation. All peril seems to have disappeared. Yet the side view again reveals Mephistopheles dangerously close. Gretchen's line from the summerhouse scene, "*Bester Mann, von Herzen lieb ich dich!*" is carefully inscribed and referenced bottom right. The precious object, no doubt specially made, is dedicated "F. Reimers to his [friend] L. Fretter | Heidelberg 1840." A student gift in token of comradeship between two members of Corps Rhenania (one of the oldest student fraternities), it belonged to Ludwig Fretter-Pico (1818–1906) who studied law at Heidelberg 1839–42. Perhaps a talisman for successful life, it inevitably reminds us of the student's verses outside the city walls in *Faust*: "A good strong beer, a puff of weed | And a fine smart lass are what I need." (F 830–31, trans. D. Luke). The rowdy student in *Faust* did not care about the devil at all. This pipe's jurist hoped perhaps that, Margaret assisting, he would out-plead the devil himself.

12.3 Moulded and Backlit

Porcelain pipes are identified as a mainly German accessory. The French say *fumer comme un Allemand* (to smoke like a German), and no other European is likely to dispute that feat, witness the wisdom (or folly) of axioms. In Alfred Crowquill's *Faust* burlesque after Retzsch, the

not only of smug ownership or mawkish sentimentality but also of innermost appropriation.

Both scenes were doubtless popular as shows their adaptation to various pipe forms. Scene details themselves evolve: in a 1830–40 Berlin adaptation, curly Faust wears

---

23 Detlef Dauer's collection online, D2479. https://www.oblivion-art.de/index.php/porzellan/motive-auf-biedermeierporzellan/literatur/item/3524-moritz-retzsch-1779-1857-gretchen-und-faust-im-gartenhaeuschen-porzellanmalerei-pfeifenkopf-d2479.
24 Peckus and Rapaport, *European Porcelain Tobacco Pipe*, 73.
25 https://www.oblivion-art.de/index.php/porzellan/porzellanmalerei-im-biedermeier/pfeifenkoepfe/item/629-d1133-faust-und-gretchen-nach-retzsch.

FIGURE 12.6A   Julius Nisle, outline of Faust and Margaret kissing in the garden combining two outlines by Moritz Retzsch, in *Göthe-Gallerie: Stahlstiche zu Göthe's Meisterwerken nach Zeichnungen von Julius Nisle*, 4th fasc., *Faust, erster Theil* (Stuttgart: Literatur-Comptoir, [June 1840]), pl. 15, steel engraved and printed by W. Pobuda
COURTESY HAAB, F 3337 (D), WEIMAR

meerschaum pipe is the hallmark of "The German in an English dress" (cf. Fig. 8.2). Faust and Gretchen after Retzsch are therefore predictable emblems for porcelain pipe bowls. They read as quintessentially German. Not so lithophanes.

To bring to life through light, to make apparent: a *lithophane* is an artefact performing photosensitively.

Grounded on chiaroscuro, it brings into view (from the Greek *phainein*, to *cause to appear*) a shape, a scene or a figure wrought in a plaque's reliefs and recesses. The first component in lithophane, *lithos*, means *stone*, but the plaque may be of glass, alabaster, or other materials, while porcelain prevails. Until light touches it from the rear, the figures recoil mysteriously in it. Once light hits it, an image

FIGURE 12.6B   Sepia painted Nathusius pipe bowl framed in gold, Margaret and Faust kissing in garden approached by Mephistopheles, 1840, 14.5 cm, Berlin form, with *Faust* quote and friendship inscription
COURTESY DETLEV DAUER COLLECTION D1133

appears. There is something creative and magical, indeed poetic, in this bringing to life through light, as if, in an ordinary, commonplace routine, Mr or Ms Run-of-the-Mill had turned creator, writer, poet or novelist, perhaps even into Deity separating light from darkness.

Patented in France by Baron Paul de Bourgoing in 1827, lithophanes were produced in France and Germany from the late 1820s onwards. The 1879 invention of the incandescent light bulb and generalized reflective lighting made them quickly recede and utterly disappear. Until then, this domestic universe of scaled glows and shades wrought a special mood accentuating favourite pictures. Lithophanes have long since been collection pieces, museum relics, and specialists' beloved hobbyhorses. Yet, in the indeterminate openings of novel or novella, when writers conjure up characters, they swiftly produced an atmosphere, and hinted at possible events or developments. Lithophanes readily responded to Honoré de Balzac's and Theodor Fontane's fiction- and symbol-making requirements. What they proffered was precisely equivalent to the writer's gift: to invent, make vivid and suggest, where there is originally nothing but a blank page.

What picture did young Camille de Grandlieu consider when, on her lover's departure, she dreamily gazed into the fire at Balzac's very opening of *Gobseck* (1830, published 1840)? She contemplated in truth a "lithophane lamp shade" (*un garde-vue en lithophanie*), not "a transparent fire-screen" as Ellen Marriage's translation has it.[26] A famous German image introducing such a scenario in *Gobseck* is fair candidate in the work of a novelist for whom detailed settings had emblematic weight in any plot's development. The picture may well have been the flower oracle with Faust and Gretchen in the garden as Balzac's story discusses the potential misalliance of the noble Camille in love with a somewhat disreputable young man whose tarnished reputation the novella will restore. Balzac dedicated *Gobseck* to his friend Baron Barchou de Penhoen, who had delved into German philosophy and the opening lithophane likely pays silent tribute to Barchou's work. Auguste Barchou de Penhoen had translated into French in 1832 Johann Gottlieb Fichte's *The Vocation of Man* (*Die Bestimmung des Menschen*, 1799) and authored in 1836 a *History of the German Philosophy from Leibnitz to Hegel*. Indeed, Balzac's very *Gobseck* may be seen as evolving along Fichte's three stages in the development of faith (doubt, knowledge, faith), as in the

Vocation of Man. Balzac's *La Peau de chagrin* (translated as *The Wild Ass's Skin*, literally *The Skin of Shagreen*) is famously enmeshed in the *Faust* legend. It was written 1831, only a year after *Gobseck*.

Theodor Fontane's *Graf Petöfy* (*Count Petöfy*, 1883) discusses a clear mismatch, the marriage in Vienna of a very young Protestant actress with an elderly Catholic Hungarian Count, but also frequently alludes to Goethe's *Faust*. The novel ends with Petöfy's suicide after taking stock of his wife's love affair with his nephew, followed by her conversion to Catholicism. Indeed, the old Count had asked from young Franziska an unattainable sacrifice, to entertain him in their *mariage blanc* with her lively conversation, tales, and presence. Despite Franziska's commitment and enthusiasm, that scenario utterly fails afore youth's claims and dissatisfaction with a rather hollow existence. Two meaningful lithophanes forecast Franziska's future destiny and vocation in Fontane's chapter 2: Correggio's *The Night* (aka *The Adoration of the Shepherds*) with Mary lovingly bending over baby Christ in a Nativity scene, and Carlo Dolci's *The Penitent Magdalen*. The first predicts Franziska's conversion to Catholicism through the Virgin, a contentious emblem she will find in her rooms after her wedding; the second refers to her future erring. Yet, in Fontane's novel, the lithophane is not just an early symbol (among others) hinting at the novel's plot. In chapter 22, it develops into the very art of Franziska's storytelling. Like the novelist, she changes the lights in the room before unravelling a key narrative of her childhood, while the count asks her to "give to her story the lighting she judges best, but give above all the story" (*Gib Deiner Geschichte jede Beleuchtung, die Du für gut hältst, vor Allem aber gib die Geschichte*).[27] Balzac's and Fontane's fictions help us understand how enchanting lithophanes were: out of the plaques' crags and hollows, they awakened silhouettes, characters, identities, a tableau; they stirred enactment, drama—a life; and like potent metaphors, they were a figure for the novelist's inventiveness.

Lithophane plaques swept across Europe and crossed the ocean, just as Victor Pavie and friends' fire screen flaunted Faust and Valentine's duel in a Parisian home. They came in all shapes: square, rectangular, oval or circular, trapezoid or with clipped corners. They made candle shields and lampshades, *veilleuses*, table screens and tea warmers, clip mounts and ornamental lights in fancy shapes, fire and hand-screens, miniatures and

---

26   The Project Gutenberg EBook of Gobseck, by Honore de Balzac, https://www.gutenberg.org/files/1389/1389-h/1389-h.htm, last updated 22 November 2016, last accessed 11 Mar 2023.

27   Fontane, *Graf Petöfy: Roman*, ed. P. Kabus (Berlin: Aufbau-Verlag, 1999), 152.

ARTEFACTS: POETICS OF EVERYDAY LIFE

commemorative memorabilia, lanterns and matchboxes. Grandly framed, they reproduced valued paintings or famed episodes. As the day waned, they suffused interiors with soft glow, escorting nocturnal thoughts. In broad daylight, they enlivened treasured views and hung in windows, as alternative to coloured or stained glass. Entire casements of lithophanes with coloured and textured cathedral glass and ornate friezes formed composite decorative mosaics.[28] Among cherished tableaux, the same *Faust* pictures, twice or thrice removed from Retzsch, were championed: Faust lovingly leaning over Margaret plucking the daisy, and above all, their kiss. Both travelled well beyond German borders.

The garden scene for instance bedecks one of the five sides of a *veilleuse théière* (cf. Fig. 12.7) attributed to Jacob Petit (1796–1868) and made in his factory established 1830 in Paris.[29] Another item of the same scene, crafted in Berlin by KPM, travelled to the United States, and is mounted today, cased in glass, in Blair Museum of Lithophanes in Toledo, Ohio.

It will come as no surprise that the attraction of "The Kiss" is even greater. It figures prominently in all known catalogues of main manufacturers, Meissen, Nymphenburg, KPM, etc. Used as a lampshade, the set sits in a frame. When again so used in a decorative holder, it is prominently advertised on a nineteenth-century commercial postcard by a Dresden firm as an "historical Biedermeier" contrivance (cf. Fig. 12.8). Characteristically, Retzsch's name appears nowhere in this ad, despite the Dresden provenance.[30] Yet again, from *c.*1872, it was made as an American replica of inferior quality from plaques in Phoenixville, Pennsylvania, imported by the Phoenix Pottery, Kaolin and Fire Brick Company.[31]

The climax of the Kiss's extensive use features as key piece in one of the so-called "Woburn windows," three large oak frames (213.36 × 91.44 × 16.51 cm) originally holding a set of 175 lithophanes of various formats in brass grids. These were auctioned in 2004 as salvaged items from the demolished east wing of Woburn, a Cistercian abbey founded in 1145, subsequently the Duke of Bedford's

private shire residence.[32] They are at present in a private collection. The lithophanes had probably been originally acquired between 1834 and 1841 in Germany by British Major-General Lord George William Russell (1790–1846). In one of the Woburn mosaics (cf. Fig. 12.9), "The Kiss" is centrally inserted, just beneath erupting *Mount Vesuvius*, an ageing Goethe's portrait, and above a lithophane after Raphael's famous *Sistine Madonna*, from the Dresden Gallery, holding Jesus in her arms.[33] Such a montage cannot be devoid of implications: however bowdlerized, Faust and Gretchen's passionate embrace still stands for the volcanic eruption of carnal love, of which the virgin-with-child motif is of natural consequence. Further surrounding religious figures, of which a penitent Magdalene, drive home the message of Margaret's guilt.

12.4 In Tin and Frail Paper

Most of the above evidence ornate homes' polished refinement, individuals enjoying culture, not merely dabbling in it. Objects were of course merchandise, which did not prevent them from being evocative, pleasant, emotional, or poetic, strongly appealing to the imagination. Apart from late American lithophane replicas, their trajectories and production blaze the trail of a European craze for Retzsch's outlines and their offshoots from the 1820s to the 1850s in Europe. Finally, two later items prove much more ordinary: tin figurines to be toyed with or advertisement booklets to be ogled may indeed elicit a reader's smile of familiarity.

Zinnfiguren, known as flats, are still very popular in Germany and elsewhere. Their precursors go back to the sixth century BC, and Herrad's *Hortus Deliciarum* (twelfth century) includes a miniature of two children playing with tin figures,[34] which Dibdin also promptly reproduced in his *Tour*. In *Dichtung und Wahrheit* (*Poetry and Truth*), Goethe himself records an enchanting episode involving such toys. It features however in a story told by an infant Goethe to a bemused child audience, which smacks of sophistication, personal pride, and perhaps influence from previous literature. As artistic objects or figurative representations of the history of humanity, tin figurines reflect intense interest in historical facts and cultural

---

28   See Karlheinz W. Steckelings, *Leuchtender Stein: Die Geschichte der Lithophanie vom 18. bis ins 20. Jahrhundert* (Düsseldorf: Hetjens-Museum; Dresden: Sandstein, 2013) with excellent reproductions, and Margaret Carney, *Lithophanes* (Atglen, Pa.: Schiffer, 2008).

29   Carney, *Lithophanes*, 38–39 with ill.

30   Ibid., 126 and 120, both with ill.

31   Steckelings, *Leuchtender Stein*, 377–78.

---

32   *Property from Two Ducal Collections*, Woburn Abbey, Bedfordshire, auction Christie, Manson and Woods, 20–21 Sept 2004, lot 396.

33   Steckelings, 177; Carney, 153 and 158 with ill.

34   Erwin Ortmann, *Figurines d'étain d'hier et d'aujourd'hui*, trans. Arlette Marinie (Paris: Stauffacher, 1973), 15, ill. 10.

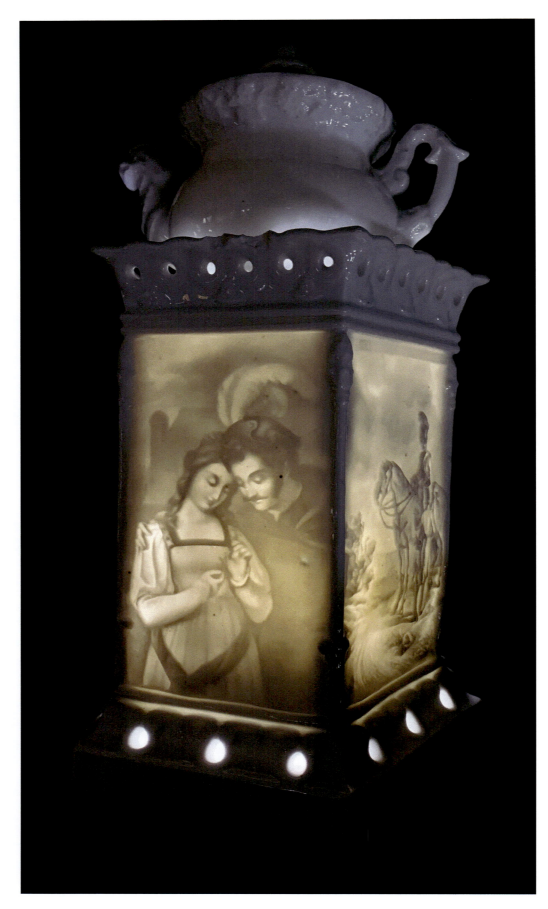

FIGURE 12.7
Jacob Petit (attributed to), five-sided *veilleuse théière*, French, 19th century. Faust and Gretchen in the garden scene after Moritz Retzsch
COURTESY BLAIR MUSEUM OF LITHOPHANES, ACC. NO. 2512, TOLEDO, OHIO

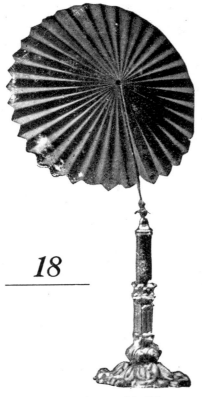

LICHT-SCHIRME

Nr. 322   Nr. 321

Nr. 321. Lichtschirm. Der seitlich verstellbare Schirm besteht aus Stoff in Gestalt eines Fächers, er ist zusammenlegbar und wird außer Gebrauch in dem mit einer Hülse versehenen Schaft des in der Höhe verstellbaren Bronzefußes aufbewahrt.

Nr. 322. Lichtschirm. Holzgestell mit lichtdurchlässigem Porzellanbild. (Lithophanie). Das Bild stellt Faust mit Gretchen dar, im Hintergrunde Mephisto. Die von den Königlichen Porzellanmanufakturen in Meißen und Berlin, sowie der Privatindustrie hergestellten Lithophanie=Lichtbilder aus Porzellan wirkten als Abblender vor Kerzen und Oellampen künstlerisch und waren zur Biedermeierzeit, als man das gedämpfte Licht bevorzugte, allgemein beliebt.

Aus den reichen Beständen von Lampen u. Leuchtkörpern früherer Zeiten der Firma Kretzschmar, Bösenberg & Co., Kgl. Sächs. Hoflieferanten, Dresden-A., Serrestraße 5 und 7

FIGURE 12.8
Kretzschmar, Bösenberg & Co., commercial postcard advertising candle screens, Dresden, 19th century, picturing screen with Faust and Margaret after Moritz Retzsch
COURTESY ARCHIVES OF BLAIR MUSEUM OF LITHOPHANES, TOLEDO, OHIO

aura.[35] As collectors' treasures, they also enjoy dedicated museums. Essentially two-dimensional, cast in low-relief slate moulds, the miniatures are made from an alloy of tin, lead and antimony, and have particularly thrived from the nineteenth century onwards in children's education. Awareness of the toxic lead compound has since prevailed and today they mainly meet aficionados' demands.

A few prominent literary figures rank with extensive militaria (over 100,000 uniforms and soldiers in historical dioramas). Even today, Berliner Zinnfiguren advertise on the internet scenes from Goethe's *Faust*, mostly not in stock, but made to order. In a few, Retzsch's branding may still be traced. It is unmistakable in Mephistopheles's tight-fitting costume (flaming red when painted), yet not in the solemn attire becoming of a medieval doctor such as Faust. Historicism has prevailed. Similarly, Gretchen's pose at the spinning wheel is typically after Retzsch's outline although the crudity of her 3 cm figure is far-fetched from its fine prototype. Most of the figurines are unsigned. Manufacturers in commercial competition did not hesitate to copy colleagues' production and engravers often worked for several. Models, figures and poses often amalgamated.

Tin flats after Goethe's *Faust* seem rather to date from the twentieth century. Such are several by engraver and lithographer Franz Karl Mohr (1896–1969), who made and

---

35 Ibid., 7.

FIGURE 12.9
Woburn window, large oak frame (213.36 × 91.44 × 16.51 cm) with a mosaic of 1834–41 acquired lithophanes in brass grids. Lithophane of Faust and Margaret's "Kiss" after Moritz Retzsch featuring under the Vesuvius eruption
PRIVATE COLL., IMAGE COURTESY ANDREW COOK

artistically painted figurines from zinc sheets in the standard diminutive 2.8–3 cm size. His compositions derive from the promenade outside the city walls or Auerbach's tavern, and mostly from a voluptuous Walpurgis Night with nothing specifically Retzschian.

Thought-provoking exceptions are the so-called showcase or display figures (*Vitrinenfiguren*) produced by Werner Fechner from July 1979. In these, the sway of one of Retzsch's 1834 additional prints is unmistakable, yet remains unacknowledged by their very manufacturer. Behind a bush Mephistopheles eavesdrops on Faust and Gretchen sitting on a bench, while Faust hands her the phial with the sleeping potion. Retzsch's print (cf. Fig. 7.1) has translated into two separate flats, Faust and Gretchen on one hand, arching Mephistopheles on the other, that may be brought together, or kept separate (Fig. 12.10). The Moosmann Collection, that comprises for instance a large number of Mephistopheles sculptures, typically elongated and Retzsch-inspired, has apparently not included the couple on the bench, retaining only the devil.[36] As in the porcelain plate of single design and painting (cf. Fig. 12.3), personal choice has again fallen on a later Retzsch print. This may have reflected a preference for tragic turning points in *Faust* (the potion will cause the death of Margaret's mother), yet the reasons may be simply technical.

Rolf Grünewald, who made these Faust moulds after a drawing by Karl Heinrichs, engraved for Fechner mostly military and civilian 3-cm tin figures for thirty-two years. The larger *Faust* items (*c*.8–10 cm) were produced as a welcome change from standard work. In tin flat production, display figures, always incidental, never dominant, are made to lodge in glass cases or sit on cabinets. A majority relates to animals or people, either mounted or on foot, such as figures from the life of Jesus, Santa Claus, famous personae, peasant couples, musicians and castles. When consulted, Mr Fechner expressed no familiarity with Goethe's *Faust*, adding that the only Retzsch print he knew, *The Chess Players*, was too complicated for a tin figure.[37] The choice of the scene may therefore rest on the shape and attitude of the models themselves or on the novelty they introduce as compared with recurrent and stereotyped *Faust* incidents. Even so, the latent antagonism between the loving pair and their wily opponent remains noticeable. The figurines synopsize Goethe's *Faust* as a conflict between trusting love and cunning snare, not so much between good and evil. If Retzsch's original conceptions were remarkably "common property" for all to enjoy at the end of the twentieth century, such goods are still available for a modicum price.

In a 4 August 1834 letter to his publisher Georg von Cotta, describing the added prints, Retzsch comments:

FIGURE 12.10   Tin showcase figurines, Faust and Margaret on bench, Mephistopheles eavesdropping, after Retzsch's 1834 insert plate 19 (cf. Fig. 7.1), produced by Werner Fechner, July 1979
AUTHOR'S COLL., PHOTO CHRISTOPHER STEAD

36   *Doctor Faustus und Mephistopheles: Bücher, Graphiken und Figuren aus der Sammlung E. P. Moosmann* (Frankfurt, Stadt- und Universitätsbibliothek, 1991), 100.

37   Werner Fechner and Barbara Rothmeier, e-mails to author, 19 and 20 Feb 2022.

No. 19. Pag: 232 Gretchen fragt besorgt, ob der Trank der Mutter auch nicht schaden werde, wärend der horchende Mephistopheles in Folge des von Gretchen früher ausgesprochenen Widerwillen Hinsichtlich seines widrigen Gesichtes, sich am Kin[n] faßend hönisch spricht "mein Mäskchen da weissagt verborgnen Sin[n]".[38]

No 19, p. 232: Gretchen asks anxiously whether the potion will not harm her mother, while the listening Mephistopheles, as a result of Gretchen's earlier expressed reluctance to see his unpleasant face, grabs his chin and says sneeringly "my little mask prophesies hidden meanings".

Mephistopheles mocks Gretchen's capacity to read evil in his features. In Albert G. Latham's translation: "My mask forebodes some mystery to unravel | I am a genius at least, she feels,— | Who knows perhaps the very Devil!" Retzsch had unambiguously leant on the tempter, not the lovers. He had turned his scheming into a demonic grin, also twisting his body into a coiling contour, even recognizable on a tin figure, by now almost a plagiarism, but still within character. Peter Moosmann, himself a sculptor and a *Faust* devotee, would not otherwise have added this spinoff Mephistopheles to his collection. Tin flat makers may have been similarly captivated.

Prints led to objects, yet objects lead us again to artefacts in print. If you were Catharine Potter Stith (see previous Chapter), would you have kept Lord Byron's rose or the book he sent on the morrow with prints copied from Retzsch? Surely both?

As we ponder over the answer, everybody is bound to need a Beecham's powder or pill. Beecham's powders today cure fevers and colds—my in-laws swear by them. A laxative pill "Worth a Guinea a Box," first marketed *c.*1842 by ex-shepherd-become-chemist Thomas Beecham of Lancashire, sold for 25 cents in the USA. Harnessing Irving's 1886 *Faust* triumph at the Lyceum, Beecham sold in the streets thousands of *Faust* booklets with Jonathan Birch's translation that advertised his wares.[39] In cream (turned brownish) paper wrappers and red print, the publication (13.5 × 10.5 cm) bears imprinted on every page of the tragedy "Beecham's Pills." In his commercial desire and rushed endeavour to succeed (*Streben*), Beecham carefully chose for his cover a well-known remediated Retzsch scene with four characters from the play: customers would

identify either with amiable and innocent Margaret, dashing Faust, unscrupulous Mephistopheles or shrewd Martha in the Eden-like garden, as provided by the comfort pills (Fig. 12.11). At the *dénouement*, when Gretchen is judged (or saved) and Faust carried away by the devil, it is instructive to read on the opposite page that Beecham's Pills are "a Remedy for Coughs in general, Asthma, Difficulty in Breathing, Shortness of Breath, Tightness and Oppression of the Chest," all of which Faust might suffer in his breakneck journey (Fig. 12.12). The ad is aptly printed in blood red. Thanks to Irving's success, the universality of Goethe's figure had made it into every family's medicine cabinet with the help (unawares) of Moritz Retzsch. The alchemist's apparel would certainly be put to good use in family cures.

12.5 Conclusion

Bourgoing, the 1827 lithophane patentee, called the wax model from which a lithophane mould is produced an *Aperçu*, in other words an *outline*.[40] This book comes thus full circle from Retzsch's initial outline engravings to three-dimensional casts. In fact, I have mostly discussed three-dimensional print and cultural artefacts, not simply texts-cum-images nor illustrations. Such artefacts are of course neither limited to Retzsch nor Goethe's *Faust*, and examples are numerous.

I have stressed here the poetic, imaginative and cultural dimension of artefacts particularly in the first half of the nineteenth century when readers were also surrounded by fictitious characters who convoyed them through life. As tough strategies imposed in commerce, and readers' scepticism and incredulity grew, wonder receded and disbelief crept in. Hard-line mercantile techniques and rivalry predominated but such obvious aspects should not obscure the fascination or magical appeal objects may have had on others' life and creations. After all, Marcel Proust may never have based *À la Recherche du temps perdu* (*Remembrance of Things Past*) on *The Thousand and One Nights* and Saint-Simon's *Memoirs*, had he not eaten off coloured porcelain plates picturing Ali Baba and Aladdin, two tales added by Antoine Galland, which do not belong to the primary *Nights*.[41]

Similarly, artefacts stemming from Retzsch may seem a far cry from his original work or Goethe's *Faust*. Yet, as the latter ebbs afore a flow of replicas, imitations are not

---

38 DLA C-R: no. 38.

39 William Heinemann, *Goethes Faust in England und Amerika*, no. 155.

40 Carney, *Lithophanes*, 14.

41 Dominique Jullien, *Proust et ses modèles: Les "Mille et Une Nuits" et les "Mémoires" de Saint-Simon* (Paris: J. Corti, 1989), 22–27.

ARTEFACTS: POETICS OF EVERYDAY LIFE

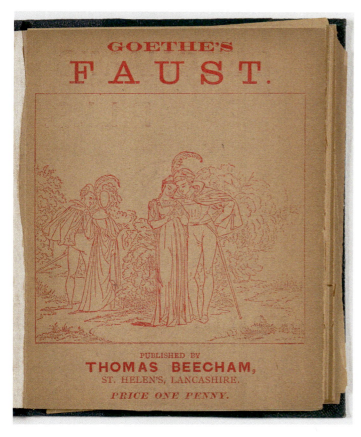

FIGURE 12.11

Cover printed in red, picturing Faust, Margaret, Martha and Mephistopheles in the garden scene after Moritz Retzsch, *Goethe's Faust Translated by J. Birch* (Lancashire, St. Helen's: Published by T. Beecham, [1886])
COURTESY HAAB, F 7665, WEIMAR

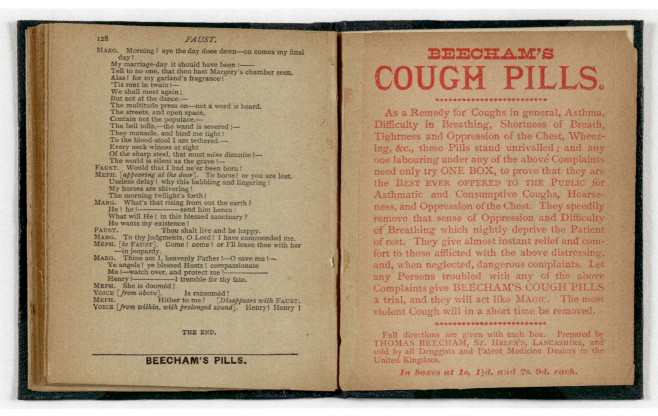

FIGURE 12.12 Last page of Goethe's *Faust* in black and advertisement of Beecham's Cough Pills in red, in *Goethe's Faust Translated by J. Birch* (Lancashire, St. Helen's: Published by T. Beecham, [1886])
COURTESY HAAB, F 7665, WEIMAR

necessarily to be deemed fake. They bear the hallmark of popularity, and the appreciation of greater numbers dims the sharpness of their original lines. Yet, they persevere remarkably, having been cut to encapsulate and compress ideas essential to Goethe's play.

Ironically, tin figurines were in the past tokens and souvenirs of venerated saints, worn by journeying pilgrims as badges (*Pilgerzeichen*). No penitent would have taken Retzsch's iconic Mephistopheles for guidance. Neither would he stand in a child's nursery, nor serve as an educational figure. Is however his tin portrait to be considered mere trivial decoration? At the very least, a Catholic tradition of *ex voto* effigies pleads against such outright dismissiveness.

CONCLUSION

Grains of Sand as Cities

Referring to eighty-eight different editions listed by Atkins in her (unpublished) thesis, Carl Schreiber states: "In the course of the decades these Outlines with their varying letterpress have girdled the world."[1] I have attempted here to assess that influence by grounding numerals in hands-on evidence, even curbing their numbers by contrasting publishers' attempts, on the one hand; and highlighting Retzsch's pioneering and extensive role, on the other, mostly on the basis of new and former evidence. Atkins's eighty-eight "different editions" prove rather to be a mixed lot, and their lump sum may be variously challenged. If the list embraces both *Faust I* and *II* editions, it includes several devoid of plates or extra-illustrated; it counts as such other formats of the very same, subcategories in fact, since publishers simply varied size and paper to meet expedient requirements; it comprises unverified entries (marked by a cross) borrowed from Engel, Kippenberg or Goedeke, occasionally erring; also Speck Collection items (named "another issue") which are rather bibliophiles' enhanced copies of the same (with additional slightly posterior material); and even includes later day compendia such as Neubert's.[2] Further, the difference between copy, exemplar and issue is not clarified, and the list embraces several end-of-the-nineteenth-century standardized *Faust* octavos, irregularly annexing Retzsch's outlines by twos or out of order. Further amendments and substantiation therefore seem necessary. The list provided in Appendix 1 synthetically records the Retzsch original portfolios and derivative copies on which the present book's first six chapters are based.

The claim that Retzsch's outlines "girdled the world" still stands. With its fifty-nine portfolios, copied sets, albums, partial or full translations with interleaved plates, and illustrated books, published in the German States, Great Britain, France, Belgium, the United States, the Netherlands, and Lithuania, and further issued in Denmark (1929), Appendix 1 validates circulation well above average for printed matter or images at the time. The outlines worked as introduction letters or visiting cards apprising in due course multiple publics for Goethe's *Faust I*. Retzsch's (reduced or levelled) outlines still

decked Russian and Italian editions in 1969, 1971 and 1987.[3] My focus, limited to the early twentieth century, has not investigated the latter in detail. By then, they had mostly entered homogenized print categories of little interest to the purpose of this study.

As explained in the introduction, this book follows Retzsch's prints in their European circulation and meaningful transformations from their first publications through to those at the onset of the twentieth century. I have scoured relevant instances of appealing cultural objects, seeking to interrelate their telling materiality, the ways they target potential reader categories with their pages, layouts and format, through representational power, symbolism, political and imaginative heft. Their first introduction to Britain shows how potent those parameters were. Wherever possible, individual readings and personal evidence have added spice to the venture. Singularity and distinctiveness of printed editions have been my guidelines in fathoming objects that seem but are not at all identical.

Two complementary paths, additionally followed, extend Retzsch's influence beyond what is usually expected from books and prints. First, his outline technique, easily adapted to reproduction, lent itself to copying and proved of exceptional resilience. Second, his compositions pervaded other arts or modes of expressions, literature, parody, the theatre, and three-dimensional artefacts in multiple ways, extending the realm of literature and art into people's very lives. Naming Retzsch "the Poet in reproduction" (*reproducierenden Dichter*), Ludwig Schorn had early captured both his poetic stature and his prints' malleability, although his intention may have ambivalently alluded also to Goethe's verse.[4]

It is the extent of such abundance, and not just of printed sets and books, that justifies Schreiber's view of the outlines as "girdl[ing] the world." True, without the prints' copying, plagiary, assorted reproduction and diffusion, such extensive circulation and permeating influence would not have been possible. To put it more clearly: we need to grasp Retzsch reproductions in the widest sense possible. This means not only as printed and copied, but also as parodied; remediated; reworked as theatre

---

1 Schreiber, "Coleridge to Boosey," 6.
2 Atkins, "Fragmentary English Translations," 44–66.

3 Siegfried Seifert, *Goethe-Bibliographie 1950–1990* (Munich: K. G. Saur, 2000), nos. 1979, 2521, 2523.
4 *Kunst–Blatt*, no. 45 (3 June 1824): 177.

© EVANGHELIA STEAD, 2023 | DOI:10.1163/9789004543010_016
This is an open access chapter distributed under the terms of the CC BY-NC-ND 4.0 license.

costumes, stage sets and back-ups; as literary props and themes; as spurs and goads for translation (George Soane, David Boileau, the 1821 *Faustus* translator or translators, Shelley); as incitements for aesthetic conversions or innovations such as silent poetry on stage (Gautier); as screens in literary creation favouring the mystery tale (Poe); as new ways of thinking the stage and the relation to the spectator (Brühl and Schinkel); or even as substitutes in courtship and literary barter (Goethe and Byron). When such a stance is adopted, their pull burgeons, offering many paths and thought-provoking vistas into the extended nineteenth-century (pre-WWI) art and literature. Appendix 2 complements Appendix 1 in this sense.

One of the most productive paradoxes of the Faust myth in modern print culture here comes to the fore: the tragedy of knowledge and the dramatic tale of a scholar, walled in by useless volumes, turn drivers of cultural capital, a key mechanism in racking up *Faust* books never more identical. Goethe's "narrow high-vaulted gothic chamber," a vertical tapered space, symbolically poised between Heaven and Hell, expands horizontally through print circulation. The Faustiana prompted by Retzsch's nonstop re-engraving of outlines prove a fluid production that shapes Goethe's reception.

Originally a brief study, as part of my wider interest in the many ways Goethe's *Faust* prompts visual culture and is furthered by it, this book's scope kept growing, every item disclosing unexpected features as meaningful parts of a bigger whole. A brief text by Jacques Derrida on Edmond Jabès's poetry, the book, and the close relation of history, literalness and writing, gave me a clue. Jabès's writing both "depicts and acknowledges in the desert an invisible labyrinth, a city in the sand" for Derrida. "In each grain of sand," writes Jabès, "a sign surprises."[5] Printed items prompted by Retzsch were as many grains disclosing surprising signs. Retzsch artefacts even resembled such sundry particles, yet each speck, in its complexity, whys and wherefores, could unveil a city. This book has tarried in detail at several, to counter Hirschberg's discouragement and decision not to investigate "wretched imitative scrawls" (*klägliche Nachkritzelungen*) and "reduced cobweb images" (*verkleinerte Spinnewebebilder*).[6]

What outcomes may such specks-as-cities reveal if closely and synthetically scrutinized?

A real bonus is the revelation of the major contribution that Retzsch made to the reception of Goethe's *Faust*, object of a rich array of valuable studies, predominantly based on textual and stage channels, primarily in one language and one cultural context. *Faust* reception has typically left aside—but for a few words or mentions—intermedial creations in circulation. Retzsch's *Umrisse*, in the several ways they spawned portfolios, sets, visual and textual prompts, albums and illustrated books, prove a crucial intermedial item. This book differs in pointing to early and productive exchanges. It is such remedial agency that turned Goethe's tough play into one of the most respected texts within the European (subsequently Western-world) canon. The establishment of literary canon thus exceeds the bounds of a specific literary work. It strongly involves, through reception, the century's flourishing visual sponsors and the wider backing of prospective commercial strategies. Recognizable iconography earns a prominent canonical pedestal for an audacious work to stand out conspicuously.

My book pleads for further well-informed studies in what still is a largely unexplored field of the nineteenth century. It has occasionally compared visual and textual translation. Within contexts largely hostile to Goethe and his poetic *alter ego*, *Faust*, a visual set works differently as ambassador and triggers translation (UK); conversely, it converts into visual aids straddling various roles in countries already rich in more than one *Faust* translation (France). As pliable visual surrogates, Retzsch's prints played remarkably diverse parts, as footnoted.[7] Their variability underscores the breadth, diversity and importance of visualisation and imagination as crucial components implementing and promoting literature. In today's media-invaded universe, such instruments of inter-mediation are more prevalent than ever.

Retzsch's early case shows to what extent the nineteenth century stands at a crucial turn in modern culture. It makes a strong claim for integrating visual investigation to comparative studies. In this one, differentiated reception principally confronts the German States to the UK and France with several extensions over the ocean and the rest of Europe. In the German States, public predilection favours both new Cotta and pirated Retzsch editions but yields scarce and reticent criticism; in the UK, the Retzschian *Faust* craze reads intense yet brief; in France, Retzsch's impact little acknowledged yet long-standing. Such results allow for better understanding a country's *Zeitgeist* and public sensibility, while similar changes in prints do not necessarily carry the same claim.

---

5 Derrida, "Edmond Jabès et la question du livre," in *L'Écriture et la Différence* (Paris: Éditions du Seuil, 1967) 105, and Jabès qtd. 104.

6 Hirschberg, *Chronologisches Verzeichniss*, 6.

---

7 I.e., visual proxies; optical elucidation tools; narrative deputies; structural back-ups; bi-medial items with a moulding agency; trappings for designing covers and decorative bindings for varied publics; productive parodies circulating between countries; theatre aids and ropes; artists' training drills; even plot underpinnings for famous writers.

Another grain-as-city invites us to consider *Faust*'s visuality and the various meanings of outline. Despite the richness and repetition in visual transmission of Goethe's *Faust*, deemed central,[8] Retzsch's key role remains largely undervalued. Apart from very few cases, Retzsch features in Goethe studies either within an array of artists whose work did not circulate as did his, or lies buried under lingering reservations and inadequately informed perception of his work's impact. This book points to his prevalence thanks to new archival evidence and fleshes out his aesthetics. I have argued that the resilience of his outlines to reproduction, indeed his deliberate and influential use of the engraving technique as endgame, forms a crucial turn in disseminating Goethe's *Faust* visually. Without refuting the valuable contribution of word-and-image studies, I further it by *reading with images* in books and prints as three-dimensional objects in circulation, and exploring readers', publishers' and collectors' attitudes. The intermedial approach meets book history, visual studies and print culture in such an interdisciplinary endeavour. Additionally, copying and reproduction are the key mainstays in spreading Retzsch as show numerous byways. Salient examples are the return of an English parody to Leipzig (Crowquill and Lachgern), early tackling the original play itself, only nine years after Goethe's demise; the impact of Retzsch's "Kiss" as Hayez's unacknowledged inspiration for an Italian national icon, ultimately hovering over *baci* chocolates; and construing iconic labels from engravings to advertisement booklets for Beecham's powders. Indeed, beyond portfolios, print sets and books, Retzsch compositions unfolded through key images and so-called by-products. In "Extensive and Intensive Iconography," I have suggested ways to deal with such expansive phenomena, pointing at stereotypification, on the one hand, and creative re-appropriation, on the other, to bear the burden of an important play.

Outlines are here threefold: visual, summary-like, and alluring. Flexible use of visual outlines as choice renderings, abridged visual translations, and enticing marketing tools fuelled such expansion. Retzsch instilled romantic stimuli and options to the classical technique he had inherited. He encouraged the flight of the imagination by cleverly mingling abstraction and narrative detail. He provided audiences with what Goethe's play lacked: a plot narrative, an action summary, character contours for assimilation. In clever publishers' hands, his prints or motifs styled books and albums as alluring objects. The potential lurked from the beginning in Retzsch's shaping and summarizing *Faust* into a continuous visual narrative that caught the eye, helped framing, and promoted a thorny script. Within the competitive early nineteenth-century market of publishing trends and print circulation, his tempting bait was easily cast "outline" fishing for customers.

Retzsch's achievements may differently appeal to personal evaluation or taste and my book's scope is not *per se* to flag up another neglected or overlooked artist. More importantly, I stress in his *Faust* work the weight of a tough and pliant iconographic matrix, upheld by intense circulation over a short period. When *Faust* editions-cum-images are seen in continuum, a lineage becomes evident from his depictions. Text alone cannot explain it. Recurrence, re-visitation and variation of scenes, and of motifs within scenes, point at a visual stereotype, fostered by prints mirroring and interpreting the text and commenting on it in dialogue. As a visual prototype poised between countries and within print genres, Retzsch's set grounded in the romantic era a staple iconography of Goethe's *Faust* through to the twentieth century.

As third outcome, typification would usefully join William Vaughan's identification of Retzsch's three main characteristics, i.e., narrative vigour, moral symbolism, and frank sentimentality. Retzsch's reduction of compositions to epitomizing contours and absence of colour also encouraged re-use, variation and reshaping at others' hands.[9] Yet sentimentality is not to be overstressed. This book has shown how wit and fancy burgeon, and how another's clever parody may undermine a stern, sober and severe view of Goethe's masterpiece, bringing out its latently humorous, ironic or caustic sides.

Identifying readership categories through print genres and differentiated items is a fourth outcome. In his founding study, William Vaughan singled out only three social categories interested by Retzsch's prints: aristocrats and other guests of elegant socialite parlours, Victorian ladies, and romantic poets or Pre-Raphaelite artists, such as Lord Byron, Percy Bysshe Shelley, John Everett Millais, Daniel Maclise or Dante Gabriel Rossetti. The Pre-Raphaelites (Rossetti excepted) were drawn rather to Retzsch's Shakespeare than *Faust* outlines, specifies Vaughan.[10] For her part, Viola Hildebrand-Schat saw his "illustrations" as an "expression of the bourgeoisie's artistic understanding" (*Moritz Retzschs Illustrationen als Ausdruck bürgerlichen Kunstverstehens*). Beyond such circles, this book shows the vast credit Retzsch's work enjoyed amongst a wider public: growing numbers of educated middle classes; subscribers to reading rooms and lending libraries; theatregoers; average readers; regular bookstore customers; more modest classes dependent on penny publications, keen

---

8   Wegner, 7; Guenther, "Concerning Illustrations to Goethe's *Faust*," 104; Forster-Hahn, "A Hero for All Seasons?" 511; Stead, "*Faust*-Bilder," 153–54; Stead, "Monumental German *Faust* Editions," 366–65.

9   Busch, *Eugène Delacroix*, 38.

10   Vaughan, *German Romanticism*, 132–54.

on cheap and colourful reproduction prints; and owners alike of expensive porcelain pipe bowls and inexpensive tin figurines. Such expansion bred on both replicas and genuine prints, without neglecting advertisement and commercial billboards. Retzsch's flimsy and lithe demon is still recognizable in such well-known advertisement posters as Leonetto Cappiello's 1907 *Thermogène* (whose green Pierrot spitting infernal fire looks suspiciously like Retzsch's Mephistopheles) and 1906 *Maurin Quina*. Not to forget royal patronage. Nagler's dictionary recalls in 1843 Mrs Jameson's quip that queens would envy Christel, Retzsch's spouse, for her husband's annual homage, i.e., the original drawing she received on every birthday.[11] Queens did even better in acquiring Retzsch's drawings. As Uwe Hellwig discovered, Retzsch entered Queen Victoria's collections.[12] His Shakespeare outlines, quality-printed in Leipzig by Ernst Fleischer in a new elegant typography from 1827, was placed under the royal patronage of the King of Great Britain and Ireland.[13] In close parallel, Goethe recommended *Hamlet*, the first of the Shakespeare series, to all superintendents of circulating libraries on 24 March 1828.[14] Victoria herself copied after Retzsch's *Faust* albums by Cotta, as did her children and husband, and their drawings are still in the Royal Collections. On 16 December 1834, she lifted Margaret imploring the Mater Dolorosa, a drawing in pencil and ink "Copied from Retzsch" that she signed "Victoria," while the Prince of Wales (later Edward VII) offered his royal mother for her birthday on 24 May 1853 an elaborate watercolour of Mephistopheles seated in the witch's kitchen. Neither he nor she were apparently daunted by such choice since the message runs: "For dear Mama, from her affectionate Son, Albert Edward." Robert Ross had decided on no other effigy in his sketch album set in a landscape (cf. Fig. 7.7 top). On the same date, Prince Albert Edward singled out Faust and Mephistopheles from the turmoil of the witches' Sabbath and outlined them ogling Margaret's spectral appearance. The prince was much taken with his evil figure since he 1853 drew and coloured again Mephistopheles's head from the witch's kitchen, stressing his malevolent mien, faunlike ears, and threatening grin next to a model watercolour by his art master, Edward Corbould. Finally, under Corbould's guidance, he again drew and coloured a ferociously smirking devil after Retzsch's *Chess Players*.[15] From

aristocrats, noblemen and gentlemen, to aficionados and enthusiasts, middle class professionals, teachers, instructors, and the popular classes, Retzsch enjoyed an extensive, variegated and internationalised fan club throughout the nineteenth century. Goethe's *Faust* earned its status concurrently, both as mass phenomenon and elite-bound work, cutting across established dichotomies. The general nineteenth-century public was visually engaged and alert.

Retzsch did not sign his *Faust* outlines. In more than one way, they were free for all to enjoy, take and use. Yet alive, he welcomed more than one hand in the process of creation. Appropriation by publishers, illustrators, adaptors, copyists, imitators, or emulators (without any of these being necessarily purloiners or plagiarists), ultimately the wider public in acquiring stencilled lithographs or lithophanes, highlights other paths in considering how art was shared in the nineteenth century. Such adoptions make both Goethe's commanding figure and Retzsch's authoritative agency recede, even fade away, while a co-operative conception of creation emerges. Actualisation of his *Faust* outlines continued, preserved, prolonged, and disseminated them through their many contributing agents. This more democratic way of dealing with a work of art or a major text grounds an intense cultural appropriation of Goethe's *Faust* and allows for anyone's (self-)projection into the tragedy. Marianne von Willemer, "the little one" (*die kleine*), early identified with humble Gretchen and her preference for Retzsch against Cornelius is telling. Thanks to Retzsch, Goethe's unfathomable masterpiece became intimate literature, everyman's capture and take, Faust being one of us. Retzsch's *Faust* was a responsive, sociable creation.

Retzsch's prints also granted Faustian lore veritable icons for two prevalent scenes (the kiss and the flower oracle in the garden), a hardwearing stage set (Margaret's bedroom), and modelled the three major characters into prototypes easy to replicate, imitate and vary. His Faust and Margaret proved perhaps not as hardy as his sinuous Mephistopheles in tight-fitting costume, snaking in red disguise, that further infiltrated twentieth-century literature, motion pictures or popular culture. But I must refrain from temptation to take this further. If only for the exploits here described, Friedrich August Moritz Retzsch's contribution to Faustian visual mythology merits full recognition.

---

11   Nagler, *Künstler-Lexicon*, 13:50.

12   Hellwig, "Studien zu Moritz Retzsch," 59–60.

13   Christine Roger, *La réception de Shakespeare en Allemagne de 1815 à 1850* (Berne: Peter Lang, 2008), 294.

14   WA 1, 49:356.

15   See Royal Collection Trust online (last accessed 11 Mar 2023) offering 17 Retzsch items, including RCIN 980113 (Margaret

imploring), RCIN 981039 (Mephistopheles seated in armchair), RCIN 981041 (Faust and Mephistopheles at the witches' Sabbath), RCIN 980477-f (Corbould's and the prince's watercolours), and RCIN 980477.r (head from *The Chess Players*).

APPENDIX 1

Moritz Retzsch's 26 *Umrisse* in Original and Copied Editions

Original Portfolios, Albums and Their Copies in the German States, Great Britain, France Etc., Object of the First Six Chapters

1816 no. 1	*Umrisse zu Goethe's Faust, gezeichnet von Retsch*. Stuttgart & Tübingen: in der Cotta'schen Buchhandlung, 1816. Small landscape buff (or yellow) portfolio with green flaps comprising a 12-p. letterpress brochure and 26 strung outline engravings. HAAB: F 3487; DLA: Cotta Hss Slg. Cotta-Archiv; Beinecke: Speck Ck99 R3 +816 Copy 1[1] Beinecke: Speck Ck99 R3 +816 Copy 2 (with Goethe's and Tsarina Maria Feodorovna's signatures)
from 1818? perhaps earlier no. 2	Hybrid copies incorporating Bohte's 1820 letterpress published as: *Extracts from Göthe's Tragedy of Faustus, Explanatory of the Plates, by Retsch, Intended to Illustrate that Work. Translated by George Soane, A. B.,* [...]. London: Printed for J. H. Bohte, 4, York Street, Covent Garden, by G. Schulze, 13, Poland Street, Oxford Street, 1820. HAAB: Ruppert 1825 (Goethe's exemplar from sundry materials put together, 1820 *Umrisse*, with inserted *Extracts*, still showing folds) BL: G. 2644. 1–2 (Glenville's exemplar, 1816 *Umrisse*) Columbia University: Rare Books, Butler, BOOKART 017.1Ge R312 1820G (added by Samuel Putnam Avery to the Avery library) Johns Hopkins University, Milton S. Eisenhower Library: PM 5923 .R44 1820a c. 1 (Leonard L. Mackall's exemplar) Beinecke: Speck Ck99 R3 +820b (anonymous exemplar in sumptuous Murton binding) University of Minnesota, Minneapolis, Elmer L. Andersen Library: Rare Books 741 R315 (anon., based on 1816 *Umrisse*) Cambridge, Sidney Sussex College: Muniment Room Bb.7.4. (Sir Austin Robinson's exemplar, based on 1820 *Umrisse*)
1818–19	Reported Cotta "Tübingen, 1818" or "Tübingen 1819" edition, advertised and imported by Bohte, still not identified however
1820 no. 3	*Umrisse zu Goethe's Faust, gezeichnet von Retsch*. Stuttgart & Tübingen: in der Cotta'schen Buchhandlung, 1820. Second Cotta edition, same conditioning as no. 1, larger margins. BMPD: 160 b 14/1; HAAB: N 28602; HAAB: F 3488; Beinecke: Speck Ck99 R3 +820; DLA: Cotta Hss Slg. Cotta-Archiv
1820 no. 4	Two-fold publication in two stages under two titles: *Retsch's Series of Twenty-Six Outlines: Illustrative of Goethe's Tragedy of Faust. Engraved from the Originals by Henry Moses. And an Analysis of the Tragedy*. London: Printed for Boosey & Sons, Broad-Street, Exchange, and Rodwell and Martin, New Bond Street, 1820. or *An Analysis of Goethe's Tragedy of Faust, in Illustration of Retsch's Series of Outlines. Engraved from the Originals by Henry Moses*. London: Printed for Boosey and Sons, Broad-Street, Exchange, and Rodwell and Martin, New Bond Street, 1820.

---

1 In the case of editions extant in multiple exemplars, I have retained either one specimen copy or only significant items.

© EVANGHELIA STEAD, 2023 | DOI:10.1163/9789004543010_017

This is an open access chapter distributed under the terms of the CC BY-NC-ND 4.0 license.

1820 no. 4 *(cont.)*	Prints issued in two batches, June and July, with or without adjacent 60-p. "Analysis." In two formats, imperial 4to before letters and 4to. Original Retzsch prints re-engraved by Henry Moses with several alterations evidencing public sensitivity but also prevalent visual models. Printed by W. Wilson, Printer, Greville-Street, Hatton-Garden, London. The two parts promote divergent readings. BL: *C.*57. h. 2. (imperial 4to, two separate title pages, wrappers, publishers' slips, plates as proofs, publisher's catalogue) Beinecke, four enhanced exemplars: Speck Ck99 R3 +820c (Murton binding); Speck Ck99 R3 +820d (Murton binding); Speck Ck99 R3 +820e (half-binding with the MS ex libris of George Frere, 45 Bedford Square); Speck Ck99 R3 +820f (imperial 4to) BnF ASP: 4-Rlc-30 HAAB: F gr 5785 (In a Murton 1822 green morocco binding with T. W. Glanville's heraldic bookplate, later acquired by M. Holzmann) HAAB: G 244; HAAB: F 8078 (sole plates in a dummy folder entitled "Retzsch's Outlines engraved by Henry Moses," used by Tille in exhibitions)
post 1820 not numbered (unique)	Unique composite volume combining the text of *Faust: eine Tragödie von Goethe*. Stuttgart: Cotta, 1816 (*Taschenausgabe*) and all re-engraved prints after Retzsch from *Series of Twenty-Six Outlines, Illustrative of Goethe's Tragedy of Faust, Engraved from the Originals by Henry Moses*. London: Boosey, 1820. A hybrid fake, mixing German and English, proficiently put together by a knowledgeable bookbinder. Cut-out and inlaid pages from the 1816 *Faust* Cotta *Taschenausgabe* in Gothic script set opposite interleaved plates from the first English Boosey edition. Followed by English "Analysis" and the two original Boosey title-pages. Contains as frontispiece Goethe's portrait engraved by H. Lips, identified as Mortzfeld A 7915. Accomplishes Bohte's idea with exactly inverse materials, and the English prints as visual translation of the German text. HAAB: F gr 5276
1821 no. 5	*Faustus: From the German of Goethe*. London: Boosey and Sons, and Rodwell & Martin, 1821. A new (partial) translation with parts in blank verse published in September. Extra plate added as frontispiece after Peter Cornelius, termed "designed by Moses." Goethe's portrait adjoined. Plates by Moses mostly interleaved. In reddish brown or dark green paper-covered boards with extra circular woodcut ornament pasted on upper cover. Retzsch's rebel pl. 18 submits to textual order (keeping its original number). Plates mounted haphazardly with captions either towards gutter or outer edge. BL: 638. i. 18 HAAB: F gr 5288 (in green paper-covered boards, circular woodcut ornament mounted on front cover, Ira A. Abbott's 1824 MS ex libris and price mentioned 17s.) Beinecke: Speck Ck99 R3 +821 (Copy 1) Beinecke: Speck Zab W 6445+Zz 821 G (Amos Niven Wilder's library) Beinecke: Speck Ck99 R3 +821 (Copy 2, Lord Byron's exemplar inscribed to Catharine Potter Stith; with publisher's slip announcing the 8vo ed. of *Faustus* without the Outlines, yet embellished with Goethe's portrait)
1824 no. 6	*Faust*. Paris: Chez Auvray, Marchand d'estampes, quai Voltaire, N° 5, n.d. [1824]. Retzsch's engravings lithographed (and retouched) by Jean-Baptiste Muret, printed by lithographer François Villain on buff paper with wide margins. No text, yet introducing brief italicized captions under the prints. Landscape prints in brown folder bearing only the title on cover. Akin to Moses in choices, yet picturing God in Heaven, probably a template for Berthoud's 1825 London edition, lithographed by Hullmandel. Beinecke: Speck Ck99 R3 +840 (Copy 1 in half-binding); Speck Ck99 R3 +840 (Copy 2 in original wrappers); BN Est. Tb. 54 in-4° (bound) Depending on the cut of paper, plate sizes may vary as in HAAB: Th N 2 11a (roughly 21.5 × 29.3, occasionally wider)

MORITZ RETZSCH'S 26 *UMRISSE* IN ORIGINAL AND COPIED EDITIONS

1824 no. 7	*Faustus: From the German of Goethe. Embellished with Retsch's Series of Twenty-Seven Outlines, Illustrative of the Tragedy, Engraved by Henry Moses. Third Edition, with Portrait of the Author.* London: Boosey and Sons, 4, Broad-Street, Exchange, 1824. Same text and visual apparel as no. 5, yet reset by printer W. Wilson in denser layout, reducing letterpress quantity by a quarter. The interleaved plates noticeably enhance text/image rotation. Probably stereotyped. "Kinetic" version subsequently used as template by publishers Septimus Prowett (1825) and Edward Lumley (1832). Beinecke: Speck Ck99 R3 +824 (in green paper-covered boards with circular ornament pasted) https://collections.library.yale.edu/catalog/16712411 HAAB: F 3494 (former Stumme Collection, rebound with circular ornament pasted on new cover) Sterling: Hkg8 020 (stereotyped ed. bound with Retzsch's outlines after Schiller's *Fridolin* and *Fight with the Dragon,* copied by Moses and published by Septimus Prowett)
1824 no. 8	*Illustrations of the Celebrated Tragedy of Faustus by Goethe, Engraved & Published by Henry Stone.* Washington City, D.C.: [H. Stone], 1824. Re-engraved outlines by American lithographer Henry Stone with alterations. Rebel pl. 18 still in its original place. Four-page unsigned introduction attributed in Speck exemplar to Jules de Wallenstein, Russian Secretary of Legation. Beinecke: Speck Ck99 R3 +824b
1825 no. 9	*Faustus: Illustrated in Twenty-Six Outlines by Retsch.* London: Published by H. Berthoud, Regent's Quadrant, 1825. Plates only, rather crude and askance to printed octavo title-page, with dramatized captions and French "Marguerite" for Margaret. Lithographed by C. Hullmandel. Reverts to picturing God in Heaven in pl. 1. Details reminiscent of Muret's lithographs (see no. 6). HAAB: F 3496 (former Stumme Collection; includes cover, with the MS note: "Hullmandel's lithographs (to accompany the 8° ~~ed of~~ <vol. of 1821 called> Faustus from the German of Goethe") Beinecke: Speck Ck99 R3 +825b (MS ex libris of Tho[ma]s Theodore Campbell Jun. | 15 Burton Crescent, the son of a surgeon; bound by "Kelly Binder," 15, Gower Place, active at this address 1836–40; cover wanting)
*c.*1825 no. 10	No title, no title-page. Lithographed copy of all 26 Retzsch prints, textual *Faust* excerpts printed in Gothic script and double column on four introductory pages, titled "Anzeige der zu den Umrisse gehörenden Stellen." HAAB: F 8099 (former *Faustbücherei* of Alexander Tille, B 602, with the MS note "Rare lithographed ed., all other German editions are engraved!")
1827 no. 11	*Retzsch's Outlines to Goethe's Faust. Adapted to Illustrate Any Edition of FAUST, But Particularly the Translation of Lord F. L. Gower to Whom They Are Most Respectfully Dedicated. Containing 26 Plates with A Portrait of the Author.* London: James Bulcock, 163, Strand, 1827. Goethe's portrait with twenty-seven prints of diminutive size by John Kennerley, crediting Retzsch and Kennerley, and Bulcock's imprint. Prints issued in two batches on 1 Aug and 22 Sept 1826. "Engraved by J. Kennerley from the large print published in Germany," under a pink cover (also used as title-page) cut in wood by J. Berryman. Several prices, papers (plain, tinted) and formats (foolscap, octavo, quarto). The diminutive size makes this ed. a probable template for Audot's booklets. Beinecke: Speck Ck99 R3 +827b (ordinary exemplar, bound with cover) Beinecke: Speck Ck99 R3 +826 (quarto, on Indian paper, limited edition of 50, at one guinea, cover wanting, with Samuel Sharp's bookplate)

n.d.
no. 12

Faust von Goethe (calligraphed MS title on inserted tissue front page)

Unique(?) exemplar pirating German originals, 18.4 × 22.5 cm. Cotta excerpts hand transcribed in Gothic script on extra insert pages opposite each copied etching. Expurgation of explicit male attributes throughout.

Bodmer (catalogue under construction)

c.1827
no. 13

Faust von Goethe in 26 Umrissen. Göttingen: In der Dieterichschen Buchhandlung, n.d.

Prints solely after Retzsch, presumably re-engraved by Riepenhausen father, strung between blue cardboard flaps irregularly cut. Title and imprint on uneven slips of paper pasted onto back cover. Small print of a modified version of Emminger's lithograph after Johannes Riepenhausen's *Faust's Meeting with Gretchen before the Church* (1811) pasted onto front cover.

Beinecke: Speck Ck99 R3 +827 and HAAB: F 3489 (as described)
Bodmer (catalogue under construction)
HAAB: Th N 2: 11 (neither wrapper nor pasted lithograph; distinctly smaller, Alfred Nicolovius's gift to the Weimar library)

end 1827
no. 14

Faust. Paris: Chez Auvray Frères, Marchands d'Estampes, quai Malaquais, N° 11, et quai Voltaire, N° 5, n.d.

Lithographic prints reissued after Muret's 1824 plates with italicized captions, size slightly reduced. Dated from announcement on back cover of Nerval's 1828 translation, advertising them as printed by "Villain and Muret from the original German." Previously flawed "Villin" on pl. 11 corrected to "Villain". Pertain to the Parisian *Faust* craze of 1828.

HAAB: F 8163 (former Tille Collection)

1828 May
no. 15

Faust. Vingt-six gravures d'après les dessins de Retsch. [Paris]: Publié par Audot, Rue des Maçons-Sorbonne, N° 11, 1828.

Retzsch's plates re-engraved by Trueb and Branche in diminutive landscape format with an 8-p. introduction on Faust legend and longer explicative captions. Illustrated tripartite cover on brown paper anonymously recomposing several motifs after Retzsch. Printed by Rignoux. Plausibly indebted to Kennerley's copies and Bulcock's cover. Affordable price for a much wider audience. Transfers English changes in images into French context.

BnF Est.: Tb. 53a in-4°; BnF: Yh. 2539 (no cover)
BnF ASP: 8- RIC-2; 8-RlC-51; P16-EGC-368 (the latter with Edward Gordon Craig's ex libris and MS notes)
Beinecke: Speck Ck99 R3 +828 (pl. 9 wanting; Bryan Waller Procter's exemplar)
Some of the above bound with other re-engraved outlines, often after Retzsch

1828 September
no. 16

Faust. Vingt-six gravures d'après les dessins de Retsch. Deuxième édition, augmentée d'une analyse du drame de Goëthe, par Mme Élise Voïart. Publié par Audot, éditeur du Musée de Peinture et de Sculpture, Rue des Maçons-Sorbonne, N° 11, 1828.

Same prints with captions under the same illustrated cover. Long interpretative introduction, a digest ersatz to Goethe's play guided by the images, by writer Élise Voïart, also a translator from German into French. Same printer (Rignoux). The second ed. synchronized with the Porte-Saint-Martin *Faust*. Advertised in the press in parallel to theatre reviews.

BHVP: 8-APO-1571 (RES) (from Guillaume Apollinaire's library, in original paper covers, plates strung, pl. 1 wanting)
BnF: 8-Yh-907; Beinecke: Speck Ck99 R3 +828b

1828 no. 17	*Faust, tragédie de Goëthe, traduite par M. A. Stapher [sic]. Nouvelle édition, ornée de 26 gravures, d'un beau portrait de l'auteur, et accompagnée de notes.* Bruxelles: À la Librairie Romantique, Rue de la Madelaine, N° 458, 1828. Considered as counterfeit, yet evidencing original intention by combining two elements from two French editions on the basis of the text-and-image prototype provided by the Motte-Sautelet ed. illustrated by Delacroix (whose prints are not retained). Issued in two parts in October and December 1828 at 1.25 Florins or 2.64 Francs per part. Printed by Weissenbruch, Imprimeur du Roi. Testifies to publisher Auguste Feuillet-Dumus's romantic and liberal credo. Blends the two French editions on the very year of their publication: the small Audot plates copied by Trueb and Branche in two versions (either with French captions or bilingual French-German ones) meet the Stapfer translation (as re-published by Motte and Sautelet). Its small format (*c.*14.1 × 9.7 cm) confirms Audot's influence abroad. HAAB: G 349 (French captions) and HAAB: F 3858 (bilingual captions)
1829 no. 18	*Faust. Vingt-six gravures d'après les dessins de Retzsch, avec une analyse du drame de Goëthe par Mme Élise Voïart, 3ᵉ édition.* [Paris]: Publié par Audot, éditeur du Musée de Peinture et de Sculpture, Rue des Maçons-Sorbonne, N° 11, 1829. Same prints, same introduction, with bilingual captions in French and German. Exemplars point severally at intercontinental exchanges. Spelling of Retzsch's name corrected. Large paper edition also probable. BnF: Yh. 2540 BnF Musique: RES-1443 (Auguste Vincent's exemplar with French-German captions and large paper plates).
n.d. *c.*1829? not numbered	Fourteen original outline prints trimmed, reframed and carefully coloured, taken to be by Retzsch himself. (Exceptional, though not sole.) Frankfurt's FDH
1830 no. 19	*Umrisse zu Goethe's Faust, gezeichnet von Retsch.* Stuttgart & Tübingen: In der Cotta'schen Buchhandlung, 1830. Engravings still in their earliest order with plate 18 (cathedral) preceding the duel. Few but mostly flawed surviving exemplars (plates missing, frayed edges, faded materials, faint impressions). Labels irregularly trimmed or older, occasionally with the indication "In 26 Plates" (*In 26 Blättern*). Beinecke: Speck Ck99 R3 +830 DLA: Glück: HH/Goethe: D; FDH: III-15979 (previously owned by Franz Glück and Hungarian politician József Ürményi)
1830 no. 20	*Faust: Esquisses dessinées par Retsch [sic].* Paris: Giard, Éditeur, Rue Pavée, St André des Arts, N° 5, 1830. Intends to both honour Goethe's *Faust* and revert specifically to the original German outlines by referring to the 1820 Cotta edition with larger margins, further enlarged, and an initial 8-page (incorporated) leaflet imitating Cotta's letterpress brochure. Anonymous writer and conceiver evidently proficient in German. Title-page frame offering complex symbolism with any reader mirroring himself in Faust's mirror. Sensational book cover lithographed by Bichebois. Hardly echoed in the press due to the 1830 July Revolution, overthrow of King Charles X, and July Monarchy under Louis-Philippe.

APPENDIX 1

1830
no. 20
(cont.)

Beinecke's several exemplars, particularly a half-morocco binding with four interlocked double Ls surmounted by a count's crown and containing 68 plates as a series of experiments in reproduction techniques, trial prints and artists' proofs, point to multi-talented Léon de Laborde, keenly interested in engraving and printing. Bound exemplar identified as from his library, proving his intense involvement in this edition (as author of summary, perhaps also of cover design involved in the trial proofs)

Speck Ck99 R3 +830b copy 1. Online at https://collections.library.yale.edu/catalog/16712419 (digitized at request)

1832
no. 21

Faustus: From the German of Goethe, Embellished with Retsch's Series of Twenty-Seven Outlines, Illustrative of the Tragedy, Engraved by Henry Moses. New Edition, with Portrait of the Author. And An Appendix Containing the May-Day Night Scene Translated by Percy Bysshe Shelley. London: Edward Lumley, 27, Chancery Lane, 1832.

With extra K, K2, L and L2 gatherings in smaller type (pp. 65–79), either inserted (between end of I and list of plates K) or added onto K to slot Shelley's translation into the Boosey template.

Beinecke: Speck Ck99 R3 +832 (translation inserted)
BL: 11746.l.4 (translation added; final plate, "Margaret Refuses to Leave the Prison," mounted as frontispiece)
HAAB: F 3495 (translation added; "Kiss" plate mounted as frontispiece)

1833
no. 22

Faust, tragédie de M. de Goëthe, traduite par M. A. Stapher[sic]. Troisième édition, ornée de 26 gravures, d'un beau portrait de l'auteur, et accompagnée de notes. Bruxelles: J. P. Meline, libraire-éditeur, 1833.

Pirates the 1828 Feuillet-Dumus *Faust* (no. 17) within Belgium, naming itself "third edition." Audot plates either on yellow paper with French titles or white paper with French-German ones. Goethe's lithographed portrait reversed in some exemplars, in others the right way round, variously signed and treated.

HAAB: F 3859 (plates on yellow paper with French captions)
Beinecke: Speck Rg13 a833 (plates on white paper with bilingual captions)

1834
no. 23

Another English ed. based on the *Faustus* template and including Shelley's translation (London: Hodgson, Boys and Graves, 1834) with the list of plates moved forward.

Available online at https://archive.org/details/faustusfromgermaoogoetuoft/page/viii/mode/thumb.

1834
no. 24

Umrisse zu Goethe's Faust, erster Theil. Gezeichnet von Moritz Retzsch, von dem Verfasser selbst retouchirt und mit einigen neuen Platten vermehrt. Stuttgart & Tübingen: in der J. G. Cotta'schen Buchhandlung, 1834.

Enlarged set of *Umrisse* after *Faust I* in larger size with wide margins (23.5 × 32.8 cm) comprising three extra plates (new pl. 5, Mephistopheles lulls Faust to sleep; new pl. 7, second scene in Auerbach's cellar; new pl. 19, Faust and Gretchen on garden bench, Mephistopheles eavesdropping). Album bound in black, lilac or grey cloth. Printed on thicker, strong paper with large margins and plates following textual order. Small Cotta advert in front pastedown.

Dates occasionally differing between label and title-page (BnF Est.: Tb. 53 in-4°); variants in label wording, with or without the indication "retouched and enlarged edition in 29 plates"; plates irregularly arrayed.

c.1835
no. 26

Illustrations to Goethe's Faust in Twenty-Six (or *Twenty-Seven*) *Outline Engravings by Moritz Retzsch.* London: W. W. Gibbings, 18 Bury Street, W.C. [c.1835].

Oblong albums of varying size in publisher's binding, front cover with decorative designs. Some include Goethe's portrait by Jagemann (attaining twenty-seven plates). Diminutive prints, recycling J. Kennerley's as issued by Bulcock, in ample margins, facing selected rhymed excerpts (unknown translations), except for pl. 1 with radiant void (instead of God) facing no translation.

MORITZ RETZSCH'S 26 *UMRISSE* IN ORIGINAL AND COPIED EDITIONS

365

1836 not numbered (*Faust II*)	*Umrisse zu Goethe's Faust, zweiter Theil. Gezeichnet von Moritz Retzsch. Elf Platten, nebst Andeutungen.* Stuttgart & Augsburg: Verlag der J. G. Cotta'schen Buchhandlung, 1836. Original edition of Retzsch's eleven plates after *Faust II* in blue portfolio with fuchsia flaps and pink label bearing dense data. Two pages of loose play summary drafted by Retzsch himself. Commercialized in Paris (Veith and Auzer [*sic* for Hauser]) and London (Black and Armstrong with a specific label and a double-sheet letterpress in English). Beinecke: Speck Ck99 R3 +836c (with two letterpress sheets in German and English)
1836 no. 27	*Umrisse zu Goethe's Faust, erster und zweiter Theil. Erster Theil neunundzwanzig Platten, zweiter Theil elf Platten.* Stuttgart: Verlag der J. G. Cotta'schen Buchhandlung, 1836. Combined edition comprising twelve pages of letterpress and forty prints. Assemblage of *Umrisse* after *Faust I* (1834) and *Faust II* (1836) in uniform album format. Commercialized with outlets in London (Black and Armstrong) and Paris (Veith and Auzer [*sic* for Hauser]). Label in treble frame with curlicues in varied colours (blue, beige, slight grey, light yellow). Exemplars show irregular order, occasionally two title-pages, and may include the original blue *Faust II* portfolio itself with new label pasted. Full-page advertisement inserted at the end of several exemplars (in at least two versions, December 1835 and October 1836). BMPR: 1927,1231.37.1–40.
1837 no. 28	*Umrisse zu Goethe's Faust, erster Theil, gezeichnet von Moritz Retzsch, neun und zwanzig Platten, mit Andeutungen.* Stuttgart & Tübingen: Verlag der J. G. Cotta'schen Buchhandlung, 1837 (not 1834 as indicated). Enlarged album of 1834 *Umrisse* reissued as *Faust I*, with 1834 still on the front cover label. BL: 506. aa. 3
1838 no. 29	*Faust, tragédie par Goethe, traduite par A. Stapfer. La traduction revue et corrigée par C. M. Friedlander.* Bruxelles: Meline, Cans et Compagnie, 1838. Counterfeit edition, still based on Feuillet-Dumus's 1828 Brussels template but with the Stapfer translation "revised and corrected by Doctor C[arl] M[artin] Friedländer, director of the German Institution in Brussels, member correspondent of the Historical Institute of France." I have not ascertained the latter's role. May have spread in France. Dissimilarity and variation may have countered publishers' possible claims.
pre-1839? nos. 30, 31	*Umrisse zu Goethe's Faust, erster und zweiter Theil gezeichnet von Moritz Retzsch. Erster Theil neunundzwanzig Platten, zweiter Theil elf Platten.* Stuttgart: Verlag der J. G. Cotta'schen Buchhandlung, n.d. Refers to an 1840 textual *Faust*. On title-page verso: Buchdruckerei der J. G. Cotta'schen Buchhandlung in Stuttgart. Hardbound album on strong paper with wide margins. Printed at Cotta's own printing works in Stuttgart. 40 plates after *Faust I* and *Faust II* under a plain printed cover. No griffin, used from 1839 as publishing mark on the title-page. The fine volume addresses a choice clientele. no. 31: Also published as a folder with plates in varying sizes (Engel, no. 1813). Not consulted as such. Beinecke: Speck Ck99 R3 +884

1839 no. 32	*Faust: a Tragedy, by J. Wolfgang von Goethe. Translated into English Verse by J. Birch, Esq., Author of "Fifty-One Original Fables and Morals," "Divine Emblems," &c. Embellished with Twenty-Nine Engravings on Steel after Moritz Retzsch.* London: Black & Armstrong / Leipzig: F. A. Brockhaus, 1839. Decisive conversion of the portfolio outlines into an illustrated book. Octavo edition marshalling 29 Retzsch plates (from Cotta's enlarged 1834 album) under tissue paper. Minuscule hard-line steel engravings of mediocre execution, with wide margins and askew to text, by John Brain. Changes satisfy decorum, yet newly numbered pl. 7 (magic mirror in witch's kitchen) eroticized. Despite royal patronage and many noble subscribers, a commercial failure. Poor translation. Beinecke: Speck Rc37 a839
1840 nos. 33, 34, 35	*Faust, ein Trauerspiel, beide Theile in einem Bande.* Paris: Baudry, 1840. also *Goethe's sämmtliche Werke,* vol. 1. *Schauspiele.* Bibliothek der besten ältern und neuern deutschen Schriftsteller, 11. Paris: Baudry, 1840. (*Faust* comprised in vol. 1 of the full edition in 5 vols) Synthetic frontispiece on the basis of eight Retzsch outlines (six from *Faust I*, two from *Faust II*), arrayed in two columns on a single sheet ($c.27.5 \times 18$ cm) with captions in German. The first (no. 33) is a single, slightly smaller one-volume *Faust.* Frontispiece used in parallel in two hefty editions for Goethe's selected (*auserlesene*) and complete works (*sämmtliche Werke*). Of the latter, the first (no. 34) is a ponderous tome, the second (no. 35) consists in five volumes, both in double-columned pages and Gothic type. All published by Baudry in Paris. Frontispiece also separately commercialized with three Goethe portraits and eight grouped subjects after other titles.
1843 no. 36	*Faust, eine Tragödie, beide Theile in einem Bande.* 8th edition. Paris: Baudry, 1843. Includes the same synthetic frontispiece. By 1843, the separate Baudry *Faust* volume had already been reprinted eight times and was widely available. BnF: Yh 407 (title page: *eine Tragödie*) Beinecke: Speck Rb41 843b copy 1 (with MS ex libris, and the half German-half French date "19. Juin 48") Beinecke: Speck Rb41 843b copy 2 (with copious notes and MS ex libris of N. J. Wyeth)
1843 no. 37, 38	Two titles (and two cover designs) for the same object. *Illustrations of Goethe's Faust by Moritz Retzsch, Engraved by Henry Moses* or *Goethe's Faust by Retzsch* London: Tilt and Bogue, Fleet Street, 1843. Album comprising Boosey's 1824 *Faustus* text and interleaved plates in only 32 pages. Boosey's template further adapted to "kinetic" form by setting text in double column. Swift and double visual/textual or textual/visual reading throughout. Printed by Josiah Fletcher, chief editor of the *Norwich News* and printer of the *Norwich Magazine.* Plates (after Moses) compete with Brain's copies in portfolio (see *infra* no. 40). Gilt compositions on embossed cover package the volume either as a magical or desirable object. On the two covers see Appendix 2.
1843 no. 39	*Faust: A Tragedy, by J. Wolfgang von Goethe. Translated into English verse by J. Birch, Esq. Embellished with Twenty-Nine Engravings on Steel by John Brain, after Moritz Retzsch.* London: Black and Armstrong / Leipzig, F. A. Brockhaus, 1839, with *Faust: A Tragedy, in Two Parts by J. Wolfgang von Goethe, The Second Part Translated into English Verse by Jonathan Birch, Esq. Embellished with Eleven Engravings on Steel by John Brain, after Moritz Retzsch.* London: Chapman and Hall, 186, Strand / Leipzic: F. A. Brockhaus, 1843. Two-volume edition of Birch's translation of *Faust I* and *Faust II* with small steel engravings by J. Brain after Retzsch. BL: 638. i. 19 (1–2); Beinecke: Speck Rc37 c

1843 no. 40	*Goethe's Faust, Complete. The Forty Outlines by M. Retzsch, Engraved on Steel for J. Birch's Translation of Faust, by J. Brain.* London: n.d. [1843]. Only prints, derivative of the 1839 and 1843 two-part illustrated *Faust* translation by Birch, 4to. Forty larger free-standing steel engravings (max. 22.3 × 30 cm) on thicker paper in royal or quarto landscape folder. For collectors. Prints vying as classy, no lettering. Beinecke: Speck Ck 99 R3 +843b (royal 4to with repaired flaps and new ribbons, acquired 4s 6d). Landscape 4to in Bow Windows Bookshop (Lewes, Sussex), catalogue 197, no. 217, £100, Mar 2015.
1844 no. 41	*Faust: Tragedya Göthego Tłómaczenie z Niemieckiego Alfonsa Walickiego. Z 26 rycinami na miedzl według Retscha, z przydaniem kilku śpiewów kompozycyi Xiążeçia Antoniego Radziwiłła. Wydanie Adama Zawadzkiego.* Wilno: Nakład i druk Józefa Zawakzkiego, 1844. Fifteen Retzsch plates re-engraved with adjustments by a certain P. Keppel with summary-like captions after Audot in Polish. Plates askance to the textual sequence. Probably reprocessing Audot's prints, inspired by Bulcock's, rather than recycling them. With four scores of *Faust* music by Polish Prince Anton von Radziwill interleaved. Beinecke: Speck Ru11 a844 Digitized <https://polona.pl/item/faust-tragedya-gothego,Mzc3MzE3/4/#info:metadata>
1850 July no. 42–48	*Faust par Wolfgang Goethe. Traduit de l'allemand par Gérard de Nerval, précédé de la légende populaire de Johann Faust, l'un des inventeurs de l'imprimerie, illustré de jolies vignettes par Éd. Frère.* Paris: J. Bry aîné, 1850. Nerval's 1840 reviewed *Faust I* translation with a partial translation of *Faust II* interspersed with abstracts and hero redeemed through divine grace. Print run of 12,000 distributed thanks to Bry's association with Maresq and Pelvey's "Librairie centrale des publications à 20 centimes." Eleven in-text woodcut illustrations copied by Édouard Frère after Retzsch perhaps via Muret. Focused on the main scene, in black and white contrast and sensational gradual shadowing, characteristic of extensive iconography. Two-column fascicle reprinted in 1852 and 1854; perhaps four reprints 1850–54, and another three 1858–64.
late 1850s? no. 49	*Outlines to Goethe's Faust: Twenty-six Etchings by Moritz Retzsch.* London: John Bumpus, 158 & 297, Oxford Street, [18—?]. Only plates. Re-engraved copies by Henry Moses with original English captions but dropping the Boosey imprint. Beinecke: Speck Ck99 R3 +888 (plates 1, 2, 8, 15, 21, and 22 wanting. Bookplate of Harry Buxton Forman [1842–1917], Victorian-era bibliographer of Percy Bysshe Shelley and John Keats. Perhaps used to extra-illustrate Shelley as suggests a pencilled note).
1855 no. 50	*Faust, eine Tragödie, die zwei Theile in einem Bande von Goethe, neue Auflage.* Paris: Vᵉ Baudry's Europäische Buchhandlung, Rue Bonaparte, 12, nahe dem Palais des Beaux-Arts, 1855. Recycles the synoptic frontispiece to all three Baudry editions "entirely revised and corrected" with a new date and imprint of Baudry's widow. Price of *Selected Works* had been reduced to 25 Francs.
1865 no. 51	*Faust: dramatisch Dichtstuk van Goethe. Nagevolgd door H. Frijlink. Met een zestal schetsen, naar teekeningen van Moritz Retzsch.* Amsterdam: Hendrik Frijlink, 1865. Dutch translation and edition by Hendrik Frijlink, young translator and enterprising publisher. Six vignettes, circularly arranged, both on cover and as compound frontispiece or ornamental title-page. Visual summary of the play after Retzsch by German lithographer and graphic artist Johann Wilhelm Frey luring customers. Below depictions small numbers refer to pages. On back cover, drawing of Faust and Gretchen in historicist costume differs from Retzsch. All figures lithographically reproduced. HAAB: F 3988; FDH: IV a 16/; Beinecke: Speck Rs13 a865

1866 no. 52	*Faust: dramatisch Dichtstuk van Goethe. Nagevolgd door H. Frijlink. Met een zestal schetsen, naar teekeningen van Moritz Retzsch. Tweede, herziene en vermeehrderde Uitgave.* Amsterdam: Hendrik Frijlink, 1866. Second edition of the Dutch version (with revised and enlarged text) a year later. HAAB: F 3989
1875 no. 53	*Outlines to Goethe's Faust: Twenty-Six Etchings by Moritz Retzsch.* London: Sampson Low, Marston, Low and Searle, Crown Buildings, 188, Fleet Street, n.d. [BM stamp 15 No 75]. Oblong 4to album in red half-binding with Moses's copies of Retzsch etchings and extracts from Anster's translation eliciting the *Athenaeum's* annoyance. Mechanical cloth binding, heavily decorated in black, red and gilt. BL: 1871. b. 1.; Beinecke: Speck Ck99 R3 +875
1877 no. 54	*Illustrations to Goethe's Faust: Twenty-Six Etchings by Moritz Retzsch with Illustrative Selections from the Text of Bayard Taylor's Translation.* Boston: Estes and Lauriat, 1877. American album with steel plates redeeming outline aesthetic. Wide margins, sparse letterpress and blanks with selected passages from Bayard Taylor's metrical translation (1870) stirring suggestive reading. Striking printed item, confectioned at Cambridge, Mass., by renowned master printers John Wilson and Son, possibly relating to the American transcendentalists' movement. Designs seen as abstracting Goethe's thought and rendering it in visual terms. Beinecke: Speck Ck99 R3 +877.
1878 no. 55	*Goethe's Faust, in Two Parts. Translated by Anna Swanwick, with Forty Illustrations Engraved on Steel after the designs of Moritz Retzsch.* London: George Bell and Sons, York Street, Covent Garden, 1878 [in fact 1879]. Revised version of Swanick's translation of *Faust I* with "Scenes from the Second Part of the Tragedy of Faustus." Industrialized meticulous 4to bound in red with gilt spine. Printed on creamy paper with wide margins for collectors. Insert steel engravings by John Brain with customary alterations, although "Publishers' Note" runs: "The illustrations are accurate copies of the original designs; they have undergone a slight reduction in size, which has tended to improve their effect." BL: 11746. k. 6.; Beinecke: Speck Rc5 c879b; HAAB F 3657
1884? no. 56	*Umrisse zu Goethes Faust, erster und zweiter Theil gezeichnet von Moritz Retzsch. Erster Theil neunundzwanzig Platten, Zweiter Theil elf Platten.* Stuttgart: Verlag der J. G. Cotta'schen Buchhandlung, n.d. Album of both parts printed in Stuttgart, "Druck von Gebrüder Kröner." With the publisher's griffin on title-page. Colourful cover made of a simple printed colour sheet by illustrator and lithographer Christian Votteler applied to robust commercial binding. Central image, copied from Retzsch's Faust's duel with Valentine. Thick paper and wide margins, lines solidified and stiffened. First plate, "Prologue in Heaven," detached as frontispiece to both sequences. Beinecke: Speck Ck99 R3 +884b; HAAB: F gr 3493

MORITZ RETZSCH'S 26 *UMRISSE* IN ORIGINAL AND COPIED EDITIONS   369

[1886]
no. 57

Faust: A Tragedy by Johann Wolfgang von Goethe. Translated, in the Original Metres, with Copious Notes, by Bayard Taylor. Authorised Edition, Published by special arrangement with Mrs Bayard Taylor, with a Biographical Introduction, and Retzsch's Plates. London, New York, and Melbourne: Ward, Lock, and Co., [1886].
Two captivating plates (*Mephistopheles conducts Faust to the summit of the Brocken to meet the Witches* and *The Witches' Festival*) detached and mounted as frontispiece). All other plates inserted in twos. Text finely typeset within red frame with four ornate crosses at corners.
HAAB: Goe: 659[4]
Another Ward, Lock and Co. edition, issued in 1887, is part of "Moxon's Library Poets" and chooses different plates for the frontispiece (*Margaret in her Chamber, Mephistopheles introduces Faust into Margaret's Chamber*).
Beinecke: Speck Re3 c887b
Subsequent octavos by this and other publishers (not recorded here) imitate grouping of plates in twos without this edition's refinement.

1893
no. 58

The First Part of Goethe's Faust. Translated by Anna Swanwick. Revised edition, with Retzsch's Illustrations. London: George Bell and Sons, York Street, Covent Garden, and New York, 1893.
Regular octavo with Brain's re-engraved plates called "Retzsch's illustrations." Title-page in red and black inks.
BL: 11746. f. 35.; Beinecke: Speck Rc5 a893; Sterling: Hkg8 177b 1

1902
no. 59

Faust, Tragedie i to dele af Goethe, Oversat og indledet af P. Hansen, Med Vignetter efter Moritz Retzschs Tegninger, Folkeudgave. København: Gyldendalske Boghandels Forlag, Fr. Bagges Bogtrykkeri, 1902.
Danish edition with Retzsch's outlines as small decorative headers combined with Engelbert Seibertz's compositions.
FDH: IV a/7/4

1929
no. 60

Goethe, *Faust, Tragedie i to dele, Oversat og indledet af P. Hansen.* København: Gyldendalske boghandel, Nordisk Forlag, 1929.
Edition of both parts of *Faust* with Retzsch's outlines turned into tiny vignette-like headers, difficult to read. One scene only (garden) retained from enlarged series of the first part, the other two discarded probably because of lack of space.
Beinecke: Speck Rn13 c929

1940
no. 61

Goethe, *Faust, avec introduction, notes et commentaires par P. Labatut.* Nouvelle collection d'auteurs allemands. Paris: Masson et Cie Éditeurs, 1940.
Educational publishing. P. Labatut's *Faust* edition in the "New Collection of German Authors" series, issued for scholastic purposes in German with abundant notes and critical apparel. Retzsch's outlines in smallish double-framed copies and Audot's captions rhythm the text alongside well-known Faust iconography. Further small alterations, two plates discarded (Prologue in Heaven and Walpurgis Night).
Published at the very beginning of World War II, it ran to at least four editions (1940, 1947, 1951, 1959); still widely used in the 1960s and 70s.

1987
no. 62

Faust, traduzione in rime e in versi con testo a fronte a cura di Roberto Hausbrandt, disegni di Moritz Retzsch. Milan: Dedolibri, 1987.
Two volumes in slipcase with German text and Retzsch compositions. (Not inspected; following images and others' descriptions).

APPENDIX 2

Moritz Retzsch's Prints Remediated

Sundry Objects Derivative of Retzschian Faust Imagery

1818–21	Thomas Frognall Dibdin, *A Bibliographical, Antiquarian and Picturesque Tour in France and Germany*. London: Printed for the Author, by W. Bulmer and W. Nicol, Shakespeare Press, and sold by Payne and Foss, Longman, Hurst and Co., J. and A. Arch, R. H. Evans, R. Triphook, and John Major, 1821. (Back of title-page: Sold at Paris, by Messrs. Treuttel and Wurtz, N° 17, Rue de Bourbon.) Three openings in vol. 3 (120–30) focus on parts from six Retzsch plates, cut out and inserted in Dibdin's text as woodcuts by John Byfield. Reportedly acquired in Cotta's Stuttgart bookshop and collaged in August 1818, they nevertheless show revisions akin to Moses's 1820 Boosey edition. Beinecke: X350 +821 (1–4) (Gift of John W. Sterling)
1818	*Kleines Geschenk zum Neuen-Jahr für 1818*. Frankfurt-am-Main: In der Jaegerschen Buch- Papier- und Landkartenhandlung. Tiny ladies' almanac (9.9 × 5.9 cm) in turquoise blue binding, including five focussed and darkened Retzsch copies accompanied by five explanatory poems by Georg Döring. Refers to 1816 *Faust* Cotta *Taschenausgabe*. FDH: XI T 124
1820	*Kleines Geschenk zum Neuen-Jahr für 1820*. Frankfurt-am-Main: In der Jaegerschen Buch- Papier- und Landkartenhandlung. Booklet for the fair sex (9.8 × 6 cm) in pink binding, including seven focussed and darkened Retzsch copies supplemented with a further array of unsigned poems. Also refers to 1816 *Faust* Cotta *Taschenausgabe*. FDH: XI T 124/2
1820	Karl Friedrich Schinkel, *Margaret's Chamber*, 1820, *décor* design, watercolour over preliminary drawing, graphite and compass on vellum, 23.5 × 36.3. Staatliche Museen zu Berlin, Kupferstichkabinett: SM 22d.95
*c.*1820?	Meissen pipe bowl, with Faust and Margaret in the garden scene with Martha and Mephistopheles passing painted after Retzsch (later?), framed in gold, 12.1 cm, Berlin form. Detlev Dauer collection D2152
*c.*1821	Delacroix's freehand copies after Retzsch's outlines, pen and ink or pencil. Louvre, Département des Arts Graphiques: RF 10214 r/v, RF 10215 r/v, RF 10340, RF 10407; Harvard Art Museums / Fogg Museum: 1929.308
1822	Königliche Porzellan-Manufaktur (KPM), painted and gilded plates with scenes after Retzsch's outlines. Twelve items remaining from the initial 24. Foundation Prussian Palaces and Gardens Berlin-Brandenburg: Inv. Nr. XII 10069–10080

© EVANGHELIA STEAD, 2023 | DOI:10.1163/9789004543010_018

This is an open access chapter distributed under the terms of the CC BY-NC-ND 4.0 license.

MORITZ RETZSCH'S PRINTS REMEDIATED

1822	Ink drawing of Faust and Gretchen kissing, 13.8 × 16.9 cm, lifted from Retzsch's pl. 15, with several supplementary details, signed "G.R. 1822." FDH: III-10749
1822–23	Königliche Porzellan-Manufaktur (KPM), twenty-four painted and gilded plates with scenes after Retzsch's outlines. One (at present in a private collection) has been replaced by a plate bearing a scene after Naeke. FDH: IV-2021–001, Adolf and Luisa Haeuser Foundation
1825	*The Decision of the Flower*, drawn by John Massey Wright after Retsch [*sic*], engraved by W. Humphreys. Printed for Hurst, Robinson & Co, London, 1825. Frontispiece to *The Literary Souvenir; or, Cabinet of Poetry and Romance*. Ed. Alaric A. Watts. London: Hurst, Robinson and Co. / Edinburgh: A. Constable and Co., 1825, with accompanying homonymous poem by L. E. L. [Letitia Elizabeth Landon]. Also as standalone print.
1825	[G. Hering, lithographic print of "The Decision of the Flower" after Retzsch, dedicated to L. E. L.] Yet untraced. *Literary Gazette*, no. 425 (12 Mar 1825): 172b.
c.1825	*Mr. Terry as Mephistopheles the Devil in "Faustus,"* portrait print after Retzsch's Mephistopheles, costume worn by actor Daniel Terry at the Drury Lane performances of Soane and Terry's *Faustus: A Romantic Drama in Three Acts* (or *The Devil and Doctor Faustus*). Harvard, Houghton Library: MS Thr 933, Box 3
1826	*The Kiss*, drawn by John Massey Wright, after Retsch [*sic*], engraved by W. Humphreys. Printed for Hurst, Robinson & Co, London, 1826. Plate inserted btw pp. 280–81 in *The Literary Souvenir; or, Cabinet of Poetry and Romance*, London. Published by Hurst, Robinson & Co, 1826, facing the beginning of Alaric A. Watts, "The First Kiss. A Poetical Sketch," pp. 280–284. Also as standalone print.
1827 November	First edition of Goethe's *Faust*, trans. Gérard de Nerval, dated 1828 on title-page with a frontispiece signed "Pineas fecit." Retzsch's pl. 4 re-engraved with the caption "Faust signe le pacte avec Mephistopheles."
1827–30	Goethe's *Ausgabe letzter Hand* published by Cotta; extra-illustrated by *Kupfersammlung* issued by Friedrich Fleischer (1828–34). Retzsch frontispiece composition for *Faust I* (vol. 12, 1828 or 1829) with Faust handing Gretchen the fatal phial while sitting on a bench (excluding Mephistopheles) after one of Retzsch's supplementary plates in the 1834 enlarged Cotta edition of his *Umrisse*. Stipple-engraved by Friedrich Wagner. Noble technique for a broader bourgeois public. The treatment hints at lovemaking.
1828 to early 1850s	Achille Devéria's "Goethe" extensive visual registry exclusively based on Goethe's *Faust* with sundry French, English and German iconography either compared with or diversely illustrating a dismantled 1828 Motte-Sautelet *Faust* volume. Traces of Retzsch in cloned images, never originals, particularly in copies of two scenes, "The Kiss" and "The Oracle of the Flower." BnF Est.: TB-55 (C)-Pet. fol.

1828?	Édouard Robert, "sourd muet," *La Décision de la fleur*, 15.5 × 12.1 cm, and *Le Baiser*, 15.3 × 12.2 cm, twin prints after Retzsch ("d'après Restech" [*sic*]), echoing the English titles, lithographed by printseller E. Ardit, who commercialized them as twin prints. BnF Est.: SNR-3 (ROBERT, Édouard)
1828	*Faust: tragédie de M. de Goethe, traduite en français par M. Albert Stapfer. Ornée d'un portrait de l'auteur, et de 17 dessins composés d'après les principales scènes de l'ouvrage et exécutés sur pierre par M. Eugène Delacroix*. Paris: Chez Ch. Motte, éditeur, et Auguste Sautelet, libraire, 1828. Several of Delacroix's 17 lithographs bear Retzsch's mark in general composition or in detail.
n.d. post 1828?	Drawing of the Witch's Kitchen, 32 cm × 25.5 cm, unsigned, n.d. Preliminary study, probably for a performance in French, 20 cm × 26 cm, with the following caption: "La Sorcière ayant tracé un Cercle le remplit d'objets étranges.—Elle apporte un Grand Livre, fait encore entrer des Singes dans le cercle, leur fait soutenir le Livre & leur donne ~~un flambeau~~ Une torche.—Faust y entre aussi.—La Sorcière verse avec beaucoup de cérémonies de la liqueur dans une tasse la présente à Faust, & au moment qu'il l'approche de ses lèvres, il en sort une vive flamme.—Méphistophélès lui dit […]age Vide—Vite—Vous vous en trouverez bien. Vous êtes l'Ami du Diable & Vous craignez la flamme." Düsseldorff, Goethe-Museum: KK 1863 and KK 1864 (preliminary study with caption)
n.d. post 1828	Re-engraved plates after the second Audot edition with French captions. Pasted on lilac backing sheets, part of the Theatersammlung, Universität Köln.
1829	Faust and Margaret in the garden scene in troubadour style by Alexandre Colin after the Retzsch template, plate 6 from *Album composé et dessiné sur pierre* by Colin issued in 1829, with a caption quoting lines from Goethe's *Faust*. BnF Est.
1830	Two sheets of thicker paper, "traced designs from the French 1829 edition or another," signed "ar 1830," with smaller grouped pen-and-ink figures after the Audot booklets. Perhaps templates for toy theatre figures or meant for decoration. FDH: VIIId-kI no. 13445 (17.1 × 19 cm) and no. 13446 (12.1 × 18.6 cm), item data files
c.1831	Louise Bertin, *Ultima scena di Fausto/Dernière scène de Faust de Goethe arrangée pour le pianoforte*. Paris: Schlesinger, [c.1831]. Cover vignette after Retzsch's pl. 26. BL, Music Collections: H.450; HAAB F 5598 (inscribed to Meyerbeer)
1833	Retzsch's pl. 19 (amorous couple under a tree) from Schiller's *Song of the Bell*, adaptable to print circulation. See 1835 under *German Lovers*.
post 1833	Pencilled sheet of tracing paper grouping instances of Gretchen after four scenes from Retzsch's original *Faust* etchings along with three details from Retzsch's 1833 compositions after Schiller's *Song of the Bell*. Crumpled sheet, often turned to lift numerous figures, with frequent little holes, pinned and re-applied repeatedly, probably for transfer purposes. FDH: VIIId-kI, no. 14847

MORITZ RETZSCH'S PRINTS REMEDIATED

1834

Faust: A Serio-Comic Poem with Twelve Outline Illustrations by A. Crowquill. London: B. B. King, Monument Yard, 1834.
Second edition within the same year, also large paper edition with coloured plates.
Twelve burlesque plates parodying Retzsch's compositions.
Beinecke: Speck Sg8a F6 +834; Beinecke: Speck Sg8a F6 +834b (large paper ed. with plates in colour);
HAAB: F 3482; HAAB: Ku 4° III S—27

1834

Das ärgerliche Leben und schreckliche Ende des vielberüchtigten Erz-Schwarzkünstlers Johannis Fausti. Erstlich vor vielen Jahren fleißig beschrieben von Georg Rudolf Widmann. Hernach übersehen und wieder herausgegeben von Pfitzer. Jetzo aber auf's Neue aufgelegt und mit 16 Holzschnitten verziert. Reutlingen: Druck und Verlag von G. B. Kurtz, 1834.
Abridged version of two historical Faust chapbooks by Georg Rudolf Widmann (1599) and Johann Nicolaus Pfitzer (1674). Two woodcuts by Wilhelm Eytel after Retzsch's plates 4 and 1 picture *Faust Handing Over the Pledge to the Devil* and *The Holy Angels as Servants before God's Throne* (obliterating Mephistopheles). Aesthetics of sixteenth-century *Faustbücher* aped in cruder style. A further image, *Under Christoph Hayllinger's Guidance, Faust Digs to Get the Crystal Mirror*, recalls the Rabenstein background in Retzsch's and Cornelius's plates.
HAAB: F 456

1834

Half-cloth landscape volume (28.9 × 34.1 cm) of a hand-cloned set of all 26 Retzsch outlines on tracing paper after the 1816 original engravings, respecting original order. Executed from 21 Jan to 3 Feb [18]36 with brief breaks by "John." Hand-copied introduction to the cloned plates after the original Cotta letterpress brochure (Huber's preface and 26 *Faust* excerpts) in regular Gothic script, dated "Muskau 3rd February 1836." Hand-drawn title page in overformal black and red Gothic script, added later, and signed "R. Jäger 1928." Could be related to Prince Pückler-Muskau's milieu.
HAAB: F gr 5019

1834
16 Dec

Queen Victoria, pen and ink drawing of Margaret imploring the Mater Dolorosa after Retzsch's pl. 17, 18.7 × 15.6 cm (sheet).
Royal Collection Trust: RCIN 980113

1834–41

Woburn windows, large oak frames (213.36 × 91.44 × 16.51) with mosaics of 1834–41 acquired lithophanes in brass grids.
Lithophane of Faust and Margaret's kissing, in prominent position below Vesuvius erupting, from previous lithographic and Schuler versions after Moritz Retzsch.
Andrew Cook collection

1835

Scenen aus Goethes Faust in acht lithographirten Bildern nach der Angabe des Fürsten Anton Radziwill zu seinen Compositionen des Faust gezeichnet von Biermann, Cornelius, Hensel, Hosemann, Fürst Ferdinand Radziwill, C. Schulz und Zimmermann. Lithographirt von Eichens, Hosemann, Jentzen, L'Oeillot de Mars und Meyerheim. Berlin: Zum ausschliesslichen Debit in Commission bei T. Trautwein, [1835].
Margaret at her table, lithographed by Meyerheim after a design by Ferdinand Radziwill, echoes in detail Retzsch's pl. 9.
Knittlingen Faust-Archiv: Moosmann, B 70; HAAB: F gr 5774

1835	*Compositionen zu Goethes Faust von Fürsten Anton Radziwill. Vollständiger Klavierauszug von J. P. Schmidt, Eingethum der Sing. Academie zu Berlin.* Berlin: Zum ausschliesslichen Debit in Commission bei T. Trautwein, [1835]. Title-page with vignettes partially following Retzsch's outlines. HAAB: F 5483
1835	*Faust: A Serio-Comic Poem with Twelve Outline Illustrations by A. Crowquill.* London: B. B. King, Monument Yard, 1835. Dated 1835 on the cover and given as "Third Edition," same inscription on title page, dated however 1834. Under "Crowquill's Faust," the back cover registers the same testimonials from the press as the second edition (1834). Beinecke: Speck Sg8a F6 +834d
1835	*The German Lovers*, after Moritz Retzsch, etching and engraving on *chine collé* by Charles Heath, after Retzsch's pl. 19 after Schiller's *Das Lied von der Glocke*. Proof illustration, 22 × 15.2 cm, to *The Keepsake for 1835*, p. 169. BMPD: 1864,0611.728 Accompanying Viscount Newark's homonymous poem, *Keepsake for 1835*, ed. by Frederic Mansel Reynolds (London: Longman, Rees, Orme, Brown, Green, and Longman; Paris: Rittner and Goupil; Berlin: A. Asher, 1835), 169–70. Also commercialized as a standalone print.
1837	*Faust und Gretchen*, kissing in enclosed space, 1837 engraving attributed to Édouard Schuler, Alsatian steel and copper engraver. Cut out by Alexander Tille without provenance. See *infra*, after 1849, steel engraving from the *Album aus der Damenzeitung Iris*. Important reworking of background enclosing Faust and Gretchen in a dark dungeon space with a menacing Mephistopheles opening the only casement. HAAB: F gr 8052 [b] (8)
1830s	Lithophane of Faust and Gretchen plucking the daisy in the garden, from remediated lithographic versions after Moritz Retzsch. Meissen 119, KPM 162. Blair Museum of Lithophanes: acc.no.547
1830s	Faust and Gretchen embracing while Mephistopheles spies, from remediated lithographic versions after Moritz Retzsch. Meissen 115, KPM 130, KPM 151. Blair Museum of Lithophanes: acc.no.516
c.1830–40	KPM pipe bowls, with Margaret and Faust kissing and Mephistopheles spying painted after Retzsch following the Schuler model, framed in gold or with a hinged lid. Peter-Christian Wegner and Detlev Dauer collections, the latter D2479
1840 June	Julius Nisle, outline of Faust and Margaret kissing in the garden imitating Moritz Retzsch, in *Göthe-Gallerie: Stahlstiche zu Göthe's Meisterwerken nach Zeichnungen von Julius Nisle*, 4th fasc., *Faust, erster Theil*. Stuttgart: Literatur-Comptoir, [1840], pl. 15, steel engraved and printed by W. Pobuda. HAAB: F 3337 (d)

1840	Sepia painted Nathusius pipe bowl framed in gold, Margaret and Faust kissing in garden approached by Mephistopheles after Julius Nisle imitating Retzsch, 14.5 cm, Berlin form, with the appropriate *Faust* quote and friendship inscription. Detlev Dauer collection D1133
1841	Anselmus Lachgern, *Bilder zu Goethes Faust*. Leipzig: C. F. Doerffling, 1841. Eleven plates lithographed after Crowquill's twelve burlesque plates, with new elements pointing at the German edition of Retzsch.
c.1841	"Faust und Gretchen," i.e., "He loves me—loves me not" (*Er liebt mich ... liebt mich nicht*), two lithographs by F[erdinand] A[ugust] Zimmermann and Karl Müller, printed and published by Eduard Pietzsch and Company in Dresden in large oblong folio format or in oblong folio. A third version, either a little later or in parallel, "executed and lithographed by H[einrich] Ferd[inand] Grünewald," made in Grünewald's own Dresden lithography studio according to the imprint, either in competition or in association with Müller. HAAB in several versions and formats
c.1841	"Faust und Gretchen," i.e., "Dearest—I love you with all my heart!" ("*Bester Mann, von Herzen lieb' ich dich!*"), lithographs after Retzsch by F[erdinand] A[ugust] Zimmermann and Karl Müller (untraced but surely extant), printed and published by Eduard Pietzsch and Company in Dresden. Also by Heinrich Ferdinand Grünewald, in his own Dresden lithography studio. Another version by self-taught reproduction lithographer Carl Friedrich Patzschke, printed in Berlin by L. Zöllner, and commercialized by C. G. Ende. In several formats and various stencil-applied colour schemes. Space and background treatment as in Schuler, 1837. HAAB in several versions and formats
1843	Two distinct titles for the same contents but differing gilt compositions on embossed covers, either as *Goethe's Faust by Retzsch* or *Illustrations of Goethe's Faust by Moritz Retzsch Engraved by Henry Moses* London: Tilt and Bogue, Fleet Street, 1843. No title on spine, meant for frontal (window) display. *Goethe's Faust by Retzsch* aggregates elements from several Retzsch outlines: two monstrous poodles (pl. 3), witchery scene with demon biting drapery, monkey with skull, snake and frog (pl. 6–7), hag with a pitchfork from witches' Sabbath (pl. 22), and Mephistopheles in profile from Auerbach's cellar (pl. 5), holding casket of jewels (pl. 10). *Illustrations of Goethe's Faust by Moritz Retzsch* is based on Faust lifting the hangings of Gretchen's bed half-hiding, half-revealing the term "Illustrations."
1847	*Le Faust de Goethe. Traduction complète, précédée d'un essai sur Goethe, accompagnée de notes et de commentaires et suivie d'une étude sur la mystique du poème par M. Henri Blaze de Bury.* 5th edition. Paris: Charpentier, 1847. Tony Johannot's flimsy and sinuous devil inspired by Retzsch. Re-used by Michel Lévy Frères in 1868; also inserted in a cost-effective *Faust* translation into Spanish decked with varied plates, including German ones (Barcelona: Olivares, 1876).

APPENDIX 2

1849

Decorative design by talented designer John Leighton, aka Luke Limner, on the spine of an industrial Josiah Westley binding for *Faust I* and *Faust II* combined, translated by Birch. Motif inspired by Retzsch's etching 10 from *Faust II*, brilliantly adapted by JL to the narrow space of the spine with inversed meaning and Mephistopheles on the brink of Hell's pit.

Beinecke: Speck Rc 37 +c839 (with bookplates by Robert Hoe III, a founding president of the Grolier Club, and American poet and literary publisher James Laughlin, founder of New Directions Publishing)

1849 Dec

Phiz (Halbôt Knight Browne), *I make the acquaintance of Miss Mowcher,* etching, 12.8 × 10.78 cm. Published in Charles Dickens, *The Personal History of David Copperfield, with Illustrations by H. K. Browne*, Ch. XXII, "Some Old Scenes, and Some New People," first issued in illustrated instalments, then in book form (1850).

post 1849

[Re-purposed copy of "The Kiss"]
Captioned "Faust und Gretchen zum *Album aus der Damenzeitung 'Iris.'* Stich und Druck d. Kunst-Anst. d. östr. Lloyd, Paris und Wien." Steel engraving.
Commercialized by E. Ludwig in Graz; further circulated in France and Austria after 1849

1850 July

Faust par Wolfgang Goëthe. Traduit de l'allemand par Gérard de Nerval, précédé de la légende populaire de Johann Faust, l'un des inventeurs de l'imprimerie, illustré de jolies vignettes par Éd. Frère. Paris: J. Bry aîné, 1850.

Nerval's 1840 reviewed *Faust I* translation with a partial translation of *Faust II* interspersed with abstracts and hero redeemed through divine grace. Print run of 12,000 distributed thanks to Bry's association with Maresq and Pelvey's "Librairie centrale des publications à 20 centimes." Eleven in-text woodcut illustrations copied by Édouard Frère after Retzsch perhaps via Muret. Focused on the main scene, in black and white contrast and sensational gradual shadowing, characteristic of extensive iconography.

Two-column fascicle reprinted in 1852 and 1854; perhaps four reprints 1850–54, and another three 1858–64.

N.B. also recorded in Appendix 1 as reworking Retzsch's plates, probably after French copies.

c.1850

August Hoffmann, *Faust*, steel engraving after Wilhelm von Kaulbach showing the impact of Retzsch's scene on a nineteenth-century German master, 13.3 × 9.3 cm (or 18.5 × 13.5 cm).

HAAB: F gr 5750 (9); https://www.oblivion-art.de/index.php/malerei-grafik/19-jahrhundert/kaulbach-w-1805-1874.

1853 24 May

Albert Edward, Prince of Wales (later Edward VII), pencil and watercolour composition of Mephistopheles seated in the witch's kitchen after Retzsch's pl. 6, inscribed to his mother Queen Victoria, 26.9 × 37.3 cm (sheet).
Royal Collection Trust: RCIN 981039

Albert Edward, Prince of Wales (later Edward VII), pencil and ink drawing of Faust, Mephistopheles and Margaret, lifted from Retzsch's pl. 22 (the witches' Sabbath), 29.1 × 38.7 cm (sheet).
Royal Collection Trust: RCIN 981041

MORITZ RETZSCH'S PRINTS REMEDIATED

1853	Albert Edward, Prince of Wales (later Edward VII) and Edward Corbould, two watercolour studies of Mephistopheles's bust lifted from Retzsch's pl. 6 (the witch's kitchen), 17.5 × 25.4 cm (sheet). Royal Collection Trust: RCIN 980477.f Albert Edward, Prince of Wales (later Edward VII), under the guidance of Edward Corbould, pen and ink drawing and watercolour showing Mephistopheles lifted from Retzsch's *The Chess Players*, 17.5 × 25.4 cm (sheet). Royal Collection Trust: RCIN 980477.r
*c.*1850–60	China plate, 22.6 cm in diameter, unmarked, seemingly from a Thuringian manufacturer. Painted with a scene signed "G. Koch" after Retzsch's supplementary plate showing Mephistopheles lulling Faust to sleep from the 1834 enlarged Cotta *Umrisse* edition. Peter-Christian Wegner collection
1859	Édouard Despléchin, stage set for Gounod's *Faust*, 5. 4, pen, watercolour and gouache highlights on blue cardboard, 26.8 × 40 cm. BMO: Esq. Desplechin-5
1859	Joseph Thierry, *Faust and Mephistopheles Riding in front of the Montfaucon Gallows*, design for the stage curtain of Gounod's *Faust*, 5. 1. Also presented in the Salon in 1866, oil on canvas, 95 × 125 cm BMO: MUSEE-655
1859	Francesco Hayez, *Il Bacio. Episodio della giovinezza. Costumi del secolo XIV* (*The Kiss. An Episode of Youth. Costumes of the 14th Century*), oil on canvas, 112 × 88 cm, first version. Painting with strong patriotic significance, exhibited at Milan's annual Brera Academy exhibition. Pinacoteca di Brera, Milan
1861	Francesco Hayez, *Il Bacio*, oil on canvas, 1861, 127 × 95 cm, second version, painting with the embracing couple's costumes alluding to the colours of the Italian flag. Private collection
1867	Francesco Hayez, *Il Bacio*, oil on canvas, 1867, 116.8 × 80 cm, third version. Exhibited at Paris's 1867 Universal Exhibition, with colour scheme of embracing couple alluding to the flags of France and Italy, allied in future Italy's unification. Private collection
post 1872	After Retzsch: free sketches with additions and changes by Ronald Ross from his sketchbook entitled "Sketches in Isle of Wight etc." LSHTM, Ross archive: GB 0809/Ross/158
ante 1878	Enlarged outlines in sepia by Hermann Bey after Retzsch ornate the lower cellar walls and vault in Auerbach's Keller in Leipzig (Moschkau 1878: 98).
1883	Champfleury, *Les Vignettes romantiques*. Paris: E. Dentu, 1883. Retzsch ("Retsch") named "a patient and cold worker." Poor imitation of plate 6 (Faust absorbed in the magic mirror) copied with the peculiar caption *Faust's Laboratory*. A manifest error although the author claims owning *Faust* "fascicles" (*cahiers*), pp. 54–56.

[1886]	*Goethe's Faust Translated by J. Birch*. Lancashire, St. Helen's: Published by T. Beecham, [1886]. Booklet (13.5 × 10.5 cm) in cream paper wrappers advertising Beecham's pills (Heinemann, 1886, n° 155). *Faust* full translation except for "Dedication," replaced by "Beecham's giving this away to you for free." All pages with the imprint "Beecham's Pills." Cover image in red after the garden scene by Retzsch, carefully chosen as stated in the back cover advertisement. Beinecke: Speck Rc37 a886; HAAB: F 7665 and F 3597
1900	Jollivet-Castelot, *Les Sciences maudites*. Paris: Édition de la Maison d'Art, 1900. Compilation on esoteric sciences, occultism and magic on pink, white and blue paper. Two in-text vignettes and a half-page illustration after Retzsch (Faust's pledge, Mephistopheles leading him to the witches' revel, and the Sabbath itself, pp. 25, 26, 27). In parallel, in November 1900, first issue of *Les Partisans. Revue de Combat, d'Art, de Littérature et de Sociologie*, reproduces the third image as full-page illustration advertising illustrated books by "La Maison d'Art," bibliophilic editions of anarchist propensity.
1904	*Le Faust de Goethe. Traduction de Gérard de Nerval. Préface de M. Frantz-Jourdain. Illustrations inédites de Gaston Jourdain*. Paris: Imprimé pour la Société de Propagation des Livres d'Art, 1904. With plates based on several influences, of which Retzsch. 420 numbered copies, of which 350 for restricted sale only.
1938	Goethe, *Faust. Traduction de Gérard de Nerval. Précédé d'une notice sur G. de Nerval par Théophile Gautier*. La Bibliothèque précieuse. Paris: Librairie Gründ, 1938. Carefully designed book on poor quality paper with various cover illustrations. One of them is an anonymous copy of Retzsch's pl. 14 with Faust leaning over Margaret and the daisy, either outlined or coloured, after Édouard Frère's refocussed composition in the 1850 Bry edition. Regularly reissued from 1936 well into 1941 and World War II.
1948	*Gretchen and Mephistopheles at Martha's*, pencil drawing after Retzsch, 1948, 14 × 16.5 cm. On the back: *Gretchen in her Room*, pencil 13.8 × 16.4 cm, unsigned, n.d. Knittlingen, Faust-Archiv: Moosmann-Böhme, no. 288
1979	W. Fechner, SHA Zinnfiguren, Schwäbisch Hall SHA 119/1 (Faust and Margaret on the bench), SHA 119/2 (Mephistopheles eavesdropping behind a bush) http://www.fechner-zinnfiguren.de/shop/katalog.php, https://www.inzinn.de/00170.html
n.d.	Coloured copy of the garden scene as an outline redrawn and coloured by an unknown hand. HAAB: F gr 9228 (1)

Bibliography

1   **Manuscripts (By Depository)**

Beinecke: William A. Speck Collection of Goetheana (Manuscripts, YCGL MSS 6)

Boosey & Sons, draft reply, pencilled on the last page of Coleridge's letter [1820]: box 2, folder 87.

Brandegee, Emily S., brief record of the meeting of Lord Byron and Mrs. Catharine Potter Stith, by her granddaughter, n.d.: box 1, folder 32.

Byron, Lord Noel, autograph letter to Mrs. Catharine Potter Stith, preserved with envelope. Dated Villa Dupuis, Pisa, 22 May 1822: box 1, folder 38–39.

Coleridge, Samuel Taylor, autograph letter to Boosey & Sons, booksellers, Broad Street, London, [1820]: box 2, folder 87 (re. the request to write the letter-press for Moritz Retzsch's copied outlines to Goethe's *Faust*).

Pückler-Muskau, Prince, to an anonymous correspondant [identified as J. F. Cotta], 20 Apr 1817: box 14, folder 546 (desiring to purchase original *Faust* drawings from Retzsch).

Retzsch, Moritz, autograph letter to Johann Friedrich Cotta, dated 9 Mar 1811: box 14, folder 555.

Deutsches Literatur Archiv, Marbach-am-Neckar

Cotta-Retzsch correspondance (47 letters mainly by Moritz Retzsch to J. F. Cotta and Georg von Cotta, from 24 Jan 1822 to 5 Jan 1837): DLA C-R—Cotta-Archiv.

Retzsch, Moritz, contracting letter to J. F. Cotta, 10 Oct 1810: DLA Co—Cotta-Archiv, Contracts (*Verträge*) 2, Retzsch, n° 265.

Doctor Williams's Library, London

Robinson, Henry Crabb, Manuscript Diary, 1817.

Dresden Prints Cabinet

Weinbergs Scenen, aus dem Leben der beiden Brüder August und Moritz Retzsch. Pictorial diary by brothers August and Moritz Retzsch: Inv. Nr. ca 53 v.

Dresden Slub (Sächsische Landesbibliothek—Staats- und Universitätsbibliothek Dresden)

[Retzsch, August,] Der Freundschaft heilig (Sacred to Friendship). Friendship album of August Retzsch. Dresden, 1800–1806: Mscr.Dresd.App. 3043.

[Retzsch, Moritz,] Denkmähler der Freundschaft (Monuments of Friendship). Friendship album of Moritz Retzsch. Dresden, 1800–1806: Mscr.Dresd.App.3044.

Retzsch, Moritz, autograph letter by Moritz Retzsch to War Secretary von Carlowitz: Mscr.Dresd.t,3097.

Retzsch, Moritz, note accompanying the last two *Faust Umrisse* plates delivered to Kummer, 29.03.1812: Mscr.Dresd.App. 1191, 600.

Dresden Stadtarchiv

Retzsch, August, manuscript journal: Hs Biogr. II 4925, notebook 25 (1810).

Freies Deutsches Hochshift, Frankfurt

[Retzsch, Moritz], presumed artist of a set of 14 coloured outlines; and item data file: VIIId-gr, 13098/13109.

380   BIBLIOGRAPHY

Goethe und Schiller Archiv, Weimar

Bohte, Johann Heinrich, to Goethe, 1 Aug 1820: S: 28/88 Bl. 362 f.

Bohte, Johann Heinrich, to Goethe, 3 June 1822: S: 28/97 Bl. 152–153.

Dawe, Mary Margaret, to J. C. Hüttner, 26 Dec 1820: S: 28/92 Bl. 110.

Hüttner, Johann Christian, 22 Aug 1820, transmitting letter by Boosey and Sons dated 19 Aug 1820: S: 28/89 Bl. 414.

Hüttner, Johann Christian, to Goethe, 28 Jan 1820: S: 28/434 Bl. 30.

Hüttner, Johann Christian, to Goethe, 4 July 1820: S: 28/88 Bl. 312.

Hüttner, Johann Christian, to Goethe, 5 June 1821: S: 28/94 Bl. 243f.

Knebel, Karl Ludwig von, to Goethe, 18 Dec 1821 (copying an extract of the *New Monthly Magazine* on Moses's copies): S: 28/517 Bl. 571f.

Köhler, Heinrich Karl Ernst von, letter to Goethe, 2 Aug 1820, from Saint Petersburg (on Goethe's present of the *Umrisse*): S 28/88 Bl. 375–380.

Lieber, Karl Wilhelm, to H. Meyer, 3 Jan 1821: S: 28/92 Bl. 12, 19.

Riemer, Friedrich Wilhelm, to Goethe, 8 Mar 1822 (invitation to *Darstellung der Scenen aus Faust* at circle Harmonie): GSA 28/96 Bl. 75.

Verlohren, Heinrich Ludwig, letter to Goethe, 2 Dec 1810 (on Retzsch engraving): GSA 28/934 St. 3.

Verlohren, Heinrich Ludwig, letter to Goethe, 20 Jan 1811 (on trial prints by Retzsch): GSA 28/934 St. 4.

Goethe-Museum, Düsseldorf

Hiller, Ferdinand, to Eckermann, Paris, 23 Mar 1829 (on Parisian life, the arts, and the Porte-Saint-Martin *Faust*): Nachlass Johann Peter Eckermann.

Herzogin Anna Amalia Bibliothek, Weimar

An artificially assembled volume of variously signed autograph material (F gr 5019) with 6 early (1811–12) autograph documents by Moritz Retzsch on his *Faust* outlines bound in. Four delivery notes to Leipzig bookseller Paul Gotthelf Kummer, payment receipt upon completion, one letter to J. F. Cotta. The nos. refer to the online digitized material, not the pencilled numbers on the docs. themselves.

Doc. 4. Last accompanying delivery note to Kummer received 21 May 1812.

Doc. 5. Autograph letter to Johann Friedrich Cotta dated 30 Apr 1812.

Doc. 6. Autograph receipt on completion of the work dated 8 Apr 1812.

Doc. 7. Accompanying delivery note to Kummer dated 7 Dec 1811.

Doc. 8. Accompanying delivery note to Kummer received on 5 July 1811.

Doc. 9. First accompanying delivery note to Kummer dated 21 Jan 1811.

Médiathèque d'Angers, Angers

David d'Angers, to Victor Pavie, 4 autographs letters: Dation Steuer, t. 1, nos. 17, 85, 101, 132.

London School of Hygiene & Tropical Medicine, Ronald Ross Archives

Ross, Ronald, *Memoirs with a full account of the great malaria problem and its solution*, typed corrected manuscript, Part 1 of the *Memoirs* (Ch. 1–7) and 2 appendices: GB 0809/Ross/178/20/16.

Ross, Ronald, landscape sketchbook in half leather, 13.2 × 25.8 cm, dated 10 Sept. 1872 and later: Ross/158, file 69.

PRESS ANNOUNCEMENTS AND ANONYMOUS PRESS ARTICLES

2 Press Announcements and Anonymous Press Articles

Eponymous or attributed articles are listed below in "Books, Articles, Dissertations"
Within the same title, entries follow chronological rather than alphabetical order

Abend-Zeitung
> N. "Bericht über die Darstellung des *Faust* von Göthe, auf der Hofbühne zu Braunschweig."
> no. 24 (28 Jan 1829): 96.
> "Nachrichten aus dem Gebiete der Künste und Wissenschaften: Correspondez-Nachrichten
> aus Wien." no. 156 (1 July 1829): 624.

Album national (L')
> R...x, E., "Bibliographie: Faust." no. 27 (14 Feb 1829): 214–15.

Art Journal (The)
> "Ornamental Bookbinding." n.s., 12 (July 1850): 228–29.
> "Obituary—Mr. C. J. Hullmandel." n.s., 3 (1 Jan 1851): 30.
> "The Royal Academy—The Eighty-Third Exhibition—1851." n.s., 3 (1 June 1851): 153–62.
> "Reviews. Dr. Martin Luther, der deutsche Reformator. In bildlichen Darstellungen von Gustav
> König. In geschichtlichen Umrissen von Heinrich Gelzer. Rudolf Besser, Hamburg." n.s. 4
> (1 Jan 1852): 35b.

Athenaeum (The)
> "Gift Books." no. 2509 (27 Nov 1875): 716 (on Retzsch's decline).
> "Sir Joseph Noël Paton." no. 3871 (4 Jan 1902): 24–25 (obituary).

Belle Assemblée (La); or, Court and Fashionable Magazine
> "Literary Intelligence: Works Recently Published." n.s., 24 (Oct 1821): 182b–86.
> "English and Foreign Drama, New Publications, etc.: A new edition of Goethe's ..." (Nov 1821):
> 183a.

Bulletin of the American Art-Union
> "The Fine Arts. Mr. Darley's Rip Van Winkle." 1, no. 14 (10 Nov 1848): 28–30. Extracted from the
> *Literary World.*

Calcutta Journal of Politics and General Literature (The)
> "Fine Arts: Outlines from Goethe's Tragedy of Faust." 3, no. 104 (1 May 1822): 7 (*Examiner* article
> abridged and edulcorated).

Cambridge Chronicle
> "John Wilson and Son." 31, no. 6 (5 Feb 1876): 5d–e.

Constitutionnel (Le)
> "*Faust*, recueil de lithographies au trait, d'après les gravures allemandes de Retsch." (8 Jan 1824):
> 4a.

Corsaire (Le). Journal des spectacles, de la littérature, des arts, mœurs et modes
> "Lithographie. *Faust.*" 2, no. 253 (19 Mar 1824): 2.
> "Théâtre de la Porte-Saint-Martin. Première représentation de *Faust.*" 6, no. 2090 (30 Oct 1828):
> 2a.

Crayon (The)
> "Maurice Retzsch." 4, no. 10 (1 Oct 1857): 305a–6 (US obituary and career recollection).

*Deutsches Kunstblatt. Zeitschrift für Bildende Kunst, Baukunst und Kunsthandwerk. Organ der
deutschen Kunstvereine*
> Th. S., "Moritz Retzsch. Ein Lebensbild." 9 (Jan 1858): 4–11.

Dresdner Geschichtsblätter
> "Aus dem Leben Moritz Retzsch's." no. 3 (1896): 280.

Écho de Paris (L')
> L. L. "Théâtre de la Porte Saint-Martin. Goethe.—*Faust*—Mme de Staël.—Frédéric." (21 Oct
> 1828): 1–2.

"Tout le monde parle aujourd'hui de *Faust*,..." (29 Oct 1828): 1 (with Audot booklet advertisement: 4).

L. L. "Théâtre de la Porte Saint-Martin. Première représentation de *Faust*." (30 Oct 1828): 1 (with Audot booklet advertisement: 4).

"Théâtre de la Porte Saint-Martin. *Faust*." (3 Nov 1828): 1.

European Magazine and London Review (*The*)

"Literary Intelligence." 79 (Apr 1821): 354–55.

"Literary Intelligence." 79 (Aug 1821): 187 (new translation of *Faustus* to be published shortly with a portrait of the author; and in 4to with 27 outlines).

"New Publications, Sold at the late James Asperne's, 32, Cornhill." (Sept 1821): 279 (*Faustus*, new analysis to accompany the series of outline etchings).

R. "*Faustus: from the German of Goethe*. London, 1821, 8vo." 80 (Oct 1821): 362–69 (1820 Analysis out of print).

Examiner (*The*)

"Retsch's Outlines to *Faust*." no. 651 (18 June 1820): 400b.

"Goethe's Faustus, A New Translation." no. 774 (24 Nov 1822): 752.

"Retsch's Designs for Schiller's *Fridolin*." no. 839 (29 Feb 1824): 144a ("to be published uniformly with Retsch's Designs to Goethe's Faust, also engraved by H. Moses").

"Retsch's Designs for Schiller's *Fridolin* Just Published." no. 841 (14 Mar 1824): 175b.

"Goethe's *Faustus* and Retsch's Outlines." no. 854 (13 June 1824): 383b.

"Goethe's *Faustus* and Retsch's Outlines. A New Edition with 28 plates." no. 871 (10 Oct 1824): 656a.

Q., "Drury Lane." no. 903 (23 May 1825): 321.

"Books of the Week." no. 3327 (4 Nov 1871): 1101.

Foreign Quarterly Review (*The*)

"Umrisse erfunden und gestochen von Moritz Retzsch (Outlines designed and engraved by Moritz Retzsch)." 18, no. 35 (Oct 1836–Jan 1837): 63–88.

Gazette de France (*La*)

"Au nombre des pièces de marionnettes qu'on joue avec le plus de succès en Allemagne." no. 7 (7 Jan 1824): 4.

M......t. "Variétés: Faust," no. 72 (12 Mar 1824): 3–4.

Gazette littéraire. Revue française et étrangère de la littérature, des sciences, des beaux-arts, etc.

"Bibliothèque des romans: Fragments du *Faust* d'Auguste Klingemann." 2, no. 18 (31 Mar 1831): 276c–79b.

Gentleman's Magazine and Historical Review (*The*)

"Mr J. H. Bohte." 136 (Oct 1824): 379 (obituary).

"Mr C. J. Hullmandel." n.s., 35, no. 189 (Feb 1851): 209–10 (obituary).

Intermédiaire des chercheurs et des curieux (*L'*)

37, no. 788 (10 Feb 1898): 166

no. 796 (30 Apr 1898): 624–25; no. 799 (30 May 1898): 760 (collectors' discussions on Nerval *Faust* frontispieces).

Journal des artistes et des amateurs

F. "Faust et Hamlet." 2nd ser., 2, no. 23 (7 Dec 1828): 353–55.

Journal des débats politiques et littéraires

[Le *Faust* de Retsch.] (7 May 1830): [2] and [3] (advertisement).

Kunstchronik. Beiblatt zur Zeitschrift für Bildende Kunst

A. R. "Nekrolog: Friedrich Eduard Meyerheim." 14, no. 18 (13 Feb 1879): 289–90.

Leipziger Literatur-Zeitung

"Bildende Künste. *Umrisse zu Göthe's Faust*, gezeichnet von *Retsch*." no. 91 (10 Apr 1818): 724–26.

Literary Chronicle

"Retsch's Designs for Schiller's Fridolin." no. 250 (28 Feb 1824): 144a ("to be published uniformly with Retsch's Designs to Goethe's Faust, also engraved by H. Moses").

"Retsch's Series of Outlines … to Fridolin." no. 253 (20 Mar 1824): 191a.

Literary Gazette (The). A Weekly Journal of Literature, Science, and the Fine Arts

"Dibdin's Bibliographical Tour (Third volume)." no. 230 (16 June 1821): 376.

"The Liberal." no. 301 (26 Oct 1822): 678–81 (carping review *inter alia* of Shelley's translation, to be concluded).

"Fine Arts." no. 425 (12 Mar 1825): 172b (G. Hering, lithographic print of "The Decision of the Flower" after Retzsch, dedicated to L. E. L.).

"Retsch's Illustrations of the Fight of the Dragon." no. 435 (21 May 1825): 329c–30a.

"Fine Arts: New Publications. Illustrations to the Keepsake." no. 929 (8 Nov 1834): 755c (on Retzsch's *The German Lovers*).

Untitled. no. 2110 (27 June 1857): 619 (brief Retzsch obituary).

Literary Panorama and National Register (The)

"Foreign Literary Gazette: Want of Character in the Devil and Doctor Faustus." 8, no. 51 (Dec 1818):col. 1490.

London Magazine (The)

"Works Preparing for Publication." 3, no. 5 (May 1821): 578.

"Literary and Scientific Intelligence." 6, no. 33 (Sept 1822): 287.

"Lord F. L. Gower's Faust." n.s., 6, no. 10 (Oct 1826): 164–73.

Magasin pittoresque (Le)

"Moritz Retzsch." 19, no. 49 (Dec 1851): 388–89. (with a wood-engraved portrait by H. Best and facsimile of the artist's signature).

Mercure du dix-neuvième siècle (Le)

H., "Faust." 10 (1825): 241–46.

Metropolitan Magazine (The)

"*Faust a Serio-Comic Poem*, with Twelve Outline Illustrations." 12, no. 45 (Jan 1835): 17.

Monthly Literary Advertiser (The)

no. 182 (10 June 1820): 41 (announcement of first batch of Boosey's 1st edition).

no. 198 (10 Oct. 1821): 75 (announcement of the *Faustus* 8vo text only translation with reference to the "Series of Twenty-seven Spirited Outlines," i.e., Boosey's 2nd edition).

Monthly Magazine; or, British Register

"New Books published in June." 49, no. 341 (1 July 1820): 558 ("Retsch's Series of Outlines of Goethe's Tragedy of Faust, engraved from the Originals by Henry Moses. Part I containing 12 plates 4to. 2s. 6d.— imperial 4to. with proof impressions, 10s. 6d.").

"New Books Published in September." 52, no. 359 (1 Oct 1821): 257–64.

New Edinburgh Review (The)

"*Faustus: from the German of Goethe*. London. Boosey and Sons. 1821, 8vo. pp. 86." 7, no. 4 (Apr 1822): 316–34 (carping review of new translation).

Nouveau journal de Paris politique, littéraire et industriel

"Théâtre de la Porte-Saint-Martin. Première représentation de *Faust*, mélodrame en trois actes et à grand spectacle." no. 457 (30 Oct 1828): 1–2.

"Théâtre de la Porte-Saint-Martin. *Faust*." no. 460 (2 Nov 1828): 1–2.

Pandore (La). Journal des spectacles, des lettres, des arts, des mœurs, et des modes

"Beaux-Arts. Faust." no. 244 (15 Mar 1824): 4b–5a.

Parthenon (The): A Magazine of Art and Literature

Φ. Χ. Ψ. "Outlines. Retsch and Flaxman." no. 1 (11 Jun 1825): 12–13.

Partisans (Les). Revue de combat, d'art, de littérature et de sociologie

"Mephistophélès et Faust au sabbat." no. 1 (5 nov 1900): 10. (advertisement for Jollivet-Castelot's *Les Sciences maudites* published by La Maison d'Art).

Phönix. Frühlingszeitung für Deutschland

"Urtheil eines Engländers über die deutschen Malerschulen." 1, no. 37 (12. Feb 1835): 146–48.

no. 38 (13. Feb): 154b–55a.

no. 41 (17. Feb): 162–64a.

Port Folio (The)

"The Fine Arts: *Illustrations of the Tragedy of Faustus*, by Goethe. Engraved and published by Henry Stone." 17, no. 266 (June 1824), 506–8 (review).

Quarterly Review (The)

"New Publications." 24, no. 47 (Oct 1820): 271 (publ. only on 19 Dec. 1820, advertisment for Boosey's 1820 *Faust*).

Revue bibliographique des Pays-Bas et de l'étranger

7, no. 37 (17 Oct 1828): 435.

7, no. 41 (11 Dec 1828): 491–92.

Saturday Review (The)

"Minor Notices." 47, no. 1224 (12 Apr 1879): 471–73.

Semaine (La). Journal hebdomadaire: sciences, arts, littérature, spectacles, tribunaux, industrie, annonces, etc.

"Le Faust de Retsch." 3 (23 May 1830): 3 ("reproduced exactly and in the same format as the original").

Tait's Edinburgh Magazine

"Faust, a Serio-Comic Poem, with Twelve Outline Illustrations." 1, no. 11 (Dec 1834): 852.

3 Books, Articles, Dissertations

Adel, Kurt. *Die Faust-Dichtung in Österreich*. Wien: Bergland Verlag, 1971.

Aign, Walter. *Faust im Lied*. Stuttgart: Ausgabe der Stadt Knittlingen / Enzkreis, 1975.

AKL—*Allgemeines Künstlerlexikon Online / Artists of the World Online*. Ed. Wolf Tegethoff, Bénédicte Savoy and Andreas Beyer. Berlin, New York: K. G. Saur, 2009. https://www-degruyter-com.

Aljumily, Refat. "The Anonymous 1821 Translation of Goethe's *Faustus*: A Cluster Analytic Approach." *Global Journal of Human-Social Science: A Arts & Humanities—Psychology* 15, no. 11, Version 1.0, 2015. PhD diss., Newcastle University, 2015.

Allert, Beate. "Goethe, Runge, Friedrich: On Painting." In *The Enlightened Eye: Goethe and Visual Culture*. Ed. Evelyn K. Moore and Patricia Anne Simpson. 73–91. Amsterdam: Rodopi, 2007.

Allevy, Marie-Antoinette. *La mise en scène en France dans la première moitié du dix-neuvième siècle*. Paris: Librairie E. Droz, 1938.

Amburger, Erik. *Ingermanland: Eine junge Provinz Russlands im Wirkungsbereich der Residenz und Weltstadt St. Petersburg-Leningrad*. 2 vols. Cologne: Böhlau, 1980.

Analysis 1820—"An Analysis of Goethe's Tragedy of Faust." In *Retsch's Series of Twenty-Six Outlines. Illustrative of Goethe's Tragedy of Faust, Engraved from the Originals by Henry Moses*. 1–60. London: Printed for Boosey & Sons, and Rodwell and Martin, 1820.

Armingeat, Jacqueline. "Un livre oublié." *L'Œil*, no. 12 (Noël 1955): 54–58.

Atkins, Lillian Espy Reed. "Fragmentary English Translations of Goethe's Faust." PhD diss., Yale University, 1937.

Auclair, Mathias, and Pauline Girard. "Les décors de *Faust* à l'Opéra de Paris (1869–1908)." In *L'interprétation lyrique de la fin du XIXᵉ au début du XXᵉ siècle: du livret à la mise en scène*. Ed. Alexandre Dratwicki and Agnès Terrier. Online: http://www.bruzanemediabase .com/Parutions-scientifiques-en-ligne/Articles/Auclair-Mathias-Girard-Pauline-Les-decors -de-Faust-a-l-Opera-de-Paris-1869-1908.

Augé, Christian, and Pascale Linant de Bellefonds. "Présentation." In Laborde, Léon de, and L.-M.-A. Linant de Bellefonds. *Pétra retrouvée: Voyage de l'Arabie Pétrée 1828*. 7–26. Paris: Pygmalion / Gérard Watelet, 1994.

BOOKS, ARTICLES, DISSERTATIONS

Bach, Max. *Stuttgarter Kunst 1794–1860: nach gleichzeitigen Berichten, Briefen und Erinnerungen.* Stuttgart: Adolf Bonz & Comp., 1900.

Baduel, Daniel, Aude Bertrand, and Christian Dauchel. *L'École d'Écouen, une colonie de peintres au XIXᵉ siècle.* Écouen: Office de Tourisme d'Écouen, 2012. 2nd enlarged ed., 2018.

Baldensperger, Fernand. *Bibliographie critique de Goethe en France.* Paris: Librairie Hachette et Cie, 1907.

Ball, Douglas. *Victorian Publishers' Bindings.* Williamsburg, Va.: The Book Press, 1985.

Balzac, Honoré de. "Avant-propos à la Comédie Humaine." In *Œuvres complètes de H. de Balzac.* Vol. 1:17–32. Paris: A. Houssiaux, 1855.

Bancroft, George. "A Day with Lord Byron." In *History of the Battle of Lake Erie and Miscellaneous Papers.* 190–210. New York: Robert Bonner's Sons, 1891.

Bann, Stephen. *Distinguished Images: Prints in the Visual Economy of Nineteenth-Century France.* New Haven: Yale University Press, 2013.

Barber, Giles. "Treuttel and Würtz: Some Aspects of the Importation of Books from France, c.1825." *Library,* 5th ser., 23, no. 2 (June 1968): 118–44. https://doi.org/10.1093/library/s5-XXIII.2.118.

Barbier, Frédéric. "Livre, économie et société industrielles en Allemagne et en France au 19ème siècle, 1840–1914." PhD diss, Paris 4, 1987.

Barbier, Frédéric. *L'Empire du livre: Le livre imprimé et la construction de l'Allemagne contemporaine 1815–1914.* Préface par Henri-Jean Martin. Paris: Les Éditions du Cerf, 1995.

Barbier, Frédéric, Sabine Juratic, and Dominique Varry, eds. *L'Europe et le livre: Réseaux et pratiques du négoce de librairie, XVIᵉ–XIXᵉ siècles.* Paris: Klincksieck, 1996.

Barbier, Frédéric, ed. *Est-Ouest. Transferts et réceptions dans le monde du livre en Europe (XVIIᵉ–XXᵉ siècles).* Leipzig: Leipziger Universitätsverlag, 2005. (*L'Europe en réseaux: Contributions à l'histoire de la culture écrite 1650–1918/Vernetztes Europa: Beiträge zur Kulturgeschichte des Buchwesens.*)

Bauer, Josephine. *The London Magazine, 1820–29.* Copenhagen: Rosenkilde and Bagger, 1953.

Bäumel, Jutta. "Vom landesherrlichen Bacchus-Triumph zum Aufzug der 'Hofewintzer.' Zur Genesis und Ausgestaltung der Winzeraufzüge in der Hoflößnitz." In Magirius, ed. 2001. 125–39.

Becker, Wilhelm Gottlieb, ed. *Augusteum: Dresden's antike Denkmäler enthaltend.* 3 vols. Leipzig: Auf Kosten der Verfassers und in Commission, C. A. Hempel et al., 1804–11.

Becker, Wolfgang. *Paris und die deutsche Malerei: 1750–1840.* Munich: Prestel-Verlag, 1971.

Benjamin, Walter. "Das Kunstwerk im Zeitalter seiner technischen Reproduzierbarkeit." Trans. "The Work of Art in the Age of Mechanical Reproduction." In *Illuminations.* Ed. Hannah Arendt, trans. Harry Zohn. 217–51. New York: Schocken Books, 1969. First published 1935.

Bennett, Shelley M. *Thomas Stothard: The Mechanisms of Art Patronage in England circa 1800.* Columbia: University of Missouri Press, 1988.

Benson, Adolph Burnett. "Catherine Potter Stith and Her Meeting with Lord Byron." *South Atlantic Quarterly* 22, no. 1 (Jan 1923): 10–22.

Bentley, Gerald Eades. *Blake Records: Documents (1714–1841) Concerning the Life of William Blake (1757–1827) and His Family. Incorporating "Blake Records" (1969), "Blake Records Supplement" (1988), and Extensive Discoveries since 1988.* 2nd ed. New Haven: Published for the Paul Mellon Centre for Studies in British Art by Yale University Press, 2004. First published 1969 by Clarendon Press.

Benz, Richard. *Goethe und die romantische Kunst mit vierzig Bildtafeln.* Munich: R. Piper & Co. Verlag, 1940.

Béraud, Antony, and *** [J.-T. Merle, Charles Nodier.] *Faust: drame en trois actes, imité de Goethe. Musique de M. Al. Piccini, ballet de M. Coraly, décors de M. Lefèvre. Paris, Théâtre de la Porte Saint-Martin, 29 octobre 1828.* Paris: J.-N. Barba, 1828.

Berg, Hartmut. *Herrn Biedermeiers Rauchvergnügen. Gesteck-Pfeifen und Porzellan-Pfeifenköpfe der 1. Hälfte des 19. Jahrhunderts: Sammlung Prof. Dr. Hartmut Berg.* Auction cat., 23 Oct 2010.

[Bertin, Louise.] *Fausto, opera semi-seria in quattro atti/Faust, opéra semi-sérieux en quatre actes. Théâtre Royal Italien, 8 mars 1830.* Paris: Au Théâtre Royal Italien / Chez Roullet, 1830.

Bertin, Louise. *Ultima scena di Fausto/Dernière scène de Faust de Goethe arrangée pour le piano-forte.* Paris: Maurice Schlesigner, n.d. [c.1831].

Biedermann, Birgit. *Bürgerliches Mäzenatentum im 19. Jahrhundert: Die Förderung öffentlicher Kunstwerke durch den Kunstverein für die Rheinlande und Westfalen.* Petersberg: Imhof Verlag, 2001. PhD diss., Göttingen, 2001.

Biedermann, Woldemar Freiherr von. *Goethe und Dresden.* Berlin: Gustav Hempel, 1875.

Bindman, David, ed. *John Flaxman, with 430 Illustrations, 4 in Colour.* London: Thames and Hudson, 1979. Exh. cat. English version of Hofmann, ed.

Blaeschke, Axel. "*De l'Allemagne*: Prolégomènes à une nouvelle édition." *Cahiers staëliens*, no. 64 (2014): 187–97.

Bleeke-Byrne, Gabriele. "French Perceptions of German Art (1800–1850): Studies in Stereotypes and their Ideological Influence." PhD diss., Brown University, 1989.

Boetticher, Friedrich von. "Retzsch, F. A. M." In *Malerwerke des neunzehnten Jahrhunderts. Beitrag zur Kunstgeschichte.* Vol. 2, 1:396b–397a. Leipzig: Schmidt & Günther, 1948. First published 1891–1901 by the author.

Böhm, Angela. *Carus Album. Die Wiederentdeckung einer Porträtsammlung.* Dresden: Städtische Galerie Dresden Kunstsammlung, 2009.

Bohte, J. H. *Verzeichniss deutscher Bücher welche um beygesetzten Preisen zu haben.* London: Gedruckt bey G. Schulze & J. Dean, 1814.

Bohte, J. H. *A Catalogue of Books in Various Languages on Sale* [With Supplement to *A Catalogue of Books in the Greek, Latin & German Languages.*] London: Printed by G. Schulze & J. Dean, 1816.

Bohte, J. H. *Extract of the Most Useful and Valuable Works Contained in the Frankfurt and Leipzig Fair-Catalogue, Just Imported by Bohte, Wilson & Glover.* London: Printed by G. Schulze & J. Dean, 1818.

Bohte, J. H. *A Catalogue of Books Now Selling by J. H. Bohte & Co.* London: Published by G. Schulze & J. Dean, 1819.

Bohte, J. H. *A Catalogue of Books Consisting Chiefly of Imported Greek and Latin Classics and Miscelllaneous Literature, in Various Languages, Including a Most Complete and Select Collection of German Literature, on Sale.* London: Printed by G. Schulze, 1821.

Bohte, J. H. *Handbibliothek der deutschen Litteratur, eine Sammlung der vorzüglichsten Werke deutscher Schriftsteller aus allen Fächern der Litteratur, welche um die beigefügten Preise zu haben sind. 1ster Theil mit einer Vorrede von August Wilhelm von Schlegel.* London: Gedruckt bey G. Schulze, 1825.

Bollert, Martin, ed. *Goethe Ausstellung: Sächsischer Kunstverein zu Dresden, Juni–Juli 1932, Brühlsche Terrasse.* Dresden: Wilhelm und Berta von Baensch Stiftung, 1932.

Bolton, Theodore. "The Book Illustrations of Felix Octavius Carr Darley." *Proceedings of the American Antiquarian Society* 61, Pt. 1 (Apr 1951): 136–82. https://www.americanantiquarian.org/proceedings/45615699.pdf.

Boosey and Sons. *A Catalogue of Foreign Engravings and Woodcuts (Ancient and Modern); also a Collection of Old Books, Ornamented with Portraits, Etchings, and Wood Cuts, which together with a Selection of the Best German Lithographic Prints Have Lately Been Imported, and Are Now on Sale.* London: Printed by J. Johnson, 1820.

Boosey and Sons. *Bibliotheca Rara et Curiosa. A Catalogue of Old Books for 1820, the Greater Part Collected on the Continent Last Autumn, Now on Sale at the Prices Affixed.* [1820].

Borchmeyer, Dieter. "Faust—Goethes verkappte Komödie." In *Die großen Komödien Europas.* Ed. Franz Norbert Mennemeier. 199–225. Tübingen: Francke Verlag, 2000.

Borges, Jorge Luis. "Nota sobre (hacia) Bernard Shaw." *Otras inquisiciones.* In *Obras completas.* Vol. 2:125–27. Barcelona: Emecé, 1996. *Otras inquisiciones* first published 1952.

Borne, Ludwig. *Briefe aus Paris.* Ed. Alfred Estermann. Frankfurt: Insel, 1986.

BOOKS, ARTICLES, DISSERTATIONS

Börsch-Supan, Helmut, and Lucius Grisebach. *Karl Friedrich Schinkel: Architektur, Malerei, Kunstgewerbe*. Berlin: Verwaltung der Staatlichen Schlösser und Gärten und Nationalgalerie Berlin, Staatliche Museen Preussischer Kulturbesitz, 1981. Exh. cat.

Boscq, Marie-Claire. *Imprimeurs et libraires parisiens sous surveillance (1814–1848)*. Préface de Jean-Yves Mollier. Paris: Classiques Garnier, 2018.

Böttiger, Karl August. "Bilder nach Wieland, Göthe und Schiller (2. in der Dresdner Ausstellung)." *Zeitung für die elegante Welt*, no. 80 (22 Apr 1811): 632–37.

Böttiger, Karl August. "Retzsch: Umrisse nach Göthe's Faust 1ster Theil." *Abend-Zeitung. Artistisches Notizenblatt*, no. 23 (Dec 1834): 92.

Brandt, Heinrich. *Goethes Faust auf der Kgl. sächsischen Hofbühne zu Dresden: Ein Beitrag zu Theaterwissenschaft*. Berlin: E. Ebering, 1921.

Bridgwater, Patrick. *De Quincey's Gothic Masquerade*. Amsterdam: Rodopi, 2004.

[Britton.] *Catalogue of the Fourth Portion of the Valuable and Extensive Library of John Britton, Esq.* Auction, 6 Apr 1846 and seven following days. [London: John Fletcher], 1846.

Brown, Eluned, ed. *The London Theatre 1811–1866: Selections from the Diary of Henry Crabb Robinson*. London: Society for Theatre Research, 1966.

Bruford, W. H. "Goethe's Reputation in England since 1832." In Rose, ed. 1949. 187–206.

Brunet, Jacques-Charles. "Goethe." In *Manuel du libraire et de l'amateur de livres*. Vol. 2:1644–45. 5th rev. ed. Paris: Librairie de Firmin Didot Frères, Fils et Cie, 1861. (With prices in the French market).

Brunsiek, Sigrun. *Auf dem Weg der alten Kunst. Der "altdeutsche Stil" in der Buchillustration des 19. Jahrhunderts*. Marburg: Jonas Verlag, 1994.

Bruson, Jean-Marie. *Théâtres romantiques à Paris: Collections du musée Carnavalet*. Paris: Paris-Musées, 2012. Exh. cat.

Buch (Das) des Goethe-Lessing-Jahres 1929. Braunschweig: F. Vieweg & Sohn, 1929.

Bühler, Roman. "Von der Konditorei zum Vergnügungspark: Ivan Ivanovič Izler, ein Petersburger Vergnügungsunternehmer um die Mitte des 19. Jahrhunderts." *Bündner Monatsblatt. Zeitschrift für Bündner Geschichte, Landeskunde und Baukultur*, no. 4 (1994): 274–82.

Burkhardt, Ramona. *Der Frauenverein in Jena im Spannungsfeld zwischen höfischen Impulsen durch Maria Pawlowna und der städtischen Gesellschaft*. Munich: GRIN Verlag, 2009. https://www.grin.com/document/130947.

Burrett, F. G. "John Massey Wright (1777–1866)." *Old Water-Colour Society's Club* 54 (1979): 42–48.

Burwick, Frederick, and James C. McKusick, eds. *Faustus: From the German of Goethe. Translated by Samuel Taylor Coleridge*. Oxford: Clarendon Press, 2007.

Burwick, Frederick. "Stage Illusion and the Stage Designs of Goethe and Hugo." *Word & Image* 4, no. 3–4 (July–Dec 1988): 692–718.

Burwick, Frederick. "On Coleridge as Translator of *Faustus: from the German of Goethe*." *European Romantic Review* 19, no. 3 (July 2008): 247–52. Online 01 July 2008 https://doi-org.janus.bis-sorbonne.fr/10.1080/10509580802211413. Adapted from his article in *Wordsworth Circle*, 38, no. 4 (Autumn 2007): 158–62.

Burwick, Frederick. "*Faust* Translations of Coleridge and Shelley on the London Stage." *Keats-Shelley Journal* 59 (2010): 30–42.

Burwick, Frederick. "Coleridge's Critique of Goethe's *Faust*." In *Goethe's Faust and Cultural Memory: Comparatist Interfaces*. Ed. Lorna Fitzsimmons, 124–45. Bethlehem: Lehigh University Press, 2012.

Busch, Günter. *Eugène Delacroix: Der Tod des Valentin*. Frankfurt: Klostermann, 1973.

Busch, Werner. "Umrißzeichnung und Arabeske als Kunstprinzipien des 19. Jahrhunderts." In Timm, ed. *Buchillustration*. 1988. 119–48.

Busch, Werner. *Caspar David Friedrich. Ästhetik und Religion*. Munich: C. H. Beck, 2003.

Busch, Werner. "Goethe, die Gebrüder Riepenhausen und deren Empfang in Rom." In *Rom-Europa: Treffpunkt der Kulturen 1780–1820*. Ed. Paolo Chiarini, Walter Hinderer et al. 43–57. Würzburg: Königshausen & Neumann, 2006.

Butler, Stephen. *The Fausts of Gérard de Nerval: Intertextuality, Translation, Adaptation.* Oxford: Peter Lang, 2018.

BwGZ—*Briefwechsel zwischen Goethe und Zelter in den Jahren 1799 bis 1832.* Ed. Hans-Günther Ottenberg, Edith Zehm. In collaboration with Anita Golz, Jürgen Gruss, Wolfgang Ritschel, and Sabine Schäfer. 3 vols. Munich: Carl Hanser, 1991–98.

[Byron.] *"In the wind's eye." Byron's Letters and Journals*, vol. 9. *1821–1822.* Ed. Leslie A. Marchand. London: John Murray, 1979.

Calloway, Stephen. "John Everett Millais, James Wyatt of Oxford and a volume of Retzsch's *Outlines to Shakespeare*: A Missing Link." In *Burning Bright: Essays in Honour of David Bindman.* Ed. Diana Dethloff et al., 160–70. London: UCL Press, 2015.

Calzabigi, Ranieri. "Lettera di Ranieri De' Calzabigi all'autore sulle quattro sue prime tragedie." In *Il teatro italiano.* Vol. 4. *Vittorio Alfieri, Tragedie. T. I. Filippo Antigone Agamennone Oreste Ottavia.* Ed. Luca Toschi. 329–64. Turin: Einaudi, 1993. Dated 1783.

Carney, Margaret. *Lithophanes.* Atglen, Pa.: Schiffer, 2008.

Carrà, Carlo. *Pittura metafisica.* Florence: Vallecchi, 1919.

Carré, Jean-Marie. *Bibliographie de Goethe en Angleterre.* Lyon: Impressions des Deux-Collines, 1920. PhD diss., Strasbourg, 1920; Paris: Plon-Nourrit, 1920.

Carus, Carl Gustav. *Lebenserrinerungen und Denkwürdigkeiten.* 4 vols. Leipzig: F. A. Brockhaus, 1865.

Catalogue de livres modernes. Livres illustrés du XIXe siècle. Éditions originales d'auteurs contemporains, publications sur les beaux-arts, composant la bibliothèque de feu M. le docteur Abel Giraudeau. 2nd Pt. Paris: Librairie Techener, 1898. Auction cat.

Catalogue des livres composant la bibliothèque de feu M. L. J. S. E., Marquis de Laborde. 2 vols. Paris: Adolphe Labitte, 1871–72. Auction cat.

Champfleury. *Les Vignettes romantiques. Histoire de la littérature et de l'art, 1825–1840, suivi d'un catalogue complet des romans, drames, poésies ornés de vignettes, de 1825 à 1840.* Paris: E. Dentu, 1883.

Chartier, Roger. "Du livre au lire." In *Pratiques de la lecture.* Ed. Roger Chartier, initiative of Alain Paire. 62–88. Marseille: Rivages, 1985.

[Chasles, Philarète.] "Beaux-Arts: Nouvelle école de peinture allemande." *La Revue britannique.* 3rd ser., 12, no. 11 (Nov 1834): 104–21. (Trans. of *German Sketches.* Adapted from an original probably by Mrs Jameson).

Chassaigne de Néronde. "La nouvelle mise en scène de *Faust* à l'Opéra." *Les Annales politiques et littéraires*, no. 1284 (2 Feb 1908): 108–9.

"Chemin (Le) du romantisme .... David d'Angers et l'Allemagne." *Saisons des musées*, no. 10 (2017).

Claes, Marie-Christine. *Répertoire des lithographes actifs en Belgique sous la période hollandaise et le règne de Léopold 1er (1816–1865).* 3rd ed. IRPA, 2022. <http://balat.kikirpa.be/lithographes/claes_lithographes.pdf>.

Clapham, John Harold. *The Economic Development of France and Germany 1815–1914.* Cambridge: Cambridge University Press, 1921.

Clayton, Tim, and Sheila O'Connell. *Bonaparte and the British. Prints and Propaganda in the Age of Napoleon.* London: British Museum Press, 2015.

Clayton, Tim. *The English Print, 1688–1802.* New Haven: Yale University Press, 1997.

Clösges, Elisabeth. "Die Illustration von Goethes Dichtung in seiner Zeit." PhD diss., Friedrich-Wilhelms-Universität zu Bonn, 1942.

Cochran, Peter. *Byron's Romantic Politics: The Problem of Metahistory.* Newcastle upon Tyne: Cambridge Scholars, 2011.

[Coleridge.] *Collected Letters of Samuel Taylor Coleridge.* Vol. 5. *1820–1825.* Ed. Earl Leslie Griggs. Oxford: Clarendon Press, 1971.

Coleridge, Samuel Taylor. *The Collected Works.* Vol. 14. *Table Talk, recorded by Henry Nelson Coleridge (and John Taylor Coleridge).* Ed. Carl Woodring. 2 vols. Princeton: Routledge / Princeton University Press, 1990.

BOOKS, ARTICLES, DISSERTATIONS

Cooke, Simon. "'If Not a Genius'? Alfred Crowquill as an Illustrator and Applied Artist." *The Victorian Web. Literature, History and Culture in the Age of Victoria*, last modified 27 May 2017 <http://www.victorianweb.org/art/illustration/crowquill/cooke.html>.

Cooper-Richet, Diana, Jean-Yves Mollier, and Ahmed Silem, eds. *Passeurs culturels dans le monde des médias et de l'édition en Europe, XIXe et XXe siècles*. Villeurbanne: Presses de l'ENSSIB, 2005.

Cooper, John Michael. *Mendelssohn, Goethe, and the Walpurgis Night: The Heathen Muse in European Culture, 1700–1850*. Rochester: University of Rochester Press, 2007.

Corvin, Michel, ed. *Goethe et les arts du spectacle*. Bron: CERTC, 1985.

[Coupin, Pierre-Alexandre.] "Paris, April 1824. Lithographie." *Morgenblatt für gebildete Stände. Kunstblatt*, no. 256 (13 May 1824): 154–55.

Creizenach, Wilhelm. *Die Bühnengeschichte des Goethe'schen "Faust."* Frankfurt: Rütten & Loening, 1881.

Crick, Joyce. "'*Faustus' from the German of Goethe translated by Samuel Taylor Coleridge*, ed. by Frederick Burwick & James C. McKusick." *Coleridge Bulletin*, n.s., 32 (Winter 2008): 70–84.

[Croly, George.] "Goethe and his Faustus." *London Magazine* 2, no. 8 (Aug 1820): 125–42.

Crowquill, Alfred. *Faust: A Serio-Comic Poem with Twelve Outline Illustrations*. London: B. B. King, 1834.

Dabezies, André. *Le mythe de Faust*. Paris: Armand Colin, 1972.

Darley, Gillian. *John Soane: An Accidental Romantic*. New Haven: Yale University Press, 1999.

Dauer, Detlef. "'Jeder erwachsene Deutsche raucht.' Pt. 1. Gemarkte Porzellanpfeifenköpfe aus Althaldensleben." *Jahresschrift der Museen des Landkreises Börde* 56, no. 23 (2016): 80–113; "Pt. 2. Berliner oder Althaldenslebener Pfeifenköpfe?" 57, no. 24 (2017): 51–61.

Daunicht, Richard. "August Klingemanns Inszenierung von Goethes *Faust 1. Teil*. Zur ersten Berufstheater-Aufführung des Stückes am 19. Januar 1829 in Braunschweig, mit 8 Abbildungen." *Braunschweigisches Jahrbuch* 61 (1980): 55–74.

[David d'Angers.] *Les Carnets de David d'Angers. Publiés pour la première fois intégralement avec une introduction par André Bruel*. 2 vols. Paris: Plon, 1958.

DCHA—*Dictionnaire critique des historiens de l'art actifs en France de la Révolution à la première Guerre mondiale*. Ed. Philippe Sénéchal and Claire Barbillon. Last modified 9 Feb 2010. https://www.inha.fr/fr/ressources/publications/publications-numeriques/dictionnaire-critique-des-historiens-de-l-art.html.

De Quincey, Thomas. "Gillies's German Stories." In *The Works of Thomas De Quincey*. Vol. 6:5–25. Ed. David Groves and Grevel Lindop. London: Pickering & Chatto, 2000. Originally in *Blackwood's Magazine* 20 (Dec 1826): 844–58.

Dédéyan, Charles. "Vocation faustienne de Gérard de Nerval." *La Revue des lettres modernes*, no. 25–26 (1er trimestre 1957): 49–98.

Dédéyan, Charles. *Le thème de Faust dans la littérature européenne*. 6 vols. Paris: Lettres Modernes, 1954–67.

Dédéyan, Charles. *Gérard de Nerval et l'Allemagne*. 3 vols. Paris: Société d'Édition d'Enseignement Supérieur, 1957–59.

Deflandre, M.-A. *Répertoire du commerce de Paris, ou Almanach des commerçans, banquiers, négocians, manufacturiers, fabricans et artistes de la capitale*. 2 vols. Paris: Au Bureau du Répertoire du Commerce de Paris, 1828–29.

Degreif, Uwe. *Eberhard Emminger, 1808–1885: Werkverzeichnis der druckgrafischen Arbeiten*. Biberach: Uwe Degreif, 2021.

[Delacroix.] *Correspondance générale d'Eugène Delacroix*. Ed. André Joubin. 5 vols. Paris: Librairie Plon, Les Petits-fils de Plon et Nourrit, 1935–38.

[Delacroix.] *Dessins d'Eugène Delacroix: 1798–1863*. Ed. Maurice Sérullaz, with Arlette Sérullaz, Louis-Antoine Prat, Claudine Ganeval. 2 vols. Paris: Ministère de la Culture / Éd. de la Réunion des Musées Nationaux, 1984.

Delacroix, Eugène. *Journal*. Ed. Michele Hannoosh. 2 vols. Paris: José Corti, 2009.

Deneke, Otto. *Die Brüder Riepenhausen*. Göttingen: Beim Herausgeber, 1936.

Deneke, Otto. *Göttinger Künstler*. Pt. 2. Göttingen: Beim Herausgeber, 1936.

Derrida, Jacques. "Edmond Jabès et la question du livre." In *L'Écriture et la Différence*. 99–116. Paris: Éditions du Seuil, 1967.

Descotes, Maurice. *Le drame romantique et ses grands créateurs, 1827–1839*. Paris: PUF, 1955. PhD diss., Paris, 1955.

Dibdin, Thomas Frognall. "Letter XXXVII. Stuttgart, August 4, 1818." In *A Bibliographical, Antiquarian and Picturesque Tour in France and Germany*. Vol. 3:120–30. London: Printed for the Author by W. Bulmer and W. Nicol, Shakspeare Press, 1821.

Dickens, Charles. *David Copperfield*. Ed. Nina Burgis. Oxford: Clarendon Press, 1981. First published May 1849–Nov 1850 in monthly parts; then *The Personal History of David Copperfield, with Illustrations by H. K. Browne*. London: Bradbury & Evans, 1850.

[Dickens.] *The Letters of Charles Dickens*. Vol. 12. *1868–1870*. The British Academy, Pilgrim Edition. Ed. Graham Story, associate ed. Margaret Brown, consultant Kathleen Tillotson. Oxford: Clarendon Press, 2002.

Dickson, Sarah. *Alfred Crowquill: A Few Words about Pipes, Smoking and Tobacco*. New York: New York Public Library, 1947.

Dictionnaire des imprimeurs-lithographes du XIXe siècle. École nationale des chartes, Éditions en ligne de l'École des chartes (ELEC). http://elec.enc.sorbonne.fr/imprimeurs/node/21884.

DiNB—Dictionary of National Biography, 1885–1900. Online. https://en.wikisource.org/wiki/Dictionary_of_National_Biography, 1885–1900/.

[Disraeli.] *The Early Novels of Benjamin Disraeli*. Vol. 1. *Vivian Grey (1826–7)*. Ed. Michael Sanders. General Introduction by Daniel R. Schwartz. London: Pickering & Chatto, 2004. First published 1826, London: Henry Colburn.

Dobbs, Brian. *Drury Lane: Three Centuries of the Theatre Royal, 1663–1971*. London: Cassell, 1972.

Dobsky, Arthur. "Moritz Retzsch, der Klassiker-Illustrator." *Bühne und Welt* 10, no. 12 (1907–8): 491–501.

Doctor Faustus und Mephistopheles: Bücher, Graphiken und Figuren aus der Sammlung E. P. Moosmann. Frankfurt: Stadt- und Universitätsbibliothek, 1991. Exh. cat.

Doin, Jeanne. "Charles Séchan et son atelier de décoration théâtrale pendant le romantisme." *Gazette des beaux-arts*, 5th ser., 11, no. 758 (June 1925): 344–60.

Dopp, Herman. *La Contrefaçon des livres français en Belgique, 1815–1852*. Louvain: Uystpruyst, 1932.

Doy, Guinevere. "Delacroix et Faust." *Nouvelles de l'estampe*, no. 21 (May–June 1975): 18–23.

Dresden. Von der Königlichen Kunstakademie zur Hochschule für Bildende Künste (1764–1989). Die Geschichte einer Institution. Ed. Hochschule für Bildende Künste Dresden. Dresden: Verlag der Kunst, 1990.

Drost, Wolfgang, and Marie-Hélène Girard, eds. *Gautier et l'Allemagne*. Siegen: Universitätsverlag Universi, 2005.

Duchartre, Pierre-Louis, and René Saulnier. *L'Imagerie parisienne. (L'Imagerie de la rue Saint-Jacques)*. Préface de Georges-Henri Rivière. Paris: Librairie Gründ, n.d. [1944].

Durrani, Osman. "*Bilder zu Goethes Faust*, by Eva Krüger." *Modern Language Review* 105, no. 3 (2010): 891–92. (Review).

Emerson, Ralph Waldo. *The Journals and Miscellaneous Notebooks*, vol. 5. *1835–1838*. Ed. Merton M. Sealts, Jr. Cambridge, Ma.: The Belknap Press of Harvard University Press, 1965.

Engel—Engel, Karl. *Zusammenstellung der Faust-Schriften vom 16. Jahrhundert bis Mitte 1884*. 2nd ed. Oldenburg: Schulze, 1885. First published 1874 as *Bibliotheca Faustiana*.

Engell, James. "Frederick Burwick and James McKusick, ed. *Faustus from the German of Goethe. Translated by Samuel Taylor Coleridge*." *Archiv* 247, no. 1 (2010): 150–52.

Erdmann, Jürgen. "Ein Stück deutscher Theaterhistorie. Zur Geschichte des ehemaligen herzoglichen sächsischen Hoftheaters Coburg-Gotha und seiner Notensammlung." In Potyra,

Rudolf. *Die Theatermusikalien der Landesbibliothek Coburg: Katalog.* Vol. 1: XI–XXXIII. Munich: G. Henle, 1995.

Erdmann, Jürgen. *Die Herzogliche Privatbibliothek Coburg als markantes Zeugnis nationaler und internationaler fürstlicher Kulturbeziehungen ab dem späten 18. Jahrhundert bis 1918.* Coburg: [Landesbibliothek], 2009.

Essen, Gesa von. "Gretchen." In Rohde, Valk, and Mayer, eds. 2018. 244–53.

Extrait du catalogue de la librairie de Dondey-Dupré père et fils; n.d. [Sept 1828]. ark:/12148/bpt6k1280205m.

FA—Goethe, Johann Wolfgang. *Sämtliche Werke: Briefe, Tagebücher und Gespräche.* (Frankfurter Ausgabe). Ed. Friedmar Apel et al. 40 (in 45) vols. Frankfurt: Deutscher Klassiker Verlag, 1985–2013.

Fairholt, F. W. "William Harvey, and the Wood Engravers of His Era." *Art Journal* 28 (1 Mar 1866): 89–90.

Fallbacher, Karl-Heinz. "Taschenbücher im 19. Jahrhundert." Special issue, *Marbacher Magazin*, no. 62 (1992).

Faustus 1824—*Faustus: from the German of Goethe. Embellished with Retsch's Series of Twenty-Seven Outlines, Illustrative of the Tragedy, Engraved by Henry Moses.* 3rd ed., with portrait of the author. London: Boosey and Sons, 1824.

Faustus 1852—*Faustus; or, The Demon of the Drachenfels.* Purkess's Library of Romance: Comprising a Series of Tales by Popular Authors. Vol. 1, no. 21 [London: G. Purkess, 1852?].

Faxon, Frederick W. *Literary Annuals and Gift Books: A Bibliography, 1823–1903.* Repr. with Supplementary Essays by Eleanore Jamieson and Iain Bain. Pinner, Mdx.: Private Libraries Association, 1973. Facsimile ed. Boston: Boston Book Co., 1912.

Fayt, René. "Les contrefacteurs belges étaient des 'étrangers'." *Cahiers du Cédic*, no. 2–4 (Jan 2003): 165–70.

Finlay, Nancy. *Inventing the American Past: The Art of F. O. C. Darley.* New York: New York Public Library, 1999.

Fischer, Bernhard. "Cottas *Morgenblatt für gebildete Stände* in der Zeit von 1807 bis 1823 und die Mitarbeit Therese Hubers." *Archiv für Geschichte des Buchwesens* 43 (1995): 203–39.

Fischer, Bernhard. "Cotta und die Brüder Riepenhausen: Zur Publikations geschichte der Riepenhausenschen Zeichnungen im *Morgenblatt*, im *Taschenbuch für Damen* und in der *Geschichte der Mahlerei*." In Kunze et al. 2001. 149–56.

Fischer, Bernhard. *Der Verleger Johann Friedrich Cotta. Chronologische Verlagsbibliographie 1787–1832. Aus den Quellen bearbeitet.* 3 vols. Marbach: Deutsche Schillergesellschaft; Munich: K. G. Saur, 2003.

Fischer, Bernhard. "Aus Moritz Retzschs unveröffentlichten Kupferstichen zur 'Bürgschaft' von Friedrich Schiller." In "Antike in Sicht: Strandgut aus dem Deutschen Literaturarchiv." Ed. Jochen Meyer. *Marbacher Magazin*, no. 107 (2004): 88–91.

Fischer, Ernst, ed. *Der Buchmarkt der Goethezeit: Eine Dokumentation.* 2 vols. Hildesheim: Gerstenberg, 1986.

Flor O'Squarr [Oscar Charles Flor.] "Édouard Frère." *Galerie contemporaine, artistique, littéraire* 1, 1st semester, 2nd ser. Paris: Ludovic Baschet, 1876.

Fontane, Theodor. *Graf Petöfy: Roman.* Ed. Petra Kabus. Berlin: Aufbau-Verlag, 1999.

Forster-Hahn, Françoise. "Romantic Tragedy or National Symbol? The Interpretation of Goethe's *Faust* in 19th-Century German Art." In *Our "Faust"? Roots and Ramifications of a Modern German Myth.* Ed. Reinhold Grimm and Jost Hermand. 82–95. Madison: University of Wisconsin Press, 1987.

Forster-Hahn, Françoise. "A Hero for All Seasons? Illustrations for Goethe's *Faust* and the Course of Modern German History." *Zeitschrift für Kunstgeschichte* 53, no. 4 (1990): 511–36.

Fouqué, Friedrich de La Motte. *Gedichte, zweiter Band. Gedichte aus dem Manns-Alter.* Stuttgart: Cotta, 1817.

Frantz, Adolf Ingram. "The English and American Faust Translators: Their Motives and Their Literary and Linguistic Backgrounds." PhD diss., Yale University, 1931.

Frantz, Adolf Ingram. *Half a Hundred Thralls to Faust: A Study Based on the British and the American Translators of Goethe's Faust, 1823–1949*. Foreword by Carl F. Schreiber. Chapel Hill: University of North Carolina Press, 1949.

Friedrich, Caspar David. *Die Briefe*. Ed. Herrmann Zschoche. Hamburg: ConferencePoint, 2005.

Fusenig, Thomas, and Giesen Sebastian. "Goethes *Faust* in Bildern." *Börsenblatt für den deutschen Buchhandel* 166. *Aus dem Antiquariat*, no. 7 (1999): A378–88.

Fusenig, Thomas. "*Faust*-Rezeption in der Bildenden Kunst." In *Goethe Handbuch*. Vol. 2. *Dramen*. Ed. Theo Buck. 514–21. Stuttgart: J. B. Metzler, 1996.

Garde, Georg, *Theater-Geschichte im Spiegel der Kinder-Theater: Eine Studie in populärer Graphik. With an English Summary*. Herning: Borgens Forlag, 1971.

GAug—*Goethes Briefwechsel mit seinem Sohn August*. Ed. Gerlinde Ulm Sanford. Weimar: H. Böhlaus Nachfolger, 2004.

Gautier, Théophile. "Revue des théâtres." *Le Moniteur universel*, no. 200 (18 July 1864): 1–2.

Gautier, Théophile. *Loin de Paris*. Paris: Michel Lévy Frères, 1865.

Gautier, Théophile. "Revue des théâtres." *Le Moniteur universel*, no. 148 (28 May 1866): 1.

Gautier, Théophile. "Joseph Thierry." In *Portraits contemporains*. 2nd ed. 340–44. Paris: Charpentier et Cie, 1874. First published 15 Oct 1866 in *Le Moniteur universel*.

Gautier, Théophile. "Gérard de Nerval." In *Portraits et souvenirs littéraires*. 1–68. Paris: Michel Lévy Frères, 1875. First published in *L'Univers illustré* 10, no. 671 (23 Nov 1867): 731, 734; no. 672 (30 Nov): 747, 750; no. 673 (7 Dec): 763–64, 766; no. 674 (14 Dec): 779–80, 782.

Gautier, Théophile. *Exposition de 1859, texte établi pour la première fois d'après les feuilletons du "Moniteur universel."* Ed. Wolfgang Drost and Ulrike Henninges. Heidelberg: Carl Winter, 1992. First published between 18 Apr and 10 Oct 1859 in *Le Moniteur universel*.

Gautier, Théophile. *Romans, contes et nouvelles*. Ed. Pierre Laubriet et al. 2 vols. Paris: Gallimard, 2002.

Gautier, Théophile. "La Toison d'or." Ed. Jean-Claude Fizaine. In *Romans, contes et nouvelles*. Vol. 1:773–815, 1429–43. First published in installments in *La Presse*, 6–12 Aug 1839, but for 10 Aug.

Gautier, Théophile. "Deux acteurs pour un rôle." Ed. Peter Whyte. In *Romans, contes et nouvelles*. Vol. 1:867–77, 1469–73. First published in *Musée des familles, lectures du soir* 8 (July 1841): 296–300.

Gautier, Théophile. "Les Roués innocents." Ed. Claudine Lacoste-Veysseyre. In *Romans, contes et nouvelles*. Vol. 1:1025–118, 1530–35. First published in installments in *La Presse*, 19–30 May 1846.

Gautier, Théophile. *Œuvres complètes*. Pt. 6. *Critique théâtrale*. Ed. Patrick Berthier et al. Paris: Champion, 2007–.

Gautier, Théophile. "Feuilleton de *La Presse*, [7 mai 1838]." In OC. Pt. 6. *Critique théâtrale*. Vol. 1:481–90. Paris: Champion, 2007.

Gautier, Théophile. *Les Beaux-arts en Europe—1855*. In *Œuvres complètes*. Pt. 7. *Critique d'art*. Vol. 4. Ed. by Marie-Hélène Girard. Paris: Champion, 2011. First published 1855–56.

Gautier, Théophile. "Feuilleton de *La Presse*, 22 août 1834. *Hamlet* illustré. *Treize lithographies*, par M. Delacroix." In OC. Pt. 6. *Critique théâtrale*. Vol. 4:353–56. Paris: Champion, 2012.

Gautier, Théophile. "Feuilleton de *La Presse* du 27 juillet 1846." In OC. Pt. 6. *Critique théâtrale*. Vol. 6:340–50. Paris: Champion, 2015. Particularly "Vaudeville. *Charlotte*, drame en trois actes précédé d'un prologue, par MM. Émile Souvestre et Eugène Bourgeois." 341–46.

Gautier, Théophile. "Feuilleton de *La Presse* du 25 mai 1847." In OC. Pt. 6. *Critique théâtrale*. Vol. 6:778–91. Paris: Champion, 2015. Particularly "*Le Comte d'Egmont*, drame en cinq actes et en vers, par M. Rolland." 782.

BOOKS, ARTICLES, DISSERTATIONS

Gautier, Théophile. "Feuilleton de *La Presse* du 17 novembre 1851." In *OC*. Pt. 6. *Critique théâtrale*. Vol. 10:42–54. Paris: Champion, 2018. Particularly "Variétés. *Mignon*, comédie en trois actes de M. Gaston de Montheau." 45–50.

Gautier, Théophile. "Feuilleton de *La Presse* du 1er décembre 1851." In *OC*. Pt. 6. *Critique théâtrale*. Vol. 10:66–77. Paris: Champion, 2018. Particularly "Théâtre de la Nation. *Vert-Vert*, ballet en trois actes de MM. Leuven et Mazilier, musique de MM. Deldevez et Tolbecque." 66–71.

Gautier, Théophile. "Feuilleton de *La Presse* du 19 avril 1852." In *OC*. Pt. 6. *Critique théâtrale*. Vol. 10:399–408. Paris: Champion, 2018. On "Opéra-Comique. *Galatée*, opéra-comique en deux actes, poème de MM. Jules Barbier et Michel Carré, musique de Victor Massé."

Gautier, Théophile. "Feuilleton de *La Presse* du 3 janvier 1853." In *OC*. Pt. 6. *Critique théâtrale*. Vol. 11:15–27. Paris: Champion, 2019. Particularly "*Orfa*, ballet-pantomime en deux actes." 15–18.

Gautier, Théophile. "Feuilleton de *La Presse* du 2 mai 1853." In *OC*. Pt. 6. *Critique théâtrale*. Vol. 11:196–205. Paris: Champion, 2019.

Gautier, Théophile. "Feuilleton de *La Presse* du 3 août 1854. Théâtre royal de Munich. *Faust*, de Goethe." In *OC*. Pt. 6. *Critique théâtrale*. Vol. 12:152–63. Paris: Champion, 2019.

Gautier, Théophile. "Feuilleton de *La Presse* du 15 août 1854." In *OC*. Pt. 6. *Critique théâtrale*. Vol. 12:165–73. Paris: Champion, 2019. Particularly "Théâtre royal de Munich. *Egmont*, de Goethe." 166–71.

GBW—Goethe, Johann Wolfgang von. *Sollst mir ewig Suleika heißen. Goethes Briefwechsel mit Marianne und Johann Jakob Willemer*. Ed. Hans-J. Weitz. Frankfurt: Insel, 1995.

GCB—*Goethe und Cotta, Briefwechsel, 1797–1832*. Ed. Dorothea Kuhn. 4 vols. Stuttgart: J. G. Cotta, 1979–83.

[Geiger, Ludwig.] L. G. "Eckermann an eine Schauspielerin." *Goethe-Jahrbuch* 17 (1896): 260–62.

Geisler-Szmulewicz, Anne. "Gautier, lecteur du *Faust* de Goethe (1831–1841)." In Drost and Girard, eds. 23–41.

Geslot, Jean-Charles, ed. *Dictionnaire des éditeurs français du XIXe siècle*. Paris, Éditions de la BnF, forthcoming. Online version http://def19.huma-num.fr/s/site/page/home.

GG—*Goethes Gespräche*. Founded by Woldemar Frhr. von Biedermann. Ed. Flodoard Frhr. von Biedermann, with Max Morris, Hans Gerhard Gräf and Leonhard L. Mackall. 2nd rev. ed. 5 vols. Leipzig: F. W. von Biedermann, 1909–11.

Giesen, Sebastian. "'Den Faust, dächt'ich, gäben wir ohne Holzschnitte und Bilderwerk': Goethes *Faust* in der europäischen Kunst des 19. Jahrhundert." PhD diss., Technische Hochschule Aachen, 1998.

Gilbert, Mary E. "Two Little-Known References to Henry Crabb Robinson." *Modern Language Review* 33, no. 2 (Apr 1938): 268–71. doi: 10.2307/3715016.

Gilmour, Joanna. *Elegance in Exile. Portrait Drawings from Colonial Australia*. Canberra: National Portrait Gallery, 2012.

Glaser, Curt. *Die Graphik der Neuzeit: Vom Anfang des XIX. Jahrhunderts bis zur Gegenwart*. Berlin: Bruno Cassirer, 1922.

GLTT—*Goethes Leben von Tag zu Tag: eine dokumentarische Chronik*. Ed. Robert Steiger, and Angelika Reimann (from vol. 6). 9 vols. Zürich: Artemis Verlag, 1982–2011.

Godfroid, François. *Aspects inconnus et méconnus de la contrefaçon en Belgique*. Bruxelles: Académie Royale de Langue et de Littérature Françaises, 1998.

Goedeke, Karl. Continued by Edmund Goetze. *Grundrisz zur Geschichte der deutschen Dichtung aus den Quellen*. Vol. 4, Pt. 2. *Vom siebenjährigen bis zum Weltkriege*. 6th bk., 1st sec., 2nd pt. 3rd revised ed. Dresden: L. Ehlermann, 1910.

Goethe. *Goethe's Faust. Pt. I & II*. Trans. Albert G. Latham. Everyman's Library. London: J. M. Dent & Sons; New York: E. P. Dutton & Co., 1908. Repr. 1914.

Goethe, Johann Wolfgang von. *Faust: A Tragedy. Interpretative Notes, Contexts, Modern Criticism*. Ed. Cyrus Hamlin. Trans. Walter Arndt. 2nd ed. New York: W. W. Norton and Company, 2001.

Goethe, Johann Wolfgang von. *Faust: Part One*. Trans. with an Introduction and Notes by David Luke. Oxford World's Classics. Oxford: Oxford University Press, 1987. Reissued 2008.

Goethe, Johann Wolfgang. "*Faust*, Tragédie de Mr. de Goethe traduite en François par M. *Stapfer*, ornée de XVII dessins par Mr. *De Lacroix*." In FA. Pt. 1. Vol. 22. Ed. Anne Bohnenkamp. 485–87, 1291–92. First published 1828 in *Über Kunst und Altertum* 4, no. 2.

Goslee, Nancy Moore. *Shelley's Visual Imagination*. Cambridge: Cambridge University Press, 2011.

Goubault, Christian. *La musique, les acteurs et le public au Théâtre des Arts de Rouen: 1776–1914*. Préface de M. Emmanuel Bondeville. Rouen: CRDP, 1979.

Gräf, Hans Gerhard. *Goethe über seine Dichtungen. Versuch einer Sammlung allen Aüsserungen des Dichters über seine poetischen Werke*. Vol. 4. *Die dramatischen Dichtungen*. Vol. 2. Frankfurt: Rütten & Loening, 1904.

Grandjonc, Jacques. *Communisme/Kommunismus/Communism: Origine et développement international de la terminologie communautaire prémarxiste des utopistes aux néo-babouvistes*. 2 vols. Trier: Schriften aus dem Karl Marx Haus, 1989.

Green, Rosalie. "The Miniatures." In Herrad of Hohenbourg, *Hortus deliciarum*. Ed. Rosalie Green et al. Vol. 1:17–36. London: The Warburg Institute; Leiden: E. J. Brill, 1979.

Gretton, Tom. "Reincarnation and Reimagination: Some Afterlives of Géricault's *Raft of the Medusa* from c. 1850 to c. 1905." In "L'Image recyclée." Ed. Georges Roque and Luciano Cheles. *Figures de l'art*, no. 23 (2013): 77–94.

Grewe, Cordula. "Outline and Arabesque. Simplicity and Complexity in German Prints, and the Allure of the Antique." In Ittmann, ed. 228–47.

Griffiths, Antony, and Frances Carey. *German Printmaking in the Age of Goethe*. London: British Museum Press, 1994. Exh. cat.

Griffiths, Antony. *Prints and Printmaking. An Introduction to the History and Techniques*. London: British Museum Publications, 1980. 2nd ed. London: British Museum Press, 1996.

Griffiths, Antony. *The Print Before Photography: An Introduction to European Printmaking, 1550–1820*. London: British Museum, 2016. Repr. 2018.

Grosse, Helmut, and Bernd Vogelsang, eds. *Faust und Mephisto: Goethes Dramenfiguren auf dem Theater*. Cologne: Theatermuseum der Universität Köln, 1983. Exh. cat.

Grovier, Kelly. "Obnoxious to Principles." TLS, no. 5472 (15 Feb 2008): 7–8a.

Guenther, Peter W. "Concerning Illustrations to Goethe's *Faust*." In *The Age of Goethe Today: Critical Reexamination and Literary Reflection*. Ed. Gertrud Bauer Pickar and Sabine Cramer. 104–12. Munich: Wilhelm Fink, 1990.

Hafferberg, Hugo. *St. Petersburg in seiner Vergangenheit und Gegenwart. Ein Handbuch für Reisende und Einheimische nebst einem Plane der Stadt*. Saint Petersburg: Buchdruckerei von Friedrich Assmann, 1866.

Haine, Heiko, ed. *Brennende Liebe: Thürigner Porzellanpfeife in alle Welt/Burning Love: Thürigner Porcelain Pipes Around the World*. Eisfeld: Museum Eisfeld, 2013. Unpublished exh. cat.

Hall, Mrs S. C. [Anna Maria.] "A Morning with Moritz Retzsch." *Art Journal*, n.s., 3 (1 Jan 1851): 20–22. With Retzsch's portrait engraved by G. Dalziel and a sketch of his cottage.

Hall, Mrs S. C. [Anna Maria.] "A Morning with Moritz Retzsch." *Harper's New Monthly Magazine* 2, no. 10 (Mar 1851): 509b–13a. Without the images.

Hall, Samuel Carter. *Retrospect of a Long Life, from 1815 to 1883*. New York: D. Appleton and Co., 1883.

Halm, Peter. "Illustrationen zu Goethes Werken." In Bollert, ed. 1932. 150–52.

Hanley, Howard J. M., Margaret Cooper, and Susan Morris. "The Mysterious Septimus Prowett: Publisher of the John Martin 'Paradise Lost'." *British Art Journal* 2, no. 1 (Autumn 2000): 20–25.

Harten, Ulrike. *Die Bühnenentwürfe*. Ed. Helmut Börsch-Supan and Gottfried Riemann. Munich: Deutscher Kunstverlag, 2000.

Harvey, John Robert. *Victorian Novelists and Their Illustrators*. London: Sidgwick & Jackson, 1970.

Haskins, Susan. *Mary Magdalen: Myth and Metaphor*. London: Harper Collins, 1993.

BOOKS, ARTICLES, DISSERTATIONS

Hauhart, William Frederic. *The Reception of Goethe's Faust in England in the First Half of the Nineteenth Century*. New York: Columbia University Press, 1909.

Hayes, Kevin J. "Retzsch's Outlines and Poe's 'The Man of the Crowd'." *Gothic Studies* 12, no. 2 (Nov 2010): 29–41.

Haymann, Christoph Johann Gottfried. *Dresdens theils neuerlich verstorbene theils ietzt lebende Schriftsteller und Künstler: Wissenschaftlich classificirt nebst einem dreyfachen Register*. Dresden: Walther, 1809.

Hayward, Abraham. "Appendix, no. II. Being an Historical Notice of the Story of Faust, and the Various Productions in Art and Literature that Have Grown Out of It." In *Faust: A Dramatic Poem by Goethe*. Translated with Notes. 4th edition. 231–45. London: Edward Moxon, 1847.

Haywood, Ian, Susan Matthews, and Mary L. Shannon, eds. "Editors' Introduction." In *Romanticism and Illustration*. 1–21. Cambridge: Cambridge University Press, 2019.

Hecker, Max, ed. "Dreizehn Briefe Mariannens von Willemer an Goethe nebst zwei Briefe an Goethes Sohn." *Jahrbuch Goethe-Gesellschaft* 2 (1915): 173–200.

Hecker, Max. "Karl Eduard von Holtei im Goethekreise." *Jahrbuch der Goethe-Gesellschaft* 4 (1917): 167–232.

Heichen, Paul, ed. *Taschen-Lexikon der hervorragenden Buchdrucker u. Buchhändler seit Gutenberg bis auf die Gegenwart*. Leipzig: Moritz Schäfer Buchhandlung / Schäfer & Koradi, 1884.

Heine, Heinrich. "Die Harzreise." In *Briefe aus Berlin. Über Polen. Reisebilder I–II (Prosa)*. Ed. Jost Hermand. In *Historisch-kritische Gesamtausgabe der Werke*. Vol. 6:81–138, notes 518–683. Hamburg: Hoffmann & Campe, 1973. Written 1824, first published 1826.

Heine, Heinrich. "Les montagnes du Harz." In *Historisch-kritische Gesamtausgabe der Werke*. Vol. 6: 233–80, notes 684–708. First published in French 1834 in *Reisebilder. Tableaux de voyage*.

Heine, Heinrich. *Tableaux de voyage*. Trans. and ed. Claire Placial. Paris: Classiques Garnier, 2019.

Heinemann, William. *Goethes Faust in England und Amerika: Bibliographische Zusammenstellung*. Berlin: August Hettler, 1886.

Heinrich, Alfred. "Charles Dickens und die *Faust Outlines*." *Anglia. Zeitschrift für englische Philologie*, n.s., 37 (Jan 1926): 353–55.

Hellwig, Uwe. "Studien zu Moritz Retzsch (1779–1857) und seinen Umrissillustrationen im verlegerischen Kontext." PhD diss., Göttingen, 2018.

[Hen, Charles.] *La Réimpression: Étude sur cette question considérée principalement au point de vue des intérêts belges et français*. Bruxelles: Auguste Decq, 1851. Gallica NUMM-109167.

Henning, Hans, ed. *Faust-Bibliographie*. 3 vols. Berlin: Aufbau-Verlag, 1966–76.

Henning, Rudolf, and Gerd Maier. *Eberhard Emminger: Süddeutschland nach der Natur gezeichnet und lithographiert*. Stuttgart: Konrad Theiss, 1986.

Hermann, L. "Moritz Retzsch und Bürger." In *Umrisse zu Bürgers Balladen. Erfunden und gestochen durch Moritz Retzsch. Neue Auflage. Mit Bürgers Text und Erläuterungen, biographischen und kunstgeschichtlichen Notizen*. 1–8. Leipzig: Ernst Fleischer, 1872.

[Hermann, L.] Translated. "Moritz Retzsch and Bürger." In *Outlines to Bürger's Ballads, Designed and Engraved by Moritz Retzsch. With Bürger's Text, Explanations, and Bibliographical Notices*. 1–7. Boston: Roberts Brothers, 1873.

Herrad of Hohenbourg. *Hortus deliciarum*. Ed. Rosalie Green, Michael Evans, Christine Bischoff, and Michael Curschmann. With contributions by T. Julian Brown and Kenneth Levy. 2 vols. London: The Warburg Institute; Leiden: E. J. Brill, 1979.

Herz, Henriette. *Ihr Leben und ihre Erinnerungen*. Ed. Julius Fürst. Berlin: Verlag von Wilhelm Hertz, 1850.

Hewitson, Mark. "Preface." In *Nationalism versus Cosmopolitanism in German Thought and Culture, 1789–1914: Essays on the Emergence of Europe*. Ed. Mary Anne Perkins and Martin Liebscher. III–IV. Manchester: Edwin Mellen Press, 2006.

Hildebrand-Schat, Viola. *Zeichnung im Dienste der Literaturvermittlung: Moritz Retzschs Illustrationen als Ausdruck bürgerlichen Kunstverstehens*. Würzburg: Königshausen und Neumann, 2004.

Hiller, Helmut, and Wolfgang Strauss. *Der deutsche Buchhandel: Wesen, Gestalt, Aufgabe.* 5th rev. ed. Mit einem Anhang von Friedrich Christoph Perthes. Hamburg: Verlag für Buchmarkt-Forschung, 1975.

Hirschberg, Leopold. "Ein Silhouettenfund. Nebst Bemerkungen über Moritz Retzsch." *Zeitschrift für Bücherfreunde* 7, no. 12 (Mar 1904): 491–93.

Hirschberg, Leopold. "Über vier wenig bekannte Kupfer der 1808-Ausgabe von Goethes Faust." *Zeitschrift für Bücherfreunde* 11, no. 4 (July 1907): 174b–76a.

Hirschberg, Leopold. *Moritz Retzsch: Chronologisches Verzeichniss seiner graphischen Werke zum ersten Mal zusammengestellt.* Berlin: Heinrich Tiedemann, 1925.

Hoe, Robert. *A Lecture on Bookbinding as a Fine Art. Delivered before the Grolier Club, February 26, 1885. With Sixty-Three Illustrations.* New York: Published for the Grolier Club, 1886.

Höffner, Eckhard. *Geschichte und Wesen des Urheberrechts.* 2 vols. Munich: Verlag Europäische Wirtschaft (VEW), 2010.

Hofmann, Werner, ed. *John Flaxman: Mythologie und Industrie. Kunst um 1800.* Munich: Prestel, 1979. Exh. cat. German version of Bindman, ed.

Holcomb, Adele M. "Anna Jameson: The First Professional English Art Historian." *Art History* 6, no. 2 (June 1983): 171–87.

Holtei, Karl, ed. *Briefe an Ludwig Tieck.* 4 vols. Breslau: Verlag von Eduard Trewendt, 1864.

[Horne, Richard.] R. H. "Fine Arts: Outlines from Goethe's Tragedy of *Faust*." *Examiner*, no. 719 (14 Oct 1821): 648–49a.

[Horne, Richard.] R. H. "Engravings." *Examiner*, no. 848 (2 May 1824): 276b–77a.

Howsam, Leslie. "An Experiment with Science for the Nineteenth-Century Book Trade: The International Scientific Series." *British Journal for the History of Science* 33, no. 2 (2000): 187–207. doi:10.1017/S0007087499003945.

[Huber, Therese.] "Vorrede." In *Umrisse zu Goethe's Faust, gezeichnet von Retsch.* 3–7. Stuttgart & Tübingen: In der J. G. Cotta'schen Buchhandlung, 1816.

[Huber, Therese.] "Bemerkungen über Goethe's *Faust* (Vorrede aus Veranlassung der trefflichen "*Umrisse zu Göthe's Faust*, gezeichnet von *Retsch*" die so eben in der Cotta'schen Buchhandlung die Presse verlassen)." *Morgenblatt für gebildete Stände*, no. 256 (24 Oct 1816): 1021–23.

[Hunt, Leigh.] L. H. "Addenda: May-Day Night." In *Faustus: from the German of Goethe, Embellished with Retsch's Series of Twenty-Seven Outlines, Illustrative of the Tragedy, Engraved by Henry Moses. New edition, with Portrait of the Author and An Appendix Containing the May-Day Night Scene, Translated by Percy Bysshe Shelley.* 65–66. London, Edward Lumley, 1832.

Illustrationen zu Goethes Werken, ed. Helga Haberland. Frankfurt: Freies Deutsches Hochstift, 1962. Exh. cat.

Important American Silver. New York, Christie's, 17 Jan 2008. Auction cat.

Introduction 1821—"Introduction." In *Faustus: from the German of Goethe.* V–VIII. London: Boosey and Sons and Rodwell & Martin, 1821.

Introduction 1877—"Introduction." In *Illustrations to Goethe's Faust: Twenty-six Etchings by Moritz Retzsch with Illustrative Selections from the Text of Bayard Taylor's Translation.* Boston: Estes and Lauriat [Printed by John Wilson and Son], 1877.

Isbell, John Claiborne. "The First French *Faust*: De l'Allemagne's *Faust* Chapter, 1810–1814." *French Studies* 45 (1991): 417–34.

Isbell, John Claiborne. *The Birth of European Romanticism: Truth and Propaganda in Staël's "De l'Allemagne," 1810–1813.* Cambridge: Cambridge University Press, 1994.

Ittmann, John, ed. *The Enchanted World of German Romantic Prints, 1770–1850.* Ed. consultant Cordula Grewe. Philadelphia: Philadelphia Museum of Art; New Haven: Yale University Press, 2017.

Ittmann, John. "Glazed and Framed: *Kunstverein* Prints for the Parlour." In Ittmann, ed. 108–23.

Jacob, Ulf, Simone Neuhäuser, and Gert Streidt, eds., *Fürst Pückler: Ein Leben in Bildern.* Berlin: Bebra Verlag / SFPM, 2020.

BOOKS, ARTICLES, DISSERTATIONS

Jameson, Anna. *Visits and Sketches at Home and Abroad, with Tales and Miscellanies Now First Collected, and a New Edition of the "Diary of an Ennuyée."* 2 vols. New York: Harper and Brothers, 1834.

Jameson, Anna. "Biographisches. Moritz Retzsch als Mensch und Künstler geschildert." Trans. Dr Vogel. *Morgenblatt für gebildete Stände*, no. 252, *Kunst-Blatt*, no. 84 (21 Oct 1834): 333–34; *Morgenblatt*, no. 254, *Kunst-Blatt*, no. 85 (23 Oct 1834): 338–39.

Jameson, Anna. "Introduction." In *Fantasien: Fancies. A Series of Subjects in Outline, now First Published from the Original Plates. Designed and Etched by Moritz Retzsch*. V–XI. London: Saunders and Otley, A. Richter and Co.; Paris and Strasburgh: Treuttel and Wurtz; Leipzig: E. Fleischer, 1834.

Jameson, Anna. *Sketches of Germany: Art, Literature, Character*. Frankfurt: Printed for Charles Jugel at the German and Foreign Library, 1837. Reprints the 1834 text on Retzsch, 338–47.

Jamieson, Eleanore. *English Embossed Bindings, 1825–1850*. Cambridge: University Press, 1972.

Jammes, André, and Françoise Courbage, eds. *Les Didot: Trois siècles de typographie et de bibliophilie, 1698–1998*. Paris: [Agence culturelle de Paris], 1998. Exh. cat.

Jeanblanc, Helga. *Des Allemands dans l'industrie et le commerce du livre à Paris (1811–1870)*. Paris: CNRS Éditions, 1994.

Jefcoate, Graham. *Deutsche Drucker und Buchhändler in London, 1680–1811*. Berlin: De Gruyter, 2015.

Jefcoate, Graham. *An Ocean of Literature: John Henry Bohte and the Anglo-German Book Trade in the Early Nineteenth Century*. Hildesheim: Olms, 2020.

Jensen, Jens Christian, ed. *Deutsche Romantik: Aquarelle und Zeichnungen. Ausstellung Deutsche Romantik im Museum Georg Schäfer*. Munich: Prestel, 2000.

Join-Diéterle, Catherine. *Les Décors de scène de l'Opéra de Paris à l'époque romantique*. Paris: Picard, 1988.

Jones, Joseph Jay. "Lord Byron on America." *Studies in English*, no. 21 (1941): 121–37. https://www.jstor.org/stable/20775390.

Jooss, Birgit. "Lebende Bilder als Charakterbeschreibungen in Goethes Roman *Die Wahlverwandtschaften*." In *Erzählen und Wissen: Paradigmen und Aporien ihrer Inszenierung in Goethes "Wahlverwandtschaften."* Ed. Gabriele Brandstetter. 111–36. Freiburg im Breisgau: Rombach-Wissenschaften, 2003.

Jourdain, Frantz. "Préface." In *Le Faust de Goethe. Traduction de Gérard de Nerval, illustrations inédites de Gaston Jourdain*. I–IV. Paris: Imprimé pour la Société de Propagation des Livres d'Art, 1904.

Jullien, Dominique. *Proust et ses modèles: Les "Mille et Une Nuits" et les "Mémoires" de Saint-Simon*. Paris: J. Corti, 1989.

Jung, Carl Gustav. *The Development of Personality*, Trans. R. F. C. Hull. In *Collected Works*. Vol. 17. London: Routledge and Kegan Paul, 1954. Originally published as "Vom Werden der Persönlichkeit." In *Wirklichkeit der Seele*. Zurich: Rascher, 1934.

Jung, Carl Gustav. *Memories, Dreams, Reflections*. Ed. Aniela Jaffé. Transl. Richard and Clara Winston. 3rd printing. New York: Pantheon Books, 1963. First published 1961. Originally *Erinnerungen, Träume, Gedanken*, drawn and ed. by A. Jaffé, 1962.

Jung, Carl Gustav. *Psychological Types*. Trans. H. G. Baynes, rev. R. F. C. Hull. In *Collected Works*. Vol. 6. London: Routledge and Kegan Paul, 1971. Originally published as *Psychologische Typen*. Zurich: Rascher, 1921.

Junod, Karen. "Crabb Robinson, Blake, and Perthes's *Vaterländisches Museum* (1810–1811)." *European Romantic Review* 23, no. 4 (Apr 2012): 435–51.

Kippenberg—*Katalog der Sammlung Kippenberg*. 2nd ed. 3 vols. Leipzig: Insel, 1928. First published 1913.

Keane, Maureen. *Mrs. S. C. Hall: A Literary Biography*. Gerrards Cross: Colin Smythe, 1997.

Kemp, Martin. "A Feverish Imagination." *Nature* 451 (28 Feb 2008): 1056.

Kerr, Matthew P. M. "Nancy Moore Goslee, *Shelley's Visual Imagination*." *Notes & Queries* 61, no. 2 (June 2014): 310–11. (Review).

Kilgarriff, Tessa Maria. "Reproducing Celebrity: Painted, Printed and Photographic Theatrical Portraiture in London, *c.*1820–1870." PhD diss., History of Art, University of Bristol, 2018. Online final copy 23 Jan 2019. https://research-information.bris.ac.uk/ws/portalfiles/portal/210737578 /Final_Copy_2019_01_23_Kilgarriff_T_PhD_Redacted.pdf.

Kindermann, Heinz. *Theatergeschichte der Goethezeit*. Wien: H. Bauer Verlag, 1948.

Kindt, Hermann. "English Versions of Goethe's *Faust*, Part I." *Notes & Queries*, 4th ser., 3 (15 May 1869): 452–54.

Kindt, Hermann. "Goethes Faust in England." *Die Gegenwart*, no. 24 (13 June 1874): 374–77; no. 25 (20 June 1874): 394–95a.

King, Edmund M. B. *Victorian Decorated Trade Bindings, 1830–1880. A Descriptive Bibliography*. London: British Library; New Castle, Del.: Oak Knoll Press, 2003.

Klussmann, Paul Gerhard. "Das literarische Taschenbuch der Biedermeierzeit als Vorschule der Literatur und der bürgerlichen Allgemeinbildung." In Mix, ed. 1996. 89–111.

Klussmann, Paul Gerhard, and York-Gothart Mix, eds. *Literarische Leitmedien: Almanach und Taschenbuch im kulturwissenschaftlichen Kontext*. Wiesbaden: Harrassowitz, 1998.

Klussmann, Paul Gerhard. "Das Taschenbuch im literarischen Leben der Romantik und Biedermeierzeit: Begriff, Konzept, Wirkung." In Klussmann and Mix, eds. 47–64.

Kopp, Heinrich. *Die Bühnenleitung August Klingemanns in Braunschweig*. Hamburg: Leopold Voss, 1901.

Krakovitch, Odile. *Les Imprimeurs parisiens sous Napoléon I*er*: édition critique de l'enquête de décembre 1810. Censure, répression et réorganisation du livre sous le Premier Empire*. With Jean-Dominique Mellot and Élisabeth Queval. Paris: Paris-Musées, 2008.

Krosigk, Hans von. *Karl Graf von Brühl, General-Intendant der königlichen Schauspiele, später der Museen in Berlin, und seine Eltern. Lebensbilder auf Grund der Handschriften des Archivs zu Seifersdorf*. Berlin: Ernst Siegfried Mittler und Sohn, 1910.

Krüger, Eva. *Bilder zu Goethes "Faust": Moritz Retzsch und Dante Gabriel Rossetti*. Hildesheim: Olms, 2009.

Kruseman, Arie Cornelis. *Bouwstoffen voor een Geschiedenis van den Nederlandschen Boekhandel, gedurende de halve Eeuw 1830–80*. 3 vols. Amsterdam: P. N. van Kampen & Zoon, 1886–87.

Kube, Karl Heinz. *Goethes Faust in französischer Auffassung und Bühnendarstellung*. Berlin: E. Ebering, 1932.

Kugler, Franz. *Kleine Schriften und Studien zur Kunstgeschichte: mit Illustrationen und andern artistischen Beilagen*. 3 vols. Stuttgart: Verlag von Ebner & Seubert, 1853–54.

Kuhn-Forte, Brigitte. "Ernst Ludwig Riepenhausen, Kupferstecher." In Kunze et al., ed. 2001. 1–6.

Kuhn, Dorothea, ed. "Quodlibet: Illustrationen aus dem Cotta-Verlag in der ersten Hälfte des 19. Jahrhunderts aus den Beständen des Cotta-Archivs." Special issue, *Marbacher Magazin*, no. 4 (1977).

Kuhn, Dorothea, Anneliese Kunz, and Margot Pehle, eds. *Cotta und das 19. Jahrhundert: Aus der literarischen Arbeit eines Verlages*. Munich: Kösel Verlag, 1980. Exh. cat.

Kuhn, Dorothea. "Johann Friedrich und Georg von Cottas Bemühungen um die Buchillustration." In *Buchgestaltung in Deutschland 1740 bis 1890*. Ed. Paul Raabe. 105–23. Hamburg: Dr. Ernst Hauswedell & Co., 1980.

Kuhn, Dorothea. "Verleger und Illustrator. Am Beispiel der J. G. Cotta'schen Verlagsbuchhandlung." In Timm, ed. *Buchillustration*. 1988. 213–40.

Kuhn, Dorothea. *Cotta und das 19. Jahrhundert: Aus der literarischen Arbeit eines Verlages*. 2nd ed. Marbach: Deutsche Schillergesellachft, 1995. Exh. cat.

Kunze, Max, ed. With Beate Schroedter and Eva Hofstetter-Dolega. *Zwischen Antike, Klassizismus und Romantik: Die Künstlerfamilie Riepenhausen*. Mainz: Verlag Philipp von Zabern, 2001.

BOOKS, ARTICLES, DISSERTATIONS

Kunzle, David. *History of the Comic Strip*. Vol. 1. *The Early Comic Strip: Narrative Strips and Picture Stories in the European Broadsheet from c.1450 to 1825*. Berkeley: University of California Press, 1973.

Kutschmann, Theodor. *Geschichte der deutschen Illustration vom ersten Auftreten des Formschnittes bis auf die Gegenwart*. Goslar: Franz Jäger Kunstverlag, n.d. [1899].

Laborde, Léon de. *Essais de gravure pour servir à une histoire de la gravure en bois*. 1st fasc. Paris: Imprimerie et Fonderie de Jules Didot l'aîné, 1833.

Lachgern, Anselmus. *Bilder zu Goethes Faust*. Leipzig: C. F. Doerffling, 1841.

Lambert, Marij. "L'illustration dans les contrefaçons belges: Une approche systémique." In "History and Theory of the Graphic Novel, special section IAWIS conference." Special issue *Image [&] Narrative*, no. 7 (Oct 2003). Online http://www.imageandnarrative.be/inarchive/graphic novel/marijlambert.htm.

Lanckorońska, Maria, Gräfin, and Arthur Rümann. *Geschichte der deutschen Taschenbücher und Almanache aus der klassisch-romantischen Zeit*. Munich: Ernst Heimeran, 1954.

[Landon, Letitia Elizabeth.] L. E. L. "The Decision of the Flower." In *The Literary Souvenir; or, Cabinet of Poetry and Romance* (1825): 1–2. (With the etching *The Decision of the Flower* by W. Humphreys, from a Drawing by J. M. Wright after Retzsch, as frontispiece.)

Lange, Victor. "The Kretzschmar von Kienbusch Germanic Collection." *Princeton University Library Chronicle* 19, no. 1 (Autumn 1957): 56–58.

Langkavel, Martha. *Die französischen Übertragungen von Goethes "Faust": Ein Beitrag zur Geschichte der französischen Übersetzungskunst*. Strassburg: Karl J. Trübner, 1902.

Laugée, Thierry. "Achille Devéria et son herbier de femmes." In *L'Invention du geste amoureux: Anthropologie de la séduction dans les arts visuels de l'Antiquité à nos jours*. Ed. Valérie Boudier, Giovanni Careri, and Elinor Myara Kelif. 91–109. Bruxelles: Peter Lang, 2019.

Le Men, Ségolène. *La Cathédrale illustrée de Hugo à Monet: Regard romantique et modernité*. Paris: CNRS Éditions, 1998.

Le Men, Ségolène. "Millet et sa diffusion gravée, dans l'ère de la reproductibilité technique." In *Jean-François Millet (Au-delà de l'Angélus)*. Colloque de Cerisy. Ed. Geneviève Lacambre. 370–87. Paris: Éditions de Monza, 2002.

Lecomte, Louis-Henry. *Un comédien au XIXe siècle. Frédérick-Lemaître, étude biographique et critique, d'après des documents inédits*. 2 vols. Paris: Chez l'Auteur, 1888.

Lehner, Gilbert. *Theater-Decorationen zu W. v. Goethe's Faust: 14 Tafeln nebst illustriertem Titelblatt und drei Erklärungs-Tafeln*. Wien: Hessling & Spielmeyer, [1891].

Lelarge, André. "La première traduction française de *Faust*." *Bulletin du bibliophile et du bibliothécaire*, n.s., 11 (20 Apr 1932): 151–60.

Lemaître, Frédérick. *Souvenirs de Frédérick Lemaître, publiés par son fils avec portrait*. Paris: Paul Ollendorff, 1880.

Lemmer, Klaus J., ed. Moritz Retzsch. *Illustrationen zu Goethes Faust*. Berlin: Rembrandt Verlag, 1980.

Lemmer, Klaus J., "Moritz Retzsch und seine Illustrationen zu Goethes *Faust*." *Börsenblatt für den deutschen Buchhandel* 44, no. 69 (1988). *Aus dem Antiquariat*, no. 8: A322–25. Same text but for the last two paragraphs.

Lempertz. Berlin. 2 May 2015. Auction 1047. Auction cat.

Leu, Philipp. "Les revues littéraires et artistiques, 1890–1900. Questions de patrimonialisation et de numérisation." 2 vols. PhD diss., Université Paris-Saclay, 2016.

Lévêque, Jean-Maxime. *Édouard Despléchin, le décorateur du grand opéra à la française, 1802–1871*. Paris: L'Harmattan, 2008.

Lever, Charles. *Roland Cashel*. London: Chapman and Hall, 1850.

Limper-Herz, Karen. "A Monument of the Love of Letters: The Right Honourable Thomas Grenville and his Library." PhD diss., University College London, 2012.

Lochnan, Katharine. "Les lithographies de Delacroix pour *Faust* et le théâtre anglais des années 1820." *Nouvelles de l'estampe*, no. 87 (July 1986): 6–13.

[Lockhart, John Gibson.] "*Faust, a Drama*, by Goethe, with Translations from the German." *Quarterly Review*, 34, no. 67 (June 1826): 136–53 (On Gower's translation).

[Lockhart, John Gibson.] *Catalogue of the Library of Abbotsford*. Edinburgh: [T. Constable,] 1838.

Lohr, Günther. "Inskription des Szenischen: Zum Kontext von Goethes 'Regeln für Schauspieler' (1803)." In Corvin, ed. 1985. 162–77.

Lohrer, Liselotte, ed. With Tilman Krömer. *Cotta in Tübingen. Dokumente, Handschriften, Bücher. Aus der Cotta'schen Handschriften-Sammlung im Schiller-Nationalmuseum, Marbach*. Tübingen: [Bürgermeisteramt], 1959. Exh. cat.

Lohrer, Liselotte. *Cotta: Geschichte eines Verlags, 1659–1959*. Stuttgart: J. G. Cotta, 1959.

Maaz, Bernhard. *Vom Kult des Genies: David d'Angers' Bildnisse von Goethe bis Caspar David Friedrich*. Munich: Deutscher Kunstverlag, 2004.

Mac Orlan, Pierre. "Daragnès et les livres." In *Œuvres complètes*. Vol. 12, 2. *Masques sur mesure*. Ed. Gilbert Sigaux. 205–7. [Évreux]: Cercle du Bibliophile, [1970].

Mackall, Leonard L. "Soane's *Faust* Translation, Now First Published, from the Unique Advance Sheets Sent to Goethe in 1822." *Archiv für das Studium der neueren Sprachen und Literaturen*, n.s., 12, no. 3–4 (1904): 277–97.

MacLeod, Catriona. "The German Romantic Reading Public: *Taschenbücher* and Other Illustrated Books." In Ittmann, ed. 198–207.

Macpherson, Gerardine. *Memoirs of the Life of Anna Jameson by her Niece*. Boston: Roberts Brothers, 1878.

Magedera, Ian H. *Outsider Biographies: Savage, De Sade, Wainewright, Ned Kelly, Billy the Kid, Rimbaud and Genet: Base Crime and High Art in Biography and Bio-Fiction, 1744–2000*. Amsterdam: Rodopi, 2014.

Magirius, Heinrich, ed. für die Stiftung Weingutmuseum Hoflößnitz. *600 Jahre Hoflößnitz: Historische Weingutsanlage fotografiert von Matthias Blumhagen*. Dresden: Sandstein, 2001.

Mahl, Bernd, ed. *Das ärgerliche Leben und schreckliche Ende des vielberüchtigten Erz-Schwarzkünstlers Johannis Fausti nach den Ausgaben von G. R. Widman [sic] und J. N. Pfitzer aufs Neue herausgegeben von Hermann Kurz*. Kirchheim: Jürgen Schweier, 1990. Facsimile of first ed. Reutlingen: B. G. Kurtz, 1834.

Mahl, Bernd. "Nachwort: Faust in Geschichte und Literatur." In Mahl, ed. 243–81.

Mahl, Bernd. "Die Bühnengeschichte von Goethes *Faust*." In *Goethe Handbuch*. Vol. 2. *Dramen*. Ed. Theo Buck. 522–38. Stuttgart: J. B. Metzler, 1996.

Mahl, Bernd. *Goethes "Faust" auf der Bühne, 1806–1998: Fragment, Ideologiestück, Spieltext*. Stuttgart: J. B. Metzler, 1999.

Maierhofer, Waltraud. "Die Titelkupfer von Moritz Retzsch zu Goethes *Ausgabe letzter Hand*." *Goethe Yearbook* 21 (2014): 219–45.

Maisak, Petra. *Johann Wolfgang Goethe: Zeichnungen*. Stuttgart: Philipp Reclam Jun., 1996.

Maisak, Petra. "Illustrationen." In *Goethe Handbuch*. Vol. 4, 1. *Personen, Sachen, Begriffe A-K*. Ed. Hans-Dietrich Dahnke and Regine Otto. 513–19a. Stuttgart: J. B. Metzler, 1998.

Malaplate, Jean. "La traduction de *Faust* par Gérard de Nerval, vérité et légende." *Cahiers Gérard de Nerval*, no. 13 (1990): 9–17.

Man, Felix H. *150 Years of Artists' Lithographs, 1803–1953*. London: Heinemann, 1953.

Mandelkow, Karl Robert, ed. *Goethe im Urteil seiner Kritiker*. 4 vols. Munich: C. H. Beck, 1975–84.

Mandelkow, Karl Robert. *Goethe in Deutschland: Rezeptionsgeschichte eines Klassikers*. 2 vols. Munich: C. H. Beck, 1980.

Marck, Jan van der. *Romantische Boekillustratie in België: Van de "Voyage Pittoresque au Royaume des Pays-Bas" (1822) tot "La Légende et les aventures héroïques, joyeuses et glorieuses d'Ulenspiegel et de Lamme Goedzak au pays de Flandres et ailleurs" (1869)*. Roermond: J. J. Romen & Zonen, 1956.

Marquardt, Hertha. *Henry Crabb Robinson und seine deutschen Freunde: Brücke zwischen England und Deutschland im Zeitalter der Romantik*. 2 vols. Göttingen: Vandenhoeck & Ruprecht, 1964–67.

BOOKS, ARTICLES, DISSERTATIONS

Marquart, Lea. *Goethes Faust in Frankreich: Studien zur dramatischen Rezeption im 19. Jahrhundert.* Heidelberg: Winter, 2009.

Marx, Karl. *Capital: A Critique of Political Economy.* Vol. 1. Introd. Ernest Mandel. Trans. Ben Fowkes. London: Penguin Books, 1990.

Masia, Luca. *Buitoni, la famiglia, gli uomini, le imprese.* Milan: Silvana Editoriale / Volumnia, 2007.

Mauss, Marcel. *The Gift.* Expanded ed. Ed. and trans. Jane I. Guyer. Chicago: Hau, 2016. First published 1950.

Max, Gabriel. *Faust-Illustrationen: Zehn Zeichnungen, in Holz geschnitten von R[ichard] Brend'amour und W. Hecht. Mit einleitendem und erläuterndem Text von Richard Gosche.* Berlin: G. Grote'sche Verlagsbuchhandlung, 1880.

Mays, J. C. C. "*Faustus* on the Table at Highgate." *Wordsworth Circle* 43, no. 3 (Summer 2012): 119–27.

Mazzocca, Fernando. "L'illustrazione romantica." In *Storia dell'arte italiana.* Pt. 3. *Situazioni momenti indagini.* Vol. 2. *Grafica e immagine.* 2. *Illustrazione, fotografia.* 321–419. Turin: Giulio Einaudi, 1981.

Mazzocca, Fernando. "Andrea Maffei patrone delle arti e collezionista." In *L'Ottocento di Andrea Maffei.* Ed. Marina Botteri, Barbara Cinelli, and Fernando Mazzocca. 96–130. Riva del Garda: Museo Civico, 1987.

Mazzocca, Fernando. *Francesco Hayez: Catalogo ragionato.* Milan: Federico Motta, 1994.

Mazzocca, Fernando. "Hayez, Francesco." In *The Dictionary of Art*, ed. Jane Turner. Vol. 14:264–67. New York: Grove / Macmillan Publishers, 1996.

Mazzocca, Fernando. "Il Bacio." *Il Sole 24 Ore*, no. 154 (7 June 1998): 28. In Mazzocca, ed. *Hayez. Dal mito al Bacio.* 178–80. Venice: Marsilio, 1998.

Mazzocca, Fernando. *Francesco Hayez: Il Bacio.* Milan: Silvana Editoriale, 2009.

McIsaac, Peter M. "Rethinking Tableaux Vivants and Triviality in the Writings of Johann Wolfgang von Goethe, Johanna Schopenhauer, and Fanny Lewald." *Monatshefte* 99, no. 2 (Summer 2007): 152–76.

Medwin, Thomas. *Medwin's Conversations of Lord Byron.* Ed. Ernest J. Lovell, Jr. Princeton: Princeton University Press, 1966.

[Meusel, Johann Georg.] "Die Künstausstellung in Dresden betreffend." *Archiv für Künstler und Kunstfreunde* 1, no. 4 (1805): 101–21.

[Meusel, Johann Georg.] "Etwas über die öffentliche Ausstellung der Churfürst. Sächs. Academie der Künste in Dresden am 5. März 1806." *Archiv für Künstler und Kunstfreunde* 2, no. 1 (1807): 86–103.

[Meusel, Johann Georg.] "Etwas über die Kunstausstellung der Königl. Sächs. Akademie der Künste zu Dresden, am 5ten März 1808. Auszug eines Schreibens, an Hrn. Gr. von L." *Archiv für Künstler und Kunstfreunde* 2, no. 3 (1808): 1–16; no. 4 (1808): 135–46.

Meusel, Johann Georg. *Teutsches Künstlerlexikon oder Verzeichniss der jetztlebenden teutschen Künstler: nebst einem Verzeichniss sehenswürdiger Bibliotheken, Kunst-, Münz- und Naturalienkabinette in Teutschland und in der Schweiz.* 2nd rev. ed. 2 vols. Lemgo: in der Meyerschen Buchhaldung, 1809.

Meyer, Alfred Gotthold. "Schinkels Theaterdekorationen." *Berliner Architekturwelt* 6, nos. 11–12 (1904): 360–68, 398–408.

[Meyer, Johann Heinrich.] W. K. F. "Neu-deutsche religios-patriotische Kunst." In FA. Pt. 1. Vol. 20. Ed. Hendrik Birus. 105–69, 818–915. Frankfurt: Deutscher Klassiker Verlag, 1999. First published 1817 in *Über Kunst und Altertum* 1, no. 2.

[Meyer, Johann Heinrich.] "Äusserungen eines Kunstfreundes." In FA. Pt. 1. Vol. 22. Ed. Anne Bohnenkamp. 487–88, 1291–92. Frankfurt: Deutscher Klassiker Verlag, 1999. First published 1828 in Über *Kunst und Altertum* 4, no. 2.

Milano, Alberto. "Change of Use, Change of Public, Change of Meaning: Printed Images Travelling through Europe." In Stead, ed. 137–56.

Mix, York-Gothart, ed. *Kalender? Ey, wie viel Kalender! Literarische Almanache zwischen Rokoko und Klassizismus.* Wolfenbüttel: Herzog August Bibliothek, 1986. Exh. cat.

Mix, York-Gothart, ed. *Almanach- und Taschenbuchkultur des 18. und 19. Jahrhunderts*. Wiesbaden: O. Harrassowitz, 1996.

Möbius, Martin Richard. "Romantik und Biedermeier." *Der Cicerone. Halbmonatsschrift für die Interessen des Kunstforschers & Sammlers* 16, no. 11 (1924): 506–9.

Mojem, Helmuth, and Barbara Potthast, eds. *Johann Friedrich Cotta: Verleger—Unternehmer—Technikpionier*. Heidelberg: Universitätsverlag Winter, 2017.

Mojem, Helmuth. *Der Verleger Johann Friedrich Cotta (1764–1832): Repertorium seiner Briefe*. Marbach: Deutsche Schillergesellschaft, 1997.

Moldenhauer, Dirk. *Geschichte als Ware: Der Verleger Friedrich Christoph Perthes (1772–1843) als Wegbereiter der modernen Geschichtsschreibung*. Cologne: Böhlau, 2008.

Michon, Jacques, and Jean-Yves Mollier, eds. *Les mutations du livre et de l'édition dans le monde du XVIIIe siècle à l'an 2000. Actes du colloque international, Sherbrooke, 2000*. Saint-Nicolas (Québec): Presses de l'Université Laval / Paris: L'Harmattan, 2001.

Mollier, Jean-Yves. "Les réseaux de libraires européens au milieu du XIXe siècle: l'exemple des correspondants de la maison d'édition Michel Lévy Frères, de Paris." In Barbier, Frédéric, ed. *Est-Ouest. Transferts et réceptions dans le monde du livre en Europe (XVIIe–XXe siècles)*. 125–39. Leipzig: Leipziger Universitätsverlag, 2005. (*L'Europe en réseaux: Contributions à l'histoire de la culture écrite 1650–1918/Vernetztes Europa: Beiträge zur Kulturgeschichte des Buchwesens*.)

Mongan, Agnes. *David to Corot: French Drawings in the Fogg Art Museum*. Ed. Miriam Stewart. Cambridge, Ma: Harvard University Press, 1996.

Moore, Evelyn K., and Patricia Anne Simpson. *The Enlightened Eye: Goethe and Visual Culture*. Amsterdam: Rodopi, 2007.

[Moore.] *The Poetical Works of Thomas Moore Collected by Himself in Ten Volumes*, vol. 6. *Lalla Rookh*. London: Longman, Orme, Brown, Green & Longmans, 1841.

Moran, Daniel. *Toward the Century of Words: Johann Cotta and the Politics of the Public Realm in Germany, 1795–1832*. Berkeley: University of California Press, 1990.

Morgenstern, Karl. *Heinrich Karl Ernst Köhler: Zur Erinnerung an den Verewigten*. St Petersburg: Buchdruckerei der Kaiserlichen Akademie der Wissenschaften, 1839.

Morley, Edith J., ed. *Henry Crabb Robinson on Books and their Writers*. 3 vols. London: J. M. Dent and Sons, 1938.

Morse, B. J. "A Note on Moritz Retzsch in England." *Anglia: Zeitschrift für englische Philologie*, no. 54 (1930): 196–98.

Moschkau, Alfred. "Die Goethe-Reliquien in Auerbachs Keller in Leipzig." *Saxonia. Zeitschrift für Geschichts-, Alterthums- u. Landeskunde d. Königreichs Sachsen* 3, no. 11 (1878): 97–100.

Motion, Andrew. *Wainewright the Poisoner*. London: Faber and Faber, 2000.

[Muret.] Digital Muret. Ed. Cécile Colonna. INHA, Online https://digitalmuret.inha.fr/s/digital-muret/page/jean-baptiste-muret-1795-1866 (last accessed 19 Mar 2023).

Murray, Chris. "'Give it up in despair': Coleridge and Goethe's *Faust*." *Romanticism* 15, no. 1 (2009): 1–15.

Murray, Christopher. "Robert William Elliston's Production of *Faust*, Drury Lane, 1825." *Theatre Research* 11, no. 2–3 (1971): 102–13.

Nachod, Hans. "Goethe in der Buchillustration." Special issue "Goethe in der Buchkunst der Welt." *Archiv für Buchgewerbe und Gebrauchsgraphik* 69, no. 11–12 (1932): 513–16.

Nagler, Georg Kaspar. "Retsch [*sic*], Friedrich August Moritz." *Neues allgemeines Künstler-Lexicon*. Vol. 13:49–52. Munich: E. A. Fleischmann, 1843. 2nd unaltered ed. Vol. 14:332–335. Linz: Zentraldruckerei, 1909.

Nagler, Georg Kaspar. "Friedrich August Moritz Retzsch." *Die Monogrammisten und diejenigen bekannten und unbekannten Künstler aller Schulen*. Vol. 4:665. Munich: Georg Franz (Ed. Lotzbeck), 1871.

NDB–Neue Deutsche Biographie. Berlin: Duncker & Humblot, 1953–. Last updated 1 Dec 2016, available to vol. 27, 2020. <https://de.wikisource.org/wiki/Neue_Deutsche_Biographie>.

BOOKS, ARTICLES, DISSERTATIONS

Neidhardt, Hans Joachim. *Die Malerei der Romantik in Dresden*. Leipzig: Seemann, 1976.

Neidhardt, Hans Joachim. "Der Scharfenbergerkreis—ein Freundschaftsbund der Romantik." In Neidhardt, *Caspar David Friedrich und die Malerei der Dresdner Romantik: Aufsätze und Vorträge*. 36–42, 98–99. Leipzig: Seemann, 2005.

[Nerval, Gérard de.] *Faust, tragédie de Goëthe [sic]: nouvelle traduction complète, en prose et en vers, par Gérard*. Paris: Dondey-Dupré père et fils, Imp.-Lib., 1828.

[Nerval.] Goethe, Johann Wolfgang von. *Faust. Traduit de l'allemand par Gérard de Nerval, précédé de la légende populaire de Johann Faust, l'un des inventeurs de l'imprimerie, illustré de jolies vignettes par Éd. Frère*. Paris: J. Bry aîné, 1850.

Nerval, Gérard de. *Œuvres complètes*. Ed. Jean Guillaume and Claude Pichois. New ed. 3 vols. Paris: Gallimard, 1989–93.

Neubeck, Ludwig. "Die Uraufführung des *Faust*." 70–80. In *Buch (Das) des Goethe-Lessing-Jahres 1929*.

Neubert—Neubert, Franz, ed. *Vom Doctor Faustus zu Goethes Faust, mit 595 Abbildungen*. Mit Unterstützung des Goethe-Nationalmuseums in Weimar. Leipzig: Verlagsbuchhandlung von J. J. Weber, n.d. [1932].

Newark, Cormac. "*Faust*, Nested Reception and La Castafiore." *Cambridge Opera Journal* 25, no. 2 (July 2013): 165–84. http://dx.doi.org/10.1017/S0954586713000050.

Nicodemi, Giorgio. *Francesco Hayez*. 2 vols. Milan: Casa Editrice Ceschina, 1962.

Nicoll, Alardyce. "Faust on the English Stage." 81–86. In *Buch (Das) des Goethe-Lessing-Jahres 1929*.

Nicolovius, Alfred. "Kupferstich-Sammlung auf Goethe's Person und Werke bezüglich." In *Ueber Goethe: Literarische und artistische Nachrichten*. 413–20. Leipzig: Johann Friedrich Leich, 1828.

Niessen—Niessen, Carl, ed. *Katalog der Ausstellungen "Faust auf der Bühne," "Faust in der Bildenden Kunst." Zur Jahrhundertfeier der Uraufführung des ersten Teiles in Braunschweig veranstaltet von der Landeshauptstadt Braunschweig und der Goethe-Gesellschaft*. Berlin: Fritz Klopp, 1929.

Niessen, Carl. "Faust auf der Bühne. Ein Jahrhundert Inszenierungsgeschichte." *Westermanns Monatshefte* 146:1, no. 871 (1929): 54–64.

Nodier, Charles. "Des types en littérature." In *Œuvres de Charles Nodier*. Vol. 5:47–66. Paris: Librairie d'Eugène Renduel, 1832. Originally published Sept 1830 in *Revue de Paris*.

Nodier, Charles. "Feuilleton: Théâtre-français." *Journal des débats politiques et littéraires* (8 July 1814): 1–3. (Not 14 July as often stated).

Norman, Frederick. *Henry Crabb Robinson and Goethe*. 2 vols. Publications of the English Goethe Society, n.s., 6 and 8. London: Alexander Moring, 1930–31.

O'Leary, Patrick. *Regency Editor: Life of John Scott*. Aberdeen: Aberdeen University Press, 1983.

Odenkirchen, Stella Esther. "Moritz Retzsch, Illustrator, with Special Reference to his Relation to England." Master of Arts diss., University of Chicago, 1948.

ODNB—*Oxford Dictionary of National Biography* Online. Oxford University Press. Last update 12 May 2021.

Orcutt, Kimberly. "The American Art-Union and the Rise of a National Landscape School: Scholarly Essay." In Orcutt, Kimberly, with Allan McLeod. "Unintended Consequences: The American Art-Union and the Rise of a National Landscape School." *Nineteenth-Century Art Worldwide* 18, no. 1 (Spring 2019). https://doi.org/10.29411/ncaw.2019.18.1.14.

Ortmann, Erwin. *Figurines d'étain d'hier et d'aujourd'hui*, trans. Arlette Marinie. Paris: Stauffacher S. A. Zurich, 1973. Originally *Zinnfiguren einst und jetzt*. Leipzig: Edition Leipzig, 1973.

Oswald, Eugene. *Goethe in England and America*. Publications of the English Goethe Society, 8. London: Nutt, 1899.

Otto, Regine. "Editionen als Instrumente der Goethe-Rezeption." In *Spuren, Signaturen, Spiegelungen: zur Goethe-Rezeption in Europa*. Ed. Bernhard Beutler and Anke Bosse. 209–23. Cologne: Böhlau, 2000.

Oxford (The) Companion to Western Art. Ed. Hugh Brigstocke. With Lori-Ann Touch. Oxford: Oxford University Press, 2001.

Oxford Dictionary of National Biography. Online version, https://doi-org.janus.biu.sorbonne.fr/10.1093/ref:odnb/19394.

Palacio, Jean de. "Décadence de Faust." In *Mythes de la décadence.* Ed. Alain Montandon. 37–46. Clermont-Ferrand: Presses Universitaires Blaise Pascal, 2001.

Pantazzi, Sybille. "A Versatile Victorian Designer: His Designs for Book Covers. John Leighton, 1822–1912." *Connoisseur,* 152 (Apr 1963): 262–73.

Parenth, Ulrich, *Wie Goethes "Faust" auf die Bühne kam.* Braunschweig: Gerd J. Holtzmeyer Verlag, 1986.

Paul, Claude. "Der Teufel in den Faust-Vertonungen von Berlioz, Gounod und Boito: Wenn Körper, Raum und Musik das Unvorstellbare darstellen." In *Von Teufeln, Tänzen und Kastraten: Die Oper als transmediales Spektakel.* Ed. Maria Imhof and Anke Grutschus. 7–38. Bielefeld: Transcript, 2015.

Paul, Claude. *Les Métamorphoses du diable: Méphistophélès dans les œuvres faustiennes de Goethe, Lenau, Delacroix et Berlioz.* Paris: Champion, 2015.

Paulin, Roger, William St Clair, and Elinor Shaffer, "Goethe's *Faust* and Coleridge. 'A Gentleman of Literary Eminence': A Review Essay." School of Advanced Study, University of London. Published online 2008. http://www.ies.sas.ac.uk/4530/.

Pavie, André. *Médaillons romantiques: Lettres inédites de Sainte-Beuve, David d'Angers, Mme Victor Hugo, Mme Ménessier-Nodier, Paul Foucher, Victor Pavie, etc.* Paris: Émile Paul, 1909.

Pavie, Victor. *Goëthe [sic] et David, souvenirs d'un voyage à Weimar.* Angers: Impr. P. Lachèse, Belleuvre et Dolbeau, 1874.

Pavie, Victor. *Voyages et promenades romantiques.* Ed. Guy Trigalot. Rennes: PUR, 2015.

Peckus, Sarunas (Sharkey), and Ben Rapaport. *The European Porcelain Tobacco Pipe: Illustrated History for Collectors. Photography by Darius Peckus.* Atglen, Pa.: Schiffer, 2014.

[Perthes & Besser.] *Verzeichnis der vom July bis December 1816 hrsg. neuen Bücher welche zu haben sind in Perthes und Besser's Buchhanlung in Hamburg.* n.d. [1816].

Perthes, Clemens Theodor. *Friedrich Perthes Leben nach dessen schriftlichen und mündlichen Mittheilungen aufgezeichnet.* 3 vols. Hamburg: F. und A. Perthes, 1848–55.

Perthes, Friedrich Christoph. *Der deutsche Buchhandel als Bedingung des Daseyns einer deutschen Literatur: Illustrierter Neudruck der Ausgabe von 1816.* Siegburg: Bernstein, 2018.

Petersen, Julius. *Goethes "Faust" auf der deutschen Bühne: Eine Jahrundertbetrachtung mit 16 Tafeln.* Leipzig: Verlag von Quelle & Meyer, 1929.

Pfäfflin, Anna Marie. "Bühnenbild und inszenierter Raum. Zum Konzept des Theatralischen im Werk von Karl Friedrich Schinkel." *Jahrbuch der Berliner Museen* 56 (2014): 111–21.

Picat-Guinoiseau, Ginette. *Une œuvre méconnue de Charles Nodier. "Faust", imité de Goethe, édition commentée, avec une introduction sur "Les deux Faust de Charles Nodier."* Paris: Didier, 1977.

Pichot, Amédée. *Voyage historique et littéraire en Angleterre et en Écosse.* 3 vols. Paris: Ladvocat & Charles Gosselin, 1825.

Pierrepont, Charles Evelyn, Viscount Newark. "The German Lovers." In *The Keepsake for 1835.* Ed. by Frederic Mansel Reynolds. 169–70. London: Longman, Rees, Orme, Brown, Green, and Longman; Paris: Rittner and Goupil; Berlin: A. Asher, 1835. (With an engraving by Charles Heath after Retzsch's pl. 19 in *Das Lied von der Glocke*).

Pieske, Christa, ed. *Bürgerliches Wandbild 1840–1920: Populäre Druckgraphik aus Deutschland, Frankreich und England.* Sammlung Dr. Christa Pieske. Göttingen: E. Goltze, 1977.

Pieske, Christa. *Bilder für Jedermann: Wandbilddrucke 1840–1940.* Mit einem Beitrag von Konrad Vanja. Berlin: Keyser, 1988.

Pinéas. *Dessin linéaire, ornement: Exercices gradués de dessin linéaire et de dessin d'ornement. Lignes droites, Lignes brisées, Lignes courbes. 1848.* 1st series. Paris, 9 Rue Sainte-Appoline: Se trouve chez l'auteur, 1848.

BOOKS, ARTICLES, DISSERTATIONS

Piper, Andrew. *Dreaming in Books: The Making of the Bibliographical Imagination in the Romantic Age*. Chicago: University of Chicago Press, 2009.

Plötz-Peters, Hannelore. "Porzellane der KPM Berlin für den polnisch-preußischen Fürsten Radziwill." *Keramos* 246 (2019): 25–34.

Poe, Edgar Allan. "The Man of the Crowd." In *Collected Works of Edgar Allan Poe*. Ed. Thomas Ollive Mabbott, with the assistance of Eleanor D. Kewer and Maureen C. Mabbott. Vol. 2:505–18. Cambridge, Ma.: The Belknap Press of Harvard University Press, 1978. First published Dec 1840 in the *Casket* and (Burton's) *Gentleman's Magazine*.

Poe, Edgar Allan. "*Ballads and Other Poems*. By Henry Wadsworth Longfellow." In *Essays and Reviews*. Ed. G. R. Thompson. 683–96. New York: Literary Classics of the United States, 1984. First published Apr 1842 in *Graham's Magazine*.

Pollock, Walter Herries. *The Picture's Secret*. In *The Picture's Secret, A Story, to Which is added an Episode in the Life of Mr. Latimer*. 3–224. London: Remington and Co., 1883.

[Pollock, Walter Harries.] "*Faust* at the Lyceum." *National Review* 6, no. 36 (Feb 1886): 833–37.

Pollock, Walter Harries. "Illustrations of *Faust*." *Temple Bar, to which is incorporated Bentley's Miscellany* 78 (Dec 1886): 528–33.

[Pollock, Walter Harries.] "Mephistopheles at the Lyceum." *Longman's Magazine* 10, no. 57 (July 1887): 294–99.

Pons, A.-J. "Notice artistique." In Goethe. *Faust, première partie, préface et traduction de H. Blaze de Bury, onze eaux-fortes de Lalauze, gravures de Méaulle d'après Wogel et Scott*. 261–70. Paris: A. Quantin, 1880.

Prause, Marianne, ed. *Die Kataloge der Dresdner Akademie-Ausstellungen, 1801–1850*. 2 vols. Berlin: B. Hessling, 1975.

Proescholdt-Obermann, Catherine Waltraud. *Goethe and his British Critics: The Reception of Goethe's Works in British Periodicals, 1779 to 1855*. Frankfurt: Peter Lang, 1992.

Proescholdt, Catherine W. "Johann Christian Hüttner (1766–1847): a Link between Weimar and London." In *Goethe and the English-Speaking World: Essays from the Cambridge Symposium for his 250th Anniversary*. Ed. Nicholas Boyle and John Guthrie. 99–110. Rochester, NY: Camden House, 2002.

Property from Two Ducal Collections, Woburn Abbey, Bedfordshire. Auction Christie, Manson and Woods, 20–21 Sept 2004.

RA—*Briefe an Goethe. Gesamtausgabe in Regestform*. Ed. Klassik Stiftung Weimar, Goethe- und Schiller-Archiv. Vol. 1–. Weimar: H. Böhlaus Nachfolger, 1980–.

Raczyński, Atanazy. *Geschichte der neueren deutschen Kunst*. Trans. from the French Friedr. Heinr. von der Hagen. 3 vols. Berlin: Auf Kosten des Verfassers, 1836–41.

Ramsden, Charles. *London Bookbinders, 1780–1840*. London: B. T. Batsford, 1956.

Reber, Franz von. *Geschichte der neueren deutschen Kunst: Vom Ende des vorigen Jahrhunderts bis zur Wiener Ausstellung 1873; mit Berücksichtigung der gleichzeitigen Kunstentwicklung in Frankreich, Belgien, Holland, England, Italien und den Ostseeländern*. Stuttgart: Meyer & Zeller's Verlag (Fr. Vogel), 1876.

Reed, Sue W. "F. O. C. Darley's Outline Illustrations." In *The American Illustrated Book in the Nineteenth Century*. Ed. Gerald W. R. Ward. 113–35. Winterthur, Del.: Henry Francis du Pont Winterthur Museum, 1987.

Reibel, Emmanuel. *Faust. La musique au défi du mythe*. Paris: Fayard, 2008.

Reifenscheid, Beate. "Die Kunst des Kupferstichs oder der Kupferstich als Kunst im Almanach." In Mix, ed. 1996. 143–65.

Retzsch's Outlines to Buerger's Ballads/Umrisse zu Buerger's Balladen. Fünfzehn Platten, Fifteen Plates erfunden und gestochen von Moritz Retzsch. Mit Buergers Text und Erklaerungen von Carl Borromaeus von Miltitz. Nebst englisher Uebersetzung von F. Shoberl. Leipzig: Ernst Fleischer; London: Sold by Black and Armstrong, 1840.

Riga, Frank P., and Claude A. Prance. *Index to the London Magazine*. New York: Garland Publishing, 1978.

Robertson, Ritchie. "*Faustus: From the German of Goethe.* Trans. Samuel Taylor Coleridge. Ed. Frederick Burwick James C. McKusick." *Translation and Literature* 17, no. 2 (2008): 247–50.

Roger, Christine. *La réception de Shakespeare en Allemagne de 1815 à 1850: Propagation et assimilation de la référence étrangère.* Bern: Peter Lang, 2008.

Rohde, Carsten, ed. *Faust-Sammlungen. Genealogien—Medien—Musealität.* Frankfurt: Klostermann, 2018.

Rohde, Carsten, Thorsten Valk, and Mathias Mayer, eds. With Annete Schöneck. *Faust-Handbuch. Konstellationen—Diskurse—Medien.* Stuttgart: J. B. Metzler, 2018.

Rohde, Carsten. "Faust populär. Zur Transformation 'klassischer' Werke in der modernen Massen- und Populärkultur." *Oxford German Studies* 45, no. 4 (2016): 380–92.

Rohde, Carsten. *Faust-Ikonologie: Stoff und Figur in der Bildkultur des 19. Jahrhunderts.* Stuttgart: J. B. Metzler, 2020.

Roque, Georges, and Luciano Celes, eds., "L'Image recyclée." Special issue, *Figures de l'art*, no. 23 (2013).

Rose, William, ed. *Essays on Goethe.* London: Cassell & Co., 1949.

Rose, William. "Goethe's Reputation in England during his Lifetime." In Rose, ed. 1949. 141–85.

Rosenbaum, Alexander. "Bildende Kunst." In Rohde, Valk, and Mayer, eds. 2018. 174–84.

Rosenblum, Robert. *Transformations in Late Eighteenth Century Art.* 3rd repr. Princeton, NJ: Princeton University Press, 1974. First published 1967.

Rosenblum, Robert. *The International Style of 1800. A Study in Linear Abstraction.* New York: Garland Publishing, 1976. PhD diss., 1956.

Rosenkranz, Karl. *Zur Geschichte der deutschen Literatur.* Königsberg: Gebrüder Bornträger, 1836.

Ross, Ronald. *Memoirs, with a Full Account of the Great Malaria Problem and its Solution.* London: John Murray, 1923.

Rümann, Arthur. *Das illustrierte Buch des XIX. Jahrhunderts in England, Frankreich und Deutschland, 1790–1860.* Leipzig: Insel, 1930.

Ruskin, John. *The Works of John Ruskin.* Library edition. Ed. E. T. Cook and Alexander Wedderburn. 39 vols. London: George Allen, 1903–12.

Ruskin, John. "Of the Imaginative Faculty." In *The Works.* Vol. 4. *Modern Painters. Vol. II.* 223–332.

Ruskin, John. "The Elements of Drawing." In *The Works.* Vol. 15: 25–228. First published 1857.

Ruskin, John. "The Art of England." In *The Works.* Vol. 33: 265–408. Published in parts 1883, in volume form 1884.

Ruskin, John. "The Black Arts. A Reverie in the Strand." In *The Works.* Vol. 14: 357–64. First published 1887.

[Russell, Charles William.] "Faust; a Tragedy." *Dublin Review* 9, no. 18 (Nov 1840): 477–506.

Russo, Wilhelm. *Goethes "Faust" auf den Berliner Bühnen.* Berlin: Emil Ebering, 1924.

Ruttmann, Irene. "Goethes Modell eines antinaturalistischen Theaters." In Corvin, ed. 1985. 180–202.

Sauer, Kurt. "Das Theater." In Bollert, ed. 1932. 166–69.

Saxl, Fritz. "Illustrated Mediaeval Encyclopaedias. 2. The Christian Transformation." In *Lectures.* Vol. 1: 242–54. London: The Warburg Institute, 1957.

Schanze, Helmut. *Faust-Konstellationen: Mythos und Medien.* Munich: W. Fink, 1999.

Schieth, Lydia, ed. *Fürs schöne Geschlecht: Frauenalmanache zwischen 1800 und 1850.* Bamberg: Staatsbibliothek, 1992. Exh. cat.

Schieth, Lydia. "'Huldigung den Frauen': Frauentaschenbücher in der ersten Hälfte des 19. Jahrhunderts." In Klussmann and Mix, eds. 1998. 83–100.

Schillemeit, Jost. "Goethe und Radziwill." In *Das eine Nation die andere verstehen möge. Festschrift für Marian Szyrocki.* 639–62. Amsterdam: *Chloe. Beihefte zur Daphnis*, 1988.

Schlegel, August Wilhelm. "Über Zeichnungen zu Gedichten und John Flaxman's Umrisse." *Athenaeum. Eine Zeitschrift von August Wilhelm Schlegel und Friedrich Schlegel* 2, no. 2 (1799): 193–246. In *Fotomechanischer Nachdruck der Ausgabe* Berlin, Frölich, 1799. Darmstadt:

BOOKS, ARTICLES, DISSERTATIONS

Wissenschaftliche Buchgesellschaft, 1960. Digitale Edition von Jochen A. Bär (Vechta 2014), http://www.zbk-online.de/texte/A0002.htm.

Schlegel, August Wilhem. "Vorrede"/"Introduction." In Bohte, J. H. *Handbibliothek der deutschen Litteratur*. Trans. John Black. IV–XXIII.

Schmidt, Otto Eduard. *Fouqué, Apel, Miltitz: Beiträge zur Geschichte der deutschen Romantik*. Leipzig: Dürr, 1908.

Schnurmann, Claudia, ed. *A Sea of Love: The Atlantic Correspondence of Francis and Mathilde Lieber, 1839–1845*. Leiden: Brill, 2018.

Schnurmann, Claudia. *Brücken aus Papier: Atlantischer Wissenstransfer in dem Briefnetzwerk des deutsch-amerikanischen Ehepaars Francis und Mathilde Lieber, 1827–1872*. Berlin: LIT, 2014.

Schöne, Albrecht. *Johann Wolfgang Goethe. Faust. Kommentare*. Berlin: Deutscher Klassiker Verlag, 2017.

[Schorn, Ludwig.] S. "Neue Kupferstiche." *Kunst-Blatt* no. 45 (3 June 1824): 177–78. (On Retzsch's *Fridolin* and *Faust*).

[Schorn, Ludwig.] S. "Neue Kupferstiche." *Kunst-Blatt*, no. 23 (21 Mar 1825): 89–90. (On Retzsch's *Kampf mit dem Drachen*).

Schorn, Ludwig. "Besuch bey Flaxman im July 1826." *Kunst-Blatt*, no. 29 (9 Apr 1827): 113–15; no. 30 (12 Apr 1827): 118–20; no. 31 (16 Apr 1827): 123–24.

Schreiber, Carl F. "Goethe, Byron, *Faust* und eine Amerikanerin." *Philobiblon. Eine Zeitschrift für Bücherliebhaber/A Magazine for Book-Collectors* 5, no. 2 (1932): 43–45.

Schreiber, Carl F. "Coleridge to Boosey—Boosey to Coleridge." *Yale University Library Gazette* 22, no. 1 (July 1947): 6–10.

Schubarth, Maria. "'… selbst nicht so vollkommen gedacht …': zeitgenössische Illustrationen Goethes." In *Goethe-Spuren: In Literatur, Kunst, Philosophie, Politik, Pädagogik und Übersetzung*. Ed. Detlef Ignasiak and Frank Lindner. 139–49. Bucha bei Jena: Quartus-Verlag, 2009.

Schumacher, Doris. *Kupfer und Poesie: Die Illustrationskunst um 1800 im Spiegel der zeitgenössischen deutschen Kritik*. Cologne: Bölhau, 2000.

Schuster, Peter-Klaus. "'Flaxman der Abgott aller Dilettanten.' Zu einem Dilemma des klassischen Goethe und den Folgen." In Hofmann, ed. 1979. 32–35.

[Scott, John.] "The Lion's Head." *London Magazine* 2, no. 7 (July 1820): 3–8.

Seeliger, Stephan. "Zur Editionsgeschichte der *Faust*-Bilder von Peter Cornelius." *Aus dem Antiquariat*, no. 7 (1988): A277–83.

Seifert, Siegfried. *Goethe-Bibliographie 1950–1990*. With Rosel Gutsell and Hans-Jürgen Malles. 3 vols. Munich: K. G. Saur, 2000.

[Shelley.] *The Letters of Percy Bysshe Shelley*. Ed. Frederick L. Jones. 2 vols. Oxford: Clarendon Press, 1964.

Siegel, Jonah. "Black Arts, Ruined Cathedrals, and the Grave in Engraving: Ruskin and the Fatal Excess of Art." *Victorian Literature and Culture* 27, no. 2 (1999): 395–417.

Sigismund, Ernst. "Moritz Retzsch." *Neueste Nachrichten. Beilage*, no. 15 (15 Jan 1901).

Sigismund, Ernst. "Retzsch, Moritz." In Vollmer, Hans, ed., *Allgemeines Lexikon der Bildenden Künstler von der Antike bis zur Gegenwart*. Vol. 28:193b–94. Leipzig: E. A. Seemann, 1934.

Sigismund, Ernst. "Zimmermann, Friedrich August." In Thieme-Becker. *Allgemeines Lexikon der Bildenden Künstler*. Vol. 36:510b. Leipzig: E. A. Seemann, 1947.

Singer, Hans Wolfgang, ed. "Retzsch, Friedrich August Moritz." *Allgemeines Künstler-Lexikon. Leben und Werke der berühmtesten Bildenden Künstler*, vorbereitet von Hermann Alexander Müller. 3rd ed. rev. and enlarged. Vol. 4:47. Frankfurt: Rütter & Loening, 1901. Unaltered 1922 in 6th ed.

Singer, Hans Wolfgang. "Die Weinbergsszenen von Moritz Retzsch." *Mitteilungen aus den sächsischen Kunstsammlungen* 5 (1914): 82–88.

Skerl, Beate. "Studien zu Leben und Werk des Dresdner Malers Moritz Retzsch." Diploma diss., Greifswald, 1993.

Sloane, William M. "George Bancroft—in Society, in Politics, in Letters." *Century Magazine* 33, no. 3 (Jan 1887): 473–87.

Soane, George. "Preface." In *Extracts from Göthe's Tragedy of Faustus, Explanatory of the Plates, by Retsch, Intended to Illustrate that Work. Translated by George Soane*. 3. London: Printed for J. H. Bohte, 1820.

[Soane George.] "Faustus. Dedication." In FA. Pt. 1. Vol. 21. Ed. Stefan Greif and Andrea Ruhlig. 447–48. Frankfurt: Deutscher Klassiker Verlag, 1998. (Erroneously attributed to Lord Leveson-Gower).

Solanki, Tanvi. "A Book of Living Paintings: Tableaux Vivants in Goethe's *Die Wahlverwandtschaften* (1809)." *Goethe Yearbook* 23 (2016): 245–70.

Spiegel, Régis J. "Réception de la peinture romantique allemande en France au XIXᵉ siècle." PhD diss., Université de Strasbourg, 2002.

Spiess, Helmut. *Goethe, Eckermann und "Faust auf der Bühne."* Dingelstädt (Eichsfeld): Gedruckt bei Josef Heinevetter, 1933. PhD diss., Iena, 1933.

Spitzer, Gerd. "Caspar David Friedrich, Johann Christian Dahl und die Professur für Landschaftsmalerei an der Kunstakademie." *Dresden Hefte. Beiträge zur Kulturgeschichte*, no. 120 (2014/4): 15–24.

Sponsel, Jean-Louis, ed. *Fürsten-Bildnisse aus dem Hause Wettin*. Königlich Sächsischer Altertumsverein. Dresden: Wilhelm Baensch, 1906.

Staël Holstein, Baroness. "Faustus." In *Germany*. Trans. from the French. 3 vols. Vol. 2:181–226. London: John Murray, 1813.

Stapfer, Albert. "Préface." In Goethe. *Faust. Tragédie de M. de Goethe, traduite en français par M. Albert Stapfer. Ornée d'un portrait de l'auteur et de dix-sept dessins composés d'après les principales scènes de l'ouvrage et exécutés sur pierre par M. Eugène Delacroix*. I–IV. Paris: Ch. Motte, éditeur, imprimeur-lithographe, et Sautelet, libraire, 1828.

Starobinski, Jean. "La vision de la dormeuse." In *Trois fureurs*. 129–62. Paris: Gallimard, 1974.

Stead, Évanghélia, and Hélène Védrine, eds. "Imago & Translatio." Special issue, *Word & Image* 30, no. 3 (July–September 2014).

Stead, Evanghelia, ed. *Reading Books and Prints as Cultural Objects*. Cham: Palgrave / Macmillan, 2018.

Stead, Évanghélia. "Les deux *Faust I* d'Engelbert Seibertz, illustrateur *in-folio* de Goethe." In "Lire avec des images au XIXᵉ siècle en Europe." Ed. E. Stead. Special issue, *La Lecture littéraire*, no. 5–6 (2002): 45–57.

Stead, Évanghélia. "Le voyage des images du *Faust I* de Goethe: Lecture, réception et iconographie extensive et intensive au XIXᵉ siècle." In *L'Image à la lettre*. Ed. Nathalie Preiss and Joëlle Raigneau. 137–68. Paris: Paris-Musées / Les Éditions des Cendres, 2005.

Stead, Évanghélia. "Les tribulations d'une série gravée d'après le *Faust I* de Goethe: le cas de Moritz Retzsch entre l'Allemagne, l'Angleterre et la France." In *Interkulturelle Kommunikation in der europäischen Druckgraphik im 18. und 19. Jahrhundert*. Ed. Philippe Kaenel and Rolf Reichardt. 689–716. Hildesheim: Olms, 2007.

Stead, Évanghélia. *La Chair du livre: matérialité, imaginaire et poétique du livre fin-de-siècle*. Paris: PUPS, 2012. Repr. 2013.

Stead, Evanghelia. "*Faust*-Bilder: Uses and Abuses of 'Illustration' in Faust Literature and Faust Collecting. The Case of Alexander Tille." In Rohde, ed. 2018. 151–74.

Stead, Evanghelia. "Introduction." In Stead, ed. 2018. 1–30.

Stead, Evanghelia. "Monumental German *Faust* Editions in International Circulation and Multimedia Modernity." *Quaerendo. A Journal Devoted to Manuscripts and Printed Books* 50, no. 4 (2020): 362–94. doi:10.1163/15700690-12341473.

Stead, Evanghelia. "Extensive and Intensive Iconography: Goethe's *Faust* Outlined." *Artl@s Bulletin* 10, no. 1 (2021): Article 4. Online. https://docs.lib.purdue.edu/artlas/vol10/iss1/4/.

Steckelings, Karlheinz W. *Leuchtender Stein: Die Geschichte der Lithophanie vom 18. bis ins 20. Jahrhundert*. Düsseldorf: Hetjens-Museum; Dresden: Sandstein, 2013.

Steig, Michael. *Dickens and Phiz*. Bloomington: Indiana University Press, 1978.

BOOKS, ARTICLES, DISSERTATIONS

Stelzig, Eugene L. *Henry Crabb Robinson in Germany: A Study in Nineteenth-Century Life Writing.* Lewisburg, Pa: Bucknell University Press, 2010.

Stith, Mrs Townshend [Catharine Potter.] *Thoughts on Female Education.* Philadelphia: Printed by Clarke and Raser, 1831. https://babel.hathitrust.org/cgi/pt?id=hvd.32044011418860&view=1up&seq=15.

Stith, Mrs Townshend [Catharine Potter.] "The Chest of Bones," *Godey's Lady's Book* (Apr 1833): 145–59a.

Stumme, Gerhard. "Über den Göttinger Nachstich der Retzschschen Umrisse zu Goethes Faust." *Archiv für Buchgewerbe und Gebrauchsgraphik* 69, nos. 11–12 (1932): 548c.

Stumme, Gerhard. *Faust als Pantomime und Ballett.* Leipzig: Druck der Offizin Poeschel & Trepte, 1942.

Stumme, Gerhard, *Meine Faust-Sammlung.* Ed. Hans Henning, Weimar: Jahresgabe der Nationalen Forschungs- und Gedenkstätten der klassischen deutschen Literatur in Weimar, 1957.

Symmons, Sarah. *Flaxman and Europe: The Outline Illustrations and Their Influence.* New York: Garland Publishing, 1984.

Taylor of Norwich, William. "Faustus, a Tragedy, by Goethe." *Monthly Review; or, Literary Journal Enlarged. Appendix* 62 (May–Aug 1810): 491–95.

Taylor, Barry. "Thomas Grenville (1755–1846) and His Books." In *Libraries within the Library: The Origins of the British Library's Printed Collections.* Ed. Giles Mandelbrote and Barry Taylor. 321–40. London: British Library, 2009.

[Teichmann.] *Johann Valentin Teichmanns literarischer Nachlass.* Ed. Franz Dingelstedt. Stuttgart: J. G. Cotta, 1863.

Tg—Goethe, Johann Wolfgang. *Tagebücher: Historisch-kritische Ausgabe im Auftrag der Stiftung Weimarer Klassik.* Vol. 1–. Stuttgart: J. B. Metzler, 1998–.

Tille, Alexander. "The Artistic Treatment of the Faust Legend." *Publications of the English Goethe Society.* No VII. *Transactions 1891–1892.* 151–224. London: Published for the Society by David Nutt, 1893.

Tille, Alexander. "Die Bilder zu Goethes *Faust.*" *Preußische Jahrbücher* 72, no. 2 (May 1893): 264–99.

Tille, Alexander. *Bilderverzeichnis der Bode-Tilleschen Faust-Galerie, zur Ausstellung im Zusstellungssaale des Archiv- und Bibliothekgebäudes der Stadt Köln vom 5. bis 30. November 1899.* Cologne: J. G. Schmitz (F. Sohn & J. F. Laué), 1899. Exh. cat.

Tille, Alexander. "Goethe und die deutschen Bilder zu seinem *Faust.* Mit zwei Einschaltbildern und sechzehn Textabbildungen aus der Bode-Tilleschen Faustgalerie." *Velhagen & Klasings Monatshefte* 15:2, no. 10 (June 1901): 393–412.

Timm, Regine, ed. *Die Kunst der Illustration: Deutsche Buchillustration des 19. Jahrhunderts.* Hannovre: Herzog August Bibliothek Wolfenbüttel; Weinheim: Acta Humaniora / VCH, 1986. Exh. cat.

Timm, Regine, ed. *Buchillustration im 19. Jahrhundert.* Wiesbaden: Im Kommission bei Otto Harrassowitz, 1988.

Todd, David. *Free Trade and its Enemies in France, 1814–1851.* Cambridge: Cambridge University Press, 2015.

Turkle, Sherry, ed., *Evocative Objects: Things We Think With.* Cambridge, Ma.: MIT Press, 2007.

Twyman, Michael. "Charles Joseph Hullmandel: Lithographic Printer Extraordinary." In *Lasting Impressions: Lithography as Art.* Ed. Pat Gilmour. 42–90. Canberra: Australian National Gallery, 1988.

Twyman, Michael. *Early Lithographed Books: A Study of the Design and Production of Improper Books in the Age of the Hand Press, with A Catalogue.* London: Farrand Press / Private Libraries Association, 1990.

Uhlig, Stefan H. "Frederick Burwick and James C. McKusick (eds), *Faustus: From the German of Goethe,* Translated by Samuel Taylor Coleridge." *Review of English Studies* 61, no. 251 (Sept 2010): 645–48. https://doi-org.janus.bis-sorbonne.fr/10.1093/res/hgq052.

Ulrich, Laurel Thatcher, Ivan Gaskell, Sara J. Schechner, and Sarah Anne Carter. *Tangible Things: Making History Through Objects. With Photographs by Samantha S. B. van Gerbig.* New York: Oxford University Press, 2015.

Vaughan, William. "F. A. M. Retzsch and the Outline Style." In *German Romanticism and English Art.* 123–54. New Haven: Published for the Paul Mellon Centre for Studies in British Art by Yale University Press, 1979.

Verweyen, Theodor, and Gunther Witting. *Die Parodie in der neueren deutschen Literatur: Eine systematische Einführung.* Darmstadt: Wissenschaftliche Buchgesellschaft, 1979.

Verweyen, Theodor, and Gunther Witting. *Die Kontrafaktur: Vorlage und Verarbeitung in Literatur, Bildender Kunst, Werbung und politischen Plakat.* Konstanz: Universitätsverlag, 1987.

Vilain, Robert. "*Faust, Part One* and France: Stapfer's Translation, Delacroix's Lithographs, Goethe's Responses." *Publications of the English Goethe Society* 81, no. 2 (June 2012): 73–135. doi:10.1179/0959368312Z.0000000006.

Villa, Luisa. "Mrs Felix Lorraine and Lady Caroline Lamb: Byronic Lore in *Vivian Grey*, Part I." *L'analisi linguistica e letteraria* 27, no. 1 (2019): 41–52.

Villeneuve-Bargemon, Bertrand de. *Alexandre de Laborde.* [Neuilly-sur-Seine]: IBAcom, 2011.

Vogel, Gerd-Helge. "Bildhafte Sprache und sprechende Bilder: Anmerkungen zum Einfluß der Werke Goethes auf Bildfindungen der Dresdener Romantiker." *Anzeiger des Germanischen Nationalmuseums* (1999): 177–202.

Vogel, Gerd-Helge. "Das Spiel der Könige. Ein Bild von M. A. Retzsch—eines in Vergessenheit geratenen Künstlers aus dem Umfeld von König Johann von Sachsen." *Sächsische Heimat Blätter,* no. 6 (1999): 359–65.

Vogel, Gerd-Helge. "Faust und Gretchen—Goethes Drama in den Umrissstichen und -zeichnungen von Moritz August Retzsch." In *"Man halte sich ans fortschreitende Leben ...": über Goethe und Goethezeitliches aus Güstrower Sicht.* Ed. Erwin Neumann, Dieter Pocher, Volker Probst. 19–25. Güstrow: Heidberg Verlag, 1999.

Vogel, Gerd-Hegel. "'Vivat Bacchus, Bacchus lebe ...' Wein, Weingott und Winzerleben. Moritz August Retzschs Winzerzug von 1840." In Magirius, ed. 2001. 154–62.

Vogel, Gerd-Helge. "Moritz August Retzschs Annäherung an Goethe im poetischen Motiv der 'exempla amoris'." *Anzeiger des Germanischen Nationalmuseums* (2008): 61–82.

Voïart, Élise. "Avertissement." In Schiller. *Fridolin: 8 dessins de Retzsch.* Trans. É. Voïart. 5–8. Paris: Audot, 1829.

Vuaroqueaux, Georges-André. "L'édition populaire au milieu du XIXe siècle: L'exemple de la famille Bry." Master diss., Université Paris X-Nanterre, 1989.

WA—*Goethes Werke* (Weimarer Ausgabe). Ed. on behalf of the Großherzogin Sophie von Sachsen. Four Pts. 143 vols. Weimar: Böhlau, 1887–1919.

Wadepuhl, Walter. "Hüttner, a New Source for Anglo-German Relations." *Germanic Review: Literature, Culture, Theory* 14 (1939): 23–27.

Wahl, Hans, ed. *Die sieben Zeichnungen Goethes zu seinem "Faust."* Weimar: Den Freunden des Goethehauses, 1925.

Waliszewski, Kazimierz. *Paul the First of Russia, the Son of Catherine the Great.* London: Heinemann, 1911. Reprint Miami, Fla.: Hardpress, [2013].

[Wallenstein, Jules de.] "Retzsch's Illustrations of Faust." In *Illustrations of the Celebrated Tragedy of Faustus by Goethe Engraved & Published by Henry Stone.* 1–4. Washington City: H. Stone, 1824.

Wartusch, Rüdiger. "Neue Spuren der ersten Aufführungen von Szenen aus dem *Faust.*" *Goethe-Jahrbuch* 113 (1996): 309–13.

Watts, Alaric Alfred. *Alaric Watts: A Narrative of his Life, by His Son.* 2 vols. London: Richard Bentley and Son, 1884.

Watts, Alaric. "The Deveria Family." *The Literary Souvenir; or, Cabinet of Poetry and Romance* (1832): 325–26.

BOOKS, ARTICLES, DISSERTATIONS

Watts, Alaric. "The First Kiss: A Poetical Sketch." In *The Literary Souvenir; or, Cabinet of Poetry and Romance* (1826): 280–84. (With the etching *The Kiss* by W. Humphreys, from a Drawing by J. M. Wright after Retzsch).

Watts, Alaric. "A Scene from Faust." In Watts, Alaric. *Lyrics of the Heart and Other Poems with 49 Engravings on Steel* (London: Brown, Green and Longmans, 1851), 141–45. (With *Gretchen at the Spinning Wheel* by Madame Colin, engraved by W. Ensom).

Weathercock, Janus [Thomas Wainewright.] "Sentimentalities on the Fine Arts (To Be Continued when He Is in the Humour) no. 1." *London Magazine* 1, no. 2 (Feb 1820): 136–40.

[Weathercock, Janus.] "Janus's Jumble: Enterlaced with Hys Iourney to Town Whereunto is Annexed a Delectable Discourse of Hys Visite to the Exhibition, and to Covent-Garden Theatre: With Sundrie Other Most Absolute Criticisms; Very Fit for Young Courtiers to Peruse, and Coy Dames to Remember." *London Magazine* 1, no. 6 (June 1820): 625–34.

[Weathercock, Janus.] "Mr. Weathercock's Private Correspondence, Intended for the Public Eye. George's Coffee House, Tuesday, 8th August, 1820." *London Magazine* 2, no. 9 (Sept 1820): 229 [*sic* for 299]–301.

[Weathercock, Janus.] "C. Van Vinkbooms, his Dogmas for Dilettanti, no. II. Giulio Romano." *London Magazine* 4, no. 22 (Oct 1821): 418–25.

[Weathercock, Janus.] "C. Van Vinkbooms, his Dogmas for Dilettanti, no. III." *London Magazine* 4, no. 24 (Dec 1821): 655–64.

Webb, Timothy. *The Violet in the Crucible: Shelley and Translation*. Oxford: Clarendon Press, 1976.

Wegner, Peter-Christian. *Literatur auf Porzellan und Steingut und in anderem Kunsthandwerk.* Lönneker, Stadtoldendorf: Verlag Jörg Mitzkat Holzminden, 2012.

Wegner—Wegner, Wolfgang. *Die Faustdarstellung vom 16. Jahrhundert bis zur Gegenwart, mit 90 Abbildungen*. Amsterdam: Verlag der Erasmus Buchhandlung, 1962.

Wegner, Wolfgang. "*Faust*, Faust-Illustration." In *Reallexikon zur deutschen Kunstgeschichte*. Ed. Zentralinstitut für Kunstgeschichte begonnen von Otto Schmitt. Vol. 7:col. 848–66. Munich: Beck, 1981.

Wende-Hohenberger, Waltraud, and Karl Riha, eds. *Faust Parodien: Eine Auswahl satirischer Kontrafakturen, Fort- und Weiterdichtungen mit einem Nachwort*. Frankfurt: Insel, 1989.

Wende, Waltraud. *Goethe-Parodien: zur Wirkungsgeschichte eines Klassikers*. Stuttgart: J. B. Metzler, 1999. First published 1995.

Weiser-Aall, Lily. "Hexe." In *Handwörterbuch des deutschen Aberglaubens*. Ed. E. Hoffmann-Krayer and Hanns Bächtold-Stäubli. 10 vols. Vol. 3:1827–1920. Berlin: Walter de Gruyter & Co, 1930–1931.

[Werner.] "Aus Zacharias Werners Nachlaß. Sonett zu einem Bilde des Gebrüder Riepenhausen, Mephistopheles, Faust und Gretchen darstellend, in dem Moment, wo der Schutzengel der lezteren davonfliegt." *Morgenblatt für gebildete Stände*, no. 16 (18 Jan 1828): 61a.

Willis, Patricia C. "'Luz y Verdad': J. Laughlin and Yale." *Paideuma* 31, nos. 1–3 (Spring–Fall–Winter 2002): 273–78.

Winzerfest (Das) der Weinbaugesellschaft im Königreich Sachsen am 25.10.1840. Dresden: Hofbuchdruckerei G. G. Meinhold & Söhne, 1840.

Wittwer, Samuel. "Betwixt Vienna and Paris: The Royal Porcelain Manufacture Berlin in the Grand European Context." In *Refinement and Elegance: Early Nineteenth-Century Royal Porcelain from the Twinight Collection. New York*. 55–95. Munich: Hirmer, 2007.

Zatti, Susanna. "Amore e morte, passione e patriottismo nell'iconografia del bacio tra Ottocento e Novecento." In *Il bacio tra Romanticismo e Novecento*. Ed. Susanna Zatti and Lorenza Tonani. 28–37. Milan: Silvana Editoriale, 2009. Exh. cat.

Zeydel, Edwin H. "Goethe's Reputation in America." In Rose, ed. 1949. 207–32.

Zschoche, Herrmann, ed. *Bilder einer Kindheit: Das malerische Tagebuch der Brüder Retzsch 1795–1809*. Husum: Verlag der Kunst Dresden, 2007.

Zucker, Paul. *Die Theaterdekoration des Klassizismus, eine Kunstgeschichte des Bühnenbildes*. Berlin: Rudolf Kaemmerer Verlag, 1925.

Index on Moritz Retzsch

Note: Given the complexity and richness of entries, this index follows the classification below rather than alphabetical order. For grouped items, image positions are indicated by line (l.) and column (col.) from left to right.

1. Family, Life, and Career
2. Personality and Characteristics
3. Choice *Faust I* Scenes Outlined, Copies and Influence
4. Additional *Faust* Outlines and Other *Faust* Drawings
5. Printed Editions of R's *Faust I* Outlines (original and copied)
6. Other Works
7. Aesthetics, Inspiration, and Technique
8. R's Distinctive Outline Treatment
9. Effect and Function of R's *Faust I* Outlines
10. Reception
11. Influence

1   Family, Life, and Career

abodes and haunts   25–28, 50, 212
    central Dresden   27, 28
    Dresden Neustadt   27
    legend of solitude/withdrawal   25, 27–28, 34, 35 (*Fig. 1.5*)
    Radebeul (Oberlößnitz)   27–28, 212
      refinement of Radebeul community   30, 30 (*Fig. 1.2*)
    Scharfenberg castle   32–33
career moves
    Dresden Academy membership   26, 50–51, 61
    Dresden Academy professorship   26, 27, 51, 61
    individual work in Academy exhibitions   33, 34, 39–40, 43, 54
    professionally tied to outline   51
    teaching and students   26, 27
      later relation to Grünewald and Zimmermann   227, 233–236
family relations
    August, elder brother and painter
      as artist   25, 27, 40
      death (1835)   36
      jolly occasions   28, 37, 270–71, 272 (*Fig. 9.2*)
      friendship album   30, 30*n*38
      MS diary   60; *see also* 6. Other Works → joint pictorial diary by R brothers
    father   25, 26
    Miersch (Mürisch or Mirisch), Johanna Christiana, aka Christel, R's wife   28–30, 29 (*Fig. 1.1*), 31 (*Fig. 1.3*), 37, 101, 358
    mother   26
    R as breadwinner   26, 27, 34, 43, 50
      drawing antiquities (*Augusteum*)   26, 40, 41 (*Fig. 1.7*)
      portraits and miniatures   26, 34, 39, 40, 44; *see also* Index → Thielmann
life markers
    blights of war   26, 43
    education and training   25–26, 39–40; *see also* career moves
    illness and ailments   27, 65, 101, 213
    lack of financial means   26
    obituaries   25
    grave   27

portrayed
    1807–08 in joint pictorial diary   28–30, 29 (*Fig. 1.1*), 31 (*Fig. 1.3*)
    1811 self-portrait in "Carus album"   34, 35 (*Fig. 1.5*)
    by Friedrich John?   220, 220*n*11
social hindrances   26, 40–42
urbane life and friendships
    Castle Scharfenberg circle   32–34, 32 (*Fig. 1.4*), 65
    Seydelmann circle and "Carus album"   34, 35 (*Fig. 1.5*)
    sociability   34, 50; *see also* Index → David d'Angers; Friedrich; Hall; Jameson; La Motte Fouqué, F.; Lieber, F.; Miltitz, C. B.; Renovanz; Vogelstein; Watzdorf

2   Personality and Characteristics

aptitudes
    craftsmanship   1, 4, 33–36, 50, 61, 65–66, 69, 71, 74–75, 96, 101–2, 333–34
    imaginative power   28, 33–34, 36, 37, 39, 40, 42, 43, 50, 71, 88–89, 302
    ingenious artist/visual translator   35–36, 37, 42, 43, 61, 62, 122, 140; *see also* Index → *geistreich*
    poetic gift/mind   2, 35–36, 37–38, 43, 87, 122, 184, 189, 190, 213, 307, 309, 310, 321
    poet in graphic art/outline   37–38, 42, 83–84, 87–88, 124, 129, 169, 206, 233, 356
    power of conception   33–34
disposition
    affinities with Goethe's *Faust*   25, 28–31, 29 (*Fig. 1.1*)
    as bipolar Janus   37
    as Pygmalionic husband   28–30, 29 (*Fig. 1.1*), 31 (*Fig. 1.3*)
    fancy   2, 25, 34, 36–39, 50, 52, 55, 69, 88, 170, 187, 247, 357; *see also* 7. Aesthetics, Inspiration, and Technique → allegory, treatment of → Fancy
    melancholy   36–37, 50

3   Choice *Faust I* Scenes Outlined, Copies and Influence

(per plate number, each outline plate followed by drawings, copies, cut-outs, copies with alterations, reworked and repurposed versions, parodies, remediated versions, influence, omissions/exclusions)

Pl. 1 Prologue in Heaven   9, 53 (*Fig. 2.1b*), 84, 87, 118, 128–29, 141 (*Fig. 5.1*), 274, 275 (*Fig. 9.3 bottom*)
preparatory drawing   69
freehand copied
    n.d. Delacroix   177, 178 (*Fig. 6.3*)
copied with alterations
    1820 Moses re-engraved as *Introduction* for Boosey   138, 142 (*Fig. 5.2*)
    1824 Muret lithograph *Méphistophélès obtient de Dieu la permission de tenter Faust*   181, 182–83, 182 (*Fig. 6.5*), 360
    1825 anon. for Berthoud   160 (*Fig. 5.15*), 161, 162, 361
    1828 Trueb re-engraving for Audot   189–90, 190 (*Fig. 6.10*), 362
    1834 Eytel's woodcut for Kurtz   117–18, 117 (*Fig. 3.17b*)
    c.1835 Kennerley recycled by Gibbings   364

INDEX ON MORITZ RETZSCH

copied without alterations
 1824 Stone re-engraving 142
detached as frontispiece to both plays in 1884? Cotta ed.
 107, 368
censored (omitted)
 1822–23 KPM porcelain plates painted 334
 1940 anon. in Labatut's ed. for Masson 205, 369
influencing
 c.1811 Goethe's drawing *Prologue in Heaven* 274, 275 (*Fig. 9.3 top*)
bypassed or suppressed
 1821 in Boosey's text 149, 154, 157
 1821 in Dibdin's *Bibliographical, Antiquarian and Picturesque Tour*
 133
 1829 Klingemann Braunschweig performance 273
Pl. 2 Poodle appearing in open country 9, 63, 151, 247, 273, 280
carefully coloured copy in R set 89, 90 (*Fig. 2.22*)
copied and repurposed
 1821 vignette in circular ornament 151, 152 (*Fig. 5.10a*), 153
 (*Fig. 5.10b*)
remediated
 1822–23 on KPM porcelain plate painted 334–38, 336 (*Fig. 12.2, l. 1
 col. 1*)
influencing
 1808–10 C. D. Friedrich's painting *Der Mönch am Meer*
Pl. 3 Faust in his study with poodle transmuting 10, 81, 89, 132, 132
 (*Fig. 4.3*), 170, 270, 274, 276 (*Fig. 9.4 bottom*), 375
preparatory drawings 68, 72
carefully coloured copy in R set 89, 90 (*Fig. 2.23 coloured*)
copied with alterations
 1824 Muret lithograph 162
 1825 anon. lithograph for Berthoud 161 (*Fig. 5.16*), 162
 1843 Tilt and Bogue "kinetic" alternate visual/textual album 169,
 175
reworked and repurposed
 1843 Tilt and Bogue combined gilt title on green binding (canine
 monsters) 170, 171 (*Fig. 5.19*), 176, 366, 375
 1865 Frey vignette for Frijlink 165 (*Fig. 5.18, l. 1 col. 1*)
remediated
 1822–23 on KPM porcelain plate painted 334–38, 336 (*Fig. 12.2, l. 1
 col. 2*)
influencing
 c.1811 Goethe drawing and wash *Conjuring the Poodle* 274, 276
 (*Fig. 9.4 top*)
 1820 Brühl with stage transformation 279–80
 1820 binding Ch. Murton 130–32, 130 (*Fig. 4.1*)
 1838 Coburg performance 287
 1849–50 Phiz in Dickens (Dr Strong's study) 319
 1968 & 1978 jokey theatre performances 301
Pl. 4 Faust and Mephistopheles in Faust's study 10, 81, 84–85, 85
 (*Fig. 2.21*)
preparatory drawings 67, 68 (*Figs. 2.4a–b*)
copied with alterations
 1820 Moses re-engraved as *Faust Makes Over his Soul to
 Mephistopheles* 84–85
 1824 Muret lithograph 84–85
 1828 Pinéas engraving *Faust signe le pacte avec
 Méphistophélés* 84–85, 181 (*Fig. 6.4*), 185, 211, 371
 1834 Eytel's woodcut for Kurtz 116 (*Fig. 3.17a*), 117, 373
 1843 recycled in Tilt and Bogue 169
 1900 vignette in *Les Sciences maudites* 208, 378
copied without alterations
 1824 Stone re-engraving 142

reworked and repurposed
 1818 anon. engraving for Jaeger 201
 1840 vignette in Baudry's synoptic frontispiece 201–3, 202
 (*Fig. 6.17, l. 1 col. 1*)
 1850 Frère cut by Rouget for Bry 204, 245, 245 (*Fig. 7.25*)
 1865 Frey vignette for Frijlink 165 (*Fig. 5.18, l. 2 col. 1*)
 1940 anon. in Labatut's ed. for Masson 206
parodied
 1834 Crowquill, *Faust Signs Over his Soul to the Devil* 259, 262, 264,
 265 (*Fig. 8.6*)
 1841 Lachgern parodying Crowquill 264, 265 (*Fig. 8.7*)
remediated
 1821 on KPM porcelain plate painted 334–38, 335 (*Fig. 12.1, l. 3 col. 1*)
 1822–23 on KPM porcelain plate painted 334–38, 336 (*Fig. 12.2, l. 1
 col. 3*)
Pl. 5 Auerbach's cellar 11, 89–90, 170, 287, 330
carefully coloured copy in R set 89–92, 296, 296 (*Fig. 9.17 coloured*)
cut-out, focussed and pasted
 1821 in Dibdin's *Bibliographical, Antiquarian and Picturesque
 Tour* 134 (*Fig. 4.4a*)
reworked and repurposed
 1850 Frère cut by Rouget for Bry 203, 204 (*Fig. 6.18*)
parodied
 1834 Crowquill 259, 262
remediated
 1843 Tilt and Bogue Mephistopheles in combined gilt title on green
 binding 170, 171 (*Fig. 5.19*), 176, 366, 375
 1822–23 on KPM porcelain plate painted 334–38, 336 (*Fig. 12.2, l.
 2 col. 1*)
 ante 1878 H. Bey sepia outlines on cellar walls, vault and menus in
 Auerbach's Keller Leipzig 212–13, 377
influencing
 1838 Coburg performance? 287
 1859 "Villa monde brillant" show 288
Pl. 6 Faust in the witch's kitchen 11, 42, 63, 81, 82, 82 (*Fig. 2.18*), 85,
 127, 142, 144 (*Fig. 5.4 bottom*), 170, 223 (*Fig. 7.7 bottom*), 240, 273,
 280, 375
preparatory drawing 67
freehand copied occasionally with alterations
 1853 Albert Edward, Prince of Wales, watercolours 358, 376–77
 n.d. Ross, Mephistopheles with owl in landscape 221, 223 (*Fig. 7.7
 top*)
cut-out, focussed and pasted
 1821 in Dibdin's *Bibliographical, Antiquarian and Picturesque
 Tour* 135 (*Fig. 4.4c*)
copied with alterations
 1820 Moses re-engraving *Faust and Mephistopheles in the Witch's
 Cave* 139, 142–43, 144 (*Fig. 5.4 top*), 149, 154, 181
 1824 Moses in "kinetic" *Faustus* 156
 1824 Muret lithograph 181, 182
 1825 anon. lithograph for Berthoud 182
 1826 Kennerley re-engraving for Bulcock 162
 1839 Brain re-engraving in Birch trans. 168, 366
 1877 finely printed by Wilson and Son 169
 1883 Champfleury with erroneous title 206, 377
copied without alterations
 1824 Stone re-engraving 142
reworked and repurposed
 1818 anon. engraving for Jaeger 112
 1828 in Audot pictorial cover (demon with drapery) 187–88, 187
 (*Fig. 6.9*), 362
 1850 Frère cut by Rouget for Bry 203, 204 (*Fig. 6.18*), 243, 243
 (*Fig. 7.23, enlarged*)

parodied

    1834 Crowquill   259, 262

remediated

    1821 on KPM porcelain plate painted   334–38, 335 (*Fig. 12.1, l. 3 col. 2*)

    1822–23 on KPM porcelain plate painted   334–38, 336 (*Fig. 12.2, l. 2 col. 2*)

    1843 Tilt and Bogue combined gilt title on binding   170, 171 (*Fig. 5.19*), 176, 366, 375

influencing

    1828 Lefèvre's matching set at Porte-Saint-Martin theatre   281

    1829 Weimar performance   280

    1838 Coburg performance?   287

    1885? W. H. Margetson painting   299

    1894 J. B. Partridge *Punch* sketch   299, 300 (*Fig. 9.19*)

    1904 G. Jourdain photogravure   245, 246 (*Fig. 7.26*)

Pl. 7 Faust drinks the potion in the witch's kitchen   12, 42, 63, 81, 82, 83 (*Fig. 2.19*), 164 (*Fig. 5.17 bottom*), 170, 222 (*Fig. 7.6 bottom*), 273, 280, 319, 332, 375

preparatory drawings   69, 70 (*Fig. 2.5*)

    in double strip   70–71, 71 (*Fig. 2.6*)

freehand copied with jokey alterations

    n.d. Kippenberg coll. with long French caption   219, 282, 372

    n.d. Ross, Faust and Mephistopheles smoking   221, 222 (*Fig. 7.6 top*)

copied with alterations

    1820 Moses re-engraving for Boosey   156

reworked and repurposed

    1827 J. Berryman cover for Bulcock   163, 164 (*Fig. 5.17 top*)

    1828 Audot demon with drapery in combined pictorial cover 187–88, 187 (*Fig. 6.9*), 362

    1843 Tilt and Bogue parts in combined gilt title on binding   170, 171 (*Fig. 5.19*), 176, 366, 375

    1865 Frey vignette for Frijlink   165 (*Fig. 5.18, l. 1 col. 2*)

parodied

    1834 Crowquill   259, 262

remediated

    1822–23 on KPM porcelain plate painted   334–38, 336 (*Fig. 12.2, l. 2 col. 3*)

influencing

    1828 Lefèvre's matching set at Porte-Saint-Martin theatre   281

    1829 Weimar performance   280

    1859 "Villa monde brillant" show   288

Pl. 8 Faust accosting Margaret   12, 25, 28–30, 46 (*Fig. 1.8*), 48, 80, 92, 110, 116, 188, 247, 248 (*Fig. 7.27 bottom*), 273, 274, 294, 319, 321, 332

preparatory drawing   67

carefully coloured copy in R set   89, 92

copied and repurposed

    1818 anon. engraving for Jaeger   112

    1821 vignette in circular ornament   151, 152 (*Fig. 5.10a*), 153 (*Fig. 5.10b*)

    1840 vignette in Baudry's synoptic frontispiece   201–3, 202 (*Fig. 6.17, l. 1 col. 2*)

    1850 Frère cut by Rouget for Bry   203, 204 (*Fig. 6.18*)

parodied

    1834 Crowquill *Faust Sees Margaret for the First Time*   256 (*Fig. 8.1a*), 259, 262

remediated

    1821 on KPM porcelain plate painted   334–38, 335 (*Fig. 12.1, l. 4 col. 1*)

    1822–23 on KPM porcelain plate painted   334–38, 336 (*Fig. 12.2, l. 3 col. 1*)

influencing

    1828 Delacroix lithograph of meeting in *Faust*   242, 247, 248 (*Fig. 7.27 top*)

    n.d. Brand print *Herr und Madame Schütz (als Faust und Gretchen)*, theatre posture   293–94, 294 (*Fig. 9.15*)

    1849 Phiz in Dickens   313–21, 314 (*Fig. 10.2*), 316 (*Fig. 10.4*), 317 (*Fig. 10.5*)

omitted

    1821 from Harmonie preparations   274

Pl. 9 Margaret musing in her chamber   13, 81, 83–84, 92, 188, 273, 278 (*Fig. 9.6*), 279, 288, 291, 307–8, 309

R's post-production replica   69

drawing in double strip   70–71, 71 (*Fig. 2.6*)

copied

    Knittlingen, Faust-Archiv   217

copied on tracing paper with other figures

    n.d. anon. FDH   218, 219 (*Fig. 7.5*)

copied with alterations

    1824 Moses in "kinetic" *Faustus*   154, 155 (*Fig. 5.11a*)

    1824 Muret lithograph *Marguerite dans sa chambre*   183, 183 (*Fig. 6.6*), 188

    1887 Ward, Lock & Co. detached as frontispiece   369

reworked and repurposed

    1818 anon. engraving for Jaeger   112, 113 (*Fig. 3.14a*)

    1835 Meyerheim lithograph in *Scenen aus Goethes Faust*   288, 289 (*Fig. 9.12*), 373

    1940 repr. 1951 anon. in Labatut's ed. for Masson   205, 205 (*Fig. 6.19*)

remediated

    on KPM porcelain plate painted   334–38, 335 (*Fig. 12.1, l. 1. col. 1*)

    1822–23 on KPM porcelain plate painted   334–38, 336 (*Fig. 12.2, l. 3 col. 2*)

influencing

    1820 Brühl with stage transformation   277–79

    1820 Schinkel watercolour *Margaret's Chamber*   277–79, 278 (*Fig. 9.5*), 370

    1828 Lefèvre's matching set at Porte-Saint-Martin theatre   281

    1829 Weimar performance   280

    1839 J. Gley's theatre costume and posture   291–93, 293 (*Fig. 9.14*)

    1859 "Villa monde brillant" show   288

Pl. 10 Faust and Mephistopheles entering/in Margaret's chamber   13, 75 (*Fig. 2.10*), 170, 188, 224, 275, 279, 375

preparatory drawings   67, 69, 73–77, 74 (*Fig. 2.9*)

copied with alterations

    1824 Moses in "kinetic" *Faustus*   154, 155 (*Fig. 5.11b*)

    1843 Tilt and Bogue "kinetic" alternate visual/textual album   169, 175

reworked and repurposed

    1843 Tilt and Bogue combined gilt title on binding (casket detail) 170, 171 (*Fig. 5.19*), 176, 366, 375

    1843 Tilt and Bogue gilt title on binding playing on *Illustrations* 170–72, 171 (*Fig. 5.20*), 176, 366, 375

    1887 Ward, Lock & Co. detached as frontispiece   369

remediated

    1822–23 on KPM porcelain plate painted   334–38, 336 (*Fig. 12.2, l. 3 col. 3*)

influencing

    1854 E. Seibertz, in-text composition   75, 76 (*Fig. 2.11*)

    1875 A. v. Kreling, in-text composition   75–77, 76 (*Fig. 2.12*)

Pl. 11 Margaret discovers the jewels   14, 75, 81, 89, 188, 224, 279, 288, 291, 307, 321

preparatory drawings   73–75, 74 (*Fig. 2.9*)

carefully coloured copy in R set   89, 91, 91 (*Fig. 2.24 coloured*), 92

INDEX ON MORITZ RETZSCH   415

freehand copied
    n.d. Delacroix (figures)   177, 177 (*Fig. 6.1b*)
copied on tracing paper with other figures
    n.d. anon. FDH   218, 219 (*Fig. 7.5*)
copied with alterations
    1821 Moses change of caption   149, 188
    1824 Moses in "kinetic" *Faustus*   154, 155 (*Fig. 5.11c*)
    1828 Muret imprint corrected in 2nd ed.   184
    n.d. Moses re-engraving *Mephistopheles Leaves Rich Ornaments in Margaret's Chamber* (in unique compound volume)   118, 118 (*Fig. 3.18*), 139, 149
reworked and repurposed
    1818 anon. engraving for Jaeger   112, 113 (*Fig. 3.14b*), 114
    1850 Frère cut by Rouget for Bry   203, 204 (*Fig. 6.18*)
    1865 Frey vignette for Frijlink   165 (*Fig. 5.18, l. 2 col. 2*)
parodied
    1834 Crowquill *Margaret Admiring the Present Left by the Devil*   260 (*Figs. 8.3a, 8.3b coloured*), 262
remediated
    1821 on KPM porcelain plate painted   334–38, 335 (*Fig. 12.1, l. 1 col. 2*)
    1822–23 on KPM porcelain plate painted   334–38, 336 (*Fig. 12.2, l. 4 col. 1*)
influencing
    1828 Maleuvre *I would never dare to adorn myself with all these jewels*, Marie Dorval as Margaret   294, 295 (*Fig. 9.16*)
    1829 Weimar performance   280

Pl. 12 Martha adorns Margaret with the jewels   14, 81, 89, 92, 188, 208, 224, 273, 296, 320, 320 (*Fig. 10.6*), 360
preparatory drawing   69
    in double strip   70–71, 71 (*Fig. 2.6*)
carefully coloured copy in R set   89, 92
freehand copied
    n.d. Delacroix (isolated figures)   177, 177 (*Fig. 6.1b*), 178 (*Fig. 6.2*)
copied on tracing paper with other figures
    n.d. anon. FDH   218, 219 (*Fig. 7.5*)
cut-out, focussed and pasted
    1821 in Dibdin's *Bibliographical, Antiquarian and Picturesque Tour*   135 (*Fig. 4.4c*)
cut-out and mounted
    n.d. in Devéria compendium   208, 209 (*Fig. 6.21 left*)
copied with alterations
    1820 Moses re-engraving *Margaret shews her Treasures to Martha*   224
    1824 Moses in "kinetic" *Faustus*   156
    1824 Muret lithograph   208, 209 (*Fig. 6.21 left*)
    1843 Tilt and Bogue "kinetic" alternate visual/textual album   169
reworked and repurposed
    1818 anon. engraving for Jaeger   112, 113, 113 (*Fig. 3.14c*)
remediated
    1822–23 KPM porcelain plate painted   334–38, 336 (*Fig. 12.2, l. 4 col. 2*)
influencing
    1849 Phiz illustration B for Dickens   313–20, 316 (*Fig. 10.4*), 317 (*Fig. 10.5*)

Pl. 13 Margaret at Martha's, Mephistopheles visiting   15, 81, 89, 91 (*Fig. 2.25 coloured*), 92, 188, 224, 273, 296
carefully coloured copy in R set   89, 91 (*Fig. 2.25 coloured*), 92
freehand copied
    n.d. Delacroix (isolated figures)   177, 177 (*Fig. 6.1b*), 178 (*Fig. 6.2*)
copied
    1836 "John" copy at Muskau   220
    1948 Knittlingen copy, Faust-Archiv   217, 378

copied with alterations
    1820 Moses re-engraving for Boosey *Mephistopheles Informs Martha of her Husband's Death*   224
    1843 Tilt and Bogue "kinetic" alternate visual/textual album   169, 175
reworked and repurposed
    1850 Frère cut by Rouget for Bry   243, 244 (*Fig. 7.24a, left*)
remediated
    1821 on KPM porcelain plate painted   334–38, 335 (*Fig. 12.1, l. 2 col. 1*)
    1822–23 on KPM porcelain plate painted   334–38, 336 (*Fig. 12.2, l. 4 col. 3*)
influencing
    1825 Terry's theatre costume   291, 292 (*Fig. 9.13*)
    1885 Irving's theatre costume   296–97, 299–301, 300 (*Figs. 9.18, 9.19*), 301 (*Fig. 9.20*)

Pl. 14 Garden scene (Margaret plucking the daisy)   15, 188, 213–14, 222–24, 291, 305, 307, 313, 315 (*Fig. 10.3*), 358
preparatory drawings   72
freehand copied
    n.d. Delacroix (Martha detail)   177, 178 (*Fig. 6.2*)
copied and coloured
    carefully coloured copy in R set   89, 92
    anon. redrawn and coloured   92, 93 (*Fig. 2.26*), 378
    copy in oils   221n15
cut-out, focussed and pasted
    1821 in Dibdin's *Bibliographical, Antiquarian and Picturesque Tour*   134 (*Fig. 4.4b*)
copied with alterations
    1820 Moses re-engraving for Boosey *The Decision of the Flower*   224, 305, 315, 319, 327–29, 328 (*Fig. 11.2*)
reworked and repurposed
    1821 vignette in circular ornament   151, 152 (*Fig. 5.10a*), 153 (*Fig. 5.10b*)
    1825 J. M. Wright *The Decision of the Flower* engraved by Ch. Heath, in *The Literary Souvenir*   224–25, 225 (*Fig. 7.9*), 371
        as standalone print   224
    1825 G. Hering lithograph *The Decision of the Flower* (untraced)   371
    1828? É. Robert, *La Décision de la fleur* reverse lithograph   225, 227, 229 (*Fig. 7.12*), 372
    1850 Frère cut by Rouget for Bry   210, 243, 244 (*Fig. 7.24a, right*)
    1938 anon. after Frère for Gründ   208–10 (*Fig. 6.22*), 243, 378
    1929 vignette in Gyldendal Danish edition   369
repurposed with patriotic overtones
    n.d. Grünewald lithograph "*Er liebt mich—liebt mich nicht*"   222–24, 227–29, 230 (*Fig. 7.15*), 375
    n.d. Müller lithograph "*Er liebt mich—liebt mich nicht*"   222–24, 227–29, 230 (*Fig. 7.14*), 375
    n.d. Zimmermann lithograph "*Er liebt mich—liebt mich nicht*"   222–24, 227–29, 230 (*Fig. 7.13*), 375
    as twin set with *Bester Mann!* (Dresden, Pietzsch)   233
parodied
    1834 Crowquill   259
remediated
    c.1820? on Meissen pipe bowl   229, 340, 341 (*Fig. 12.4*)
    1822–23 on KPM porcelain plate painted   229, 334–38, 337 (*Fig. 12.2, l. 1 col. 1*)
    1840 on Nathusius pipe bowl after Nisle (← R)   343, 345 (*Fig. 12.6b*), 370, 375
    as lithophane (Meissen 119, KPM 162)   347, 374
    ante 1868 as lithophane *veilleuse théière* by J. Petit   347, 348 (*Fig. 12.7*)

remediated (*cont.*)

    1886 as advertisement on Beecham's *Faust* booklet   352, 353
       (*Fig. 12.11*), 378

    *c.*1907 as embossed postcard   229–31, 231 (*Fig. 7.16*)

original or copies influencing

    1816 Marianne v. Willemer   332

    1823 Byron's gift   327–29

    1826 Disraeli in *Vivian Grey*   305

    1828 Porte-Saint-Martin performance   290

    1829 Colin lithograph in troubadour style   225–26, 226 (*Fig. 7.10*),
       372

    1849 inserted in Phiz final plate C for Dickens   313–21, 314
       (*Fig. 10.2*)

    1849 Phiz in sketch A for Dickens (?)   316 (*Fig. 10.4*), 318–21

    1852 Gautier in press review   307

    1859 "Villa monde brillant" show   288

    1850 Ch. Lever, *Roland Cashel*   318

    n.d. N. Maurin lithograph *Marguerite consulte une fleur pour savoir
       si elle est aimée de Faust*   226–27, 228 (*Fig. 7.11*)

Pl. 15 Faust and Margaret kissing   16, 49, 73, 80, 188, 222–24, 232–33,
    232 (*Fig. 7.17*), 242, 247, 357, 358

preparatory drawings   77, 78 (*Figs. 2.13, 2.14*), 79 (*Figs. 2.15, 2.16*)

carefully coloured copy in R set   89, 92

redrawn in ink

    1822 G. R.   217–18, 218 (*Fig. 7.4*), 371

copied with alterations

    1820 Moses re-engraving for Boosey specially offered with 1st batch
       of prints   138, 224

    1820 Moses re-engraving for Boosey *Margaret Meets Faust in the
       Summer House*   224, 232–33, 327–29, 328 (*Fig. 11.3*)

    1824 Muret lithograph *Faust et Marguerite dans un pavillon*   183,
       233, 234 (*Fig. 7.18 bottom right*)

       post 1847 cut-out and mounted by Devéria   233, 234 (*Fig. 7.18
       bottom right*)

reworked and repurposed

    1826 J. M. Wright *The Kiss*, engraved by W. Humphreys in
       The Literary Souvenir   224–25, 225 (*Fig. 7.8*), 371

       as standalone print, 224

       post 1847 cut-out and mounted by Devéria   233, 234 (*Fig. 7.18
       top left*)

    1828? Édouard Robert, *Le Baiser* reverse lithograph   225, 234
       (*Fig. 7.18 top right*), 372

       post 1847 cut-out and mounted by Devéria   233, 234 (*Fig. 7.18
       top right*)

    1828 in Audot's combined pictorial cover   187–88, 187 (*Fig. 6.9*),
       362

    1832 as choice frontispiece in Lumley exemplar   157, 157*n*84, 158
       (*Fig. 5.13*), 233, 364

    1840 vignette in Baudry's synoptic frontispiece   201–3, 202
       (*Fig. 6.17, l. 2 col. 1*)

    1843 Tilt and Bogue "kinetic" alternate visual/textual album   169

crucially modified and repurposed

    1837 Schuler engraving Faust und Gretchen   236–38, 237
       (*Fig. 7.21a*), 374

       steel engraved in *Album aus der Damenzeitung Iris*   237
       (*Fig. 7.21b*), 238, 376

       reworked and repurposed in historical attire

          n.d. Zimmermann lithograph "*Bester Mann, von Herzen lieb'
          ich dich!*"   223–24, 233–36, 236 (*Fig. 7.20*)

          n.d. Müller lithograph "*Bester Mann, von Herzen lieb' ich
          dich!*"   223–24, 233

          n.d. Grünewald lithograph "*Bester Mann, von Herzen lieb' ich
          dich!*"   223–24, 233–36

          *c.*1880 Patzschke coloured lithograph "*Bester Mann, von
          Herzen lieb' ich dich!*"   238–39, 238 (*Fig. 7.22*)

          as twin set with *Er liebt mich* (Dresden, Pietzsch)   233

parodied

    1834 Crowquill   259

remediated

    1821 on KPM porcelain plate painted   334–38, 335 (*Fig. 12.1, l. 2
       col. 2*)

    1822–23 on KPM porcelain plate painted   334–38, 337 (*Fig. 12.2, l. 1
       col. 2*)

    1834–41 as lithophane in Woburn window   347, 350 (*Fig. 12.9*), 373

    *c.*1830–40 on KPM pipe bowls painted   340–43, 342 (*Fig. 12.5a*),
       343 (*Fig. 12.5b*)

    1840 on Nathusius pipe bowl combined with garden scene   343,
       345 (*Fig. 12.6b*), 370, 375

    as candle screen on advertisement postcard   347, 349 (*Fig. 12.8*)

    as lithophane   340*n*20, 347

R original or 1820 Moses's *Margaret Meets Faust in the Summer House*
    influencing

    1822 P. B. Shelley   1, 154, 233, 247

    1823 Byron's gift?   327–29

    1826 A. Watts, "The First Kiss: A Poetical Sketch"   224, 224*n*23, 371

    1826 Disraeli in *Vivian Grey*   305

    1840 Nisle print combined with garden scene   343, 344 (*Fig. 12.6a*),
       374

    post 1847 further French romantic versions mounted by
       Devéria   233, 234 (*Fig. 7.18*), 371

       n.d. N. Maurin, lithograph *Réunis dans un pavillon du jardin*
       233, 235 (*Fig. 7.19*)

    *c.*1850 W. v. Kaulbach steel engraved by A. Hoffmann   233,
       233*n*34

    1859 Hayez, *Il Bacio. Episodio della giovinezza. Costumi del
       secolo XIV*   242, 247–51, 249 (*Fig. 7.28*), 357, 377

       reproduction prints of *Bacio* in paintings   250

    1861 Hayez, *Il Bacio*   250–51, 251 (*Fig. 7.29*), 377

    1867 Hayez, *Il Bacio* or *Il Bacio del volontario*   250–51, 251
       (*Fig. 7.30*), 377

       Bacio reworked and repurposed   251–54, 252 (*Fig. 7.31a*), 253
       (*Fig. 7.31b*)

Pl. 16 Margaret at the spinning wheel   16, 80, 98 (*Fig. 3.1b*), 188, 279,
    288, 291, 332

    1830 in later Cotta ed.   98 (*Fig. 3.1a*), 99

preparatory drawings   72 (*Fig. 2.7*), 73

    in double strip   70–71, 71 (*Fig. 2.6*)

carefully coloured copy in R set   89, 92

freehand copied

    n.d. Delacroix   177, 177 (*Fig. 6.1a*), 298

cut-out, focussed and pasted

    1821 in Dibdin's *Bibliographical, Antiquarian and Picturesque Tour*
       134 (*Fig. 4.4b*)

as trial etching

    anon. *c.*1830 in Laborde exemplar   196 (*Fig. 6.15b*)

copied with alterations

    1824 Moses in "kinetic" *Faustus*   156

reworked and repurposed

    1850 Frère cut by Rouget for Bry   243–45, 244 (*Fig. 7.24b, far left*)

    1865 Frey vignette for Frijlink   165 (*Fig. 5.18, l. 3 col. 1*)

remediated

    1822–23 on KPM porcelain plate painted   334–38, 337 (*Fig. 12.2, l. 1
       col. 3*)

INDEX ON MORITZ RETZSCH

influencing
    1820 Schinkel's watercolour *décor*   278 (*Fig. 9.5*), 279, 288
    theatre décors   308
    tin figurines   349
Pl. 17 Margaret imploring the Mater Dolorosa   17, 80, 97, 279, 334
preparatory drawing   69
carefully coloured copy in R set   89, 92
hand copied
    1834 Queen Victoria   358, 373
copied with alterations
    1824 Moses in "kinetic" *Faustus*   156
remediated
    1822–23 on KPM porcelain plate painted   334, 334n10
Pl. 18 Cathedral scene   17, 80–81, 270, 271 (*Fig. 9.1*), 272–73, 307
as rebel plate   80, 99, 103, 138, 175, 181, 182, 195, 219, 361, 363
as subjugated print   103, 138, 149, 154, 168, 192, 360
preparatory drawing   69
    in double strip   70–71, 71 (*Fig. 2.6*)
carefully coloured copy in R set   89, 92
freehand copied
    n.d. Delacroix, isolated figures   177, 177 (*Fig. 6.1a*), 178 (*Fig. 6.2*)
copied
    1836 "John" copy at Muskau   219
    n.d. on tracing paper with other figures
    n.d. anon. FDH   218, 219 (*Fig. 7.5*)
copied with alterations
    1820 Moses re-engraving for Boosey *The Evil Spirit Whispers Despair to Margaret while at Mass*   138
    1824 Moses in "kinetic" *Faustus*   156
reworked and repurposed
    1850 Frère cut by Rouget for Bry   244 (*Fig. 7.24b, left*), 245
remediated
    1822–23 on KPM porcelain plate painted   334–38, 337 (*Fig. 12.2, l. 2 col. 1*)
influencing
    Braunschweig performance (following R's order)   178–80
omitted
    1821 from Harmonie preparations   274
Pl. 19 Rigged duel with Valentine   18, 80, 99, 103, 273
freehand copied
    n.d. Delacroix   177, 178 (*Fig. 6.3*)
    as trial lithograph in *c.*1830 Laborde exemplar   195
copied with alterations
    1820 Moses re-engraving for Boosey *Valentine Fights with Faust*   138
    1824 Muret lithograph   181
    *c.*1827 in Riepenhausen pirated copy   110
    1843 Tilt and Bogue "kinetic" alternate visual/textual album   169, 175
reworked and repurposed
    1840 vignette in Baudry's synoptic frontispiece   201–3, 202 (*Fig. 6.17, l. 2 col. 2*)
    1850 Frère cut by Rouget for Bry   244 (*Fig. 7.24b, top right*)   245
    1884? C. Votteler, coloured lithographic cover   106–7, 107 (*Fig. 3.9*), 368
parodied
    1834 Crowquill   259
remediated
    1822–23 on KPM porcelain plate painted   334–38, 337 (*Fig. 12.2, l. 2 col. 2*)
    as fire screen?   333, 346

Pl. 20 Valentine dying upbraids his sister   18, 73, 73 (*Fig. 2.8*), 80, 82, 92
preparatory drawings   69, 73
    in double strip   71, 71 (*Fig. 2.6*)
carefully coloured copy in R set   89, 92
reworked and repurposed
    1820 anon. engraving for Jaeger   114
remediated
    1822–23 on KPM porcelain plate painted   334–38, 337 (*Fig. 12.2, l. 2 col. 3*)
omitted
    1821 from Harmonie preparations   274
Pl. 21 Faust and Mephistopheles ascending the Brocken   19, 157, 159 (*Fig. 5.14*), 247, 273
preparatory drawings   67, 69
copied with alterations
    1820 Moses re-engraving for Boosey   140, 157
    1824 Moses in "kinetic" *Faustus*   156
copied and repurposed
    1886 Ward, Lock & Co. detached as frontispiece   369
    1900 vignette in *Les Sciences maudites*   208, 378
remediated
    1821 on KPM porcelain plate painted   334–38, 335 (*Fig. 12.1, l. 4 col. 2*)
    1822–23 on KPM porcelain plate painted   334–38, 337 (*Fig. 12.2, l. 3 col. 1*)
influencing
    1822 P. B. Shelley "The May-Day Night Scene"   157–59
    1824 Heine *Harzreise*   303–4
    1828 Delacroix, lithograph 14 in *Faust*   247
Pl. 22 Walpurgis Night/the witches' revel   19, 42, 82–83, 145, 147 (*Fig. 5.7*), 170, 303, 307, 311, 375
preparatory drawing   69
freehand copied
    n.d. Delacroix   177, 178 (*Fig. 6.3*), 245
    1853 Alfred Edward, Prince of Wales   358, 376
copied with alterations
    1820 Moses re-engraving for Boosey   140, 145, 146 (*Fig. 5.6*), 154
    1821 Moses re-engraving for Boosey (read by Shelley)   154
    1824 Stone re-engraving, naked witches clothed   142
    1843 Tilt and Bogue "kinetic" alternate visual/textual album   169, 175
copied and repurposed
    1886 Ward, Lock & Co. detached as frontispiece   369
    1900 half-page illustration in *Les Sciences maudites*   208, 378
reworked and repurposed
    1843 Tilt and Bogue combined gilt title on green binding (hag detail)   170, 171 (*Fig. 5.19*), 176, 366, 375
    1850 Frère cut by Rouget for Bry   244 (*Fig. 7.24b, bottom right*), 245
influencing
    1824 Heine *Harzreise*   303–4
    1824 stage sets for Milner's *Faustus*   281
    1828 Lefèvre's matching set at Porte-Saint-Martin theatre   281
    1828 Porte-Saint-Martin performance   290
    1855 Gautier in art criticism   307
    1859 "Villa monde brillant" show   287–88
    1883 Pollock, *The Picture's Secret*, plot and character construction   311–13
censored (omitted)   157
    1821 in Dibdin's *Bibliographical, Antiquarian and Picturesque Tour*   133
    1822–23 in KPM plates   334
    1940 in Labatut's ed. for Masson   205, 369

missing

    from *c.*1830 Laborde trial exemplar   195

Pl. 23 Faust confronting Mephistopheles 20, 83, 169, 188, 221, 262, 263 (*Fig. 8.4*)

as trial lithograph

    Magnenat, *Faust accable Méphistophélès de reproches*, in *c.*1830 Laborde trial exemplar   196 (*Fig. 6.15a*)

copied and modified

    Ross, Faust fighting Mephistopheles   221

copied with alterations

    1843 Tilt and Bogue "kinetic" alternate visual/textual album   169

reworked and repurposed

    1820 anon. engraving for Jaeger   114 (*Fig. 3.15a*)

    in combined pictorial cover (Mephistopheles), Audot, 1828   187–88, 187 (*Fig. 6.9*), 362

parodied

    1834 Crowquill *Faust Hears that Margaret Is in Prison*   259, 262, 263 (*Fig. 8.5*)

    1841 Lachgern parodying Crowquill   263 (*Fig. 8.5*), 264

remediated

    1822–23 on KPM porcelain plate painted   334–38, 337 (*Fig. 12.2, l. 3 col. 2*)

influencing

    1825 Terry's theatre costume   291, 292 (*Fig. 9.13*)

    1885 Irving's theatre costume   296–97, 299–301, 300 (*Figs. 9.18, 9.19*), 301 (*Fig. 9.20*)

Pl. 24 Faust and Mephistopheles riding past the Rabenstein 20, 83, 84 (*Fig. 2.20*), 284, 285 (*Fig. 9.11 bottom*)

copied and repurposed

    1820 anon. engraving for Jaeger   114 (*Fig. 3.15b*)

    1821 vignette in circular ornament   151, 152 (*Fig. 5.10a*), 153 (*Fig. 5.10b*)

    1840 vignette in Baudry's synoptic frontispiece   201–3, 202 (*Fig. 6.17, l. 3 col. 1*)

remediated

    1822–23 on KPM porcelain plate painted   334–38, 337 (*Fig. 12.2, l. 3 col. 3*)

influencing

    1834 Eytel's iconography for Kurtz   118, 373

    1859 Thierry design for stage curtain (later painting)   284, 285 (*Fig. 9.11 top*), 377

    Faustian romantic iconography   204

Pl. 25 Margaret prostrate in prison 21, 81, 83, 273, 298, 298 (*Fig. 9.8*)

    carefully coloured copy in R set   89, 92

copied with alterations

    1843 Tilt and Bogue in "kinetic" alternate visual/textual album 169

reworked and repurposed

    1820 anon. engraving for Jaeger   114 (*Fig. 3.15c*)

remediated

    1822–23 on KPM porcelain plate painted   334–38, 337 (*Fig. 12.2, l. 4 col. 1*)

influencing

    1828 actors' performance at Porte-Saint-Martin theatre   290

    1828 Béraud, Merle, and Nodier's *Faust* stage directions   282

    1828 Lefèvre's matching set at Porte-Saint-Martin   281

    *c.*1831 L. Bertin's stage directions in score   283

    1859 É. Despléchin's stage set   283–84, 284 (*Fig. 9.10*)

    romantic prison iconography   204

Pl. 26 Faust exhorts Margaret to leave the prison 22, 72–73, 80, 81, 81 (*Fig. 2.17*), 84, 273, 291, 307

preparatory drawings   67, 72–73

copied with alterations

    1843 Tilt and Bogue "kinetic" alternate visual/textual album   169

reworked and repurposed

    *c.*1831 cover vignette for Bertin, *Ultima scena di Fausto*   282–83, 283 (*Fig. 9.9*)

    1832 choice frontispiece in Lumley   364

    1840 vignette in Baudry's synoptic frontispiece   201–3, 202 (*Fig. 6.17, l. 3 col. 2*)

    1865 Frey vignette for Frijlink   165 (*Fig. 5.18, l. 3, col. 2*)

parodied

    1834 Crowquill *Margaret Refuses to Leave the Prison*   256 (*Fig. 8.1b*), 259, 261, 268

remediated

    1822–23 on KPM porcelain plate painted   334–38, 337 (*Fig. 12.2, l. 4 col. 2*)

influencing

    1828 Lefèvre's matching set at Porte-Saint-Martin theatre   281

    1847 T. Johannot's Mephistopheles   206 (*Fig. 6.20*), 207

    1859 "Villa monde brillant" show   288

    romantic prison iconography   204

omitted

    in 1841 Lachgern *Bilder zu Goethes Faust*   264

4   Additional *Faust* Outlines and Other *Faust* Drawings

1834 *Faust I* additional plates in Cotta album *Umrisse zu Goethe's Faust*

    insert pl. 5 Mephistopheles lulls Faust to sleep   22, 103, 104 (*Fig. 3.7*), 364

        n.d. R's post-production replica   69

            *c.*1850–60 G. Koch unmarked painted plate   338–40, 339 (*Fig. 12.3*), 377

    insert pl. 7 second Auerbach scene   23, 103, 364

        n.d. R's post-production replica   69

    insert pl. 19 Faust handing Gretchen the phial   24, 103, 213–14, 214 (*Fig. 7.1*), 351–52, 364

        n.d. R's post-production replica   69

        *c.*1829 refocussed by R for extra-illustrated *AlH*   213–14, 215 (*Fig. 7.2*)

        1929 vignette in Gyldendal Danish edition   369

        1979 Fechner tin showcase figurines   351–52, 351 (*Fig. 12.10*)

1836 sq. *Umrisse zu Faust, zweiter Theil* (*Faust II*)   36, 99, 101–2, 106

    1836 Cotta original blue and fuchsia portfolio   54, 101–2, 103, 103 (*Fig. 3.6*), 105, 105 (*Fig. 3.8*), 365

        1837 Black and Armstrong English release with add-ons   105–6, 105 (*Fig. 3.8*), 167

        reworked and repurposed plates

            pl. 4 (Classical Walpurgis) 1840 vignette in Baudry's synoptic frontispiece   201, 202 (*Fig. 6.17, l. 4 col. 1*)

            pl. 10 (death of Faust)   172, 173 (*Fig. 5.22*)

                1849 Leighton decorative spine   172–75, 172 (*Fig. 5.21*), 376

                1840 vignette in Baudry's synoptic frontispiece   201, 202 (*Fig. 6.17, l. 4 col. 2*), 366

    1836 Cotta combined *Faust I* and *Faust II* album   54, 105–7, 365

    pre-1839? combined Cotta album printed in Stuttgart   106, 365

    1884? combined Cotta album with Votteler cover printed by Kröner   106–7, 107 (*Fig. 3.9*), 368

Other R drawings after Goethe's *Faust*

    1810 "Outside the City Walls" sent to Goethe(?)   63

    1810 "Witch's Kitchen" sent to Goethe(?)   63

    1847 Faust and Gretchen in the garden, pencil drawing (FDH)   100 (*Fig. 3.5*), 101, 213

INDEX ON MORITZ RETZSCH — 419

Other R drawings after Goethe's *Faust* (*cont.*)
  n.d. cathedral in uneven octagonal shape (FDH) 101
  n.d. Faust and Gretchen(?), double portrait in pencil (HAAB) 100
    (*Fig. 3.4*), 101, 233
  n.d. Faust and Gretchen on garden bench (Berlin) 101, 213
  n.d. Faust and Margaret, full-length portrait in pencil outline
    (Beinecke) 100 (*Fig. 3.2*), 101
  n.d. *Faust*, pencil and chalk double portrait (HAAB) 100 (*Fig. 3.3*),
    101
  n.d. three artworks on Faust and Gretchen in historical costume
    (Berlin) 101n30

5   **Printed Editions of R's *Faust I* Outlines (original
      and copied)**

copied foreign editions
  in Belgium   *see* Index → Feuillet-Dumus; Meline; Meline, Cans
    and Co.
  in France   *see* Index → Audot; Auvray; Baudry; Bry; Giard; Gründ;
    Masson et Cie
  in Great Britain   *see* Index → Bell; Berthoud; Boosey; Bulcock;
    Gibbings; Lumley; Prowett; Sampson Low, Marston & Co.; Tilt
    and Bogue
  in Lithuania   *see* Index → Zawadzki
  in the Netherlands   *see* Index → Frijlink
  in the USA   *see* Index → Estes and Lauriat; Stone
original German editions   *see* Index → Cotta, J. F., and Cotta, G.
pirated editions (*Nachdrücke*)
  c.1825 lithographed duplicate (former Tille coll.) 108, 361
  1827 Jäger *Nachdruck* (?), unidentified 108
  c.1827 engraved copy involving the Riepenhausens 109–12, 111
    (*Figs. 3.10a, 3.10b*), 362
  n.d. copy with expurgated male attributes (Bodmer coll.) 108, 362
unique copied exemplars
  1836 "John" hand-made copy at Muskau 219–21, 373
  1820 Moses English prints inlaid with 1816 German pocket *Faust*
    118–19, 118 (*Fig. 3.18*), 360

6   **Other Works**

albums of drawn reveries 36
designs for objects
  Intemperance Tankard for Tiffany 333–34
joint pictorial diary by R brothers 28–30, 29 (*Fig. 1.8*), 31 (*Fig. 1.3*), 44,
    89, 270–71, 272 (*Fig. 9.2*)
paintings
  c.1810 life-size portraits of J. A. Thielmann and wife Wilhelmine
    34, 60
  1824? *Die vier Jahreszeiten* after Fouqué 37
  Carl Boromäus von Miltitz and Auguste von Miltitz, double portrait
    32–33, 32 (*Fig. 1.4*)
  Diana canvas with drawings 39–40
  Egmont after Goethe 35
  Erlking (*The*) after Goethe 35
  Faust and Gretchen in half figure 101
  Fisherman (*The*) after Goethe 35
  Idylls after Gessner 34–35
  Sintram after Fouqué 34
  Undine after Fouqué 30, 33, 34
  Wilhelm Meister's Apprenticeship after Goethe 35

R's outlines after other literary works (followed by copies)
  Bürger
    1840 *Umrisse zu Buerger's Balladen* 33, 36, 40, 67, 85, 85n
      1840 *Retzsch's Outlines to Buerger's Ballads* 85n
      ballad of Leonora 88
    1872 *Umrisse zu Bürgers Balladen* 60, 60n41
      1873 *Outlines to Bürger's Ballads* 60, 60n41
  Schiller
    1814? **Der Kampf mit dem Drachen* (Dieterich) 109
    1814? **Fridolin* (Dieterich) 109
    1823 *Fridolin* (Cotta) 42, 54, 95, 96, 189
      1824 *Fridolin, or The Road to the Iron-Foundery: A Ballad*, re-
        engraved by Moses (Prowett) 123, 156, 361
      1829 *Fridolin*, French copy (Audot) 188, 189, 307, 309
      1829 *Fridolin*, trans. by J. W. Lake (Ackermann and Tilt)
        170, 179, 189
    1824 *Der Kampf mit dem Drachen* (Cotta) 42, 54, 96, 104, 156,
      189
      1825 *Der Kampf mit dem Drachen*, German prints imported
        by Boosey 156
      1825 *The Fight with the Dragon: A Romance*, re-engraved by
        Moses (Prowett) 123, 151n68, 156, 361
      1829 *Le Dragon de l'île de Rhodes*, French copy (Audot) 188,
        189
    1833 *Umrisse zu Schiller's Lied von der Glocke nebst Andeutungen*
      (Cotta) 36, 67, 101, 214, 216 (*Fig. 7.3a*), 218, 372, 374
      parts of pl. 1 & 2 anon. copied on tracing paper with other
        motifs (FDH) 218, 219 (*Fig. 7.5*)
      pl. 19 214, 216 (*Fig. 7.3a*)
        1835 Heath *The German Lovers*, re-engraved and
          repurposed in *Keepsake for 1835* 214–15, 217
          (*Fig. 7.3b*)
    1833 *Pegasus im Joche nebst Andeutungen* (Cotta) 36, 101
    1833–37 *Bürgschaft* (unpublished) 36, 44n111
  Shakespeare
    1827 *Hamlet* (16 pl. and a title vignette) 60, 97, 99, 109, 110, 358
      1828 French copy in steel (Audot) 187n46, 188, 189
    1827–46 *Shakespeare Gallery* 27, 42, 96, 97, 99, 101, 102, 189,
      357, 358
      French version (Audot) 189
    1833 *Macbeth* 101
    1836 *Romeo and Juliet* 33
    1838 *King Lear* 33; *see also* Index → Dante
R's own outlines and outlines in own albums
  1810 "Mythologische Darstellungen" known in one exemplar 39,
    61
  1831 trilingual *Phantasien und Wahrheiten/Fancies and Truths/
    Fantaisies et Réalités* 37, 101
    Der Kuß: Altes und neues Coelibat (*Old and New Celibate*)
      77–80
  1831 (1834) trilingual *Die Schachspieler* (*The Chess Players*) 33,
    89n123, 101, 310
    1853 copied by Albert Edward, Prince of Wales 358
    as *tableau vivant* for R's birthday 271
  1834 trilingual *Fantasien: Fancies. A Series of Subjects in Outline*
    27, 27n26, 37
    The Genius of Poetry/The Fate of the Poet, pl. 3 33, 88
  1840 *Winzerzug* (*Parade of the Vinedressers*), 8 lithographic
    prints 37, 40, 70, 212, 271, 334
    n.d. unsigned wood-carved relief 212
  1852 *Fancy* from "Selections from the Portfolio of MR" 38–39, 38
    (*Fig. 1.6*)
R's visionary drawings 37; *see also* 1. Family, Life, and Career → R as
  breadwinner → portraits and miniatures

7   Aesthetics, Inspiration, and Technique

allegory, treatment of   28, 33, 36, 37–38, 50, 310
    Fancy   37–39, 38 (*Fig. 1.6*); *see also* 6. Other Works → 1831
       trilingual *Phantasien und Wahrheiten*; 1831 (1834) trilingual *Die
       Schachspieler* (*The Chess Players*)
colour
    absence in outlines   1, 357
    use in –ed set   88–92, 90 (*Figs. 2.22, 2.23*), 91 (*Figs. 2.24, 2.25*), 296,
       296 (*Fig. 9.17*); *see also* Index → colour → symbolic use
drawing
    –s used for etching   67–69, 74–75, 74 (*Fig. 2.9*), 75 (*Fig. 2.10*)
    early equivalent of painting   37, 38, 39–40, 43, 50
    vs. imitative drawing (*Nachzeichnen*)   26, 40
etching
    as calque   298
    as endgame   4, 357; *see also* as reproduction vehicle
    as intercultural tool   3
    as own art   33–34, 38, 40, 48, 52, 69–70, 101
       cleaning and retouching *Faust* plates   40, 66, 69, 95, 101–2
       drawings as preparatory to –   77
       drawings used in –   64, 66, 67–69
       etching by trial and error   69
    as reproduction vehicle   3, 4, 42, 48–49, 51, 64, 69–71, 96, 213, 233,
       298
       R as "Poet in reproduction"   42, 355; *see also* 9. Effect and
         Function of R's *Faust* I Outlines → upshots → reproduction
painting   28, 32–33
    commissions   26–27, 34
    graphic art vs. painting   37, 39–40, 43, 50, 54, 180
    history and literature   26, 34–35, 39–40, 101
    imitative – (*nachmalen*)   25–26
    –s lost through wars   32, 32 (*Fig. 1.4*), 34; *see also* colour

8   R's Distinctive Outline Treatment

adapting Flaxman   122, 123–24
    adapting/modifying –   4, 49, 61, 86–89, 240, 357
    compared to   42–43, 48, 50, 54, 77, 88, 121*n*13, 121–24, 180, 189, 213,
       279
    conforming to   48
distinct features
    eroticism/sexual yearning   25, 39, 50, 52, 67, 73–77, 80, 82, 85, 88,
       103, 141, 145, 172, 203, 213–14, 224, 232, 327–29
    fanciful/playful disposition   25, 50, 52
    from classical to romantic   50
    grotesque   25, 37, 38–39, 38 (*Fig. 1.6*), 50, 82, 82 (*Fig. 2.18*), 88
    humour/wit   28, 44, 50, 62, 82, 83, 88, 110, 357
    imaginative brio   62
    metamorphosis   25, 39
    moral symbolism   80, 357
    personal reading of G's *Faust* through drawings   28–31, 67–86
    sentimentality   25, 80, 115, 120, 269, 343, 357
    (misleading) simplicity   89, 94, 162, 291, 298, 330
specific outline treatments
    anon. multiple set free for all   108, 357, 358
    propagation vehicle   42, 69, 71, 94, 355
    details stirring interpretation   2, 73, 82–84, 87, 110, 115–16, 124, 189,
       190, 240, 273, 279, 306, 308, 321
    fluidity of line   39
       frame dimensions per scene location   81, 96, 102, 273

    independence from text   36, 80–81, 149, 169, 189, 291
    line weight (reinforced contours)   67, 92, 168, 195
    vs. academic canon   26, 43

9   Effect and Function of R's *Faust 1* Outlines

assets
    bordering *Faust* in sharp contours   5, 6, 80, 258, 271–72, 273, 286,
       298
    explanation   273
    initiatory/allusive   48, 87, 110, 162, 169, 305, 321; *see also* Index →
       outline, aesthetic medium → by Schlegel → and initiation
    interpretation through visual media   4, 5, 6, 36, 45, 80, 82, 83, 84,
       87, 89, 93, 94, 116, 122, 124, 129, 136, 206, 213, 242, 257; *see also*
       Index → picture story
    narrative vigour   80, 357
    overall image planning   37
    R's prints as archetypes   *see* Index → printed items → as
       archetypes/templates
    resilience/adaptability   42, 45, 50, 51, 66, 68–69, 106, 108–15, 125,
       136, 139–45, 166, 175, 184, 201, 212, 216, 242, 245, 279, 284, 286, 321,
       338, 355, 356, 357
    stimulating symbolism   73, 87, 310, 312–13; *see also* Index →
       symbolism
    stirring emotions   62, 87–88, 92, 136, 273, 329–330, 332
    stylization and characterization   43, 80, 189
    synoptic summary   5, 6, 136, 149, 167, 169, 213, 214, 281, 291
    theatricality   241, 270–73
       pull of etching on stage   189, 274–76, 286–87
functions
    creating stereotypes   84, 206
    drill tools for copying   184, 185–86, 210, 216, 356*n*7
    empowering interactive reading   1, 2, 6, 48, 87, 92, 357
    marketing tools   52–54, 55, 162–63, 170–72, 357; *see also* Index →
       marketing
    model etchings for the stage   50, 186–87, 271–72, 273–74, 279–80,
       281, 286, 290–91, 296–97, 298
upshots
    conversions
       cultural mediation   115, 163, 255, 304–13
          beyond outlines   254–354
          multimedia dissemination   112
          templates for objects   334, 347
       ingenious interlingual translations   1, 3, 35–36, 50, 122, 130, 136,
         137, 166, 179, 358
       steering translation   127, 167; *see also* Index → translations
         (textual); translations (visual)
    diffusion across cultures   40, 45, 48–49, 50, 54, 58, 62, 95–112, 136,
       137–66, 175–76, 181–211, 212–45, 254, 355–57
    making R known   3, 40, 54
    mediation card for Goethe's *Faust*   1–3, 39, 40, 45, 51, 54, 58, 89,
       115–17, 120, 122, 126, 137, 159, 163, 166, 175–76, 179, 183, 201, 206,
       208–11, 213, 227, 229–31, 268, 297, 306–7, 338, 340, 356, 357
       Faust as democratic work shared by all   136, 240, 250, 358; *see
       also* Index → reader categories of R's outlines; reception of
       Goethe's *Faust*
    reproduction
       and aura   252–54; *see also* Index → aura
       and diffusion   4, 28, 242, 357–58; *see also* Index → diffusion (of
       prints/print culture)

INDEX ON MORITZ RETZSCH

upshots, reproduction (*cont.*)

    and remediation   3, 77, 136, 137, 163, 227, 255, 277, 286, 291, 298, 355

    and replication culture   89, 108, 212; *see also* Index → copying; pirating R

    and typification   297–98; *see also* Index → typification/typifying

    shifting rules in appreciation   115, 115*n*87, 136; *see also* Index → engravings/etchings

    silent poetry on stage (Gautier)   2, 3, 309, 321, 356

10   Reception

as gifted artist (seen by others)   30, 34, 35, 36, 62, 81, 88, 286; *see also* Index → *geistreich*

disparaged/redeemed   44–45, 88–89

name misspelt

    "d'après Restech"   225, 372

    "J. Retsch" (in Bohte's catalogues)   97, 124

    Kretzch   307, 309

    Reitsch   201

    Reschz   306, 307

    Reshtz   306, 307

    Retsch (as published by Cotta 1816 & 1820)   8, 36, 52, 60, 64, 66, 97, 99, 108, 123, 127, 138, 142, 147, 154, 156, 159, 161, 162, 166, 179, 186, 188, 191, 206, 220, 221, 281, 291, 307, 308, 309[1]

    Retzch   189

    Reztch   307

    Rœtzsch   307, 309

reception   80, 95, 96, 120, 121, 157, 180, 181, 200, 206, 210, 242, 356

    comparative   3, 5, 95

    underrated by copies   4–5, 107, 190, 206, 253, 257, 356–58, 368

    uneven/negative   39, 45; *see also* Index → Goethe, Johann Wolfgang v., and R

per area and country

    Australia   137, 169, 175, 369

    Belgium   99, 181, 197–200, 210, 215, 355, 364

    Britain (mainly England)   3, 25, 36, 39, 40, 48–49, 59, 60, 62, 99, 120–76, 179, 180, 215, 224–25, 255–62, 264–68, 281, 291, 294–97, 299–301, 304–6, 311–21, 352, 355, 358

    Denmark   200, 355, 369

---

1   This list does not include occurrences in captions or appendices.

Europe (including comparative –)   1–3, 39, 40, 54, 60, 62, 99, 106, 122, 163, 166, 170, 179–81, 200, 210, 215–16, 222, 227, 231, 255, 299, 347, 355–56

France   3, 36, 39, 42, 49, 99, 137, 159, 162, 166, 177–97, 200, 201–11, 215, 225–27, 233, 238, 242–47, 257, 279, 281–85, 290–91, 294–95, 299, 301–2, 306–9, 333, 346, 347–48, 355, 356

German States   2, 3–4, 25, 26, 35–36, 37, 39–51, 52–62, 63–67, 80–81, 85–94, 95–119, 122–23, 138, 156, 179–80, 189–90, 200, 201, 215–21, 222–24, 227–31, 233–40, 255, 257, 261–69, 271–81, 286–87, 288–94, 298, 301, 303–4, 329–32, 333–52, 355, 356

Hungary   99, 363

Italy   242, 247–54, 355, 357, 377

Lithuania   137, 159, 163, 166, 215, 355

Netherlands (the)   137, 159, 163–66, 197, 215, 355, 367–68

Poland   137, 163, 200, 215, 220, 367

Russia   58, 200, 287–88, 355

United States of America   3, 25, 28, 37, 80, 137, 142, 153, 169, 173–75, 189, 200, 203, 210, 240–42, 299, 310–11, 323–24, 325–29, 333–34, 347, 355, 361, 368, 376

11   Influence

Cornelius

    R compared to –   39, 45–49, 59–60, 61–62, 332

    – compared to R   25, 39, 42, 43, 45, 48–49, 50, 60, 61, 62, 65, 87, 240, 247, 280–81, 332, 358

    R influenced by –   97, 103

R influenced by Chodowiecki?   71

R influencing

    entrepreneurs   *see* Index → Beecham; Berliner Zinnfiguren; Fechner; Petit

    French romantic circles   *see* Index → Colin; Devéria; Delacroix; Gautier; Nerval

    Goethe   274, 275 (*Fig. 9.3 top*), 276 (*Fig. 9.4 top*)

    literature/men of letters   *see* Index → Béraud, Merle, and Nodier; Byron; Craig; Dickens; Disraeli; Gautier; Heine; Laborde; Poe; Pollock; Ross; Shelley, P. B.

    other artists   176, 239; *see also* Index → Berryman; Corbould; Darley; Delacroix; Frère; Friedrich; Hayez; Jaeckel; Johannot; Kaulbach; Kreling; Leighton; Phiz; Seibertz; Stothard; Votteler

    theatre (the)   270–302   *see also* Index → Brühl; Craig; Gley; Holtei; Irving; Kladzig; Lefèvre; Schütz-Höffert; Schinkel; Schütz; stage (the) and R's impact; Terry; Tieck

General Index

Abend-Zeitung (Dresden)   279, 288n75
   Abend-Zeitung. Artistisches Notizenblatt (Dresden)   104n45
abstraction   52, 86–87, 169, 190, 250, 322, 357; *see also* outline,
   aesthetic medium → by Schlegel → and abstraction
Ackermann, Rudolph   170; *see also* Tilt
Adam, Adolphe, 1852 *Orfa*, mime and ballet   309
Adelaide of Saxe-Meiningen   *see* Queen Dowager
Aders, Eliza (wife of K.)   123
Aders, Karl (Charles)   121, 123
advertising   95, 102, 103–4, 105 (*Fig. 3.8*), 106, 108, 120, 122, 124, 126, 135,
   136, 138, 139, 148n48, 149n59, 156, 161n93, 163, 169, 179, 184, 185
   (*Figs. 6.7a–b*), 187, 191, 203, 208, 251, 282, 288, 299, 305, 347, 349,
   352, 357, 358, 359, 362, 364, 365, 378
   buyers' psychology   54, 66, 126, 148, 149, 170, 189; *see also*
      Beecham; Berryman; posters
Aeschylus   48, 86, 122, 213
aestheticism   206, 208
Aign, Walter   257n7
Albert Edward, Prince of Wales (later Edward VII)   358, 376–77
Albert of Saxe-Coburg and Gotha (Prince Consort to Queen Victoria)
   287, 299, 358
Album aus der Damenzeitung Iris (post 1849)   237 (*Fig. 7.21b*), 238, 374,
   376; *see also* Schuler
Album national (*L'*)   281n50
albums   3, 4, 5, 73, 77, 95, 99, 102–7, 163, 168–72, 175, 176, 240, 241, 255,
   262–68, 291, 302, 305, 308, 309, 333, 355, 356, 357, 358, 368
   as symbolic objects   170–72, 171 (*Figs. 5.19, 5.20*)
   combined   52, 54, 96, 105–7, 116, 181; *see also* industrialized
   friendship – (*Stammbücher*)   30, 30 (*Fig. 1.2*)
   industrialized   220, 288, 358, 364, 365, 366, 368; *see also* *Album*
      aus der Damenzeitung Iris; Colin; Darley; formats; *Scenen aus*
      Goethe's Faust in acht lithographirten Bilder
alchemy
   as graphic or poetic process   40, 297
   as practice   208, 221; *see also* Rembrandt
   by analogy   352
   visual allusions to –   170, 171 (*Fig. 5.19*), 204
Aldebert, Isaac, friend of H. C. Robinson   123
Alfieri, Vittorio   288, 289n82
Aljumily, Refat   149n60
Allan, David   240
allegories
   by Cornelius   45, 150, 150 (*Fig. 5.8*)
   by Leighton   172–75, 172 (*Fig. 5.21*)
   by Riepenhausen   110, 111 (*Figs. 3.10b, 3.11, 3.12*)
   in *Hortus deliciarum*   133–35
   in poetry   224
   in theatre (Holtei)   286
   political   197, 212; *see also* Index on MR → 7. Aesthetics,
      Inspiration, and Technique → allegory, treatment of
Allegra, Byron's daughter   327
Allert, Beate   238n46
Allevy, Marie-Antoinette   281n48
allusions
   textual   184, 303–4, 307, 325, 330, 332
   visual   115, 115 (*Figs. 3.16a–b*), 305
   visual/textual   302, 302 (*Figs. 9.21a–b*)
      btw. Dickens and Phiz   319–21

almanacs   33, 36, 71, 110, 115, 116, 212
   and moral message   112–14
   and patriotic verse   113
   Kleines Geschenk zum neuen Jahr für 1818   95, 109, 112–13, 112
      (*Fig. 3.13*), 113 (*Fig. 3.14a–c*), 323, 370
   Kleines Geschenk zum neuen Jahr für 1820   95, 109, 112 (*Fig. 3.13*),
      114 (*Fig. 3.15a–c*), 115 (*Fig. 3.16a–b*), 323, 370; *see also* keepsake
      literature
Amable, set designer   279
Amburger, Erik   287n73
Amyot, Thomas Edward, friend of H. C. Robinson   123
analogies, visual   48, 143, 144–45 (*Figs. 5.4, 5.5*), 170, 171 (*Fig. 5.20*), 247,
   248 (*Fig. 7.27*), 313, 314–15 (*Fig. 10.2–10.3*), 320, 320 (*Fig. 10.6*), 321
   and poetry   87
   and reading   48, 287
   as neoclassical principle   288
"Analysis" (1820 Boosey)   36n62, 118, 128, 133, 137, 138–40, 147, 148,
   154n74, 166, 299n112, 359–60
Anster, John, *Faust* trans.   169, 368
Apel, Johann August   32, 33; *see also* Scharfenberg circle
apes/aping   *see* imitation
Apollinaire, Guillaume   197
arabesque   44n112, 50, 75, 76 (*Fig. 2.11*), 86, 112 (*Fig. 3.13*), 114, 130, 130
   (*Fig. 4.1*), 192 (*Fig. 6.12*), 193–94, 221n18, 250
Ardit, E.   225, 372
archives
   Blair Museum of Lithophanes   349 (*Fig. 12.8*)
   Cotta (DLA, Marbach)   27nn21–22, 40n88, 59n36, 60n42, 63n58,
      65n69, 69n81, 95nn2–3, 96, 96nn10–11, 99n28, 101nn33–35,
      102nn36–41, 103n, 106n51, 220n12, 352n38, 359
   Deutsches Literatur Archiv (DLA, Marbach)   44, 65, 98 (*Fig. 3.1a*),
      99n26, 363
   Dresden Stadtarchiv   60n40
   Knittlingen Faust-Archiv   217, 373, 378
   Knittlingen Faust-Museum   229, 231 (*Fig. 7.16*), 289 (*Fig. 9.12*)
   KPM (Berlin, Charlottenburg)   334
   Ross (LSHTM, London)   221, 221n17, 222 (*Fig. 7.6 top*), 223 (*Fig. 7.7*
      top), 377
   Weimar (GSA)   44, 58n27, 59n31, 62n54, 64nn60–61, 125n47,
      148n42, 274nn17–18, 277n19, 283n58
Ariosto   259
Aristophanes, *The Frogs*   258
Arkas (mythology)   39
Armingeat, Jacqueline   254
Arndt, Walter, *Faust* trans.   5, 31, 74, 170, 261, 287
Art Journal (*The*)   27, 28nn30–31, 38, 38 (*Fig. 1.6*), 160, 163n101, 173n126,
   240
art societies   112, 229, 236n36, 240
   American Art-Union   241–42
   Art Union of London   240
   Saxon Art Association   27
   Stuttgart art club (Württembergischer Kunstverein Stuttgart)   112
Art Union Monthly Journal   27
art hierarchies   3, 4, 26, 37, 39–40, 43, 45, 51, 133, 135, 180, 239
artefacts   3, 52, 117, 125, 166, 168, 169, 175, 176, 189, 192, 213, 239, 286,
   307, 333–54, 355, 356
   and emotional lives   62, 330, 334, 338, 347
   and everyday poetics   330, 333, 334, 346, 347, 352

GENERAL INDEX

artefacts (*cont.*)
as "mysterious items" (Marx) 338
as provocation to thought 334, 335 (*Fig. 12.1*), 336–37 (*Fig. 12.2*), 339 (*Fig. 12.3*), 341 (*Fig. 12.4*), 342 (*Fig. 12.5a*), 343 (*Fig. 12.5b*), 345 (*Fig. 12.6b*), 347, 348 (*Fig. 12.7*), 350 (*Fig. 12.9*), 351 (*Fig. 12.10*), 371; *see also* home decorations; lithophanes; porcelain plates; pipe bowls; tin figurines; Ulrich
Artemis (mythology) 39
asyndeton 333
Athenaeum (1799 Schlegel essay) 86, 87*n*103, 310
Athenaeum (*The*) 169–70, 240, 368
Atkins, Lillian Espy Reed 59, 139, 140*n*23, 142*n*31, 146, 148*n*53, 149, 180, 212–13, 355
Auclair, Mathias, and Pauline Girard 279*n*32, 284*n*
auctions 55–56, 56 (*Fig. 2.2*), 57*n*20, 123, 195, 197, 200, 221, 333, 334, 336–37 (*Fig. 12.2*), 340*n*17, 347, 350 (*Fig. 12.9*)
audiences *see* reader categories of R's outlines
Audot, Louis-Désiré (son of L.-E.) 190
Audot, Louis-Eustache, bookseller and scribbler 187–89, 190
1826–29 announcements-cum-catalogues 190
1828 *Faust. Vingt-six gravures d'après les dessins de Retsch* 141, 179–81, 183, 184–90, 186 (*Fig. 6.8*), 187 (*Fig. 6.9*), 190 (*Fig. 6.10*), 191, 210, 362
alluring cover 187–88, 187 (*Fig. 6.9*)
blunted copies by Branche and Trueb 218
booklets owned by artists and writers 197, 297
outlets 201*n*89
theatre vogue 186–87, 198, 282, 372; *see also* Voïart
1828– *Shakespeare Gallery* 170, 189
1828 Shakespeare, *Hamlet* 188, 189
1828–34 bilingual *Musée de peinture et de sculpture* 187
1829 *Faust. Vingt-six gravures d'après les dessins de Retsch* 186 (*Fig. 6.8*), 190, 363
1829 Schiller, *Dragon de l'île de Rhodes*, with R re-engraved 189
1829 Schiller, *Fridolin* probably after Ackermann and Tilt 170
and relations
15 prints with Polish captions 367
Bulcock 163, 198, 361
Kennerley's copies 163
Librairie Romantique 198, 363
Meline 364
Audot, Louis-Joseph (son of L.-E.) 190
Augé, Christian, and Pascale Linant de Bellefonds 195*n*65
Augusta, Princess, future Queen of Prussia 56, 109, 110
Augustus II, aka Augustus II the Strong 27, 85
aura 138, 242, 347–49
as in W. Benjamin 252–54
enhanced
by replicas/reproduction 149, 253, 298
in circulation 3, 40, 59
Auvray Frères 184–85, 185 (*Fig. 6.7a–b*), 362
Auvray, printseller 181, 182 (*Fig. 6.5*), 183 (*Fig. 6.6*), 184, 188, 210
1824 lithographed *Faust* after R *see* Muret
avant-garde genres 184, 309
Avery-Quash, Susanna 135*n*89
Axmann, J., engraving Ramberg's 1828–29 *Faust* plates 209 (*Fig. 6.21*)

Bacchus (mythology) 37, 40, 212, 271, 333; *see also* Dionysus; Pan; Silenus
Bach, Max 95*n*1; 97*n*17
Baci Perugina, chocolates 251–52, 252 (*Fig. 7.31a*), 253 (*Fig. 7.31b*), 357
Baduel, Daniel, Aude Bertrand, and Christian Dauchel 203*n*95

Baldensperger, Fernand 203, 204*n*96
Ball, Douglas 172–73*n*125, 175*n*129
Ball, J. Meredith, 1887 *Mephistopheles: March* 299
Balzac, Honoré de 204
1830 pub. 1840 *Gobseck* 346
1831 *La Peau de chagrin* 346
1842 foreword to the *Human Comedy* 297
Bancroft, George 324–25
bande dessinée 120; *see also* strip cartoon
Bann, Stephen 180
Barber, Giles 179*n*13
Barbier, Frédéric 180
Barbier, *Faust* adaptor 187
Barchou de Penhoen, Auguste 346
Batrachomyomachia (*Battle of the Frogs and Mice*), mock epic of the *Iliad* 258
Baudelaire, Charles 203
1863 *Le Peintre de la vie moderne* 227, 311
Baudry, Louis-Claude, bookseller and publisher 201–3, 206, 210
1840 *Faust, ein Trauerspiel, beide Theile in einem Bande* 201, 366
1840 synoptic frontispiece for all *Faust I* and *Faust II* editions 201, 202 (*Fig. 6.17*)
1843 *Faust, eine Tragödie, beide Theile in einem Bande* 201, 366
1855 new ed. 203, 367
European Bookstore (*Baudry's europäische Buchhandlung*) 201
outlets 201
reading room 201; *see also* series
Baudry's widow 203
Bauer, Josephine 126*n*51, 126*n*53, 126*n*58
Bäumel, Jutta 37*n*72
Bechstein, Ludwig, 1832, 1833 *Faustus* 118
Beck, Andreas 264
Becker, Wilhelm Gottlieb 26, 40, 41
1804–11 *Augusteum: Dresden's antike Denkmäler enthaltend* 26, 40–41 (*Fig. 1.7*)
Beecham, Thomas, of Lancashire, powders and pills 352, 353 (*Figs. 12.11, 12.12*), 378
Beethoven, Ludwig van, *lied* of 1803 *Margaret at the Spinning Wheel* 257
Belgian counterfeit editions (*contrefaçons/préfaçons belges*) 197–200
aesthetic and commercial effect of R 198, 200
set ideas nuanced 200, 210
Bell, George, and Sons, *Faust* editions 168, 368, 369; *see also* Swanwick
Belle Assemblée (*La*) 154, 159*n*89
Bellotto, Bernardo 27
Benjamin, Walter 252; *see also* aura
Bennett, Shelley M. 240*n*49
Benoit, Charles, Adam West, and Roland Weibexahl, 1857 *Neue Bilder zu deutschen Dichtern* 267; *see also* parodies of *Faust I*
Benson, Arthur Burnett 324, 329*n*19; *see also* Stith, C. P.
Bent, William *see Monthly Literary Advertiser* (*The*)
Bentley, Gerald Eades 123*n*35
Bentley, S. and R., printers 156
Benz, Richard 45, 50, 84, 109*n*75, 240
Béraud, Antony, Jean-Toussaint Merle, and Charles Nodier, 1828 *Faust* (or *Le Docteur Faust*) 186, 281–82, 290; *see also* Dorval; Lefèvre; Lemaître
Berg, Hartmut 340*n*17, 342*n*22
Berliner Zinnfiguren 349; *see also* tin figurines
Berlioz, Hector 185, 206*n*100
Bern Treaty 231

Bernardt, Käthe   212

Bernhard II, Duke of Saxe-Meiningen   58

Berryman, John, wood engraver   163
   pink cover   162–63, 164 (*Fig. 5.17 top*), 176, 187–88, 361

Berthier, Patrick   286*n*65, 306*n*10, 306*n*13, 309*n*29

Berthoud, Henry, Jr, painter and engraver   159, 166
   1824 *Tartini's Dream* by Boilly   162
   1825 *British Theatrical Gallery* by Daniel Terry   162
   1825 *Faustus: Illustrated in Twenty-Six Outlines by Retsch*   159–62,
      160 (*Fig. 5.15*), 161 (*Fig. 5.16*), 180, 182, 361
      and Muret's French copy   162, 179, 182, 182 (*Fig. 6.5*), 360; *see
         also* Hullmandel

Berthoud, Henry, Sr (printseller, father of H., Jr)   159, 162

Bertin, Louise, 1831 *Fausto: Opera semi-seria in quattro atti* (Théâtre
      Italien)   282–83, 283 (*Fig. 9.9*), 372

Besser, Johann Heinrich, Perthes's associate   37, 122

Bewick, William, painter   59

Bey, Hermann   377

Bible   130, 176
   Book of Job   140, 141
   John's Gospel   130
   multiplication of loaves and fishes   330
   Proverbs   321

bibliophiles   148, 154, 204
   as Faust in their libraries   162
   bibliophilic protocols   4, 96, 118 (*Fig. 3.18*), 118–19, 124–25, 128,
      129–30, 130 (*Fig. 4.1*), 147, 160–61, 162, 355
      boundaries shifting   133–35, 136; *see also* bookplates; books
         and prints as cultural objects; collectors; connoisseurs; ex
         libris; Dibdin; Grenville; Hoe

Bichebois, Louis, Pierre, Alphonse, lithographer   194, 195, 210
   1828–29 title-page for J. Milbert, *Itinéraire pittoresque du fleuve
      Hudson*   193–94
   1830 Blanc, *Protestation des députés réunis chez Alexandre de
      Laborde*   195
   1830 Giard *Faust* cover   192, 193, 193 (*Fig. 6.13*), 194–95, 197, 203,
      363–64

Biedermeier   32*n*47, 213, 347, 349 (*Fig. 12.8*), 343*n*23, 343*n*25
   post-Biedermeier   107

Bielmeier, Katrin   26*n*13

Bierman, draughtsman?   288, 289 (*Fig. 9.12*), 373

bindings   3, 356*n*7
   cloth – in red, black and gilt   170, 368
   half-leather publisher's – with gilt spines   201
   in Mephistophelean red   168, 368
   industrialized –   172–73, 172 (*Fig. 5.21*)
   Japanese –   200, 241, 301, 340
   R on alluring commercial –   77, 170–75, 171 (*Figs. 5.19, 5.20*), 172
      (*Fig. 5.21*), 176, 379; *see also* Leighton; Murton; spine designs

Birch, Charles Bell, artist   240

Birch, Jonathan, *Faust I* and *Faust II* trans.   137, 163, 167–70, 172,
      172 (*Fig. 5.21*), 173, 174 (*Fig. 5.23*), 200, 352, 353 (*Figs. 12.11, 12.12*),
      366–67, 376, 378

Black and Armstrong, publishers
   1837 English *Umrisse zu Faust, zweiter Theil* by R   102, 365
   1839 Birch's *Faust I*   167, 168*n*115, 172 (*Fig. 5.21*), 173, 174 (*Fig. 5.23*),
      366
   commercializing R's *Umrisse zu Goethe's Faust, erster und zweiter
      Theil*   105, 365

Black, Young and Young, London publishers   101, 103

Blackwood's Magazine   129

Blaeschke, Axel   1*n*2, 120*n*7

Blair Museum of Lithophanes   347, 348 (*Fig. 12.7*), 349 (*Fig. 12.8*), 374

Blake, William, and H. C. Robinson   121*n*18, 122–23
   Illustrations of the Book of Job   88, 123

Blanc, *Protestation des députés réunis chez Alexandre de Laborde*
      195

Blaze de Bury, Henri, 1847 *Faust I* trans. into French   180*n*24, 207
      (*Fig. 6.20*), 233, 307, 375

Blocksberg (location)   304
   in Goethe's *Faust I*   286, 290

Bluebeard   318

Bobée, Auguste, French publisher   183

Boès, Karl, ed. of *La Plume*   208

Bogue, David, Tilt's associate   170; *see also* Tilt

Böhm, Angela   34*n*54

Böhme, E., printer   212

Bohte, Johann Heinrich, German bookseller in London   62, 95, 97,
      124, 125, 128, 138, 139, 148, 156, 167
   1820 *Extracts* letterpress (hybrid assortments)   124–25, 129, 130
      (*Fig. 4.1*), 137, 139, 143, 147, 359
   1821 (failed) bilingual landscape *Faust* with R interleaved   119, 125,
      128, 156, 163, 175, 360
   1823 *Faust, eine Tragödie* (in German)   163, 163*n*100
   and Cotta   126
   catalogues   97, 124, 126
   importing R's *Umrisse*   95, 97–99, 121, 124–25, 129, 136, 139, 141, 148,
      359
   launching R   125, 126–27; *see also London Magazine*; Scott, J.;
      Wainewright
   obituary   129
   reading room (*Deutsche Lesebibliothek*)   125

Boieldieu, François-Adrien   185

Boileau, Daniel, *Faustus* trans.   128, 139, 140, 148, 356

Boisserée, Sulpiz   45, 48, 59, 61
   1823 *Geschichte und Beschreibung des Doms von Köln*   49

Bonington, Richard Parkes   226

book as
   cathedral   172
   emotion-laden possession   62, 154
   memento   325, 329
   monitor of life   173
   rose   323, 324, 325–29, 352; *see also* artefacts; books and prints as
      cultural objects

book history   5, 357

book trade
   Anglo-German –   99, 124–25, 124*n*40
   British –   156, 159, 166, 175, 175*n*131
   Brussels –   197–200
   Dutch –   166
   European –   166, 180, 215–16
   French –   180, 187–88, 190–91, 201–6
   German –   45, 106–8, 121, 122
      and national literature   108, 122; *see also* Cotta; Perthes
   shifting rules   136
   to relate to print trade (and stage)   3, 166, 180, 186, 338
   triangular relations in –   179–81; *see also* circulation; diffusion;
      distribution

book lovers   *see* bibliophiles; bookplates; collectors; Dibdin; ex libris;
      Hoe; Laughlin; reader categories of R's outlines; Wilder

bookplates   162
   Evans, Lawrence B.   105*n*47
   Forman, Harry Buxton   367
   Glanville, T. W., heraldic –   147*n*40, 360

GENERAL INDEX

bookplates (*cont.*)
Hoe, R., III   173, 174 (*Fig. 5.23*), 376
Laughlin, James, gift of –   173–75, 174 (*Fig. 5.23*), 376
Sharp, Samuel   361; *see also* ex libris
books and prints as cultural objects   2, 5, 5*n*11, 128, 176, 252–54, 355;
see also artefacts; objects; printed items; things
Boosey, Thomas and Sons, publishers, and Rodwell and Martin,
printsellers   137, 138, 139, 162, 189, 305
1820 twofold ed.   58, 62, 118, 126, 128, 133, 135, 136, 137–39, 146
(*Fig. 5.6*), 151 (*Fig. 5.9*), 154, 175, 188–89, 221, 224, 264, 328
(*Figs. 11.2, 11.3*), 359–60, 367, 370
adapted to English *Zeitgeist*   139–45, 142 (*Fig. 5.2*), 144 (*Fig. 5.4
top*)
and Coleridge   120, 139, 140, 148, 151, 324; *see also* Coleridge
debate
enlarged end-users   139
"food for thought" to Goethe   58, 62, 80, 85–86, 138, 140
1820 ed. re-issued?   146–47
1821 *Faustus: from the German of Goethe* with 27 pl.   148–54, 166,
175, 224, 281, 323, 324, 360
Moses frontispiece adapting Cornelius to R   149–51, 150
(*Fig. 5.8*), 151 (*Fig. 5.9*), 180, 360
carping reviews of trans.   148–49
circular ornament   151, 151*n*68, 152 (*Fig. 5.10a*), 153 (*Fig. 5.10b*),
176, 360, 361
marketing strategy   149
1821 *Faustus* as text octavo with Goethe's portrait   148, 149, 160,
161, 162, 163
read by publisher W. Heinemann   149, 149*n*65
Boosey, Thomas and Sons, publishers   154, 156
1824 *Faustus from the German*, stereotype ed.   154–59, 158
(*Fig. 5.12*), 169, 175, 305, 361, 364, 366
as shared reference   157–59
"kinetic" dimension   154–56, 155 (*Figs. 5.11a–c*)
bootlegging   *see* copyright; pirating R
Borchmeyer, Dieter   89
Borges, Jorge Luis   5, 30
Borne, Ludwig   283
Börsch-Supan, Helmut, and Gottfried Riemann   277*n*20
Börsch-Supan, Helmut, and Lucius Grisebach   277*n*23
Bosch, Hieronymus   172
Böttiger, Karl August, on R   43, 65, 104, 108, 156, 188
Boucher, Antoine, Nerval's uncle   190
Bouffé, Hugues, actor   333
Bourbon Restoration   179, 195, 227
Bourgoing, Paul de, lithophane patentee   346, 352
Bracebridge, Charles Holte (Holt)   56, 57, 58
Bracebridge, Selina, née Mills (wife of C.)   56–58
Brain, John, steel engraving R   137, 163, 168, 366, 368
diminutive illustrations   168, 369
in portfolio   169, 366, 367; *see also* Birch
Branche, Jean-Antoine, engraver
1828 Audot *Faust* copies (with Trueb) after R   187, 198, 218, 362,
363; *see also* Audot; Trueb
1828 Audot *Hamlet* copies on steel after R   189
1831 outline lithographs of *Robert le Diable* sets   187
Brandegee, Emily (granddaughter of C. P. Stith)   325, 327
Brentano, Clemens   323
Bresc-Bautier, Geneviève   195*n*65
bricolage   *see* Lévi-Strauss
Bridgwater, Patrick   125*n*44
Britton, John   123

Brocken
Heine's – tour   303–4
– spectre (*Brockengespenst*)   304; *see also* Index on MR →
3. Choice *Faust 1* Scenes Outlined → Pl. 21 & 22
Brockhaus, Friedrich Arnold   167, 168, 172 (*Fig. 5.21*), 174 (*Fig. 5.23*), 366
Brown, Eluned   281*n*45
Browne, Hablôt Knight   *see* Phiz
Brühl, Karl Friedrich v., theatre manager   277, 279, 286, 338, 356
Brunet, Jacques-Charles   180
Brunsiek, Sigrun   50, 273
Bry, Joseph (J. Bry aîné), French publisher
1848 *Werther*   203, 204
1850 *Faust*   203–4, 204 (*Fig. 6.18*), 210, 242–45, 243 (*Fig. 7.23*), 244
(*Figs. 7.24a, 7.24b*), 245 (*Fig. 7.25*), 253, 367, 376, 378
turning point in French reception   203, 206
inventor of *roman de quatre sous*   203; *see also* Frère; Nerval;
Maresq and Pelvey; series
Bühler, Roman   287*n*73
Bulcock, James, British publisher   162
1826 *Faust* prints in batches   162
1827 *Retzsch's Outlines* re-engraved by Kennerley   162–63, 164
(*Fig. 5.17 top*), 188, 361
and Audot   163, 187, 198, 362, 367
extensive influence   163, 166, 218; *see also* Berryman; Kennerley
Bulletin of the American Art-Union   241
Burckhardt, Jacob   43
Bürger, Gottfried August   33, 36, 40, 60, 67, 85, 85*n*, 287*n*72; *see also*
Index on MR → 6. Other Works → R's outlines after → Bürger
Buri, Christian Karl Ernst Wilhelm   113
Burkhardt, Ramona   56*n*19
burlesque   245, 254–55, 268–69, 308, 313, 343, 373, 375
and tragedy   259, 261
vs. jingoism   269
vs. sentimentality   269
Burns, Robert, compared to Goethe   123
Burty, Philippe   177, 245*n*75
Burwick, Frederick   92*n*125, 149*n*60, 272, 281*n*44
Burwick, Frederick, and James McKusick, eds., 2007 *Faustus. From the
German of Goethe. Translated by Samuel Coleridge*   124*nn*39–40,
125*n*64, 128*n*65, 128*n*70, 139, 149, 166*n*107; *see also* Coleridge
debate
Busch, Günter   45, 50, 239, 240*n*52, 240*n*55, 357*n*9
Busch, Werner   32*n*45, 86*n*99, 109–10*n*75, 239
Butler, Samuel, *Hudibras*   261
Butler, Stephen   186*n*41
Byfield, engravers' family   135
Byfield, John, wood engraver   134–35, 134 (*Fig. 4.4a–b*), 135
(*Fig. 4.4c*), 184, 370
Byron, George Gordon (Noel)   2, 120, 197, 203, 221, 240, 304, 305*n*8,
322, 323, 356, 357
Byron's rose   154, 323–27, 326 (*Fig. 11.1a, 11.1b*), 352; *see also*
Stith, C. P.
his *Faustus* ed.   55, 137, 148, 151, 154, 323–27, 329, 352, 360
politics/visit to USS Constitution   329
works by
Cain   120
Don Juan   324
Manfred   221
Lara   240

Cadmus (mythology)   39
Calcutta Journal of Politics and General Literature (The)   154

426 GENERAL INDEX

Caldesi, Leonida   299
Caleb (Bible)   212
Callisto (mythology)   39
Calloway, Stephen   176*n*133
Cambridge Chronicle   169*n*121
Campe, Joachim Heinrich, *Theophron*   113, 140
Canaletto   27
Canova, Antonio, outlines   187
Cappiello, Leonetto
   1907 poster *Thermogène* and 1906 poster *Maurin Quina*   358
captions
   absence of – to R's outlines   2, 52, 54, 74, 87, 112, 122, 138
   agency of   188–89, 205, 210, 233, 255, 360, 361, 362, 367, 369, 371
   bilingual   170, 187*n*45, 189, 198, 363, 364
   carved (*Winzerzug*)   212
   changes in   149, 154, 179, 188–89
   classy absence of   169, 192
   compared   188
   descriptive   138, 162
   eccentric   161, 170, 361, 377
   faulty   139, 149, 154, 204, 206
   Faust I lines as –   110, 111 (*Fig. 3.12*), 113 (*Figs. 3.14 a–c*), 114 (*Figs. 3.15 a–c*), 226, 231, 231 (*Fig. 7.16*), 372
   in parody   264, 267
   later introduction of –   3, 138, 162, 181, 186, 187, 188, 360
   superfluous   198
   translated   163, 188, 367
   uses of –   137, 154, 167, 168, 181, 186, 187, 188, 195, 201, 204, 205, 210, 219, 264, 282, 360, 362, 366, 369, 372, 376
caricature   180, 255, 257, 268, 301
   reviving the original   259–61, 262–64, 268; *see also* burlesque; parody
Carlowitz, Carl Adolf v., War Secretary   26
Carlyle, Thomas   57, 167
Carney, Margaret   347*nn*28–29, 347*n*33, 352*n*40
Carrà, Carlo   247, 250*n*79
Carré, Jean-Marie   140*n*23
Carus, Carl Gustav   43
   "Carus album"   34–35, 35 (*Fig. 1.5*)
cathedrals   88*n*115, 180*n*23
   Cologne   48–49
   Frankfurt *Kaiserdom*   270
   in *Faust I* and Faust iconography   46 (*Figs. 1.9, 1.10*), 47 (*Figs. 1.11, 1.12a–b*), 48, 80, 110–12, 111 (*Fig. 3.11, 3.12*)
   Meissen   270
Cayet, Pierre Victor Palma, 16th-c. trans. of anon. Faust legend   203
censorship   122, 197
   "impious" prologue   140–41, 142 (*Fig. 5.2*), 205; *see also* Coleridge; Protestant → reserve in images; Roman Catholicism
   censored male crotches   85, 108, 135, 141–42, 143, 162, 168, 221, 224, 362
      vs. overt female charms   62, 85, 141–43, 144 (*Fig. 5.4*), 145, 162, 168, 182, 243
   codpieces historical costume detail   143, 162, 201, 213–14, 215 (*Fig. 7.2*), 221; *see also* Index on MR → 3. Choice *Faust I* Scenes Outlined → Pl. 6, 7, 8, 15; → 8. R's Distinctive Outline Treatment → distinct features → eroticism/sexual yearning
Cerrito, Fanny, ballet dancer   309*n*26
Champfleury, 1883 *Les Vignettes romantiques*   206, 208, 377
Chapman and Hall, publishers   168, 173, 366
   1843 Birch's *Faust II* trans. (with F. A. Brockhaus)   168, 366
Charles X, French monarch   197, 363

Charles, Duke of Mecklenburg   298, 334–38
Charlet, Nicolas-Toussaint, artist   184
Chartier, Roger   120*n*2
   "intensive and extensive reading"   242
Chauvet, J.   245, 246, 246 (*Fig. 7.26*); *see also* Jourdain, G.
Chesterfield, Philip Dormer Stanhope, Earl of, 1774 *Letters to His Son on the Art of Becoming a Man of the World and a Gentleman*   140
Chodowiecki, Daniel   71, 86
Ciartes, portrait of Faust   208
cinema, early   322, 358; *see also* "kinetic" versions
circulation   48, 49, 268
   and copying/replication   108, 184, 212–15, 355–56
   and extensive/intensive iconography   49, 242–54
   and *Faust I* appropriation   5, 147, 175, 356
   and typification   108
   comparative/triangulated   3, 5, 179–80
   European   54, 55, 166, 175, 215–16, 355–57
      and beyond   241
   from prints to objects   334–54
   image –   48, 54, 252–54
   in Britain   59, 121, 124–27, 175–76
   in German States   51, 55, 71, 95, 109–12, 111 (*Figs. 3.10a–b, 3.11, 3.12*), 115–18
   of reproductions and media   3, 48, 75*n*84, 356–57; *see also* copying; distribution; diffusion; loose/scattered leaves; reception of Goethe's *Faust I*
Claes, Marie-Christine   198*n*78
Clairmont, Claire   327
Clapham, John Harold   179
Clark, Lewis Gaylord, ed. of *Knickerbocker*   324
classicism   39, 45, 49, 60, 86, 88
   and romanticism   49, 50, 87, 206, 288, 289–90, 357; *see also* neoclassical; neoclassicism
Clayton, Tim, and Sheila O'Connell   180
Clösges, Elisabeth   50, 52*n*1, 86*n*95, 97
Cochran, Peter   329*n*8
Colburn, Henry   305
Coleridge, Samuel Taylor   2, 120, 121, 126, 140, 151, 166, 281*n*44, 288, 324
   – debate (*Faustus* trans.)   55*n*17, 124*n*39, 136, 137, 149, 149*n*60, 166, 324; *see also* Boosey → 1821 *Faustus*
   Rime of the Ancient Mariner outlined   240
Colin, Alexandre   208, 372
   1829 *Album composé et dessiné sur pierre*   225, 372
      Faust and Margaret in the garden   225–26, 226 (*Fig. 7.10*)
Colin, Madame, *Gretchen at the Spinning Wheel*   224*n*23
collages   39, 118–19, 118 (*Fig. 3.18*), 135–36, 135 (*Figs. 4.4a–b*), 136 (*Fig. 4.4c*), 170, 171 (*Fig. 5.19*), 187–88, 187 (*Fig. 6.9*), 213, 370
collections
   private
      Dauer, Detlef (Magdeburg)   341 (*Fig. 12.4*), 343, 343 (*Fig. 12.5b*), 345 (*Fig. 12.6b*), 370, 374, 375
      Kasten, Hans (Bremen)   221
      Puppel (Berlin)   236*n*36
      Wegner, Peter-Christian (Lübeck)   237 (*Fig. 7.21b*), 338, 339 (*Fig. 12.3*), 340, 342 (*Fig. 12.5a*), 374, 377; *see also* Aders, K.; Britton; Hoe
   private→ institutional
      Berg Collection, NYPL (New York)   316 (*Fig. 10.4*), 318
      Bodmer, Martin (Geneva)   57 (*Fig. 2.3*), 108, 362
      Devéria, Achille (BnF, Paris)   206–8, 209 (*Fig. 6.21*), 225, 226 (*Fig. 7.10*), 227, 228 (*Fig. 7.11*), 229 (*Fig. 7.12*), 233, 234 (*Fig. 7.18*), 235 (*Fig. 7.19*), 371

GENERAL INDEX

private→ institutional (cont.)

Gabrielle Enthoven (V&A, London) 300 (*Fig. 9.18*), 301 (*Fig. 9.20*)
Goethe's music collection (Weimar) 283
Kippenberg (Düsseldorf) 219, 282n51, 282n53, 372
Kretzschmar v. Kienbusch, Carl Otto (Princeton) 200
Lahmann, Johann Friedrich (Dresden) 69
Moosmann-Böhme (Knittlingen) 231 (*Fig. 7.16*), 289 (*Fig. 9.12*), 351, 352, 373, 378
Speck (Beinecke, Yale) 99, 146–47, 184, 195, 200, 329, 355[1]
Tille, Alexander (HAAB, Weimar) 48n120, 108, 221n18, 237 (*Fig. 7.21a*), 238, 361, 362, 374; *see also* Grenville, T.; Stumme

institutional (public)

British Museum Prints and Drawings 97
Charlottenburg Palace (Berlin) 334
Goethe-Haus (Frankfurt) 334
Harvard's Theatre Collection (Boston, Ma.) 291, 292 (*Fig. 9.13*)
Kupferstichkabinett (Berlin) 101n30, 278 (*Fig. 9.5*), 370
Modena (→ Dresden) 26–27
Paris Opera "Prints after *Faust* scenes" 203
Prints Cabinet (Kupferstich-Kabinett, Dresden) 44, 67, 70
Royal Collection Trust 358n15, 373, 376–77
Saint Petersburg (Hermitage) 58, 67
Theatersammlung, Universität Köln (Cologne) 189n49, 372
Theatre and Performance (V&A, London)
V&A (Victoria and Albert Museum) 58, 62; *see also* libraries

collectors

R's prints tempting – 4, 54, 106, 108, 125, 126, 127, 129, 136, 137, 139, 143, 151, 154, 159, 162, 168, 169, 175, 176, 179, 181–84, 191, 204, 210, 216, 220–21, 236, 255, 277, 349, 357, 367, 368; *see also* bibliophiles; collections; connoisseurs; Dibdin; Robinson, H. C.; Sigismund

Collier, John D., ed. of *Monthly Register* 123, 156
Collier, John Payne (son of J. D.), Schiller trans. 123, 156, 170

colour

–ed lithographic prints after R 106, 107 (*Fig. 3.9*), 238–39, 238 (*Fig. 7.22*), 358, 368, 375
–ed version of Crowquill 255, 256 (*Figs. 8.1a, 8.1b*), 260 (*Fig. 8.3b*), 373
expressive/symbolic use of 89–92, 90 (*Figs. 2.22, 2.23*), 91 (*Fig. 2.24, 2.25*), 93 (*Fig. 2.26*), 250, 262, 287, 363, 378
of porcelain wares 338, 340, 352
on R portfolios and editions 52, 53 (*Figs. 2.1a-b*), 54, 96, 97, 102, 103 (*Fig. 3.6*), 105, 166, 212, 213, 365; *see also* bindings; devil; Mephistopheles

comic/comedy 37, 89, 192 (*Fig. 6.12*), 193–94, 258, 264n21, 301, 319
and (impure) tragedy 89, 103, 133, 135, 175, 184, 192 (*Fig. 6.12*), 193–94, 210, 213, 279, 339
– relief 83; *see also* burlesque; parody

commercial strategies 159, 356; *see also* marketing
commodities 107, 241, 338; *see also* Marx
comparative literature 5, 356
comparison as method 5, 38, 39–43, 45–49, 50, 52, 115, 356
brief – with music 257
btw. artworks 133–35, 136, 144–45, 146 (*Fig. 5.6*), 147 (*Fig. 5.7*), 227, 233, 247, 262–68, 307
by Flaxman 123
by Marianne v. Willemer 332

btw. lookalike exemplars and prints 4–5, 52, 95, 106, 120, 137, 138, 175–76, 179–81, 355
in language 38, 58–59
in visual analysis 28–30, 67–73, 87
compendia of Faust images 4, 49, 50, 208, 225, 233, 245, 355; *see also* Devéria; Neubert

competition (commercial)
btw manufacturers 349
btw. printmakers 169, 227, 375
btw publishers 5, 95, 102–6, 128, 136, 137, 147–48, 156, 179, 184, 190, 201, 210, 268, 352; *see also* marketing

Colnaghi, print publishers and art dealers 291
Concanen, Alfred 299
Concanen, Hugh (son of A.) 299
connoisseurs 49, 58, 60, 112, 121, 123, 139, 168, 183, 184, 200; *see also* collectors; reader categories of R's outlines
Constant, Benjamin 197
Constitutionnel (Le) 182n29
consumer goods 3, 154, 229
consumerist culture 3, 124, 166, 241, 245; *see also* commodities; objects
Cooke, Simon 258
Cooper-Richet, Diana, Jean-Yves Mollier, and Ahmed Silem, 180n14
Cooper, John Michael 44
Cooper, Thompson 167n112
copperplates 95, 96, 99, 108, 138, 169
vs. steel engravings 106, 168
vs. woodcuts 135

copying
and copies of copies 5, 137, 321
and originals 58, 62, 115–17, 137
as process 4–5, 89, 108, 176, 179–80, 180n18, 184, 198, 212, 215–21, 268, 298, 355–57
experimental – 195, 196 (*Fig. 6.15a–b*), 364; *see also* circulation; distribution; diffusion; duplicates/duplication; imitation; loose/scattered leaves; reception of Goethe's *Faust I*; remediation; reproduction

copyright 200, 224, 236
1814–15 Vienna congress 108
lack of – 107, 109, 115, 122
Coralli, Jean 290
Corbould, Edward 358, 377
Cornelius, Aloys 48
Cornelius, Peter (son of A.) 3, 43, 45, 50, 59, 67, 97, 110, 115, 118, 180, 268, 272, 277, 343, 373
1816 (fully 1826) *Bilder zu Goethe's Faust* 264, 280
and the gallery model (*Bildreihe*) 48–49, 52
dedication pl. 2 ("Prelude on the Stage") 150, 150 (*Fig. 5.8*)
adapted by Moses to R 149–51, 151 (*Fig. 5.9*), 180, 360
Faust meeting Gretchen 46 (*Fig. 1.10*), 48
prison scene 280–81, 280 (*Fig. 9.7*)
title-page 274
1841 smaller *Bilder zu Goethe's Faust* (Mey and Widmayer) 49
Faust drawings 45
on relation to R *see* Index on MR → 11. Influence → Cornelius
Corps Rhenania 343
Correggio 42
The Night (aka *The Adoration of the Shepherds*) as lithophane 346
Corsaire (Le) 182n29, 184, 281n50, 290n86
cosmopolitan/cosmopolitanism 122, 261

---

1 This entry does not include caption, footnote and appendices references, easy to follow by interested readers.

428 GENERAL INDEX

Cotta firm   189, 208, 213, 356[2]
  commercial announcements (*Circulaire*)   66, 67, 95, 109
  griffin mark (from 1839)   106, 365, 368; *see also* Seibertz
  order book (*Auftragbuch*)   95
  printing works in Stuttgart   106
  Stuttgart bookshop   54, 133, 370
  Württemberg seat   60; *see also* Kröner
Cotta, Georg v. (son of J. F.)   27, 40, 54, 65, 67, 69, 96, 101–6, 109, 126,
    168, 208, 214, 220, 241, 339, 351, 358
  1834 enlarged and retouched *Faust I* album (29 pl.)   8, 36, 54, 55,
    69, 95, 96, 99, 102–5, 106, 108, 213, 216, 220, 241, 288, 339, 364,
    365, 366, 371, 377
    extra plates   22–24, 103, 104 (*Fig. 3.7*), 213, 214 (*Fig. 7.1*)
    random order   103
    delayed   99, 101
    divergent/wanting dates   95, 99, 102, 104–5
  1836 colourful *Faust II* portfolio   36, 54, 102, 103 (*Fig. 3.6*), 105, 105
    (*Fig. 3.8*), 106, 167, 168, 365
    pl. 10   172, 173 (*Fig. 5.22*)
  1836 joint *Faust I* and *Faust II* album (40 pl.)   4, 54, 105, 106, 168,
    220, 241, 288, 358, 365
    divergent dates   52, 54, 105
    random combination   105–6
  n.d. *Faust I* and *Faust II* album   106–7
    pre-1839? (or *post* 1840) printed by Cotta (no griffin)   4, 106,
      106n54, 365
    1884? printed by Kröner   4, 106–7, 107 (*Fig. 3.9*), 368
  and R   101–5
    decrying *Faust I* diverse frame sizes   102, 102n37
    disputing price for re-engraving *Faust I* plates   101–2
  as art publisher   104, 106
  European connexions   102, 103, 106
Cotta, Johann Friedrich   2, 27, 35, 36, 39, 40, 42, 45, 49, 52, 59, 60–61,
    62, 63–66, 67, 69, 96–99, 101, 106, 108, 109, 112, 122, 126, 133, 138,
    156, 179, 323, 338, 359
  1816 *Umrisse zu Goethes Faust*, R's original portfolio   2, 8, 35,
    36n62, 40, 42, 48, 56, 56 (*Fig. 2.2*), 65, 66, 67, 95–96, 97, 99, 101,
    102, 103, 104, 121, 122, 124, 125, 125n48, 129, 137, 138, 175, 213, 220,
    227, 307, 323, 338, 339, 359, 373
    as twofold device   52–54, 53 (*Figs. 2.1a–b*)
    "prints on demand"   96, 99
  1818? alleged Tübingen ed.   95, 97–99, 124, 359
  1820 *Umrisse zu Goethes Faust*, 2nd impr.   2, 8, 56, 57 (*Fig. 2.3*),
    59, 87, 93, 95–97, 99, 108, 109n73, 125, 126, 128, 130 (*Fig. 4.1*), 138,
    191–92, 334, 359, 363
    improved paper quality   96, 97, 138; *see also* plate margins
  1828? putative ed.   43, 96, 97
  1830 extra impr.   96, 97, 98 (*Fig. 3.1a*), 99, 108, 363
  and R   63–67, 99–101
Cottin, Madeleine   306
Coudray, Clemens Wenzeslaus   101
Counter-Reformation   182; *see also* Roman Catholicism
Coupin, Pierre-Alexandre   42, 49
Courrier des théâtres (*Le*)   290n86
covenant vs. wager   84–85, 85 (*Fig. 2.21*), 116 (*Fig. 3.17a*), 117, 128, 181
    (*Fig. 6.4*), 186, 201, 208, 245, 245 (*Fig. 7.25*), 259, 264, 281, 371, 373,
    378
  signing with blood   127, 168, 352; *see also* Mephistopheles

─────────
2   Undecidable references to Cotta either father or son

covers after R
  alluring
    colour and ivy in Nerval trans.   184, 185, 185 (*Figs. 6.7a–b*), 211,
      362
    see Audot; Frère; Tilt; Votteler
  devout   *see* Riepenhausen, E. L.
  magic related   *see* Berryman; enigmatic ornaments; Tilt
  on scores
    c.1831 piano – after Bertin   283, 283 (*Fig. 9.9*), 372
    publicizing Irving's silhouette   299
  sensational   *see* Bichebois
  sentimental   *see* Beecham; Librairie Gründ
  synoptic   *see* Frey, J. W.
covers for Goethe's *Faust I*
  sensational   *see* Devéria
  pretend/reverse   *see* Lachgern
Craig, Edward Gordon   197, 197n67, 296–97, 298, 299, 362
Crayon (*The*)   25
Crick, Joyce   149n60
Croly, Rev. George   126, 139
croquis   180, 258, 306
crossbreed (items)   *see* hybrid printed assemblages
crow, a/to crow   255, 258–59
Crowquill, Alfred (pseud. of brothers Alfred Henry and Charles Robert
    Forrester)   258
Crowquill, Alfred (pseud. of Alfred Henry Forrester)   206, 255–57,
    258, 269, 357
  1834 *Faust: A Serio-Comic Poem with Twelve Outline
    Illustrations*   123n31, 255, 258–62, 343, 373, 374, 375
    as spiced-up trans.   259, 262
    parodying R   256 (*Figs. 8.1a, 8.1b*), 259, 260 (*Figs. 8.3a, 8.3b*), 263
      (*Fig. 8.5*), 265 (*Fig. 8.6*)
    "The German in an English dress" (self-portrait)   259, 259
      (*Fig. 8.2*), 261, 262, 266, 268, 344
    turned into 1841 German album   262–68; *see also* burlesque;
      heroic-comic; Lachgern
  1854 *A Bundle of Crowquills*   258–59
Cruikshank family   318
  Cruikshank, George   258
cultural history   43, 45, 115, 116, 175–76, 254, 332, 338
cultural practices   3, 5, 59, 176, 333
  embodied in books and other items   30, 56, 147, 149, 154, 170,
    175–76, 340
cultural transfers   54, 122, 132, 157, 179, 189, 257, 261, 340
Cupid (mythology)   38; *see also* Eros

Dabezies, André   296n100
Danae (mythology)   39
Dante, Alighieri, works by
  Inferno   77
  Divina Commedia   86, 89, 110, 122, 189, 213
    1793 *Paradise* outlined by Flaxman   141, 143, 143 (*Fig. 5.3*)
    1833, 1840 outlined by R   36; *see also* Flaxman
Darley, Felix Octavius Carr, outlines   240–42
  1843 *Scenes in Indian Life*   241
  1848 after W. Irving, *The Legend of Sleepy Hollow*   241
  1849 after W. Irving, *Rip Van Winkle*   241
  1856 (published) after S. Judd, *Margaret*   240
  1879 *Compositions in Outline from Hawthorne's Scarlet Letter*   241
Darley, Gillian   127n64
Daunicht, Richard   279n37, 280n39

GENERAL INDEX

David d'Angers, and R   27, 37, 42, 92, 290
Davison, Simmons, and Co, printers   157
Dawe, George (son of P.)   58
Dawe, Mary Margaret (daughter of P.)   58–59
Dawe, Philip, mezzotint engraver   58
De Quincey, Thomas   125n44, 129
   "On the Knocking at the Gate in *Macbeth*"   233
Debreux, Marguerite (Mademoiselle Debreux)   299
Dédéyan, Charles   186, 190n55
Deflandre, M.-A.   191n57
Degreif, Uwe   112n83
Delacroix, Eugène   2, 50, 60, 128, 168, 177, 179, 206, 208, 226, 247, 284,
      290, 291, 298, 333
   1827 painting *Mephistopheles Appearing to Faust*   184
   1828 lithographed Goethe portrait (← Schmeller) repurposed
      198–200, 199 (*Figs. 6.16a–b*), 208, 363
   1828 in-folio *Faust* lithographs   49–50, 54n10, 60, 62, 92, 180, 181,
      184, 187, 189, 198, 204, 205, 208, 245, 254, 270, 272, 273, 299, 333,
      372; *see also* Motte-Sautelet 1828 in-folio *Faust*
   1843 *Hamlet* lithographs   307
   1862 letter to Burty   177, 245n75
   and R   84, 177, 206, 210, 239, 245, 247, 270, 291, 370
      Faust meeting Gretchen compared   48, 242, 247, 248 (*Fig. 7.27
         top*)
      freehand copies of R   177–79, 177 (*Fig. 6.1a–b*), 178 (*Fig. 6.2, 6.3*),
         216, 270, 298, 370
Delpech, François   162
Deneke, Otto   109
Denon, Dominique-Vivant, 1816–20 *Monuments des arts du dessin*
      182
dénouement   172, 280–81, 313, 352
Deschamps, Léon, ed. of *La Plume*   208
Despléchin, Édouard, stage set designer   283–84, 284 (*Fig. 9.10*), 377
Derrida, Jacques   356
Deutsche Miscellen, Perthes's newspaper project   122
Devéria, Achille   208, 208n106, 225, 226
   1824–50s "Goethe" visual compendium   206, 209 (*Fig. 6.21*), 226
      (*Fig. 7.10*), 227, 228 (*Fig. 7.11*), 229 (*Fig. 7.12*), 233, 234 (*Fig. 7.18*),
      235 (*Fig. 7.19*), 371
   1828 *Faust* cover as "the pencil's Walpurgis"   206–8
Devéria, Eugène   208, 226
devil, the   262, 332
   as censor in book of universe (Staël → Nerval)   211
   as fearful spirit   298
   as man and interiorised   127, 290–99
      civilized   298–99, 304, 305, 309, 338
      parallel btw. Faust and –   46 (*Fig. 1.8*), 48, 247, 248 (*Fig. 7.27
         top*)
   as typesetter and printer   297
   depiction of   77, 80, 84, 351–52
      and sexuality   74–75, 74 (*Fig. 2.9*), 75 (*Fig. 2.10*), 232 (*Fig. 7.17*)
      in red   296
      R model for –'s type   59, 162, 281, 291, 292 (*Fig. 9.13*), 296,
         297–301, 302, 351
      the –'s prying eye   72, 85–86, 92, 227, 229, 231, 233
   in R's *The Chess Players*   310, 358
   is in the details   262; *see also* Delacroix; irony; Johannot;
      meerschaum pipe; Mephistopheles; Momus; Old Nick
Dibdin, Thomas Frognall   2, 43–44, 54, 133–36, 139, 184, 213, 347, 370
   1821 *Bibliographical, Antiquarian and Picturesque Tour in France
      and Germany*   43, 133–35, 134–35 (*Fig. 4.4a–c*), 139, 184

Dickens, Charles   2, 203, 303, 315, 318
   1848 *Dombey and Son*   319
   1850 *David Copperfield*   303, 313–21, 314 (*Fig. 10.2*), 316 (*Fig. 10.4*),
      317 (*Fig. 10.5*), 376
   and R   319
Dickson, Sarah   258n11
Diderot, Denis   289, 311
Didot, Jules, alias J. Didot aîné   191, 193, 195
Didot, Pierre, alias P. Didot aîné (brother of J.)   191, 193n59
Dieterich, Johann Christian, publisher   109–11, 111 (*Fig. 3.10a*), 362
diffusion (of prints/print culture)   3, 45, 48, 50, 86, 89, 89n123, 93,
      108, 112, 115–16, 175, 257, 279, 301, 309, 310, 355, 357, 358; *see also*
      circulation
digitization reducing effect   4, 5, 52, 166, 245n71; *see also* remediation
Diodati group   32
Dionysus (mythology)   40; *see also* Bacchus
Disraeli, Benjamin   2, 4, 303, 304, 305, 308, 311, 321
   1826 *Vivian Grey* and R   304–6, 308, 311, 321
distribution (of prints/print culture)   108, 112, 175, 179, 200, 203–4,
      215, 229, 367, 376; *see also* book trade; circulation; diffusion
Dobbs, Brian   290n84
Dobsky, Arthur   49, 97n17
Doerffling (Dörffling) Carl Friedrich, Leipzig publisher   262, 264–67
   1837 or 1839 *English Novelist (The)*   264n19
   c.1844 *Unter-Italien*, panoramic prints   264
   and Franke   264
Dolci, Carlo, *The Penitent Magdalen*   346
Don Quixote (the character)   261
Dondey-Dupré, publishers   *see* Nerval
Dopp, Herman   197n70, 197n73, 200n82
Doré, Gustave   284
Döring, Georg   113, 114, 370
Dorval, Marie, as Marguerite   186, 281, 290–91, 294, 295 (*Fig. 9.16*)
Doy, Guinevere   177n2, 247nn76–77
Doyle, John (H. B.)   318
Dresden
   Academy of Arts   25, 26
   Armoury (*Rüstkammer*)   85
   as Florence of the Elbe   27
   court   26, 27, 34, 59, 212, 271
   Gallery (*Gemäldegalerie*)   25, 26, 40, 44, 347
   Gallery of Antiques   40
   Green Vault   40
   Prints Cabinet (*Kupferstich-Kabinett*)   44, 67, 70
Dresdner Geschichtsblätter   26n7
Dresen, Wolfgang   301
Drost, Wolfgang, and Marie-Hélène Girard   306n11
Dublin Review   167
Duchamp, Marcel, *The Bride Stripped Bare by her Bachelors, Even*   327
Duchartre, Pierre-Louis, and René Saulnier   184n33
Duke of Bedford   347; *see also* Woburn
dumb shows/ballet as silent poems (Gautier)   309, 311
duplicates/duplication   5, 108, 110, 162, 166, 212, 213, 215, 218, 220, 297;
      see also copying; reproduction
Dürer, Albrecht   61, 123
   1498 *Apocalypse*   88
   1514 *Saint Jerome in his Study*   130–32, 131 (*Fig. 4.2*)
Düsseldorf Association for the diffusion of religious images   227

Ebner, Georg, art publisher   110, 111 (*Fig. 3.12*); *see also* Emminger
Écho de Paris (*L'*)   189n48, 290n86, 290n89

Eckermann, Johann Peter   49, 186*n*43, 272, 273, 282, 288*n*80
editions/prints
  deluxe/fine   4, 5, 6, 96, 97, 102, 103, 106–7, 112, 138, 139, 148, 149, 159, 162, 167, 168, 169, 191–97, 204, 241, 245, 365, 369
  large paper   138, 139, 187, 241, 255, 256 (*Fig. 8.1a–b*), 363, 373
  pirated   96, 99, 107–12, 136, 137, 149, 154, 161, 307, 356
  popular   5, 6, 49, 51, 108, 118, 157, 197, 200, 203–4, 210, 240, 247, 255, 264, 299–301, 343; *see also* Belgian counterfeit editions; illustration
Eilfer wine (1811)   55, 330
Elkan, David Levy, painter and lithographer   267
"embellishments" period term for *illustrations*   138, 148, 155 (*Fig. 5.11a–c*), 158 (*Figs. 5.12, 5.13*), 167, 168, 222, 360, 361, 364, 366
Emerson, Ralph Waldo   169, 189, 240
Emminger, Eberhard   109, 110, 110*n*81, 112*n*83, 362
  chalk lithograph after J. Riepenhausen, *Faust's First Meeting with Gretchen*   110–12, 111 (*Fig. 3.12*), 362
Ende, C. G., printseller?   238, 238 (*Fig. 7.22*), 375
Engel, Karl   49*n*122, 97, 106*n*54, 166*n*104, 180*n*19, 201*n*88, 288, 333, 355, 365
Engelhardt, Christian Moritz, 1818 ed. *Hortus deliciarum*   133, 135
Engell, James   149*n*60
Engelmann, Godefroy, Franco-German lithographer   162
Engelsing, Rolf   242*n*69
engravings/etchings
  as art and reproduction vehicle   64, 69, 70–71, 71 (*Fig. 2.6*), 89
  imprinted onto minds   252–54, 290–91, 296–97, 298, 306–7; *see also* metaphors; Index on MR → 7. Aesthetics, Inspiration, and Technique → etching
enigmas in fiction   310–11, 321
enigmatic ornaments   151, 151*n*68, 152 (*Fig. 5.10a*), 153 (*Fig. 5.10b*), 176, 360, 361
ephemera   333; *see also* artefacts; trivial, triviality
epigram   38
epithalamium   330
Erdmann, Jürgen   287*n*71
Ernst I, Duke of Saxe-Coburg and Gotha   287, 299
Ernst, Max   39
Eros   114–15, 115 (*Fig. 3.16a*)   323; *see also* Cupid
Essen, Gesa v.   86
Estes and Lauriat, Boston publishers, 1877 *Illustrations to Goethe's Faust*   169, 368
etchings   *see* engravings/etchings
Europe (mythology)   39
European Magazine and London Review   148*n*45, 149
European Magazine and Monthly Review   147
ex libris (MS)
  Abbott, Ira A.   360
  Bagot, Harry   163*n*100
  Byron, George Gordon (Noel)   154*n*75, 329
  Campbell, Tho[ma]s Theodore, Jr   361
  Craig, Edward Gordon   362
  Heinemann, William   149*n*65
  Frere, George   360
  L.   201
  Parsons, Henry G. J.   149*n*65
  Wilder, Amos Niven   153 (*Fig. 5.10b*), 360
  Wilder, Thornton Niven   360
  Wyeth, N. J.   201–3, 366; *see also* bookplates
Examiner (*The*)   149*n*59, 154, 156*n*80, 161*n*93, 167, 170, 281*n*47
exchanges
  commercial   59, 64, 124; *see also* book trade
  cross-cultural   58, 121–23, 136, 338, 356

cultural   121–23, 150–151
  images as major currency in –   4, 58, 122
  intellectual   189, 324
  transnational   121–24, 136, 166, 180, 189, 264, 356; *see also* gifts
exhibitions
  Brera Academy annual – (Milan)   250, 377
  Crystal Palace World – (1851 London)   28, 172, 240
  Dresden Academy annual –   34, 39, 40, 43
  Goethe centenary – (1932 Dresden)   236
  Leipzig international – on Goethe illus. editions (1932)   50
  Royal Academy annual – (London)   28
  Tille –s (1899 catalogue)   227, 238, 360
  Universal – (1867 Paris)   250, 377
  Weimar –s   61
extra-illustration   36, 147, 149*n*66, 151, 153 (*Fig. 5.10b*), 159, 163*n*100, 209 (*Fig. 6.21*), 213, 215 (*Fig. 7.2*), 226 (*Fig. 7.10*), 227, 228 (*Fig. 7.11*), 229 (*Fig. 7.12*), 234 (*Fig. 7.18*), 235 (*Fig. 7.19*), 355, 371
Eytel, Wilhelm, amateur woodcuts after R   116 (*Fig. 3.17a*), 117, 117–18 (*Fig. 3.17b*), 373

Fairholt, F[rederick] W[illiam]   163*n*101
Fallbacher, Karl-Heinz   115*n*86
fancy vs. imagination   88; *see also* imagination; Index on MR → 2. Personality and Characteristics → aptitudes → imaginative power; disposition → fancy
Fashionable (*Le*)   290*n*86
Faure, Jean-Baptiste, in Gounod's *Faust*   299, 311
Faust (the legendary character)
  and *Bilderbogen*   210
  and carnival   268
  and Don Juan   324
  and magical books   189
  as magician (*Hexenmeister*)   55, 87, 168
  as old/genuine Germanic figure   2, 4*n*6, 48, 61, 117–18, 122, 140, 168, 184, 210, 261, 268*n*25, 269, 296
Faust (the character) as inventor of printing   184, 192–93, 210–11; *see also* Fust
Faust/*Faust I* iconography   4, 43, 45, 50, 208, 239, 274
  and German art clubs   112
  and inclusive studies   50, 108, 205, 225, 369; *see also* compendia
  and monumental editions   49, 75, 75*n*84, 149, 208, 268
  and mythical past   116 (*Fig. 3.17a*), 117–18, 117 (*Fig. 3.17b*)
  Goethe's theatre *Faust* drawings   274, 275 (*Fig. 9.3*), 276 (*Fig. 9.4*)
  heroic/Germanized –   4*n*6, 261, 268
  R's leading –   2–3, 6, 43, 75–77, 115, 176, 205, 239, 274, 298, 301, 331, 357
Faust as Man/everyman   2, 122, 140, 189, 192 (*Fig. 6.12*), 194, 224, 261, 270, 272–73, 297, 340, 342, 352, 358
Faust, die (German *the fist*), pun   193 (*Fig. 6.13*), 194
Faustus: or, The Demon of the Drachenfels (1850)   299
Fayt, René   200*n*81
Fechner, Werner, tin figurines   351, 378
  and Barbara Rothmeier   351*n*37
  Mephistopheles, Faust and Gretchen after R   351–52, 351 (*Fig. 12.10*)
Feldman, Theo, book dealer   200
Fénelon, François, *Telemachus*   113, 140
Ferniot, Paul   208
Feuerbach, Anselm   250
Feuillet-Dumus, Auguste (Auguste Feuillet), co-dir. of La Librairie Romantique   197–98, 364
  1828 *Faust: Tragédie de Goëthe*   197–200, 199 (*Figs. 6.16a–b*), 363
Fichte, Johann Gottlieb, 1799 *Die Bestimmung des Menschen*   346

GENERAL INDEX

fine printing 102–4, 159, 169, 190–95; *see also* editions/prints →
    deluxe/fine
Finlay, Nancy 240*n*58, 241*n*61
Fischer, Bernhard 44–45, 95, 96*n*12, 97, 99, 108, 112*n*82
Flaxman, John 2, 86, 110, 123, 169, 238, 240, 241, 274, 286, 310
    and Goethe 61, 86, 124, 274, 275 (*Fig. 9.3*)
    and Moses 137, 141, 142 (*Fig. 5.2*), 143 (*Fig. 5.3*)
    major literary works outlined
        Aeschylus's tragedies 48, 86, 110, 122, 213
        Dante, *Divina Commedia* 86, 110, 122, 189, 213
            Circle of Angels around the Sun (*Paradiso*, X) 141, 143
                (*Fig. 5.3*)
            The Lovers Surprised (*Inferno*, V) 77
        Hesiod 86, 110, 122, 213
        Homer, *Iliad* 48, 86, 87, 110, 122, 123, 213, 238, 274
            Jupiter Sending the Evil Dream to Agamemnon 274
            The Council of the Gods 274
        Homer, *Odyssey* 48, 86, 110, 122, 123, 213, 238; *see also* Index
            on MR → 8. R's Distinctive Outline Treatment→ adapting
            Flaxman
Fleischer, Ernst, Leipzig bookseller and publisher 89*n*122, 96, 97, 99,
    101, 102, 103, 241, 358
Fleischer, Friedrich, Leipzig bookseller and publisher
    Kupfersammlung zu Goethes sämmtlichen Werken 213–14, 317
Fletcher, Josiah, Norwich ed. and printer
    Norwich Magazine (*The*) 169, 366
    Norwich News 169, 366
Flor O'Squarr, Charles-Marie (Oscar-Charles Flor) 203*n*95
Fontallard, Henri-Gérard *see* Gérard
Fontane, Theodor, 1883 novel *Count Petöfy* 346
formats
    competition btw. 168–70, 175
    evocative 48, 52, 61, 110, 137, 138, 154, 175, 176, 191, 215, 355
    homogenized 49, 103
    landscape 2, 129, 148, 169, 227, 241, 262
    landscape vs. portrait 129, 154, 160, 168, 175
    large 70, 138, 227, 240
    modified 3, 95, 96, 112
    monumental 49, 52, 75, 149, 208
    small/diminutive 168, 198, 241
    unpretentious 48
    varying 51, 149, 151, 163, 176, 213, 227, 238; *see also* albums; octavos;
        portfolios; quartos
Forrester, Alfred Henry *see* Crowquill
Forrester, Charles Robert (brother of A. H.) *see* Crowquill
Forster-Hahn, Françoise 4, 52*n*3, 116, 261*n*14, 357*n*8
Förster, Karl 27
Français peints par eux-mêmes (*Les*) (1840–42) 297; *see also*
    physiologies
Frantz, Adolf Ingram 167, 168*n*115
Frederick William IV, King of Prussia 167
Frère, Édouard, French artist
    alluring cover 245, 245 (*Fig. 7.25*)
    copying R 203, 204, 204 (*Fig. 6.18*), 210, 210 (*Fig. 6.22*), 242–43, 243
        (*Fig. 7.23*), 244 (*Figs. 7.24a, 7.24b*), 245*n*71, 253, 367, 375, 376, 378;
        see also Bry
Fretter-Pico, Ludwig, student, Corps Rhenania 343
Frey, Jean George, printer and lithographer 195
Frey, Johann Wilhelm, graphic artist 163–66, 165 (*Fig. 5.18*), 367
Friedländer, Carl Martin 200, 365
Friedrich August I, aka Frederick Augustus the Fair 26
Friedrich Wilhelm III 334

Friedrich, Caspar David 25, 26, 28, 42, 239*nn*45–46
    and Goethe's *Faust I* 31
    and R 31–32, 37, 62, 239
    1808–10 painting *Der Mönch am Meer* and R's pl. 2 31, 239
    c.1830 "Statements" 37
Frijlink, Hendrik, Dutch publisher and trans. 166, 367, 368
    1865 *Faust* into Dutch with 6 vignettes after R 163–66, 165
        (*Fig. 5.18*)
frogs, unpoetic animals *see* Aristophanes; *Batrachomyomachia*
frontispieces as mediating devices 107, 137, 360, 368, 369
    1820 *Kleines Geschenk* 114, 115, 115 (*Fig. 3.16a*)
    1821 Moses after Cornelius beckoning readers 149–51, 151
        (*Fig. 5.9*), 180, 360
    1825 J. M. Wright, *The Decision of the Flower*, in *The Literary
        Souvenir* 224–25, 225 (*Fig. 7.9*), 371
    1828 Pinéas after R in Nerval trans. 85, 181 (*Fig. 6.4*), 185–86, 211,
        307, 371
    1829 R's – for *Faust* in *AlH* 213–14, 215 (*Fig. 7.2*), 371
    1832 "Kiss" plate mounted as – 157, 158 (*Fig. 5.13*), 233, 360
    synoptic
        1840 in Baudry ed. 201–3, 202 (*Fig. 6.17*), 366
        1865 in Dutch ed. 165 (*Fig. 5.18*), 166, 367
Fugger v. dem Rech, Simone 26*n*15
Funès, Louis de 301
Fusenig, Thomas, and Sebastian Giesen 239*n*44
Füssli, Henry
    and Retzsch 143
    The Nightmare 143, 145 (*Fig. 5.5*)
Fust, Johann, printer and Gutenberg's associate 211, 192

Galignani, Giovanni Antonio's succrs 201
Galland, Antoine 352
Gallimard, Paul 245
Garde, Georg 298*n*108, 301*n*115
Garibaldi, Giuseppe Maria 250
Gaudin, Charles, 1868 *Faust* stereoscopic views 206
Gautier, Théophile 2, 184, 186, 208, 279, 284, 286, 287*n*69, 291*n*95, 303,
    306, 307, 311, 378
    fascinated by R's prints 307–8
    outlines paralleled to avant-garde performances 309, 321–22, 356
    works by
        1835 *Mademoiselle de Maupin* 307
        1839 "La Toison d'or" 307, 308
        1841 "Deux acteurs pour un rôle" 308
        1841 *Giselle* 309
        1846 *Les Roués innocents* 308–9, 321
        1855 *Les Beaux-arts en Europe* 307
        1865 *Loin de Paris* 306
        1874 *Portraits contemporains* 284
Gazette de France (*La*) 179*n*4, 182*n*29, 184
Gazette littéraire 193
Geiger, Ludwig (L. G.) 272*n*4, 273*n*80, 288*n*80
Geisler-Szmulewicz, Anne 307*n*18
geistreich (*geistvoll*), qualifying R 35–36, 37, 44, 59, 61, 62, 80–86, 124
    spirit/spirited in reception 5–6, 59, 62, 124, 138, 156, 310
Gentleman's Magazine 129*n*74, 160*n*90, 162
George IV *see* King of Great Britain and Ireland
Gérard (Fontallard, Henri-Gérard) 184, 184*n*34
Géricault, Théodore 160, 252
    The Raft of the Medusa reproduced 252
Gessner, Salomon, *Idylls* 34–35
Giard book trade lineage 190–91

Giard, Paris publisher   181, 190, 192, 195, 197, 210, 363
    1830 *Faust: Esquisses dessinées par Retsch* reverting to German
        original   142, 179, 180, 184, 190, 191–93, 195, 197, 203, 211, 233,
            363–64
        cover lithograph by A. Bichebois   193 (*Fig. 6.13*), 195
        etched title-page   192 (*Fig. 6.12*)
        Speck exemplar of trial prints   195; *see also* Laborde
Giard, Antoine   190
Giard, François   190
Gibbings, W. W., London publisher
    1830s *Illustrations to Goethe's Faust in Twenty-Six* (or *Twenty-Seven*)
        Outline Engravings by Moritz Retzsch   163, 169, 175, 364
Gibson, John, sculptor   28
Giesen, Sebastian   50, 61*n*44, 65, 86, 239; *see also* Fusenig
gift books   169–70, 224–25, 238, 323; *see also* almanacs; keepsake
        literature
gifts
    and aesthetic message   57–59, 112, 121, 123–24, 136, 229
    and art treasures   58
    and charity   55–56
    and circulation mechanisms   2, 55, 58, 121–24
    and commercial symbolism   120, 122, 136
    and cultural dialogue   59, 121–24
    and literary value   121, 136, 324
    and national/political symbolism   55–56, 120, 121–22, 136
    and publicizing   55
    birthday – 37, 338
    by poets   55, 154, 254, 323–32
    friendship/comradeship –   30, 30 (*Fig. 1.2*), 55, 343, 345 (*Fig. 12.6b*)
    of pirated goods   109, 362
    royal –   334–38, 335 (*Fig. 12.1*), 336–37 (*Fig. 12.2*); *see also*
        exchanges; Goethe offering R's *Umrisse*; Mauss
Gilbert, Mary E.   121*n*21
Gilmour, Joanna   126*n*54
Giraudeau, Abel, med. doctor and bibliophile   200
Giro d'Italia (Il), racing event   302
Gisborne, John   1, 154, 324; *see also* Shelley, P. B.
Glaser, Curt   44
Gley, Julie, actress, as Margaret   293, 293 (*Fig. 9.14*)
Globe (*Le*), open letters on Goethe   185
Gluck, Christoph Willibald   288
Glück, Franz   98, 98 (*Fig. 3.1a*), 99, 363
Godey's Lady's Book   324
Godfroid, François   197*n*71
Goedeke, Karl   97, 355
Goethe, August (son of J. W.)   277
Goethe, Christiane v., née Vulpius (wife of J. W.)   323, 330
Goethe, Johann Wolfgang v., and R   59–62, 63–64, 65, 66, 67, 97, 109,
        110, 124, 273, 358
    drawings sent to Weimar   63, 66
    Dresden visit   34, 60–61
    English copies triggering R appraisal   60, 62
    Goethe offering R's *Umrisse*   see Bracebridge, C. H.;
        Bracebridge, S.; Dawe, M. M.; Jena Patriotic Women's
        Association; Köhler; Sophia Dorothea of Württemberg;
        Vigoureux; Willemer, J. J.; Willemer, M.
    indirect relations   59–62, 64, 65
    R commented by Meyer   61–62; *see also* geistreich
Goethe, Johann Wolfgang v., and print technologies   54–55
    and monumental editions   106, 213, 214, 268
    Faust merged with printed object   55
    in translated series vs. defeat of R's prints   175
    steering his works' publication   106

Goethe, Johann Wolfgang v., compared to venerated poets   40, 122,
        189, 213, 329
Goethe, Johann Wolfgang v., *Faust I* German editions
    1790 *Faust: Ein Fragment*   1, 55, 308
    1808 *Faust, eine Tragödie*   1, 2, 25, 30, 45, 52, 54, 63, 80, 213, 242,
        255, 261
    1816 *Faust* pocket ed. (*Taschenausgabe*)   52, 54, 113, 114, 118, 118
        (*Fig. 3.18*), 128, 360, 370
    1829 pocket *Faust* (*AlH*)   97
    1830 pocket *Faust*   99
    1833 *Faust*   104
Goethe, Johann Wolfgang v., *Faust I*
    and explanations   113, 127, 138, 147, 156, 166, 168, 188
    as (intellectual) chaos   1, 54, 55, 62, 157
    as disguised comedy   89
    as gloomy fantasy/nocturne   89, 332
    as national/heritage tragedy   2, 4*n*6, 6, 45, 54, 118, 175, 253, 287, 304
        revised   261, 269; *see also* Faust (the legendary character)
    as puzzling text   1, 89
    as splinter/fragment   1–2, 3, 89, 133
    as theatre within the theatre within the theatre   268, 272
    impossible to stage   271–73
    parodied   206, 255, 257, 259, 261, 262, 264, 266–69, 357
Goethe, Johann Wolfgang v., portraits used/inserted   104, 109; *see*
        also Delacroix; Jagemann; Kiprinksi; Lips; Schmeller; Seibertz;
        Vincent, D.; Williaume; Woburn windows
Goethe, Johann Wolfgang v., works by (excepting *Faust I*)
    Ausgabe letzter Hand (*AlH*)   36, 97, 106, 213, 215 (*Fig. 7.2*), 371
    Dichtung und Wahrheit   347
    Egmont   35, 168, 306
    Elective Affinities   274, 286, 287
    Erlking (*The*)   35
    Faust II   2, 54, 106, 167, 168, 172–73, 201–2, 203–4, 307, 366, 367,
        368, 378; *see also* Index on MR → 4. Additional *Faust I* Outlines
        and Other *Faust* Drawings
    Fisherman (*The*)   35
    Götz von Berlichingen   59
    Hermann and Dorothea   58
    Iphigenia in Tauris   168
    Italian Journey   303, 332
    Letters from Switzerland   303
    Tag- und Jahres-Hefte als Ergänzung meiner sonstigen Bekenntnisse
        61, 274
    Tasso   168
    The Sorrows of Young Werther   60, 120, 203, 204, 205
    Über Kunst und Altertum   42, 60, 61, 62, 128, 148, 325
    West-östlicher Divan   55, 323
    Wilhelm Meister's Apprenticeship   35
    Works (issued by Cotta)   55, 106, 213
Goethe, Ottilie v. (daughter-in-law of J. W.)   57
Goethe's *Faust I* read in text and by image (per textual order)
    Prelude on the Stage   128, 150–51, 150 (*Fig. 5.8*), 151 (*Fig. 5.9*), 192
        (*Fig. 6.12*), 193–94, 200, 268, 272
    Prologue in Heaven   1, 2, 69, 107, 117–18, 117 (*Fig. 3.17b*), 127, 133,
        140–41, 141 (*Fig. 5.1*), 142 (*Fig. 5.2*), 149, 154, 157, 186, 189–190,
        190 (*Fig. 6.10*), 193 (*Fig. 6.13*), 194–95, 200, 205, 270, 272, 273, 275
        (*Fig. 9.3*), 334
    night in Faust's study   80, 89, 90 (*Fig. 2.23*), 128, 130, 133
    outside the city walls   343
    two souls   304, 305–6
    Mephistopheles's second appearance   130–32
    entbehren   30–31

GENERAL INDEX 433

Goethe's *Faust I* (cont.)
  wager scene   2, 67, 68 (*Figs. 2.4a–b*), 84–85, 85 (*Fig. 2.21*), 116
    (*Fig. 3.17a*), 117–18, 181 (*Fig. 6.4*), 185–86, 211; *see also* covenant vs.
    wager; Pinéas
  Auerbach's tavern   296, 296 (*Fig. 9.17*), 330
  Faust rejuvenated   141–42, 291
  Faust meeting Gretchen   28–30, 45–49, 46 (*Figs. 1.8, 1.9, 1.10*), 47
    (*Figs. 1.11, 1.12a–b*), 100; *see also* Riepenhausen
  in Margaret's chamber (Faust musing/Mephistopheles hiding the
    jewels)   73–75, 74 (*Fig. 2.9*), 75 (*Fig. 2.10*), 279; *see also* Kreling;
    Seibertz
  garden scene   30, 224–31, 225 (*Figs. 7.8, 7.9*), 231 (*Fig. 7.16*), 327–29,
    332, 351; *see also* Colin; Grünewald; Maurin; Müller; Robert;
    Zimmermann
  kiss in the summerhouse   1, 77, 78 (*Figs. 2.13, 2.14*), 79 (*Figs. 2.15,
    2.16*), 217–18, 218 (*Fig. 7.4*), 222–24, 232–39, 232 (*Fig. 7.17*), 234
    (*Fig. 7.18*), 327–29; *see also* Maurin; Patzschke; Schuler; Wright;
    Zimmermann
  Margaret at the spinning wheel   72 (*Fig. 2.7*), 73, 257
  Margaret at the cathedral   80, 270–73, 271 (*Fig. 9.1*)
  Mephistopheles's sarcastic serenade   330
  Walpurgis Night   1, 143–45, 146 (*Figs. 5.6, 5.7*), 149, 154, 157, 167, 205,
    287, 303–4, 307, 312, 335, 351; *see also* Shelley, P. B.
  Faust confronting Mephistopheles   262, 263 (*Figs. 8.4, 8.5*), 264
  galloping past the Rabenstein   83, 84 (*Fig. 2.20*), 204, 284, 284
    (*Fig. 9.11*)
  finale in prison   2, 72–73, 80, 81, 81 (*Fig. 2.17*), 84, 89, 92, 169, 170,
    256 (*Fig. 8.1b*), 259, 261, 264, 280–81, 280 (*Fig. 9.7*), 283, 283
    (*Fig. 9.9*), 284, 284 (*Fig. 9.10*); *see also* Index on MR → 3. Choice
    Faust I Scenes Outlined → Pl. 25 & 26
Goethe's *Faust I* translated
  in verse   1, 128, 135–36, 139, 148, 149, 157, 167, 168, 169, 323–24, 360,
    366, 368
  into Dutch   *see* Frijlink; Vleeschouwer
  into English   *see* Anster; Arndt; Birch; Boileau; Gower; Coleridge
    debate; Hayward; Latham; Luke; Shelley, P. B.; Soane; Swanwick;
    Taylor, B.
  into French   *see* Blaze de Bury; Nerval; Sainte-Aulaire; Stapfer
  into Polish   *see* Walicki; Zawadzki; *see also* translations (textual)
Goethe's *Faust I*, reception   *see* reception of Goethe's *Faust I*
Goethe's library   58, 125, 126, 128, 138, 148n50, 359
Goldsmith, Oliver   203
Göschen, Georg Joachim, Leipzig publisher   220
Goslee, Nancy Moore   157n87
Gotter, Pauline   63
Goubault, Christian   301n116
Goujon, Jean   187
Gounod, Charles
  1859 opera *Faust*   204, 206, 257, 279, 283, 284, 284 (*Fig. 9.10*), 285
    (*Fig. 9. 11*), 299, 301, 302, 311, 377
  1861 German version *Margarete*   257
Goupil and Co.   241
Gower, Francis Leveson, 1823, 1825 *Faust* trans. into English   148n52,
    149n61, 162–63, 361
Gradiva complex   306
Gräf, Hans Gerhard   273n11, 283n58
Grandjonc, Jacques   197n74
graphein (ancient Greek), to *draw* and to *write*   38
Grassi, Josef   25, 39, 40
Green, Rosalie   133nn85–86, 135n88
Greif, Stefan, and Andrea Ruhlig   148n52
Grenville, George, British prime minister   128

Grenville, Thomas (son of G.), bibliophile and diplomat   125, 128–29
Gretton, Tom   252
Grevedon, H., lithographer   208
Grewe, Cordula   44, 86
Griffiths, Antony   97n15, 180n18
Griffiths, Antony, and Frances Carey   180n18
Griffiths, Ralph, founding ed. of *Monthly Magazine*   126; *see also*
    Wainewright
Grillparzer, Franz   266n22
Grolier Club   179, 376
Gros, Jean-Antoine   227
Grosse, Helmut, and Bernd Vogelsang   298n108, 298n110
grotesque (the)
  and commodities (Marx)   338
  in *Faust I* editions
    1830 title-page in Giard ed.   192 (*Fig. 6.12*), 193
    1884? cover by Votteler   106–7, 107 (*Fig. 3.9*)
  L. Laborde's interest in –   195–97
  vs. sublime   257; *see also* Crowquill; Index on MR → 8. R's
    Distinctive Outline Treatment → distinct features → grotesque
Grovier, Kelly   149n60
Gründerzeit   281
Grüner, Vincenz Raimund, engraver and writer   43, 115
Grünewald, Heinrich Ferdinand   227, 230 (*Fig. 7.15*), 233, 238, 375
Grünewald, Rolf, moulder and engraver   351
Guenther, Peter W.   89n121, 357n8
Guiccioli, Teresa   325
Gulliver and the Brobdingnagians (*Gulliver's Travels* by J. Swift)   319,
    321
Gutenberg, Johannes   192, 205, 211
Gutzkow, Karl   298n110

Hafferberg, Hugo   287n73
Haine, Heiko   340n17
Hall, Anna Maria   27–28, 36, 37, 38, 54, 92
Hall, David D.   242n69
Hall, Samuel Carter (husband of A. M.)   27–28, 240
Hamilton, Lady Emma, née Amy Lyon (wife of Sir W.)   286
Hamilton, Sir William   286, 287
Hanley, Howard J. M., Margaret Cooper, and Susan Morris   156n78
Harmonia (mythology)   39
Harmonie (Weimar), social circle   274
Harper's New Monthly Magazine   28
harpies   193 (*Fig. 6.13*), 194
Harrington, Peter, book expert   132
Harten, Ulrike   277n20, 277n23, 279
Hartmann, Christian Ferdinand   26, 60–61, 63, 227
Hartmann, Johann Georg (father of C. F.)   60
Hartmannsche(s) Haus, influential Stuttgart salon   60
Harvey, John R.   313, 318–20
Haskins, Susan   262n17
HathiTrust cyber-library   52, 54, 200
Hauhart, William Frederic   97n20, 120n4, 124, 167n113, 168n116
Hautecœur, Herménégilde-Honorat, printseller   294, 295 (*Fig. 9.16*)
Hayes, Kevin J.   80n87, 304n6, 310–11
Hayez, Francesco   242, 247, 250–52, 254, 357
  1823 *L'ultimo bacio dato a Giulieta da Romeo*   247
  1859 *Il Bacio. Episodio della giovinezza. Costumi del secolo* XIV
    242, 247–51, 249 (*Fig. 7.28*), 377
    as reproduction print in paintings   250
    reworked and repurposed   251–54, 252 (*Fig. 7.31a*), 253
      (*Fig. 7.31b*)
  1861 *Il Bacio*   250–51, 251 (*Fig. 7.29*), 377

Hayez, Francesco (*cont.*)
 1867 *Il Bacio* or *Il Bacio del volontario*   250–51, 251 (*Fig. 7.30*), 377
 and German painters   250
 as illustrator and printmaker   250
Haymann, Christoph Johann Gottfried   40
Hayward, Abraham, 1833 first full *Faust* trans. into English   49*n*124, 167
Haywood, Ian, Susan Matthews, and Mary L. Shannon   138*n*8
Heath, Charles, engraver   214, 217 (*Fig. 7.3b*), 224, 225 (*Fig. 7.9*), 374
Hecker, Max   286*n*62
Heichen, Paul   106*n*55
Heidelberg website   52
Heine, Heinrich   2, 306, 321
 1824 *Die Harzreise*   109*n*74, 303–4; *see also* Brocken
 1834 *De l'Allemagne*   304
 1847 *Der Doktor Faust, ein Tanzpoem*   304
 and R   109*n*74, 303, 304
 vs. Goethe   303
Heinemann, William, critic   140, 143, 352*n*39
Heinemann, William, publisher   149, 149*n*65
Heinrich, Alfred   319*n*46
Heinrichs, Karl, draughtsman   351
Heinz, Adolf   301
Hellwig, Uwe   25, 26*n*4, 26*n*6, 26*n*10, 26*n*14, 27*n*18, 27*n*28, 50, 59*n*35, 89*n*122, 109*n*65, 110*n*78, 287*n*72, 358
Hen, Charles   197*n*70
Henning, Hans   166*n*104, 204
Henning, Rudolf, and Gerd Maier   110*n*81
Hera (mythology)   39
Hergé (born Georges Remi)
 1956 *L'Affaire Tournesol* (1956 trans. *The Calculus Affair*)   302
 1958 *Cock en stock* (1960 trans. *The Red Sea Sharks*)   302, 302 (*Fig. 9.21a–b*)
Hermann, L.   60, 287*n*72
Herment, Georges   340
heroic-comic poetry   261, 267
Herrad of Landsberg (Herrad of Hohenbourg), 12th c. *Hortus deliciarum* (*Garden of Delights*)   133–35, 136, 347; *see also* Dibdin; Engelhardt
Hervé, 1869 *Le Petit Faust*   301
Hesiod   *see* Flaxman
Hessling, Bruno   279*n*31
Hewitson, Mark   122*n*26
Hildebrand-Schat, Viola   3, 45*n*116, 50, 65, 80, 87, 92, 96, 99*n*28, 239, 273, 357
Hildebrand, J. M. C.   67
Hill, Jane Seymour, dwarf chiropodist (Dickens's Miss Mowcher)   318
Hiller, Ferdinand   282
Hirschberg, Leopold   4, 33*n*50, 36*n*63, 39, 49, 54*n*12, 105, 109, 223*n*, 227, 340, 356
historicism   43, 349
 and Faustian iconography   166, 239, 268, 349, 367
History of Dr Johann Faust (1587)   122, 268
 1608 *History of Dr Faust*, trans. P. F. Gent   129*n*75
 1696 rhymed English *History of Dr John Faustus*   129*n*75; *see also* Cayet; Eytel; Pfitzer; Widmann
Hoe, Robert, III, printing-press maker and book lover   173, 174 (*Fig. 5.23*), 376
 1885, pub. 1886 *A Lecture on Bookbinding as a Fine Art*   173
Höffner, Eckhard   108*n*57
Hofgarten, August Ferdinand   239

Hoflößnitz   40, 212
 – Museum of Saxon Viticulture   212; *see also* Oberlößnitz; Radebeul
Hogarth, William   70–71, 86, 110, 122, 127, 266, 318
 1732 *The Harlot's Progress*   70
 1735 *The Rake's Progress*   70, 127
 mock-Hogarth by Lachgern   264–66, 266 (*Fig. 8.8*)
Holdermann, Carl, painter, engraver and actor   274
Holst, Theodore v.   37, 176
Holtei, Karl Eduard v.   27*n*24, 286
Holy Roman Empire   2, 270; *see also* Reich
home decorations   222; *see also* artefacts; objects; trivial, triviality
Homer   *see* Flaxman
Horace (Vernet, Horace)   184, 184*n*34
Horne, Richard   154
Hosemann, Theodor, painter and lithographer   239, 373
Houghton, Mifflin and Co., Boston publishers   241
Houghton, Osgood and Co., Boston publishers   241
Howsam, Leslie   175*n*131
Huber, Therese, ed. Cotta's *Morgenblatt*   36, 42, 52, 66
 German preface of R's *Umrisse*   35–36, 42, 66, 113, 220, 298–99, 373
 affecting English prefaces   35, 36, 127, 140, 299
 demon and Faust as one   127, 140, 298–99
 Faust as any man's guide   113, 122, 140
 female almanac version   113
Hudibras, wandering knight   *see* Butler
Hugo, Victor   92*n*125, 204, 272*n*5
 1830 *Hernani*   194, 197
Hullmandel, Charles Joseph   159–62, 180, 182, 360, 361
 1824 *The Art of Drawing on Stone*   160; *see also* Berthoud, H., Jr
 c.1824 Boilly's *Tartini's Dream*   162
 printing Géricault's lithographs   160
Humoristich-satirisches Bilder-Album (1849)   267–68; *see also* parody
Humphreys, aka Humphrys, William, engraver   208, 224, 225 (*Fig. 7.8*), 233, 371
Hunt, Leigh   157
Hurst, Robinson and Co., British publishers and printers   224, 225 (*Figs. 7.8, 7.9*), 371
Hüttner, Johann Christian, literary agent in London   58, 60, 62, 125, 138, 148
hybrid printed assemblages   3, 52, 114, 119, 124–25, 126, 128, 129, 132, 136, 137, 156, 360

Iago (character in Shakespeare's *Othello*)   291, 297
iconography   109, 200, 203, 272, 321, 334, 356
 burlesque/satirical   255–69
 emotional   3–4, 48, 62, 114–15, 136, 204, 214, 222–39, 250–52, 340
 extensive   49, 117, 176, 203, 206, 212, 242–45, 250–54, 357, 367, 376
 intensive   117, 176, 206, 212, 242, 245–47, 252, 253–54, 357
 lit. *writing with images*   4
 Republican   183, 189–90, 191 (*Fig. 6.11*)
 reworked/derivative   1, 6, 95, 112, 120, 166, 203, 206, 208–10, 214–18, 224–25, 227–31, 233–36, 247, 253, 257, 355, 356–57
 romantic   204, 210
 synthetic   206; *see also* Faust/ *Faust I* iconography
illuminism   190
Illustrated London News (*The*)   258, 299
illustration
 as term
 ahistorical   48, 48*n*120, 138, 166
 as used in the 19th c.   49, 59, 129, 166, 240, 255, 306, 307, 309, 311

GENERAL INDEX

435

illustration
  as term (*cont.*)
    common/literal sense 4
    improper/levelling 5, 166, 239, 313, 352
    pervasive in scholarship 36, 43, 48, 49, 86, 166, 176, 239, 252
    referring to text-bound images 36, 49, 54, 88, 138, 166–68, 169,
      170, 195, 203–6, 208, 243–45, 301, 313, 315, 318
  challenged 4, 5, 36, 166–67
  effect of
    and visual imagining 313–21
    enticement 170, 171 (*Fig. 5.20*)
    revealing political/cultural fabric 116
    tantalizing screen 320
  functions of
    as depiction 127, 273
    as textual explanation 127, 138, 166
    as translation 127, 138
    embellishment and lustre 138, 167, 213, 283 (*Fig. 9.9*)
    historical – 25, 26
    in counterfeit Belgian editions 197–200
    in Germany 44, 86, 115
    literary – 213
  seen as
    lowly category 43, 44; *see also* embellishments; extra-
      illustration; translations (textual); translations (visual)
image and text
  analogies btw 48
  combined 3, 4, 54, 99, 105, 118–19, 124–25, 138–39, 147, 166, 169, 175,
    198, 255, 257, 259, 315, 319, 324, 360, 363, 365; *see also* Crowquill;
    Motte-Sautelet 1828 in-folio *Faust*
    and performing arts (Gautier) 309–10
  competition (visual/verbal divide) 86, 175; *see also* Lessing
    image vs. text 137, 175
    text vs. image 86, 262
  dependence from text 54, 80–81, 137, 138, 166, 149; *see also*
    illustration
  independence from text 52, 80–81, 94, 318
  plates askance text 163, 168, 175, 198, 361, 367
  reading in-between 4, 87, 150–51, 150 (*Fig. 5.8*), 151 (*Fig. 5.9*), 255
  text subservient/ancillary to prints 104, 133, 138–39, 166–67, 175
image frames
  and reading 195, 227, 232, 233, 273
  double 89, 99, 129, 138, 205, 264, 363, 369
  elaborate 105, 106–7, 107 (*Fig. 3.9*), 130, 130 (*Fig. 4.1*), 132, 160,
    163n103, 193, 211, 226, 227, 363, 365, 369
  in pipe bowls and lithophanes 341 (*Fig. 12.4*), 342 (*Fig. 12.5a*), 343,
    343 (*Fig. 12.5b*), 345 (*Fig. 12.6b*), 347, 350 (*Fig. 12.9*), 370, 373, 374,
    375
  plain and thin 2, 52, 54, 70, 75, 81, 87, 89, 101, 181, 192
  within an image 313, 318; *see also* formats; margins
imagination 1, 157
  and power of images 175, 252, 254, 291, 310, 312–13, 312 (*Fig. 10.1*),
    318, 330, 357
    visual – (Shelley) 1, 157, 157n87, 356
  and printed artefacts 6, 176, 213
  collective orientation of – 48, 62, 83, 87, 107, 213, 232, 242, 254,
    298, 301, 302, 306, 309, 310, 320, 325, 330, 356
  kinds of – (Ruskin) 88
  objects' effect on – 347; *see also* bindings; covers after R; covers
    for Goethe's *Faust I*; fancy vs. imagination; outline, aesthetic
    medium
imitation (aesthetics of) 186, 212
  ars simiae/aping 186, 264, 268

  in graphics 192
  in *tableaux vivants* 286–87
  mocking – *see* parody
  R – craze 4, 212, 240, 298, 356
    as hallmark of popularity 352–54
    customized 137
    with variation 179–80
  replication (*Nachahmung*) 212, 216, 241
import taxes 97, 125, 139
importation
  to Britain (England) 95, 97, 99, 120, 121, 124–29, 136, 139, 141, 148,
    156; *see also* Bohte
  to France 49, 189, 201, 281
  to the German States 264, 269
  to the United States 240, 347
impressionism 206
Induno, Gerolamo, 1862 painting *Triste presentimento* 250
industrial
  era 2, 124, 242
  products/applications 4, 173, 216, 251
  revolution 198
industrialisation/industrialized 4, 69, 108, 169, 180, 197, 220, 251, 261,
    338
Ingres, Jean-Dominique 284
interactions
  and circulating images 252–53; *see also* image and text; outline,
    aesthetic medium
  born from circulating prints 3, 186
    btw book, print trade, and stage 166, 186
    btw media 255
    btw original and copies 119, 175, 221
interdisciplinarity 5, 43, 252, 357
Intermédiaire des chercheurs et des curieux (L') 180n21
intermedial (combining several art media)
  approach 357; *see also* hybrid printed assemblages; multimedia
  creations in motion 163, 255, 277, 356
  dialogue 112
irony
  and critical distance 255, 257, 261
  fin-de-siècle – 253
  in Goethe's *Faust I* 89, 357
  in texts (Disraeli, Gautier, Heine) 303–4, 304–5, 308, 321
  perceived – in R's prints 291
  symbolic 157
  the devil's – 127, 167, 211, 221, 268, 296, 298; *see also* devil; Momus;
    theatre productions →tongue-in-cheek *Faust*
Irving, Henry, as Mephistopheles 297, 299–301, 300 (*Figs. 9.18, 9.19*),
    301 (*Fig. 9.20*), 311, 352
Irving, Washington 241, 308
  1848 *The Legend of Sleepy Hollow* 241
  1849 *Rip Van Winkle* 241; *see also* Darley
Isbell, John Claiborne 1n2, 120n7, 247n78
Isler, Johann Luzius (Ivan Ivanovič Izler), leisure entrepreneur
  287–88
Italy, as key artistic destination 25, 26–27, 30, 40, 45
Ittmann, John 44n112, 112n84, 115n86
ivy (*hedera*) and printing 211

Jabès, Edmond 356
Jackson, John 264
Jacob, Ulf, Simone Neuhäuser, and Gert Streidt 220n10
Jaeckel, Willi, 1925 *Faust, eine Tragödie von Goethe* 239

Jaeger (Jäger), Johann Christian (son of J. W. A.)   109
Jaeger (Jäger), Johann Wilhelm Abraham, Frankfurt bookseller and
    publisher   108–9, 112–15, 112 (*Fig. 3.13*), 113 (*Fig. 3.14a–c*), 114
    (*Fig. 3.15a–c*), 115 (*3.16a–b*), 370; *see also* almanacs
Jagemann, Ferdinand, Goethe's portrait   148, 149, 160, 162, 163, 360,
    361, 364
Jäger, R.   219, 220, 373
Jameson, Anna   26–27, 30, 36, 37, 39, 42, 43, 62, 101, 104, 358
    1834 *Fancies* preface   27
    1834 trans. chapter on R in *Kunst-Blatt*   39n82, 42, 104
    1834 *Visits and Sketches*   27, 30n41, 36n64, 36n67, 37n71, 37n77,
        62n56
Jammes, André, and Françoise Courbage   193n59
Janin, Jules, 1840 *Pictures of the French*   297
Janus (mythology)   37, 126
Janus Weathercock   126–28, 140, 143; *see also* Wainewright
Jeanblanc, Helga   180, 201n87
Jefcoate, Graham   49n125, 124n40, 126n52, 126n62, 179n13
Jena Patriotic Women's Association   55–56, 56 (*Fig. 2.2*)
Jensen, Jens Christian   110n79
Job (Bible)   44
Jocelyn, Percy   57n22; *see also* Vigoureux
Johannot, Tony   206, 207 (*Fig. 6.20*), 210, 233, 301, 375
    1847 title vignette cut out and mounted by Devéria   233, 234
        (*Fig. 7.18 bottom left*)
John or Johne, (Carl) Wilhelm, architect   220n10
John, (August) Wilhelm, landscape painter   220n10
John, Eugenie, pen name E. Marlitt   220n10
John, Friedrich, printmaker and stipple etcher   220
"John," MS signature   220, 373
Join-Diéterle, Catherine   187n47
Jollivet-Castelot, François, 1900 *Les Sciences maudites*   208, 378
Jooss, Birgit   286n67
Jouaust, Charles, French publisher   204
Jouaust, Damase (son of C.), bibliophilic editions   204
Jourdain, Frantz, architect and author   245, 378
Jourdain, Gaston (brother of F.), artist, and R   206, 242, 245, 246
        (*Fig. 7.26*), 253, 378
Journal des artistes et des amateurs   187n46, 189
Journal des débats   179n12, 191n58, 203, 282, 289n83
Judd, Sylvester, 1856 pub. *Margaret*   *see* Darley
Jullien, Dominique   352n41
July Monarchy   197, 363
Jung, Carl Gustav   127, 140
    1934 *The Development of Personality*   140
    1968 *Memories, Dreams, Reflections*   140
    1971 *Psychological Types*   140n19
Jung, Marianne   *see* Willemer, Marianne v.
Junod, Karen   121n18, 122n25, 123n27
Jupiter (mythology)   274; *see also* Zeus

Kaenel, Philippe, and Rolf Reichardt   3n4
Karl August, Grand Duke v. Saxe-Weimar-Eisenach   58, 60
Kaulbach, Wilhelm v.   205, 239, 250, 261, 376
    "Kiss" scene influenced by R   233, 233n34
Keane, Maureen   28n29
Keepsake for 1835 (The)   214, 217 (*Fig. 7.3b*), 374
keepsake literature   224–25, 225 (*Figs. 7.8, 7.9*); *see also* almanacs
Kemp, Martin   221
Kennerley, John, line- and stipple engraving artist   162–63, 168, 189,
        218, 361
    and Audot   163, 187, 362
    extensive influence   163, 218, 364; *see also* Bulcock
Keppel, P., copying R's plates for Zawadzki   163, 367

Kerr, Matthew P. M.   157n87
Kilgarriff, Tessa Maria   162n97
Kindermann, Heinz, theatre historian   280n40, 291, 293n96
Kindt, Hermann   59
"kinetic" versions of R's outlines   81, 154–56, 155 (*Fig. 5.11a–c*), 169, 170,
    175, 361, 366
King of Great Britain and Ireland (George IV)   358
King, B. B., London publisher   258, 259, 373, 374; *see also* Crowquill
King, Edmund M. B.   175n129
Kinnaird, Douglas   325
Kiprinksi, Obrest, Goethe's portrait lithographed by H. Grevedon
    208
kiss in literature and art
    1831 R's *Der Kuß: Altes und neues Coelibat*   77–80
        Huldbrand and Undine   77
        Paolo and Francesca   77
        Romeo and Juliet   247; *see also* Hayez; Index on MR → 3. Choice
        Faust 1 Scenes Outlined → Pl. 15
Kladzig, Auguste, actress   272, 273
Klingemann, Ernst August   273, 290
    1815 *Faust* popular romantic play   193
    1829 *Faust* Braunschweig performance   89, 97n16, 273, 279–81
Klinger, Friedrich Maximilian, 1791 *Fausts Leben, Thaten und
    Höllenfahrt*   257
Klopstock, Friedrich Gottlieb, *Works*   220
Klussmann, Paul Gerhard   115n86
Klussmann, Paul Gerhard, and York-Gothart Mix   115n86
Knickerbocker (The), New York journal   324
Koch, Carl Wilhelm, trans. and theatre adaptor   286; *see also*
    Zschokke
Koch, G., signatory painter of a R scene   338–40, 339 (*Fig. 12.3*),
    377
Köhler, Heinrich Karl Ernst v. (Egor Egorovič Köhler)   58
Köhler, Heinrich Ludwig Andreas (son of H. K. E.)   58
Kollwitz, Käthe, *Gretchen*   331 (*Fig. 11.4*), 332
Konewka, Paul, 1871 English *Faust* silhouettes   170
Königliche Porzellan-Manufaktur (KPM)
    lithophanes   347, 374
    pipe bowls   340, 342 (*Fig. 12.5a*), 343 (*Fig. 12.5b*), 374
    plates   334, 335 (*Fig. 12.1*), 336–37 (*Fig. 12.2*), 338, 370, 371; *see also*
        artefacts; objects
Kopp, Heinrich   97n16
Körner, Christian Gottfried   61
Körner, Theodor (son of C. G.)   113
Krakovitch, Odile   197n68
Kraus, Karl   99
Kreling, August v.   75–77, 76 (*Fig. 2.12*), 239
Kretzschmar v. Kienbusch, Carl Otto, American collector   200
Kretzschmar, Bösenberg & Co., Dresden firm   349 (*Fig. 12.8*)
Kröner brothers, Adolf and Paul, acquiring Cotta's firm   106, 368
Kröner, Adolf   106
Krüger, Eva   50, 77, 80, 176n133
Kruseman, Arie Cornelis, Dutch publisher   166n105
Kube, Karl Heinz   180n20
Kugler, Franz   43–44
Kuhn-Forte, Brigitte   110n76
Kuhn, Dorothea   54n8, 61, 66
Kuhn, Dorothea, Anneliese Kunz, and Margot Pehle   220n9
Kummer, Paul Georg   59n36
Kummer, Paul Gotthelf   59, 64–66, 219
Kunst-Blatt, *Morgenblatt*'s art supplement   39n82, 42, 104, 355n4
Kunzle, David   70n81
Kutschmann, Theodor   43

GENERAL INDEX

L. E. L.   *see* Landon, Letitia Elizabeth
L. G.   *see* Geiger, Ludwig
La Motte Fouqué, Caroline de (second wife of F.)   33
La Motte Fouqué, Friedrich
   1811 *Undine*   30, 32, 33, 34, 77, 129
   1813 *Der Zauberring*   33–34
   1814 *Die Jahreszeiten: Ein Cyclus romantischer Dichtungen*   37
   1814 *Sintram und seine Gefährten*   34
   1817 *Gedichte, zweiter Band*   33*n*53
   and R   30, 33–34, 37
Labatut, P.
   1929 *Werther* with silhouette illustrations   205
   1940s → 1970s educational *Faust* with controlled R images   205–6, 205 (*Fig. 6.19*), 210, 369
Laborde, Alexandre   191, 195, 197; *see also* Blanc
   1816–36 *Monuments de France*   191
   1871–72 *Catalogue des livres composant la bibliothèque de feu...*   195*n*66, 197
Laborde, Léon de (son of A.)   195, 197, 210
   1830 Giard *Faust* ascribed to   191–97, 211, 364
     trial prints   196 (*Fig. 6.15a–b*); *see also* Bichebois; Giard
   1830 *Voyage de l'Arabie Pétrée*   195
   1833 *Essais de gravure*   195
   1871–72 *Catalogue des livres composant la bibliothèque de feu...*   195, 195*n*66, 197
Lachgern, Anselmus (pseud.)   206, 262, 357
   1841 *Bilder zu Goethe's Faust*   264–69, 265 (*Fig. 8.7*), 375
     covers   262, 264, 266, 266 (*Fig. 8.8*), 267 (*Fig. 8.9*), 268; *see also* Crowquill; Philogelos
   and R   264, 266
Lacroix, Paul (Bibliophile Jacob)   204
Ladvocat, Pierre-François   183
Laheen, Kevin   57*n*22
Lamb, Charles   121
Lambert, Marij   198
Lanckorońska, Maria, and Arthur Rümann   113*n*85, 115*n*86
Landon, Letitia Elizabeth (L. E. L.)
   1825 "The Decision of the Flower"   224*n*21, 371
   1825 *The Improvisatrice*   224
   1825 *The Troubadour*   224; *see also* Watts, A. A.; Wright, J. M.
Lange, Victor   200*n*85
Langkavel, Martha   180*n*20
Lappenberg, Hamburg family   122
   Lappenberg, Hans   122
   Lappenberg, Johann Martin   121–22
LaRoche, Karl v., actor   290
Latham, Albert G., *Faust* trans.   5, 77, 84, 306, 352
Laugée, Thierry   206–8, 208*nn*105–6
Laughlin, James, poet and publisher   173–75, 174 (*Fig. 5.23*), 376
   1949 ed. with R. Smyth of Goethe's *Faust*   175
layouts
   and reader categories   168, 355
   in R's compositions   247
     imitated (Crowquill)   262
   ironed-out differences in –   49
   on standalone sheets   218–19
   significant – in R editions   81–82, 135, 136, 154, 176, 361
     imitated (Darley)   241
Le Men, Ségolène   180, 253
   "extensive and intensive culture of the image"   242

Lecomte, Louis-Henry   290
Lecouvey, "great vault" close to Palais-Royal   184
Leda (mythology)   39
Lefèvre, Charles, theatre set designer   281, 283; *see also* Tomkins
Lehár, Franz, *The Merry Widow*   301
Lehner, Gilbert   279
Leighton, John, aka Luke Limner, book designer   175, 176
   book spine   172–73, 172 (*Fig. 5.21*), 175, 376
   tomb mosaic   175
Leipzig   37, 42, 50, 59, 64, 66, 97, 101, 167
   book fair   65, 125, 126, 128
   book fair catalogues (*Messekataloge*)   66, 67
Leipziger Literatur-Zeitung   42, 43
Lemaître, Frédérick, actor, as Mephistopheles   186, 281, 290, 333
   Souvenirs de Frédérick Lemaître   290*n*90
Lemmer, Klaus J.   27*n*20, 34*n*56, 44*n*109
Lessing, Gotthold Ephraim   192
   1766 *Laocoon*, visual/verbal divide   86
   questioned   286
Leu, Philipp   208*n*110
Lévêque, Jean-Maxime   283*n*60
Lever, Charles, Irish novelist, 1850 *Roland Cashel*   318
Lévi-Strauss, Claude, 1966 *The Savage Mind*   334
Lévy, Michel, French publisher   306; *see also* Michel Lévy Frères
Lewald, August   298*n*108
Lewis, George Robert, artist   135; *see also* Dibdin
Liberal (*The*)   157; *see also* Hunt; Shelley, P. B.
Librairie Gründ, publishers
   1938 cover of *Faust* after Frère (← R)   208–10, 210 (*Fig. 6.22*), 243, 378
libraries
  private
     Abel Giraudeau's   200
     Achille Devéria's   208
     Alexandre and Léon de Laborde's   194 (*Fig. 6.14*), 195*n*66, 195–97
     Antoine Boucher's (uncle to Nerval)   190
     Auguste Vincent's   197
     Bryan Waller Procter's   197
     Edward Gordon Craig's   197
     Franz Glück's   98 (*Fig. 3.1a*), 99
     John Britton's   123
     Walter Scott's (Abbotsford)   59; *see also* Goethe's library
  private → institutional
     Thomas Grenville's   124, 128–29
  institutional
     Beinecke Rare Book and Manuscript Library (Yale)   65, 109, 146, 147, 168*n*115, 175, 323
     Bibliothèque nationale de France (Paris)   180, 182, 227
     British Library (London)   129, 283
     Elmer L. Andersen Library (Minneapolis)   124, 125
     Free Library of Philadelphia   318, 320
     Herzogin Anna Amalia Bibliothek (HAAB), Weimar   66, 92, 97, 109, 118, 119, 168*n*115, 221
     Institut catholique de Toulouse (ICT)   205*n*98
     King's Library (British Library)   129
     Library of the University of Michigan   25*n*6, 105*n*47
     Royal Library (Paris)   49
     Widener Library (Harvard)   200
     Weimar (historic) library   109, 274; *see also* HathiTrust cyber-library

library as theme in *Faust* 130, 130 (*Fig. 4.1*), 136
   influenced by R 274, 276 (*Fig. 9.4*)
   represented
      after R 116 (*Fig. 3.17a*), 117, 161 (*Fig. 5.16*), 162, 165 (*Fig. 5.18 top left*), 181 (*Fig. 6.4*), 202 (*Fig. 6.17 top left*), 211, 264, 265 (*Figs. 8.6, 8.7*), 319, 335 (*Fig. 12.1, l. 3 col. 1*), 336 (*Fig. 12.2 l. 1 col. 2–3*), 339, 339 (*Fig. 12.3*)
      by R 10, 22, 50, 68 (*Fig. 2.4b*), 72, 84, 85 (*Fig. 2.21*), 89, 90 (*Fig. 2.23*), 103, 104 (*Fig. 3.7*), 123–24, 132, 132 (*Fig. 4.3*), 270, 356
Lieber, Carl, painter, engraver and restorer 274
Lieber, Francis, R fan 37, 44
Lieber, Mathilde (wife of F.) 37
Lilith (in Goethe's Walpurgis Night and after R) 311–13
Limper-Herz, Karen 129*n*71, 129*n*80
Linant de Bellefonds, Louis Maurice Adolphe, 1830 *Voyage de l'Arabie Pétrée* 195; *see also* Laborde, L.
Lips, Johann Heinrich
   1790 *Faust* frontispiece after *The Alchemist* by Rembrandt 55, 274
   1791 Goethe's portrait 118–19, 360
Literary Chronicle 156*n*80
Literary Gazette (*The*) 179, 224, 371
Literary Panorama and National Register (*The*) 99
Literary Souvenir; or Cabinet of Poetry and Romance (*The*) 208, 224, 225 (*Figs. 7.8, 7.9*), 233, 371; *see also* keepsake literature; Watts, A. A.
literature
   blending with life 28–31, 33, 50, 329; *see also* types
   as ethnic bond 2, 45, 54, 108, 118, 122, 129
   in individual lives 332, 333, 342, 355
lithographs, lithographic prints 47 (*Fig. 1.12b*), 48, 49, 54*n*10, 70, 84, 85, 92, 95, 99, 108, 109, 110, 111 (*Figs. 3.10b, 3.12*), 112, 128, 160–61, 160 (*Fig. 5.15*), 161 (*Fig. 5.16*), 162, 166, 177, 179, 180, 181, 182, 182 (*Fig. 6.5*), 183, 183 (*Fig. 6.6*), 184, 185, 187, 193, 193 (*Fig. 6.13*), 194, 195, 196 (*Fig. 6.15a*), 197, 198, 199 (*Figs. 6.16a–b*), 200, 206, 208, 209 (*Fig. 6.21 left*), 210, 212, 223, 225–26, 226 (*Fig. 7.10*), 227–29, 228 (*Fig. 7.11*), 229 (*Fig. 7.12*), 230 (*Figs. 7.13, 7.14, 7.15*), 233, 235 (*Fig. 7.19*), 236, 236 (*Fig. 7.20*), 241, 245, 247, 248 (*Fig. 7.27 top*), 250, 257, 258, 264, 266, 266 (*Fig. 8.8*), 267 (*Fig. 8.9*), 270, 271, 283, 283 (*Fig. 9.9*), 288, 289 (*Fig. 9.12*), 293, 299, 307, 334, 340, 360, 361, 362, 363, 364, 367, 368, 371, 372, 373, 374, 375
   colour lithographs 106–7, 107 (*Fig. 3.9*), 238–39, 238 (*Fig. 7.22*), 240, 241, 251, 258, 299, 358
lithography (technique) 42, 88, 95, 110, 159, 181, 182, 184, 195, 210, 213, 251, 333, 375
   typolithography 88
lithophanes 236, 333, 340, 344, 346–47, 348 (*Fig. 12.7*), 349 (*Fig. 12.8*), 350 (*Fig. 12.9*), 352, 358, 373, 374
   and art of storytelling 346
   and creation 344–46
Lochnan, Katharine 54*n*10
Lockhart, John 59
Lohr, Günther 288*n*81
Lohrer, Liselotte 95*n*1, 106*n*55
London Gazette (*The*) 172
London Magazine (*The*) (*LM*) 34*n*55, 97, 99, 124, 125, 126–27, 128, 129, 138*n*3, 139, 140, 148*nn*46–47, 149, 163, 233
London Stereoscopic and Photographic Company 299
Longfellow, Henry Wadsworth 200, 241
   Ballads and Other Poems 310*n*31
Longman and Co., early compared to Cotta 133
Loos, Adolf 99
loose/scattered leaves (*fliegende Blätter*) 212–13, 215–21, 241, 242

Lorentz, Alfred 156*n*82
Lorraine (*Lothringen*) 321, 333
Lost Art Internet Database 34*n*60
Louis-Philippe, last king of France 187, 197, 201, 363
Lowder, Gerald 221
Lowell, James Russell, American poet 200
Ludwig I of Bavaria 45
Ludwig, E., publisher in Graz 237 (*Fig. 7.21b*), 238, 376
Luise v. Baden 56
Luke, David, *Faust* trans. 5, 74, 291, 332, 343
Lumley, Edward, British publisher 175
   1832 *Faustus: from the German of Goethe* with Shelley trans. 156–57, 158 (*Fig. 5.13*), 167, 233, 361, 364; *see also* Shelley, P. B.; stereotype edition
Luther, Martin, pictorial life of 240
Lycaon (mythology) 39

Mabbott, Thomas M. 310*n*33, 311
Mac Orlan, Pierre 269
Mackall, Leonard L. 124, 128*n*70, 148*n*51, 359
MacLeod, Catriona 115*n*86
Maclise, Daniel 176, 357
Maffei, Andrea, Schiller trans. into Italian 250
Magasin pittoresque (*Le*) 25, 26, 54, 206, 264
Magdalene (aka Mary Magdalene) 262, 262*n*17, 281, 307, 346, 347; *see also* Dolci; Rembrandt
Magedera, Ian H. 126*n*53
magic lantern *see* optical effects
Magnenat, C.?, draughtsman 195
Mahl, Bernd 117*n*, 271, 279*n*34, 279*n*37, 280*nn*42–43, 290*n*92, 294*n*97, 298*n*109, 301*n*117
Maierhofer, Waltraud 96*n*7, 213
Maisak, Petra 242*n*70, 274*nn*15–16
Maison d'Art (La), publishing firm 208, 378
Malaplate, Jean 186*n*41
Man, Felix H. 162*n*96
Marck, Jan van der 197*n*69, 197*n*72, 200*n*82
Maresq and Pelvey 203, 367, 376; *see also* Bry
Margetson, William Henry 299
Maria Pavlovna, Grand Duchess of Saxe-Weimar-Eisenach 55–56
marketing 73, 125, 126, 170
   strategy 149, 203, 251
   tools 54, 56, 93, 102, 106, 149, 357
Markham, Sandra 327*n*16
Marlowe, Christopher 127, 128, 151, 154, 157, 168, 221, 259
   The Tragicall History of *Dr Faustus* 127, 128, 148, 221, 259
Marquardt, Hertha 121*nn*12–13, 121*n*17, 122*n*22, 123*n*29, 123*n*33, 123*n*36
Marquart, Lea 180, 181*n*25
Marriage, Ellen 346
Martin, John 156
Marville, Charles 201
Marx, Karl, *Capital: A Critique of Political Economy* 338
Masia, Luca 251*n*87
Masson et Cie, French publishers 200, 203, 205–6, 205 (*Fig. 6.19*), 210, 369
materiality (material bibliography)
   and cultural trends 5, 5*n*10, 59, 136, 216, 257, 334, 338, 355
   and publishing trends 4, 93, 125, 156, 176, 198, 200
   and reading practices 5, 77, 93, 120, 128, 136, 176, 216, 355
   and symbolical or poetic value 5, 56–59, 120, 154, 157–59, 158 (*Fig. 5.13*), 176, 198, 233, 355
   as vehicle of ideas 5, 59
Matisse, Henri, *Luxe, calme et volupté* 212

GENERAL INDEX

Maurin, Nicolas, artist   208, 226–27, 228 (*Fig. 7.11*), 233, 235 (*Fig. 7.19*)
Mauss, Marcel   338; *see also* gifts
Max, Gabriel, 1880 *Faust-Illustrationen: Zehn Zeichnungen*   245, 312 (*Fig. 10.1*)
Maximilian I, King of Bavaria   133
May, Phil   299, 301 (*Fig. 9.20*)
Mays, J. C. C.   149*n*60, 151*n*70
Mazzocca, Fernando   247, 250
McIsaac, Peter   286
Meadows, Kenny   258
   1839–40 *Heads of the People*   297
media   5, 6, 38, 124, 126, 224, 239, 255, 257, 297, 299, 315
   – circulation   3
   – culture   3, 222
   – negotiation   3
   media-driven modernity   268, 356
   visual –   36, 45, 48; *see also* multimedia; printed items; remediation; Index on MR → 9. Effect and Function of R's *Faust I* Outlines → upshots → reproduction
Medwin, Thomas   120*n*10
meerschaum pipe
   and translation   259, 259 (*Fig. 8.2*), 262, 267 (*Fig. 8.9*), 268, 343–44
   the devil with –   262, 263 (*Fig. 8.5*), 268–69; *see also* Crowquill; devil; Mephistopheles; Old Nick
Meissen, locality   227, 270
Meissen, porcelain factory   227, 340, 341 (*Fig. 12.4*), 347, 370, 374
melancholy   42, 250, 307
   and Faust   2, 84, 89, 90 (*Fig. 2.22, 2.23*), 342
   and Margaret   91 (*Fig. 2.24*), 92, 257, 298
Meline, Jean-Paul, counterfeit Belgian publisher
   1833 pirating the Feuillet-Dumus *Faust*   200, 364
   supplying Germany, Poland, Denmark, Russia   200
Meline, Léon Cans et Co., counterfeit Belgian publishers and exporters   200, 365
   1838 re-issuing pirated Feuillet-Dumus *Faust*   200
   popular in learned contexts   200
melodrama   206, 281, 290
   and sensational images   208, 281
   commercially successful   281, 291
melodramatic (manner, way)   290, 312–13, 321
Mengs, Anton Raphael   34
Méphisto (Le): Journal théâtral, musical, fantaisiste, illustré (Rouen)   301
Mephistopheles, treatment of   46–47 (*Figs. 1.8–1.12a–b*), 48
   and sexuality   91 (*Fig. 2.25*), 103, 104 (*Fig. 3.7*), 224, 233, 339 (*Fig. 12.3*), 339–40
   as (traditional) hellish spirit   48, 110, 111 (*Figs. 3.10b, 3.11, 3.12*), 140, 172, 172 (*Fig. 5.21*), 173 (*Fig. 5.22*), 183, 224, 236, 236 (*Fig. 7.20*), 245, 245 (*Fig. 7.25*)
   as cunning schemer   67, 68 (*Figs. 2.4a–b*), 84, 107, 107 (*Fig. 3.9*), 133, 188, 214 (*Fig. 7.1*), 224, 308, 340, 341 (*Fig. 12.4*), 342 (*Fig. 12.5a*), 343 (*Fig. 12.5b*), 345 (*Fig. 12.6b*), 351, 351 (*Fig. 12.10*), 352
   as Faust's double   92, 140, 247, 248 (*Fig. 7.27*), 296, 304, 305
   as man   42, 299, 309, 338
   as stage director   150–51, 150 (*Fig. 5.8*), 151 (*Fig. 5.9*)
   female   305–6, 315, 319, 321
   hallmarked as sinewy after R   59, 67, 74–75, 74 (*Fig. 2.9*), 75 (*Fig. 2.10*), 84, 162, 206, 207 (*Fig. 6.20*), 217, 239, 290–91, 292 (*Fig. 9.13*), 297–302, 300 (*Figs. 9.18, 9.19*), 301 (*Fig. 9.20*), 351, 354, 358; *see also* devil
   in parody   255–68
   Mephistophelean red   296, 296 (*Fig. 9.17*), 299–301, 334, 352, 363; *see also* bindings

Mercure du dix-neuvième siècle (Le)   179*n*6
Mérimée, Prosper   197
metaphors   154, 213, 241, 306, 321, 323
   etching/printing   307
   expressive/potent   167, 239, 346
   pictorial   307
   romantic   157
   visual   75, 75 (*Fig. 2.10*), 81 (*Fig. 2.17*), 84, 247
   weaving – as trap   113
Metropolitan Magazine (The)   258*n*10
Mettais, Charles, draughtsman   204
Meusel, Johann Georg   39–40
   1808 *Archiv für Künstler und Kunstfreunde*   39*nn*83–84
   1809 *Teutsches Künstllexikon*   40
Meyer, Alfred Gotthold   277*n*23
Meyer, Johann Heinrich, Swiss painter and connoisseur   61, 62, 115, 274, 286
   on R   42, 60, 69, 115
Meyer, Kuno, Celtic philologist   200, 210
Meyerbeer, Giacomo   185, 283, 283 (*Fig. 9.9*), 372
Meyerheim, Friedrich Eduard?, lithographer   239, 288, 289 (*Fig. 9.12*), 293, 373
mice, unpoetic animals   *see Batrachomyomachia*
Michel Lévy Frères, publishers   206*n*104, 375; *see also* Lévy
Michelangelo   182
Middleton, Thomas   157
Mignon (character from *Wilhelm Meister's Apprenticeship*)   35, 306
Milano, Alberto   179*n*9
Milbert, Jacques, 1828–29 *Itinéraire pittoresque du fleuve Hudson*   194
Millais, John Everett, and R   176, 357
Millet, Jean-François   242, 253
Milner, Henry M., 1824 *Faustus; or, The Demon's Victim*   281
Miltitz, Auguste v. (wife of C. B.)   32–33, 32 (*Fig. 1.4*), 34
Miltitz, Carl Borromäus v.   32–33, 32 (*Fig. 1.4*), 34, 36*n*69, 85; *see also* Scharfenberg circle
Milton, John   88, 127
   Paradise Lost   156
Minkus, Ludwig, 1864 ballet *Néméa*   309*n*29
Mix, York-Gothart   115*n*86
Möbius, Martin Richard   32*n*47
Mohr, Franz Karl, tin figurines after Goethe's *Faust*   349–50
Mojem, Helmuth, and Barbara Potthast   54*n*7, 95*n*1
Moldenhauer, Dirk   121*nn*18–19, 122*n*24
Mollier, Jean-Yves   180
Momus, god of derision   259, 261, 262, 266, 268; *see also* Old Nick
Mongan, Agnes   177*n*3
Moniteur universel (Le)   284, 291*n*95, 309*n*29
Monnier, Henry Bonaventure, 1826 *Marchand d'estampes*   184
Monstre et le Magicien (Le), 1826 melodrama after *Frankenstein* by M. Shelley   281
Monthly Literary Advertiser (MLA) (*The*)   138, 148
Monthly Magazine   126, 148, 149*n*57
Monthly Review   120
Moore, Thomas   325, 327
   1817 *Lalla Rookh*   325
Moosmann, Peter   352
Moran, Daniel   54*n*7, 95*n*1
Morgenblatt für gebildete Stände   35, 36, 39, 42, 66, 112
Morgenstern, Karl, German philologist   58*n*26
Morley, Edith J.   121*n*15, 140*n*26
Morlon, A.   299
Mortzfeld, Peter   119*n*92, 360
Moschkau, Alfred   377

Moses (Bible) 140, 182
Moses, Henry, English engravings after R 35, 42, 58, 60, 62, 83, 84, 96, 118, 118 (*Fig. 3.18*), 123, 126, 128, 133, 135, 136, 137, 138–39, 146 (*Fig. 5.6*), 148, 149, 154, 155 (*Fig. 5.11a–c*), 156, 157, 158 (*Figs. 5.12, 5.13*), 161, 162, 167, 168, 169, 170, 171 (*Figs. 5.19, 5.20*), 176, 179, 181, 182, 183, 221, 224, 233, 243, 262, 264, 281, 305, 319, 323, 327, 328 (*Figs. 11.2, 11.3*), 359, 360, 361, 364, 366, 367, 368, 370, 375
   adapting Cornelius to R 149–51, 150 (*Fig. 5.8*), 151 (*Fig. 5.9*), 180, 360
   adapting R to English *Zeitgeist* 140–45, 141 (*Fig. 5.1*), 142 (*Fig. 5.2*), 144 (*Fig. 5.4*)
   mushrooming of copies 136; *see also* Boosey
Moshofer, Theres 231
Motion, Andrew 126*n*53
Motte-Sautelet 1828 in-folio *Faust* 180, 187, 198, 210, 227, 242, 248 (*Fig. 7.27 top*), 363, 371, 372; *see also* Delacroix; Devéria
Motte, Charles 181, 198, 208, 225, 245
Moultrie, John 151
Müller, Carl, close to the Nazarenes 227
Müller, Friedrich v., Weimar chancellor 58, 101, 186, 290
Müller, Hermann Alexander 44
Müller, Karl, lithographer 227–29, 230 (*Fig. 7.14*), 233, 340, 375
multimedia/multimedial 75*n*84, 112, 115, 163; *see also* intermedial
Münderloh, Johann Gabriel Wilhelm, Weimar merchant 57
Muret, Jean-Baptiste, French artist, first to copy R in France 42, 49, 85, 210
   1824 *Faust* lithographs (Auvray) 179, 180, 181–84, 182 (*Fig. 6.5*), 183 (*Fig. 6.6*), 188, 208, 209 (*Fig. 6.21*), 233, 360
   1828 2nd ed. (Auvray Frères) 185, 185 (*Fig. 6.7b*), 362
   and England 161, 162, 182–83, 361
   Muret's copies copied 195, 203, 205, 206, 211, 243, 367, 376
Murray, Chris 149*n*60
Murray, Christopher, theatre historian 247*n*76, 281*n*46
Murray, John, publisher 325, 327
Murton, Charles, bookbinder 129–32, 146–47, 151*n*69, 154, 173, 221, 359, 360
   Faust in his study 130–32, 130 (*Fig. 4.1*), 176
   and visual/textual translation 130–32
Musset, Alfred de 311

Nachdruck (German), both *reprint* and *pirated copy* 108, 108*n*61, 108–12
Naeke, Gustav Heinrich 34, 39, 40, 43, 115, 239, 270, 334, 340, 371
   1811 lost painting *Faust and Margaret* 46 (*Fig. 1.9*), 48, 334
     engraved and lithographed 47 (*Fig. 1.12a–b*), 48, 334
     preliminary sketches 47 (*Fig. 1.11*), 48
     remediated on KPM porcelain painted plate 334–38, 337 (*Fig. 12.2, l. 4 col. 3*)
   1811 painting *Faust and Margaret in the Garden* 43
Nagler, Georg Kaspar 40, 43, 44*n*109
   1843 *Neues allgemeines Künstler-Lexicon* 39, 43, 97*n*17, 227, 358
   1871 *Monogrammisten (Die)* 43*n*105
Napoleon Bonaparte 58, 195, 261, 323
Napoleon III 250
Napoleon, Prince (Napoléon-Joseph Bonaparte, cousin of N. III) 241
Nash, John, Regent's Quadrant 159
nations competing in Europe 2, 5, 242, 252, 254, 261, 268, 321
   Franco-British dispute in parody 261
   Franco-German rivalry 106–7, 107 (*Fig. 3.9*), 321
Nauwerck, Ludwig 43, 115, 274
Nazarenes, the 45, 227
   Nazarene style 58

Neefe, Hermann 279
negotiations
   aesthetic 121–22, 124, 175
   artistic 121–22, 322
   commercial 63, 102, 121–22, 175
   cultural 3, 4, 123, 127, 141–42, 179
   political 322; *see also* nations competing
Nehrlich, Gustav 239, 240
Neidhardt, Hans Joachim 32*n*46, 37*n*76, 45
neoclassical
   ideal/style 40, 87, 151, 152 (*Figs. 5.10a*), 153 (*Fig. 5.10b*), 273, 277
   motifs 84, 160
   prints 54
   theories of art 86
neoclassicism 42, 288
Nerval, Gérard de 2, 189, 190, 192, 203, 210, 244, 245, 253, 307, 362
   1828 trans. *Faust, tragédie de Goëthe* 85, 180, 181, 184, 186, 188, 190, 193, 200, 210, 371
     covers' visual appeal 184, 185, 185 (*Figs. 6.7a–b*), 211, 362
     frontispiece copying R 180, 181 (*Fig. 6.4*), 211, 257, 307, 371
   1840 last *Faust I* and partial *Faust II* trans. 203, 242–43, 245
   1850 Bry's popular *Faust* 203, 367, 376
   1936 *Faust* trans., preface by Gautier 208–10
   1938 Gründ cover after Frère copying R 208–10, 210 (*Fig. 6.22*), 243, 378
   and theatre 184–85, 186
   legend of Goethe's praise 186; *see also* Bry; Frère; Fust; Jourdain, G.; Librairie Gründ
networks 99, 112, 121, 154, 162, 180; *see also* book trade; circulation; diffusion; distribution
Neubert, Franz 49, 50, 52*n*2, 96*n*4, 180*n*19, 210*n*111, 355
Neureuther, Eugen Napoleon 50
New Directions Publishing 175, 376
Newark, Cormac 302
Nicholas I, Tsar 55
Nicolai, Friedrich, as "Buttock Fantasist" (*Proktophantasmist*) 304
Nicolovius, Alfred 109, 362
   1828 *Über Goethe: Literarische und artistische Nachrichten* 109*n*73
Niessen, Carl 89, 221*n*13, 271, 287
Nightingale, Florence 57
Nisle, Julius 239, 240, 343
   1840 *Göthe-Gallerie* steel engraved by W. Pobuda 239, 343, 344 (*Fig. 12.6a*), 374
   1840 pl. remediated as pipe bowl picture 343, 345 (*Fig. 12.6b*), 375
Nodier, Charles 197, 289
   on types 297–98; *see also* typification/typifying
Norman, Frederick 121*n*14, 123
Norton, Caroline Sheridan 264*n*19
Notes & Queries 59, 157*n*87
Nouveau journal de Paris 290*n*87
Nymphenburg, porcelain factory 347
Nyx or Night (mythology) 259

O'Leary, Patrick 126*n*52
Oberlößnitz 25, 26, 27, 30; *see also* Hoflößnitz; Radebeul
objects 3, 242, 254, 333, 339, 343, 347, 354
   books and prints as commodities 107, 241, 338
   emotional – 334, 342–43, 347, 352–54; *see also* artefacts; books and prints as cultural objects
octavos 170, 175, 187, 210
   domesticating the plates 167–68, 175, 355
   standard – as illustrated books 167, 168–69, 241, 366, 369
   text – 148, 149, 160–61, 162, 163

GENERAL INDEX

441

Odenkirchen, Stella Esther   50, 96*n*5, 97, 120, 124
Old German masters   45
Old Germanic style   109, 110
Old Nick   262; *see also* devil; meerschaum pipe; Mephistopheles; Momus
Oldach, Julius, 1828 *Mephistopheles and the Student*   206
optical effects   299, 346
   gas lighting   92
   light bulb, invention of   346
   limelight   92, 298
   magic lantern   92, 288
   phantasmagoria   104 (*Fig. 3.7*), 286, 294, 338–39, 339 (*Fig. 12.3*); *see also* lithophanes
Orcutt, Kimberley   241*n*59, 242*n*65
Orcutt, Kimberley, and Allan McLeod   241*n*59
Ortmann, Erwin   347*n*34
Osiander, Christian Friedrich   54, 115
ottava rima   259
Otto E., lithographer   212
Otto, Regine   106*n*52
Oury, Gérard, 1966 film *La Grande Vadrouille*   301
outline style (history of)   86, 86*nn*97–99
   and art hierarchies   40, 42–43, 51
   as key interpretation of literary works   3–4, 33, 36, 129, 213
   eclipsed   43, 89, 92, 206
   in Germany   26, 40, 42, 44, 89
   vogue of –   86, 89, 176
outline, aesthetic medium
   by Schlegel
      and abstraction   86–87, 167, 169; *see also* abstractions
      and initiation   86–87, 103, 169, 250, 309, 310, 321, 330; *see also* allusions
      and poetry   36, 87, 184, 330
      evocative   5–6, 86–87, 136, 162, 190, 213, 250, 301–2, 309, 310, 315; *see also* imagination
      vs. painting   87
   by Starobinski
      stirring dream, fantasy, desire   87, 325–29
   Schlegel overturned/extended
      enriching covert plans/riddles   311, 312, 313–21, 325
      conveying visual ciphers/veiled messages   310–11, 313, 315, 322
      predicating avant-garde genres (Gautier)   309–11, 321
outline, meanings of
   Aperçu, wax model for lithophane mould   352
   bait of outline   253, 357
   epitome/summary   149, 357
   in this book   5–6, 357
   texts into linear compositions   5, 6, 36, 77, 120, 122, 149, 154, 291; *see also* picture story
   uncertain naming in French   54, 180, 184
Overbeck, Johann Friedrich   43
   1828 *Italia und Germania*   250
Ovid   39, 154
oxymoron   308, 321

Palacio, Jean de   206
Pan (mythology)   40
Pandore (La)   179*n*5, 182*n*29, 183
paragone   *see* Lessing
Parenth, Ulrich   280*n*43
Parinet, Élisabeth   194*n*62, 195*n*64

parodies of *Faust I*   206, 254, 55
   textual   *see* Grillparzer; Vischer
   textual and visual   *see* Crowquill
   visual   *see* Benoit, West and Weibexahl; *Humoristich-satirisches Bilder-Album*; Lachgern
parody   255, 268, 355
   and cultural tradition   255–57
   and – of parody   262–68
   as refined reading of Goethe's *Faust I*   255, 257, 261, 268–69
   as spiced-up translation   259–62
   vs. nationalistic appropriation   261, 264–69; *see also* burlesque
parody in Goethe's *Faust I*   127, 168, 186
Parthenon (The): A Magazine of Art and Literature   88; *see also* Φ.Χ.Ψ.
Partisans (Les). Revue de combat, d'art, de littérature et de sociologie   208, 210, 378
Partridge, John Bernard, English illustrator   299, 300 (*Figs. 9.18, 9.19*)
Paton, Joseph Noël
   1847 painting *The Quarrel of Oberon and Titania*   307
   1863 outlines for *Coleridge's Rime of the Ancient Mariner*   240
Patzschke, Carl Friedrich, printmaker   238, 238 (*Fig. 7.22*), 375
Paul I, Tsar   55
Paul, Claude   206*n*100
Paul, Howard (George Henry Howard)   299
Paulin, Roger, William St Clair, and Elinor Shaffer   148*n*44, 149*n*60, 149*nn*63–64
Pavie, André, *Médaillons romantiques: Lettres inédites*   273, 296*n*101
Pavie, Victor (son of A.), *Voyages et promenades romantiques*   42, 60, 273, 290, 291*n*93, 296, 333, 346
Pavlovna, Maria, Grand Duchess of Saxe-Weimar-Eisenach   56; *see also* Jena Patriotic Women's Association
Pays (Le)   306
Peach, Annette   126*n*53
Peckus, Sarunas (Sharkey), and Ben Rapaport   340*n*16, 343*n*24
Penny Magazine (The)   264
Pereira-Arnstein, Louis v.   239
Perthes and Besser, booksellers' firm   37, 122; *see also* Besser
Perthes, Clemens Theodor   122*nn*22–23
Perthes, Friedrich Christoph (father of C. T.)   37, 55, 109
   and H. C. Robinson   121–23, 176
   German book trade representative   108, 121
   1816 *Der deutsche Buchhandel*   122
Perugina (La), Italian firm   *see* Baci Perugina
Petersen, Julius   271, 272*n*3, 279, 286*n*64, 288*n*79, 294*n*98, 298*n*111
Petit, Jacob, French ceramist   347, 348 (*Fig. 12.7*)
Pfäfflin, Anna Marie   277*n*23
Pfennig-Magazin (Das)   264
Pfitzer, Johann Nicolaus, 1674 *Faust* chapbook, 1834 Eytel illus. after R   116 (*Fig. 3.17a*), 117, 117 (*Fig. 3.17b*), 373
phantasmagoria   *see* optical effects
Philogelos (3rd or 4th c. CE)   262; *see also* Lachgern
Phiz (Hablôt K. Browne), Dickens illustrator   2, 258, 303, 313
   1848 frontispiece Dickens, *Dombey and Son*   319
   1849 *I make the acquaintance of Miss Mowcher*, illus. Dickens, *David Copperfield*   313–21, 314 (*Fig. 10.2*), 316 (*Fig. 10.4*), 317 (*Fig. 10.5*), 376
Phoenix Pottery, Kaolin and Fire Brick Company   347
Phönix: Frühlingszeitung für Deutschland   42
photographs   299, 301
photomechanical reproduction   112, 213
   heliotype printing   241
   photogravure (*héliogravure*)   241, 245, 246 (*Fig. 7.26*)
physiologies (literature on)   297

Picat-Guinoiseau, Ginette   185n38, 187n44, 290n88
Pichois, Claude   184n37
Pichot, Amédée, 1825 *Voyage historique et littéraire en Angleterre et en Écosse*   179, 291, 297, 298
picture story (visual narrative)
    silent (in outline)   2, 3, 6, 9–21, 48, 54, 62, 70–71, 71 (*Fig. 2.6*), 80, 81–82, 87, 93, 103, 115, 120, 154, 169, 288, 309, 356n7, 357
    captioned   54, 139, 210; *see also* captions
Piéri-Bénard, Antoine-François   103
Pierrepont, Charles, styled Viscount Newark   214
Pieske, Christa   227n29, 229
Pietzsch, Eduard and Company, publishers/printers   223, 227, 229, 230 (*Figs. 7.13, 7.14*), 233 (Pietsch), 236 (*Fig. 7.20*), 375
Pillet aîné, printer   184
Pinéas
    1828 pirating R   180, 181 (*Fig. 6.4*), 185, 211, 307, 371
    1848 *Dessin linéaire, ornement: Exercices gradués*   185n40
pipe bowls   229, 333, 340–43, 358
    c.1820? after R   340–43, 341 (*Fig. 12.4*), 370
    c.1830–40 after R   340–43, 342 (*Fig. 12.5a*), 374
    c.1830–40 after R   340–43, 343 (*Fig. 12.5b*), 374
    1840 after Nisle influenced by R   343, 345 (*Fig. 12.6b*), 375; *see also* artefacts; objects
Piper, Andrew   175
pirating R   96, 99, 107–12, 137, 149, 154, 307, 356, 362
    via an intermediary   136, 137, 161; *see also* copyright; *Nachdruck*
Piroli, Tommaso, engraving Flaxman   48, 86, 110, 143 (*Fig. 5.3*)
plate margins of R editions and copies
    close-cropped (1816 R portfolio)   52, 96
    differing   110, 181
    large
        for diminutive prints   162, 163, 364, 366
        in 1878 Bell & Sons quarto   168, 368
        in Cotta albums   103, 106, 107, 364, 365, 368
        in industrialised items   169
    wide
        in 1824 Muret   181–82, 360
        in 1877 Estes & Lauriat   169
    wider (1820 R portfolio)   96, 124, 125, 138, 191, 359
        in 1830 Giard ← 1820 Cotta   363
        lithographed pirated copy   108
Plaskitt, Emma   127n64
Plötz-Peters, Hannelore   334n11
Plume (La)   208
Poe, Edgar Allan   2, 303, 321, 356
    1836 "Metzengerstein"   310
    1840 "The Man of the Crowd" and R   80n88, 304–5n6, 310–11, 313
    1845 "The Purloined Letter"   311
Polignac, Jules de   195, 197
Pollock, Walter Herries   297, 298, 299, 303
    on Irving and R   297, 299, 311
    1883 *The Picture's Secret*   310, 311–13, 321
Pons, A.-J., "Notice artistique" on Faust   180
popular *Faust*-based entertainments   273, 279–82, 286–88, 289–91, 293–97, 299–301, 301–2
porcelain plates, painted   352
    after Naeke   334, 337 (*Fig. 12., l. 4 col. 3*)
    after R   334–40, 335 (*Fig. 12.1*), 336–37 (*Fig. 12.2*)
        for greater numbers   338–40, 339 (*Fig. 12.3*), 351
        scenes rejected   334; *see also* artefacts; objects; things
portfolios of prints   264, 333, 356, 357, 359, 365, 366
    artists' –   110, 245, 307; *see also* Darley
    copied R – turned albums   169–72, 171 (*Figs. 5.19, 5.20*)

copied R – turned illustrated books   3, 137, 166–75
for collectors   48, 159, 162, 168, 169, 204, 216
for gentlemen   184, 204
original R – turned albums   3, 102–7, 175, 176
uses of –   149, 304–5
postcards   229, 258, 301
    commercial   347, 349 (*Fig. 12.8*)
    picture   229–31, 231 (*Fig. 7.16*)
posters   208, 258, 288, 299, 301; *see also* Cappiello
    title-page as –   163, 164 (*Fig. 5.17 top*)
Potyra, Rudolf   287n71
Pre-Raphaelites   357
Presse (La)   286n65, 287n69, 306nn13–15, 307, 308, 309nn27–28
prices   42, 49, 55, 63, 102, 104, 107–8, 114, 126, 137, 139, 156, 160, 161, 163, 164 (*Fig. 5.17 top*), 183, 184, 188, 189, 203, 204, 213, 351, 360, 361, 362
print culture   3–5, 216, 254, 356, 357
    and Faust myth   211, 239, 356
    by focus
        comparative/triangular relations   180
        France, French   180, 201–11
        in Britain   137–76, 201
        in diffusion   3, 5, 50, 356
        in Europe   3, 4, 215–16
    nature of
        and new technologies   5; *see also* engravings/etchings; lithography; reproduction; woodcuts
        beyond outlines   254
        bourgeois/industrial   2, 4, 69, 80, 99, 108, 112, 124, 139, 169, 172–73, 172 (*Fig. 5.21*), 197–98, 203, 216, 220, 222, 261, 338, 357, 368, 371, 376
        fluidity of – vs. set ideas   204
        mediating and tempting   80, 112, 122, 151, 154, 163, 357
        myth of unaltered –   175–76, 179, 179n9
        visual turn in   138
printed items
    and literary readings   179
    as ambassadors   55, 62, 59, 175, 322, 356
    as archetypes/templates   54, 87, 149, 154–57, 167, 169, 170, 175, 184, 200, 213, 214, 218, 219, 220, 251, 271, 297, 301, 305, 306, 307, 339, 360, 361, 364, 365, 366, 372
    as international language   37, 89, 95, 102, 106, 122, 123, 179, 358; *see also* translations (textual); translations (visual)
    remediated into objects/things   334–54
Procter, Bryan Waller (pseud. Barry Cornwall)   197, 362
Proescholdt-Obermann, Catherine Waltraud   120n8, 141
Proescholdt, Catherine W.   60n37
Protestant   197–98, 346
    reserve in images   334; *see also* Roman Catholicism
Proteus (mythology)   40
Proust, Marcel, *À la Recherche du temps perdu*   352
Prout, Samuel   58
Prowett, Septimus, publisher   156, 170, 361
Proyart, Jean-Baptiste de, book expert   195
Pückler-Muskau, Hermann v., Prince   220, 373
Pujoulx, Jean-Baptiste   277
Punch; or, The London Charivari   258, 299, 300 (*Fig. 9.19*)

Quarterly Review (The)   138n1, 139n13, 163
quartos   124, 129, 139, 148, 149, 154, 157, 162n99, 168, 203, 208, 361, 367
    imperial   138, 139, 146, 175
    oblong/landscape   128, 169, 175, 367
    ordinary   138, 175
    royal   156n79, 169, 175, 367

GENERAL INDEX

443

Queen Dowager (Adelaide of Saxe-Meiningen)   168
Quérard, Joseph-Marie   180
Quesnel, Jean   190; *see also* Giard

Rabelais   203
Racine, *Britannicus*   289
Raczyński, Atanazy   43, 49*n*125
Radebeul   27, 37, 212, 271; *see also* Hoflößnitz; Oberlößnitz
Radziwill, Anton v., Prince   163, 220, 239, 273, 279, 288, 302, 334, 367
    1819–20 *Faust* as intermedial performance   277–79, 278 (*Figs. 9.5,*
        9.6)
    1835 score *Compositionen*   163*n*103, 374; *see also* Scenen aus
        Goethe's Faust in acht lithographirten Bildern; Zawadzki
Radziwill, Ferdinand (son of A.)   288, 289 (*Fig. 9.12*), 373
Radziwill, Luise v., Princess (wife of A.)   277, 338
Rahl, Karl Heinrich   43
Ramberg, Johann Heinrich   220, 272, 273, 280
    1828–29 *Faust* plates in *Minerva* engraved by Axmann   208, 209
        (*Fig. 6.2 right*)
Ramsden, Charles   129*n*81, 146*n*39
Ranieri de' Calzabigi, theatre theoretician   288, 289*n*82
Raphael, *Sistine Madonna*   347
Rapp, Gottlob Heinrich   112
reader categories of R's outlines across time (overview)   116, 139, 154,
        168, 184, 197, 201, 204, 210, 216, 357–58
    by occupation
        aesthetes   210
        art lovers   112, 120
        artists and draughtsmen   120, 176, 179, 181, 184, 197, 204, 210,
            215, 227, 233, 239, 240, 274, 298, 303, 357
        book lovers   120
        book traders   77, 201
        bookbinders   120, 172
        booksellers   120, 357
        critics   139
        intellectuals/literati   139, 195, 201, 210, 245
        lycée pupils and undergraduates   210
        men of letters   197, 210, 356*n*7
        poets   139, 151–52, 159, 175, 254, 303, 324, 357
        print collectors   125, 139, 176, 181, 184, 204, 210, 216
        printers   201
        printsellers   176
        publishers   176
        stage directors   210
        theatre-goers   210, 357
        translators   120
    by social distinction
        aristocrats   56, 106, 115, 121, 129, 139, 167, 168, 184, 195, 204, 210,
            220, 245, 279, 304–5, 357, 358
        bourgeoisie   80, 112, 203, 357
        continental and German expats   125, 210
        cultivated gentlefolk   201, 303, 304, 321
        middle-class   37, 50, 52, 95, 106, 115, 168, 184, 208, 210, 227, 315,
            338, 358
        modest or popular classes   56, 201, 204, 210, 357, 358
        royalty   358
        upper and middle educated classes   56, 106, 115, 139, 198, 210,
            357, 358
        Victorian   37, 357
        young girls of the bourgeoisie   309
    other groups
        art club subscribers   112
        bookstore customers   357

connoisseurs   139, 184
enthusiasts   112, 125, 139, 184, 210, 216, 358
general/average   181, 184, 210, 357
non-Germanophone   127
reading circles and literary societies   201, 357
subscribers to reading rooms and lending libraries   357, 358;
    see also Apollinaire; bookplates; bibliophiles; connoisseurs;
    collectors; Craig; Darley; Dibdin; ex libris; Giraudeau;
    Grenville; Hoe; Kretzschmar v. Kienbusch; Laughlin; Lowell;
    Meyer, K.; Procter; Vincent; Wyeth
readers' reception   122–24, 305, 331–32
reading protocols
    reading text   4
    reading with images   4, 264, 307, 357; *see also* image and text
    interactive –   48, 52–54, 87, 127, 322; *see also* hybrid printed
        assemblages
    second-degree – (parody)   155–68
readymades   333
realism   43, 190, 206, 310
Reber, Franz v.   43
reception of Goethe's *Faust I*   5, 45, 50, 97*n*20, 120*n*5, 120*n*8, 123,
    140*n*23, 180, 185–86, 200, 203, 257, 356; *see also* readers'
    reception
    comparative   3, 5, 60
    dependent on images   1–3, 55, 59, 122, 163, 188, 192, 242, 255; *see*
        also image and text; imagination → collective orientation of –;
        reading protocols
        vs. lingual translation   *see* translations (textual); translations
          (visual)
    iconography as influential –   4, 116, 200, 356
    negative (19th c.) –   1–2, 4, 120
    R's prints as reception matrix   2–3, 106, 156, 247, 257, 297, 340, 356,
        357
    typification as passport in –   *see* typification/typifying
Recueil des monuments antiques   182; *see also* Muret
Redonnel, Paul   208
Reed, Sue W.   240*n*58, 241*n*61
Reibel, Emmanuel   185*n*39, 206*n*99, 257*nn*7–8, 283*n*54
Reich
    1806 dissolved   2, 108
    imperial Germany's resentment   107; *see also* Holy Roman Empire
    second –   299, 333
Reichardt, Rolf   180
Reifenscheid, Beate   115*n*86
Reimers, F., student, Corps Rhenania   343
Reina, Giuseppe, 1862 painting *Triste novella*   250
Reinhard, Karl Friedrich   101, 148, 186, 290, 291, 298
Rembrandt
    1790 etching *The Alchemist* (renamed *Faust*)   180, 205, 274, 308
        copied by Lips   55, 274
    Mary Magdalene   307
remediation   5, 52, 93, 95, 120, 136, 184, 213, 215, 216, 227, 338, 340, 352,
    355, 370–78; *see also* objects; pipe bowls; porcelain plates; tin
    figurines
    Renovanz, Julianne Henriette (Julie)   28, 29 (*Fig. 1.1*), 30,
        30 (*Fig. 1.2*)
reproduction
    as unequally mapped research area   239
    invention vs. reproduction (Nodier)   297–98
    techniques   51, 88, 195, 210, 212, 213, 242, 298: *see also* copying;
        duplicates/duplication; photomechanical reproduction;
        Index on MR → 9. Effect and Function of R's *Faust I* Outlines →
        upshots → reproduction

Rethel, Alfred, dances of death   88
revolutions
    1848 uprisings   201, 261
    Belgian Revolution   197
    French Revolution   2, 180, 198
    industrial –   198
    July Revolution   197
    technological –   154
Revue bibliographique des Pays-Bas et de l'étranger   198n75
Richardson, Samuel   203
Richter, Adrian Ludwig   26, 89
Riedel, A., artist   239
Riemer, Friedrich Wilhelm   66, 274, 286
Riepenhausen, Ernst Ludwig, engraver   110n76
    and Goethe   109
    copied cover?   110–12, 111 (*Fig. 3.10b*)
    R's *Faust* copied   109–10, 112, 362
Riepenhausen, Franz (Friedrich Franz, son of E. L.)   43, 61, 112, 112n82
    c.1810? 14 chalk drawings after *Faust*   109–10
Riepenhausen, Johannes (Christian Johann, brother of F., son of E. L.)
        43, 61, 112n82
    c.1810? 14 chalk drawings after *Faust*   109–10
    1811 *Faust's Meeting with Gretchen in front of the Church*   110, 111
        (*Fig. 3.11*), 112, 362
        outline copy attrib. to Riepenhausen father   110, 111 (*Fig. 3.10b*);
            see also Emminger
Rignoux, Thomas-François, Audot's printer   170, 187, 189, 362
Rittner and Goupil   217 (*Fig. 7.3b*), 374
Ristori, Ernesto   291
rituals
    amorous   327–29, 328 (*Fig. 11.2*)
    and identification   217, 333
    give-and-take   2, 59, 122; see also gifts
    romantic pranks and –   28–30
    social   28, 55, 121, 176
    symbolic   121
    trade/commercial   121; see also smoking; symbolism
Riverside Press (The)   241
Robert, Édouard, lithographer
    Le Baiser after Retzsch   225, 229 (*Fig. 7.12*), 233, 234 (*Fig. 7.18*), 372
    La Décision de la fleur after Retzsch   225, 372
Robertson, Ritchie   149n60
Robinson, Anthony (friend of H. C.)   123
Robinson, Henry Crabb   2, 133, 136, 140, 156, 176
    and Flaxman   54, 87, 121, 123–24
    as art connoisseur   54, 122–23
    as mediator   121–24
    as theatre-goer   281
Rodwell and Martin, printsellers   137, 142 (*Fig. 5.2*), 144 (*Fig. 5.4 top*),
        146 (*Fig. 5.6*), 148, 224, 328 (*Figs. 11.2, 11.3*), 359; see also Boosey
Roger, Christine   358n13
Roget, Peter Mark, future lexicologist   123
Rohde, Carsten   333n2, 338n13
Rohde, Carsten, Thorsten Valk, and Mathias Mayer   61n46
Roman Catholicism   27, 175, 182–83, 198, 205, 290, 303, 346, 354; see
        also Counter-Reformation; Protestant → reserve in images
roman de quatre sous (dime brochures)   203
romantic
    art   86, 206, 227, 233, 247, 357
    characters/motifs   83, 206, 274
    iconography   210, 245
    ideas   34, 140, 197, 225, 363

literature   33, 39, 43
myth   247
sensationalism   25
sensibility/emotions   157, 214, 290
style   197, 277
theatre   128, 162, 187, 193, 273, 281, 288, 289–91, 333; see also gifts;
        metaphors; rituals
romanticism   49, 50, 54, 87, 121, 126, 129, 183, 194, 198, 357
    American   200
    and printed editions   193, 198
    English   1, 151, 166, 324, 329n18, 357
    French   60, 185, 197, 208, 227
    German   32–33, 39, 80, 109, 123, 240n48, 304
        German vs. French   206
    Italian   250
Roque, Georges, and Luciano Celes   115n87, 252n88
rose, as symbol   38, 154, 172, 172 (*Fig. 5.21*), 173 (*Fig. 5.22*), 175, 176, 318,
        323–29, 326 (*Figs. 11.1a, 11.1b*), 332, 352
Rose, William   120n5
Rosen, Gerd, bookseller   89
Rosenbaum, Alexander   61n46, 96n8
Rosenblum, Robert   86n98, 124n38
Rosenkranz, Karl   189, 190n54
Ross, Ronald, and R   217, 221, 222 (*Fig. 7.6 top*), 223 (*Fig. 7.7 top*), 358,
        377
Rossetti, Dante Gabriel, and R   50, 77n84, 80, 176, 357
Rothbart, Ferdinand   239
Rouen-Gazette   301
Rouget, François   203, 208, 210, 243, 243 (*Fig. 7.23*), 244 (*Figs. 7.24a,
        7.24b*), 253
Rousseau, Jean-Jacques   203
    La Nouvelle Héloïse   233
Rousset, 1829 *Faust* adaptor   187
Rümann, Arthur   49, 109n74, 239, 255n3, 257, 267, 273
Runge, Philipp Otto   37, 46, 92, 121, 239n46
Ruscheweyh, Ferdinand   49
Ruskin, John, on R   2, 88
    1846 *Modern Painters*   88
    1857 *The Elements of Drawing*   88
    1883 *The Art of England*   88
    1887 "The Black Arts: A Reverie in the Strand"   88–89
Russell, Charles William   167n114
Russell, George William   347
Ruttmann, Irene   288n81

Saint-Léon, born Charles Michel   309n26
Sainte-Aulaire, Louis-Clair Beaupoil de, 1823 *Faust* trans.   183
Salvat, Joseph, clergyman   205n98
Sampson Low, Marston & Co., publishers
    1871 Paul Konewka's *Faust* silhouettes   170
    1875 *Faust* album with Moses prints and Anster trans.   169, 368
Sand, George   204
Sanders, Michael   304n4, 306n9
Sarony & Major, lithographic partnership   241
Sarony, Napoleon   241
Sartorius v. Waltershausen, Georg   66
satire   1, 37, 38, 43, 258, 266–68, 301, 304; see also burlesque;
        grotesque; parody
Saturday Review (The)   240
Saunders and Otley, co-publishing Retzsch's trilingual
        Fancies   27n26, 101
Sautelet, Auguste   183, 193; see also Motte-Sautelet 1828 in-folio *Faust*

GENERAL INDEX

445

Saxl, Fritz   133*n*87

Saxon Art Association   27

Saxonia, Dresden periodical   227

Scenen aus Goethe's Faust in acht lithographirten Bildern (1835)   239, 288, 289 (*Fig. 9.12*), 373

Schacky v., Baroness   231

Schanze, Helmut   268*n*25

Scharfenberg circle   32, 65

Scheffer, Ary   270

Schelling, Friedrich Wilhelm   63

Schieth, Lydia   113*n*85, 115*n*86

Schiller, Friedrich v.   36, 39, 43*n*100, 44*n*111, 54, 65*n*66, 67, 95, 96, 99, 101, 104, 109, 123, 151*n*68, 156, 170, 179, 188, 189, 214–16, 216 (*Fig. 7.3a*), 218, 227, 250, 307, 309, 324, 361, 372, 374
   works by
      1781 *The Robbers*   42
      1801 *The Maid of Orleans*   113; *see also* Index on MR → 6. Other Works → R's outlines → Schiller

Schinkel, Karl Friedrich, as set designer   277–79, 278 (*Fig. 9.5*), 284, 288, 289, 293, 308, 338, 356, 370

Schlegel, August Wilhelm
   1799 "Über Zeichnungen zu Gedichten und John Flaxman's Umrisse"   86–87, 88, 136, 169, 213, 250, 309, 310, 315, 330
   as Shakespeare trans.   168*n*115, 169
   on Bohte   125, 139

Schlegel, Friedrich, *Lectures on Dramatic Art and Literature*   120

Schleiermacher, Friedrich Daniel   92

Schmeller, Johann Joseph, Goethe's portrait later lithographed by Delacroix   198

Schmidt, Otto Eduard   32*n*46, 33*n*48, 33*n*51, 36*n*69

Schney, porcelain factory   343

Schnorr v. Carolsfeld, Julius (son of V. H.)   250

Schnorr v. Carolsfeld, Ludwig Ferdinand (son of V. H.)   239

Schnorr v. Carolsfeld, Veit Hans   220

Schnurmann, Claudia   37*n*74

Schorn, Ludwig   42, 87, 355

Schreiber, Carl F.   55*n*17, 139*n*11, 140*n*23, 355

Schröder, Friedrich Ludwig   277

Schubert, Franz, 1814 *lied Margaret at the Spinning Wheel*   257

Schuler, Édouard, engraver
   1837 *Faust and Gretchen* engraving after R   236–38, 237 (*Fig. 7.21a*), 340, 373, 374, 375
   post 1849 *Faust and Gretchen* steel engraving after R   236–38, 237 (*Fig. 7.21b*), 373, 375, 376; *see also Album aus der Damenzeitung Iris* and Flaxman   238

Schultze, Carl Friedrich, c.1818 outlines after Fouqué's *Undine*   77, 129

Schulze, Gottlieb, Bohte's printer   124, 125, 128, 163, 359

Schumacher, Doris   50, 54*n*12, 61*n*45

Schuster, Peter-Klaus   86*n*102

Schütz-Höffert, Sophie, actress   293–94, 294 (*Fig. 9.15*)

Schütz, Eduard, actor (husband of S.)   279, 293–94, 294 (*Fig. 9.15*)

Schwerdgeburth, Carl August, painter and court engraver   47 (*Fig. 1.12a*), 48, 274

Schwind, Moritz v.   118, 239

Scott, John, ed. of *London Magazine*   126, 136, 138

Scott, Sir Walter   121, 203, 204
   1799 trans. of *Götz von Berlichingen*   59
   1819 *Ivanhoe*   250
   c.1820? R exemplar   59

Seeliger, Stephan   49*nn*121–22, 67

Seibertz, Engelbert   75, 76 (*Fig. 2.11*), 239, 261, 369
   image of griffin-riding Goethe   208

Seifert, Siegfried   355*n*3

Semaine (*La*)   191*n*58

Semele (mythology)   39, 329

Semper, Gottfried   283

Seneca, Federico   251
   Perugina logo   251–52, 252 (*Fig. 7.31a*)

Senefelder, Aloys   160

Senft, Didi, as red "Devil"   302

sentimental genre   49, 189, 203, 308

sentimentality   25, 52, 59, 80, 82, 88, 115, 120, 126*n*55, 133, 140*n*27, 150*n*67, 170, 233, 269, 308, 343, 357

series
   Ausgabe letzter Hand (*AlH*)   96*n*7, 97, 106, 213, 215 (*Fig. 7.2*), 371
   Baudry's "European Bookstore"   201
   Baudry's "Foreign Languages Library"   201
   Baudry's "Library of the Best Old and New German Writers"   201
   "Bohn's Standard Library"   168
   "Booklets of German Theatre"   239
   Bry's "Les Veillées littéraires illustrées"   203, 242, 245
   "Everyman's Library"   5
   Ladvocat's "Chefs-d'œuvre des théâtres étrangers"   183
   Librairie Gründ's "Bibliothèque précieuse"   208–10, 210 (*Fig. 6.22*), 378
   Librairie Romantique's "Théâtre romantique"   197
   Maresq and Pelvey's "Librairie centrale des publications à 20 centimes"   203, 367, 376
   Masson et Cie's "Nouvelle collection d'auteurs allemands"   205, 369
   "New Directions College Books"   175
   "Oxford World's Classics"   5

sexuality   *see* devil; Mephistopheles; Index on MR → 8. R's Distinctive Outline Treatment → distinct features → eroticism/sexual yearning

Seydelmann Apollonia, née de Forgue (wife of J.), Dresden artist   34

Seydelmann Jacob (Josephus Johannes Crescentius), Dresden artist   34

Seydelmann, Carl (or Karl), actor   280, 289, 298, 301

Seymour, Robert   258

Shaffer, Elinor   148*n*44; *see also* Paulin, St Clair, and Shaffer

Shakespeare
   Hamlet (the character)   291
   King Lear (the character)   261
   Lady Macbeth (the character)   162
   works by
      King Lear   261*n*16
      Othello   291; *see also* Index on MR → 6. Other Works → R's outlines → Shakespeare

Shelley, Harriet, née Westbrook (first wife of P. B.)   233

Shelley, Mary (second wife of P. B.)
   1818 *Frankenstein*   32
   1824 ed. *Posthumous Poems* by P. B. Shelley   157

Shelley, Percy Bysshe   1, 2, 357, 367
   1821 *Faustus* ed. read by   1, 36, 137, 138, 148, 151–54, 324
   1821 trans. "Prologue in Heaven"   120*n*5, 154, 157
   1821 trans. "The May-Day Night Scene"   1, 83, 120*n*5, 145, 146 (*Fig. 5.6*), 154, 156–57, 159 (*Fig. 5.14*), 281
   1824 *Posthumous Poems*   157
   1832 symbolism of Lumley ed.   157–59, 158 (*Figs. 5.12, 5.13*), 364
   and Goethe   1, 83, 157, 356
   visual imagination and R's plates   1, 138, 154, 157*n*87, 157–59, 159 (*Fig. 5.14*), 175, 232–33, 232 (*Fig. 7.17*), 233*n*32, 247

Sherwill, Markham   258, 258*n*9

Siddons, Mrs   162

Siegel, Jonah   88*n*116

Sigismund, Ernst, R connoisseur   27, 30*n*39, 36, 45, 61, 67, 69, 227*n*28

silence (aesthetic parameter)   89, 189, 324, 346

Silenus (mythology)   40, 41 (*Fig. 1.7*), 212

Silvanus (mythology)   40

Singer, Hans Wolfgang   44
    1901 *Allgemeines Künstler-Lexikon*   44
    1914 "Die Weinbergsszenen von Moritz Retzsch"   44*n*108

Singing Academy (Berlin)   277

Sloane, William M.   325, 327

Smith, Raphael, father to Eliza Aders   123

smoking
    as diminutive theatre performance   340–43
    as social habit/ritual   342

Smyth, Richard   175

Soane, George (son of Sir J.)   127, 136, 140, 143, 356
    1818 *Undine* by Fouqué, free trans. and stage adaptation   129
    1820 *Extracts from Göthe's Tragedy of Faustus*   124, 127–28, 130, 137, 139, 359
    1821 *Faust* partial verse trans.   128, 128*n*70, 148
        "Dedication" 1823 published in *Über Kunst und Altertum*   148
        praised by Goethe   148

Soane, George, [and Daniel Terry]
    1825 *Faustus: A Romantic Drama*, aka *The Devil and Dr Faustus* 128, 162, 180, 281, 290, 371
    1829 Cumberland ed.   291; *see also Faustus: or, The Demon of the Drachenfels*; Terry

Soane, Sir John, architect   127

Société des Amis des Livres   200

Södergran, Edith   176

Solanki, Tanvi   286*n*66

Sophia Dorothea of Württemberg, Tsarina Maria Feodorovna   55–56, 56 (*Fig. 2.2*)

Sophia, Grand Duchess of Saxe-Weimar-Eisenach (daughter-in-law of S. D.)   56

Spagnoli, Luisa   251

Spenser, Edmund, *The Faerie Queene*   259–61

Spiess, Helmut   280*n*41, 286*n*63, 286*n*43

Spiess, Johann, 1587 printer of *History of Dr Johann Faust*   122

spine designs (*Faust 1*)
    as lay stained-glass window   172–73, 172 (*Fig. 5.21*), 175, 176, 376
    gilt   147, 168, 195, 201, 368
    implication of   162, 175, 211
    no lettering (frontal display)   170, 375
    ornate   170, 211

Spitzer, Gerd   26*n*11

Spohr, Louis, 1813 opera *Faust* (1830 Paris production)   187, 257

St. Petersburger Zeitung   287*n*74

Staël, Germaine de   80, 184, 186, 197, 304
    1813 *Germany* (1814 *De l'Allemagne*)   1, 120
        Goethe's *Faust 1* as "intellectual chaos"   1, 55, 157, 211

stage (the) and R's impact   219, 254, 273–74, 277–81, 278 (*Figs. 9.5, 9.6*), 281–86, 283 (*Fig. 9.9*), 284 (*Fig. 9.10*), 285 (*Fig. 9.11*), 288, 289 (*Fig. 9.12*), 291–94, 292 (*Fig. 9.13*), 293 (*Fig. 9.14*), 294 (*Fig. 9.15*), 298, 301, 302, 307–8, 355–56, 358
    English –   59, 129, 162, 247, 281, 291, 292 (*Fig. 9.13*), 296–99
    French –   179–80, 184–88, 281–85, 283 (*Fig. 9.9*), 284 (*Fig. 9.10*), 285 (*Fig. 9.11*)
    German/Austrian –   50, 181, 187, 189, 203, 277–81, 278 (*Figs. 9.5, 9.6*), 288, 289 (*Fig. 9.12*), 293, 293 (*Fig. 9.14*), 338, 356
    pleasure-ground *Faust*   287–88

stage → printed media   299–301, 300 (*Figs. 9.18, 9.19*), 301 (*Fig. 9.20*)

stage → curios   333

stage designs/sets and the visual arts   2, 92, 108, 271–72, 273–74, 278 (*Figs. 9.5, 9.6*), 280–81, 280 (*Fig. 9.7*), 284; *see also* Brühl; Despléchin; Schinkel; Terry; Thierry

standalone prints   48, 112, 116, 213, 215, 216, 221, 224, 229, 255, 371, 374

Stanhope, Philip Dormer, 4th Earl of Chesterfield   *see* Chesterfield

Stapfer, Albert (son)
    1823 *Faust* trans.   183, 186, 193, 200
    1828 Motte-Sautelet in-folio *Faust* (Delacroix)   189, 193, 198, 208, 248 (*Fig. 7.27 top*), 372
        mentioning R   180
    1828 republ. with Audot copies by Librairie Romantique   198, 199 (*Figs. 6.16 a–b*), 363
    1838 Meline *Faust*, revised trans. by C. M. Friedländer   200, 365

Starobinski, Jean   87, 87*n*106

Stassen, Franz   239

Stead, Evanghelia   3*n*4, 5*nn*10–11, 48*n*120, 75*n*84, 108*n*59, 112*n*84, 120*n*3, 166*n*106, 208*n*108, 238*n*37, 242*n*67, 253*n*90, 261*n*15, 357*n*8

Stead, Évanghélia, and Hélène Védrine   4*n*7

Steckelings, Karlheinz W.   347*n*28, 347*n*31, 347*n*33

steel engravings   106, 137, 162, 163, 168, 169, 189, 197, 213, 233, 236–39, 237 (*Fig. 7.21b*), 241, 258, 264, 343, 344 (*Fig. 12.6a*), 366, 367, 368, 374, 376

Steig, Michael   318, 319, 320

Stelzig, Eugene L.   121*n*11

stereoscopic views   *see* Gaudin; London Stereoscopic and Photographic Co.

stereotype edition (1824 Boosey *Faustus* print template)   154–56, 155 (*Figs. 5.11a–c*), 360, 361; *see also* Wilson, W.

stereotypes   298, 308, 351
    and outlines   206, 301, 357
    copying and – (coined typecasts)   298, 321, 357
    myth and –   298
    national –   297
    playful use of – (Gautier)   306, 308, 309
    reversible use of – (Gautier)   321; *see also* typification/typifying

Stern, Ernst, 1920 coloured *Faust* ed.   239

Stieglitz, Christian Ludwig   115

Stieler, Joseph Karl   60, 61, 83, 273

stipple engravings   87, 145 (*Fig. 5.5*), 162, 213–14, 215 (*Fig. 7.2*), 220, 371

Stith, Ann Florence (daughter of C. P.)   327

Stith, Bolling Buckner Africanus (son of C. P.)   327

Stith, Catharine Potter   154, 323–29, 326 (*Figs. 11.1a, 11.1b*), 332, 352, 360
    1830 song "Our Friendship"   324
    1831 *Thoughts on Female Education*   324
    1833 "The Chest of Bones" in *Godey's Lady's Book*   324*n*6
    unsigned translations   324

Stith, Townshend (husband of C. P.)   323, 329

Stith, Victorina Sprague (daughter of C. P.)   327

Stone, Henry, American lithographer   142
    1824 *Illustrations of the Celebrated Tragedy of Faustus*   142*n*30, 240, 361; *see also* Wallenstein

Stothard, Thomas, and R   240

strip cartoon   54, 70, 82, 201; *see also bande dessinée*

Strixner, Johann Nepomuk   47 (*Fig. 1.12b*), 48

Stubenrauch, Philipp v.   293, 293 (*Fig. 9.14*)

Stumme, Gerhard   89, 109, 110, 138, 145, 160, 161, 220–21, 361

Sue, Eugène   204
    1842–43 *The Mysteries of Paris*   203

Supreme Being (cult and iconography)   189–90, 191 (*Fig. 6.11*)

GENERAL INDEX

447

Surrealists   39
surrogate prints   175, 236, 240, 305, 338, 356
Swanwick, Anna
    1850 *Faust I* verse trans. in *Dramatic Works of Goethe*   168
    1878 revised *Faust I* trans. with "Scenes from the Second
        Part"   168, 368
        pub. 1878 as *Goethe's Faust, in Two Parts*   368
    1893 *The First Part of Goethe's Faust* ("with R's illustrations")   369
symbolism   80, 83, 87, 157, 167, 247, 270, 296, 303, 310, 311, 313, 318, 321,
        355, 357, 363
    commercial and political   120
    patriotic/nationalistic   250, 251
    religious   109, 172; *see also* colour
symbols   5, 84, 85 (*Fig. 2.21*), 221, 253, 270, 322
    in ancient Greece   333
Symmons, Sarah   86*n*99, 86*nn*102–3

tableaux vivants/lebende Bilder
    1787 Caserta performance of Emma, later Lady Hamilton   286
    1821–22 *Tableaux from Faust* (Harmonie, Weimar)   274
    1838 *Lebende Bilder aus Faust* with recitatives (Coburg)   286–87
    and reading analogy   287
    as hybrid creations   287
    in Goethe's *Elective Affinities*   274, 286–87
    in Pollock's *The Picture's Secret*   313
    R's *Chess Players* performed   271
Tait's Edinburgh Magazine   255*n*6
Tallis, John, 1852 *Tallis's History and Description of the Crystal Palace*
        172*n*124
Talma, François-Joseph   289
Tasso, Torquato   203, 259
Taylor of Norwich, William   120
Taylor, Arthur   123
Taylor, Barry   129*n*73, 129*n*77
Taylor, Bayard, American poet and 1870 trans. of *Faust*   169, 368, 369
Taylor, John (father of A.), Unitarian hymnist   123
Temperance movement, American   334
    R's *Intemperance Tankard*   333–34; *see also* Tiffany
Terry, Daniel, actor
    1825 author of *British Theatrical Gallery*   162
    1825 co-author of *Faustus: A Romantic Drama*, aka *The Devil and
        Dr Faustus*   128, 162, 180, 281, 290, 299, 371; *see also* Soane, G.
    as Mephistopheles after R   59, 162, 247, 281, 291, 292 (*Fig. 9.13*),
        299, 371
Terry, Ellen   299
text and image   *see* image and text
texts accompanying R's prints
    as captions   3, 38, 110, 111 (*Fig. 3.12*), 113 (*Figs. 3.14a–c*), 114, 115 (*Figs.
        3.16a–b*), 137, 138–39, 149, 154, 161, 255, 267, 300, 359, 360, 361,
        362, 363, 364, 366, 367, 368, 369, 371, 372, 376, 377
    as excerpts   1, 3, 4, 52, 54, 67, 80, 87, 99, 103, 104, 106, 108, 124,
        127–28, 136, 137, 139, 154, 163, 169, 175, 220, 241, 255, 267, 288, 334,
        361, 362, 364, 373
    as introductions   35, 36, 52, 54, 60, 128, 139, 166, 167, 168, 175, 188,
        192, 195, 219, 220, 255, 327, 361, 362, 363, 373
    as synopses/summaries   1, 3, 4, 6, 62, 102, 135, 139, 140, 149, 154, 167,
        195, 255, 323, 327, 364, 365, 367; *see also* image and text; outline,
        aesthetic medium
Th. S.   25, 26, 27, 28, 30, 31*n*43, 34*n*59, 36*n*68, 37*n*73, 65, 101, 271*n*1
Thaeter, Julius, German printmaker   49, 118
theatre productions (often derivative of R)
    Goethe's *Faust*

1819–20 Radziwill's *Faust* (Berlin, Monbijou)   277, 278
        (*Fig. 9.5*), 279, 288, 289 (*Fig. 9.12*), 298, 302, 338; *see also*
        Charles, Duke of Mecklenburg; Radziwill; *Scenen aus
        Goethe's Faust in acht lithographirten Bildern*
    1821 *Tableaux from Faust* (Harmonie, Weimar)   274
    1829 *Faust* (Braunschweig) → Dresden, Hanover, Leipzig,
        Weimar, Bremen, Hamburg, Magdeburg, Munich,
        Stuttgart   89, 97, 273, 279–80, 293–94, 294 (*Fig. 9.15*)
    1832 (Vienna)   291–93
    1832 *Faust* (Stuttgart)   180
    1838 (Berlin, Royal Theatre)   279, 280, 298
    1838 *Faust* in six parts (Berlin Opera)   279
    1839 (Vienna)   293, 293 (*Fig. 9.14*)
    1854 (Munich, Royal Theatre)   279, 306, 307–8
    1891 (Vienna, Hofburgtheater)   279
Goethe's *Faust* adapted
    1824 *Faustus: or, The Demon's Victim* (London)   281
    1825 Soane [and Terry], *Faustus: A Romantic Drama* (London,
        Drury Lane)   128, 162, 179, 247, 281*n*47, 289–90, 291, 294,
        296, 299, 371; *see also* Soane, G. [and Terry]
    1827 *The Devil and Dr Faustus* (New York)   281
    1827 Théaulon, *Faust, drame lyrique en 3 actes* (Paris, Théâtre
        des Nouveautés)   185
    1828 Béraud, Merle, and Nodier, *Faust* (or *Le Docteur Faust*)
        (Paris, Porte-Saint-Martin)   186, 189, 220, 281–82, 283, 290,
        294, 362; *see also* Béraud, Merle, and Nodier
    1829 *Faust* (Vienna, Prater)   287–88
    1829 Rousset, *Faust, ou Les Premières Amours d'un métaphysicien
        romantique* after Barbier (Paris)   187
    1831 Bertin, *Fausto: Opera semi-seria* (Paris, Théâtre Italien)
        187, 282–83, 283 (*Fig. 9.9*)
    1832 Lesguillon, *Méphistophélès*   187
    1838 *Lebende Bilder aus Faust* with recitatives (Coburg Court
        Theatre)   286, 287
    1851 *The Devil and Dr Faustus* (New York, Broadway
        Theatre)   281
    1859 Isler's summer show and musical attraction (Saint
        Petersburg, Villa monde brillant)   287–88
    1885–88, 1894–1902 *Faust* with Irving as Mephistopheles
        (London, Lyceum Theatre, etc.)   297, 299–301, 300 (*Figs.
        9.18, 9.19*), 301 (*Fig. 9.20*), 311, 352
Gounod, *Faust*
    1859 *première* (Paris, Théâtre Lyrique)   204, 206, 257, 283–84,
        284 (*Fig. 9.10*), 285 (*Fig. 9.11 top*)
    1861 *Margarete* (Darmstadt)   257
    1864 (London, J.-B. Faure as Mephistopheles)   299
    1869 (Paris, Académie Impériale de Musique)   299
    1908 (Opéra de Paris)   279
tongue-in-cheek *Faust*
    1829 *Le Cousin de Faust* (Gaîté extravaganza)   187
    1870 *Le Petit Faust* (Lyceum Theatre)   299
    1968 merry *Faust* (East Berlin)   301
    1978 *Faust* (Stuttgart)   301
theatre innovations   273, 277–79, 284, 288, 338, 356; *see also* Brühl;
        Schinkel; stage (the) and R's impact; stage designs/sets and the
        visual arts
Théaulon, Emmanuel, 1827 *Faust, drame lyrique en 3 actes*   185, 193,
        210
Thelwall, John, British orator and poet   123
Thielmann (Thielemann), Joseph Adolf   34, 60, 61
Thielmann (Thielemann), Wilhelmine (wife of J. A.)   34, 60, 61
Thierry, Joseph, French painter   284, 285 (*Fig. 9.11 top*), 377

things   333–34, 338, 340; *see also* artefacts; home decorations; objects; Ulrich
Thomson of Edinburgh, George   240
Thousand and One Nights (The)   352
Tieck, Ludwig   27, 280, 288, 289
Tiffany and Co., *Intemperance Tankard* by R   333–34
Tille, Alexander   48n120, 50, 108, 140, 141n28, 221n18, 227, 237 (*Fig. 7.21a*), 238, 333, 360, 361, 362, 374
   1899 *Bilderverzeichnis der Bode-Tilleschen Faust-Galerie*   108, 227n27
Tilt, Charles, British publisher   170, 175
   1828–32 R's *Gallery of Shakspeare* (T. and Ackermann)   170
   1829 *Fridolin* album with new trans. (T. and Ackermann)   189
   1843 *Goethe's Faust by Retzsch* (T. and Bogue)   170, 171 (*Fig. 5.19*), 176, 366, 375
   1843 *Illustrations of Goethe's Faust* (T. and Bogue)   77, 169, 170, 171 (*Fig. 5.20*), 176, 366, 375; *see also* Ackermann; Audot
tin figurines or flats (*Zinnfiguren*)
   and history   347–48
   and cultural aura   349, 354, 358
   display – (*Vitrinenfiguren*) after R   351–52, 351 (*Fig. 12.10*); *see also* Berliner Zinnfiguren; Fechner; Mohr
title-pages
   aesthetics   106, 115 (*Fig. 3.16a*), 163, 163n103, 164 (*Fig. 5.17 top*), 165 (*Fig. 5.18*), 166, 192 (*Fig. 6.12*), 197, 201, 283, 283 (*Fig. 9.9*), 361, 367, 368, 374
   in red and black inks   168, 219, 241, 368, 369, 374; *see also* Mephistopheles; covenant vs. wager → signing with blood
   interpreting Goethe's *Faust I*   192 (*Fig. 6.12*), 193–94, 195, 197, 363
   tampered –   157, 158 (*Figs. 5.12, 5.13*)
Todd, David   179
Tomkins, English sceneshifter   281; *see also* Lefèvre
Töpffer, Rodolphe, 1833 *Story of Mr. Jabot*   82
Toscani, Caetano (Cajetan)   25
Tour de France, racing event   302
toy theatres   218, 298, 299, 372
transcendentalists   169, 240, 368; *see also* Emerson
translation (as mutating concept)   136
   applied to R's copied images (Ruskin)   88, 155, 188
   rule of textual over visual –   167, 169, 179
   visual vs. textual/interlingual –   122, 136, 179, 210, 356
translations (textual)
   boosting illustrated books   49, 50, 85, 167–68, 169–70, 242–45, 243 (*Fig. 7.23*), 244 (*Figs. 7.24a, 7.24b*), 245 (*Fig. 7.25*)
   calling for extra-illustration   159
   of Goethe's *Faust I*   1, 3, 4, 5, 49, 59n32, 62, 85, 115, 119, 120, 126, 127, 128, 128n70, 129n75, 135, 136, 137, 139–40, 147, 148–49, 151, 154, 156–57, 159, 163, 167–68, 169, 172, 180, 183, 183n32, 184, 185, 186, 188, 192, 193, 198, 200, 203, 204, 206n104, 208, 210–11, 233, 245, 253, 255, 257, 259, 281, 307, 352; *see also* Goethe's *Faust I* translated
   of texts accompanying R's prints   35, 188
   of texts on R   37, 43
   promoting/urging visual –   159, 162–3, 163–66, 164 (*Fig. 5.17 top*), 180, 181 (*Fig. 5.4*), 185, 185 (*Figs. 6.7a–b*), 208, 211, 233, 307, 355
   vs. illustration   138, 139
translations (visual)
   R's prints as –   1, 3–4, 36, 50, 75, 75 (*Fig. 2.10*), 115, 122, 123, 124, 357
   accompanying textual –   163, 179, 356
   adapted to textual –   162–63, 164 (*Fig. 5.17 top*)
   as poetry/poetic comment   35–36, 206
   levelled as textual –   166

promoting textual –   163–66, 165 (*Fig. 5.18*), 190
   steering textual –   127, 137, 166, 167, 175, 179, 273, 281, 356
   turned into illustrated books   163, 166, 167–68
Trelawny, Edward John   324
Treuttel and Würtz, publishers   179, 179n13, 370
   co-publishing R's trilingual *Fancies*   101
trivial, triviality   254, 261, 286n68, 333, 338, 354; *see also* artefacts; home decorations; objects; Ulrich
Trollope, Anthony   318
Trueb, engraver
   1828 Audot copies (with Branche) after R   187, 190 (*Fig. 6.10*), 198, 206, 218, 362, 363; *see also* Branche
Turkle, Sherry, *Evocative Objects*   334, 338n14
Turner, J. M. W.   88
Twyman, Michael   88n111, 160n91, 162n96
types
   and etching/printing/reprinting   306–7, 321
   and/vs. live creatures   62, 307
   creating –   240, 279, 297–99, 301, 306–7, 311
   psychological – (Jung)   140n19
typification/typifying   6, 48, 49, 62, 84, 108, 136, 214, 229, 240, 242, 270, 301, 357; *see also* Nodier; printed items → as archetypes/templates; types; stereotypes

Über Kunst und Altertum   60, 61, 62, 128, 148, 325
Uhlig, Stefan H.   149n60
Ulrich, Laurel Thatcher, Ivan Gaskell, Sara J. Schechner, and Sarah Anne Carter, *Tangible Things*, Harvard exh. and seminars   334n6, 334n8
Universal Post Union   232
Ürményi, József, Hungarian politician   99, 363
USS Constitution, "Old Ironsides," frigate   323, 324, 325, 329
ut pictura poesis   307

Van de Weyer, Sylvain   197
Van der Post, C.   166n104
Vaterländisches Museum   121n18, 122
Vaughan, William   3, 25, 26, 28, 45, 80, 88, 89n123, 120, 121, 125, 167, 176, 240, 255, 257, 303, 304nn5–6, 357
Veith and Hauser (qdt. as Auzer), Paris print publishers   102, 105, 365
Venus (mythology)   30
Verlohren, Heinrich Ludwig   59, 64, 65, 69
Vernet, Horace   *see* Horace
Verweyen, Theodor, and Gunther Witting   266n22
Vicaire, Georges   180
Victoria, Queen   287, 299, 358, 373, 376
vignettes   99, 114, 115 (*Fig. 3.16a*), 151, 152–53 (*Figs. 5.10a–b*), 163–66, 165 (*Fig. 5.18*), 169, 176, 193, 197, 201, 203, 204 (*Fig. 6.18*), 205 (*Fig. 6.19*), 206, 208, 233, 234 (*Fig. 7.18 bottom left*), 240, 243, 243 (*Fig. 7.23*), 250, 266, 367, 369, 372, 374, 376, 378
Vigoureux, L. John   57, 57 (*Fig. 2.3*), 57n22, 97
Vilain, Robert   183n32, 198n77, 198n79
Villa, Luisa   305n8
Villain, François, French printer   181, 184, 360, 362
Villeneuve-Bargemon, Bertrand de   195n65
Villiers de L'Isle-Adam, 1886 *L'Ève future*   288
Vincent, Auguste, French composer and bibliophile   187n45, 197, 363
Vincent, Dominique (later Meulenbergh), half-brother of Frères Williaume   198
   lithograph of Goethe's portrait after Delacroix (← Schmeller)   198–200, 199 (*Fig. 6.16a*), 363
Vischer, Friedrich Theodor   266n22

GENERAL INDEX

Vittorio Emmanuele II   250
Vitzthum v. Eckstädt, Heinrich   26, 32, 61
Vleeschouwer, Lodewijk Joachim, 1842 *Faust* trans. into Dutch
    166*n*104
Vogel v. Vogelstein, Carl   38, 239
Vogel, Dr, translator   39*n*82
Vogel, Gerd-Helge   37*n*72, 40, 50, 80, 88, 101, 212*n*1
Voïart, Élise   179, 186 (*Fig. 6.8*), 189, 362, 363
    and pull of pictures   188
    1828 Audot long *Faust* "Introduction"   188
Votteler, Christian, 1884? cover for Cotta   106–7, 107 (*Fig. 3.9*), 368

Wadepuhl, Walter   60*n*37
Wagner, [Friedrich], German engraver   213–14, 215 (*Fig. 7.2*), 371
Wagner, Richard   283
Wahlen, Adolphe, Belgian printer/bookseller   200
Wainewright, Thomas Griffiths   125, 126; *see also* Janus Weathercock
Walicki, Alfons, 1844 *Faust* trans. into Polish   163, 368; *see also*
    Zawadzki
Waliszewski, Kazimierz   55*n*18
Walker, Henry, 1868 *Faust in Five Minutes*   299
Wallenstein, [Jules de], 1824 pref. *Illustrations of the Celebrated
    Tragedy of Faustus*   142, 361; *see also* Stone
Walpurgis Night (classical, in *Faust II*)   201; *see also* Index on M R →
    4. Additional *Faust I* Outlines
Walpurgis Night (in *Faust I*)   *see* Goethe's *Faust I* read in text and
    by image; *see also* Index on M R → 3. Choice *Faust I* Scenes
    Outlined → pl. 22
Walpurgis Night (traditional)   303, 304
Ward, Robert Plumer, 1825 *Tremaine; or, A Man of Refinement*   305
wars
    American civil war   169
    American War of Independence   241
    Franco-Prussian War   107, 133, 250, 333
    Napoleonic wars   2, 26, 56, 58, 96, 113, 120, 121, 122, 167, 179, 255,
        277, 321
        German war of liberation   34, 261
        Hundred Days war   309
    World War I   251, 287
    World War II   32, 32 (*Fig. 1.4*), 34, 50, 206, 210, 270, 369, 378
Wartusch, Rüdiger   277*n*21, 277*n*25
Watts, Alaric A.
    1825–35 ed. of *Literary Souvenir* (*The*); or, *Cabinet of Poetry and
        Romance*   208, 224–25, 225 (*Figs. 7.8, 7.9*), 371
    1826 "The First Kiss: A Poetical Sketch"   224, 371
        later renamed "A Scene from Faust"   224*n*23
    1832 "The Deveria Family"   208*n*107
    1851 *Lyrics of the Heart: And Other Poems*   224*n*23
Watts, Alaric Alfred (son of A. A.), *Alaric Watts: A Narrative of his Life*
    224*n*22
Watzdorf, Luise v.   33, 36; *see also* Scharfenberg circle
Webb, Timothy   120*n*5, 154*n*71, 157, 157*n*83, 233
Webster, John   157
Wegner, Peter-Christian   61*n*45, 236, 237 (*Fig. 7.21b*), 239, 338–40, 339
    (*Fig. 12.3*), 342 (*Fig. 12.5a*), 374, 377
Wegner, Wolfgang   50, 118*n*90, 221, 225*n*25, 239, 240, 268*n*27, 357*n*8
Weiser-Aall, Lily   296*n*99
Weissenbruch, August Karl Wilhelm   197–98
Weissenbruch, Louis (son of A. K. W.), printer   197–98, 199
    (*Figs. 6.16a–b*), 363
Wende-Hohenberger, Waltraud, and Karl Riha   266*n*22
Wende, Waltraud   266*n*22

Wengler, F., publisher in Aachen   267
Wenner, Johann Friedrich, publisher/printer   46 (*Fig. 1.10*), 49, 67, 110,
    150 (*Fig. 5.8*), 280 (*Fig. 9.7*)
Werl, Adolph, bookseller and lithographer   267
Werner, Zacharias   112; *see also* Riepenhausen
Wertheimber, Palmyre   307
Westley, Josiah, bookbinder   172, 376
Westleys and Co. (Westley, J., Frederick Westley, and William Clark,
    Partners)   172–73*n*125
Widmann, Georg Rudolf   184, 203
    1599 *Faust* chapbook, 1834 Eytel illus. after R   116 (*Fig. 3.17a*),
        117–18, 117 (*Fig. 3.17b*), 373
    on Faust and printing   184, 210–11
Wieland, Christoph Martin, *Works*   220
Wilde, Oscar, 1891 *The Picture of Dorian Gray*   313
Wilder, Amos Niven   153 (*Fig. 5.10b*), 360
Wilder, Thornton Niven (brother of A. N.)   153 (*Fig. 5.10b*)
Willemer, Jakob Johann v.   55, 154, 323, 325, 329–30, 331, 332
Willemer, Marianne v., born Jung (third wife of J. J.)   55, 154, 323, 324,
    325, 329–32
    as *die kleine*   323, 329, 358
    as Suleika   55, 323
    self-identification with R's Gretchen   329–30
Willemer, Rosine v. (daughter of J. J.)   330
Willemin and Aubert fils, engravers   133
William I, German Emperor   109
William I, King of The Netherlands   197, 198
William II, Elector of Hesse   195
Williams, Edwin   28
Williaume brothers, Joseph and François, lithographers   198
    Goethe's portrait after Delacroix (← Schmeller)   198–200, 199
        (*Fig. 6.16b*), 363
Willis, Patricia C.   175*n*128
Wills, William Gorman, Irish dramatist and *Faust* adaptor   299
Wilson, John, and Son, Boston master printers   169, 169*n*121, 368
Wilson, W., English printer   137, 149, 154, 156, 360, 361; *see also*
    stereotype edition; "kinetic" versions of R's outlines
wit, witty   28, 44, 50, 88, 110, 221, 261, 299, 361; *see also geistreich*
Wittwer, Samuel   334*n*11
Woburn, Cistercian abbey   347
Woburn windows (mounted lithophanes)   347, 350 (*Fig. 12.9*), 373
Wolff, Pius Alexander, actor   274
women
    and charity   55–56
    and emancipation   329
    and writing   332
    as weak creatures in almanacs   112–15
    bluestockings in Heine   304
    cryptic authorial status   324
    education of –   324
    fallen –   262; *see also* Magdalene
    Goethe "the greatest painter of –" (Gautier)   307
    in *tableaux vivants*   286–87
    scheming – in *Vivian Grey*   305–6, 321
woodcuts (wood engravings)   38, 38 (*Fig. 1.6*), 39, 43, 55, 75, 76 (*Figs.
    2.11, 2.12*), 116 (*Fig. 3.17a*), 117, 117 (*Fig. 3.17b*), 118, 134–35 (*Fig. 4.4a–
    b*), 135, 151, 152 (*Fig. 5.10a*), 153 (*Fig. 5.10b*), 184, 189, 195, 197, 203,
    204, 204 (*Fig. 6.18*), 243, 243 (*Fig. 7.23*), 244 (*Figs. 7.24a, 7.24b*),
    245 (*Fig. 7.25*), 264, 360, 367, 370, 373, 376
word-and-image   *see* image and text
    – studies   357
Wordsworth, William   28, 121

Wright, John Masey, reworking R   208, 224–25, 225 (*Figs. 7.8, 7.9*), 233, 371; *see also* Heath; Humphreys; Landon; Watts
Wright, Thomas   58–59; *see also* Dawe, M. M.
Wyeth, Nathaniel Jarvis   203, 210

Xenophon, *Cyropaedia*   140

Young, Charles Mayne, actor   291, 297

Zahn, Johann Karl Wilhelm   277
Zatti, Susanna   250*n*84
Zawadzki, Józef, 1844 Vilnius *Faust* publisher   163, 367; *see also* Radziwill; Walicki

Zeitung für die elegante Welt   43, 65
Zelter, Carl Friedrich   66, 273, 277, 279, 290*n*85
Zeus (mythology)   39; *see also* Jupiter
Zimmermann, Friedrich August   223, 227, 229, 233, 236, 238, 239*n*38, 373
Faust and Gretchen lithographed after R   227–29, 230 (*Fig. 7.13*), 233–36, 236 (*Fig. 7.20*), 238, 340, 375
Zöllner, Ludwig Theodor, printer   227, 238–39, 238 (*Fig. 7.22*), 375
Zschoche, Herrmann   28*n*34, 28*nn*36–37, 31*n*44
Zschokke, Heinrich, "Love and Hate"   287
Zucker, Paul   277*nn*23–24

Φ.Χ.Ψ., cryptic signatory in the *Parthenon*   88